Educational Psychology
for Tomorrow's Teacher

Educational Psychology for Tomorrow's Teacher

Paul S. Kaplan

Suffolk Community College

West Publishing Company

St. Paul   New York   Los Angeles   San Francisco

To
Mark and Sharon Kaplan
Steven and Elaine Pliskin
Four Great Teachers

Production Credits

COPYEDITOR Deborah Cady
DESIGN Diane Beasley
COMPOSITION G & S Typesetters, Inc.
ILLUSTRATION Alice Thiede and Kay Peterson
COVER ART "White Patio with Red Door" by Georgia O'Keeffe
Courtesy of The Regis Collection, Minneapolis, MN

COPYRIGHT ©1990   By WEST PUBLISHING COMPANY
50 W. Kellogg Boulevard
P.O. Box 64526
St. Paul, MN 55164-1003

All rights reserved

Printed in the United States of America

97 96 95 94 93 92 91 90   8 7 6 5 4 3 2 1 0

Library of Congress Cataloging-in-Publication Data

Kaplan, Paul S.
  Educational psychology for tomorrow's teacher / Paul S. Kaplan.
     p.   cm.
  ISBN 0-314-66572-2
  1. Educational psychology. 2. Teaching. I. Title.
LB1051.K273   1990
370.15--dc20   89-29659
                                         CIP ∞

Photo Credits

3 © 1985, Barbara Rios/Photo Researchers; 5 © 1989, Elizabeth Crews/Stock Boston; 7 © 1981, Elizabeth Crews/Stock Boston; 9 © James L. Shaffer; 20 © 1989, Sven Martson/Comstock; 27 © James L. Shaffer; 30 Bill Anderson/Monkmeyer Press; 35 © James L. Shaffer; 37 George Zimbel/Monkmeyer Press; 38 © Elizabeth Crews/Stock Boston; 40 Mimi Forsyth/Monkmeyer Press; 45 © 1988, Bob Daemmrich/Stock Boston; 48 © James L. Shaffer; 51 © James L. Shaffer; 56 © Rick Smolan/Stock Boston; 61 © 1986, Gale Zucker/Stock Boston; 69 © 1989, Sven Martson/Comstock; 72 © 1978, Elizabeth Crews/Stock Boston; 73 © 1988, Michael Weisbrot/Stock Boston; 75 © James L. Shaffer; 77 © James L. Shaffer; 82 © 1983, Peter Menzel/Stock Boston; 88 © 1986, Bob Daemmrich/Stock Boston; 92 © 1986, Peter Menzel/Stock Boston; 93 © 1989, Maureen Fennelli/Comstock; 94 © 1989, Sven Martson/Comstock; 97 © 1989, Sven Martson/Comstock; 105 © 1989, Sven Martson/Comstock; 109 © 1986, Gale Zucker/Stock Boston; 115 © James L. Shaffer; 125 © 1981, Anestis Dia- kopoulos/Stock Boston; 128 © 1989, Sven Martson/Comstock; 130 © James L. Shaffer; 132 © James L. Shaffer; 133 Jim Anderson/Woodfin Camp and Associates; 145 © 1989, Sven Martson/Comstock; 148 © James L. Shaffer; 150 © 1988, Elizabeth Crews/Stock Boston; 152 © James L. Shaffer; 156 © 1988, Rob Crandall/Stock Boston; 158 © James L. Shaffer; 164 © 1989, Sven Martson/Comstock; 173 © 1981, Christopher S. Johnson/Stock Boston; 185 © Hella Hammid/Photo Researchers, Inc.; 187 © 1989, Elizabeth Crews/Stock Boston; 191 Tom Ballard/EKM-Nepenthe; 192 © 1989, Maureen Fennelli/Comstock; 197 © James L. Shaffer; 198 © James L. Shaffer; 199 © 1986, Michael Weisbrot/Stock Boston; 200 © 1981, Karen Rosenthal/Stock Boston; 203 © 1985, Gale Zucker/Stock Boston; 207 © James L. Shaffer; 208 © James L. Shaffer; 209 © 1989, Sven Martson/Comstock; 211 © 1989, Maureen Fennelli/Comstock; 212 © 1989, Sven Martson/Comstock; 219 © 1989, Sven Martson/Comstock; 222 © 1981, Patricia Hollander Gross/Stock Boston; 227 © 1988, Billy E.

(Continued following Subject Index)

Contents in Brief

Contents

II SOCIAL AND MORAL DEVELOPMENT   183

III THE TEACHER-STUDENT INTERACTION 251

Preface

The underlying theme of this text presents the teacher as an informed decision maker. Using an activist approach, this text seeks to demonstrate how educational psychology can be of help to the classroom teacher in making decisions in many challenging situations. The teacher must be aware of the nature of the challenges and the possible alternatives and consequences of each choice. While respecting teachers' individuality and creativity, this book suggests alternatives available to teachers who are faced with daily challenges. Other professionals' research and experiences can be of great help to the teacher, but the teacher must adapt the suggestions to meet his or her own needs, ability, and style. If one approach does not seem to work, the active teacher searches for another. These themes, the teacher as a decision maker and as an active researcher of new and better ways to improve his or her teaching are the underpinnings of this text.

This text has been designed especially to help students identify the challenges involved in teaching, analyze them, present possible alternatives for meeting these challenges, and evaluate the consequences of choosing one strategy over another. In addition, the text is organized in a way that will hopefully allow professors to use it more effectively and somewhat differently from other texts. This text is designed not only as a resource providing a basic understanding of the research and scope of educational psychology, but also as a source of discussion material. It contains many short cases and examples of the challenges teachers face, and it asks students to think and consider the nature of the decisions teachers must make in a number of areas. To accomplish this, the text has been written and organized with the following features.

Content. All texts in educational psychology present the basic principles. However, I have found that many of the most interesting, current, and challenging issues are often slighted or not mentioned at all. This text presents not only the basic principles of educational psychology but also the latest areas of concern for teachers. The text devotes an entire chapter to the use of technology in education, discussing the use of computers, instructional television, and the interactive video. Chapter 9 on communication focuses on such topics as teacher clarity in communication, specific questioning skills, methods for praise and correction, applications of listening skills and writing, communication with parents, and conflict management. This text also presents a number of specific topics of interest for teachers including study skills, social skills training, test anxiety, teacher-parent communication and conferences, moral/value education, and the latchkey or self-care situation. Other subjects addressed are: curiosity, goal setting, competition and cooperation in the classroom, the effects of divorce and stepfamily situations on schooling, classroom demonstrations, test–taking skills, alternative testing for students who require it, learned helplessness, teaching critical and higher level thinking, homework, peer tutoring, cooperative learning, and bilingual education.

Theoretical Approach. All decisions are based upon some theoretical approach. In this text, a number of different theoretical approaches are discussed and evaluated. The text illustrates how various decisions lead to different implications for teachers. The text recognizes theory as a useful tool.

Organization. This text is organized into five parts. The text begins with an introductory chapter describing educational psychology and its relevance to the classroom teacher. Part One contains chapters devoted to cognitive and language development, information processing, creativity, thinking, problem solving, and cognitive styles, and the behavioral approach to education. Part Two examines social and moral development. It explores the school's role in developing students' values and attitudes, the effects of social changes (such as divorce) on students, the latchkey situation, and day care. Part Three focuses on the dynamics of teacher-student interaction, and contains chapters on motivation, communication with students and with parents, and classroom managment. Part Four surveys effective teaching techniques, including objectives and modes of teaching, the uses of technology in education, and effective ways to teach children with exceptional needs. Part Five examines evaluation methods through the use of standardized tests and classroom testing and grading.

Pedagogical Devices and Features. This text offers a number of special features that will be helpful to the professor and the student. Each chapter begins with twelve true-false motivational statements with the answers on the following page. In addition, the questions are repeated following the paragraphs in the body of the text where the answers can be found. Another feature is called "Connections." After the text discusses research on a topic and analyzes the topic's implications for classroom use, the Connections feature presents specific ideas about how this material can be used to improve classroom instruction. All key terms appear in boldface and are defined at the end of each chapter and again in the glossary found at the end of the text. In addition, each chapter concludes with a point by point summary. Two additional features found at the end of the chapter deserve special mention. The Activities and Exercises feature presents various activities, which encourage the student to go beyond the text and actively seek out more information. It presents the student with suggestions for things to do that directly deal with the material covered in the text. The Scenarios feature presents short cases, which ask the student to identify how he or she would react in similar circumstances and to find constructive ways to deal with each situation.

Tables, Figures, and Appendix. Great care and attention has been given to the tables and figures throughout the text. Some of the tables are summaries of material that will help students. The figures graphically present material in a way that will make it easier for students to learn. An appendix on research methods can be found at the back of the book.

Research, Examples, and Practical Applications. Research in educational psychology can be useful to the classroom teacher. The research must

be presented clearly and its implications for the classroom teacher noted. This text presents the research in each area and discusses its relevance for the classroom teacher. The implications of the research are noted in the Connections features. In addition, whenever any topic is discussed, a number of examples directly related to instruction are noted. For example, Piaget's ideas are discussed and examples relating Piaget's ideas directly to teaching at various levels are presented immediately after that section.

Emphasis on Secondary as well as Elementary School. Throughout this text, the reader will notice that secondary schools are given considerable attention. This includes not only high school but the commonly forgotten intermediate and junior high levels.

Instructor's Manual, Test Bank, and Study Guide. An instructor's manual with test bank is available. The instructor's manual also contains 32 transparency masters which may be used in the classroom. A study guide written by Eileen Kelble of the University of Tulsa is also available. Within the study guide, important issues and people are emphasized with thought-provoking study questions.

A great many people are involved in the process of developing and writing a text. I wish to thank Peter Marshall, Christine Hurney, Jane Bacon, Maralene Bates, and Angela Deadwiler at West Publishing Company whose expertise, professionalism, and encouragement made this project possible. I also wish to thank Dr. Sheldon Gordon and Dr. Florence Gordon for their invaluable help during the course of this project. In addition, I would like to thank David Quinn, Joyce Malik, and the entire staff of the Suffolk Community College Western Campus library for their help in locating and obtaining some hard-to-find sources required for this text. The reviewing process is a vital one in the development of a manuscript, and I have been fortunate to receive the constructive feedback from a number of professionals. I would like to express my personal gratitude to the following members of the academic community:

Kenneth Ahrendt
   Oregon State University
Kay Alderman
   University of Akron
Tom Boman
   University of Minnesota-Duluth
John Eliot
   University of Maryland

Meryl Englander
  Indiana University
Philip Faticandi
  American International University
Mark Grabe
  University of North Dakota
Harold Jones
  Purdue University-Calumet
Verne Keenan
  University of Colorado
Eileen Kelble
  University of Tulsa
Charles LaBounty
  Hamline University
Ludwig Mosberg
  University of Delaware
Edward Morris
  Kentucky State University
Richard Mueller
  Northern Illinois University
John Newell
  University of Florida
Karen Piepmeier
  Linfield College
Joy Rogers
  Loyola University-Chicago

Stephanie Salzman
  Idaho State University
Tom Sherman
  Virginia Polytechnic Institute and State University
Fred Teague
  Southwest Baptist University
Joan Timm
  University of Wisconsin-Oshkosh
Mack Wedel
  Central State University
Donald Yarbrough
  University of Iowa

Finally, writing a textbook is a very exhausting, time consuming activity. In many ways it becomes a group effort, involving everyone in the family in some way. When writing this text, I have frequently discussed various issues and questions with my wife and children who are all involved in education at one level or another and who have naturally had their own opinions about the educational process. I deeply appreciate their understanding and patience during the development of this text and take this opportunity to thank my wife, Leslie and my children, Stacey, Amy, Jodi, and Laurie for their help and understanding during the writing of this project.

To the Student

Teaching seems so simple. A teacher, possessing superior knowledge, stands in front of a classroom and transmits the information to students who sit at their desks and learn. This is how teaching must appear to people who have never tried to teach. However, appearances are deceiving. The educational process is one of the more complicated phenomena of human interaction. Actually, in order to be successful, the teacher has to take a number of variables into consideration and make many decisions.

Surveying the classroom, we can see a group of students usually comparable in age and possessing certain age-related similarities. First-graders differ in their interests and in the way they think and process information from fifth-graders who again differ greatly from junior or senior high school students. The teacher must understand these age–related abilities and interests and decide how to teach material in a developmentally appropriate manner. You certainly would not teach a lesson the same way to students at different grade levels.

However, a teacher must see more than a class of students. Students differ from each other in ability, learning skills and prior experience in the subject matter being taught. Some students have a good knowledge base and know how to learn and study, while other students do not. Some students can easily sift the important from the not so important points in the lesson, while other students cannot. The teacher must decide how to present the material while taking these individual differences into account. If the teacher does not, then a good portion of the students will not succeed.

The teacher's day is filled with decisions. Imagine planning a lesson on the economy of New England or the nature of tornadoes. How you approach planning and teaching the lesson partially depends upon the goals and objectives of the lesson. Frequently our goals include not only the transmission of factual material but also the cultivation of reasoning abilities including critical thinking. In addition, students may not always be interested in certain topics, so the teacher must find some way to motivate students and maintain their attention. Armed with knowledge of the students' abilities, skills and background, and an understanding of the objectives of the lesson, the teacher chooses an instructional strategy. The teacher has many choices, each alternative having strengths and limitations, and each more or less useful in particular circumstances. Even after the lesson, the teacher must decide which practice activities to assign and finally, how the learning is to be evaluated.

Looking more deeply into the teacher-student interaction, the teacher must be an expert in communication. Even here, the teacher faces a number of decisions. The teacher must know how to organize and present the material clearly as well as communicate on a personal level with students. The teacher must know when and how to praise, give correction, and how to ask questions.

It would be wrong to confine the teacher's interests and expertise to the cognitive realm. The schools are involved in developing attitudes and encouraging both moral development and the development of health related skills. In addition, the schools have a primary responsibility to help students develop social skills and a positive self-concept. In these areas as well, the teacher must make decisions about how to approach nutrition, drug, or sex education, and how to focus on questions dealing with ethics and morality.

The teacher must also be able to manage a classroom containing thirty or more students. The teacher's skills as a classroom manager prevent problems from starting in class. The teacher must also effectively deal with these problems when they do arise.

The educational process is a complicated matter in

which the teacher is making many informed choices. Educational psychology gives the teacher the basic information needed to make decisions in all educational areas. When a teacher must decide, for instance, the best way to give correction, the research performed in educational psychology offers not only basic principles that can guide the use of correction but also provides research on what methods do and do not work. Educational psychology helps make teachers aware of factors to take into consideration and possible consequences of following particular strategies. The teacher does not have to rediscover the wheel. The painstaking research efforts of many social scientists provide the teacher with a foundation on which to make his or her decisions.

However, the purpose of educational psychology is not to turn the teacher into a type of robot who applies the tricks of the trade to one class after another. It is not the purpose of this discipline to make the decisions for teachers. Educational psychology does not oversimplify matters and claim that if the teacher follows path A, he or she will always succeed and never have any conflicts with students. Educational psychology promises that help is available for making these decisions. The teacher adapts this knowledge to the special needs of the class and to his or her own abilities and style. This reflects an active orientation, emphasizing the need to constantly try new ideas, use those that work and discard or modify those that do not. If a teacher knows that a particular lesson has not worked, then he or she must find a way to improve it. Examined in this way, teaching is both a science based upon research and a very personal and creative enterprise.

This text specifically focuses on how educational psychology can help the new teacher in many areas of interest. As you read the text, try to imagine yourself faced with the challenges that are discussed and consider how you would deal with them. There is never just one way to approach a challenge. By using the research and experience of others presented in this text, you can consider some of the practical issues that arise in teaching and think about ways to solve them.

Educational Psychology
for Tomorrow's Teacher

1

Are These Statements True or False?

Turn the next page for the correct answers. Each statement is repeated following the paragraph in which the information can be found.

1. Educational psychologists are more concerned today with practical application than they were in the past.

2. Elementary schoolchildren spend more than half their time in class doing seatwork, that is, drill or practice exercises designed to be performed at the child's seat.

3. When doing practice exercises, lower-achieving students are more likely to carefully choose a problem solving strategy and ask themselves whether their answers make sense than higher-achieving students.

4. Teachers usually wait too long after asking a question to give students a chance to answer.

5. Educational psychologists are more interested in the cognitive processes of perception, memory, reasoning, and problem solving than they were in the past.

6. Giving background information to students about what they are going to read is a poor strategy, because it eliminates the important aspect of surprise from the reading material.

7. More than half the parents of schoolchildren consider their local schools good or excellent.

8. American adults see discipline as the greatest problem facing education in the United States.

9. The public receives a balanced view from the news media of how students are doing in school.

10. About 75 percent of all disabled students are mainstreamed, that is, placed for some time during the schoolday in a regular classroom.

11. The idea that the schools should play an active part in developing the morals and values of students has been increasing in popularity among the public.

12. Most teachers hold positive attitudes toward education research.

Educational Psychology and the Classroom Teacher

Answers to True-False Statements

1. *True*
2. *True*
3. *False* Correct statement: Low-achieving students are less likely to carefully choose problem solving strategies or to ask themselves whether their answers are reasonable.
4. *False* Correct statement: Just the opposite is true. Teachers do not wait long enough after they ask a question for students to answer it.
5. *True*
6. *False* Correct statement: Giving students background information about what they are going to read is recognized as an excellent strategy.
7. *False* Correct statement: About 40 percent of the people surveyed rate their local schools as good or excellent.
8. *False* Correct statement: Today, Americans see drug use as the single greatest problem facing the schools.
9. *False* Correct statement: Criticisms and stories of failure are much more likely to find their way into print and be covered on television than news of success.
10. *True*
11. *True*
12. *False* Correct statement: Unfortunately, teachers do not hold positive attitudes towards education research.

A teacher gives a regularly scheduled mathematics test on Monday. The class is not doing well and complains to the teacher. The teacher collects the papers after the test and throws them in the garbage, telling a relieved class that the test will take place on Wednesday and warning them to study. One student objects. She studied for the test. She demands that her test be marked, since she thinks she answered all the questions correctly. The teacher tells her that if she did well on this test, she ould be able to do well on Wednesday. Was the teacher's behavior correct?

A third-grade teacher is told that a child with cerebral palsy who is in a wheelchair will be placed in her class the next day. The child has not been in a public school before and seems shy and reserved. The teacher must decide how to introduce the student to the class and how to tell the students something about the child's disability. How should the teacher proceed?

A seventh-grade teacher trying to teach a lesson on police procedure and constitutional law through a lecture format feels that he is talking to a wall. The students show no interest, and the teacher finds that he has failed to get the main points over to the class. The teacher has scheduled one more session on the subject and wants to find some way to motivate the class. What plans might he make for that final lesson?

THE DECISION MAKER

Teachers play a number of roles throughout the schoolday, including instructional specialist, class leader, expert communicator, counselor, executive manager of a group called a class, motivator, and role model. One constant factor in successfully fulfilling each role is the teacher's ability to make decisions. Teachers are constantly making decisions: Is Mary ready to learn multiplication? How can I best encourage John to do his homework more carefully? What is the best way to present to the class the concept of erosion? Such decisions are made during the course of a day, in which the teacher has at least 1,500 interactions with individual students while often supervising thirty or more students at one time (Billups & Rauth, 1987).

Teaching is not an automatic process of simply lecturing to students who are thirsting for knowledge. It involves a teacher with particular skills attempting through a variety of means to teach students who differ widely in ability and background. The material to be learned may include factual knowledge, concepts, skills, ideas, or even values and attitudes. Teachers constantly must make decisions about what to teach and how to teach it. To make such decisions, teachers must understand their students' abilities and backgrounds as well as the nature of the material to be taught. No one is a born teacher. Teachers develop their skills through experience and training, and some of this training is in psychology.

EDUCATIONAL PSYCHOLOGY

Educational psychology is the field that applies psychology to education. Paraphrasing the new definition prepared in 1987 by the American Psychological Association's Division of Educational Psychology, it is the field of psychology concerned with the development, evaluation, and application of theories and principles of human learning and instruction that can enhance lifelong learning (Wittrock & Farley, 1989). The scope of its concerns includes basic research in learning, cognition and instruction, applied research leading to more effective instruction, program evaluation, the development of instructional materials, creating new types of tests, preparing effective curricula, and investigating learning strategies (Bardon, 1989). Its goal is a practical one of helping teachers make decisions, using the research that has been conducted over the years, about what to teach, how to teach, how to deal with specific classroom situations, and how to test. The three problems described at the beginning of the chapter are examples of the many daily challenges that teachers face. Psychology is the primary source of information about handling such challenges.

Educational Psychology and the Classroom Teacher

Educational psychologists face a difficult challenge. For their experimentation to be considered "scientific," it must satisfy the scientific demand for precision and control. However, to be truly effective, educational psychologists must communicate their findings to the teacher and influence education in the classroom (Schulman, 1982). More than ever before, educational psychologists recognize the need for communicating their results to the classroom teacher

educational psychology   A field of psychology that applies psychology to education. It is concerned with the development, evaluation, and application of theories and principles of learning and instruction that can enhance lifelong learning.

and providing answers to practical problems not only for teachers but also for parents and the public at large.

True or False   Educational psychologists are more concerned today with practical application than they were in the past.

Unfortunately, educational psychology has not always received credit for some of the positive changes that have taken place in schools. For example, educational psychologists have taken a long look at textbooks and, finding that many lacked a rational

At least 1,500 separate interactions with students take place in the course of a teacher's day.

organization, stressed the recall of facts often unconnected to each other, and rarely asked students to think, have suggested changes. Some states, such as California, now reject both texts that do not measure up to specific literary standards and mathematics texts that do not focus on problem solving (Jones, 1989). Educational psychologists have also recommended that more emphasis be placed on developing thinking skills. Many states, such as Connecticut, have implemented research-based plans for teaching such skills (see Chapter 4). This does not mean that factual information is unimportant. However, information is best remembered when it makes sense to the student and is understood in a larger context.

Educational psychology's practical contributions in the area of classroom practice have been many. Recently, a new appreciation of the learner as an active participant in the learning situation has arisen. Students are not simply recipients of information but learners who redefine and interpret the information. Such factors as their reasoning process, memory, and prior knowledge determine how much they will learn. This new emphasis on the student's cognitive (intellectual) processes impacts on a number of classroom activities, such as the use of seatwork in elementary school. Seatwork involves students individually performing drill or practice exercises at their seat. It is

estimated that more than half an elementary school student's time is spent on seatwork, more time than is devoted to any other school-related activity (Rosenshine & Stevens, 1986).

True or False Elementary schoolchildren spend more than half their time in class doing seatwork, that is, drill or practice exercises designed to be performed at the child's seat.

Seatwork, however, is sometimes ineffective. Students are less attentive to seatwork than to actual instruction. In addition, the major goal in seatwork of both high- and low-achieving students is simply to finish the work, and both groups don't understand the instructional goals related to each exercise (Anderson, 1981). Low-achieving students, who need extensive practice, tend to use any strategy they can just to finish the work, and they don't seem to consider whether or not their answers make any sense. They do not monitor their own strategies for solving the problems, nor do they ask themselves such important questions as What does the problem require? or Does my answer make sense? High-achieving students know when they don't understand what is required of them and immediately seek out the teacher's help. They monitor their own problem-solving processes better. Furthermore, most students don't understand

Based upon work conducted by educational psychologists, many states now want texts to meet increasingly severe literary standards and focus on problem solving and thinking.

CHAPTER 1
Educational Psychology and the Classroom Teacher

Researchers have noted that many students do not understand the purpose of seatwork and simply try to finish it as soon as possible.

The importance of understanding the purpose behind the work is evident in another area—computer-aided instruction (CAI), discussed in Chapter 12. Conventional wisdom says that students should be challenged, but certainly not to the point of frustration. Computers can often be programmed so that as a student succeeds at one task, other, slightly more challenging tasks arise for the student. This certainly makes sense. However, this may not be as simple as first thought. One researcher tells the story of a student who was working on a computer program and became quite frustrated (Lepper, 1985). When questioned, the student replied that each time he was able to solve the problems, the computer would begin to give him new problems that he would miss. He did not experience any sense of achievement. He obviously did not understand the nature and purposes of the task.

Other useful studies have focused on teacher-student communication, especially questioning. Think of how often your teachers stopped after presenting some material and simply asked, "Any questions?" How often did students raise their hands and inquire? The teacher probably would wait only a second and, not seeing any hands raised, proceed with the lesson. Studies have repeatedly demonstrated that teachers do not wait long enough after asking a question for students to answer. Waiting at least three seconds is recommended. In addition, asking a specific question about the material will give a teacher a better understanding of the comprehension level of the students than a simple request for questions.

True or False   Teachers usually wait too long after asking a question to give students a chance to answer.

We also know that just because children say they understand the material does not automatically mean they actually do. Children often do not really know whether or not they understand the material. This is a common problem and is much misunderstood by both parents and teachers. Asked whether she understood the paragraph she was assigned to read, fourth-grader Sarah said yes; but when asked a question about it, she answered it incorrectly. Did Sarah read the paragraph carefully? The first impression may be no, but it's possible that Sarah read it, thought she understood it, but really didn't. Children can be taught self-monitoring skills to help them understand what they know and don't know, a concept called meta-cognition (see Chapter 4).

why they are doing the work, and some students don't understand *what* they are supposed to do (Berliner, 1987).

True or False   When doing practice exercises, lower-achieving students are more likely to carefully choose a problem solving strategy and ask themselves whether their answers make sense than higher-achieving students.

Taken together, these research findings lead to the practical suggestion that the teacher use guided practice whereby the teacher takes the students through the first few problems to be certain the students know what to do and how to do it and are ready to work on their own (Rosenshine & Stevens, 1986). Students also should be told why they are doing the work; that is, they need to understand the purpose of the work.

Isn't It Just Common Sense?

But, isn't it just common sense? is frequently asked of educational psychologists. No, it isn't. Many commonly held beliefs about learning and teaching are actually incorrect or are half truths. Consider the following ten statements:

1. Since students change more answers from right to wrong than from wrong to right on multiple choice tests, they should stick with their first choices.

   This commonly believed statement is incorrect. Studies do not show that a student is better off staying with his or her first answer, and telling students to do so is a disservice (Hanna, 1989; Feder, 1979).

2. Since teachers would like every student to answer questions, pupils should be called upon randomly and not in a regular rotation.

   Anderson and colleagues (1979) found that first-grade students whose teachers used ordered turn taking did better than those who did not. This is counter-intuitive. Perhaps when teachers think they are randomly choosing students they really aren't, and some students are still being given more opportunities than others to answer. Another possibility is that students spend a great deal of time trying to figure out the method the teacher is using to call on students, thus reducing the attention they are paying to the lesson (Schulman, 1982).

3. Giving students frank, honest, and comprehensive information about sexuality and contraception reduces the teen pregnancy rate.

   Unfortunately, this is only one part of the possible solution to the problem. Just giving information is relatively ineffective. Successful programs include discussions of morals and values and encourage sexually active students to seek out contraceptive advice.

4. Good classroom managers jump right into the work at the beginning of the term, showing their students that the single purpose of the class is learning.

   Studies show that good classroom managers spend a substantial amount of time at the beginning of the term working out procedures and rules. During the early elementary school years, practicing these procedures is especially important.

5. When students tell the teacher that they understand some fact, it is relatively certain that they do.

   As already noted, studies have repeatedly found that students may not know when they know something and when they do not.

6. Children who are bilingual (speak two languages) often have difficulty in school because of their confusion between the languages.

   Bilingual students do not have difficulty because they speak two languages, and studies show that being bilingual may even be an advantage.

7. The law now actively requires disabled students to be placed in regular classrooms.

   This is false. The law requires students to be placed in the least restrictive environment, which may or may not be the regular classroom.

8. Elementary schoolchildren who return to a home after school in which no parent is present are likely to do poorly in school and get into trouble.

   Many teachers blame the latchkey situation for children's poor academic grades and other conduct problems. Studies show, however, that if the student comes directly home after school and the parents exercise even long-range supervision over the telephone, the self-care situation need not lead to problems.

9. Very bright students often have social problems.

   Studies show that gifted and talented students usually have good interpersonal relationships.

10. If students who suffer from a great deal of test anxiety engage in activities or exercises that relax them, their grades will improve.

    This is often not the case. Studies show that although students who are anxious about tests can become less anxious by engaging in relaxation exercises, such exercises may not by themselves lead to better grades. Such students' study skills must also be taken into consideration.

All of the preceding statements are either untrue or, at best, half true. They are still believed by many to be true, even after research has demonstrated them to be false. Each of them might lead to an incorrect decision on the part of the teacher. For example, a teacher might stop the lesson, ask for questions, get none, and assume the students understood the material, only to find on the next exam that they didn't. Other misconceptions, such as those involving latchkey children and bilingual students, might lead to giving parents false information or expecting less from such students.

Who Influences the Direction of Educational Psychology?

The focus of interest in educational psychology is affected by progress in other disciplines of psychology as well as allied fields such as sociology. It is also affected by the changing interests of both the public and government leaders. For example, after the Russians launched the first space satellite in the late 1950s, an outcry from the public and government leaders led to more emphasis on science education. The many comparisons between American and Japanese students in the area of science and mathematics are leading once more to an emphasis on the sciences.

Changes in social structure often affect education, and the public expects psychologists and educators to discover how such changes affect educational achievement. Lately, there has been much research aimed at discovering the effects of early day-care and nursery school experiences on later academic achievement, and more interest has been shown in morals and values education as well.

Educational psychology is also affected by its realization that the interests and concerns of classroom teachers should be a central focus. A look at how scientists in allied fields, the public, and teachers in general influence the field is instructive.

The Cognitive Revolution

Perhaps the greatest change in psychology in the past few decades is the growth of interest and research in cognitive psychology. **Cognition** refers to all the intellectual functions of the mind, including sensation, perception, concept development, problem solving, decision making, critical and creative thinking, memory, and metacognition (a person's understanding of

> **cognition** The process of thinking, knowing, or processing information.

what he or she knows or does not know). Cognitive theorists see learning as an activity that is under the control of the individual and involves these cognitive processes (Letteri, 1985). In the cognitive view, learners are involved in an active process whereby they review what they know, link new information to prior information, form and test hypotheses about the meaning of a problem, assess the strategies that are necessary to solve the problem or do the assignment, and revise concepts as new information is learned. Learning requires sustained and conscious effort. Researchers have adapted this cognitive view of learning to techniques of instruction.

True or False Educational psychologists are more interested in the cognitive processes of perception, memory, reasoning, and problem solving than they were in the past.

Cognitive instruction refers to any effort on the part of the teacher to help students process information in meaningful ways and become independent learners (Jones, 1986). From the practical viewpoint, cognitive instruction has changed some aspects of reading instruction and has led to the following recommendations. Before reading, teachers should discuss the vocabulary, help students make predictions about what they will be reading based on surveys of the titles and text features, and plan how they will attack the assignment. The idea is to actively relate what they are reading to prior knowledge. During reading, students monitor their own comprehension by clarifying the

New research on cognition has helped change the way we teach reading.

information, summarizing text segments, evaluating predictions, and separating important from unimportant information. After reading, the students organize the material through summarizing and categorizing (Jones, 1986).

True or False Giving background information to students about what they are going to read is a poor strategy, because it eliminates the important aspect of surprise from the reading material.

The advances in cognitive psychology have caused educators to teach thinking and reasoning skills along with strategies to monitor students' progress and generally to teach students how to learn. Cognitive psychology has influenced every area of education. In 1987, the U.S. Department of Education published a booklet called *What Works: Research About Teaching and Learning.* Anyone looking through it must be impressed by how extensively it has adopted the cognitive emphasis. For example, when discussing effective reading comprehension, the booklet states:

> Young readers, and poor readers of every age, do not consistently see connections between what they read and what they already know. When they are given background information about the principal ideas or characters in a story before they read it, they are less apt to become sidetracked or confused and are more likely to understand the story fully. Afterwards, a question-and-answer discussion session clarifies, reinforces, and extends their understanding (p. 20).

Later, when discussing the difficult task of solving word problems, the booklet states:

> Good mathematical problem solvers usually analyze the challenges they face and explore alternative strategies before starting work. Unsuccessful problem solvers often act impulsively when given a problem and follow the first idea that occurs to them. Too often, school instruction emphasizes and rewards the rapid solving of problems and fails to recognize and reinforce thoughtful behavior (p. 29).

This does not mean that other models, such as the behavioral model, which looks at the environment, its reinforcers, and punishments as most important, are necessarily wrong or "dead" or that the social learning model, which emphasizes the importance of observational learning, does not offer anything of value. On the contrary, these other views remain valuable even though, at the present time, the cognitive model is most influential. Another view, the developmental

model, which argues that teachers must understand the nature of both cognitive and social developmental changes that occur, remains a necessary basis for understanding how students reason at different ages. These other models are not neglected. They will be discussed in Part One of this text, and are summarized here in Table 1.1.

Educational Psychology Meets the Public's Challenge

The American public has a keen interest in education. When people from the United States, Japan, and Western Europe were asked to rank the importance of different aspects of their lives, their children's education ranked first among the American and European sample but fifth among the Japanese (U.S. News and World Report, August, 1988). What is the American public's attitude toward public education?

For the past twenty years, *Phi Delta Kappan* magazine has conducted a poll of the public's view of education. In the 1988 poll, more than 2,000 adults were interviewed across the country. As Table 1.2 shows, 40 percent of the sample believed that their local schools were either good or excellent, a slight drop from 1987's total but a considerable increase since the low in 1983 (Gallup & Elam, 1988). People living in large cities gave their public schools lower grades than people living in the suburbs or rural areas. When asked to rate the nation's schools, only 23 percent gave the schools a good or excellent rating. People tend to see their own local schools as better than the nation's schools.

True or False More than half the parents of schoolchildren consider their local schools good or excellent.

When asked what they thought were the biggest problems in the public schools in their local communities, people most often mentioned use of drugs, lack of discipline, lack of proper financial support, difficulty getting good teachers, poor curriculum/poor standards, parents' lack of interest, and moral standards (see Table 1.3). In the seventeen Gallup polls taken before 1986, the public identified discipline as the biggest problem (except in 1971, when lack of proper financing was first). Today, the public clearly sees drug use as the greatest difficulty facing schools.

True or False American adults see discipline as the greatest problem facing education in the United States.

Table 1.1 Comparisons of Models

These four theories have the greatest impact on educational psychology. They can all be useful to the classroom teacher.

	Behavioral Theory	Social-Learning Theory	Informational-Processing Theory	Developmental Theory
Knowledge	When two behaviors occur together many times, they are associated with one another. Later, when one occurs, the other is recalled.	We observe the actions and the reactions of others. One learns by imitating physical, cognitive, and social skills.	People actively select sensory information for attention. Some of the stimuli are encoded into long-term memory. Others are not retained.	We are biologically programmed to learn through genetic structures. Through maturation and through interaction with the environment, we develop more complex knowledge structures.
Environment	Learning is a function of the environment. Stimuli that reinforce other events or other stimuli facilitate learning. Events that are not reinforced are not learned.	Behaviors that are observed are models for subsequent behavior. The available models in the environment shape what is learned.	The individual imposes meaning on the environment. Given the same environment, two different people will have different perceptions.	Although the individual interacts with the environment, the interpretation of the interaction changes as the individual matures.
Teacher's Functions	Learning controlled through manipulation of learning experiences. Teachers must reinforce desirable learning behaviors.	Teachers serve as role models for learning. Therefore, they must consciously demonstrate desirable learning behavior.	Teachers must focus students' attention on meaningful environmental stimuli and then monitor students' perceptions of those stimuli.	Teachers must design tasks that are appropriate for students' level of development and guide students' progress.

Adapted with permission from *Touch the Future: Teach!* by W. R. Houston, R. T. Clift, H. J. Freiberg, and A. R. Warner, p. 76. Copyright © 1988 by West Publishing Company. All rights reserved.

If the public's rating of education has improved since 1983 and now seems to have hit a plateau, this is not the case with the press. The other day I was looking through the education section of my local library, and almost every title seemed to scream the message that the schools are failing and that there is a continuing crisis in education. Almost weekly, the public is bombarded by the disappointing findings from research studies showing that students are not learning effectively. Many of these findings appear in newspapers. When American 13-year-olds were compared with their cohorts in six other countries in mathematics and science knowledge, Americans fared poorly. Only 40 percent of the U.S. students could perform two-step mathematics problems, while 78 percent of South Korean pupils succeeded on this task (Rothman, 1988).

In a study conducted of 8,000 high school juniors by the National Endowment for the Humanities National Assessment of Educational Progress, one in three did not know when Columbus discovered America. The students were not asked to identify the exact year; their answers had to be within fifty years of the correct date. About one in three could not recognize the two countries that were the United States' principal enemies in World War II, and more than a third did not know what checks and balances are. About 90 percent could not identify "To be or not to be" as a quotation from *Hamlet* (Finn & Ravitch, 1987).

Another study of high school students conducted

	National Totals %	No Children in School %	Public School Parents %	Nonpublic School Parents %
A + B	40	37	51	33
A	9	8	13	8
B	31	29	38	25
C	34	34	36	37
D	10	10	8	21
FAIL	4	4	4	4
Don't know	12	15	1	5

	Ratings Given the Local Public Schools										
	1988 %	1987 %	1986 %	1985 %	1984 %	1983 %	1982 %	1981 %	1980 %	1979 %	1978 %
A + B	40	43	41	49	42	31	37	36	35	34	36
A	9	12	11	9	10	6	8	9	10	8	9
B	31	31	30	34	32	25	29	27	25	26	27
C	34	30	28	30	35	32	33	34	29	30	30
D	10	9	11	10	11	13	14	13	12	11	11
FAIL	4	4	5	4	4	7	5	7	6	7	8
Don't know	12	14	15	13	8	17	11	10	18	18	15

by the Joint Council on Economic Education found that most students don't understand basic economic terms, and another study found that 20 percent of Americans in their twenties could not read at an eighth-grade level (Newsday, Jan. 27, 1989).

The study that had the greatest impact, however, was entitled *A Nation at Risk*, which publicized the results of eighteen months of study by a panel called the National Commission on Excellence in Education appointed by the Secretary of Education in 1981. The commission documented many problems in the educational system and recommended, among other things, stricter requirements for graduation, especially in English, mathematics, science, foreign language, and social studies; a lengthening of the school year; and curricula reform. It is clear that there has

never been more public scrutiny of education at any time in our history.

The newspapers and many reports tend to focus on the negative aspects of the educational situation. Sometimes these reports give the impression that things were better in "the good old days," when everyone could read and solve mathematics problems and graduated with honors and teachers were more dedicated. However, this is not so. In "the good old days" segregation was rampant, students with disabilities were often denied an equal access to education, and the graduation rates from high school were low. Studies show that creativity and reasoning skills have improved since the 1960s (Flanagan, 1983). In addition, the country's commitment to equal opportunity has not been adequately covered. The public hardly gets

Table 1.3   The Public's Opinion of the Nation's Problems
What do you think are the biggest problems with which the public schools in this community must deal?

	National Totals %	No Children in School %	Public School Parents %	Nonpublic School Parents %
Use of drugs	32	34	30	29
Lack of discipline	19	20	15	25
Lack of proper financial support	12	10	17	11
Difficulty getting good teachers	11	10	11	13
Poor curriculum/poor standards	11	11	11	14
Parents' lack of interest	7	7	7	6
Moral standards	6	6	7	2
Large schools/overcrowding	6	4	10	9
Pupils' lack of interest/truancy	5	6	4	5
Drinking/alcoholism	5	5	6	6
Low teacher pay	4	3	7	5
Integration/busing	4	4	3	3
Teachers' lack of interest	3	3	3	8
Crime/vandalism	3	3	2	1
Lack of needed teachers	2	1	3	2
Lack of respect for teachers/other students	2	2	1	2
Fighting	1	2	1	1
Lack of proper facilities	1	1	3	3
Mismanagement of funds/programs	1	1	1	1
Problems with administration	1	1	1	1
Communication problems	1	1	1	*
Parents' involvement in school activities	1	1	1	*
Lack of after-school programs	1	*	1	1
Too many schools/declining enrollment	1	*	1	*
School board politics	1	1	1	1
There are no problems	2	2	4	3
Miscellaneous	5	4	6	4
Don't know	10	12	4	5

*Less than one-half of 1%.
(Figures add to more than 100% because of multiple answers.)
Reprinted with permission from "The 20th Annual Poll of the Public's Attitudes Towards the Public Schools," *Phi Delta Kappan.* Copyright © 1988 Phi Delta Kappan, Inc.

a balanced view of the schools from the media, because negative information seems to receive more attention than positive achievements.

True or False The public receives a balanced view from the news media of how students are doing in school.

Almost all states have initiated reforms in response to the recommendations made by the National Commission on Excellence in Education and to other task force reports. These reforms often have meant greater emphasis on monitoring student achievement and teaching the basics. Some evidence exists that such efforts are having some effect, since the scores on the Iowa Test of Basic Skills that began to decline in 1963 have now improved (Stedman & Kaesle, 1985). Scores on the SAT and ACT have also reached their lowest point and some improvement has been noted. However, the reforms have been test driven; that is, the emphasis on accountability and showing that education is working is more dependent upon results of certain tests than ever before.

Although objectively measuring improvements in reading or mathematics is certainly in order, many teachers now complain that all they are asked to do is "teach to the test." It seems that we may be in danger of entering a phase of "if you can't directly measure it, it doesn't exist." In addition, this test-driven success or failure concept means that the technical construction of the test becomes crucial and more arguments concerning the nature of various tests can be expected.

These critical studies are often reported in the newspapers without much comment, and criticisms of the studies are not given equal time. Many of the reports have concentrated on distinct factual information which no doubt is important but is only one part of the educational process. Ayers (1987) suggests that one report that received a great deal of attention, entitled "What Our Seventeen-Year-Olds Know," amounted to little more than a trivia test. Others suggest that even the famous *A Nation at Risk* report overgeneralized and emphasized only the welfare of college-bound students as the criterion for judging success (Albrecht, 1984). Many of the remedies pointed out are either very expensive or unrealistic (Ornstein, 1985). Last, these reports paint a negative picture of education with a broad brush, ignoring the fact that many schools do work well and many teachers work very effectively.

Despite the emphasis on the negative in the media and in some reports, the public seems to have gained confidence in their local schools. States and local districts have taken action to tighten up requirements. It must be remembered, however, that the school is asked by society to do much more than impart facts. Schools are also asked to encourage positive attitudes, tolerance, and good health habits in their students and to help students develop morals and values. Such virtues are not always easily measured. After looking at the diverse forces bombarding the schools, it is clear that teachers have the attention and some measure of support from, in addition to the scrutiny by, the community.

Educational Psychology and the Concerns of Teachers

Imagine that you have landed the job you want. You are going to teach your subject in the school of your choice. What are your chief concerns? The eight most often noted concerns of beginning teachers are classroom discipline, motivating students, dealing with individual differences, assessing students' work, relationships with parents, organizing classwork, insufficient or inadequate teaching materials and supplies, and dealing with problems of individual students (Veenman, 1984). These concerns are similar for both elementary and secondary teachers.

When teachers who subscribe to the publication *Learning* were sent a questionnaire concerning their professional concerns, they reported that finding time to accomplish all their objectives, having too many nonprofessional duties, teaching children who have problems outside of school, working in overcrowded classrooms, and getting support and cooperation from parents and administrators were their greatest problems (Turner, 1987a, 1987b) (see Figure 1.1).

Educational psychologists have long realized the importance and difficulty of the transition from student, or even student-teacher, to teacher. The reality shock is well documented in the literature. Two problems causing this shock are classroom management and motivating students (Kearney et al., 1988). Elementary schoolteachers seem to have less reality shock than secondary schoolteachers, and teachers in urban areas experience more than teachers in suburban and rural areas (Marso & Pigge, 1987). Many new teachers state a desire for more practical help in

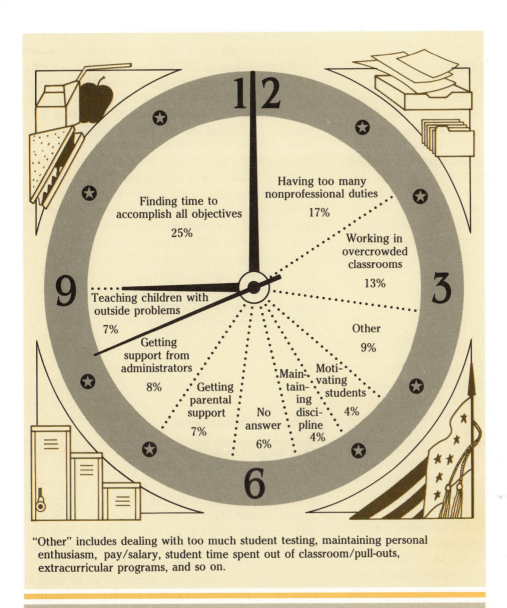

Finding time to accomplish all objectives 25%

Having too many nonprofessional duties 17%

Working in overcrowded classrooms 13%

Teaching children with outside problems 7%

Other 9%

Getting support from administrators 8%

Getting parental support 7%

No answer 6%

Main-tain-ing disci-pline 4%

Moti-vating students 4%

"Other" includes dealing with too much student testing, maintaining personal enthusiasm, pay/salary, student time spent out of classroom/pull-outs, extracurricular programs, and so on.

Figure 1.1   Teachers' Biggest Problems
Teachers respond to the question, "What is your single greatest problem?"

Adapted with permission from the March issue of *Learning 87*. Copyright © 1987. Springhouse Corporation, 1111 Bethlehem Pike, Springhouse, PA. All rights reserved.

their educational training and report their relationships with other teachers and administrators more helpful and better than they had expected (Marso & Pigge, 1987). Educational psychologists have listened and, more than ever before, have related research results directly back to the teacher as a way of offering practical help in the classroom. In addition, some schools have begun mentoring programs in which an experienced teacher is asked to help a new teacher. These programs may help the new teacher cope with the problems often encountered in the first year of teaching.

EMERGING AREAS OF EDUCATIONAL PSYCHOLOGY

Educational psychology is a dynamic area that has been responsive to changes in both the educational environment and society. New areas are emerging while older, more traditional areas continue to evolve. As we've already seen, one emerging theoretical/research area that has affected education is the cognitive revolution. Six other emerging areas are the use of technology in the classroom, teaching children with exceptional needs, classroom management, morals/values education, testing and evaluation, and parent-teacher relationships.

Computers and Education

For children growing up today, a knowledge of computers is more than just valuable, it is absolutely necessary. It is estimated that in 1985, there were one million computers in schools; in 1986, two million computers were being used. In 1987, that figure jumped to four million, and the trend continues (Callison, 1988). Computers have obviously affected every aspect of our lives, and more and more people will use computers in their jobs. Computer instruction can be seen as either teaching about computers or teaching with computers (Brownell, 1987). The first involves knowing what a computer can do, learning how to operate one, and understanding how the computer can aid in particular tasks. It may also include a knowledge of the limitations of computers. Teaching with computers—sometimes called computer-aided instruction (CAI)—involves presenting new material or performing drill, practice, tutorials, simulations, and instructional games with the aid of a computer. CAI may also include the use of computers as word processors for both teachers and students. Because of the importance of the use of technology in education, an entire chapter (Chapter 12) is devoted to the topic, including a discussion not only of computers but also of instructional television and films.

Teaching Children with Exceptional Needs

To receive an appropriate education, a little more than 10 percent of all children in our public schools require a modification of their educational environment. The three most common groups of students with exceptional needs are those with learning disabilities, language and speech impairment, and mental retardation. If the gifted were placed in these ranks of exceptional children, they would rank third, after learning disabilities and language and speech impairment and before mental retardation (Heward & Orlansky, 1988).

About 75 percent of all learning-disabled students are mainstreamed to some degree. That is, they spend at least part of their time in a regular classroom setting. Almost every elementary schoolteacher and most secondary schoolteachers can expect to serve children with exceptional needs during their career. Teachers are also expected to refer students for evaluation. Chapter 13 discusses ways to work in the regular classroom setting with students with exceptional needs.

True or False About 75 percent of all disabled students are mainstreamed, that is, placed for some time during the schoolday in a regular classroom.

Classroom Management

Over the past thirty years, interest in classroom management and teacher-student interaction has increased greatly (Ash & Love-Clark, 1985). This interest is partly a response to the public's interest in school discipline and the concern expressed by both new and experienced teachers. The research in this field is divided into two parts. First, a number of studies have investigated the differences in the way effective and ineffective classroom managers try to prevent difficulties. These studies point to some very practical and realistic measures that teachers can take. Second, new techniques from both the behavioral and cognitive viewpoints for handling misbehavior once it has occurred have been advanced. Chapter 10 discusses both prevention of and strategies for coping with classroom management problems.

Morals/Values Education

After a relatively long absence, morals and values education is in the headlines again. The public seems ready to give the school an increasing role in developing morals and values in their children. This readiness is more a rediscovery of mission than anything else, because almost every state charter cites one responsibility of the schools as instilling morals and values. The difference is that educators have gone beyond mere lecture and have now formulated some promising techniques that are quite controversial.

Health and welfare concerns have also taken center stage with the advent of AIDS, the concern of teenage pregnancy and drug abuse, and the recognition that teachers have a responsibility in identifying child abuse. Morals and values education and health and welfare concerns are covered in Chapter 7.

True or False   The idea that the schools should play an active part in developing the morals and values of students has been increasing in popularity among the public.

Testing and Evaluation

The traditional concern of educational psychology for testing and evaluation has had a new infusion of life poured into it lately. As noted, much of the educational reform in the 1980s is test driven. Minimum competency tests and standardized achievement test results are of great importance to teachers and their school districts. More interest is also being taken in the classroom measurement of learning and grading as well as teaching test-taking skills. Evaluation is covered in Chapters 14 and 15.

Parent-Teacher Relationships

When 2,000 intermediate and secondary schoolteachers were surveyed, one of the glaring problems they identified was their lack of communication with their students' parents (Chase, 1986). They felt they did not know many parents and that parents did not know much about the school. It comes as no surprise that the home makes an important contribution to the educational success of the child. Parents are often interested in their children's progress but may not know what to do or how to help their children. Teachers often ask parents to help by reading aloud to their children, signing homework papers, and drilling their children in mathematics and spelling. They also encourage parents to discuss school activities with their children. Help with problem behavior is often required. However, communicating with parents and

gaining their support is a skill. Some necessary communication skills are discussed in Chapter 9.

The family situation of many children in the 1990s is not what it was in the 1950s. Many present-day students come from one-parent families and stepfamilies, and increasing numbers of students will be called upon to care for themselves and their younger siblings after school. The school-family relationship is discussed extensively in Chapter 6.

THE VALUE OF RESEARCH IN EDUCATION

In all of the preceding areas, teachers can use information gleaned from research. In addition, a great deal of research has been performed relating specific teaching practices to improved student achievement (Brophy & Good, 1986). Some of this research is discussed in Chapter 11. Teachers can use the research to improve their skills (Erickson, 1986), although some unfortunately do not.

Instructor magazine published the responses of experienced teachers who were asked what their experiences had taught them. Teachers offered a number of comments, among them, "I've learned to give kids time to think after I ask a question," "I call parents when children do something well," and "I've learned to be consistent, to offer students routines and discipline" (Lynn, 1986). Such practices have been extensively researched and suggested by educational psychologists for years. Research in educational psychology can be of use to teachers. Specific research methods and problems faced by researchers are reviewed in the appendix.

 **CONNECTIONS**

How to Tell Good Research from Poor Research

If teachers are to use research, they must be able to differentiate between good research and research that is poorly designed and conducted. Using research isn't always easy, and people reading studies are often put off by the statistics. One student asked, "Since I am not an expert in statistics, how can I be expected to evaluate research?" In many cases, one doesn't have to be an expert in statistics to evaluate research. A person can ask a number of questions to enable him or her to separate good from poor research.

1. **Is the problem well stated?** Each study is designed to answer some research question. The statement of the problem should be clear and to the point.

2. **Is the research review coherent, and does it cover the topic?** Studies usually have extensive reviews of the literature on the topic. These reviews should be relatively easy to follow and organized in a way that shows that the present study is based upon other work in the field.

3. **Are the hypotheses clear?** Many researchers base their hypotheses on the theoretical view they are taking and an analysis of past research. The hypotheses should not take you by surprise. They should come directly from the reasoning shown in the description of the problem and review of the literature.

4. **Are the major elements in the study defined in such a way that they can be easily tested?** You should have no difficulty picking out the variables and defining them in a way that allows easy measurement. If the definitions are "fuzzy" or incapable of independent measurement, the study is open to misinterpretation.

5. **How was the sample chosen? Is the sample representative of the population?** The answer to these questions will determine to what extent the results can be generalized to other groups.

6. **Is the method clear?** The method by which the study is conducted should be so clear that you could easily replicate the study without having to ask any further questions of the researcher.

7. **Are the measurement devices being used described?** Some background as to the usefulness of the measuring instruments should be discussed. In addition, there should be no doubt that the devices measure what the researcher is trying to measure. For example, if a study is measuring the effects of praise on grades, it is reasonable to look at end-of-term marks or even students' scores on standardized achievement tests. However, the use of an intelligence test would not do, since intelligence tests purport to measure aptitude, not achievement.

8. **Are the results organized so that they are easily understood?** Although not everyone will have the sophistication to evaluate the statistical treatments used, the organization of the results should be logical and the results reported in an orderly fashion.

9. **Do the researcher's discussions of the results and implications of the study realistically reflect what the study has actually shown?** In the discussion portion, researchers do exactly that—they discuss their results. They write about the implications of the study and discuss applications. They may also give some tentative reasons for their findings or lack of findings. All opinions should be labeled opinions and should reflect the results of the study.

Teachers and Research

After demonstrating that research can be useful to the classroom teacher, it is only fair to ask, "How do teachers feel about educational research?" Unfortunately, not very positively, according to most attitude research (Isakson & Ellsworth, 1979). The public also is skeptical about research in education and educational psychology, and research rarely gets any credit for improving education in America (Finn, 1988). Often, teachers find research reports long and difficult to get through, and some research simply is not directed toward practical classroom situations. Classroom teachers also sometimes perceive researchers as having little understanding of the daily classroom problems.

True or False Most teachers hold positive attitudes toward education research.

On their side, researchers admit that they have no easy recipes or magic pills for making classroom teachers more effective. Researchers also admit that they seem to have some difficulty talking the language of classroom teachers and adequately communicating with them. In addition, not all educational psychology research is aimed at practical classroom help. Some is directed at investigating basic learning processes and is vital to the future well-being of the field. Often such research forms the basis for more practical future research. Finally, researchers receive comparatively little feedback from teachers.

In this state of affairs, it is clear that both the researcher and the classroom teacher need to communicate better. Teachers need to remain open-minded about the help the researcher can provide, while researchers must find better ways to communicate with the classroom teacher and show they understand the realities of the classroom situation.

Research can help teachers, but research findings should not be turned into rigid directives. The problem in doing this is aptly described by Myers (1986), using the example of "time on task," which has become a popular phrase in American education. The amount of time the students spend attending to academic tasks (engaged time) depends on the amount of time the teacher assigns to such tasks (allocated time) as well as a number of other factors, including the nature of the interactions between teacher and student and the way the lesson is presented. The concept of time on task has a great deal to offer but was turned into mandated policy, with one state training administrators and teacher evaluators to record on-task and off-task behavior in the classroom. This policy required the school principal to make four sweeps of the classroom using a checklist type of instrument. Administrators were so busy checking one thing or the other that they could not watch for the quality or the substance of the lesson. Research advice should not turn into rigid mandates.

Research can offer teachers specific and valuable advice. If it's known that teachers often go from one topic to another and back (a flip-flop) and that this practice leads to confusion, instructors can eliminate the practice. If it's known that going over the rules and practicing procedures, such as lining up in elementary school, is important to maintaining discipline, teachers can find ways to do it. If it's known that teachers do not use praise very often, teachers can be encouraged to increase the use of praise. But is this type of scientific research the answer to improving teaching?

Teaching: An Art, A Science, or Both?

The debate over whether teaching is an art, a science, or both has been raging for many years. The implications are important. If education is a science, then through the process of scientific inquiry insights can be gained that can be used to guide teachers. In other words, certain definite principles can be used in a number of classrooms that may differ in many ways. Teachers then would be seen as having a set of specific skills and knowledge that can be taught and measured (Billups & Rauth, 1987). On the other side, some argue that the classroom is too dynamic to yield to scientific inquiry and that teaching is an art based upon style and creativity. Which viewpoint is correct?

There *is* science in education. Research has demonstrated principles, many of which are not "common sense" that can be applied to the classroom. A number of scientifically devised principles of classroom management that have been formulated and can be taught to new teachers may serve to prevent classroom misbehavior. The practical implications of research concerning ways to begin a new term (Emmer et al., 1980), teacher praise (Brophy, 1981), direct instruction, cooperative team learning, and student motivation have been useful when taught to new teachers.

On the other side, the search for significant principles involved in teaching has led some to complain that the art of teaching is being ignored. Some see the intangibles of teaching as being artistry, and these intangibles go beyond charisma and style.

Great teachers may neither teach in the same way nor embrace the same beliefs about education. The qualities that form the basis of teaching are intangible because they are imprecise, yet they still exist. If they cannot be easily found, can they be taught or cultivated? The answer, according to one writer in the field, is yes (Rubin, 1983). Teachers who are given some training in theatre arts and staging, humor, and the use of novelty and creativity to heighten interest are able to improve in these areas. Teachers who attain the highest level of artistry make teaching decisions intuitively, are confident in their competence, and are imaginative. Teachers can also gain from watching creative and imaginative teachers teach and can learn through communicating with such teachers. Perhaps the greatest objection to the scientific look at education is that it may lead to a group of do's and don'ts and the art and creativity of teaching will be glossed over.

By looking at fragments of good teaching, we may lose our understanding of the integrity of the whole lesson. In teaching, the whole may be greater than the sum of its parts. According to this view, the skills of teaching cannot be treated as discrete elements and formed together to show what teaching is. The artist in the classroom invents new ways of doing things, and teaching will never be routine.

With these seemingly opposing viewpoints, can we find some harmony? Even those who wish to emphasize the personal, the creative, and the art of teaching believe that scientific research can play a role in educational progress. They mostly fear overdependency, fragmentation, and the lack of appreciation

Teachers certainly possess many skills, but is teaching too dynamic to yield to scientific inquiry?

for creativity. Scientific researchers often note that their research can be used to identify features of practices and processes that teachers need to consider. The question of how to apply these rules or principles, however, is up to the individual teacher (Evertson, 1987). For example, research shows that teachers do better when they plan rules and procedures for general classroom organizations, present rules to students in some way along with expectations for appropriate performance, monitor students, and provide feedback. However, there are many ways in which this can be done, and what may work for one teacher may not work for another.

Research provides the information, but the artistry in teaching determines how each teacher will utilize it. Even while appreciating the science of teaching, the specific art of the teacher who tries to help Sarah learn her multiplication tables in a creative way should be appreciated. It is for that reason that reading what other teachers have done and found successful may be important, even if these ideas have not been subjected to scientific scrutiny. If you try something new, you may find that it works for you or that it is a dismal failure. You may also find that you must modify it to work for your style and your goals. Thus, teaching is both a science and an art.

THE PLAN OF THIS BOOK

This text presents the scientifically derived principles and research in educational psychology as well as the practical implications and suggestions that come directly from this work. At the same time, the unique creativity of the teacher is appreciated. Although suggestions are given, they are offered not as something to imitate blindly but as something to try and to adapt to individual style and needs.

This book is divided into five parts. Part One covers cognitive development, information processing, language, creativity, thinking and cognitive styles and, the behavioral approach to education. Part Two investigates social and moral development, including the school's role in social development; the meaning for the teacher of social changes such as divorce, the latchkey situation, and day care; and the school's role in developing students' values and attitudes. Part Three looks at the dynamics of teacher-student interaction, including motivation, communication both with students and with parents, and the area of classroom management that emphasizes both preventing classroom problems and dealing with those problems that do arise. Part Four looks at effective teaching techniques, including objectives and modes of teaching, the emerging area of the use of technology in education, and effective ways to teach children with exceptional needs. Part Five examines evaluation through the use of standardized tests and classroom testing and grading.

Each chapter begins with twelve true-false statements. You are asked to note whether these statements are true or false. The answers are found on the following page. The statements are repeated following the paragraph in the body of the text where material relating to these statements can be found. Throughout the chapter, the material is organized in such a way that the research and its implications are discussed. At intervals within the chapter, a "Connections" feature discusses specifically how the material can be used to improve classroom instruction. All key terms are presented in boldface and defined in a running glossary, and then a consolidated glossary is presented at the end of the text. A point-by-point summary can be found at the end of each chapter. In addition, "Activities and Exercises" and "Scenarios" features are presented at the conclusion of each chapter. The "Activities and Exercises" feature suggests ways that you may go beyond the text and find out more for yourself. The "Scenarios" feature presents brief cases and asks you to figure out some constructive ways to deal with each situation. For many of these cases, there is no single answer, but they will all serve to encourage you to think about what you would do in similar circumstances.

One of the most challenging aspects of teaching is the constant variety of circumstances and decisions that arise in the course of an average day. The fifth-grade teacher teaching a class on the American Revolution must take into consideration students' developmental level, prior knowledge, and interests, and consider the variety of ways that the material can be taught. The high school teacher teaching American history must do the same. It is this variety of experience, the activism of trying new approaches, and the conscious decisions that surround the activity of teaching that are celebrated in this book.

SUMMARY

1. Educational psychology is the field of psychology concerned with the development, evaluation, and application of theories and principles of human learning and instruction that can improve lifelong learning. Educational psychologists perform basic research in the areas of learning, cognition, and instruction as well as applied research aimed at providing answers to classroom teachers' concerns.

2. Teachers must make many decisions each day in their interactions with their students, and research from educational psychology can help teachers make wise, rational decisions.

3. The focus of educational psychology is influenced by advances in other areas of psychology and allied fields as well as the changing interests of the public and government leaders.

4. The greatest change in psychology in the past few decades is the growing interest in cognitive psychology. Cognition refers to the intellectual functions of the mind, including perception, memory, concept development, thinking, and problem solving. However, other models such as the behavioral model, which emphasizes the importance of the environment and its reinforcers; social learning, which emphasizes the importance of observational learning; and the developmental approach, which focuses on developmental changes that occur both socially and cognitively in childhood are also important.

5. The public ranks drugs, lack of discipline, lack of proper financial support, difficulty getting good teachers, poor curriculum/poor standards, parents' lack of interest, and moral standards as the most important problems facing education today.

6. A number of recent research studies have reported the inadequacies of education. Most states have initiated reforms in response to these reports, usually involving greater emphasis on monitoring student achievement and teaching the basics. More of an emphasis is being placed on testing than ever before.

7. The schools are asked to do more than teach facts, and developing attitudes, tolerance, good health habits, and morals and values are important goals of schooling as well.

8. Six emerging areas of educational psychology include the use of technology in education, teaching the child with exceptional needs in the regular classroom, classroom management, morals/values education, testing and evaluation, and parent-teacher relationships. These areas combine with the traditional areas of concern, such as motivation

and teaching methods, to cover many areas of practical interest to the teacher.

9. Through scientific research, we gain an understanding of the principles that may serve as guides in the classroom. However, the artistry of teaching and its creativity should not be forgotten.

ACTIVITIES AND EXERCISES

1. **Attitudes Toward Education.** Take a poll of your friends and acquaintances concerning their attitudes towards education. Three questions that should definitely be included are, How would you rate the nations' schools (excellent, good, fair, poor)? How do you rate your local schools? What are the three most serious problems that the nation's schools face? These questions are similar to those used in the Gallup poll described earlier in the chapter. Ask any other questions that might interest you.

2. **Is It Just Common Sense?** Ten statements were offered in this chapter to demonstrate that educational psychology is not just "common sense." It would be interesting to see just how many people believe these statements. Select people from all age groups and ask them to answer true or false to the statements. Determine which statements are believed by a majority of people you question. If you have a sufficient sample, you may want to analyze the answers by age.

3. **How Have You Changed?** If you have the opportunity, speak with experienced teachers and ask them, "What have you learned through your _____ years of teaching?" Other possible questions are, What do you wish they had taught you in your education and educational psychology courses that you learned during the actual experience of teaching? and How have you changed since you began teaching? As noted in the chapter, getting practical advice from teachers in the field is often helpful.

4. **Education Bashing.** When you find yourself in the public library, make a list of the titles in the education section. When you look at the list, see how many involve "crisis" or "failure" and how few seem to emphasize the positive aspects of schooling.

5. **What's New?** Seven emerging areas were noted in this chapter: the cognitive revolution, the use of technology in education, teaching children with exceptional needs, classroom management, morals/values education, testing and evaluation, and parent-teacher relationships. Leaf through some of your favorite newspapers or magazines, such as *Time, U.S. News and World Report,* and *Newsweek,* cut out the articles concerning education, and see how many fit into these emerging areas. Note any other areas where interest seems to be increasing.

6. **Parent-Teacher Relationships.** Communication between the school and parents is certainly an important issue. Parents want to know what is happening in the classroom and are generally interested in their children's progress. Some school districts and school PTAs sponsor a number of programs that offer parents an opportunity to learn about what is going on in the schools. These programs can include not only the familiar open-school week but also perhaps a night at the beginning of the year on which teachers tell parents what is going to be covered during the semester. In addition, numerous workshops may be offered. Find out what programs are available in your district, how they are publicized, and how well they are attended. If possible, interview an officer in the PTA and/or a person within the district who formulates school programs, asking specifically about the goals of the programs and any difficulties encountered in running the programs.

7. **Interviews.** Interview teachers with special responsibilities within a school that seem to flow from the emerging issues listed in number 5. For example, interview the computer coordinator of the school or district or a special education teacher. Focus the interview on what services are available for the classroom teacher.

8. **Attend a Conference.** Many conferences are held that may be of interest to teachers. Some are listed in journals, while others can be found in such publications as *Education Week.* Choose a conference that mirrors your area of interest and attend it.

9. **Where Can I Find the Research?** There are many journals and magazines of interest, and the only way to find which are most interesting and relevant to you is to leaf through them and read one or two articles. This is especially important, since such journal and magazine articles can help keep you in touch with what other teachers and re-

searchers are saying and doing after you enter the field. Some journals and interesting magazines include *Adolescence, American Educational Research Journal, Arithmetic Teacher, Childhood Education, Clearing House, Computers and Education, Educational Leadership, Elementary School Journal, High School Journal, Journal of Alcohol and Drug Education, Journal of Educational Research, Journal of Home Economics, Journal of Research in Science Teaching, Journal of Social Studies Research, Phi Delta Kappan, Review of Educational Research, Education Digest, Science Education,* and *Young Children.* There are many others. In addition, familiarize yourself with *Education Index,* which may be used to research an area of particular interest.

10. **Analyzing Research.** This chapter suggests nine questions that can be used to evaluate a research study. Using these nine questions, look up a research study in one of the journals mentioned and analyze it.

Cognition, Development, and Learning

2

Are These Statements True or False?

Turn the next page for the correct answers. Each statement is repeated following the paragraph in which the information can be found.

1. Students who are in one stage of cognitive development may either proceed to the next one or regress to an earlier one depending upon the environmental stimulation available.

2. The stage of cognitive development a student is negotiating is accurately determined by considering the student's chronological age.

3. During the preschool years, the child reasons in a manner that is qualitatively different from that of the average adult.

4. Young preschoolers believe that even inanimate objects are capable of being alive and conscious.

5. Elementary school students can solve abstract, hypothetical problems if they are given enough time to do so.

6. If a student is not reasoning at the same advanced level of his or her classmates, the best thing for a teacher to do is to wait for the child to mature.

7. Fifth- or sixth-grade elementary school students can be taught grammar because they have the cognitive ability to classify words into such categories as noun, verb, and adjective.

8. A child's understanding of numbers is reflected in the ability to count from one to twenty.

9. The ability to interpret proverbs or political cartoons develops during adolescence.

10. High school students suffer from an overly practical, down-to-earth way of viewing the political process and social problems.

11. It is normal for young children to use the incorrect forms of words, such as *goed* and *drinked* instead of *went* and *drank*.

12. Bilingualism itself leads to cognitive difficulties and academic problems.

Cognitive and Language Development

Answers to True-False Statements

1. *False* Correct statement: People cannot regress to an earlier stage, nor can they skip stages.
2. *False* Correct statement: Children enter and leave a particular stage at different times. Ages noted by most theorists are averages and are meant only as rough guides.
3. *True*
4. *True*
5. *False* Correct statement: Elementary school students cannot solve abstract, hypothetical problems even if they are given plenty of time to do so.
6. *False* Correct statement: Teachers may be more active by presenting students with challenging problems and need not simply "wait" for the child to mature.
7. *True*
8. *False* Correct statement: Children often learn to count through imitation. Counting itself does not necessarily demonstrate an understanding of numbers.
9. *True*
10. *False* Correct statement: Just the opposite is often the case. High school students tend to construct elaborate, hypothetical models without taking reality into consideration.
11. *True*
12. *False* Correct statement: Bilingualism itself does not lead to cognitive difficulties and academic problems.

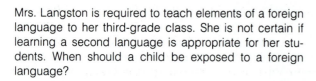

Mrs. Langston is required to teach elements of a foreign language to her third-grade class. She is not certain if learning a second language is appropriate for her students. When should a child be exposed to a foreign language?

Mr. Ioria has asked his fourth-grade class to bring in political cartoons and discuss them. He is disappointed that his students cannot understand the message behind the cartoons.

Mrs. Ennis claims that her five-year-old child can count from one to twenty and is now ready for addition and subtraction. She believes that the teacher is not teaching mathematics properly in kindergarten.

Mr. Leonard is teaching English to high school students. He is discussing *Hamlet* and compares it to other stories these students have read in the past. Are his students ready for discussions of character analysis and hypothetical discussions of plot alternatives?

Mrs. Green finds that her fourth-grade students use one or two words to answer her questions. They do not seem able to express themselves well. What can Mrs. Green do to encourage their linguistic abilities?

COGNITIVE FUNCTIONING AND TEACHING DECISIONS

Suppose in the midst of a teaching job interview you were asked to go into the next room and design a lesson on the causes of the American Revolution. If you were allowed to ask only one question concerning this task, what would it be? If you think about it, one vital piece of information you'd need is the students' level of cognitive functioning. You wouldn't teach the lesson the same way to fourth-graders as you would to junior high school students or to high school students. You would not expect students at different cognitive levels to reason in the same manner. Students at various developmental stages think differently and have varied abilities to process information. However, when asked to describe specifically what these differences are, many people lapse into silence. Yet, teachers must take these differences into account when planning lessons.

This chapter looks at children's cognitive and language development. It discusses in detail Jean Piaget's theory of cognitive development. Although Piaget's theory is not the only one to cover this important area, it is the most complete theory available at the present time. The chapter also looks closely at language development. Linguistic abilities are certainly essential to academic success. We use language to solve problems, express ourselves, and question and explore concepts. The goal of this chapter is not just to describe the general developmental trends that serve as useful guideposts for teachers but also to translate these trends into recommendations for teaching.

PIAGET'S THEORY OF COGNITIVE DEVELOPMENT

Children are not little adults! Perhaps you shrug your shoulders at this rather banal statement, but for years people did not understand that a child's way of thinking and dealing with problems is different from an adult's. They interpreted the differences between the thinking of children and that of adults as "mistakes" or as signs of stubbornness against growing up. Jean Piaget devoted his adult life to studying the cognitive (intellectual) development of children, including how children think and develop their notions of time, space, mathematics, and reality. Piaget's work is monumental, and his discoveries have a number of important implications for teaching.

Caution Ahead

A couple of cautions are required whenever Piaget's theory is discussed within the framework of educational psychology. First, Piaget did not write "how to" books for educators. There are very few references to reading in Piaget's work, and Piaget never conducted any research into the mechanism behind children's learning to read (Wadsworth, 1978). Piaget did not, then, directly write about how to teach reading or science but rather described in detail the development of children's cognitive abilities from infancy through adolescence. When he did discuss education, he advocated that educators take advantage of the "new" knowledge about cognitive development that he and others had discovered (Piaget, 1970). In this area, Piaget had some very definite beliefs. It remained for others to take his ideas and apply them directly to curricula development and classroom instruction.

Second, no program of instruction can be purely Piagetian, because the theory does not encompass all aspects of development or of educational practice (DeVries & Kohlberg, 1987). Piagetian theory as applied to education has much to recommend it, but it should not be thought of as complete in and of itself. Even so, Piaget's ideas are so challenging that they deserve a prominent place in educational psychology.

Basic Concepts in Piaget's Theory

An appreciation of Piaget's ideas must begin with an explanation of the basic concepts of his theory.

What Is Knowledge?

For most people, knowledge is a set of facts or concepts that an individual has been taught. This rather static view of knowledge allows only for adding more facts to one's storehouse. To Piaget, though, knowledge is equated with action. As Robert Thomas (1979, p. 29) notes, "To know something means to act on that thing, with the action being either physical, mental or both." The second-grader's knowledge of a crystal is based upon the interaction between the child and the object. Therefore, the relationships between a child and any object is not stable (Piaget, 1970, p. 196). It changes as the child matures and becomes more experienced. Knowledge, then, is a process rather than some stable state. To try to put a number on intelligence ignores the changing nature of a child's interaction with the world. Piaget was interested in discovering the different ways children interacted with their world to create knowledge. As children mature, their ways of knowing the world change.

The Three Types of Knowledge

Piagetians believe that there are three types of knowledge: physical knowledge, logico-mathematical knowledge, and social-arbitrary knowledge (see Table 2.1). Each type of knowledge is dependent upon the active interaction of the child with his or her environment. **Physical knowledge** includes the

physical knowledge Knowledge about objects acquired through acting on objects and observing the result of the actions.

	Physical Knowledge	Logical-Mathematical Knowledge	Social-Arbitrary Knowledge
Defined	knowledge about the physical properties of objects	abstract knowledge	knowledge made by people
How acquired	discovered by actions on objects; objects are the source	invented from actions on objects; actions are the source	obtained from actions on and interactions with others; people are the source
Reinforcer	objects	objects	other people
Examples of areas of knowledge	size, color, texture, thickness, taste, sound, flexibility, density	number, mass, area, volume, length, class, order, time, speed, weight	language, moral rules, values, culture, history, symbol systems

From *Piaget for the Classroom Teacher* by B. J. Wadsworth. Copyright © 1978 by Longman Inc. Reprinted with permission of Longman Inc.

Jean Piaget's theory of cognitive development has had a major impact on educational thought.

nature of objects and learning how objects operate. Examples are knowing that a car has wheels that roll and that some objects sink and others float. Physical knowledge results directly from the child's acting on the objects. Such actions include, among others, touching, lifting, throwing, looking, and listening.

Physical knowledge is obtained through the process of discovery. The educational implication here is that students acquire knowledge about the physical attributes of objects by actively manipulating the objects. There are other ways of learning about objects, such as being told about them or even reading about them. However, these are not as potent, according to Piaget. Whenever possible, it is better for students to experience and actively discover than to be passively told about something.

Physical learning requires that the child have experience with concrete items, and the role of the teacher is to provide a number of opportunities for children to learn through discovery. This does not mean that all physical learning must occur through active manipulation. Telling a child that if he goes too near the kiln he will be burned is more practical than allowing students to learn this painful lesson for themselves.

The second type of knowledge is **logico-mathematical knowledge.** This type of knowledge involves

logico-mathematical knowledge   Knowledge acquired through creating and inventing relationships between objects and symbols.

inventing relationships between objects and symbols. It is the type of knowledge involved in understanding mathematics concepts. For example, let us say that a child is given seven buttons and from her own interaction she begins to understand that whether they are placed in a circle or a straight line there are still seven buttons. She has begun to understand the concept that no matter what display is made the number remains the same.

Logico-mathematical knowledge is involved when students classify objects (round ones and square ones), compare them (which is bigger or smaller), and evaluate different points of view. Piaget (1970) argues that the child gains this knowledge through invention; that is, the child deduces the relationships from his or her interactions with the objects in different circumstances. This cannot be taught by others. It is a complex process in which the child imposes an order upon the world. To invent such relationships, the child requires experience. Although Piaget differentiates discovery from invention, both of these components of knowledge require the active participation of the student, and the role of the teacher is one of facilitator and guide. Later in the chapter, we describe some activities that teachers can structure to provide the experiences necessary to encourage discovery and invention.

The third type of knowledge is **social-arbitrary knowledge.** This knowledge is based upon the child's active interactions with other people. Through social experience the child learns language, values, rules, and morals. Sometimes this type of knowledge results from being told a fact: that a test tube is used for laboratory purposes and not as a cup. Social-arbitrary knowledge involves learning social customs in addition to learning skills, facts, and dates (Peterson & Felton-Collins, 1986). This requires active teaching and corresponds to the more traditional framework of education. Piaget's theory does not deal extensively in this area. In fact, Piaget deemphasized the importance of learning facts, dates, and rules.

Traditionally, education has not differentiated

---

social-arbitrary knowledge Knowledge acquired from other people including their customs, language, and values.

---

among these three components of learning. Educators have been much more interested in the last component. Although Piaget relegated it to a distinctly secondary status, we need not always do so. As discussed in a number of sections in this text, providing students with a knowledge base is an important area of concern for educators. However, knowledge of facts and rules is not enough. Often studies of educational outcomes have measured discrete knowledge, such as "Who was the President of the United States during World War I?" As noted in Chapter one, the results of such studies have not always been favorable. However, Piaget reminds us that discrete knowledge is not the sole goal of all education. Nor is it the only type of knowledge, and educators have a responsibility in other areas as well. Each of the three types of knowledge requires a different process of learning by the student.

Piaget emphasized the importance of active experience both with objects and with other people. Although Piaget did deemphasize the learning of facts, he realized that specific content was important. What he was really advocating was a "balance being struck, varying from subject to subject between the different parts to be played by memorization and free activity" (Piaget, 1972).

Piaget argues that it is through students' experience that knowledge exists. For instance, perhaps students are going to study different classes of birds. Active experiences with birds—holding them, feeding them, watching their behavior—will form the basis for this knowledge. In fact, many people, when asked what they remember most positively from their school experiences, often mention some active experience. The area of experiential learning is now becoming more popular both in the academic and morals/values areas (see Chapters 11 and 6). The teacher, then, in the Piagetian perspective, encourages students to interact and discover. These are the general methods through which children learn about their world.

Cognitive Development in Children

If knowledge is based upon the child's ever-changing interactions with the world, then as the child develops, these interactions will change. No one seriously believes that the infant, the preschooler, the school-age child, or the adolescent sees the world in the same way or interacts with objects in the exact same manner. Therefore, to understand how the child's interactions change, one must understand development. According to Piaget, development involves continuous alteration and reorganization of the ways in which people deal with the environment (Piaget, 1970), and all learning rests on development.

Development is defined by four principal factors: maturation, experience, social transmission, and the process of equilibration. **Maturation** involves the unfolding of the genetic plan for life (Hottinger, 1970). This master plan, which functions as a timetable of sorts, largely (but not entirely) determines when a certain event will occur. The genetic master plan may also place limits on the speed of progress. For example, before a baby can walk, he or she needs to have strength and balance, which are determined largely by maturation. A child is ready to walk only after these prerequisites are met. A student can learn to read only when his or her eyes are developed to a point that they allow the student to focus on the words and the student's brain is able to process the information. Maturation is a most important factor in infancy and becomes somewhat less important from a Piagetian point of view with age (Gorman, 1972) as other factors become more important.

The second factor, experience, involves the active interaction of the child with the environment. It is this factor that Piaget believes is so important. The third factor, social transmission, refers to the information and customs that are transmitted from parents and other people in the child's environment. This is what is commonly meant by education and learning, but as we've seen, Piaget argues that the provision of facts and rules is only one—and not the most important—part of development.

Finally, the process of equilibration defines development. **Equilibration** is the process by which children seek a balance between what they know and

---

maturation A term used to describe changes that are due to the unfolding of the genetic plan.

equilibration The process by which children seek a balance between what they know and what they are experiencing.

---

what they are experiencing. When children are faced with information that calls for a new and different analysis or activity, they enter a state of disequilibrium. When this occurs, they must change the way they deal with the information to establish a new, more stable state of equilibrium. In this way, children progress from a very limited ability to deal with new experiences to a more mature, sophisticated level of cognitive functioning. For example, let us say that a child believes that heavy things are big and light things are small. The child is introduced to a styrofoam beam. The beam looks like wood but isn't. The child is forced into disequilibrium and is motivated internally to find out more and establish a new equilibrium. This he does by changing his ideas.

To Piaget, children are not simply passive receivers of stimulation. Children actively interact with the environment, and their active experiences impel them to new heights in cognitive functioning and action. Therefore, the child's cognitive development is based not only on information directly and formally transmitted from parents and teachers to the child but also on the child's personal experiences. It again follows that teachers must provide activities that will challenge students to think and experience rather than simply supply students with facts and information. Learning, then, is something that students actively do for themselves, not something that is done to them by others.

Organization and Adaptation

Two of the most important concepts in Piagetian theory are organization and adaptation. First, people must organize their knowledge in a way that makes the knowledge useful. Second, every organism must adapt to its environment to survive (Phillips, 1975). Adaptation can be understood in terms of adjustment. As the forces in the environment change, so must the individual's ability to deal with them.

Organization: Cognitive Structures and Schemata

Watch a three-year-old try to pick up a block. The child easily uses thumb and fingers, examines the block, and places it on top of another block. The blocks are combined in a primitive way to form a building. It is easy to forget the tortuous steps that led to the child's behavior. Hand the block to an infant, and the infant places it in her mouth. Infants explore their environment in their own way by sucking on it. Sucking is an example of what Piaget calls a schema.

As children develop, they perceive and deal with the world in more sophisticated ways. Piaget uses the term **schema** to describe an organized system of actions and thoughts useful for dealing with the environment that can be generalized to many situations (Piaget, 1952). These schemata (the plural of schema) are the cognitive structures that underlie patterns of behavior.

Younger children have qualitatively different schemata from those of older children. That is, their way of organizing material and responding to the environment differs as they progress through various stages of development. For instance, the infant given a block may place it in her mouth and suck on it. This is the sucking schema. When given other items, she may suck on them too. The infant is also the master of other schemata, including looking, listening, grasping, hitting, and pushing. Preschoolers and school-age children have developed still other schemata, some involving language.

Schemata are tools for learning about the world, and they become more involved as the child matures and develops new schemata. These cognitive structures can be thought of as actions and strategies that children use to understand and deal with their world and that form the bases for later thought. For Piaget, development is the gradual and continuous change in schemata. In infancy, the schemata are all basic and involve types of overt behavior, such as sucking and picking things up, while later on they become more symbolic and mental. The eight-year-old given a block can mentally operate on the block. He can imagine placing two blocks together and taking them apart. He does not always have to physically do so. These symbolic schemata that characterize older children are referred to as operations.

An **operation** is an internalized action that is part of the child's cognitive structure. Such actions include plans or rules for solving problems (Piaget, 1974). For example, Piaget wrote extensively about the operational schema of reversibility, that is, being able to return to one's point of origin. If 3 plus 5 equals 8, then subtracting 5 from 8 will leave 3. You can add something to the 3 and then take it away and think your way from one condition to another and then return to the starting point (Phillips, 1975). Such an understanding is very important in mathematics where we want students to be aware of the relationship between addition and subtraction.

As children develop, their cognitive structures become more and more similar to those of adults. For instance, consider what happens when a magnet is given to children at different stages of development. The infant merely puts the magnet in his mouth or perhaps bangs it against the floor. The three-year-old might realize that some objects stick to or want to stay with the magnet. The nine-year-old child realizes that certain objects with certain characteristics are attracted to the magnet, and she tests out which ones and at which distances. The adolescent forms an abstract theory of magnetism that involves the size and shape of the magnet and distance from the object (Miller, 1989). As children develop, then, their cognitive structures or abilities to deal with the outside world change, and they develop more and more sophisticated strategies for dealing with information.

Adaptation

The second major concept in Piagetian theory is adaptation, which involves two complementary processes: assimilation and accommodation. In the process of **assimilation,** input is filtered or modified to fit already existing structures (Piaget & Inhelder, 1969). When we assimilate something, we alter the form of an incoming stimulus to adapt it to our already existing actions or structures (Piaget, 1983). A child who sees an odd-shaped piece of paper and uses it as an airplane has assimilated the paper into his or her structure and knowledge of an airplane.

The process of **accommodation** involves modifying internal existing schemata to meet the require-

schema   An organized system of actions and thoughts useful for dealing with the environment that can be generalized to many situations.

operation   An internalized action that is part of a child's cognitive structure.

assimilation   The process by which information is altered to fit into one's already existing structures.

accommodation   The process by which one's existing structures are altered to fit new information.

ments of a new experience (Piaget & Inhelder, 1969). When we accommodate, we create new schemata or change old ones. For example, a child may be very good at using a one-handed pickup schema—such as lifting a small ball with one hand—but when faced with a beach ball, the child must accommodate and use a two-handed pickup schema.

Assimilation and accommodation work together. Suppose you are teaching a lesson on how to determine the area of particular geometric figures. The children learn that the area of a rectangle is length times width. Whenever the children see rectangles of different sizes, they assimilate them and, despite the rectangles' different dimensions, they know how to find the area of these figures. When faced with a trapezoid, however, they find that the formula does not work, and they are forced to accommodate, that is, to change strategies. They cannot directly fit the trapezoid into the old schema and thus adopt a new schema to deal with this discrepant information. If faced with various trapezoids and given a strategy for finding their areas, they can then solve these area problems as well. The children have separated the concepts of how to determine the area of a rectangle from the area of a trapezoid. Students use both assimilation and accommodation in their attempts to understand challenges in their environment.

Piaget's Goals of Education

Armed with an understanding of Piaget's view of knowledge and the importance of active experience, we are not surprised that Piaget believed that many of the more traditional methods of teaching involve simply transferring information from teacher to child. The learner's role is, according to Piaget, essentially passive in such endeavors. The student simply responds, receives, repeats, or memorizes. At best, this type of learning is incomplete and very short lived (Piaget, 1974). The goals of education for Piaget are more active, namely, to create people who can do new things and can verify things for themselves (Duckworth, 1964). Piaget was interested in fostering self-motivated, independent learning rather than merely transmitting facts and rules. Piaget (1973) argues that the school's primary task is to develop reasoning, and the best way to do so is through an active, discovery type of method in which students are challenged with problems that help them develop their thought processes.

Piaget's work shows a certain realism. Piaget does not argue that the child needs to discover or invent all knowledge. Some knowledge is based upon convention and can be effectively taught through standard lessons. For example, students need not discover the correct spelling of the word *expedite*. Spelling is a matter of convention and can be taught in a more direct manner.

To summarize, Piaget sees knowledge as a process, not an end result. Knowledge is gained through active interaction with the environment. The goals of education are not simply transmission of knowledge but rather helping people to become more independent learners and developing students' reasoning abilities. The teacher, in this conception, is expected to design lessons that give students an opportunity for discovery. Some of these discoveries must be guided by the teacher, while others may be totally a matter of individual progress. Knowledge is constructed from the interaction between the person and the environment. A student can be told what will happen if a cork is placed in water, but a child's active experimentation with the cork will teach the child more. Such active experimentation is useful at all levels of education, whether it be preschoolers experimenting with mirrors to discover their properties or high school students learning about the laws of aerodynamics using models and a fan. However, Piaget believed that his concept of active methods was sometimes misinterpreted to mean that all activities had to be physical. This is not true (Piaget, 1970). As students develop, they can work on problems that do not require the physical manipulation of the environment and that are essentially mental and, later, abstract in nature.

The activities designed by the teacher depend upon the cognitive level of the student. Such activities are to be challenging though not so advanced that students cannot do them. Students learn by being challenged, and this optimal mismatch can cause disequilibrium which motivates students to seek answers to problems and develop their reasoning abilities (Furth & Wachs, 1975).

PIAGET'S STAGES OF COGNITIVE DEVELOPMENT

Piaget (1954) argued that children's cognitive development occurs in a sequence of four stages. However, Piaget as well as many other developmental psychologists use the term *stage* in a way that differs from common usage.

What Are Stages?

"He's only going through a stage." How many times have we heard this statement? Parents use it to talk about a temporary interest, such as collecting bottle caps, or a type of behavior, such as being argumentative. However, Piaget and developmental psychologists look at the concept of a stage differently. Piaget argued that children develop their cognitive abilities in stages, and each stage represents a different way in which children deal with the world. Stage theories present development in terms of age-related periods in which people show particular abilities.

Stages of cognitive development as delineated by Piaget describe qualitative differences in structures or modes of thinking. Simply stated, as children develop from stage to stage, their way of thinking changes qualitatively. Progression from stage to stage occurs in an invariant manner. In other words, children develop from stage one to stage two, and so on. They do not regress nor can they skip a stage. Cultural and environmental factors may speed up or slow down de-velopment, but they do not change the sequence. New skills develop from skills acquired in previous stages.

True or False Students who are in one stage of cognitive development may either proceed to the next one or regress to an earlier one depending upon the environmental stimulation available.

Perhaps the most misunderstood idea about stages, though, is that each person may enter or leave a particular stage at different times. It is incorrect to equate ages with stages. The ages given throughout this chapter are nothing more than averages and guides and should not be thought of as absolutes. The educational implications of this last point are crucial. There is a tendency to state that if a student is six, he or she is in the preoperational stage. This may not be true. A student might enter the next stage earlier than his or her classmates or, for that matter, later. In addition, even within the same stage, children do not always reason in exactly the same manner. Children develop many different schemata within a stage, and they develop some schemata before others.

Putting this all together, we are cautioned not to take a student's cognitive level of sophistication for granted. We cannot categorize the student just by knowing the student's age. If we are to understand

Some of these children are in the preoperational stage, while others are in the stage of concrete operations. You cannot simply use age as a determinant of cognitive level.

Figure 2.1 Through the Child's Eyes
The first road looks longer than the second road, causing the preschooler to think that it will take longer for the driver of the first car to get to the end of the road than the driver of the second car.

how a student is thinking, we must observe the student and perhaps give him or her challenges that will show his or her reasoning abilities.

True or False The stage of cognitive development a student is negotiating is accurately determined by considering the student's chronological age.

Stage theories like Piaget's are especially good at describing what to look for in the student's functioning and at predicting what will happen next. They are not especially strong in indicating, on an individual basis, just when the student will enter the next stage.

One last point of explanation is needed before looking at Piaget's four stages of development. When children reason differently from adults, such differences do not show "mistakes" but rather the children's prevailing mental abilities. Let us say that you lay six sticks end to end and then take six other sticks and lay them out in a jagged fashion (as in Figure 2.1). The first display appears longer than the second because it is laid out straight while the other is crooked. Now tell preschoolers that these displays are two roads and ask them who makes the longer trip—the person who drives a car the entire length of the first road or the one who drives the second road. The preschoolers are fooled by the appearance of the road and say that the straight road is longer (Flavell, 1977).

How do we interpret the preschooler's answer? Those who see the reasoning as mistaken have missed Piaget's point. Piaget's stages show the prevailing cognitive structures of the child. The preschooler really sees the roads as being different lengths. The child's perception is not a case of a mistake in reasoning but rather a reflection of the way the preschooler is reasoning at the present time. It is for this reason that Piagetian stages are of such importance for the teacher.

Imagine the same preschoolers dealing with measurements. If they judge by appearance, they will be fooled constantly. When Piaget noted that preschoolers interpret everything they see in terms of appearance and that school-age children do not reason using a scientific deductive logic, he did not mean that these traits were failings. Indeed, Piaget argued that the reasoning that children show at different levels of development is true for them, even if it does not match adult reasoning processes.

When the characteristics of each stage are discussed, it is easy to understand why it is important to appreciate the way in which children think. After all, understanding how students reason and appreciating their prevailing mental abilities are necessary if we are to teach in a way that our students can understand. To show how children reason at different stages, Piaget presented challenges to children and observed how the children dealt with these problems and often questioned them in order to understand how they arrived at their answers. This laboratory work demonstrates very well how children develop their reasoning abilities, and some of it is described here. In addition, after each stage is described, with the exception of the stage covering infancy, some of the ways that Piaget's ideas translate directly into classroom teaching are noted. Piaget's ideas can be applied to science, mathematics, English, and social studies, although Piagetian theory does not provide us with an all-encompassing theory of instruction. The goal is to show that Piagetian theory does more than just suggest general guidelines for teaching. It can be applied to decisions about what to teach, when to teach it, and how to teach it.

The Sensorimotor Stage

Between birth and about two years of age, infants progress through the **sensorimotor stage.** They investigate their world using the senses (seeing, hearing, touching, smelling, and tasting) and motor activity. They develop **object permanence**—the understanding that objects and people do not disappear merely because they are out of sight. Very young infants believe that when a parent leaves the room, the parent has disappeared. As infants mature, they develop object permanence and know this is not so. The child's abilities in this stage are limited by an inability to use language or symbols—things that represent other things. Children must experience everything directly through their senses and through feedback from motor activities. Schoolteachers, of course, do not deal with infants. However, about half the mothers of infants under one year of age are in the labor force. With the advent of infant day care, we may eventually see professionals who require knowledge of how to stimulate these children and develop their cognitive abilities.

The Preoperational Stage

From about ages two through seven, children negotiate the **preoperational stage.** At this stage, the child

In early infancy, babies do not show object permanence—the understanding that objects exist even though they are out of sight. Children develop object permanence in later infancy.

can use one thing to represent another, such as a piece of wood to symbolize a boat (Mandler, 1983). This ability is evident in pretend play. Children can also use language which allows them to go beyond their own direct experience and opens up a new world. Another manifestation of the ability to use symbolism is known as deferred imitation. The child can see something occur, store the information about it, and perform the action at a later date. Therefore, the great advance in this stage is an understanding of the **symbolic function.** However, a child's understanding of the world in this stage is limited. The stage is marked by many advances while at the same time has many limitations.

If you ask preschoolers to put a series of sticks in order from biggest to smallest, an operation called **seriation,** they simply cannot do it. Nor can they

Seriation involves the ability to place things in size order. It is a necessary skill underlying a number of mathematics concepts.

classify items, at least at the beginning of the pre-operational stage. When young children are given a number of plastic shapes that include squares, triangles, and rings of different colors and are asked to put things that are alike into a pile, most children younger than five do not organize their choices on any particular logical basis. They may put a red triangle and a blue triangle together but then throw in a red square. No central organizing principle is evident. Some young children do not even understand the task at all (Ault, 1977). Later in the preoperational stage, children make some progress in classification. They can sort items on the basis of one overriding principle—most often form—but they fail to see that multiple classifications are possible.

Children also have difficulty with problems that require a knowledge of **conservation,** the principle that quantities remain the same despite changes in their appearance. You can demonstrate this for yourself with a child in the preoperational stage. Take two equal lumps of clay and roll each one into a ball. The child has no difficulty telling you they are the same size. Then, with the child watching, roll one ball into a long, thin shape and ask the child which clay form has more clay. The youngster will fail to understand that the two pieces are still equal in size and believes that one piece has more clay. A second demonstration is to present a young child with two identical glasses partly filled with water. The child will tell you the glasses contain equal amounts of liquid. Now transfer the water from one glass to a squat glass and ask the child which container has more water. The answer will usually be that the taller glass contains more liquid (see Figure 2.2).

symbolic function   The ability to use one thing to stand for another.

seriation   The process of placing objects in size order.

classification   The process of placing objects in different groupings.

conservation   The principle that quantities remain the same despite changes in their appearance.

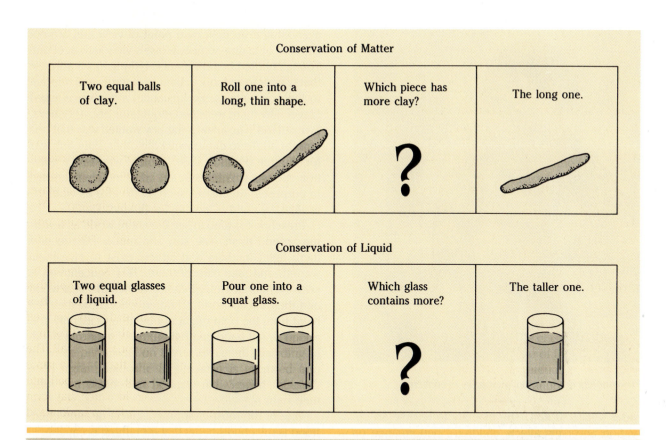

Figure 2.2 Conservation
Conservation is the principle that quantities remain the same in spite of changes in their appearance.

Most children do not exhibit an understanding of these conservation tasks until they are about eight years of age. As we will see shortly, the fact that many children do not understand these basic processes even during the early years of elementary school has a number of important implications for teachers.

True or False During the preschool years, the child reasons in a manner that is qualitatively different from that of the average adult.

Many reasons are offered to explain a child's difficulties understanding these basic ideas. First, such children can concentrate on only one dimension at a time (Piaget & Inhelder, 1969). This is known as **centering.** Try, for instance, to explain to a preschooler that a cup and a glass hold the same amount of liquid. Because the containers are shaped differently, the child believes that one is larger than the other. Nor can these children **reverse** operations. If a clay ball is rolled into a thin, wormlike shape in front of them, the children cannot mentally rearrange the shape back to its original form. Show a child three balls of the same size, each of which is a different color. Place the balls in a cylinder in a certain order (e.g., blue, green, yellow). The child has no difficulty understanding that the balls will come out of the bottom in the same order they went in. Rotate the cylinder 180 degrees, however, and the child will continue to predict the original order and will be surprised when the balls leave the cylinder in the opposite

centering The tendency to be able to concentrate on only one dimension at a time.

reversibility Beginning at the end of an operation and working one's way back to the beginning.

Preschoolers do not show the ability to conserve.

order (Piaget, 1967). The inability to reverse an operation adversely affects children's performance on mathematical tasks. Such children do not understand, for example, that subtraction is the reverse of addition.

Generally, young children confuse how things look with what they really are, judging things on the basis of their outward appearance. For example, show a three-year-old a red toy car and cover the car with a green filter that makes it look black. Now hand the car without the filter to the child and put the car under the filter again. When the child is asked what color the car is, the child says black (Flavell, 1986). Preschoolers have difficulty going beyond the visual information given.

Underlying all the child's reasoning is a basic **egocentrism.** Piaget (1954) argued that children see

egocentrism A thought process in which young children believe everyone is experiencing the environment in the same way they are. Children who are egocentric have difficulty understanding someone else's point of view.

everything from their own point of view and are not capable of taking someone else's view into account. Young children believe that everything has a purpose that is understandable in their own terms and relevant to their own needs. For instance, a boy once asked Piaget why there were two mountains above Geneva, Switzerland. The answer the boy wanted was that one was for adults to climb while the other, little one was for children (Pulaski, 1980). A child who asks a question such as why the sun shines is mostly interested in purposes. An answer such as "to give us warmth" is what the child is looking for (Elkind, 1987).

Preschoolers tend to see the entire world as revolving around them. The sun and moon exist to give them light; mothers and fathers exist to give them warmth and take care of them. This egocentrism is seen in children's interpretation of their physical world and their social world. Children who know their left hand from the right might not be able to identify correctly the left hand and right hand of a person standing opposite them. Nursery schoolteachers are aware of this and, when facing preschoolers, often raise their left hand when wanting the children to raise their right.

One of the most charming aspects of early childhood is the child's belief that everything is capable of being conscious and alive, known as **animism.** A paper turtle can be alive; a hammer has a life of its own. If you step on the paper turtle, you've just killed something, not just smashed a small toy. Preschoolers may bump into a desk, smack it, and say bad desk. A balloon that has soared to the ceiling does not want to be held.

True or False Young preschoolers believe that even inanimate objects are capable of being alive and conscious.

Animism is more characteristic of the early part of the preoperational stage. It becomes less evident as children reach the age of four or five (Bullock, 1985). Another aspect is **artificialism,** the belief that natural phenomena are caused by human beings. For example, when asked why a particular event occurred, many preschoolers will explain it in terms of their own experience. The half moon occurs because someone cut the moon in half; the lake was made by someone digging a hole and filling it up with water.

Putting all this together, we get a picture of how the preschool child—and to some extent the first- and second-grader—look at the world. The characteristics of preoperational thinking are summarized in

> **animism** The preschooler's belief that inanimate objects are conscious or alive.
>
> **artificialism** The belief that natural phenomena are caused by human beings.

Table 2.2. Children in this stage are egocentric—not able to take someone else's perspective—and they see things only from their own point of view. They are easily fooled by the appearance of objects and believe that natural phenomena are caused by human beings. However, their improvement in language in this stage makes verbal communication possible, and they can now use words and other symbols to represent what they are thinking or doing.

The Teacher and Students Negotiating the Preoperational Stage

Much of Piaget's theory was formed as he presented problems to children of different ages. The value of understanding the way children at different ages reason cannot be emphasized too greatly. The fact that these methods of reasoning are not errors but rather that they show the child's prevailing mental structures allows educators to deal with a student on the student's level. There is nothing "wrong" with a preschooler looking at the sun as if it were placed there to keep him warm or believing that two mountains are in a picture so that one is for children and the other for adults. These are not errors to be corrected by instruction.

The preoperational stage is a long stage. Obviously, the six-year-old has different abilities from the two-year-old. Preoperational thinking is often linked with preschool education, including nursery school. It is often forgotten, however, that kindergarten, first-, second-, and perhaps even some third-graders may also show preoperational thinking. Therefore, many elementary schoolteachers will be dealing with students who do not yet show conservation, have difficulty understanding reversibility, and depend upon the *appearance* of the object when making judgments. In understanding how preoperational-stage thinking affects early childhood teachers and first- and second-grade teachers, it is necessary to again note that Piaget was more interested in facilitating development and reasoning than in the learning of facts and figures.

Before discussing how all of the preceding affects the teacher, we need to differentiate between the early and late part of this period. In the early part, from about two to four, preschoolers tend to show animism, artificialism, and egocentrism more than in the later part. This can even be noted from children's speech patterns. Between four and seven years, children's speech becomes less egocentric. Five-year-olds will now pay attention to the statements of their playmates and disagree with them, showing that they are at least becoming aware of and attending to a perspective that is not their own (Siegler, 1986). We should also remember that children pass through the stage at their own rate. As we've noted so often, some children the same age will function at a higher level than others who take more time to reach that level.

Sometimes Piagetian concepts such as conservation, seriation, and classification seem very abstract and unrelated to learning specific academic skills. However, this need not be the case. Students must be able to perform Piagetian operations such as conservation, seriation, and classification in order to do well in science, mathematics, and reading (Bybee & Sund, 1981). In fact, an understanding of these operations can serve as a measure of a child's readiness for reading and certain mathematical work (Arlin, 1981).

In the early years, learning mathematics requires interaction with objects that will develop a child's concept of more and less. Children learn most basic mathematics concepts by interacting with objects before they formally learn the subject through the use of symbols. If students can't group or classify, adding two apples and two apples rather than two apples and two oranges has little meaning.

If a child cannot add, a teacher well versed in Piagetian theory looks for the cause in terms of the child's reasoning. Perhaps the child can't seriate or classify. The teacher can then help the child with this operation by designing activities that enable the child to develop these skills. For example, classification activities for preschool children between the ages of four and six might include labeling the attributes of things and noting and describing how things are similar yet different (Peterson & Felton-Collins, 1986). Seriation activities might involve comparing which stick is bigger, heavier, softer, or narrower. Piagetian theory tells the teacher to look for *why* a student may not be able to do something by investigating the

Table 2.2 The Preoperational Stage

In this stage, children can use symbols, and can judge on the basis of appearance. However, they cannot perform mental operations such as reversibility. This stage is a long one lasting from about two to seven years of age. Children in the later part of the stage are much more advanced than those in the earlier part. Remember, it is incorrect to simply use age to judge cognitive abilities because children enter and leave a stage at their own individual rates.

Characteristic	Explanation	Example
Symbolic function	The ability to use one thing to represent another.	A child can use a spoon to represent a hammer. The ability to use words also requires the use of symbols.
Deferred imitation	The ability to observe an act and imitate it at a later time.	A preschooler can see the teacher exercising and can imitate similar actions at a later time without the teacher's presence.
Inability to seriate	The process of placing objects in size order.	Preschoolers cannot place ten blocks of wood in size order.
Inability to classify	The process of placing objects in different groupings.	Younger preschoolers can not group plastic objects of varying shapes and colors by shape or color.
Appearance and reality	The tendency to judge on the basis of appearance.	A child shown a red car will correctly identify the color. If a filter which makes it look black covers the car, he will say the car is black. When the filter is removed, he will now identify it as red again.
Inability to conserve	The inability to understand that quantities remain the same despite changes in their appearance.	If shown two equal size lumps of clay the preschooler will know they are equal. If one is flattened out, she will believe that they are no longer the same size.
Centering	The tendency to attend to only one dimension at a time.	When comparing the contents of a small thin beaker and and a short fat beaker, the preschooler will do so by comparing only one dimension of each, probably height, and will ignore the differences in width.
Irreversible Thinking	The inability to begin at the end of an operation and work back to the start.	Preschoolers do not understand that if you add 4 to 2 to make 6, then you can take 2 away from 6 to make 4 again.
Egocentrism	The inability to understand someone else's point of view.	If shown a display and asked how someone standing opposite them is seeing it, preschoolers will not be able to visualize the other person's perspective. Preschoolers believe that the world revolves around them.
Animism	The belief that inanimate objects have a consciousness or are alive.	A young preschooler believes that the balloon soared to the ceiling because it did not want to be held.
Artificialism	The belief that natural phenomena are caused by human beings.	A preschooler will see a lake and say it was made by a group of people digging and then filling it up with water from hoses.

student's prevailing reasoning ability. Such a technique is useful throughout the grades.

A number of programs use Piaget's ideas in some way. The basic model of a Piagetian curriculum is often described as a PWRE model, signifying plan, work, represent, and evaluate. In this model, the children plan the work they will be doing. The teacher invites the children to think about, communicate verbally or in pictures, or even later write about where the activity will take place, the materials and amount of time needed, the sequence to be followed, and possible problems encountered in, for example, planting a cutting or getting a fishbowl ready for fish. The students then carry out the activity and do their "work." Representation involves depicting in some manner what is going on, such as through taking photographs, making drawings, telling about the activity, painting pictures, writing stories, or even performing a play. Since language is incorporated into the activity, you can see the importance of the children's ability to represent and use symbols. Last, the students evaluate the activity by describing the finished product—what they have done and how they did it. They may also ask questions about what other students did (Morrison, 1988).

A Piagetian approach to early education, then, would employ the abilities young students have in the areas of representation and symbolic function. If a five-year-old draws a picture, the teacher can ask the student to give the drawing a title and write the title at the top of the picture, thus showing how words can be used to represent the student's thoughts. Activities in the areas of classification and seriation are also important. In the science realm, observation can be used (Bott et al., 1970). Children's observations develop their conceptual awareness. Observing the behavior of a guinea pig and listing the behaviors can induce students to ask why, leading to further study. The emphasis in the early years is in teaching a child *how* to learn more than *what* to learn (Peterson & Felton-Collins, 1986).

The Concrete Operational Stage

Students in the first two years or so of elementary school are experiencing the end of the preoperational stage and are entering the stage of **concrete operations.** This shift is gradual, however, and young elementary schoolchildren show some of the character-

> **concrete operational stage** Piaget's third stage of cognitive development—lasting from about seven through eleven years of age—in which children develop the ability to perform logical operations, such as conservation.

istics described previously. A child does not go to sleep one night in the preoperational stage and wake up the next morning in the concrete stage. The child does not go to sleep egocentric and unable to fully understand classification and conservation and wake up with fully developed abilities in these areas. The skills develop gradually over the years.

During the concrete operational stage (approximately ages seven through eleven), children deal with concrete objects rather than abstractions when they consider change (Forman & Kuschner, 1977). They must either see or be able to imagine objects. For example, terms such as democracy, liberty, and justice are just too abstract for these children, although such children can understand democracy in terms of voting and majority rule, and justice in terms of fairness. If students in this stage are presented with purely verbal problems that involve hypotheses, they cannot solve them. However, if you explain the problems in real, concrete terms, the students will have no difficulty with the challenge (Wadsworth, 1971).

True or False Elementary school students can solve abstract, hypothetical problems if they are given enough time to do so.

Children in this stage become less egocentric, understanding that other people see the world differently than they do. This is accomplished through social interaction during which they can share their thoughts and verify their views of the world. In addition, they can now take the perspective of the other person and imagine what others are thinking of them in a relatively simple way (Harter, 1983). They are capable of being more sensitive to the feelings of others. Children slowly develop the ability to reverse operations—to realize that if you roll a clay ball into a long, wormlike shape you can reverse your operation and recreate the ball of clay. They develop the ability to decenter—to take into consideration more than one dimension at a time. Children now realize that the increase in the length of the clay worm compensates for the decrease in its width. Therefore they begin to understand conservation (Piaget & Inhelder, 1969).

Although the ages at which children can solve different types of conservation problems is variable, this ability is developed in a specific order (Piaget, 1952). Conservation of number comes first, followed by substance, weight, and finally the ability to solve conservation of volume problems at about age 11 or 12 (refer to Figure 2.2). Trying to teach young children the law of buoyancy before they have an understanding of conservation of volume simply will not work.

Elementary schoolchildren develop the ability to seriate. They can easily arrange a series of sticks by length, later by weight, and finally by volume. Their ability to classify also improves greatly. In fact, school-age children are known for their propensity to collect things (Kegan, 1982). They will collect anything and everything, thereby practicing their skills of classification. They begin to realize that an item can be classified in many ways and can belong to a great many classes at one time. The child in this stage realizes that a dog is an animal and a mammal at the same time. During this stage, students are also often unaware of their inconsistencies in their reasoning. They may use hunches to solve problems rather than rely on logic.

Table 2.3 summarizes the characteristics of concrete operational thought. The child in the concrete stage of operations has made great progress, although limitations still exist. For instance, ask a seven-year-old to interpret a proverb such as "You can lead a horse to water but you can't make him drink," and you will be very surprised at the answer. The child may say something about not being able to force an animal to drink, show a puzzled expression, or attempt a literal interpretation of the saying. Children in this stage do not understand the more general, abstract meaning of the saying. Political cartoons also require the ability to think in the abstract, and young children do not understand them very well. Teachers who are aware of this may attempt to explain difficult concepts in more concrete terms that children can readily relate to.

Children in this stage also have difficulty with hypothetical situations. Ask a child, "If all dogs were pink and I had a dog, would my dog be pink, too?" Children often rebel at such statements (Ault, 1977). They insist that dogs are not pink, and that's that! Children in the concrete stage of operations have difficulty accepting hypothetical situations. In a Piagetian framework, Bybee and Sund (1982) suggest that teachers use many concrete experiences and examples as the basis for their educational strategies and refer to events or situations that are familiar to the children.

Table 2.3 The Concrete Operational Stage
In the stage of concrete operations, children can deal with information that is based upon something they can see or imagine. They can mentally operate on objects, but cannot deal with abstractions.

Characteristic	Explanation	Example
Conservation	Children in this stage understand that things remain the same despite changes in appearance.	A child develops the ability to understand that a ball of clay can change shape and still contain the same amount of clay.
Ability to classify	Students can place objects into various categories.	Elementary school students can now group different animals as mammals.
Ability to seriate	Students can place things in size order.	Children can arrange a series of sticks in terms of length or weight.
Ability to reverse operations	Students can follow a process from beginning to end and then back again.	If a teacher rolls a ball of clay into a long worm-like structure, a child in this stage can mentally recreate the ball of clay.
Inability to use abstractions	Students cannot deal with material that is abstract such as ideas and statements not tied to something observable or imaginable.	Children may find political cartoons and proverbs puzzling because they cannot understand their abstract meaning.

Educational Implications of Concrete Operational Thinking

Piaget has greatly influenced early childhood education. His emphasis on active discovery techniques has formed the basis for many preschool programs. However, children in the concrete operational period (seven though eleven years of age) are now expected to learn to read, write, solve mathematical problems, and achieve competence in science and social studies. We now have basic school skills to impart and a knowledge base to teach. In such an atmosphere, Piaget's theory has sometimes mistakenly been relegated to a simple idea: understand the material from the student's point of view. However, this is unfortunate, since Piaget's discoveries have much to say about teaching in the elementary school years. True, Piaget does not give us point-by-point instruction concerning how to teach reading or how to impart to students the facts about, say, the Revolutionary War. However, Piaget's discoveries can help guide teachers and avoid mistakes that are commonly made. As previously noted, it is important to recognize that students in the lower grades of elementary school are often in a transition from preoperational thinking to concrete operational thinking. Some children will reason preoperationally, while others will be able to reverse operations and conserve. Some will have great difficulties with classification and seriation; others may not.

One of the reasons that children have problems with reading—especially in first or second grade—is that they cannot conserve. When they come across a vowel, they sometimes fail to understand that an *a* can have a number of sounds and still be an *a*. There is a significant correlation between the ability to conserve and reading achievement. As the child develops conservation abilities, this problem should recede.

Many states have undertaken a policy to introduce foreign languages in the elementary schools. Some wonder how appropriate it is to do so. Piagetian theory answers this practical question. Piaget's findings would encourage teaching a foreign language as early as possible. Since the prerequisite for understanding a foreign language is possessing the ability to use symbols—an ability that children possess at this age—learning a foreign language should present no cognitive difficulties for such children.

In the area of mathematics, Piaget's ideas are challenging (they are covered separately in the section

At what age should students be exposed to a foreign language? Piaget believes that even young students can learn a foreign language.

that follows). Concrete operations such as classification and seriation are required if the child is to understand mathematical operations. Children learn mathematics from their interaction with concrete objects, and they learn mathematical operations inductively using objects. Therefore, using pennies or other concrete displays is certainly reasonable. After much practice, students at this level will then generalize these operations. Students gain their understanding of mathematics concepts from working with real objects (Copeland, 1984).

What if a teacher finds that second-graders cannot understand subtraction? Some people have misunderstood Piaget's ideas and offered the advice to just wait. This is not what Piaget argued. Piaget argued that experience is also important. Thus, when children are nearing the end of one stage, we don't have to simply wait but can challenge the children by involving them in problems or exercises designed to give them experience at the next level. Activities in classification and seriation can help. Students in the concrete operational stage can learn some geometry, because they can classify figures according to their attributes. Because they understand conservation, measurements are possible and comparing geometric forms is practical.

True or False If a student is not reasoning at the same advanced level of his or her classmates, the best thing for a teacher to do is to wait for the child to mature.

Generally, it is important to continue the policy of encouraging students to investigate problems using real objects. Because it is also possible for children at this level to mentally manipulate objects, it is reasonable to ask them questions that require performing a mental operation such as comparison as long as the questions relate to real objects or something that can be imagined by the students.

The elements of concrete operational thought can also be applied to English and social studies. In both literature and social studies, the material should be linked to people and events that are more real and meaningful to the students, since these do not depend upon abstract thinking. When studying geography, students can learn about life in villages, cities, and rural areas by understanding the characteristics of each, such as transportation and styles of life. This approach stresses learning the basic characteristics and requires classification skills. Piaget would deemphasize memorizing the fifty largest cities and towns in a country. When teaching a unit on, say, Native Americans, Piagetian thought would lead to an emphasis on the characteristics of their societies. Because students reasoning at this stage can classify and understand relationships, it would also emphasize the relation of Native Americans to other peoples, perhaps in the Far East.

When reading a book, students can grasp the characteristics of the people in the book and classify the type of book as comedy or tragedy (we see classification again). What about teaching grammar? Grammar also depends upon classification, and so students can be taught the elements of grammar in this stage.

True or False Fifth- or sixth-grade elementary school students can be taught grammar because they have the cognitive ability to classify words into such categories as noun, verb, and adjective.

Students can use their ability to classify things in the science area, also. They can place elements into different categories and understand how animals are related to different species. Classifying animals as mammals and nonmammals, vertebrates and invertebrates, is possible. Students can now use inductive reasoning to generalize. In other words, after studying a number of concrete examples, they now understand the general rule. Students can then actively perform an experiment, take in data, and use inductive reasoning to generalize.

Again, Piaget emphasizes the importance of active methods of discovery that are based upon exploration of problems and physical and mental manipulation and social interactions. The manipulation can be internal and mental or external and physical. Roleplaying in social studies and using projects and active experimentation in science are examples of such methods.

However, the limitations associated with this stage of learning should also guide teachers. Students can manipulate objects in their minds, but the objects must be related to what the students can see or imagine. Anything that is abstract or too complex will lead to frustration and bewilderment. Explanations are certainly possible for students who can mentally manipulate objects, but again, such objects must be linked to something students can see or imagine. Piaget's ideas lead to many practical ideas about teaching basic subjects, although they certainly do not give us all the answers. The skills of classification, seriation, and conservation and the reduction in egocentrism have many important implications for educators. However, students in this stage will still have difficulty with material that is too complex, too vague, and too abstract.

The Interesting Case of Mathematics

Perhaps the most interesting application of Piaget's ideas is in the area of mathematics. We've noted that logico-mathematical knowledge is necessary for understanding concepts in mathematics, science, and logic. This type of knowledge cannot be taught in the traditional sense but must be invented by the student. It includes spatial relations, time concepts, number concepts, understanding a one-to-one correspondence, classification, seriation, and conservation.

If the preceding is so, how do we explain the fact that young children can count? Children can be taught the names of the numbers—one, two, three, etc. This is seen even in very young children. A two-year-old may produce a smile on her mother's face when she "counts" from one to ten. This is essentially the rote learning of facts—or part of social-arbitrary learning in Piagetian theory—and does not imply an understanding of number. It is common to find young children who can recite the numbers in a rising pitch, as they do on "Sesame Street," but who cannot do it in an even tone (Peterson & Felton-Collins, 1986). Counting may not be of much help to preoperational children. If you present two rows of seven pennies each—one that is more spread out than the other— the child may count both rows and get seven each time but will continue to say that the longer row has more pennies. This is because the child judges the rows of coins by their overall appearance.

True or False A child's understanding of numbers is reflected in the ability to count from one to twenty.

Mathematics concepts are more important than merely knowing the names of the numbers. We take for granted many number concepts, for instance, that ten pennies are ten pennies whether they are arranged in one way or another. If we rearrange a particular display of ten pennies, the shape may change, but the number stays the same.

The concept of number depends upon the student's knowledge of classification and seriation. Classification allows one to represent a collection of objects and is necessary if students are to understand the statement that, for example, there are seven pennies but two dimes. This relates to the cardinal property of numbers. Seriation is vital because it relates to the ordinal property (first, second, third). Another important understanding relates to conservation, which involves understanding what is called a one-to-one correspondence. Perhaps the easiest way to understand this is to try an experiment. Take six buttons and place them in a row. Ask the youngster to do what you have done, and you will find that even very young children will make a display that corresponds in length but will not necessarily use the same number of buttons. At about age five or six, the child will use your display as an exact model. However, if you now make a pile of the buttons, the child below the age of six or seven may say that the pile has fewer buttons. Conservation of number occurs at about six or seven years of age. The problems many youngsters in the earliest years of elementary school have with mathematics can be explained by such children's inability to understand the basic processes that underlie mathematics concepts.

Again, the teacher does not just sit and wait for the students to invent the knowledge on their own. Classification activities can be very helpful. For example, if you have a tray of many different buttons of various sizes and colors, very young students can classify the buttons according to any single attribute you choose. Students in the early concrete operational stage may improve their classification skills by categorizing things that are more complex, such as things that are animate and inanimate. The attributes of living things can be tricky, and the class can get into a discussion of whether plants are alive and how we know that. Older students can also classify according to negative attributes, such as classifying things that are not squares or not hard.

Seriation is more difficult for young children than classification, because to place things in some sort of order, a comparison must be made. When classifying, we must decide whether an object possesses a particular characteristic (is it round or is it blue?). When placing things in size order, comparisons must be made. Students may arrange rocks on the basis of weight or sticks on the basis of length. Students may discuss the order in which various ingredients for preparing a recipe must be used or the sequence of steps in getting dressed. Both seriation and classification involve relationship learning.

One of the difficulties students have with mathematics in the junior high and perhaps even early high school years involves the fact that much of the mathematics work at this level is hypothetical and abstract and many students may not be able to understand these abstract ideas. These students may still require some concrete materials to understand mathematics concepts, at least in some areas. These students may be able to understand that x stands for an unknown— a relatively simple abstraction—but unable to understand more abstract material, such as nondecimal base systems. As we shall see, the transition from concrete operations to formal operations has a number of implications for the classroom teacher.

The Stage of Formal Operations

Between the ages of about 11 or 12 and 15, students enter the **formal operational stage.** They now become able to reason in a very scientific manner. Give elementary schoolchildren a science problem in which they must find all the possible alternatives and solutions, and you may be surprised to find that they do not approach the task in a scientific manner. The ability to find all possible alternatives to answer a problem is called **combinational logic.** Inhelder and Piaget (1958) presented children of varying ages with five jars, each containing a colorless liquid, and told the children that some combination of the chemicals would yield a yellow liquid. Preschoolers in the preoperational stage simply poured one into another, making a mess. Children in the concrete stage of operations combined the liquids but did not approach the task with a systematic strategy. They would combine jars one and two and then jars three and four. Adolescents, however, formed a strategy for making all the possible combinations of liquids and finally solved the problem.

Adolescents can also accept a proposition and separate themselves from the real world (Ault, 1977). They can form hypotheses and test them, which entails separating themselves from the real and considering the possible (McKinney et al., 1982). Adolescents can reflect on a verbal hypothesis even though the elements of the hypothesis do not exist in real life. Some teachers may have difficulty with adolescents who can and do suggest alternatives that may not be feasible or that teachers simply do not like. The separation of what is from what can or could be allows adolescents to begin to think about a better world. However, adolescents' answers to the world's prob-

Students in the stage of formal operations can now handle abstractions, opening up a new and rich type of learning.

lems are often based on possibilities sometimes divorced from reality. Their lack of experience in the real world sometimes limits their ability to consider these possibilities in practical terms.

The ability of adolescents to separate themselves from the trappings of what is real stems partly from their newfound ability to create and use abstractions. Adolescents begin to be able to understand political cartoons and adages and deal with problems that are abstract and hypothetical. The ability to deal with abstraction also allows them to develop internal systems of overriding principles. They can now deal with such concepts, ideals, and values as freedom, liberty, and justice. Unlike the concrete operational thinker, however, adolescents can discuss these ideas divorced from any firm, real-world example. These abstract concepts, ideals, and values take on added significance when separated from their specific situational meaning.

True or False   The ability to interpret proverbs or political cartoons develops during adolescence.

Their emerging abilities allow adolescents to engage in what Piaget called **hypothetical-deductive reasoning.** Basically, this is the ability to form a hypothesis which then leads to certain logical deduc-

---

formal operational stage   The last Piagetian stage of cognitive development, in which a person develops the ability to deal with abstractions and reason in a scientific manner.

combinational logic   The ability to produce all the possible alternatives to answer a problem.

hypothetical-deductive reasoning   The ability to form a hypothesis, scientifically test the hypothesis, and draw conclusions using deductive logic.

tions. Some of these hypotheses may be untestable, such as "What if all humans were green?" Others, however, may be capable of scientific investigation. This type of reasoning is necessary for scientific progress: Although no one has ever seen an atom, the developments in atomic theory have greatly affected our lives (Pulaski, 1980).

The ability to use combinational logic, separate the real from the possible, interpret abstractions, and use scientific logic allows adolescents to deal with problems at a higher level than they could during childhood. Adolescents can accept assumptions in the absence of physical evidence, develop hypotheses involving if-then thinking, test out these hypotheses, and reevaluate them (Salkind, 1981). The thinking of adolescents is also more flexible, because they can consider a number of alternatives, weigh them, and discard those that do not fit the situation. The ability to attack problems more logically has great value in science, mathematics, and social studies.

Teaching the Student Who Can Use Formal Operational Reasoning

The changes in cognitive abilities during the stage of formal operations are very important, and they are summarized in Table 2.4. However, two caveats are especially useful here for secondary schoolteachers. First, Piaget may have underestimated the age at which children enter this stage (Copeland, 1984). Especially in the early part of this stage, formal operational abilities are spotty and have a "here one minute, absent the next" quality about them. It is only after about age 15 that these abilities become more stable. This is why some late junior high school students may have difficulty with more abstract subject matter. Second, not all students will have these abilities even at 16. Most of life's problems can be solved on a concrete basis. Many students will not consistently show the sophisticated abilities even in high school.

Even so, the appearance of formal operational abilities in many students leads to some interesting possibilities in high school education as well as in understanding student behavior. High school students are often very critical of existing social, political, and religious establishments and may show a cynical attitude towards government. This is because they may be constructing a highly theoretical and elaborate alternative system. These students may want to discuss theoretical issues such as Why must there be poverty? or Why does an economy have to be based on money? The problem here is that many of

Table 2.4	The Formal Operational Stage	
In the stage of formal operations, adolescents develop the ability to deal with abstract information and theoretical propositions. They can formulate and test hypotheses in a scientific manner.		

Characteristic	Explanation	Example
Combinational logic	The ability to find all the possible alternatives.	When asked what the president could have done in a certain situation, a student will produce a great many alternatives, some real, some impractical. If given five jars of colorless liquid and told that some combination will yield a yellow liquid, a student will use an efficient and effective strategy that will produce all possible alternatives.
Separating the real from the possible	The ability to accept propositions that are contrary to reality and to separate oneself from the real world.	A student can discuss propositions such as, "What if all human beings were green?"
Using abstractions	The ability to deal with material that is not observable.	A student understands higher level concepts such as democracy and liberty as well as the abstract meaning in proverbs.
Hypothetical–deductive reasoning	The ability to form hypotheses and use scientific logic.	A student uses deductive logic in science to test a hypothesis.

these students' alternatives lack a real-world feeling. Now that students at this stage are capable of finding all the alternative paths and dealing with hypothetical situations, they are likely to become less realistic about evaluating solutions. Everything is food for thought, and often ideas are accepted only to be rejected a bit later.

True or False High school students suffer from an overly practical, down-to-earth way of viewing the political process and social problems.

The influence of formal operations can be seen in political philosophy and values. Values and attitudes affect one's view of politics. Adolescents see law and politics differently from the way younger students see them. When adolescents and younger students were asked: What is the purpose of laws?, Adelson (1972) found striking differences between the answers of adolescents and those of preadolescents. Younger students answered that laws are necessary so that people don't get hurt or so that people won't kill or steal. Adolescents about 15 or 16 years old viewed law in more abstract and principled terms: Laws ensure safety, enforce government policy, and act as guidelines for determining right and wrong. Subjects younger than age 11 focus on the consequences of law and order for themselves, while older adolescents go beyond this and see the legal system from the point of view of the community as a whole (Adelson & O'Neil, 1966).

Preadolescents look at law and government in terms that are concrete, absolute, and authoritarian and evaluate them on the basis of how they affect particular individuals. For example, seatbelts are necessary to protect the driver and passengers. Older subjects are less authoritarian and more sensitive to individual rights and personal freedom. Adolescents may see the conflict between requiring seatbelts for the good of everyone and the loss of personal freedom that comes with regulation—a conflict that younger children do not see. When Gallatin and Adelson (1971) asked these younger children what they thought of a law requiring men to have a yearly medical checkup, they noted the good the law might do and frequently were willing to accept the idea. Older children believed that the good must be weighed against the loss of individual freedom. Preadolescents see government in personal terms, personifying it in terms of the president, the mayor, or the police officer, while older adolescents see it in

terms of abstract properties (Sprinthall & Collins, 1984). Children see government as powerful and good, but by about the eighth grade, they have become more skeptical (Merelman, 1971).

High school social studies and English teachers will then be facing students who can and do see conflict in abstract terms, may be cynical, and may argue a point that they may even agree with if there are flaws in the teacher's argument. High school students can understand symbolism and can analyze political cartoons, which are largely abstract. Discussions that begin on a concrete level can easily then expand to a more abstract level.

High school students can see the conflicts between individual rights and societal needs and may wish to argue questions of basic principles, such as whether legislators should follow their own opinions or vote for things the people they represent want. Social studies teachers may make use of this propensity. It is possible to talk about various alternatives and what could have been done within a historical framework. A discussion of "Should we have dropped the atomic bomb on Hiroshima?" is more abstract and analytical than the more concrete, simplistic manner in which younger students deal with history. However, the information available at the time of the actual incident should be emphasized. Too often adolescents are able to use their hindsight without attempting to understand what was known at the time the actual event occurred.

In English, the high school student's ability to use logical, abstract strategies means that the student can understand symbolic meanings, metaphors, and similes (Sprintall & Collins, 1984). Adolescents can understand the symbolism in novels, and any controversial issues raised in these writings can be divorced from the real world or even from something they can imagine, as was the case in concrete operations. If the student reads a book such as *Gulliver's Travels, The Scarlet Letter,* or *Animal Farm,* he or she may enjoy the story. In addition, however, the formal operational thinker will also understand the political satire and allegorical meaning behind it, something concrete operational thinkers cannot do. Formal operational thinkers are also more likely to respond to abstract ideas contained in artwork, dance, and theater.

This ability to deal with abstractions is important in some high school science courses. Certainly, biology can be taught in the younger grades, but the more abstract principles, especially genetics and ecosystems,

Adolescents are particularly good at pointing out logical flaws in arguments.

require the ability to use abstractions, which is difficult for younger teens and more appropriate for older students. In fact, a relationship exists between being able to do well in physics and chemistry and formal operational abilities.

Students in the period of formal operations can understand propositional logic and are capable of finding logical flaws. This allows such students to reason in a scientific manner. For example, an experiment that requires a proposition such as "If A or B is true, then C is true" can be used by a student who has formal operational skills. Such logic may be important in advanced mathematics, logic, and science courses (Steinberg, 1985). As noted earlier, some students may have difficulty in algebra and geometry if they cannot handle abstractions and engage in scientific logic. Remember that quadratic equations and many algebraic problems are basically hypothetical. Students who have difficulty with these abstract problems may first need some additional experience with concrete problems. They may not be aware of characteristics of geometric shapes or many mathematics concepts—a prerequisite for this more abstract work.

No one doubts that by high school, students can learn concepts and structured knowledge through direct instructional means. However, active methods still have their place. Students may well want to put their own feelings and understandings, many of which are abstract, on paper or communicate them in some way besides reading and watching films. Writing poems, making films, and taking part in theater may all encourage students to communicate their ideas— often abstract—to others.

Students at this stage can now compare ideas and positions, evaluate evidence, and arrive at conclusions using scientific deductive logic. They can evaluate verbal arguments as to their validity and analyze a stream of reasoning for inconsistencies. For example, a high school biology course may include not only the concrete aspects of various categories or taxonomies but also experiments demonstrating the deductive reasoning used in the field, including controlling variables and examining all possibilities. Questions such as How else could we explain this outcome? and What can we do to control for it? require the ability to deduce. Students who are 15 or 16 are far better at deducing than students who are in the transitional phase to formal operations and who are about 11 or 12.

Active methods can promote the development of formal operational reasoning. Renner and colleagues (1976) compared junior high school science classes using traditional methods of teaching with experimental classes using more active methods, including actual experience in solving laboratory science problems and the use of open inquiry and self-directed problem solving. They found a substantial increase in formal thinking abilities in the experimental group. The methods of teaching used during this transition from concrete to formal operations that consist of more student-directed inquiry and problem solving encourage the development of formal operational reasoning skills.

The American Question: Should We Accelerate?

American educators and parents often ask how fast or how early a child can accomplish a certain academic task. We are impressed by the child who is reading at the age of three or solving algebraic equations at age eight. Reflecting this fascination with speed, researchers have raised the question of whether children should be accelerated through these various developmental periods. The entire idea actually runs counter to Piaget's ideas.

Piaget was reluctant to make any recommendations to teachers or parents concerning how to maximize a child's potential, let alone how to accelerate the child (Vernon, 1976). Psychologists and educators sympathetic to Piaget have written a number of guides on how to help students develop the ability to think within their developmental stage (Furth & Wachs, 1975). Remember that Piaget's theory emphasizes the importance of giving children an opportunity to interact with the environment. Parents and teachers can help their children by providing an environment that allows for interaction with a variety of materials and gives children plenty of opportunity for discovery. For instance, when presenting children with objects of different textures, it is best to have a variety of such objects in the environment and to allow the children to explore the objects at their own rate. This does not mean that parents and educators remain passive. In fact, students who are in a transitional phase between two stages may be aided by being challenged. Educators interact extensively with students, but the emphasis is on discovery. In addition, if the child is ready, it makes sense to accelerate the curriculum to meet the child's needs. It is incorrect to suggest that we must always structure the curriculum a particular way for every ten-year-old. If a student is ready for more advanced mathematics or reading assignments, the student should be given such work.

Perhaps we should present the question a different way. The purpose of challenging the student and designing a stimulating and appropriate atmosphere is to provide an environment that allows children to develop their cognitive potential. At certain stages, particular experiences are beneficial. For example, to help a child develop the ability to seriate, we might present the child with some sticks of different lengths and ask the child to properly arrange the sticks. Perhaps the next day the child may be given disks, eventually asking the student to set the disks up from largest to smallest. The goal is not to see how fast a child can progress through these stages but to provide experiences that will help the child develop the ability to think, using his or her individual abilities defined by the developmental stage.

CONNECTIONS

What Piagetian Theory Means to the Teacher

Piaget's theory has much to say to educators. The following points show how we can apply the theory to the concerns of the classroom teacher.

1. **The teacher needs to see the material to be taught from the student's point of view.** Consider the teacher who may believe that students in the concrete stage of operations should be able to understand the symbolism behind a story. These students can read and understand the story but will not be able to make the cognitive leap to understanding abstractions. I can remember one of my teachers trying to get us to appreciate political cartoons in elementary school. Most of us found them very difficult or impossible to understand. It is most important to consider the child's cognitive developmental level when formulating lessons, units, and curricula.

2. **It is cognitive level, not grade level, that counts.** It is easy to read a description of Piaget's stages of cognitive development and then consider any child who is eight as functioning in the concrete operational stage and any fourteen-year-old as being in the formal operational stage. This is not so, and such thinking fails to appreciate and respect the fact that children develop at their own rate. Although children all pass through Piaget's stages, they may enter and leave a particular stage at different times. In addition, the preoperational and concrete operational stages are quite long, and some students in the same stage will be more advanced than others. Since students enter and leave these stages at various times, it is a mistake to think of students in terms only of grade level. Some students in the same grade will be more or less advanced than others.

One common misconception of stage theories is that they place children into neat categories. However, Piaget as well as other stage theorists emphasizes the fact that students may begin and end a particular stage at their own rate. Therefore, knowledge of the individual's reasoning strategies becomes important. Teachers who are working closely with students may begin to understand students' cognitive levels by observing how they attack problems and reason. For instance, junior high school teachers often have students in the midst of the transition between concrete and formal operations. Some students may have little problem with symbolism in English literature, while others may not understand it very well. Some students may find the meaning of an unknown in algebra relatively easy to understand, while others may require a more concrete explanation. In such cases, teachers must be prepared to help those students still at the concrete operational stage by presenting a variety of examples.

3. **Learning rests upon development.** Even a short review of Piaget's stages of cognitive development is enough to demonstrate that learning rests upon a developmental framework. Piaget would argue that the educational process should involve helping students develop their thinking and reasoning abilities.

4. **Some areas of knowledge cannot be taught but must be experienced.** Traditionally, we have been interested in efficiently and effectively transmitting facts and concepts to students. This is an important concern. However, Piaget reminds us that there are other types of knowledge that may need to be taught by allowing students the opportunity to explore and try out new things. The teacher does not teach the child conservation or classification but rather engineers experiences that allow the child to discover these concepts.

5. **The teacher's role is not only as a dispenser of information but also as a facilitator of learning.** Teachers have a role to play as dispensers of information. However, since Piaget would like students to become independent learners and capable of verifying things on their own, students need to know how to learn. Therefore, experimentation and activity-based education at all levels is required, although obviously the activities will differ as students mature. The student who learns through experimentation in a water tank about what floats and what does not float will understand this concept much better than the student who is merely told about it. The student who makes careful observations about plant life will not only understand the facts but also be able to use observation as a technique of learning on his or her own. The teacher helps the child to focus attention on the process by asking such questions as What do you think happened? What did you do to make this happen? What do you think would happen if . . . ? The teacher in this way encourages children to think about and predict the outcomes of particular actions and to assess predictions in terms of the outcomes.

6. **Using surprise is a way of producing disequilibrium.** One way to motivate students to discover is to provide them with experiences that cause disequilibrium. If students are shown something surprising—for example, an object that looks heavy but floats—they may be motivated to look more deeply into the phenomenon.

7. **Student differences in thinking at different cognitive levels do not show "errors" but rather show students' prevailing mental abilities.** Piaget has done more than any other theorist to rid us of the idea that children are just less-sophisticated adults. You might be surprised that many people who deal with children do not understand that children see the world differently and, more importantly, deal with information very differently than adults do. If we are to effectively teach children, we must understand how students think. When children do not come to the same conclusions that adults do, it does not mean that they are thinking "incorrectly." Put another way, students will have different explanations of reality at different times in their lives (Bybee & Sund, 1982). To understand where a student is and to encourage active participation, teachers should encourage students to justify their conclusions and inferences and explain their reasoning through such questions as Could you explain that? and Why do you think that is so? (Karplus & Arnold, 1982).

8. **Memorization is not understanding.** It has become very popular for children to show off what they know at earlier ages. Often children who are very young can recite the alphabet or count to twenty. This enthralls parents and grandparents but should not be interpreted to mean that the child understands the number system. Teaching children to memorize the names of states makes sense only if the child knows what a state is as well as the state's relationship to the country.

Piaget emphasized the importance of understanding, not just memorizing facts and names. This does not reduce the need for a knowledge base. A reasonable case can be made that memorization is necessary in some areas and that a knowledge base that includes, for example, a country's principal rivers, mountain ranges, and cities, is important. In fact, many Americans were surprised when a study showed that many young adults ages 18 to 24 could not answer relatively simple questions about geography (New York Times, July 28, 1988). However, such memorization is not all there is to education. Piagetian theory leads to the conclusion that understanding relationships and meaning is also important.

9. **Students need to be actively involved.** Children develop their reasoning through experiences that stimulate thinking (Bybee & Sund, 1982). They require interaction and experience. They are active learners, not merely passive receivers of information. Some of their experiences are social, and Piaget believed that social interaction is crucial to overcoming egocentrism. Other experiences involve games, puzzles, problems, and experimentation. If this is true, lessons can be designed to involve students through active exploration, both physical and mental. In some classrooms, students are passive receivers of information, which is then repeated at the appropriate times. Piaget did not agree with this concept of education. Since thinking is such an important part of education, children should be challenged to think, to consider, and to explore.

10. **When teaching elementary school students, teachers should use concrete examples.** Elementary school students in the concrete operations stage do best when offered concrete examples. Visual aids, including pictures and charts, and other audio-visual material are very effective. Hands-on experiences should be designed into the lesson whenever possible.

11. **Junior high school students are frequently in a slow transition to formal operational logic.** Certainly many changes take place during early adolescence. One of them involves the gradual change from concrete to formal operational abilities. Junior high school teachers often note the huge individual differences among the students in their classes. This is partly because some of the students will be able to understand symbolism and scientific logic and accept hypothetical problems while others who don't have such skills

struggle with activities that require those skills. The junior high school teacher must be armed with many concrete examples as well as the ability to challenge students to go beyond the concrete.

12. **When teaching high school, teachers should remember that students are sometimes interested in possibilities over reality.** Teens in the stage of formal operations develop the ability to use abstractions and separate the real from the possible. They are interested in possibilities, some of which are divorced from reality. They are likely to be idealistic and impractical. When suggestions for solving complex problems become too unrealistic, teachers should not hesitate to bring out the practical problems or the ramifications of actions and behaviors to others.

Criticisms of Piaget

It would be incorrect to give the impression that Piaget's ideas are completely accepted or that they remain unchallenged. Piaget's studies exploring how children think, reason, and solve problems allow us to understand how a child progresses cognitively from infancy through adolescence. However, Piaget's theory has also been criticized. Critics of the theory argue that Piaget underestimated the influence of formal learning on intellectual development. In addition, there is evidence both for and against the idea that children progress through a series of stages in cognitive development (Flavell, 1982).

Some Piagetian concepts, especially egocentrism, have also come under fire. For example, Flavell (1975) showed some children in the preoperational stage a number of proposed gifts for their fathers and asked the children to choose the appropriate gift. Most of the children chose the appropriate gift, demonstrating that they are able to take the point of view of others when they have had the experience in a particular activity.

There are also some technical objections to Piagetian theory. Most researchers find that when you test students in Piagetian tasks exactly the way Piaget did, you get Piaget's results. However, if the method of testing is changed, children can do quite a bit more than Piaget's method showed. For example, Inhelder and Piaget (1964) argued that children can seriate if they can place the items in correct order, put additional items into the series, and correct any errors. But Piaget used a total of ten sticks in his studies and concluded from this that true seriation did not occur at this stage. Barbara Koslowski (1980) used a similar approach, but instead of ten sticks she used four. Using the same criteria, she found that three quarters of the three- and four-year-olds could put the sticks in size order, about four fifths could insert new sticks into the order, and all the children could correct the incorrect insertions. The ability to seriate is present in these children, but ten sticks is simply too many for preschoolers to deal with. This does not mean that Piaget was wrong, only that we should be very careful about stating categorically what a child can or cannot do without looking at the experience children have with the task and the nature and requirements of that task.

PIAGET RECONSIDERED

Now that we've looked at Piaget's theory and applied it to some basic questions, it is difficult not to marvel at Piaget's discoveries. The basic ideas of understanding how students reason at different stages, appreciating the importance of different types of knowledge, helping students learn how to learn, taking on the role of facilitator as well as provider of information, and using surprise to create interest and encourage curiosity are all important and have implications that will arise again and again as you teach.

The importance of Piagetian theory as one base for teaching does not lie in the completeness of the theory as a mode of instruction (see Kuhn, 1979). The importance is that the theory serves to remind us that teachers have a duty to encourage the development of a student's reasoning capacity. The cognitive structures of the student serve as a base allowing material to be assimilated and accommodated. If that cognitive structure is understood and appreciated, the material presented will be congruent with the student's abilities and needs, thus making school a more meaningful experience for the student and a more pleasant and rewarding one for the teacher.

LANGUAGE SKILLS

Listen to a child discuss a trip to the zoo or tell a story. We can wonder at the originality and creativity of the child's language. Language allows us to express our thoughts, our ideas, and our desires to one another. It allows us to show what we know and to influence others. Language skills are obviously crucial to success in school.

The relationship between cognitive development and language is intimate but very complex. Cognitive development certainly underlies linguistic abilities (Flavell, 1985). For example, words are symbols, and the development of symbolic function and deferred imitation—concepts described by Piaget—are necessary for language to develop. A child cannot use language until he or she has acquired the ability to use one thing to refer to—or symbolize—another. A child must listen to adult speech and learn words to use at a later time. Cognition and language are also linked by a simple truism—that people can talk about only what they know. A child who does not understand abstract ideas cannot talk about them.

On the other hand, linguistic skills facilitate cognitive functioning. When children possess a good vocabulary and an ability to express themselves well, they can better communicate their understanding of concepts, understand new concepts, and explore ideas. The process is cumulative, and new words allow students to master new areas of knowledge (Clark & Clark, 1977). By the time elementary schoolteachers meet the student, the child has already learned basic skills in this area. However, teachers can still do much to improve student language skills.

The Development of Language

Language development begins in infancy. Obviously, communication between infants and their caregivers does not require language, since smiles, cries, gestures, and eye contact all form the basis for later communication. Although very young infants cannot understand words, they do respond to the caregiver's language, and some linguistic abilities are present almost from birth (Molfese et al., 1982). One-month-old infants are able to discriminate between certain vowels, such as the *u* from an *i-a* and *pa* from *pi* (Trehub, 1973).

The infant's ability to respond to language and to other nonverbal cues leads to a kind of turn taking. A parent speaks, and the baby responds by smiling or cooing. The parent then says something else, and the pattern continues. These interactions are the beginning of a conversation mode and form the basis for later communication. The infant is also an expert at cooing, which involves production of single-syllable sounds such as *oo*. Vowel sounds are often led by a consonant, resulting in a sound like *moo.*

The next step in language development is babbling, which involves both vowel and consonant sounds stuck together and repeated often. Babbling may begin as early as three months, and it gradually increases until about nine to twelve months of age. It then decreases as the child begins to use words (deVilliers and deVilliers, 1978).

Children usually utter their first word anytime between ten and fifteen months of age, but there is considerable individual variation. Children's first words are not usually those they hear most often. Katherine Nelson (1973) studied early word acquisition in a number of children and was able to divide the children into two categories. Expressive children used words that were involved primarily in social interactions such as "bye-bye" and "stop it." The early language of referential children involved the naming of objects, such as dog and penny. These different styles followed the linguistic style used by the child's caregivers. The parents of referential children named objects very frequently, while those of expressive children used words that directed their children's activities and emphasized social interactions. Notice that even at this tender age, the environment has a potent influence on the type of language developed in young children.

Children then begin to use single words to represent an entire thought. This is called a **holophrase.** For instance, a child says "up" to mean "pick me up." The child's early speech, whether it is constructed of two- or three-word sentences, leaves out small words like *a, to,* and *from* and concentrates on the more important words. This is called **telegraphic speech,** because it is similar to the language found in telegrams, where the sender includes only the words absolutely necessary to communicate the message. For example, "mommy go store" may mean mommy is going to the store, or it may be thought of as a command: "Mommy, go to the store." Whatever this utterance means, the child has used only the words that are absolutely necessary for conveying meaning.

By about three-and-a-half years of age, children begin to use sentences of approximately four or five words, and by five years of age, their syntax is quite good. The three-year-old has a vocabulary of about 900 words and begins to use plural nouns and the past tense. By age four, children are using conjunctions and their sentences are much more complex. By age five or six, syntax has improved and approaches that of an adult (Smith & Neisworth, 1983), although tense errors and other grammatical irregularities still occur in speech until eight to ten years of age.

As their linguistic competence develops, children make certain predictable mistakes (Griffiths, 1986). If you listen even casually to the speech patterns of young children, you will find some striking differences between their use of language and that of adults. Young children overextend and underextend their use of words and follow grammatical rules with what

holophrase   One word used to stand for an entire thought.

telegraphic speech   Sentences in which only the basic words necessary to communicate meaning are used, with helping words such as *a* or *to* left out.

"I drinked the waters!" Once children begin to master the rules of grammar, they often overgeneralize them.

seems to be blind devotion. For example, a young child looking at a magazine might label every picture of a man "daddy" and every four-legged animal "dog," even though the child knows his or her father and is probably aware of the difference between a cat and a dog. This type of error in which children apply a term more broadly than is correct is called an **overextension** and is probably a problem of production more than of comprehension (Whitehurst, 1982). That is, children understand the difference, but they have difficulty producing the correct labels. Children also **underextend;** that is, they use a term to cover a smaller universe than it should (Anglin, 1977). Young children often use "animal" to define only mammals and may deny that people, insects, or birds are also animals.

Once children begin to acquire some of the basic rules, they overuse or, as psychologists say, **overgeneralize** (Goodluck, 1986). For example, to pluralize a noun, we ordinarily add an *s* to the word, as in dogs or pencils. However, exceptions abound, and the plural of man is not mans but men. When creating the past tense, we normally add the suffix *ed,* as in walked or talked. But again, exceptions are plentiful: The past tense of go is not goed but went, and the past tense of see is not seed but saw. Children will often overuse these rules and use words like *seed* or *goed.* They may have used the word correctly in the past, but once they know the rule, they apply it in every case, producing such grammatically incorrect forms. With experience, children correct themselves and most gradually learn the exceptions with little or no formal training.

True or False   It is normal for young children to use the incorrect forms of words, such as *goed* and *drinked* instead of *went* and *drank.*

How We Learn Language

The simplest questions are often the most difficult to answer. For years, psychologists have been struggling over the question of how a child develops from a being that understands and produces no language to one that can use language with great ease. At first glance, it appears that children learn language through imitation. The vocabulary of each language differs, and children do learn vocabulary through imitation. Children learn the word *cookie* when they have the need for the word. They master words in an

overextension   A type of error in which children apply a term more broadly than it should be.

underextension   A type of error in which children apply a term more narrowly than it should be.

overgeneralization   A type of error in which children overuse the basic rules of language. For instance, once they learn to use plural nouns they may say "mans" instead of "men."

attempt to communicate with others (Hoff-Ginsberg, 1986). When they finally say "chair," they have imitated what they have heard in their environment and attached a meaning to the word. The growth in vocabulary, especially between the ages of one-and-a-half and six-and-a-half, is great.

The effect of imitation on word acquisition is evident, and parents who label common, everyday items are more likely to have a child who has a superior early vocabulary (Nelson, 1973). According to B. F. Skinner (1957), operant conditioning—including the processes of reinforcement, generalization, and discrimination—is responsible for language development. Children learn language the same way they learn about everything else. They are reinforced for labeling the environment and for asking for things. Through the process of generalization and discrimination, children come to reduce their errors and use appropriate forms of language.

It is a mistake, however, to think that because the child learns vocabulary through these processes, all language development can be explained by imitation and reinforcement. There is more to it. To use language correctly, children must learn the rules of language, such as changing tense or creating word order (called syntax). Although learning must be involved in language acquisition, the theory does not seem sufficient to explain totally how a child acquires language. It is difficult to explain the simple but brilliant creativity and originality of a child's sentences using learning theory. All children create original sentences they have not heard before. In addition, how could a child of limited cognitive abilities master the complicated rules of grammar that even adults cannot explain—and do this without formal training (Bloom, 1975). Finally, if only the processes of learning are involved, why do children make the same mistakes as they develop their language abilities and produce such childish speech patterns as telegraphic speech, which they do not hear spoken?

A different approach, called the **nativist approach,** was taken by Noam Chomsky (1972), who argued that human beings are preprogrammed to learn language. Children require only exposure to the language prevailing in their own culture. Human beings are born with an innate biological ability to learn language, called a language acquisition device. Children acquire the grammar of the particular language because their brain is biologically patterned to understand the structure of languages.

Although human beings may be "prewired" to learn language, the weaknesses of the nativist position are evident. For example, the existence of a language acquisition device has not yet been demonstrated. In addition, even if we agree that a neurological basis for language exists, it does not explain the processes involved in learning language. Finally, although the similarities between how children learn language around the world are impressive, some differences exist. Although some biological foundation for learning language is probable, the nativist position does not fully explain language acquisition either.

The child's cognitive abilities certainly must be taken into account if we are to understand language acquisition. Learning language involves such cognitive processes as attention, information processing, and retention. For instance, paying attention to stimuli that are loud or attached to some vital activity (such as feeding), remembering them, and making discriminations and judgments about them (such as whether they are the same or different) are all cognitive processes related to learning language (Peters, 1986). Children must also develop some intuitive understanding of the rules of language which, in itself, is a cognitive process.

Another important ingredient is the child's social environment. Children do not acquire language in a vacuum. They are affected by their total environment, including the home and day-care center or school they may attend. Language is purely functional. The purpose of speech and language is to communicate thoughts, ideas, and desires to one another and to direct the actions of other people. The child learns that communication involves signaling meaning, sharing experiences, and taking turns. Jerome Bruner (1978) sees language development in terms of problem solving. Children must solve the problem of how to communicate their wishes and thoughts to others. They learn language through interactions with others and by actively using language. The opportunity to engage actively in communication is necessary. Children acquire grammar and vocabulary to accomplish their aim of getting across to others what they want and what they are thinking. Language is learned as an extension of nonlinguistic communication.

Children learn language through an active process that involves exposure to a particular linguistic environment and active language usage. The finding that the nature of this early linguistic interaction determines the child's later language abilities comes as no surprise. Children who are encouraged at an early age to verbalize and expand on their language skills develop superior language abilities as they get older (Hoff-Ginsberg, 1986).

A number of studies have found that language usage among middle-class and working-class people differs. Middle-class youngsters use more expansive language and do better in language activities in school. Children of working-class parents use simpler sentences and more commands (Olim et al., 1967). But we must remember that language is functional and that children of working-class parents are not deficient in their native environment (Menyuk, 1977). What is somewhat lacking are the specific language abilities required in school.

▶▶▶ CONNECTIONS

How Teachers Can Help Students Improve Their Language Skills

The school is a significant part of the child's social and linguistic environment. Although children obviously have developed their basic language skills before entering school, teachers can do much to improve children's language skills through direct involvement in classroom activities and by helping parents to expand their children's language abilities. The following suggestions can be of some help in this regard.

1. **Encourage and improve teacher-student communication.** Children develop their linguistic abilities as active participants. This is true in the classroom as well as in the home. Many studies indicate that teachers do most of the talking in the classroom and most students simply answer questions using only one or two words. Research also indicates that as students interact with teachers, their linguistic skills are improved (Cooper & Stewart, 1987). Therefore, teachers can improve students' language skills by encouraging verbal interaction. There are many ways to do this. Asking more open-ended questions is one way. Asking students for details when they speak is another. With younger students, using a show-and-tell procedure may help. In addition, students may be encouraged to speak in front of the class if asked questions such as Who did something this morning that made you feel proud? or What did you do this morning? (Oken-Wright, 1988). The class can be encouraged to ask questions and participate as well. Asking students to make up their own stories or to tell a story based upon a photograph is still another way to improve language skills (Hough et al., 1987). Roleplaying is yet another possibility.

2. **Talk about student concerns.** What to talk about is often a problem. Students are rarely fluent in the new material that may have just been presented. They will, however, talk about their own concerns and ideas. Teachers can improve linguistic skills if they talk with children about topics of interest to students that are related to the learning outcomes sought (King, 1987).

3. **Provide a friendly, warm atmosphere in which students are not afraid to make a mistake.** Extensive verbal interactions are more likely to occur when the atmosphere is relaxed, students have a warm relationship with their teacher, and students are not afraid to participate (Christensen, 1960).

4. **Beware of paying less attention to children low in linguistic ability.** It is natural for teachers to hesitate to call upon students whose verbal abilities are limited. Such students rarely participate on their own. However, it is important to understand this tendency and realize that these students can be drawn into conversations through questions, assignments that require verbal interaction, or discussions about topics of interest to the student.

5. **Do not evaluate everything.** One reason students tend not to participate and practice their verbal skills is that they fear evaluation. Some teachers will correct and evaluate everything, making students frightened to participate. In a conversation, it is best *not* to correct everything.

6. **Listen to the students.** If students ask or answer questions or comment on the material, both the teacher and other students must listen. If you are an active listener, which involves giving feedback and dealing with what students are saying, students are more likely to feel that their input is important and accepted and to participate in class discussions. Teachers should not ignore student comments because this communicates to the class that student input is unimportant. Then, students may not listen to their fellow students. However, if teachers pay attention to students' comments, other students will listen. One way to make certain they are listening is to ask one student to comment on or summarize what another student has said. If the student who is called on says that he was not listening, ask the student who spoke to repeat what she said.

7. **Model good language usage.** Because children tend to copy the way their parents and teachers express themselves, reasonably good linguistic models are important. Finishing sentences, answering questions in an expanded way, and using adjectives can contribute to children's language development.

8. **Avoid sexism in language activities.** Teachers sometimes show a tendency to call on male students for verbal interaction that often requires critical thinking and on females for more factual answers. This should be avoided.

9. **Help parents to encourage their children's language skills.** Especially in the elementary school years, teachers can provide parents with various ideas for language-related activities that may encourage more extensive verbal interaction, such as reading to children, making up stories, or discussing something the child did during the day. Parents can actively help their children develop their linguistic abilities. (One drawback, however, can exist when the dialect or language spoken at home or in the neighborhood is not the same as that spoken by teachers in the school.)

Black Versus Standard English: Deficit or Difference?

"By the time I get there, he will have gone."
"Time I git dere, he be done gone."

If you were asked which of these sentences would be best received by an English teacher, you would certainly choose the first. While the first sentence illustrates Standard English, the second is **Black English**—a dialect spoken throughout the United States by lower-income blacks (Raspberry, 1970) that contains a consistent, logical, and coherent grammar (Labov, 1977).

At one time it was thought that Black English was simply mispronounced and poorly spoken Standard English, and the dialect was accorded no respect. In fact, because children from ghetto areas have many language difficulties, it was thought that their problems were caused in part by their initial exposure to, and learning of, this dialect. This belief led to what has been called the **linguistic deficit hypothesis.** The dialect was considered to be a deficit—i.e., something wrong—not merely different. It was something that a child should give up somewhere on the educational ladder.

Beginning in the 1960s, however, social scientists began to reconsider this position. After all, if Black English is understood in the black child's environment and has a consistent set of rules, why treat it differently from Spanish or French? In some ways, it is even more precise than Standard English. When a teacher asks a black child why her father couldn't make a meeting the night before, the child might answer, "He sick." But when asked why the father has not attended any of the meetings during the year, the child says, "He be sick" (Raspberry, 1970). Inclusion of the word *be* shows an ongoing, chronic status. In Standard English, the answers to both questions might simply be, "He is sick."

Black English is a valid dialect of Standard English. Black children do not suffer from linguistic deficits, but they do experience some academic difficulties because of **linguistic differences,** and differences are not necessarily deficits. Raspberry (1970) presents a nice analogy. He notes that the reason we want children to learn Standard English is that Black English is less negotiable than Standard English, just as trading stamps are less negotiable than cash. What is needed is to help children develop Standard English without forcing them to give up their own dialect, just as a child can learn English as a second language without giving up his or her original language.

If teachers consider Black English to be inferior to Standard English, however, they may reject black children's ideas, essentially turning these students off and reducing communication between teacher and student. Such students may develop feelings of inferiority. This can be minimized if teachers accept the child's ideas without reacting negatively to the dialect. This is true of regional dialects as well.

Whether it is called a deficit or a difference, Standard English represents difficulties for lower-income children from ghetto areas. Perhaps both the deficit hypothesis and the difference hypothesis miss the mark in one regard. Children need to be able to deal with their environment, and Black English is useful for this. However, even though Black English may be generally accepted as a dialect, children need to learn Standard English if they are to succeed in school and in the work world. When six Black college women were sent for job interviews, those who spoke Black English were given shorter interviews and received fewer job offers. The offers that were made were for lower-paid positions (Raloff, 1982). Thus, for both academic and economic reasons, students need to learn Standard English.

Most people who accept Black English as a dialect agree that Black children still need to learn to speak Standard English. What is lacking is sufficient information on how one teaches children a different dialect—one the children will not hear very much around their own neighborhoods. One promising approach is to point out the differences between students' speech and Standard English without criticizing students' speech. Students exposed to these differences show no resentment as long as their speech is not called incorrect (Cooper & Stewart, 1987).

The Bilingual Puzzle

Black English is a dialect of English, but what of the tens of thousands of children in the United States who

---

Black English   A dialect spoken throughout the United States by lower-income blacks.

linguistic deficit hypothesis   The belief that a dialect such as Black English is a hindrance to learning.

linguistic difference hypothesis   The belief that a dialect such as Black English is different from Standard English but not a deficit.

Cognition, Development, and Learning

Should bilingual children be taught subjects other than English in their native language or in English?

come from homes in which a foreign language (most commonly Spanish) is the primary language. These **bilingual** children, who often come from impoverished backgrounds, face many of the same problems blacks do, although their language itself is accepted as a true language. English is the second language for these children, and their success in the United States depends partly on learning Standard English.

What is the best way to educate these children? Some educators propose that a bilingual program be introduced in the school—that subjects such as mathematics and social studies be taught in Spanish to Spanish-speaking students until the children gain sufficient ability in English to function effectively in that language. At the same time, these children would receive instruction in Standard English. Evaluations

---

bilingual A term describing people who can communicate in more than one language.

---

of such programs have been mixed. Some evidence shows that the programs have helped students achieve scholastically (Willig, 1985; Crawford, 1987). Other researchers disagree, noting that the programs have not been as successful as hoped (Baker & de Kanter, 1981).

Some researchers note that there is a strong need to emphasize English instead of the child's native language through a process similar to immersion. In such programs, students are taught in English by teachers who know another language but use it only to help students who do not understand the material being taught. The students are encouraged not only to use English but also to ask questions in their native language when necessary (U.S. News and World Report, March 31, 1986).

Other detractors note the difficulty in recruiting effective bilingual teachers. They additionally point out that problems arise when more than one foreign language is used by various children in a class.

The debate over the best way to teach English to bilingual children is ongoing, and more research is needed (August, 1986). Bilingual education is a fact of life in the United States, although it is increasingly under attack, and the debate over the consequences of bilingualism continues.

At first glance, people who can function in society using more than one language would seem to be at a great advantage. However, research in the 1950s indicated that bilingual children did poorly in school and suffered retarded language development in both languages (Segalowitz, 1981). These studies have been criticized for their poor methodology and questionable testing devices.

Recently, however, an about-face on the issue of bilingualism has occurred. McLaughlin (1977, 1978) found no clear evidence that being bilingual leads to intellectual or cognitive problems in school. Some of the difficulties encountered by bilingual students are due not to their bilingualism but to poverty, poor housing, lack of intellectual stimulation, and other socioeconomic variables (Diaz, 1985). In fact, there is evidence that bilingual children are high in verbal and nonverbal intelligence when tested in an appropriate manner and show more cognitive flexibility (Segalowitz, 1981). Some have argued that this is so only in a balanced bilingual situation in which both languages are encouraged and taught. However, often bilingual students are not given any opportunity to continue their native language studies, which means that they are relatively poor in their primary language (Crawford, 1987).

True or False Bilingualism itself leads to cognitive difficulties and academic problems.

What can we conclude about the bilingual child? First, there is nothing inherently inferior about bilingualism, and there is evidence that bilingual children have certain advantages over their monolingual peers. Second, poverty and bilingualism are often confused. Many minorities in the United States who speak a language other than English suffer from the degradation of poverty and all that it entails—including poor self-concept, disillusionment, discrimination, and poor opportunity. It may be that these problems rather than bilingualism itself actually cause many of the difficulties experienced by students in the public schools. Finally, we still do not know the best way to teach English to children, and there is probably room for many different approaches.

If bilingual programs in the schools are to work, they must ensure that all children learn English in a way that will allow them to function reasonably well, not only in the outside world but also in academic settings. If children leave school knowing some mathematics and social studies but functioning poorly in language-related areas, such as reading, writing, and speaking, their prospects for educational advancement will be poor and their vocational opportunities limited. To be certain that these children are learning English, bilingual programs must be continuously evaluated.

LANGUAGE DEVELOPMENT RECONSIDERED

Linguistic skills are certainly one key to academic success. Although students already have learned their primary language by the time they meet their first schoolteacher, there is much teachers can do to encourage students to develop their linguistic skills.

We will undoubtedly see increasing emphasis placed on developing linguistic skills. Language developed in childhood is carried over into adulthood. Adults are frequently judged on their linguistic abilities, including their vocabulary and ability to express themselves. Adults who have limited linguistic abilities may find themselves limited in the job market and in certain interpersonal interactions, such as dealing with supervisors or making a positive impression at job interviews. Thus, language abilities take on an importance for the entire lifespan.

SUMMARY

1. Children think in a qualitatively different manner from adults. Jean Piaget described the qualitative differences in reasoning among children as they develop.

2. Piaget differentiated between three different types of knowledge. Physical knowledge involves understanding the nature of objects and is acquired through discovery. Logico-mathematical knowledge involves the understanding of relationships between objects and is acquired through a process called invention. Social-arbitrary knowledge is the understanding of facts and rules and is learned from others.

3. Piaget argues that the school's main task is to promote reasoning. Learning rests on development. Development is defined by four principal factors: maturation, experience, social transmis-

sion, and the process of equilibration. Equilibration is the process by which children seek a balance between what they know and what they are experiencing.

4. Two important Piagetian concepts are organization and adaptation. A schema is an organized system of actions and thoughts useful for dealing with the environment that can be generalized to many situations. At first, schemata are physical and include sucking, looking, and touching. Later, schemata become more symbolic, internal, and mental. These mental schemata are called operations. Adaptation involves assimilation and accommodation. In the process of assimilation, input is filtered or modified to fit already existing structures. The process of accommodation involves modifying internal existing schemata to meet the requirements of new experience.

5. Piaget argued that children's cognitive development could be understood as occurring in four stages, each of which is qualitatively different from the last. People cannot skip stages, and they do not regress. However, since children can enter or leave stages at different times, equating age with stage is incorrect.

6. In the first stage, the sensorimotor period, infants must explore their world through their senses and motor activity. They gradually develop a sense of object permanence—the understanding that things do not disappear when they are out of view.

7. In the preoperational stage, lasting from about ages two through seven, children can use symbols and begin to use language. Preschoolers cannot seriate, classify, solve problems that require a knowledge of conservation, or reverse processes. Children in the preoperational stage center—concentrate on only one dimension at a time—and judge everything on the basis of appearances. They are egocentric—believing that everyone sees things from their point of view—and at the beginning of the stage, they are animistic—believing that everything is animate. Teachers employ the children's ability to represent and encourage students to discover the properties of physical objects and the relationship between objects.

8. The third stage is the concrete operational stage, during which many of the limitations of the preoperational stage slowly fade. Children in this stage can conserve, reverse operations, classify,

and seriate. However, they cannot handle abstractions or hypothetical examples and have difficulty with scientific reasoning.

9. Piaget argues that just because a child can count from one to ten does not mean that the child understands the concept of number. Number concepts depend upon logico-mathematical knowledge, and students need experience to attain this knowledge. Teachers can design classroom activities that provide students with experiences that encourage them to focus on the nature of the relationships that underlie mathematics concepts.

10. In the stage of formal operations, teens gradually develop the ability to use scientific logic, deal with abstractions, and separate what is from what can be. High school teachers can make use of the student's ability to use hypothetical deductive logic and abstractions to go beyond the concrete and discuss aspects of science, mathematics, social studies, and English that are divorced from any concrete occurrence.

11. Piaget's theory has many important implications for teachers. According to Piaget, teachers should see the lesson from the student's point of view and take the student's reasoning abilities into consideration when planning and teaching. This requires an understanding of the cognitive level of students, not just their grade level. Piaget advocated the use of active methods to facilitate learning. The teacher is not simply an information giver but has the responsibility of guiding the students to use their abilities and discover new ideas. Students must be actively involved in their learning.

12. Critics of Piaget claim that he underestimated the importance of formal learning and that there is evidence both for and against the idea that people progress through stages. In addition, some of Piaget's concepts, such as egocentrism, have been the subject of dispute.

13. By the time elementary schoolchildren meet their teachers, they have already learned language. The infant can discriminate certain sounds from birth. Infants coo, babble, and utter their first word at about one year. They then begin to use holophrases—single words that stand for entire thoughts. At about eighteen months, they show telegraphic speech in which they leave out small words like *a* and *to*. Children speak in full sentences by about three and a half. Children over-

generalize the rules of language, using them consistently even when exceptions are grammatically correct.

14. Behaviorists such as Skinner use the processes of reinforcement and imitation to explain language acquisition. Chomsky argues that a human being is preprogrammed to learn language and merely requires exposure to a language to master it. The nativist position sees language acquisition as having a biological basis. Cognitive psychologists argue that such factors as attention and memory are involved in language acquisition. Social interaction is also important, because children learn language through interaction with caregivers who fine tune their language to the developmental level of the child. Environmental influences are important, and teachers may improve the linguistic abilities of their students by encouraging parents to help develop better skills in their children and by improving teacher-student verbal interaction.

15. Black English is a dialect spoken by lower-income blacks. It has a consistent, logical, and coherent grammar. Many authorities believe that it should be accepted as a valid dialect and that teachers should not reject the ideas of students using this dialect. But children who use Black English sometimes have difficulty with Standard English, which is necessary for success in the academic and vocational world.

16. Early studies seemed to show that bilingualism was a deficit to learning, but more recent studies stress the advantages the bilingual child has. A great deal of controversy surrounds bilingual programs, and much research concerning the best way to teach English remains to be performed. It is important that every child learn Standard English.

ACTIVITIES AND EXERCISES

1. **Conservation.** Piaget noted that young children do not understand the principle of conservation: that quantities remain the same despite changes in their appearance. Try this experiment. Place equal amounts of liquid into two identical glasses and ask the child if the glasses have the same amount of liquid. Then pour the contents of one glass into a short, squat container and ask the child which container has more. Children in the preoperational stage say that the taller container has more. Try to "test" children as young as four and go up through eleven-year-olds. You will notice that the very young children can't do it and the older children seem to have little difficulty with it. However, you will also note that not all children ages seven and eight or so will answer the same way, thus demonstrating that there are individual differences among children. In the early grades of elementary school, these individual differences are especially important. ONE CAUTION THOUGH. Whenever performing a Piagetian experiment, do not surround yourself with an audience. "Test" one child at a time. If you have older and younger children you may find that the older children "can't believe" that the younger ones can't get it right and may ridicule them.

2. **Proverbs and Adages.** Many elementary school students have difficulty understanding adages and proverbs. Piaget argued that this is because children at that age can't handle abstractions. Ask children of various ages to interpret the simple proverb, "You can lead a horse to water, but you can't make him drink" and note the interpretations. You will probably find that children in elementary school interpret the proverb in a very concrete manner. Try this with other proverbs as well.

3. **Appearance and Reality.** Children in the preoperational stage often make judgments based on the way things appear. An easy way to demonstrate this is to take twelve short sticks of equal size. Lay six sticks end to end in a straight line and next to this display lay six sticks in a jagged formation. The first display of six sticks looks longer, because it is straight. Place a toy car at the start of each "road" and ask children of different ages which car will travel farther—the car on the straight road or the car on the jagged road. Most children in the preoperational stage will say the car on the straight road. By the end of the preoperational stage some children will get this right and some will not, and older children will easily answer the question.

4. **Visit a Nursery School or a Kindergarten.** There is no doubt that Piaget has had a greater impact on the early childhood education curriculum than on the later elementary school and secondary

school areas. Visit an early childhood class and take note of those activities that seem guided by Piaget's theory. For example, look for tasks that may give children practice in classification and seriation and for teaching strategies that create disequilibrium in some way. If you can, ask the teacher if he or she was affected by any of Piaget's ideas.

5. **Use of Surprise.** Piaget argued that when a teacher creates disequilibrium in a child through surprise, the student is motivated to find out more about the area and reestablish equilibrium. Design three activities in your area of expertise in which surprise may be used. If you have the opportunity, try the activities out on a few students.

6. **Read a Section of Piaget's Work.** Piaget wrote many books and articles. To gain a better understanding of his method of research and his ideas about education, read one of his books or articles. For example, Piaget's book entitled *The Science of Education and the Psychology of the Child* (1970, Grossman Publishers, Inc.) is certainly a relevant work.

7. **Investigate How the Teaching of Mathematics Has Changed.** If there is one subject where the curriculum and emphasis seems to change periodically, it is mathematics. Recent studies showing that American students do not always measure up to students in other countries may provide the impetus for even further change. Interview an experienced elementary schoolteacher or a mathematics coordinator for a school district and ask her or him what changes she or he has noticed in teaching mathematics and whether she or he believes any other changes are on the horizon. Evaluate the comments in the light of Piaget's ideas. Another possibility is to interview a specialist in mathematics education who may be engaged in research on teaching mathematics. Ask the researcher whether Piaget's ideas about the development of mathematics concepts have affected the teaching of mathematics.

8. **Use of Observation.** One active method of learning is through observation. In many classrooms, students are encouraged to observe animals or different physical phenomena and report what they see. Design a project requiring observation for students who are functioning at the cognitive level at which you hope to teach.

9. **Analyzing English Literature.** Piaget notes that students in the concrete and formal operational stages may both read the same books but the concrete operational reasoner will not be aware of the underlying abstract symbolic meaning. Ask students or an English teacher what books are required reading in their high school. If you can talk to an English teacher, ask to what extent abstract symbolism enters his or her lessons.

10. **Visit a Bilingual Classroom.** Bilingual programs are relatively common but still controversial. Perhaps you can arrange a visit to a bilingual classroom to observe how a bilingual program is conducted. Or you might want to speak to a bilingual teacher to learn the teacher's aims and strategies for teaching bilingual children. Be certain you cover the question of evaluating the students' progress in English.

11. **The Nature of Student-Teacher Interaction.** Teachers ask many questions, but often their questions can be answered by students in one or two words. Observe some classes and make a note of how questions are answered in the class. If students answer in one or two words, note whether the teacher asks them to expand upon their answers, thereby helping them develop their skills. If so, how does the teacher do it?

12. **What Do Teachers Do to Help Parents Foster Language Skills?** Many teachers, especially in elementary school, try to encourage parental involvement in language activities. Ask elementary schoolteachers how they encourage parental involvement and make a list of the activities they suggest. Sometimes, teachers or districts send suggestions for language-building activities directly to students' homes. If this is the case, ask for a copy of these suggestions.

SCENARIOS

Here are eleven scenarios. Try to apply the information you have learned in the chapter to each situation.

1. Mr. Edwards is trying to teach his third-grade class the difference between democracy and dictatorships. After giving the two different definitions of the terms, he wants to discuss the advantages of democracy but finds that his students do not seem to understand the concepts. This has happened in the past, and his friend who teaches science has found that his fourth-grade students

don't seem to be able to reason in a scientific manner. What can these teachers do to teach these concepts to their students?

2. Mr. Bender enjoys his tenth-grade English students very much. They are a lively group, always seemingly ready to argue or discuss a point with him. After reading a short story or discussing some problem related to the story, however, the students raise solutions to problems that are quite unrealistic; they don't seem to understand the practical problems involved. Mr. Bender sometimes finds himself arguing with his students. He does not believe this is very educationally sound, but he is concerned about their inability to handle problems realistically. He asks you whether his class is "unusual" and what can be done to "bring them down to earth." How would you reply?

3. Mrs. Ortiz's problem is not her student Stan, who is a first-grader with a relatively slow maturation rate and who is making slow but steady progress. Her problem is Stan's mother, who claims that her child is stubborn and seems not to reason as a "regular person." Stan's mother has read some of Piaget and knows that her child is now at the end of the preoperational stage and will soon be entering the concrete operational stage. However, she wants to speed up Stan's progress somewhat. She argues that only by speeding up her son's development can he compete successfully with the other children in the class. If you were Mrs. Ortiz, how would you react to Stan's mother, and what would you do for the child?

4. Mr. Arthur is proud to be seen as a "tough" teacher who stresses the basics. He believes that students in the fourth grade must be encouraged to develop a knowledge base, and he emphasizes memorization of material such as names of cities, states, different animals, flowers, mathematics facts, and definitions. Lately, he has noticed that although his students may do well on tests of these materials, they do not seem to be able to apply their knowledge and often show a lack of knowledge concerning the relationships between these pieces of information. Mr. Arthur believes a knowledge base is important but does not know what to do now that he has encountered this problem. If you had to advise him, what would you say?

5. Ms. Falco believes that her sixth-grade classroom should offer students an opportunity to become more active and involved learners rather than allow them to simply sit back and passively accept the information she provides. She agrees with Piaget that students need to be actively involved. She would like to provide this active involvement in mathematics, English, science, and social studies but does not know what she can do. She asks you, her colleague. What would you tell her?

6. There is disagreement concerning the importance and relevance of Piaget's work to planning and teaching lessons. In one of your college psychology class discussions, Don states that after his analysis of the nursery school years, Piaget really does not have anything very useful or specific to say to elementary schoolteachers and nothing to say to high school teachers. Sherry disagrees, claiming that if schools were run using Piagetian principles of active education, they would be more successful and little else would be needed. She argues that the way we test would have to be changed, but the use of more active means of teaching would enhance both the elementary and high school experiences of students. As others give their opinion, it is plain that the question of what Piaget means for the elementary and secondary schoolteacher is a matter of controversy within the teaching ranks. If you were asked to give your opinion of how Piaget's theory applies to the everyday concerns of the teacher, what would you say?

7. You are at a parent-teacher association meeting when one parent notes that the curriculum of the early elementary school grades does not seem to emphasize formal learning. The woman's daughter, who is in second grade, does not receive much, if any, formal homework, and there appears to be no urgency to learn mathematics or master social studies. The daughter does not know the names of the states and "still does math using disks." The mother argues that these students should be going as fast as they can and should be engaged in more formal learning. You are asked to present an answer to her. What would you say?

8. Mr. Leopold has become somewhat concerned over David's problems in mathematics. David is in second grade and does not seem to grasp numbers very well. When David's parents visited school, they noted that David had always been

slow (but within the normal range of development) and argued that all he needed was time. They did nothing at home with David to develop any skills, because they did not want to frustrate him. They again told Mr. Leopold that in time, David would catch up. They argued that maturation is very important and cannot be rushed. If you were Mr. Leopold, how would you answer David's parents? What could you do (if you choose to do anything) to help David?

9. Mrs. Polanski would like to teach a unit on American government to her fifth-grade class. She shows a chart covering the judicial, the executive, and the legislative branches of government. She goes through the idea of checks and balances and finds her students have some difficulty with this. She asks the students questions about the branches of government and finds that they can answer them. Although students performed fairly well on the test measuring knowledge of the system, she is disturbed that they do not seem to understand the idea of checks and balances. Evaluate Mrs. Polanski's method of teaching. How else could these ideas have been taught to the students?

10. Ms. Carlino is concerned about Alana, a student who comes from another country and is having some difficulty with English. Alana's parents speak English hesitantly, and although Alana is a very bright youngster, she is not achieving well. The school has a bilingual program where social studies, science, and mathematics are taught in Alana's native language. Alana's parents believe, however, that this will retard her progress in English. They ask you for your advice and how they can be certain Alana learns enough English to finish school. What advice would you give Alana's parents?

11. Mr. King has been asked by the P.T.A. to conduct a workshop for parents to discuss ways in which parents can help the school improve their children's language skills. Mr. King works in an elementary school in a working-class neighborhood. He is warned that the parents attending this workshop want specifics. Outline some suggestions that Mr. King can use.

3

Are These Statements True or False?

Turn the next page for the correct answers. Each statement is repeated following the paragraph in which the information can be found.

1. Children below the age of six focus mostly on color, while children older than six focus on shape and form.

2. Children's ability to control where they place their attention improves up to age nine and then actually shows a slight decline from ages ten to fifteen.

3. Telling students to pay attention to a particular concept is counterproductive, as students usually ignore the direction and pay attention instead to other areas.

4. The ability to recognize information is better than the ability to recall information throughout life.

5. Most people can keep about twenty separate pieces of information in their working memory at one time.

6. Students who already know something about the topic to be studied usually have more difficulty learning new information compared with children who are completely unfamiliar with the topic.

7. Preschoolers are more rigid than elementary schoolchildren in their understanding of what should take place and the order in which events should occur in school.

8. If material is rehearsed after an individual already knows it well, the result is a reduction in the amount of material remembered.

9. Children in the later years of elementary school will often spontaneously—that is, without the teacher's prompting—use memory strategies such as rehearsal.

10. When elementary schoolchildren claim they understand something, a parent or a teacher can be reasonably certain that they do.

11. The study skills techniques used by good and poor students are quite similar.

12. Taking notes while reading text material is an ineffective learning technique.

Information Processing

Answers to True-False Statements

1. *True*
2. *False* Correct statement: The ability to voluntarily control one's attention increases up to age 15.
3. *False* Correct statement: Giving students information that directs their attention to a particular concept is a very useful strategy.
4. *True*
5. *False* Correct statement: Most people can work with only about seven bits of information at a time.
6. *False* Correct statement: Students who already know something about the material to be taught have an easier time learning than students who have no background in the area.
7. *True*
8. *False* Correct statement: Overlearning increases the amount of material remembered.
9. *True*
10. *False* Correct statement: Students often do not know when they understand and when they do not understand material.
11. *False* Correct statement: Studies have repeatedly shown that study techniques used by good and poor students differ.
12. *False* Correct statement: Note taking can be an effective learning technique depending upon the nature of the learning task.

Jennifer seems to pay attention to the lesson but cannot differentiate between important details and unimportant details. She is doing poorly in class and is becoming frustrated.

Jimmy says he knows his work. If you ask him questions using almost the exact words used in the text or in class, he can answer them. If the questions are altered even a little, though, he cannot.

Rashid's notebook is filled with notes, both from his readings of the text and from class. He tries to copy almost everything. He complains that it is too much work.

THE INFORMATION PROCESSING APPROACH

Consider a fifth-grade student with his notebook open listening to his teacher give information and ask questions. We expect him to pay attention to the relevant information, take it in, process it in some way so it is placed into memory, and have it instantly ready in response to some question. Understanding the process by which this occurs is the chief task of specialists who adopt the **information processing approach.**

Information processing specialists investigate the way people take in information, process it, and act on it. Such factors as attention, perception, memory, the mediating process by which people do something to the information in their mind, and their response system are important. The information processing approach looks at each of these factors for clues to how best to present information to students. It also investigates reasons for students' lack of comprehension.

The students in these vignettes have difficulties that can be understood using the information processing approach. For example, what if you were to ask Jimmy who the President of the Union was during the Civil War and Jimmy answered incorrectly. There

information processing approach An approach to cognition which investigates the way people take in information, process it, and act on the information.

are many possible reasons for his failure to give the right answer. Perhaps it was the way the question was asked. Perhaps the question was not phrased in a way Jimmy could understand. Were the words too difficult? Did Jimmy understand what you were referring to? Could he process the words quickly enough? Could Jimmy's memory be at fault? Could there be an attention problem? In this case, Jimmy was aware that Lincoln was the president of the United States at the time of the Civil War. He just didn't know that the Union was the United States.

Information processing specialists often use the computer as an analogy for the workings of the human mind, but this does not mean they see human beings as computers or robots. The computer analogy helps us to understand how people solve problems and use information.

What we type into the computer, called the input, is roughly analogous to information we gather from our environment through our senses. Some operations are performed on the information according to the program, and the information is encoded and stored so that it can be retrieved. Some processes must occur in our minds, enabling us to attend to a particular stimulus, organize it, and remember it so we can use it in the future.

The information that is produced when the proper command is given can be considered output. The output could be some motor activity, such as moving your arm to catch a baseball, or a verbal response, as when you come up with the answer to a mathematics problem.

Finally, an individual receives feedback, information noting whether the response was effective. Just as the title of a computer program gives some clue as to the general results of the program, human beings may have an upper executive plan that coordinates the activities described above and guides purposeful behavior. Perhaps the student voluntarily pays attention to key words spoken by the teacher and ignores disruptions and irrelevant information. Information processing theorists are interested in following the information through the system to learn how it is encoded, processed, and retrieved (Sternberg, 1985). Thus, they look at cognition on a very detailed level.

The information processing approach is not always seen in a developmental context, but it can be. As we shall see, each of these processes exists in all children, but children's abilities in the areas of paying attention, encoding, and retrieving memories, and controlling these abilities develop as children mature.

ATTENTION

Why didn't Jimmy answer the question correctly? One of the most obvious reasons is that Jimmy didn't pay attention either to the question or to the information when it was being taught. It is easy to relate a lack of attention to a lack of learning (Berliner, 1987), and children who are easily distracted from the learning task learn less than those who pay attention (Wittrock, 1986).

Attention has been used in at least two different ways. Early concepts of attention looked at it in terms of a bottleneck or filter in the information processing system. As Jimmy listens to the teacher, he is exposed to a large number of other stimuli, including extraneous sounds, objects in the classroom, and the whispers of his classmates. Some of this information is relevant and important to the material being learned, while much of it isn't. Since we cannot process all of this information simultaneously, attention acts as a filter to screen out the less relevant and select the more important stimuli for further processing. People have the ability to selectively attend to stimuli in their environment (Klatzky, 1980). Although the concept of **selective attention** is valuable, the filter theory has been deemphasized, because no one has been able to determine where the bottleneck is (Daehler & Bukatko, 1985).

More recently, attention has been used to describe mental effort, which can be applied to a task in varying degrees (Daehler & Bukatko, 1985). Instead of looking at attention as a filter that funnels information through a narrow channel, this newer approach looks at it as a cognitive resource (Best, 1986). We can choose to place effort on particular information and allocate it as we think best. Attention involves concentrating and focusing our mental efforts. However, not all information requires primary use of this ability.

selective attention   The capacity to focus attention on a narrow band of sensory stimulation.

Attention is surely one of the important elements in learning. Children who are easily distracted learn less.

The better we are at something, the less of this resource we must use. A student who knows the multiplication tables very well does not have to use the same mental effort as a student who is just mastering it. A student who knows how to read very well need not spend as much effort on sounding out the words as someone who is just learning phonics. As people become better at a task, they allocate fewer resources to it and become less aware of it.

This last example is of great importance in understanding reading. Students who have to use all their attention to sound out the words very slowly may not be able to comprehend the material very well. The decoding takes almost all of this resource. However, once the students are able to do so, they can then attend more to the meaning of the material. This also will affect their attitude towards reading, as reading yields little enjoyment if every voluntary bit of attention must be placed into decoding. Poor readers need an opportunity to read the material after they have mastered the vocabulary at a given level. It is not sufficient that these students be able to read the material with a low error rate. Comprehension requires that capacity be available for interpreting the material as well.

Attention, however, is not always at the beck and call of the individual. Certain stimuli may attract a child's attention. Imagine that Jimmy is trying to listen to the teacher but at the same time is attracted by his friend's chatter or a fly crawling on his desk. Jimmy may find it more difficult to concentrate on what his teacher is saying, especially if the material is new.

However, what if Jimmy were older? Would he then have more control over his attention and be able to use his concentrative abilities better? The answer is yes. In fact, to understand attention, we must look both at the nature of the stimuli and at the development of a child's ability to voluntarily use this cognitive resource.

The nature of the stimuli affects attention. Jimmy may not have attended to the teacher's recitation because it was boring, he was lost, or other stimuli attracted him. Younger children are often more easily distracted by those stimuli around them, and their attention span is shorter. Teachers recognizing the importance of keeping children's attention will vary their presentation and their voice intensity, highlight the important points, and sometimes use surprise in their presentation. Questioning can serve this purpose of focusing attention on the stimuli. Certain specific features of stimuli attract young children, including color, movement, surprise, and novelty. Anyone who has ever watched "Sesame Street" can understand how, by using motion and variety and by not overtaxing a young child's attention span, attention may be secured and to some degree maintained. Although these features may attract everyone, they are more likely to attract younger children, who are less able to direct their attention away from distracting stimuli.

Teachers, then, can use visual displays to attract and hold young children's attention. However, it would be incorrect to view young children merely as beings who are passively manipulated by their environment. Preschoolers attend to messages that they understand and that are focused on their interests (Anderson & Field, 1983). Some elements of attention are more important for young children. For instance, children under the age of six focus mostly on color, while children older than six focus on shape and form (Koran & Lehman, 1981). Children between 10 and 13 years of age can discriminate relevant from irrelevant information and develop the ability to focus attention much better than younger children.

True or False Children below the age of six focus mostly on color, while children older than six focus on shape and form.

As children mature, their ability to control their attention, to discriminate between what is and is not most important, and to adapt their attention to the demands of the situation improves. Their ability to plan what they are to attend to also shows improvement

The children's television program "Sesame Street" uses constantly changing stimuli and color to get the attention of its audience.

(Flavell, 1985). These abilities are primitive in the preschooler and develop over the elementary school years. Children's ability to control their attention increases between 12 and 13 years of age. It continues to increase, though at a slower rate, through at least age 15 (Wittrock, 1987). Children are also able to maintain their attention for longer periods because they are becoming less easily distracted (Anderson & Lorch, 1983).

True or False   Children's ability to control where they place their attention improves up to age nine and then actually shows a slight decline from ages ten to fifteen.

The gradual development of voluntary planned attention is shown in a study by Vurpillot (1968; Vurpillot & Ball, 1979). Children between the ages of four and nine were asked to compare two different pictures of a house, each house containing at least six windows, with objects such as flowerpots, hearts, curtains, and socks in the windows. The children's task was to judge whether the two houses were identical. As the children inspected the houses, their eye movements were tracked. Preschoolers often made their decisions based on incomplete information, using only seven of the windows instead of all twelve, which the older children used. The best way to ac-

complish the task was to first focus attention on window one of house one and then switch attention to window one of house two, and so forth. This requires planning. Not one child in the preschool group did this, but almost all of the eight- and nine-year-olds did.

 CONNECTIONS

What the Research on Attention Means to Teachers

Most teachers see attention as a crucial aspect of learning (Houston et al., 1988). Paying attention is a necessary but not a sufficient condition for understanding. Some students who do pay attention may not learn because they have other difficulties, but most students who do not pay attention will not learn. The research shows that teachers must be concerned both with creating classroom lessons that will gain and hold children's attention and with helping students to focus their attention on the relevant areas. At the same time, teachers must keep in mind the developmental level of the students, understanding the approximate attention span of the children they are teaching. The younger the children, the more help they will need in focusing their attention and the more likely they are to be distracted by other stimuli in the classroom. The following suggestions are based upon the research.

1. **Discover the interests of your students—what grabs their attention and how long they can keep their attention focused.** Give examples that relate to their interests as material is covered. Challenging students with a problem is one way to do this. One junior high school mathematics teacher asked the students in a class to be managers of a baseball team who had to determine which batter to send to the plate, knowing that one batter had 135 hits in 454 appearances while the other had 72 hits in 234 appearances. Many of the students were on baseball teams, and this problem served to gain their attention.

2. **Select materials and design lessons that focus children's attention on the most important aspects of the lesson.** (Koran & Lehman, 1981) Spend more time on the most important points and use more than one example to explain the points. As you plan the lesson, underline or in some way highlight those points that are most important. Something that will focus children's attention, such as an interesting question, example, problem, or activity, can be planned for each point.

3. **Highlight those topics that merit special attention.** In the stream of information that often flows from teacher to student, it is often difficult for students, especially younger students, to differentiate between the relevant and the not so important information. Highlight the important topics by writing them on the blackboard, repeating them, or directing student attention to them.

4. **Vary the presentation.** School is principally an auditory experience. Varying the presentation to include more sense modalities can help to gain and keep attention. This is especially important with younger children.

5. **Prepare students in advance.** Since students are more likely to attend to relevant information when they are told what the objective of the lesson is, it is a good strategy to communicate the goals of the lesson to the students.

6. **Minimize distractions.** Poorer learners are especially vulnerable to distractions, and reducing unnecessary competing stimuli is important.

7. **Use questions to focus student attention.** Questioning is an effective means of directing student attention (Andre, 1979).

8. **Use the questions in the text for focusing student attention while reading.** The data indicate that students will attend to the most important information if questions are presented either before or after the written work, because such questions focus students' attention on particular aspects of the chapter (Wittrock, 1987).

9. **Use surprise to gain attention.** Sometimes, especially in science class, surprising things may be shown by engaging in experimentation. This helps to gain student attention by promoting interest.

10. **Watch the pacing and look for signs of inattention.** If the pace of the lesson is too slow, students become bored and inattentive. If the pace is overly quick, their attention is lost. It is difficult to find the best pace, especially when dealing with students with a wide range of individual abilities. Be aware, however, of the signs of inattention, including increased movement, gazing out the window, and low-level but constant chatter.

11. **Take attention span into account while teaching.** Young children have a shorter attention span than older children, and better students seem to attend to lessons for a longer period of time than do the less proficient students.

12. **Be certain that simpler, prerequisite processes are mastered before progressing to more complex skills that utilize these basic skills.** As previously noted, if students cannot decode words, it is difficult for them to attend to their meanings.

True or False   Telling students to pay attention to a particular concept is counterproductive, as students usually ignore the direction and pay attention instead to other areas.

MEMORY: ENCODING, STORAGE, AND RETRIEVAL

One of the most satisfying aspects of teaching is to hear a student tell you how she used something you taught her in her daily life. Nothing can be used, however, unless the information or skill is remembered. The memory process includes encoding or laying down new memories, storing them, and finally retrieving them at the appropriate time.

Even if a student is paying attention to the lesson, he or she may be having difficulty differentiating the important from the not so important facts and concepts.

Measuring Retrieval

There are three principal ways in which memory is measured. First, there is **recall,** which involves producing the correct response on the basis of very limited cues. For example, if you asked a student to recite the Pledge of Allegiance, define a particular term,

or name the sixteenth president of the United States, you'd be measuring recall. This is similar to the task faced by the student taking an essay test or being asked to fill in the missing word when presented with a statement with a key word missing. **Recognition** involves the ability to choose the correct response from a group of answers and is similar to the multiple-choice questions on a test. As a rule, our ability to recognize is far better than our ability to recall information throughout life (Wingfield & Byrnes, 1981). A third technique, used mostly in laboratory settings, is called **relearning** and involves measuring the amount of time a student would save if he or she had already learned material at some earlier time and is trying to master it for a second time. In this method, a student is taught something, allowed time without rehearsing it to forget it, and then allowed to relearn the information. It normally takes less time to learn something a second time, and this time savings is measured and reflects what was still in memory at the time of the second learning. This leads to the conclusion that students should be encouraged to learn their work as it is assigned and then review it before the test rather than try to learn it the night before the exam. It will take less time to relearn it than to learn it the first time.

True or False   The ability to recognize information is better than the ability to recall information throughout life.

A Model of Memory for the Teacher

A model of human memory was developed by Atkinson and Shiffrin (1968) which is now more or less accepted (see Figure 3.1).

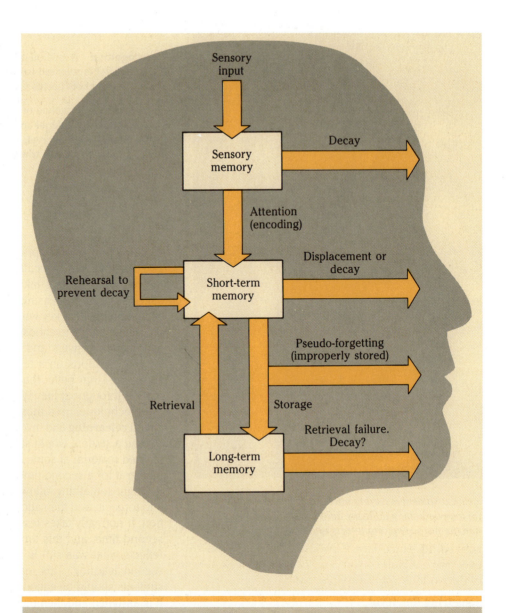

Figure 3.1 A Model of Human Memory
In the first stage of memory, sensory input registers in the sensory memory. Sensory memories decay very quickly unless they are attended to. Paying attention to sensory memories encodes them into the short-term memory, where they can be held by rehearsal or lost through decay and displacement. To enter the long-term memory, short-term memories must be processed and stored.

PART I

Cognition, Development, and Learning

Memory processes are important to learning.

The Sensory Register

An incoming stimulus first enters the **sensory register,** where it is held in their exact form for a very brief amount of time, certainly less than two seconds (Klatzky, 1980). If you wave your hand in front of your face, the trace that remains after your hand is gone is evidence of the sensory register (Norman, 1982). There is probably a different register for each sense, and the capacity appears unlimited. The sensory registers are not overwhelmed, because most of what enters simply fades away, since it is not attended to. Sensory registers allow some continuity in your sensory world, since momentary blanks are smoothed over. For example, when you blink, your perception of the world is not disrupted, since the sensory memory keeps the images together. In addition, sensory memory allows you to keep the material in mind before determining whether it should be processed further.

Short-Term Memory

If the material is attended to, it enters short-term, or working, memory. **Short-term memory** has a very limited capacity and is of short duration, not more than thirty seconds (Shavelson et al., 1986). It is called working memory because it consists of what you have in mind at the present time. A child trying to solve mathematics problems on a test has the ele-

ments of the problems in mind. Ten minutes after taking the test, the child may not be able to tell you much about each individual problem. If working memory duration is so short, how do we keep things in mind? The secret is rehearsal: by repeating something, you can keep it in memory.

The small capacity of short-term memory can create problems for both teachers and students. Most people can keep about seven items in mind at a time (Miller, 1956). Some can handle only five, and a few can handle as many as nine. Suppose you were asked to remember a string of twelve numbers. How can you remember them all? You can do so if you use the technique called **chunking,** which involves collapsing the information into seven or fewer pieces of information. In this case, you might create six bits of information by combining numbers 32, 64, 87, 43, 52, 67. You could further reduce the number by using three-digit numbers.

True or False Most people can keep about twenty separate pieces of information in their working memory at one time.

The two characteristics of working memory—its short duration and limited capacity—should make teachers wary of presenting too much material too quickly. Teachers must allow enough time for rehearsal and not overload the student's system. With young children, it is easy to overload the system, and frequent checks must be made to be certain the speed at which a teacher is instructing the students matches the students' ability to use the material. Short-term memories are soon forgotten, either because they are displaced by new items or because they decay with time. Developmentally, short-term memory improves from ages five to ten. The typical five-year-old can

---

sensory register   A type of memory that retains an almost complete representation of sensory stimulation for a very brief period of time.

short-term memory   A type of memory that has a short duration and a very limited capacity.

chunking   A technique for remembering many bits of information by combining them.

recall four or five numbers after a single presentation; a ten-year-old can recall six or seven (Williams & Stith, 1980).

We have a visual and an auditory channel for processing information. When you look at something—for example, a tree—you are using your visual system. However, the word *tree* can also be encoded acoustically. Since the systems are different, we know that it is best to use both systems for remembering information. In fact, people best remember words they hear when at the same time they have in mind a visual image that the word represents (Paivio, 1971).

Long-Term Memory

If information is to be remembered for a longer period of time, it must be encoded into **long-term memory.** Long-term memory has a large—perhaps an unlimited—capacity and a long duration. To transfer material to long-term memory, rehearsal is necessary. We need to differentiate, however, between **maintenance rehearsal,** in which we merely repeat the item to ourselves, and **elaborative rehearsal,** in which we search for meaning in what we are learning. If I read a paragraph concerning superconductor technology, I will be able to remember it far better if I search for the meaning rather than just repeat the words to myself.

We can understand long-term memory better if we differentiate between three different classes of memory. The first involves procedures—the steps required to execute a particular skill such as riding a bicycle, solving a quadratic equation, or giving cardiopulmonary resuscitation. Procedures have to do with knowing how to do something. **Procedural memory** very often does not require much, if any, thought after the procedure has been learned (Ellis & Hunt, 1989).

long-term memory   Memory storage that has a large—perhaps an unlimited—capacity and a long duration.

maintenance rehearsal   A type of rehearsal in which information is simply repeated.

elaborative rehearsal   A type of rehearsal in which information is processed in some meaningful way.

procedural memory   Memories concerning how to do something.

episodic memory   Memories concerning specific events that happened to a person at a specific time or place.

semantic memory   Memories consisting of general knowledge.

Have you ever tried to explain how to tie a shoe? It is very difficult to do so because you never access this procedural memory in a verbal manner. This is also one reason it is so easy to leave out a step when you are trying to teach students how to do something. Demonstrating how to tie a shoe while you explain it in a step-by-step process is more effective than simply orally explaining the process.

The other two types of memories are episodic memories and semantic memories and involve knowing that something exists or has occurred (Tulving, 1972). **Episodic memories** are personal, autobiographical memories that are sensitive to the effects of context. These memories are organized by time and place. On the other hand, **semantic memory** is composed of general, encyclopedic knowledge of the world and language. It is organized on the basis of class membership. Obviously, both are often involved in a process of remembering something. If I ask you where you bought your belt, I am requiring you to access an episodic memory, but your understanding of what I mean by the word *belt* is certainly semantic. Many of your long-term memories are encoded automatically and are stored without much effort. These are mostly things that happen to you. Most school-related learning requires a more active type of processing if it is to be processed into long-term memory.

How is long-term memory organized? The structure of memory is still somewhat of a mystery, but research now has determined that our mental connections are laid down in networks. Each fact or concept is called a node, and some nodes are associated with others. Strong associations are made between closely related concepts, weaker ones between loosely related concepts, and no associations at all between others. For instance, if we are thinking about Columbus, such things as discovering America and being an Italian might be strongly related. A bit less strongly related is that Columbus sailed for Spain, and unrelated to Columbus might be that the capital of New York

State is Albany. Therefore, long-term memory is a dictionary organized by meaning rather than by alphabet (Klatzky, 1980).

In a dictionary, words are connected, whereas in memory concepts are interconnected. One interesting example of this also shows the difference between organization of memories in short-term and in long-term memory. If students are shown a list of words and asked to recall them hours later, they will make what memory specialists call intrusion errors, which involve recalling words that are not actually on the list. The intrusions are very likely to be similar in meaning to rather than sounding like the original words on the list. For example, if one of the original words on the list was *boat,* the intruding word is more likely to be ship than bud or boar (Baddely & Dale, 1966). On the other hand, if we are testing short-term memory and ask students to immediately repeat the list back, students are much more likely to list acoustic intruders.

Many cognitive scientists now believe that these memory networks are more complicated and involve more than simple bits of information. These networks include **propositions**—the smallest units of knowledge that can be either true or false. For example, the word *Columbus* is not a proposition, but the statement, "Columbus discovered America" certainly is. Many statements, however, contain more than one proposition. Propositional theorists argue that memory can best be understood in terms of individual propositions linked together. For example, consider the statement: "Joey kissed the beautiful girl, whom he had recently met." This statement actually consists of three different propositions:

Joey kissed the girl.
The girl was beautiful.
Joey recently met the girl.

Each of these propositions can be verified separately. Figure 3.2 shows how each can be diagrammed and then combined to form a propositional network. Notice that in the first sentence, Joey is the agent and the girl is the recipient. The kiss is the verb or relation

(adjectives can also be relations), and the time frame is shown as the past. When these individual propositions are placed together, they form a network. When information is required, the individual does not remember the exact proposition but rather generates the information in a meaningful though not verbatim manner. In addition, you can readily see how one thought can easily lead to another, since propositions are linked.

The important point to be retained from this detailed look at how material is stored in long-term memory is an understanding that what is stored is seldom what is actually heard or seen. It is the meaning of the material that is stored. In addition, this explains why one phrase, term, or idea often leads to our remembering others.

Schemata: The Importance of Prior Knowledge

If long-term memory is structured using networks of knowledge and propositions with vast interconnections, when we lay down memories we do not do so in a vacuum. We often have a framework on which to hang our memories. For instance, before hearing about Columbus, we may have seen a film about explorers or know what an explorer does. This makes learning about Columbus easier. Psychologists have recently focused much attention on the importance of what people know—their knowledge base—to what people are trying to know or remember (Chi & Glaser, 1985). Their findings show that the more people know, the easier it is for them to lay down new memories. This may occur because people who have some prior knowledge have what cognitive psychologists call schemata already formed. The term as used by Piaget was introduced in the last chapter. Its use by information processing psychologists is a bit different.

A **schema** is an organized body of knowledge that functions as a framework describing objects and relationships that generally occur. Schemata (the plural of schema) can contain both knowledge about and rules for using knowledge. A schema for a dog may

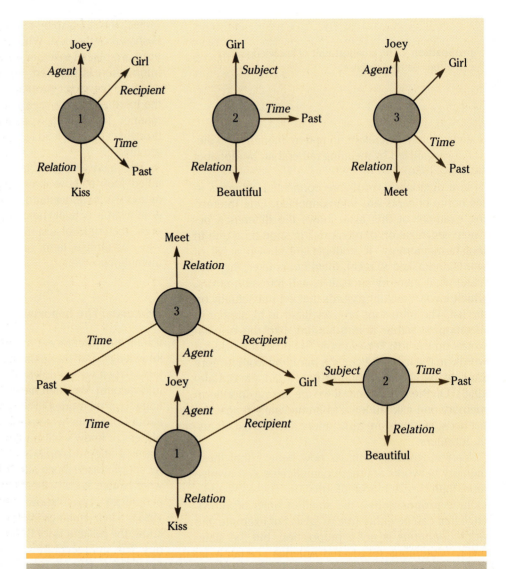

Figure 3.2   A Small Propositional Representation of the Sentence "Joey kissed the beautiful girl, whom he had recently met."
Many cognitive psychologists believe that long-term memories are organized in an array of interconnected propositions.

Adapted with permission from *Cognitive Psychology*, 2/e by J. B. Best, p. 198. Copyright © 1988 by West Publishing Company. All rights reserved.

contain ideas about the dog's physical features and activities and different aspects of a dog's behavior as well as ways of treating dogs.

We can think of schemata as sets of propositions that form a base allowing people to receive and organize information. This is easiest to understand through an example. Consider a teacher talking about hospi-

tal procedures and telling students about a nurse taking a patient's blood pressure. It would be easier for students with some prior knowledge of hospitals to understand or visualize this scenario than students without this knowledge. Such prior knowledge might involve the roles of various people at the hospital, various hospital procedures, and knowledge of the types of instruments used in hospitals. Many cognitive psychologists believe that memory structures (that is, schemata) underlie our understanding of events and allow us to interpret and clarify what we are experiencing or learning (Chi & Glaser, 1985). The more we know about hospitals and their procedures, the easier it is to understand the occurrence.

Schemata allow us to encode additional information more meaningfully, since new information can be linked to already encoded information. It also allows us to fill in gaps and to infer. As children progress through school, their schemata become more complicated, richer, and more flexible. A child's background may contain a rich amount of information in one area and a poor amount in another. It will be much easier, then, for students to learn information in the areas where they already know something than in areas where they know less. In one study, students were asked to read a selection on baseball. Those who knew more about baseball initially obtained more information from the reading (Recht & Leslie, 1988). If readers have advanced knowledge, they do better in comprehending what they are reading. Therefore, prior knowledge is crucial, because it gives students an adequate schematic scaffolding on which to place new memories.

True or False Students who already know something about the topic to be studied usually have more difficulty learning new information compared with children who are completely unfamiliar with the topic.

A concept that is similar to schema is script. A **script** is a "structure that describes an appropriate sequence of events in a particular context" (Schank & Abelson, 1977, p. 41). We have numerous scripts, including those for birthday parties, job interviews, and a schoolday. Both adults and children show a great deal of agreement on these scripts. For instance, if you were asked what happens when you visit a restaurant, you probably would have no difficulty constructing a sequential series of events. You enter the restaurant, sit down, order the food, eat the food, pay the check, and leave.

script A structure that describes an appropriate sequence of events in a particular context.

Four-year-olds describe daily events at home, in a day-care center, or at a McDonald's restaurant in much the same way as adults do (Nelson, 1978). Preschoolers, though, are rather rigid in their ideas of what should take place and when (Wimmer, 1980). They will often rebel if people do things that are not in keeping with their idea of the script. Older children begin to produce more alternative paths in their scripts. For instance, when describing activities, such as making a campfire, they will offer many more possible paths to accomplishing the task than younger children would. Scripts, then, become more flexible and more complex as children develop (Mandler, 1983).

True or False Preschoolers are more rigid than elementary schoolchildren in their understanding of what should take place and the order in which events should occur in school.

Scripts form the base for remembering stories and events that are familiar. If we are given information and are familiar with the script, we can fill in missing information (Chi & Glasser, 1985). Prior knowledge represented by the script makes the story easy to follow. When young children are presented with a script that contains an event that is out of order and are asked to recall it, they either omit the misordered event or put it in the place that is in keeping with their knowledge of how it usually is (Nelson & Gruendel, 1981). Children recognize deviations from the proper script and correct them (Wimmer, 1979, 1980). Youngsters misremember stories if the stories differ from their familiar scripts. For instance, children invent and put appropriate materials in stories when they cannot recall what they were told (Mandler & Johnson, 1977).

The knowledge of scripts also affects how children make inferences. Children who are told that José went to a restaurant or is drinking milk in the kitchen do not need to be told that he probably looked at a menu or had a glass that held his milk. They understand this is so, and they infer it because they are familiar with the script. Scripts show how prior knowledge affects the way new material is processed. One's prior knowledge makes new material meaningful, suggests how one can bridge gaps in what one knows, and helps to organize material (Salomon, 1983). Some of the differences in memory between older children and younger children are caused by the more extensive knowledge base of the older children. In summary, the child's knowledge base is an important variable in understanding how the child functions. Knowledge facilitates memory and affects performance on a variety of tasks.

The Controller

There is still something missing in our model—a mechanism for controlling how we encode the material. Let's say you ask your students to read a chapter in their health book concerning the various food groups. You tell them that you will be testing them on the contents of the chapter. It would not surprise you that even if they all spent the same amount of time on the reading, some would do better than others on the test. Remembering material for retrieval is not a haphazard phenomenon; it is coordinated and controlled by the individual. The student determines what strategies to use to encode the material. These controlling

This student has to make a decision about how to encode this technical material.

processes enable us to attend to what is important and do what is necessary to place the material in long-term storage.

Memory and Learning Strategies

If you were one of the students referred to above— that is, a student having to remember the material from the chapter—how would you go about it? Perhaps you would list important terms. Perhaps you would look for questions at the end of the chapter. Perhaps you would try to relate the information in the chapter to something already in your memory. But what would you do with the list of foods for each category (carbohydrates, protein, etc.)? Here you might try a different strategy, perhaps visualizing a plate with each type of food on it or making a word out of the first letter of the various foods.

Since memory is so important in learning, helping students develop strategies for encoding information efficiently is very important. Knowledge that is encoded more deeply is retrieved more quickly (Craik & Lockhart, 1972). This reflects the **levels of processing** model that states that the richer the meaning of the material encoded, the more deeply the material is encoded and the easier it is to retrieve. Think of students being asked to remember some body of information. If they just learn it by rote, they are not processing it at a deep level. However, if they think about the meaning of the material or relate the material to other information in memory, they process the material more deeply and encode it more efficiently. Some techniques for encoding are superior to others.

Simple Rehearsal

This is a most common method of encoding new information and, although useful, is not usually the best. In this method, the material is simply repeated over and over again until it is learned well. Perhaps you have studied the names of states or definitions in biology or science class or words of a foreign lan-

> **levels of processing view**   A view of memory as a system with many levels of processing. How well an item is remembered is purported to be a function of how deeply and elaborately information is processed.

guage again and again. Although this is certainly useful, it may not be very effective if the material is not very meaningful and thus is not connected to other meaningful material in your memory. If it need be done, an approach using overlearning is advised. **Overlearning** involves practicing the material even though a student already knows it. For example, if students practice the names of the state capitals, they should be taught to continue practicing them even though they know them. This will improve their memory of the material.

True or False   If material is rehearsed after an individual already knows it well, the result is a reduction in the amount of material remembered.

Clustering and Categorizing

Another useful method is to cluster or categorize information so that various pieces of information are meaningfully associated with one another. For example, in learning the list of foods, you might categorize them into different food groups.

Paraphrasing and Summarizing

This is one of the simplest activities that can be used to encode material more deeply. Teachers often see the results of students who memorize definitions or simply read the material. These students often do poorly on tests because they do not connect the new material to information already encoded in memory or integrate it with other already known material. When a test is given, unless the question asks for the remembered material in the exact same way as presented, the student may not retrieve the material. For instance, a student who learns the definition of *photosynthesis* but does not understand it may be able to place the word correctly if the question reads: _____ is the synthesis of complex organic materials by plants from carbon dioxide, water, and inorganic salts using sunlight as the source of energy and with the aid of a catalyst such as chlorophyll (The American College Dictionary, 1969). However, if a simple application is required or if the question is worded differently, the student may not be able to an-

swer the question correctly. If the student learns to paraphrase or summarize material, the material will be encoded on a deeper level. How can this be accomplished? Summarizing paragraphs or paraphrasing definitions by saying them out loud to oneself can sometimes accomplish this (Muth et al., 1988). Other effective devices are teacher-generated questions or review questions found in texts that encourage students to put the material into their own words.

Advance Organizers

Teachers can help their students encode more efficiently if they present some organizational framework that provides students with the cognitive scaffolding on which to place new learning. One idea, advanced by David Ausubel (1968), is that teachers provide that scaffolding through the use of **advance organizers**—topical introductions that orient students to the subject matter and relate new learning to material students already know. These advance organizers are presented at a higher level of abstraction and are more general than the material to be read or discussed (Ausubel, 1968).

A concept organizer is often a general statement. For example, in a lesson on computer crime and its prevention, the concept organizer could be a paragraph describing the idea that new inventions often give rise to new abuses, which in turn give rise to new methods for controlling these abuses (Kloster & Winne, 1989). A lesson on the effects of technology on the environment might begin with a generalization such as "the more technology and knowledge a person acquires, the less limiting are the influences of nature on a person's life" (Eggen et al., 1979, p. 263).

Analogies can also serve as advance organizers. For the computer crime lesson, comparing misuses of office photocopiers and efforts to control them might be interesting. For a lesson on waterways, an advance organizer consisting of a paragraph comparing waterways to the circulatory system of the body might be in order.

Advance organizers might involve the use of charts and diagrams that show how the material in the lesson fits in with other material. It may also entail the presentation through written or oral means of a general conceptual framework into which the current day's lesson can fit (Borich, 1988). A literature teacher might present an introduction to the meaning of tragedy before discussing *Hamlet.*

Advance organizers are effective in some instances but not all. They are more effective for students who know little about the material (White & Tisher, 1986; Kloster & Winne, 1989). It is also a help only when the material to be encoded is conceptual. It does not aid students in encoding details (Mayer, 1979; Kloster & Winne, 1989). As with all the other instructional aids we will discuss, advance organizers are effective only if students use them (Corkill et al., 1988).

Use of Instructional Objectives and Outlines

Students can be helped to encode material by being encouraged to attend to the most important areas of the lesson or text reading. This can be accomplished through the use of instructional objectives (see Chapter 11) or an outline showing how the parts of the chapter or lesson are connected.

Beginning- or End-of-Chapter Questions

Another device that helps students better encode the material is the practice of presenting students with questions before reading a chapter or providing them with review questions following the chapter. This helps to focus student attention on specific points, thus aiding the process of encoding.

Mnemonic Devices

A **mnemonic device** is a memory aid that makes the information to be learned more meaningful through interactive imagery or association with well-learned information (Glover et al., 1987). These devices facilitate encoding. For example, making a word using the first letters of a list of items can help. To remember the colors of the spectrum (red, orange, yellow,

---

mnemonic device   Memory aid that helps to organize new material through interactive imagery or by relating it to existing, well-learned information.

---

green, blue, indigo, and violet), many students are taught to use the first letter of each color which translates to Roy G. Biv.

Another such device that has been heavily researched is the keyword method. In this method, a familiar word is used to establish an acoustic (similar sound) key, and this word is then visually linked to the unfamiliar term. For example, to learn the French word *couteau,* meaning knife, one might take *toe* as the keyword because it sounds like the last syllable in couteau and because it can be easily imaged in some meaningful interaction with knife, such as a knife cutting someone's toe. On a test, the word *couteau* will prompt *toe* through the acoustic link, and *toe* will enable the learner to recall the image and decode the word into knife (Paivio & Desrochers, 1981). In trying to remember the Spanish word *huevo,* meaning egg (pronounced wave-oh), one might use the word *wave* and then imagine the egg bobbing on the crest of a wave (Jones & Hall, 1982).

The keyword method has been useful in foreign language learning as well as in learning social studies facts, such as pairing countries with products (Pressley & Dennis-Rounds, 1980), and in other subjects such as biology (Shriberg et al., 1982). In one fascinating study, Debra Veit and colleagues (1986) used the keyword method to teach dinosaur vocabulary, the attributes of dinosaurs, and the reasons for their extinction to learning disabled students in sixth, seventh, and eighth grade. Dinosaur names are easily divided into two word parts. For the word part *ornith,* meaning bird, the keyword was "oar" and the picture was a bird carrying an oar (see Figure 3.3). For teaching dinosaurs' attributes, such as the geological period during which the dinosaur existed and the dinosaur's eating habits, cards were made and presented to students. An early-dinosaur card included a picture of a rooster, indicating the morning; if the dinosaur was from the middle period, a hot midday scene was shown; and the later period was indicated by a night scene that included an owl (see Figure 3.4). If it was a carnivore, the dinosaur was red; a plant eater, green. Students learned these dinosaur facts very well.

Another mnemonic method is the peg word method. What if you wanted students to remember a list, for example, of directions. In the peg word system, the students first memorize a set of number-word rhymes that act as the pegs on which other ideas can be hung as images. They then associate

Figure 3.3 Mnemonic Representation of Ornith
The researchers used the keyword method to teach children the names of dinosaurs.

From "Extended Mnemonic Instruction with Learning Disabled Students" by D. T. Veit, T. E. Scruggs, and M. A. Mastropieri in the *Journal of Educational Psychology*. Copyright © 1986 by the American Psychological Association. Reprinted by permission of the American Psychological Association and the author.

Figure 3.4 Mnemonic Representation of Geologic Time
Using a series of cards such as the one pictured above, researchers taught children the attributes of various dinosaurs.

From "Extended Mnemonic Instruction with Learning Disabled Students" by D. T. Veit, T. E. Scruggs, and M. A. Mastropieri in the *Journal of Educational Psychology*. Copyright © 1986 by the American Psychological Association. Reprinted by permission of the American Psychological Association and the author.

each rhyme visually with something else. The most common is the "one is a bun, two is a shoe" mnemonic rhyme.

One is a bun.
Two is a shoe.
Three is a tree.
Four is a door.
Five is a hive.
Six is sticks.
Seven is heaven.
Eight is a gate.
Nine is a pine.
Ten is a hen.

For example, if the first direction is to turn on the switch, a student could imagine a turned-on switch placed in the middle of a bun. If the second direction is to place the paper over the sprockets, a person might imagine a sheet of paper with sprockets sticking out of the edges of a shoe. This is very useful for remembering things in order, because it forces the student to elaborate on the material (Pressley & Levin, 1986). In the dinosaur study, Veit used the "one

is a bun" in teaching students nine reasons that dinosaurs may have become extinct. The first was that the earth turned cold, and Veit presented students with a card showing a freezing dinosaur with a bag of frozen buns (see Figure 3.5). Many mnemonic devices involve the use of visual imagery.

The Development of Control Processes

Students' voluntary control over their memory strategies shows a developmental progression. As children mature, they develop the ability to use these strategies on their own. Students of different ages may not possess the abilities and skills necessary to use all these memory strategies.

Preschoolers and children in the very early grades of elementary school are limited by their inability to spontaneously use memory strategies that many of us take for granted. Suppose you were shown a group of pictures and asked to remember them. You might first separate the pictures into categories (food, buildings, people), then rehearse them. Preschoolers do not use

Figure 3.5 Mnemonic Representation for Extinction Lesson
Researchers used the pegword method to teach children the possible reasons that dinosaurs became extinct.

From "Extended Mnemonic Instruction with Learning Disabled Students" by D. T. Veit, T. E. Scruggs, and M. A. Mastropieri in the *Journal of Educational Psychology*. Copyright © 1986 by the American Psychological Association. Reprinted by permission of the American Psychological Association and the author.

these strategies on their own (Kail & Hagen, 1982). When preschoolers were asked to remember a string of digits, they did not spontaneously use any rehearsal—the simplest strategy—but when they were instructed in the use of rehearsal, their ability to remember the numbers improved greatly (Flavell & Wellman, 1977). Children can be taught to use rehearsal; however, at a later time, young children will not spontaneously use this strategy when confronted with the same task without being instructed to do so (Keeney et al., 1967). In other words, young children apparently can use the strategy but do not unless they are told to do so.

The memory of young children is often considered nonstrategic and unplanned (Brown et al., 1983). However, if we look more deeply, we can see the beginning of strategy use, and at times children will surprise us with their memories. The characteristics of the task and the meaning the task has to young children are important variables. Many memory strategy studies have used artificial situations that require remembering new information for its own sake (Paris & Lindauer, 1982).

When information and situations are more familiar and the goals of remembering are clear, preschoolers and young elementary schoolchildren show the beginnings of memory strategies, and the ability to recall improves markedly. For instance, children three to seven years of age were asked to remember a list of five words under two different conditions. Under one condition, the children played a game of grocery store and had to recall the items so they could buy them. Under the second condition, children were simply told to remember the items. Children recalled significantly more items in condition one than in condition two (Istomina, 1975). When children were tested on the task of remembering a list, young children did quite well when the words were made up of familiar categories, such as names of their teachers and television shows (Lindberg, 1980).

Preschool and early elementary schoolteachers thus need to be certain that children of this age level find the material meaningful and useful and understand the purpose of the exercise. Teachers should also provide students with the organization that will allow easy encoding, since these students will not spontaneously cluster, categorize, or—at least for the younger children—rehearse effectively.

No matter how it is measured, memory improves as children approach and move through middle childhood. Short-term memory continually improves from five to ten years of age. The typical five-year-old can recall four or five numbers after a single presentation; a ten-year-old can recall six or seven (Williams & Stith, 1980). Recognition is generally good at all ages, but it also shows improvement with age (Dirks & Neisser, 1977). Recall improves with age as well. The ability to retain knowledge for long periods of time also shows improvement as students progress through the elementary school years.

Children in middle childhood begin to use verbal memory strategies on their own. Flavell and colleagues (1966) showed pictures to five seven- and ten-year-olds. They pointed to certain pictures that were to be remembered and measured the rehearsal strategies used by the children. Only 10 percent of the five-year-olds showed any rehearsal; 60 percent of the seven-year-olds did so once, but only 25 percent used the strategy regularly. Some 85 percent of the ten-year-olds verbalized at least once, and 65 percent did so consistently.

True or False Children in the later years of elementary school will often spontaneously—that is, without the teacher's prompting—use memory strategies such as rehearsal.

Two points stand out here. First, notice that the percentages do not approach 100 percent, showing that individual differences must be taken into consideration. Some children will need help in developing memory strategies used by others in their age group. Second, even if students use a strategy once, it does not necessarily mean that they will use it consistently. Elementary schoolteachers thus need to remind students when to use particular strategies.

As children progress through middle childhood, they become aware that some strategies are superior to others. In one study, second-graders showed no preference for categorization over rehearsal, while sixth-graders demonstrated a clear preference for categorization, a more sophisticated strategy (Justice, 1985). Progress in understanding the relative effectiveness of different strategies continues throughout the elementary school years. The developmental progression in the use of strategies is quite clear. Preschoolers may occasionally name an item to be remembered, point at it, or pay greater attention to it, but they do not yet use any verbal strategy spontaneously. Children in the middle years of childhood rehearse, use repetition, and later demonstrate planning and flexibility in their use of strategies (Brown et al., 1983). However, these children may not always use these strategies every time they are required, although consistency increases with age.

Metamemory

Nowhere is the control process so obvious as in the case of **metamemory**—a person's knowledge of his or her own memory process. The idea that children may not be aware of what they remember and don't remember is the cause of some parent-child and teacher-child conflict. Consider the following cases:

"After you study the names of the presidents and know them well, come downstairs and I'll test you," said Rachel's mother. With that, nine-year-old Rachel ran upstairs to study. A little while later she thought she was ready and when asked whether she knew the presidents, she confidently answered yes. However, it soon became apparent that she knew very few of them. Rachel's mother got angry, and Rachel ran upstairs in tears.

Mrs. Cammeron asked Roger whether he understood how to add two fractions together. After a few seconds he said yes, and with that, the teacher continued. Unfortunately on Roger's test, Mrs. Cammeron found that Roger did not know the material. When she mentioned it to him, Roger said he thought he knew it.

These situations are not uncommon, and both Rachel's mother and Roger's teacher would have an easier time if they understood the concept of metamemory. Children's knowledge of their memory processes increases with age. Neither Rachel nor Roger knew that they did not understand the work. It is a mistake to take a student's claim that he or she understands something at face value.

True or False When elementary schoolchildren claim they understand something, a parent or a teacher can be reasonably certain that they do.

A pioneer in metamemory research, John Flavell (1985) suggests that metamemory should be understood in terms of two major categories. The first is

Many students who say they understand the material actually may not be aware that they don't.

sensitivity. Children need to understand—that is, be sensitive to—the meaning of instructions, which often involve words such as *remember*. Although this may be a problem with very young children, most school-age children have little problem with such instructions. The second category involves three types of variables that interact to determine how well an individual performs on memory problems (Flavell, 1985). The first is knowledge of one's own memory abilities. Young children tend to overestimate the number of items that they can remember (Flavell et al., 1970). In one study, Ellen Markman (1973) found that second-graders and fourth-graders were better than kindergartners and first-graders in understanding whether they knew items after studying them.

The second variable involves the nature of the task. Young children often have difficulty separating the important material from the not so important

---

metamemory A person's knowledge of his or her own memory process.

material (Brown & Smiley, 1977). In addition, children must understand what is required of them. Barbara Rogoff and colleagues (1974) told six-, eight-, and ten-year-olds that they would be tested on their recognition of forty pictures after either a few minutes, a day, or a week. Only the older children studied longer when told they would have to remember the material for a longer period of time.

The third variable is knowledge of strategies. As we've seen, as children mature, they gain the ability not only to use more strategies but also to understand the situations in which one strategy is more useful than another.

Metamemory is a promising area of research and one that has a number of implications for teachers and parents. John Holt, in his influential book *How Children Fail* (1964), noted that part of being a good student is understanding one's level of comprehension. Good students may be those who often say they do not understand because they are aware of their level of knowledge. Poor students may not really know whether they understand the material. Holt (1964, p. 29) notes "the problem is not to get students to ask us what they don't know; the problem is to make them aware of the difference between what they know and what they don't."

Can anything be done to improve a student's metamemory? A number of studies have demonstrated that children can be taught to use specific strategies that increase their ability to know when they know something and when they don't (Short & Ryan, 1984; Cross & Paris, 1988). One way to do this is to (1) ask students right before the material is taught or read what they think they should know, what they need to know, and what they would like to know and (2) help students to focus their attention on these areas (Gray, 1987). Another is to have students working in pairs read a section and write down three questions about the material that they feel are important. Then have one pair of students exchange questions with another pair of students who answer the questions without referring back to the material. Finally, have the second pair of students return the questions to the first pair and have the two pairs of students discuss the questions (Fitzgerald, 1983). Another technique is to teach students the SQ3R method of reading, discussed later in the chapter. Other strategies relating to specific areas of teaching and learning are described as these areas are discussed throughout this text.

Forgetting

"I forgot it." A student comes up to your desk and tells you that he studied the material but can't remember it. He shows you a log that reflects his study time. Still, he can't answer the questions in class. This is a most frustrating situation. We know that much of what is learned is forgotten within the first day unless it is rehearsed. There is a catch, however. You can't forget something you have never learned. Many students study and do not efficiently and effectively encode the material, claiming they forgot the material when, in fact, they never encoded it properly in the first place. Assuming, though, that the student did know the material and was able to answer the review questions in the text, why does forgetting occur?

The most common explanation for forgetting is the disuse theory. We forget the eighteen exports of Brazil or the names of the bones in the hand because we don't use the material. This seems reasonable but does not explain why we remember so many things we haven't thought about for so long. For instance, can you remember the names of your elementary schoolteachers? Most people can remember at least a few of them. Yet we haven't thought about them for years. In addition, certain motor skills such as riding a bicycle or bowling don't seem to fade very rapidly. That's not to say that if you don't ride a bike for a few years you'll be as good as ever. However, you probably will still be able to handle the bicycle.

The second theory of forgetting involves interference. If you study two different subjects that are similar, you may confuse the material from one with the material from the other. New material can interfere with the retrieval of already known information, and older information can interfere with the learning of new material. If we are teaching material that is fairly similar to material already encoded, some interference may take place. It is therefore important for teachers to differentiate new material from older material. In addition, elementary schoolteachers who teach many different subjects could more profitably plan their use of time so that similar subjects are not taught back to back, thus reducing the chances that interference will take place.

A third theory is a failure of retrieval. Sometimes the memory is there, but for some reason we can't quite retrieve it. This is similar to the tip-of-the-tongue experience in which we know we understand something but just can't get to it. There are many reasons for this. We may depend upon certain cues that are no longer present. Perhaps the questions on a test are asked using different terms. If we learned the material under one set of circumstances but are asked to recall it under a different set, we may have difficulty with it.

A fourth theory accounts for the forgetting of emotionally charged material. We are sometimes motivated to forget material that may be emotionally unpleasant. This theory might explain why a student forgets that a big test is forthcoming, but it has little relevance to normal classroom learning.

As you can see, no single theory can account for all examples of forgetting, and the possibility remains that failure to encode properly is the student's real problem.

⫸⫸⫸ **CONNECTIONS**

Educational Considerations and the Process of Memory

Memory is such a basic function that it is easy to take it for granted. The study of memory cannot, however, be easily isolated from the entire process of learning itself. Memory involves encoding or laying down new memories, storing them, and retrieving them. We've seen how the organization of material can affect how material is encoded and remembered. The new information on memory processes leads to a number of important strategies for teaching.

1. **Do not overload students' short-term memory.** We know that short-term memory is severely limited. If students are asked to do too many things at one time or work with too many concepts, they cannot process the material. Younger students' short-term memory is more limited than that of older students.

2. **Provide overviews and advance organizers for students.** Information is best remembered if it is organized in such a way that all the parts of the lesson relate to other parts and they all make sense. This can be accomplished by providing students with an overview or using advance organizers, such as analogies. Organizing the material so that students can understand how various facts and concepts are related can also help.

3. **Show students how different facts are connected within the lesson.** We now know that long-term memory is organized in networks with concepts and propositions connected to one another. Teachers can make use of this fact by continually showing students how various concepts are linked.

4. **Students with rich knowledge bases will learn material faster than students with poor knowledge bases.** Since a student's prior knowledge influences the student's ability to encode new material, teachers should understand that a student who knows a great deal about the Civil War will have an easier time with material pertaining to the Civil War than students who have less background on the subject. Teachers, then, must ascertain what students know in a particular subject. If students know very little, the teacher will have to provide the bases.

5. **If possible, present the terms using more than one modality.** Some authorities believe that students will remember material better if it is presented using more than one modality. Therefore, showing a picture of an oak tree and describing it verbally may be better than simply showing pictures or lecturing on oak trees.

6. **Teach students active forms of rehearsal.** Although simple rehearsal has its place, we know that it is not as effective as more active forms, such as paraphrasing or summarizing. Students often try to use the terminology of the book and the examples and learn them verbatim. This is very difficult and, as noted earlier, can lead to problems, since the material being studied is not necessarily connected to other material in memory. In addition, the lack of understanding can become a problem if test items do not exactly mirror the wording that the students have memorized. Also, students who are taught to paraphrase and summarize will encode the material at a deeper level, making retrieval much easier. Suggesting to students to talk out loud to themselves or to come up with new examples are ways that will help students more actively and more deeply encode material.

7. **Teach students to use mnemonic devices.** Mnemonic devices are especially useful when students must memorize lists. Students need to learn how to make a word from the first letters of the items on the list and to use the keyword or peg word method when necessary.

8. **Remind students of which memory devices to use.** Younger students, especially, may not be aware of when to cluster or paraphrase and need to be reminded.

9. **Teach students to monitor their memory processes.** Metamemory—students' knowledge of their own memory processes—can be improved by asking students to write questions about the material they feel are important and giving students questions to focus upon.

10. **Students require practice.** Students must be taught how to review notes. There are, of course, a number of ways to practice and review, and students must discover which study methods are most effective for them. Without effective study methods, students will quickly forget, or possibly never really learn new material.

11. **Teach to reduce interference.** We know that the more similar the material is to other material being taught, the more likely one will interfere with the other and confuse students. Make clear the differences between two similar concepts and, if possible, try not to teach similar subjects back to back.

Memory is a vital area of concern in education. If students do not remember the material, they cannot use it either as a basis for other learning or to solve problems. Students cannot, however, simply rely on what they hear in class. They must actively participate to give themselves a better chance of success in school. They must read material in textbooks, take notes in class, and review for an upcoming exam. Lately, there has been a surge of interest in how students study and what they do to improve their classroom learning.

INFORMATION PROCESSING AND STUDY SKILLS

"But I studied, and I still didn't do well," Carlene complained. This has to be one of the most difficult situations for teachers to handle. The student's disappointment shows as she tells you that she did read the chapter, did do her homework, or reviewed her notes. There is a tendency to either shrug one's shoulders or just say, "I guess you have to study more." Perhaps all the student needs is more time studying, but it is just as likely that the problem lies with the student's study skills. Studying can be seen in terms of a problem-solving exercise. The goal is to learn the material and be able to demonstrate this learning. The methods by which this problem can be solved are called study skills.

Study skills are methods students use to study, including reading, outlining, summarization, or locating materials (Carter & Good, 1973). Study skills are often divided into two major categories. First, there is knowing how to find information that is necessary to complete an assignment. For instance, a child who is asked to define the word *volcano* might do so by looking the word up in the dictionary or the glossary of the text. A student who is assigned to do a report on volcanos must have reasonably good library skills. Indeed, such skills are a part of many curricula, and knowing the components of a textbook or a newspaper is important.

More commonly, study skills relate to the techniques a student uses to learn the material once it is presented. These techniques relate to organization of the material, effective use of time, specific reading skills, essay and report writing skills, memory-enhancing techniques, note-taking skills, and test-taking skills (Percival & Ellington, 1988). Such skills are so important that many colleges and some high schools are offering courses in study skills, sometimes called "school survival skills."

Studies show that different study skills are used by good and poor students and that good skills can be taught. Good students adjust the way they study to the demand of the material, the time available, what they know about the topic, and the purpose and importance of the assignment. They tend to space their learning over a number of time periods and do not study the same topic continuously; they identify the main idea of the new material, connect new material to what they already know, and appraise their own progress (U.S. Department of Education, 1987). Poor students, on the other hand, tend to focus on less relevant details and do not use strategies that can help them learn and remember (Schmidt et al., 1989). For example, a student might be able to give you all the details of the sufferings at Valley Forge but not know the causes of the Revolutionary War. Another student may believe that studying a chapter in a text means reading the chapter quickly from beginning to end without stopping to consider the meaning of what she is reading (Schmidt et al., 1989).

study skills   Methods students use to study.

Many schools have begun study skills or school survival skills classes. These classes cover a number of skills, including time-scheduling, note taking, and organizational skills.

True or False   The study skills techniques used by good and poor students are quite similar.

The student who studies but does not do so effectively is a student who is likely to be frustrated. Although all students may need study skills training, the student who studies but does not do well requires more intensive training. However, a teacher must be certain where the problem lies. If the student's decoding skills are very poor and he cannot read the words in a book, this needs to be the prime source of intervention. We, then, begin from the premise that the child is able to read the material he is responsible for or is able to pay attention to the material taught in class.

There has been much attention given to separate areas of study skills. Before looking at some of the areas of interest and some of the most common mistakes students make in studying, one caveat is necessary. Proper study skills are often handed down in terms of rigid statements of right and wrong, and certainly, as we shall see, some practical rules for studying exist. However, students have different styles, and teachers can help students find the most effective style and method of studying for them. This may involve suggesting and modeling different ways to study and showing students how to change their strategies to match the requirements of the learning task. For example, a student who is asked to memorize a poem or the exports of the Soviet Union would use a different type of procedure than the same student who was asked to comprehend a story and put it into his or her own words. And both assignments differ in demand from one that asks the student to read material in a science book on the principles of genetics and be able to apply the information to various cases.

Some Common Study Problems

It isn't possible to delve deeply into all the study skills areas where students may have difficulties. The major areas, however, are time scheduling, physical factors, organizational skills, specific study techniques, reading skills and note taking. (Test-taking strategies are covered in Chapter 15.)

Time Scheduling

Many students do not budget their time effectively. This is seen in a number of areas. For example, many students have difficulty doing long-term assignments. Other students cannot estimate how much time they should allot to a particular subject. Others will cram for an examination rather than study on a regular basis. Keeping a record of study time can help, as can scheduling a particular time for studying each night.

Physical Factors

It is important for students to study in a place that will allow them to concentrate and do their work well. However, as we shall see in Chapter 4, new information on student learning styles means that we must be careful about describing the specific conditions under which a student will do best. For example, some students who like music can study with some background noise, while others cannot. Some like strong light; others find it a problem. Some like to read while sitting on the floor, some prefer working at a desk.

Organizational Skills

Some students are plainly disorganized. Often these students forget materials necessary for class, may try to remember assignments rather than write them down, have notebooks that are poorly organized, and always seem to miss details because they do not

Many students are disorganized, and helping students organize their notebooks is one way to help students achieve more.

follow directions properly. In this area, teachers and parents can work with students. Teachers can help students organize their notebooks by suggesting a desirable format for the books. For example, a teacher may want one section devoted to class notes and another for assignments. Or, teachers may require students to write their homework assignments on an assignment pad. It is good practice for teachers to hand out a written statement describing their homework and notebook policies to be read by the students and signed by the parents. The statement should include information about the format in which assignments are to be completed and should suggest that parents periodically check their children's notebooks and homework assignments.

Students must also organize the material so it makes sense. Some students see history or science as nothing but an endless stream of facts and dates unrelated to any overall theme. Because students do not see the overall theme or the relationships between the pieces of information, they see the ideas and facts as being equally important. Nor can they choose the most important facts. Successful students understand what is most important and how facts are used. Teachers can aid this process in their classes by specifically identifying the important ideas and directing student attention to them. In addition, before having the students read the chapter, teachers might give the students some overviews, questions, or information concerning the overall relationship of the sections of the chapter to one another and the themes that are most important (Schmidt et al., 1989). Writing an outline is also sometimes very helpful.

Students might also need help in organizing the material for studying. They sometimes look at a whole book to be read or at twenty-five problems to be solved for mathematics class and become overwhelmed. They may need help in breaking these assignments down to manageable segments, such as reading one chapter a night or doing a few problems at a time.

Specific Study Techniques

Within each subject, students must learn to use techniques that will work. Students often make mistakes in their study techniques that doom their studying to failure from the beginning. Consider the student who memorizes a list, only to discover that he will be tested on how well he comprehends the material or on its application. Good students adapt their study techniques to the task requirement. For example, taking verbatim notes may be an effective technique if students are to be tested only on lists or definitions or words or phrases. However, summarizing and paraphrasing are better techniques if the information has to be applied. Students should be aware of the goals of the assignment and of the learning process and adjust their study skills to these goals.

Reading Skills

Another area of study techniques includes different types of reading. Again, different tasks require different reading strategies. Reading a novel for the express purpose of understanding the characters and the plot is one type; reading a science text requires quite a different kind of reading. Students must be taught to analyze different types of assignments and use different skills for each type.

Note Taking

The best-known study skills technique is note taking. Students may take notes from written material, such as a text, or from classroom lessons. Note taking has two main functions. First, it can help students encode the new material by giving them an opportunity to connect new material to older material already in memory. Second, notes have a storage function; that is, having notes available for later use makes reviewing more efficient. But does note taking make a difference? Do students who take notes do better than those who do not? These questions are not easy to answer for a number of reasons. Some students take notes that are more lengthy than the passage they are reading. Others cannot take notes because a lesson proceeds too fast. Other students may read a text and not know what material is most important and what is less important and thus may take unnecessary notes or fail to take pertinent notes. Still other students may copy the exact words of a definition from the text, know it well, but then fail because they were asked questions that required application or conceptual relationships.

Stome studies have found definite advantages for students' taking notes; these advantages are related to better encoding of information (Aiken et al., 1975). Di Vesta and Gray (1972) found that students who were allowed to take notes recalled more than did those

How should this student take notes? Should the student paraphrase (or summarize) or take verbatim notes?

students not allowed to take notes, even though they were given no opportunity to review their notes. Other studies have not found such impressive results for taking notes (see Peper & Mayer, 1978).

Perhaps the reasons for the differences in the findings lie in the manner in which notes are taken and the match between the notes and the test. Note taking seems to improve encoding of new material, provided the notes taken match the material on the test (Bretzing & Kulhavy, 1981). In other words, if the test material is found in the notes, the notes are of help. If not, the notes may not be very helpful (Barnett et al., 1981). For instance, what if a student writes down the exact words of text definitions but is tested on applications. The verbatim exercise will not help much. However, if the student elaborates on the material by paraphrasing and summarizing it, creating analogies, and answering questions, the notes will help. At the same time, if a teacher tells students that they will be responsible for a list of items or for exact recall from the text, underlining or perhaps verbatim copying (although it is a very time consuming process) may help. However, students who merely memorize the words may have difficulty with test items that differ even in a small way from the text's words. Material that is memorized but not understood in one's own words is useful only if it is tested on the basis of straight memorization. Other studies have found that note taking is even more successful if students are allowed and encouraged to review their own notes (Carter & Van Matre, 1975).

What type of note taking is best? Bretzing and Kulhavy (1979) performed an interesting experiment with high school students in which the students were divided into five groups. One group was told to summarize the material they were asked to read, the second group to paraphrase the most important ideas, the third group to take verbatim notes, the fourth group to copy all the words that began with a capital letter, and the last group to read the material without taking any notes. They were all then tested on the material. What would you hypothesize would be the results of this experiment and why?

The researchers found that those students who summarized or paraphrased did the best, and in fact, the group that took verbatim notes did not do any better than the group that did not do anything special. The results can be explained in terms of information processing theory. As noted earlier, in the levels of information processing theory, students remember ma-

terial better the deeper the material is processed and the better it is understood and can be related to previous knowledge. Summarizing and paraphrasing essentially force students to process material more meaningfully and more deeply. Other studies have also shown that students who actively organize the material when taking notes do better, especially when they are asked questions that require understanding rather than mere rote memorization (Barnett et al., 1981).

In yet another study, Doctorow and colleagues (1978) asked elementary schoolchildren to read and remember written material. Four groups of children were used. One group was asked to write a summary sentence about the main idea of each paragraph; the second group was given a heading for each paragraph that essentially summarized the material; the third group both received headings and was told to summarize; the fourth group read the material without either being asked to summarize or being given the headings. For both good and poor readers, the groups that used either summaries or headings did better than group four, and the group that used both summaries and headings did even better. It seems that for many, but not all, functions, elaborating is superior to rote memorization.

To summarize, then, note taking is effective when the notes match the manner in which students will be asked to retrieve the information. Elaborative methods are better than verbatim methods in most, but not all, situations. In addition, note taking may help more if the student later uses the notes. Students can be taught to take notes more effectively if also taught such strategies as telling the difference between the more and the less important information, abbreviating terms, paraphrasing, and using an outline (Carrier & Titus, 1981).

True or False   Taking notes while reading text material is an ineffective learning technique.

The SQ3R

One of the most common reading and studying techniques used is the **SQ3R,** which stands for survey, question, read, recite, and review. This approach, first advanced by Francis Robinson, is very useful for mastering reading material, especially text material.

Survey: The student first previews the chapter by looking over a chapter outline, thumbing through the chapter and looking at the headings, or reading a summary. This takes only about a minute after some practice (Cohn, 1979) and gives the student an overview of what he or she will be reading. The student pays attention to the order of the headings, which contain useful clues to the content of the chapter.

Question: The student then converts each title or subtitle into a question. For example, if the subtitle is "The Extinction of the Dinosaurs," the student might turn it into a question: Why did dinosaurs die out? This gives the reading more focus and links what a student knows about the subject to what he or she will be learning. Sometimes more than one question is useful.

Read: The student then reads the section with an eye to answering the question. The student may take some notes during this reading. It is also important for students to continue to ask themselves whether they understand what they are reading. Students may read for the main ideas as well as for details. If a technical term is italicized or placed in bold type, it is important that students make certain they know what the term means.

Recite: Once students have finished reading the section, they then answer the question in their own words. I have found that it is also somewhat helpful if students are able to put any definitions or unusual terms into their own words. Recitation is a good way to improve recall, since the material is then encoded at a deeper level. It may also help students learn whether or not they understood the material. If students are learning a subject that contains a great deal of detail or facts, they may need more time for recitation.

Review: The student then writes the major points or states them after reading all the sections. This can be done by reviewing his or her notes and finally by stating the major points and terms without referring to any material.

CONNECTIONS

Working with Students on Their Study Skills

To some extent, each student has his or her own methods of studying. In fact, students should be encouraged to discover what works for them when studying different types of material. It is not as important to detail one rule for everyone as it is to encourage students to find out what factors improve their own ability to study. However, to be successful, students must be willing to change their ways of studying if their current methods do not work. In my experience, the students who are having difficulties studying have the most difficulty changing their study habits. Simply put, many students continue to study in ineffective ways because either they do not know how to change or change would take too much effort. For instance, students might be taught to use a study technique such as the SQ3R and then abandon it because it is too time consuming. This is especially likely to happen if students do not realize that studying a chapter in a text differs greatly from reading a novel.

The following suggestions are not meant to be rigid directives about how to study but are based both upon research and upon this understanding of the individual student's needs.

1. **Analyze why the student's study strategies have not worked.** Students may not be able to identify their weak points. Asking students questions about their study skills can yield important information in the areas of physical setting, organization skills, memory aids, time scheduling, note taking, and study strategies. Of course, this is predicated on the assumptions that the student is studying and has the basic abilities to read and master the material.

2. **Provide group instruction on study skills.** Students, especially in the younger grades, must be taught how to organize their notebooks and assignment notepads and where and how to allot their time. They must also be taught study strategies such as the SQ3R.

3. **Emphasize a student's awareness of what the learning task entails.** Different learning tasks require different study strategies, and students must be made aware of this. Students may continue to memorize words and do poorly on tests of comprehension and application if they are not taught that different learning tasks require different study strategies.

4. **Students should be encouraged to encode material at deep levels.** Since material encoded more deeply is remembered better, students should be encouraged to paraphrase and summarize in their own words and to seek application of the material where it is required.

5. **Have parents check study skills.** Parents can help improve study skills if they check homework and assignment notebooks and make certain that students keep to their time schedules. Often, if students do not have much homework they do not review, and teachers can make parents aware of the need for students to review their notes.

6. **Teach students how and when to take notes.** Students need instruction on when and how to take notes both from class lessons and from their written assignments. This can be done in a number of ways. The note-taking skills involved in summarizing, outlining, and paraphrasing are most important. Students also need practice in learning to identify the most important facts and details. One way to do this is to first give the students some idea of what note taking is all about. Then give the students a few paragraphs or a five-minute lesson and ask them to take notes. The next step is to give the students some idea of how the notes might look. With some students, a more detailed type of note taking is required and providing the students with an outline at the beginning of a lesson may be helpful (see Chapter 13). Discuss with students the problem of taking too many notes as well as taking too few notes. In addition, prepare students to take notes differently when the requirements of the learning task change.

7. **Teach the SQ3R approach.** Teach students skills of reading from a text. Impress upon students that reading from a text differs greatly from reading from a novel. It takes longer, and students should expect it to do so. However, if they encode the material in a more meaningful manner, the material will stay with them longer.

8. **Make certain students understand library skills.** Students must understand how to find the answers to questions by using such resources as indexes and dictionaries.

9. **Encourage students to talk to one another about how they study.** Sometimes, students can make suggestions that allow other students to understand new ways of studying or organizing their work.

10. **Realize that students do not always understand when they know or do not know something.** Many students do not know when they know or do not know something. Any study skills material is useful only if students understand that they need more help in a certain area. The suggestions made in this chapter's discussion of metamemory and in the next chapter's discussion of metacognition are viable.

11. **Make certain students use these strategies.** Students often will begin to use a study strategy, such as organizing their notebook or paraphrasing or outlining notes, and quickly fall back into bad habits. The strategies must be checked. One of the problems with study skills is that they often initially take more time than the student is used to putting into the reading or the work. Teachers must check that students are using these strategies.

Library skills are part of a study skills course. Students must learn how to find the information they seek.

THE INFORMATION PROCESSING AND PIAGETIAN VIEWS: SEEKING HARMONY

The last chapter looked at the cognitive developmental approach typified by Jean Piaget's work. It may seem at first glance that the Piagetian view and the information processing approach are opposites, but this is not so. The information processing approach allows us to delve more deeply into the same kinds of phenomena that interested Piaget. The Piagetian and information processing viewpoints can complement each other, giving parents and teachers new ways to analyze a child's cognitive growth.

If we look closely, we will see that information processing theory specifically analyzes in great detail the way children perceive, attend to, encode, process, and retrieve information. Piaget may not have examined these processes with as much detail, but he has presented us with splendid descriptions of the ways children think at different ages and look at the same phenomena but from different angles. When a child answers a question, Piagetian theory allows us to understand how the child is reasoning and what his or her limitations are. An information processing approach might delve into the specific manner in which the material is taken in, processed, and retrieved. Both approaches give us valuable information about how children reason and see their world. A teacher who understands such abilities is more likely to plan lessons that interest students, deliver the lessons effectively, and, in the end, be more successful.

SUMMARY

1. Information processing specialists investigate the way people take in information, process it, and act on it. Such factors as attention, perception, memory, the mediating process by which people do something to the information in their mind, and a person's response system are important.

2. Attention is sometimes thought of as a filter that allows the most important elements to be processed while allowing the unimportant elements to be ignored. People select what they want to attend to. A more modern conception views attention as mental effort applied to the task by the learner. The better we know something, the less attention we need to pay to it. As children mature, they become better at voluntarily directing and allocating this cognitive resource.

3. Memory processes involve encoding or laying down new memories, storing them and retrieving them at the proper moment. Memory is measured in the classroom most often through recall—in which students are asked to retrieve information using very few cues—or recognition—in which they must choose the correct answers from a number of choices. People are better at recognition than they are at recall through life.

4. Information first enters the sensory register, where it is held in its exact form for two seconds or less. It has a short duration but a large capacity. If the material is attended to, it continues on into short-term memory or working memory. Short-term memory has a short duration, about thirty seconds, and a small capacity, about seven items. If material is not rehearsed, it is lost. If it is rehearsed, it may continue to be processed into long-term memory, which has a huge capacity and a long duration. Long-term memories can be understood in terms of networks, where concepts or propositions are related to other concepts or propositions. The richer these networks, the easier it is to lay down new memories.

5. The student's knowledge base affects memory. Students possess a number of schemata—organized bodies of knowledge that function as frameworks for describing objects and relationships that generally occur. Scripts are structures describing the sequence of events in a particular situation that form the basis for understanding events. Scripts and schemata form the framework that allows students to learn new information by relating the information to already stored information.

6. Various strategies can be used to encode material efficiently. The levels of processing theory states that the more deeply the material is processed, the more easily it will be retrieved. Therefore, connecting new information with older information or thinking about the meaning of the material rather than merely repeating it are sound strategies. The use of paraphrasing, summarizing, advance organizers, and mnemonic devices allows students to encode material more effectively. Preschoolers and children in the early years of ele-

mentary school have difficulty using verbal strategies spontaneously, although they may use them if they are directed to do so by the teachers.

7. Metamemory involves an individual's knowledge of his or her own memory processes. Students often do not know when they know something and when they do not. Metamemory abilities increase during the elementary school years.

8. There are a number of different theories of forgetting. Decay of the memory trace theory notes that forgetting takes place when information is not used. Interference theory suggests that new learning interferes with older learning or older learning interferes with new learning. The failure in retrieval explanation notes that the material is stored but cannot be retrieved, possibly because it was encoded under a different category or in a different way. In addition, some material is forgotten because it is very anxiety provoking and the individual is motivated not to remember.

9. Many students who have the ability to do well in school might not because they lack the study skills to succeed. Study skills involve the ability to use effective reading techniques that change with the learning task at hand, test-taking skills, organization skills, locating material, outlining, summarizing, paraphrasing and taking notes. Good students usually have effective study skills, while poorer students often are disorganized, do not know how to get the necessary information from their texts or the classroom lesson, and do not budget their time effectively. Study skills can be learned.

10. One effective way to read text material is to use the SQ3R technique, which involves surveying the material, formulating questions using subheads, reading the material, using recitation, and reviewing the material.

11. Studies generally, but not universally, show that note taking can be an effective learning skill. It can be useful in encoding information and helping students relate new facts to facts already in their memory and as a resource for review. Students who take notes generally do better at remembering the central concepts and in using the material to answer questions or solve problems that are not exactly like those they are reading about. Paraphrasing and summarizing are more effective in these situations than are underlining

and studying the exact words, because they allow students to process the material more deeply. However, if the material to be learned is a long list or the student will be required to recall verbatim the exact definitions of the terms, the latter strategies can be effective.

ACTIVITIES AND EXERCISES

1. **Capturing Student Attention.** Seek out teachers in your own specialty and ask them how they gain and keep their students' attention. Make a list of the techniques they use.

2. **"Sesame Street" Reconsidered.** One of the most interesting aspects of "Sesame Street" is its ability to hold young children's interest. Watch a twenty-minute segment of "Sesame Street" and list the ways the program's producers use movement, color, music, action, and other elements to capture attention.

3. **Short-Term Memory.** An item of information in short-term memory or working memory lasts only about thirty seconds unless it is rehearsed. To demonstrate this, try the following demonstration based upon an experiment performed by Peterson & Peterson (1959). Ask a colleague if she thinks she can remember a telephone number for a minute without rehearsing it. She'll most likely say she can. Give her a telephone number and wait a little more than thirty seconds. She will easily recall the telephone number. However, she *has* rehearsed it, even if she doesn't admit it. To keep her from rehearsing, ask her to remember another telephone number, but this time after giving her the number, ask her to count backwards from one hundred by threes or fours. This simply prevents her from rehearsing it, and she will probably not be able to remember the number.

4. **Recognition and Recall.** It is easy to demonstrate the superiority of recognition over recall. Make a list of one hundred names of politicians, including senators and vice presidents, both present and past, and make certain the names of *all* the presidents of the United States are sprinkled randomly throughout the list. First ask people to write down all the presidents they can remember from memory. After they finish, give them the list and ask them to place a check next

to the presidents on the list. You will find that people can recognize many more presidents than they can recall.

5. **Information Processing and Encoding.** Plan a lesson on any topic in your specialty and after doing so, analyze the lesson in an information processing manner, answering the following questions:

Will it capture and keep attention? How?

Does it take into consideration the information processing abilities of the students (attention span, memory abilities)?

Is the pacing too slow or too fast?

Does the lesson encourage elaborative encoding rather than simple rehearsal?

Does the lesson highlight the important features?

6. **Demonstrating Scripts.** One of the more recent discoveries in the area of cognition is the use of scripts and schemata as guides by even the youngest children in their understanding of their world. Interview children of different ages, asking them to describe what happens at a McDonald's restaurant, during a schoolday, or at a birthday party. You may be surprised to find that their scripts are all very similar. Older children's scripts may show somewhat more flexibility.

7. **The Keyword Method.** The keyword method involves making an acoustical link between a word and something that can be easily imagined and then connecting that image with another word, creating a more vivid image. For example, as described in the chapter, to remember the Spanish word *huevo,* meaning egg, you could remember wave, which is easily imaged, and imagine an egg bobbing on a wave. Prepare a list of foreign words and their English equivalents. Then have some children study the words while helping others use the keyword method to remember the meanings. Test both groups, and as an interesting additional experiment, wait a few days and test both groups again to see which group still remembers the words.

8. **The Pegword Method.** You can do a similar experiment using the pegword method and the "one is a bun" rhyme. Simply make up two lists of directions or things to do for a day (such as errands). Have some people try to memorize all ten directions or things in order. Then have the other people do the same using the "one is a bun" de-

vice. Write the rhyme on a piece of paper and help the second group create mental images as described in the chapter. You will find that using the pegword method, the students do much better.

9. **Metamemory.** Knowing when you know something and when you don't is a fundamental problem in education. Ask children of various ages to study a page of text from their books until they say they know it. Then test them on it by asking questions about the material. You may find that some of the children do not know when they know the material and when they do not.

10. **Study Skills Training.** It was noted in the chapter that some schools have study skills courses sometimes called student survival skills. Find some high schools or even colleges that give such courses and ask for a copy of the curriculum, course outline, and/or text that is being used. Examine the material. List the important study skills that are discussed and the techniques used to teach students study skills.

11. **How do you study for _____.** Ask your colleagues how they study for a particular test. The research on study skills demonstrates that good students study differently depending upon the learning task, so you will have to ask about the subject of the test, the form of the test (essay or multiple choice), the need to memorize any lists, as well as the amount of time needed for study.

SCENARIOS

Here are nine scenarios. Try to apply the information you have learned in the chapter to each situation.

1. There is a discussion in the teachers' lunchroom about keeping student attention. Some teachers have suggested that junior high school students should be able to pay attention to lessons in forty-minute periods, and if they can't, there is little the teacher can do on an everyday basis. Other teachers suggest that the curriculum is the problem and is just not very interesting. A third group claims that there are things teachers can do on a daily basis to capture and keep students' attention. Which group would you join and why? If your answer is the third group, discuss some of the strategies you could use to capture and hold students' attention at the grade level you will be teaching.

2. Lorraine always tries. She puts a great deal of time into her work but still does not do well in fifth grade. Her mother has told Mr. Timmons, her teacher, that Lorraine studies the assigned material at home, thinks she knows it, but often does not. In addition, she has difficulty memorizing some of the material. Lorraine has been extensively tested, and her tests show that she has no identifiable learning problems and her reading ability is at grade level. Her parents have asked for help, especially since Lorraine is becoming frustrated. How would you analyze Lorraine's problem, and what can be done about it?

3. Mrs. Yamamoto's ninth-grade science class just did poorly on an examination. Because most of the students claim that they studied and know the subject matter, Mrs. Yamamoto has decided to show them that they really don't know the material. She has them take out a piece of paper and gives them five terms to define. To her surprise, most of the class gets them correct. This confuses her, since she is under the impression that the class simply does not know the material. One student tells her that this is not what she asked for on the test. When Mrs. Yamamoto looks over the test, she notices that the wording is changed a bit from the book's definitions and that some relatively simple applications are required. She doesn't understand why there is a problem, since her students seem to know the definitions. If this happened in your class, could you explain the results? How?

4. Mr. Ianello has found that when his students know something about what they are going to learn and he focuses their attention on the important points, his fourth-graders do better. He also reminds his students of the memory strategies they should use. He has made it a practice of giving an overview, thought questions, and review questions. However, one of his colleagues has told him that he is "babying" his students and he will retard their progress. He is having second thoughts about his procedures. Evaluate his colleague's criticisms and Mr. Ianello's procedures.

5. "I read the chapter three times," sixth-grader Jennifer told Mr. Franklin. The chapter in social studies on westward expansion was a relatively long chapter but not an intensely difficult one. "I also took notes," Jennifer said, showing Mr. Franklin some very well written notes. When Mr. Franklin looked them over, he noted that they were written in almost the exact words as the book. They also covered everything and seemed not to have any focus. His tests are essay tests that measure conceptual information, much of which comes from the chapter. Mr. Franklin would like to help Jennifer, but has two problems. First, he is not certain how to go about helping Jennifer take effective notes. Second, his time is limited, and whatever he can do to help Jennifer cannot take a tremendous amount of time. If Jennifer were a student in your class, how would you try to help her? In addition, Mr. Franklin has not obtained all the necessary information from Jennifer to conclude that note taking is her problem. What other questions or additional information would you want?

6. Lisa is taking a biology course in which her worst problem is her inability to remember the many terms for various parts of the body. No matter how hard she tries, she just can't seem to remember them. When she receives a test in biology, the test items that she answers incorrectly are based almost exclusively upon the facts that she cannot remember. Labeling diagrams, placing the correct answer in a blank space, and other such test items are very difficult for Lisa. She does understand the overall concepts but not the details that appear to be so important. Mr. Greenspan, her biology teacher, is sympathetic. He has heard this problem before. What can Mr. Greenspan do to help Lisa learn this material?

7. Mrs. Krastin has noted that her eighth-grade science class seems to lack the study skills necessary to succeed. She has discussed this problem with a number of teachers in different subjects, and many of them agree that the study skills abilities of their students leave much to be desired. She has noticed that some students simply leaf through the pages of their texts or read them very quickly. Other students in her class have notebooks filled with scraps of paper and cannot seem to find anything. Others do not seem to be familiar with the parts of the text. Other teachers have made these and other observations. Mrs. Krastin mentioned her problem to the principal, who noted that she, too, was becoming concerned. The principal asked Mrs. Krastin to come up with both a list of skills she and her colleagues believe students require and some mechanism for teaching students study skills. Mrs. Krastin has a number of choices and has some misgivings. She is not certain that

the study skills necessary in her subject are the same as those necessary in social studies or English. In addition, there is a question whether skills should be taught after school, during a special school week, or as part of the curriculum. Last, what role should parents play? As a colleague, she asks you for your input. How would you answer her questions? What would you like to see taught? How should the program be structured?

8. Few of Mr. Cowens' students have ever studied Chinese history. They have very little experience with this new material, and to be honest, Mr. Cowens realizes the difficulties the students will face. The curriculum has been changed to give students some background in non-Western cultures. Students are unfamiliar with the names of the people, the geography of China, Chinese culture, and just about everything else that Mr. Cowens is supposed to teach. Everything is different. Many of Mr. Cowens' students, although pleased to study a new area, are having difficulty with it for various reasons, including the cultural differences, the concept of ancient Chinese government, and the name problem. Mr. Cowens believes that teaching some non-Western culture and history is good policy but would like some understanding of why these students are having so much difficulty and would like to help them learn more efficiently. Using concepts from information processing theory, such as schemata, suggest some ways that Mr. Cowens might approach teaching radically new material to his students.

9. Mrs. Watson believes that since students in the last year of junior high school (ninth grade in her district) will be going on to high school next year, they require some help in learning how to read a textbook. The textbook in her area is quite good, and she feels that it is both clear and concise. It contains a number of subheads, introductory questions, and summary questions and is written at a reasonable level of understanding. To test her students' skills, Mrs. Watson announces that a test will be given on Friday on one and only one chapter. She tells her class that the major concepts will be tested as well as the meanings of the major terms in the chapter. To her amazement, her class does very poorly on the test. The students did not complain that the text was too difficult, and all the students were surprised at their low grades. Mrs. Watson believes that most of the students read the text, and she is puzzled about what to do now. She believes that these students should be able to master the material in the text and sees no point in having a text if students can't make use of it. She has read that many students do not know how to read a textbook. After discussing this with a few students, she finds that some of the students simply skimmed the material while others read the material quickly as if they were reading a novel or a short story. If you were Mrs. Watson, how would you confront this problem? In addition, if you were to teach certain skills, note specifically which ones you would teach and how. Lastly, if students complain that using these skills "takes too long," how would you answer their complaints?

4

Are These Statements True or False?

Turn the next page for the correct answers. Each statement is repeated following the paragraph in which the information can be found.

1. At present, there is no universally accepted definition of intelligence.
2. The majority of states have mandated that thinking skills be taught in the classroom.
3. When thinking skills are taught in school, children show not only improvements in their ability to think but also increases in their scores on achievement tests.
4. In an attempt to show interest in a student's reasoning, teachers should never ask students why they think something is so, because this type of question injures the student's self-concept.
5. Having extensive knowledge in a particular area, such as economics or astronomy, facilitates solving problems in that field.
6. Trying to visualize a problem in some way is a useful strategy for solving problems.
7. When students learn a skill in one class, the teacher can be fairly certain students will transfer that skill to other situations.
8. The sole criterion for determining creativity is originality of response.
9. The more intelligent an individual is, the greater the chance that he or she will be creative.
10. Students who are impulsive—that is, take very little time to answer—make more mistakes than those who take more time to reflect on the question or problem.
11. If students' learning style preferences are not followed, it is the very bright, creative, well-behaved student who suffers the most.
12. Since the right and left hemispheres seem to control different facets of behavior and thinking, it is desirable to educate the hemispheres separately.

Thinking Skills, Problem Solving, and Creativity

TAKING ME BY SURPRISE

When I first began teaching, I was assigned to teach an eighth-grade social studies curriculum on urban studies that included, among other things, a detailed look at the many facets of urban life, including culture, housing, health care, education, and the environment. After teaching these elements individually, I reasoned that it was time to combine them into some kind of project. I divided the students into groups and asked each group to design a city that would provide adequate services for the population. The students were to use their imaginations, draw their plans, and write a group report that would define their ideas. They were also required to describe their designs to the other students in the class.

The students seemed pleased at the prospect of designing their ideal city, and I offered guidelines and discussed possible ways of approaching the task. One student, John, asked if he could do it by himself. I hesitated, but the look on his face made me believe that he was serious about it.

When the time came for John to turn in his report, I had no idea what to expect. John had done some work

in class—just as the groups were doing—mostly sketches, diagrams, and some reading. I was unprepared for his final product, which contained a diagram that measured five feet by four feet, with three acetate overlays and a report about a quarter of an inch thick.

I was astounded. John's project was not only a work of art, it was conceptually superior to anything I had seen. John had limited the density of each neighborhood by making certain that all types of housing existed. Each neighborhood had its own park system, and each park had a different theme, such as pirate rides or a fairy tale motif. John had strategically placed ambulances in each neighborhood so that they would not have far to travel. He had designed a bus system and worked out the stops so that by taking no more than two buses a person could get from one part of the city to every other part. The overlays showed these systems.

John was an average student who hardly ever participated in class. If called upon, he answered the question, and that was all. He never elaborated and never asked any questions. His scholastic average was somewhere around 75. He was reading a bit lower than grade level and had taken an intelligence test that showed his intelligence to lie within the average range.

I arranged a meeting with his mother, who described her son as quiet. His mother was pleased that her son's project was so well received. I asked John's mother about her son's work, and she told me that she thought the project was nice but that John was always doing things like that. During the summer, John had earned a couple of hundred dollars, which he had converted to pennies. After cleaning each penny, he constructed a large elephant-shaped bank from these pennies. On another project, he had cut up old carpets from which he designed a scene from the Middle Ages of two knights fighting while a crowd, including kings and other royalty, watched. Here was a student with an average school record that did not mirror what obviously were a number of superior abilities in critical thinking and creativity.

I have often thought about John and wondered how many other students like him go through our schools without having their talents noticed. This chapter explores the areas of intelligence, thinking skills, creativity, and learning styles. Our conceptions of these areas have changed substantially over the past decade or so, and research in these areas has considerable implications for teachers.

CONCEPTIONS OF INTELLIGENCE

I can remember looking at John's intelligence test results and wondering why he had not done better on the test. Judging from his project and other activities, John was certainly bright. However, he did not show it on the intelligence test, perhaps because his linguistic skills were average at best, and most intelligence tests emphasize verbal abilities. This begs an important question. Was John very intelligent? The answer depends solely on how intelligence is defined. It's clear that, at least in our society, language proficiency is linked to intelligence, but intelligence may be far more than a collection of verbal skills.

Intelligence has been defined as the ability to profit from one's experiences, a cluster of cognitive abilities, the ability to do well in school, and whatever an intelligence test measures. Howard Gardner, a respected expert in this field, defines intelligence as "an ability to solve problems or to fashion a product

intelligence The ability to profit from experience. A cluster of abilities, such as reasoning and memory. In the Piagetian view, any behavior that allows the individual to adapt to the environment.

Theory of Multiple Intelligences A conception of intelligence advanced by Howard Gardner, who argues that there are seven different types of intelligence.

which is valued in one or more cultural settings (1987, p. 25)." Piaget viewed intelligence not as a "thing" but rather as an ongoing process by which children use qualitatively different ways to adapt to their environment. There is no universally accepted definition for intelligence.

True or False At present, there is no universally accepted definition of intelligence.

An important question to ask about intelligence is whether it is one quality or is composed of a number of separate and distinct components (Kail & Pellegrino, 1985). If it is one quality, one would expect people who are "intelligent" to show this quality across a wide variety of tasks. This is referred to as the g factor (general intelligence factor). On the other hand, some psychologists argue that some people perform much better on some tasks than on others and that in addition to having this general factor, people possess specific abilities (the s factor). Still others deny that any general factor for intelligence exists, insisting that a number of primary abilities are present. For example, Thurstone (1938) argued that there are seven primary abilities: verbal comprehension, word fluency, number, spatial abilities, associative memory, perceptual speed, and general reasoning. Today, this viewpoint has been expanded in a new approach by Howard Gardner (1983, 1987a, and 1987b), who advanced the **Theory of Multiple Intelligences,** that is, the theory that a number of different types of intelligence exist (see Table 4.1), as follows:

Linguistic Intelligence. This is the ability to use and interpret words.

Logical-Mathematical Intelligence. This involves scientific and mathematical ability. Gardner believes that Piaget's concept of intelligence actually

Table 4.1 Gardner's Conception of Intelligence

Linguistic

Language skills include a sensitivity to the subtle shades of the meanings of words

Logical-Mathematical

Both critics and supporters acknowledge that IQ tests measure this ability well

Musical

Like language, music is an expressive medium—and this talent flourishes in prodigies

Spatial

Sculptors and painters are able accurately to perceive, manipulate and re-create forms

Bodily-kinesthetic

At the core of this kind of intelligence are body control and skilled handling of objects

Interpersonal

Skill in reading the moods and intentions of others is displayed by politicians, among others

Intrapersonal

The key is understanding one's own feelings—and using that insight to guide behavior

From "7 Ways to be Bright," *U.S. News and World Report.* Copyright © November 23, 1987, U.S. News and World Report.

Spatial Intelligence. This is the ability "to form a mental model of a spatial world and to maneuver and operate using that model" (Gardner, 1987, p. 190). Sailors, engineers, surgeons, sculptors, and painters require this type of intelligence.

Bodily-Kinesthetic Intelligence. This is the ability to solve problems or to fashion products using one's body. Dancers, athletes, surgeons, and craftspeople exhibit this type of intelligence.

Interpersonal Intelligence. This is the ability to understand other people, how they work, what motivates them, and how to work with them. Salespeople, politicians, teachers, and religious leaders have (or should have) this type of intelligence.

Intrapersonal Intelligence. This is the ability to understand one's own feelings and then use this insight to guide behavior. Intrapersonal intelligence also includes one's knowledge of all the other intelligences.

Gardner thinks of the preceding as seven different intelligences that we all possess to some extent though not on equal levels. Therefore, one of the responsibilities of the school is to assess students on all their individual abilities and then to find ways of enriching the students' education by challenging all of their talents.

Another new approach is based on an information processing model. Here, investigators try to understand intelligence in terms of the mental processes that relate to performance on a task. For example, Robert Sternberg (1984, 1985) advanced the **Triarchic Theory of Human Intelligence,** arguing that intelligence involves purposeful adaptation to the real world. What is adaptive in one culture may not be in another. An intelligent person in the United States

measured logical and mathematical intelligence. Both linguistic and mathematical intelligence are highly valued in society, and students who possess these types of intelligence will do well on intelligence tests and the SAT and ACT exams. However, whether students do well after they leave college may depend upon the other intelligences.

Musical Intelligence. Music is a method of expressing oneself, and Gardner considers it an intelligence of its own.

Triarchic Theory of Intelligence   A theory of intelligence based on information processing considerations advanced by Robert Sternberg, who postulates the following mechanisms of intellectual functioning: metacomponents, which involve the individual's skills used in planning and decision making; performance components, which relate to the basic operations involved in actually solving the task; and knowledge acquisition components, which involve processes that are used in acquiring new knowledge.

Howard Gardner suggests that the ability to express one-self musically and the ability to create products using one's hands are examples of intelligence.

might be quite unable to cope with the requirements of living in a mountainous Asian country.

According to Sternberg, intelligence has three components. First, there are metacomponents or executive skills used in planning and decision making, including recognition of the problem, knowledge of the various processes involved in selecting a solution strategy, allocation of time, and the monitoring of the solution attempt. Second, there are the performance components, the basic operations involved in actually solving a problem, such as encoding information, inferring relationships between different aspects of the problem, and comparing and contrasting different answers. The third component of intelligence is knowledge acquisition. This involves processes useful in acquiring new knowledge, including selective encoding (sifting the relevant from the irrelevant), selective combination (integrating the knowledge in a meaningful way), and selective comparison (rendering the information meaningful by appreciating its relationship to other information).

Most intelligence tests emphasize verbal intelligence and ignore other types of intelligence or information processing skills. They are frequently defended because there is a high correlation between school achievement and performance on intelligence tests, about .6 or so. Children who score very low may

have difficulty in school, and those who score very high may do better. Because the correlation is not perfect, however, other factors such as motivation and study skills play a part. However, while intelligence tests are decent predictors of academic success, they are poor predictors of job success. One study found that one third of all professionals it tracked had below-average childhood intelligence scores (*U.S. News and World Report,* 1987).

The currently popular intelligence tests are discussed in Chapter 14 following an introduction of a number of considerations about testing. Here, we are interested in understanding the concept of intelligence rather than the problems involved in its measurement. These two new approaches to intelligence have much to offer. First, Gardner's multiple intelligences lead us to look beyond language and logic and examine other skills that have been slighted. Students need to be evaluated on each of these seven intelligences and to have their abilities encouraged. Gardner is now preparing new ways of measuring students' skills. Sternberg's theory leads us to look at the thinking processes that underlie problem solving. These processes can be taught and improved.

How does all this relate to John? If we look at the traditional definitions of intelligence, John possesses average intelligence. But if we look at intelligence in terms of multiple intelligences or thinking processes, then John may be considered highly intelligent. He certainly showed kinesthetic and spatial intelligence, and his ability to reason, plan, and execute as shown in his project were exceptional. In the end, we must expand our idea of intelligence so that people like John are not forgotten. As we've seen, there are new approaches that are doing just that.

THINKING SKILLS

John's project showed an ability to critically analyze a difficult problem and solve it. Lately, there has been a public outcry that our schools must teach students to think in better ways. The National Commission on Excellence in Education noted that many 17-year-olds did not possess the higher order reasoning skills expected of their age group. About 40 percent could not draw inferences from written material, and only one in five could write a persuasive essay (McTighe, 1985).

In 1987, the Michigan Board of Education issued a

policy statement stating that educational institutions at all levels should address the dimensions of thinking in all content areas from kindergarten through grade 12 (Palincsar & Brown, 1988). About ten states or so have mandated that thinking skills be taught in the schools (Grice & Jones, 1989). Many school districts have now focused their attention on teaching particular thinking skills.

True or False The majority of states have mandated that thinking skills be taught in the classroom.

A close relationship exists between thinking, language skills, and verbal intelligence. A well-known authority in the field of thinking, Edward de Bono defines thinking as the "operating skill with which intelligence acts upon experience" (1983, p. 703). The relationship between thinking and language is obvious, since language is one tool for thinking. However, we need not limit thinking to language (Eisner, 1988). Some people think by visualizing. For example, a science student might visualize the atomic structure of a particular compound. In our daily lives, we might try to solve the problem of where we left our keys by visualizing the room and our movements. Nevertheless, much of our reasoning and thinking requires language.

Why Teach Thinking?

Many reasons exist for teaching thinking in the schools. Many authorities dissatisfied with student achievement argue that at least part of the problem can be attributed to a deficiency in higher reasoning skills (Presseisen, 1986). Numerous studies have linked performance on tests of reasoning to grades on traditional achievement tests (Strahan, 1986). There is evidence that when thinking skills are taught as part of the curriculum, test scores in academic areas as well as scores on intelligence tests improve (Whimbey, 1985; Matthews & Lin-Odom, 1988).

True or False When thinking skills are taught in school, children show not only improvements in their ability to think but also increases in their scores on achievement tests.

There is more to teaching thinking skills, however, than an attempt to boost test scores. Today, we are facing a glut of information. Teachers are called upon to teach more material as the sheer amount of knowledge increases. Any parent who remembers science class may look at what his or her child is learning and realize that much of it is new. With this information explosion, we are more than ever being forced to evaluate and compare, to decide and act. Having information is not enough, people need to be trained to do something with the information (Presseisen, 1987). They need to learn to think independently. Preparing students for this is part of the school's responsibility.

Unfortunately, the evidence indicates that many students cannot properly use the information they possess (Nickerson, 1987). Many people are biased in their decision making and do not see long-range consequences, nor do they consider all alternatives. Good thinking involves, among other things, the ability to use evidence skillfully and impartially, to organize thoughts consistently, to suspend judgment in the absence of evidence, to anticipate consequences, to see similarities and analogies that are not superficial, to apply problem-solving techniques in fields other than those in which they were learned, to listen carefully to other people, and to look for unusual approaches to complex problems (Nickerson, 1987). Good thinking does not occur naturally (Glaser, 1985). It is not usual for people to wait until the evidence is in before forming conclusions or considering all the alternatives. These are skills that must and can be developed.

What Types of Thinking Are Needed?

If we can agree that teaching students to think is an important concern, the next step is to evaluate what types of thinking are required. Some argue that each discipline has its own logic and reasoning skills and that reasoning skills do not bridge subject differences. However, most authorities today do not agree with this argument, claiming that there are thinking skills that can be developed and that are necessary and valid for use in a great many different disciplines (Ennis, 1987).

Many lists of the thinking skills that students need are available, and no list can be seen as complete. Table 4.2 shows twenty-seven different thinking skills that are commonly found in the literature. The term **higher order reasoning skills** is often used to describe elaborate and complex thinking skills such as analyzing, comparing, inferring, interpreting, and evaluating. Higher order thinking is not routine and often leads to multiple solutions to problems, each with costs and benefits. Table 4.3 shows the applications of higher order reasoning skills in science, social studies, and literature. The term **critical thinking** refers to thinking that is involved with analyzing and focusing on what to believe or do in a particular situation.

Approaches to teaching thinking skills can be divided into two camps. There are those who argue that teachers should write their own thinking skills material, perhaps together with other colleagues, and those who argue that a professionally designed, commercially available program is best. There is also no accepted answer to whether these thinking skills programs should be separated from or injected into the rest of the curriculum (Sternberg, 1987). Some even argue in favor of a mixed model in which thinking skills are taught as a separate course and at the same time are infused into the entire curriculum.

Table 4.2 Twenty-seven Thinking Skills
There is more emphasis today than in the past on developing student thinking skills.

Comparing	Translating	Using analogies
Classifying	Reorganizing	Imagining
Estimating	Setting priorities	Logical deducing
Summarizing	Setting criteria	Identifying pros/cons
Hypothesizing	Goal setting	Identifying propaganda
Synthesizing	Problem solving	Identifying consequences
Sequencing	Decision making	Observing
Predicting	Justifying	Creating/designing
Evaluating	Making assumptions	Interpreting

From "Teaching the Process of Thinking, K-12" by K. R. Chuska, *Phi Delta Kappan*, p. 11. Copyright © 1986, Phi Delta Kappa Educational Foundation. Reprinted with permission.

---

higher order reasoning skills (higher order thinking skills)   Term used to describe elaborate and complex thinking skills such as analyzing, inferring, and evaluating.

critical thinking   Thinking that involves analyzing and focusing on what to believe or do in a particular situation.

Table 4.3 Examples of Applications of Higher Order Reasoning Skills in Three Subject Domains
This table shows specifically how higher order reasoning skills can be applied to science, social science, and literature.

	Science	Social Science	Literature
Analyze	Identify the components of a process or the features of animate and inanimate objects	Identify the components of an argument or the elements of an event	Identify the components of literary, expository, and persuasive discourse
Compare	Compare the properties of objects or events	Compare the causes and effects of separate events and of social, political, economic, cultural, and geographic features	Compare meanings, themes, plots, characters, settings, and reasons
Infer	Draw conclusions, make predictions, pose hypotheses, tests, and explanations	Predict, hypothesize, conclude	Explain characters' motivations in terms of cause and effect
Evaluate	Evaluate the soundness and significance of findings	Evaluate the credibility and significance of arguments, decisions, and reports	Evaluate form, believability, significance, completeness, and clarity

From *Teaching Thinking Skills: Theory and Practice* edited by Joan Boykoff Baron and Robert J. Sternberg, p. 91. Copyright © 1987 by W. H. Freeman and Company. Reprinted by permission.

Table 4.4 Twenty-eight Principles of Critical Thinking
This table shows strategies teachers can use to help students develop critical thinking skills.

	Examples of Characteristics
Affective Strategies	
to think independently	encourage children to find out for themselves, to test, to try out
to develop insight into ego/sociocentricity	encourage children to question their own immediate beliefs and those of their peer group
to exercise reciprocity	encourage children to roleplay the thinking of parents and other children
to explore thoughts and underlying feelings	encourage children to think about *why* they feel as they do
to think so as to avoid stereotyping	present children with common stereotypes and, through open discussion, help them critique them
to suspend judgment	present children with "evidence" and help them practice avoiding conclusions that go beyond it
Cognitive Strategies—Macro-Abilities	
to develop insight into mechanical skills	encourage children to reflect on why we invent this or that routine, rule or process
to explore underlying purposes	encourage children to express and think about their reasons and purposes
to recognize reasons underlying categories	encourage children to explore different ways to classify things
to clarify issues	provide many opportunities to discover and discuss different ways to express problems
to clarify ideas	encourage children to give examples and to elaborate on their ideas
to develop criteria for evaluation	give children practice in setting up standards or ideals and discuss how they might use them to test something
to evaluate source credibility	identify sources for belief (gossip, TV news, advertisements) and have children discuss which they would believe
to evaluate arguments	give children various reasons to justify getting what they want and help them to discuss which reasons are better
to evaluate solutions	give children various proposed solutions and help them to discuss which are better and why
to evaluate actions	describe a problem and ask children to decide what they feel would be the right thing to do and why
to critique text	encourage children to question what they read
Cognitive Strategies—Micro-Skills	
to distinguish facts from ideals	give children practice in identifying the differences between what is so and what they wish were so
to use critical vocabulary	give children practice in using words like assume, infer, prove
to distinguish ideas	give children two similar words or phrases and have them explain the difference (small vs. tiny)

Table 4.4 Continued

Examples of Characteristics

Cognitive Strategies—Micro-Skills continued

to make assumptions explicit	encourage children to recognize what they and others take for granted
to distinguish relevant from irrelevant facts	ask children to explain which information is relevant to a problem, which is not, and why
to make inferences	ask children to make inferences from a wide variety of statements and actions and encourage them to distinguish their inferences from their observations
to supply evidence for a conclusion	routinely ask children *why* they say what they say
to recognize contradictions	give children practice in telling which pairs of statements couldn't both be true and have them explain why
to explore implications	give children statements and ask them, "If this were true, what else would have to be true?"
to evaluate assumptions	give children an opportunity to explain which of two assumptions is better to make
to use probability qualifiers	encourage children to qualify what they say ("Do you mean *all* girls, or *most* girls?")

Adapted with permission of the publisher, Early Years Inc., Norwalk, Connecticut 06854. From the April 1988 issue of *Teaching/K-8* magazine.

CONNECTIONS

How Can Thinking Skills Be Injected into the Classroom?

If you as a teacher were asked to develop a thinking skills program for your own classroom, how would you go about doing it? One way would be to seek the help of those who have already done so. For example, Richard Paul (1988) suggests that no matter what grade or subject is taught, lesson plans can be modeled to encourage critical thinking. He has formulated twenty-eight principles of critical thinking (see Table 4.4) and argues that once teachers know these principles they can apply them on their own. The following suggestions can help introduce thinking skills materials into the classroom.

1. **Identify which thinking skills should be taught and emphasized.** Some of the thinking skills that are on the many available lists can be found in Tables 4.2 and 4.4. Choose a set of thinking skills that are important to your discipline.

2. **Identify comprehension pitfalls in your subject.** Diane Halpern (1987) suggests that teachers think about the pitfalls that commonly occur in students' understanding of the work. For instance, a common problem in mathematics and science is overreliance on formulas that are not understood. You may find that in reading, students understand the literal meaning of a paragraph but have difficulty making inferences from it. A thinking program may benefit students by addressing such pitfalls.

3. **Know the process by which the skill is to be taught.** What if you were teaching a lesson on comparisons and a student had difficulty understanding exactly how to compare things in a reasonable fashion. If you hope to teach a lesson on this skill, you would have to demonstrate a series of steps that must be taken to compare. For example, the steps of comparing may include the following:
   a. Present the objects or ideas to be compared.
   b. Have the students observe and describe them one at a time.

c. Compare the objects or ideas and make a list of their similarities.

d. Repeat the process, making a list of differences.

e. Identify the criteria used in making the comparisons.

f. Summarize the significant similarities and differences (McTigue, 1985).

4. **Encourage active student participation in reasoning.** This can be accomplished in a number of ways. A teacher might ask questions requiring students to consider the pros and cons of each issue and specifically point out the reasoning skill being used. Students might be asked to compare or show their understanding of a skill such as making analogies. Not all methods need to be verbal, and students can show their ability to reason through class projects and challenges.

5. **Make abstract concepts concrete and relevant.** Whenever dealing with an abstract concept, ask students to apply the concept to relevant, everyday occurrences and generate many examples to show where the concept can be applied. Analogies are also effective in this area.

6. **Think aloud when you solve a problem to show students your own thought processes.** When working on a problem in the class, think out loud, showing the steps you go through to solve the problem (Beyer, 1987). Students learn through observation, and this think-aloud process might help students develop their abilities to think.

7. **Use probing questions.** Not all teacher questions encourage thinking. Often, questions require no more than one- or two-word answers and usually require only recall. Teachers can ask probing questions, however, and these questions can be built into the lesson. This is not to say that questions that deal with facts and information are not important. They are. However, after asking factual questions about Columbus, ask students age-appropriate questions that require them to think. Such questions might take the form of "What if. . .?" For example, "What if Columbus had not believed the world was round?" Or, the question might also take the form of "If this is true, then what else might be true?"

8. **Actively involve the children in generating questions.** Student-generated questions can stimulate thinking. One possibility is to ask students when reading to translate heads and subheads into questions.

9. **Provide an atmosphere in which students are not afraid to think.** Student thinking will be most evident when students feel free enough to think, disagree, and participate without being ridiculed. This involves respecting students' opinions and tolerating dissent. Teachers can show interest in students' thoughts in a number of ways such as asking students for their opinions, and asking students why they think something is so.

10. **Use simulations and roleplay.** Roleplaying and simulations can be of help in teaching thinking. However, teachers must emphasize the thinking processes involved. For example, students might argue the cause of the Civil War by taking on the roles of people from both the North and the South (Levitsky, 1987).

11. **Develop listening skills.** Listening skills are basic to communication and thinking. Students may need help in developing the ability to actively listen to their fellow students during class.

12. **Encourage parents to help develop their children's thinking skills.** Parents can encourage their children to generate questions and ask their children to imagine what will happen next in a story, to explain why they feel a particular way, and to support their opinions (Heiman & Slomianko, 1987B).

True or False In an attempt to show interest in a student's reasoning, teachers should never ask students why they think something is so, because this type of question injures the student's self-concept.

Prepackaged Programs to Promote Thinking

Some school districts have found it desirable to use one of the more than thirty commercially available programs for teaching thinking skills (Beyer, 1987). One advantage of a packaged program is that it has already been worked out for the teacher. The disadvantages are that the program may not fit readily into the time slot that has been allotted to it or fit the exact needs of the teacher. The program may also require extensive teacher training. The following programs are a sampling of what is available.

Cognitive Research Trust. Cognitive Research Trust (CoRT), developed by Edward de Bono, concentrates on the importance of perception (1983, 1987).

Thinking can be encouraged through the use of role-playing.

De Bono argues that many people are good at processing but poor at perception. He gives the following example:

> Imagine a man holding a small block of wood and it falls to the ground. When he releases it a second time, the wood moves upward. The third time, it remains exactly where it is. This seems strange, but if you were told that the second time the person was under water and the third time in outer space, it now makes sense.

In other words, things seem logical if we define the context in which they are taking place.

De Bono argues that stimuli are patterned and self-organized in a very efficient manner. However, this also makes it difficult for people to see things in different ways. He argues that we need to teach the ability to see things more clearly and more broadly. This is accomplished in the CoRT program through the use of a number of tools or exercises. The CoRT program has six sections, each consisting of ten lessons covering breadth, organization, interaction, creativity, information, and feeling and action. For example, one tool is the PMI method, which means plus, minus, and interesting. The thinker looks at the good points, the bad points, and the interesting points in a statement. Another tool is CAF (consider all factors), in which students are required to generate increasingly longer lists of aspects of a given situation or proposition. De Bono's program is independent of any content class, and

de Bono believes that thinking abilities can be transferred to many situations.

Reuven Feuerstein's Instrumental Enrichment. This program is specifically designed for students, including learning disabled students, who are experiencing problems in school. Feuerstein and colleagues (1981) argue that intelligence is an expression of two kinds of learning. First, there is learning that occurs as a direct result of exposure to the environment. Second, human learning involves learning how to learn, which Feuerstein calls cognitive modifiability, and is a function of what Feuerstein calls mediated learning experience. Mediated learning occurs when a mediator interposes himself or herself between the learner and the learner's environment and interprets the world to the learner. Feuerstein gives the example of the mother-child interaction where the mother selects the stimuli for presentation and attaches specific meaning to objects and events in the child's world. Mediated learning provides the experience necessary for building cognitive structure. Whether a child learns to build a rowboat or a television set, he or she must learn to plan ahead, employ appropriate strategies, understand how the parts are related to the whole, and draw logical inferences. Children have difficulty learning because they lack the cognitive structures that connect, organize, integrate, and relate information.

To remedy this deficiency, Feuerstein has constructed a program consisting of fifteen instruments containing pencil-and-paper exercises that cover organization of dots, analytic perception, orientation in space, comparisons, categorization, family relations, illustrations, and syllogisms, to name some. The program is content free; that is, the exercises are seen as vehicles to accomplish the overall goal to enhance the ability of the child to learn how to learn. Figures 4.1 and 4.2 illustrate the first and last instruments listed. Figure 4.1 presents the organization of dots and is similar to the connect-the-dots material found in children's books. Children are asked to mentally perceive the dots as figures that are identical to those in the models. In Figure 4.2 (syllogisms), relations are imposed on a set of elements according to an abstract model. Both figures deal with the need to impose order on the world. Through these exercises, the thinking processes of children can be improved.

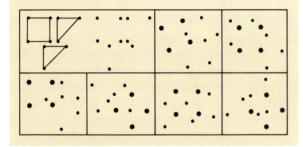

Figure 4.1 Example from Organization of Dots
The student must perceive the dots in an amorphous, irregular cloud so as to project figures identical in form and size to those in the given models. The task becomes more complicated by density of the dots, overlapping, increasing complexity of the figures, and changes in their orientation. Successful completion demands segregation and articulation of the field.

Among the cognitive functions involved are

Projection of virtual relationships
Discrimination of form and size
Constancy of form and size
across changes in orientation
Use of relevant information
Discovery of strategies
Perspective
Restraint of impulsivity

The thickened dots aid in projecting the square but also serve as a distractor and prevent the perception of similarities between frames. In addition to the functions and operations listed on the title page (above), the tasks involve labeling, precision and accuracy, planning, determination of starting point, systematic search, and comparison to model. Successful completion aids in creation and maintenance of motivation.

From "Cognitive Modifiability in Adolescence: Cognitive Structure and the Effects of Intervention" by R. Feuerstein, R. Miller, et al. Reprinted with permission from the *Journal of Special Education*. Copyright © 1981.

Learning to Learn. A third program, called Learning to Learn (LTL), takes those skills that research has shown successful students to have and translates them into a program to teach them to all students (Heiman & Slomianko, 1987; Heiman, 1985). For example, successful students identify the components of complex principles; break down major tasks into smaller ones; ask questions about new materials and engage in an internal dialogue, forming hypotheses and reading and listening for confirmation; and focus on instructional objectives. Although it began as a program for disadvantaged college students, LTL has been used for students reading as low as fifth grade.

Philosophy for Children. This program, advanced by Matthew Lipman (1987), aims at turning the classroom into a community of inquiry based upon philosophical thinking principles. The program offers a series of novels, beginning with Pixie and Kio and Gus, written for kindergarten through fourth grade, and concluding with others aimed at higher grade levels, ending with early high school. For example, the Pixie program contains a children's novel of about 100 pages with a 400-page instructional manual crammed with exercises and discussion plans. The novel, *Harry Stottlemeier's Discovery*, is written for fifth- and sixth-graders and introduces the basic principles of logic. Books for older children emphasize ethical reasoning and thinking, writing, and social studies.

Each of these programs can point to some success. The important question, though, is whether students learning these reasoning skills will use them in other contexts. One major use for thinking skills is in the solving of problems.

PROBLEM SOLVING

A mother St. Bernard had two pups. She ate ten pounds of dog food per day, and each pup ate two pounds per day. The dogs' owner bought a 100-pound bag of dog food. One pup was sold after the third day. The other pup was sold after the seventh day. How many days did the 100 pounds of dog food last? (Karmos & Karmos, 1987)

You are selected by the president of the United States to examine the plight of the homeless in the United States and advance cost-effective solutions that will solve the problem. You came to present your plan to the president and his cabinet, and you must be able to defend your program.

You are given three pegs and a set of discs of different sizes. The discs are all stacked on the first peg by order of decreasing size. Your goal is to move all the disks to the third peg as they now appear on the first. However, you are not allowed to place a larger disk on top of a smaller one, and you can move only one disk at a

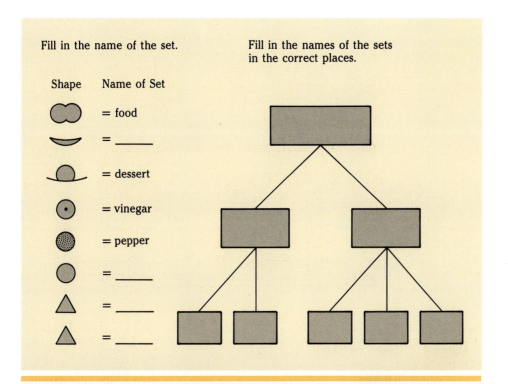

Fill in the name of the set.

Fill in the names of the sets in the correct places.

Shape   Name of Set

= food

= ____

= dessert

= vinegar

= pepper

= ____

= ____

= ____

Figure 4.2   Example from Syllogisms

Each one of the shapes above represents a set. Every set has a name.

The names of the sets are salt, spices, food, ice cream, dessert, cake, pepper, vinegar.

Logico-verbal reasoning becomes highly abstract. Meaning is based on the rules that have been acquired regarding members of sets and subsets. The task involves encoding and decoding, use of signs, finding relationships, discovering the principle upon which categories have been formed, choosing and processing relevant data, and thinking logically.

From "Cognitive Modifiability in Adolescence: Cognitive Structure and the Effects of Intervention" by R. Feuerstein, R. Miller, et al. Reprinted with permission from the *Journal of Special Education*. Copyright © 1981.

time. (This is called the Tower of Hanoi problem—see Figure 4.3.)

The preceding are examples of problems. A problem is a situation in which you are trying to reach a goal and must find a way to do so. John's project showed considerable evidence of problem-solving skills. John was aware of the central problems discussed in class, and through his urban design, he found ways to deal with many of them.

Educational psychologists and information processing theorists have been very interested in the en-tire area of problem solving, including why some people are better than others at solving problems, how people solve problems, and even how teachers can improve the problem-solving capabilities of their students. There has been some concern about student problem-solving abilities, since tests show that students have great difficulty using their knowledge to solve problems (Confrey, 1987).

Some basic difficulties exist, however, in investigating problem solving. First, there is the question of the type of problem to be presented to the students. The three problems described above differ widely

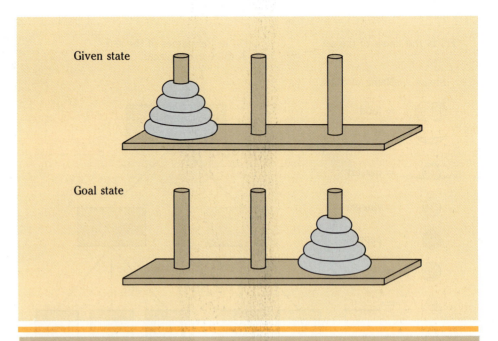

Figure 4.3   Tower of Hanoi
In this problem, the person is asked to move all the disks to the third peg just as they now appear on the first. The problem solver is not allowed to place a larger disk on top of a smaller one and can move only one disk at a time.

from one another. Some problems, such as the third one, are actually puzzles; some, such as the first one, are mathematical problems; others are personal difficulties; and some, such as the second problem, are related to political and social issues often examined in social studies classes.

Problems can be classified according to whether they are well defined or ill defined (Chi & Glaser, 1985). **Well-defined problems** are those that are clearly described, whose definitions are evident, and whose desired end states are clear. **Ill-defined problems** are those that offer unclear descriptions or that do not have directly available the information needed

to solve the problem. Problems in mathematics and science tend to be very well defined, while problems in the social sciences often, though not always, are less well defined. All problems, however, share some common features. They all have an initial state and some goal, and to solve them, some operations must be performed. In addition, they have rules, called constraints, that tell the problem solvers what they can and cannot do when finding the solution.

A Look at How We Solve Problems

We can investigate problem solving by using an information processing model that considers how information about the problem is taken into the organism, interpreted, represented, and acted upon. Attention is an initial concern. Obviously, if a student does not attend to the problem, the problem cannot be solved. The student also must attend to the important parts of the problem. Then the problem must be represented. This essentially refers to how the student understands and interprets the problem. For example, one study found that the reason preschoolers tend to have diffi-

well-defined problems   Problems that are explicitly described and whose end states and constraints are clearly defined.

ill-defined problems   Problems whose descriptions are vague or for which the information needed to solve them is not directly available.

culty with the Tower of Hanoi problem is that they do not remember that a disk is not to be placed on a disk that is smaller and they forget their goal (Klahr & Robinson, 1981). At other times, a problem solver may actually add constraints that are not there.

The teacher's responsibility is to be certain that students understand the initial status, the constraints, and the desired end state of the problem. This is an easier task when the problem is well defined. When a problem is not well defined, students must find ways to supply the missing information. For example, in the problem concerning the plight of the homeless, students would have to define the problem's initial status through a series of questions such as, How many homeless are there? What are the ages of the homeless? Where are the homeless located? The constraints are also vague. What does cost-effective or realistic mean? The end state or final goal state must be better stated. Through this type of analysis, which students can be taught, problems can be better conceptualized. Simply stated, students can be taught to analyze problems in an orderly, sequential way so that the nature of the problem is understandable.

Once the problem is comprehended, the question of how to proceed to solve it arises. The student begins by generating a hypothesis, that is, an educated guess about how to solve it. This will be partially determined by the experience the student has with other similar problems as well as by the nature of the student's knowledge base. Students who have had experiences with similar problems and can remember them can focus on the relevant strategies and ignore the irrelevant ones, a process called strategy focusing (Fry & Lupart, 1987). Of course, the student who has extensive problem-solving experience with similar problems will need little time to choose the correct solution.

The real challenge is how the student ought to proceed if he or she does not have extensive experience with the type of problem presented. We cannot possibly expose students to every type of problem they will eventually encounter. For educators, the question therefore is one of teaching general problem-solving strategies that work. To do so, many information processors have looked at the differences between good problem solvers, that is, successful ones, and poor problem solvers. The research shows that good problem solvers are more active than poor problem solvers. They do more with the problem, including creating mental pictures, relating problems to familiar

experiences, thinking aloud, and asking themselves questions (Karmos & Karmos, 1987). Better problem solvers also have more knowledge in the area of the problem (Bell-Gredler, 1986).

It is sometimes thought that problem solving is a general skill completely independent of knowledge. Although there may be general skills involved, studies repeatedly show that one's knowledge base and ability to use the knowledge base (memory functions) are important. You cannot solve the problem about how much dog food is needed unless you understand numbers and can use them. Studies of problem-solving techniques in social studies show the importance of specific knowledge. More sophisticated problem solvers use a great deal of domain-specific knowledge to solve their problems (Armento, 1986). The implications of this finding are important. First, students must have the prerequisite skills necessary to solve problems. This means that if students are given written problems, they must be able to read. Thus, before giving students problems, teachers need to understand what specific skills the students might need and teach these skills. Second, if problems are to be given in specific domains, such as science or social studies, the state of the students' knowledge will make a difference. Sometimes, this knowledge is factual or conceptual, while at other times, it may be procedural. Secondary school students given the problem of the plight of the homeless must be able to find the necessary information needed just to define the problem adequately.

True or False Having extensive knowledge in a particular area, such as economics or astronomy, facilitates solving problems in that field.

Algorithms and Heuristics

A number of general strategies are useful in many areas of problem-solving. Best of all, they can all be taught. Two classes of strategies used to solve problems are algorithms and heuristics. An **algorithm** is a procedure guaranteed to produce the solution to your

algorithm A procedure that guarantees a solution to a problem but may not be the most efficient way to do so.

problem (Best, 1986). It may be time consuming and not always efficient, but it always works. Algorithms are especially useful in mathematics problems. For example, suppose you were offered two choices: You can receive one million dollars today, or you can begin with one cent today and have it doubled each day for a month. Which would you take? An algorithm here would simply be to calculate the total accumulated over thirty days and then compare the amount to one million dollars. Notice it would take a great deal of time.

A **heuristic,** on the other hand, is a rule of thumb that is developed from experience. Best notes that in changing a tire, you probably know that loosening the bolts slightly before you jack up the car is helpful. If you play chess, keeping the queen in the center of the action is advantageous. Heuristics don't guarantee a solution, but they are useful. The following general problem-solving strategies are included under the heading of heuristics.

Thinking Aloud. This strategy encourages people to say their thoughts aloud when trying to solve a problem. When students do this, they sometimes avoid skipping steps or omitting important information. This strategy is also very useful as a diagnostic device when a teacher needs to discover why a particular problem is giving a student difficulty. If as the student is asked to work on the problem, he or she thinks out loud, the teacher can readily see where the difficulties with the problem-solving process lie.

Working Backwards. At times, working from the goal backwards to the beginning of the problem is a good strategy. Consider the following problem:

> It is 4:00 p.m., and you have just received notification that you are expected for an important company meeting in Chicago at 8:00 the next morning. There are two flights open. One is a dinner flight that leaves at 6:00 p.m. and arrives in Chicago at 6:00 a.m. the next day. The other flight departs at 7:30 p.m. and arrives in Chicago at 7:30 a.m. the next day. When you arrive in Chicago you will need to wait twenty minutes for your luggage and it will

take twenty minutes by taxi to get to your meeting. Which flight should you take? (Bransford et al., 1987)

If you work backwards, the problem is much easier and you will realize the first flight is better (Bransford et al., 1987). In the homeless problem, an effective strategy in defending your ideas is to ask yourself what questions others might ask at the meeting.

Using Trial and Error. Trial and error involves trying different methods of solving a problem until one works. It has been underestimated as a problem-solving strategy (Karmos & Karmos, 1987). When using trial and error, we do not try every solution. Usually, by representing the problem well, we can reduce the number of probable solutions to a few and then try them out.

Considering All the Possibilities. Suppose there are four marbles in a bag, numbered 1, 2, 3, 4. What are all the ways to draw out the marbles one at a time if, once a marble is drawn, it is not returned to the bag? Perhaps the best way is to draw a tree (see Figure 4.4). While doing so, not only are all the possibilities exhausted but also one can see that we could find answers to similar problems by multiplying 4 by 3 by 2 by 1. It would then be easy to solve this problem (Karmos & Karmos, 1987).

Using Means/Ends Analysis. The idea of a means/ends analysis is to find what differences exist between the current state and the final desired state and then to find some way that will reduce those differences. If there is more than one operation that will work, the one that reduces the largest difference is the one to be used. This is especially good when dealing with problems that may have more than one solution or perhaps where the desired end state cannot be produced. We may not be able to completely solve the problem of the homeless, but we can come close. Means/end analysis may not always provide a solution, because if there is no available means, this type of analysis will not work (Chi & Glaser, 1986).

Subgoaling. Sometimes if problems are very difficult it may be necessary to choose a subgoal and then use a means/end analysis. For example, in the homeless situation, we may be able to choose a goal of providing housing for a particular group of homeless people, such as families with young children, or housing for half the homeless population within three years.

---

heuristic   A rule of thumb for solving problems or for reasoning in everyday situations.

PART I

Cognition, Development, and Learning

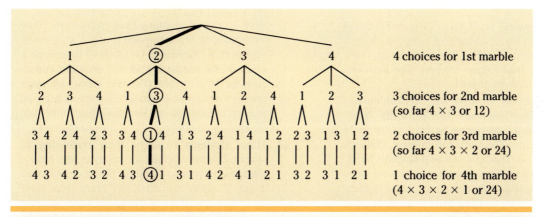

	4 choices for 1st marble
	3 choices for 2nd marble (so far 4 × 3 or 12)
	2 choices for 3rd marble (so far 4 × 3 × 2 or 24)
	1 choice for 4th marble (4 × 3 × 2 × 1 or 24)

Figure 4.4   Finding All the Possibilities
Drawing a "tree" is an effective way of systematically listing all the possible outcomes of some occurrence.

From *Thinking Skills Instruction: Concepts and Techniques,* edited by M. Heiman and J. Slomianko. Copyright © 1987, National Education Association. Reprinted with permission.

Using Win-Stay, Lose-Shift. Active problem-solving techniques are best. Students should be taught to stay with strategies that work and to shift away from the strategies that fail.

 CONNECTIONS

Teaching Problem Solving

Students face a number of problems each day. Some are teacher-constructed classroom problems, some are no more than puzzles, while others are encountered in the day-to-day life of the student. Sometimes the problems are well constructed and easily understood, with all the necessary information provided; at other times, this is not the case. We know that problem solving does not occur in a vacuum and that the student's experience with problems as well as his or her information store and memory is important. Although puzzles and mathematics problems do differ from social studies or practical personal problems, such as how to drive from Philadelphia to Montreal, certain problem-solving strategies do work best, and they can be taught to students. The following ideas can help.

1. **Teach students how to define the problem properly.** Any problem, whether it is well defined or poorly defined, requires an analysis of its initial state, its desired end state, and whatever constraints and limitations exist. Teaching students to set problems up in this way will help.

2. **Teach problem-solving strategies.** A number of such strategies are described previously. None of these strategies will be successful in every instance. However, teaching students means/ends analysis, working backwards, and subgoaling will help them to gain some valuable background in strategies.

3. **Be certain students have the background necessary to successfully solve the problem.** Many problems require background knowledge. If students are asked to solve problems without such knowledge, it is impossible for them to do so. Analyze the type of knowledge necessary before presenting the problem.

4. **Encourage students to transform the problem.** Encourage students to transform the material in some way, such as visualizing the problem, circling important features in a verbal problem, drawing a diagram, or writing a list of the information known, to make working on the problem easier.

5. **Encourage students to actively "play" with problems.** Problem solving can be an enjoyable and creative activity. Better problem solvers are active in all aspects of the problem. Encourage students to try solutions and to clarify the problem by asking questions.

6. **Keep the anxiety level low.** Some students are afraid of making a mistake or taking a chance. This is counterproductive. Try to encourage problem solving based upon interest. The activities need not always be graded.

7. **Expose students to fairly simple problems at first and then increase the difficulty level.** Students need experience working with problems. If the problems are too difficult, students simply give up. Teachers can help students by exposing them to simple problems, making them aware of the steps they should use to solve these problems, and then urging them to go on to more difficult problems.

8. **Model problem solving.** To give students some experience with problem solving, the teacher can focus on a problem and verbalize his or her reasoning, thus demonstrating the steps necessary to solve the problem. Modeling problem-solving behaviors can help students understand how to approach problems.

9. **When directly teaching problem-solving skills, use a step-by-step approach.** Teachers can ask students to provide the steps necessary to solve a problem by asking them, "What should we do now?" This is especially useful for well-defined problems. If you are trying to teach problem solving in steps, explain each step and give students practice in using this problem-solving strategy.

10. **Encourage students to ask questions about the problems.** Suppose you have just raised a specific problem in class; perhaps you've asked students to determine which wing design of a paper airplane is best. Encourage students to ask questions about the problem, such as the meaning of "best," which will help clarify the problem.

11. **Consider using a guidance and discovery approach to problem solving.** Using this approach, students are asked to discover some principle, given a set of exercises. The student may also be given a principle and encouraged to apply it to a number of problems. Fry and Lupart (1987) give the example of students being presented with the principles or rules that can be used to determine what is or is not a balanced meal. Students can then be asked to create balanced meals by using these rules.

12. **Allow students to brainstorm solutions or show their reasoning to others. Brainstorming** involves presenting a problem and allowing students to suggest as many possible solutions without fear of criticism or evaluation at that point.

After all the suggestions have been made, they are evaluated. Brainstorming is useful when seeking the steps that might be followed to achieve a goal and in suggesting all the possible consequences of an event (Penrod, 1986). Although brainstorming was originally created as a group activity, individuals can also use brainstorming as a means of coming up with many alternatives.

13. **Allow students to show their reasoning to others.** It is very helpful for students who have a solution to a problem to show how they reasoned it out. Students can therefore learn from their peers, ask questions of them, and become more involved.

14. **Teach students to evaluate their strategies.** Once students have decided on a strategy, they should try it out and evaluate it. If it works, they should stay with it. If not, they need to change it.

15. **Problems should be appropriate for the child's cognitive level.** Even young students can enjoy puzzles and problems. However, the young student's ability to solve problems in a logical manner is limited by many factors, including his or her relatively poor information background, attention span, and tendency to be distracted. Younger students need more modeling, direct instruction, and simpler problems.

True or False   Trying to visualize a problem in some way is a useful strategy for solving problems.

THE PROBLEM OF TRANSFER

If students are taught thinking skills, such as deductive reasoning and creating analogies, and problem-solving skills, such as subgoaling and means/end analysis, will they use them in mathematics, science, and social studies? The problem of **transfer**—the gen-

brainstorming   A technique for generating a large number of solutions to a problem in which people suggest many possible solutions that are not evaluated until the group (or individual) is finished proposing solutions.

transfer   Learning in one situation that is carried over to another situation.

eralization of skills from one particular circumstance to another that requires the same skill—plagues not only the thinking skills area but also all other areas of education. Most experts now agree that transfer may not automatically occur. Even if children have the knowledge and skills, they do not necessarily put them to work. Imagine a child who learns addition, subtraction, multiplication, and division but cannot use them appropriately in situations in which they apply. The problem of lack of transfer is the concern of every teacher.

True or False When students learn a skill in one class, the teacher can be fairly certain students will transfer that skill to other situations.

Perkins (1987) suggests that there are really two types of transfer. **Low road transfer** occurs when a skill that is well learned is automatically transferred to a very similar situation. If you know how to drive a Chevy, you can probably drive most cars. The more practice you have in driving different cars, the more likely you will be able to drive all other cars. Slight differences can easily be negotiated. However, major differences, such as trying to drive a car that has a stick shift when you can drive only an automatic, are likely to cause major difficulties.

High road transfer involves the abstraction of a principle from one context and the conscious application of the principle to another context. High road transfer requires conscious effort. The person must understand what the principle is and be able to see the need to apply it to the new context, which may not look similar at first. Students may be taught problem solving skills and strategies in one subject. However, for these strategies to be of the greatest use, students must be able to apply these skills to other situations that may be quite different from the original one. School learning must provide for high road transfer.

low road transfer The transfer that occurs spontaneously when material learned in one circumstance is carried over to very similar situations.

high road transfer Transfer that requires the abstraction of a principle from one context and the conscious application of the principle to another context.

 **CONNECTIONS**

Encouraging Transfer

Teachers can encourage transfer in the following ways:

1. **Be aware that transfer may not automatically take place.** Many teachers become angry or upset when they find that they teach a skill in one subject or in one context and the students do not apply the skill to another setting in which it is appropriate. However, this may be because transfer-related activities were not built into the lesson. If you are teaching a skill that you hope will generalize— comparisons, for example—structure the lesson to encourage transfer.

2. **Use many different examples from a variety of disciplines.** If you hope to have students transfer material, you must present examples from many different areas that expand the circumstances in which a strategy may be used. Unfortunately, lessons often contain examples from only one field.

3. **Vary the examples and circumstances of transfer from academic to practical settings.** Students often complain that what they learn in school is not useful outside or is not relevant to their lives. If we want transfer to occur, we need to use examples that are both academic and practical (Sternberg, 1987).

4. **Be receptive to students' original thinking.** If we want transfer to occur, we need to encourage students' thinking (Ennis, 1987). This is also a part of improving thinking skills and encouraging creativity. When students attempt to transfer skills, they require encouragement as well as direction and feedback.

5. **Focus student attention on themes and patterns.** Transfer may be improved if general themes and patterns are identified. For example, the reasoning of Sherlock Holmes involves deductive reasoning, which can be transferred to many situations.

6. **Ask students to deliberately seek applications for what they are learning.** This can be accomplished through homework assignments and group work.

7. **Encourage students to become aware of what they are doing to solve problems.** This awareness, called metacognition, is especially important in encouraging high road transfer. When students are aware of their own thought processes, they can transfer principles from one situation to another (Perkins, 1986).

METACOGNITION

How much is one half of two plus two? Arthur Costa (1984) suggests that as people attempt to solve this question they begin to talk to themselves and try to decide if they should take one half of the first two and add two or add the twos first and take one half of that sum. As you solved this problem, you probably checked your reasoning and logic to make certain your answer was correct. **Metacognition** is the conscious monitoring and regulation of the way a person approaches and solves a problem or a challenge (Bondy, 1984). It involves becoming aware of the way we produce information that is needed to solve a problem and the steps and strategies we use during the problem-solving stage as well as how we evaluate whether or not we have correctly solved the problem (Costa, 1984).

Metacognitive abilities are important. Studies show that students who can monitor and regulate their learning strategies are more successful than those who cannot (Owings et al., 1980). Teachers can do much to improve the metacognitive abilities of their students.

Providing instruction in self-questioning techniques is quite effective. Students can be taught to interrogate themselves and ask themselves questions or offer self-instructions (Bondy, 1984). For example, students can be told to ask themselves "Is this solution reasonable?" Students often arrive at answers that are unreasonable. For instance, consider the following problem, "if twelve prices of candy cost $1.44, how much does each piece of candy cost?" If a student multiples instead of divides, he or she would come up with an answer of $17.28. By asking him or herself if this answer is reasonable, the student will realize that the method of solution should be re-evaluated. Other self-instructions might involve saying to oneself, "What do I know?" or "What do I need to find out?" In addition, teaching students to summarize the material in their own words can help them become aware of what they know. If they cannot do so

or if something is missing, they can be taught to refer back to their notes or book or to ask for help.

Metacognitive abilities can be demonstrated to a student by having a fellow student test the first student after he says he knows the material. Teaching students to check their results for plausibility also works. As noted, often students come up with decidedly questionable and sometimes ridiculous answers to questions because they do not ask themselves whether their answers are reasonable and they do not check their results.

Other metacognitive improvement strategies are similar to those advocated for teaching thinking. For example, teachers can serve as models by showing their own metacognitive activities, including discussing their own difficulties in understanding some material, and encouraging students to show theirs. This teaches students to become watchers, analyzers, and evaluators of their own knowledge.

Metacognition and Reading

Metacognition can also be applied to the reading process. Some students are aware of the strategies they use when reading, while others are not. It is one factor that separates good from poor readers. Paris and colleagues (1983) suggest that metacognition as it applies to reading involves "knowing that," "knowing how," and "knowing when and why." The knowing that, called declarative knowledge, involves knowing that there are different ways to read. Procedural knowledge involves knowing how to read the material and includes the strategies that the reader has available, such as skimming and outlining. Conditional knowledge involves using these strategies in different contexts (knowing when and why). Many studies have shown that good and poor readers differ on these dimensions, with good readers knowing more about reading strategies, detecting errors more often, and having better recall (Paris & Myers, 1981). Knowing when and knowing why to use strategies are keys to the transfer of skills as well (Paris & Oka, 1986).

A number of teaching approaches are available to improve metacognition. One is called Informed Strategies for Learning, or ISL. The program emphasizes the awareness of reading strategies and provides practice in these skills, including dialogues that stimulate students to think and share their ideas. The package includes twenty modules arranged in groups

---

metacognition The conscious monitoring and regulation of the way people approach and solve a problem or challenge.

of five aimed at planning and preparing to read, identifying meaning, reasoning about text content, and comprehending material. Strategies include elaboration, creation of inferences and summaries, and comprehension monitoring (rereading, self-questioning, checking consistencies, and paraphrasing). Instruction is faded; that is, children slowly take on more and more responsibility from the teacher. Results from the use of ISL are quite positive (Paris & Jacobs, 1984; Cross & Paris, 1988).

Another promising approach was developed by Brown and Palincsar, called **reciprocal teaching,** which involves students and teacher in a dialogue for discovering the meaning of a written passage (Palincsar, 1986; Palincsar & Brown, 1984). The approach uses four activities: summarizing, question generating, clarifying, and predicting. Each day before beginning the dialogue, the students review the strategies they are learning and the context in which the strategies are to be used. The students are then presented with the title of the text; they are encouraged to make use of all the background information they have about the topic under discussion and to make predictions about what they will learn and what they would like to learn about the topic. A teacher is appointed from the students, and all the students read the material. The student teacher then asks a question which is answered by the other students, summarizes the answers, asks for elaborations on the summary, and leads a discussion aimed at clarifying the meaning of the passage. The group finally discusses predictions about what might happen next, and a new teacher is appointed.

In the initial days, the adult teacher is responsible for keeping the dialogue moving as he or she models and provides instruction in the four strategies. As the process continues, the teacher tries to give more and more responsibility to the student teachers while providing feedback and coaching. An example of such a dialogue is found in Figure 4.5. The results have been quite favorable, with most of the research

performed with junior high school students in remedial reading classes who were poor readers.

The metacognitive revolution has really just begun. As students become more aware of what they are doing and how they are doing it, they become more autonomous learners and better able to function when faced with an unfamiliar task.

CREATIVITY

Name some people who you think are creative. If you are like most people, you will name either people in the arts or perhaps a very creative scientist such as Albert Einstein. We tend to consider creativity in terms of musicians or artists or mental genuises who seemingly have made quantum leaps in contributing to our ability to understand our world. Yet, this conception of creativity may be too narrow. We would all

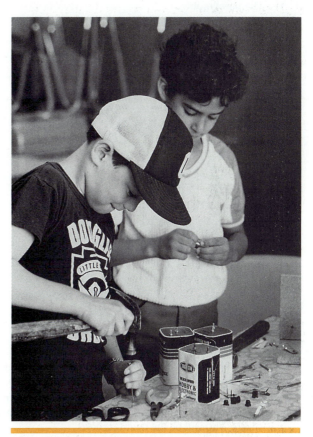

Whenever the term creativity *is mentioned, the arts come to mind. However, creativity can occur in every area of life.*

reciprocal teaching   An approach to teaching reading strategies that involves summarizing, question generating, clarifying, and predicting and requires students and teacher to enter into a dialogue for discovering the meaning of a written passage.

Text from which students are working:

Crows have another gift. They are great mimics. They can learn to talk and imitate animal sounds. Some have been known to learn one hundred words, and even whole phrases. They can imitate the squeak of a chicken, the whine of a dog, or the meow of a cat.

Games have a certain fascination to crows. In a game of hide-and-seek, a crow hides in the hollow of a tree and then sounds distress caw. The others rush to the spot, look around, then flap away. This may be done over and over, after which the young crow pops out of its hiding place and caws gleefully. Far from being annoyed at this, the flock bursts into loud cawing themselves. They seem to like the trick that has been playing on them.

T   Chantel, you're our teacher, right? Why don't you summarize first? Remember, just tell me the most important parts.

S1   Crows have a hundred words they can learn by imitation. They can imitate chickens, the whine of a dog, and cats.

T   Okay. We can shorten that summary a bit.

S2   You could say they can imitate other animals.

T   Oh! Good one! There's a list there, Chantel, did you notice that? It says they can imitate the squawk of a chicken, the whine of a dog or the meow of a cat; and you could call that "animal sounds." Can you ask us a question?

S1   Ain't no questions here.

S3   The words (sic.) that need to be clarified are (sic.) "mimics."

S4   That means imitate, right?

T   Right. How did you figure that out, Shirley?

S4   The paragraph.

T   Show us how somebody could figure out what "mimic" means.

S5   They are great mimics. They can learn to talk and imitate animal sounds.

T   Yes, so the next sentence tells you what it means. Very good. Anything else need to be clarified?

All   No.

T   What about that question we need to ask? (pause) What is the second paragraph about, Chantel?

S1   The games they play.

S3   They do things like people do.

S4   What kinds of games do crows play?

S3   Hide and seek. Over and over again.

T   You know what, Larry? That was a real good comparison. One excellent question could be, "How are crows like people?"

S4   They play hide and seek.

T   Good. Any other questions there?

S2   How come the crows don't get annoyed?

S5   What does annoyed mean?

T   Irritated, bothered.

S5   Because they like it, they have fun. If I had a crow, I'd tell him he was it and see what he'd do.

T   Let's summarize now and have some predictions.

S1   This was about how they play around in games.

T   Good for you. That's it. Predictions anyone?

S2   Maybe more tricks they play.

S4   Other games.

T   Maybe. So far, they have told us several ways that crows are very smart; they can communicate with one another, they can imitate many sounds, and they play games. Maybe we will read about another way in which they are smart. Who will be the next teacher?

Figure 4.5   Sample Reciprocal Teaching Dialogue
This sample dialogue demonstrates how students and teachers can become involved in discovering the meaning of written work by using summarizing, question generating, clarifying, and predicting.

From "Metacognitive Strategy Instruction" by A. S. Palincsar, in *Exceptional Children*, 1986, 53, 118–124. Copyright © 1986 by The Council for Exceptional Children. Reprinted with permission.

agree that John was creative, not only because his artwork was excellent but also because his conceptions were novel.

Defining creativity has never been an easy task. **Creativity** involves a "person's producing a novel response that solves the problem at hand" (Weisberg, 1986, p. 4). To be creative, the response cannot be simply a repetition of something an individual saw or heard. Also, it must be appropriate; that is, it must solve the problem it is designed to solve. If a student hopes to solve the problem of increasing the efficiency of a kite, throwing a baseball at the kite may be novel, but it will not solve the problem.

True or False   The sole criterion for determining creativity is originality of response.

Conceptions of Creativity

The most popular way of looking at creativity is to consider it to be a type of thinking. Guilford (1967) differentiated between two kinds of thinking—convergent and divergent. **Convergent thinking** involves arriving at an answer when given a particular set of facts and is the type of thinking measured by intelligence tests. **Divergent thinking** involves the ability to see new relationships between things that are still appropriate to the situation.

The most common test of creativity was developed by E. Paul Torrance and is called the **Torrance Tests of Creative Thinking** (TTCT). The test measures creativity by considering four criteria: (1) fluency, the production of a large number of ideas; (2) flexibility,

the ability to produce a variety of ideas; (3) elaboration, the development and embellishment of the ideas; and (4) originality, the production of ideas that aren't obvious (Hennessey & Amabile, 1987). Figure 4.6 shows some questions that illustrate the TTCT. Sometimes, a test measuring just one of these criteria (ideational fluency—the production of a large number of ideas) is used by itself, because it is highly correlated with other factors, such as originality and flexibility but is easier to work with (Kogan, 1983).

Problem 1 List all of the questions you can think of concerning the figure shown below. Ask all of the questions you need to know for sure what is happening. Do not ask questions that can be answered just by looking at the drawing. (Give yourself three minutes to list your questions.)

Problem 2 Suppose that all humans were born with six fingers on each hand instead of five. List all the consequences or implications that you can think of. (Give yourself three minutes.)

Problem 3 List as many white, edible things as you can in three minutes.

Problem 4 List all the words that you can think of in response to *mother*. (Give yourself 3 minutes.)

Problem 5 List all the uses that you can think of for a *brick*. (Give yourself 3 minutes.)

Figure 4.6   Problems from the Torrance Tests of Creative Thinking
Try these sample problems testing creative thinking.

From *The Journal of Creative Behavior*, 1968, 2(3) with permission from the publisher, the Creative Education Foundation, Buffalo, NY. Copyright © 1968.

---

creativity   The production of a novel response that appropriately solves a given problem.

convergent thinking   A type of thinking in which people solve problems by integrating information in a logical manner.

divergent thinking   A type of thinking marked by the ability to see new relationships between things that are still appropriate to the situation.

Torrance Tests of Creative Thinking   A test of creativity that measures the fluency, flexibility, ability to elaborate, and originality of a person's thinking.

Tolerating dissent and disagreement produces an atmosphere of free expression and creativity.

Not everyone is satisfied with the idea that creativity is solely a type of thinking or is the same as divergent thinking (Mansfield et al., 1978). Some consider this a rather narrow definition and point out that evidence shows that divergent thinking in childhood is not highly correlated with creative activities in adulthood (Feldhusen & Clinkenbeard, 1987).

Some see divergent thinking as one, but only one, of the components that creative activity comprises. Daniel Keating (1980) expands the definition of creativity to include content knowledge, the ability to communicate, and the ability to critically analyze, along with divergent thinking. Content knowledge is important because it is difficult to think creatively if one does not understand the area in which creativity is taking place. Communication skills are required in the broad sense, since an idea must be communicated to others. The element of critical analysis has rarely been identified with creativity. However, it is an integral part of the process. If an individual has fifteen ideas about what could occur and what should be done to solve a problem, how should that person proceed? A judgment needs to be made so that some avenues can be explored and others left behind. Critical analysis allows one to follow the most promising approach. With this in mind, the relationship between teaching thinking skills and creativity may be positive.

But why cover creativity here instead of in the chapter that focuses on teaching the student with exceptional needs. Many people feel that if you measure a student's intelligence, you will get a fair estimate of the student's creativity. However, that is not the case, and some school districts that simply look at intelligence scores and academic achievement as criteria for entrance into their "gifted and talented" programs are actually doing students like John a disservice. In reality, the relationship between intelligence and creativity is hardly simple. Studies show that people with low intelligence scores do indeed show low creativity, but once an average intelligence score is evident, there is little relationship between intelligence and creativity (Hennessey & Amabile, 1986). Intelligence tests, then, are poor indicators of creativity. We also tend to think only of people who open new frontiers of knowledge as creative. However, creative performance can be found in many people if the atmosphere encourages creativity.

True or False   The more intelligent an individual is, the greater the chance that he or she will be creative.

 CONNECTIONS

Encouraging Creativity

There are many ways to encourage creativity and creative thinking in children. Some commercially prepared programs are designed to foster divergent thinking, while other suggestions attempt to build opportunities to be creative into classroom activities. Some general suggestions for encouraging creativity in the classroom include the following.

1. **Use divergent questions whenever possible.** Convergent questions call for a limited number of correct answers. Examples are What is a figure with three sides called?, Name three parts of speech, and name the last three presidents. Instead, ask divergent questions in which there are a number of possible correct answers. For example, you could ask, What are some similarities between baseball and football? or What conditions led to war in the colonies? Answering this type of question requires more thought (Montague, 1987).

2. **Provide an opportunity for creative expression.** Some students receive little or no encouragement or opportunity to create. One teacher always added a few questions or challenges to his lesson to create an opportunity for students to express themselves in an open-ended manner. You can ask students to suggest different ways to do something or to solve a problem.

3. **Allow students to try new things without fear of failure.** Often students are afraid that everything will be graded, and they choose the safe alternative.

If students are to be "daring" in their thoughts, they must feel that doing so will not adversely affect their grades.

4. **Allow students to work together to create something.** Some students like to work alone to solve a problem, while others prefer to work in groups.

5. **Allow students to brainstorm solutions to problems.** This suggestion (noted when we discussed problem solving) can be used to encourage creativity. Remember, though, that it need not take place in a group situation. Individual students can learn to first generate many possible solutions to a problem or many ideas and evaluate them later.

6. **Encourage disagreement and constructive dissent.** The toleration of dissent and disagreement generates an atmosphere of free expression and creativity.

7. **Show creativity yourself.** If you do this, students may follow your lead. In one study, a model named a number of ways to use a cardboard box. When subjects were then asked to do the same for a tin can, their creativity scores improved (Navarick, 1979). Most did not use the model's words; they had learned to use their imagination.

8. **Give students things to do not just to read.** Many students enjoy working with their hands or "doing" something. Projects and invention can be made part of certain units. This is what brought out John's special abilities. Terry Borton (1986) notes that children do not think in terms of invention, often believing that everything has already been invented. He suggests that encouraging invention is possible if you, among other things (a) explain what an invention is, (b) convince children that invention is possible, (c) focus on improving something by asking children to consider how they would improve something in their environment, (d) look for a problem that needs solving while stressing reality over science fiction, and (e) encourage imagination.

9. **Fight the conventional wisdom that creativity is for the few.** As previously discussed, creativity is not the sole domain of the brilliant or talented.

Prepackaged Programs to Promote Creativity

As in the case of thinking, a number of professionally developed packages aim at improving divergent thinking. For example, the Purdue Creativity Program consists of twenty-eight audio tapes and a set of printed exercises to accompany each tape. The tapes consist of two parts: a three- to four-minute presentation designed to teach a principle or idea for improving creative thinking and an eight- to ten-minute story about a famous American pioneer. The exercises consist of problems or questions designed to provide practice in creative thinking in areas measured by the TTCT (Feldhusen et al., 1970).

Covington and colleagues' Productive Thinking Program (1966) offers a set of programmed instruction booklets designed to foster creative problem-solving abilities and favorable attitudes towards problem solving. The program consists of a number of booklets using a cartoon format that provides instruction in a variety of problem-solving skills. The characters are Jim and Lila and Uncle John, a science teacher who is also a part-time detective known as Mr. Search. The uncle leads the children through each mystery and stresses such skills as recognizing puzzling facts, asking relevant and important questions, and solving problems in new ways. Studies of this program show some evidence for its effectiveness, but it is unclear if the effects are sufficiently generalizable to real-world situations (Mansfield et al., 1978).

The Parnes Program uses, among other techniques, brainstorming, in which students are encouraged to generate as many ideas as possible. It is used with high school and college students and has been successful in improving divergent thinking.

Creativity Reconsidered

A number of conclusions are clear from the literature on creativity. First, although creativity has been linked to divergent thinking, it is not the only element in the creative process. Knowledge of subject matter and critical thinking are also important. Second, it is possible to increase divergent thinking through direct instruction, although the question of transfer still haunts these programs (Feldhusen & Clinkenbeard, 1986). Third, creativity is found in all areas of life. It is incorrect to relate creativity to one field, such as the arts or to "geniuses." Finally, teachers can encourage creativity or discourage it in their own classrooms. If creativity is a goal, open-ended challenges must be structured into the curriculum.

One way to encourage creativity is to have students actually do something, not just talk about it.

LEARNING AND COGNITIVE STYLES

Do you prefer to learn when the room is quiet or when there is some background noise?

Do you prefer to learn through lecture or through films?

Do you prefer bright light or a light of low intensity when you are trying to learn?

Do you prefer a formal or an informal setting when you learn?

Do you consider yourself a persistent learner?

Do you learn best when you are alone or when you are with people?

Do you learn best in the morning, in the afternoon, or in the evening?

We all have our preferences for learning, our own learning styles. John preferred to work alone and in a quiet atmosphere. Recently, educational psychologists have begun to concentrate on the importance of learning styles. **Learning styles** can be defined as "the normal variations in internal and external preferences for the setting and manner in which learning takes place" (Bireley & Hoehn, 1987, p. 437). Another term, **cognitive style**—the characteristic manner in which people perceive, organize, and evaluate information—is also important in this area (Kagan, 1987, p. 393).

Learning Styles: Individual Preferences in Learning

If you were asked to learn about the various types of Australian animals, would you prefer to attend a lecture by an expert, read about the animals, or visit a zoo? You probably have a preference, as do students. Some students would prefer any one of these methods or combinations of them, and these preferences should be taken into account when lessons are planned and taught. The concept of learning style is one that is intuitively familiar to many students. After all, everyone has preferences for studying. Some like noise, while others can't stand any noise. Some like to hear lectures, some prefer discussion, and some would rather personally experience the thing being studied.

How can we conceptualize learning styles? There are many systems, and they can become confusing. One popular way is illustrated in Figure 4.7. The

learning style Normal variations in internal and external preferences for the setting and manner in which learning takes place.

cognitive style The characteristic manner in which people perceive, organize, and evaluate information.

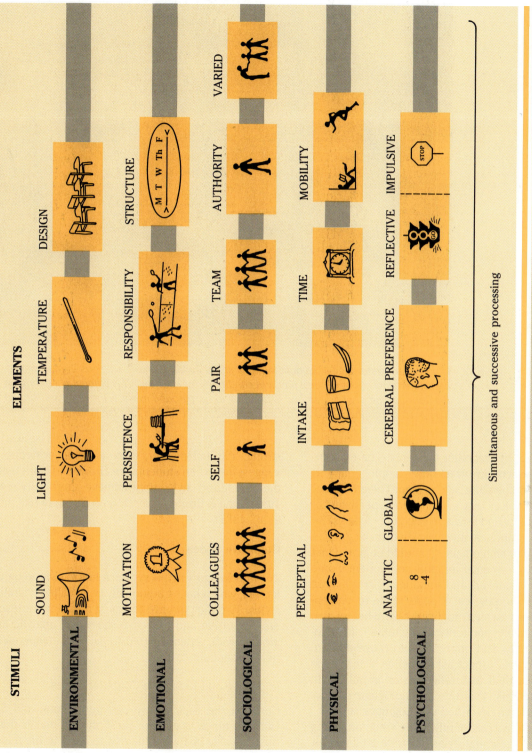

Figure 4.7   Diagnosing Learning Styles

Students differ in their preferred learning styles. While looking over this figure, consider your own learning preferences and how they might affect your teaching.

From *Teaching Students to Read Through Their Individual Learning Styles.* Designed by Drs. Rita and Kenneth Dunn.

Our new understanding of student learning styles makes us more cautious in making general statements about the best physical conditions for studying. This student is reading on the floor instead of at a desk and is listening to background music rather than studying in a very quiet atmosphere. The important question is, Does it work for the student?

system consists of five major elements. The environmental component involves how people adapt to sound, light, temperature, and design. The emotional component involves one's motivation, persistence, and responsibility and how one structures a task. The sociological component involves whether one prefers working alone or with others. (It should be noted that cultural factors may enter into this component. Some cultures value teamwork and working in a group more than others.) The physical aspects relate to perceptual preferences (which might involve whether you learn best visually, auditorily, or tactually), food intake, time of day, and opportunity to move around. The psychological aspect asks whether a learner is analytical or global and reflective or impulsive in learning situations. It is this psychological component that has been described as a cognitive style.

One mistake is consistently made when analyzing learning styles. Learning styles illustrate preferences, and it is wrong to think that a student with a visual preference cannot learn from a lecture. Students need not always operate in their preferred mode (Arm-

strong, 1987). However, there is some evidence to suggest that when students are allowed to learn using their preferred style, they achieve more (Cotterell, 1982; Dunn & Bruno, 1985; Dunn & Dunn, 1978; Carbo et al., 1986).

Cognitive Styles

The fifth category in this system refers to psychological factors, which have traditionally been called cognitive styles. Two factors have the most meaning for teachers: impulsive and reflective styles and analytic and global styles, often referred to as field independent-field dependent styles.

Impulsive and Reflective Cognitive Styles

Consider the case of two children, Glenn and Sal. Glenn is quick to answer questions but makes many mistakes. He is always the first to hand in his paper. Sal thinks things through and takes his time before answering. Which child do you think will do better in school?

The **reflective-impulsive** continuum shows the degree to which a subject either delays or responds rapidly to tasks on which the answer is uncertain (Stuart & Pumfrey, 1987). Glenn is impulsive. He does everything fast and consequently makes many mistakes. Sal is reflective. He takes his time and reflects on his work. Children who have a reflective cognitive style generally make fewer errors on a variety of different tests, including those involving recognition memory, inductive reasoning, and visual discrimination (Borkowski et al., 1983). Impulsive children make more errors in reading (Kagan, 1965). Impulsive children have more difficulty learning, and studies indicate that underachieving children tend to be impulsive when compared with normally achieving students (Blackman & Goldstein, 1982). Reflective children can adapt to a faster pace if necessary, whereas impulsive children are locked into a less adaptive style (Kogan, 1983; Bush & Dweck, 1975).

Students who are impulsive and who do not think through their answers tend to make more mistakes than students who are reflective.

True or False Students who are impulsive—that is, take very little time to answer—make more mistakes than those who take more time to reflect on the question or problem.

Where differences are found, reflective children seem to be superior (Messer, 1976), although extremes of either can cause problems. One study found that students who were very impulsive or very reflective did not do as well as students who were judged moderate on the impulsive-reflective continuum when solving problems that required the consideration of unusual or unlikely hypotheses (Duemler & Mayer, 1989). Most people, though, are not found at the extremes.

Although these styles are rather stable, they can be altered. For example, children who are very impulsive can be taught to be more reflective (Kogan, 1983). One way is to teach such children to utter certain self-statements in which the children monitor their own progress and remind themselves to go slow (Meichenbaum & Goodman, 1971). Some of the suggestions concerning metacognition are also helpful.

Analytic-Global or Field Independent-Field Dependent Styles

Another dimension of cognitive style involves what psychologists called **field independent-field dependent** (analytic versus global) styles. People with a

> **reflective cognitive style** A cognitive style marked by first thoroughly exploring the problem, then considering various alternatives, and finally answering the question or performing the task.
>
> **impulsive cognitive style** A cognitive style marked by cursory examination of a problem and answering questions very quickly.
>
> **field independent cognitive style (analytic cognitive style)** The use of internal, independent factors as guides in processing information.
>
> **field dependent cognitive style (global cognitive style)** The use of information absorbed from the environment as the principal guide in processing information.

field independent style are likely to use internal, independent factors as their guides in processing information. Field dependent people are more likely to use information gleaned from the outside world (Witkin et al., 1977). Field independent people are less influenced by context and other people, relying more on their own judgment, than are field dependent people. Field dependent people are more likely to look to others in social situations to define their own attitudes and are more socially sensitive than field independent people (Witkin & Moore, 1974). They are also less attentive to detail. This is especially true in situations where the available information is unclear or vague. Field dependent people are more likely to describe themselves as interested in people and to be socially outgoing than field independent people (Witkin et al., 1977).

These dimensions are measured in several ways. One way is to discover the extent to which an individual can overcome distracting background elements. A person is presented with a figure that is embedded in a complex geometric pattern. People who are field independent or analytical perform better on this test than people who are more global and field dependent.

In the learning area, field independent people perform better in mathematics (Vaidya & Chansky, 1980). Field independent children are also likely to do better on unstructured tasks, because they can impose their own structure on the learning situation (David & Frank, 1979). Field dependent children require more detail and clarity in order to do well. They may also form concepts differently. Field independent children prefer a more active discovery approach than field dependent children (Saracho & Dayton, 1980). Field dependent people learn better with more structure and organization, while field independent people do better when given more freedom (Roetter, 1987). Field dependent students are better at material with a social content, whereas field independent people may require help in material with social content.

Field dependent learners are often referred to as global learners, because they concentrate on the whole, while field independent learners are often called analytic, since they solve problems systematically and concentrate on small parts of the problem. Marie Carbo (1982) suggests that this global/analytic style difference is important, since most students who are at risk for dropping out and who are doing poorly are global learners (Carbo & Hodges, 1988).

Teachers' Cognitive and Learning Styles and Styles of Teaching

It is certainly fair to ask what difference cognitive style and general learning style makes to the teacher. Fortunately, we now have some of the answers to this question. A number of studies (but not all) have shown that problems may arise when students have a definite preference for one style but their teachers teach from a different style. For example, consider the impulsive teacher who presents material very rapidly and expects rapid-fire answers. The reflective child, though more adaptive, is likely to experience some difficulty. Field dependent teachers are more socially oriented, preferring class discussion, while field independent teachers favor either the lecture or discovery techniques. The teacher's learning style is reflected in how the teacher teaches (Kuchinskas, 1979).

A mismatch between teaching style and students' learning style can cause difficulty, and children and teachers who are matched on this dimension like each other better than those who are mismatched (Witkin et al., 1977). In addition, mismatched students do not seem to learn as much (Packer & Bain, 1978). Matching learning and teaching styles with instructional strategies improves concentration and learning (Carbo & Hodges, 1988). Most studies show that when instructional strategy and learning and cognitive style are similar, educational outcomes are better.

However, a mismatch seems to be most important in the educational experience of students who are having difficulty, are at risk for dropping out, or are constantly misbehaving. At-risk youngsters are less visual and auditory and have higher preferences for tactile/kinesthetic tasks. They also have greater needs to be mobile and to eat or drink liquids while they learn. They are unmotivated or strongly adult motivated, can concentrate and learn best with an adult or with peers, are most alert in the late morning or early afternoon, and are global learners (Carbo & Hodges, 1988). These students react poorly to mismatches, experiencing great anxiety and stress.

True or False If students' learning style preferences are not followed, it is the very bright, creative, well-behaved student who suffers the most.

Practical Implications of Cognitive Style and Learning Style

Educational psychologists have identified a number of learning and cognitive styles. Studies have demonstrated that students with a definite preference for one style may be academically at a disadvantage if asked to perform under a different set of circumstances. Students performing poorly in school tend to be the most sensitive to radical mismatches in teaching and learning styles. This makes attention to cognitive and learning styles necessary.

Stylistic preferences can be treated in three possible ways. First, we can opt to change students' learning or cognitive style. With students who seem to be at the extremes, this may be necessary. For example, an extremely impulsive student may need some help. However, this is very difficult in some of the other areas, and since learning style variables are preferences, it is doubtful that this is the best strategy.

The second strategy is to match teachers with students. Students who work best auditorily might get a teacher who lectures; students who learn best visually might be taught by a teacher who uses a more visual style. A student who is extremely field dependent may be helped by a teacher who gives a great deal of structure; a student who is analytical may be given a teacher who allows more freedom.

Major problems exist with matching, however. First, it treats these styles not as preferences but as absolutes. Second, from a practical viewpoint, it is probably not possible to match teachers and students in most cases. Third, students may benefit from being exposed to information taught using a number of learning approaches, not just their own preferences. There is more to be said for matching for students who are at risk for dropping out or who have behavior problems than for most normally achieving students.

The third, and much more practical, approach that has gained much support is the process of **style flexing,** which involves teachers determining the learning styles of their students and using a variety of approaches that increase the range of their teaching techniques (Cornett, 1983). Sometimes, this is a relatively simple procedure. For example, when teaching mathematics to field dependent subjects who need structure, circling relevant information can help (Bien, 1974).

---

style flexing   A term used to describe the use of a variety of teaching techniques to accommodate varying student cognitive and learning styles.

▶▶▶ CONNECTIONS

The Classroom Teacher and Learning Styles

The following suggestions can be used by the classroom teacher to modify instruction to make it more compatible with students' learning styles.

1. **Become sensitive to learning styles.** Learning styles inventories are available in some schools. In schools without such inventories, teachers can learn a great deal about students either through speaking with them or observing them work. Becoming aware of how a particular student prefers to learn can help the teacher adapt instruction to the student's needs. In fact, teachers who are aware of their students' cognitive styles adapt to the students' styles, resulting in an increase in student performance (Doebler & Eike, 1979). A knowledge of learning styles allows the teacher to be sensitive and allows students, when possible, to learn in the manner that they prefer.

2. **Vary teaching techniques with an eye to involving all students.** A teacher may allow some choice in assignments that match students' learning styles. Using a number of teaching techniques, such as discussion, music, pictures, books, charts, maps, and games, helps bring students of different styles into the lesson.

3. **Become sensitive to which students require more freedom and which ones need more structure.** Some students will require step-by-step help and a great deal of organization, while others will not.

4. **Share information on learning styles with students.** Students can be asked relatively easy questions, such as those at the beginning of this section, and they can be encouraged to use their learning styles to the fullest. For example, a student who prefers to learn through discovery might like to do an experiment to fulfill an assignment.

5. **Remember that many at-risk students are global learners, and if tasks are overly fragmented, such students do not do well.** Global learners en-

joy listening to and acting in plays, drawing pictures, and using puppets. It is also a good idea to begin lessons globally, and starting with anecdotes and visual aids helps. Providing concrete experiences such as interviews, skits, model construction, and trips is in keeping with global preferences. After the context and importance of the task are understood, youngsters are capable of learning rules and performing exercises. A chapter might be introduced by showing a related film, telling students what the chapter is about and arousing their interest with personal anecdotes, or reading aloud. These learners are also tactile and kinesthetic and require hands-on learning, including painting, playing games, typing, working with computers, taking trips, building, and doing photography. They also need a highly organized environment with limited choices (Carbo & Hodges, 1988).

6. **Allow students to work with peers, alone, with a friend, or however it is most comfortable.** Although this may not always be practical, it is sometimes possible, and it takes individual students' sociological preferences into account.

7. **If possible, design your room to respond to the children's strengths.** Allow for student physical comfort preferences whenever possible. Some may prefer to sit one way; another a different way. Some may prefer to read while sitting on the floor; others, while sitting in chairs. Place students who need a great deal of quiet away from noisier areas.

8. **Take into consideration students' perceptual strengths.** This can be accomplished by using a number of modalities to teach a particular point. Students who prefer the auditory mode may prefer lectures; students who are more visually oriented may prefer either to read aloud or to create pictures. Students with a tactual preference may prefer to manipulate concrete materials (Cuccia, 1986). Remember, however, that students can learn through all modalities, and cognitive styles are a matter of degree of preference.

9. **Become aware of your teaching style.** This is the most important area of concern. Teachers have cognitive styles and learning styles that affect their teaching styles. For example, a teacher who is comfortable learning from lectures may tend to lecture and have difficulty with class discussion. A teacher who likes discussion may be uncomfortable teaching students who may prefer a more discovery oriented or a more direct approach. If teachers are to style flex, they must be aware of their preferences and their limitations.

The recent attention that learning and cognitive styles have received is no fad. "Meeting the individual needs of the student" is a phrase often used in education. The new attention to learning styles and cognitive styles holds the promise for addressing the individual needs of students in a practical and realistic manner.

BRAIN RESEARCH AND TEACHING

The new approaches to intelligence, thinking, problem solving, creativity, and learning styles parallel some new and exciting work in brain research. The most interesting brain research concerns hemispheric specialization within the cerebral cortex. The cerebrum is responsible for, among other things, our executive functions, including reasoning, thinking, planning, and problem solving. The cerebral cortex (the top portion of the cerebrum) is divided into two hemispheres—the right and the left. The right and left hemispheres are connected by the corpus callosum, a collection of nerve fibers. Years ago, it was discovered that the left side of the cerebral cortex controls the right side of the body. It is responsible for language in most people and responds best to verbal, abstract, and sequential material (Mannies, 1986). The right hemisphere of the cerebral cortex controls the left side of the body and is superior in processing visual imagery, spatial perception, and recognition of faces and patterns.

This research has given rise to a number of suggestions concerning people who are right brain or left brain dominant. According to the theory, people differ in their styles of thought, depending on which half of the brain is dominant. The right brain was thought to be dominant when an artist painted, while the left brain was allegedly dominant when an author was writing a book. Logic was supposedly to be found in the left hemisphere, whereas creativity and intuition were to be found in the right hemisphere (Levy, 1984). If we glance at Figure 4.8 which shows left brain and right brain characteristics, it seems evident that instruction significantly emphasizes left brain capabilities. This belief led to a claim that subject matter and teaching strategies should be developed to educate one hemisphere at a time.

However, people have more recently moderated their stand. Although the idea of the capabilities of each hemisphere is supported by the literature, the

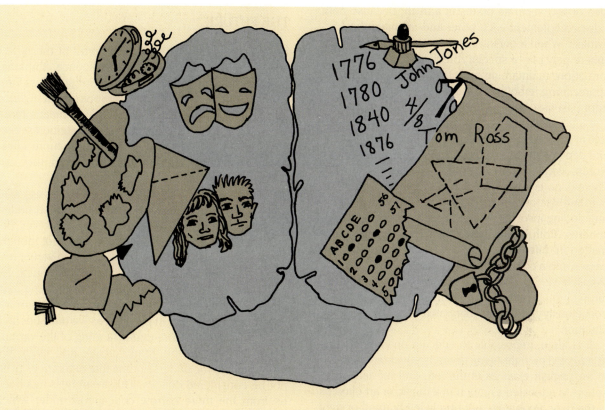

Right Brain Characteristics

- Remembers faces

- Responds to demonstrated, illustrated, or symbolic instructions

- Prefers solving problems by looking at the whole or the configurations rather than approaching problems through patterns, using hunches

- Prefers open-ended questions

- Is free with feelings

- Writes metaphorically or makes up stories to tell

- Gets lost in the present moment rather than keeping track of time

- Acts spontaneously to change plans on the spur of the moment

- Easily does geometry and graphing

- Senses moods of individuals and groups quickly and accurately

Left Brain Characteristics

- Remembers names

- Prefers solving problems by breaking them down into parts rather than by approaching the problem sequentially, using logic

- Is planned and structured

- Prefers talking and writing

- Prefers multiple choice tests

- Controls feelings

- Remembers jokes accurately, including punch lines

- Recalls chronological events in history

- Remembers small details in what is seen or heard

- Easily works fractions, percentages, algebra, and statistical math

---

Figure 4.8   Characteristics of Left and Right Hemisphere of the Brain
Although scientists have identified different characteristics of the left and right brain, the hemispheres cannot be educated separately. Our brains produce a unified and coherent view of the world.

From "Brain Theory and Learning," by N. Mannies, *The Clearing House*, 1986, 60, 127–130. Adapted with permission of the Helen Dwight Reid Educational Foundation. Published by Heldref Publications, 4000 Albemarle St., N.W., Washington, D.C. 20016. Copyright © 1986.

idea of two separate brains is a myth, because both sides complement each other and integrate their activities. "When a person reads a story the right hemisphere may play a special role in decoding visual information, maintaining an integrated story structure, appreciating emotional content, deriving meaning from past associations and understanding metaphor. The left hemisphere at the same time, plays a special role in understanding syntax, translating written words and deriving meaning from complete relations among words, concepts and syntax" (Levy, 1984, p. 43). There is no evidence that either creativity or intuition is found exclusively in either hemisphere. Cognitive functioning involves the collaboration between hemispheres. Both hemispheres process the same information in different ways and then integrate both processes into a coherent, conceptual whole (Springer & Deutsch, 1981). We do not receive conflicting interpretations from the two hemispheres. Rather, we consciously receive an integrated view of the entire situation.

It is, then, impossible to educate one hemisphere at a time. The right hemisphere is educated as much in an English class as is the left, and the left hemisphere is educated as much in a music or art class as is the right. People are not purely left brained or right brained but rather show a preference for one type of processing.

True or False. Since the right and left hemispheres seem to control different facets of behavior and thinking, it is desirable to educate the hemispheres separately.

Despite the misunderstanding, this research has much to say to teachers. Some people are more likely to learn by using shapes and patterns and by visualizing, while others are more analytic and verbal. This is well in keeping with our ideas about multiple intelligences and learning styles and again may demonstrate that a biological basis underlies these qualities. For example, students who prefer right brain processing would learn more about dinosaurs by visiting a museum, whereas left brained students would learn more from a lecture. Again, though, it is important not to lose sight of the fact that one can learn details as well as patterned images from a museum display. The suggestions for redesigning lessons and teaching strategies to fit the learning styles of students are germane. However, it is undesirable and incorrect to view people as having two separate brains that do not interact when, in reality, the opposite is true.

THE FUTURE

In this chapter, we've looked at some of the newer conceptions in the areas of intelligence, thinking, problem solving, creativity, and learning styles. Educational psychologists no longer look at intelligence only in terms of verbal skills. Thinking means more than simply parroting the teacher's statements. Students can be taught to solve problems more effectively, and under the proper circumstances, they can demonstrate creativity.

Our new appreciation of these areas opens up exciting vistas and opportunities. These newfound understandings have come too late for John, however. Because he was an average student, he was not thought to be creative. Because he did not excel in verbal reasoning, he was not thought to be very intelligent. He was never given the training in critical thinking, and his more kinesthetic and visual styles of learning were not appreciated. In these areas we have become more flexible and more understanding of the various ways in which people think, create, and learn. We have come to the understanding that differences need not be considered deficits. This awareness has freed us from the more narrow conception under which we've operated and has given us a truer appreciation of the ways in which people use their resources to learn about and improve the world around them.

SUMMARY

1. Today we have gone beyond the traditional notions of intelligence that are reflected solely in linguistic and mathematical abilities. There is no universally accepted definition of intelligence, and there is much debate over whether intelligence is one quality or a number of different qualities. Howard Gardner argues in his theory of multiple intelligences that there are seven different intelligences. Robert Sternberg argues that intelligence can be best understood from an information processing perspective.

2. There is a movement towards teaching thinking skills in the schools. Teachers can develop their own materials or use one of the commercially available programs. Teachers need to know what specific thinking skills they wish to teach their students.

3. Problems have an initial state, a goal, and constraints that tell what can and cannot be done in solving them. Some operation must be performed to solve them. Some problems are well defined; that is, they have a definite initial status and goal and the constraints are known. Other problems are ill defined, and these facts are not directly stated. Good problem solvers actively work on the problem, creating mental pictures, relating the problem to their past experiences, and organizing data, and have more knowledge of the area covered by the problem.

4. An algorithm is a strategy that will always work to solve a problem, although it may not always be the most efficient strategy. Heuristics are rules of thumb, more general strategies that may or may not solve the problem. General problem solving strategies that can be taught to students include thinking aloud, working backwards, using trial and error, considering all the possibilities, using means/end analysis, and subgoaling. Students can learn to solve problems better if they are taught to organize information according to its initial status, goal, and constraints and are taught problem-solving strategies.

5. The question of transfer—the generalization of skills learned in a class to other subjects and to the outside world—is an important concern to educators. Studies show that transfer may not just happen. Strategies that encourage transfer must be an integral part of the lesson if transfer is to occur.

6. Metacognition is the conscious monitoring and regulation of the way a person approaches and solves a problem or a challenge. Metacognition can also be applied to reading. Students who understand that different strategies exist for reading can identify the nature of these strategies, and know when to use them are better readers. Two promising programs that aim at improving metacognitive abilities are ISL and reciprocal teaching.

7. Creativity involves a person's producing a novel response to solve the problem at hand. Traditionally, creativity has been viewed as a kind of thinking. Divergent thinking involves the ability to see new relationships between things that are still appropriate to the situation. The most common test of creativity is called the Torrance Tests of Creative Thinking (TTCT) and looks at creativity in terms of four criteria: fluency, the production of a large number of ideas; flexibility, the ability to produce a variety of ideas; elaboration, the development and embellishment of the ideas; and originality, the production of ideas that aren't obvious. Some believe that this conception is too narrow and that subject knowledge, communication skills, and the ability to critically analyze a problem and solutions are important factors as well.

8. Learning styles refer to the internal and external preferences for the setting and manner in which learning takes place. Cognitive styles are the characteristic manner in which people perceive, organize, and evaluate information. One of the most commonly used systems of describing learning styles consists of five major elements; environmental components; emotional components; sociological components; the physical aspects of the learning situation, including perceptual preferences; and psychological components, sometimes referred to as cognitive style. Two important cognitive styles are the reflective-impulsive continuum and the field independent-field dependent style, sometimes called the analytic-global style. The teacher's learning style influences his or her teaching style. It is recommended that teachers adopt flexible teaching styles so as to accommodate as many learning styles as possible.

9. New breakthroughs in brain research parallel the new approaches to many cognitive functions. The discovery that the left hemisphere of the cerebral cortex is most concerned with verbal and analytic material while the right hemisphere is more involved with spatial perception and patterning led to some suggestions concerning educating the two hemispheres separately. However, the hemispheres of the brain act together in concert and cannot be educated separately.

ACTIVITIES AND EXERCISES

1. **Intelligence and the Popular Press.** Many newspapers and magazines have become interested in the new theories of intelligence. As you look through the popular press, cut out articles that discuss intelligence and note what controversies are being raised and how the question of what is intelligence is being addressed.

2. **Lessons Using Thinking.** Look at Table 4.4, which describes Robert Paul's twenty-eight principles of

critical thinking. This table names the strategies and the characteristics of exercises or assignments that reflect these strategies. For example, one of these strategies is to distinguish facts from ideals, and Paul suggests that children practice identifying the differences between what is real and what they wish were real. Children may also be given help with their use of words such as *assume, infer,* or *prove.* Look through this table and choose a few of these strategies that may be appropriate to something you might teach. Describe some practical ways that these strategies could be worked into the lesson.

3. **Teaching Thinking Skills.** Many schools and school districts are now encouraging or mandating some approach to teaching thinking. Find out how this works in your particular school district by asking administrators or teachers if there are any such programs in the district. One question to ask is whether teachers work thinking skills into their own subject or whether it is a schoolwide or districtwide program. If it is a commercially prepared program, take a look at the materials and ask teachers about their experience with the thinking skills curriculum.

4. **Diagnosing Problem-Solving Difficulties.** One way to determine where the difficulties lie in the students' abilities to solve problems is to have students solve a problem out loud. Give the students a problem. The problem might be a simple verbal mathematics problem, or it might even be some questions to answer after the students have read a written selection. Ask the students to verbalize what they are telling themselves as they solve the problem. At first, it may be somewhat difficult to do so, but the effort is worth it, as it will demonstrate where the students' difficulties lie.

5. **Building Transfer into the Lesson.** We've stressed that transfer may not happen unless the teacher builds in examples from many fields and, in the case of high road transfer, specifically looks at the principle and abstracts it for use in other fields. Choose one skill or concept that is useful outside the classroom and outline some ways you could attempt to build transfer into your lesson.

6. **Observing Creativity.** Usually, the most creative teachers are relatively well known within a school. Observe one or more of these teachers and try to discover why they are considered creative. Discuss their techniques with them. Take special notice of their projects and assignments.

7. **Your Most Creative Assignment and Teachers.** Who were your most creative teachers? Ask a few of your friends to tell you about their most creative teachers. Try to understand the criteria that are being used (even if they aren't verbalized). What were the most creative assignments that you were given while you were a student in elementary or secondary school?

8. **Learning Styles.** The concept of learning styles is quite useful. Using the five components described in Figure 4.7, consider your own learning style. For instance, under the environmental component, what sound, light, temperature, and design conditions enhance your learning? Under the emotional component, such questions as, How are you motivated? and Do you consider yourself persistent? are important questions. The sociological component can be noted by answering the question, Do you prefer to work in a group, on a small team, by yourself, or in a pair? The physical component involves mobility and food or drink intake as well as whether you are an auditory, visual, or tactual learner.

9. **Learning and Teaching Styles.** Some teachers feel right at home in a discussion, while others prefer to lecture. The text suggests that teachers try to accommodate a number of learning styles. As you observe other teachers, make a note of the styles they use in teaching.

SCENARIOS

Here are ten scenarios. Try to apply the information you have learned in the chapter to each situation.

1. Mrs. Santos assigned her eighth-grade students to compare and evaluate the soundness of two arguments in a particular written selection. To her surprise, the students did not seem to understand how to tackle the problem in an organized fashion. Mrs. Santos would like to work out a way to teach students how to compare and evaluate but does not know how to start. She asks you, her colleague, for advice. What would you tell her?

2. "I'm frustrated," Mr. Parkinson says over lunch in the cafeteria of the high school in which you both teach. "I teach something, such as the scientific

method, and find that students can understand the stages. When I ask students at a later time how to handle another problem, it is as if they never heard of the scientific method. I don't know what I'm doing wrong, since students do well on the exam. They show they know the material but don't seem to be able to use it at a later time when it would be appropriate." Evaluate Mr. Parkinson's problem and offer some specific ideas as to how he could solve it.

3. Dennis is in fifth grade. He can add, subtract, and multiply. Whenever he is given a mathematics example, he does it quickly and accurately. He does have one difficulty that threatens his achievement in mathematics: He cannot solve verbal problems. Although he can multiply 12 by 7, he can't seem to solve problems such as, "Ken buys twelve pieces of candy. The candy costs 7 cents apiece. How much does all the candy cost?" Dennis's parents are aware of the problem and have asked for advice on how to help Dennis. They have high expectations for Dennis and are a bit frustrated at their inability to help him. Mrs. Wilson, Dennis's teacher, would like to help Dennis and also give Dennis's parents some advice. If you were Mrs. Wilson, what specifically would you do, and what advice would you give Dennis's parents?

4. Ms. Elias has been working with Linda, a bright sixth-grade girl who does her work but often comes up with ridiculous answers. At times, Linda says she knows her work but does not. This is causing Linda to begin to lose her confidence. The other students are beginning to snicker, and Ms. Elias is afraid that Linda will stop trying and participating in class. Ms. Elias has a good relationship with Linda and would like to help Linda overcome this tendency. What can Ms. Elias do?

5. Mr. Green would like to encourage some divergent thinking in his sophomore social studies class. He decides to say something outlandish and wait for the students to react, disagree, and, he hopes, come up with some original and appropriate solutions to a problem. To his horror, not one student in the class responds, and some even take down his ridiculous statement in their notes. He doesn't understand why the students did not react and wonders where he might have gone wrong. What can Mr. Green do to encourage divergent thinking?

6. Part of Ms. Valencia's job is to discover those students who are "creative" in order to help them develop their talents. Ms. Valencia is now forming a class for these students. She believes that creativity and intelligence are related. She looks at student scores on an intelligence test, choosing those students who have scored over 125. She then administers the TTCT to these students. Those who score high on the TTCT are included in her special class. Evaluate Ms. Valencia's method of identifying "creative" children.

7. It is rare for an entire school district to become completely involved in a program that stems from one idea, but that is what happened in your district. After a presentation on Gardner's Theory of Multiple Intelligences, the faculty and administration have decided to reevaluate their concept of intelligence and to look at Gardner's seven intelligences. They find that their course work values and deals only with linguistic and mathematical-logical intelligences, and they would like to expand their evaluation and curriculum to encourage the other intelligences. Some voices of dissent may be heard, arguing that the school's main mission is in teaching subjects that reflect the first two intelligences and that any other emphasis will endanger academic standards. After reviewing Gardner's ideas, discuss how the theory might be used and give your view of the dissenters' opinion.

8. Adapting our knowledge of learning styles to the classroom may not be easy, but Mr. Waters believed it was worth a try. He first discussed the concept of learning style with his class of sixth-graders and then explained the first four components of the model (environmental, emotional, sociological, and physical). He asked the students to evaluate themselves on these elements and, after discussing their responses, decided to try to style flex. He offered assignments that could be approached from a number of perceptual angles and allowed students some freedom to eat while working and to work in pairs. Although environmental factors were difficult to work out, he did allow those who said they needed quiet to sit in the quietest part of the room and varied whatever other environmental elements were possible. Evaluate Mr. Waters' approach to taking learning styles into account.

9. "I prefer to use a lot of class discussion and teamwork," Miss McGhee said proudly to parents gathered to hear how she approached teaching her fourth-grade class. The parents all seemed very pleased except for Mr. Bell, who privately told Miss McGhee that his son Brett did not like that much discussion and preferred to work alone and discover things for himself. Miss McGhee nodded but told Mr. Bell that such class discussion and cooperative work gave his son valuable lessons in sociability and teamwork. Mr. Bell told the teacher that his son has friends but does not feel he is learning that much in her class. Mr. Bell then dropped the subject but later suggested that perhaps it would be best if Brett were switched to another class. Miss McGhee noted that Brett did well on tests but did not participate in the discussion and seemed to put in the minimum effort in the teamwork exercises. Evaluate the problem that has arisen here, especially as it relates to learning style. Should Brett's class be changed?

10. Kelly is an impulsive seventh-grader who works very fast, is always finished first, but usually makes a great many mistakes in her work. Mr. Gillam, her mathematics teacher, is certain that Kelly is a good student, but Kelly's grades in mathematics don't show it, since Kelly makes so many errors. What can Mr. Gillam do to help Kelly overcome this problem?

5

Are These Statements True or False?

Turn the next page for the correct answers. Each statement is repeated following the paragraph in which the information can be found.

1. A student's emotional responses to various aspects of school, such as experiencing anxiety in mathematics class, are innate rather than learned.

2. Giving students a reward even though they may not have earned it may encourage students to work harder.

3. Today, teachers use edible rewards less often than they did in the past.

4. Teachers use reprimands far more often than they use praise.

5. The practice of rewarding good work by increasing the amount of recess time or allowing students to play games should be discouraged, since it undermines the message that the primary purpose of school is learning.

6. Positive reinforcement can be used to increase desirable behaviors, whereas negative reinforcement is the mode of learning responsible when students learn undesirable behaviors.

7. Students can be taught to reinforce themselves.

8. Reinforcement programs in which teachers ask parents to reinforce students when they have achieved a certain level each day have generally been successful.

9. Feedback—information following a behavior telling students about their performance—should be given sparingly, since it emphasizes student errors.

10. Ignoring the undercurrent of noise in the class caused by student conversations is not a technique that will lead to the reduction or elimination of this undesirable behavior.

11. After a behavior has been learned, the number of reinforcements given should be increased to maintain the behavior.

12. For students to learn, they must be reinforced directly.

The Behavioral Approach

Answers to True-False Statements

1. *False* Correct statement: A student's emotional responses such as anxiety in mathematics class are learned, often through classical conditioning.
2. *False* Correct statement: Students should not be given reinforcers unless they have reached the standard. However, standards must be reasonable if any program to improve or increase a behavior is to work.
3. *True*
4. *True*
5. *False* Correct statement: The use of activities as rewards should be encouraged, since such rewards are potent sources of reinforcement within the classroom.
6. *False* Correct statement: Both positive and negative reinforcement increase the likelihood of a behavior's occurring. Students can learn both desirable and undesirable behaviors through either type of reinforcement.
7. *True*
8. *True*
9. *False* Correct statement: Feedback is necessary if students are to correct their mistakes. In addition, feedback need not be targeted only at errors, as it can also tell students what they have done correctly.
10. *True*
11. *False* Correct statement: After a behavior is well learned, the reinforcements should be decreased or faded slowly.
12. *False* Correct statement: Students may learn by observing others, especially when positive models are reinforced.

There are five students in your class who do not finish their written assignments. When you press them to do so, they rush through the work and make many mistakes.

Ken is a student in your sixth-grade class. He is about eight months behind in reading and, according to his mother, never reads at home. You notice that whenever he has free time in school, he rarely spends it looking at a book. Both you and Ken's parents are afraid that Ken will fall further behind.

You notice that Jane does not seem to volunteer much during discussions or question-and-answer periods even though she seems to know her subjects fairly well. You have a reasonably good relationship with Jane, and she finally raises her hand to answer a question. Unfortunately, her answer is wrong. You are in a bind. You can't leave her answer as is, since it is not correct. On the other hand, you are concerned that a correction may cause Jane not to volunteer anymore. What can you do?

You are asking a number of parents to work with their children on particular aspects of mathematics. You know that their participation is important. At first, the parents help their children, but soon there is a significant reduction in

their help. You would like to keep it going. How could you accomplish this?

THE BEHAVIORAL APPROACH

Chapters 2 and 3 discussed the Piagetian and information processing approaches to learning. Cognitive approaches are surely in the forefront of research today. However, two other schools of thought—the behavioral and social learning approaches—have much to offer teachers. In the rush of educational interest that surrounds cognitive psychology, the usefulness of these other approaches is sometimes obscured. This is most unfortunate, since the behavioral approach and social learning theory rest on solid research bases, and mountains of practical applications await rediscovery.

What Is the Behavioral Approach?

When the word *behavioral* is used, such terms as *reinforcement* and *punishment* and such names as B. F.

Skinner and John Watson come to mind. The behavioral view involves more than these identifications, however. It is an approach as well as a philosophy. It involves identifying the changes one wants to make and proceeding in a planned, organized way to adopt a program that will lead to the desired changes. According to Charles Maher and Susan Forman (1987), the approach involves five elements.

1. **A Focus on Current Behavior as It Relates to School Performance.** Behavioral approaches look at improving both current academic behavior and student conduct in the school. The first step is to define in a measurable way the level of student functioning. This may involve recording the frequency of a behavior, such as the number of times a student participates in class discussion, or determining the accuracy of academic work. The behavioral view uses only observable, measurable behavior to define school performance. All learning involves behavior change. For example, if a student can answer five algebra problems correctly after attending a special program but could answer only two before the program, learning has occurred.

2. **An Emphasis on Precision in Assessing Behavior and in Setting Goals.** Whatever the methods of assessing behavior that are used, they must be both valid (that is, measure what they are supposed to measure) and reliable (that is, dependable or consistent). A specific type of objective called a behavioral objective describes the precise expected student performance following instruction (Axelrod, 1983). Behavioral objectives are addressed at length in Chapter 11. For example, if we want Jane to participate more, we would not simply state that we want her to do so. We would have to be more precise, and the goal might be for Jane to raise her hand to volunteer to answer two questions during the discussion session following silent reading.

3. **Reliance on Prior Experimental Research as a Basis for Program Design.** The behavioral approach to education utilizes previous empirical research on learning in the design of programs. Such studies, some of which derive from laboratory work, serve as the foundation for creating programs. As such, behavioral programs are always designed using principles that have been demonstrated to be effective in controlled basic and applied research.

4. **A Focus on Specificity in Defining Programs and Procedures.** The behavioral approach demands a careful description of any program aimed at changing behavior. After the problem is assessed, the goals and objectives clearly noted, and information from previous research analyzed, we can then look at which activities, methods, and materials have a reasonable chance of success. All parts of the program are specified, including such factors as appropriate rewards, duration of the program, and how the program will be administered.

5. **Inclusion of Routine Evaluation of Program Effectiveness.** One hallmark of the behavioral approach is the emphasis on constant evaluation. Evaluation procedures come directly from the behavioral objectives. The information derived from the evaluation can then be used to determine the success or failure of the program.

The behavioral approach, then, is an objective attempt to identify a problem, write goals for changing behavior in such a way that they can be measured, use research from learning theory to help design programs, predict the probable success of the programs, and evaluate the programs once they have been implemented.

MODELS OF LEARNING

Behaviorists design their programs to take advantage of what they know about three principal modes of learning. Classical or respondent conditioning involves changing the conditions under which an innate response takes place. Operant conditioning is a mode of learning in which the frequency of a behavior is increased or decreased depending upon its consequences. Observational learning explores how people learn through watching others.

In this chapter, we'll look at these processes of learning and investigate the implications of the behavioral view for the classroom teacher. Many of the techniques described in detail in Chapter 10 ("Classroom Management") come directly from behavioral research. Many behavioral techniques have been successfully used by classroom teachers to improve behavior and the quality of student work in class. This chapter looks at how the behavioral approach can aid the classroom teacher in the academic as well as behavioral areas.

Classical or Respondent Conditioning

Classical conditioning involves the pairing of a neutral stimulus with a stimulus that elicits a particular response until the originally neutral stimulus elicits that response (Reese & Lipsett, 1970). For example, suppose your teacher walked into the room with a businesslike expression on her face. She asks you to clear your desk and begins to hand out paper. You feel your throat tightening, your heart pounding, and anxiety rising. Why are these reactions occurring? If the same event occurred in a kindergarten classroom, the students would probably simply be excited. Why the change? The answer is found in classical conditioning. From years of experience, you know a test is coming, and you have associated the teacher's actions with a test; this elicits the anxiety.

The learning process known as classical conditioning explains some of the emotional reactions students experience. For example, students may develop a negative attitude towards their teacher, Mr. Evans, if school-related activities are linked with some painful event. Suppose we first say that the students in Mr. Evans's class originally had no opinion of the teacher. However, when the students did poorly, Mr. Evans criticized and yelled at them, causing them to feel inadequate, embarrassed, and anxious. Eventually, just the sight of Mr. Evans may be sufficient to arouse negative feelings in these students.

To understand classical conditioning, some definitions need to be introduced. An **unconditioned** stimulus is the stimulus that elicits the response prior to the conditioning. In the example presented, the continuous criticism by Mr. Evans is the unconditioned stimulus, because it caused the aversive feelings in the students before the conditioning took place. The **unconditioned response** is the response to the unconditioned stimulus. A child's feelings of inadequacy after being criticized is the unconditioned response. The **conditioned stimulus** is the previously neutral stimulus that acquires the ability to elicit a response when it is associated with the unconditioned stimulus. In this case, Mr. Evans is the conditioned stimulus. Only when he was paired with the criticism did he cause negative feelings. Finally, the **conditioned response** is the learned response that becomes attached to the conditioned stimulus. In this case, it is the child's experience of anxiety, dread, and pain when entering Mr. Evans's class.

If this occurs with a few other teachers, these students may react with fear to all aspects of school. This is called **stimulus generalization.** However, let us say that the children do not receive such treatment in other classes. They may then show this fear and anxiety only in Mr. Evans's class. They have discriminated between Mr. Evans and the rest of the staff and react only to Mr. Evans in this manner. This is called

These students can feel their hearts pounding and anxiety rising because they associate handing out paper with taking a test.

classical conditioning   A learning process in which a neutral stimulus is paired with a stimulus that elicits a response until the originally neutral stimulus elicits that response.

unconditioned stimulus   The stimulus that originally elicits the response.

unconditioned response   The response to the unconditioned stimulus.

conditioned stimulus   The stimulus that is neutral before conditioning and after being paired with the unconditioned stimulus will elicit the desired response by itself.

conditioned response   The learned response to the conditioned stimulus.

stimulus generalization   The tendency of an organism that has learned to associate a certain behavior with a particular stimulus to show this behavior when confronted with similar stimuli.

stimulus discrimination. Will the fear of Mr. Evans ever end, or will the students always hate going to his class? Perhaps, after many experiences in which being in Mr. Evans's class does not mean criticism, the response will be **extinguished,** that is, the students will no longer respond with anxiety.

Classical Conditioning and the Classroom Teacher

Classical conditioning is especially useful for understanding students' emotional responses to various aspects of the school environment. The example just described involved anxiety and fear, but it could just as easily have been framed in a way that would have led to the formation of positive emotions, such as self-satisfaction and joy. What if Mr. Evans had encouraged his students instead of engaging in constant criticism and the students had succeeded? In such a case, the students might have developed positive feelings towards their teacher. Many emotional responses are classically conditioned. An understanding of classical conditioning can allow a teacher to understand the genesis of a student's emotional reactions.

Conditioned emotional responses may arise from experience with a given subject. Many students have math anxiety (Harris & Harris, 1987). Perhaps such anxiety arises when a student always has difficulty with mathematics and low grades follow. Mathematics lessons become linked to failure, and the child reacts to mathematics with anxiety. Stimulus generalization may then occur as the anxiety associated with early failure is generalized to all areas in which arithmetic is used and leads to poor attitudes toward mathematics at all levels.

True or False   A student's emotional responses to various aspects of school, such as experiencing anxiety in mathematics class, are innate rather than learned.

This is easy to understand using a classical conditioning model. Let's presume that in first grade, mathematics is not associated with either positive or negative emotions. The student persistently fails and

stimulus discrimination   The process by which a person learns to differentiate among stimuli.

extinction   The weakening and disappearance of a learned response.

receives criticism from the teacher. This criticism is an unconditioned stimulus. After many pairings between mathematics and failure, the student develops anxiety and a dislike of mathematics. After a while, the student will show an active fear of mathematics, which will lead to such undesirable behaviors as giving up easily and avoiding the subject whenever possible.

The same analysis can be used to explain some students' dislike of reading aloud. Perhaps Jack is having difficulty reading and is asked to read aloud. If reading aloud brings snickers from his classmates and constant criticism from his teacher, Jack will develop anxiety concerning reading aloud. This can even generalize to anxiety whenever Jack is called upon in class. Just anticipating reading aloud (or doing mathematics, as in our other case) could be sufficient for experiencing anxiety.

The fact that students develop many conditioned emotional responses from their experiences in school—and that these experiences can be generalized—should make teachers more aware of the possibilities for developing both favorable and unfavorable attitudes towards learning and towards the entire school experience. If a teacher has an unpleasant demeanor, makes unflattering statements, especially publicly, or uses criticism constantly, a student might develop an undesirable emotional response, such as anger or anxiety, towards school in general. The student may then find that school tasks elicit anxiety, which leads to lack of persistence and withdrawal (Ringness, 1975). Indeed, misbehavior can sometimes be linked to anxious reactions to taking tests, talking in front of the class, or being judged (Gnagey, 1981). The student may act out to mask his or her anxiety or may adopt an I-don't-care attitude to save face and avoid embarrassment.

Students are frequently conditioned to show emotional reactions to words. In late elementary school, and certainly in junior and senior high school, when teachers announce a test, an oral report, or some challenging homework assignment, behaviors relating to anxiety, such as murmurs and restlessness, are frequently noted. Words can be a conditioned stimulus for fear and anxiety. Therefore, certain words, such as *test,* or certain phrases, such as "clear your desks," or even having one's name called by the teacher can be linked with an unpleasant unconditioned stimulus and eventually may elicit a conditioned emotional response of anxiety.

Perhaps the emotional reaction this student is experiencing can be explained through classical conditioning.

We've been largely considering the conditioning of undesirable emotional reactions. However, it is also possible that we may be able to condition positive emotional responses to school challenges. If teachers provide many stimuli that elicit positive emotional reactions, students will relate school tasks to these positive reactions, with more positive attitudes towards school as a result. The emotional tone of the classroom is dictated by the teacher. A calm voice, enthusiasm, humor, and accepting students as individuals can lead to desirable emotional responses. If the teacher is pleasant and schoolwork is linked with success and praise, students may develop a positive attitude towards the teacher and towards school in general.

How can the conditioning of undesirable emotional responses be prevented? If teachers are aware that they might be creating conditioned emotional responses such as anxiety, it is possible for them to avoid delivering the unconditioned stimulus, for example not making deprecating remarks to students who have done poorly. Had Mr. Evans realized that he has the tendency to criticize and embarrass students, he might have been able to avoid embarrassing the students or making negative comments.

Many secondary schoolteachers will face students who already have negative attitudes towards their school subjects. The challenge for such teachers is not only how to prevent the establishment of new negative emotional responses but also how to change such responses once they've been established. One way is to provide activities and experiences that lead not to negative emotions but rather to more positive ones. For example, understanding that his students may have had poor experiences with mathematics in the past, Mr. Evans might have tried to build success into his students' work, and the students might not have reacted so negatively.

Certain classroom activities, such as taking tests and giving speeches in front of the class, tend to be rather stressful. In such situations, trying to ensure success as much as possible is important. If teachers diagnose a student's problems and help the student overcome them, the student is more likely to associate the class with success than with failure. Whenever possible, the student should be introduced to a potentially stressful situation gradually. Consider the teacher's problem when dealing with a student suffering from great anxiety around the requirement of giving a speech in front of the class. Asking the student to answer a question from his or her seat would serve as a good introduction to speaking before the class. The student may then be asked to stand up at his or her seat and say a few words, then perhaps write the answer to a question on the blackboard and explain it while standing in front of the classroom. These and other activities might gradually lead up to the student's giving a speech. Positive support is also important. The teacher can give gentle encouragement which may enable a student to approach these potentially stressful situations with more confidence.

Conditioned emotional reactions can be modified using a variety of approaches. One possibility is to use an extinction procedure. A student who is afraid of writing compositions because he had been told that he is terrible at writing or is "dumb" will undoubtedly develop a conditioned emotional reaction of anxiety or anger. However, if the negative comments stop and only factual corrections are given, the conditioned stimulus (the composition) is no longer followed by the unconditioned stimulus (personal criticism), and the reaction may be extinguished. Since this approach can take a long time to take effect, a different procedure can be used that might be both quicker and more effective. Consider the example of the student with math anxiety. Suppose we build success in mathematics into the equation. Knowing that the student will react negatively because he has failed in the past, we teach him carefully in small steps, making certain he is successful at each step. The student's emotional reaction to mathematics may then be altered. By pairing the anxiety-provoking event with a pleasurable one such as success, we may begin to see changes in the child's attitude and behavior towards the subject.

Some students react negatively to any correction at all. All stimuli that are not glowing approvals of their work are interpreted as criticisms. In this case, the student must be taught to discriminate between personal criticism—"you're dumb"—and factual correction—"example number three is incorrect." The teacher may need to point out the difference to the student.

Another method of altering fears is to expose the child with the fear to a similar child who does not have this fear and allow the fearful child to observe the other child. Sometimes, however, strong emotional reactions require more help than a classroom teacher can provide, and a referral to the guidance counselor may be necessary. Many counselors use a method of reducing anxiety, called systematic desensitization, in which the student first constructs a hierarchy listing the situations in which anxiety is present and then places a numerical value on each situation, thereby ranking the situations as to the amount of anxiety experienced. The student is then relaxed, and small amounts of the anxiety-provoking stimulus are presented to or imagined by the student until the student can successfully overcome each small amount of anxiety. The student is then ready to proceed to the next level (Emery, 1969). Relaxation is often used to reduce anxiety in general, and relaxation seminars are sometimes held for test anxiety as well. Although relaxation does reduce anxiety, other factors, such as test-taking skills and study habits, must be addressed before it has much of an effect on academic achievement (see chapter 14).

Operant Conditioning

Most of the behavior that interests classroom teachers, however, is not classically conditioned. Such behavior as volunteering in class, doing homework, paying attention, and following instructions cannot be understood in terms of emotional reactions. To understand these voluntary behaviors, we need to look at **operant conditioning,** in which behavior is followed by some event that increases or decreases the frequency of that behavior. If the event increases the likelihood that the behavior will recur, the action is said to be **reinforced.**

In operant conditioning, then, behavior is governed by its consequences. If the consequences are positive, the behavior is likely to occur more frequently. If the consequences are aversive, the behavior will occur less frequently. This all seems rather simple and obvious. However, it may not be. Let's take a look at a classroom situation. Mr. Evans has assigned some seatwork when he notices that Jimmy is not doing his work. He asks Jimmy if he has finished, and Jimmy says no. As soon as Jimmy seems to return to his work, Mr. Evans turns away, only to hear a muffled voice say "and I'm not going to," followed by a laugh. As Mr. Evans turns back around, the other children return to their work. Mr. Evans scolds Jimmy. As he turns to help another youngster, two of Jimmy's friends begin laughing at a face Jimmy has just made. Mr. Evans this time gives Jimmy an extra assignment. Mr. Evans has constant trouble with Jimmy but can't figure out why. After all, he reasons, he is not reinforcing Jimmy's behavior, and he actually is punishing Jimmy. What is Mr. Evans doing wrong?

First we could say that Mr. Evans's attention could be reinforcing Jimmy's poor behavior. Ignoring the behavior, however, is not a practical course. The real reinforcers may be the other students. There are many reinforcers both in the classroom and in a child's life. The peer group is a significant reinforcer, and gaining attention from his peers may be keeping Jimmy in his pattern of inattention and fooling around.

Generalization and discrimination are also important concepts in operant conditioning and explain many behaviors. If a student is reinforced for aggression, as when he gets to keep the pen he snatched from another student, he may show this same behavior in similar contexts. The student probably will learn when the behavior will work and when it leads to unfortunate consequences. In other words, he learns to discriminate.

operant conditioning The learning process in which behavior is governed by its consequences.

reinforcement An event that increases the likelihood that the behavior that preceded it will recur.

Reinforcement techniques have been successfully applied to a wide array of classroom situations. For example, Taylor and Hoedt (1966) divided over 100 fourth-graders into two groups. In one group, the teacher praised the students by highlighting the best portions of the students' written assignments. The students in the other group were simply told which sections needed additional work. The number of comments was the same for both groups. The quality of both groups' work improved, but those in the praise group improved significantly more.

In another experiment, students who obtained perfect scores on spelling tests were allowed to engage in some enjoyable activity, such as listening to records. The percentage of fourth-graders who obtained scores of 100 percent increased from 24 to 64 percent (Christie, 1971). However, teachers should beware of setting the standards too high. It might be better to set a lower goal and then raise it gradually (Piersel, 1987). In another study (Tribble & Hall, 1972), a student named John, who completed less than 25 percent of his work, was told that if he finished at least 60 percent within a specified time, the entire class would receive extra free time and John would be allowed to be the leader in the class's recreational games. John's level of completion improved dramatically.

In still another interesting study using reinforcement, Glover and Gary (1976) used a group-based program to increase creativity in class. The experimenters defined creativity in terms of fluency (the production of large number of ideas), flexibility (the production of a variety of ideas), elaboration (the embellishment or filling out of ideas), and originality. Fourth- and fifth-grade students were exposed to a gamelike situation in which they were told that many common items have unusual or uncommon uses that do not occur to people. Fluency, flexibility, elaboration, and originality were explained to the students. Two teams were formed and various objects presented to them. Each team member was awarded points based on the four criteria. The team with the greater number of points was allowed ten minutes additional recess, and each member received milk and extra cookies. Both teams could win if the lower score met or exceeded 80 percent of the winning team's score. Creativity as measured by these four criteria increased.

Many studies show the power of positive reinforcement. In a few schools, however, positive reinforcement has become a schoolwide effort. In one Oregon

Many parents hear from teachers only when teachers have something critical to say about their children. Teachers can use telephone calls to compliment or praise students.

middle school, a "think positive" attitude pervades the school, and a number of reinforcement activities are designed into the schoolday. For example, teachers make many positive phone calls to parents about their children; students who say "thank you" or who are polite in other ways are given "courtesy cards" that can be turned in for free treats; good-grades parties are held; and students who display good citizenship and attendance are given VIP passes, allowing them to leave class a minute early or receive special treats (Hering & Nys, 1988).

This approach is especially noteworthy, because too often the classroom and the school itself present students with many potential punishments but few reinforcers. Students are constantly told what punishments will be administered for failing to turn work in on time and for misbehaving. Certainly, students should be informed of the consequences of their actions. However, overemphasizing these punishments can create a situation in which students are working simply to avoid punishment (Skinner, 1968). Such students will find ways to escape or avoid work. For example, a student may be very slow in doing his or her work, may not pay attention, and may do just enough work to avoid punishment, but no more. It is easy for teachers to create classrooms devoid of positive reinforcement where punishments are emphasized and students are mainly motivated to avoid them. This aversive classroom atmosphere is often combined with the undesirable conditioned emotional responses learned through classical conditioning discussed earlier. It is easy, then, to understand why some students develop behavior patterns in which they do very little work—just enough to avoid punishment—and react to school so negatively. Using positive reinforcement is one way to combat the overly aversive nature of the classroom.

How Teachers Can Use Reinforcement

Imagine that Mr. Evans wants to use a reinforcement strategy on Jimmy to improve Jimmy's behavior. He chooses as his reinforcer a piece of candy, after receiving Jimmy's mother's permission to do so. Jimmy begins to improve until the end of the day. Then, seeing that Jimmy is falling back to his old behaviors, Mr. Evans tells Jimmy, "Up to now, you've been good. Don't ruin it." Jimmy's behavior gets worse. However, since Jimmy has tried, Mr. Evans gives him the candy. Again Mr. Evans is frustrated. His technique did not work, but he can't understand why.

Mr. Evans made a number of mistakes. In fact, he violated four basic rules of reinforcement (Axelrod, 1983).

Rule Number 1. For a reinforcer to be effective, it must be made contingent upon a specific desired behavior. That is, before the reinforcer is given, the desired behavior must be exhibited. Giving students a reinforcer when they did not show the appropriate behavior will not result in any improvement. Mr. Evans did not make the candy contingent upon Jimmy's finishing his assignment. In fact, since he gave the candy after Jimmy was not showing the correct behavior, Mr. Evans may even be reinforcing Jimmy's poor work habits.

True or False Giving students a reward even though they may not have earned it may encourage students to work harder.

Rule Number 2. The reinforcer should be delivered as soon after the desired behavior is shown as possible. This is especially important when working with younger children. In this case, Jimmy had shown the desired behavior throughout the day, and he should have been reinforced immediately after completing each assignment.

Rule Number 3. The reinforcer needs to be appropriate for the individual child. A reinforcer might be rewarding at one time and not at another and be rewarding to one child and not to another. Mr. Evans

used candy as a reinforcer for Jimmy. But what if Jimmy had all the candy he ever wanted at home, didn't like candy, or got enough of it at lunch? For the reinforcer to be effective, Jimmy should not have much access to it outside the classroom and it should be something that will motivate him to finish his work. In addition, children do become satiated on edible reinforcers.

Rule Number 4. Reinforcers should be varied. It would be best if Mr. Evans varied the reinforcers, perhaps using praise or free time as well as food (Egel, 1981).

How Often Should Reinforcers Be Given?

How often should a child be reinforced? Should Jimmy be reinforced every time he completes his assignments on time, every second time, or just once in a while? Reinforcing a behavior each time it occurs is called **continuous reinforcement.** Each time Jimmy completed his assignments on time, he would receive a treat. Under such circumstances, Jimmy should learn to complete his work quickly, since each correct behavior is reinforced. However, what would happen after the reinforcement stopped? Jimmy would probably stop doing his work on time. Behaviors that are learned under continuous reinforcement are learned quickly but are also extinguished quickly.

Other alternatives exist, however. What if Jimmy weren't reinforced each time he completed his work but was reinforced for some fraction of the times that he did? Such reinforcement procedures are known as **partial reinforcement schedules,** and there are four types. In a **fixed ratio reinforcement schedule,** the

continuous reinforcement A reinforcement schedule that involves reinforcing each instance of the desired behavior.

partial reinforcement schedules A group of reinforcement schedules in which the reinforcer is administered after a portion of the total responses in a particular situation rather than after every response.

fixed ratio reinforcement schedule A schedule of partial reinforcement in which a predetermined number of responses must be made before the reinforcer·is administered.

teacher would choose the desired ratio, let's say two correct responses for each reinforcer, and reinforce Jimmy's correct behavior every second, fourth, sixth, eighth time, and so on. Mr. Evans would save reinforcers, but soon Jimmy would probably catch on and expect the reinforcer.

We could also deliver the reinforcer on a **variable ratio reinforcement schedule,** in which, again, we choose two correct responses for each reinforcer but vary the number of correct answers between reinforcers. For instance, let's say that ten assignments are given during the day and we want to deliver the reinforcer on a variable ratio reinforcement schedule consisting of two correct behaviors for one reinforcer. Instead of giving the reinforcer after every second behavior, we might give it after the first and then not again until the fourth, then give it the fifth and the sixth, and then again the ninth time the correct behavior is shown. On the next day, we might give the reinforcer after each of the first three assignments is completed correctly and then not again until the eighth and the tenth. Notice that Jimmy still receives the reinforcer five times for ten correct behaviors, but he never knows when it is coming. He just knows if he does his work, the reinforcer will be delivered. Of course, it takes longer to learn behaviors under partial reinforcement schedules, because some correct behaviors will not be reinforced. However, behavior learned under partial reinforcement schedules—and especially under variable ratio—is resistant to extinction, and it will continue after the reinforcer has been withdrawn. In addition, we can easily maintain Jimmy's behavior by giving him a reinforcer once and a while.

Two other possible options are fixed interval and variable interval reinforcement schedules. In a **fixed interval reinforcement schedule,** the reinforcer would be given after standard intervals of time. The reinforcer is given only when the interval has elapsed and the first correct behavior shown is reinforced. In a **variable interval reinforcement schedule,** the reinforcer is given on the basis of the first response that occurs after a period of time, which varies from one reinforcement situation to the next. Just as in variable ratio, the person cannot figure out when the reinforcer is coming.

The difference between fixed and variable interval schedules can be seen in the use of home reports. Let's say that we want to let Jimmy's parents in on our program. We tell them that we will be sending home letters each day letting them know how Jimmy is doing

variable ratio reinforcement schedule   A partial reinforcement schedule in which the number of responses required to obtain a reinforcer varies.

fixed interval reinforcement schedule   A partial reinforcement schedule in which the reinforcer is administered following a fixed period of time after the previous reinforcer has been delivered.

variable interval reinforcement schedule   A partial reinforcement schedule in which the time period between the administration of reinforcers is varied.

and how many assignments he finished. Jimmy's parents then give Jimmy, say, extra television time as a reinforcer. Perhaps the amount of time depends on the number of assignments he does correctly. This is an example of a fixed interval reinforcement schedule, since it occurs each day. After a while, we could change it to once a week. However, what if we told the parents that we would send home progress reports averaging once a week for the term (sixteen or so reports) but that we would be sending them home at irregular intervals. Sometimes we would send two reports a week or even three to the student's home, and sometimes none. This is an example of a variable interval reinforcement schedule. Under such schedules, students perform even better than on fixed interval reinforcement schedules (Saudargas et al., 1977).

When teachers read about these schedules, they sometimes react with displeasure. The idea of counting or timing is difficult to accept when a teacher has thirty students. However, that isn't necessary. Mr. Evans is in a situation where he can reinforce Jimmy for each correct single behavior; but if he were reinforcing another behavior of Jimmy's—perhaps raising his hand—he probably couldn't.

It is important to understand that learning will be more rapid the more often the reinforcer follows the desired behavior. It is also possible that poor behavior may be reinforced, especially on a variable ratio reinforcement schedule. Consider what might happen if Mr. Evans decides to ignore some behavior, such as calling out four or five times during the day, but then calls on Jimmy occasionally when Jimmy calls out. This will reinforce Jimmy on a variable ratio reinforcement basis and will be more difficult to extinguish.

What Reinforcers Can Be Used in the Classroom?

Teachers can use a great many different reinforcers, and choosing the proper one is vital to the success of any attempt to change a student's behavior. These reinforcers can be placed into three categories: edible and tangible, social, and activity reinforcers. Each has its advantages and disadvantages.

Edible and Tangible Reinforcers

The picture many people have of the process of reinforcement is that of the teacher or psychologist giving a student candy, such as M&Ms, for the desirable behavior. Today, **edible reinforcers** are used infrequently, although they remain effective, especially when working with younger children or severely handicapped students. The same can be said to some extent of the use of **tangible reinforcers,** such as stickers and banners. The problems of immediate and contingent delivery, satiation, and the fact that school policies limit the application of such reinforcers have restricted their usage (Nelson, 1987). As we shall see, some tangible reinforcers can be useful as backup reinforcers when a program is designed whereby students receive tokens that can be saved up or used immediately to "purchase" tangible reinforcers.

True or False   Today, teachers use edible rewards less often than they did in the past.

Social Reinforcers

Social reinforcement processes involve the use of smiles, praise, attention, and signs of approval, including hand or facial signals. Certainly, we've all had teachers who use these **social reinforcers.** However, research studies show that teachers do not use them consistently. Teachers utter fifteen times as many reprimands as praise statements (Walker, 1979), and

---

edible reinforcers   Reinforcers that involve any type of food.

tangible reinforcers   Material reinforcers such as stickers.

social reinforcers   Behaviors such as praise and attention that can be used as reinforcers.

---

they do not use social reinforcers as often as one would think (White, 1975). Two reasons for this stand out. First, good work, adequate attention, and conduct do not stand out in class. What stands out is the opposite—incomplete work, inadequate attention, and fooling around. We frequently are told to expect good work, and this is certainly necessary. However, expecting good behavior and good work does not mean that they should not be reinforced. Just the opposite is true. It is best to search out the positive acts, such as finishing work on time, and reinforce them with a positive statement. Second, some teachers feel insincere giving praise or attention for good work. However, these feelings fade as teachers use social reinforcers with their students. Social reinforcement techniques do not require the teacher to gush over a student. Praise should always be specific and provide detailed information, such as "I like the way you . . ." (McDaniel, 1987). (Much more about the use of praise is found in Chapter 9.)

True or False   Teachers use reprimands far more often than they use praise.

Praise is a very potent type of reinforcer, with the added benefit that it is economical, meets with general public approval, is easy and quick to give, and normally does not lead to satiation (Forman, 1987). In one study, Kirby and Shields (1972) used the social reinforcer of praise to change the behavior of a seventh-grade boy who was doing poorly in arithmetic and did not pay attention to the lesson without constant reminders. Each day the child was praised for correct answers on his arithmetic worksheets after he completed them. At first, every two or so correct answers were praised, but eventually the number of correct answers needed to receive praise was increased. Both the student's attention and the number of correct answers increased dramatically. In fact, some investigations show that reinforcing good academic performance both improves academic achievement and attention and reduces disruptive behavior (Kazdin, 1984).

Social reinforcers do have their drawbacks. First, although these reinforcers are powerful, they are conditioned reinforcers; that is, they take their meaning from being paired in the past with other desirable circumstances. Not everyone reacts positively to praise, and not everyone understands that a wink can be a compliment. At times, students may be embarrassed or may believe that they did not deserve the praise. If

A variety of activity reinforcers can be used with students, including allowing them free time to do their favorite activities and giving them additional time at recess.

the praise is offered too profusely, the student may not believe the teacher is sincere. (More is said about this in the chapter on communication.)

Activity Reinforcers

Activity reinforcers include free time, playing games, reading magazines or comics, listening to records, drawing, painting, or extra time at recess. These are extremely effective reinforcers and deserve more use than they get. Of course, not every student will find reading magazines a reinforcer, but it is easy to figure out which activity reinforcers are effective with which classes or students. As you observe your students, their favorite activities will become evident. Some students love to play games, others to read comics, still others to have free time to draw; others simply want to run around at recess for a couple of extra minutes.

True or False   The practice of rewarding good work by increasing the amount of recess time or allowing students to play games should be discouraged, since it undermines the message that the primary purpose of school is learning.

A teacher can use the more frequently engaged in activities as reinforcers for less frequently engaged in activities. This is called the **Premack principle** after the discoverer David Premack (1965). Basically, this principle means that if students spend a great deal more time playing games than reading, game playing might be used as a reinforcer for reading. In some elementary schools, it may be possible to devote a small part of the classroom as a reinforcement area where behaviors that are being reinforced through activity can take place.

In one study, Long and Williams (1973) used free time to alter disruptive classroom behavior. During this free time, students could talk to peers, play games, or read magazines if they cooperated and obeyed

activity reinforcers   Any reinforcer that allows students to engage in a preferred activity as a reward for the desired behavior.

Premack principle   A principle of learning that states that a behavior that appears more often can be used as a reinforcer for a behavior that occurs less often.

PART I

Cognition, Development, and Learning

classroom rules. Behavior improved greatly. In another study, third-grade hyperactive boys received colored tokens that could be exchanged for fifteen minutes of play on video games which they earned by completing academic assignments and other tasks. Task completion increased dramatically (Robinson et al., 1981).

Activity reinforcers have a number of advantages. Students usually do not become satiated by them, they are easily varied, and they are readily available. They also have their limitations. Sometimes they cannot be given immediately, and some very young children may not be able to tolerate the delay that might be necessary. In addition, activity reinforcers sometimes cannot be given in small quantities. That is, either the children get free time or they don't, either they get to read a comic book or they don't, either they can go on a trip or they can't. It may be possible in some circumstances to modify the amount of time given towards these activities, but not always.

The Misunderstood Concept of Negative Reinforcement

So far, whenever a student performed the target behavior, something positive happened. The student was given free time for finishing his assignments on time or praise for raising his hand. However, there is another possibility. What if something unpleasant was taken away as a reward for performing the correct behavior? My daughter's fifth-grade teacher used this concept. Students who did their homework responsibly for four nights a week did not receive homework on Fridays. This had the effect of increasing the probability that students would do their homework. Since homework is aversive (that is, students often find it unpleasant), the teacher was taking away something unpleasant (homework) if the students performed the correct behavior (doing homework for the first four days). **Negative reinforcement** involves reducing or eliminating an aversive stimulus and acts as a reinforcer for the desired behavior.

A common mistake is to equate negative reinforcement with punishment. Negative reinforcement is *not* punishment. It is a type of reinforcement, since it increases the probability that a certain response will occur. In positive reinforcement, the reward for the target behavior is providing something desirable, while the reward in negative reinforcement is a reduction or elimination of some unpleasant stimulus.

True or False   Positive reinforcement can be used to increase desirable behaviors, whereas negative reinforcement is the mode of learning responsible when students learn undesirable behaviors.

Special Reinforcement Procedures

The use of operant conditioning to alter behavior is called **behavior modification.** A number of special techniques can be used by the classroom teacher to increase a desirable behavior. Some of the most common are token reinforcement, contracts, self-reinforcement, contingency and home-based reinforcement.

Token Reinforcement

The students in the class have been told that each time they finish an assignment with a predetermined level of accuracy they will be given a star. These stars can be used to "purchase" free time, reduced or no homework, or other privileges. This type of system is called a **token economy,** or **token reinforcement system.** It involves the use of some symbol, such as a star, that can be used immediately to purchase reinforcers or saved up to purchase larger reinforcers, called **backup reinforcers.**

Tokens can include chips, stars, play money, stamps, points, or check marks (Forman, 1987). Token economies have been successfully used for a wide variety of purposes, including improving reading and writing skills, encouraging cooperation, and finishing

negative reinforcement   A type of reinforcement in which the reward for the desired behavior is a reduction or elimination of an aversive condition.

behavior modification   The use of the principles of learning theory to alter behavior.

token economy (token reinforcement system)   A system of reinforcement in which students receive a token (such as a star) for performing the desired behavior and can either use it immediately or save it and add it to previously earned tokens to "purchase" reinforcers.

backup reinforcers   The reinforcers that can be purchased by students who have earned tokens in a token economy.

work on time (Presbie & Brown, 1985). For example, in one study, five fifth-grade boys were identified as discipline problems. The teacher observed the students for some time to discover the boys' average level of disruption—a procedure known as forming a **baseline.** A token reinforcement program was applied to reading performance, which was measured by the percentage of correct answers in daily performance sessions of fifteen minutes each. The students were required to produce written answers to test material selected daily by the reading teacher for which they were awarded points. Table 5.1 shows the point

Although token reinforcement procedures are often involved and take much time, they can be very useful in changing student behavior.

baseline A measure of the frequency in which a specific behavior is demonstrated.

Table 5.1 Back-up Reinforcers

Points Earning Criteria for Fifth-Grade Reading Class

1. 80% correct on workbook assignments	= 2 points
2. 100% correct on workbook assignments	= 5 points

Back-up Reinforcers

Daily

1. Access to game room (per 15 minutes)	2 points
2. Extra recess time (10 minutes)	2 points
3. Buy a ditto master	2 points
4. Have ditto copies run off (per copy)	1 point
5. Review grades in teacher's book	5 points
6. Reduce detention (per 10 minutes)	10 points
7. Change cafeteria table	15 points
8. Have the lowest test grade removed	20 points
9. Become an assistant teacher	Auction

Weekly

1. See a movie	6 points
2. Have a good work letter sent to parents	15 points
3. Become the classroom helper for one week	Auction
4. Become the ball captain for one week	Auction
5. Do bulletin board (will remain up for three weeks)	Auction

From "Eliminating Discipline Problems by Strengthening Academic Performance" by T. Ayllon and M. D. Roberts, *Journal of Applied Behavior Analysis.* Copyright © 1974. Reprinted by permission of *Journal of Applied Behavior Analyses* and author.

system and lists the backup reinforcers. Such a system improved academic performance, but what is most interesting is that it greatly reduced classroom disruptions (Ayllon & Roberts, 1974).

To establish such a program, the teacher first must specify the behavior that is to be performed (e.g., students must finish the mathematics assignment in twenty minutes with either one error or no errors). The teacher then needs to determine the number of tokens a student obtains for correctly doing the behavior (e.g., one token) and formulate a list of reinforcers that the tokens can buy. For example, five tokens might entitle the student to fifteen minutes of free time, while ten tokens might entitle the student not to have to do homework for a night.

Token economy systems sometimes fail because teachers do not adequately establish the criteria for receiving a token or specify the nature of the rewards. The target behavior necessary to receive a token must be reasonable yet challenging. This can be determined by observing the students and finding out how often or with what accuracy they exhibit the targeted behavior. Asking students for 100 percent accuracy when they're obtaining only 20 percent accuracy during the baseline period will not work. Instead, allowing for 40 percent accuracy at first and slowly increasing the percentage is reasonable. Also, for such a system to succeed, the backup reinforcers must be something that children want.

Token reinforcement procedures have many advantages. Tokens can be given immediately after the correct behavior is exhibited. They can be saved for larger reinforcers that would not be practical if given for every correct response, such as taking a trip. There is little danger of satiation, and tokens can be given for many different tasks, such as improvements in both mathematics and reading, and can be exchanged for a variety of reinforcers. Tokens are also concrete symbols of success, and the system encourages students to set goals that would allow them to obtain the reinforcer they want (Stephens & Cooper, 1980). The results also seem to last, although it is best to plan for maintenance (Kazdin, 1982) (discussed shortly). Some people argue that if only one teacher uses the system, student performance in classrooms in which token procedures are not used will suffer. There is no evidence, however, to support this assumption (Kistner et al., 1982).

Token reinforcement systems have their disadvantages, some of which are serious. Such systems require a great deal of bookkeeping, and the system can become a burden. In addition, teachers can become so encouraged by the results that they forget to fade out the system so that students will continue to work for other reinforcers. Tokens can sometimes be lost or stolen, and systems are not always easy to set up. Despite these problems, token economies can be useful. However, because they are so complex, the teacher may first want to try other, simpler procedures, such as a program of social reinforcement, before considering setting up a token reinforcement program. Giving social reinforcement with the tokens is a good policy. If a token reinforcement system is set up properly, it can be very effective in increasing desired behaviors.

Self-Reinforcement

Another approach to reinforcement is to teach students to reinforce themselves. **Self-reinforcement** is the process by which people increase and maintain their behavior using rewards that they control whenever they attain a standard (Dickerson & Creedon, 1981). The key to this process is that the student is the agent of his or her own reinforcement (Goldiamond, 1976). The advantages are many. The approach teaches the student responsibility and independence and takes less teacher time. In addition, normal teacher-administered programs require teachers to notice each time a certain behavior is exhibited, which is not always possible. A teacher may simply not be aware of one student's time spent on a task if he or she is working with another student.

True or False Students can be taught to reinforce themselves.

Self-reinforcement procedures involve teaching students to monitor their own behavior, record it, and reinforce themselves when appropriate. Students can monitor, for example, the number of times they raise their hands or the number of correct answers on a mathematics practice sheet and give themselves reinforcers, such as free time. Self-monitoring by itself leads to small improvement, probably because the

self-reinforcement   A process in which students reinforce themselves for desired behaviors.

student learns how often he or she is engaging in a specific behavior. For example, a student who does not finish his work may not be aware of how often this happens. If he monitors himself, however, he may begin to appreciate the problem. However, awareness results in only a temporary improvement. The reinforcement is necessary as well.

Self-reinforcement is certainly not appropriate for every student, and it does present problems. Recording is more likely to be accurate if the behavior is clearly defined, and teachers must periodically check for accuracy. The teacher may do this by choosing one portion of the desired behavior, keeping a record of it, and comparing it with the student's record.

Contingency Contracts

Contingency contracts are fully written contracts between a teacher and a student (and sometimes a parent) that specifies the rewards for a particular behavior. They may involve bonuses and penalties. The contract can cover academic work, classroom behavior, or homework. A student, teacher, and parent may enter into a contract that says that if the child does her homework with at least 90 percent accuracy, she may stay up an extra half hour that night, and if she meets the standard every day for two weeks, she may have a friend sleep over. A sample contingency contract can be found in Figure 5.1. In one study, Kelley

> **contingency contract**   A contract between teacher and student specifically noting the exact behavior desired and the consequences for performing and perhaps not performing the behavior.

and Stokes (1982) used contingency contracts with disadvantaged youths in a vocational training program. Students were paid contingent on contract fulfillment of academic productivity goals set by mutual agreement between student and teacher. Student productivity more than doubled.

Contingency contracts offer some clear advantages. Students have input into the contract, and the contingencies are specified and can be negotiated. Contracts are flexible and, at times, may be adjusted (Kazdin, 1984). It is best if the payoff is immediate at the beginning and provides for frequent small rewards for improvement. The contract should be clear and reasonable for both parties. (Contingency contracts and self-reinforcement are discussed in greater detail in Chapter 10.)

Home-School Programs

Many teachers would like to set up a behavior-modification program but are afraid that it will take

---

Homework Contract

Every school day Ms. Johnson will check Walter Brown's mathematics homework. If Walter gets 90 percent of the homework examples correct, Ms. Johnson will initial the homework and Ms. Brown will allow Walter to stay up an additional half hour after his traditional bedtime. If Walter gets 90 percent of the homework examples correct for one month, Walter can go to the amusement park for the entire day the following Saturday.

Date: September 15
Expires: December 23

Walter Brown (Student)

Ms. Brown (Parent)

Ms. Johnson (Teacher)

Figure 5.1   Contingency Contract
Contracts can be adapted to meet the specific requirements of the situation.

PART I

Cognition, Development, and Learning

a great deal of time and may even engender some feelings of jealousy in those students who are not participating. In addition, with some children, it may not be easy to identify potent reinforcers in the school environment (Axelrod, 1983). The answer may be a home-school reinforcement program. In such a program, the teachers outline the behavior to be reinforced and are responsible for specifying rules, evaluating the student's work, and communicating with the parents. The parents are asked to dispense the reinforcer. Such home-school reinforcement programs have been used to improve student attention, schoolwork and homework completion, punctuality, classroom preparation, and accuracy (Gresham & Lemanek, 1987).

Evaluations indicate that such programs are quite successful (Atkeson & Forehand, 1979). For instance, in one study, Lahey and colleagues (1977) used the daily report card system in kindergarten classes to increase schoolwork completion. A letter was sent to parents explaining the daily report and telling them *not* to punish the child if the child did not receive positive evaluations. The report just noted, among other things, whether the child followed directions well, completed his or her work, and played well with others. Parents were told to praise their children for positive reports, and this led to improvements in the areas covered. Parents also liked receiving the information.

True or False Reinforcement programs in which teachers ask parents to reinforce students when they have achieved a certain level each day have generally been successful.

In another study, Schumaker and colleagues (1977) used a daily report for three students that included both praise and a token reinforcement system that led to snacks and privileges, such as staying up late. The academic areas targeted included, being punctual and bringing the correct materials to class. Again, the system was successful.

Daily report cards can also be used in the secondary school. Figure 5.2 shows a sample daily report card for a junior high school student. The teacher sends the card home daily at first and later on a weekly basis. The parents' job is to praise the child or administer any other reinforcements agreed to by the parents.

For any home-school program to be successful, the parents must be willing and able to reinforce the child. To determine this, two questions need to be answered: Are the parents willing to do so? and How much training will be required? (Graham-Clay & Reschly, 1987). As for the first question, the parents must be willing to give the praise or the reward, such as staying up later or going to a ball game. It is important to emphasize the need for consistency once the program has begun.

The second question is more difficult to answer. Some parents do not know how to praise their children. In addition, notice that at no time has punishment been mentioned. Punishment is not a part of this procedure. If a child does not measure up to the standards for reward, he simply isn't praised or given the privilege. Parents must not punish, or a number of problems result, including antagonism towards the teacher, a spiral toward worse behavior, and avoidance of both parents and schoolwork. Some parents cannot restrain themselves, and the possibility for verbal or actual physical abuse when a poor report is sent home is present. Parents need to be told that punishment should never be given as a consequence for failure to meet standards, and praise or privileges should be delivered without sarcasm, such as "At last, you finally did good work!" As the child improves, the report cards can be sent home at less frequent intervals, every two or so days, then weekly, then perhaps only occasionally.

Using Prompts or Cues

There are times when we can prevent problems from occurring if we know that a particular environmental cue will lead to an unwanted behavior. We may know, for example, that when we say, "Take out your math books" after students have finished a science assignment, a great deal of talking takes place. We may want to control the situation and offer a different cue. A **cue** (or prompt) is nothing more than a stimulus that provides information to the students that leads them to the desired behavior. For example, we may say to a class, "I know that changing subjects some-

cue (prompt) Any event that helps initiate a desired response.

| Date: _____ | | | | | |
Period	Came to Class on Time	Came to Class Prepared	Homework Completed	Test/Quiz Grades	Cooperation
Science					
Home Economics					
Social Studies					
Gym					
Lunch					
Math					
Spanish					
English					

Comments:

_____
Teacher's Signature

_____
Parent's Signature

Figure 5.2 Sample Daily Report Card for a Junior High School Student
On this daily report card, the teacher simply makes a check mark or writes yes or no where appropriate. If there is a problem or if the teacher wants to indicate a special positive comment, the teacher can do this in a brief manner. Daily report cards can be tailored to fit the individual needs of the student and teacher. This student had shown difficulty completing work, coming to class on time, and did not tell his parents about his grades. Please notice that this daily report card contains only one general heading for behavior marked "cooperation." However, if the student had problems in this area, the general heading might not be used and more specific headings such as stays in seat, raises hand for attention and speaks courteously, might be used.

times leads to a great deal of noise. We waste a lot of time because it takes you too long to settle down. Let's see how quietly we can take out our math books." If the desired behavior occurs, the teacher must reinforce the class.

Cues or prompts are helping aids commonly used in teaching. For example, a teacher might make a big mark on a child's right hand to give the child lots of practice when learning the right hand from the left hand. The mark is a helping aid that eliminates the need for the teacher to correct a student again and again. The size of the mark can be reduced gradually until it is not there (Presbie & Brown, 1985).

Sometimes students require cues to help them control their own behavior. For example, charts that remind students of what is expected in each different lesson help children to improve on task behavior. A short list of behaviors, such as look at the teacher, stay in your seat, write in your books, or read instructions on the blackboard, can often be helpful in reminding students of the proper classroom procedures (Glynn & Thomas, 1974).

Some cues may be physical. Eye contact is an aid that facilitates correction and increases compliance. Teachers sometimes must demand eye contact. If you say the student's name and wait two seconds, the

PART I

Cognition, Development, and Learning

child should respond through eye contact, and the instruction can then be given. If not, the teacher might say, "_____, look at me, please" (Hamlet et al., 1984). However, the teacher must take subcultural differences into account. In some subcultures, it is usual for a person to lower one's eyes when an authority figure is speaking, especially when admonishing someone. The teacher should always be aware of a student's subcultural background and customs. In addition, watching for those stimuli that lead to problems can help teachers change the stimuli and reduce the problems. Providing cues or prompts may help remind students of what is required of them.

The Use of Feedback

Reinforcement has two basic functions. First, it motivates the student, and second, it informs the student that he or she has performed correctly (Axelrod, 1983). The second function is known as **feedback**—information following a behavior that students can use to modify their performance (McClenaghan & Ward, 1987). The corrections on compositions, a statement telling the student that he or she solved the problem correctly, a nod that tells the student that the teacher has noticed his or her hand is raised are all examples of feedback.

Feedback, itself, can be a powerful modifier of behavior, and before a more involved procedure is tried, feedback is a reasonable course. For example, sometimes marking a problem wrong and showing the student how to work the problem correctly is sufficient to help a student learn to solve problems. Feedback encourages students to continue working, ensures that effort is recognized, reduces error, focuses students' attention on a particular area, and shows students what they do and do not know (Chilcoat, 1988). Feedback affects not only the student receiving it but also other students in the vicinity at the same time (Drabman & Lahey, 1974). If one student receives feedback, others hear it and sometimes use it to correct their own work.

> **feedback** Information that helps a student correct his or her behavior.

True or False Feedback—information following a behavior telling students about their performance—should be given sparingly, since it emphasizes student errors.

Sometimes more elaborate feedback procedures are required. For instance, Van Houten and colleagues (1975) found that if a teacher posted the number of comprehension problems that students answered correctly, noting personal highs, the number of problems that students correctly solved doubled. Fink and Carnine (1975) gave students feedback in the form of a note telling them how many errors the students made on mathematics worksheets and plotted the numbers on a graph. The number of errors fell.

There is no doubt that feedback can sometimes be very effective. Feedback is most effective when it is given immediately and is precise. Immediacy is important, since we do not want students practicing the wrong way to solve some problem. The feedback must be precise, since its prime purpose is to give information to the student.

There are two types of feedback: affirmative feedback and corrective feedback. Affirmative feedback is intended to strengthen a desirable response or to improve accuracy. Verbal affirmative feedback for new learning or for students who are hesitant often combines information with social reinforcement. There are four types of affirmative feedback; praise plus praise, praise plus reason, praise plus integration, and personal citation (Chilcoat, 1988). The first method—praise plus praise—signifies approval or correctness and encourages students. This method involves two general affirmative statements back to back, such as "Good," "You are doing better." The second method—praise plus reason—is a statement first identifying the correctness of a response and then explaining why the response is correct, such as "Good going. Those are the four steps used to solve this theorem." The third method—praise plus integration—is a statement by the teacher indicating how a student's response applies to the objective of the lesson, such as "Right, Jimmy. Those are the ways animals defend themselves." The fourth method—personal citation—is a statement that recognizes and appreciates what a student has done as special. It begins with the student's name, followed by a statement that describes how well the student performed the behavior. For example, "Karen, your painting shows great use of perspective."

Feedback gives students information about their work and allows students to modify their performance if necessary.

Corrective verbal feedback is a teacher-made statement identifying something that is incorrect and giving the student information as to how to correct it. It does not indicate disapproval of the person. George Chilcoat suggests three different types. The most common is to give correction and information, such as "No, the battle took place at Saratoga, not Boston." One problem with this method is that some students find it difficult to accept this type of correction, and the second method praise plus correction may work better. "Good for you for trying, but the answer is 5," or "That's very close; his name was Woodrow not William Wilson." Some hint of improvement can be communicated by "That's getting better; you've identified the noun and verb, but 'quickly' is an adverb, not an adjective."

Correction plus reason is the third possibility. Feedback that the answer is wrong is given in addition to a reason. For example, "No, you have given the definition of a pronoun. Nouns are people, places, things, and events." This response first explains why the student's response is wrong and then gives the correct answer.

Feedback can also be used to show students that they have been noticed and must wait their turn. For example, what if you are helping a student or answering a question and three other students have their hands up? If you do nothing, they may call out impatiently. However, if you say something like: "Herb, then Lynn, then Tom," you have given each feedback that tells the students that you know they are waiting.

Feedback is a most useful way of improving academic work and behavior, but it must be done correctly. It must inform students and give them exact information without putting them down or embarrassing them.

Procedures to Reduce the Frequency of a Behavior

All of the procedures so far (with the exception of corrective feedback) are aimed at increasing some response, be it hand raising, study time, time on a task, or accuracy. At times, though, teachers may want to reduce some behavior or substitute a different behavior for one that is shown.

Using Reinforcement to Reduce a Behavior

Although it may sound contrary to the definition of reinforcement given previously, reinforcement can also be used to reduce the frequency of a behavior. Consider for a moment the student who continually bothers the teacher with unnecessary questions or, despite the fact that nothing is wrong with him physically, continually asks to go to the bathroom or to get a drink of water. The teacher often does not want to get rid of these behaviors completely but just wants to reduce them. Reinforcement can be used in three different ways to accomplish this goal.

First, there is **differential reinforcement of low rates of responding** (DRL), which provides for a reinforcer to be delivered when the response is separated from the most recent response by a minimum amount of time (Deitz & Repp, 1974). This is used when reduction but not complete elimination of the behavior is desired. In this technique, the student is reinforced if he or she shows that behavior at or below a specific number of times or amount of time. Using a DRL technique, Deitz and Repp (1974) reduced talking-out behavior of an eleven-year-old when nonexchangeable gold stars were made contingent on two or fewer responses per session.

Another technique, called **differential reinforcement of other** (DRO), demands that an individual completely refrain from a behavior to receive a reinforcer. It is a schedule in which a reinforcer is delivered if a particular response has not been emitted (Repp et al., 1983). In other words, students are reinforced for not performing some behavior. In one class, if children did not display aggression for a specific period of time, they were rewarded with stars that were exchangeable for tangible rewards (Repp & Deitz, 1974). DRL and DRO are relatively easy and do not produce troublesome side effects. The problem with DRO is that behaviors other than the targeted behavior can be reinforced, and it is therefore possible—but certainly not desirable—to reinforce poor behavior.

Another procedure, called **differential reinforcement of an incompatible behavior** (DRI), answers this problem. The teacher reinforces a specific desirable behavior that cannot coexist with the undesirable behavior. For example, a child may be reinforced when in his seat rather than out of his seat. Since the child can't be in two places at once it

differential reinforcement of low rates of responding (DRL) A process in which the reinforcer is delivered for a reduction in the frequency in the target behavior.

differential reinforcement of other (DRO) A process in which the reinforcer is delivered after any response other than the target response is shown.

differential reinforcement of an incompatible behavior (DRI) A process in which a reinforcer is delivered after a response that is incompatible with the target response.

is a reinforcement of an incompatible response. A teacher may reinforce a behavior such as reading, which is incompatible with talking out. Notice that the reinforcement in DRO and DRI procedures are reducing the unwanted behavior by increasing other behaviors.

Extinction Procedures

Extinction involves withholding the reinforcer that is maintaining some behavior (Nelson, 1987). It requires teachers to identify the reinforcer and control it. It is used only when teachers realize that they themselves are reinforcing the poor behavior, perhaps by giving attention for poor work. Let's say that when Jimmy doesn't do his work, he receives a great deal of attention and coaxing. The attention, itself, may be a reinforcer, and the teacher may choose to ignore the poor work itself and use positive reinforcement to increase the accuracy and amount of Jimmy's work. For this to work, the teacher must be certain that the act is being reinforced by his or her own attention. What if calling out is reinforced not only by teacher attention but also by student attention? In such a case, extinction procedures will not work.

Extinction procedures are not as useful in the classroom as are other behavioral procedures (Nelson, 1987). First, they cannot easily be used if the behavior of the child is annoying others. Ignoring talking in class will not lead to extinction of the problem, because it is reinforced by students. Second, even when extinction is working, it is not uncommon that the behavior first becomes worse, a phenomenon known as

extinction burst (Axelrod, 1983). A student may then interrupt the teacher more often during a lesson before extinction begins to take effect. In addition, **spontaneous recovery** may occur. That is, after a rest period, the response may return. The behavior may be extinguished again, but the recurrence is unnerving. Last, consistency is required if a teacher is to ignore a behavior. The teacher who gives in "once in a while" to such behaviors as calling out or doing poor work simply reinforces the behavior under a variable ratio schedule of reinforcement. Extinction, though, can be used as part of a process in which the undesirable behavior is ignored as long as the behavior does not affect other students and the desirable behavior is reinforced. It is, however, of limited usefulness to the regular classroom teacher.

True or False Ignoring the undercurrent of noise in the class caused by student conversations is not a technique that will lead to the reduction or elimination of this undesirable behavior.

Verbal Reprimands

One of the more common ways to reduce a behavior is through a verbal reprimand, such as "Please stop talking" or "Jane, don't turn around." For such reprimands to be effective, they must be delivered right after the targeted misbehavior occurs. The reprimand should be short, businesslike, and aimed directly at the behavior the teacher wants changed. It should give information about the behavior. For example, "Jimmy, stop talking," is reasonable, but a statement such as "Jimmy, you are always disturbing others" does not direct the student's attention to the offending behavior but rather focuses attention on the student. Other important factors include making eye contact, using gestures or facial expressions that indicate disapproval of a behavior, and giving positive reinforcement for appropriate behavior and work (Van Houten et al., 1982; Jones & Miller, 1974). If used moderately for mild behavior and work problems, such teacher response can be useful (Kerr & Nelson, 1983). However, reprimands are often given too frequently and in such a way that they disrupt the class.

Response Cost

Response cost involves taking away a reinforcer—often points or tokens—if the undesired behavior is exhibited. For example, suppose a student receives two points for completing mathematics practice sheets with only one mistake per sheet. However, if there are

extinction burst An increase in the frequency of the response that often occurs when an extinction procedure is begun.

spontaneous recovery The phenomenon in which after extinction has taken place and a rest period ensues, the response thought to be extinguished returns.

response cost A procedure in which a positive reinforcer is lost if an undesirable behavior is exhibited.

more than four mistakes, the student loses a point. In this type of system, the student receives points when the desired behavior is exhibited and loses points only when he is careless. If he makes two or three errors, he does not gain or lose. A student might receive tokens for each time homework is done according to criteria and be penalized when he does not do the homework. A class might be awarded extra recess time if the students do not call out more than twice in a period and might lose some time if they do. This entails some practical problems, however, since both those who are given more recess time and those who are not have to be supervised, necessitating the help of others.

In one study, Rapport and colleagues (1978) used response cost to reduce off-task behavior. Each time an incident of off-task behavior occurred, the teacher removed one minute of a possible thirty minutes of free time that the students were allowed.

Response cost can be administered in various ways. Students can be given free reinforcers and lose them for undesirable behaviors. For example, a student may receive five points at the beginning of the class session and lose a point for a well-publicized infraction. Students can work under a system in which they earn reinforcers for desirable behavior and lose them for undesirable behaviors, such as gaining points for accuracy and losing them for inaccuracy. For example, students can be awarded a total of four points, one point each for accuracy, neatness, organization, and completeness, and lose one point for each one of these not demonstrated on a homework assignment.

Response cost can also be used with a group. For example, specific rules can be presented to a class, and students might be told that they have fifteen minutes of free time but will lose a minute for each violation.

Response cost systems can work but only if the criteria and scoring system are reasonable. If it is very difficult to gain reinforcers but easy to lose them, the situation becomes frustrating. In addition, if errors are to be the reason for losing tokens, students must know the work and be able to do it accurately. This is not a procedure to be used when students are just learning the material and mistakes can be expected.

Other techniques can be used to reduce the frequency of behavior (See chapter 10). However, problems can occur when teachers focus on punishment and ignore the possibilities of using reinforcement procedures. All techniques for reducing the frequency of a behavior are best if they are performed swiftly and are combined with reinforcement for the correct behavior.

But Will It Last?

Imagine that Mr. Evans has just successfully increased Jimmy's time on a task and number of correct answers in mathematics and reduced Jimmy's irritating calling out. Now that Mr. Evans is satisfied with Jimmy's behavior, he ends the program. The result: The problems return. To maintain the new behavior, specific procedures that are usually not very difficult must be incorporated into the program. Maintenance does not just occur; it must be planned (Forman, 1987). In fact, if a teacher has been successful using a behavior-modification program and finds that after the program stops the student returns to his or her old ways, it does not mean that the program has been unsuccessful but merely that the teacher has failed to see it through.

Once the desired behavior has been established, it can be maintained in a number of ways. First, the prompts and reinforcers can be **faded,** meaning that the prompts or reinforcers that help a student perform a behavior are gradually removed. Let's say that for a

fading   The gradual removal of a prompt or reinforcer.

child to learn to do a multiplication word problem, a number of verbal prompts are necessary, including, perhaps, statements such as read the problem, ask yourself what the problem asks, and set up the example. After the child shows that she knows the material, you might take away one of these prompts, then two, then three, until the child no longer requires the prompts. When the teacher who is trying to teach a child left from right places a crayon mark on the right hand of the child and each day makes the mark smaller and smaller, he is using fading.

Reinforcers are also faded. What if, at the beginning of a procedure, you had to reinforce the child each time she showed the response? Once she knows the response, you can use a partial reinforcement schedule, perhaps beginning with one reinforcer every second correct answer and then further reducing reinforcement. In addition, if a tangible reinforcer is being used, introducing the practice of giving a social reinforcer such as praise and then reducing the use of the tangible reward can be effective. If you are using token reinforcement, you can slowly increase the severity of the criteria required for the reward and at the same time add social reinforcement each time the correct behavior is shown.

True or False   After a behavior has been learned, the number of reinforcements given should be increased to maintain the behavior.

Delaying reinforcement is another approach that is sometimes used. When something is learned, at first the reinforcer is given immediately. When the child has mastered the task, the reinforcer can sometimes be gradually withdrawn by lengthening the time between action and reinforcement.

The use of feedback alone may be sufficient at times to maintain the level of performance. However, it should be understood that occasionally special rewards may still be required.

Of course, not all behaviors require maintenance procedures. A child who learns to read well may find reading enjoyable. A child who learns to interact with other children in a positive manner may continue even after the program is withdrawn. The child who feels good about his or her achievement may not require much more incentive to continue the new behavior. In such cases, other reinforcers have taken over. However, many behaviors require a maintenance procedure.

But Is It Ethical?

At times, I've heard teachers complain about using reinforcement procedures. Why reinforce students for what they should be doing anyhow? After all, students should do their work to the best of their ability, behave reasonably in class, and act in a responsible manner. Why use reinforcement? Isn't this akin to bribing students?

These are sound questions, but answers are readily available. Objections are much more likely to be raised regarding the use of token or tangible reinforcement than they would be for social reinforcement. No one seriously questions the desirability of showing students approval when they do something right, and all the behavioral technique does in this case is to ask teachers to do it on a more regular and contingent basis. The ethical questions surrounding the use of token or tangible reinforcement are more pressing. However, the term *bribery* is a poor one, loaded with bad connotations. When someone is bribed, it usually involves doing something unnatural or illegal. None of the uses we've looked at here fit that category. In addition, as teachers, we enjoy getting a paycheck or even a letter from a parent saying that the family discusses around the dinner table the same topics we've talked about in the classroom. These are also rewards.

Also remember that it is always our aim to eventually obtain the desired behavior without the use of external reinforcers. Note, too, that at no time in the discussion of reinforcers did we talk about using a reinforcer that was involved in the child's total well-being or health. For example, we may use food as a reinforcer, but no one ever advocated using an entire meal as a reinforcer for students.

Another concern is coercion. This does not arise so much when an individual student is the target for the reinforcers we are using, such as praise or tokens for free time. However, it can arise when using group contingency procedures. One such procedure is called the *good behavior game*. Barrish and colleagues (1969) divided a regular fourth-grade class into two teams. After discussing specific class rules, the teacher told the teams that if she saw any student breaking a rule, the team would receive a check mark. The team with the fewest check marks would receive privileges and free time at the end of the day. If both teams had fewer than five marks, they would both receive the rewards. But what of the pressure exerted on the few individuals who may cause the group to lose? Such individuals are likely to be open to bullying or ridicule or worse. The answer here is for the teacher to be fully aware of the coercion problem and attempt to devise group strategies where both groups can win. If coercion and social problems develop, programs must be redesigned immediately.

Home-based reinforcement programs have some ethical difficulties as well (Graham-Clay & Reschly, 1987). An ethical problem arises with a parent who, despite admonitions from the teacher, punishes the child or humiliates the child for not succeeding. The best answer here is for teachers to individually get to know the parents and design the program to fit the ability level of the parents. If the parents punish the child despite being told not to punish, the program should be discontinued immediately.

▶▶▶ CONNECTIONS

Behavior Modification and the Teacher

Teachers use reinforcement and some forms of punishment frequently but often inconsistently. Sometimes, teachers begin programs of reinforcement without adequately planning them out, find the programs fail, and incorrectly argue that the programs are too unwieldy or difficult to administer. Some behavior-modification programs are relatively simple to design and use, while others, such as token reinforcement, may be more involved and should perhaps be used only after some of the easier techniques have not worked.

How does a teacher go about using behavior-modification programs? It involves the following procedures.

1. **Target the behavior.** The first step is to specify the behavior that the teacher wants to change. Although this may seem simple, it is not. Such statements as "I want the child to act better," "I want the child to work harder," or "I want the child to act more maturely" may make sense to us, but they do nothing to target the behavior. Specific behaviors must be targeted, such as improving accuracy in seatwork from 40 percent to 60 percent, spending more time on a task by reducing talking by 10 percent, reducing calling out to once (or not at all) per period, doing homework each night, or bringing a pencil, pen, and notebook to class each day. These are specific behaviors that teachers can observe and measure.

2. Obtain a baseline. Let's suppose we want to encourage Jimmy to bring his materials to school. To see the improvement, we must have some idea of what was happening before the behavior-modification program was introduced. If good records are not kept, it is impossible to evaluate the success of the program. In addition, what if we want to improve the accuracy of a child's seat-work? The child probably has already done some work correctly before we begin the behavior-modification program and probably will not always receive a perfect score even after the program is operating. It is best to be able to say that Armand usually does half the work correctly in mathemat-

ics, one quarter in science, and so on. Then if there is improvement to, say, 80 percent in mathematics and 50 percent in science, we know that our procedures are working.

Sometimes charts are kept and the material is graphed as in Figure 5.3 which shows a child's talk-outs counted during one half hour each day. The solid line shows the number of talk-outs for a child, while the dotted line shows the teacher's self-count of verbal praises given to any child in the class during another class period. The first section entitled "baseline" provides a basis for comparing the student's behavior before and after the procedures designed to reduce talk-outs are implemented. In

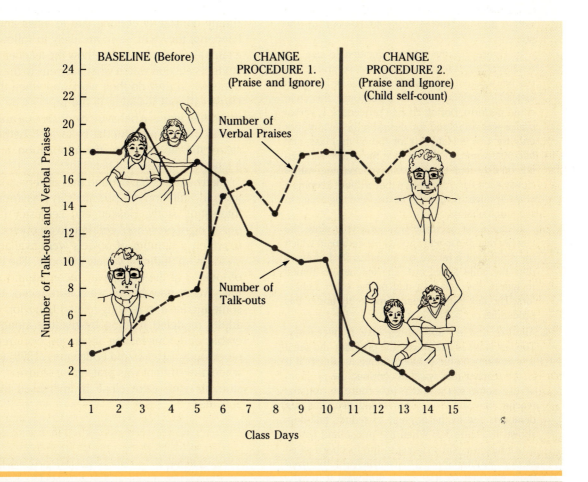

Figure 5.3 Graph of Child's Talk-Outs

In this graph, notice the pattern of both the student's talk-outs and the teacher's use of two strategies, praise and ignore and praise and self-count, over the course of about two weeks.

From *Behavior Modification*, 2d ed., by R. J. Presbie and P. L. Brown. Copyright © 1987 by the National Education Association. Adapted with permission.

this case, you may notice that in the last two days of the baseline, the teacher's praise increased and the student's calling out decreased. Such changes occur because baseline activities force teachers to become aware not only of the student's behavior but also of their own behavior, and sometimes the teachers begin to change. This may cause the baseline to change and should be considered when evaluating the effectiveness of the program.

3. **Choose a procedure.** Now the teacher is ready to change the environment in some way. The procedure must be worked out carefully and be practical. The criteria for receiving the reinforcer(s) must be precise and communicated clearly to the student. The reinforcement procedure must require a response that the student can attain, such as improving from 40 percent correct to 70 percent rather than improving from 40 percent to 100 percent.

In Figure 5.3, the teacher decided to use the reinforcer of teacher praise. The response the teacher wanted, the child's raising his or her hand instead of calling out was a response the child could perform. During change procedure 1, verbal praise was increased for desirable behaviors, not only for this student but for the entire class, and talk-outs were ignored. Notice the praise rate rising quickly and the talk outs decreasing rather slowly each day. Also notice that without keeping a chart, it might be difficult at the very beginning to see much change.

Because the decrease was somewhat slow, the teacher decided to add another procedure in which the child kept a record on an index card of every time the child talked out. The teacher continued to ignore the talk-outs and praise other behaviors. The talk outs decreased markedly under this procedure.

4. **Analyze and try something else if necessary.** The last stage is to evaluate the program and see if it is working. Is the behavior being modified? If it is, the teacher may want to continue the program or use some maintenance procedure. If not, the teacher may want to try something else. This was demonstrated in the attempt to reduce talk-outs shown in Figure 5.3. When the praise and ignore procedure was not working to the teacher's satisfaction, another approach was tried which proved more effective. Most teachers first want to try the least intrusive method, and only if it does not work will they inaugurate a more involved procedure. The aim is to not take up too much of the class's time. However, if something doesn't work, teachers should be prepared to try something else that might be more involved but may have a greater chance of success. It may be necessary, and in fact even desirable, to ask another teacher or the school psychologist who may be more experienced in this area for help in improving the procedures and suggesting alternatives.

Social Learning Theory: Learning Through Observation

We don't need to experience everything ourselves. We can learn from watching others. If students see Jimmy constantly coming late to class and nothing happens, they will be more likely to follow Jimmy's example. Students observe how the teacher and other students act and watch what happens to the other students when they do their work and when they don't. **Observational learning** is the process by which an individual learns a behavior by observing another person (a model) perform the behavior. The person observes the model, stores the information, and may at a later time imitate the behavior.

Many studies have found that observational learning and imitation are prevalent in classrooms. In an interesting study, Haskett and Lenfestey (1974) exposed eight preschool children to an open classroom in which a number of objects were available to the children, including a variety of books. The initial rate of looking at the books was recorded and was quite low. When new books were introduced, there was some increase in reading-related behavior, but when adults modeled reading by reading aloud, considerable and long-lasting increases occurred. In another study, Broden and colleagues (1970) found that when one student was praised for studying, the other students who were close by increased their study activities.

observational learning   Learning by observing others.

We are justly concerned about the models children have around them. When I was coaching a roller hockey team, I witnessed some very aggressive behavior—dropping gloves to fight and stick-related infractions, such as slashing. One wonders what effect these same behaviors shown on television in professional hockey may have had on these youngsters.

Imitation has always been part of the behavioral tradition. However, the study of observational learning, called **social learning theory,** has added a cognitive dimension (Bandura, 1986). Behaviorists tend to treat imitative learning as a case of matching one's behavior to the behavior of a model who is reinforced for some behavior. However, the leading authority in this field, Albert Bandura, believes that this conception is too restricted and fails to account for novel responses. People may learn a behavior through observation but not perform the acts in exactly the same way. Children do more than merely mimic. They often derive some information from what they see. Children who witness a great deal of aggression may not aggress in the same way. They may simply learn that aggression is a way to solve one's problems. Children who are exposed to creative adults may not copy the model's exact creative behaviors but will learn that creativity is acceptable and perhaps will learn to use their imagination.

The Process of Imitation

We can understand imitation as a four-step process (Bandura, 1977; 1986) involving attention, retention, motor reproduction, and motivational processes.

Attention. The first step is paying attention to the model. The child cannot learn unless he or she attends to the model. Attention, though, has a number of aspects to it. A student may be attending to the model but not to the model's particular behavior that is being encouraged. For example, a teacher may be modeling a method of reading out loud while the student is attending to the teacher's

hand tapping against the desk. To obtain relevant attention, it may be necessary to use a prompt and tell the student, "Now listen carefully to the way I _____." Second, whether the student pays attention or not depends upon the characteristics of the model, the functional value of the behavior, and the characteristics of the observer. Models who are regular associates and peers, who are personally engaging and prestigious, and who are seen as deserving trust or credibility gain attention. Models that have high status, are successful at what they do, and show competence and power are also effective. The functional value of the behavior is also an important consideration. If the behavior is relevant and understandable, it is likely to garner attention. The characteristics of the learner, including his arousal status (is he drowsy?), interest level, and past performance, also influence attention. Attention, then, is no simple phenomenon (see Chapter 3).

Retention. If the behavior that the child has noticed is to be used, it must be encoded and stored. The process of memory was discussed in Chapter 3.

Motor Reproduction. In this step, the individual selects the behavior and executes it. Motor reproduction is, of course, influenced by the developmental level of the child as well as by the child's history. Even if a child wants to hit a baseball like his or her favorite ballplayer, he or she may not physically be able to. In addition, people learn a number of things through observation that they may never exhibit in their behavior. Children witness hundreds of murders on television as well as all sorts of other behaviors, including poor behavior in the classroom, but may never perform these acts. The behaviors may be stored, but inhibitions against doing them may prevent a person from acting on the information.

Motivational Processes. After the child produces the behavior, some reinforcement must be available. According to Bandura, reinforcement provides children with information about what might happen in the future if they perform the particular behavior. It can also motivate children. Children may remember the consequences of the behavior and then later on use the information to attain their own ends. They do not have to experience the reinforcement personally. Three processes function as motivation: direct reinforcement, vicarious

social learning theory A theory of learning emphasizing the importance of imitation and observational learning.

reinforcement (i.e., seeing others reinforced), and self-reinforcement. Students who anticipate that if they study they will be reinforced are more likely to study. But direct reinforcement is not necessary. Vicarious reinforcement can also affect the probability of performance. If the model is reinforced for doing something, it could encourage such behavior in the observer. Observing others being punished conveys information about which behaviors are and are not tolerated. The third motivator is self-reinforcement, which was discussed previously.

True or False For students to learn, they must be reinforced directly.

Bandura also noted that in the acquisition of very complex skills, self-efficacy and self-regulation are important. Self-efficacy is the belief that one can successfully perform the behavior and produce the necessary outcome. Self-regulation involves establishing standards for oneself, observing one's own behavior, and evaluating it. These areas are discussed in Chapters 8 and 10.

▶▶▶ CONNECTIONS

Using Social Learning Theory in the Classroom

Social learning theory has a number of implications for the classroom teacher.

1. **Models are important.** Social learning theory emphasizes the importance of models in a child's life. The teacher is one such model. Since the teacher represents authority and the community, his or her deportment and sincerity are likely to be observed carefully by students. More specifically, the teacher models problem-solving behaviors that students can follow. For example, it was noted in Chapter 4 that teachers can model thinking processes that show how they solve a problem and model cognitive flexibility when changing from one problem-solving method to another.

2. **Teachers should be aware of the possibility of incorporating models into instructional activities.** It may be possible to have doctors, nurses, firefighters, or business executives speak at the school. Such people are especially effective if their work is connected to the work in class.

3. **Teachers should plan demonstrations carefully.** Teachers planning to demonstrate some academic skill that they hope students will carefully observe and follow sometimes make the mistake of going too fast, not emphasizing the steps, or not noting why a decision was made to do A rather than B. Demonstrations are more effective when the steps taken are clearly noted and logically presented and when students are told why one strategy was used over another. In addition, if the procedure is complex, students require considerable practice, and fading may be necessary. That is, if the procedure requires, say, five steps, the teacher could take the students through all the steps at first, then gradually reduce his or her participation by demonstrating only four steps, then three, etc. Demonstrations are discussed in more detail in Chapter 11.

4. **Teachers should be aware that how they handle a situation for one student will affect the other students.** If a student does not do his or her homework or—on the positive side—works well in class, other students will attend to how the teacher treats the student. If no sanction is applied to the students who do not do their homework, the others will follow. In addition, if students who do their work are praised, this will have an effect on the other students.

5. **Teachers should use the process by which people learn through observation in instruction.** Bandura noted that the process of learning through observation involves attention, retention, motor reproduction, and motivational processes, each of which needs to be taken into consideration. Since attention is so important, it is necessary to give cues telling students where and when to attend. Younger students especially need such cues. The functional value of a behavior can be raised by directly reinforcing peer models for appropriate behavior and making material relevant to students. In addition, if students are to use what they have learned, practice in motor reproduction is vital to success. Too little practice will lead to inadequate performance.

6. **Modeling can be used in an attempt to transfer responsibility for learning from the teacher to the students.** You may recall that in the method of teaching called reciprocal teaching (refer to Chapter 4), the teacher modeled a method of conducting a reading lesson after which various students were given the task of doing the same. Students can also be trained to give presentations and help other students when teachers model and demonstrate these skills.

USING A LEARNING THEORY APPROACH TO TEACHING

Behavior modification is a strong approach to improving academic performance and student behavior. There seems to be no doubt that such procedures can be used by teachers. Social learning reminds us of the importance of models and learning through observation. The question that is frequently asked is, What does the behavioral approach have to say about instruction? The great behaviorist, B. F. Skinner (1987), addressed this question, arguing that we could solve major problems in education and students could learn more without longer schooldays, longer school years, or more homework if we would adopt four procedures:

B. F. Skinner is the most prominent behaviorist. His writings on many topics, including education, are both controversial and thought provoking.

1. Be clear about what is to be taught. Teachers, students, and parents must all understand what is to be taught. This also involves understanding the standards for being reinforced. Too often the objectives are fuzzy, which causes infinite problems in trying to measure what students have learned. The behavioral approach stands for objectivity and precision. Without understanding the goals, it becomes difficult to demonstrate meaningful progress.
2. Teach first things first. Skinner claims that we are too quick to move to final products without explaining where to start. The end goal of excellence (whatever that might be) or even of creativity does not tell students where to start. Students must be taught the basics, and we, as educators, must become responsible for understanding and teaching the progression of steps leading towards the end result. This is essential to the educational process.
3. Stop making all students advance at essentially the same rate. We pay lip service to individual differences in rate of progress, but Skinner argues that we cannot succeed if we expect every student to work at the same pace. Tracking is a feeble remedy, and Skinner advocates the use of individual instruction and new technologies that allow students to proceed at their own pace.
4. Program the subject matter. This is partially the translation of the first three procedures into action. Skinner argues that material must be organized so that students are first told what they will be doing, then prompted, and finally given immediate correction and reinforcement on an individualized basis.

INSTRUCTION USING BEHAVIORAL IDEAS

The preceding ideas have led to the call for more instruction that would allow students to proceed at their own pace, would have well-thought-out and measurable goals, and would carefully present first things first. A number of such programs have been advanced, including programmed instruction, personalized instruction, and precision teaching.

Programmed Instruction

The need for individualized pacing, immediate feedback, teaching in organized small steps, specific objectives, and reinforcement are all satisfied in a type of instruction long advocated by Skinner called programmed instruction. **Programmed instruction** (PI) is a self-instructional process in which material is presented to the student either through a computer or in book form in a step-by-step progression from easier to more difficult and provides immediate feedback to the student (Maher et al., 1987). In PI, the student is exposed to a well-thought-out, rational sequence of steps, beginning with what he or she knows and slowly taking the student to the desired objective. Instruction is broken into small pieces called frames. The student is often presented with a statement, asked a question about the statement, and given immediate feedback.

There are two types of programs. Linear programs

programmed instruction A self-instructional process in which material is presented to students in a step-by-step progression from easier to more difficult and provides students with immediate feedback.

are instructional materials in which all students, regardless of ability, proceed through the program in the same way (see Table 5.2). If the student makes an error, he or she repeats the steps until the mistake is corrected. Linear programmed instruction uses small bits of information—generally one or two sentences—and requires students to compose their own answers rather than selecting from a number of possible an-

---

Table 5.2   Linear Programs

Part of a program in high school physics. The machine presents one item at a time. The student completes the item and then uncovers the corresponding word or phrase shown at the right.

Sentence to be completed	Word to be supplied
1. The important parts of a flashlight are the battery and the bulb. When we "turn on" a flashlight, we close a switch that connects the battery with the _____.	bulb
2. When we turn on a flashlight, an electric current flows through the fine wire in the _____ and causes it to grow hot.	bulb
3. When the hot wire glows brightly, we say that it gives off or sends out heat and _____.	light
4. The fine wire in the bulb is called a filament. The bulb "lights up" when the filament is heated by the passage of a(n) _____ current.	electric
5. When a weak battery produces little current, the fine wire, or _____, does not get very hot.	filament
6. A filament which is *less* hot sends out or gives off _____ light.	less
7. "Emit" means "send out." The amount of light sent out, or "emitted," by a filament depends on how _____ the filament is.	hot
8. The higher the temperature of the filament the _____ the light emitted by it.	brighter, stronger
9. If a flashlight battery is weak, the _____ in the bulb may still glow, but with only a dull red color.	filament
10. The light from a very hot filament is colored yellow or white. The light from a filament which is not very hot is colored _____.	red
11. A blacksmith or other metal worker sometimes makes sure that a bar of iron is heated to a "cherry red" before hammering it into shape. He uses the _____ of the light emitted by the bar to tell how hot it is.	color
12. Both the color and the amount of light depend on the _____ of the emitting filament or bar.	temperature
13. An object which emits light because it is hot is called incandescent. A flashlight bulb is an incandescent source of _____.	light

From "Teaching Machines," Table 2, vol. 128, p. 973, 24 October 1958 by B. F. Skinner. Reprinted by permission of *Science* and the author. Copyright © 1958 by the AAAS.

swers. No frames are skipped. Students can proceed at their own pace, with some proceeding through the programs faster than others.

A branched program is more complex and works differently. In this program, the order in which material is presented varies depending on the student's success or failure. The student is offered a number of answers to a question and must choose one answer. If the answer is correct, the learner is directed to the next step. An incorrect answer leads to other frames that may explain the error and give additional instruction or review. A branched program allows slower learners to go through the material in smaller steps than faster learners would take (see Figure 5.4). Usually, the learner is presented a paragraph or two and then asked a series of questions. If the learner selects the correct responses, she goes on to the next piece of information. If not, she is told to go to a remedial section or loop that will explain why her answers are wrong and is then referred back to the original questions to select an alternative response.

The advantages and disadvantages of programmed instruction have been extensively researched. Active involvement is one advantage. Students involved in programmed instruction must actively participate, whereas in many classes only a few students are actively involved. Programmed instruction is individualized and self-paced, which allows faster students to go faster and slower students to go at their own pace. These programs also offer immediate reinforcement for correct responses (Skinner, 1986). In addition, making an error is not a public humiliation. Programmed instruction presents material to students in small steps and in a very rational manner. It provides review, since review is written into the program. Last, it frees the teacher for helping other students and attending to other tasks.

Disadvantages (or perhaps criticisms would be a better way of putting it) have been noted as well. First, programmed learning is obviously only as good as the program itself, and programs are relatively expensive to write. Since this is not the type of material that a teacher could sit down and continually compose, programs have to be purchased. They may not all match the instructional objectives of the school. In addition, students do become bored with the technique, and motivation is a problem (Borich, 1988). This last objection is answered by many proponents. Motivation and challenge can be built into the sequence through branching techniques and humorous

or unexpected responses within the program format (Maher et al., 1987). However, this is not easy to do.

A number of programmed learning workbooks are available. In addition, many tutorial programs that are delivered via computer are based upon the principles of programmed learning and are discussed extensively in Chapter 12. Today, programmed learning is used, especially for slower students, as an adjunct to regular instruction.

The Keller Plan: Personalized System of Instruction

Another instructional technique using behavioral methods is Fred Keller's Personalized System of Instruction (PSI) (Keller, 1968). Keller's method differs from conventional teaching because it is mastery oriented and self-paced and uses printed study guides to direct student learning and occasional lectures to stimulate and motivate the student. It has become somewhat popular at the college level.

Work in PSI courses is divided into topics or units. At the start of the course, the student receives a study guide to direct the work on the first unit. The student may work anywhere, including the classroom, to achieve the objectives and may come to class during regular class hours to receive individual help or simply to take a quiz on the unit. Quizzes are evaluated immediately. There is no penalty for failure to pass a quiz, but the student must pass the quiz demonstrating mastery before going on to the next unit. Some students meet the course requirements before the term is over, while others require a longer period of time. Students who fail to achieve at a preestablished level of mastery (80 or 90 percent) may work with fellow students who have achieved mastery, or they may study until they do.

Studies show that PSI does work. One review of seventy-five studies shows that students do better in PSI than in conventional classes and rate the classes as more enjoyable although more demanding. The overall completion rates are similar as well (Kulik et al., 1979).

Precision Teaching

Precision teaching is another technique based on behavioral concepts that is used with students with dis-

Frame 1

When issued a driver's license, the driver is granted the privilege of using Wisconsin streets and highways as long as he obeys the traffic laws and drives in a safe manner.

Question 1

Upon obtaining a Wisconsin driver's license, the driver

(a) is permitted to drive in any manner he chooses, (p. 5)
(b) should remember his responsibilities for safety. (p. 7)
(c) is obligated to renew his license periodically. (p. 6)

Student Answers

(p. 5) Upon obtaining a Wisconsin driver's license, the driver is permitted to drive in any manner he chooses.

   Whoops! Obviously, this is wrong. Whether a driver has just received his license or is an experienced driver, he never has the right to drive as he pleases. One of the remaining two answers is better than this one. Go back to the question on page 1 and see if you can find it.

(p. 6) Upon obtaining a Wisconsin drive's license, the driver is obligated to renew his license periodically.

   While this is true, it is not the answer for which you are looking. Return to page 1 and select a better answer.

(p. 7) Upon obtaining a Wisconsin driver's license, the driver should remember his responsibilities for safety.

   Right you are! A driver must always assume responsibility when operating a motor vehicle. This means obeying the traffic laws and driving in a safe manner. Now you are ready to go to additional information in Frame 2 (page 2).

Frame 2

Special attention must be given to traffic violators, to drivers involved in accidents, and to those whose physical condition makes safe driving questionable. The Driver Improvement Bureau was created to deal with such people. If this cannot be achieved, the Bureau has no alternative but to suspend or cancel the driver's license.

Question 2

The agency created to deal with drivers whose physical condition is questionable is the

(a) Highway Patrol. (p. 8)
(b) Department of Public Safety. (p. 10)
(c) Driver Improvement Bureau. (p. 9)

Student Answers

(p. 8) The agency created to deal with drivers whose physical condition is questionable is the Highway Patrol.

Figure 5.4 Branched Program
Note that if the person responds with the incorrect answer the individual is directed to the page in the book where the correct answer can be found. The learner must answer the question correctly before continuing.

Adapted by permission from *Introduction to Educational Psychology* by Herschel D. Thornburg, pp. 412–413. Copyright © 1984 by West Publishing Company. All rights reserved.

No, not in this case. Of course, the Highway Patrol will apprehend a driver whose physical condition obviously is interfering with safe driving. But this agency was not created for the improvement of the individual's driving. With this clue you should return to page 2 and select another response.

(p. 9) The agency created to deal with drivers whose physical condition is questionable is the Driver Improvement Bureau.

Excellent! This is the correct answer. The Driver Improvement Bureau was specifically created to deal with traffic violators, drivers involved in accidents, and those whose physical condition is in question. The basic purpose of this agency is to create self-improvement in the licensed driver. Now that you have successfully answered this question, let's try Frame 3 (page 3).

(p. 10) The agency created to deal with drivers whose physical condition is questionable is the Department of Public Safety.

Incorrect! This answer is too general. The Department of Public Safety has many functions, but it was not specifically created to deal with drivers whose physical condition is questionable. Go back to page 2 and select a more appropriate answer.

Figure 5.4 continued

abilities who are newly mainstreamed, placed into a regular class. In this system, the teacher first finds a target behavior that the student must master and then charts the student's progress in learning that single skill. Perhaps the skill is to know how to use a particular number of vocabulary words or to be able to read at a particular rate. The student's mastery of the targeted behavior is tested, usually on a daily basis, and the number of correct and incorrect responses given in a specified time period (sometimes one minute) is charted. These tests are called probes (Raybould, 1984). Mastery is defined in terms of a certain rate of correct responses, for example, reading 100 to 140 words per minute with two or fewer errors.

Precision teachers record the daily performance of each student and chart the results. The value of the daily charting lies in the fact that it offers a direct, continuous, and precise measurement system. Teaching in this model is direct and simple. It can involve a number of materials and methods, including commercially prepared materials, drill sheets, flash cards, and games. The results are impressive (Mercer, 1986).

What Teachers Can Take with Them from the Behavioral Model

We've now looked at the possible uses of the behavioral model in both improving student academic per-

formance, behavior, and its use in instruction. Of course, the many behavioral techniques are valuable. However, the behavioral model reminds us of the importance of stating objectives precisely, teaching in small steps in logical order, of active responding, the necessity for recitation and practice followed by feedback, and the need to use reinforcement.

In the midst of the cognitive revolution, it is easy to forget strategies that have worked in the past. Sometimes these strategies have seemed cold and distant, but this need not be the case. In fact, nothing is warmer than a smile from the teacher, the feeling of success that comes when one has reached a goal, or a compliment from a parent. The behavioral approach to teaching and behavior modification has much to offfer teachers, and behavioral methods present teachers with useful strategies for improving both behavior and academic skills.

SUMMARY

1. The behavioral view emphasizes objectivity in defining problems, writing measurable goals for behavior change, the use of research from learning theory to design programs, and continuous evaluation of these programs.
2. Classical or respondent conditioning involves the pairing of a neutral stimulus with a stimulus that

elicits a particular response until the stimulus that was originally neutral elicits that response. It is useful for explaining emotional reactions.

3. In operant conditioning, behavior is determined by its consequences. If the consequences are positive, the action is likely to recur. If the consequences are aversive, the behavior is less likely to occur again. Any event following a behavior that increases the probability that the behavior will recur is called a reinforcer. Reinforcement should be made contingent upon some desired behavior, be delivered as soon after the desired behavior as possible, and be individualized and varied.

4. Reinforcers may be delivered on a continuous basis, that is, each time the correct response is given. Behaviors learned under continuous reinforcement are learned quickly but are extinguished rather quickly. Reinforcers may also be given under a partial reinforcement schedule; that is, not every correct behavior will be reinforced. It takes longer to learn a response under partial reinforcement, but when learned, it is more resistant to extinction. There are four types of partial reinforcement schedules: fixed ratio, fixed interval, variable ratio, and variable interval. Teachers may use edible or tangible reinforcers, social reinforcers, and activity reinforcers.

5. In negative reinforcement the reward for the correct behavior is a reduction or elimination of an aversive stimulus. For example, the reward for an A on a test is no homework that night.

6. The use of operant conditioning techniques to alter behavior is known as behavior modification. Token reinforcement involves rewarding students for correct behavior with tokens that can then be turned in immediately or saved up and later used to obtain larger reinforcers. At times, contracts might be written that precisely state what behaviors will lead to specific reinforcers. Students may also be taught to reinforce themselves, and at times, parents might be partners in a reinforcement program by delivering an agreed-upon reinforcer when instructed to do so by the teacher.

7. Feedback is information that students can use to modify their performance. Feedback is most effective when it is immediate and precise.

8. There are many behavioral techniques for reducing the frequency of a particular behavior. A teacher using differential reinforcement of low rates of responding (DRL) will reinforce a student if the response is separated from the preceding response by a minimum amount of time. Differential reinforcement of other responses (DRO) demands that a student completely refrain from a behavior and other behaviors are reinforced. Differential reinforcement of an incompatible behavior (DRI) is used when a behavior that is incompatible to the undesirable response is reinforced. Extinction procedures are effective only if the reinforcement is under the direct control of the teacher. Verbal reprimands are most effective if they are delivered immediately and are short and businesslike and if positive reinforcement is administered for the appropriate behavior. In response cost, a reinforcer is taken away if an undesired behavior is exhibited.

9. It is often necessary to plan maintenance into a program. One way is through fading, that is, gradually removing the reinforcers or prompts being used. Teachers designing a behavior-modification program should target the behavior, obtain a baseline, choose a procedure, and evaluate it.

10. Social learning theory emphasizes the importance of learning through observing others. It involves four processes: attention, memory, motor reproduction, and motivational processes.

11. B. F. Skinner argues that we could improve education if we were clear about what is to be taught, if we taught material beginning with the basics and slowly moved up to more difficult material, if we stopped making all students advance at the same rate, and if we programmed the subject matter.

12. Programmed instruction is a self-instructional process in which material is presented to the student in a step-by-step progression from easier to more difficult and immediate feedback is delivered. Linear programs are programs in which each student proceeds through the program as small bits of information are presented and no frames are skipped. If students make mistakes, they return to previous frames. In a branching program, the order of presentation varies depending on the student's success or failure. Students who make an incorrect response are directed to a loop in which additional instruction and correction are given. In the personalized system of instruction, students work individually and take tests as they feel competent to do so. Precision teaching uses precise daily measurements of

achievement on a given objective to improve performance.

13. The behavioral approach to instruction involves defining objectives precisely, teaching in small steps, encouraging active responding, and emphasizing the importance of practice and feedback and the need to use reinforcement.

ACTIVITIES AND EXERCISES

1. **Using Reinforcement in the Classroom.** Three types of reinforcers—edibles and tangibles, social reinforcers, and activity reinforcers—were discussed in this chapter. The first and third are more likely to be used in elementary school, while the second might be used at all levels. As you observe a class, take note of the use of reinforcers in the classroom. If a teacher has a reputation for using reinforcement, ask the instructor how he or she sets up the program.

2. **Social Reinforcement—How Often Is it Used?** One of the surprising findings in a number of studies is that teachers do not use social reinforcement as much as one would think. In addition, sometimes students reinforce a fellow student for a behavior that might be the opposite of the one the teacher wants. Last, teachers sometimes reinforce students with attention for poor behavior. Taking these facts into consideration, observe a class with the aim of identifying the social reinforcers used. Answer the following questions: Are the reinforcers given contingent upon certain behaviors? Are the students reinforcing one another for behaviors different from those the teacher wants to reinforce? Is the teacher reinforcing students for poor behavior?

3. **How Were You Rewarded or Punished?** List the names of four of your past teachers. They can be elementary, junior high, or high school teachers. Write down what you remember about their use of reinforcement and punishment. From what you remember, were the methods effective? If not, why not? Do you remember the punishments better than the rewards? If so, why? Discuss with some of your classmates how their former teachers used reinforcers or punishments.

4. **Designing a Reinforcement Program.** As an exercise, design a behavior-modification program to

a. increase the percentage of correct answers on mathematics practice sheets of a student who usually gets only one or two correct out of ten.

b. increase the number of students in your class who do their homework each night.

c. increase the frequency with which students raise their hands instead of shouting out answers.

d. decrease the number of students who come to class unprepared for work.

e. improve the spelling proficiency of students in the class.

5. **The Experience of Using Reinforcement Techniques.** There is no substitute for personal experience. If you are in a position to do so, choose a student who shows a behavior at a low frequency that you would like to increase. For example, perhaps the student obtains only a moderate score on mathematics practice sheets and you want the pupil to improve by 30 percent. Design a reinforcement procedure and carry it out. The reinforcement may be as simple as the use of praise or attention. It is advisable to check your procedure with your educational psychology professor as well as the student's teacher before you begin.

6. **Using Prompts and Cues.** Prompts can be considered reminders and cues as information that lead the student to the desired behavior. Design prompts or cues to handle the following situations:

a. Students make a great deal of noise when switching from one subject to another. Much time is wasted until students attend to the new lesson.

b. Students have a great deal of difficulty solving word problems.

c. Students don't seem to remember the rules of the classroom.

d. Students do not seem to know what information they need to write down in their notebooks.

7. **Practice Using Feedback.** Feedback is information that follows a behavior and that students can use to modify their performance. Feedback can be divided into two categories: affirmative and corrective. Affirmative feedback includes praise plus praise, praise plus reason, praise plus integration, and personal citation. Corrective feedback includes correction and information, praise and correction, and correction plus reason. Write

a feedback message for the following behaviors and note which type of feedback you are using.

a. Terry is trying very hard but still can't get his adverbs and adjectives straight. He confuses them in his compositions.

b. Enid does not volunteer to answer many questions in class. Today she did, but she said that the capital of New York is New York City, not Albany.

c. You are giving a lesson on temperature when Jimmy tells you that it can be measured in both Fahrenheit and Celsius.

d. Juan, Sue, and Andrew raise their hand to ask a question at the same time. They all want your attention immediately.

e. Randy makes the comment to the class in an oral report that Abraham Lincoln was the fifteenth president when Lincoln actually was the sixteenth.

8. **Step-by-Step Teaching.** Choose some procedure that entails teaching in a detailed, step-by-step procedure. It might be a type of mathematics problem (verbal problems), a laboratory demonstration, or instructions on how to do an assignment. The steps needed to do a comparison are listed in Chapter 4 and you may use them in this exercise. Detail the exact steps you want students to use.

9. **Programmed Instruction.** Many schools use programmed instruction, mostly as an adjunct to regular instruction. Some programs are found in workbooks, while others are in the form of computer programs. Look over these programmed materials and ask teachers who use them about their value. Who do the teachers think receive the most help from using the programs? What are some of the problems in using these programs?

10. **The Keller Plan.** Many colleges offer Personalized Systems of Instruction (PSI), and there is a good chance that the college you attend does so. Ask the professor in charge of the program about his or her experiences with PSI. If you know students who have tried PSI, ask them about their experiences. Do you think PSI could be used in high school? Why or why not?

11. **Token Reinforcements.** Token reinforcement is an involved procedure but one that can be useful. Imagine yourself a teacher of a sixth-grade class. You would like to raise the quality of homework and test grades. Devise a token reinforcement

system for the class, with the backup reinforcers being going on a trip to see a professional baseball game which you can consider reinforcing for each student. Other backup reinforcers are activity reinforcers such as free time, playing games with the students, and working puzzles.

SCENARIOS

Here are eleven scenarios. Try to apply the information you have learned in the chapter to each situation.

1. Each time Mrs. Gonzalez begins a class in mathematics, her fifth-grade students show their displeasure vocally. This bothers Mrs. Gonzalez terribly for a number of reasons. First, mathematics is a very important subject. Second, most of the class does well, but there seems to be almost a fear of mathematics in the class. Third, many students in the class seem to give up on the problems when they are close to solving them. What can Mrs. Gonzalez do to reduce the students' negative emotional reactions to mathematics?

2. Mr. Wilkins has had a number of conferences with Jeffrey's parents about Jeffrey's inability to come to class prepared. Jeffrey is a bright sixth-grader but is always seeking a pencil from one student and a piece of paper from another. He often must share a book because he "forgets" to bring the materials to school. Mr. Wilkins has given Jeffrey demerits that count against his grade and reprimanded him on many occasions. Even reprimands from his parents and having a privilege taken away do not seem to help. Mr. Wilkins believes that a home-school reinforcement program should be used. Jeffrey's parents are willing and able to participate. However, Mr. Wilkins has never tried anything like this before and asks you for help. Briefly outline such a program for your colleague.

3. Mrs. Lang has a problem in library class. After she teaches the seventh-grade class something about the library, she gives them an assignment to do by themselves to show their knowledge of what she has taught them. It is during this time that the students make a great deal of noise. Mrs. Lang tries to go around the library helping each student, but as she is helping one, some of the others are fooling around and not doing their work. She has read that she might try a group-

based contingency reinforcement program, and a colleague suggests that she use a variation of the "good behavior game." Briefly discuss how Mrs. Lang could set up such a program.

4. Mr. Campese has begun a program to raise the vocabulary test scores of one group of students. The students are the weakest in the class and are in a special group. For the first three weeks, Mr. Campese took a baseline for each student which gave him some idea of the percentage of correct answers that each student obtained on the test. All five students averaged about five correct out of the fifteen words. Mr. Campese then told the students that if they obtained eight right, they would receive ten minutes of free time to talk or do puzzles at the end of the day. All students would have to obtain this score. He allows the group time to help one another. After a few weeks, the program seemed to be working, so Mr. Campese raised the goal to eleven correct answers and intends to raise it again to thirteen later in the semester if everything works out. Evaluate Mr. Campese's program.

5. Students in Mrs. Eddington's eighth-grade science class do not seem to complete their assigned homework, and when they do, she has noticed that it is inaccurate. Students are writing anything down on paper just to reduce the possibility of getting a zero if she collects the homework that day. Mrs. Eddington has two problems. First, she wants to improve homework accuracy and completion. Second, she does not want to have to spend hours each night reading these assignments. She can correct the papers once or twice a week but no more. She asks you for help in designing a reinforcement program that may be of help in this matter.

6. You are a third-grade teacher who must deal with Susan, a girl who is very sensitive to correction. Whenever any corrective feedback is used, Susan seems to give up and refuses to do anything but the easiest material. The most unusual aspect of this case is that Susan doesn't make all that many errors and writes fairly well. If she is called upon in class and she answers the question incorrectly, she gets very upset and sometimes closes her book. How could you deal with Susan's problem?

7. Mr. Anderson's reinforcement strategy seems to have worked with his class. The students received activity reinforcement if they finished their seatwork with 90 percent accuracy. Mr. Anderson has made certain that the students could do the work, and according to his chart, they have improved from 70 percent accuracy to the present 90 percent. Mr. Anderson decides to end the program, since it has worked so well. Almost immediately, the accuracy rate goes back to where it was before the program. He complains that the program was not a success because the students returned to their old habits, and he vows not to use such a program again. Briefly analyze why Mr. Anderson's program was not a complete success and suggest what he could have done to improve it.

8. Mrs. Kent has been working with Michael, a fourth-grader who is very disorganized and does not arrive in class on time, constantly asks to go to the bathroom, and does his work carelessly. She believes that Michael has the ability to do the work and so begins a social and activity reinforcement program with him. She will allow him to have ten minutes free reading time at the end of the day and will give him praise if he completes nine of the ten daily assignments correctly. She is surprised that this is not working and asks you why. Briefly describe Mrs. Kent's mistakes in her program and what she could do to improve her program.

9. You like to have a great deal of discussion in class, and this works in most cases but not with your last-period class. These high school juniors do not seem very involved. Any question you ask is greeted with silence. The students dutifully take down some notes, but they do not participate even when the questions relate to their own experience. At times, one or two students will volunteer, but two out of twenty-five is hardly what you would like to see in class. Using reinforcement and any other techniques or approaches you wish, describe how you would deal with this problem.

10. Mr. Edwards has decided to use stickers as a reinforcement for his first-grade class. After he teaches the class, Mr. Edwards gives his students seatwork practice sheets that he wants completed. He then goes around the room trying to help those who need help. Unfortunately, the students do not seem to care whether they receive these rewards or not and he does not understand why. He asks you what the problem might be.

11. Kevin lags behind. That is the problem. While the other students all finish their work, Kevin daydreams and slowly does his work. His work is fair, but no better. Kevin seems to have the ability but not the motivation to finish his work on time. He complains often about not having enough time, but you often notice that he wastes time and is often engaged in off-task activities. Meanwhile, Kevin's tardiness is becoming a problem, as other students waiting for him to finish often get bored and the class becomes noisy. On the other hand, if you go on with the class and let Kevin finish his work in his own time, he requires quite a bit of individual instruction to compensate for the material he has missed. You've sent a note home to his parents, who simply punished Kevin which was ineffective. How would you help Kevin to improve his time on tasks and the prompt completion of his work?

Social and Moral Development

6

Are These Statements True or False?

Turn the next page for the correct answers. Each statement is repeated following the paragraph in which the information can be found.

1. Comparing children is a healthy activity, since it gives students realistic feedback about their rank in class.
2. If children who are not achieving well are given tutoring that improves their scholarship, their self-esteem will be raised as well.
3. Early maturing boys have a social advantage in adolescence.
4. The earlier a student makes a commitment to a career path the better, so teachers should actively encourage students in high school to commit themselves to a career.
5. Introducing students to many career choices does little more than confuse teens and should not be attempted by school personnel.
6. Aggressive children tend to be unpopular and rejected.
7. Children with poor social skills usually outgrow their problem.
8. Generally, children who attend day care have moderately serious social and emotional problems during their elementary school years.
9. Elementary schoolchildren who regularly return home from school to an empty house and call their parents are no more susceptible to peer pressure nor do they have lower self-esteem than children who have a parent present when they get home from school.
10. Children from one-parent families have less academic ability than children from two-parent families.
11. Boys receive more attention from elementary schoolteachers than girls do.
12. The best way to encourage cross-racial and cross-ethnic friendly interaction is to desegregate classrooms and let students work out their own relationships.

Social and Personal Development

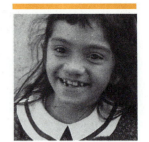

Answers to True-False Statements

1. *False* Correct statement: Comparing students can give the children who come out the worse a sense of inferiority.

2. *True*

3. *True*

4. *False* Correct statement: Early commitment reduces flexibility, and some students may not be vocationally mature enough to make such commitments, so teachers should encourage exploration but not necessary commitment.

5. *False* Correct statement: Schools should actively introduce students to various career choices.

6. *True*

7. *False* Correct statement: Children with social skills deficits do not usually outgrow these problems.

8. *False* Correct statement: Elementary school students who have attended day care programs do not suffer from moderately severe social and economic problems. There are differences between children reared at home and those who spent part of their day regularly in day care, but these differences are neither great nor necessarily negative.

9. *True*

10. *False* Correct statement: Children from one-parent families do not have lower academic ability than children from intact families.

11. *True*

12. *False* Correct statement: Just leaving students to their own devices leads to segregation within classrooms. To encourage friendly interaction, both groups must be of equal status and have shared goals and the interaction must be encouraged by authority figures.

CHILDREN TODAY: THE SAME OR DIFFERENT?

If you were asked to check one of these statements, which one would you choose?

Children today are the same as they were thirty years ago.

Children today are much different than they were thirty years ago.

On the one hand, children have the same social and personal needs and desires as they have always had. The need for a positive sense of self and good interpersonal interactions did not start with the current generation. As children develop through the various stages of childhood, they face identifiable social and personal challenges that have not changed much from one generation to the next.

On the other hand, a case can also be made for differences between children today and children of thirty years ago. Today's children are more likely to experience the divorce of their parents and perhaps a remarriage. They are much more likely to have both parents working. They face a world with less permanence, one that is changing at a faster rate. They are more likely to spend some time outside their parents' care when young and to experience less parental supervision.

Look at the changes over the past thirty years. In 1960, nine percent of the children were living with one parent. By 1990, the figure is expected to rise to 25 percent. In 1960, 73 percent of all children lived with two parents who were married only once. In 1990, that figure will be reduced to 56 percent (Hernandez, 1988). In 1960, 8.6 percent of the children lived with a natural parent and a stepparent. In 1990, that percentage is expected to increase to 16 percent.

Why Are Teachers Interested in Personal and Social Development?

School is more than a place where children learn facts and concepts. It is also a place where much personal growth and social interaction occurs. Children meet many new people in school and develop new friendships. School also plays a part in the development of the self-concept and the personal identities of adolescents. Although the school is not the only influence in these areas, it plays a major role in the child's social development, and often the school as a social institution is forgotten.

Why are teachers concerned about the child's personal and social development? First, we can easily make a case that a child's self-concept, self-esteem, and social development are important parts of life, and one responsibility of the school is to help children build a healthy self-concept and improve their relationships with others. Because the ability to relate to others is necessary if a child is to fully participate in life, helping children develop social skills may be part of the school's agenda (Hatch, 1987). This point of view argues that the school has a direct responsibility in these areas.

Second, the child's self-concept, self-esteem, and interpersonal relationships mediate between the learner and his or her ability to learn and get along in school. In other words, these areas greatly influence a child's academic achievement and behavior. There is much evidence to support this argument. Children who possess strong self-concepts volunteer their ideas more often in class, while those with a low estimate of themselves are often overwhelmed by school tasks (Berne, 1987). Positive self-esteem is related to better adjustment in school, more independence, less defensive behavior, and greater acceptance of others. It is also associated with school achievement (Gurney, 1987). Low self-esteem is implicated in the lower academic performance of minority group children (Minuchin & Shapiro, 1983). Children with a positive academic self-concept see themselves as more competent, and the relationship between perceived competence and scholastic achievement increases between grades three and six (Entwisle et al., 1987). A child's interpersonal relationships also affect learning. Seventh graders who see themselves as making a good start in junior high school attribute their success to the presence of old friends and their ability to make new friends (Mitman & Packer, 1982). Children who

School is a place where much social interaction occurs, friendships are made, and students learn to get along with others.

are unpopular and rejected are at risk for poor adjustment and poor academic achievement (Shantz, 1983).

Influences outside of school, most importantly the family, also affect the child's self-concept, interpersonal relationships, and academic achievement. The changing nature of the family and new child-care patterns may affect children's schoolwork and adjustment. For example, a child whose family is in the throes of dissolution may find it difficult to concentrate on geography. A child in a stepfamily situation may be dealing with demands from two families. In addition, many children today enter school with a background of extensive preschool experience, which may affect the child's social behavior in elementary school. The teacher has little control over any of these experiences. However, as we shall see, understanding the nature of these experiences and laying aside prejudices is necessary if teachers are to deal effectively with such students. In addition, teachers can do much to help students deal with the challenges in their social environment and to improve relations between the school and parents in alternative family situations.

The first portion of this chapter investigates the development of the child's self-concept and interpersonal relationships. The second part looks at some of the changing aspects of the family system, including divorce, latchkey children, and stepfamilies. Finally, we will look at sex roles and social relationships among ethnic groups, two areas that are also rapidly changing. The purpose of this chapter is to examine how these social factors affect learning and to look at the way schools can aid in developing the child's social skills.

ERIKSON'S PSYCHOSOCIAL THEORY OF DEVELOPMENT

One of the most popular ways of viewing the psychosocial aspects of human development was offered by Erik Erikson, and it can serve as a handy guideline for understanding how children are challenged as they progress through childhood and adolescence. Erikson (1963) argued that human beings develop according to a preset plan called the **epigenetic principle,** which consists of two main elements. First, personality develops according to predetermined steps that are maturationally set. Second, society is structured in a way that invites and encourages the

epigenetic principle   The preset developmental plan in Erikson's theory consisting of two elements: personality develops according to maturationally determined steps and each society is structured to encourage challenges that arise during these times.

challenges that arise at particular times. Each individual proceeds through eight stages of development from cradle to grave. Each stage presents the individual with a crisis. If a particular crisis is handled well, the outcome is positive. If it is not handled well, the outcome is negative. Few people emerge from a particular stage with an entirely positive or negative outcome. In fact, Erikson argues that a healthy balance must be struck between the two poles, although the outcome should tend toward the positive side of the scale. People can reexperience these crises during a life change, but by and large, the crises take place at particular times in life. The resolution of one stage lays the foundation for negotiating the challenges of the next.

Trust vs. Mistrust. The positive outcome of the stage of infancy is a sense of trust. If children are cared for in a warm, caring manner, they are apt to trust the environment and develop a feeling that they live among friends. If the parents are anxious, angry, or incapable of meeting a child's needs, the child may develop a sense of mistrust. Trust is the cornerstone of the child's attitude towards life. For example, children with a sense of trust are inclined to believe that others will come through for them and that people are generally good, while people with a low sense of trust focus on the negative aspects of other people's behavior (Hamachek, 1988).

Autonomy vs. Shame or Doubt. Two- and three-year-olds are no longer completely dependent on adults. Toddlers practice their new physical skills and develop a positive sense of autonomy. They learn that they are persons in their own right. Children of this age who either are not allowed to do the things they can do or are pushed into doing something for which they are not ready may develop a sense of shame or doubt about their own abilities and fail to develop self-confidence. People with a sense of autonomy have a basic attitude of "I think I can do it" and "I have something of value to offer" (Hamachek, 1988).

Initiative vs. Guilt. By the time children reach about four years of age, they can begin to formulate a plan of action and carry it through. The positive outcome of this stage is a sense of initiative, a sense that one's desires and actions are basically sound. If parents encourage children of this age to form their own ideas, the children will develop a sense of initiative. If a child is punished for expressing his or her own desires and plans, the child develops a sense of guilt, which leads to fear and a lack of assertiveness. Children with a sense of initiative accept new challenges, are self-starters, and have a strong sense of personal adequacy, while those with a sense of guilt show the opposite patterns (Hamachek, 1988).

Industry vs. Inferiority. During the elementary school years, children must learn the academic skills of reading, writing, and mathematics as well as social skills. If a child succeeds in acquiring these new skills and if the accomplishments are valued by others, the child develops a sense of industry. But children who are constantly compared with others and come up a distinct second may develop a sense of inferiority. Children with a sense of industry enjoy learning about new things and experimenting with new ideas, persevere, and take criticism well (Hamachek, 1988).

True or False Comparing children is a healthy activity, since it gives students realistic feedback about their rank in class.

Identity vs. Role Confusion. During adolescence, children must investigate various alternatives concerning their vocational and personal future and develop a sense of who they are and where they belong. The adolescent who develops a solid sense of identity formulates a satisfying plan and gains a sense of security. Adolescents who do not develop this sense of identity may develop role confusion and a sense of aimlessness and being adrift. Those with a sense of identity are less susceptible to peer pressure, have a high level of self-acceptance, are optimistic, and believe they are in control of their own destinies, while those with a sense of confusion can be described in the opposite manner (Hamachek, 1988). More is said about identity later in the chapter.

Intimacy vs. Isolation. In young adulthood, the psychosocial crisis involves attainment of intimacy. Intimacy requires a sense of identity, because identi-ties are shared in marriage. Although marriage is not the only vehicle for achieving intimacy, most people in this age group do marry. An individual who is fearful or opts not to enter into very close interpersonal relationships may develop a sense of isolation and of being alienated from society—essentially lonely and alone.

Generativity vs. Stagnation. In middle age, most people have set routines and can easily become stagnated, absorbed only with their own needs and comforts. This negative outcome may be avoided by giving oneself to the community and to the younger generation. Helping other people is a means of remaining productive and achieving the positive outcome of generativity.

Integrity vs. Despair. The last psychosocial stage, that of old age, revolves around integrity and despair. Older people must cope with the death of others, increasing illness, and their own approaching end. Yet, if they can look back with pride at the life of accomplishment, they can develop a positive sense of ego integrity. If, on the other hand, all they see is missed opportunities, they become depressed and bitter, developing a sense of despair.

Teachers are most concerned with early childhood (initiative vs. guilt), middle childhood (industry vs. inferiority), and adolescence (identity vs. role confusion). According to Erikson, the resolution of the psychosocial crises is based upon one's interactions within the culture. Through these interactions, children develop a sense of self, an understanding of their strengths and weaknesses, and an appreciation of how they fit into the group.

SELF-CONCEPT AND SELF-ESTEEM

A person's **self-concept** is the picture the individual has of him or herself. The term **self-esteem** refers to the value people place on various aspects of the

self-concept The picture people have of themselves.

self-esteem The value people place on various aspects of the self.

self (Kaplan & Stein, 1984). Self-esteem is related to the self-concept but is slightly different. Two children may think that they are good in mathematics but not good in art. However, one may think that mathematics is much more important, while the other may value art more than mathematics (Searey, 1988). A child's self-concept colors how the child interprets situations and influences behavior and attitudes (Burns, 1979). Consider a nine-year-old presented with a difficult division problem. If the child believes that she is a poor mathematics student she may react with displeasure and not persevere. If she has a positive view of herself as a good mathematician, she approaches the problem with a positive attitude and shows more persistence. Children with a positive view of their physical self will join in and play baseball with the other children, while those who do not think they are good enough in this area will refuse to join the group to avoid embarrassment. A vicious circle may ensue, for children who do not practice their motor skills will not develop such skills to their fullest. They fall further behind their peers, until they do not measure up to them. This causes them again to refuse to play, leading to a further lack of development.

Various aspects of the self affect one another. Students with a poor physical sense of self who refuse to play ball may place themselves at a social disadvantage, because such games form a part of the social scene at an early age. They interact with fewer children and therefore may find it more difficult to develop social skills.

The self-concept also affects how information is processed. If children believe they are "bad," they will believe such feedback from other people. In this way, the self-concept can cause a self-fulfilling prophecy to develop. Believing that someone will say something negative causes children to anticipate poor evaluations and even to interpret neutral feedback as negative.

How Does the Self-Concept Develop?

The self-concept evolves from a combination of the feedback a child receives from others and the child's evaluation of his or her own subjective experiences. The child gets feedback from many people, including peers, parents, and teachers. Children whose parents or teachers tell them that they have no mechanical

ability may believe it, and the vicious cycle described previously ensues. However, children are not just passive recipients of feedback. They also evaluate their own experiences. They experience themselves as being good, bad, aggressive, calm, and honest and compare their experience against a standard set by the society, parents, peers, and finally themselves. Even in the absence of direct feedback, they evaluate these experiences. Children whose experience is not in keeping with their sense of self may reject their subjective experience. For instance, children may believe that they are honest yet have difficulty coming to grips with the fact that they copied from a friend during an exam. Their experience of dishonesty does not match their conception of themselves as honest.

During middle childhood, a number of factors make this situation more complex. First, children receive feedback from many sources. They encounter more children and adults, not all of whom will like them. Some of this feedback is likely to be negative, or at least conflicting. The child who has been the center of attention at home may find that is not the case in school (Williams & Stith, 1980). Second, children's newly developing cognitive skills affect the development of their self-concept. Children in the concrete operational stage (Chapter two) can reason more logically, allowing them to verify the attributes of their self. Children now develop the ability to take another person's point of view and can imagine what others are thinking of them (Froming et al., 1985). Children are especially good at developing a self-theory from inductive (specific) experiences. They may conclude that they are smart because they are good at reading and mathematics (Harter, 1983) or honest because they returned something they found.

The School and the Self-Concept

By the time children enter elementary school, their self-concept is partially formed. However, in school they get more feedback from a variety of new sources. The feedback may be contradictory, as peers may reinforce one behavior and teachers another. Sometimes, even teachers and parents may be in conflict. Children may have been taught to think for themselves at home, while the teacher wants them to obey orders without question, and vice versa.

How a child performs in school affects the child's self-concept. Children who do well in music and not in science may see themselves in terms of these skills. Some children must cope with failure for the first time. School failure leads to feelings of shame and distress, embarrassment and incompetence. Negative effects are likely to be greatest when children have studied but still fail, convincing them that they lack ability in a particular area. This illustrates how important study skills may be. Children may do poorly on a test because they studied the wrong material or did not know how to study effectively. They may then incorrectly conclude that they are not capable in mathematics and reading and develop a negative concept of their academic self in these areas. This, in turn, reduces the amount of time such children devote to learning the material. Self-esteem is likely to be greatest when one is convinced that one's success is due to ability and effort.

The Teacher's Role in Developing a Child's Self-Concept and Building Self-Esteem

Research evidence clearly indicates the importance of a child's self-concept and self-esteem. The question, though, is what can be done realistically by the teacher to help children build positive self-concepts and improve their self-esteem.

Searey (1988) divides attempts to improve self-esteem into four categories: helping children feel more capable, more significant, more powerful, and more worthy. Children will feel more capable if their school papers are displayed, they are encouraged to teach something they are good at to other children, and they are allowed time to pursue interests and abilities. Children will feel more significant if we listen to them, help them to participate in groups such

Students who participate in clubs or scouting feel more significant than those who do not.

as scouting or clubs, encourage them to volunteer to help others, and celebrate their successes. Children will feel more powerful if we give them more responsibility by allowing them to make certain choices, perhaps in assignments or selecting a schedule. Children will feel more worthy if we value some quality that makes them special (such as sensitivity to animals or regard for others), promote their hobbies, and discuss their ideas openly.

We also know that when children achieve academically their self-esteem rises (Silvernail, 1987). High levels of achievement are related to high levels of self-esteem for both boys and girls (Robison-Awana, 1986). Research shows that special remedial reading programs, if successful, lead to improvements in self-esteem (Gurney, 1987). Some of the gain may be due to success in academic areas, but the special attention itself seems to increase self-esteem, especially for those who have low self-esteem.

True or False   If children who are not achieving well are given tutoring that improves their scholarship, their self-esteem will be raised as well.

Sometimes teachers can adversely affect a child's self-esteem through poor communication practices. For example, teachers may give more attention to good students than to poorer ones. In addition, only about six percent of teachers' communication with students involve praise. Even in kindergarten, teachers use reprimands significantly more than praise (Entwisle et al., 1987). This can be avoided by being aware of this propensity, praising children for their positive achievements, and focusing on a child's strengths rather than weaknesses (Magee, 1987).

Parents can also be involved in improving a child's self-esteem. Many parents do not use praise or value their children's accomplishments. They emphasize the negative aspects of the child's behavior or they give the child the message that what they did was good but they could do better. Parents can be reminded to praise their children for their accomplishments and follow some of Searey's suggestions outlined above, leading to activities that make the child feel more capable, significant, powerful, and worthy.

SPECIAL CONCERNS OF ADOLESCENCE

A child's self-concept becomes more complicated in adolescence as rapid physical and social changes challenge the adolescent's ability to adjust.

Physical Development and the Self-Concept

Most adolescents are acutely aware of their physical selves. Early adolescence is a time of tremendous physical change that affects the adolescent's self-concept and behavior. Although the sequence of this physical change is predictable, the timing of the change varies considerably from person to person. The physical changes that occur in adolescence are well known to almost everyone. For females, shortly after the growth spurt begins, girls develop breast buds, pubic hair appears, and the breadth of their hips increases. Then, when the growth spurt is at its maximum, changes in the genital organs take place. When growth slows considerably, menarche takes place. At this point, a number of other changes in fat and muscle composition also occur. Following menarche, most of the changes are nonsexual, including further changes in body shape and voice (Krogman, 1980).

The first signs of puberty in males are the growth of the testes and scrotum along with the appearance of pubic hair. This is followed about a year later by a spurt in height and the growth of the penis. The prepubertal growth spurt in males occurs approximately two years after the average female has experienced her growth spurt and takes the average male well beyond the height of the average female. As is often the case, we can predict the sequence of events, but the time at which the events occur varies from person to person. The trunk and legs elongate. Leg length

Early adolescence is a period during which tremendous physical changes occur that affect the self-concept.

reaches its adult proportions before body breadth. The last growth change to occur is a widening of the shoulders. The male's voice deepens, and facial hair appears. Muscles develop, in part because of the secretion of testosterone, and the heart and lungs increase dramatically, as does the number of blood cells.

Teenagers' bodies are changing quickly. Although some teens cope very well with these changes, many are not always comfortable with their new bodies. Many want to change some aspect of their physical selves—mostly their height, weight, and complexion. For example, in one sample of teenage girls, although 81 percent of the subjects were assessed to be within the ideal weight range or even underweight, 78 percent wanted to weigh less, and only 14 percent were satisfied with their current weight (Eisele et al., 1986). In adolescence, a good part of one's self-esteem is determined by body image. A link exists between physical attractiveness and self-esteem and between dissatisfaction with one's body and low self-esteem (Grant & Fodor, 1986). The combination of peer pressure and media advertising encourages teens to try to change what can be changed and to meet some stereotyped, socially approved image. It may take time for teenagers to become comfortable with their bodies and accept those elements such as height that cannot be changed. During these years, parents and teachers sometimes forget what it was like to experience these changes and lose patience with their teenage children.

Early and Late Maturation

Most people are neither very early in maturing or very late. They fall somewhere in between. Some evidence exists, however, that teens who mature either very early or very late may be affected by the experience. Early maturing males seem to have a substantial social advantage over late maturers. Adults rate early maturers more positively than late maturers. Early maturing boys are considered more masculine, more attractive, and better groomed. Late maturers are considered tense and childish and are seen as always seeking attention. Peers see them as bossy, restless, and less attractive and as having less leadership ability (Jones and Bayley, 1950).

True or False Early maturing boys have a social advantage in adolescence.

In adolescent girls, the effects of early and later maturation are less clear. Some studies find that early maturing girls are better adjusted in young adulthood (Peskin, 1973) and that late maturing girls are more likely to suffer from anxiety (Weatherley 1964). Other studies, however, do not show any advantages for early maturing females (Jones & Mussen, 1958; Jones, 1949). Some evidence indicates disadvantages for the early maturer. Staffieri (1972) found that early maturing girls are not considered attractive, because they are fatter, whereas later maturers are thinner and are judged more conventionally attractive. Perhaps whether the changes take place in elementary or junior high school makes a difference (Faust, 1960). Early developing girls in elementary school receive fewer positive comments, but the situation is reversed in junior high school, where early developing females receive more positive feedback. Adolescents are very aware of how their physical development compares to that of their peers, and the reactions of others may affect how they see themselves.

Adolescent Thinking and the Self-Concept

Chapter 2 discussed the adolescent's cognitive advancement during Piaget's formal operational stage, including the ability to use abstractions, reason in a deductive manner, and separate the real from the possible. These emerging formal operational abilities greatly affect an adolescent's social behavior and self-concept.

The self-consciousness of adolescents, especially early adolescents, is legendary. In fact, early adolescent eighth graders in one study were found to be significantly more self-conscious than both younger children and older adolescents (Elkind & Bowen, 1979). Adolescents often look at themselves in the mirror and imagine what others will think about them. Adolescents can now think about thoughts—both their own and those of others. However, a logical error occurs. Teenagers can understand the thoughts of others, but they fail to differentiate between the objects towards which the thoughts of others are directed and those that are the focus of their own thoughts (Peel, 1969). Because teens are concerned primarily with themselves, they believe everyone else is focusing on them too and is as obsessed with their behavior and appearance as they are. The inability to differentiate between what one is thinking and what others are thinking constitutes what David Elkind (1967) called **adolescent egocentrism.** This leads to two interesting phenomena: the imaginary audience and the personal fable.

The Imaginary Audience

Adolescents often believe that when they walk into a room everyone focuses their attention on them. They anticipate the reactions and create an **imaginary audience,** believing that everyone is looking at and evaluating them. The *people* in this audience are real, but the audience is imaginary, because most of the time the adolescent is not the focus of attention. The imaginary audience phenomenon leads to self-consciousness and the adolescent's mania for privacy. The self-consciousness stems from the conviction that others are seeing and evaluating them in the same way that they see and evaluate themselves. The mania for privacy may come either from what Elkind calls a reluctance to reveal oneself or from a reaction to being constantly scrutinized. Privacy becomes a vacation from evaluation.

Adolescents are deeply involved with how others will evaluate them. As they dress, act, and groom, they imagine how others will see them. Elkind notes that when the boy who combed his hair for hours meets the girl who carefully applied her makeup, each is more concerned with being observed than with being the observer. During later adolescence, the imaginary audience disappears considerably as teens realize that people may not react to them the way they've imagined they do.

The Personal Fable

"You can't know what it is like to fail," said one adolescent to his biology teacher. He was convinced that the feelings he was experiencing were unique. As adolescents reflect on their own thoughts and experiences, they come to believe that what they are thinking and experiencing is absolutely unique in the annals of human history. The belief that what they are experiencing and thinking is original, new, and special is known as the **personal fable.** The personal fable declines somewhat as the adolescent enters young adulthood, but it may never be completely extinguished.

adolescent egocentrism The adolescent failure to differentiate between what one is thinking and what others are considering.

imaginary audience A term used to describe an adolescent's belief that he or she is the focus of attention and is being evaluated by everyone.

personal fable The adolescent's belief that his or her experiences are unique and original.

The Teacher and Adolescent Development

In the midst of discussing the general aspects of adolescent physical development, the subjective experience of the adolescent should not be forgotten. The junior high school student who is sensitive about his or her lack of development or who believes that everyone will notice and judge his or her clothing requires understanding and patience. As dean of a junior high school, I received a number of complaints about students who would not change for gym. Often these students were sensitive about their physical development. In one case, a student cut school for the day because she did not like how her hair was cut and thought students would laugh at her. One late developing boy was concerned because although he was among the tallest before his peers experienced their growth spurt, he was now quite short. He felt better when he learned that when he experienced his growth spurt he would probably regain his relative height (Tanner, 1970).

Many of the concerns students have about their physical changes are handled in health class, and we will discuss issues concerning sex education extensively in the next chapter. However, the classroom teacher can avoid problems by realizing how important it is that young adolescents appear acceptable to their classmates. Adolescents' concern over their appearance is normal. Even a remark made in jest concerning their appearance can cause young adolescents anxiety. In addition, teachers may prefer early maturers who are more adult looking and may give them more attention and select them for leadership positions. This only increases the feelings of insecurity experienced by later maturers. Last, secondary school students who believe the personal fable are often surprised, interested, and pleased when they find that other students are experiencing similar thoughts and feelings. When this occurs, students may become more attentive, and even if it means going off on a tangent occasionally, such discussions are well worth the time.

Identity

Who am I?
Where am I going?
Where do I belong?

Erikson (1959) saw the positive outcome of adolescence as the formation of a solid, personal **identity** while viewing the negative outcome of adolescence as an aimlessness known as role confusion. Adolescents cannot simply be carbon copies of their elders, nor can they discard the values and attitudes they have been taught in childhood as totally dysfunctional. They must blend the old with the new and create their own individual identity.

The Four Identity Statuses

Achieving an identity depends on two variables: crisis and commitment (Marcia, 1967). In a crisis, one actively faces and questions aspects of one's personal identity. For example, a student may have to choose which college to attend and feel pressure concerning his or her vocational choice. In the personal sphere, the student may be dating someone for a while and have to decide whether or not to get more deeply involved. The second aspect, commitment, involves making a firm decision concerning a question and following a plan of action that reflects the decision. A person who investigates many vocational choices and decides on a business career will follow the appropriate course of study.

Adolescents differ in the extent to which they have experienced crises or made commitments. A prominent researcher in this field, James Marcia (1980, 1967), grouped adolescents into four categories according to their experiences with crises and commitments. One group of adolescents, termed **identity diffused,** consists of adolescents who may or may not have experienced a crisis but have not made any commitments. Identity diffused people may actively seek noncommitment, actually avoiding demanding

situations. They may also appear aimless, aloof, and drifting (Osofsky et al., 1973). Their self-esteem is not very high. Many people go through such periods, and identity diffusion is negative only when a person leaves adolescence without making any commitments. In fact, a period of confusion often precedes establishment of a firm identity (Erikson, 1959).

The **identity foreclosed** group consists of teens who have not experienced a crisis but have made commitments anyway. These people appear to have it all together. They seem to know what they want at an early age and appear confident and secure. These seemingly lucky people have formed a commitment perhaps to go into some vocation, but the decision may be premature and not even of their own making. It may be one handed down to them by their parents. For example, some people may go into their parents' business because it was always expected of them. They were not permitted, or did not permit themselves, to search for other alternatives.

Identity foreclosure can be a secure status. The people in this group appear to function well and do not suffer periods of crisis. They show little anxiety (Marcia & Friedman, 1970). Identity foreclosed people are often envied by their classmates. After all, they have a direction in life and are following a definite path. But this security is purchased at a price. The path is not one they might have chosen, and foreclosed individuals sometimes find themselves later on mired in an unhappy lifestyle (Petitpas, 1978).

True or False The earlier a student makes a commitment to a career path the better, so teachers should actively encourage students in high school to commit themselves to a career.

Another side exists to identity foreclosure. Some adolescents may be foreclosed because they do not have the opportunity to search for or to know what is available. Many poor and minority group youths do

---

identity   The sense of knowing who you are.

identity diffusion   An identity status resulting in confusion, aimlessness, and a sense of emptiness.

identity foreclosure   An identity status marked by a premature identity decision.

not believe they have many choices. Some must enter the labor force as soon as possible to support themselves and their families. Others may not have the basic academic skills necessary for more advanced study that would allow them to explore alternative vocational opportunities. For these teens, foreclosure is forced on them by circumstances, by lack of knowledge about their choices, or by their belief that they do not have any control over their own destinies.

The third group—the **identity moratorium** group— contains adolescents who are presently experiencing a crisis but have not yet made any commitments. This is a period of delay in which a person is not yet ready to make definite commitments (Erikson, 1968). Many possibilities are being explored, some of them radical, but final commitments tend to be more conservative. The moratorium state is not a happy one. The adolescent may be dissatisfied with everything and everyone. The teen may be searching for something. He or she may see everything that is wrong but be less successful when it comes to suggesting what realistic steps can be taken to alleviate the problems. People in this status are active and troubled. They are quick to debate and frequently in opposition to authority (Donovan, 1975). A moratorium may be necessary for a person to experience, for when a person does make a commitment, the commitment is his or her own, made after a period of searching for answers.

The **identity achievers** group consists of adolescents who have already experienced crises and made their commitments. Their goals are realistic, and they can cope with shifts in the environment. These independent personal identities are not carbon copies of their parents' values and attitudes nor are they totally the opposite. Their identity includes some of the parents' values and attitudes while omitting others. They are well adjusted (Bernard et al., 1981) and have good relationships both with peers and with authority figures (Donovan, 1975).

Two keys to identity formation are searching and exploring. The process of identity formation requires

identity moratorium   An identity status in which a person is actively searching for an identity.

identity achievement   An identity status in which a person has developed a solid, personal identity.

a person to combine considerations from the past, the present, and the future. Before the age of 18, the overwhelming number of young people are either foreclosed or diffused (Archer, 1982).

The Teacher and Identity Development

It is easy to argue that the schools encourage foreclosure, since conformity and submission to authority are highly valued. Foreclosure students are the most comfortable in school and hold positive attitudes toward school, while those who are in the moratorium status evaluate their experience most negatively (Waterman & Waterman, 1971). The very structure of the school, including curricula and grades, encourages foreclosure rather than exploration. This argument is too simplistic, however. The school can, and often does, play some part in a student's search for identity, although it is only one influence in this area. Some vital identity issues in the sexual, interpersonal, vocational, and political arenas can be explored in the classroom, especially if students are encouraged to participate in discussions. Such topics as drug education, human development, sex education, consumer economics, and interpersonal relationships can be made academically rigorous and still allow for exploration (Muuss, 1982). It is possible not only to teach the facts but also to discuss underlying values. For example, many biology courses may present the use of technology and ethical problems along with academic facts. Erikson emphasized the importance of occupational identity. Students are often sheltered, however, especially from some of the newer fields. Schools can introduce students to many occupations through a number of programs, including on-the-job experience, community work, and various tours and lectures (Miller, 1978).

True or False   Introducing students to many career choices does little more than confuse teens and should not be attempted by school personnel.

Many adolescents are ready and willing to discuss some rather difficult material. Their newfound cognitive abilities (discussed in Chapter 2) allow them to consider their own morals and values. When discussing plays and novels, students may be able to talk about such matters as self-definition and feelings.

Communication is also a key. Teachers and parents often lecture rather than listen to adolescents. Adults are often more interested in presenting their

It is important to listen to students. Unfortunately, adults are frequently more interested in explaining their points of view to teens than in listening to them.

own values and points of view than in listening to others. Yet adolescents must be made to feel free to explore areas of concerns, and active listening (discussed in Chapter 9) by adults can help.

INTERPERSONAL RELATIONSHIPS

During middle childhood, the influence of peers and friends grows substantially. Elementary schoolchildren form their own groups and interact extensively with other children. Friends take more of a central position, and being popular and accepted are more important. In adolescence, the peer group takes on even greater influence. Peer interaction is very different from adult-child interaction. Child-child interaction involves companionship and amusement; adult-child interaction involves protection, care, and instruction (Furman & Buhrmester, 1985). Children have more power with friends as well.

Children learn a great deal from their peers. They learn social skills and obtain information by comparing themselves with one another. Such interaction fosters a sense of group belonging (Rubin, 1980). Peer interaction allows children to gain a better understanding of social events and to learn self-control. However, a peer and a friend are not the same. Although peer once meant someone of equal status, the word is now used to indicate anyone of similar age (Hartup, 1983). Friendship connotes a positive, reciprocal relationship (Shantz, 1983). Children in the same class are peers, yet a particular child may have few, if any, friends. In fact, five to ten percent of all elementary schoolchildren are named by no one in their class as a friend (Asher & Renshaw, 1981), and about twelve percent are named by only one person as a friend (Gronlund, 1959). Such a lack of popularity can have many undesirable consequences for the child.

Popularity and Unpopularity

Certain characteristics lead to popularity and unpopularity in school. For example, children quickly learn society's standards of beauty. Children as young as three years old reflect adult standards when asked to choose which children are prettier (Dion, 1973). Physical attractiveness is related to acceptance. In elementary school, stereotypes of beauty are well established, and children deviating substantially from the norm are likely to be rejected. Children also relate best to others who share their interests (Byrne, 1961). Those who have the same interests are more likely to start a conversation and play together. In addition, if children share similar attitudes and backgrounds, they meet on common ground and accept one another.

Peer acceptance is also related to friendliness (Hartup, 1970). Children who are outgoing, know how to give positive reinforcement, and are enthusiastic and accepting are popular. Deviant and negative reactions to others are related to rejection (Hartup, 1983), and unpopular children often show social skills deficits (Asher & Renshaw, 1981). Late in middle childhood, such traits as loyalty and empathy become important. Not everyone has the social skills necessary to interact successfully with peers. These skills include giving positive social responses, attending to what others are saying, giving affection and acceptance, sharing, and being able to communicate (Asher et al., 1977). Unpopular children do not interact well with other children, are aggressive, and criticize others. Those who are most rejected are often aggressive (Coie & Dodge, 1988), and both rejected boys and girls often play with other ostracized children (Cairns et al., 1988; Pellegrini, 1988). One way to help unpopular children is to teach them the social skills they lack. Although popularity in class is beneficial, having a few close friends is probably more important to a child's overall development.

Students who do not know how to resolve conflict and reinforce others are often rejected.

True or False   Aggressive children tend to be unpopular and rejected.

Friendships and Interpersonal Influence

Although children interact with other children from infancy, they begin to form friendships in early childhood. Like all preschool interpersonal relationships, these friendships are fragile (Corsaro, 1981) and fleeting. Preschoolers see friends in terms of playmates, and friendship is defined by momentary interactions. The qualification for friendship is simply being physically present and willing to play (Rubin, 1980). Friendships form and disintegrate very quickly, and relationships are not based on any real intimacy.

In the early elementary school years, a gradual change takes place. Between the ages of four and seven, common activities, affection, support, and closeness are all important, but expectations concerning affection and support increase with age while references to physical characteristics decrease (Furman & Bierman, 1983). Older children see support, helping, sharing, and affection as more important than common activities. Friendships become more stable as children progress from grade one to grade four (Berndt & Hoyle, 1985). As children mature, they begin to look at psychological compatibility (Rubin, 1980) and see friends as people with whom they can share both good times and problems. Friendships become based on deeper values, such as intimacy, trust, loyalty, and faithfulness (Berndt, 1981).

Same-sex friendships are the rule during middle childhood. Boys and girls do talk with one another, but their relationships lack intimacy and involvement and are less stable than same-sex friendships (Tuma & Hallinan, 1979). Active rejection of the opposite sex is rare; avoidance is the usual course of action (Hartup, 1983). This segregation reaches its peak during the late elementary or early junior high school years (Schofield, 1981). Of course, individual differences do exist, and some fast-developing seventh graders may be ready to develop cross-sex friendships.

Peer influence increases throughout middle childhood and into adolescence. The amount of time spent with parents declines, and the sheer quantity of time spent with friends increases. In early adolescence, dependence on parents decreases while dependence on peers increases. Adolescents become more emotionally autonomous; they idealize their parents less and relinquish some of their childhood dependence on them. This is accompanied by increased susceptibility to peer influences (Steinberg & Silverberg, 1986). Adolescents in late junior high and early high school (eighth and ninth graders) are most influenced by peers (Berndt, 1979).

Teaching Social Skills

A child may not have friends, may be unpopular, or may be unable to interact effectively with other students for many reasons. Both teachers and students can easily point out the unpopular students in the classroom (Coie & Dodge, 1988). Often these students lack the **social skills** needed to succeed in interpersonal relationships, and they carry this problem with them from interaction to interaction (Mergendoller & Marchman, 1987). When they enter a new group, they become unpopular rapidly and remain so (Coie & Kupersmidt, 1983). In addition, such students do not usually outgrow their deficits. Specifically, social skills include the ability to follow instructions, accept criticism, disagree appropriately, greet someone, make a request, and reinforce and compliment others as well as using acceptable ways of getting attention (Kail et al., 1988). Nonverbal skills, such as looking at the listener when talking, are also included.

True or False   Children with poor social skills usually outgrow their problem.

social skills   Skills necessary for good interpersonal relations, including the ability to follow instructions, accept criticism, disagree appropriately, greet someone, make a request, and reinforce and compliment others.

The teacher hoping to improve a child's social skills must first assess the extent to which particular skills are used by an individual or a class (Keefe, 1988). A target skill is then identified and taught. Students learn such skills best when a number of examples are given. Stories and movies can be used to set the stage, and roleplaying is especially helpful (Manning, 1986). For example, a student may roleplay how to ask a teacher to change a grade or how to disagree with an authority figure. Special attention should be paid to facial expressions, gestures, and intonations. Teachers can also model these techniques. A number of commercially prepared social skills training programs are available (Epstein & Cullinan,

During the elementary school years, boys' and girls' groups normally separate. Avoidance rather than rejection is the rule.

1987). These programs cover both problems and opportunities for friendly interaction and focus on different ways to solve problems using such tools as compromise, communication, cooperation, and support rather than power (Mergendoller & Marchman, 1987). Opportunities for rehearsal are important, and generalization should be encouraged. Social skills are an important area of concern and one that must be addressed, especially for those who lack such skills.

Even the unpopular child who has learned some social skills may still have difficulty in social interactions. Unpopular children not only need to learn these skills but also need an opportunity to show them off, because their peers continue to reject them out of habit (Bierman & Furman, 1984). In addition, a child may be unpopular for other reasons, such as not having the same interests as other children his or her age. The teacher can help by suggesting activities in which the child can meet other children of similar interests. For example, a teacher may encourage a child interested in stamp collecting to join a stamp club. In addition, teachers can give children the opportunity to practice these skills by using cooperative learning strategies (see Chapter 8) and peer tutoring (see Chapter 11) and by planning activities that increase communication among students. For the truly unpopular student, a relationship with the teacher may be the child's only hope for understanding, and it may be that the only way to help this child is by building a special relationship with him or her. Such simple activities as meeting the child at the door and saying "hello," speaking to the child on the playground, and remembering the child's birthday may build such a relationships and encourage the student to seek out help (Manning, 1986). Last, some students will join the class well into the school term. These latecomers must break into established groups. Each new student must be introduced to the others, although this may not be sufficient. Sometimes assigning another student to help a new student get to know his or her way around can get the new student involved in social interactions.

THE CHANGING FAMILY AND THE SCHOOL

Social skills, the self-concept, and self-esteem arise in large measure from the child's experience at home. The family is naturally the greatest influence on the child's life, and family problems and changes can affect the child's academic and social abilities. The American family today, however, is a far cry from what it was even thirty years ago, and many parents now believe that the school does not understand the new family and its needs.

The structure of the modern family has changed. Today, the traditional family consisting of a mother who is a homemaker, a father who works, and two children is less common. In fact, only five percent of the families have a working father and a homemaker mother (Barney & Koford, 1987). The number of single-parent families has increased substantially, and one million children each year are affected by divorce. As many as three quarters of all divorced people will remarry, but children will spend on the average of six years in a family headed by a single parent (Hetherington, 1979).

Many more women are working. Between 1973 and 1986, the number of working mothers with children under six rose from 33 percent to 57.4 percent. Over 72 percent of all women with children from age six to age seventeen are in the labor force, and 54.8 percent of all women with children under three are employed outside the home (U.S. Department of Commerce, 1989). Most women work because they have to. Two thirds of all women in the labor force are single, widowed, divorced, separated, or married to husbands who do not earn much money (Maymi, 1982). In other

The traditional family consisting of a working father, a mother who is a homemaker, and two children is declining.

words, most women work out of economic necessity. Partly because of this trend, teachers will be seeing many more students who have experienced day care in their classes. In addition, many elementary school students will have to take care of themselves before and after school.

Since the teacher cannot change these social trends, why discuss them here? First, it is important for the teacher to understand the child's experiences and the family's needs. Second, many teachers blame these social changes for some of the problems children experience in school, and these beliefs may affect the teacher's behavior. Therefore, looking at the evidence concerning how these experiences affect children is appropriate.

Day Care

What is the effect of day care on a child's subsequent behavior in school? We might assume that if a child went from a stimulating environment at home to a good day-care center, little gain or loss should occur. But if a child came from a nonstimulating environment to a stimulating environment, some gain should result. If a child came from a stimulating environment to a poor quality day-care center, negative effects should be apparent. Indeed the research supports these notions (Belsky & Steinberg, 1979).

Day care seems to have no injurious effects on the cognitive development of low-risk children (Belsky & Steinberg, 1978). For disadvantaged children, an enriched day-care program may encourage cognitive development (Kaplan, 1988). The evidence on the effects of the day-care experience on social development shows that generally the overall social and emotional adjustment of day-care children is good and compares well with that of children raised at home (Watkins & Bradbard, 1984; Etaugh, 1980). Some differences have been noted, however. Children who experience day care are more outgoing, but they are also more aggressive and boisterous (Clarke-Stewart, 1982). Children enrolled in day care are inclined to be more impulsive and egocentric as well (Belsky & Steinberg, 1978). Children in day care interact more with their peers. However, the type of program makes a difference. Children enrolled in a cognitively oriented day-care establishment were more aggressive in the early years of elementary school

than were children who had attended more typical programs that focus on social skills. These children, however, were not considered difficult to manage, and the aggression decreased over time (Haskins, 1985). When more attention is given to prosocial behaviors in these programs, aggression is reduced and cognitive gains are not affected (Finkelstein, 1982). In summary, although differences exist in the social-emotional area, there is no evidence that day care causes serious emotional or social problems for children.

Much depends, however, on the quality of the day-care center (Phillips et al., 1987). High-quality, stable child care is associated with positive school outcomes (Howes, 1988). All the effects described above are mediated by the characteristics of the day-care center and the home. In one study, four-year-olds were observed during play at both good and poor-quality day-care centers and again four years later in play. Those from good day-care centers had more friends, showed more friendly interactions with peers, and were rated as more socially competent and happier at eight than those who attended poor-quality day-care centers (Vandell et al., 1988). Certain factors are especially important in evaluating the quality of a center. One such factor is the nature of the program. Although day care should not be thought of in terms of school, such activities as reading to children and playing social games can contribute to social and intellectual growth. Other factors such as the child-to-caregiver ratio, safety, ventilation, security, cleanliness, convenience, staff turnover, and cost should also be taken into consideration.

True or False Generally, children who attend day care have moderately serious social and emotional problems during their elementary school years.

Nursery School

It is sometimes difficult, if not impossible, to know where day care ends and nursery school begins. The growth in nursery school attendance has been impressive. Nursery school enrollment of three- and four-year-olds doubled between 1970 and 1983. In 1970, 14.3 percent of the three- and four-year-olds were attending nursery school, while in 1983 the percentage stood at 33.6 percent. In 1986, about 29 percent of the three-year-olds and 49 percent of the four-year-olds attended nursery school (U.S. Department of Commerce, 1989). The trend towards increased enrollments in nursery school is continuing. The need for many women to work and the increase in one-parent families account for part of this increase. In other cases, parents worry that unless their children receive a preschool education they will enter elementary school at a disadvantage.

There are many approaches to preschool education. Some emphasize the importance of social skills and emotional development and include in their programs telling stories, listening to music, looking at art, taking trips, and encouraging cooperation and sharing (McClinton & Meier, 1978). Others are more cognitively oriented. Generally speaking, nursery schools accomplish their purposes. Children who attend nursery school are more advanced than their nonattending peers. This is especially true for children in lower-income groups (Minuchin & Shapiro, 1983). Children who attend preschool programs are more socially competent, outgoing, self-assured, curious, independent, and persistent on a task than those who do not attend. In elementary school, such children are better adjusted and more task oriented, goal directed, persistent, cooperative, and friendly (Clarke-Stewart & Fein, 1983).

Project Head Start

The finding that children, especially those from poor backgrounds, are likely to benefit from the preschool experience is important. If children from poverty backgrounds enter school behind their middle-class counterparts, they are likely to fall farther behind as they progress through school. Perhaps if these children could attend a preschool that would help compensate for their different experiences, this cycle could be stopped and the children would have a reasonable chance for academic success. This was partly the thinking behind one of the greatest educational and social experiments of the past fifty years: **Project Head Start** (Cooke, 1979).

Project Head Start   A federally funded education program aimed at reducing or eliminating the differences in educational achievement between poor and middle-class youngsters.

The original hope of this project was that a program instituted early enough could give children living in poverty a head start in school and reduce or eliminate the social class differences in educational achievement (Zigler & Berman, 1983). Project Head Start had both cognitive and social goals (Washington, 1985). Children were to learn to work and play independently, become able to accept help and direction from adults, learn competence and self-worth, sharpen and widen their language skills, be curious, and grow in ability to channel inner destructive impulses. The program also had health goals.

Recent research demonstrates the beneficial effects of the Head Start experience. Students who had taken part in Head Start were significantly less likely to be held back a grade or to be found in special education classes. The results of studies on reading and mathematics achievement of children who attended a Head Start program are mixed, with some showing Head Start children achieving more in mathematics and reading (Lazar et al., 1982; Darlington et al., 1980). In fact, recent study showed that Head Start was superior to other preschool programs (Lee et al., 1988).

Should Four-Year-Olds Go to Public School?

If the research shows that preschool experiences may enrich a child's cognitive and social growth, why not require all preschoolers to attend school? The movement to open public schools to four-year-olds is gaining strength (Hymes, 1987) for many reasons. The increased number of children whose parents work and who must attend day care, the increased popularity of nursery schools, and the fact that special groups of children attending preschool programs gain from such programs have all added to the arguments for beginning public education at a younger age than we do today. On the surface, this seems reasonable. However, there are problems. For example, the data on middle-class, preschool-age children indicate that high-quality out-of-home care has neither an adverse nor a beneficial effect. The greater benefits are found for lower-income children (Kagan, 1985). In addition, any universal public four-year-old school program will be very expensive. Most important, there are possible dangers, especially of pushing children to read and write before they are ready and overselling to the public what can be taught to four-year-olds. These dangers are well brought out in David Elkind's 1987 book, *Miseducation.* No educator or psychologist is opposed to teaching children to read or write when such children are ready. However, "only between 1 and 3 percent of the children are reading with comprehension before entering kindergarten and the majority of children do not show interest in how to read until ages five or six" (Elkind, 1987, p. 185). We are miseducating our children if we push youngsters into academic situations in which they are not ready. Too often, educational programs that are designed for school-age children are being written down to the level of four-year-olds. Elkind believes that we place these young children at a risk for short-term stress and long-term personality damage and that these programs do not serve any useful purpose or have any lasting benefits. Some of these programs communicate inappropriate expectations, and little attention is given to individual differences in development and learning styles. Similar questions are being asked about the kindergarten curricula as well (Egertson, 1987).

The question of universal education for preschool children is controversial. Elkind reminds us that any such program must be developmentally related to the child's needs and abilities, and he encourages us to question the appropriateness of academic training for young children. Others argue that appropriate education can be offered to preschoolers and that the public schools ought to get involved. The controversy is an ongoing one with no clear answer in sight.

Overall, we can conclude that high-quality, developmentally appropriate preschool experiences do not injure the child or cause later academic problems. As noted, the evidence shows that such experiences may even aid children, especially those from lower socioeconomic backgrounds. Yet, the public should not be oversold on what can be accomplished with such programs, which may constitute a danger if too much pressure is placed on young children to develop academic skills before they are ready.

Latchkey or Self-Care Children

When Mark comes home from the fourth grade, no one is waiting for him. Both his mother and his father work, and he spends two hours a day alone. Will this experience affect him socially and academically? No one really knows how many such children exist in the United States. Estimates of the number of elementary

Many elementary schoolchildren return home from school to an empty house. New research has discovered the importance of parents knowing where their children are and communicating with them on a regular basis.

schoolchildren who are home alone after school range from two to ten million, and it is estimated that about 15 percent of children from six to nine years of age and about 45 percent of children from nine to eleven fall into this category (Goleman, 1988). These children are called **latchkey children** or, more recently, **self-care children** (Rodman et al., 1985). The public is greatly concerned about the safety and development of these children (Campbell & Flake, 1985). A nationwide poll found that teachers look to the lack of supervision at home after school as a major reason for lack of achievement (Flax, 1987). They cite the latchkey situation more often than poverty or single-parent families. Many parents agree.

Are these opinions substantiated by research? Rodman and colleagues (1985) compared forty-eight self-care children with forty-eight matched children with adult care on such variables as self-esteem, locus of control, social adjustment, and interpersonal relationships, and found no significant differences.

latchkey children (self-care children) Elementary schoolchildren who must care for themselves after school hours. (Some add junior high school students to the definition.)

However, Steinberg (1986) criticized this research, since Rodman used only children who usually went directly home after school. Steinberg also argued that the public was more concerned about the possibility that these unsupervised children might get into trouble, especially since other studies have shown that parental monitoring deters delinquent activity. Instead, Steinberg measured susceptibility to peer pressure in children grades five through nine, finding that adolescents who report home after school were not significantly different from other children but that children who were removed from adult supervision were more susceptible to peer pressure to engage in antisocial activity. Adolescents whose parents knew their children's whereabouts were less susceptible, even if the supervision was somewhat lax. Unfortunately, nearly half of the self-care youngsters seem not to go directly home (Steinberg, 1988). Steinberg concludes that parental monitoring is most important and that even long-distance monitoring, as when children call their parents at work to tell them that they're home, can be useful.

True or False Elementary schoolchildren who regularly return home from school to an empty house and call their parents are no more susceptible to peer pressure nor do they have lower self-esteem than children who have a parent present when they get home from school.

Some organizations have begun to institute survival courses for these children and their parents. The courses encourage parents to evaluate the maturity level of their children and the ability of their children to be alone. They also teach children safety and survival skills, such as how to talk to strangers on the phone, discriminating between emergencies and nonemergencies, and caring for younger siblings. One study of a thousand children found that after such courses, children felt more confident about handling both emergencies and everyday situations. However, the children strongly wished that a parent were home with them or would call them. They experienced a sense of independence and accomplishment, but they also felt frightened, lonely, and bored (Gray & Coolsen, 1987).

Divorce

Teachers also consider divorce and the "broken family" reasons for lack of achievement in school. Di-
vorce is not just an event; it is an experience that affects the entire family forever. Divorce brings many changes. Not only is the child's world torn asunder, but his or her entire lifestyle may be disrupted. Financial problems may force the family to move to a new neighborhood, altering the daily routine. Most children do not see these changes in a positive light even years after the divorce (Wallerstein et al., 1988).

Almost all children find divorce a painful experience. The early symptoms may differ from child to child, but they include anger, depression, and guilt (Hetherington, 1979). Children often show such behavior changes as regression, sleep disturbances, and fear (Wallerstein, 1983). Parent-child relationships also change. The custodial parent—usually the mother—becomes stricter and more controlling, while the other parent becomes permissive and understanding though less accessible. Both parents make fewer demands on children to mature, become less consistent in their discipline, and have more difficulty communicating with the children (Hetherington et al., 1978). Parents' discipline practices become poorer (Forgatch et al., 1988), and conduct problems are not uncommon (Brody & Forehand, 1988).

Children react in different ways to divorce depending upon the child's age. Preschoolers are often very distressed and show regressive behavior and separation anxiety. Children in elementary school feel powerless and frightened and frequently are angry at one or both parents and may support one parent. About one half show severe drops in achievement during the year. Adolescents often show acute depression, acting-out behavior, emotional and social withdrawal, and anxiety about their future (Wallerstein et al., 1988).

How quickly a child recovers from the initial shock depends upon whether a stable environment is created and whether the divorced parents can act with civility as well as on the social supports available to the child (Kurdek, 1981). Although many of these initial reactions either become less severe or disappear by the end of the first year (Hetherington, 1979), the long-term effects of divorce on children can be severe. In one study of children whose parents divorced during their middle childhood years, the functioning of half had improved while about one quarter of the subjects had become significantly worse (Kelly & Wallerstein, 1976). Children from one-parent families do not differ in academic ability or intelligence, but they are absent from school more often, are more disruptive, have lower grades, and are viewed by teachers as less motivated (Minuchin & Shapiro, 1983).

True or False Children from one-parent families have less academic ability than children from two-parent families.

Children recover best when both parents are involved and there is a minimum of conflict (Abarbanel, 1979). Unfortunately, conflict does not end with the divorce. One study found that 66 percent of the exchanges between ex-spouses two months after the divorce were marked by conflict (Hetherington et al., 1978). When there is less conflict, the outcome is better (Forehand, et al., 1988). In addition, at a time when children require more social support, less is offered. Parents are often confused and must rearrange their own lives. Peer relationships may suffer, as some children feel guilty about what is happening. Family friends may be forced to take sides and maintain contact with only one parent. The main social supports are weakened at a time when increased support is required.

Sometimes the divorce itself is blamed for the children's problems, but family turmoil, whether or not it ends in divorce, creates problems for children (Emery, 1982). The more open and intense the hostility, the more serious the children's difficulties. Marital turmoil is also related to underachievement in school, and evidence indicates that some of the problems that can be considered consequences of divorce may be present before divorce (Block et al., 1986).

The Stepfamily Experience

Most parents who divorce will remarry. About one in six children is now a stepchild (Strong & DeVault, 1989). When positive relationships exist between stepparents and stepchildren, the children are less aggressive, and females in particular show higher levels of self-esteem (Clingempeel & Segal, 1986). In addition, it is commonly believed that children do not thrive in stepfamilies because the adjustments are so difficult. However, the most common finding of studies comparing stepfamilies with nuclear families on adjustment or cognitive functioning is that there is little or no difference (Clingempeel & Segal, 1986). In fact, when stepfamilies and single-parent families are compared, the presence of a stepfather reduces some of the negative effects of divorce for boys, and males

score higher both on measures of cognitive development and on measures of adjustment (Oshman & Manosevitz, 1976; Santrock, 1972).

There is no doubt that stepchildren are faced with many adjustments. However, research in this area shows that living in a stepfamily can be a positive experience depending upon the quality of the relationship between parents and children.

>>> **CONNECTIONS**

The School and the "New" Family

The experience of many youngsters today is different from what it was years ago. The changes are great, and no doubt the educational experience of the child is affected by the home situation. Yet, as shown, before we make any wild suppositions about the latchkey situation causing this problem or stepfamilies causing that one, we ought to look at the research and put our prejudices aside. The following suggestions might be helpful in dealing with some of the challenges these changes raise.

1. **Consider your attitude towards stepfamilies, single-parent families, day care, and self-care children.** Teachers sometimes possess negative stereotypes of the stepfamily or the latchkey child. It is important to be aware of your attitudes towards these changes that may influence your dealings with both students and parents.

2. **Don't assume all children live in two-parent families.** Since single-parent status is more common, use "parent/guardian" or "family" on forms.

3. **Make appointments and communicate with parents when it is practical and convenient for all parties.** It is not easy for working parents to take a day off. Some teachers advocate evening conferences (Barney & Koford, 1987), although this may not be practical. Still, telephone calls and regular communication channels can be established.

4. **Consider how families are portrayed in stories and textbooks.** Many texts still emphasize a working father, a homemaker mother, and two children. This is not the case for 95 percent of children. It is helpful to find stories that deal with stepfamilies and working mothers in a positive manner.

5. **Consider survival skills training.** Many students will be involved in self care. Although more research is needed, the available studies do not

indicate that self care inevitably leads to difficulties. Two keys seem most important. First, parents must know where the child is and monitor the child at home even from a distance. Second, children require survival skills training. Teachers may become involved by running such seminars in the evening, perhaps together with some community organization.

6. **Be aware of changes in student conduct, work habits, or grades that may signify a deterioration of the home situation.** Teachers often do not know that a divorce is occurring in the home and do not understand that behavioral changes may be due to the family breakup (Wallerstein & Kelly, 1980). If the child's behavior or academic work shows a precipitous change, contact the parents immediately.

7. **Be sensitive to the child's reaction to divorce.** Children going through a parental divorce often show symptoms, especially withdrawal. The child may need support, and cooperative activities can keep the child involved.

8. **When dealing with parents going through a divorce, encourage the parents to keep communication with their children open.** Children experiencing a parental divorce often show a decrease in academic performance, but a good relationship with at least one parent can prevent some school-related problems (Forehand et al., 1987).

9. **Be ready to refer the student to counseling if necessary.** A student going through a divorce or having difficulties in a stepfamily may require counseling. Sometimes the child will feel more comfortable talking to a teacher, but a teacher may believe that he or she cannot provide the counseling necessary, and some referral to the guidance counselor may be in order.

10. **Involve the noncustodial parent when appropriate.** Many noncustodial parents are eager to learn about their children's progress (Colson, 1987). However, regular channels of communication may not be open. The district's policies in this area should be checked, and when appropriate, noncustodial parents should receive progress reports if they want them.

11. **Communication with the home should not always be critical of the student.** When a parent receives letters or telephone calls from the school it is normally a complaint about his or her child. Sometimes a teacher must be critical of a student, but it is important for the teacher to balance criticism with positive feedback about the student's progress whenever possible.

12. **Understand the unique challenges of the stepfamily and the divorce situation.** Manning and Wootten (1987) asked stepparents what they would like the school to know and do about the challenges of stepfamilies. Many suggestions were made. Among the most important was being sensitive to basic stepfamily issues involving stresses, establishing better communication with the family, and recognizing that the child has two families. These parents felt that the school should learn about the family situation and send reports to both sets of parents when appropriate. New stepchildren may need special attention during the early transitional phase. In addition, noncustodial parents and stepparents often want to be actively involved but do not feel welcome. There should be room for stepparents at graduations and open houses. Parents would like school personnel to communicate to their classes that the blended family is a viable family unit and would like visitation and special problems taken into consideration. Some children may not be able to finish an assignment or study if Tuesday, for example, is the only day a student can visit a parent. Schools should also be sensitive to the work schedules of parents and should not side with one natural parent or the other. It should be realized that many stepchildren in the younger grades must make more than one set of gifts. Generally, stepparents' suggestions centered around improved communication, a desire for teachers to show greater understanding, a change in curricula to show that these family structures are viable, and a desire to be more involved.

The modern family is more varied and teachers may be dealing with children who face a number of challenges at home. Yet, these children can and do succeed, and the teacher can play a positive role not only in teaching academic skills but also in helping children with their adjustment to their new family situation, their self-esteem, and their interpersonal relationships.

GENDER AND CULTURAL ISSUES

The family does not exist in a vacuum. Two overriding factors that affect a child's self-esteem and interpersonal relationships are gender and culture.

Many children in stepfamilies may have to make two gifts, one for their biological mother or father and one for their stepmother or stepfather.

Sex Roles

"Sally, you pass out the candy; Sam, you wash the blackboard."

"Jim, you go to woodshop; Cindy, you go to home economics."

"Peter, you should be taking trig; Jannette, do you want to take intermediate algebra?"

Our interactions and self-concepts are partially based upon our concepts of sex roles. **Sex roles** consist of the behaviors expected of people in a given society based on a person's gender. These roles may serve to limit an individual. For example, people who believe that truck drivers are men and nurses are women are limiting themselves. How one perceives sex roles acts as a mediator informing boys and girls

about what they should or should not do (Fennema, 1987). For example, a girl who believes that doing well in mathematics is not feminine may not be as persistent in math as she could be.

Of course, teachers and schools are not totally responsible for a child's understanding of sex roles. Certainly, the family, one's peer group, and the media influence this aspect of life, and students begin school with a knowledge of sex roles (Nash, 1979). However, the school also affects the social roles assumed by students. There are four areas in which the school has been criticized for sexist practices (Minuchin & Shapiro, 1983); (1) bias in teacher-student interactions, (2) sex stereotypes in the curricula, (3) inequality in access to programs, and (4) a lack of role models. The first two areas are of special importance to the classroom teacher.

Differences exist in the way teachers interact with boys and girls. Although elementary schoolteachers interact more with boys than with girls, much of this interaction is critical. Teachers are more likely to reprimand boys (Serbin et al., 1973). Boys are more likely to be seen as causing trouble, and girls do not receive as much harsh discipline in school as boys. When teachers attend to task-oriented activities in class, boys still receive more attention than girls (Fagot, 1977). In addition, when children demand attention, teachers respond to boys with instructions and to girls with nurturance. Girls are also given more attention when physically close to teachers, while boys are given more attention when they are far away. Perhaps teachers expect good behavior from girls but feel that boys require encouragement. Male and female teachers are not very different in their views of student behavior. Perhaps these interactions reinforce physical proximity and conformity in girls and more task-oriented behaviors in boys.

True or False Boys receive more attention from elementary schoolteachers than girls do.

Books may also contribute to the perpetuation of traditional sex roles. An interesting exercise is to go to the library and analyze the sex roles shown in

Both boys and girls should be encouraged to do all chores in the classroom. Chores should not be divided on the basis of gender.

Could these sex role stereotypes affect achievement? Even though no sex differences exist in intelligence, girls perform better than boys in reading, spelling, and verbal skills, while boys—at least in the later elementary school years—do better in mathematics and problems involving spatial analysis (Busch-Rossnagel & Vance, 1982). Why should these differences exist? Perhaps girls are more ready for school, and this physiological readiness gives them a push toward academic achievement (McGuinness, 1979). Perhaps the atmosphere of school is considered feminine, with its great percentage of female teachers and its emphasis on obedience and sitting still. Boys and girls experience school in very different ways, and both male and female teachers value the stereotyped feminine traits of obedience and passivity rather than aggressiveness and independence (Etaugh & Hughes, 1975).

At least in the early grades, boys may find school achievement more difficult and not in keeping with their view of the masculine role. One reason put forward for male superiority in mathematics in the later grades is that males expect to do better. These higher expectations are found as early as the first grade, even though boys' grades and abilities are not superior to those of girls (Entwisle & Baker, 1983). Attitudes towards mathematics are particularly important, because they are related to math performance in both sexes (Paulsen & Johnson, 1983). Differences in performance are not inevitable, especially when females have positive attitudes toward mathematics.

Adolescent girls and boys do not achieve identically in secondary schools either. Girls' achievement levels slip. The gap between males and females closes rapidly in high school. Perhaps some of the change occurs not only because males begin to value school achievement but also because teachers now value the sex role competencies of males more than females. Females may be more comfortable in elementary school and find that their noncompetitive, highly social, more obedient behavior brings them praise and is greatly valued by teachers. However, in secondary school, males become more aware of their future and take school more seriously. Perhaps teachers also be-

children's books. A number of the books are blatant, not only in their narrative but also in their pictures. But bias does not have to be obvious, as when men are pictured as scientists and engineers and females are depicted as elementary schoolteachers and nurses. Some mathematics books give verbal problems that involve action sequences that are sex stereotyped. Tom mixes chemicals or fixes his bicycle, while female names are used when something is being done to someone else. Evidence indicates that children are aware of the sex roles of the characters in stories and especially remember if the sex roles run counter to expectations. Children resist change. Jennings (1975) reversed some stories, allowing a girl to be a mail carrier and a boy to be a ballet dancer. The children remembered this switch and preferred the traditional sex roles in their stories. Sexist materials include those in which one sex appears as the main characters or is illustrated far less frequently, the sexes are gin to value more the aggressiveness and competitiveness of males.

The fact that males catch up and females lag in high school does not tell us anything about the reasons this happens. There are many theories but few real facts. Women have an achievement orientation equal to that of men. They are also as persistent as men. The evidence on self-esteem is mixed, with some studies showing it to be very similar (Richmond-Abbott, 1983) while other studies show moderately higher levels in males (Robison-Awana et al., 1986). It is possible that sex-role orientations and expectations affect and sometimes limit academic plans and achievement.

We are all probably aware of the scene in which a bright adolescent female is advised not to take an advanced mathematics course because it's a waste of time. After all, what is she going to do with it anyway? This type of blatant sexism has been held up to public scrutiny and criticized, as it should be. But such statements are probably less common than the subtle communication of expectations. In many schools and homes today, females are not actively restricted from these areas, they are simply not encouraged to take such courses. Females do not have to be actively dissuaded from achieving. Lack of encouragement produces the same result.

Because of societal biases, female teenagers frequently need encouragement to continue their studies in science and mathematics.

Reducing Sex Role Stereotyping in the Classroom

The school has a responsibility to eliminate sexual stereotyping and sexist practices. It also can play a role in expanding children's ideas about what is appropriate for males and females. The following ideas are just some ways in which the classroom teacher can help.

1. **Become aware of your stereotyping both in communication and behavior.** Statements such as "I need two strong boys to carry . . ." and "Girls are so artistic" are limiting (Shapiro et al., 1981). In addition, take special notice of your tendencies to place students in sex-stereotyped jobs around the classroom, having the boys do one thing and the girls another.

2. **Target all groups for broadening sex roles, not just girls.** Fennema (1987) asserts that if girls are targeted to help change their mathematics attitudes and nothing is done to change the attitudes of boys that mathematics is strictly a masculine domain, it is much more difficult to succeed in expanding sex roles perceptions.

3. **Try to evenly distribute leadership roles in the classroom.** When organizing group work, equalize the number of male and female leaders.

4. **Show examples of sex stereotyping used in the media and in school materials.** Make students aware of the problem. For example, many advertisements are sexist, such as those showing action-oriented toys as meant only for males.

5. **Be aware of your expectations for students.** Expect high achievement for all subjects from both males and females.

6. **Review instructional materials for bias.** Although there has been an improvement in many instructional materials in this regard, some bias may still exist.

7. **Show nontraditional models in a positive light whenever possible.** When discussing literature, science, or history note nontraditional role models.

8. **Be aware of the everyday casual remarks that unnecessarily differentiate boys and girls.** Some authorities suggest that classroom seating and lunchroom seating separating boys and girls is unnecessary (Shapiro et al., 1981).

9. **Look for gender-stereotyped practices in school, such as girls taking cooking and boys taking shop.** Children should be exposed to both.

Race and Ethnicity

Another significant variable affecting social development is one's cultural background. There are two areas of interest here. First, it is important for students to understand and value not only their own culture but also other people's cultures. Second, one social goal of schooling is to reduce prejudice and improve interpersonal relationships across racial and ethnic groups. To do so, we must find effective ways of encouraging such interactions.

Multiethnic or Multicultural Education

One way to reduce prejudice is to understand and appreciate the cultural heritage and contributions of other cultures. A movement called **multiethnic** or **multicultural education** aims at giving individuals some knowledge and understanding of one another's culture in the hope that respect will ensue. It also seeks to show how history can be seen from other perspectives. American history is sometimes seen as affecting only Anglo-Americans, and the movement tries to show how different events may have affected other cultural groups as well. If only one viewpoint is given in the class, the students are denied a knowledge of the music, literature, values, lifestyles, and culture of other groups. Such education also attempts to reduce prejudice through the realization that people may at the same time retain their cultural background and contribute to American culture. Proponents of such an approach ask for a change in philosophy and the curriculum. However, much can be done by the regular classroom teacher.

>>> CONNECTIONS

The Teacher and Multicultural Education

1. **Stress the understanding that people from all ethnic groups have contributed to America's culture and history.** It is important to demonstrate that Americans are a diverse people.
2. **Help students see history though the eyes of other people.** (Benjamin, 1985) In discussing some historical event, try to see it from both sides. Giving assignments that encourage students to look at some issue from different perspectives is valuable.

3. **Do not overemphasize differences between groups.** Although an understanding of differences is obviously important here, all groups have similar hopes, wants, and needs but different ways of satisfying them.
4. **Do not allow your multicultural activities to hinge only on heroes.** (Banks, 1977) One easy and fashionable way of giving lip service to multiethnic education is to concentrate on heroes. Heroes can be role models, and showing how particularly important people have contributed to American history and culture is reasonable. However, too often that has been the extent of it, and it is far too easy to consider these people exceptions to the rule. In addition, often the same heroes are discussed over and over, giving the impression that only they have contributed. The multiethnic approach means more than introducing a few heroes. It means understanding the experience of people and their daily contributions.
5. **Discuss misunderstanding of culture in class.** Sometimes newspapers and television programs discuss cultural misunderstandings. Speakers can also be used here. In one high school class, the teacher emphasized business and culture, bringing in some business executives to discuss how the culture affects international trade and how understanding can help.
6. **Be sensitive to the different meaning holidays may have to particular ethnic groups.** Columbus Day may mean something very different to Native Americans, while Christmas and Easter may have very different significance to Jewish Americans. Understanding the discomfort that may be there does not mean that these holidays should not be noted; it does mean that some sensitivity should be shown.

Relationships Among Ethnic and Racial Groups

Consider this problem. You are a teacher of a class where the ratio of white to black students is about

multiethnic education (multicultural education) Multidisciplinary approach to education that aims at teaching students about the cultural heritage of various groups and the many contributions each group makes to society.

It is good to discuss the contributions specific people have made to American society, but care should be taken to be certain students are taught the daily contributions minorities make to American life and history.

60:40. You notice that although there is little overt prejudice expressed, the two groups do not interact very much. Each group ignores the other, with only a few exceptions.

This situation is not at all unusual. When many schools were integrated, it was assumed that physical proximity would encourage interaction, dispel prejudice, and reduce intergroup problems. However, the results have not been particularly promising (Weyant, 1986). We have not seen the expected precipitous drop in racial prejudice or the increases in interaction between blacks and white. Studies have not shown that desegregation has reduced prejudice or resulted in increases in self-esteem (Stephan, 1978).

The lack of progress could have been predicted. Gordon Allport (1954) argued that to succeed in reducing prejudice, contact needs to be planned to fulfill three characteristics. First, the groups must have equal status. Second, they should share a common goal. Third, they should engage in activities that are supported by authority figures. Unfortunately, these three components have often been lacking. Status differences between majority and minority students are often maintained, and systems in many classrooms do not encourage cooperation. In addition, many communities have not reacted positively to racial desegregation. Finally, there has been little attempt to bring the groups together.

Under these circumstances, it is not surprising that little or no social interaction occurs, and there is less than sufficient evidence for better understanding. Yet this does not mean it cannot happen. It just means that we cannot simply throw children together and expect them to do what we think is necessary. One answer is to provide situations in which cooperation is needed between people of different groups (Slavin, 1980). Studies show that if cooperative learning programs are used in which mixed groups of students help one another towards common goals, the result is more harmony and less conflict (Weigel et al., 1975). One very interesting technique developed by Elliot Aronson and colleagues (1978; 1980) is called the **jigsaw technique,** a method of instruction in which children from different ethnic groups work cooperatively to learn new material. In the first stage, teachers attend a workshop on the technique. Then the students are introduced to the instructional method. At first, they work at simple, nonacademic exercises that help them learn certain cooperative skills. They are then divided into racial and ethnic heterogeneous groups of five or six students, and each group meets for a few hours a day and works on some academic topic. The topic is divided into several sections, and each member of the group is given the responsibility of learning his or her own section and then teaching it to the other group members. Students from different groups who are responsible for the same sections are encouraged to help one another learn the material. The method fosters intergroup cooperation, intragroup

jigsaw technique   A method of instruction in which students from different ethnic groups work cooperatively to learn new material.

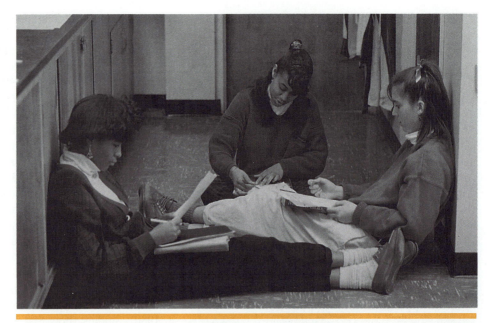

The challenge of integration is not necessarily the avoidance of conflict but rather how to encourage constructive interaction.

cooperation, and interdependence. Students are tested individually so that one child is not penalized because others have not learned the material. The groups are periodically changed. The research on such a technique is encouraging (Blaney et al., 1977). Studies report increases in both self-esteem and a liking for students' jigsaw group partners, little difference in content knowledge, and a decline in negative ethnic stereotypes (Weyant, 1986).

True or False The best way to encourage cross-racial and cross-ethnic friendly interaction is to desegregate classrooms and let students work out their own relationships.

 CONNECTIONS

Encouraging Social Interaction

Teachers can improve interaction and reduce conflict in the following ways:

1. **Use cooperative strategies.** The jigsaw technique and other cooperative learning techniques can help. In addition, two students may be assigned to research an item and report to the class.

2. **Do not allow homogeneous groups to participate in competitive activities.** In physical education class, five white students should not play against five black students. This violates the assumptions Allport noted for successful integration.

3. **Do not segregate within classes or schools.** Minority group members should not be segregated by being placed within one class. Within the classroom, try to encourage integrated seating.

4. **Promote understanding by emphasizing shared goals and concerns.** Encourage students to become involved in cooperative activities, such as collecting money for charity.

6. **Share leadership jobs.** Equal status must be maintained and leadership jobs should be shared.

7. **Actively fight racism, anti-Semitism, and negative stereotypes.** The teacher should not remain neutral in the face of prejudicial statements. The teacher must demonstrate that certain attitudes are out of the mainstream and are not acceptable.

8. **Some high schools have special programs aimed at improving communication and understanding among children of different groups.** If such a program exists in the school, support it and urge students to participate in the program.

> When there is greater tolerance and understanding and an increase in social interaction, conflict is reduced and everyone benefits. It is then that people can feel free to like or dislike one another, based not on some ethnic stereotype but upon personal characteristics and behaviors.

SOCIAL DEVELOPMENT AND THE CLASSROOM TEACHER REVISITED

Whenever people talk about better ways to teach subject matter or curricula reform, people listen intently. After all, the primary duty of the teacher is to teach the curriculum in the best way possible. Sometimes the importance of social factors in academic achievement and the social and personal life of the child are forgotten. Perhaps this is because teachers and the schools have a more limited influence on this area of life and they cannot easily change family and societal problems. However, research not only shows the importance of social interaction, the self-concept, and self-esteem in their own right, it also shows that these social factors have a direct influence on academic achievement. In addition, although teachers cannot make the unpopular child popular or the child who is suffering through the divorce of her parents forget her problems, the school experience can serve to reduce the problems and improve the child's self-esteem and social abilities. It is not a question of whether one should stress the cognitive or the social. Each affects the other, and teachers cannot teach the curricula and avoid the social aspects of schooling.

SUMMARY

1. Educators are interested in the social and personal development of children because helping children to build a positive view of themselves and good interpersonal relationships is a part of the school's purpose. Evidence indicates that the self-concept and interpersonal relationships mediate between the learner and what the student achieves in school.
2. Erik Erikson argued that each person proceeds through eight stages from cradle to grave. Each stage has a positive and a negative crisis. If the crisis is handled well, the resolution is positive. Each crisis sets the stage for the next crisis.
3. A person's self-concept is the picture one has of oneself. Self-esteem refers to the value one places on different aspects of the self. The self-concept and self-esteem affect behavior as well as how information is processed. Children develop a self-concept from the feedback they receive from others as well as from their evaluation of their own experience. Efforts to build a positive self-concept revolve around helping children feel more capable, more significant, more powerful, and more worthy.
4. The physical changes in adolescence affect the teen's self-concept. Early maturation in males is a social advantage during adolescence. The evidence concerning the effects of early maturation on females is mixed.
5. Adolescents often have difficulty differentiating between their own thoughts and those of others, leading to egocentric thinking. Out of this egocentrism comes the imaginary audience, in which adolescents often believe everyone else is looking at them, and the personal fable, in which adolescents believe their experiences and thoughts are absolutely unique in the annals of human history.
6. Erikson viewed the formation of a personal identity as the positive outcome of adolescence. Identity confusion—the failure to answer the fundamental questions of identity—is the negative outcome of the stage. Marcia extended Erikson's conception of identity to include four identity statuses. Identity diffusion is a status in which a person has not begun to make any commitments. This status is considered negative only when an individual leaves adolescence without making reasonable progress toward finding an identity. Identity foreclosure is a status in which a person has made commitments prematurely. Identity moratorium is a temporary status in which an individual is not ready to make commitments but may be exploring possibilities. Identity achievers have gone through their crises and made their commitments.
7. Children who are popular tend to be friendly, have good social skills, share interests with their peers, and be physically appealing. Children who are aggressive tend to be rejected. The school

can help children by actively teaching social skills. Children's ideas about friendship change over time as they become more cognitively sophisticated.

8. Many teachers blame social changes in the family and child care for academic problems, but research does not permit such generalizations. The day care experience may be positive, neutral, or negative depending on the quality of the day care. Studies show that in general, day care does not injure the child and in some instances may actually promote development. Children who experience nursery schools are more advanced compared with those who have not. This is especially true for children from low socioeconomic status groups. Children who attended Project Head Start are less likely to be held back or found in special education classes, and some evidence indicates that they achieve more in school.

9. Anywhere between two and ten million children take care of themselves after school. These children are called latchkey or self-care children. Evidence indicates that if the child comes right home after school and parents monitor the child even from a distance, the experience does not yield negative results. However, many children do not go home straight from school and are not monitored. Some schools and social agencies offer training for self-care children.

10. Children's immediate reactions to divorce involve anger, depression, and guilt. Normally, children recover from the initial shock after a year or so, but the long-term effects can be serious if parents continue to argue, if serious financial problems exist, and if social supports are unavailable. Teachers can help children of divorce by giving them emotional support and understanding.

11. Although children in stepfamilies face many challenges, a good relationship between a stepparent and a child can have a positive influence on the child's development.

12. There are differences in the ways teachers interact with boys and girls. Boys are given more attention, but much of it is negative. Girls receive more attention when they are physically close to the teacher. Some books still show sex stereotypes.

13. Multicultural or multiethnic education attempts to expose children to the cultures and values of others, hoping that respect will follow. History and other subjects may be taught from the point of view of many groups.

14. The evidence on desegregation shows that we cannot simply place students together and expect them to interact with one another in a friendly manner. Such interaction occurs best when the groups are of equal status, when they are engaged in activities that have shared goals, and when these interactions are encouraged by authority figures. Cooperative activities such as the jigsaw classroom approach are effective in reducing prejudice and increasing friendly contacts among children.

ACTIVITIES AND EXERCISES

1. **Helping the Child with Poor Social Skills.** Ask teachers how they deal with the children in their classes who do not seem to be liked by their peers. Do they ignore the situation, or do they have a method of their own for dealing with it? In addition, ask a special education teacher how social skills are integrated into the curriculum for learning disabled students.

2. **A Message to Parents About a Child's Self-Concept and Self-Esteem.** Although the school is an important source of information that influences the self-concept and self-esteem, parents may not understand that their statements and actions may affect their children's view of themselves. Suppose you were asked by your principal to compose a list of ten things that parents could do to improve their children's self-concept. This list is to be used as the basis for a parents' seminar and later to be sent home to all parents of elementary schoolchildren in your district. Write the ten (or so) solid suggestions.

3. **The "New" Family and Academic Achievement.** Research indicates that many teachers blame divorce, day care, self care, and stepfamilies for the lack of academic achievement. Construct a questionnaire concerning this issues. Some possible statements include the following:

   Children who go home after school without a parent being present are less likely to achieve in school than children who have a parent present.

   Children who spend two years in day care are

more likely to show behavior problems in elementary school.

Parents who leave their children at home without after-school supervision are neglecting them.

Children in stepfamilies usually have more problems than children from single-parent families.

Children whose parents have been divorced for as long as five years will still show poorer academic achievement.

A good practice in any such poll is not simply to ask people whether they agree or disagree but to ask whether they strongly agree, agree somewhat, are neutral, disagree somewhat, or strongly disagree. Interview parents, college students, and, if possible, some teachers to gather the opinions of three different groups.

4. **Visit a Day Care Center and a Nursery School.** Day care and nursery schools have become major sources of controversy in a number of areas. The long-term effects of preschool care on elementary school achievement and behavior is one issue, and the question of what programs should be instituted in such preschools is another. Should social skills be emphasized? Should academic skills be presented? Visit a day care center and a nursery school and observe the teacher-child ratio, the nature of the child-child interactions, and the types of activities that children are encouraged to engage in.

5. **Programs for Latchkey Children.** Many children now must take care of themselves after school. As the text states, a number of groups have taken an active interest in helping these children and their parents. Find out whether the PTA, a social services agency, the school, or any other community groups are involved in training children for self care. If there are such groups, try to attend one meeting.

6. **Policies Concerning the Noncustodial Parent.** One of the areas that many noncustodial parents complain about is the lack of cooperation they get from the school in their desire to become involved in their child's education. Certainly, not every noncustodial parent wants involvement, but many do. Find out the school or district policies concerning giving information to the noncustodial parent.

7. **Sex Roles in Textbooks.** Take a stack of texts and look through them with an eye towards the way each sex is represented. You may not find gross caricatures, but more subtle forms of sexism may be present. For example, do the texts show pictures of males as active and females as passive? Do the texts show women as being homemakers and men as working? Do the texts show sex stereotypes of any kind?

8. **Encouraging Social Interaction.** Just placing children of different ethnic and racial groups in proximity does not seem to work. Instead, as Allport suggests, for such interaction to work, the groups must be of equal status, share a common goal, and engage in activities that are encouraged by authority figures. Many newspaper articles discuss racial conflict or, at least, the lack of friendly interaction among children of different groups. Analyze the situations described in these articles for the presence or absence of Allport's three criteria.

SCENARIOS

Here are ten scenarios. Try to apply the information you have learned in the chapter to each situation.

1. Mr. De Fino is a fourth-grade teacher. In October, a new student, Sheila, enters the class. Mr. De Fino introduces Sheila, as he does all new students, but notices that she does not seem to be able to gain entrance into a group of children. Sheila has no friends in the class and does not seem to talk to anyone. She is absent for a week and does not have any assignments finished when she returns to school. When he asks her why she has not done any of the work, she tells him that she has no one she can call in the class because she has no friends in the class. Mr. De Fino would like to help. What steps could he take to help Sheila?

2. Ms. Thomas is concerned about Horace, a student who is achieving approximately an 80 percent average in most academic subjects. Although Horace is doing relatively well and seems well adjusted in class, he sometimes makes self-disparaging remarks. Upon investigation, Ms. Thomas discovers that Horace has a brother who is a year older and is a solid 95 percent student in all his subjects. Horace's parents tell Ms. Thomas

that they try not to compare the two boys, but Horace still compares himself to his brother. It bothers them as well, since Horace has shown signs of giving up when he finds something difficult. Horace's parents are very willing to help but do not know what to do. What could Ms. Thomas and Horace's parents do to help Horace?

3. Jon is a good art student but unfortunately is not very good in math or science. He sees himself in these terms and is disappointed in his abilities. He considers math and science much more important than art. His sixth-grade teacher, Mr. Drucker, is aware of his feelings and would like him to value his strengths. How can Mr. Drucker help Jon to improve his self-esteem?

4. Curt is a late developing eighth grader. He is shorter than most of the students and has lately had to deal with his peers calling him "Shorty." When students are selecting teammates, Curt is not chosen until they have to include everyone. Curt is frequently unhappy. Mr. Kelly has a good relationship with Curt, but the boy believes that no one can really understand his plight. The situation is becoming more urgent since Curt is beginning to act out in his classes. Mr. Kelly thinks it is to gain attention. What can school personnel do to help Curt?

5. Mrs. Davis entered her seventh-grade music class to find Kevin, a very slow and learning disabled student, sitting in the back of the room isolated from the other students. As Mrs. Davis observes him, she is finding that Kevin turns the other students off. Kevin does not seem to be able to converse easily with his peers, and they now ignore him. Mrs. Davis does not believe it is due to Kevin's condition but rather to a lack of social skills. Mrs. Davis would like to help Kevin but does not know how to begin. She asks you, her colleague, for advice. What would you tell her?

6. Mrs. Lang teaches high school English. She finds that many students do not seem to know what they want to be, and some appear aimless, with little motivation. One student told her that it is hard to study or care when you don't have a goal. Some students have challenged her asking why they have to learn Shakespeare or the parts of speech. "What good will it do me in life?" Mrs. Lang is concerned about these attitudes and asks you whether she should be? How would you answer her.

7. Jerry, a fifth grader, is supposed to go home every day right after school. His mother works full-time, and Jerry's father does not live with them. Mrs. Ellington is concerned because she believes that the lack of supervision is responsible for Jerry's lack of achievement and poor conduct. Jerry's mother came up to school, and it was clear that she is rather disorganized and is having a difficult time with Jerry. She asks Mrs. Ellington what she can do? Discuss Mrs. Ellington's beliefs in the light of current research and suggest some things both the teacher and Jerry's mother could do in this situation?

8. Mr. Henderson has been watching Kim, a second grader in his class, since the beginning of September. Kim was a fairly happy, popular child, but lately she has been moody and withdrawn. Mr. Henderson asks Kim's mother for an appointment and discovers that Kim's parents are going through a divorce. Kim's mother is having difficulties of her own and is not fully aware of Kim's reactions. Kim's father calls the next day, says that he wants to be informed of Kim's progress in school, and gives you his address and phone number. He also states that if Kim is acting up in class, he wants to know about it. Mr. Henderson believes that both parents should be involved but does not want to get in the middle. In fact, Kim's mother tells Mr. Henderson that she feels the reason he is interested in Kim's progress is to make a custody case against her. She does not want any information to go to the father. Mr. Henderson continues to see a lack of academic progress and further problems with Kim. What can Mr. Henderson do without involving himself in the divorce?

9. Mrs. Cummings is a high school teacher in a newly integrated school. Despite some community misgivings, the integration plan was put into practice without much overt opposition. The administration made certain that the students would not be segregated in school, and some minority students can be found in every class. In addition, a student-faculty committee was set up to serve students who have complaints about unequal treatment, and a dialogue was established in a once-a-week class meeting where topics concerning tolerance and understanding are stressed. Still, Mrs. Cummings notices that children from the ethnic groups do not interact very much in her class. When she asks her colleagues, they

have much the same story to tell. Although there is seemingly little tension, there is also little interaction. Mrs. Cummings would like to see more interaction, for she believes that without such interaction, eventually racial problems will surface. Whether you agree or disagree with Mrs. Cummings reasons for trying to improve interaction, what steps can she take to accomplish her goals?

10. Mr. Sizemore's students were reading a story about a child's day spent with his father at work. When the story mentioned that the father's boss was a woman, the children laughed a little. A few pages later, the students were uneasy when the person in charge of the company's day care center was a man. Mr. Sizemore has never considered sex roles much of a problem in his classroom. He treats all his students equally. He gives both boys and girls all classroom jobs in his fifth-grade class, makes certain leadership positions are evenly divided, and encourages students of both sexes to try every activity. However, his students seem to resist these changes in sex-role stereotypes and he would like to do something to broaden his students' horizons. What would you suggest?

7

Are These Statements True or False?

Turn the next page for the correct answers. Each statement is repeated following the paragraph in which the information can be found.

1. Moral education is traditionally and historically a part of the school's purpose.
2. Schools are more effective at teaching students what to do than in teaching them what not to do.
3. Preschoolers often understand that rules can be changed by mutual consent.
4. Boys experience more conflict with their peers than do girls.
5. The majority of parents oppose sex education courses in school.
6. When sex education is offered in the schools, about a quarter of the parents refuse to allow their children to remain in class.
7. Giving students frank, honest, and comprehensive information about sexuality and contraception will reduce the teen pregnancy rate.
8. Drug abuse prevention programs have generally not been very successful.
9. Showing the dramatic fatal aftermath of drug abuse is an effective way to reduce drug use.
10. The majority of referrals for child abuse are made by educators.
11. Teachers have a legal responsibility to report instances of child abuse.
12. People who talk about committing suicide rarely make a suicide attempt.

Moral Development, Values, and Attitudes

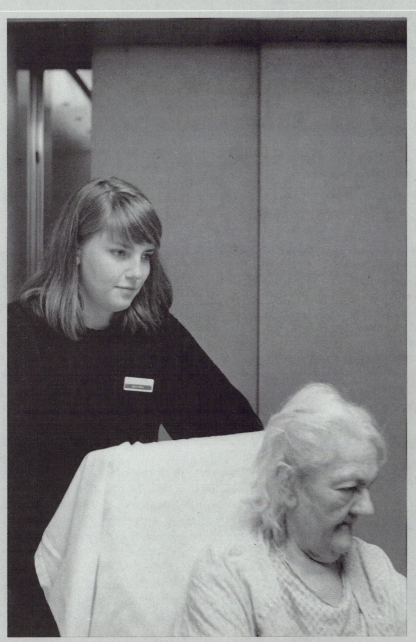

Answers to True-False Statements

1. *True*
2. *True*
3. *False* Correct statement: Preschoolers see rules as fixed and not subject to change by mutual consent.
4. *True*
5. *False* Correct statement: The majority of parents favor sex education courses in the schools.
6. *False* Correct statement: Only about three.percent of all parents refuse to allow their children to take sex education courses in school.
7. *False* Correct statement: Most studies find that just giving honest information about sexuality does not reduce the teen pregnancy rate. Programs that include discussions of morals and values and that encourage sexually active students to seek out birth control advice are more successful in this regard.
8. *True*
9. *False* Correct statement: Scare tactics do not reduce drug use.
10. *False* Correct statement: Educators account for only about 13 percent of all child abuse referrals.
11. *True*
12. *False* Correct statement: People who talk about committing suicide are more likely to make a suicide attempt.

Large-scale reports of cheating and poor conduct appear in the press, and the schools are told they must be leaders in improving moral conduct.

A study shows that most students do not seem to understand "democratic" values, and the schools are told they must provide education in democracy.

One million teenage girls become pregnant every year, and the schools are told that they must find some way to reduce the rate of teen pregnancy.

The AIDS epidemic gets front-page coverage almost daily, and the schools are told that they have a definite responsibility in AIDS education.

Suicide is now the second leading cause of death among adolescents in the United States, and the schools are told that they have responsibility in this area.

A child is abused to death in a large urban area, and teachers are asked why they did not recognize the symptoms of child abuse.

THE SCHOOL'S INVOLVEMENT IN MORAL EDUCATION

More demands than ever are being placed on schools to become active in moral, values, and health education. Historically, moral education was one of the school's great responsibilities. Most state education charters refer to moral education, including the teaching of values and skills of citizenship (Ryan, 1981). Currently, surveys of the general public and school personnel show that large majorities favor the school's involvement in these areas. The mandate exists. Yet this area is fraught with cautions and tensions. Although the aims may be clear—a belief in democratic institutions, encouraging such values as honesty and integrity, reducing the chances of students developing AIDS or becoming pregnant—the methods to accomplish these goals are controversial. For example, the public favors sex education classes by a large margin, but people disagree on what should be taught in these classes.

This chapter examines moral development and moral education and looks at sex and drug education. The schools have been asked to take a leading role in combatting psychological and physical health problems, especially in the areas of child abuse and suicide prevention. These areas are loosely tied together by two threads. First, we are now more concerned with providing students with the skills necessary to make important decisions in their lives, and students are faced with momentous decisions in some of these areas. Second, the schools share the burden of responsibility with parents to develop healthy attitudes and behaviors in their children.

Evaluating Programs in Moral and Health Education

Measuring achievement in mathematics involves testing the student's ability to solve a problem. If she can add two numbers together, we know she has that skill. Despite the problems inherent in testing, we can usually agree on some method of measuring the degree to which a child has mastered a skill. Unfortunately, this is not so in the areas of moral and health education. Programs in these areas are difficult to evaluate for a number of reasons.

First, such programs often have multiple objectives that are rather broad, making evaluations difficult. For example, is a sex education program that has not reduced the incidence of teenage pregnancy useful if students now possess more accurate information? If one of the objectives of the program was to reduce the incidence of pregnancy, this particular program has not been successful. Yet, if one of the objectives was to give students correct information, the program was at least partially successful.

Second, since most programs in these areas do not use control groups, evaluating their success or failure becomes difficult. If you institute a program to enhance moral reasoning and you find out the incidence of severe misconduct declines, can you actually state that the decline was due to this program? After all, the attention drawn to the problem of, say, vandalism and perhaps better enforcement of vandalism laws may also have contributed to the reduction in vandalism.

Third, although many moral and health education programs seek to provide information, change attitudes, or improve reasoning, even if they are successful, they may not lead to changes in behavior. A student may know it is dangerous to drink and drive, yet may drink and drive. A student may memorize the dangers of using cocaine, yet still may use the drug. A student may reason that it is best not to cheat, yet may yield to temptation. A student may know that it is dangerous to engage in sex without contraception, yet may do so anyway. In the areas of moral and life skills education, a cognitive component of knowledge, an attitudinal component, and a behavioral component exist. Unfortunately, changing the cognitive component does not always lead to attitudinal and behavioral changes.

Fourth, schools are much better at teaching students to do something than they are at teaching them *not* to do something (Nevi, 1988). If teachers can teach students to perform a particular skill or learn a particular body of knowledge, the educational process can work relatively well. However, educators are not very effective at teaching students *not* to act in a particular way. We do not seem to have developed successful long-term avoidance techniques, and unfortunately, some of what we must teach in the areas of morality and health involves not doing something that is often immediately gratifying and easy.

APPROACHES TO MORAL DEVELOPMENT

The school joins with friends, family, and the mass media in transmitting values to children. During middle childhood, children are challenged by situations that demand that they decide what behaviors are morally correct. Consider the following situations:

Cynthia sits next to her best friend in mathematics class. During the last mathematics test, her friend signalled that she didn't know some of the answers. All Cynthia would have had to do was to uncover her paper and put it on her desk in such a way that her friend could get a good look at it.

Everyone has been teasing Henry because he can't catch a ball very well. Tyrone likes Henry and really doesn't like all this teasing, but he also wants to fit in with the other boys. He doesn't know what to do.

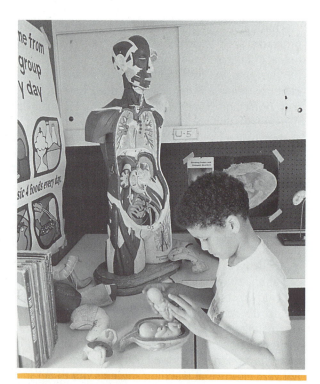

Health concerns and moral development are now major educational concerns.

We would all like our children to develop a solid sense of right and wrong, the ability to think for themselves, and an orientation toward helping people. Children are faced with moral decisions every day. Cheating, lying, and stealing are daily temptations in school. Decisions about when to obey and when to disobey, when to fight back and when to turn away, and whether to return a lost article are fairly common. Such issues have recently become the focus of much attention.

Moral Questions

A question involving morality arises anytime a person can do something that helps or injures another individual (Carroll & Rest, 1982). Two distinct approaches to the study of morality are especially important to teachers. The first approach studies children's **moral reasoning**—their ideas about justice and right and wrong. This approach is typified by the work of Jean Piaget and Lawrence Kohlberg. The second approach is a rather diverse social-learning and behavioral tra-

dition, which emphasizes how such values as honesty and altruism are learned. Each approach looks at moral development in a different way and is perhaps tapping different elements of morality.

Piaget on Moral Reasoning

Piaget (1965/1932) looked at morality in terms of how a child develops a sense of justice and a respect for the social order. He argued that children's understanding of rules follows a general sequence. Preschoolers and children in the early school years consider rules sacred and untouchable and created by an all-powerful authority figure. In this stage, called **moral realism,** rules are viewed as inflexible, and justice is whatever the authority or law commands. At about age seven or eight, children reach the intermediate stage. They now interact more with their peers and develop some type of reciprocal give-and-take understanding. What is fair is more important than the position of authority. Punishments may or may not be fair, depending on the crime committed. In the stage called **moral relativism,** emerging at about 11 or 12, children take extenuating circumstances into account and weigh them in their moral judgments. Children become more flexible, and rules are changeable. In the same way, children in the stage of moral realism do not take intent into account when assessing moral questions. For instance, ask a young child, "Who was naughtier—the child who broke one dish trying to sneak into the refrigerator to get some jam or the child who broke five dishes trying to help her mother?" Children in the stage of moral realism claim that the second child was naughtier,

moral reasoning   An approach to the study of moral development stressing the importance of the child's ideas and reasoning about justice and right and wrong.

moral realism   The Piagetian stage of moral reasoning during which rules are viewed as sacred and justice is whatever the authority figure says.

moral relativism   The Piagetian stage of moral reasoning in which children weigh the intentions of others before judging their actions as right or wrong.

but children in the stage of moral relativism argue that the first child committed the worse act. Children younger than seven years old, then, rely primarily on the consequences when evaluating another person's actions. Children older than age ten or so rely on intentions. Between ages seven and ten, children rely on either one of these (Ferguson & Rule, 1982).

True or False Preschoolers often understand that rules can be changed by mutual consent.

Piaget's ideas in this area are rather narrow. Making judgments about who is naughtier is a very special type of moral judgment. Piaget does not deal with questions about what a child *should* do (Rest, 1983). It remained for another social scientist, Lawrence Kohlberg to formulate a broader theory of moral reasoning.

Kohlberg's Theory of Moral Reasoning

Heinz's wife has cancer. There is a drug that might cure her, but the only dose is owned by a pharmacist who wants a great deal of money for it. Heinz doesn't have the money. Should he steal the drug? Lawrence Kohlberg (1969) presented dilemmas like this to many subjects, and after careful study, he proposed a model that describes the development of moral reasoning. Kohlberg sees moral reasoning as developing in a three-level, six-stage sequence (summarized in Table 7.1). The stages are universal and sequential— that is, they are applicable to every culture, and no stage is ever skipped. Each stage requires more sophisticated cognitive skills than the one that preceded it.

How would you have answered the dilemma just described? Most students state immediately that Heinz should steal it. However, Kohlberg is not interested in the answer itself. It is the *reasoning* behind the choice that is of interest and that determines what stage of moral reasoning a person is in.

Let's take a more relevant example. Suppose Karen found a wallet with ten dollars in it. She could use the money, but she discovers that the owner is a wealthy business executive. Karen's best friend Linda is very poor and could use some slacks; Karen also believes it would be nice to go to the movies. What should she do? As Kohlberg's three levels and six stages are reviewed, keep in mind that it is the moral reasoning,

not the answer itself, that determines one's stage of moral development.

Level One: Preconventional Morality. At the **preconventional level,** people make decisions based on reward and punishment and the satisfaction of their own needs. If Karen reasoned at this level, she might keep the wallet because it satisfied her immediate desires. On the other hand, she might not, because she is afraid of getting caught and being punished. Morality is defined strictly by the physical consequences of the act.

Stage One: Punishment and Obedience Orientation. An individual in stage one avoids breaking rules because doing so might lead to punishment. This person shows a complete deference to rules. The interests of others are not considered.

Stage Two: Instrumental Relativist Orientation. In Stage Two, the right actions are those that satisfy one's own needs and only sometimes the needs of others. However, the only reason for helping others is that they will then owe you something, to be collected at a later time. There is a sense of fairness in this stage, and a deal is acceptable.

Level Two: Conventional Morality. At the **conventional level,** conformity is the most important factor. The individual conforms to the expectations of others, including the general social order. Karen might keep the wallet if she reasons that anyone would keep it—and it's just too bad for the owner. On the other hand, she might not keep it if she reasons that it is against the rules and she would not be doing the "right" thing or being a good girl.

Stage Three: Interpersonal Concordance, or "Good Boy/Nice Girl" Orientation. Living up to the expectations of others and being good are the important considerations for a person in Stage Three. The emphasis is on gaining approval from others by being nice.

preconventional level Kohlberg's first level of moral reasoning in which satisfaction of one's own needs and rewards and punishment serve as the bases for moral decision making.

conventional level Kohlberg's second level of moral reasoning in which conformity to the expectations of others and society in general serves as the basis for moral decision making.

Table 7.1 Kohlberg's Stages of Moral Reasoning

Lawrence Kohlberg views the development of morality in terms of moral reasoning. The stage of moral reasoning at which people can be placed depends upon the reasoning behind their decisions, not the decisions themselves.

I. Preconventional Level

The child is responsive to cultural rules and labels of good and bad, right or wrong, but interprets these either in terms of the physical or hedonistic consequences of action (punishment, reward, exchange of favors) or in terms of the physical power of those who enunciate the rules. This level has two stages:

Stage 1: Punishment and obedience orientation. The physical consequences of action determine its goodness or badness regardless of the meaning or value of these consequences. Avoidance of punishment and unquestioning deference to power are valued in their own right, not in terms of respect for an underlying moral order (the latter being Stage 4).

Stage 2: Instrumental relativist orientation. Right action is that which instrumentally satisfies one's own needs and occasionally the needs of others. Human relations are viewed in terms of the marketplace. Fairness, reciprocity, and equal sharing are present but are always interpreted in a physical, pragmatic way. Reciprocity is a matter of "you scratch my back and I'll scratch yours," not of loyalty, gratitude, or justice.

II. Conventional Level

Maintaining the expectations of the individual's family, group, or nation is perceived as valuable in its own right, regardless of consequences. The attitude is not only one of *conformity* to personal expectations and social order but also of loyalty to it, of actively *maintaining*, supporting, and justifying it, of identifying with the persons or group involved in it. This level has two stages:

Stage 3: Interpersonal concordance or "good boy/nice girl" orientation. Good behavior is that which pleases or helps others and is approved by them. There is much conformity to stereotypical images of what is majority or "natural" behavior. Behavior is frequently judged by intention— "he means well" becomes important for the first time. One earns approval by being "nice."

Stage 4: "Law and order" orientation. Orientation is toward authority, fixed rules, and the maintenance of the social order. Right behavior consists of doing one's duty, showing respect for authority, maintaining the social order for its own sake.

III. Postconventional, Autonomous, or Principled Level

The person makes a clear effort to define moral values and principles that have validity and application apart from the authority of the groups or persons holding these principles, and apart from the individual's own identification with these groups. This level has two stages:

Stage 5: Social-contract, legalistic orientation. Generally with utilitarian overtones. Right action is defined in terms of general individual rights and standards that have been critically examined and agreed upon by society. The person is clearly aware of the relativism of values and opinions and so emphasizes procedural rules for reaching consensus. Aside from what is constitutionally and democratically agreed upon, right is a matter of personal "values" and "opinion"; emphasis is thus on the "legal point of view" but with the possibility of changing law in terms of rational considerations of social utility rather than freezing in terms of Stage 4. Outside the legal realm, free agreement and contract is the binding element. This is the "official" morality of the American government and Constitution.

Stage 6: Universal ethical principle orientation. Right is defined by the decision of conscience in accord with self-chosen *ethical principles* appealing to logical comprehensiveness, universality, and consistency. These principles are abstract and ethical (the Golden Rule, the categorical imperative); they are not concrete moral rules like the Ten Commandments. At heart, these are universal principles of *justice of the reciprocity and equal of human rights* and of respect for the dignity of human beings as individual persons.

From "Definition of Moral Stages: Kohlberg's Stages" in *Cognitive Development and Epistemology*, T. Mischel, ed. Copyright © 1971 by Academic Press, Inc.

Stage Four: "Law and Order" Orientation. A person in Stage Four is oriented toward authority and maintaining the social order. The emphasis is on doing one's duty and showing respect for authority. Sometimes people in this stage reason, "If everyone did it then . . ."

Level Three: Postconventional, Autonomous, or Principled Morality. People in the **postconventional level** have evolved moral values that have been internalized. These values are individualized and do not depend on membership in any particular group. Usually, since such moral reasoning does not occur until adolescence at the earliest, we would not expect Karen to show such reasoning. However, if this dilemma occurred at a later age, Karen might return the wallet because she, herself, values honesty and integrity, even if it means she has to do without something. In Karen's case, the reasoning for keeping the wallet is admittedly strained. However, Karen might reason that the wealthy person who lost the wallet does not need the money as much as she and her friend do and that even if she were caught, she would be helping another human being in need—her friend. Karen's values of friendship, loyalty, and giving to others would become more important than honesty and integrity.

Stage Five: Social-Contract, Legalistic Orientation. In Stage Five, correct behavior is defined in terms of individual rights and the consensus of society. Right is a matter of personal values and opinions, but the emphasis is on the legal point of view. Here, people might offer the Bill of Rights as an explanation for their reasoning.

Stage Six: Universal Ethical Principle Orientation. In this highest stage, Stage Six, the correct behavior is defined as a decision of conscience in accordance with self-chosen ethical principles that are logical, universal, and consistent. These are very abstract guidelines (Kohlberg & Kramer, 1969).

People rarely reason solely in one stage. More often, they are predominantly in one stage but are also partly in the stages just before and just after. A person may be 40 percent in Stage Three, 30 percent in Stage Two, and 30 percent in Stage Four. Change involves a gradual shift in the percentage of reasoning from one stage to the next rather than a wholesale switch from one stage to the next higher stage (Carroll & Rest, 1982). Kohlberg's theory has been applied successfully to many cultures (Snarey et al., 1985), and evidence shows that the stages are indeed sequential (Walker, 1982; Kohlberg et al., 1978). People do not skip stages, although they enter and leave them at varying times.

postconventional level Kohlberg's third level of moral reasoning in which moral decisions are made on the basis of individual values that have been internalized.

Moral Reasoning and Gender

If you look at the descriptions of Kohlberg's stages, it is clear that the emphasis in the higher stages of moral reasoning is on justice and individual rights. Higher moral reasoning seems to have little to do with interpersonal relationships. According to Carol Gilligan (1982), women learn a different orientation to moral questions than men learn. Women see moral dilemmas in terms of how such issues affect interpersonal relationships rather than in strictly individualistic terms. They are raised to be concerned with the rights and needs of others and to be interested in interpersonal relationships (Hotelling & Forrest, 1985). The emphasis in male reasoning is on individual rights and self-fulfillment. For example, boys learn to be independent, assertive, achievement-oriented, and individualistic and to attach great importance to the rule of law. This is similar to the Stage Four perspective. Females, on the other hand, are oriented toward interpersonal connectedness, care, sensitivity, and responsibility to other people rather than toward abstract principles of justice (Muuss, 1988). They tend to see moral difficulties as conflicts between their own wants and needs and the wants and needs of others. They may thus base their decisions on how their relationships with others will be affected. Harmony rather than justice may be the guiding principle. Sensitivity to the needs of others rather than strict individual rights becomes the criterion that women apply in such dilemmas. This seems more like the Stage Three perspective. Gilligan notes, however, that neither reasoning is superior—the perspectives simply differ from each other, and the differences should be understood and respected.

Kohlberg's theory fails to take these differences into account. Karen may look at how her actions might affect her relationships with others rather than simply examine some abstract rule of justice. Some interesting evidence in favor of this point of view comes from studies showing that five- and seven year-old-boys and girls settle their disputes differently. Boys are more likely to use threats and physical force and to pursue their own goals, while girls try to reduce conflict with a goal of improving harmony (Miller et al., 1986). Boys also experience more conflict with peers than do girls.

True or False Boys experience more conflict with their peers than do girls.

Gilligan's ideas have become popular, but they are not completely accepted. For instance, Walker (1984) reviewed the literature in the field and failed to find evidence of consistent sex differences in moral development. Others have criticized Walker's research (Baumrind, 1986), while Walker (1986) has steadfastly defended it. All we can say at the present time is that sex differences in moral reasoning may exist and that we should take care when stating that a particular type of reasoning is higher or lower—the reasoning may simply be different. Even if consistent sex differences are subsequently not supported by research, Gilligan's contribution lies in broadening our view of moral reasoning to include the idea that the moral person may integrate concepts of abstract justice and the concern for others (Muuss, 1988).

Is Moral Reasoning Related to Moral Behavior?

Would a person reasoning at a Stage Five level act differently from a person reasoning at the Stage One level? As the individual progresses toward Stage Six, we would think that moral behavior such as honesty and resisting temptation would increase. Indeed, most studies do find a relationship between moral reasoning and moral action (Kohlberg, 1987; Blasi, 1980), but the strength of the relationship varies from area to area. Some support is found for the idea that people at higher moral stages are more honest, but there is little support for the idea that people at the postconventional level resist social pressure to conform in their actual moral actions. Only relatively weak associations are found between progressing to higher levels of moral reasoning and whether or not a child will cheat, yield to temptation, or behave altruistically if there is personal cost attached to such behavior (Maccoby, 1980). In one study, college students were found to cheat less as their level of moral reasoning increased. However, although subjects low in moral judgments cheated more, those higher in moral judgment also cheated when the temptation became strong (Malinowski & Smith, 1985). Therefore, although a relationship between moral reasoning and moral behavior exists, other factors help determine whether a person will perform a particular act.

Evaluating Kohlberg's Theory

Although Kohlberg's theory offers a valuable framework for understanding moral development, it has been criticized. One problem is the discrepancy between the level of moral reasoning and action. For whatever reason, people sometimes proceed in ways they think are theoretically best, and sometimes they do not (Chandler & Boyes, 1982). In addition, it is possible to reason at any level and still find a reason to cheat, lie, or steal. More predictability is needed. Last, moral reasoning is perhaps only part of the process by which people convert environmental information into an action sequence. How people perceive the situation and people's learning history are also important factors.

The Learning Theory Approach to Morality: The Study of Behavior Itself

Some psychologists approach moral development by studying the behavior itself—including sharing, helping, and giving as well as lying, stealing, and being aggressive—rather than looking at the moral reasoning of the individual. They explain moral behavior in terms of the situation, the child's background, the models available to the child, and the reinforcements that are present in the environment.

Learning theorists argue that moral behavior is learned like any other behavior. Operant conditioning explains some of it. Children who are reinforced for giving and sharing are more likely to give and share. Social learning theorists add imitation and observation to the picture. Much behavior is influenced by watching how others—both adults and peers—deal with life's challenges (Bandura, 1986). If we observe people we respect helping others or giving to charity, we are more likely to do so ourselves. Of course, we do not imitate everything we see. Such factors as the characteristics of the model, the consequences of the behavior, and our own characteristics affect imitation (Bandura, 1977). Cognitive factors, such as how we perceive the situation and process the information, are also important. For instance, aggressive children are more likely to believe that aggression will get them what they want and find it easier to be aggressive than will nonaggressive children (Perry et al., 1986). Another factor is competence to deal with a particular situation (Mussen & Eisenberg-Berg, 1977). A person who feels competent may act one way; a person who is bewildered may act in a totally different manner.

It is impossible to review all the literature on the behavioral aspects of each different type of moral behavior. The most important things to remember about the behavioral approach to morality is that the approach is based upon what a person actually does rather than the way he or she reasons and that it emphasizes models, rewards, and punishments as well as the child's background.

What Moral Training Occurs in the Schools?

The school's influence on the moral development of children cannot easily be measured, and most of it is not consciously planned by educators. Children learn that conforming to rules is important in school and being part of the crowd is desirable if they are to be accepted by their peers (Power & Kohlberg, 1987). A hidden curriculum in school is imparted to students through their experiences (Ryan, 1986). Children learn that differences exist between ideals and practices. For instance, students may learn that a teacher will accept certain excuses for not doing their homework and will use those excuses even though they still believe that honesty and truthfulness are important. The value of avoiding the consequences of not

doing one's homework may become paramount in such circumstances. I can remember a junior high school where democratic values were taught in every social studies class, but not one democratic value was practiced in the school. The student government never made decisions of any importance, nor were students given explanations for administrative action. Such conflicts are real, and students are keenly aware of them.

The teacher is a model in some ways, and children learn much about such values as honesty, integrity, truthfulness, and fairness through their interactions with teachers. As authority figures, teachers demonstrate how authority is used. At the same time, teachers may use coercion to foster certain values, such as punctuality and responsibility. School is also a place where students interact with other students. The values of the peer group have an influence on the student, and these values sometimes—though not always—run counter to the values teachers and parents hold. For example, the teacher may teach the values of honesty and truthfulness, but when asked whether someone in the class did something, a child may place more importance on loyalty to the group than

There is a need for the schools to train students in the democratic process. This does not mean that students are given the power to determine everything in the school but that some areas of decision making should be shared with students.

on answering a question truthfully. School is also a place where students must interact with students who may have different value orientations.

PROGRAMS TO FOSTER MORAL DEVELOPMENT

In an attempt to formalize moral and ethical educational experiences, a number of educational programs have been advanced. We will discuss three here: values clarification, Kohlberg's cognitive-developmental approach, and character training. Each arises from a different outlook on moral education and poses significant challenges to the teacher.

Values Clarification

Values clarification courses became popular in the 1970s, though recently they have become controversial. In the book *Teaching and Values* (Raths et al., 1966) that defined the movement, the authors emphasized the importance of experiencing the process of valuing rather than treating values as objects. The process of valuing involves choosing, prizing, and acting. After careful consideration from a number of alternatives, values are freely chosen. Prizing involves the public affirmation of the values. Acting involves behaving in accordance with the values.

In values clarification courses, students are challenged to discover their own values. The teacher does not try to inculcate a set of values into the students. The teacher offers a number of anecdotes, simulations, and other activities that aim at getting students to freely adopt and clarify their own values (Ringness, 1975). Teachers may play devil's advocate, but they do not force their own values onto students.

Many techniques are used in values clarification. For example, students are asked to make choices and identify their priorities or preferences in an exercise called rank-ordering. In values-voting, the teacher offers the students a series of questions by asking, How many of you . . . ? Students respond with hand signals showing whether they are in favor or against the idea and to what extent. In the spread-of-opinion activity, the teacher draws a line on the blackboard and identifies the issue, labeling each extreme position and asking students to place their initials on the line to indicate where they stand on the issue. Moral

dilemmas are also used in which students are asked what they would do in a certain circumstance and to generate possible alternatives. A values inventory is sometimes performed in which students take stock of their beliefs and become aware of their preferences in activities. Items are listed on some topic—perhaps what a student might like to do in life or which people are important to the student—and students analyze their responses, finally drawing conclusions from the inventories (Read et al., 1977). In the public interview, the teacher may list a number of topics involving such issues as money, sports, and politics and ask for volunteers to be interviewed on a topic chosen by the student. The teacher interviews the student, who can pass on a question that he or she does not wish to answer. If the student does answer the question, the student may then ask the teacher the same question. In the values-sheet strategy, a student is given a statement outlining some value—perhaps civil liberties—and is asked to write a response to the statement. As you can see, values clarification offers many techniques that can be used in the classroom.

Lately there has been a reaction against values clarification. There seems to be an overemphasis on the process and little stress on the results or the end product (Ryan, 1981). Nor is information given to the students relating to what our culture has discovered about moral and ethical questions (Ryan, 1986). There is no right and no wrong (Bauer, 1987). The neutrality required by the teacher is also troublesome. At times, teachers may experience problems when they must remain neutral in the face of questionable decisions on the part of the students. The values clarification approach also assumes that all values are equal and of similar importance and that values are equally false, equally true, and equally useful. Many authorities argue that fostering democratic values such as tolerance and understanding cannot be left to self-discovery and that students cannot be allowed to find their own values without input from adults.

Kohlberg's Approach: Cognitive-Developmental Approach

Teachers using Kohlberg's approach present a number of dilemmas, such as the case of Heinz, to classes allowing students to dissect the cases. Students are encouraged to play the role of different characters within the dilemmas. A dilemma is offered to the class in the form of a story, and the students determine how the dilemma should be resolved, giving reasons for their solutions which are then shared in group discussion. Specially written dilemmas can be used with young children. For example, consider the case of Holly, a young girl who likes to climb trees and who, after falling from one, promised her father she would not climb trees again. She then comes upon a friend whose kitten is in a tree and can't get down. None of the other children are good enough climbers to climb up to get the kitten, and they ask Holly to do so. Should Holly break her promise (Kohlberg & Likona, 1987)? A number of other possible dilemmas are suggested by Mark Pitts (see Table 7.2). Remember that Kohlberg is interested in improving the moral reasoning of the children, not necessarily in teaching children right and wrong (Kohlberg, 1987). According to Kohlberg, students reasoning at lower stages will be influenced by the reasoning of students in the higher stages, causing cognitive conflict eventually leading to improvements in moral reasoning. The teacher probes, explains, and suggests (Hersh et al., 1979). Although there is a preferred type of reasoning, there is not necessarily a preferred answer. Kohlberg is not morally neutral and argues that there

are universal moral principles that ought to be held that include respect for the individual and tolerance. These principles arise not from lecture but through rational argument and thoughtful decisions about values that may be in conflict (Power & Kohlberg, 1987).

Kohlberg's approach is not entirely verbal and cognitively oriented, for he understands that moral reasoning—and morality itself—is based upon experience. Thus, Kohlberg argues for transforming schools into just communities. This involves establishing democratic structures and student participation in making and enforcing rules and policies. Kohlberg argues that schools must provide students with the opportunities to examine the values of the hidden curriculum, such as competition and achievement at all costs, and to relate them to basic values of justice and caring. In some schools that have adopted some participatory democratic practices, students were given a real voice and decided to mandate restitution for victims of theft, to voluntarily switch classes to achieve greater racial integration, and to enforce no-cutting rules by accepting responsibility to help students get to class (Kohlberg & Lickona, 1987; Power & Kohlberg, 1987). Teachers are encouraged to be democratic and especially to explain the reasons behind rules. There are limits, of course, to student participa-

Table 7.2 Moral Dilemmas

This table offers some moral dilemmas that can be presented to students for discussion.

- A friend confides that she stole a marker from another student. Will you tell your teacher?
- A friend who had to go out with her parents the night before asks to copy your homework. Do you let her?
- Your boy/girlfriend asks you to write a paper for him/her. You are overloaded but are "nuts" about this person. Would you do it?
- You have just seen your least admired classmate cheat on a test you studied all evening for. Should you tell?
- Your brother is taking the same class from the same teacher you had last year. He wants an A. Do you show him your copy of last year's tests?
- You receive an F on a progress report that must be signed by your parents. They have warned you that low grades will result in restriction. Will you forge their signatures?
- A classmate you don't like very much hits you for no reason. Do you hit back?
- You forget your lunch ticket. While going to lunch you see a ticket on the floor. Do you use it?
- The principal calls you in to ask you if you saw your best friend fighting in the hall. You know you were the only uninvolved witness and that your friend was fighting. Do you say so?
- You ride your bike across town to get a record album on sale for $5.99. The store is out of that record, so you buy another for $10. As you leave, you notice that the clerk charged you only $7.99. Do you say anything?

From "Values Declaration: An Alternative for Classroom Values Discussion," *The Clearing House,* 1987, 61, 169–171. Reprinted with permission of the Helen Dwight Reid Educational Foundation. Published by Heldref Publications, 4000 Albemarle St., N.W., Washington, D.C. 20016. Copyright © 1987.

tion, but students need to feel that they have some power to submit grievances and get things done—a feeling that few students have in today's schools.

Criticism of Kohlberg's attempts at moral education through dilemmas centers around the highly verbal nature of Kohlberg's dilemma-based approach. Kohlberg's program does not necessarily lead to action (Ryan, 1986). In addition, some authorities disagree on the basis for Kohlberg's theory and argue that the relationship between moral reasoning and moral behavior may be positive but low. Last, it is not clear whether such a program will lead to the values that Kohlberg himself valued so greatly, including social justice, tolerance, and integrity.

Values clarification and Kohlberg's cognitive developmental education seem to have a great deal in common, and indeed they do. Both are verbal, challenge students to reason, and focus on process rather than product. However, whereas values clarification is essentially a neutral strategy whose purpose is to allow students to discover for themselves how they feel about some issue, Kohlberg's goal is to help students achieve higher levels of thinking through cognitive conflict (Mills, 1987). In an interesting exchange of opinions between Kohlberg and Sidney Simon (an originator of values clarification), the former argued that values clarification strategies were useful but that Simon's theory is inadequate in supplying objectives, while Simon argued that Kohlberg's theory is important but lacks strategies for implementation (Learning, 1972).

Character Building: The Directive Approach

Ray Wilcox (1988) describes the observation of a student teacher in a junior high school giving a lesson on alcohol use. One student gave a speech presenting the arguments against alcohol. After the speech, the class members began to argue with the student, making points that drinking alcohol is cool and fun. They seemed to be winning. When Wilcox asked the student teacher why he didn't say anything, the teacher said "There's no way I wanted to indoctrinate these students" (p. 249). Wilcox notes that by remaining neutral and quiet, the teacher avoided teaching the students and the discussion could just as well have occurred in the locker room.

Somewhat of a rebellion has taken place against the moral reasoning and values clarification ap-

proaches in favor of a more teaching-oriented approach (Bauer, 1987). Perhaps this is a reaction to the neutrality of the other approaches. As Harriet Tyson-Bernstein puts it, "Complaints about the value-neutral curriculum have been mounting amid a growing sense that the schools are leaving students morally adrift" (1987, p. 15). It is now argued more frequently that schools have the responsibility to build character and to teach morality and values. It isn't enough for students to clarify their feelings or improve their moral reasoning. Schools and teachers need to actively plan to transmit societal values to their students.

The first question is, What are these values to be? Although there may be some differences of opinions, there is general agreement on the many values—including loyalty, responsibility, and a sense of civic duty—that can serve as the bases for character teaching (Goldberg, 1987a). The values that underlie our political and economic system—including freedom, individual initiative, and tolerance—can be added to the list. Although there may be some grey areas, describing the values schools and teachers wish to impart is not very difficult.

How can we instill such values in students? The teaching approach is conducted through what Kevin Ryan (1986) calls the five E's. The first is *example*. Teachers are role models and must act in accordance with that responsibility. In addition, the literature of our culture and historical figures can teach by example (Rothman, 1988; Moline, 1983). For instance, the biographies of Martin Luther King and Helen Keller may help to broaden a student's horizons. Even children's stories can serve the same purpose. Preschoolers often enjoy *The Little Engine That Could*, a story that teaches perseverance (U.S. Department of Education, 1987b).

The second E is *explanation*. If rules are to be established and enforced, students deserve to know the reasons behind them. Often, the answer in class and at home is "because I say so," which mixes coercion with irrational use of power. Explanations are desirable for two reasons. First, students begin to understand that rules are not arbitrary, that they are based upon reason. Second, most teachers and parents would like children to reason in a way that is similar to their own and to agree with—and comply with—their rules. This is much easier if students understand the reasons behind the rules. Students may not always agree with the rules or a particular ruling, but they need to understand the thinking behind the rules.

The third E is *exhortation.* There are times when teachers must encourage and exhort students to persevere or, in some cases, to change. Ryan notes that a student who may be flirting with racism may need to realize that his views are undesirable, and heart-to-heart talks may be necessary.

The fourth E is *environment.* The teacher must create a moral environment, which may not always be easy. This includes a balance between competition and cooperation and individual and community responsibility along with the discussion of what ought to be.

The last E is *experience,* an area that is being increasingly emphasized. Students require experience, which puts values into action. Within the school, students can help out and tutor one another. They can volunteer to help teachers and librarians. Community-based programs that enable students to put their stated values into practice are valuable. Such programs may involve community service, working in day care centers, with the physically challenged, or helping the elderly. Through such volunteer work, students can experience the values of responsibility and helping others.

The teaching approach to values education stresses the necessity of teaching societal and democratic values, and it is becoming more popular (Rodman, 1987). However, there are some problems with this approach. At times, society has merely paid lip service to its values, and students see hypocrisy in teaching values that may not be echoed in their neighborhoods, their families, or the classroom. Students may rightly realize that these values are not practiced in our society. Students may also tell their teachers what they want to hear but never think about their own values. Sometimes approaches based upon moral reasoning are criticized as too verbal, but the teaching approach may also suffer from the same fate unless a concerted effort is made to structure in situations in which students can put their values into practice.

There is a new emphasis on students putting their values into action.

CONNECTIONS

What Do These Approaches to Moral Education Mean to Teachers?

The calls for programs on moral education are becoming louder and more frequent, and everyone seems to agree that there is a need for the programs. The question is, How best to promote values in students? Should teachers stay neutral or actively transmit values using a teaching perspective? These are not easy questions to answer. Many students in my classes have felt that there is something incomplete about the values clarification approach with its neutrality, something unsatisfying about emphasizing moral reasoning, and something unrealistic about the teaching approach. Yet, each may offer something important.

1. **A need exists for programs that emphasize putting one's values into action.** All programs require an action component that may involve school and community service. Without an action component, values are merely words.

2. **There is merit in students' understanding their own values and discussing moral dilemmas.** Values education must be something more than moralizing and preaching. It needs to have an element of self-discovery. Some of the exercises ad-

vocated in values clarification not only are interesting but also can encourage students to ask questions and think.

3. **One needs to be aware of how the school's moral environment works.** One of the difficulties in the teaching approach is the possibility that educators preach but do not practice such values as hard work, perseverance, tolerance, and democracy. While few people believe that schools or classrooms can be totally democratic, there is room for participation, explanation, and questioning. In addition, being sensitive to the hidden agenda—the morals and values that are being taught in school but are not discussed—is important.

4. **Teaching decision-making skills needs to be stressed.** When students are faced with moral dilemmas in daily life, they can gain through being taught to identify the alternatives and predict the consequences of various courses of action.

5. **One needs to understand the values orientation that students bring into the classroom.** Often the values that educators want to instill may not be practiced in the home. For instance, toleration is important, but a student may be getting a steady diet of sexism or racism at home. A teacher may encourage a student to become friends with a child who is physically challenged, but the student's parents may discourage the student from doing so. There is no easy way to counter such contradictions, but a student ought to be encouraged to recognize that such values as toleration and understanding do exist.

6. **Educators need to be aware of moral issues in the curriculum.** Too often moral education is seen in terms of a particular subject. It need not be. Many subjects offer opportunities to discuss moral questions. For instance, social studies is replete with questions concerning the rights of others and individual rights. English teachers can easily find moral principles and problems in their literature. Science teachers may most often run across moral issues in the use of technology and scientific discoveries.

7. **Educators need to take the developmental level of children into consideration.** Adolescents may possess certain cognitive abilities that allow them to develop their own internal conceptions of right and wrong. They are also better than younger children in seeing moral and values conflicts. High school students may be very involved in understanding how one's rights interfere with society's rights. For instance, if you ask students of various ages the question of whether everyone past 40 should have to submit to a physical examination for early detection of disease or whether seat belts should have to be worn, younger students just see the benefits while older students tend to see the value conflict between the general good and individual freedom (Adelson, 1972; Adelson & O'Neil, 1966; Gallatin & Adelson, 1971). Such developmental differences need to be taken into account when developing a lesson in the area of morals or ethics.

8. **Educators need to have respect for student opinions.** Both values clarification and Kohlberg's approach show tremendous respect for student opinions and values. To discuss values, students must feel that their opinions will be respected. This is an absolute necessity in both values clarification and Kohlberg's approach. However, there is a tendency in the teaching approach to coerce students into agreeing with the teacher. Students may feel that they cannot disagree with a teacher who takes such a stand and may merely mouth what they think the teacher wants to hear.

SEX AND DRUG EDUCATION

Whenever moral education is discussed, questions concerning sex and drug education are raised. Most students are faced with challenges in these areas, and student decisions concerning sex and drugs may have profound consequences.

Sex Education

I wish my parents had canned the stork story and fairy tale explanations and told me the truth.

I wish my parents had sat me down and told me about sex instead of just saying, "Don't let no one in your pants."

I wish my parents had been more open about sex and not treated it as a big dark secret to be discovered and experienced after marriage.

I wish my parents spoke to me more about birth control and let me know that in trouble I could turn to them.

These are just a few of the responses from a questionnaire given to 450 Syracuse University undergraduates. About 90 percent indicated that sex was not honestly discussed in their homes (Gordon, 1981). In fact, only about ten percent of the students were satisfied with their parents' efforts at sex education.

The majority of teens have had no formal sex education from either teachers or parents; they learn about sex from their peers (DeLora et al., 1981). Parents favor sex education in the schools by a wide margin. Some surveys show that as many as 80 percent of all Americans are in favor of sex education in the schools (Barron, 1987). When sex education is offered in school, less than three percent of all parents refuse to let their children participate (Scales, 1978). Although some parents may be opposed to sex education, most favor it, and only a very few will forbid their children to take part in it. The truly controversial question is, What should be taught?

True or False   The majority of parents oppose sex education courses in school.

True or False   When sex education is offered in the schools, about a quarter of the parents refuse to allow their children to remain in class.

Most parents want their own values taught, and there is a great difference of opinion as to what should be included in the sex education curriculum. Once we get past the standard biological content, questions concerning contraception and values arise. Although some parents do not want contraception taught or birth control devices made available to students, most do (Rinck et al., 1983). Other parents are afraid that the teacher will encourage sexuality or teach values that differ from those "taught" at home.

Sex education programs are becoming more common, but it is estimated that fewer than 15 percent of the U.S. children receive comprehensive sex education—now often called family-life education—that covers such diverse areas as reproduction, getting along with others, understanding one's emotions and development, knowing what to do about sexual abuse, and AIDS education.

Everyone agrees that the family is the basic transmitter of education about sexuality (Tatum, 1981). Indeed, sex education programs in the schools can be seen as a way to supplement the family's efforts and not as an attempt to take over what is, and continues to be, a parental responsibility. However, the statistics show that parents are *not* talking to their children in an honest and open manner about sex. A recent poll conducted by Planned Parenthood found that although teens cite their parents as the most important source of information on sex, pregnancy, and contraception, only a third had discussed sex and contraception with their parents. Those who had discussed them were about twice as likely as those who hadn't to use contraceptives if they were sexually active (Wattleton, 1988). Only about a third of the teens in this survey had taken school sex education courses, and again, sexually active teens who had had comprehensive sex education were more likely to use contraceptives than were those who hadn't.

Although there may be some vocal opposition at school board meetings, most parents are in favor of sex education courses in the school. The big question is, What should be taught?

Those who harbor the most misconceptions and myths about sex are those who have not had comprehensive sex education. Adolescents whose parents talk to them about sex tend to be less sexually active. When a great deal of communication occurs, teens are more likely to share the sexual values of their parents (Fischer, 1986). Although the evidence is clear that sex education conducted by parents can be very effective in transmitting values and encouraging the use of contraception if the teenager becomes sexually active, the evidence indicates that most parents do not provide comprehensive sex education for their children.

The consequences of this omission are serious. The birthrate among teenagers in the U.S. is higher than any in other developed country (Compton et al., 1987). About one million teenage pregnancies occur each year, and early pregnancy is related to dropping out of school, early marriage, poverty, and a potential loss of educational and occupational opportunities. The high risk-factors for children of teen parents include increased infant mortality and prematurity, a high incidence of abuse, and many cognitive and developmental problems (Compton et al., 1987).

The need for sex education is also shown by many attitude surveys and informational tests given to teens. Although we often think that the sexually active teen is a well-informed person knowledgeable about the facts of conception, that is not what the research shows (Morrison, 1985). Between 10 and 25 percent of teens questioned did not believe they could become pregnant the first time they had intercourse. When adolescents were asked to identify the time during the menstrual cycle when the greatest risk of pregnancy existed, fewer than half answered correctly. Fewer than half the teens sampled know that sperm could live for three days; one third believed that sperm lives less than one day. About one third of the respondents in one major survey believed they couldn't get pregnant if they didn't want to, even if they had sex without using some contraceptive method, while one quarter of another sample believed that a woman must have an orgasm to become pregnant (Sorenson, 1973).

Teen sexual behavior does not show the responsibility that we would like teens to have. Many sexually active teens do not use contraception. Between one third and two thirds used no contraception during their first sexual intercourse (Morrison, 1985), and in one study, Zabin and Colleagues (1979) found that the majority of teens do not look for any contraceptive assistance until they have been sexually active for about a year. This is distressing, because so many pregnancies occur during the first six months after teens begin engaging in sexual intercourse. Most sexually active teens have had intercourse at least once without using any form of birth control (Dreyer, 1982). Perhaps adolescents do not use contraception regularly because of erroneous beliefs about fertility, indifference to becoming pregnant, not knowing where to get contraceptive help, and negative attitudes toward using contraceptive devices (Morrison, 1985). Most methods of birth control demand that the person acknowledge that he or she is sexually active and views sexual encounters realistically (Pestrak & Martin, 1985). The personal fable (refer to Chapter 6) causes many adolescents to believe they are immune to danger and cannot get pregnant.

The need for sex education, then, is great, but what are its purposes? Some see sex education as a way of reducing the teenage pregnancy problem, while others simply believe students should be given correct information about sex. Still another group argues that sex education should stress personal responsibility. It is the nature of the objectives that should determine the type of program offered. If all we wish to do is to offer students correct information, a biologically based program is sufficient. However, studies have demonstrated that such programs will not lead to a reduction in teen pregnancy, because they ignore moral and value issues. The High School and Beyond Survey, which examined the attitudes of 10,000 high school females, found a relationship between personal and parental attitudes and sexual behavior. Teens who have high educational expectations or who believe they have control over their lives are much less likely to have an out-of-wedlock child. Teenage girls whose parents show concern for where they are, their grades, and their future are also less likely to bear children. The report did not find a relationship between having had sex education classes and bearing children, but an earlier study by Zelnik and Kim (1982) found that sexually active young women who have been exposed to sex education courses are less likely to become pregnant. No support at all was found for the oft-made statement that having had sex education or birth control information increased sexual activity (Goldberg, 1987b). While opponents of sex education have used this study to show that sex education courses don't work, advocates stress that knowledge of contraception is necessary but not sufficient, that decision-making abilities and values must be discussed.

True or False   Giving students frank, honest, and comprehensive information about sexuality and contraception will reduce the teen pregnancy rate.

Most students want more than biological information in sex education courses; they also want to discuss values. Parents also want values discussed, especially abstinence. School programs are better off admitting to parents from the beginning that there is no such thing as a value-free program and discussing the values that will be stressed. This honest approach is best and is most likely to gain public support (Scales, 1982).

For sex education to work, it must be structured so that students can ask questions in a way that does not embarrass them. In one class, the teacher passes out small slips of paper for anonymous question-and-answer sessions so that students do not have to be embarrassed by their questions (Barron, 1987). Parents may become involved by being given input into what is being taught. In an attempt to reduce teenage pregnancy, some communities, realizing that more than frank information is required, have made counselors from clinics available in the school and discussed with students where to go for contraceptive counseling (Zabin et al., 1986). The more ambitious the objectives, the more comprehensive programs must be.

Does sex education work? Evaluating sex education programs is difficult, because so many different programs exist. A short program covering nothing but a bit of biology cannot be compared with a program that includes discussions of values and offers information concerning contraception and where contraceptive counseling is available. In addition, any program based on the ideas that it relieves parents and the religious establishment of the responsibility to educate children about values, that simply giving the facts will automatically reduce the pregnancy and venereal disease rates, or that any sex education course will reduce sexual activity once it has started is unrealistic (Dale & Chamis, 1981). However, studies do show that those students who have taken a comprehensive sex education course have more factual knowledge about sex (Kirby et al., 1979).

There is no evidence that sex education alters personal values in any way that increases sexual behavior (Zelnik & Kim, 1982). Studies show that comprehensive sex education leads neither to higher levels of teen pregnancy nor to greater sexuality, and some (but not all) studies find it increases the likelihood that teens will use birth control (Wattleton, 1988; Select Committee on Children, Youth, and Families, 1985). One study showed not only that 15- and 16-year-olds who had taken a course in sex education were less likely to experiment at that young age but also that parental roles are not undermined by sex education programs (Furstenberg, 1985). Finally, one interesting experimental program was conducted in Baltimore in which junior and senior high school students received not only sex education but also information presented by social workers in their homerooms dealing with the services offered at a clinic. For several hours each day, staff members assigned to each school made themselves available for individual counseling. After school, a special clinic across the street or a few blocks away offered open group discussions and individual and group counseling that

In many sex-education classes, students are encouraged to submit questions in writing anonymously.

emphasized personal responsibility, goal setting, parental communication, and health care, including contraception. The results showed better contraceptive and sex knowledge (something other studies have shown) as well as a delay in the age of first intercourse. Students attended the clinic sooner after initiating sexual activity, and there was an increased use of contraception among those who were sexually active. This behavior was especially noticeable among the younger teens, who usually show less responsible sexual behavior. The program altered behavior partially because access to high-quality free services, including professional counseling, was assured (Zabin et al., 1986).

Drug Education

Drug education is not nearly as controversial as sex education. No one denies the need for it; everyone is for it. In fact, in a survey of elementary school principals, 89 percent said drug education should begin by the third grade, and 65 percent would favor starting it in kindergarten, while only 52 percent favored teaching third graders about sex education, and only 23 percent believed sex education should begin in kindergarten (Viadero, 1987a). The public is often aroused to anger by the figures showing the extent of teenage drug use. The school is not exactly a drug-free oasis in a drug-taking society. Over half the users say they buy their drugs in school, and one third who smoke marijuana do so in school (U.S. Department of Education, 1987a). Studies also show that students are using drugs at an earlier age, making elementary and junior high school students prime targets for drug education (Minix, 1987). On the average, a high school teacher will confront a student body in which one in four of his or her students smoke pot and two out of three use alcohol (Tower, 1987a). In the area of drug education, there is little question concerning the need to teach or even what should be taught. The key question is the effectiveness of drug education.

Any drug abuse program can be divided into drug abuse prevention and identification and treatment of drug users. Drug abuse prevention programs have generally not been very successful (Goodstadt, 1987). One reason is that these programs cannot remove the social problems that may lead to drug abuse. A student may abuse drugs for immediate pleasure, as a means of experimentation, to show rebelliousness,

and because of peer pressure to use drugs. These reasons are easy to understand. However, drugs may also be used as an escape from the harsh realities of life, such as failure, rejection, and family problems (Tower, 1987a). Personality characteristics consistently related to drug use are low self-esteem and feelings of not being competent or wanted (Heron, 1988). Of course, some students with these characteristics will not become drug users. In order to be effective, drug education programs must deal with the issue of how to help students find alternative ways of dealing with their problems. We also need more research on why some students with these problems become attracted to drug use and become drug users and why some students do not. However, these complicated family, societal, and personal problems cannot be addressed very well with only the resources available in the schools, and society must address the social problems that lead to drug abuse (Forbes, 1987).

True or False   Drug abuse prevention programs have generally not been very successful.

Another problem is the assumption that just giving students the information about the dangers of drug abuse is sufficient to reduce drug use. We've seen the same type of programs fail in sex education. Information is important, and teaching students the facts about drugs is necessary but not sufficient in itself to reduce drug use. Information is frequently accompanied by the use of scare tactics, which are ineffective

Drug education is an important educational concern. However, many drug-education programs have not been successful.

(Minix, 1987; Sagor, 1987). Programs that use recovering addicts or police or narcotics agents who try to scare students with lurid stories just don't work, perhaps because the recovering addicts often reinforce students' beliefs that tough people, like themselves, can use drugs and not become addicted.

True or False Showing the dramatic fatal aftermath of drug abuse is an effective way to reduce drug use.

With the preceding in mind, many drug prevention programs have changed their emphasis from giving information to teaching personal decision-making strategies and focusing on personal goals (Minix, 1987). One project that emphasizes abstaining from alcohol, called Project Smart (self-management and resistance training), is designed for students in the fourth through eighth grades. The project does not focus on content—only two of eleven sessions teach what alcohol and other drugs are and how they work. The rest of the sessions are spent discussing the social situations in which students find themselves, methods of resisting peer pressure and refusing drugs, getting peer reactions to saying "no," and finding out what approaches work and why they work (Barron, 1988b). Peer counselors are also used to help students who drink, and being a peer counselor is prestigious and requires training.

Many modern programs, then, besides giving the facts, emphasize the social aspects of life and focus on social skills training and decision-making skills. Some programs advocate targeting students at high risk for abusing drugs, including those who show poor relationships with their parents, a history of abuse, low self-esteem, delinquency, low academic motivation, tolerance for risk taking, family or peer use of drugs, early nicotine use, and psychological problems (Brenna, 1983).

Many drug education programs also focus on helping the drug user. Here, identification is most important. Table 7.3 lists some of the signs that a student may be abusing drugs. Although some of these signs, such as short attention span and difficulty concentrating, may be due to other problems, they suggest a possibility that drug use is present.

Many schools have policies concerning referral of students thought to be using drugs, and each teacher needs to be aware of such policies. A teacher who believes that a student may be using drugs can express his or her concern with a statement such as, "I'm really worried about you, Anne. Your behavior seems

Table 7.3 Signs of Drug Use
Changing patterns of performance, appearance, and behavior may signal use of drugs. The items in the first category listed below provide direct evidence of drug use; the items in the other categories offer signs that may indicate drug use. For this reason, adults should look for extreme changes in children's behavior, changes that together form a pattern associated with drug use.

Signs of Drugs and Drug Paraphernalia

- Possession of drug-related paraphernalia such as pipes, rolling papers, small decongestant bottles, or small butane torches.
- Possession of drugs or evidence of drugs, peculiar plants, or butts, seeds, or leaves in ashtrays or clothing pockets.
- Odor of drugs, smell of incense or other "cover-up" scents.

Identification with Drug Culture

- Drug-related magazines, slogans on clothing.
- Conversation and jokes that are preoccupied with drugs.
- Hostility in discussing drugs.

Signs of Physical Deterioration

- Memory lapses, short attention span, difficulty in concentration.
- Poor physical coordination, slurred or incoherent speech.
- Unhealthy appearance, indifference to hygiene and grooming.
- Bloodshot eyes, dilated pupils.

Dramatic Changes in School Performance

- Distinct downward turns in student's grades—not just from C's to F's, but from A's to B's and C's. Assignments not completed.
- Increased absenteeism or tardiness.

Changes in Behavior

- Chronic dishonesty (lying, stealing, cheating). Trouble with the police.
- Changes in friends, evasiveness in talking about new ones.
- Possession of large amounts of money.
- Increasing and inappropriate anger, hostility, irritability, secretiveness.
- Reduced motivation, energy, self-discipline, self-esteem.
- Diminished interest in extracurricular activities and hobbies.

From "What Works: Schools Without Drugs." United States Department of Education, 1987.

different. You know, if you would like to get some help, I'd be willing to work with you or to put you in touch with people who can help. Would you like to talk about what's going on?" (Tower, 1987a). While some teachers may mention the possibility of drugs, others are not comfortable doing so and simply express concern over the student's behavior. Discussions should *not* be initiated if students show signs they are under the influence of drugs, including glazed eyes, extreme lethargy, sleepiness, or extremes in mood. When consulting parents, teachers may not want to mention their fears of drug use immediately. A teacher may inform the parents of the symptoms, asking them what they think it is. If the parents ask if you think it could be drugs, the opening is present. Such indirect approaches may not always work, and teachers are urged to speak to the school's guidance staff and administration about the situation, since handling these cases is not easy, and it is wise to search for help and support in this area.

Americans identify the drug problem as one of the most important in society and are willing to support drug abuse prevention programs in school. As in the area of sex education, though, giving the facts is not enough, and developmentally appropriate programs that prepare students with the skills to make sensible decisions in social situations are required.

AIDS Education

No disease in the past 100 years has had the shocking effect that AIDS (acquired immune deficiency syndrome) has had on the American public over the past several years. By the end of 1986, more than 29,000 Americans had contracted AIDS, and it is projected that by 1991 the figure will be close to 270,000 (U.S. News and World Report, 1987). AIDS cripples the body's natural defenses, leaving the body vulnerable to opportunistic diseases that healthy bodies fight easily (Schram, 1986). The disease is caused by a virus that some call the lymphadenopathy virus (LAV) and others call the HTLV-111 virus (the human t-cell lymphotrophic virus) (Gong, 1985). But not everyone who comes in contact with the virus will immediate develop AIDS. An estimated 1.5 million Americans now carry the virus but display no symptoms, and no one knows for certain what percentage of these people will eventually exhibit symptoms of AIDS. However, even if these people are not presently showing symp-

toms, they can pass the virus on to others. Although relatively few teens today have the virus, teen sexual and drug-taking behavior makes teenagers a group at risk for coming into contact with the virus. The two most common means of transmission are through sexual contact and through the use of infected drug syringes. Decisions in the areas of sex and drugs initiate patterns of behavior that affect the student for years to come (Flax, 1987; Drotman & Viadero, 1987). A third method of transmission is prenatal, in which an infected pregnant mother transmits the virus to her unborn child (Pinching & Jeffries, 1985). Some of these infected children will be attending school, which raises other questions for teachers.

Teens do not seem to know the basic facts about AIDS. According to a 1986 study of teens, 30 percent believed that AIDS could be cured if treated early, and one third thought that AIDS could be transmitted by merely touching someone. In another study of 860 teens, 22 percent did not know that AIDS could be transmitted by semen, and 29 percent did not know it could be transmitted by vaginal secretions. Even when students know the facts, their behavior does not seem to change much. Studies of AIDS education programs in the schools have not been many, but the federal report "How Effective Is AIDS Education?" found that few have changed their behavior, and those who modified their conduct did not make effective changes. This may be the "it can't happen to me" syndrome. So, again just teaching the facts may not be enough. The goals of many AIDS programs include convincing students to delay sexual intercourse, reduce the number of sexual partners, and use birth control techniques such as condoms.

AIDS education is now mandated in most states, and the Surgeon General advocates that it begin by nine or ten years of age (Flax, 1987). One area of difference is how explicit the education should be. For example, many people advocate emphasizing abstinence (Viadero, 1987b), while others advocate teaching about the use of condoms, which provide some protection. Should the emphasis be placed on explicitly teaching the sexual techniques that are most and least likely to cause contact with the AIDS virus? Or should it simply be placed on abstinence as the only "certain" way to prevent the spread of AIDS? For example, in the U.S. Department of Education's booklet entitled *AIDS and the Education of our Children*, only a paragraph is devoted to the use of condoms: "Research also shows that most teenagers are not using condoms, which provide some but by no means complete protection from the AIDS virus" (1988, p. 5). Rather, the booklet's emphasis is on the moral area of sexual behavior and abstinence.

AIDS education can take place within the sex education or family life classes, but teachers need to be informed in order to answer questions (McCormick, 1987). As in the case of sex education, community involvement is best, and the instruction must be educationally sound and developmentally appropriate (McCormick, 1987). Unfortunately, much AIDS information is written at a level of the college sophomore, way too high for many younger students (Education Week, Sept. 16, 1987).

AIDS education programs must offer students the facts and discuss prevention, including sexual abstinence and fidelity as well as the use of condoms, careful selection of sex partners, and the dangers of using needles and syringes. It must deal with knowledge, attitudes, and behavior. Taking responsibility for one's own health and the health of others are values that must also be addressed (Yarber, 1988). AIDS education is a necessary part of the curriculum, but more research is needed before we can discover the most effective approach to changing attitudes and behavior in this area.

The second area of AIDS education is rarely discussed—the terrible discrimination against AIDS victims. Some of this discrimination is due to misinformation. For example, some people believe that casual contact can transmit the disease. However, studies of health care professionals and families living with AIDS victims find that these people do not catch the virus from casual contact (Friedland et al., 1986). Still, the general public is frightened of even casual contact with an AIDS victim (Altman, 1986). Some parents have reacted violently to the knowledge that a child with AIDS will be admitted to school. The school can do much to counter the sufferings and ostracism of children with AIDS, but only if it offers the facts as we know them and its teachers are trained to handle these difficult situations and to disseminate accurate information about the disease. The help of the medical community is also required.

What the Evidence on Sex and Drug Education Means to Teachers

No one claims that school-based sex and drug education programs by themselves will eliminate the problems of teenage pregnancy and drug abuse in our society. These programs are simply messages added to the ones offered at home, by peers, and in the media. However, some general findings are now becoming accepted. First, programs in these areas do not lead to increased sex or drug use; nor do they undermine the transmission of parental values. Second, scare tactics do not seem to work very well. Third, although giving accurate information is vital, it is not sufficient to reduce experimentation or to change behavior in these areas. Fourth, courses must deal with attitudes, values, individual goals, and decision-making abilities. Fifth, every program is based upon values, and communicating these values to parents is necessary if community support is to be generated. Sixth, parents can and should have input into the curriculum, but educators must accept the fact that a few parents will always be opposed to sex education programs and expect such opposition. The vast majority of parents, however, will support broad-based, well-taught curricula in the family life area.

MODERN CONCERNS: CHILD ABUSE AND SUICIDE PREVENTION

Social problems impinge on the school and teachers are often given responsibilities for identifying conditions that can be life threatening. Two such areas are child abuse and suicide prevention.

Child Abuse

After the death of a six-year-old child in New York City, many concerned people wondered why this child was not helped. Why didn't someone, presumably in the school, notice (Goldberg, 1987a)? All states have mandatory reporting laws, and since all children must attend school, educators could be expected to be in the forefront of identifying and reporting child abuse cases. Yet, only 13 percent of all the child abuse reports are made by school personnel (Meddin & Rosen, 1987), and only the most obvious cases are reported (Camblin & Prout, 1983). Why this seeming lack of response? First, many teachers do not know how to recognize the symptoms of possible child abuse, or they may not understand their responsibilities under the law. Second, except for the most obvious cases, many of the manifestations of child abuse or neglect are only possible symptoms, and teachers are reluctant to act on probability or possibility, even though the law in many states holds a person making a mistaken report in good faith harmless from suit. Third, many teachers are afraid of the strained relationship that may occur if a report is made to a social services agency that later turns out to be false (Turbett & O'Toole, 1983). Yet, the physical and psychological harm of child abuse requires educators to play a greater role in the identification and referral of such abuse.

True or False The majority of referrals for child abuse are made by educators.

Child abuse occurs when adults responsible for the child intentionally injure the child. **Neglect** refers to a situation in which the physical care and supervision of the child is inadequate or inappropriate, for example, a child who comes to school each day dressed inadequately for bitterly cold weather. Sexual abuse can involve forcible rape, statutory rape, sodomy, incest, or "indecent liberties" such as genital exhibition and physical advances (Sarafino, 1979). About 56,000 cases of sexual abuse were reported in 1984 (Child Welfare League, 1986), but the incidence of such abuse is underreported, and it is the least reported type of child abuse (Schultz & Jones, 1983). Because states vary in their definition of abuse and neglect, each teacher needs to become familiar with his or her state's definition. There were over 1,900,000 cases of child abuse and neglect reported in 1985 (U.S. Department of Commerce, 1989).

Emotional Abuse

Child abuse does not have to be physical. Some parents constantly yell at and berate their children. Imagine a six-year-old who has just spilled some juice hearing a parent shout, "You're a stupid, rotten kid. If I had any sense, I'd give you away!" It has been argued that some teachers indulge in psychological maltreatment when they engage in such behaviors as corporal punishment, verbal abuse, or rejection (Hart, 1987).

It is difficult to define **emotional abuse** (sometimes called psychological maltreatment) (Rosenberg, 1987). Certain parental actions can lead to loss of self-esteem in the child and interfere with emotional development, but defining such actions and describing remedial steps are difficult. Conceptually,

child abuse A general term used to denote an injury that is intentionally perpetrated on a child.

neglect A term used to describe a situation in which the care and supervision of a child is insufficient or improper.

emotional abuse (psychological maltreatment) Psychological damage perpetrated on the child by parental actions which often involves rejection, isolation, terrorizing, ignoring, or corrupting.

such behaviors as rejecting, isolating, terrorizing, ignoring, and corrupting constitute psychological maltreatment (Garbarino et al., 1986), and these forms of abuse frequently produce emotional and behavioral problems in children (Hart & Brassard, 1987).

What Are the Signs of Child Abuse?

The range of symptoms that *may* indicate child abuse is wide. The problem is that often these symptoms are suggestive, not absolute. Many children have bruises or broken bones or may come to school inappropriately dressed because they run out the door before their parents can check to see if they are wearing a coat in cold weather. However, repeated injuries, new injuries before previous ones have healed, welts, evidence of lack of nutrition, and burns on the palms of the hands are causes for concern. Table 7.4 lists physical and behavioral indicators of physical abuse and neglect, sexual abuse, and emotional maltreatment. Teachers should ask children who arrive with a physical injury how the injury occurred. For example, children are often innocently injured on their knees, forehead, or hands when they attempt to break a fall. It is possible to determine whether the injuries could have been sustained the way the child suggests.

Reporting Child Abuse

In every state, educators are required to report suspected child abuse. In most states, teachers can make a report orally to a governmental agency such as social services. However, many school districts encourage or require teachers to report to the principal, who then will notify the authorities. Many states require the oral report to be followed by a written report, and

Table 7.4   Physical and Behavioral Indicators of Child Abuse and Neglect

A child may show some of the listed symptoms but may not be a victim of child abuse. However, this list may be useful in suggesting those behaviors and conditions that may indicate that child abuse has occurred.

Type of Child Abuse/Neglect	Physical Indicators	Behavioral Indicators
Physical Abuse	Unexplained bruises and welts —on face, lips, mouth —on torso, back, buttocks, thighs —in various stages of healing —clustered, forming regular patterns —reflecting shape of article used to inflict (electric cord, belt buckle) —on several different surface areas —regularly appear after absence, weekend, or vacation —human bite marks —bald spots Unexplained burns —cigar, cigarette burns, especially on soles, palms, back, or buttocks —immersion burns (socklike, glovelike, doughnut-shaped on buttocks or genitalia) —patterned like electric burner, iron, etc. —rope burns on arms, legs, neck, or torso Unexplained fractures —to skull, nose, facial structure —in various stages of healing —multiple or spiral fractures Unexplained lacerations or abrasions —to mouth, lips, gums, eyes —to external genitalia	Wary of adult contacts Apprehensive when other children cry Behavioral extremes —aggressiveness —withdrawal —overly compliant Afraid to go home Reports injury by parents Exhibits anxiety about normal activities, e.g., napping Complains of soreness and moves awkwardly Destructive to self and others Early to school or stays late as if afraid to go home Accident-prone Wears clothing that covers body when not appropriate Chronic runaway (especially adolescents) Cannot tolerate physical contact: or touch
Physical Neglect	Consistent hunger, poor hygiene, inappropriate dress Consistent lack of supervision, especially in dangerous activities or long periods Unattended physical problems or medical needs Abandonment Lice Distended stomach, emaciated	Begging, stealing food —Constant fatigue, listlessness or falling asleep States there is no caretaker at home Frequent school absence or tardiness Destructive, pugnacious School dropout (adolescents) Early emancipation from family (adolescents)
Sexual Abuse	Difficulty in walking or sitting Torn, stained, or bloody underclothing Pain or itching in genital area Bruises or bleeding in external genitalia, vaginal, or anal areas Venereal disease Frequent urinary or yeast infections	Unwilling to participate in certain physical activities Sudden drop in school performance Withdrawal, fantasy, or unusually infantile behavior Crying with no provocation Bizarre, sophisticated, or unusual Anorexia (especially adolescents)

Table 7.4   Continued

Type of Child Abuse/Neglect	Physical Indicators	Behavioral Indicators
Sexual Abuse	Frequent unexplained sore throats	Sexual behavior or knowledge
		Sexually provocative
		Poor peer relationships
		Reports sexual assault by caretaker
		Fear of or seductiveness toward males
		Suicide attempts (especially adolescents)
		Chronic runaway
		Early pregnancies
Emotional Maltreatment	Speech disorders	Habit disorders (sucking, biting, rocking, etc.)
	Lags in physical development	Conduct disorders (antisocial, destructive, etc.)
	Failure to thrive (especially in infants)	Neurotic traits (sleep disorders, inhibition of play)
	Asthma, severe allergies, or ulcers	Behavioral extremes
	Substance abuse	—compliant, passive
		—aggressive, demanding
		Overly adaptive behavior
		—inappropriately adult
		—inappropriately infantile
		Developmental lags (mental, emotional)
		Delinquent behavior (especially adolescents)

Reprinted with permission from *How Schools Can Help Combat Child Abuse and Neglect,* 2d ed. by Cynthia Crosson Tower. Copyright © 1987, National Educational Association.

school officials may then become involved. It is very important that each teacher know the procedure to follow within his or her school and district in reporting child abuse cases. Some districts have clear rules, while others don't. Some districts also have a school team composed of counselors, nurses, administrators, and teachers who discuss the potential report. Such a system partially relieves the teacher of the pressure and offers support (Tower, 1987b).

True or False   Teachers have a legal responsibility to report instances of child abuse.

What if a teacher feels that he or she has enough evidence that a report should be made and brings this evidence to the administrator, who then refuses to report it. This is a difficult situation for two reasons. First, even if a teacher has reported suspected abuse to an administrator, this does *not* relieve the teacher of his or her responsibility under the law (Tower, 1987b; Education Week, Nov. 25, 1987). Second, some administrators may not be aware of their responsibility in this area, and the teacher may have to work hard to convince the administrator that the report is necessary. After a report is made, the social services agency will investigate the complaint and take the appropriate action.

Programs to Prevent and Deal with Child Abuse

Programs to deal with child abuse have centered on two general approaches. Primary programs of prevention enroll parents in educational programs, have professionals visit the homes, and offer courses on child development in high schools. In such courses, students are taught child-care techniques, given information concerning children's nutritional and emotional needs, and told where parents can turn for help. The results of such programs are encouraging (Starr, 1979).

Help is available for families as well. Many approaches have been used to treat child abusers. Social work, individual and family therapy, self-help groups such as Parents Anonymous that provide emotional support, and group treatment can all claim some success. The figures for improvement range widely from about 40 percent to 80 percent (Starr, 1979). Generally, about half the parents involved in abusive situations can be helped at least to stop physically abusing their children. This means that in most cases, children will stay within the school environment.

The victims of abuse need help. Abused children show many behavioral disturbances that, of course, affect learning and development. Many improve even when there is only a mild to moderate improvement in the home situation (Jones, 1979). Early identification is one factor in successful treatment.

There are also programs to help students recognize abuse, and some filmstrips are available. Many schools now teach students that they do not have to allow anyone to touch them if they do not want to be touched, they shouldn't take candy from strangers, they do not have to agree to demands for physical closeness even from relatives, and they should report instances of people touching them in intimate areas or asking them to do the same to them. One concern of sexual abuse prevention programs is that they may have a negative effect on children by making children frightened of strangers or uncomfortable about physical affection. Studies generally show that this does not occur (Wurtele & Miller-Perrin, 1987a, 1987b).

Identifying possible cases of child abuse is definitely part of a teacher's job both legally and morally. Being alert to the possible signs of abuse is of primary importance, but teachers must also be familiar with the school's policies and procedures. It is hoped that more districts will become involved in setting up programs and committees to help teachers in this very difficult area of concern. The stakes are high, since 1,300 children nationwide were reported to have died from abuse or neglect in 1986, and one wonders in how many of those cases some intervention might have made the difference (Education Week, Nov. 25, 1987).

Suicide Prevention

Suicide is the second leading cause of death among people between the ages of 15 and 21 (accidents are first). Nationally, suicide increased by more than 200 percent between 1960 and 1980, although the suicide rate has leveled off in recent years (Viadero, 1987c; Frederick, 1985). It is the eighth leading cause of death among children between the ages of 5 and 14 (Bernhardt & Praeger, 1985). It is estimated that 11 percent of all youths in the 15- to 19-year-old age group have attempted suicide, with more than 5,000 succeeding in taking their own lives during 1985 (Hobart, 1986; Frederick, 1985).

Whenever a suicide occurs in a community, people start looking for answers and clues. Indeed, in the majority of cases, clues are found. About 80 percent of the adolescents communicate their feelings and intentions to other people before attempting suicide (Shafii, 1985). Teachers and fellow students can play a role in identifying and seeking help for these students.

Two different elements highlight suicide prevention programs. The first is teacher recognition of the signs of possible suicide. Second, there are programs—a few of them mandated by states, such as in New Jersey and California—that attempt to educate students on the signs of possible suicide, discuss suicide itself, and inform students of the help that is available.

Recognition of the possible signs of intended suicide is the foremost responsibility of the teacher in this area. The most common indication preceding suicide, according to most experts, is depression (Gispert et al., 1985). However, not all people who are depressed will try suicide, and many suicide victims are not depressed (Allen, 1987). A sense of hopelessness seems to pervade suicide victims (Farberow, 1985). Those who attempt suicide often have a family history of breakdown, divorce, and suicide in the family; have few friends; and suffer from rejection (Wenar, 1982). Many experience a large number of stressful events in childhood, with a marked increase in stress in the year preceding the suicide attempt (Gispert et al., 1985). Other predisposing factors include early death of a parent, rejection in love, academic pressure to achieve, and failure (Hardin, 1985). Familial determinants include divorce, poor communication, conflict, unavailable parents, high parental expectations, mental illness, job loss, suicide of a family member, and alcoholism (Allen, 1987). Sometimes parents have a "do your own thing" or an "I come first" attitude that affects children. The loss or lack of a confidant is another problem, since these potential victims lose the one person in whom they could confide.

Suicide prevention is hampered by the numerous myths about suicide that the general public believes to be true. For instance, many believe that people who talk about suicide never actually do it. This is not so. People who talk about suicide are actually more likely to attempt it. Other myths involve the belief that suicide happens without warning, improvement after suicide means that suicide risk is over, and suicide and depression are synonymous (McGuire, 1983). A number of signs may be of help in identifying potential suicide victims. There is no absolute agreement, but the following list is useful:

1. Preoccupation with themes of death or expressing suicidal thoughts.
2. Giving away prized possessions or making a will or other "final arrangements."
3. Changes in sleeping patterns—too much or too little.
4. Sudden and extreme changes in eating habits or losing or gaining weight.
5. Withdrawal from friends and family or major behavioral changes.
6. Changes in school performance, lowered grades, cutting classes, dropping out of activities.
7. Personality changes, such as nervousness, outbursts of anger, or apathy about appearance and health.
8. Use of drugs or alcohol.
9. Recent suicide of a friend or relative.
10. Previous suicide attempts (People, 1985, p. 87).
11. Feelings of hopelessness and depression (Allen, 1987).
12. Recent loss of people who are close to them.

True or False People who talk about committing suicide rarely make a suicide attempt.

Some districts offer classes in which students are taught how to recognize the warning signs and help their troubled friends; such classes also introduce students to the community resources available. The California program is a four-hour curriculum. Evaluations show a significant gain in the understanding of suicide prevention techniques, and school staff and parents completing suicide awareness seminars appreciate the practical advice. Over 40 percent of the students say that they liked learning how to help themselves and others with feelings of depression. The program has had a positive impact on the knowledge and attitudes of the students, who have thus become better able to recognize the signs and symptoms of potential suicide (Nelson, 1987). One interesting outcome of the New Jersey evaluation is that most of the teens questioned reported that because of the program they were more likely to use a hotline to help themselves or their family deal with problems (Viadero, 1987d). The evaluation also indicated that most students already held what were considered "desirable" attitudes about suicide, such as taking seriously a friend's stated intention to commit suicide. Not all students see these programs as desirable, and some describe them as upsetting or boring. Disagreement exists on the total effect that these programs and films on suicide may have on already troubled students. Could they cause a troubled student to consider suicide? The studies in this area are difficult to interpret. Some question the repetition of the suicide theme, while others claim that the conclusion that these programs or films on the subject may encourage suicide in troubled students is premature (Viadero, 1987d). More research is certainly needed on this subject, but no one denies the need for teachers to be alert to the signs of potential suicide and for students to know where help is available.

THE SCHOOL AND SOCIAL PROBLEMS

As we've seen, more and more pressure is being placed on schools in the areas of values and health education. As we look for solutions to problems that arise in our society, one response always seems to be the same—teach about these subjects in the schools. But the schools are only one part of the child's day. The influence of a child's peers, parents, and neighborhood are strong, and schools are much better at teaching positives (doing something) than at teaching a negative (not doing something). It may be unfair to expect the schools to do something about society's problems in a vacuum. However, the schools have a role to play in values education and sex and health education as well as in the identification of child abuse and the prevention of suicide. However, if we are to succeed, we must use a realistic approach.

Preaching and scare tactics don't work. Education that gives the facts in a developmentally appropriate manner is important but, as we've seen, does not necessarily change attitudes and behavior. The current movement toward arming students not only with the facts but also with the social skills and values needed to make responsible decisions is promising.

At the same time, there has been somewhat of a change from allowing students to clarify their own values to an increased emphasis on more directly transmitting certain values to students. Encouraging students to take responsibility for their acts, gain moral lessons from history and literature, and understand the values that underlie our democratic system are reasonable goals. However, it is doubtful that such goals can be accomplished through a series of lectures devoid of reality or through preaching from role models who indulge in the very behaviors they are condemning or who are not respected.

From an overemphasis on process in the 1970s, we may now be seeing too much stress on the content of what is delivered. Character education does not take place in a vacuum, and in the midst of communicating positive values directly, we should not forget the importance of process. As Haim Ginott once said (1969, p. 243),

> Character traits cannot be taught directly; no one can teach loyalty by lectures, courage by correspondence, or manhood by mail. Character education requires presence that demonstrates and contact that communicates. A teenager learns what he lives, and becomes what he experiences. To him, our mood is the message, the style is the substance, the process is the product.

If education in this area is to be successful, it must be concerned with both product *and* process and concentrate on knowledge, attitudes, and behavior.

SUMMARY

1. The demands that schools become more active in the realm of moral, values, and health education have increased. It is frequently difficult to evaluate programs in these areas, because the goals of the programs are not only to increase knowledge but also to change attitudes and behavior. Schools are better at teaching students to do something than not to do something.

2. Piaget and Kohlberg both advanced theories of moral reasoning. Piaget noted that young children do not take intention into consideration when judging actions and see rules as unchangeable. Older children are more flexible and consider intent when judging actions. Kohlberg explained the development of moral reasoning in terms of three levels, each of which contains two stages. It is the reasoning behind the moral decision and not the decision itself that determines the level of moral reasoning.

3. Carol Gilligan argues that males and females reason differently on moral issues. While males are oriented toward individual rights and legal issues, women are more concerned with how their decisions will affect their social and interpersonal relationships. A positive relationship exists between moral reasoning and moral behavior, but it is far from perfect.

4. Behaviorists are more interested in studying moral behaviors, such as cheating and altruism, than they are in the reasoning behind the behaviors. The environment, the child's learning history, and the situation itself affect moral behavior.

5. Values clarification courses emphasize students choosing, prizing, and acting upon their own values. Students are encouraged to discover their own values while their teachers remain neutral. Instructors provide the means to discovery by using a variety of exercises. In recent years, criticism of values clarification courses has increased as many people argue that students cannot simply be allowed to discover their own values and that input from adults is important.

6. Kohlberg's approach to moral education involves offering students moral dilemmas, encouraging students to see the dilemmas from all sides, and stimulating discussion concerning possible alternatives. Kohlberg believes that during this verbal give-and-take, students reasoning at higher stages will influence those reasoning at lower stages, thereby encouraging improvement in moral reasoning. Kohlberg also advocates the formation of a just community in schools in which democratic values are put into action.

7. Recently, a movement to teach moral values has arisen. Teachers become actively involved in showing the values that underlie history, literature, and the U.S. political and economic system. This movement is typified by the five E's:

example, explanation, exhortation, creating an environment that reflects desirable values, and providing experience for students to put their values into action.

8. Most parents favor sex education, although exactly what to teach remains controversial. Family-based sex education can be very effective, but most parents do not talk realistically with their children about sex. It is relatively easy to teach students the facts of sexuality, but discussions of values are necessary if attitudes and behavior are to be altered. Some programs also offer access to comprehensive contraceptive counseling. There is no evidence that sex education courses increase sexual activity.

9. Everyone agrees that drug education is necessary. The key question is, What type will be successful? Again, information itself, while valuable, does not change attitudes and behavior, and scare tactics do not work. Some current programs not only give information but also concentrate on decision-making skills and preparing students to counter the social influences that surround drug taking. Identifying drug abusers and assisting them in getting help is also an important part of the drug education effort.

10. AIDS (acquired immune deficiency syndrome) is a fatal disease that reduces the body's ability to fight off infection. AIDS education is now mandated by law. While everyone advocates giving students the facts, the degree of emphasis placed on prevention through abstinence and reduction in the number of sexual partners and encouraging the use of condoms is controversial. Information itself may not change attitudes and behavior, and discussion of values is required. At this point, we do not know the most effective way to change behaviors that threaten to spread the AIDS virus. AIDS education can also serve to reduce discrimination against AIDS victims that is based upon ignorance.

11. Teachers are required by law to report suspected cases of child abuse. Child abuse can be physical, sexual, or emotional. Child neglect involves inadequate or inappropriate supervision. A wide range of symptoms can suggest possible abuse, and teachers should know both state law and school policy in reporting abuse. Educators have also started programs to prevent abuse, often giving child development courses in high school

and offering information to students about sexual abuse.

12. Suicide is the second leading cause of death among adolescents, and teachers who can recognize the signs of impending suicide may save lives. Some states are mandating suicide education that deals with recognizing the signs of suicide, knowing where to go for help, and helping students deal with stress.

ACTIVITIES AND EXERCISES

1. **Piaget's Theory of Moral Reasoning.** Piaget's ideas about the difference between younger and older children's ability to take intention and motivation into account before judging another person's behavior are interesting. If you have access to children of different ages, ask preschoolers, school-aged children of various ages, and a couple of young adolescents the question, Who was naughtier, Juan, who broke three dishes trying to help his mother clear the table, or Tina, who broke one dish while trying to sneak some cookies from the cookie jar? Piaget argues that children younger than about seven should not be able to take intention into account and would say that Juan was naughtier, while children above the age of ten or so would understand the importance of intention and choose Tina. Children between these two ages would choose either. One caution, though, as was noted in Chapter 2: Ages are just guidelines in stage theories, so avoid the reasoning that a child who is seven years of age should reason a certain way. Children enter and leave stages at their own rate. Do your findings support Piaget's ideas in this area?

2. **Kohlberg's Dilemma.** Kohlberg's theory of moral reasoning is broader than Piaget's. You can use the technique of studying moral judgment by presenting people with moral dilemmas. This will give you a general idea of how people reason about various moral questions. Write your own moral dilemma or use the case of Heinz or Holly described in the chapter. Dilemmas should be developmentally appropriate. Present your dilemma to a number of people but remember that it is not what the people would do but their reasoning behind doing it (the "why" that Kohlberg's theory deals with in great detail). Write a sen-

tence or two describing each person's answer and reasoning and see which type of reasoning is most popular.

3. **Moral "Training" in the Schools.** Some school districts have become more interested in the moral education of students and offer programs dealing with values. Speak to a number of administrators and teachers and find out if there has been any movement in the area of moral education in their school. The movement may be in the form of curricula emphasis, as social studies teachers may be asked to emphasize democratic values or English teachers to bring out morals from literature. In addition, ask teachers whether they deal in their lessons with morals and values and, if so, to tell you about one of their lessons in this area.

4. **What Else Should the Schools Do?** Whenever a societal problem such as drug abuse, teenage pregnancy, child abuse, or suicide becomes the focus of attention, the school is asked to play a role in dealing with it. As you read the newspapers, cut out articles stating or hinting that the schools should be more involved or have failed in some endeavor not related to teaching what we might call the regular school subjects and skills. While listening to television, jot down the same sentiments. You may be surprised at the broad spectrum of "nonacademic" goals the schools are asked to achieve.

5. **Teacher Training in Sex Education, AIDS Education, and Drug Abuse Prevention.** The schools' responsibilities in the areas of sex education, AIDS, and drug abuse prevention are well established, but what sort of training do teachers have in these areas? Find out who is responsible for such programs in a district and ask the individuals what training they have had and how they received their position. If every teacher in elementary school is involved in drug abuse prevention, ask the teachers what sort of training they have had and whether they thought their training was adequate.

6. **Curricula Review.** Many different curricula are used in the areas of sex and drug education. Ask a principal or a teacher in charge for a curriculum in these areas. If the school has a course or a set of lesson plans for moral education, request to see it as well. Review the curricula, taking notice of how comprehensive they are, whether they are

developmentally appropriate, and how much time is devoted to each topic.

7. **Attend a School Board Meeting—Confrontation, Confusion, or Cooperation.** Education in the areas discussed in this chapter is sometimes discussed at school board meetings, where parents with definite opinions who are involved in the development of curricula may report to the community or community residents and may present their opinions forcefully to the school board. The experience of listening to the residents is valuable, as is examining the methods by which the school board or district administration tries to gain community support for programs and handle the opposition they may encounter.

8. **AIDS Instruction.** AIDS education is now mandated in most states. Ask teachers at all levels what materials on AIDS they have received, if they are required to teach about AIDS, and what they teach? In addition, ask if any health-related procedures have changed, such as directions on handling students' bruises or cuts.

9. **Your Own Poll.** Take a poll of how people feel about sex education, AIDS education, and drug education in schools. First divide your inquiries into the three different areas (sex education, AIDS education, and drug education). The first question might be whether the subject believes the schools should offer education in that particular area. If the answer is no, ask why and end the poll. If the answer is yes, as it will be in the majority of cases, ask detailed questions concerning what should be taught. For instance, ask if the biological facts of life should be taught, whether contraception should be covered, and whether contraceptives should be made available in the school.

10. **What Kind of Sex Education or Drug Education Did You Receive in School?** Interview your classmates and other students, asking them to describe what sort of drug or sex education programs they were exposed to in school? In addition, ask them to evaluate whether they thought these programs were effective and what they would do to make them more effective.

11. **School Procedures.** Some schools have specific procedures about reporting cases of suspected child abuse and drug abuse. Ask teachers and administrators in various schools whether their schools have such procedures and, if they do,

what they are. If they do not, ask the administrators how they would want a teacher to handle such cases. A teacher can save him or herself much trouble and be more certain of gaining support by being aware of the school's procedures.

12. **What Community and School Resources Are Available?** Almost every community has resources to help students cope with problems in the areas described in the chapter. Find out what is available in your community and ask the guidance counselors, school psychologist, or drug counselor which community resources are used by the school.

13. **An Interview With . . .** There are experts in drug education, sex education, suicide prevention, and child abuse who are often very willing to be interviewed. Prepare a set of questions to ask these authorities, emphasizing the school's role in these areas.

14. **Observe a Lesson on Sex Education or Drug Abuse.** If possible, observe a teacher instructing his or her students on one of the topics covered in this chapter. Take special note of how students react to the lesson.

SCENARIOS

Here are eleven scenarios. Try to apply the information you have learned in the chapter to each situation.

1. Mr. Philips has been discussing the dangers of drugs, including cocaine and heroin. Students don't seem to have any comments and accept the information well. When Mr. Philips talks about alcohol, there is a smile on a number of faces and a snicker from the back. Students tell him that their parents drink and their older brothers enjoy drinking. When one student said that it was just a way to look grown up, he was hooted down. "Don't you ever take a drink or have a beer?" his students yell out. Mr. Philips is not a heavy drinker, but he does occasionally have a beer or a glass of wine. How should Mr. Philips handle this situation?

2. Ms. James has been asked by her administrator to teach a developmentally appropriate sex education or family life course in junior high school. She is a biology teacher and feels competent to deal with the biological aspects of reproduction and AIDS but not the values and feelings aspect of sexuality. After relating her concerns to her su-

pervisor, Mrs. Daily, the assistant principal, told her that she has great confidence in Ms. James's ability and not to worry. Ms. James began dealing with love and its relationship to sex, and one of the student's parents appeared the next day to question her about her values and what she is going to teach. Although the parent was polite, Ms. James doesn't know what to do. She is an excellent teacher but is not prepared for this. She might just preach abstinence and get around the subject, but she doesn't feel that is what should be done. On the other hand, she wants no more problems with parents or the administration. What should she do?

3. Mr. Mandel has noted that Jon is always dirty and usually depressed. He often has bruises on him but no more than you would expect from an active nine-year-old. However, Jon has recently had a spate of injuries, which he claims are due to falls and playing ball roughly with his friends, but Mr. Mandel is not quite satisfied with Jon's explanations. At the recent parent-teacher conference, Mr. Mandel noticed that Jon's mother was angry and was very short with Jon. Jon's mother was also very nervous and anxious. When Mr. Mandel reported the situation to his supervisor, Ms. Taylor, he was told that there was not enough evidence to make a report on child abuse. If you were Mr. Mandel, what would you do?

4. Ms. Perkins has been worried about Kathy for a while. Kathy always seems tired and not able to concentrate, her eyes sometimes show a glazed expression, and she experiences excessive mood swings. Ms. Perkins suspects drug abuse but is wary about saying anything. Kathy's mother is well known and well respected in the P.T.A. and has organized programs on drug abuse. Ms. Perkins doesn't know how to approach the situation. If she asked you, what advice would you give her?

5. Mr. Kaye's supervisor in high school has just asked Mr. Kaye to design a curriculum in the area of family life. Mr. Kaye easily found a comprehensive curriculum and modified it to meet local needs. Within a few months, he presented the program to his supervisor, who thought it was great. Now he is asked to present it to the school board and obtain community backing for the ambitious program. How should Mr. Kaye proceed?

6. A parents group has just lost its lawsuit to keep a six-year-old with AIDS out of school. Some parents

have accepted the decision, some have threatened a boycott, and others are plainly frightened at the prospect of "exposing" their children to a child who carries the AIDS virus. You are asked to speak as a first-grade teacher to a group of parents on this subject. How would you handle the situation?

7. Few people objected to sex education in the district, and when the district wanted to create a more comprehensive program, it met with little objection. The community is rather sophisticated in this area, and the staff teaching the family life program is skilled and competent. However, the teenage pregnancy and venereal disease problem has not been reduced. The staff has suggested a partnership with a birth control clinic in which access to contraception would be easy. A counselor from the clinic would be available and would talk to each class about what services were available at the nearby clinic. Some parents object to this program because they think it will encourage early sexual experimentation and lead to a reduction of the school's emphasis on delaying sexual intercourse and the value of abstinence. The principal has asked you to speak to the parents gathered at a meeting in the school library about this program. What would you say?

8. Mr. Williams is discussing the American Revolution and its heroes. One student in the tenth-grade class asks Mr. Williams if it was true that some of these heroes owned slaves and may have joined the rebellion for economic reasons. Another student states that many of these heroes didn't want the Bill of Rights as the law of the land. Still another student notes the conflict between what ought to be and what is in the country, pointing out that people pay lip service to the values in the Constitution and the Declaration of Independence. How should Mr. Williams handle these questions and comments?

9. Mrs. Tomasetti has a problem with Kevin, an eighth-grade student who makes a number of racist comments. Kevin sees the world in terms of "them" and "us." Mrs. Tomasetti has spoken with Kevin's father, who does not seem concerned at all about Kevin's attitudes, and she thinks that Kevin is picking up the attitudes from his parents. Mrs. Tomasetti has presented her class with a number of exercises to help her students clarify their values, but instead of getting an outcry from the class when Kevin spouts off, she gets silence. If you were Mrs. Tomasetti, what would you do?

10. Mr. Jones believes that the school has the responsibility to try to transmit values to students, but every approach he uses seems to rely on words and more words. He finds that values are being "taught" or "discovered" in a vacuum. After bringing this out to his administrator, he is encouraged to create an action-related program. Mr. Jones has the opportunity to create a program that puts values into action but does not know where to start. He asks you as his colleague for suggestions. What would you say?

11. Lois, a student in your high school English class, asks to speak to you and tells you that her friend, who is a schoolmate, has been acting strangely, giving things away, and seems to be depressed since his parents' divorce. Lois's friend has said that "things would be better without me," and Lois is frightened by such talk. She does not want to tell you the student's name but asks you what to do. How would you respond?

The Teacher-Student Interaction

Are These Statements True or False?

Turn the next page for the correct answers. Each statement is repeated following the paragraph in which the information can be found.

1. Students who are considered troublemakers in school often have a positive self-concept that interferes with their ability to conform to school rules.

2. Students with a high fear of failure lack achievement motivation.

3. If students attribute their failure to lack of effort, they are likely to put in more effort at a later date.

4. High-achieving students usually attribute their successes to internal factors such as ability and effort and their failures to external factors such as luck.

5. Teachers should not relate past effort and success to a student's present challenge because it is unrealistic to assume that effort will always lead to success.

6. Poor readers have the same expectations for success in school and show more perseverance when faced with a difficult task than more competent readers.

7. About half the achievement differences among students can be attributed to how much their teachers expect them to achieve.

8. Teachers wait longer for students with lower ability to answer questions than they do for higher achieving students.

9. Providing hands-on experiences is an effective way to stimulate curiosity.

10. Competition should never be used in the classroom to improve student performance.

11. Extrinsic incentives given by the teacher, such as free time, stickers, or being exempted from homework, are best used when a student is not good at a particular task.

12. Rewarding students with something material such as a prize can reduce a student's natural interest in the activity.

Motivation

1. *False* Correct statement: Students who are considered troublemakers in school usually have a low self-concept and little self-respect.

2. *False* Correct statement: Students with a high fear of failure may not lack achievement motivation but may opt for very safe or almost impossible tasks because of their desire to avoid failure, or at least failure that would be attributed to their ability.

3. *True*

4. *True*

5. *False* Correct statement: Teachers should relate past effort and success to a student's present challenge.

6. *False* Correct statement: Poor readers have lower expectations for success in school and give up more quickly when faced with a difficult task than more competent readers.

7. *False* Correct statement: Between five and ten percent of the academic achievement differences among students can be attributed to teacher expectations.

8. *False* Correct statement: Actually, teachers wait less time after asking a low-ability student a question than they do when they ask a higher ability student a question.

9. *True*

10. *False* Correct statement: Although there are many problems in using competition, it can be used effectively in the classroom if all the students have the necessary skills to succeed, success is based upon effort, and the consequences of winning and losing are minimized.

11. *True*

12. *True*

Carlos tries hard but gives up easily. When presented with a problem requiring some thought, Carlos looks at it, tries it, and quickly announces to the teacher that he can't do it. Carlos's teacher, Mr. Turpin, believes that Carlos has the ability to do the work. What can he do to help Carlos?

Ms. Moore is teaching a class of fourth-grade students who vary greatly in their reading ability and enjoyment of reading. Some students will go to the back of the room, choose a book or magazine, and read when they have free time. Others avoid the class's book collection entirely. Ms. Moore would like to create a reward system in which the students will receive some tangible reward for their extra reading. She is concerned, however, that such a reward may dampen the already-interested students' enthusiasm for reading. Is her concern warranted?

Mr. Ozawa is teaching history to a class of high school juniors. He plans his lessons carefully but finds that the students don't seem interested in the work. Most of his students do their work but are just going through the motions. After talking with a few students, Mr. Ozawa discovers that one of the reason they lack interest is that they have already studied the American Revolution several times. What can Mr. Ozawa do to motivate his students?

A QUESTION OF MOTIVATION

According to one ten-year-old, to motivate is to "convince someone he always wanted to learn something he never even knew he wanted to learn" (Dunn, 1981, p. 37). Teachers often identify the failure to motivate as their primary problem in discipline and control (King-Stoops & Meier, 1978). Students often question why they have to learn certain material or complain that their classes are boring.

Motivation is the process by which a person is aroused, thus directing his or her behavior towards attaining some goal (Kaplan & Stein, 1984). However, we can't see motivation; we infer it from behavior. When a child acts out in class to get attention, does her homework to get an A, or performs an experiment at home because she wants to find out what hap-

Teachers can sometimes know that their teaching is effective by evidence of student interest and motivation.

pens when paper airplanes of different wing designs are thrown, we say that the child is motivated to do these things. Psychologists have viewed motivation from different perspectives, and each perspective has something important and practical to say to teachers about how to motivate students.

MOTIVATION AND NEEDS: MASLOW AND THE HUMANISTIC APPROACH

Whether the need is for food, for companionship, or for respect, people are motivated to try to meet their needs. However, the learner's agenda of needs does not have to match that of the teacher. The teacher may feel the necessity for learning the sixteen exports of Brazil, memorizing the multiplication tables, or mastering the use of the comma in writing. It doesn't mean that the student does. Children may be absorbed by other needs and interests, such as working out their own problems or getting attention from classmates.

The relationship of needs and motivation was best described by Abraham Maslow (1968, 1970), who

noted that people were constantly striving to satisfy their needs. When one set of needs was satisfied, people would turn their attention to their next set of needs. Maslow's hierarchy of needs is shown in Figure 8.1. Maslow divided needs into two distinct categories. The first category of needs is **deficiency needs** (also called maintenance needs). These needs disrupt a person's psychological or biological balance, causing the person to respond to the discomfort. These needs include such physiological requirements as food, water, sleep, and pain reduction; they also include security, belongingness, and esteem needs. The physiological needs are the most basic and, if

motivation   The process by which behavior is activated and directed towards some goal.

deficiency needs (**maintenance needs**)   Maslow's term for needs that disrupt a person's psychological or biological balance, causing the individual to respond to the discomfort.

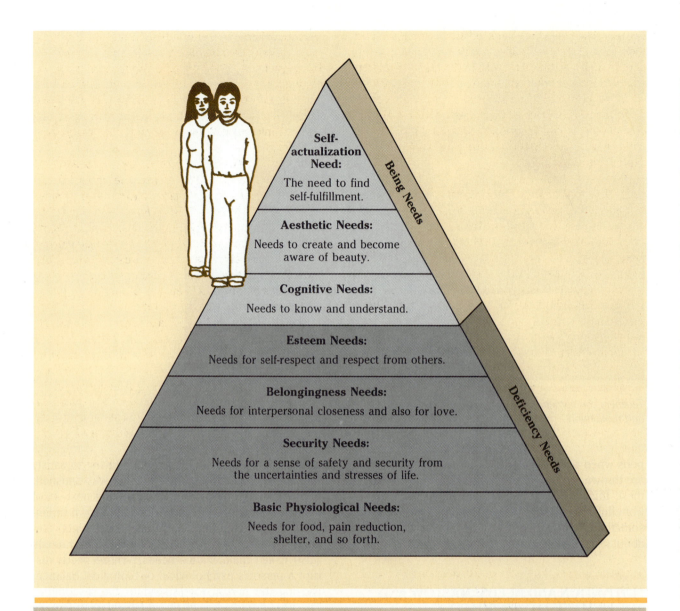

Figure 8.1 Maslow's Hierarchy of Needs
Maslow suggests that needs can be placed in a hierarchy. Only when the deficit needs are satisfied can people's being needs come into focus.

not satisfied, dominate all others. However, what if they are satisfied? The individual then turns to the next level—safety needs. Children whose world is threatened will be preoccupied with the threat, and the threat will consume their attention. Certain events such as family fights, separation, divorce, or illness, or death of a family member can make a child's search for safety paramount. Children who are bothered by such home problems will find it difficult to concentrate on schoolwork. Studies show that children whose families are in turmoil due to divorce or a death in the family show more misbehavior and poorer achievement (Block et al., 1986; Emery, 1982).

Most people have their safety needs satisfied and move to the third level of needs, those that involve love, affection, and belongingness. At this level, people cope with their lack of friends or love from their family. They want affectionate relationships with people and a stable place within the group. Children who desperately want acceptance by a group may do whatever they think is necessary, including refusing to do their homework or misbehaving. If it is not acceptable in the child's group to be a good student, the child may decide that it is more important to be accepted than to achieve.

If one's belongingness needs are satisfied, esteem needs take center stage. These needs include the need for self-esteem and self-respect as well as the need to receive esteem and respect from others. Maslow divided these esteem needs into two categories. First there is the need for achievement, feelings of adequacy, independence and confidence. The second category involves the need for prestige, recognition, and appreciation. When these needs are satisfied, a person has a feeling of self-confidence and worth and a personal sense of adequacy. If the needs are thwarted, they produce feelings of inferiority, weakness, and helplessness. Indeed, students who are identified as troublemakers in school often lack self-respect and self-esteem and have a low self-concept (Gnagey, 1981). Children who have failed in many of their academic areas may switch their attention to other areas in pursuit of adequacy.

True or False Students who are considered troublemakers in school often have a positive self-concept that interferes with their ability to conform to school rules.

Maslow's second category of needs is **being needs**, (also called growth needs). These needs are associated with the fulfillment of an individual's potential. The three levels of growth needs are cognitive, aesthetic, and self-actualization. Relatively little is known about the first two needs, and Maslow does not say much about them (Liebert & Spiegler, 1987). Cognitive needs include the need and desire to know, to understand, and to solve problems. Here curiosity, exploration, and novelty influence the behavior. Students who are interested and curious about a particular subject have a motive and direct their attention to getting infor-

mation. When this sort of desire is seen by teachers, they experience an immediate feeling of success. When Jackson (1968) asked a group of outstanding elementary schoolteachers how they knew they were teaching effectively, they cited evidence of motivation, namely signs of student interest during the lesson as well as interest that endured after the lesson was completed.

Aesthetic needs involve an awareness of beauty and artistic endeavors. Students may be motivated to create beautiful things of their own to satisfy their need to create. The highest need is for self-actualization, which involves the desire to become all that one is capable of becoming. When we think of self-actualized people, we usually think of great musicians or scientists, although this is not necessarily the case. Each person has abilities that can be nurtured if given the right environment and opportunity.

Maslow estimated that self-actualization is attained by only about one percent of the population for two reasons. First, in many cases, lower needs remain unsatisfied. Second, growth needs are delicate and are not easy to nurture. They require an environment in which people can express themselves and explore. In addition, whereas the satisfaction of deficiency needs reduces tension and stress, the satisfaction of growth needs actually increases tension and stress. It is certainly easier not to think or experiment than to do so. It is safer to parrot what the textbook or teacher says then to challenge ideas. Teachers often complain that students don't want to think or go beyond the text. Maslow explains that security and safety are rather attractive—even seductive—while growth can be rather frightening. If a teacher does not accept and encourage challenge, students will take the safe course, which is often repetitive and boring.

What Does Maslow's Theory Mean to the Teacher?

Maslow's theory suggests that since lower level needs must be satisfied before higher level needs can be met, it is possible for a student who has been functioning at a higher level to become concerned once again with a lower level need. A child who has been curious and interested in schoolwork may become preoccupied with safety and security as problems arise at home. A student who is very concerned with being accepted by a particular group of students may sacrifice his work to be accepted in the group.

being needs (growth needs) Maslow's term for needs that are associated with a person's fulfillment of potential.

Although teachers cannot alter a difficult family situation, they can make every effort to assure that students have their lower needs satisfied. Breakfast and lunch programs are available for hungry students. The student who is not popular in class may need social skills training. Even within the classroom, students who are made physically comfortable will become more relaxed and feel safer, allowing them to concentrate on their work. Using Maslow's formulations, we thus become aware of the possibility that basic needs can interfere with academic achievement and learning. In some cases, these needs can be satisfied through the intervention of the teacher.

Satisfying the lower level needs is only part of Maslow's theory. The theory has some practical and positive things to say about the higher growth needs. Children must be encouraged to think and not be penalized for being different and creative. Instead of just giving fifty historical terms to learn and spew back, teachers need to give some thought to their assignments for which students will have to venture into the unknown, where there may be no completely right or wrong answer. For instance, asking students whether they would have joined the American revolutionary army and how such a choice would have changed their lives requires students to think beyond the text. An activity such as having a student act the part of a revolutionary war recruiter or a British governor may force students to go beyond the points taught in the history book.

Maslow reminds us of the need to be aware of the teacher behaviors that encourage curiosity and challenge students and those that turn students off. Since growth needs are so delicate, even a hint that a teacher is impatient when students ask questions or is fixated on book answers and does not want to explore ideas will be enough to quash inquiry and curiosity. A teacher, then, must be careful not to punish exploration by simply reinforcing safe answers but to encourage curiosity.

A Need for Achievement?

Some students always seem to be motivated to work and achieve. Even when there is little or no payoff, they work to their fullest. Other students rarely respond to challenges in school. Do people have a specific need to achieve?

According to researchers in the field (McClelland et al., 1953), people do have such a need. It is a need to excel or to perform according to higher standards and is found in varying degrees in people. Some people have a very high need to achieve; some have very little achievement motivation; and most people lie in the middle, showing a moderate need to achieve. People with a high need to achieve do not respond to every task with a need to excel. They are motivated to work hardest only at tasks that are moderately difficult and on which there is some doubt as to their success (Atkinson, 1964). In other words, they seek challenge.

People with a high achievement motivation are more intrinsically motivated, ambitious, competitive, and independent in decision making than people with a low need for achievement. They do not require immediate rewards and can work for larger, future rewards (Kukla, 1972). In addition, people with a high need for achievement work hardest when told that a task is difficult, while people with a low achievement motivation work hardest when they are told that the task is easy (Kukla, 1975). Studies show, not surprisingly, that students with a high achievement motivation earn better grades in high school and college and are more likely to attribute their successes to their own ability and their failures to a lack of effort (Klienke, 1978).

Fear of Success

Does everyone want to succeed? Is it possible that some students fear success? For example, is it possible that a female student would not want to do well in mathematics because she thinks it is not feminine to do so? Is it possible that a male student would not try very hard in home economics because he sees the subject as basically concerned with feminine matters? If the answer to either of these questions is yes, a student's gender might affect how much effort the student puts into a particular course or perhaps even whether the student will take a course when allowed a choice.

The possibility that females show a fear of success was demonstrated in a study conducted by Matina Horner (1968). Horner asked female college students to write a story about Anne, a top student in her medical school class. Male college students were asked to write a story about John, also a top medical student. Horner found that 65 percent of the women wrote stories showing that Anne was not happy with her success or had negative experiences. Only 10 percent of the men wrote stories indicating that such academic success led to negative consequences for John.

The early research on fear of success considered such fear a problem mostly for women, and not all studies attempting to show fear of success have been able to do so (Zuckerman & Wheeler, 1975). Newer research shows that fear of success can also be found in men. In one study, although only 41 percent of the men indicated any fear of success for John in medical school, about 63 percent of the men saw him as having problems if he were to enter nursing school (Cherry & Deaux, 1975). Some 50 percent of the women wrote fear-of-success stories for Anne in medical school, but only 13 percent wrote such stories for her in nursing school. Still other studies have found no difference between fear of success in men and in women (Condry & Dyer, 1976). Both males and females will avoid success if they believe the consequences will be disagreeable. Fear of success seems to be situational (Cook & Chandler, 1984). It depends on the field one enters (Popp & Muhs, 1982; Feathers, 1975). It may be that women fear succeeding in male-stereotyped occupations and vice versa (de Charms & Muir, 1978).

Apart from the question of gender, why do some people fear success? David Tresemer (1977) believes that people fear success because they are afraid that success will place extra demands upon them, their peers will reject them if they stand out, or success will require a stressful shift in their self-concept.

Some studies find that fear of success is declining, especially among women whose mothers work. Patricia Gibbons and Richard Kopelman (1977) found that when asked to write a story about Anne, women whose mothers work showed much less of fear of success than daughters of nonworking mothers. Because more women are working than ever before, fear of success will probably decrease even further.

Fear of success, then, can be found in both sexes when people are entering areas that they do not see as reflecting society's sex-role expectations for them. Because of changes in social attitudes and values, teachers can expect to see less of this problem in class. However, teachers will still have to deal with women who believe that science and mathematics are male domains and with men who believe that

home economics is for females. Teachers can encourage males and females to partake in all school activities. As we will see in Chapter 9, students require extra encouragement if they are to enter fields or take courses in areas traditionally thought of as the domain of males or females.

Fear of Failure

People are motivated not only to succeed and achieve but also to avoid failure. There are students who, despite being bright and relatively successful in school, never take a chance and won't volunteer for a special assignment when challenged unless they believe no one else could possibly succeed (Birney, 1968). These students may not lack achievement motivation but may be afraid of failing. Students with a high need to achieve and a high fear of failure avoid challenging problems, opting for very easy or almost impossibly difficult ones. These people may take on almost impossible tasks because if they fail they cannot be criticized, since no one could have done it anyway. In a study of procrastinators, Jane Burka and Lenora Yuen (1982) found that people would put off tasks until the last minute and then work as hard as possible. Perhaps these people feared failure, and their last-minute efforts could no longer be viewed by themselves or others as reflecting their true ability. They can even earn some praise for pulling themselves together at the last minute.

True or False Students with a high fear of failure lack achievement motivation.

Achievement orientation is a learned motive. Studies show that children learn by observing their parents and other significant authority figures cope with challenges (Bandura & Walters, 1963). Expectations also play a part in achievement, since parents who expect their children to strive for success and praise them for achieving have children who are highly motivated and independent (Eccles, 1983). Looking at the different patterns that produce either high or low fears of failure, Richard Teevan and Paul McGhee (1972) found that mothers of both groups expected independence and achievement at an early age. However, the mothers of high-fear-of-failure students gave neutral responses for their sons' achievement and punished their sons for unsatisfactory behavior. The mothers of low-fear students rewarded achievement but were not as critical for failures. It is not the early demand for achievement that causes this fear of failure to occur but the punishment and reinforcement given. When positive achievement receives little praise and failures result in considerable punishment or criticism, the outcome is high fear of failure. The same analysis may be useful in the classroom. Teachers who punish students for failure and do not praise students for good work may also promote a fear of failure.

Achievement Motivation and Fear of Failure: What They Mean for the Teacher

Teachers who want students with high achievement motivation to work at their fullest potential must give moderately challenging assignments. Students who have a high need for success and a low fear of failure will not show their best efforts if the assignment is too easy or too difficult. These students need assignments that go beyond the book and offer a challenge. For students with a high fear of failure, the teacher must praise the effort and use a failure, not as a time for excessive criticism but rather as a time to reevaluate learning strategies. Students who are praised for their best efforts and whose failures are minimized may begin to volunteer in class even though they may not always have the correct response.

COGNITIVE VIEWS OF MOTIVATION

Needs are not the only influences on motivation. Cognitions are also important. There are two major cognitive theories of motivation that are of importance to teachers: the value/expectancy theory and the attribution theory.

The Value/Expectancy Theory: He Wants to Be a Lawyer but Doesn't Do Homework

What about the students who say they want to do well and would like to become lawyers yet do little or no work for the class? We could say that they really don't have that great a desire to do well in school or to become lawyers; that is, the strength of the value or the goal is not great. However, another possibility exists.

What if the goal is valued but the students don't expect to succeed no matter how hard they try? Students who don't believe they can become lawyers or get A's despite their best efforts will not put the effort into their work. Students must have hope that they can realize their dreams and obtain the grades necessary to do so. Expectation is dependent upon a number of factors, including a person's background and reinforcement history (Green, 1984).

Attribution Theory: Why I Didn't Bother to Work

I remember taking a major statewide exam in high school when the school's roof was being repaired. Every minute or so, construction workers would throw sandbags from the roof that would fly past the window and land with a thud in the schoolyard. It was later found that those students who took the exam on the side of the building near the schoolyard received lower grades than those who were on the other side of the school. Everyone (students, parents, and administrators) attributed the poorer grades to the external distraction, to a situational factor outside of their control, and not to students' own lack of study or ability. When the students who failed were given an alternative examination at a later date, most expected to pass and, in fact, did. Because everyone attributed their failure to events outside their control, they were given another chance, and the previous failure did not affect their expectation of passing the next exam.

An approach that is gaining many adherents today looks at motivation in terms of how people ascribe the causes of their successes and failures. **Attribution theory** attempts to discover how people perceive the cause of their behavior and then looks at the way their perception might affect their later behavior (Fiske & Taylor, 1984). Causal attributions can be understood in terms of three dimensions. First, the action may be ascribed to either *internal* or *external causes*. For example, if you did poorly on a test, you could tell your-

attribution theory   An approach that seeks to explain how people make sense of events occurring both within and about the individual by ascribing the causes of these events.

self that it was due to internal factors such as poor effort or lack of ability. On the other hand, you could simply attribute doing poorly to external factors by saying that the work or test was too difficult or that you just had bad luck. This internal-external dimension is important because it leads to emotional reactions concerning achievement outcomes. When success is attributed to ability or effort (internal factors), a sense of pride and positive self-esteem results. If a student attributes success to external factors, there is little gain in self-esteem. When a failure is ascribed to internal factors, such as lack of effort or lack of ability, a person experiences negative self-esteem. Failure that is attributed to external factors does not result in negative self-esteem.

Stability/instability is the second dimension. You can attribute your success or failure to some factor that is almost always going to be there or to a temporary factor. Ability is a rather stable attribute, while effort is unstable; luck is an unstable quality, while task difficulty tends to be stable. When people did not do well on the statewide test because of the outside noise, they ascribed their failure to an unstable or temporary condition. The stability/instability dimension underlies student expectations for future success or failure (Weiner et al., 1983). Students who ascribe their success to a stable factor that is relatively fixed will expect to succeed at the same task the next time it is presented. Students who attribute success to an unstable factor, such as lack or unusual help from the teacher, will have little or no expectation of later success. Failure ascribed to a stable cause, such as low ability, decreases the expectation of future success. Failure ascribed to a temporary illness or bad luck or too much noise should not affect expectations for later success.

The third dimension, which has not always been accepted as separate by all authorities (Parsons & Ruble, 1977), is the *controllable/uncontrollable* dimension. This relates to whether the success or failure is ascribed to factors that are under the student's control or under someone else's control. You really can't control your luck, but you certainly can control your effort. If you believe that your failure was due to low ability, which is an uncontrollable factor, rather than to lack of effort, a controllable one, you are more likely to give up. If you believe that effort is the problem and you know you can do it, you can change. This dimension influences interpersonal evaluation.

Individuals anticipate more punishment from others when failure is attributed to personally controllable causes than when it is attributed to uncontrollable ones (Graham & Long, 1986).

A student who attributes success to an internal, stable dimension, such as ability, expects success in the future and will continue to strive (Fennema, 1987). A student who attributes success to an external cause, such as a teacher, or to an unstable one, such as luck, will not be as confident of success in the future. Failure works differently. A student who attributes failure to an unstable cause, such as effort, has a tendency to try harder. Attribution of failure to stable causes, such as lack of ability, will lead a person to believe that failure is inevitable. Therefore, success leads to more success depending on how one attributes his or her success. Failure may or may not lead to more failure, also depending upon the attributions (Bardwell, 1984a). Attributions, then, are critical to later performance (Weiner, 1979; 1972).

True or False If students attribute their failure to lack of effort, they are likely to put in more effort at a later date.

Children differ in the way they attribute their successes and failures. High-achieving children attribute their success to internal factors, such as ability and effort, whereas they attribute their failure to a lack of effort or to external causes (Whitehead et al., 1987). Low-achieving children attribute their successes to factors beyond their control, such as luck or easy tasks while attributing their failures to lack of ability (Bar-Tal, 1978).

True or False High-achieving students usually attribute their successes to internal factors such as ability and effort and their failures to external factors such as luck.

There is also a developmental trend in attribution, as some studies of reading achievement show (Hiebert et al., 1984). As children age, they are more and more likely to ascribe their achievement—or lack of achievement—to ability. Teachers want students to work harder and to plug at their work despite occasional failure. Since effort is voluntary, unstable, and internal, it is important to encourage children to ascribe most of their failures and successes to their efforts. A person who ascribes past failures to low effort may do more in the future but only by assuming that increased effort will produce success (Weiner, 1979). In one study, children who did not know how to subtract received two types of feedback concerning their effort: attributional feedback for *past* or present achievement, such as "You've been working hard," or attributional feedback for *future* achievement, such as "You need to work harder." Attributional feedback for past and present achievement led to more progress and an increased perception of self-efficacy which, as we shall see later in the chapter, involves the belief that one can handle a particular situation or challenge (Bandura, 1986; Schunk, 1982). Therefore, teachers who simply tell students to work harder in the future are not as successful as those who relate past effort to achievement in a subject.

True or False Teachers should not relate past effort and success to a student's present challenge because it is unrealistic to assume that effort will always lead to success.

What happens when a student puts in a great deal of work and still fails? Many students have had the unfortunate experience of believing they could succeed (i.e., they have the ability), studying very hard, and nevertheless failing. When students put in a great deal of effort and fail, they feel defeated, whereas when students put in low effort and fail, they are less emotionally affected (Covington & Omelich, 1979). The latter group can always tell themselves that they could have passed if they had only tried. Effort, then, is a double-edged sword. Some students may save their self-esteem by not trying, at the cost of their learning. Such failure could result from poor study habits, inadequate knowledge about what would appear on the test, or lack of feedback about the true state of one's knowledge. Teachers should look carefully into instances in which children continually say they study but do not succeed.

CONNECTIONS

What Does Attribution Theory Say to Teachers?

Attribution theory emphasizes the importance of linking success and failure to the work ethic. However, this is all predicated on the assumption that the student has the ability to succeed. In most classrooms, content is taught and work assigned so that ability will not be the cause of the failure. Attribution theory leads to a number of points for teachers to keep in mind:

1. **Become aware of how students are attributing their successes or failures.** Students who attribute their failures to lack of effort or successes to their own effort are more likely to try harder. Students who attribute their successes to luck or easy tasks will not put forth more effort. Ask students privately why they think they succeeded or failed.

2. **Be aware of subject differences in attribution.** Students may attribute their success in one subject to luck and in another to skill.

3. **Attribute success to past and present rather than future effort.** Teachers should point out how effort has led to improved achievement. Rewards may not motivate students to work if they attribute success to factors that are either unstable or uncontrollable. Teachers can encourage effort attributions. In one study, Andrews and Debus (1978) reinforced all effort attributions by saying "very good," "O.K.," or "good." If students did not attribute their success or failure to effort, the researchers would say, "We usually fail because we don't try hard enough, don't we?" Researchers found that students could be taught to make effort attributions and that such training increased achievement later on. The key is for teachers to find out how students are attributing their successes and failures and to encourage students to attribute the outcome to effort.

Learned Helplessness: The Child Who Gives Up

In a special case of attribution, students simply give up trying. Balk (1983) suggests that we imagine a classroom filled with busy students. In this atmosphere, some have difficulty with the work and can correct themselves, while others need extra help from the teacher. One child, however, has completely stopped trying because he has made a mistake. Some children react to failure to such an extreme that they are paralyzed from further action. How can teachers identify such children, who fail, not because of poor academic abilities, but because of self-defeating responses to their own errors? Diener and Dweck (1978) found that such children (1) have low expectations for their own performance, (2) make self-deprecating remarks, (3) very quickly link failure to ability, and (4) are constantly thinking of causes of their failure rather than concentrating on finding effective ways to deal with their problems.

Sometimes students learn that they cannot succeed no matter how hard they try. Such learned helplessness is difficult to remedy.

Consider these attributions from students who give up on themselves very quickly. "I just received a D on the exam. That is a very low grade. (This generates feelings of frustration and upset.) I received this grade because I have little ability. (This is followed by feelings of incompetence.) There is really something lacking in me which I probably will always lack. (This is ensured by low self-esteem and hopelessness.)" (Weiner et al., 1983, p. 116).

Individuals who find themselves in an unpleasant situation in which they are convinced there is nothing they can do to improve may simply give up and passively endure the situation. This condition is called **learned helplessness** and has been viewed as an underlying cause of some cases of depression (Selig-

> **learned helplessness** The learned inability to overcome obstacles that involves the belief that one cannot do anything to improve one's lot.

man, 1975). People suffering from learned helplessness see no relationship between what they do and the consequences of their actions (Miller, 1986). If they later have an opportunity to exercise control, they behave as if they were helpless (Phares, 1988). A person who believes that any action is futile might as well give up; learned helplessness is the result of this belief.

The concept of learned helplessness is readily applied to the classroom. Teachers often describe poor readers in terms of passivity, lack of persistence, negative self-attitudes about intellectual performance, and low self-esteem, symptoms that match descriptions of people suffering from learned helplessness. In a sample of fifth-grade boys, Butkowsky and Willows (1980) found that poor readers had lower expectations for success, gave up more quickly in the face of difficulty, tended to attribute failures to internal and stable causes, and attributed successes to more external causes. The boys' confidence was easily shaken. Low perceptions of competence and control translate into helplessness in achievement settings and reduced motivation and effort (Boggiano & Barrett, 1985).

True or False   Poor readers have the same expectations for success in school and show more perserverance when faced with a difficult task than more competent readers.

>> **CONNECTIONS**

Working with Children Who Give Up

Working with children who believe that failure means that success is beyond their capability takes patience and care, but the teacher can do much to help these children.

1. **Learn to identify the children.** Look for children who show apathy, give up easily, and attribute their successes to external sources and their failures to internal sources.

2. **Teach children to interpret failure as feedback that they need more information.** (Balk, 1983) If a child has difficulty with mathematics because she fails to read the problem, the teacher can tell the student to put the problem into her own words.

3. **Focus children's attention on needed effort, not on ability.** A number of studies have sought to change the attributions of the learned helpless. In

one, Sowa and Burks (1983) describe a three-phase cognitive restructuring program. In the educational phase, students received an explanation of the relationship between cognitions and behavior and how such a relationship affects performance in mathematics. A list of negative or self-defeating statements related to attributions to ability were given to the students, who were asked to list their own self-defeating statements. Finally, a list of positive self-statements was generated that contradicted these negative ones. For instance, a student who says, "I can't do the work because I'm stupid" might generate, "I couldn't do the work because I have to work harder." In the rehearsal phase, negative self-attributions about ability were contradicted aloud by positive statements. In the application phase, students were asked to substitute positive self-statements in actual stressful situations without the trainer's being present. To help students do this, they were asked to practice while working on mathematics homework or solving problems in mathematics class. These students had much more positive attitudes toward mathematics and performed quite well. Teachers who identify these children might try a similar strategy of helping students restructure their cognitions by (1) teaching children the relationship between thoughts and performance, (2) finding out the negative self-statements that children make and countering them with other, more positive ones, (3) helping students rehearse the positive statements, and (4) writing the statements on cards and encouraging students to use them when they encounter a difficult assignment.

4. **Teach children new strategies to deal with their academic problems.** For example, if a child has difficulty spelling, Balk suggests concentrating on the word, thinking before speaking, and then spelling the word.

5. **Teach children to perform self-instructions that pertain to accomplishing the task.** Some children are impulsive, and teaching students to say to themselves, "slow down" and to follow a list of steps can be helpful.

6. **Provide children with experiences that mix failure with success rather than providing only success experiences.** Then speak with the children to discover how they dealt with the failure (Craske, 1985).

7. **Model ways of coping with difficulties.** Teachers can help children learn to cope with problems by modeling strategies and appropriate attitudes. Hoy

(1986) suggests that teachers faced with a difficult problem might say, "The way I'm doing this isn't working. What's another way to try it?" Teachers should avoid expressing frustration. Instead, failure should indicate a need to investigate other strategies or to seek appropriate help.

Preserving Self-Worth

The concept of learned helplessness gives us some understanding of students who give up. However, what about students who have the ability but do only just enough work to pass? These students always have a reason for not studying. Perhaps they were ill before the big test or were involved in something more important and could not turn in that major assignment on time. These students have the ability but do not put in the effort necessary to do well.

Self-worth theory can be helpful in understanding this particular behavior pattern (Covington, 1984; Covington & Beery, 1976). This theory assumes that students need to protect their own sense of worth or personal value. Self-worth theory combines elements of some of the approaches to motivation examined earlier. It maintains that self-perceptions and self-attributions of causality are important in understanding motivation and achievement. It also accepts the idea that people have a need to succeed as well as a need to avoid failure.

In our society, personal worth depends largely on one's accomplishments. Ability is perceived as a critical component of success and accomplishment, while inability is often perceived as a prime cause of failure. Students in elementary school tend to believe that both effort and ability are important factors in achievement, but they see these factors as related. Students who are bright work harder. Most secondary students believe that ability is the most important aspect of success in school (Covington, 1984). There-

self-worth theory A theory of achievement motivation whose central postulate is that students need to protect their own sense of worth or personal value and will act in a way that minimizes the implications of failure with respect to ability.

fore, as students progress through their school careers, they see ability as more important and as the single greatest factor in achievement (Covington & Omelich, 1979).

Self-worth theory stresses that although people have some drive to achieve and succeed, they have a powerful need to remain competent and to avoid anything that might imply low ability. Feelings of low ability translate into feelings of worthlessness. If success is in doubt, one's first priority is to act in a way that minimizes the implications of failure with respect to ability. Students will experience feelings of worthlessness if failure means that they are incompetent and lack ability. The basic postulate of self-worth theory is that students will protect themselves against any implication that they lack the ability to achieve.

Where does the effort fit into this model? Consider the student who has doubt about his or her ability to succeed. If the student tries very hard, studies every night, does all the extra work allowed, and still fails, the failure reflects poorly on his or her ability and causes feelings of worthlessness to arise. Therefore, it becomes a safer policy not to work so hard. If little effort is expended, the student's opinion of his or her own ability may stay constant. A student who puts in no work may experience feelings of guilt and risk punishment, but a student who puts in a great deal of effort and still fails may risk feelings of incompetence. To resolve this dilemma, students may exert some effort to avoid punishment, failure, and personal feelings of guilt, but not so much as to risk incompetence should they try hard yet still fail. Martin Covington believes that when students have to choose between feeling guilty and experiencing the humiliation that comes from feelings of incompetence, they will choose the guilt and therefore will put less effort into their work. Putting in a great deal of effort, then, can be a possible threat to self-worth, because not succeeding implies lack of ability.

Self-worth theory assumes that achievement behavior is best understood in terms of attempts to maintain feelings of competence and self-worth. To maintain such feelings, students must avoid failures that imply a lack of ability. How can students do this? One possible strategy is to select very easy goals that ensure success. This might involve taking the easiest courses and, generally, avoiding all challenges. The second possibility is to select impossible course work and challenges, given the student's background and ability. Although this makes failure very likely, it does not necessarily reflect on ability. As noted earlier in the chapter, the sense of failure is diminished because a person can tell him or herself that few people could have succeeded at the work (Beery, 1975).

These two strategies may not be available to students, since many students do not have a choice of course. A more popular way to avoid failure is to use a variety of protective techniques that involve a reduction in effort. Such techniques include studying too little, too late, or very inefficiently, along with offering plausible excuses for the lack of effort. These and other failure-avoiding strategies afford temporary relief. However, Covington argues that their repeated use may destroy a student's will to learn (Covington, 1984). When this happens, a shift occurs from avoiding failure to accepting failure. As the student's excuses become less and less believable, the evidence for low ability becomes more pronounced and the student begins to accept failure. Therefore, these failure-avoiding strategies fail in the long run.

Understanding the importance of students maintaining their self-worth is one thing. Doing something to help students who are engaging in failure-avoiding strategies is something else. The teacher's task is to help students become less preoccupied with ability implications so that they will be willing to try to learn. Covington mentions a number of possible ways to do this. He advocates that teachers use noncompetitive learning structures whenever possible. Mastery learning is one such structure that is covered in Chapter 11. In mastery learning, standards of performance are high and constant, but students are given a flexible amount of time to achieve such standards. Since everyone is expected to achieve mastery, mastery learning leads to feelings of adequacy. Covington also advocates the use of cooperative learning strategies discussed later in the chapter. Contracts in which students formulate with their teachers agreements that reflect reasonable goals that the student can reach also lead to feelings of adequacy. All these strategies strengthen a student's perception of the importance of effort and promote realistic goal setting.

Another strategy that aims at improving a student's sense of ability is to teach students problem-solving strategies as well as ways to learn so that students will see that ability can improve. In addition, any strategy that shows students that their self-worth goes beyond the mere possession of ability will be helpful. A student who sees self-improvement or gains satisfaction from a job well done is likely to feel worthy.

Another important strategy is to build success into a program and increase the possibility that effort will lead to success (Covington & Omelich, 1979).

Self-worth theory gives us a better understanding of a student's need to maintain a positive view of him or herself as competent. It also explains why some students may habitually use failure-avoiding strategies and why some students may not work very hard. Self-worth theory gives us a new and valuable perspective on achievement motivation.

THE BEHAVIORAL VIEW OF MOTIVATION

Behaviorists argue that behaviors that show motivation can be understood in terms of the principles of conditioning. When they talk about motivation in the behavioral sense, they are speaking of certain behaviors, including paying attention, studying, and participating actively in class. These behaviors are the result of prior experience. Behaviorists view problems in motivation as difficulties in environmental reinforcement and punishment, not as signs of some problem within the student. When students do not learn, it is because of an inappropriate learning environment.

Although some needs, such as food, sleep, and thirst, are biological, many needs, such as those for power, and achievement, are learned. Even those motives that are biologically based are satisfied in ways that are learned. We learn to eat with utensils and at particular times. Motivation, then, is based on internal needs that give rise to learned actions as well as by external reinforcers and punishers. Since the usefulness of the behavioral view has been shown throughout the text, the extensive coverage as found in Chapter 5 is not repeated here.

SOCIAL LEARNING THEORY: SELF-EFFICACY EXPLAINED

Social learning theorists argue that the behavioral view of motivation and behavior is too narrow. Albert Bandura (1982, 1986) divides behavior into two different processes: learning and performance. We learn—that is, we acquire knowledge—through a number of processes, including observing others. However, whether or not a person will show the behavior depends partly upon what Bandura calls self-efficacy.

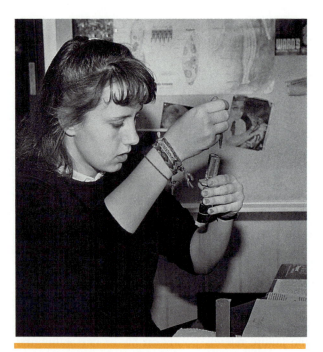

It is important for students to believe they can *do something.*

Self-efficacy is a term describing one's beliefs about what one can and cannot do in a particular situation. It answers the central question, Do I really believe I can do it? Self-efficacy judgments, whether accurate or not, affect one's choice of activities. People who believe a task is within their capabilities will try it, while people will avoid activities that exceed what they consider their capabilities (Bandura, 1982).

Self-efficacy affects just how much effort a person will expend. People with a high degree of self-efficacy will place more effort into a particular task than those who have a low degree of self-efficacy. Self-efficacy also affects persistence. When faced with an obstacle, people with low self-efficacy give up, while those with a high degree of self-efficacy show greater effort. Dale Schunk (1981) found that children be-

self-efficacy A term describing people's beliefs about what they can and cannot do.

tween the ages of nine and eleven who had a high degree of self-efficacy regarding how to do division problems were more persistent than were children with a low degree of self-efficacy.

It is important to remember that self-efficacy is dependent upon the task. A person may have a high degree of self-efficacy in solving mathematics problems, a low degree of self-efficacy concerning giving a speech in front of a class, and a moderate degree of self-efficacy concerning his or her ability to perform well on the athletic field.

To Bandura, the key question is whether or not the person believes that he or she *can* perform the behaviors necessary to obtain the desirable outcome. Here we must differentiate between efficacy expectations and outcome expectations. An *efficacy expectation* is a belief that one can successfully perform a behavior required to produce the desired outcome (Bandura, 1977). For instance, students may believe that they can study efficiently or write a good essay. An *outcome expectation* is the belief, for example, that studying or writing well will lead to a desired outcome, in this case, a good grade. Students may know that some behavior leads to some outcome but may doubt their ability to perform the behavior. A student may realize that studying will lead to better grades but doubt that he or she can study effectively.

In another area of life, a person might believe that eating low-calorie foods will lead to weight loss but not believe he or she is capable of abstaining from junk food (Desmond & Price, 1988). People who believe that they cannot adequately do something—and that even if they try they will not succeed—will avoid the task even though they realize the relationship between the behavior and the outcome. Of course, self-efficacy will not totally determine whether the behavior will take place, since a person must have the skills necessary and the incentives must be in place to actually perform the required behavior.

Efficacy expectations vary in magnitude, generality, and strength. Magnitude refers to the level of difficulty for a particular task (Desmond & Price, 1988). Lattie may believe that she can pay attention in class—a relatively easy task for her—but may not believe she can write the essay necessary to do well on the test. Generality is the second factor. Some experiences create a sense of self-efficacy only for a specific activity, while others extend to many areas. For instance, Lattie may believe that she can study and suc-

ceed in mathematics but not in English. On the other hand, she may believe that she has the study skills necessary to succeed in any subject. Last, the strength of these efficacy expectations varies. Lattie may hold a strong or a weak expectation for her ability to perform some behavior. She may strongly believe that she can solve mathematics examples but believe only slightly that she can write a poem.

What influences self-efficacy? Self-efficacy judgments arise from past experiences, observations of others, verbal persuasion, and one's physiological state (Bandura, 1982). Past experiences in similar situations are one key. Successes raise one's perception of self-efficacy, while repeated failures lower it. People with a strong sense of self-efficacy due to a string of successes in a particular area do not let an occasional failure affect their view of their ability to do something. People also are affected by watching others succeed or fail. They persuade themselves that if others can do it, they can too.

Verbal persuasion can also be a factor but should be approached with care. People can be persuaded that they have certain capabilities in reading or mathematics, for example, especially if they have some reason to believe that this is so. However, raising unrealistic expectations for success may undermine a student's self-efficacy as well as lower the teacher in the student's view. People also rely in part on information from their physiological state in judging their capabilities. Lattie may read the increase in her heart rate and the fact that she is sweating as signs of vulnerability. High arousal when one is engaged in a complex task is associated with poorer performance. Bandura notes that people are inclined to expect success when they are not experiencing great tension and agitation.

Self-efficacy is an important concept that mediates between knowledge and performance. Bandura (1982) notes that many studies have found that perceived self-efficacy is a significant determinant of performance, one that is at least partially independent of underlying skills. For example, in one study, children who perceived themselves to be high or low in mathematical self-efficacy were presented with difficult problems to solve. While certainly mathematical ability contributed to their ability to solve the problems, those who thought themselves efficacious were quicker to discard incorrect strategies, solved more problems correctly, reworked more of those they did not get correct and did so more accurately, and displayed more positive attitudes toward mathematics than those low in self-efficacy (Collins, 1982).

Self-efficacy is being examined as an important factor in motivation in other areas. A number of studies in the health area show that self-efficacy is an important factor when people try to stop smoking cigarettes, lose weight, or control their alcohol consumption (Strecher et al., 1986). Self-efficacy is a consistent predictor of both successful short- and long-term behavioral changes. For example, people trying to lose weight must believe not only that if they eat a particular diet they will lose weight (a short-term outcome expectation) but also that they can stay on the diet (a long-term efficacy expectation).

Goal Setting and Self-Evaluation

Bandura does not believe that self-efficacy is the only cause of motivation. Other causes include biological or socially based motives (money, power, status). People are also motivated by their expectation of reward. Reinforcement is seen as serving an informational function determining what a person expects will happen the next time the behavior is performed.

Still another important motivator is goal setting. Perhaps a student has a particular goal in mind, such as to receive an A in the course or to master a particular type of problem in mathematics. The goal can act as a motivator for the student. As the student works, he or she evaluates his or her performance against the goal itself. Bandura believes that it is not the goal itself that motivates people but rather the fact that people with goals evaluate their own behavior. These goals then specify the requirements for positive self-evaluation.

Obviously, one's sense of self-efficacy will affect the goals that are set and vice versa. If we do not believe we can master the work, we probably would not set the goal. But attaining a goal can sometimes lead to setting a higher one as self-efficacy is increased (Bandura, 1982).

Certainly not all goals increase motivation. For example, if a student has the capability of doing excellent work but sets a low goal, the goal will not motivate the student to expend more effort studying. At the same time, if impossible goals are set, a student may give up. What, then, are the characteristics of goals that lead to self-evaluation and are, thus, motivational?

Bandura argues that goals that are specific, have clear standards attached to them, and are attainable motivate students. Goals that are moderately challenging are best. If goals are not challenging, they tend not to be motivating. If the goals are too difficult, a student's performance tends to be poor. There is another danger inherent in goals that are too difficult to reach. Repeated failure may reduce perceived self-efficacy, thereby actually reducing motivation further. Last, effective goals must be attainable in a reasonable amount of time.

Goals that are very far off into the future do not tend to be motivational and do not exert much control over present behavior. Therefore, if a goal seems very distant, it is best to break the major goal into subgoals that can be reached in a reasonably short amount of time. This is also true for goals that may be initially beyond the scope of a student's ability. For example, during a keyboarding class, the teacher may want a particular standard of excellence that may be stated in a number of words correctly typed in a particular amount of time by the end of the term. Such a goal will not be very motivating by itself for beginners. However, if subgoals are given and attained, the march towards the final goal can be accomplished. The attainment of each subgoal (which may be moderately challenging) increases self-efficacy. Therefore, if goals initially appear too distant or too difficult, creating moderately challenging subgoals is an effective strategy.

>>> **CONNECTIONS**

What Does Self-Efficacy Theory Mean to Teachers?

We are just beginning to appreciate the importance of self-efficacy. Bandura's arguments can be translated into the following recommendations:

1. **Try to increase students' feelings of efficacy as they approach a task.** Students must feel they can do a thing before they will invest much effort in it. If students feel a sense of self-efficacy concerning a particular task, they are more likely to try and to persevere despite setbacks. One way to increase self-efficacy is by building success into the experience of the student. Past experience affects self-efficacy. In addition, attributing the success to past or present effort ("You've been working hard") is

far superior than stressing the value of future effort ("You need to work hard") (Schunk, 1982).

2. **Model persistence.** Children who observe other people persisting learn to persevere.

3. **Encourage students to set goals that are likely to be effective motivators.** We know that goals that are moderately challenging, attainable, clearly stated, and able to be attained in a fairly short time frame are more likely to motivate students.

4. **Use subgoals when the final goal is too distant or very difficult.** If a goal seems too far off into the future or is much too high and students cannot really see themselves being able to reach the goal, consider creating a number of subgoals. As students attain these subgoals, newer challenging subgoals can be established.

5. **Use persuasion with care.** If a student is persuaded that he or she can do something but fails, the teacher is diminished in the student's view. Verbal persuasion concerning competency should be given only when the student does have the skills and the teacher believes the student has some idea that he or she can do it.

6. **Be aware of creating situations that diminish a student's sense of self-efficacy.** This is especially true for slower students, who are sometimes lost as the teacher instructs the class as a group. These students may feel that they lack the ability to succeed. Diagnosing problems and giving extra help when needed can reduce this problem. Slower students may also find themselves in the lowest reading and mathematics groups and may have to deal with negative evaluations, which can reduce self-efficacy judgments. Their efficacy expectations can be improved if they have success and see progress. Seeing students in their group working hard, persevering, and progressing, sometimes even into other higher groups, can have a positive effect on their sense of self-efficacy. Competitive situations in which students are certain to come in last will reduce feelings of self-efficacy. (The use of competition is discussed later in the chapter.)

7. **Do not compare students publicly.** When students are frequently compared and do not compare well to their peers, they tend to see their ability as poor (Rosenholtz & Rosenholtz, 1981).

Self-efficacy is a useful concept that demonstrates the importance of a student's belief that he or she can successfully perform a particular task.

LOOKING AT MOTIVATION THROUGH DIFFERENT EYES

The preceding views of motivation each differs from the other, yet they all have something practical to say to the teacher. In an attempt to make sense out of the vast array of theoretical approaches, Raymond Wlodkowski (1981) formulated the time continuum model of motivation, which offers a relatively simple way to understand how each element enters the motivational equation. The educational process is divided into three time periods, which Wlodkowski labels beginning, during, and ending. Wlodkowski suggests specific questions and motivational strategies for each time period.

The first time period encompasses the *beginning* of the lesson. Here, two important motivational factors stand out: the students' attitudes toward the subject, and understanding and meeting the needs of the student. Wlodkowski suggests that teachers ask themselves two questions:

What can I do to guarantee a positive student attitude for this activity?

How do I best meet the needs of my students through this activity?

Some attention should be addressed to developing a positive student attitude toward the subject matter. This can be accomplished in many ways. For example, asking an interesting question or giving students a challenging problem to solve can spark initial interest in the subject matter. In addition, teachers need to confront any misunderstandings or erroneous expectations students may have about the subject. Some students may enter the classroom with a fear of failure or a belief that they cannot succeed (discussed earlier in the chapter.)

During the course of the lesson, the major motivational factors are stimulation and affect. Wlodkowski suggests that teachers ask themselves the following questions:

What is it about this activity that will continuously stimulate my students?

How is the affective or emotional climate for this activity a positive one for my students?

Teachers can stimulate their students by planning challenges into the lesson, either through interesting questions and problems or through planning some project. Varying the presentation of material is essential, and various ways of presenting material are discussed in Chapter 11. Teachers can deal with the affective climate by considering aspects of the material that may be of specific interest to students and by having students suggest aspects of the material they may want to learn.

At the *end* of the lesson, the main factors are competence and reinforcement. Wlodkowski suggests teachers ask themselves these questions:

How does this activity increase or affirm the students' feelings of competence?

What is the reinforcement that this activity provides for my students?

Competence can be maximized by providing consistent feedback regarding the students' mastery of the material. Students also require praise for good work and, when necessary, other reinforcers (refer to Chapter 5).

Wlodkowski's ideas are interesting because they show the need for teachers to consider motivational factors throughout the lesson. Many of these factors have been covered adequately when discussing a particular theory, but two major factors—attitudes (and expectations) and stimulation—require additional explanation.

EXPECTATIONS: THE HIDDEN AGENDA

Students enter the classroom carrying more than just their books and pencils. They enter with a set of needs as Maslow showed, with a history of success or failure in school and in the particular subject, and with expectations about how they will do and what will happen in the class. Parents also have expectations about their children's progress, and their attitudes can affect student achievement. Teachers have expectations, too, and the nature and effect of teacher expectations on student behavior has been extensively researched.

A Modern Look at Teacher Expectations and the Self-fulfilling Prophecy

Today, few authorities seriously question that teacher expectations can affect student achievement and be-

havior in the classroom (Dusek & Joseph, 1983). But how are these expectations communicated, and how important are they?

In 1968, Robert Rosenthal and Lenore Jacobson performed the most famous study on the subject. They chose 20 percent of the children in an elementary school serving a lower income community and then told the children's teachers that according to tests, the children were likely to bloom academically during the following year. They planted expectations in the teachers' minds as to the expected academic performance of the children. Their sample included 20 percent from each of three tracks—low, average, and high achievement. Their results showed that within a year, those labeled late bloomers showed higher academic achievement and greater gains in IQ than those who were not so labeled (see Figure 8.2). They were also rated as having greater potential; being more interested, curious, and happy; and being more intellectually promising. When teachers rated children who were not labeled late bloomers but nevertheless gained substantially during the year, they did not give them as much credit or rate them as highly. This was especially true of children in the low track.

At the end of the second year, some difference favoring the group of "late bloomers" still existed, but most of the differences had decreased substantially. The effects were greater in the younger groups than the older groups, but the effects of expectations on the younger students faded much more than the effects on older students. The older children's self-concepts were more resistant to change, but once altered, the change persisted. The results of this study have been explained by invoking the **self-fulfilling prophecy**—the phenomenon that expectation increases the likelihood that a particular event will occur. If you expect students to do well, they are more likely to achieve; if you do not, they are less likely to achieve.

This study's conclusions have, at times, been blindly accepted. However, numerous criticisms and doubts have been raised. The methodology and statistical procedures have been challenged (Elashaff &

self-fulfilling prophecy The concept that a person's expectations concerning some event affects the probability that it will occur.

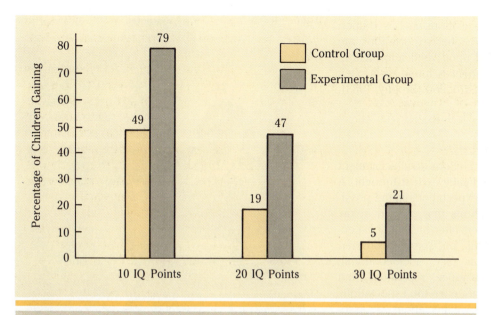

Figure 8.2   Percentage of First- and Second-Graders Gaining Ten, Twenty, or Thirty Total IQ Points

Robert Rosenthal and Lenore Jacobson's famous experiment concerning the self-fulfilling prophecy is widely quoted. This figure graphically presents some of the results of this study.

Figure 7.2 from *Pygmalian in the Classroom: Teacher Expectations and Pupil's Intellectual Development* by Robert Rosenthal and Lenore Jacobson. Copyright © 1968 by Holt, Rinehart, and Winston, Inc. Reprinted by permission of the publisher.

Snow, 1971), and attempts to replicate this study have yielded mixed results (Cooper, 1979). Others argue that although the self-fulfilling prophecy does exist, it is less widespread than the study would have us believe (Proctor, 1984). However, despite these problems, the proposition that teacher expectations can and do affect student achievement has been validated by much research. In a four-year study of over 5,000 children, Crano and Mellon (1978) found that teacher expectations based on social characteristics unrelated to academic capabilities had a strong impact on children's achievement. Other studies have found that even when matched for prior achievement, teacher expectations were related to student achievement (Lockheed, 1976). Rutter and associates (1979) found that in secondary schools in which high level of achievement and better behavior were found, teachers communicated more positive expectations for student achievement than in low-achieving schools. The belief that students can learn—which is then commu-

nicated to students—can lead to higher achievement (Good, 1981).

If we grant that teacher expectations can affect achievement, the next question is, How important are these effects? The proposition that severely inaccurate initial expectations substantially alter academic achievement in students is not supported by the research (Cooper & Tom, 1984). Brophy (1983) notes that expectations do not always affect student achievement, but even when they do, the effects make only a 5 to 10 percent difference on the average in academic achievement. This of itself is important, but it also means that low student achievement cannot be explained exclusively or predominantly by blaming low teacher expectations. More interestingly, teacher expectations seem to sustain rather than set the existing achievement level (Cooper, 1979). Therefore, if students who are not expected to show interest do, teachers may not notice or may respond inappropriately because of their previous expectations. In addition, not all teacher expectations are based upon irrelevant characteristics. Teacher expectations are largely accurate and based upon valid information, and when differential treatment is found, it is often because of individualized instruction (Brophy, 1983).

True or False About half the achievement differences among students can be attributed to how much their teachers expect them to achieve.

In summary, teacher expectations do affect student achievement but not as radically as first thought. A larger problem than initial expectations is the possibility that teacher expectations may sustain a low level of achievement. Teachers often base their expectations on valid observations, but sometimes other, extraneous factors, such as race, socioeconomic background, physical appearance, reputation, and sibling performance, may influence the expectations (Dusek & Joseph, 1983). Low expectations are associated with minority group membership, a nonconforming personality, physical unattractiveness, and nonstandard speech (Proctor, 1984). However, the expectations vary from teacher to teacher, and any blanket condemnation is unsubstantiated by the evidence (Brophy & Good, 1974).

How are these expectations communicated in the students? After all, teachers do not say, "Peter, you're dumb" or "Jane, you can't pass math." In one study, Chaikin and colleagues (1974) videotaped forty-two undergraduates tutoring ten-year-old students. After studying the lesson plan for ten minutes, the tutors were given one of three different descriptions of the children to be tutored. All the descriptions stated that the child was highly motivated and got along well with his peers, but one description mentioned that the child was very bright, another said that he was slow, and another made no assessment at all. Analysis of the tapes indicated a definite difference in the treatment of those children thought to be bright from the treatment of those labeled neutral or slow. Tutors who thought their students bright used more eye contact, nodded their heads more, and smiled and leaned forward more often. When teachers expect students to do well, their nonverbal cues change so that they communicate more approval. These effects were present only with the bright students, which shows that the tutors tried not to show their disapproval with the slower students.

Teachers may also communicate expectations by treating high- and low-achieving students in ways that

Teachers communicate expectations through their facial expressions and gestures.

discriminate unnecessarily between the two groups of students. Teachers treat high- and low-achieving students differently, seating the lower achieving students farther away from the teacher, paying less attention to slower students, calling on slower students less frequently, waiting less time for them to answer questions, failing to ask follow-up questions, criticizing slower students more frequently for giving incorrect answers, praising slower students less for giving correct answers, giving slower students less feedback and less detailed feedback, and demanding less work from the slower students (Good, 1981). The result is that slower students become less willing to volunteer. Such students are discouraged from taking risks and participating in class and are less motivated to do their work. Instead, they are motivated to be safe, reduce risks, remain passive. Many of these students are afraid to approach the teacher to ask questions, especially if the material has already been covered, because teachers may react with annoyance. Students know that some teachers are more approachable than others. And students do see these differences in teacher behavior. They perceive high-achieving students as having more choices and being given more time to complete their work (Weinstein & Middlestadt, 1979). However, there is great variability in teacher behavior toward high- and low-achieving students. Some teachers do criticize slower children more frequently, while others will praise marginally correct answers. Some teachers are very protective and bend over backwards to help a slow student. Some teachers spend more time working with the highest reading group, while others spend more time with the lowest.

True or False Teachers wait longer for students with lower ability to answer questions than they do for higher achieving students.

>> CONNECTIONS

What Does the Research on Teacher Expectations Mean to the Teachers?

We know a great deal about the effects teacher expectations have on students. We also know that expectations vary from teacher to teacher and that teachers with the same expectations do not always behave similarly towards students. The following suggestions can minimize the extent to which expectations can negatively affect achievement.

1. **Try to understand where your expectations are coming from and avoid forming inaccurate expectations.** Expectations based on how a student's older brother or sister did are unfair to a student. When expectations are based upon race or socio-economic status, teachers do a gross disservice to their students.

2. **Understand that expectations may sustain a level of achievement and be aware that low-achieving students can show sparks of interest.** Sometimes, teachers may not encourage a low-achieving student as much as a high-achieving one. Be careful in grouping students, since sometimes a premature grouping can lead to a self-fulfilling prophecy.

3. **Keep expectations fluid and current by monitoring students' progress closely and stressing present performance.** (Brophy, 1983) Avoid forming expectations before students even enter the class, or even during the first few weeks of school.

4. **Do not set upper ceilings as goals.** In other words, let group or individual progress, not the teacher, set the limits.

5. **Stress a student's own improvement and progress rather than comparing the student with other children.** Such comparisons often have a negative effect on a student's self-concept and self-esteem.

6. **Be aware of the differences in behavior toward high- and low-achieving students.** It is especially distressing that teachers give low-achieving students less time to answer questions and provide them with less accurate and less detailed feedback. Although no one is advocating that low- and high-achieving students be treated identically, it is important not to discriminate unnecessarily between the groups.

7. **Focus as much as possible on the areas of competence.** Downing (1986) suggests making known the desired behavior, such as taking out a book, looking for children who are doing what is asked, and verbally providing positive reinforcement such as saying, "Jorge has his book out and is ready to go." This communicates positive expectations.

8. **Watch your nonverbal behavior.** Teachers tend to smile more at brighter students, and nonverbal behaviors can communicate expectations.

9. **Have one standard for everyone.** Students are very sensitive to differential treatment and often resent it. Teachers should be aware of treating high achieving students differently by letting them off more easily when they misbehave or giving them more time to finish an assignment.

10. **Communicate positive expectations for every student.** It is important to communicate the fact that every student can learn by encouraging all students to improve and by not comparing students.

Parental Involvement: Motivating Unmotivated Parents

Parents also hold expectations for their children's schooling and may communicate their expectations to their children. Many teachers complain that the parents they see during parent-teacher conferences are never those that they want to see. There are many reasons that parents may seem uninterested or don't hold high expectations for their children's achievement. A parent may be having difficulty making ends meet, may be working three jobs, or simply may be overwhelmed by parenting responsibilities. Some parents may not be aware of their children's behavior, have the ability to question, or have the background to help their children in school. In addition, many parents do not understand their role in the education of their children, seeing their children's education as solely the school's responsibility (Fredericks, 1984). Then again, parents who are uneducated or feel uncomfortable in the school environment may not know how to join with teachers in a partnership. They may feel intimidated. However, parents are not only important reinforcers for their children but also models for them. If parents don't seem to care about learning, their children will pick up this attitude. Parents' attitudes towards learning and the need for education create an atmosphere at home and an attitude that carries over to the school. Anything the teacher can do to create a healthy parent-teacher partnership can help student achievement. The following suggestions are just a few ways this can be done.

1. Keep in mind that communication with parents is important. As much as possible, the communication should be positive. Too many times, the only letters or phone calls from teachers to parents are to complain about something or to tell the parents their child spoke back in class or failed an exam.
2. Reinforce any interest parents show with a note of thanks or a phone call if practical. Fredericks (1984) suggests that a note of thanks for checking a homework paper is appropriate reinforcement. This is especially important if you have asked the parent to do this.
3. Parents may be afraid to ask about their child's progress because they are afraid the child is doing poorly. Ask parents about their goals for their child and pose such questions as, How do you feel about your child's progress so far? Do you feel good about what your child is doing? What would you like to see your child accomplish in this subject this year? Do you feel that this represents your child's best work? Such questions involve parents but also encourage a positive dialogue. Of course, the teacher must think through the possible responses the parent may give and have a course of action and alternatives planned. For instance, what if the parents say that they are not satisfied with their child's work and ask for suggestions? The teacher must be able to suggest solid recommendations for improvement and, it is hoped, to involve the parents.

Student Expectations

Students have expectations for their own achievement as they enter class, and certainly as the months unfold. These expectations are based on such factors as the student's past experience and the reputation of the individual teacher. In one study, students in high school who believed that a particular teacher had great ability and motivation misbehaved less and received higher final grades (Jamieson et al., 1987). A student's own expectations affect many aspects of behavior, including attention in class, persistence in the face of challenge and disappointment, and the amount of effort put into schoolwork. These expectations are important, since students with higher expectations perform at higher levels than students with lower expectations, even when their abilities are similar (Motowidlo, 1980).

The effect of prior failure is crucial. Failure lowers a student's estimation of his or her ability and triggers negative emotions and lower expectations for success (Covington & Omelich, 1981). Failure, then, is especially a problem for students with little self-confidence who enter school doubting their ability. Such students are more vulnerable.

What are students' expectations for themselves? High achievers tend to underpredict, and low performers tend to overpredict their future academic performance. Expectations increase after success and decrease after failure (depending upon attributions). Young children have unrealistically high expectations, but accuracy increases with age (Bardwell, 1984b; Bigelow, 1977).

>>> **CONNECTIONS**

Dealing with Student Expectations

Teachers who must deal with students who have low expectations of their success or who are nervous about doing well in class can help their students.

1. **Get to know your reputation with students.** Students will be entering your class with expectations about you. After teaching for a few years, teachers gain a reputation, and it can be helpful to know how students will be perceiving you at the beginning of the term.
2. **Set clear standards and offer clear explanations about each assignment.** Students do much better when they know what you want. In addition, knowing what you want may help to correct students' initial misimpressions. Also, the students' work will reflect the true level of learning only when the

assignments are clear and no misunderstandings about form exist.

4. **Reduce anxiety.** Students can be rather frightened in class, especially if they have not been successful in the past. A teacher can reduce anxiety by setting clear standards, using humor, and reducing the consequences of doing poorly on a single test.

5. **Show students that you believe they can succeed.** If students do not expect to succeed, teachers may need to restructure their cognitions or attributions.

6. **Give students the feeling that this is a new ball game.** Sometimes students see their current classes as merely an extension of how they did in the past. Teachers can help students try harder at the beginning of school by convincing them that their class is different and that previous problems do not have to recur.

7. **Give personal attention to those students with poor expectations.** Students with a history of failure may require personal attention, including some special program such as peer tutoring or cooperative learning groups.

MOTIVATING STUDENTS DURING THE LESSON

No matter what expectations students arrive with, they can be changed as students experience the classroom. Teachers can do a great deal to stimulate and motivate students during their lessons. Traditionally, motivation has been divided into two types: intrinsic and extrinsic. Motivation is said to be **intrinsic motivation** when it emanates from *within* the person, as when the child's curiosity about the weather causes her to conduct an experiment at home. Motivation is said to be **extrinsic motivation** when it comes from *outside* an individual, as when a child does his homework just to pass the course or to be liked by his

intrinsic motivation   Motivation that flows from within the individual.

extrinsic motivation   Motivation that comes from outside the individual, as when a student does his work to get a reward from his teacher.

teachers. A behavior can also be a mixture of intrinsic and extrinsic motivation, as when a student is interested in the work but is also motivated by the desire to get good grades.

Intrinsic Motivation

Intrinsically motivated work is exhibited when the learning is motivated by curiosity, the incentive is to work for one's own satisfaction, the preference is for challenging work rather than easy work, and there is a desire to work independently and to satisfy internal criteria for success rather than external criteria (Harter, 1981).

A fair question to ask is, Why are we interested in intrinsic motivation? Some would argue that intrinsically motivated, self-directed learning is the ideal model for education. There is much research to back up the importance of this type of motivation. For instance, a study of fourth graders and seventh graders found that children who report higher academic intrinsic motivation have significantly higher school achievement, more favorable perceptions of their academic competence, and lower academic anxiety (Gottfried, 1983; 1985). Just how can teachers stimulate students and encourage intrinsic motivation?

Developing Student Interests

Interest must head the list. When the work is interesting, students will show more initiative. Thomas McDaniel (1985) suggests that teachers begin planning for their units or curriculum with the guiding question, What would my students enjoy doing that will also correlate to my learning objectives? Even if the curriculum is predetermined, the way it is presented is usually the teacher's decision. One way to discover students' interests is to involve the students in the planning process. However, an open-ended questionnaire is counterproductive, because students need some structure to provide the teacher with the answer to the above general question. Bruce Brombacher (1983) suggests that teachers use a webbing process that begins with the teacher's writing the main topic or concept at the center of the blackboard and, in a spider-web fashion, writing the objectives and skills that need to be covered to satisfy the basic curriculum. The teacher then adds areas of personal interest that relate to the topic. After that, students begin to write down aspects of the topic they would like to study as well as any other interests they may have. Sometimes these seem unrelated. The final product may appear somewhat busy, but most of the topics will be pertinent to the curriculum. The second step involves identifying the major areas of interest and making a list of topics to consider. The third step involves creating an individual study plan for each student. This does not mean that the teacher never lectures or covers topics with the whole class. However, students are given an opportunity to look into areas of personal interest and to take on individual projects. Under this system, the teacher has some idea of what interests the students.

Curiosity and Learning

Curiosity is the ideal motivator, because it leads to active participation and perseverance in a task. Material learned out of curiosity is remembered longer than material learned for the sake of satisfying others (Erickson, 1984). There are three basic types of curiosity: perceptual curiosity, in which students' curiosity is piqued by what they see around them; manipulative curiosity, in which students' curiosity is awakened through active manipulation of some ob-

ject; and conceptual curiosity, in which curiosity involves the desire to know or to solve a mystery (Kreitler, 1975).

R. Stewart Jones (1985) identified teachers who were especially good at stimulating student curiosity and, through using a questionnaire, found that these teachers considered providing hands-on experience most important in stimulating curiosity (see Table 8.1). One successful teacher suggested such activities as building model rockets and demonstrating them to another school; designing and building kites; making maple syrup; and recycling paper, glass, and aluminum as a continuing project. Teacher questions that required the students to stretch their minds beyond the factual material presented is important. Sometimes outrageous statements were used to stimulate curiosity. At other times, questions were generated from student activities. One teacher noticed a student making a paper airplane and asked the student if he would like to make a better one. Since aerospace was a unit in the school's curricula, the teacher was provided an opportunity to use the student's interest and curiosity to begin the unit. Teacher enthusiasm was also mentioned as being important.

True or False Providing hands-on experiences is an effective way to stimulate curiosity.

Students may become curious when something they see around them stimulates their interest.

Table 8.1   Methods Used to Stimulate Curiosity by Forty Teachers Judged by Their Principals to Be Effective

Curiosity is an important motivator. Here, teachers list the methods they use to stimulate curiosity in their students.

Method Reported	Frequency
Hands-on experience	14
Asking questions, particularly those that are perplexing, paradoxical, and un-expected	11
Displays of homemade materials on bulletin boards and elsewhere in the classroom	11
Using concrete and personal examples relevant to students' lives	7
Roleplaying and simulation	5
Playing devil's advocate	5
Being enthusiastic	4
Varying activities	4
Using open-ended topics	4
Accepting all questions	3
Other	12
Total	80

From "Teachers who Stimulate Curiosity" by R. S. Jones, in *Education*. Copyright © 1985. Reprinted by permission of *Education*.

A teacher can use all three types of curiosity to stimulate students. Perceptual curiosity can be stimulated through the use of attractive and meaningful classroom displays, manipulative curiosity through allowing students to examine real objects, and conceptual curiosity through questioning techniques and raising issues that have some bearing on the students' lives.

Relevance and Meaningfulness

Relevance is certainly an overused term. One high school teacher once asked me, "How do you make the Thirty Years' War relevant?" He thought he could make it interesting as he described the changes of alliances and the intrigue, but he scoffed at making the historic event relevant. He happened to be an excellent teacher and was very concerned with student interest, but he did not see the possibilities of using a parallel with religious differences and present-day in-

tolerance. Such an approach could have led to discussions of power and interpersonally relevant themes.

Generally, teachers can make their lessons more relevant by considering the everyday experiences and backgrounds of their students. For example, when learning percentages, students can be assigned to calculate batting averages or to figure store discounts to determine whether 30 percent off one price is better than 23 percent off another as shown in a newspaper advertisement.

Variety, Surprise, and Adventure

"What happened in school today?" one parent asked. "Nothing special," was the answer. Varying classroom presentations affects interest and motivates students to do more work in a particular area. Student familiarity with classroom routines is desirable. However, when nothing special ever occurs, a type of boredom can set in and students will begin to just go through the motions. Varying the presentation by using such aids as films, roleplay, and case studies can add interest and can motivate students to learn. Teachers have many opportunities to do this. Instead of giving a lecture, the teacher can do something unusual that will get the students involved and perhaps working on their own. When teaching a unit on product safety, allowing students to investigate their homes for unsafe products and reporting back to the class can be interesting. Using surprise is another possibility. I've had good success with beginning a lesson with ten or so very unusual true-false questions. The answers are sometimes surprising, and as the class discusses the questions, a number of issues of interest arise. I sometimes use students' comments as the basis for student projects or student research.

Another noteworthy attempt is to make something a mystery and at times add adventure to the topic being studied. Students can see themselves as detectives as they track down an answer to a question or learn about, say, how a baseball bat is made. This type of learning may involve going to other resources, such as the library or a local legislator's office.

Allowing for Going Off on Tangents

Sometimes the most interesting and satisfying parts of a lesson are hardly what the teacher had intended them to be. Not a teacher exists who cannot tell you of how a student's question or a quip made by a student has led to a mammoth discussion and student involvement. I remember teaching a lesson in junior high on the political process that involved monitoring the role of radio, television, and the newspapers. One student reacted with a statement to the effect that the media wasn't fair to the candidates. The class got into a heated debate on what is fair for a reporter to do and say to a candidate. The discussion took up the entire period and led to some individual work on the part of some of the students. One student wrote a letter to a reporter, another interviewed a reporter, a third researched the legal aspects of reporting, while others listened to and taped some political discussions.

This is not to imply that teachers should turn each lesson into a bull session. That would be counterproductive. However, some teachers are so focused on their lesson that they miss opportunities to explore valuable and interesting areas that can stimulate student interest and lead students to independent work.

Encouraging Students to Begin

"Take out your history books and turn to page. . . ." is not a technique that leads to involvement on the part of the students. Thomas McDaniel (1985) suggests that some interesting question or statement be made that focuses student attention on what is to be learned. For example, if the class is going to read about Thomas Edison, asking a question such as Who can guess how many light bulbs Edison invented before he got one to work? is a good ploy. The teacher can follow up by saying, "Now let's read the story about an inventor who wouldn't give up, no matter how many times he failed. Ask yourself how long you would have stayed with this experiment." Another strategy is to set the stage by bringing up an event that has happened in school or in the news or blindfolding someone as a prelude to studying the life of Helen Keller.

Age-Appropriate Work

Giving age-appropriate examples and work is not often a problem with high-achieving students. It is, however, a considerable problem with lower achieving students and students who are placed in special education (Gleason, 1983). For these students, different work has often meant not only simpler work but also work whose basic content is not age appropriate.

A twelve-year-old who is a poor reader and is asked to read a story that would interest a seven-year-old is likely to rebel. It reinforces his or her sense of worthlessness and failure. Reading material must contain content that is age appropriate. This is sometimes a problem in high school when teaching a lesson on a topic that students may have covered many times in the past, such as the causes of the American Revolution. When dealing with high school students, a more adult approach is required, including perhaps looking into the real lives of the heroes of the Revolution instead of merely telling the stories students have heard so often throughout grade school and junior high school.

Setting Goals

Students will work towards educational goals when they are aware of what the goals are and where the teacher is going. However, the students may want to set some of the goals or cooperate in forming them. This is a natural outgrowth of interest forming policy. The goals (both class and individual) may be set both by the teacher and in cooperation with the students and should be stated in behavioral terms whenever possible. While everyone shares in the class goals (e.g., to learn techniques of persuasion), a student may also set individual goals (e.g., to learn how to debate).

Challenging Students

Challenging students to prove something is another effective motivational device. It creates excitement. Again, such challenges arise from the topic or unit being studied and should, obviously, challenge students. Asking "Can you find out?" . . . or "What do people do when?" can be challenges. Again, be alert to student interests leading to challenges that are self-made and of interest to the students yet related to the work in class.

Don't Just Talk About Things: Do Something

One junior high school student once told me that he doesn't do anything; he merely sits, listens, reads, and writes. He wanted to *do* something. Students can sometimes see learning as a passive rather than an active process, and this is a problem. Some students would rather learn through an action-oriented project. For example, after discussing the court system, students were asked to participate in a mock trial. Taking surveys or creating something to accompany a presentation can be more action oriented and can encourage student curiosity and learning.

Encouraging Questions

What if Mark Antony hadn't been allowed to give his speech in Shakespeare's *Julius Caesar?* Much interest comes out of questioning, including "what if?" questions. Encouraging questions from students can lead to a more interesting class lesson. Questioning techniques will be discussed in Chapter 9.

Providing a Relaxing Atmosphere with Little Anxiety

"Now this will be on the next test" is certainly one way to motivate *some* students but certainly not *all* students. Learning takes place best when students are not anxious about taking chances, asking questions, and making mistakes. The use of anxiety or fear to motivate learning has many pitfalls. Students who learn only for the sake of passing a test and avoiding failure will tend to listen only to those parts of the lesson that involve the test material. Interest is no longer important. The goal is to avoid failure, not to learn for the sake of interest or to participate in class. Students who do not care about grades for whatever reason will not be motivated by the desire to score well on examinations. In addition, failure or success is totally measured by external criteria.

Offering a Choice of Assignments

Whenever possible, students should be given a choice of assignments and projects. They can then follow their interests while investigating something related to the subject being covered. Having everyone research the same question or do the same project brings up a number of problems. One is competition. Children may give up if they know that their project or assignment will not match that of the best student in the class. In addition, there may be more than one way to attain the same desired result. Some children can build and use their hands, others may use art work, while still others may write or interview some-

one. Allowing students some choices within a targeted framework allows students to follow their interests.

Teacher Enthusiasm and Belief in One's Own Subject

One of my supervisors used to tell me that to be effective you had to be in love with your own particular discipline. You had to have a passion for it and believe it was important and had something to offer people. While others may not feel so strongly, the basic premise holds true. Enthusiasm is contagious, and teachers who believe that their subject is important and interesting will communicate this belief to their students (Johnson, 1981, Gray, 1981). Add humor to enthusiasm. In a symposium on motivation, a number of teachers mentioned using humor as a way to motivate students. For example, Frances Spielberg (1981), a high school mathematics teacher, notes that when a student presents a theorem that isn't in the text, she labels it, using the student's name.

THE STRUCTURE OF THE CLASSROOM

The structure of the classroom also affects learning and motivation. Some classrooms are structured so that each individual student's progress is compared to some external criterion. Other classrooms emphasize either competition or cooperation.

Competition

We can all remember classroom competition. The best get the rewards; the rest sit and stare. It is hard to feel good about a classmate's success if that person's success reduces your chances of getting a good grade. In one study, students were given puzzles to solve. Competing children were told that the one who solved the most puzzles would be the winner and could select a prize. Noncompeting children were told they would both get a prize for participating. The result was that the children who competed and lost put themselves down, saw themselves as incapable, and experienced negative emotions. Competition thus produced failure and low self-concepts. Competing children who won devalued the losing person and had inflated ideas of their own abilities. Competitive

Under what circumstances does competition improve or impede performance?

success, though, was more valued than noncompetitive success (Ames & Ames, 1978).

The results of many studies warn us against indiscriminate use of competition. There are times, however, when competition can be effectively used. Competition works best when everyone has the ability to succeed, that is, when all students have the necessary skills (Michaels, 1977). In addition, if winning reflects effort, as when the students with the five neatest correct homework assignments receive a special privilege, it may have a positive effect on the class. The consequences of winning or losing must be weighed carefully. If they are too high, anxiety and less learning may result. Competition can be used to increase performance in simple drill activities once everyone has the ability, as well as in areas where speed and the sheer quantity of work are desired on a project. When winning does not generate much anxiety and a sense of pleasure results, it can be useful (Johnson & Johnson, 1974). In fact, making some lessons into a competitive game can be helpful. Children are used to playing games and frequently enjoy such fun-related competition. That is, children enjoy such games as long as the rewards for winning and the punishments for losing are not great.

True or False   Competition should never be used in the classroom to improve student performance.

An additional area where competition is useful is in competing against oneself and one's own prior score. Many video games work this way. This strategy is similar to goal setting. Thus, a student who gets 80 out of 100 on a multiplication drill can compete against his or her own past grade to improve a score.

Cooperation

What if you were faced with an anti-academic atmosphere in your high school class, where the students were more interested in socializing than working and seemed to fear looking "too smart" or being "too interested." What would you do? Such a problem is not unusual, especially in junior and senior high schools. One possible solution is to adopt a **cooperative learning strategy**—a strategy that involves two or more students working together to reach some academic goal.

Robert Slavin (1984) developed two methods that illustrate cooperative learning strategies: STAD (Student Teams and Achievement Division) and TAI (Team Assisted Individualization). In STAD, the teacher presents a lesson, and then the students study worksheets in teams comprising students of different ability levels. The students quiz each other, compare answers, and discuss problems within their groups. They then take individual quizzes, and team scores are computed based upon the degree to which each student improved over his or her past records. The scores are recognized in the class newspaper. This strategy is similar to handicapping in golf in that low achievers can score points while performing at a lower level while high achievers need to perform at a higher level (Weyant, 1986).

In TAI, students work in heterogeneous teams, but they work on individualized curriculum materials at their own levels and rates. Students are encouraged to help each other and to check each other's work.

cooperative learning strategies   Learning strategies that require two or more students to work together to reach some academic goal.

Cooperative learning strategies have become more popular as research has demonstrated its many benefits.

Teams receive certificates based on the number of units completed and the accuracy of all team members' assignments. In a twenty-four week mathematics experiment using third-, fourth-, and fifth-grade students, the TAI students achieved significantly more than students taught using traditional mathematics instruction (Slavin et al., 1984).

In study in Israel, Sharan (1980) found that STAD and other cooperative teaching methods increased academic achievement and led to better interpersonal relationships. Students in cooperative learning systems achieve more than those in competitive structure (Slavin, 1983). Cooperative work promotes higher achievement in high-, medium-, and low-skill students (Skon et al., 1981). Under a cooperative learning system, peer norms support achievement, and the perception by students that their classmates want them to excel has a strong positive effect on achievement. In addition, cooperative strategies can reduce intergroup antagonism and improve interpersonal relationships. There is also evidence that cooperative learning can promote positive relationships among students of different ability levels as well as

between handicapped and nonhandicapped students (Warring et al., 1985; Johnson et al., 1983).

How does a teacher go about establishing cooperative learning environments? The following guidelines (Knight et al., 1982) can help:

1. Specify the objective of the task.
2. Select the group size most appropriate for the lesson.
3. Cluster the groups.
4. Provide appropriate materials.
5. Explain the tasks and the cooperative goal structure.
6. Observe student-student interactions.
7. Intervene and consult when necessary.
8. Evaluate the group product.

A cooperative learning group can be composed of only two individuals. Some studies have paired an excellent student with a student of lower ability. The students were told to read a passage silently. The better student was to explain the passage while the other student listened for mistakes and omissions. The students were then instructed to discuss the material and to continue with the next selection. Under such a system, both low-ability and high-ability students learn more than in a traditional framework (Lambiotte et al., 1987). This system works because the lower achieving student gets more attention while the high-achieving student has an opportunity to verbalize his or her knowledge (Van Oudenhoven et al., 1987).

Power and Powerlessness in the Classroom: Origins and Pawns

Intrinsic motivation requires initiative and choices. However, students often feel powerless in the classroom. They help to make few decisions, initiate little, and are safer keeping quiet and following exact instructions than thinking for themselves. For intrinsic motivation to surface, autonomy is needed. However, can such autonomy exist within a classroom setting? If so, how can educators foster it? It's not easy. The teacher who is used to directing and controlling everything, to acting as a benevolent despot, may feel threatened. Although some believe that sharing power and control leads to chaos, this is simply not the case, as Richard de Charms (1976) showed in his classic study on enhancing motivation.

To understand de Charms' study, we have to differentiate between a pawn and an origin. A *pawn* is a chessman of least value, and de Charms refers to a pawn as a person who is pushed around by others. An *origin* is someone who originates his or her own behavior. A pawn is externally motivated, while an origin is internally motivated. A child in the more traditional classroom is a pawn, responding to the dictates of the teacher. If encouraged to originate his or her own behavior, the child becomes an origin in school. A pawn is defensive and irresolute, avoids challenges, and feels powerless. The origin is optimistic and confident, accepts challenges, and feels more potent.

The plan of de Charms' study was relatively simple. A group of teachers were trained in motivation-enhancing techniques, with special emphasis on treating students as origins. These techniques were to be used in the classroom. De Charms and his colleagues were to assess the effect of such training on both motivation and achievement by comparing students treated as origins with a group of students who did not have teachers trained in motivation-enhancing techniques. The project was extended for four years,

beginning in the fifth grade. The teachers and students were from one large inner-city school district.

The teacher training involved helping teachers to understand their own motives through self-study. The training included how to teach children to set goals, choose activities that help lead to these goals, assume personal responsibility, believe in their own ability, and assess their progress. Fundamentally, teachers were asked to learn how to actively encourage and treat students like origins.

The ultimate aim of the workshop was to apply the origin concept to practical concerns in the classroom, using a number of exercises. For example, to introduce the origin-pawn concept, staff members assembled in a room equipped with large tables and Tinkertoys and were told to build anything they liked for fifteen minutes or so. They were then asked to show what they had built to the others and to tell about it. The staff members then became more serious and told participants to disassemble what they had built and put the pieces back into the boxes. When this was done, specific instructions for arranging, sitting, not talking, raising the hand, listening, and following directions were given. As this occurred, the instructor gave some contradictory directions. When the participants corrected the trainer, the trainer refused to listen to the criticism and criticized the teachers for not obeying directions.

Following this exercise, the teachers were asked about their reactions. Most had felt free and involved during the first part of the exercise. When strictly controlled, they felt constrained and powerless. The teachers were asked what they could do to create a sense of personal responsibility in their students. Some of their suggestions involved avoiding arbitrary rules with no explanations, busywork that requires no thinking, and threats of punishment. Such policies lead to passive acceptance, conformity, and sometimes rebellion, but not to creativity and productive energy.

The results of the study showed the importance of training students to be origins. Students of the trained teachers showed more commitment to task, were more work oriented, took more personal responsibility, and showed higher academic achievement than those of the untrained teachers. In a later study, de Charms (1980) found that more trained students than untrained students graduated from high school.

The study shows that it is possible to create an atmosphere that encourages students to take responsibility for themselves and that an atmosphere that fosters autonomy can lead to improved motivation and achievement. Such an atmosphere, however, is anything but chaotic. In an allied study of 140 elementary school students, Ryan and Grolnick (1986) found that the more students perceived themselves as origins within their classroom, the higher they saw their self-worth, cognitive competence, internal control, and mastery motivation. In another study, Deci and colleagues (1981) found that elementary schoolteachers' orientation towards being controlling rather than supportive of autonomy was related to their students' lower intrinsic motivation to learn and lower feelings of perceived competence.

EXTRINSIC MOTIVATION

In 1987, Asher Edelman, a New York businessperson, was teaching a course at the Columbia University Business School. As a final exam, he told his students to find a company that he could take over. The reward for finding such a company was not just an A in the course but also a $100,000 finders fee. The dean of the school vetoed the proposal, because he feared that students would be so motivated by the money that they would neglect their other studies (New York Times, October 17, 1987). Since Mr. Edelman was not allowed to continue with the project we cannot say what the quality of the students' work would have been. However, it certainly well illustrates the concept of extrinsic motivation.

Obviously, few teachers will be in Mr. Edelman's position, but it does raise some interesting questions. Under what circumstances should rewards be offered? How does the giving of an external reward affect intrinsic motivation?

Unfortunately, the desirability of intrinsic motivation sometimes prevents people from appreciating the importance of extrinsic motivation to learning and performance. Extrinsic motivation gets a reputation as something impure. This is not the case, though. There are numerous times when extrinsic rewards such as extra privileges, attention or praise from the teacher, stars or tokens, and awards are desirable and can aid in motivating students. It all depends upon how and when such rewards are used.

In two distinct cases, extrinsic motivation is useful. First, extrinsic incentives are very useful when children are first learning a skill or are not very good at it

(Bandura, 1986). For instance, it is certainly not enjoyable just to practice the scales of the piano or to read when you are not a good reader. These activities take on intrinsic incentives only when you can play the piece of music you want to play or read well enough to enjoy the content of the book. Until the feeling of satisfaction can take over, there must be some reason for developing skills, especially when they are not in themselves enjoyable. In addition, the lack of enjoyment or immediate success could lead to a cycle of continued failure. Take the example of the child for whom reading is very difficult. She spends an inordinate amount of effort trying to put the sounds together to make words and the words together to give sentences meaning. We know from experience that the more she reads (under the proper teaching), the better she will read. Eventually she may come to enjoy reading. On the other hand, the less she reads, the more likely it is that she will fall further behind in class and feel frustrated. This will lead to even less reading and more failure. Success breeds success, and failure often breeds more failure (depending on the attributions, of course).

True or False Extrinsic incentives given by the teacher, such as free time, stickers, or being exempted from homework are best used when a student is not good at a particular task.

An incentive program could help a slow reader. For instance, it is possible to set up a token reinforcement system for increasing effort in reading (Kazdin, 1984; Stephens & Cooper, 1980). Tokens can be given for each appropriate book read. The tokens can then be traded in for some larger reward, such as a ticket to a movie, the opportunity to play, or a special party. As noted in Chapter 5, such token economies should be used only after less intrusive extrinsic incentives such as praise have not worked.

There are a number of ways to distribute these rewards. In one case, a cabinet was divided into fifteen drawers, and a desirable item was placed in each drawer. When a student met the desired goal, he or she could then select a paper numbered from one through fifteen. Then, the student could keep the item in the corresponding drawer. Some drawers contained stickers or trinkets, while others contained cards that gave the student the right to engage in a preferred activity. Special cards were sprinkled throughout the cabinet, allowing the student to get an extra prize.

This system can be used in secondary school as well, but with some age-appropriate changes. For adolescents, a touchdown triumph package was used in which a miniature football field was constructed with first-down markers, some of which were colored a special green. When students reached a criterion, they moved their piece toward the teacher's goal line (they began on the fifty-yard line). If the student did not meet the criterion within a stipulated time, the student's piece was moved ten yards toward his or her own goal. When the student made a touchdown, he or she received a card that allowed six minutes of free time for the day, up to a maximum of sixty minutes (ten cards). Variations are, of course, possible. When a student's progress is such that a student's piece is moved to the green yard marker, the student can receive special play cards that range from a rest, less homework, or a poster of some kind. Using these systems, Raschke and colleagues (1987) claim significant improvements in students' sight reading and mathematics knowledge.

Extrinsic incentives are often successful at motivating a student to become involved in some activity in which the student would normally not participate. Giving additional credit for attending a special lecture or watching a television program may be necessary to introduce a student to a particular activity. The student may have originally not wanted to participate in the activity because of its reputation, the time and effort involved, the lack of certainty for success, or because it had a lower priority on his list of needs and activities than other activities. Yet, the introduction of new activities can be encouraged through such incentives as praise and additional credit.

Many of the most common extrinsic motivators are praise and grades, and they are discussed specifically in Chapters 9 and 15. Extrinsic incentives are tools that can be used to heighten student motivation under certain circumstances.

Extrinsic Incentives and Intrinsic Motivation

How does the use of extrinsic incentives affect intrinsic motivation? A number of studies have found that when rewards are given to children performing tasks that they already enjoy, the children's intrinsic motivation is reduced. This is called the **overjustification effect**—the loss of interest that occurs when an individual shifts from an intrinsic to an extrinsic motiva-

overjustification effect The loss of interest that occurs when an individual shifts from an intrinsic to an extrinsic motivational orientation.

tional orientation. In one now famous study, Lepper and colleagues (1973) observed nursery schoolchildren playing with felt-tip pens—an intrinsically interesting activity. The children were divided into three groups: expected-award, unexpected-award, and no-award. The children were then individually asked if they would help the experimenter out by drawing some pictures. The children in the expected-award group were shown a good-player award consisting of a gold star and ribbon on an index card which they were told they would receive for their efforts. Children in the unexpected-award and no-award groups were told nothing. All the children drew pictures for several minutes. Afterward, the children in the unexpected-award group were told that since they had done a good job, they would be rewarded. Children in the expected-award group received the award as promised.

Between one and two weeks later, all the children were again observed playing, and among the toys and games available were felt tip-pens and paper. The expected-award children spent about half as much time drawing as did the children in the other two groups because, according to the authors, the awards undermined the intrinsic interest in the task. The children in the unexpected-award and no-award groups spent about the same amount of time playing. This means that something more than just rewards themselves are involved. Only when the reward was interpreted as the reason for drawing did it affect the intrinsic motivation.

True or False Rewarding students with something material such as a prize can reduce a student's natural interest in the activity.

Why do extrinsic rewards interfere with intrinsic motivation? One explanation is that people engaging in a task for its own enjoyment or satisfaction see themselves as the focus of the activity. On the other hand, if a powerful external reward is applied, such people switch their perception of the reason for undertaking the task from internal control to external control, and they become extrinsically motivated. Removing the reward decreases both motivation and subsequent activity (Greene & Lepper, 1974). Other studies have found that it also results in a preference for tasks that are less challenging and more easily accomplished (Pittman et al., 1982) and produces work of lower quality that contains more errors (Condry, 1977).

The overjustification effect has enormous implications for everyone from employers to teachers. After all, it seems to cast doubt on the benefits of using rewards in class at all. However, additional experimentation has shown this is not always the case. First, notice that the overjustification effect occurs when intrinsic motivation is already high. No behaviorist suggests using token economies or material rewards for behavior that is intrinsically motivated (Morgan, 1984). The effect is not found when there is little or no intrinsic reward. When intrinsic motivation and interest are initially low, extrinsic motivation can actually increase intrinsic motivation (McLloyd, 1979).

Second, under certain conditions, external rewards do not reduce intrinsic motivation. For instance, as Fiske and Taylor (1984) suggest, no one argues that a singer likes to sing less because he or she gets a great deal of money or that the skills of a basketball player decline as his or her salary goes up. The key is to look at how one views the external reward. If rewards emphasize success or competence, they do not undermine intrinsic motivation and actually increase it (Morgan, 1984). If they are given just for performing the behavior, they reduce the intrinsic motivation perhaps because they are seen as an attempt at control. If the rewards are given to control behavior, to make students do what the teacher wants and when he wants it, they will undermine intrinsic motivation. However, when rewards communicate that the student is competent, extrinsic rewards will not reduce intrinsic motivation (Fiske & Taylor, 1984). In fact, there is some evidence that praise can lead to increased intrinsic motivation (Blanck et al., 1984; Anderson et al., 1976) if it is informational, as in "You're doing a good job." Positive verbal feedback, then, is beneficial to intrinsic motivation if it is definitely related to the task (Bates, 1979). Feedback in the form of praise—and even some criticism if it is informational, such as "What you wrote was correct, but you could have used more examples. Look for more examples in. . . ."—can enhance intrinsic motivation when compared to receiving no feedback or receiving just grades (Butler & Nisan, 1986).

Do Extrinsic Rewards Reduce Intrinsic Motivation? The Teacher's View

Many people who read the studies on extrinsic rewards and intrinsic motivation overgeneralize the effects of this technique. Even its two great advocates, David Greene and Mark Lepper (1974), admit that when children have no intrinsic interest in the activity there is no intrinsic motivation to lose, or if the child does not possess basic skills necessary to enjoy the activity, such as reading, the use of extrinsic rewards may be necessary. Finally, if rewards provide the student with information about his or her ability in a particular task, the child's feelings of competence and intrinsic motivation may be bolstered.

CONCLUSION

Some students are easily motivated, perhaps because they are successful, interested, or achievement oriented. Other students are not so easily motivated. Although no teacher can motivate every student, it is part of the teacher's responsibility to present lessons in a way that will motivate students to want to learn or to work hard and develop necessary skills. There is no end to the techniques that will work, and methods that work should be shared. Teachers can help one another by discussing what has worked for them in presenting certain units or topics. Teachers can thus expand their ability to present work in the most effective manner. To do so requires the teacher's willingness to take a chance and try something new. Administrative support for innovation is also necessary. However, such techniques can also help teachers to remain fresh and to avoid the repetition that comes with teaching the same subjects year after year. Such variety makes school more pleasant and challenging for both teachers and students.

SUMMARY

1. Abraham Maslow argued that people were motivated to satisfy their needs. Needs can be arranged in a hierarchy, and only when the lower needs are satisfied can people turn to upper level needs. Maslow divided needs into two categories: deficiency needs and being needs. Deficiency needs involve physiological needs and the needs

for security, belongingness, and esteem. Being needs are cognitive, aesthetic, and—to be all one can be—self-actualization. Teachers can help students satisfy their basic needs and create an atmosphere where they can feel secure enough to be creative and to go beyond the safety of textbook answers.

2. People have a need to achieve and to excel, which varies among individuals. People with a high need for achievement will work hardest when tasks are challenging. People with a high need for achievement but a high fear of failure will choose work that is either very easy or impossibly difficult. Children with a high fear of failure often are punished for their failures and receive little reward for their successes. Teachers must give moderately challenging assignments to get the best work from students with a high need for achievement. When faced with students with a high fear of failure, teachers should praise effort and minimize punishment for failure.

3. The value/expectancy theory of motivation argues that both the value of the goal and the expectation of success are important motivational factors.

4. Attribution theory emphasizes the importance of how students perceive and explain the causes of their successes and failures. Attributions can be made along three dimensions: internal/external, stability/instability, and controllable/uncontrollable. If students attribute successes to internal factors such as ability and effort, they are more likely to feel confident of future success. If students attribute failure to effort, they may increase their efforts; but if failure is attributed to ability, students may not try very hard. Teachers should become aware of how students attribute their failures and help students to attribute success to effort.

5. Some students see no relationship between what they do and the outcome. They give up quickly and are quick to link failure to ability. They suffer from learned helplessness and require a great deal of help. Such students must be identified and taught to interpret failure as feedback that a new strategy must be used and to focus on effort.

6. Behaviorists see motivation in terms of conditioning principles and look at the nature of the reinforcers and punishers in the environment to pinpoint problems in student motivation. Using such reinforcers as praise and prizes can sometimes help motivate students.

7. Social learning theorists note that a student may know how to do something but still not perform a behavior. One reason for the disparity between knowledge and action lies in self-efficacy, or the belief people have about what they can or cannot do. People with a high degree of self-efficacy believe they can do a particular thing, while people with a low degree of self-efficacy do not. Children should be encouraged to set personal standards, and teachers must model persistence in task performance.

8. Teacher expectations can and do affect student achievement. Teacher expectations can be communicated in many ways, some of them nonverbal. Teachers nod and smile more to the more intelligent students. In addition, teachers treat high- and low-achieving students in ways that unnecessarily differentiate between the two groups. However, expectations explain only between 5 and 10 percent of the differences between students' achievement. Often teacher expectations are based upon factual differences, such as intelligence and effort. However, the evidence that teacher expectations are sometimes based on extraneous factors such as race and socioeconomic status is a definite cause for concern. In addition, teacher expectations may serve to lock students into a particular achievement level. Teachers should try ot keep expectations fluid, not jump to conclusions, be aware of the source of the expectations, and be aware of the differences between how they act to high- and low-achieving students.

9. Parents may not be motivated to help their children in school because of pressing home considerations, a lack of understanding concerning the role of the home in education, or feelings of intimidation from professionals. Communicating with parents the need to compliment their children, asking parents about their children's progress, and reinforcing interest are steps teachers can take to motivate parents to participate in their children's education.

10. Students have expectations for their own achievement, depending upon their past achievement, the teacher's reputation, and their view of their own ability. Setting clear standards, reducing anxiety, showing students that they can succeed, and giving personal attention to those experienc-

ing more difficulty in a subject can help alter student expectations for achievement.

11. Motivation is said to be intrinsic when it emanates from within the person. Teachers can increase intrinsic motivation by developing student interests; encouraging curiosity; making learning more meaningful; using variety, surprise, and adventure; allowing time for going off on tangents; teaching age-appropriate work; setting goals; challenging students; allowing students to do things and not just talk about issues; encouraging questioning; creating a relaxing atmosphere; giving students whenever possible a choice of assignments; and being enthusiastic.

12. Competition in the classroom must be used with great care, since research shows that students who lose see themselves as inadequate and incapable. Competition is best used when all students have the necessary skills to succeed, when winning reflects efforts, when the consequences of winning or losing aren't great, and when the competition is in areas where sheer quantity of work is important, such as spelling and vocabulary.

13. Many studies show that cooperative learning systems—where students work in groups to reach some goal—can succeed in improving learning. Cooperative learning strategies vary greatly. In STAD (Student Teams and Achievement Division), teachers present a lesson, the students study in groups and quiz each other, and team scores are computed based upon student improvement. In TAI (Team Assisted Individualization), students work at their own levels or on individualized curriculum materials but help each other. Teams receive certificates based upon the accuracy and quantity of work completed.

14. An important study by deCharms showed that students who see themselves as having some power in the classroom to set goals and choose activities show more intrinsic motivation and superior achievement than those who don't. Teachers can aid in fostering autonomy by discarding arbitrary rules, not giving busywork, not issuing threats, and giving students some power to influence their own learning experience.

15. Motivation is said to be extrinsic if it originates from outside the individual. Extrinsic incentives include measuring up to someone else's expectations and earning rewards. Extrinsic incentives are most useful when students are first learning a

skill or when a teacher tries to get students involved in an activity in which they would not normally participate.

16. Extrinsic rewards may reduce intrinsic motivation when prizes are given as a reward for performing activities students already enjoy and when these rewards are seen as controlling students' actions. The interference of extrinsic rewards with intrinsic motivation is called the overjustification effect. If the reward is seen by students as a measure of competence, it does not lead to a reduction in intrinsic motivation.

ACTIVITIES AND EXERCISES

1. **Maslow's Hierarchy of Needs.** People are motivated to satisfy their needs. This is as true in school as it is outside of school. You can become aware of how school fits into one's needs by spending a week listing your activities in school and noting which needs they satisfy. For instance, belongingness may be satisfied through interpersonal relationships and the aesthetic need through creativity.

2. **Safety and Growth.** One of the more challenging aspects of Maslow's theory is the possibility that safety needs interfere with being or growth needs. It is sometimes safer not to volunteer in class or to show interest. Keep a log of the times you could have taken a chance and offered something in class, done a different assignment, or shown curiosity and didn't. Consider your reasons for continuing on the safe side. In addition, ask teachers how they encourage students to take a chance and volunteer in class. See if they use extrinsic rewards and, if so, whether such rewards work.

3. **Attributions.** As the chapter indicates, how one attributes success or failure has an enormous effect on later achievement and one's emotional reaction to success or failure. Ask your friends what they attributed their success or failure to on a particular test (ability, luck, effort, task difficulty). According to attribution theory, if they attribute their success or failure to effort, they will try harder. If they attribute their failure to task difficulty or lack of ability, they will not put in more time. See if these hypotheses hold by asking your friends after they take the next test whether they

put in more work and, if so, how much more work.

4. **Teacher Expectations.** Most students have had the experience of being in a teacher's classroom and feeling that the teacher liked or disliked them or expected a certain level of achievement from them. Teacher expectation is a variable affecting the quality of student work in class. Interview six students (three boys and three girls) in elementary school, junior high, and high school and ask them:

a. Do you remember a teacher who liked you very much? If the answer is yes:

How did the teacher let you know it?

Did the teacher expect you to do more work than, the same amount as, or less work than the other students?

How did you feel about the teacher?

What grade did you receive in the subject (class)?

b. Do you remember a teacher who didn't like you very much? If the answer is yes:

How did the teacher let you know it?

Did the teacher expect you to do more work than, the same amount as, or less work than the other students?

How did you feel about the teacher?

What grade did you receive in the subject (class)?

For the interviewer. Do you see any pattern linking students who liked a teacher and ratings of students' effort in class or final grades? In addition, look at the teacher behaviors described by the students that denote a student's being liked or disliked and see if there are any patterns that might communicate different expectations for student achievement.

5. **Do Teachers Treat High- and Low-Achieving Students Differently?** A distressing finding is that high- and low-ability or achieving students (they're not the same) are sometimes treated differently in ways that are unnecessary. Observe a teacher in elementary, junior high, or senior high school and check whether this is so. You might even use a college classroom as your object of study. First, identify a few students who you know to be doing well and a few you know are not achieving. Observe whether the teacher (a) calls on the poorer students less often, (b) pays less attention to slow students, (c) waits less time for them to answer questions (d) asks follow-up questions less frequently, (e) criticizes poorer students more for incorrect answers, (f) gives slower students less detailed feedback. While doing this observation, you may notice other differences as well.

6. **Tutoring with a Nonverbal Bias.** One way students pick up teacher expectations is through the teacher's nonverbal behavior, such as nodding, smiling, frowning, or increasing or decreasing the distance between the students and the teacher. Perform a variation of Chaikin et al.'s experiment. Chaikin asked undergraduates to tutor ten-year-old students who were labeled bright or slow and observed the nonverbal behavior of the tutors. If possible, you might be able to do the same. During your observation, take special note of the nonverbal behavior of the teachers toward the students labeled slower or faster.

7. **Curiosity Seeking.** There are three types of curiosity: perceptual, manipulative, and conceptual. Choose one or two of the following topics and think of ways you could stimulate student curiosity when teaching a lesson on the topic or topics:

a. adding fractions

b. the nature of checks and balances in government

c. the solar system

d. writing a business letter

e. slavery before the Civil War

If you plan to teach in high school, think of ways to stimulate curiosity in the following lessons:

a. whether the government should require industries to supply day-care facilities for their employees

b. Adding fractions (teaching in high school, remember)

c. The circulatory system

d. Hamlet or any other Shakespearean play

8. **Initial Motivations.** It is good idea to begin each lesson with some motivational activity that will grab students' attention and interest. Pick a topic you will be teaching and think of an initial activity that would get students immediately involved.

9. **Cooperative Learning Groups.** Cooperative learning groups such as STAD and TAI take much planning and require the use of group rewards. However, you can gain some understanding of the cooperative group experience by forming your own learning group. Select two or three

other students in the class and make up a study schedule. Meet as a group, read the material in the text, discuss it briefly, and test each other. It isn't easy to set up a group reward, but it can be accomplished. Discuss the type of reward (such as attending a play or going to a restaurant together) that would be appropriate. Discuss also the grade on the next test that each would like to achieve. The grades should be an improvement over previous grades. See if your score both individually and as a group increases compared to some standard (a prior test or your performance in a previous, similar class). In addition, evaluate the experience of being in the group. Of course, this does not prove that cooperative learning groups are superior, since you may spend more time studying with the group than you would on your own, but the learning group does serve to give you some idea of the group experience.

10. **The Anti-Achievement Orientation.** This is an especially important problem in junior high and high school. I have spoken to many of my classes in college about the junior and senior high school norm, which is to not show much interest in class. To see if this is a correct observation and to look at it from both sides of the table, ask teachers whether they see an anti-achievement bias and, if so, what they do to counter it. Ask high school students whether they perceive or have experienced such a bias and ask them what effect it may have had on their achievement.

11. **What Works for You?** Every teacher has his or her favorite techniques for motivating students. At the conclusion of the chapter, I suggested that sharing these techniques is important for all teachers, but most of all for inexperienced teachers. Ask ten teachers how they motivate students when teaching a specific lesson. Report these ideas back to some of your fellow students in the course and see if you find any similarities in teachers' approaches.

SCENARIOS

Here are eight scenarios. Try to apply the information you have learned in the chapter to each situation.

1. Mr. Kennedy is confused by Lee's progress in fifth grade. Lee is a ten-year-old whose performance in school has sharply declined from the first marking period. He seemed to be a good student in September, but now in February he is failing. He daydreams and seems not to be motivated to do his work. When Mr. Kennedy asks Lee about his problems, Lee says, "Nothing is wrong." Yet, he seems to be getting worse and does not seem to care. What steps can Mr. Kennedy take to help Lee?

2. Simon has high ability and seems to want to succeed in class. However, he is always picking the least challenging assignments, those that are so easy they take him only a few minutes to complete. He rarely takes any chances, often repeating the teacher's words on tests or assignments, and rarely participates in class discussion. Although his teacher, Miss Black, finds that he is getting reasonably good grades, she is perturbed by his desire to avoid challenge. How can Miss Black encourage Simon to try challenging work?

3. Mrs. Schumacher doesn't understand Kelly at all. Although Kelly appears to be a bright young girl, she does the bare minimum and doesn't participate in class. When Mrs. Schumacher asked her students what they want to be, Kelly confidently said she wants to be a doctor. Mrs. Schumacher believes that Kelly is just mouthing this aspiration, because if Kelly truly wanted to be a doctor, she would study and work harder since she knows how important grades are. When Mrs. Schumacher expressed her doubt regarding Kelly's aspiration, Kelly shot back that she really does want to be a doctor. Mrs. Schumacher can't reconcile Kelly's aspirations with her work habits. If Mrs. Schumacher asked you about Kelly's behavior, how could you explain it?

4. Mrs. Rodriguez feels some ambivalence about her third-grade class. Although the students are well behaved and their achievement is relatively good, they show little self-direction or individual initiative. They constantly require extensive teacher direction, and after finishing a task, they sit and simply wait for directions. Mrs. Rodriguez would like the students to show more individual responsibility and initiative. What can Mrs. Rodriguez do?

5. Students in Mr. Huggins' class vie for their A's because Mr. Huggins gives only the top 15 percent the best grades. Mr. Huggins has a percentage that receive B's, C's and so on. He feels that this is a way to avoid grade inflation. The students in

the class do not share information with one another or help one another. Yesterday, Mr. Huggins found Terry sabotaging Carl's science experiment by placing the wrong fluid into Carl's test tube. He was shocked by this, and asks you, his colleague why this occurred. Explain this to him and discuss the use of competition in the classroom.

6. Ms. Davison is frustrated with Josette. Although Josette appears to have average intelligence and has good interpersonal skills, she becomes so easily discouraged that she just gives up when she does not understand something and tells Ms. Davison, "I just can't do it." Although Ms. Davison has tried to structure the work so that Josette gets everything correct, it doesn't seem to increase Josette's ability to deal with challenging work. What can Ms. Davison do to help Josette?

7. Mr. Dawkins is an eighth-grade social studies teacher who believes that parents have the responsibility to monitor their children's work. He also believes that parents should watch the news with their children and discuss it with them. Most parents have cooperated with Mr. Dawkins' idea, but Pam says that her mother and father don't have the time to watch the news and besides, they consider the news too violent. Mr. Dawkins knows that Pam's mother and father are home at five o'clock (when the news is on) and that there is only one other child in the family. He believes that Pam's parents just don't want to help out. He would like to motivate her parents to help. What, if anything, can Mr. Dawkins do to enlist Pam's parents' cooperation?

8. In an effort to increase intrinsic motivation, Ms. McNally told her seventh-grade students to do a five-page report on any country of their choosing. She had the students color the flag of the country they had picked and hung the flags on the walls. She was looking forward to some good reports. She was very surprised and disappointed by the quality of the work and by the fact that the students were not very excited about doing the work. She thought the assignment gave the students a great deal of freedom and encouraged their creativity, but now she wonders how to spark interest in her students. How could the teacher have improved the assignment and increased student interest?

9

Are These Statements True or False?

Turn the next page for the correct answers. Each statement is repeated following the paragraph in which the information can be found.

1. Teachers do about two thirds of all the talking done in the classroom.
2. Most of the questions teachers ask involve testing students' ability to apply knowledge to practical situations.
3. Asking students whether they understand the material when a teacher finishes a topic or lesson is a poor way to check student understanding.
4. The choral answer, a questioning technique that requires the class to answer a question in unison, is a reasonably efficient and effective way to measure students' understanding of the material just taught.
5. If a student gives a ridiculous answer to a question, the question should be redirected to a different student.
6. Teachers normally wait too long after asking a question for their students to answer.
7. The average student asks about one substantive question per half hour of class time.
8. Teachers use praise very extensively in their classrooms.
9. Teachers perceive students who choose seats close to them as more competent than students who choose seats farther away from the teacher.
10. Boys receive more criticism from teachers, but girls receive more praise.
11. Most teachers want more communication with the parents of their students.
12. Most teachers say they would welcome parent cooperation in curriculum planning and the establishment of school rules.

Communication and Teaching

Answers to True-False Statements

1. *True*
2. *False* Correct statement: Most of the questions teachers ask are factual in nature.
3. *True*
4. *False* Correct statement: Choral answers are ineffective as a means of checking student understanding.
5. *True*
6. *False* Correct statement: Teachers usually do not wait long enough before calling on students to answer the question.
7. *False* Correct statement: The average student asks about one question per month.
8. *False* Correct statement: Research shows that teachers do not use praise extensively in their classroom.
9. *True*
10. *False* Correct statement: Boys receive both more criticism and more praise than girls.
11. *True*
12. *False* Correct statement: Teachers would like parents to monitor their children's progress but do not want parental cooperation in curriculum planning or the establishment of school rules.

After finishing the lesson, Mr. Hillman asks, "Does anyone have a question?" When his question is met with silence, Mr. Hillman says "good" and goes on to the next topic. He becomes upset when most of his students do poorly on a test covering the material he has just taught.

Ms. Marcus thinks Jeff is an excellent student, and she often chooses him to work on special problems and praises him publicly for his work. She is astounded when Jeff doesn't hand in some easy seatwork and laughs about not doing the assignment.

Mr. Rodriguez frequently has difficulty with Larry. They seem to have a personality clash. Larry sees everything Mr. Rodriguez does as unfair, and Mr. Rodriguez finds that Larry is always challenging him. Their conflict is becoming a problem for both of them.

COMMUNICATION: THE FIRST SKILL OF TEACHING

Communication is such an important skill that it sometimes is taken for granted. Whenever a teacher explains material or gives instructions or questions, praises, or criticizes students, communication skills come into play. Some communication is nonverbal. A teacher's smile or frown can communicate different meanings to students. This chapter examines communication—not only between teachers and students

but also between teachers and parents—by analyzing specific types of communication, with an emphasis on ways to optimize one's communication skills.

What sort of communication takes place in the classroom? One way to analyze the various types of communication that occur in the classroom can be found in Table 9.1 (Flanders, 1970). The typical American classroom has 68 percent teacher talk, 20 percent pupil talk, and 12 percent time spent in silence or confusion. More than two thirds of all the talk, then, is done by the teacher. Although it is fair to ask whether teachers need to talk so much (Delamont, 1976), this chapter concentrates on what messages are communicated and how teachers communicate with students.

True or False Teachers do about two thirds of all the talking done in the classroom.

Communicating Facts, Procedures, and Directions

Teaching requires the communication of information directly to the student. Some communication is content oriented and involves talking about a particular subject. Teachers also give directions and evaluate student work or conduct. Although such communications differ, the are unified in the one requirement for effectiveness—clarity. When teacher communication is clear, students are more likely to understand it (Borich, 1988). Research demonstrates that behaviors that signify clarity are related to positive learning outcomes and student satisfaction (Hines et al., 1985). But what are these behaviors?

Behaviors that lead to clarity include orienting and preparing students for what is to be taught, providing sufficient examples and demonstrations, using a variety of teaching materials, teaching in a logical step-by-step manner. They also include repeating and stressing directions and difficult points, adjusting teaching to the learner and topic, helping students to organize material in a meaningful way, and providing students with sufficient practice and feedback concerning how well they are doing (Cruickshank, 1985). Taken in sum, clarity requires preparation, logical instruction at a reasonable pace with practice and examples, and adequate feedback.

Misunderstandings frequently arise when directions and requirements about an assignment are not clearly communicated to the students. The problems lie in two main areas: (1) the lack of explicit directions and (2) the inability to see problems from a student's point of view. To reduce such problems, the teacher's first requirement is to consider what the students will need to do to complete the assignment (Carter & Doyle, 1987). This entails forming a set of

Table 9.1   Flanders' Interaction Analysis Categories*

These categories will give you some idea of how communication in the classroom may be classified.

		1. *Accepts feeling.* Accepts and clarifies an attitude or the feeling tone of a pupil in a nonthreatening manner. Feelings may be positive or negative. Predicting and recalling feelings are included.
	Response	**2.** *Praises or encourages.* Praises or encourages pupil action or behavior. Jokes that release tension but not at the expense of another individual; nodding head or saying "um hm?" or "go on" are included.
		3. *Accepts or uses ideas of pupils.* Clarifying, building, or developing ideas suggested by a pupil. Teacher extensions of pupil ideas are included, but as the teacher brings more of his own ideas into play, shift to category five.
Teacher Talk		**4.** *Asks questions.* Asking a question about content or procedure based on teacher ideas, with the intent that a pupil will answer.
		5. *Lecturing.* Giving facts or opinions about content or procedures; expressing *his own* ideas, giving *his own* explanation, or citing an authority other than a pupil.
	Initiation	**6.** *Giving directions.* Directions, commands, or orders to which a pupil is expected to comply.
		7. *Criticizing or justifying authority.* Statements intended to change pupil behavior from nonacceptable to acceptable pattern, bawling someone out, stating why the teacher is doing what he is doing, extreme self-reference.
	Response	**8.** *Pupil-talk—response.* Talk by pupils in response to teacher. Teacher initiates the contact or solicits pupil statement or structures the situation. Freedom to express own ideas is limited.
Pupil Talk	**Initiation**	**9.** *Pupil-talk—initiation.* Talk by pupils that they initiate. Expressing own ideas, initiating a new topic, freedom to develop opinions and a line of thought such as asking thoughtful questions, going beyond the existing structure.
Silence		**10.** *Silence or confusion.* Pauses, short periods of silence, and periods of confusion in which communication cannot be understood by the observer.

*There is *no* scale implied by these numbers. Each number is classificatory; it designates a particular kind of communication event. To write these numbers down during observation is to enumerate, not to judge a position on a scale.

From Flanders' Interaction Analysis Categories, *Analyzing Teacher Behavior.* Addison-Wesley, 1970, p. 34.

Clarity of communication is important in communicating material to students or in giving directions for an assignment.

explicit instructions and telling the students what is to be done and what is required to succeed at the assignment.

Many student questions and concerns arise from the lack of specific instructions for performing an assignment. You probably can remember receiving an assignment that was not explained correctly or in enough detail. I find that an effective way for me to assign work is to first ask myself what I want, in what form do I want it submitted, what date do I want it submitted, and will there be any penalty for late submission. I then ask myself what else a student might want to know. Many students ask such questions as whether the assignment needs to be typed, what heading the teacher wants, and how long it should be.

Some teachers are rather irritated when faced with such questions, since they may be more interested in explaining the content of the assignment than the form. However, this is a failure to view the assignment from the students' perspective and to fully understand the students' experience. Many students have had teachers who are more concerned about form than content. Losing points for content is one thing, but losing them because you did not put a heading on your paper, placed footnotes in the wrong place, or wrote two and a half instead of three pages is intolerable to many students.

Another means of improving clarity when giving assignments is to demonstrate just how the work

is to be accomplished. The more complex the directions, the more necessary it is to give examples and demonstrations of how to go about doing the assignment.

A third area of improving clarity involves monitoring students' work by asking students questions whose answers demonstrate student understanding as well as observing students working at their desks. Last, student accountability needs to be explicitly explained. If students are told that they will be graded on the accuracy of their problem solving and are expected to check their division examples, holding them accountable for such work is reasonable. If they are not, having points deducted for not checking their work is likely to cause teacher-student problems.

 CONNECTIONS

The Teacher and Clarity

Clarity is a necessary prerequisite for effective classroom communication. Table 9.2 lists some of the indicators of good and poor clarity and gives some solutions to clarity problems. The following suggestions can be useful for improving clarity.

1. **Try to see what you are communicating from your students' point of view.** Anticipate their problems and questions.

Table 9.2 Indicators for Clarity

This table shows the ways in which a teacher's clarity and lack of clarity are demonstrated in the classroom and provides useful suggestions for improving clarity.

Being Clear (An effective teacher . . .)	Poor Clarity (An ineffective teacher . . .)	Solutions
1. Informs learners of the lesson objective (e.g., describes what behaviors will be tested or required on future assignments as a result of the lesson).	Fails to link lesson content to how and at what level of complexity the content will be used.	Prepare a behavioral objective for the lesson at the desired level of complexity (e.g., knowledge, comprehension). Indicate to the learners at the start of the lesson in what ways the behavior will be used in the future.
2. Provides learners with an advance organizer (e.g., places lesson in perspective of past and/or future lessons).	Starts presenting content without first introducing the subject with respect to some broader context.	Consult or prepare a unit plan to determine what task-relevant prior learning is required for this lesson and what task-relevant prior learning this lesson represents for future lessons. Begin the lesson by informing the learner that the content to be taught is part of this larger context.
3. Checks for task-relevant prior learning at beginning of the lesson (e.g., determines level of understanding of prerequisite facts or concepts and reteaches, if necessary).	Moves to new content without checking for the facts, concepts, or skills needed to acquire the new learning.	Ask questions of students at the beginning of a lesson or check assignments regularly to determine if task-relevant prior knowledge has been acquired.
4. Gives directives slowly and distinctly (e.g., repeats directives when needed or divides them into smaller pieces).	Presents too much clerical, managerial, or technical information at once, too quickly.	Organize procedures for lengthy assignments in step-by-step order and give as handout as well as orally.
5. Knows ability levels and teaches at or slightly above learners' current level of functioning (e.g., knows learners' attention spans).	Fails to know that instruction is under or over heads of students. Seems not to know when most learners have "tuned out."	Determine ability level from standardized tests, previous assignments, and interests and retarget instruction accordingly.
6. Uses examples, illustrations, and demonstrations to explain and clarify (e.g., uses visuals to help interpret and reinforce main points).	Restricts presentation to routine verbal reproduction of text or workbook.	Restate main points in at least one modality other than the one in which they were initially taught (e.g., visual v. auditory).
7. Provides review or summary at end of each lesson.	Ends lesson abruptly without "repackaging" key points.	Use key abstractions, repetition, or symbols to help students efficiently store and later recall content.

From *Effective Teaching Methods* by Gary D. Borich. Copyright © 1988 by Merrill Publishing Company, Columbus, Ohio. Reprinted by permission of Merrill Publishing Company.

2. **Give your directions and information at a reasonable pace.** Beware of covering assignments too fast.

3. **Orient students.** Give them an introduction to what they are to do or learn.

4. **Use examples, illustrations, and demonstrations when appropriate.** These are often useful in clarifying a point.

5. **Write the main points or directions for an assignment on the blackboard or present them in**

6. **Monitor student understanding.** Question students to be certain they understand the work or the directions. If the work is to be done in class, you can see if the students understand it as you walk around the classroom. If it is a long assignment that entails doing research or reading a book, check with students periodically about their progress.

THE ART AND SCIENCE OF QUESTIONING

"To know how to question is to know how to teach" (Dillon, 1982). Questioning has always been a major part of teaching, but in the past few decades, interest in the art and science of questioning has increased. A look at the purposes behind questioning explains this increased interest.

Teachers ask questions for a variety of reasons. Some questions elicit information from students that demonstrates the students' level of understanding.

Others focus attention on the important areas of a lesson. Still others aim at encouraging students to become involved or interested in the lesson. Finally, some questions aim at encouraging students to use the more advanced thinking skills of analysis, synthesis, and evaluation.

Questioning is a popular teaching technique. In elementary school social studies and science classes, teachers ask an average of about two questions per minute (Susskind, 1969). About 60 percent of these questions involve recalling information, 20 percent focus on higher level thinking skills, and the remaining questions are organizational or procedural (Gall, 1984).

True or False Most of the questions teachers ask involve testing students' ability to apply knowledge to practical situations.

Questioning is a process involving the question itself, a response, and a reaction to the response. Questioning in the classroom differs greatly from questioning at home, and that is one reason classroom questioning is a unique skill (Morine-Dershimer & Beyerbach, 1987). When people ask questions at home, they usually want information they do not already have. A

Questioning is a popular teaching method. Teachers ask on the average of about two questions per minute.

question such as "Where are the flower seeds?" or even a more personal question such as "Did you and Steve have a fight"? shows a desire to obtain new information. Teachers normally know the answers to their own questions. At home we acknowledge the answer, while at school the teacher's reaction communicates an evaluation of the student's response. A positive evaluation terminates the three-part question cycle, whereas a negative evaluation extends it as teachers repeat or simplify the question.

Questions That Check Student Understanding

When teachers finish a topic, they too often simply ask, "Are there any questions?" or they merely say, "Okay?" Students don't respond to such questions, and their resulting silence may be taken by the teacher as meaning that the students understand the material. This is a false assumption. First, the material on meta-memory and metacognition discussed in Chapters 3 and 4 shows that children may think they understand something when in fact they do not (Kaplan, 1986). Second, many students who do not understand are reluctant to ask questions because they do not want to be embarrassed in front of their peers. Third, these questions are often asked in haste and in passing, leading students to believe that their questions are not really welcome. Last, students who are truly lost may not be able to formulate their own questions. When a teacher asks "Does anyone have a question?" it carries the implication that if the student does, he or she wasn't listening or isn't very bright (Hunter, 1982).

True or False   Asking students whether they understand the material when a teacher finishes a topic or lesson is a poor way to check student understanding.

There are many effective ways to use questioning to check students' understanding. One way is to use signaled answers, that is, to pose a question or a statement and have every student signal the answer. Sometimes these answers can be signaled using some nonverbal sign, such as holding up a specific number of fingers. Madeline Hunter (1982) suggests that students be asked to give a thumbs up if the statement made is true, thumbs down if false, or thumbs to the side if the students are not certain. The answers to multiple-choice questions can be signed by placing the number of fingers under the chin to indicate the number of the correct answer. This is a quick way to

check student knowledge, although teachers must be on the lookout for students who are copying other students. This problem can be countered somewhat by asking the students to close their eyes before signaling their answers. These techniques appear more useful in the younger grades, but Hunter's experience is that if the purpose is explained, even older children will gladly participate. One simple device with older children is to explain that it is better to find misunderstandings now than later on a test.

Another way of checking students' understanding involves posing a brief question and asking students to write a brief response. You can then circulate among the students and help those who are having difficulty. Still another way is to sample individual responses by posing a question and calling on individual students. Based upon their responses, you can infer the class's level of understanding.

Some teachers use choral responses as a way of checking students' understanding. This technique involves asking a question such as, Is this triangle isosceles or equilateral? Teachers can gauge the class's knowledge not through the correctness of the response (it is almost always correct) but by the strength of the class's response. However, choral responses have some rather obvious problems. Some students simply do not answer, and it is difficult to determine which children are not answering and why. Second, some of the students who do respond may be copying others. Third, choral answers refer to a choice or a simple question, and students may be chanting without understanding (Fairbairn, 1987). Although choral answers may give the teacher some idea of the class's knowledge of a subject, they are not recommended for the purpose of checking understanding.

True or False   The choral answer, a questioning technique that requires the class to answer a question in unison, is a reasonably efficient and effective way to measure students' understanding of the material just taught.

In summary, there are a number of ways to check for student understanding using questioning.

1. Before presenting the lesson, prepare a large number of oral questions that can be used at strategic times throughout the lesson to monitor understanding.
2. Call on students whose hands aren't raised in addition to those who volunteer, since those who volunteer normally know the answers and may not be representative of the class.

3. Have all students write the answers while the teacher circulates.

4. Require all students to write the answers and check a representative group of student answers.

5. Some attempts at monitoring student understanding can be cooperative. At the end of a lecture/discussion (especially with older students), write the main points or the questions that have been answered by the lesson on the blackboard and have the students meet in small groups and summarize the main points to one another (Rosenshine & Stevens, 1986).

6. Ask students to summarize the rule or process or define a term in their own words. I believe this to be crucial. A question such as What is osmosis? checks a student's understanding. But what if a student merely uses the words memorized from a written definition in the text? Requiring that a student answer a question in his or her own words is superior, since it checks a student's understanding and not simply the pupil's memory. Some students are proficient at memorizing a definition or a statement. If you ask for the exact words on a test, such students do well. However, if the test question requires a more thorough understanding, perhaps an application, these students are often lost. Teachers should be alert to students who demonstrate this problem and should not equate memorization with understanding.

Questions That Stimulate Interest and Thinking

Questions can also be used to stimulate student interest and thinking. To do so, questions must be phrased in such a way that answers are not automatic. For instance, Silberman and colleagues (1976) suggest that teachers prepare what they call thought questions before the lesson. If the topic is Shakespeare, the following questions are possibilities:

How could Shakespeare write so many plays?

Why did Shakespeare use such fancy language?

How did Shakespeare know what Julius Caesar and Brutus said to each other?

If Shakespeare were alive today, do you think he would be famous, and why?

Such questions can be used in almost any discipline. I can remember one of my social studies teachers asking us to consider what would have happened if the South had won the Civil War? It sparked an interesting discussion and a great deal of thought.

But how does a teacher form such questions? One way is to use Benjamin Bloom's taxonomy of educational objectives for the cognitive domain as a start which will be discussed in more detail in Chapter 11. When a teacher asks a student to name the sixteen exports of Brazil, the student's knowledge is being tested. If comprehension is to be measured, a teacher might ask a student to define some term in his or her own words or to give examples of something specific.

Going to a higher level, we arrive at application of information. At this level, a teacher might ask the students to generalize, estimate, or in some way apply the material to a particular situation. Such questions as How would you use your knowledge of area to find out how much carpeting is needed to cover a room? What are the metaphors in the story?, are examples of questions seeking application. This is the beginning of higher level thinking.

When teachers speak of higher level reasoning, however, they usually are talking about analysis, synthesis, and evaluation. Analysis involves the ability to organize and reorganize information. One must be able to understand the relationship among the parts. Asking a student to list the arguments that support the position that a person should be required to have a yearly medical examination is one example. Asking In what ways is Native American culture unique? is another example of such questions. To answer them, information must be taken apart and reorganized.

Questions that involve synthesis require invention or creation of something new. Synthesis often involves divergent thinking (refer to Chapter 4). Asking students to design their own experiment, write a poem, or create something are examples of synthesis. Such assignments can be put into question form: How would you design an experiment to demonstrate whether body build was influenced by genetic endowment? How could you solve your neighborhood's pollution problem?

The last level—evaluation—involves making judgments when there is no single correct answer. If students are asked to evaluate Edgar Allan Poe's poetry or to critically discuss Martin Luther King, Jr.'s greatest contributions, evaluation is required. Note that the teacher is not just asking an opinion, since the students are being asked to base their views on reason, logic, and knowledge.

It is appropriate at this point to ask two separate questions. First, do students benefit from being asked questions? Second, is there any special benefit to asking higher level questions? There is evidence that teacher questioning in general leads to better student achievement (Gall, 1970). However, the research on the effects of various types of questioning is mixed and controversial (Dillon, 1982). Some studies link the use of higher questioning techniques with improvements in academic achievement, while others do not. After reviewing the literature, Philip Winne (1979) found no significant difference when teachers used higher or lower level questioning. In a detailed study, Meredith Gall (1970) also did not find the benefit to higher level questions. Using a different procedure, however, Doris Redfield and Elaine Rousseau (1981) found that higher order questions did indeed lead to better academic achievement. They argue that an eighth-grade social studies student who would normally score at the fiftieth percentile on an achievement test with a teacher who asks mostly lower order questions would score at about the seventy-seventh percentile if taught by a teacher who used predominantly higher level questions. One obvious conclusion is that more research is needed on this question. Another possible conclusion is that although higher level cognitive questions are important, questions that elicit facts are also valuable (Brophy, 1986).

Questions That Increase Student Participation

Questions can be an effective device to get students involved. However, not all questions accomplish this. Factual questions such as Who discovered America? and At what temperature does water boil? require one-word answers and do not really involve the students. In addition, such questions are usually answered by the same children all the time (Morine-Dershimer & Beyerbach, 1987). Calling on students randomly to check their understanding is a possible way of increasing participation, but this method has its limitations. Calling on students randomly can yield an embarrassed silence or a one-word answer and may not encourage these students to participate on their own later in the lesson. Factual questions may show that some students possess this knowledge, but if the purpose is to involve students, factual questions will not accomplish this. True class participation occurs when many students join in and even answer each other's questions or react to each other's statements. When students participate, time seems to fly by for both students and teachers, and student participation is a fair measure of student interest and involvement.

What type of questioning involves students? Open-ended questions are more likely to encourage students to participate. Such questions have no correct

Questioning can be an effective teaching device for getting students involved in the lesson.

or incorrect responses and require more than a one- or two-word answer. For example, What might happen if people's life expectancy increased to 150 years? or How would society be different if the telephone had never been invented? The only requirement for a student to answer this type of question correctly is that the student's answer relate directly to the question (Montague, 1987). Another method that I have found successful at the junior high level and beyond is to place a student into a particular situation and ask the pupil to consider a way out of a dilemma or ask the student what he or she would do in a particular case. For example, "You are asked to write a letter giving a recommendation to a neighbor you don't particularly like. How would you handle the situation?" or "You're trying to get public support for your position against mass incineration of garbage. You want recycling to be considered. What would you do?" This technique can be used with the younger grades if the situations are somewhat simple. If you want a student who never volunteers and who may not be very proficient to participate, try to ask a question that involves an opinion that does not require much information. It is also possible, once you get the answer to the question, to delve more deeply into why the student would do something. It is easy to give positive reinforcement in such circumstances, since the answers are neither right nor wrong.

What Constitutes a Poor Question?

Different types of questions, then, accomplish different tasks. But not all questions are useful and productive. For example, a mathematics teacher giving a lesson on angles points to the angles of a triangle and says, "What about these angles?" One student pipes up, "I don't like them." This is an example of an elliptic or ambiguous question, one of the types of questions Donald Fairbairn (1987) argues are poorly designed. This type of question does not give students enough information to know what you are talking about (Fairbairn, 1987). It is better to ask, "How are these two angles related?"

Another mistake is asking overlaid or multiple questions (Posamentier & Stepelman, 1981). This type of question contains more than one question, such as Who fought the Civil War, and which state was most fought over? This can confuse students and does not focus their attention.

Questions are also poorly designed that are actually statements ending in a question mark which Fairbairn calls whiplash questions. For example, The slope of this line is what? (Fairbairn, 1987). The beginning of this sentence forms a statement while the end is a question.

Don't you agree? and This is okay, right? are leading questions. Students are not going to disagree with you, and such questions are not really meant to be questions.

Unfortunately, these questions are rather commonly used in the classroom. They add nothing and can inhibit students from answering questions and participating in the lesson. To be useful, questions need to be clear and precise and formulated according to the purpose the teacher has in mind.

Responding to Answers

You are teaching a lesson on nouns and verbs. Lester, a fourth grader who rarely raises his hand, does so. You call on him, and he tells you that "goes" is a noun. What do you do now?

Incorrect or incomplete answers are a part of the questioning process, and dealing with them can be tricky. After all, it took some courage for Lester to raise his hand, and now the ball is back in your court. You face a dilemma. You cannot let his incorrect response pass, and at the same time you want to reinforce him for participating. If you say "That's incorrect," Lester may become embarrassed, especially if you show impatience.

Hunter (1982) suggests that when a student gives an incorrect answer, there are two questions the student does not know the answer to. The first is the question you asked, while the second is the question to which the student's answer belongs. Hunter suggests turning the situation into a learning experience.

A reasonable response to Lester's mistake would be supplying the question or statement to which Lester's answer belongs, for example, telling Lester that he would be correct if we were looking for examples of verbs. You could also give Lester an assist or a prompt that provides additional information, or you could ask him probing questions. You could tell Lester that a noun is a person, place, or thing; thus, "rabbit" is a noun. Asking the student again will often give you the correct answer. You might also ask another simpler question that would direct Lester's attention to the correct answer (Berliner, 1987). If, after a second question, the student still doesn't get the correct answer, you should redirect the question to another student. You could then say, "It's a good try; let's see if we can get some help from Tomas." Students are accountable for learning, and a gentle statement such as "Let's go over that one again so you'll remember it" or "I'll check with you tomorrow to be sure you remember this" is reasonable. If a student gives a completely ridiculous answer, the best strategy is to redirect the question to another student without reacting to the ludicrous response.

True or False   If a student gives a ridiculous answer to a question, the question should be redirected to a different student.

Wait Time

Teachers don't wait long enough after asking a question. This is the unanimous finding of a number of studies (Rowe, 1974, 1978, 1986). Nathan Swift and Thomas Gooding (1983) found that if elementary schoolteachers increased their wait time from the usual average of about one second to at least three to five seconds, a number of "good things" occurred. For example, the students increased the length of their responses, student-student exchanges increased, failures to respond decreased, the number of questions asked by students increased, the number of students participating in discussions increased, the students offered more alternative answers, and achievement on written measures improved. In secondary schools, the evidence is similar. Increasing wait time increases student responsiveness, and students perceive the lesson as less difficult, although they also may view the lessons as slower moving (Anderson & Fowler, 1978).

True or False   Teachers normally wait too long after asking a question for their students to answer.

In another study, Kenneth Tobin and William Capie (1982) found that increasing the wait time along with the use of clear high-level cognitive questions enhanced attention and achievement in middle school science courses. It isn't hard to wait, either; the teacher simply counts to three before choosing a student (Morine-Dershimer & Beyerbach, 1987). This technique has benefits for the teacher as well. Teachers who wait longer show greater continuity in their lessons (Rowe, 1986). Unfortunately, not all students

receive the advantage of longer wait time. Teachers often give students who are more able a greater amount of time to answer (Good, 1983). Each student, no matter what his or her academic level, should be given the benefit of longer wait times.

Student Questions

Earlier we noted that teachers ask an average of about two questions per minute. How often do students ask questions? According to a study by Susskind (1969), the entire class asks about one question per hour, which is about one question per pupil per month. Teachers underestimated the number of questions they asked by almost 300 percent and felt that students asked only about one-sixth the number of questions that were considered optimal.

True or False   The average student asks about one substantive question per half hour of class time.

Why don't students ask questions? It may well be the traditional social situation of the classroom itself that does not encourage questioning (Dillon, 1982). In the standard classroom situation, the teacher asks the questions and the students answer them. The teacher reserves the right to speak after the student answers. In some cultures, it may be inappropriate to ask questions directly of teachers. Students are also afraid of feeling dumb or looking stupid, and this fear dissuades them from asking questions. Students may also find it difficult to put their questions into words. Students are put off by teachers who ask for questions but may not really want them or by teachers who react verbally or nonverbally with scorn or impatience when students do ask questions. A teacher may answer the student's question but demonstrate irritation or impatience. The teacher may frown or say, "Weren't you paying attention?" (van der Meij, 1988). Such reactions dissuade students from asking questions. Last, some students have learned to be passive in class and not to answer or ask questions. In one study of students from kindergarten through the senior year of high school, Thomas Good and his colleagues (1987) found that requests for explanations were rare at all grade levels, while procedural questions were relatively frequent at all levels. Low-achieving students, however, asked fewer questions over time, perhaps because these students are called on less frequently, are given less time to respond, are less likely to be

Studies show that students do not ask many questions in class.

praised, and are criticized for their failures. They learn through painful experience that it is safer to be passive.

How can teachers increase the number of student questions? First, the teacher must create an atmosphere that promotes questions. The better your relationship with the class and the more students who think your desire for questions is genuine, the more likely the students are to ask questions. Most teachers do ask for questions from students and are disturbed when none are asked. Another way to bring forth questions is to reinforce student questioning, perhaps by saying, "That's really a good question" or even offering extra points for a good question.

Some children require training in asking questions, especially those who are low achievers or perhaps have some learning disability. Anne Bengfort (1987) suggests that such students need to be taught through roleplaying and practice of asking questions. For young children, the process might be (1) raise your hand, (2) say Excuse me, Ms._____," (3) say "I can't _____," (4) say "Can you please help me?" and (5) after the teacher answers, say "Thank you, Ms. _____."

However, what the teacher does with these questions is just as important as prompting the student to ask them. If a student asks a question, the teacher's response will be watched by the other students. If the teacher is impatient, makes a joke of the question, or ridicules it, he or she can be reasonably certain it will be the last question the student will ask for a while. Also, if the teacher penalizes the student asking the question by saying, "Why don't you look it up?", the teacher is merely giving the student extra work. However, if the teacher responds by offering the student extra credit or an excuse from homework if the student researches the question in the school library, he or she may encourage questioning.

One additional technique that works is to ask students to prepare questions on a topic after reading the material. For example, if students are assigned to read their text's chapter on the War of 1812, asking the students to write questions on this topic may be one way to get them to think in a questioning mode. These questions can be used the next day in class.

Questioning: What It Means for the Teacher

It is an axiom that teaching involves questioning students. However, questions can be used for many purposes, including focusing students' attention, encouraging student participation, checking understanding, and encouraging thinking. As we've seen, teachers should avoid asking multiple, vague, or leading questions and should use straight, factual questions, yes-no questions, and questions that involve choral responses with care. Even questions that are educationally sound may not accomplish their purposes if teachers dominate the interaction too much (Dillon, 1984).

Since questions are an integral part of the lesson, preparing questions is part of preparing the lesson (McCullough & Findley, 1983). This is especially important for teachers who wish to tap higher order cognitive skills or increase student participation in class. In addition, teachers need to vary their questions so that they cover various levels of Bloom's taxonomy. Asking only factual questions will not bring about much thinking or participation. Yet asking factual questions does serve the important purpose of determining the students' factual base.

The literature on wait time leads to some practical conclusions. Teachers do not wait sufficient time to allow students to think about their answers. This is especially true of questions that tap higher order cognitive skills, and counting to three after asking a question seems to help. Last, teachers ask more questions than they think they do, and students ask very few questions in class. Teachers can encourage student questioning through a number of methods and should be aware of their reactions to student questions.

FEEDBACK FROM TEACHERS

Whether students are asking questions, answering them, or making a comment, teachers must respond to student communication. There are many ways teachers can respond. Two ways are through praise and criticism, both of which can be communicated to students in writing, orally, or through gestures or facial expressions.

Praise

The conventional wisdom on the use of praise does not match the facts. Conventional wisdom dictates that praise is used extensively by teachers, that it is an effective reinforcer and motivator in the classroom, that it leads to better work and behavior, and that stu-

dents always respond positively to praise. Unfortunately, each of these assertions is either untrue or, at least, a half-truth.

Teachers do not use praise very much. In one study, first-grade teachers praised only about 11 percent of their students' correct answers during reading group work and gave praise only 18 percent of the times when students read aloud (Anderson et al., 1979). Carolyn Evertson and colleagues (1980) observed that junior high school teachers praised only about 10 percent of the correct responses. Praise for good conduct was rare in first grade and almost non-existent in junior high school. Jere Brophy (1981) suggests that if a classroom teacher praises once every five minutes, the rate of praise for an individual student would be something in the neighborhood of once every two hours.

Praise is most effective when it is contingent on performance and the student is told specifically what he or she is being praised for doing.

The low rate of praise would not be troublesome if it were directed at lower achieving students to encourage them. However, as Brophy (1981) notes, this is not the case, and research is split on whom teachers praise. While some studies show that teachers praise students with whom they are concerned—usually lower achieving students—others show no difference between children of differing ability groups, and still others show the opposite patterns—that higher achieving students are praised more.

Is there a relationship between the use of praise and higher academic achievement? The studies here again are mixed. Some studies show that praise in early elementary school, especially for students from lower socioeconomic backgrounds and for low-achieving students, does correlate slightly with academic achievement as measured in grades (Brophy, 1981; Cantrell et al., 1977). However, apart from these rather weak findings, little relationship is found.

Why does praise seem to be so ineffective? One reason is that it is often poorly used. Praise contains two components: what the teacher says and what the student says to him or herself (Ginott, 1972). For instance, Haim Ginott offers the case of a student named Alice who was shown an apple and asked what family it belonged to? Alice didn't know the answer, so the question was redirected to Carol, who replied correctly. The teacher praised Carol by saying "good girl, good girl." The teacher was unaware of how Alice felt. If Carol was good for answering the question, what does that make Alice? Knowing a fact doesn't make someone good or bad. In another case, Ginott tells us about a young student named Ben who threw a dart at a target and hit the bull's eye. His gym teacher said, "You're great. You have a perfect eye. You are a marksman." The teacher was surprised when Ben walked away. Ben was thinking to himself, "This teacher now expects my every dart to hit the bull's eye. The bull's eye happened by chance, and if I try once more I may not even hit the target. I'd better quit."

These examples show that praise is not as easy to deliver effectively as many people think. Praise that does not evaluate character or personality but rather is directed at specific acts, describing a child's efforts and accomplishments and our feelings about these acts, is effective. Ginott suggests that the cardinal rule

of praising is "describe without evaluating: report—don't judge" (1972, p. 298). Using these ideas, what might the teachers in the examples have said? In the first example, the teacher could simply have supplied additional information to Alice or repeated Carol's reply with no evaluation of Carol as a person. In the second case, the teacher only had to say, "I see the dart hit the bull's eye," so that Ben might not have inferred that the teacher's expectations were so high. Guidelines for effective and ineffective praise are listed in Table 9.3.

For praise to serve as a reinforcer, it must be contingent on the performance of some behavior, be specific, and be credible (O'Leary & O'Leary, 1977; Madsen et al., 1968). However, the evidence reviewed by Brophy (1981) shows that teacher praise often is not contingent on a behavior, lacks specificity, and sometimes lacks credibility.

If praise does not function as a reinforcer, what does it do for students? Praise communicates to the other students that the pupil who answered the question or performed the behavior did so correctly. In other words, it serves an informational purpose (Brophy, 1981).

Another reason that praise may be ineffective is that it is often targeted at the wrong students. As noted earlier, it is more effective with lower ability students, with students who possess an external locus of control, and with young students who are eager to please the teacher (Wittrock, 1986). It can be counterproductive when a student is intrinsically motivated, that is, doing something for personal enjoyment (explored in detail in Chapter 8). If praise is given to high-achieving students for very easy successes, it is often seen as undeserved by the very students the praise is intended to help.

What Does the Research on Praise Mean to the Teacher?

Unfortunately, after reading this sobering account of praise, it is easy but incorrect to conclude that praise is not a useful technique in the teacher's arsenal. What the literature shows is that praise can be effective, but only if used correctly and judiciously (refer to Table 9.3). Praise is best when it is contingent on performance and the student is told specifically what he or she is being praised for. Praise should be given for achievement and prosocial behavior and for follow-

Table 9.3   Guidelines for Effective and Ineffective Praise

Effective Praise	Ineffective Praise
1. Is delivered contingently.	**1.** Is delivered randomly or unsystematically.
2. Specifies the particulars of the accomplishment.	**2.** Is restricted to global positive reactions.
3. Shows spontaneity, variety, and other signs of credibility; suggests clear attention to the student's accomplishment.	**3.** Shows a bland uniformity, which suggests a conditioned response made with minimal attention.
4. Rewards attainment of specified performance criteria (which can include effort criteria, however).	**4.** Rewards mere participation, without consideration of performance processes or outcomes.
5. Provides information to students about their competence or the value of their accomplishments.	**5.** Provides no information at all or gives students information about their status.
6. Orients students towards better appreciation of their own task-related behavior and thinking about problem solving.	**6.** Orients students toward comparing themselves with others and thinking about competing.
7. Uses students' own prior accomplishments as the context for describing present accomplishments.	**7.** Uses the accomplishments of peers as the context for describing students' present accomplishments.
8. Is given in recognition of noteworthy effort or success at difficult (for *this* student) tasks.	**8.** Is given without regard to the effort expended or the meaning of the accomplishment (for *this* student).
9. Attributes success to effort and ability, implying that similar successes can be expected in the future.	**9.** Attributes success to ability alone or to external factors such as luck or easy task.
10. Fosters endogenous attributions (students believe that they expend effort on the task because they enjoy the task and/or want to develop task-relevant skills).	**10.** Fosters exogenous attributions (students believe that they expend effort on the task for external reasons—to please the teacher, win a competition or reward, etc.).
11. Focuses students' attention on their own task-relevant behavior.	**11.** Focuses students' attention on the teacher as an external authority figure who is manipulating them.
12. Fosters appreciation of and desirable attributions about task relevant behavior after the process is completed.	**12.** Intrudes into the ongoing process, distracting attention from task relevant behavior.

From "Teacher Praise: A Functional Analysis" by J. Brophy. *Review of Educational Research, 51,* 5–32. Copyright © 1981 by the American Education Research Association. Reprinted by permission of the publisher.

ing group rules. It is best delivered when using a variety of expressions and when nonverbal messages such as smiling occur along with the verbal expression of praise (Madsen et al., 1968). Such statements as "Freddie, that's the right answer," "Theresa, you're working very well," and "Bill, thank you very much for helping José wash the blackboard" meet these criteria (O'Leary & O'Leary, 1977). Above all, statements of praise should not evaluate a student's character or set up unreasonable expectations about a student's ability.

Criticism

The opposite of praise is criticism, and like praise, it is used rather infrequently in the classroom (Brophy, 1981). If you take into account praise and criticism for conduct along with work, criticism is used a bit more frequently than praise (Heller & White, 1975). There tends to be more criticism in low-ability classes than in high-ability classes, even when taught by the same teacher (Heller & White, 1975), probably because there are so many more instances of poor work and behavior in these classes. More effective teachers generally criticize less, probably because they structure the classroom to prevent discipline problems (Kounin et al., 1970). Even when looking only at schoolwork, we find that teachers praise high-achieving students more and give them less criticism when incorrect or unable to respond (Brophy & Good, 1974).

Criticism itself need not be injurious to the pupil's self-concept. In fact, the rules for reasonable criticism are similar to those for praise. The criticism should be specific, be contingent upon some activity, describe the problem, and be sincere. However, criticism is more likely to sting the child than is praise given ineffectively, since by its very nature, it is an unpleasant type of communication.

People have a tendency to criticize the child rather than the child's action, especially when they're angry (Ginott, 1969). If a child's grammar on a test is poor, a criticism of the child's grammar would be in order, but an over-general statement such as "You don't seem to be able to write at all" is not. When criticizing behavior, it is best to avoid labeling the child. "You're the worst behaved kid in the class" is not likely to help much, but telling the child that his behavior of throwing spitballs is unacceptable and will be followed by some consequence (see Chapter 10) is reasonable.

Keeping the criticism light is a skill, especially when criticizing work in which the student has put in a great deal of effort. Saying something that demonstrates your appreciation for the student's efforts, followed by some corrective statement directed at the behavior, is one way to show students you recognize their work. It is also important for a teacher to avoid communicating anger, frustration, or sarcasm by his or her tone of voice or facial expression (Petti, 1987). In addition, after noticing the problem targeted for criticism, the teacher should be prepared to offer some solid way of rectifying the problem. Just telling a student that his or her grammar requires more work does not tell the student what to do about it. However, showing the student some exercises demonstrates that the teacher's interest is in improving the student's work and not just in criticizing the student. Criticism is also more effective if it is combined with praise for the correct behavior or good work and if the teacher's relationship with the student is good. Furthermore, praise should follow improvements in the criticized areas. Last, the teacher should try to place him or herself in the child's shoes when criticizing a student, especially when doing so in public. Students do not like to lose face, and teachers should be sensitive to a student's feelings.

Nonverbal Behavior

What would happen if a teacher were to praise a child while frowning or criticize a student for throwing paper clips around the classroom while smiling? After receiving relatively little attention, interest in the role of nonverbal behavior in teaching is growing for two reasons (Casonova, 1987). First, the research on nonverbal behavior outside of education shows how important such behavior is to communication. Although people have differences of opinion regarding the relative contribution of verbal and nonverbal messages to total communication, the importance of the nonverbal domain is beyond question (Smith, 1979). Second, there is now some evidence showing that nonverbal communication in the classroom can affect teacher-student relationships, participation in class discussions, and classroom behavior.

Gestures, facial expressions, tone of voice, and the use of space to communicate are all aspects of nonverbal communication. Almost everyone who writes about the subject suggests that it is important for teachers to become aware of what they are nonverbally communicating and to not give out dual messages—one verbal and one nonverbal. A person who is shouting "I'm not angry!" is sending two messages (Bolton, 1979). The person is saying one thing verbally and another nonverbally. Most of the time, we believe the nonverbal message over the verbal one, because we all know that it is easier to control the words we say than the nonverbal aspects of our speech (Gazda et al., 1977). Awareness of our gestures, facial expressions, tone of voice, and use of space is the key in eliminating the possibility of giving off dual messages. There is some evidence that teachers—at least in the elementary schools in both low- and middle-class areas—are unaware of their nonverbal influence on young students (Davis, 1974).

Teachers often use space to show their feelings and communicate messages to students, although they may not be aware that they're doing so. In one study, Douglas Brooks and Barry Wilson (1978) found that when students answered questions, teachers stood farther away from students who were labeled rejected by their teachers than they did from students labeled accepted, concerned, or indifferent. Raymond Adams and Bruce Biddle (1970) found that pupils were more likely to participate in class if they were seated in the first three seats of the center rows. Most, although not all, studies have found some bias in student participation (Smith, 1979). Studies have also looked into how students perceive desk arrangement. Zick Rubin (1973) found that students of higher ability prefer a horseshoe seating arrangement in which everyone feels free to participate. Participation improved in the horseshoe arrangement, which is easiest to use in small classes (Hurt et al., 1978). Studies have also found that in elementary school, students preferred closeness over farness from the teacher (Sherman, 1973). Closeness seems to indicate friendliness, warmth, approval, and liking, at least in elementary school (Woolfolk & Brooks, 1982).

Teachers use many gestures and facial expressions to communicate messages to students. Smiles can be reinforcers; frowns communicate a different message. Teachers who use gestures are often perceived as more friendly and more enthusiastic. These two characteristics are related to student liking for the teacher and excitement toward the class (Smith, 1979). Students see teachers who smile often as being warmer than teachers who do not smile much (Bayes, 1970). A teacher who slouches or twitches shows students that he or she is not composed (Hurt et al., 1978). Voice quality rather than simply presenting subject content is also important, especially for younger children who may not be as aware of the subtle nonverbal messages but who have considerable experience in finding meaning in adult speech through interpretation of voice tone. A teacher communicates confidence and authority through voice tone, and whether or not the teacher really possesses these traits, they are an important aid to classroom management.

The teacher is also affected by nonverbal messages sent by students (Brooks & Woolfolk, 1987). Teachers view pupils who choose to sit in the front of the class—and therefore closer to them—as more attentive and responsive than those who sit in the rear (Woolfolk & Brooks, 1987; Schwebel & Cherlin, 1972). In addition, student nonverbal behaviors such as good posture, eye contact, and smiling lead to positive teacher evaluations of a student's competence and attitude (Brooks & Woolfolk, 1987). Thus, at the same time, the teacher is giving off nonverbal messages that affect students, students are giving off their own nonverbal messages that affect their teachers.

True or False Teachers perceive students who choose seats close to them as more competent than students who choose seats farther away from the teacher.

Nonverbal Behavior and Culture

Perhaps the most controversial and potentially important aspects of nonverbal communication are the possibility that a teacher will misread the nonverbal messages of minority students or treat students differently because of racial or ethnic characteristics. In the first case, evidence shows that students belonging to different cultural groups do exhibit different nonverbal behaviors that can be misunderstood by the teacher. For instance, Edward Hall and Mildred Hall (1987) suggest that blacks tend to communicate more directly with less fear of hurting other people's feelings, while whites tend to be more indirect. They therefore suggest that blacks might give the impression of being more aggressive or rude, while whites appear to blacks as seeking to avoid issues. Blacks often do not look directly at authority figures when listening, while whites normally do. This nonlooking does not signal inattention, although it is frequently seen as such (Hall, 1969). Even when black children look at their white teachers, they make eye contact far less often than when white teachers interact with white children (Byers & Byers, 1972). Somehow the signals necessary for timing eye contact are misunderstood.

Some research does indicate the potential for teachers to treat students differently on the basis of race or ethnicity, though the research should be approached with caution. First, much of this research concerns behavior in tutorial sessions, often with undergraduates playing the part of teachers. Second, there is ample evidence that teachers act differently towards high- and low-ability students, and any study of differential treatment would have to take this aspect into consideration as well (Heller & White, 1975). One would have to ask, Is the teacher acting differently towards James because he belongs to a particular racial or ethnic group or because he is not doing well in class? Third, evidence exists that teachers reinforce students from middle-class backgrounds more positively than those from lower income backgrounds, even when race is not a factor (Friedman, 1976).

Keeping all this in mind, the research shows the possibility for such differential treatment. In one study, undergraduate "teachers" were asked to give a test and offer feedback concerning "student" performance on test items. The differences in nonverbal behavior were judged by black and white undergraduates from videotapes of the sessions. Both whites and blacks behaved more positively towards students of their own race, although only the judges of the same race could distinguish the differences in behavior (Feldman & Donohoe, 1978). In another experiment, these authors found that highly prejudiced teachers were more likely to show differential reinforcement based on a student's race than were not so prejudiced teachers (Feldman & Donohoe, 1978), thus reminding us of the importance of individual differences in determining nonverbal behavior. The possibility exists that teachers who hold low expectations for students based on extraneous factors such as race and ethnicity interact with students in a different manner, and this may affect student achievement.

What Does the Research on Nonverbal Behavior Mean to Teachers?

Taken as a whole, research shows that teachers' nonverbal behavior affects their students while at the same time their students' nonverbal behavior affects them. Teachers cannot always be aware of their nonverbal behavior. However, they can increase their awareness and understanding of both how they are affecting their students and what their students' nonverbal behavior really means. By videotaping their classrooms while they are teaching, teachers can become more aware of their nonverbal gestures, the different tones of voice they use for students who are doing well or poorly, and their tendency to call on students who sit in certain areas of the classroom. Later, they can review the tape and take special notice of their nonverbal patterns.

The second area of understanding requires some research. Students' cultural and ethnic backgrounds might affect their nonverbal behavior and attitudes towards classroom interaction. A teacher might misunderstand student behaviors. For example, many Americans of Spanish descent are uncomfortable with competing or standing out. Although hard work is expected, competition at the expense of others is not accepted (Hall & Hall, 1987). Native American students are frequently unwilling to respond in class, especially as they mature and tend to gaze at one another more than they look at the teacher. Susan Philips (1983) suggests that this trait may be due to some extent to their cultural background in which communication is more likely to be directed towards a group than an individual, immediate response to a speaker is not required, and speakers are never interrupted. In the usual classroom, teachers determine who speaks and when the turn to speak is over. To understand how such nonverbal factors can work to the teacher's advantage, it might be useful to observe some very successful teachers of particular eth-

nic groups and take special note of the classroom teacher's use of nonverbal behavior and style.

Teacher Communication and Student Gender

With all this information concerning the use of questions, praise, criticism, and nonverbal behavior, it's reasonable to ask whether teachers interact differently with boys than with girls. Admittedly, this is a question in which individual differences in teachers become most important. The evidence does suggest that teachers do interact differently with boys than with girls. Boys receive more discipline, more criticism, and more praise (Fennema, 1987). In addition, boys and girls are criticized for different things—boys for lack of effort and girls for the poor quality of their work (Dweck et al., 1978). Boys receive about half their criticism for poor conduct or lack of neatness and motivation, while 90 percent of negative feedback directed towards girls involves the quality of their work. According to Carol Dweck (1986), this differential pattern explains why girls are more likely than boys to exhibit what is known as learned helplessness, a condition in which a person sees failure as unavoidable, gives up, and passively accepts defeat (see Chapter 8). Since the nature of the criticism directed at girls involves the quality of their work, girls are more likely to believe that a negative evaluation indicates their ability level. Since most of the criticism directed at boys involves lack of motivation and neatness, boys perceive the criticism as unrelated to intellectual performance. It is no wonder that boys may persevere more and girls are more likely to exhibit learned helplessness.

True or False   Boys receive more criticism from teachers, but girls receive more praise.

Teachers interact more with high-achieving boys than with high-achieving girls (Good et al., 1973). When boys and girls are disruptive and aggressive, teachers are three times more likely to respond to the behavior of boys than of girls. Boys are also reprimanded in a louder voice (Serbin et al., 1973). Even at the nursery school level, boys are treated differently. Teachers disapprove of the behavior of boys more, but they also listen to them more and give them more individualized instruction (Serbin & O'Leary, 1975). Teachers accept more wrong or poor answers from boys than from girls (Good, Sikes, & Brophy, 1973). Boys are also more likely to be criticized by teachers if they participate in cross gender activities, such as doll play (Fagot, 1977). Observations in second grade showed that teachers had more contacts with boys in mathematics and girls in reading, and by the end of the year, girls were better in reading and boys in mathematics, though their initial abilities were the same (Leinhardt, et al., 1979). There is also some evidence that girls are more often reinforced for dependency than boys (Serbin, 1973), although there is ample evidence that both boys and girls are reinforced for dependent and quiet behavior (Doyle, 1985; Richmond-Abbott, 1983).

It would be easy to conclude that boys and girls are reinforced for totally different behaviors, but this is not the case. Boys and girls experience school in different ways, and both male and female teachers value the stereotyped feminine traits of obedience and passivity rather than aggressiveness and independence (Etaugh & Hughes, 1975). This may reinforce society's pressure for girls to be more docile (Busch-Rossnagel & Vance, 1982).

The conclusion seems inescapable that teachers do treat boys and girls differently (Fennema, 1987). However, it is difficult to determine whether some of the differences are due to the greater activity level and disruptive behavior of boys (Bank, et al., 1980). In addition, individual differences among teachers are great, and some teachers do not show these patterns of differential treatment.

Despite these caveats, the probability exists that some teachers treat boys and girls differently without adequate cause. It is possible that girls are more likely to be reinforced for passivity and that boys and girls are given different types of feedback for their work which leads girls to exhibit more learned helplessness.

Again, it seems reasonable for the teacher to monitor the treatment of students in order to be certain that both boys and girls are chosen for various chores around the classroom or for leadership assignments. Just as in the case of possible differential treatment due to race and ethnicity differences, awareness and a willingness to change are the keys to reducing gender discrimination.

THE TEACHER AS LISTENER

Teachers do more than speak. To be effective as communicators, they must also listen, not only in the classroom but also outside the classroom. Listening skills are part of one's total communication skills.

Have you ever spoken to someone who showed no interest in responding to what you were saying? For most of us, behaviors that show interest and respect seem so simple that we are often surprised when we hear someone complaining that someone was rude or did not show interest at a particular time. Some people are excellent listeners, while others have to learn these skills and approaches. Listening skills are especially troublesome in teaching, where evidence shows that the teacher does most of the talking and where the position of authority is very well defined. The following listening skills encourage students to communicate both in the classroom and in one-on-one interactions.

Attention. Have you ever found yourself speaking to a teacher who is busy putting away books or whose attention is focused elsewhere? It is annoying. Nothing communicates interest more than attention, and nothing communicates lack of interest more than inattention. Many of these attentional cues are nonverbal, including eye contact, posture, and facial expression. Often teachers are required to attend to two things at once. Despite this, good communication skills demand teachers' answering students by looking at them and excusing themselves when they need to attend to pressing classroom business.

Active Listening. When a student says something to a teacher, the teacher has a number of choices concerning how to respond. One possibility is silence (Benjamin, 1974). This is a natural response and can indicate anything, including that the teacher didn't hear the student, the teacher is preoccupied, the teacher is ignoring the student, the teacher doesn't feel well, etc. Another response is the "mm-hm," which indicates that the teacher is asking the student to continue. It has a number of meanings but is one way of keeping the student talking. A more active form of listening is called restatement, in which the teacher repeats the same words that the student has just used. Restatement does communicate that the teacher is listening. If the student says that he feels that he can't pass the test, the teacher merely changes the pronoun and echoes back, "You feel you can't pass the test." This can be used if a student is telling you that another student is doing something. If Tom tells you, "Richard took his shoes off," repeating the statement "Richard took his shoes off" shows that you have listened, and nothing more is required. Another possible response is clarification, in which the teacher simplifies the statement to make it clearer. Suppose the student says, "How am I going to do all this homework? I have to do the chores at home, go to work, help my grandmother, and practice baseball." You might say, "You have so many things to do that come before your homework." This again encourages a student to continue communicating.

Reflection. The most difficult and yet potentially most useful technique—reflection—involves being empathic and serving as a mirror to reflect back the student's feelings and attitudes. Reflection shows that the teacher is hearing more than the content and is aware of the student's feelings and attitudes. If a high school student were to say "I don't know what I want to be, and without a goal I can't seem to get motivated," how would you answer her? One way would be to concentrate on the emotion and reply, "It sounds like you're disturbed because you do not know what to do with your life." This response communicates empathy and again encourages the student to continue the communication but, in this case, to concentrate on her feelings.

Communication is a two-way process. When teachers talk, they expect students to listen and then respond. When students speak to their teachers, they have the right to expect the same courtesy. Good two-way communication requires active listening, which communicates understanding and interest. Teachers can adversely affect the learning process if they are defensive, try to lecture, or are careless when responding to student comments and questions. On the other hand, if teachers actively listen to what their students are communicating to them, the learning process can be enhanced.

CONFLICT AND COMMUNICATION

Whenever people come into contact with one another, the possibility of conflict exists. Conflict occurs when people are committed to incompatible courses of action or goals (Hurt et al., 1978). Conflict always creates tension and anxiety. When the teacher wants to do something one way and the students another, conflict will occur. But why cover conflict in the dis-

cussion of communication rather than in the chapter on classroom management and discipline? Although conflict can lead to discipline problems, it is not always negative and does not always signal behavioral difficulties. Conflict is, however, an aspect of communication, especially in the classroom.

There are four types of classroom conflict. **Conceptual conflict** occurs when there is a spirited argument over philosophy or subject content. This type of conflict can be a very positive, interesting, and valuable element of the learning situation. When students disagree with one another or feel they can disagree with the teacher over some aspect of learning, discussions become livelier and students are more likely to become involved in the discussion. For example, a conflict over what causes poverty in society or whether a character in a book is really a hero promotes learning. However, in handling such often delightful conflict, two rules need to be kept in mind. First, students must learn to react to what the others are saying rather than criticize the persons saying it. Denigrating remarks such as "you're crazy" just make a student less willing to participate. Second, the teacher must ask him or herself whether he or she is secure enough to accept student criticism and encourage such cognitive conflict in the classroom. When a student challenges a teacher's opinion, a neutral question such as Why do you think that? and acceptance of the student's opinion will keep such challenges coming. Of course, if a student makes a factual error, the error must be corrected using the techniques discussed earlier.

Procedural conflict involves a disagreement over what action should be taken to reach an agreed-upon goal. Often administrators and teachers disagree on the best way to teach something or to achieve order in the school. Students and teachers may have different ideas about such things as how and when classroom chores should be performed and the nature of assignments. Teachers can easily handle most procedural conflict by making students clearly aware of what the

conceptual conflict   Conflict that occurs when there is a disagreement over philosophy or content.

procedural conflict   Conflict over what action is necessary to reach an agreed-upon goal.

procedures are, the reason for the procedures, and the consequences for not following them. Sometimes a teacher will follow a student's suggestion. For instance, consider the science teacher who gives an assignment to research how dams are designed by going to the library and looking up the information. One student wants to build a model dam. The teacher must decide upon the real purpose of the assignment. If the purpose of the work is exclusively to learn how to use the library, the teacher will say no. If the purpose is to learn something about designing dams, the teacher might agree. If the teacher has both purposes in mind, some agreement might be reached in which the student's suggestion is incorporated into the assignment. Much procedural conflict can be minimized by clearly communicating the procedures and knowing the goals.

A third type of conflict is **substantive conflict,** which involves a disagreement over goals. Students may want a weekend free from homework; the teacher may see the need for study. A common example occurs in junior high school, where students may see acceptance and popularity in their peer group as more important than academic achievement. Unfortunately, students don't always know or tell teachers what their goals are. In this area, some negotiation may be necessary. It may be possible to meet both the students' and the teacher's needs through some meeting of the minds, a process of negotiation that takes place in the classroom or in individual conferences. A teacher might allow students a free weekend if the students measure up to a particular standard, such as doing their homework the other four days.

A fourth and more serious type of conflict is **interpersonal conflict,** which involves differences in style and personality (Schmuck & Schmuck, 1983). Such conflict often involves high emotions and sometimes a refusal to be cooperative. Personal dislike enters into the situation, and both the teacher and the students are likely to interpret each other's actions in the most negative light possible. The idea that the two

just can't get along can cause academic problems as well.

Interpersonal conflict is difficult to handle. First, it has to be identified. Student-teacher interpersonal conflict can be identified by its emotional impact and its generalized negative pattern of interaction. If events are blown out of proportion, annoyance or anger is high, or the student, the teacher, or both experience animosity towards each other, interpersonal conflict may exist. In such cases, disagreements and misinterpretation of each other's actions are common. The word *always* is frequently used, as in "The teacher always picks on me" or "The student always challenges me." One way of handling such conflict is to reduce one's emotional involvement and to stay calm. In addition, the teacher and the student can have a frank discussion concerning their feelings that begins perhaps with the teacher asking, "Do you feel our relationship isn't what it should be? What can we do to improve it?" Sometimes negotiation and a contract in which each agrees to reduce the offending behavior can help to improve the relationship.

Conflict can be prevented or controlled through actively listening, being aware of what actions trigger the conflict, and accepting others (Bolton, 1979). When conflict does occur, it is best to deal with one issue at a time, start with issues that can be most easily resolved to the satisfaction of all parties, break down the issues into smaller units, define the dispute in nonemotional terms, and establish procedures for handling disputes (Bolton, 1979). Notice that in such conflict, the teacher usually takes the stand that there is a need for both the teacher and the student to improve. It is easy for a teacher to see any type of conflict as a direct assault upon the teacher's position. However, conflict is part of even our closest interpersonal relationships. Although it cannot always be avoided, conflict does not have to lead to interpersonal and classroom problems. The key is to find a procedure to handle it.

One set of procedures is offered by Thomas Gordon (1974), who sees conflict resolution in terms of a problem-solving process. However, before the process begins, some important prerequisites are required. First, teachers must be willing to listen to students and express their own feelings using "I" statements (*I* feel frustrated when you don't come to class on time). Second, the student must be convinced that the teacher is serious about wanting to resolve the conflict and about using the conflict-

substantive conflict Conflict that occurs when people disagree over goals.

interpersonal conflict Conflict arising from differences in style or personality.

resolution method to do so. Third, the method requires some equality between student and teacher, which is difficult to achieve. Basically, the teacher is entering into a negotiation procedure with the student, the aim of which is to arrive at a solution that they can both live with. Gordon advocates a six-stage method, as follows:

1. **Defining the Problem.** It is important to understand how the student sees the problem and how the teacher sees the student.

2. **Generating Possible Solutions.** Both students and teachers can offer possible solutions. At first, the solutions should not be evaluated, and solutions and ideas should be encouraged.

3. **Evaluating the Solutions.** The ideas can be evaluated at this stage.

4. **Making the Decision.** Often a solution emerges that can satisfy both parties. Gordon advises teachers involved in group conflict not to vote on the solution, since voting yields winners and losers. The purpose is to get a consensus. The question at this stage is, Would it work for everyone? The solution should be put in writing.

5. **Determining How to Implement the Decision.** This is a crucial and often forgotten stage. Such questions as What do we need to get started? and Who is responsible for what? need to be answered.

6. **Assessing the Success of the Solution.** This need not be formalized, but in some way the success or failure of the solution should be assessed.

One question that always arises whenever a problem-solving or conflict-resolution procedure is used is, Why go through it at all? Why not just tell a student that this is the rule and that's it? Why try to resolve conflicts? Indeed, there are times when a teacher's authority must be used. For example, emergencies that require immediate action are not candidates for the use of such procedures. In addition, after explaining the reasons for a procedure and listening to any suggestions, the teacher should implement a rule if he or she thinks it is necessary.

Although both teachers and parents have the responsibility to explain the reasons behind a procedure—since this shows children how the adults are thinking and may serve to enlist the children's active support—they do not require the active approval of children. However, the continuous use of power to solve interpersonal problems can produce resentment and reduce the motivation to carry a task out

and requires constant enforcement vigilance. Ignoring the conflict is a poor approach, since the conflict may arise again and, if it is noticeable, children will lose respect for the adult who is unwilling or unable to handle conflict.

Conflict resolution is not a process by which students run the classroom or in which students vote not to do the work. It is rather a process in which different types of conflict may be dealt with in an effective manner. The teacher and the students seek peaceful resolutions to conflicts in which the needs and requirements of both are taken into consideration. No one loses face, and the teacher does not lose the respect of the students.

COMMUNICATION THROUGH STUDENT WRITTEN WORK

Students and teachers also communicate through writing. Interest in student writing increased throughout the 1980s and will continue to grow in the 1990s. Writing is a very useful medium of communication as well as an important academic skill. Teachers in all areas and at all grade levels are now being encouraged to emphasize writing in their classrooms. Students are writing in social studies and science as well as in English, and in both elementary and secondary schools.

Students may write for a number of reasons, which Marlene Scardamalia and Carl Bereiter (1986) group under three headings. First, there is writing as a self-contained activity. This involves writing personal letters, reaction papers, and journals whose entries serve as a form of communication between students and teachers. Writing in this context is intrinsically satisfying and assumes that the audience (the teacher or fellow students) has an interest in the writer's opinions and feelings. The teacher may ask the students to keep a daily diary or to respond to a poem and share their responses with the class as the basis for a class discussion. Students may be asked to write on a topic of interest to them and submit their papers to the teacher, who then writes back to each student, forming a dialogue in writing. Such writing helps to develop better writing skills and encourages communication among students and between students and teachers.

The second heading is writing as a contributory activity. The phrase "writing across curricula" or "writing across disciplines" is often found in today's educational literature, and the way to accomplish such writing is through using writing as a contributory activity. Here, writing is incidental to some other academic activity, such as giving a report or taking a test. Students might write to demonstrate their knowledge of a topic as reflected in an essay or a research paper that may tap higher level cognitive skills (see Chapter 15). Students might be asked to write a report about a science experiment or to analyze the similarities and differences between the American Revolution and the French Revolution. Writing is simply the vehicle for demonstrating one's understanding of an academic area. Sometimes this type of writing can be made more exciting to students. For example, one of my daughters was given an assignment to test different paper towels and write her results. Other students were busy testing other commercial claims. The reports were read to the class and commented upon by the other students and then attractively displayed around the classroom.

Last, there is writing as an exercise of skill. This involves writing for the express purpose of developing a particular writing skill. The writing that is assigned is meant as an exercise that will improve various aspects of the writer's skills. The emphasis here is on performance rather than inner satisfaction or writing as a practical means of demonstrating knowledge. This type of writing has come increasingly under attack for a number of reasons. Writing, like all forms of communication, has the purpose of communicating a message and therefore is generated with some knowledge of the audience and the intent of the communication. Many of the assignments that aim at focusing on writing as a skill are artificial and lack a communicational purpose.

What do we know about how teachers use writing in their classrooms? In a summary of the research on student writing, Susan Florio-Ruane and Saundra Dunn (1987) concluded that students generally write in response to teacher demands and the teachers select both the purpose and the format of the writing. In other words, the teacher initiates the writing and makes the decisions about what is to be written and how it is to be written. Most student writing is done for evaluation purposes, and the evaluation often focuses on surface features of language rather than meaning. In addition, the researchers found that little or no technical support is offered to students while they are writing, that time available is limited, and

that any interaction with peers during the writing process is discouraged. Last, they found that little time is spent on revision and that most writing done in school stays there and is never read by a wider audience. For most written work, then, the teacher gives the assignment, the student follows the teacher's rules, and the teacher evaluates the student's work.

These findings are troublesome. Writing does not seem to be used as a form of practical communication. It is frequently divorced from what is going on inside or outside the classroom. In addition, there is little focus on the process of writing. Revision and rewriting are not emphasized, and the final product is often seen by no one else, nor does it serve as the basis for any further study or discussion.

Our understanding of the process of writing is admittedly limited, although we are making strides in understanding the process. The most common model used in understanding the process of writing divides the process into three phases: planning, translating, and reviewing (Hayes & Flower, 1980). During the planning phase, students collect information, organize their ideas, and think about their goals. During the translating phase, students write the material based upon the plan. During the reviewing phase, the students read their own material over and edit it. Most authorities today argue that writing instruction would be more effective if it were taught as a process and if the instruction focused on the communicational value of writing.

Writing instruction is more effective when it is tied to something real, when the process is recognized, when students are helped to produce their best work, and when students and teachers cooperate in forming goals and improving skills. In a very valuable report, George Hillocks (1984) analyzed experimental studies on writing instruction and divided such instruction into four general methods. In the natural process mode, students shoulder the responsibility for the entire writing process, writing about whatever interests them. The teacher acts as a facilitator of ideas. In the presentational mode, the most common, the teacher defines the topic, discusses what students should concentrate on, and gives feedback. In the environmental mode, students are given a problem such as writing a description of a person so that other students may recognize the individual. The students work on particular tasks in small groups before working independently. High levels of student interaction and involvement are required. In the individualized mode, students receive instruction through tutorials. Hillocks found that the environmental mode was superior to the other methods of teaching writing.

How can these ideas be used by the teacher, and what mistakes are commonly made in teaching writing? Consider the following teacher's method of the development of writing skills in a class. The teacher informs the students the day before that she will ask them to write something. The next day the teacher writes the topic on the board and reminds the students about the importance of such things as complete sentences and good grammar. She distributes paper and thirty minutes later suggests that the students finish and check their papers for errors. Students then recopy the material and are told that they must submit their compositions the next day. The teacher marks the papers at home, correcting all the errors. After returning the papers to the class, the teacher asks several students who have done well on the assignment to read their papers aloud to the class (Daigon, 1982).

How would you critique this teacher's efforts? According to Daigon (1982), the teacher is well-meaning, but the instructional technique runs counter to what we know is important in teaching writing skills. First, the assignment came from out of the blue. Writing should come from experience, from something that is going on in the classroom. If a class of second-graders sets up a small community store, the students might be asked to write to the candy company requesting stock. Since various types of writing have different purposes, writing can emphasize a number of aspects of thinking, including persuading, defining, comparing, and contrasting (Slater, 1982). Writing a story differs from writing a letter to a company complaining about a poorly manufactured toy, and both differ from writing that tries to change someone's opinion or communicates one's feelings about a poem.

Second, the teacher's reminders about proper form are poorly timed and probably a waste of time. The first task in any assignment is not form and grammar but the formation of a plan to tackle the assignment. The teacher would have been more helpful had she discussed the subject and the objectives of the assignment and helped the students to generate ideas. At this stage, students should think and talk about the purposes of their writing, collect information, organize their material, and consider what they want to say (U.S. Department of Education, 1987).

Third, the teacher's suggestion that after thirty minutes the students check for errors and make a final draft is also ill-timed. It would have been better if the teacher had encouraged the students to jot down their ideas freely, uninterrupted by attention to mechanical or grammatical blunders. Maintaining the creative flow of ideas is more important at this stage. Daigon (1982) admits that punctuation, capitalization, and grammar are crucial, but these elements are best attended to later.

In addition, the teacher assumed that after thirty minutes the children could merely check their papers. No time was allowed for revision. Most writers consider revision the real task of writing. Revision entails a reorganization and an extensive reevaluation of the product, not mere proofreading. Students probably need more help in this area than in the others. The most useful teacher responses to an early draft focus on what students are trying to say, not the mechanisms of writing. The teacher can help by asking the students for clarifications and by suggesting ways of improving the material. The students then consider the feedback, decide how to use it, and revise their paper. On the next draft, the teacher might focus on particular aspects of good writing that can improve structure. Here, the emphasis is on alternatives to using the same words, the importance of writing clearly, and some of the technical areas of writing (U.S. Department of Education, 1987). One of the last processes in the technical area is proofreading, where errors in spelling, grammar, and punctuation are corrected.

Asking the top students to read their own masterpieces is also a mistake. This only emphasizes the other students' inadequacies. A better idea is to allow the students to draft, revise, and draft again until a good product emerges, and then publish the papers in some form. Letters may be mailed, or stories may be placed in booklet form and given to other classes or displayed perhaps in the classroom or the school library.

Daigon also believes that evaluation is critical and should be a learning experience and suggests that teachers comment on a composition's strengths and weaknesses, provide time for student conferences, and allow students to show their best work. Writing conferences have become more popular. Instead of covering a student's composition with red marks, the teacher can sit down with the student and discuss the work, its purposes, and any problems the student may be having. In this way, the teacher can listen to the student author and try to understand the student's intentions and problems and respond with questions and suggestions. The teacher can then guide the student through the judicious use of comments and questions such as, What is the next step in planning your essay? (Scardamalia & Bereiter, 1986).

The writing conference idea is a good one, although it does have some limitations. One problem is the tendency of teachers to take over such a conference instead of asking students questions and guiding them. Another is the time problem involved when teachers have so many students to serve. However, some work can be accomplished in small groups.

For some, these ideas about writing may seem like heresy, but no one is supporting slipshod and ungrammatical writing. What many authorities are now suggesting is that we know that successful writers have a purpose, draft and redraft their writing, and only at the end make the technical corrections that are so important to a good final draft.

The changes in the way we look at the writing process hold the promise of helping students develop better skills in this important area of communication. It takes a great deal of time and effort on the part of both the teacher and the student to develop good writing skills, and teachers in every subject and at every grade level share some responsibility in this area.

PARENT-TEACHER COMMUNICATION

A final area of communication involves not the students but their parents. Most teachers have some contact with parents, although communication is relatively slight (Feinman-Nemser & Floden, 1986). In one survey, over 90 percent of teachers from all parts of the country wanted more home-school interaction (NEA, 1982). The public agrees, with most people wanting more communication as well.

True or False Most teachers want more communication with the parents of their students.

Does increased communication lead to better school outcomes? The greatest positive findings are in schools composed of predominantly black students where high parental involvement is associated with greater achievement (Brookover et al., 1979). The research on the effects of parental involvement is very limited (Becker & Epstein, 1982), but most stud-

ies do indicate that parents can help students either by monitoring their work or by helping them at home (Lightfoot, 1978).

Parent-teacher contact can be divided into two forms. First, there are the contacts in which the children's performance is evaluated and more information is sought from the parents. Second, there are those activities in which teachers desire active parental participation, such as watching and discussing a particular television program or reading to each other (Moles, 1982).

Teachers are rather definite about the kind of relationship they want with parents. They see the ideal relationship with parents as one in which the parents support teacher practices, carry out teacher requests, and do not interfere with the teacher (Feinman-Nemser & Floden, 1986). They do not want parental input into curriculum. In one survey, Williams (1981) found that teachers did not want parents participating in curriculum development or instruction or making school rules. Rather, they wanted parents to assist with homework and believed that they should be active in showing parents how to help their children. You can see where some conflict might exist between parents who are very active in the community and want some input into educational planning and teachers who do not feel that this is the place for parents.

True or False Most teachers say they would welcome parent cooperation in curriculum planning and the establishment of school rules.

Almost all teachers want parents to monitor their children's work and support teachers' policies at home (Epstein & Becker, 1982). However, the extent to which parents can participate in the teaching process at home is often questioned. This was amply shown in a survey of 3,700 teachers from 600 Maryland schools. Teachers wondered whether the effort it took to prepare workshops that aimed at teaching parents how to work with their children was worth the time (Becker & Epstein, 1982). Teachers held varied opinions on the question of how involved parents should be in teaching their children, with some believing that parents might put too much pressure on their children which might adversely affect parent-child relationships. However, despite these doubts, most teachers sought parental involvement to improve their children's basic skills, help students retain skills, especially over the summer, and improve behavior and general cooperation in school. Many

Teachers can sometimes give parents instructions that allow parents to work more effectively with their children.

teachers doubted that parental involvement in the teaching or tutoring area was reasonable for older students. The most popular formal program involved reading on a regular basis. Two thirds of the teachers asked parents to read with their children.

Communicating with Parents

Parent-teacher communication is not easy. Flyers often do not get home, and telephone calls can be difficult, since many parents work during the day and have to be called at night. Parents and teachers often have conflicting time schedules as well as different perceptions of the educational process. Teachers may use a variety of ways to communicate with parents, including sending notes, holding conferences, making home visits, encouraging joint participation in workshops, making telephone calls, and having daily papers and weekly folders signed.

When a face-to-face conference is not required, telephone calls and written communication are fre-

quently used. Telephone calls are more personal than written communication and allow parents and teachers to enter into a dialogue without having to make an appointment to see each other. Telephone calls have their limitations, however. Many parents work during the day and may wish to be interrupted only in emergencies. In addition, it is frequently difficult for teachers to make phone calls at night. Even if a teacher does contact a parent, it may prove to be an inconvenient time, perhaps while the parent is making dinner or giving the baby a bath. Last, although a telephone call is more personal, it still does not allow for the face-to-face interaction that a conference does.

Written communication suffers from being less personal and sometimes too structured. If parents have a number of questions or need more information, writing notes back and forth between teachers and parents is time consuming and does not allow the give-and-take necessary to come to some conclusion about what should be done to help the student. In addition, since such letters are sometimes intercepted by others before parents receive them, it is a good idea to require parents to sign the letters and send them back or have their children bring them back.

Written communication has the advantages of efficiently transmitting the exact information the teacher desires and allowing those parents who need more information to respond appropriately in a structured manner. In addition, since many of these informational letters are standardized, they are a less time consuming method of communication than the telephone and allow teachers to transmit information to more parents than they could reach by telephone. A teacher can routinely fill in the blanks on such letters and send out five or ten letters in the time it might take to make only two or three phone calls. Last, with the availability of word processing, teachers can personalize such letters in less time than ever before.

Written communication can inform parents that their child is not doing well or is misbehaving; that the teacher wishes a parent-teacher conference; or that their child is progressing in a particular subject, improving his or her behavior, or generally doing well. It is very important that teachers communicate to parents a student's positive achievements as well as problems. Many parents moan whenever they receive a letter from school because they "know" it contains some complaint about their child. They are pleasantly surprised when they receive a letter informing them of something positive. Informing parents that their child has shown considerable improvement, has written a very interesting composition, or has helped another student in some capacity will help improve the teacher's relationship with both the parents and the student. Such communication demonstrates to parents that the teacher has noticed the positive achievements of their child. Students will be pleased that their teacher has taken the time to compliment them to their parents.

What should a letter to parents include? Obviously, this depends upon what the teacher is trying to communicate. However, the following guidelines suggested by Fred Chernow and Carol Chernow (1981) may be helpful:

1. Especially for secondary school students who have a number of teachers, the letter should introduce the teacher to the parents. A phrase such as "I am your child _____'s English teacher" is appropriate.

2. The letter should give parents specific information. If a teacher wishes to tell parents that the student has violated rules, the parent should be specifically informed that the student was late to class without a pass twice, missed his or her homework on Wednesday, or received a failing grade on a test. The same principle applies to letters that inform parents of positive deeds.

3. The letter's tone should be positive and contain a sentence noting that improvement is possible. Even if the teacher is informing parents of poor achievement, it is reasonable to include some phrase noting that there is still time for improvement.

4. The formality of the form letter should be reduced as much as possible. Form letters are by their very nature formal. Certainly, personalized letters are best, but a teacher may not be able to write all the letters he or she would like to write. Therefore, the best alternative is to reduce the formal tone of these letters. This can be accomplished by avoiding any educational jargon and making the tone of the letter somewhat personal. Many teachers have access to word-processing packages that can help to personalize these letters.

5. Parental comments should be encouraged. Letters should include a request for parental questions or comments if appropriate.

6. Letters should be signed and returned. Some letters are intercepted by others and never get to the parents. Later, perhaps during a conference, the parents are surprised to learn something about their child. The teacher tells the parents that a letter was sent to the home, to which the parents reply that they did not receive the letter. This can be avoided by requiring such letters to be returned with a parent's signature. These letters should be kept in a file.

These principles are reflected in the following sample letter informing a parent of a student's last two mathematics grades that were poor (Chernow & Chernow, 1981).

Dear _____:

I am _____'s mathematics teacher, and I would like to share with you some information concerning your child's progress in school. _____ has earned grades of __ and __ on the last two math tests given this marking period. I thought you would like to be informed about your child's progress so that _____'s math achievement can be improved.

If you would like to discuss your child's progress in more detail, please feel free to make an appointment to see me by calling _____. Please sign the bottom of this letter and return it to the school. Feel free to write any comments you wish on the back. I'm certain that with some additional effort, _____ can improve.

Sincerely yours,

_____

There is no single, accepted style, and with experience, teachers can create written communications that fit their particular needs.

Parental Conferences

Teachers have the most contact with parents of children who have learning and discipline problems and with parents who are most active in the school. It is not surprising, then, that teachers sometimes have difficulty dealing with parents. Parents of children experiencing difficulties are likely to be defensive about their children. Many parents will be veterans of such conferences, while others may be overwhelmed by the problems. These conferences, though, can be important and beneficial. The information that parents and teachers can give each other may help the student and clear up communication problems and misunderstandings. For example, a child may be telling his parent that he has no homework. The parent may want to know why. The parent may then learn during a conference that the child does have homework but is doing it during a study period.

Some school systems have found parent-teacher conferences so valuable that such conferences are considered a vital part of the educational process. In Houston, conferences for all grade levels are held twice a year, and schools are recessed for this purpose. Teachers have computer printouts of student test scores. These printouts also tell parents how to help their children in areas where they haven't done well. In high school, occupational information is also given. Most parents are satisfied with this program (Tangri & Moles, 1987).

Parent-teacher conferences may also fail to help, however, especially if they are not handled properly. Interpersonal skills such as warmth, attentiveness, and responsiveness are always important, but they are crucial to success, especially when dealing with resistant or angry parents (Rotter & Robinson, 1982).

Practical Suggestions for Parent-Teacher Conferences

There is no substitute for teacher preparation. Whether the conference is called by the teacher to discuss some aspect of a child's work or is requested by the parents, being ready is crucial to the success of the conference. This translates into having the child's work, hard data on tests, and examples of homework at one's fingertips. If the conference concerns conduct, having the records of when and where the incidents occurred is necessary. A teacher does not need to overwhelm parents with data but should have some hard facts available.

Fred Chernow and Carol Chernow (1981) offer some practical suggestions for holding a conference. The conference should take place while both parents and teacher are sitting in adult-sized chairs. The authors suggest that teachers not take notes about what the parents tell them, if possible, and take the attitude of accepting the parents as equals in an effort to help the child. If the teacher wants cooperation from the parents, the attitude that "we are going to help John together" is best. I have always found that avoiding blame is most important, especially with parents who are already defensive.

Teachers can easily anticipate the three most important questions parents will ask at most conferences: How is my child doing? How is my child behaving? Does my child get along with others? One way to reduce defensiveness is to use a PNP, or positive-negative-positive, approach whenever possible, beginning the conference with a positive statement about the child.

To further decrease defensiveness, A. Stuart Losen and Bert Diament (1978) suggest that teachers acknowledge a parent's anger and convey concern about it and at the same time assure parents that they themselves are concerned, too. Listening in an empathic manner to parents while withholding judgment is also a way for teachers to show parents their concern. Using open-ended questions to encourage parents to talk and active listening techniques is recommended (Losen & Diament, 1978). Last, teachers should make solid and realistic suggestions and design procedures to keep in touch with parents to follow up on the suggestions.

Consider the teacher in conference who has introduced him or herself to the parents, greeted the parents, told the parents what they will cover, asked the parents if they have anything they want to cover, showed the parents some of their child's work, and discussed the child's problems. The parents may ask a simple but devastating question: How can I help? Teachers who want to involve parents must have some ideas in mind. In the work area, it may involve practice or checking homework. In the behavioral area, it may involve weekly report cards or weekly telephone calls. Parents can be asked if they have any suggestions, but teachers should be prepared to give some as well. Tables 9.4 and 9.5 list elements of effective conferences (Rotter et al., 1987).

COMMUNICATION RECONSIDERED

If communication is the primary skill in teaching, improving communication should be a priority. In this chapter, we've investigated specific elements of communication, including questions, praise, criticism, nonverbal behavior, conflict resolution, listening skills, and communication with parents. Improving one's ability to communicate requires constant monitoring. It is easy to fall into the pitfalls of not being attentive or actively listening, asking poor questions,

Table 9.4 Elements of Effective Parent-Teacher Conferences

How can the teacher plan and conduct effective parent-teacher conferences? This list points out elements of successful conferences as initiated by the teacher and the parent.

Teacher-Initiated	Common Elements	Parent-Initiated
—Prepare for conference in advance.	—Allow enough time.	—Positively identify parent requesting meeting.
—Give parent(s) some idea of topic.	—Determine whether student should be present.	—If parent shares topic, collect necessary background information.
—Specify points to be made.	—Do not become defensive; maintain open mind.	—Have pertinent student records accessible for conference.
—Prepare written progress report to include survey of student progress, areas of concern and areas of strength	—Listen to all parent is saying, specifically and implied.	—Do not make assumptions; invite parents to express concerns.
—Don't wait for regularly scheduled conference if a matter arises; deal with it.	—Seek clarification when necessary.	—Get complete story before suggesting action or solutions.
—Structure conference for parent(s): why, what, when; explain purpose.	—Avoid overwhelming parent with presence of nonessential school personnel.	
—Allow parent(s) time to read and/or discuss written summary.	—Avoid overwhelming parent with irrelevant material or use of jargon; be thorough.	
	—Meet parent(s) at building entry point if possible.	
	—Show parent concern and respect—respect as person, concern as patron of school; maintain positive professional demeanor.	
	—Make environment for conference conducive to open communication; avoid physical barriers.	
	—Attempt to part on positive note; set up future conference or referral procedures before parent leaves.	
	—Be sure to carry out any promised followup.	

From Parent-Teacher Conferencing, 2d ed. by J. C. Rotter, E. H. Robinson, and M. A. Fey. Copyright © 1987, National Educational Association. Reprinted with permission.

Table 9.5 Effective Conferencing Scale

This scale can help teachers to evaluate how effectively they plan and conduct parent-teacher conferences.

	Always	Sometimes	Never
1. Prepare for conference in advance.			
2. Give parent(s) some idea in advance of topic to be discussed.			
3. Allow enough time for conference.			
4. Avoid becoming defensive when parents question judgment.			
5. Maintain an open mind to parent ideas.			
6. Listen to all parent is saying (verbal and nonverbal) before responding.			
7. Avoid overwhelming parent(s) with presence of other school personnel.			
8. Avoid overwhelming parent(s) with irrelevant material or use of jargon.			
9. Avoid physical barriers such as desk, uncomfortable chairs.			
10. Follow up on commitments.			

From Parent-Teacher Conferencing, 2d ed. by J. C. Rotter, E. H. Robinson, and M. A. Fey. Copyright © 1987, National Educational Association. Reprinted with permission.

giving praise incorrectly, or criticizing in a way that does not serve a corrective purpose. Although some people are better communicators than others, communication is a set of skills that can be improved with practice, awareness, and preparation. Judging by the research on the importance of communication to the educational process, improving one's communication skills is certainly worth the effort.

SUMMARY

1. Teachers talk more than two-thirds of the time in the average classroom. One factor that differentiates effective from ineffective communication is clarity. Clarity involves teaching in a logical manner, preparing students for what they will be taught, using examples and demonstrations, reviewing the material, adapting the level of communication to the students, and giving adequate feedback. When assigning work, the importance of procedural questions should not be minimized.

2. Questioning has many purposes, including checking students' understanding, focusing their attention on aspects of the lesson, encouraging participation, and promoting thinking. Asking if there are any questions after finishing a lesson is a poor way to check student understanding, since the silence that often greets a teacher's bid for questions does not demonstrate that the students understand. Student understanding can be checked by asking the students to signal answers nonverbally or write the answer to a question or by choosing representative students to answer some questions. Asking students to define a word or explain something in their own words is an excellent way to check their understanding of material.

3. Questions that are used to encourage thinking and higher level skills must be carefully formulated. One suggestion is to prepare questions using Bloom's taxonomy of educational objectives as a base and to ask questions that not only measure knowledge, comprehension, and application but also require analysis, synthesis, and evaluation. Evidence exists that questioning can improve student skills. The research on the effects of using higher level questioning is mixed.

4. Questions can be used to encourage student participation. To do so, teachers need to expand their questioning techniques by asking questions whose answers require little book knowledge. Poor students, especially, will find such questions less threatening, and since there are no right or wrong answers, teachers can give reinforcement for class participation without being forced to correct these students.

5. When a student answers a question incorrectly,

the teacher has a number of alternatives available. The question can be redirected to another student, or the teacher might simplify the question or provide information so that the student can answer the question correctly. The teacher might also supply the question that the student's incorrect statement answered and then either redirect the question or give additional clues.

6. Teachers often do not wait long enough after they ask a question to call on students. When teachers increase their wait time, a number of benefits accrue, including improvements in participation and the quality of student answers.

7. Students do not ask many questions, perhaps because they do not want to stand out, do not wish to be seen as "dumb," or believe the teacher really does not want questions. Students can be encouraged to ask questions if teachers create an atmosphere in which questions are accepted, reinforce questioning, assign students to formulate questions, and train students—especially low-achieving students—to ask questions.

8. Praise is not used very often in most classes, and under some conditions, students may not react positively to praise. Praise given incorrectly does not reinforce the desired behaviors. Praise is most effective if it is contingent on specific behaviors, is genuine, and does not generally judge the student's personality or character but rather describes the behavior and the teacher's feelings towards the behavior. Unfortunately, praise often does not meet these criteria.

9. There is more criticism than praise used in many classes, especially those with lower achieving students. Criticism is most effective if it is contingent on particular undesirable behaviors, is specific, is combined with praise for the correct behavior, does not overtly judge the student's character, and is sincere. Teachers are responsible for giving some suggestions on how to improve an area that they criticize.

10. Teachers should be careful not to send double messages—one message on the verbal channel and a counter message on the nonverbal channel. Examples of a teacher's nonverbal behavior include gestures, facial expressions, voice tone, and the use of space to communicate. Teachers often stand farther away from students they do not like. Teachers are affected by the nonverbal behavior of their students.

11. Listening skills are essential for good communication. Teachers signal their interest through both verbal and nonverbal channels and can actively promote student communication by using restatement, clarification, and reflection.

12. Whenever people are in contact with one another, conflict can arise. Conceptual conflict occurs when people disagree on their interpretation or analysis of content. Such conflict is often healthy, as long as people respect each other's opinions. Procedural conflict involves disagreements over how to reach a goal. Such disagreements can be reduced by improving the clarity of instructions and offering honest explanations for classroom rules and procedures. Substantive conflict involves disagreements over goals, many of which are unstated. Sometimes negotiations can allow people to meet their needs and those of other people. Interpersonal conflict involves a conflict in style and personality. This often involves high emotionality and lack of cooperation. Sometimes a contract can be negotiated in which the teacher and the child agree to cease certain behaviors that bother the other. Conflict can be handled by using a set of procedures that are similar to those used to solve other types of problems.

13. Teachers want a relationship with parents where parents will support their classroom efforts and, especially in the early grades, help their children at home. They do not want parent involvement in curriculum or school rules. Teachers disagree on the degree to which parents can help their children as teachers or tutors. Preparation is most important to the success of parent-teacher conferences.

ACTIVITIES AND EXERCISES

1. **Teacher Talk.** Flander's Interaction Analysis Categories (refer to Table 9.1) offers us a very useful way of categorizing classroom interaction. A number of students are surprised that teachers talk as much as they do and praise so little. Using the categories listed, tape record perhaps fifteen minutes of a class session (with the teacher's permission) and analyze the talk by dividing it into various categories.

2. **Teacher Clarity: How Clear Are Your Explanations?** Teacher clarity is essential for good communication. Formulate directions or instructions for doing one of the following:

   a. A book report for a junior high school English course.

   b. An explanation of how to use some type of laboratory setup or equipment.

   c. A series of interviews for sixth-graders to carry out with friends and neighbors on their feelings towards the homeless.

   d. How to use the protractor.

   You may also want to outline how you would teach some topic in your specialty and analyze it for clarity in the following way:

   Is it presented logically, in a step-by-step manner?
   Is there an introduction to it?
   Are questions that monitor understanding built into the lesson?
   Have you anticipated the areas where students might have the most difficulty by giving additional examples and perhaps demonstrations?

3. **Analyzing Questions.** Since questioning is so important, it is always interesting to discover just how teachers use questioning. This can be accomplished in a number of ways. Perhaps you could observe an elementary schoolteacher or secondary schoolteacher and note whether the teachers' questions are used to focus the students' attention on a particular area, monitor understanding, promote thinking, or encourage interaction. To do this, divide a sheet of paper into five columns headed "Questions that focus students' attention," "Questions that check understanding," "Questions that promote thinking," "Questions that encourage student involvement," and a fifth category, "Miscellaneous questions—those that are procedural." Also note how often the questions are factual in nature or higher level.

4. **Writing Higher Level Questions.** Choose any topic in your specialty and prepare two or three questions that would fall into the categories of knowledge, comprehension, application, analysis, synthesis, and evaluation.

5. **How Do Teachers Handle Wrong Answers?** An incorrect answer is a challenge to a teacher. It is easy to say "wrong" or "no," but this simple strategy reduces participation and is not educationally sound. The text suggests asking other questions that give clues that show the student what question he or she answered or redirecting the question. Ask a group of teachers how they handle a student who has answered a question incorrectly.

6. **Wait Time.** Next time you are tutoring someone or even testing a friend in preparation for a test, become aware of how long you wait for an answer once you have asked a question. If you are observing a teacher, see if he or she waits the desired three seconds or so.

7. **Encouraging Student Questions.** You don't have to go into an elementary or secondary school to appreciate the fact that students don't ask many questions, even when they do not understand the work. You can see this in many of your own classes. Interview a number of students at random as to whether they ask questions in their classes. If they do, find out in which classes they do and why they do not in others.

8. **Working with a Student Who Does not Ask Questions.** The text notes the problem of students, especially lower achieving pupils, who just don't ask questions. Bengfort's (1987) suggestion of roleplaying and teaching students to raise their hand and say excuse me, I can't, or can you please help me and to say thank you after the help is given is a reasonable procedure. Choose a student who has some difficulty in asking questions, and through roleplaying, teach the child how to ask questions.

9. **Praise and Criticism.** The rules for praise and criticism involve being specific, being genuine, describing an action, and not evaluating the student's character. Praise is not common in classrooms. However, we don't have to look at classrooms to analyze the use of criticism and praise. Choose a particular behavior and try to praise a friend or an acquaintance for some action and observe the person's behavior. Keep a log of the behavior and see if your praise acts as a reinforcer. At the same time, if you are observing a class, notice the extent to which praise and criticism are used and their effects on the students. Last, keep a record of the use of praise and criticism in your home. How often are you or other family members praised or criticized?

10. **Nonverbal Behavior.** Videotape yourself tutoring a student or lecturing. Then become aware of your gestures, voice tone, facial expressions, and use of space. For instance, do you move closer to the

student who gives you a correct answer or farther away from the student who answers incorrectly?

11. **Developmental Differences in Nonverbal Behavior.** Cut out magazine or newspaper pictures of people showing different expressions or different gestures. Show the pictures to children of different age groups (from three years up) and see if there are any developmental age-related differences in reading these people's messages.

12. **Active Listening.** The use of various listening techniques can encourage people to talk both in and out of the classroom. The techniques can also be used to focus a communicator's attention on some aspect of the communication. For example, reflecting feelings back usually encourages the communicator to focus on his or her own feelings. More active listening techniques such as clarification, summarizing, and reflection tend to encourage communication. Try to use these techniques when conversing with someone and note whether this increases communication.

13. **How Do You Handle Interpersonal Conflict?** Teachers have all had to deal with students with whom they have personality clashes. Ask several teachers to relate case histories of such students and ask them how they dealt with the conflict. In addition, ask the teachers as well as other students at what point a student should be assigned a different class because of a personality clash.

14. **Parent-Teacher Communication Within the District.** How do school administrators communicate with parents? Many school districts are concerned about their community relations. In your own district, interview some school administrators on the subject, asking them to name the most and least effective types of communication. Then interview some teachers and ask them the same question.

15. **Writing to Parents.** Design letters to parents that communicate the following information:
    a. A student has failed the last test.
    b. A student has just successfully completed a research report and received an A.
    c. A student has come late to class and without completed homework three times in the past week with no excuse.
    d. You would like to schedule a conference with a parent to discuss a student's work.

16. **Parent-Teacher Conferencing.** A number of different activities and studies are useful in more fully understanding the area of parent-teacher conferences.
    a. Ask teachers to discuss their methods of handling such conferences.
    b. Try to roleplay such a conference, using the standards and suggestions noted in the text.
    c. Speak to some parents concerning what they want to get out of such conferences.

SCENARIOS

Here are nine scenarios. Try to apply the information you have learned in the chapter to each situation.

1. Mr. Whitman is teaching a class on solving equations to his seventh-grade class. After explaining the material, he asks his students if they have any questions, waits a second or so, and continues with the next section of his lesson. He argues that at this age, students should be able to discuss the material and form their own questions. If they don't ask questions, it is their loss. Discuss Mr. Whitman's technique and his philosophy and use of questions.

2. Ms. Henriques would like to have more student interest shown in her lessons on the French Revolution. She has asked a number of questions, such as "Who was Voltaire?" and "In what year did the revolution take place?" However, she doesn't get much of a response. When she calls on people who do not have their hands raised, she often gets an embarrassed silence. To improve participation, she has told her class that those students who answer questions correctly will get a half a point added to their next test for each question answered correctly. This has proven effective with some of the higher ability children but has not succeeded with the other students. Evaluate her policy and make suggestions on how to increase student participation.

3. Mr. Tatum has a particular problem with Robert. Robert often raises his hand and wants to answer the question but usually gets it wrong. Mr. Tatum does not want to ignore Robert's hand but on the other hand has difficulty handling the wrong answers. After ignoring Robert's hand for most of the period, Robert asked Mr. Tatum why he didn't call on him. Mr. Tatum said that other people needed a chance as well. How might Mr. Tatum handle Robert's wrong answers?

4. When Ms. Canter gave her fifth-grade class a test on division, she did not expect Joyce to do well; nevertheless Joyce received a grade of 95 percent. To lift Joyce's confidence, Ms. Canter told Joyce that she was a great math student. She was surprised when Joyce just sloughed the compliment off. Ms. Canter was trying to reinforce Joyce, but her praise didn't work. Where did she go wrong?

5. Working with a child with a fragile ego is not an easy task but one that Mr. Brownstein has to face. Jerry is a rather fearful and anxious child whose work is about average but who reacts poorly to any criticism. Yet, his papers must be corrected, and since Mr. Brownstein does write comments on compositions, he must write criticisms on Jerry's rather poor work. He wrote on Jerry's paper that he thought Jerry's ideas were good and that Jerry should do the exercises on pages 13–15 in his grammar book because he didn't seem to know the difference between "there" and "their." He made some other points on Jerry's paper and told Jerry that if he handed in the paper again with the correct grammar he would raise Jerry's grade. Evaluate Mr. Brownstein's way of presenting criticism.

6. Tina just does not get along with Miss Crawford. In fact, there is not one thing about Miss Crawford that Tina likes. Tina feels that Miss Crawford gives too much work, yells too much, is too strict, and does not like her. Miss Crawford understands the dislike Tina feels for her but notes that Tina does not do her homework well and is generally rude and negative. She has tried to warn this junior high school student that she has to change her attitude. Tina has asked her mother to take her out of the class. If you were Miss Crawford, what would you do? If you were Tina's parents, would you accede to Tina's request?

7. Mr. Ennis was looking forward to seeing Peter's parents. Peter has not been doing his work and has performed poorly in his eighth-grade studies. Mr. Ennis gathered examples of Peter's work and achievement test scores and prepared answers to the questions he thought Peter's parents would ask. Peter's parents agreed that Peter isn't doing the work, but they did not know what to do. Mr. Ennis and Peter's parents agreed that Peter's parents were to check Peter's homework each night. At first, there was some improvement, but three weeks later Peter had regressed to a point where his work was again unacceptable. Why is the cooperative program failing?

8. The Brinsons are angry. Mrs. Brinson has had to take off a day of work to meet with her son John's teacher. John's mother does not understand what the problem could possibly be, since John has always done well in elementary school. After shaking hands with Mr. Anderson, Mrs. Brinson makes it clear that this visit is an imposition. Mr. Anderson acknowledges the imposition, shows Mrs. Brinson the dates of John's misconduct, and asks her if she has any suggestions. Mrs. Brinson asks why she was not informed before, to which Mr. Anderson replies that he thought a personal conference was best. They agree that Mr. Anderson will send a weekly report home discussing John's behavior, and Mrs. Brinson will sign the note and return it to school. How did Mr. Anderson handle the conference? Can you make any additional suggestions?

9. Ms. Carson believes strongly that parents can help their children by reading to them. She has sent a note home imploring parents to read with their children, but it seems that most of the parents of her second-grade students are not doing it. Ms. Carson sees two possible alternative explanations: The parents may not be interested in their children's progress, or they may not have the time. Evaluate Ms. Carson's position and discuss the problems with her reading program.

10

Are These Statements True or False?

Turn the next page for the correct answers. Each statement is repeated following the paragraph in which the information can be found.

1. Both the general public and teachers view discipline as one of the greatest problems in schools.
2. Most teachers become more authoritarian with experience in the classroom.
3. Teachers should present about ten rules to their classes at the beginning of the term.
4. Good class managers jump right into the work on the first day to show the students that the main focus of the class is learning.
5. Teachers should not publicly correct every misbehavior, since this interferes with learning.
6. Effective class managers can do more than one thing at a time.
7. Teachers should routinely repeat a student's response so the class will understand that it is worth the class's attention.
8. Teachers should use sarcasm with high school students but not with elementary school students.
9. Teachers are more likely to have time left over at the end of the class in high-ability classes than in classes of lower ability.
10. When students are asked to keep track of how often they interrupt the class, they tend to interrupt the class more.
11. Teaching children to reward themselves does not work, since children are incapable of choosing the appropriate times to reinforce themselves.
12. One effective way of handling defiant behavior is to ignore it.

Classroom Management

Answers to True-False Statements

1. *True*
2. *True*
3. *False* Correct statement: Teachers should limit their rules to between three and six.
4. *False* Correct statement: Good class managers do not jump right into the work but spend more time presenting the rules and practicing them.
5. *True* Teachers should not publicly correct every misbehavior but, whenever possible, should use techniques that do not interfere with the lesson.
6. *True*
7. *False* Correct statement: Effective teachers do not routinely repeat student responses, since that teaches the rest of the class that they do not have to listen to other students.
8. *False* Correct statement: Teachers should never use sarcasm to discipline students.
9. *False* Correct statement: Teachers are much more likely to have time left over at the end of a period when teaching students of lower ability than students of higher ability.
10. *False* Correct statement: Self-monitoring tends to decrease the troublesome behavior over the short term.
11. *False* Correct statement: Although any self-reinforcement procedure requires monitoring by the teacher, self-reinforcement can be used successfully in schools.
12. *False* Correct statement: Defiant behavior cannot be ignored and must be dealt with calmly and swiftly.

Mr. Monroe is looking forward to his first year of teaching. He has heard that many first year teachers have some difficulties with classroom management and student discipline. What can he do to prevent these problems?

Ms. Ryan has difficulty with Victoria, a sixth grader who does her work inaccurately and in a sloppy manner. Victoria also likes to talk to whoever is around her. The situation has worsened as Victoria now gives Ms. Ryan "smart" answers. A few days ago, when Ms. Ryan asked her to move to another seat, Victoria refused. How can Ms. Ryan work with Victoria?

Mr. Dempsey is very frustrated. He has one class of high school sophomores who constantly talk to each other and do not pay attention to the lesson. The class constantly argues with his rules and standards for work, and he is not satisfied with their progress. How can Mr. Dempsey deal with this class?

DISCIPLINE: EVERYONE'S CONCERN

What does a teacher do if a student talks out in class, turns in poor work, fights with another student, defies an order to sit down, or breaks a classroom rule?

Most teachers are concerned about discipline in the classroom, and new teachers are especially vulnerable to discipline problems. When the problems of beginning teachers in a number of developed countries were surveyed, discipline was the number one problem identified by the teachers (Veenman, 1984). The general public is also concerned about discipline problems in the schools. Year after year in the annual Gallup poll reflecting the public's view of education, discipline is named as one of the greatest problems (McDaniel, 1986).

True or False Both the general public and teachers view discipline as one of the greatest problems in schools.

Too often, though, discipline is viewed only in terms of handling problem behavior, such as talking out of turn and disobedience (Weber & Sloan, 1986). It is more than that, however. According to Edmund Emmer, "Discipline indicates the degree to which students behave appropriately, are involved in activities, are task-oriented, and do not cause disruptions (1987, p. 233)." Discipline, then, involves something more than punishing students for misbehavior. It involves providing an atmosphere that is conducive to learning and preventing problems from arising. It also involves helping students to develop internal controls that allow them to monitor their own behavior (Kohut & Range, 1986).

Some Cautions and Concerns

Before we begin, however, some basic concerns need to be mentioned. First, the degree of classroom control desired by teachers differs from teacher to teacher. In some classrooms, a child calling out or any classroom noise is a sign of impending chaos to the teacher, and no talking is permitted. In other classrooms, a lighter type of discipline exists, with the teacher encouraging self-regulation, and discipline is less punitive. A silent classroom does not necessarily mean that learning is going on. Students may not dare to misbehave in a class from fear of ridicule or punishment, but this same unquestioned compliance may not teach students self-control and may inhibit active participation in the learning process (Kindsvatter & Levine, 1980). On the other hand, a classroom in which chaos reigns, misbehavior is common, and the rights of others are denied is one in which learning cannot take place. As teachers gain experience, they tend to become more authoritarian. Bergmann et al. (1976) reported that more than half the beginning teachers changed their original student-centered teaching behaviors to more authoritarian ones as a result of their classroom experiences. Discipline, then, is very much a personal matter and depends upon the type of classroom the teacher wants.

True or False   Most teachers become more authoritarian with experience in the classroom.

Second, for any discussion of discipline to be helpful it must present realistic alternatives for new teachers (Brophy, 1983). I have never been impressed with the idea that each teacher can be, or should be, a therapist or an expert in complex psychological techniques. However, every successful teacher has his or her own methods that do work, and some cognitive and behavioral techniques can be used successfully by the teacher.

Third, too often discipline has been viewed using a "circle the wagons" orientation in which teachers are seen as student adversaries (Curwin et al., 1980). In such an orientation, the teacher thinks of him or herself as there primarily for control and secondarily for teaching. Teaching is part of discipline, and discipline is part of teaching (Morris, 1981). In addition, setting up a more cooperative "we need discipline so we can learn" attitude is better than establishing a "you're going to behave or else" attitude. Discipline, then, is a means to an end, not an end in itself.

Fourth, in looking at classroom discipline, the overall school climate and organization cannot be ignored (Short & Short, 1987). It is difficult for students to concentrate while the halls are filled with students milling about, constant interruptions are occurring, and fights are breaking out just outside the room (Smith, 1987). Also, each teacher within a school is affected by every other teacher. Each school has its own "feeling." While some schools are orderly, others have a carnival atmosphere (Kaplan, 1986). Teachers argue that the school administration must back them up in their attempts to create an orderly environment (Tjosvold, 1980). Individual teachers within their own classrooms cannot unilaterally solve the very serious problems of drug abuse (including alcoholism) and violence in the schools. These problems require schoolwide action and coordinated districtwide policies. No discussion of discipline can give new teachers "easy" methods that work when confronted with such problems. However, even within troubled schools, one can find some classrooms in which misbehavior is relatively infrequent and students are learning at a reasonable pace.

Last, most teachers decry the lack of practical help that they are given—both in their teacher education classes and in their schools—for maintaining discipline. What is presented is often in the form of cliches (McDaniel, 1986) or theories (Lasley, 1987). This chapter looks not only at the "what" of discipline but also at the "how." However, a clear theoretical basis exists for discipline choices (Glickman & Wolfgang, 1979). The teacher who believes in a behavioral viewpoint is more likely to use behavior modification; a teacher who is more humanistically inclined is more likely to use a technique such as active listening.

PREVENTING PROBLEMS THROUGH EFFECTIVE CLASSROOM MANAGEMENT

I can remember my first day teaching in a junior high school. I was ill prepared to deal with the problems I was to encounter. As I look back, it wasn't my

Discipline in the classroom is affected by the climate that exists within the school itself.

inability to handle the student who didn't do his homework or who talked out of turn that I remember so vividly as the fact that some of the misbehavior that occurred in my class could and should have been prevented.

Research Perspectives on How to Prevent Problems

Studies in elementary school and junior high and high school have consistently found differences in classroom management between effective and ineffective teachers (Emmer, 1987; Evertson & Emmer, 1982; Cruickshank et al., 1981). The measures of effectiveness can be classtime on task, student recommendations, and observations of pupil behavior. Most effective teachers manage and monitor their classes in a way that prevents discipline problems. The search continues for teaching strategies that differentiate effective from ineffective teachers, but a variety of such factors have already been discovered. Moskowitz and Hayman (1976) found that junior high school teachers who were rated best by students were more successful on their first day, used the time to establish control, spent more time orienting and setting the class climate, and had less off-task time. Edmund Emmer and colleagues (1980) found that third-grade teachers who were more effective managers had more

workable systems of rules, taught their rules and procedures systematically and thoroughly, and carefully monitored pupil behavior, reacting swiftly to rule breaking and immediately stopping such behavior. Studies have shown that these techniques can be taught to new teachers to make them more effective (Evertson et al., 1983; Borg & Ascione, 1982).

What the Research on Teacher Management Means to Teachers

Research shows that advanced planning, formulating and teaching students classroom rules, communicating to students the consequences for breaking the rules as well as effective use of the first few days of school and consistent monitoring are the keys to preventing discipline problems. Classroom management is aimed at achieving order through gaining the cooperation of students in reaching the goal of learning (Doyle, 1985). Some aspects of management must be undertaken before the class begins and some during the first few class sessions. Monitoring the class is a constant procedure.

Before the Class Meets

Prevention of discipline problems begins before the class meets. Three areas are especially important: the physical layout of the classroom, the rules and procedures necessary for the smooth functioning of the class, and the system of consequences for both proper behavior and misbehavior.

The Physical Layout of the Room

How should desks be arranged? Where should students sit? Is the room in good order? These are basic questions. Normally, this area is more relevant to elementary schoolteachers who spend more time in one room with their class and have more freedom to arrange the desks. Junior high and senior high schoolteachers often share the room with other teachers and are faced with a potentially difficult problem of shifting desks at the beginning of some class periods, a situation that can cause disruption.

All rooms should be checked to be certain they are ready for the class. If the lights don't work, a window is broken, there is no lock on the closet, or there are not enough desks, such problems should be corrected before the first day. If you have twenty desks and twenty-five pupils in your class, five students have to stand, or you may have to waste important time during the first class session dealing with the situation. This could lead to problems as the rest of the class waits while you send for what you need.

The choice of room arrangement (where to place the teacher's desk, whether to place student desks in rows, circles, or clusters) is determined by individual needs, and no single arrangement meets all needs. Teachers need not fear that choosing a less orthodox desk arrangement such as a circle or a cluster leads to disruptive behavior, because the evidence indicates that this is not so (Rosenfield et al., 1985). However, whether a teacher likes a traditional or a nontraditional setting, certain precautions should be kept in mind. First, students must be able to see clearly from every seat to all instructional areas. If you plan to perform demonstrations in one area of the class and more directive instruction in another (perhaps near the blackboard), both areas must be easily seen by students. If students cannot see from their seats, they will have to move in order to see the board or the demonstration or they will not pay attention. Second, the teacher must be able to monitor the students from every area of the classroom (Emmer, 1987). Third, teachers need to consider the traffic patterns in the room. Sometimes desks are placed too close to a window, making it difficult to open or close the window, or the aisles are not wide enough. Fourth, the particu-lar physical needs of any handicapped students in the class must be taken into consideration. A child in a wheelchair needs sufficient aisle space; a deaf child with an interpreter will require an unobstructed view of the person signing to him or her. For specific instructions on the physical needs of the child, the guidance counselor or special education teacher is a good source of help.

Planning Rules and Consequences

Most teachers want to present the rules and procedures to their students on the first day. Whether a teacher intends to ask the class for help in formulating classroom rules or to explain the rules him or herself, the teacher must plan what rules are to be implemented. Experienced teachers know what they want to do, but a new teacher must plan rules carefully. It is good practice to ask effective, experienced teachers what rules they establish, how they present them to the class, what the consequences are for breaking the rules, and what their grading system is.

Classroom rules can be roughly divided into two areas: classroom procedures and rules for decorum. Classroom procedures include step-by-step statements that focus on the way a particular goal is accomplished in the classroom, such as lining up for recess, heading one's paper, or what to do if absent from school. Such procedures also entail beginning- and end-of-period activities, such as what students should do when they enter the room and how to leave their desks at the end of class. Having the homework assignment or a "do now" problem on the blackboard at the beginning of the class is one such activity. Rules for decorum involve those regulations that protect everyone's right to participate in an active learning process and might include rules for calling out in class or getting out of one's seat. These rules should be written out and the consequences of following or disobeying them noted. For example, what will happen if a student does not do the homework or gets out of his or her seat without permission? Consequences can include demerits for poor work leading to failure or detention for lateness. Some thought should also be given to rewards or positive consequences for following some of the more important rules, such as an extra few points if all homework is done. One effective way to highlight the importance of rules is to issue them in writing and have them signed by parents.

Along with having his or her own rules, every teacher must enforce school policy. New teachers should familiarize themselves with school policies concerning administrative details and discipline. For example, record keeping concerning attendance, cutting class, and the like are often covered by firm school policy.

What sort of rules should a new teacher adopt? To some extent, this depends upon the subject and school level. A science teacher working with equipment may require different rules than an English teacher. Procedural rules should cover bringing all needed materials to class and being in one's seat and ready to work as well as rules concerning being recognized in class and leaving one's seat. Decorum rules cover having respect for people and property, including no name-calling and picking up litter (Emmer et al., 1982).

THE FIRST FEW DAYS OF SCHOOL

The students quietly file into your classroom on the first day. They all sit down, and the late bell rings. They look at you. Now it's your turn. What do you do?

Teachers place great importance on how they handle the first class meeting, and much evidence supports their concern. In some cases, year-long discipline difficulties can be traced back to problems that would have been prevented if enough thought had been given to the first few meetings of the class. Effective managers use the first day of class to explain what they expect from the class. Good managers are not in a great rush to get right down to work. They take the time to explain the procedures and rules that will govern the classroom.

CONNECTIONS

Teaching the Rules

Both good classroom managers and poor ones have rules and present them. However, good managers can be differentiated from poor ones by the way in which they present the rules to their classes (Emmer, 1987).

Teachers can be tempted to have a rule for everything, to enforce rules selectively, not to explain why a rule is necessary, to want to go directly into the work instead of rehearsing the rules, or to give messages that students don't have to obey a rule. The following guidelines can help make the process of rule making easier and more effective.

1. **Three to six rules are necessary for most classes** (Emmer, 1987). Too many rules overload students, making it difficult for them to deal with the rules. Any rules that are made must be enforced. If there are too many rules, it becomes difficult to enforce them, and the teacher becomes nothing more than a law enforcement officer.

2. **Explain only those rules and procedures that are needed at the beginning of the first class.** Some rules concerning raising one's hand, when a student can get up to get a drink of water, procedures for going to the bathroom, or what to do if a student doesn't understand something can be explained. However, since you probably won't be doing any small-group reading instruction on the first couple of days, it makes little sense to discuss such rules right away.

3. **Explain the reasons behind the rules.** Students are more likely to cooperate if they understand the reasons for rules or procedures.

4. **Make rules explicit, not general.** Rules such as "Don't talk" or "Do your work" communicate little. However, rules such as "Stay in your seat unless you have permission from me to leave" or "Raise your hand and wait to be recognized before speaking" are better. Some elementary schoolteachers may have a special sign that a student can use for asking to sharpen a pencil or go to the bathroom so that the student does not need to disrupt the class discussion to make such requests.

5. **Whenever possible, state rules positively.** It's better to say "Arrive on time" rather than "don't be late" or "raise your hand when you want to say something" rather than "don't call out."

6. **Rehearse your rules whenever possible.** Rehearsing certain procedures, such as lining up in elementary school, is often necessary. Rehearsing procedures in secondary school involving science labs may be necessary, but practicing other routines probably is not required.

7. **Create rules to govern transitions.** About 15 percent of a student's time is spent in transitional activities between two major activities, such as switching from social studies to science or from checking papers to doing seat work (Doyle & Carter, 1987). Discipline problems increase greatly during these transitions, and teachers need to give transitions greater attention. Give a particular amount of time, such as a minute, to make the transition, compliment students who are ready,

and ignore the one or two children who may be taking a little longer. Saying "I see Randy is ready" is sometimes effective.

8. **Enforce all rules.** Even kindergarten children can tell you the difference between real rules—those that are enforced—and paper rules—those that are stated but not enforced (Kounin et al., 1961). If you make a rule, enforce it.

9. **Repeat rules when necessary.** Effective teachers remind students of the rules, especially during the first week or so (Emmer et al., 1980).

10. **Make rules relevant to the learning situation.** Some teachers persistently criticize students for their hair styles, clothing, the way they walk, or other educationally irrelevant areas. Students are more likely to keep rules that are relevant to the learning situation.

11. **Make penalties and rewards known to students.** Students deserve to know what will happen if they do not finish their homework or if they persistently talk to their neighbors during class. A violation of an academic rule should result in an academic penalty. Breaking a non-academic rule should result in a consequence other than lowering grades. For example, if a student persistently talks to other students, a non-academic violation, he or she might lose free time. If a student fails to submit assignments on time, an academic violation, his or her grade might drop. At the same time, a teacher should give some thought to rewards for good work and good behavior. Whatever rewards or penalties are used, students should be familiar with the teacher's policies.

True or False Teachers should present about ten rules to their classes at the beginning of the term.

Student Help in Forming Rules

Some teachers feel that students can help to form rules (Gnagey, 1981). This can increase student acceptance and promotes a sense of responsibility (Emmer, 1987). On the other hand, since students don't always identify all the areas teachers deem important, teachers may have to prompt students. In addition, some of the procedures, such as those for lining up, don't require much debate. When student input is desired, it should be limited to general classroom rules and a few procedures. If a teacher suggests a rule, he or she can ask the student what the reasons for such a

Some teachers present the rules, while others ask students for help in establishing rules. Whichever system is used, classroom rules should include both procedures and rules for decorum.

rule are, especially in elementary school. This communicates to the students that each rule has a reason behind it.

Rule Making in Elementary, Junior High, and High School

Elementary schoolchildren often require extra practice in some classroom procedures, whether it's passing out paper or lining up. These students may also be unfamiliar with general classroom rules, especially in the early elementary school grades. Explanations to these children must be explicit, and rehearsals are especially important. At the same time, peppering these youngsters with one rule or lengthy procedure after another may result in an overload in which nothing is learned. A relatively slow, rational explanation combined with rehearsals and reminders is best.

Junior high school students come to school with six or seven years of elementary school training. They require less or no rehearsal in the more mundane classroom matters. Presenting a written list of rules to the class once the rules have been established, and perhaps even posting them, is a reasonable strategy. Robert Houston and colleagues (1988) suggest that teachers can begin a discussion of rules using such questions as Are there rules in everyday life? What would a football game be like without rules? Why were rules established for sports? or What is the purpose of traffic signals? This can be followed by a discussion of the class's specific rules.

Junior high school students may have some difficulty following rules and procedures because they encounter so many different teachers, each with his or her own rules. This differs from their elementary school experience. The junior high school is often the first school in which the student has a different teacher for each subject. Since it is sometimes difficult for students to deal with the different procedures, some repetition may be required. Written rules can be placed in a student's notebook.

In high school, the teacher has a special need to explore work-related rules and academic standards. Specific standards of work must be communicated directly and accurately. For example, the teacher may want reports typed or a specific style of bibliography on a report. In addition, the grading system should be explicitly explained and any consequences for missed assignments or tests discussed. Some high schools and most colleges require or recommend that a course outline be given to the students that outlines the grading system, classroom procedures, and other policies. High school students are especially proficient at questioning the need for a procedure, and the teacher must be able to answer such questions without getting into a debate. The procedures can be modified if students have a good suggestion, but teachers should be wary of being argued out of sanctions for tardiness because the student had something else to do or for missed assignments because of too many other tests. Constant arguing or changing requirements makes the teacher look weak. In addition, teachers should be aware of school rules, especially those concerning tardiness and cutting class. Teachers usually cannot influence school procedures or penalties, and stating that it is a school rule and therefore must be enforced should end any discussion.

A New Look at Rules: Three-Dimensional Discipline

Richard Curwin and colleagues (1980) advocate an interesting use of rules in urging a system of class management called **three-dimensional discipline.** They see the classroom as a social contract in which

three-dimensional discipline A system of classroom management based upon the establishment and refinement of classroom rules that form the basis for a contract binding both students and the teacher.

rules and the consequences for breaking them are generated, discussed, refined, and tested by members of the class. The teacher first develops rules for students and proposes consequences for violations. The consequences need not be the classic type of punishments that Curwin believes are only a way of "getting even" with the student. Instead, the consequence for throwing paper on the floor may be an apology to the class and picking up the paper. There are no exceptions to the rules, and violations are never overlooked. As infractions of the rules occur more frequently, the sanctions become greater. For example, the first violation of the rule that the student will arrive for class on time results in a conference with the student, the second in an after-school class, and the third in a parent-student-teacher conference. Rewards such as free time and allowing students their choice of activities are given to students who always follow the rules.

For most teachers, the development of rules is the end of the rule formation process, but Curwin doesn't see it that way. A second procedure calls for students to develop rules for the teacher and consequences for the teacher for violating them. This is not as radical as you might think. After the teacher presents his rules, he gives an example of a rule the students might make for him. One possible rule is that the teacher must give all homework for the upcoming week on Friday so that students can plan. If the teacher breaks the rule, the consequence may be that the teacher cannot give homework over the weekend. Of course, all such rules must conform to state, local, and school regulations.

Students then make rules for themselves and discuss violations. These rules govern student-student relationships. Such rules might involve name calling or using profanity, and the consequences may require a written apology.

These rules form the basis for a contract binding both teachers and students. Of course, the teacher is final arbiter of the rules and cannot allow overly harsh rules to be adopted. The contract can be used for a month and then updated. The final set of rules can be adopted through a vote after this trial period. Each rule should be discussed, and Curwin suggests that a test be given to make certain everyone understands all rules. The rules can be posted in the classroom. Curwin claims that this social contract approach reduces the amount of time teachers spend on discipline problems, although it is a time-consuming and sometimes tedious task.

A Sample First Day

What does a teacher do on the first day of school? Emmer and colleagues (1982) make many useful suggestions. Before the bell rings, the teacher should be in the hall or by the door, make eye contact, be pleasant, but above all, be visible. Students may be invited to sit where they want at the beginning, but the teacher should make it clear that this is a temporary situation. When the bell rings, the teacher should begin promptly, and if a student continues talking, a gentle reminder that the bell has rung and it's now time to begin is sufficient.

Good classroom managers begin by introducing themselves and perhaps mentioning something about what they like to do or what they did during the summer. This should be kept short. An introduction to the course and an overview that is positive in tone is also a good idea. At this point, such administrative tasks as taking the roll or filling out class forms should be performed. Each administrative task should be announced to the class and any procedures specifically stated. The teacher can make a statement such as "I'm going to call the roll now. Please say 'present' when you hear your name. If I mispronounce your name, please correct me." When filling out class cards, the teacher should tell the students to raise their hands if they have a question. A temporary seating chart is a reasonable idea so that the teacher can begin to learn students' names quickly.

Next comes the presentation of the class rules. Emmer suggests that each rule be read and an example given and the rule's rationale and the consequences for breaking the rule noted. Whether the teacher specifically wants to discuss grading practices on this first day is a personal choice and depends upon the time available. The teacher may want to wait until the second day in elementary school

and, perhaps, junior high school to avoid overloading students.

True or False Good class managers jump right into the work on the first day to show the students that the main focus of the class is learning.

Assuming there is time, an initial content activity should be planned. This activity should be interesting, perhaps reading a short story and answering questions, presenting a brief experiment, or working some examples. The activity should be easy and the potential for success very high. The object of the activity is to encourage good work habits and to practice work-related procedures. This first activity allows the teacher to show how the rules work. It must be checked and reviewed so that students will obtain a sense of accomplishment and success. If time is too short, telling the students that the class will go over the material tomorrow is appropriate.

Monitoring Compliance

It does little good to have a meaningful, relevant set of rules only to ignore them by the second or third class session. Compliance to rules must be constantly monitored and consequences imposed (Spettel, 1983). There should be no excuses allowed and no exceptions made. When a rule is broken, the teacher should ask the student to state the appropriate rule.

The consequences for breaking the rules should be progressive. That is, students who fail to complete their homework only once should be penalized less severely than students who habitually break the rule. Consequences should fit the behavior, and teachers should be aware of taking too much class time talking to one student about his or her behavior while the other students look on bored.

The progressive aspect of discipline means that the teacher must keep accurate records of student misbehavior and rule breaking. This becomes extremely important in parent conferences when teachers are often asked to demonstrate that the student has not done his or her homework x number of times. Having the dates makes a teacher look professional and more organized.

What sort of consequences can teachers use? There are many, but the simplest are often the most effective. For example, if a class comes in late from recess, David Adamson (1987) suggests subtracting the amount of time from the next recess. Detention, demerits, loss of free time, loss of points on one's grade, loss of a privilege, especially in elementary school, a letter home to a parent, and parent-teacher conferences are all consequences. Each student should know that the first forgotten homework means a demerit, which combined with other demerits means a loss of points on one's grade. The second forgotten homework means something else. Each teacher must devise his or her own system, and the system must be explained to the students.

When teaching junior high school, I found that sometimes using a reward system of "pluses," in which two pluses caused a point to be added to a test grade, did much to help reduce the punitive nature of discipline. A student who had lost a point or two because of not doing homework could improve his or her grade by working harder. Discipline involves the use of positive consequences as well as negative ones. Thus, sometimes rewarding students for doing an extra chore like picking up a piece of paper from the floor when you didn't ask or complimenting a child for being ready to work is appropriate.

What Does Rule Making Mean to the Teacher?

One area that differentiates good managers from poor ones is the ability to think through rules and procedures and communicate them, monitor them, and reinforce them when necessary. The emphasis on rules does not have to be overly authoritarian, and the teacher can use a number of ways to develop rules. Some teachers simply supply the rules, other teachers might ask students why a rule is necessary or ask for student input, while still others might try a process such as Curwin's social contract. Rules and procedures are not ends in themselves, but they allow the teacher the opportunity to create an atmosphere in which learning can occur.

MAINTAINING DISCIPLINE

Rules are aids that help prevent discipline problems. With so much emphasis on the first day or two of class, it is easy to forget the importance of maintaining a program that prevents discipline problems throughout the school year.

Jacob Kounin's Research into Discipline

To try to discover the differences between teachers whose classrooms were racked with misbehavior and those that had few cases of misbehavior, Jacob Kounin (1970) videotaped eighty first- and second-grade classes, each of which contained at least one emotionally disturbed child. Kounin found, however, that there were few significant differences in this area. He found instead that effective teachers create environments in which misbehavior is minimized. In other words, the differences between the two groups of teachers were found to be not so much in how the teachers dealt with disruptive students but in the ways in which their management techniques prevented misbehavior from arising in the first place. Kounin described the major differences using terms such as *withitness*, *momentum*, *overlapping*, and others that have become a part of the new vocabulary of preventative discipline.

Withitness

Does the teacher know what is going on at all times? This is the basic question defining **withitness.** Some teachers notice the note passing in the back of the room, the fidgety behavior on the side, and everything else that is going on. Teachers who are "withit" know what is going on and who did what and deal with misbehavior before it becomes more troublesome. They do not make timing errors, that is, wait too long before intervening, or target errors that involve blaming innocent students. Withit teachers scan the room and gain eye contact, especially at the beginning of the term (Brooks, 1985). Withit teachers do not publicly correct every little misbehavior, since this detracts from the time students work on tasks. These teachers sometimes use nonverbal methods, such as walking towards the offender or pointing (Emmer et al., 1984). However, if nonverbal signals are being used, teachers must be certain that the student has stopped the misbehavior before going on to something else.

withitness Jacob Kounin's term for teachers who constantly know what is going on in the classroom.

Withit teachers move around the room and are vigilant in monitoring compliance and following through with reminders when necessary (Brophy & Good, 1986).

True or False Teachers should not publicly correct every misbehavior, since this interferes with learning.

Momentum

We've all been in classes in which the teacher either goes too fast or too slowly. If a teacher proceeds too slowly, students become fidgety and lose interest and misbehavior results. If a teacher goes too fast, the slower students are left behind, and again, misbehavior results. Momentum can be disrupted by overdwelling or fragmentation. In behavioral **overdwelling,** a teacher makes a mountain out of a molehill. This can occur when the teacher spends five minutes lecturing a student on some small misbehavior, such as whispering to a neighbor. A teacher may overdwell in other ways, such as spending too much time explaining a piece of apparatus.

Fragmentation is the tendency to have individuals do something one at a time that could be better done as a group. Explaining a procedure to a few students at a time when everyone needs to know it is one example.

Smoothness

Some teachers are able to move through their lessons smoothly without a hitch. Their transitions are easy, and they make no abrupt changes. When teachers clearly break the momentum of one activity and start another with a minimum of disruption, a smooth transition is achieved (Arlin, 1979). About thirty-one major transitions occur every day in elementary classrooms and account for about 15 percent of classroom time (Doyle, 1986). Transitions take less time at the secondary school level. Internal distractions account for nearly 90 percent of all distractions, but their average length is only about ten seconds. External interruptions are infrequent but can disrupt the lesson for several minutes (Behnke, 1979).

The smoothness of transitions can be affected by many things, including thrusts, flip-flops, dangles, and being stimulus bound. **Thrusts** are intrusions that disrupt the progress of the lesson. Some are external, such as the public address announcer's un-

necessary announcement about yearbooks, while others are caused by the teacher him or herself when calling attention to a typographical error during seatwork (Partin, 1987). A **flip-flop** occurs when a teacher moves from one topic to another and then returns to the first. A teacher might complete spelling, make the transition to social studies, and then ask how many students got a perfect score on their spelling test. Sometimes a teacher destroys the lesson's smoothness by starting one activity and then reacting to other stimuli that occur to them. This is what Kounin calls a **dangle,** since the class is left dangling while the teacher unloads his or her thoughts about something unconnected to the lesson. Such a teacher might be presenting a lesson on cancer prevention and then ask the students if they know how many inches of rain are expected that evening. The class if left dangling. Kounin also found that some teachers are **stimulus bound**, that is, they cannot resist reacting to anything that pops into their mind.

At the secondary level, when class periods are exactly forty-five or fifty minutes long, making certain that the work fills up the available time and the lesson is completed within the time frame is a concern (Doyle, 1984). Screaming the homework assignment at students as they are fleeing out the door to go to their next class is a disaster. Sometimes teachers tend

overdwelling Teacher behavior that involves spending too much time on a small point.

fragmentation The tendency to have students learn something individually that could better be learned in a group context.

thrusts Any intrusion whether internal or external that unnecessarily disrupts the lesson.

flip-flop A term used to describe an instructional behavior in which a teacher goes from one topic to another and then returns to the first.

dangle An instructional behavior in which students are left dangling while teachers talk about something essentially unconnected with the lesson.

stimulus bound Jacob Kounin's term for a state in which teachers react to anything that momentarily enters their mind.

to run out of work, especially with classes containing students of lower ability (Evertson, 1982), perhaps because they have difficulty getting these students involved in a discussion and these students ask fewer questions. A teacher should guard against this, since when there is no task to perform, misbehavior can result.

Overlapping

Teachers who are effective managers can do more than one thing at a time, an ability called **overlapping**. When conferring with one pupil, they can monitor other events going on. When instructing a small reading group, an effective teacher can deal with a student from another group who needs help without stopping the group activity.

Signalling

Teachers must be able to read students' signals as well as give students signals. It is not enough just to monitor the class and know what is going on. Some sensitivity to the meaning of what is going on is important. I can remember observing a lesson in which the students obviously were lost. They were restless, some of the books were closed, and a few students were looking out the windows. The teacher noticed it (he was "withit") but did not interpret these signals correctly. They were signals of boredom, but the

Effective teachers recognize the signs of student lack of interest and boredom.

> **overlapping**   Jacob Kounin's term for a teacher's ability to do more than one thing at a time.

teacher did not read them as such. Understanding the signals is important.

Teachers also signal students and let them know that they see what is going on. Such signals may end inattention without allowing it to escalate into bigger problems. For example, a teacher might move near inattentive students, make eye contact, direct a question to them, or make a brief comment (Brophy, 1983). Such signals do not interrupt the lesson but are effective.

Group Alerting and Accountability

Good classroom managers use strategies and techniques that keep the class alert and accountable, including looking around the group before calling on someone to recite, getting around to everyone frequently, interspersing choral responses with individual responses, asking for volunteers, throwing out challenges by saying that the next question is tricky, calling on a student to comment on or correct another student's response, and presenting novel or interesting material (Brophy, 1983). One aspect I have always found important is to keep students' attention on the comments of other students. Some teachers repeat what a student has said, which just teaches students not to listen to one another. To keep students tuned into other students, a teacher might consider asking students to repeat in their own words what a fellow student has said. Students are kept accountable for understanding what is said because they know it will be checked often.

True or False   Teachers should routinely repeat a student's response so the class will understand that it is worth the class's attention.

Challenge in Seatwork

Many teachers, especially in elementary school, assign seatwork to their students. That is, the students are working on their own. To be most useful, seatwork must have some interest value and a reasonable level of difficulty. It must have enough variety to keep the students interested. Seatwork should be matched to students' abilities. However, since we want students to work independently for a fairly extended period of time, the potential success rate should be high, certainly more than 80 percent correct. Seatwork will be discussed in detail in Chapter 11.

The Ripple Effect

Kounin first saw the ripple effect when teaching a course on mental hygiene. As he reprimanded a student for reading a newspaper during class, he noticed the effect the reprimand had on the other students. Their eyes went from the window to their work. The **ripple effect** is the effect the teacher's behavior towards one student has on the entire class. When a teacher tells a student to stop talking, it has an effect on the other students. Students also are affected by the inability of a teacher to stop a troublesome behavior. Misbehavior that is not monitored and stopped can lead to other outbreaks in the class.

Preventing Discipline Problems: What It Means to the Teacher

The research on preventing discipline problems has expanded greatly over the past two decades, and for good reason. The work conducted by Kounin and his colleagues (Kounin & Doyle, 1975; Kounin & Gump, 1971) as well as others shows that teachers can prevent discipline problems by planning effectively before the class begins, communicating a set of meaningful and relevant rules to students during the first days, monitoring compliance with the rules, and enforcing the rules.

Teachers can become good classroom managers if they make it a practice to notice what is going on; watch the pacing of their lessons; become sensitive to student signals; avoid flip-flops, dangles, fragmentation, and overdwelling; understand and use the ripple effect; and learn how to overlap.

> **ripple effect**   The effect that a teacher's behavior towards one student has on other students.

COPING WITH DISCIPLINE PROBLEMS: SOME STRATEGIES THAT WORK

Although it is possible to prevent some misbehavior through effective planning and management, misbehavior is unfortunately a fact of classroom life. Misbehavior is anything but uncommon. In one study of first- and fifth-graders, Doyle (1979) found that teachers made sixteen conduct statements to students per hour. Ever since Kounin's work, it has become somewhat popular to blame the teacher for misbehavior within the class. However, this is a misreading of Kounin's work. Although teachers can do much to prevent discipline problems, Kounin never said that discipline problems would completely disappear if classroom management improved.

This section concentrates on what to do when a discipline problem presents itself, specifically offering suggestions for dealing with some of the more common behavior problems. But no matter how well a teacher practices a particular strategy, the strategy is doomed if it violates some of the general guidelines for disciplining students listed below.

⟫ CONNECTIONS

These Hints Could Save Your Class

When serving as the behavioral dean of a large urban junior high school, I found that some teachers were able to isolate discipline problems and deal with them while others challenged with a relatively simple problem, such as a child talking to his or her neighbor, would soon become embroiled in a situation that threatened to disrupt the entire class. Some of the mistakes teachers made were relatively simple, and the following guidelines are helpful in handling any kind of classroom problem and can prevent a small problem from becoming a bigger one.

1. **Never embarrass students or make them lose face in front of their friends.** All students, but especially those in late elementary school and junior high school, have great social needs. If the teacher's statements back a student into a corner and it becomes a choice between accepting the teacher's insults or losing face in front of friends, the student will often choose to save face. For instance, a teacher who says, "Your work is so poor, Edward, I don't think you have time to fool around

with Joseph," is likely to get a smart answer in return, and a debate may ensue. A student will respond better to a reprimand that is given in private where he or she does not have to impress his or her peers.

2. **Don't debate with students.** Some students will try to debate and find the fine points of law. This may gain them points with the other students or extra attention or show the teacher up. The student who gets a teacher to debate the fairness of a rule that has been laid down months ago makes the teacher look weak and irresolute. A statement from the teacher such as "We can discuss this rule later in private" or "I'll hear your complaint later when it does not affect class time" is better than debating.

3. **Don't use sarcasm.** Young children don't understand sarcasm, and older children don't like it. Sarcasm adds nothing to your discipline procedure and will only serve to anger students more.

4. **Don't lose your temper.** Defuse anger, don't add to it. Many of the hardest discipline problems involve student anger. Sometimes such anger is the result of problems at home that the teacher cannot solve. In other words, some students come to school angry. At other times, something in school, such as frustration at not being able to do the work properly or anger at an insult from another student, may be the cause. The teacher who remains calm can defuse the situation more easily.

5. **Be consistent, fair, and unbiased.** If you have a rule such as bringing a notebook to class and having it open at the beginning of the period and there is a penalty for not having the notebook, the rule must be consistently followed. As discussed in the chapter on motivation, some teachers treat good students and poor ones differently, such as giving good students more latitude in handing work in late. Students are very sensitive to exceptions being made, and this can lead to problems.

7. **Use small punishments and be as unobtrusive as possible.** Many problems are relatively minor, such as talking or fooling around, and are more of an annoyance than a danger. Sometimes unobtrusive discipline techniques such as standing closer to a student, moving around the room, looking at the student and shaking your head or pointing or placing your finger to your lips ("sh") are sufficient and do not interrupt the lesson.

8. **Don't continually threaten students.** Teachers who threaten punishments that they cannot or will not carry out lose the respect of their stu-

dents. Don't threaten to suspend a student or give three hours of extra homework if you cannot or do not wish to carry out the threat.

9. **Have enough to teach.** Teachers are more likely to have time left over in classes that contain many students of lower ability than in classes where most of the students possess high scholastic ability. Always have some activity in reserve in case your lesson does not fill the entire period.

10. **Handle as much of your own discipline problem as possible.** Certainly, there are events that are serious enough to require the assistance of the dean or principal, the school psychologist, or the guidance counselor, including fistfights, criminal behavior such as extortion, drug-related problems, self-abuse, and severe aggression. Many schools require teachers to report to deans certain infractions, such as excessive lateness. Generally, however, such day-to-day problems as talking in class, not finishing work, and fooling around with other students should be handled by the classroom teacher.

11. **Be aware of your relationship with your students.** All types of discipline procedures are more effective if you have a good relationship with your students. In addition, you want misbehaving students to return to work. Shouting at students for poor behavior often causes a problem, because even if you get a student to stop misbehaving, you may lose the student.

12. **Discipline the student's action, not the student.** Students who misbehave need to have their actions corrected. As long as a teacher's comments remain fixed to an undesirable action, such as talking out, students are not likely to feel personally injured. However, if the teacher tells a student, "You're the worst behaved person in the school," "I can't understand why you didn't get this right when everyone else did," or "You're really not college material," it impacts on the student as a person and is not likely to be effective.

13. **Whenever possible, look for ways of teaching self-control and self-discipline.** Sometimes, there is too much emphasis on teachers as law enforcement agents. As we will see shortly, it is possible to teach students to control their own behavior, and this is normally an effective way of limiting troublesome behavior.

True or False Teachers should use sarcasm with high school students but not with elementary school students.

When dealing with misbehavior, it is important not to embarrass students, debate with them, lose your temper, or use sarcasm.

True or False Teachers are more likely to have time left over at the end of the class in high-ability classes than in classes of lower ability.

Focus on Specific Techniques

With these general guidelines in mind, let's look at some techniques that work. These techniques have been researched and used by teachers. Most teachers are activists and try a number of techniques until they find the one that works.

Problem Ownership

One approach to misbehavior is to identify who "owns" the problem. Thomas Gordon (1974), whose work on conflict was discussed in Chapter 9, suggests that classroom problems can be divided into teacher-owned and student-owned problems. **Teacher-owned** problems are those in which student behavior interferes with teachers meeting their own needs and sometimes causes the teacher to feel frustrated or angry. The most common problems in the classroom,

including fooling around and getting out of one's seat, are owned by the teacher. A student who is scratching a desktop, interrupting another student, leaving books unshelved, is late, is caught smoking, or argues incessantly has caused the teacher a problem.

Student-owned problems are those in which a student's needs are frustrated by other people or events that do not directly involve the teacher. They include lack of friends and rejection from peers as well as problems with parents and can affect the student's performance in class.

Gordon suggests that one way to handle discipline problems is to differentiate between student-owned and teacher-owned problems and to handle them differently. To help students with student-owned problems, Gordon suggests passive listening, acknowledgement responses, door openers, and most importantly, active listening. In passive listening, the teacher listens silently to the student, which shows a willingness to listen. However, although not interrupting students while they communicate is helpful, acknowledgment through nodding, leaning forward, smiling, and giving verbal cues such as "uh-huh" is important. Door openers involve such encouragement as "Would you like to say more about that?" "That's interesting," or "Want to go on?"

However, active listening is also important. **Active listening**, which involves giving the student feedback that you understand, is similar to reflection in that it involves reflecting the feeling the student is showing.

In handling teacher-owned problems, Gordon suggests using "I" messages rather than "you" messages. Instead of saying "Stop that noise," he suggests saying how you feel about the behavior and how the

teacher-owned problems   Problems in which student behavior interferes with teachers meeting their own needs and at times cause the teacher to feel frustration or anger.

student-owned problems   Problems in which a student's needs are frustrated by other people or events that do not directly involve the teacher.

active listening   Providing the student with feedback that demonstrates that the teacher understands the student's difficulties.

behavior is affecting you. An example is to say, "I'm frustrated by this noise and I can't work when I have to wait for quiet." "I" messages have a high probability of promoting a willingness to change, do not negatively evaluate the student, and do not injure a teacher's relationship with the student. A message such as "When you put your feet in the aisle, I'm afraid of falling and tripping" is likely to communicate and correct the behavior.

Do teachers use these techniques? Jere Brophy and Mary Rohrkemper (1981) examined how ninety-eight elementary schoolteachers interpreted problems by presenting teachers with vignettes involving failure, perfectionistic behavior, underachievement, and hostility. Teachers saw internal student factors rather than themselves as causes of teacher-owned problems. Students with teacher-owned problems were seen as responsible for their own behavior, acting intentionally and being blameworthy. Those with student-owned problems were not seen as responsible. Teachers were pessimistic about changing students with teacher-owned problems and focused on immediate control strategies. They were more likely to be motivated to try long-term remedies, including support, encouragement, and extended talk for student-owned problems. They responded sympathetically to students with student-owned problems but offered suggestions and advice, not active listening. In teacher-owned problems, they were punitive and did not use the problem-solving strategies covered in Chapter 9. In other words, these potentially effective ways of handling problems were rarely used by educators.

Direct but Nonintrusive Discipline Methods

Minor misbehavior is relatively common, and it is a mistake to continually stop a lesson to deal with minor off-task misbehavior. When teachers do this, they ruin the smoothness of their lesson and open themselves up to a number of problems. Continually scolding children magnifies the behavior, and effective teachers must learn to discipline a student for minor offenses without stopping the lesson, a type of overlapping. A teacher can do this through a number of nonintrusive methods.

1. **Move closer to the student.** If you close the distance between you and the student and stand near the offender, you will often find minor misbehavior stops.

2. **Point to the work.** If a student seems to be looking around and inattentive, one way to reduce such inattention is simply to point at the book. It isn't necessary to be overly serious in doing this.

3. **Make eye contact.** If teachers practice withitness, they are looking around the room, and establishing eye contact can reduce small instances of misbehavior.

4. **Call on a student.** If a student is not paying attention or is whispering, occasionally calling on the student is sufficient to encourage him or her to get down to work.

5. **Note good behavior in the classroom.** Sometimes, especially during transition periods, some increase in noise occurs. A teacher can reduce the problem by simply saying, "Thomas is ready for work, and so is Tina."

6. **Shake your head.** If you are looking at the student, at times a simple shaking of the head to signify disapproval is sufficient. It reminds students of their misbehavior.

Techniques That Are Slightly Intrusive

Sometimes these techniques may not be sufficient, or they may not provide enough information for the student. Some additional directive techniques that may be effective are as follows:

1. **Remind students of the rule.** "Jonah, what is the rule for getting out of your seat?" This should be asked in a matter-of-fact tone and without sarcasm. This has two advantages. First, it is brief and to the point, and second, it allows the other students to know that you will enforce the rules. If Jonah says he does not know the rule, another student may be asked to give the rule.

2. **Request the students to stop the misbehavior.** It is generally effective to tell students, "Please stop talking" or "Pick the paper up that you threw on the floor." However, a teacher must know who he or she is saying it to. A student who does not respond easily to such urging may require a different discipline approach, and after reminding a student to stop talking, dropping paper clips on the floor etc., a teacher must be ready for the next step.

3. Separate students. Some students simply seem incapable of sitting next to each other, and separating the student, especially by placing an offender nearer to the teacher, can be effective. This allows you to monitor a student who causes problems more easily.

4. A verbal "Please see me after class" can be effective. This is most effective when the misbehavior is minor but obvious.

The key to these procedures is that they are quick and produce only a small interruption of class time. Again, teachers should avoid harping on minor misbehavior, making a mountain out of a molehill, becoming angry, or making statements that show that they are exasperated, such as "Didn't I tell you fifty times not to throw spitballs" or "You're never doing what I tell you." Such statements tell the student nothing and only lead the class to believe that the teacher lacks self-control. However, minor misbehavior still has the potential for disrupting the class, and teachers must deal with it.

Behavioral Methods

If all misbehavior could be solved through simple directive means, teachers probably would not see discipline as a significant problem. Sometimes these simple means are not effective, and something more is required. The bases for behavioral approaches were described in Chapter 5 as well as some of the techniques such as contingency contracting, response cost, and the daily report card. Here we will be involved only with describing how these and other techniques can be used specifically to reduce misbehavior. However, it should be remembered that at the same time that a teacher is trying to reduce student misbehavior, the student ought to be reinforced for the correct behavior. The following discipline techniques have been effectively used in schools by teachers.

Contingency Contracting

How can a teacher encourage students to do their homework correctly each night and arrive in class on time? One method is the **contingency contract**. This is an actual contract signed by both teacher and student indicating agreement on its terms. The contract specifies the exact behavior desired and the conse-

quences for both performing and not performing the behavior. Contingency contracts often but not always contain five elements. They detail what each party expects to gain. The teacher may want Reggie to complete his homework, and Reggie may want free time. Second, the behaviors must be observable and specifically spelled out in the document. Third, the contract may provide sanctions for failing to meet its terms. Fourth, the contract may provide a bonus clause that reinforces compliance with it by including extra privileges for consistent performance. Fifth, the contract provides for a way of monitoring compliance with the terms of the contract.

Contingency contracting can be used in a number of instances. In one study, Bristol (1976) hoped to reduce the fighting of an eight-year-old student. The contract involved both the parents and the teacher. Each morning Andrew received a card with a face on it. The teacher signed the card three times a day if Andrew didn't fight. The teacher's signatures served as points toward the purchase of a reward. Andrew's parents used praise and extra little rewards such as staying up later at night as well. This procedure was successful in reducing the number of Andrew's fights in school.

Response Cost

One way of reducing such bothersome behavior as students leaving their seats or speaking during tests is through a technique known as **response cost**. In this technique, misbehavior results in the loss of previously earned rewards (Gelfand et al., 1982). For example, a child could lose a point on a test for speaking to another student during the test. A student is punished by losing something that he or she has already earned. Obviously, the teacher must be certain that the child has the reward that is to be taken away. For example, the teacher might have a list of procedures for handling science equipment and add five

---

contingency contract A contract between teacher and student specifically noting the exact behavior desired and the consequences for performing and not performing the behavior.

response cost A behavior modification technique in which misbehavior results in the loss of previously gained rewards.

points to the grade of each student who handles the equipment correctly. Each time a student mishandles the equipment, the student loses a point (Axelrod, 1983). Another variation allows students to earn reinforcers for desirable behaviors and lose them for misbehavior. The teacher may give out token reinforcement for good behavior and remove tokens for incorrect behavior.

Still another type of response cost involves the entire class. Here the whole group loses reinforcers for undesirable behavior. For example, if the class gets extra free play two days a week, misbehavior could result in less free time for the entire class. Of course, this procedure should be used with care. Although it does get the other students to reinforce the teacher's discipline, it also could cause a multitude of interpersonal problems.

Response cost is effective in reducing undesirable behavior (McLaughlin & Scott, 1976), and most evidence shows few negative side effects. However, as Axelrod suggests, some problems can arise. Imagine a student who loses a point on a test for talking when all he did was to ask the student next to him to move his leg so he could pick up his pencil. This student may feel that the punishment is unfair and refuse to try his best on the test. Sometimes the technique is so easy to use that teachers overuse it and do not depend upon positive alternatives for managing their classrooms.

Time Out for Misbehavior

Two students are constantly trying your patience by fooling around in the back of the classroom. Another student talks to her friend, bothering the other students in the class. **Time out** involves placing such students for a period of time in a less reinforcing environment following misbehavior. Sending a child who is misbehaving to sit in the hallway for a few minutes is an example. It is similar to the penalty box in hockey (Axelrod, 1983).

Sitting in the hallway is sometimes a problem and not well received by the school administration, since students may fraternize or leave the vicinity. Moving

---

time out A technique in which a student who misbehaves is placed for a short period of time in a less reinforcing environment.

---

the student to a more isolated area of the classroom is a possibility. If two children are playing with blocks and one is misbehaving, removing the child from the blocks for a few minutes is possible. Time-out periods should be short—no more than five minutes.

The Daily Report Card

The daily report card is an effective device for encouraging students to do their assignments and to arrive in class promptly and prepared to work. In this technique, introduced in Chapter 5, the teacher notes the student's behavior, homework, and test grades on a sheet of paper, which is then brought home for the parents' signatures. There are many variations. Sometimes only behavior is recorded, sometimes only grades or homework. If it is to be used for classroom management purposes, the behavioral category may be divided into subheadings such as stays in seat, speaks courteously, and pays attention to the lesson. In junior high school, each teacher may sign the form, and the guidance counselor may coordinate the procedure. This procedure is often effective and has the added benefit that it involves parents who often complain that they are not aware that their children are going to school unprepared. It also can lead to the use of rewards for doing all the homework or for getting a good grade in conduct.

Using Positive Reinforcement

Throughout this text, we've echoed the oft-stated maxim that teachers should seek ways to reward students. Since consequences for misbehavior are emphasized so greatly, it is especially important to deliver positive reinforcement for the preferred behavior. At times, an improvement in everyone's effort may lead to a reward. For instance, if all the students do their homework, no homework is assigned over the weekend.

Self-Control

Behavior modification procedures described here and in Chapter 5 are dependent upon an outside agent—the teacher—to monitor the behavior and work habits of the student. Recently, a new emphasis has been placed on teaching children to monitor their own progress and take an active part in making behavior changes. This certainly makes sense for a number of reasons (O'Leary & Dubey, 1979). First, teachers want students to act independently. Second, the teacher or parent may not always be available to give the rewards. Third, if children control their own behavior, teachers can spend more time teaching. Fourth, teaching children to control their behavior may lead to more durable behavior changes. In addition, as agents of socialization, teachers are partially responsible for teaching students how to act under various circumstances.

New techniques have recently been suggested that aim at helping students develop internal strategies for controlling their own behavior. Many of these strategies begin with some behavior-modification procedure delivered by the teacher, such as a token reinforcement procedure or response cost, and then switch to a self-control strategy (McLaughlin, 1976).

Self-Monitoring

"I don't interrupt the class that much," said Susan to her seventh-grade teacher. The teacher suggested that Susan keep track of how often the teacher had to stop the lesson to wait for Susan to stop talking, take out her books, and get settled. After a week or so, Susan was surprised at how often her behavior affected the lesson.

Sometimes students do not realize how they are affecting others, and **self-monitoring** can help. When students agree to keep track of the number of times they talk out in class or leave their seats, positive changes can occur. In another realm, students can keep track of the time they spend preparing for an exam or studying. The change that occurs when people monitor their own behavior is known as **reactivity** (Spiegler, 1983).

True or False   When students are asked to keep track of how often they interrupt the class, they tend to interrupt the class more.

To teach students to monitor a specific behavior, the behavior that is chosen must be relatively easy to observe. It is important to define the unit of behavior, such as number of pages read or total minutes or hours spent studying. A convenient recording device such as an index card is necessary so that the student can keep track and plot the frequency of the behavior.

Some students are quite good at monitoring their own behavior, while others are not so good. As an occasional check on the students, the teacher should keep a running count when the behavior involves classroom discipline. Self-monitoring is similar to creating a baseline, as discussed in Chapter 5, except

the student does it. Although changes in behavior often occur through self-monitoring, they tend to be temporary. Self-monitoring is most useful when combined with other techniques, such as self-reinforcement.

Self-Reinforcement

The major factor in self-reinforcement is the student's ability to reinforce him or herself at the appropriate time (Rosenbaum & Drabman, 1979). In one case, Humphrey and colleagues (1978) used self-reinforcement and self-punishment to deal with behavior problems in a second-grade classroom. The self-reinforcement involved children administering tokens for accurate performance in reading. Children corrected their work and awarded themselves with tokens based on how well they worked. The work was randomly checked by the teacher to monitor the accuracy of checking and reward. Response cost was used for self-punishment. Each day, children began with a number of tokens and fined themselves for inaccurate work. Both self-reward and self-punishment improved the amount of work completed and reduced disruptive behavior, but the improvement was superior under self-reward.

True or False   Teaching children to reward themselves does not work, since children are incapable of choosing the appropriate times to reinforce themselves.

Alternate Response Training

Alternate response training is a self-control procedure that has become increasingly popular, consisting of teaching students responses that either interfere with or replace an undesired response. Students are taught to replace a troublesome response with a different one. To do so, a student must recognize the

---

self-monitoring   An activity in which students keep track of some aspect of their own behavior.

reactivity   Changes that occur when people monitor their own behavior.

alternate response training   A self-control procedure in which students are taught to use responses that either interfere with or replace an undesirable response.

circumstances in which a troublesome response may occur as well as have an alternate response ready. Arthur Robin and colleagues (1976) developed the turtle technique, which uses as its model the image of the turtle withdrawing into its shell when provoked by something in the environment. Young children are taught to react to their aggressive impulses by imagining that they are turtles withdrawing into their shells and actually pull their arms close to their bodies, put their heads down, and close their eyes. They are also taught to relax and to use problem-solving strategies to generate other responses. This problem-solving training involves roleplaying and discussions in which children are offered alternate strategies for coping with problems. Peers are taught to support the use of the turtle technique. In Robin's study, six children who were highly aggressive were taught how to emit the turtle response in circumstances in which they believed that an aggressive interchange was about to occur. If a teacher noticed that the child was about to throw a tantrum, the teacher called out "turtle." Even a classmate could do so. Results showed a significant decrease in aggressive behavior.

Cognitive Behavior Modification: Self-Instructions and Self-Statements

When you are trying to perform some intricate maneuver, do you ever find yourself talking out loud to yourself? Developmental psychologists argue that people use language to control their actions, and this ability develops in three clear stages (Harter, 1983). First, other people, such as parents, control and direct a child's behavior during early childhood. Then the child learns to say things out loud that describe a course of action. Finally, the self-verbalization is internalized, and covert "thought" controls one's behavior. In self-instruction training, a student is taught to control behavior by making suggestions and comments that guide behavior as if the student were being instructed by someone else.

In a famous study, Donald Meichenbaum and Joseph Goodman (1971) succeeded in altering the impulsive behavior of children. The experimenters asked teachers to model careful performance on such tasks as solving problems. The teachers then talked out loud, verbalizing questions about the task, answers to the questions, and self-instructions such as "go slow." They finally used self-reinforcement. The children were asked to do this just the way the teachers had. They learned first to whisper the instructions

and finally to say them privately without lip movements. Using this technique, a significant reduction in impulsive behavior was shown.

In another study, Philip Bornstein and Randal Quevillon (1976) trained preschoolers who were highly disruptive to ask themselves, What does the teacher want me to do? and to answer the questions and give themselves praise. For example, the answer might be "I'm supposed to copy the picture." First, the children were taught to say it out loud, then in a whisper, and finally to themselves. Again, behavior was significantly improved.

Self-instructions are also useful in helping students to resist temptation. In one study, students were taught to say to themselves, "No, I will not bother the animal" when tempted to do so. This simple procedure was effective. It can also be useful in helping students to wait for rewards by telling them to pretend there is a wall between them and a forbidden object (Patterson & Mischel, 1975).

Sometimes, these techniques are used together, as in the interesting program called Think Aloud (Camp & Bash, 1981). In this program self-verbalizations, developing alternative responses, and helping students understand cause and effect are used to help students control their behavior.

What Does the Emphasis on Self-Control Mean to Educators?

The relatively new emphasis on self-control certainly makes sense. As in the case of behavior modification, a self-control strategy requires much advanced planning and checking. However, it can be effective (O'Leary & Dubey, 1979). The research that shows it to be effective as a concluding portion of an external behavior-modification program is important, because it means that teachers using praise, tokens, or anything else as rewards should consider allowing students to deliver the rewards at the appropriate times and fade external reinforcements out slowly. This strategy will improve self-management.

To be successful, the teacher must first determine the exact behavior to be charted and how it is to be measured and then select the procedure (instructional statements, self-reinforcement, etc.) to be used. In most of these strategies, teachers model the correct way to do something and then slowly teach it to the student. Finally, compliance must be monitored.

Teaching self-control strategies has its pitfalls, however. One is the problem of depending upon students to determine when the situation is ripe for using a "turtle behavior" or for giving themselves a reward. Since studies demonstrate that children become more lenient over time and reinforce themselves for relatively disruptive behavior (Rosenbaum & Drabman, 1979), teachers must check students relatively frequently. Second, although self-monitoring is an important step in many of these procedures, the behavior change frequently gained is temporary, and self-monitoring thus should not be thought of as the permanent solution to a problem. Third, when using a procedure such as self-statements, it is important to identify the situation and to instruct students precisely concerning the very words to use. Despite these cautions, self-control strategies can be effectively used to improve discipline in the classroom.

WHAT DO I DO WHEN . . . ?

For most new teachers, the question of how to handle specific discipline problems takes center stage. As we've seen, teachers can often prevent problems. However, even in the best of classes, misbehavior occurs. In this last section of the chapter, some techniques that are effective in handling some of the more common classroom misbehaviors are discussed. Note that there is no one way to handle these situations and there is no substitute for knowing your students. Walking towards a student might easily stop one student yet be ineffective with another student who is more frustrated.

How Do I Handle Defiant Students?

TEACHER: Please sit down.
STUDENT: No, make me.

TEACHER: Why didn't you do your homework?
STUDENT: I didn't feel like it. I'm not doing it tomorrow either.

Few things sting a teacher as much as student defiance, especially if it is public. Defiant behavior cannot be ignored, because it can become a model for others. It must be handled quickly.

True or False   One effective way of handling defiant behavior is to ignore it.

Preventing defiance is sometimes a matter of understanding your students. If you know a student is

likely to defy you, try not to get into a test of wills in public. In addition, when students are very angry, they are much more likely to defy the teacher, so it may be wise to deal with the student's anger. For example, the student may not want to sit down because someone took his pencil and he is looking for it and wants to punish the culprit. If you notice the anger, defiance can be prevented by reducing your distance from the student and acknowledging his anger. "I know you're angry and upset, but please sit down anyway." This is less public and may prevent some defiance, at least from becoming too public.

A second method is to improve your relationship with students by encouraging communication, as discussed in Chapter 9. Students are much less likely to defy your authority if you have a reasonably good relationship with them.

What if a defiant action or statement has occurred? Try to give the student an out by calmly asking the student to reconsider.

TEACHER: Please sit down.
STUDENT: Make me.
TEACHER: It's up to you, but think it over for a minute.

Another way of handling it is to ask the student to step out in the hall for a minute.

TEACHER: Please sit down.
STUDENT: Make me.
TEACHER: It's up to you to do it or not, but I suggest you step out in the hall to think about it.

If the student will not comply with any suggestion, another student should be sent to get assistance from the dean or assistant principal. Even if the student does comply before help arrives, some punishment should be exacted after class. First, speak to the student and find out the reason for his or her defiance. The student should be told how the behavior caused a problem and how it interfered with learning. If the behavior continues, a conference with the parents and the continued involvement of guidance counselors, deans, and the administration are required. It may also be necessary to begin a positive behavior-modification program to reward the student for changing his or her behavior.

Of all the misbehaviors possible, defiance can cause teachers to become overly emotional and can add to the problem. If the teacher being told to "Make me" replies with idle threats or increased hostility, such a response just adds to the tension. Keeping one's emotions under control is thus very important.

How Do I Handle Students Who Don't Pay Attention?

Students who don't pay attention are frequently a problem. In the youngest grades, short attention span may be the cause. That is, young children may lack the ability to pay attention for a long period of time. In any grade, however, lack of attention can mean that the child is lost or bored. The first priority is to make certain that the child understands the work. This can be accomplished by perusing the child's work or asking questions. At times, simple, nonobtrusive methods such as making eye contact, pointing, and sometimes asking students "What page are we on"? can be sufficient.

A student who is not paying attention may also not know what is required of him or her. This can be handled through asking the student a question such as "Jeff, when we finish our reading, what are we supposed to do?" At other times, the student who is not paying attention may be concerned with other things, such as home problems. A teacher should try to find out whether something is wrong and use the active listening approach advocated by Thomas Gordon (discussed earlier).

If the child is easily distracted, the teacher might consider having the child sit at the front of the room or away from distractions. It may also be possible to use a reinforcement program by praising the student when he or she is paying attention and doing his or her work.

How Do I Deal with Students Whose Work Is Usually Poor?

Sloppy assignments, incomplete work, fooling around during seatwork assignments, lack of effort, and not turning in homework are relatively common problems that most teachers must face at one time or another. Emmer and colleagues (1982) suggest that teachers keep accurate records of students' work, contact parents to monitor the children's work, contact other teachers for suggestions, and converse with students to identify reasons for poor work. Above all, they suggest, don't pass students because you think they are smart and could pass if they did their work, for this only encourages such slack behavior. All of this is predicated on the assumption that such students have the ability to do the work.

There are other things that teachers can do. For example, some students, especially if they are bright, are used to sliding through courses and may react negatively if they are faced with a demanding teacher. It is important to communicate the standard of work that is acceptable in your class. For example, if cross-outs are not permitted in your class, this should be made clear to the student. If handing in an assignment late has a consequence—perhaps some points off—this should be made clear to the student and the punishment tacked on when the inappropriate behavior is exhibited. In addition, monitoring work is of great importance. Sometimes parents are surprised when they are told that their children are handing in work that is not up to standard. The daily or weekly report card can be of help. Still another approach is to use a behavior-modification procedure for students who do not finish their work, perhaps allowing them more time for free play or less homework if their work measures up to your standards. Even a response cost approach, where students begin with a certain amount of credits towards free time and lose them for poor work, is appropriate. Whatever the approach used, making certain the student has the ability to perform, communicating to your students your standards of work, closely monitoring student work, and involving parents when necessary are steps that can help.

What Can I Do with Students Who Constantly Break the Rules?

There are comparatively few students who consistently break the rules, although almost every student breaks them at one time or another. Some students may habitually call out, others talk to their neighbor, and some simply forget their books or paper and pencils. Emmer and colleagues (1982) suggest some general rules which are helpful. Teachers can try to catch students before the make trouble by reminding them to bring in their books or raise their hand before speaking. Another strategy is to use self-monitoring and perhaps self-reinforcement. Again, holding a conference with a student concerning the breaking of rules and seeking parental help when needed are appropriate. Asking the student to state the rule is helpful as well. James Levin and colleagues (1985) offer an interesting procedure for resolving chronic problems. They suggest keeping an anecdotal record each day of the behaviors and following each class with a short conference in which both the positive behaviors and misbehaviors are discussed. The misbehaviors are listed on the daily record, and the student is encouraged to recognize how the behavior impacts on the class and what the student's chances are for success. A verbal commitment to improve is requested. Last, the student is asked to sign the anecdotal record.

Of course, each type of rule breaking requires its own action. For example, the student who calls out answers without raising his or her hand is a common problem. Sometimes, a gentle reminder is sufficient. However, at other times, either the impulsiveness of the child or the child's desire for attention may make it difficult for the child to wait to be recognized. In such cases, the student's answer should not be recognized until the student raises his or her hand. It is difficult to extinguish the behavior by simply refusing to notice it, since it still bothers the rest of the class and interferes with the lesson. When students do raise their hand, they should be recognized. Breaking the rules based on impulsiveness can be handled through the use of cognitive behavior modification, including self-statements.

When students are successful in meeting the rules, some private statement could be made to the student such as "I'm glad you brought your book so we can work with it today."

What Do I Do with the Student Who Talks to Other Students All Day?

This problem is a special case of rule breaking because it is so common and understandable that it requires some additional explanation. After all, the constant undercurrent of noise in a classroom is a significant problem to other students trying to work or listen to the teacher. Teachers differ on the noise level they will tolerate during the class. Certain activities, such as small-group work, require some student-student interaction, but the noise level must be constantly monitored.

In a recitation class setting, the undercurrent of talking can be reduced if the students are involved in the lesson or in their seatwork. Especially in elementary school, some signal that requires students to look up and give teachers their undivided attention is a possible way of breaking through this undercurrent without trying to talk it over. Some teachers will

One of the most common and annoying examples of misbehavior is constant talking during class.

simply say, "I have to wait until it's quiet enough to start." Other teachers look at the class and mention the name of a "talker" while writing a zero in their grading book. Students are told that a particular number of zeros will cause a reduction in conduct grade and a loss of some privilege. Still other teachers give pluses and minuses and mention the names of the students who are ready for work (i.e., are not talking).

When one particular student cannot seem to keep quiet, moving the student to the front of the room or at least away from his or her friend is quite effective. In addition, having the student monitor the number of times he or she is interfering is also a possibility, and such self-monitoring can be combined with self-reinforcement or self-instruction.

How Do I Handle Fighting?

Much of the daily misbehavior that bothers teachers and interferes with class work is relatively minor. Violence, however, is not. Violence not only has the potential for bodily and property damage but also changes the atmosphere in the classroom and the school. Many violent episodes occur outside the classroom in the hallway or in the schoolyard.

The extent of a teacher's involvement in a fight can be determined by an evaluation of the physical danger as well as by the school rules. No teacher is required to place him or herself in physical jeopardy by separating two combatants if he or she believes that doing so will result in physical injury. In addition, there are often school rules in this area concerning whom to contact, and sometimes an investigation is performed by the dean. This is true of other behaviors, such as carrying a dangerous weapon or setting a fire.

When two students are fighting, they should be isolated as much as possible so that other students will not get hurt or get involved, since there is always the potential for the situation to spread to other students. A student should immediately be sent to the dean's office for help, since it often takes more than one adult to break up a fight. Getting the names of any witnesses and the participants is a good procedure.

The preceding are good policies whether the incident takes place in the halls or in the classroom. Of course, what takes place in the hall or schoolyard is a school problem, and the teacher may not know the people involved. In the classroom, minor aggressive behavior such as hitting may occur. Separating the students who are not getting along is a must, as is settling the dispute after class. The goal is to reduce the effects on the other students and to deal with the situation at the teacher's leisure. The help of a dean or an assistant principal may be necessary.

DEVELOPMENTAL CONCERNS

Although there are many similarities between discipline in elementary schools and discipline in secondary schools, there are some differences as well. Many of these differences are based upon the developmental level of the students.

Discipline in Elementary Schools

In elementary school, students often need more reminders concerning rules and regulations as well as extensive practice in some relatively simple administrative procedures, such as lining up. In addition, some of the behavior-modification procedures using stickers and small material rewards are often sufficient and successful. Young students differ in their ability to self-monitor their behavior, and their reasoning abilities in the first few years may be limited. They may say they agree with your reasoning and not understand it at all. Therefore, checking to see that the student really does understand your rule or your expectations is of paramount importance.

The elementary schoolteacher has a considerable size and strength advantage, and combined with the student view of teachers as substitute parental figures, this advantage makes maintaining discipline somewhat easier. Elementary schoolchildren are more likely to accept commands and less likely to question than older children. They are also more likely to accept simple alternate behaviors such as the turtle concept. At about the age of ten, children have a tendency to be a little more rebellious and to talk back as they begin to realize that teachers are not infallible and do make mistakes (Kaplan, 1986). This leads to some additional difficulties with defiant behavior that are often short-lived. There is also an increase in classroom chatter. For the elementary schoolteacher, forming clear rules, practicing them, using positive reinforcement whenever possible, and making certain that students understand the teacher's reasoning are the keys to better discipline.

Discipline in Junior High Schools

Discipline in junior high school is complicated by two factors. First, the developmental changes are so radical that students trying to cope with puberty and all that it entails (refer to Chapter 6) may have difficulty making the transition from child to teenager. The junior high school student does not want to stand out, and fitting into a group may be of prime importance to the child. In some cases, the achievement and conduct of some high-achieving elementary school students may decline as social needs take center stage. These students may respond best to private conversations, and it is most important not to maneuver the student into a point where he or she will be losing face.

Second, for many students, junior high school means having six or seven teachers for the first time, and sixth- or seventh-graders may need help in remembering which teacher requires what. In elementary school, students had to satisfy only one teacher. In junior high, because students may become confused, keeping a written sheet of rules and procedures in the front of their notebooks for reference is important. Sometimes mentioning a rule or two may be helpful. At the same time, the increased freedom of junior high school students in passing from one

In elementary school, it is a good policy to practice procedures.

class to another may require more monitoring not only of their work but also of their attendance. A policy of sending warning letters home to the parents of students who do not finish their work is one approach. Some parents are taken aback when they get the report card and have not been told sooner that their child was not performing up to par.

Discipline in High School

High school students often see themselves as grown up and close to adult status and rebel against being treated like children. Here, it is most important that the teacher's standards and expectations be conveyed to the students and reviewed. However, high school students come with many years of socialization and do not require the constant review of procedures that elementary school students and early junior high school students may need.

Disciplinary procedures in the high school classroom may also be based upon behavior-modification and self-control procedures but must be modified and made age appropriate. Older students will still respond to praise and a reward of free time or no homework, but not to stickers. In fact, self-monitoring may be more effective, and self-reinforcement may work

better in the high school. In addition, since high school students may not accept because-I-say-so reasoning as readily as younger students, the reasons for procedures must be explained to them. A balance must be struck between allowing feedback from the class and not getting into a debate.

DISCIPLINE AS A NECESSARY STEP TOWARDS LEARNING

In this chapter, we've steered a middle course between two extremes. One extreme sees the teacher as a therapist, able to "treat" and solve student problems. Often, this approach explains the cause of misbehavior in terms of poor teaching. The problem with this extreme is that teachers are not therapists, nor are they supposed to be. They are teachers. In addition, while teachers can do much to prevent misbehavior, the idea that misbehavior is always caused by poor teaching is false. Students sometimes enter a classroom angry or involved in other things, and personality conflicts do occur.

The other extreme sees the teacher as a type of law enforcement officer who must keep a stringent discipline in order to keep the enemy (students) from overwhelming the teacher and causing anarchy. This view sees any misbehavior as simply a challenge to the teacher's authority and calls for severe consequences even for slight misbehavior. The problem with this view is immense. First, students aren't the teacher's enemies, and successful teachers often have a cooperative "we" attitude rather than a "you against me" perspective. Second, a classroom in which students are afraid of the teacher is not necessarily one in which students will participate. A very quiet classroom in which you can hear a pin drop does not necessarily mean that meaningful learning is going on. Last, teachers who see themselves as police officers may have forgotten that their primary responsibility is to teach.

The view that I take of discipline is that it is necessary for establishing an effective learning environment. Discipline consists of fair, well-thought-out rules and procedures that are reasonable, whose compliance is monitored, and whose application is uniform. It involves dealing with misbehavior in an objective, nonthreatening manner. Under such a system, misbehavior is viewed as behavior that does not allow the class or the student to learn, and discipline is seen as a set of behaviors that allow efficient learning to take place in the classroom.

SUMMARY

1. Discipline is viewed as a major problem not only by teachers but also by the general public. The climate in the school greatly affects discipline in the classroom.
2. Studies consistently find differences between effective and ineffective teachers on how they manage their classes. This includes teaching rules to students, structuring the classroom so there is little time away from tasks, immediately responding to misbehavior, and using the first few days of school for orientation purposes.
3. Before the school term begins, the teacher should survey the physical layout of the room and establish the seating arrangement. Teachers should consider the procedural and conduct rules they wish to present, the consequences for breaking the rules, and the way to handle the first few days of school.
4. Rules for decorum in late elementary school and beyond should be written out. During the first day of class, rules should be explained. A number of

ways of presenting rules to students exist. In three-dimensional discipline, students and teachers form a contract that contains their rules. The teacher develops rules for the class, and the class develops rules for themselves and the teacher. Class rules must be enforced without exception, and the consequences for breaking the rules must be communicated and delivered to the students. Consequences for misbehavior should be progressive and fair.

5. Jacob Kounin's famous research study demonstrated the many ways effective and ineffective teachers differ in classroom management. Effective managers are "withit," which means that they know what is going on every second in their classroom. They also keep their lessons flowing at a reasonable pace, and their transitions are smooth. Effective teachers also are able to attend to two things at once—a skill called overlapping—and give students clear signals as well as interpret student signals. They also keep the class accountable for their learning.
6. All discipline actions should be governed by guidelines, such as never embarrassing students; not debating with students; not using sarcasm; being consistent, fair, and unbiased; using small amounts of punishment for minor infractions; not threatening students; disciplining the student's actions and not the student; and focusing on ways to teach self-control and self-discipline.
7. Thomas Gordon suggests dividing problems into student-owned and teacher-owned problems. Teacher-owned problems are behaviors that cause the teacher distress, while student-owned problems are those that do not directly involve the teacher but cause the student difficulties, such as unpopularity and peer rejection. Gordon suggests using listening techniques, especially active listening, to help students with student-owned problems and using "I" statements for teacher-owned problems.
8. Minor misbehavior can be reduced through techniques that do not interfere with the lesson, such as moving closer to the student, pointing, making eye contact, and calling on the student. Other techniques include reminding students of the rules and separating students.
9. Many successful behavioral methods can be used by the teacher to reduce misbehavior. They include contingency contracting, in which student

and teacher agree on a contract; response cost, in which misbehavior leads to the loss of previously gained rewards; time out, in which children are separated from the source of reinforcement for a short period of time; daily report cards to be signed by parents, and positive reinforcement.

10. Teachers today are very interested in promoting self-control. Some of the techniques being used successfully are self-monitoring, alternate response training, cognitive self-statements, and self-instructions.

11. Defiance can sometimes be prevented by knowing one's students and not entering into a test of wills with the students. When defiance does occur, responding without anger and asking if he or she would like to reconsider his or her actions is appropriate. If the defiance continues, conferences with the student and parents as well as action by the dean may be required.

12. Lack of attention may be due to many reasons. The teacher must be certain that the child understands the work. Sometimes gentle reminders concerning on-task behavior or behavior modification can be helpful. Such behavior may have little to do with schoolwork and may reflect some problem at home.

13. To reduce poor or sloppy work, teachers should keep a record of such work, make certain their standards are known, and use a behavior-modification approach such as a home report card. Students who constantly break the rules may be helped through the use of signed daily anecdotal records, self-monitoring, and parental conferences. Continuous talking can be reduced by using a demerit system or moving the student to another part of the classroom.

14. Discipline procedures and problems differ in elementary, junior high, and senior high school. In elementary school, students are socialized into behavior patterns, and children need training in proper behaviors. Children respond well to praise and behavior modification. In junior high school, private discipline is more effective, since losing face with their peers is a serious problem for students at this level. In the high school, communicating standards is most important, and self-monitoring and self-control strategies can be very effective.

ACTIVITIES AND EXERCISES

1. **Most Common Problems in Classrooms and Schools.** Ask ten elementary schoolteachers, ten junior high teachers, and ten high school teachers, "What are the most common discipline problems you face in your schools and in your individual classrooms?" You would expect differences between elementary and secondary schoolteachers, but are there any differences between the junior high and high school teachers?

2. **A New Teacher's First Year.** Interview a few second-year teachers about their experiences during their second year of teaching. Some possible questions include the following:
   a. How did you plan for your first few days of school?
   b. What were the major problems you encountered?
   c. What changes are you planning to make this year?
   d. What advice would you give to a new teacher entering the school?

3. **What Are Your Rules?** Much of the literature on classroom management speaks of the importance of forming rules and teaching them to the students. Ask as many teachers as possible to list the rules they have for their classes, how they formulate them, and how they teach them to their classes. Also ask whether any of their rules have changed much since they began to teach.

4. **Observation and Kounin's Work.** Jacob Kounin and his colleagues have invented a new vocabulary of classroom management that includes such terms as withitness, smoothness, and signalling. Observe a class and note how the teacher's behavior shows evidence of these areas.

5. **Transitions.** One of the most difficult areas to manage for many teachers is the transition, the time between the end of one activity and the beginning of another. Misbehavior is more prevalent at these times. Ask teachers how they manage smoothness in transitions and observe and note the manner in which transitions are facilitated.

6. **Dealing with Misbehavior.** This chapter has looked at some of the more common forms of misbehavior, including talking out, not finishing work, talking to one's neighbor, not paying

attention, fighting, and talking back. Ask experienced teachers to describe how they deal with these problems.

7. **School Policies on Misbehavior.** Many schools have policies on how to handle certain types of misbehavior, such as unexcused absences, fighting, and drug-related incidents. Ask either teachers or administrators what policies their schools have concerning major types of misbehavior.

8. **Interview with a Dean.** Most secondary schools have people whose job is to deal with the more serious types of misbehavior. Such people's points of view are often interesting, since they are more likely to deal with the most difficult cases. Ask the dean to give you his or her impression of school discipline, the problems teachers encounter, and especially how he or she deals with particular types of behavior problems.

9. **How Did You and Your Friends Behave in Schools?** It may have been quite a while ago, but a round table discussion with friends concerning the school-related misbehavior in your past can be interesting. This might include discussions of notorious troublemakers in your class. The discussions should focus on the why of the misbehavior—why it occurred in certain classrooms and not in others—and how such misbehavior was handled.

10. **Dealing with the Home.** One of the ways to deal with recurrent misbehavior is to involve the parents. However, sometimes the parents have other things on their mind more immediately important than their child's misbehavior in school. At other times, parents' reaction may be out of proportion to the offense. Ask teachers, administrators, and deans how they explain misbehavior to parents and what type of program (if any) they try to institute with the parent to reduce the child's misbehavior.

11. **Follow a Child Through the Process.** If you are working in a school, ask permission from the dean or assistant principal to follow a child who has a history of misbehavior through the process that may be involved with the child's suspension. Look into what techniques were used to help the child and why they failed or succeeded and what the school officials intend to try in the future.

12. **The Substitute's Lament.** Being a substitute teacher is a difficult job, especially since the substitute does not know the class procedures or the students' names. Ask someone in the school who the best substitute teachers are and ask these substitute teachers how they are able to maintain discipline and teach.

13. **Plan Your First Day.** You are given your first teaching job and must plan out your opening day's activities. Specifically outline what you intend to do and how you will do it. You may want to use the model discussed in the chapter, although there is no single correct way to do this.

SCENARIOS

Here are nine scenarios. Try to apply the information you have learned in the chapter to each situation.

1. Mr. Simpson is a mathematics teacher who has been having difficulty with three of his sixth-grade students. Two are friends, Ken and Will, who are constantly teasing a third boy, Stu, who does not seem to be able to fight back. Stu has no friends, and now other students are joining Ken and Will in picking on Stu. The other day Stu just placed his head in his hands. In addition, Ken and Will aren't doing their work completely. Although they turn in their work, it is often sloppy and poorly done. Ken is the fifth in a family of eight children. Both parents work, and they are rather overwhelmed by the problems of taking care of two elderly parents who live with them. Will's parents are going through a rather messy divorce, and Will has one sister who is much older. Will's parents care but are involved in a very difficult time. Stu's parents don't know what to do, since Stu has no friends and spends each day after school watching TV cartoons. What could Mr. Simpson do to help Stu?

2. Alexandra is a junior high school student who shows a history of being a good student. However, now in seventh grade, she does as little work as possible, often comes late to class, and talks incessantly to her neighbors. According to her parents, she has hit puberty like a brick wall, and her social concerns are more important than anything else. Her parents have punished her for bringing home 75s on her report cards, since they think she can do better. They've just received a warning letter from her social studies teacher, Mr. Franco. Mr. Franco claims that Alexandra is late twice a week, sometimes does not do her homework, and always seems to have a "smart" answer for every-

thing. She primps in the middle of the class session and does not seem to be paying attention, although when asked a question, she usually understands it and sometimes gets it right. She always answers the question in a bored voice. How can Mr. Franco best deal with this situation?

3. Mr. Morgan has a difficult time with his science class. He does not seem to be able to get his points across to his students, and he loses his temper when students misbehave. Every time he turns to the blackboard, the noise level increases. If he tries to deal with one problem, such as the note passing between Ed and Simon, another problem, such as Bill's dislike for Gene, surfaces in the form of an argument. Mr. Morgan feels he is losing his students and has lost control of the situation. What advice would you give Mr. Morgan?

4. Ms. Thompson's problem can be voiced in one word—Dennis. Dennis never seems to break any rule twice but has broken every rule once. He always has an excuse for everything and is always making a joke, often behind Ms. Thompson's back. Ms. Thompson contacted Dennis's mother, who told her that Dennis feels that she does not like him. Dennis's mother has accepted Dennis's account of all his misbehavior, but Dennis is blaming his misbehavior on others and is not being held accountable for it. At this point, what can Ms. Thompson do to improve Dennis's conduct?

5. When Mr. Beech asked Kevin to stop talking, Kevin didn't answer. When Mr. Beech went over to Kevin, Kevin just stared at him and bolted from the room. Kevin's behavior has been a problem all year. As a sophomore in high school, he has not been doing much in school and has gotten into a few fistfights on the school grounds. What are Mr. Beech's alternatives? How should he handle Kevin when the student returns to class?

6. This is Ms. Tuttle's first year teaching elementary school. Ms. Tuttle seemed to start the year off all right, giving her rules and then getting right into her work. Occasionally, she reminded the students of the rules and procedures. The first challenge was Judith, who did not bring in her homework and was caught talking to Jean when she should have been working. Ms. Tuttle walked over to Judith and told her that she would get two zeros: one for talking during the lesson and one for missing her homework. She warned Judith that one more zero and she would fail. A few days later,

Judith was out of her seat, a
"Okay, now you've failed."
Tuttle—that's for certain—
no work. At the same timhome for chewing gum incalled out an answer, sheother day, Kayla was scipal's office for talking back.
week of school, and Ms. Tuttle thinks she
fair and consistent. She doesn't know where she went wrong. Analyze Ms. Tuttle's process and suggest improvements.

7. Mr. Philips has a difficult time going from one subject to another. The class will finish a mathematics lesson, and then it will take an inordinate amount of time to get the students into reading groups. During this time, there is commotion, and the noise level increases. What can Mr. Philips do to reduce this problem?

8. Mr. Karlin is talking to you about the disaster he encountered during third period. This is how his story goes:

I was reviewing a test with the class. I was short a few, so I went to the closet and got the ones I needed. That took only a minute. As I turned around, I noticed John dropping some paper on the floor. I don't like litter, so I told him a thing or two about neatness, and he did pick up the paper. Then we went over the test. When we had finished, Samantha had an example marked wrong that was right, and of course, I had to check it, and it took a minute. The class didn't cooperate at all, and I had to quiet them a few times. Then I said it was time to discuss the American Revolution and that they should open their books to page 128. They were noisy, and it took them a while to get started. We read a page or two and then discussed the causes of the war. Then I remembered that there was a special class trip next week and asked the students if they had their permission notes in and not to forget them. It took a while to get back to the revolution. George and Louis weren't paying attention, so I called on them. When they didn't get the answer right, I showed the class how inattention leads to not knowing the answers. Then Tina asked a good question about how people felt about George Washington, and as I was answering her, the students were very restless and made it difficult to continue. As the lesson ended and the bell rang, I gave them the homework assignment.

Analyze Mr. Karlin's "disaster" by referring to known research.

9. Delores has always been a good student, courteous,

operative, and until last week the same be said for Don. In the past few weeks, Don's avior has gone from bad to worse. Delores ad a family problem and could not do her homework. Ms. Davis, understanding that these things happen, did not give Delores a zero but gave her another chance. However, when Don, who had missed a few homework assignments in the past week, was given a zero, he exploded. "She didn't do her homework and you didn't give her a zero, but I got one." Ms. Davis explained that Delores had a good reason for not doing her homework and that it was the first time she had missed. At that point, Richard piped up that he got a zero for the first time he didn't do his homework when he had to go with his parents to the ball game. Don said that he got a zero his first time as well. Should Ms. Davis have made an exception for Delores? What should she do now?

Effective Teaching Techniques

11

Are These Statements True or False?

Turn the next page for the correct answers. Each statement is repeated following the paragraph in which the information can be found.

1. One reason teachers write instructional objectives is to help communicate what they are trying to accomplish to parents, administrators, and students.

2. Instructional objectives should not influence testing procedures because their primary purpose is to introduce a new unit of study.

3. The form of teaching called direct instruction is another name for lecture.

4. Teachers using the discovery method of teaching give students a problem and then allow students to solve it in their own way without interfering with student activity.

5. While conducting a demonstration, teachers should tell their students why they have chosen to do it one way rather than another.

6. Seatwork is actually a type of self-teaching.

7. Seatwork should be assigned as long as students are certain to get half of the examples or problems correct.

8. The amount of homework assigned by teachers has increased in the past decade.

9. Most parents want teachers to assign homework regularly.

10. Peer tutoring is an effective way of providing practice for students.

11. One of the most effective methods of peer tutoring is apportioning rewards to the tutor on the basis of how well the tutee performs on an examination.

12. Small-group instruction is usually superior to whole-class instruction.

Objectives and Teaching Strategies

Answers to True-False Statements

1. *True*
2. *False* Correct statement: Instructional objectives should be used as a basis for testing.
3. *False* Correct statement: Direct instruction is not another term for simple lecture.
4. *False* Correct statement: Teachers using the discovery method do not just give students a problem and allow them to tackle it on their own. They also clarify the problem for students, guide students, and make certain students can obtain the necessary materials.
5. *True*
6. *False* Correct statement: Seatwork is a type of practice, not self-teaching.
7. *False* Correct statement: When seatwork is assigned, students should be able to do at least 80 percent of the work correctly.
8. *True*
9. *True*
10. *True*
11. *False* Correct statement: Rewards should not be apportioned to tutors on the basis of how well the tutee performs on an examination.
12. *False* Correct statement: Teachers tend to use small groups and whole-class instruction for different purposes. It is not possible at the present time to make any generalization about which method is superior.

CHOOSING GOALS AND METHODS

Imagine you are a high school history teacher who is teaching a unit on the Civil War. Your students have already studied the Civil War for years and think they know a great deal about the subject. How would you approach the task?

A number of alternatives are available. You could lecture, show a film, assign readings on the subject, or begin a discussion with a question or controversial issue. You could try something different by dividing the class into two groups and having each group present position papers from the North's or South's point of view concerning various national issues surrounding the war. You might also organize a project that involves looking into how the students' town or village functioned during the Civil War. Although there are many possibilities, the methods you use will depend in part upon your goals. If one of your goals is a working background knowledge of the Civil War, you may be more directive. If, on the other hand, understanding the reasoning of the North or South was important, you might approach the subject dif-

ferently. If an appreciation of the experience of going to war was your goal, still another method may be needed. This chapter looks at two of the most basic decisions that a teacher must make: choosing goals and deciding what methods of teaching to adopt.

GOALS OF EDUCATION

Educational goals are broad statements about what is to be accomplished in education (Houston et al., 1988). These goals tend to be timeless and very general and offer little or no guidance concerning how to measure the outcome. For example, the goals of an elementary school education are attaining basic literacy, providing citizenship education, and enhancing personal development (Jarolimek & Foster, 1989). They have not really changed much over the years. Of course, these goals can be divided into a number of subgoals. For example, basic literacy can be considered in terms of reading, writing, science, mathematics, and, today, even computer literacy.

Lists of educational objectives have meaning as broad statements of purpose. They may also serve to direct attention to the amount of time scheduled for activities that are devoted to securing these goals. In the 1960s and early 1970s, additional emphasis was placed on personal development, while in the 1980s and 1990s, more emphasis is being placed on the fundamental literacy skills. To be useful to the classroom teacher, however, these general goals must be translated into more specific objectives that can guide a teacher's lesson planning.

INSTRUCTIONAL OBJECTIVES

Consider an art teacher about to teach a lesson on the impressionist artist, Claude Monet. What are her objectives? Perhaps she wants to improve her students' knowledge of Monet's style, life, and ideas; perhaps she simply wants to introduce students to Monet's art. Perhaps appreciation of Monet's paintings is one of her objectives. On the other hand, she may want the students to be able to contrast Monet's style with that of other artists.

Instructional objectives are descriptions of what students are expected to do after completing some unit of instruction (Reisman & Payne, 1987). They are formulated by the teacher and reflect the instructor's own belief about what students should gain from instruction.

Why bother formulating such objectives? Instructional objectives have three purposes (Gronlund, 1985). First, they provide direction for instruction. The art teacher would use very different techniques if her objective was stated in terms of art appreciation than if her aim was to improve her students' knowledge about Monet's life. Second, objectives provide guidelines for testing. When composing a test, teachers use their objectives to decide which test questions ought to be included. If the objective was to teach about Monet's life, the teacher might use a multiple-choice test; if the objective was to teach how to paint using an impressionistic style, the teacher might test the students on their ability to do so. In addition, as teachers compose test questions, they want the questions to reflect as many of the goals as possible and do not want too many questions covering one objective and too few another (see Chapter 15). Last, instructional objectives allow educators to tell others what they intend to do. Teachers have a responsibility to communicate their objectives to students, parents,

administrators, and the community. Many schools have inaugurated special evenings at the beginning of the term during which teachers tell parents what they hope to accomplish.

True or False One reason teachers write instructional objectives is to help communicate what they are trying to accomplish to parents, administrators, and students.

General Objectives and Behavioral Objectives

There are two types of instructional objectives: general objectives, sometimes called nonbehavioral objectives, and behavioral objectives, sometimes called performance objectives.

General Instructional Objectives

General instructional objectives state the general learning outcomes a teacher can expect from teaching a particular unit. For example, the teacher may want her students to understand the nature of Impressionism, to know Monet's background, and to identify various paintings as impressionistic. These objectives are often expressed in statements such as "Students will learn to interpret symbols on a map." "Students will understand how bears prepare for winter." "Students will appreciate the need for cooperation in sports."

It is not difficult to write such objectives, providing the teacher is aware of some common mistakes. First, sometimes the objectives are described in terms of teacher performance rather than student performance. Objectives should state expected outcomes as they relate to students. For example, "To understand the meaning of operant conditioning" would be a general instructional objective written from a student's point of view, while an objective stating "To teach the definition of operant conditioning" is not. Second, the

instructional objectives Descriptions of what students are expected to do after completing some unit of instruction.

general instructional objectives Statements of the general learning outcomes expected after teaching a particular unit.

Teachers have a number of choices when planning a lesson. Their instructional goals will guide their choice of how to present the material.

objectives should be stated in terms of product rather than learning process. For example, "Students will apply basic principles of operant conditioning to education" would be a product, whereas "Students will gain some knowledge of the basic principles of operant conditioning" would emphasize process. Other problems include not giving enough detail and trying to cover more than one objective in a single statement. When writing general objectives, then, the teacher focuses attention on the student outcome and the type of performance expected. Although these objectives are flexible, they lack specificity. For example, "Students will know word meanings" does not tell us much. How many word meanings should a student know, and in what time period? As useful as these general instructional objectives may be, something more definitive is required.

Behavioral or Performance Objectives

Given a list of twenty-five words, students will be able to spell 90 percent correctly on the spelling test at the end of the week.

Without referring to the periodic chart, a student will be able to list the symbols and full name of fifty elements on a test on Thursday.

Students will be able to identify the verb in each of four simple sentences on practice sheets on Wednesday.

When given ten sentences in French, students will be able to translate at least eight into English without error on a unit test.

These objectives include much more detail than the general objectives discussed previously.

Behavioral objectives have three distinguishing characteristics (Mager, 1962). First, they contain the condition under which the behavior will occur. Second, the behavior is described in observable terms, usually including a verb or an infinitive. Third, the criterion for successful performance is noted. The parts of behavioral objectives are illustrated in Table 11.1. Consider the following objective:

After reading the story "The Lady and the Tiger," students will correctly answer nine of ten multiple-choice questions, showing a literal understanding of the story.

The condition is reflected in the first part of the statement: that students will read the story. The observable behavior is answering the questions, while the criterion is getting 90 percent correct.

The most important aspect of a behavioral objective is the *terminal behavior* that is desired. Such behavior must be specific. For example, knowing, appreciating, understanding, learning, and thinking about are too general and do not point to something that can easily be observed or measured. On the other hand, choosing, defining, describing, writing, and comparing are more specific.

Behavioral or performance objectives have some obvious advantages over less precise objectives. They leave very little doubt concerning what is to be accomplished. They provide more structure, making planning easier, and allow the teacher to demonstrate success or determine the need to reteach the material. They can be shaped to the needs and abilities of the class or the individual student.

On the other hand, there is much resistance to writing objectives this rigorously. One objection is that not every outcome can be so easily measured (Furst, 1981). It would be difficult though (as we shall

behavioral objectives Specific statements of learning outcomes defining the behavior expected of students after completing a unit in observable terms, the conditions under which the behavior is to be shown, and the criterion for successful performance.

Table 11.1 Behavioral Objectives

Behavioral objectives are very specific and state the behavior desired, under what conditions it is to be shown, and the criterion (or criteria) for success.

Condition	Behavior	Criteria
Given a set of 220 flash cards from the Dolch sight word list,	the student will orally read each word	correctly within three seconds, on first attempt, for three consecutive days by September 14.
Given a worksheet with ten English measures of weight (in pounds and ounces) and the formula for conversion into metric units,	the student will write the metric equivalents	with 90 percent accuracy within twenty-five minutes on two consecutive days by December 11.
Given any three selections from the text, *Be a Better Reader,* Level A,	the student will orally read	with a correct rate of at least 110 wpm and an error rate of no more than 4 wpm for two consecutive days by March 28.

From *Behavior Modification for the Classroom Teacher,* 2d ed. by Saul Axelrod. Copyright © 1983 by McGraw-Hill Publishing Company. Used by permission of the publisher.

see a bit later) not impossible, to assess whether students now appreciate art more after receiving instruction. There are other, less obvious objections. One is that their use may lead to an emphasis on objectives that can be easily measured rather than goals that reflect higher level learning. After all, it is easier to measure a student's knowledge of art than his or her ability to contrast two styles. Since higher order thinking is sometimes difficult to place into this type of objective, it might be omitted. Others argue that this level of specification reflects a rigidity of purpose that does not allow the teacher to take advantage of special circumstances to cover other material. In addition, this type of objective is cumbersome to write, and some authorities maintain that omitting the setting condition and criterion for success, leaving only the specific description of the objective, is sufficient for classroom use (Gronlund, 1985).

Each of these objections can be countered. If high-level outcomes are being ignored, what better way to discover this than to look at the teacher's objectives? Second, behavioral objectives are not meant to be rigid directives that do not allow for the necessary flexibility. Stating the objectives in this way simply allows for greater clarity of thought. Last, there is a great advantage to thinking about objectives and the behaviors that are desired of students and how these behaviors can be measured accurately.

Domains of Concern

What areas should these objectives cover? Basically, there are three domains of interest: the cognitive, the affective, and the psychomotor. Each area has its own objectives. The cognitive domain involves the intellectual components of learning, the affective domain reflects the emotional and attitudinal components, while the psychomotor domain involves those objectives concerning body movement. Let's look at a unit on exercise. We may want students to learn something about the physiology of exercise and be able to compare different types of exercise. These are cognitive goals. We may also want students to change their attitudes toward exercise and people who exercise. This would represent the affective component. We may want students to actually begin to exercise. This represents the psychomotor area. Often, objectives that are stated in one area of concern actually overlap the others (Furst, 1981). The manner in which students perceive people who exercise may affect their willingness to participate in exercise, and students' knowledge of different types of exercise and the benefits of exercising may affect their attitudes. Although in common practice we separate these three domains, in reality they interact with one another.

Understanding Taxonomies

Would you say it was more difficult to describe an event or analyze it? Is it more difficult to get a student's attention or to motivate him or her to actively participate? Is it easier to get a student to copy something or to originate or create something? Obviously, some objectives are more difficult to attain than others. In fact, the skills and objectives involved for all three domains can be placed onto a list of objectives from simple to complex, from least difficult to most difficult. Such lists are called taxonomies, which are arranged in a hierarchy and are cumulative. Taxonomies are hierarchical in that each level is more complex than the previous one. They are cumulative because each presumes the ability to perform all the behaviors described in the levels that precede it.

Educational Objectives in the Cognitive Domain

Benjamin Bloom and his colleagues (1956) constructed a **taxonomy of educational objectives for the cognitive domain.** These objectives include knowledge, comprehension, application, analysis, synthesis, and evaluation. A short description will make their differences apparent.

Knowledge. The knowledge component involves retrieving previous knowledge. It is measured, for example, when reciting the alphabet, knowing who the president and vice president of the United States are, and defining the word *influential.*

Comprehension. Comprehension involves translating knowledge into one's own words. It requires understanding the meaning of material and includes summarizing a story and predicting what will happen to a character in the story. This goes beyond the simple retrieval of the material, for the student must show understanding.

Application. Application involves the ability to use learned material in new situations. A child taught the rule of how to find the area of a geometric figure will need to use the rule in a new situation in which the rule is appropriate.

taxonomy of educational objectives (cognitive domain) Bloom's hierarchical listing of educational objectives covering the cognitive (intellectual) domain.

Analysis. Analysis is the ability to break a concept down into its basic parts and show how each part relates to the others, how the parts are organized, or which part is most important. This involves identifying parts, analyzing relationships, and understanding organizational principles. For example, a student may be asked to analyze and compare two different chemical reactions.

Synthesis. Synthesis involves putting elements together in a unique and creative manner. Writing a story, using certain materials to build something new, or proposing an experiment that will demonstrate some principle are examples of synthesis.

Evaluation. Evaluation involves the ability to judge value for a specific purpose. Evaluation is based upon standards that students may first have to determine. This is not simply opinion, as evaluation may require a student to draw conclusions from data. Evaluating the trends in poverty over the past two decades and writing a critique of a poem are examples of the evaluation component.

Bloom's taxonomy is widely used, and Table 11.2 illustrates some of the descriptive phrases that can be used to write instructional objectives for the cognitive domain. However, there are objections to the taxonomy. The most serious objection is that the taxonomy is not really a hierarchy, and making one objective "higher" than another does not fit the facts. For example, history in secondary school often involves a long list of events tied together by a narrative. David Moore (1982) gives the example of the explanation of manifest destiny that is often used to tie together facts about westward expansion. Moore claims that the narrative corresponds to synthesis, while the facts correspond to knowledge. He argues that we cannot artificially separate one from the other. Both are necessary. It would perhaps be better to view the taxonomy as a listing of parallel objectives rather than as a hierarchy (Furst, 1981). Others argue that the separation of the cognitive from the affective and

Table 11.2 Examples of General Instructional Objectives and Clarifying Verbs for the Cognitive Domain of the Taxonomy

Illustrative General Instructional Objectives	Illustrative Verbs for Stating Specific Learning Outcomes
Knows common terms Knows specific facts Knows methods and procedures Knows basic concepts Knows principles	Defines, describes, identifies, labels, lists, matches, names, outlines, reproduces, selects, states
Understands facts and principles Interprets verbal material Interprets charts and graphs Translates verbal material to mathematical formulas Estimates future consequences implied in data Justifies methods and procedures	Converts, defends, distinguishes, estimates, explains, extends, generalizes, gives examples, infers, paraphrases, predicts, rewrites, summarizes
Applies concepts and principles to new situations Applies laws and theories to practical situations Solves mathematical problems Constructs charts and graphs Demonstrates correct usage of a method or procedure	Changes, computes, demonstrates, discovers, manipulates, modifies, operates, predicts, prepares, produces, relates, shows, solves, uses
Recognizes unstated assumptions Recognizes logical fallacies in reasoning Distinguishes between facts and inferences Evaluates the relevancy of data Analyzes the organizational structure of a work (art, music, writing)	Breaks down, diagrams, differentiates, discriminates, distinguishes, identifies, illustrates, infers, outlines, points out, relates, selects, separates, subdivides
Writes a well-organized theme Gives a well-organized speech Writes a creative short story (or poem or music) Proposes a plan for an experiment Integrates learning from different areas into a plan for solving a problem Formulates a new scheme for classifying objects (or events or ideas)	Categorizes, combines, compiles, composes, creates, devises, designs, explains, generates, modifies, organizes, plans, rearranges, reconstructs, relates, reorganizes, revises, rewrites, summarizes, tells, writes
Judges the logical consistency of written material Judges the adequacy with which conclusions are supported by data Judges the value of a work (art, music, writing) by use of internal criteria Judges the value of a work (art, music, writing) by use of external standards of excellence	Appraises, compares, concludes, contrasts, criticizes, describes, discriminates, explains, justifies, interprets, relates, summarizes, supports

Reprinted with permission of Macmillan Publishing Company from *Stating Objectives for Classroom Instruction,* 3d ed. by Norman E. Gronlund. Copyright © 1985 by Norman E. Gronlund.

psychomotor is too artificial. Despite these criticisms, Bloom's taxonomy can prove helpful in clarifying cognitive objectives.

Educational Objectives in the Affective Domain

Educational objectives go well beyond the cognitive realm. Educators are interested in feelings and emotions, tastes and preferences, appreciation, attitudes, and values (Ringness, 1975). Objectives that measure these qualities lie within the affective domain. Obviously, it is more difficult to objectively measure outcomes in this area.

Some classes, such as art and music, may openly state such objectives, but classes in other subjects rarely do. However, these objectives do fit into other subjects. For example, we may want students to not only understand the Holocaust during World War II but also empathize with the victims. We may want students to both understand various aspects of technology and have positive attitudes toward the use of computers. We may teach students about the Bill of Rights, but we also want them to treasure their individual rights.

A **taxonomy of educational objectives for the affective domain** was formulated by Krathwohl, Bloom, and Masia (1964). The levels for these objectives are receiving, responding, valuing, organization, and characterization. They can be described in the following manner.

Receiving. At this lowest level in the affective domain, students are sensitized to certain phenomena, are aware of them, and, most importantly from a teaching point of view, pay attention to them.

Responding. This next level requires active student participation. Here the student must show some simple response, be it volunteering in class discussions or showing some pleasure during reading. However, there is no commitment required, and the learner is neither expressing nor internalizing any values.

---

taxonomy of educational objectives (affective domain) A hierarchical listing of education objectives covering the affective domain (attitudes, values, and emotions).

Valuing. This is the first level in which students are asked to assign worth to a particular activity or object. Students now must show that they have internalized some set of values. These values and attitudes may be reflected in students' answers to questions, in their comments in class, or through their behavior itself. A student who values freedom or equality may speak out on an issue even though the issue may not be popular.

Organization. Once students internalize and express their values, they may find that values are in conflict with one another. At this level, students must build a consistent and organized value system and resolve conflicts between values. Values are compared, and some become more dominant than others. When students are choosing a vocation, they must understand their values, for example, money and community service, and relate their values to their choice.

Characterization by a Value or Value Complex. At this highest level, the individual's value system has been in place for some time and his or her responses consistently based upon these values. These values typify the individual and are descriptive of the person's philosophy of life. The individual shows a consistent relationship between these values and his or her behaviors.

As you can see, the taxonomy is structured along a continuum of internalization and involvement. At first, students are only aware of their feelings, while at later stages they become more deeply involved, internalize the value, and finally make it part of the fabric of their belief system, using it to direct their actions. For instance, the student at the first level may become aware of racism, show some interest in it, and perhaps later even choose to read an article about it over doing some other activity. At the second level, the student adopts an opinion and later may be willing to state it in public and defend it. At the higher levels, the value is integrated into the student's value system, and the student may become active in a cause. At still higher levels the value's meaning expands and may be linked to other values, such as civil rights. Last, the value may characterize the student's whole way of life.

Note that the lower levels of the affective taxonomy involve simply attending and responding. When writing objectives for this level, it is common to use the phrase "Students will show a willingness to _____."

For example, "Students will demonstrate a willingness to pay attention to the lesson by completing assignments." At the response level, the term *voluntarily* is often used. For example, "Students will demonstrate their attitude towards helping others by volunteering to tutor their friends in a peer-tutoring program" (Houston et al., 1988). It is not difficult to state that we would like students to value honesty or integrity or to feel personal responsibility. Table 11.3 shows some of the descriptive phrases that can be used to write instructional objectives for the affective domain.

Table 11.3   Examples of General Instructional Objectives and Clarifying Verbs for the Affective Domain of the Taxonomy

Illustrative General Instructional Objectives	Illustrative Verbs for Stating Specific Learning Outcomes
Listens attentively Shows awareness of the importance of learning Shows sensitivity to human needs and social problems Accepts differences of race and culture Attends closely to the classroom activities	Asks, chooses, describes, follows, gives, holds, identifies, locates, names, points to, selects, sits erect, replies, uses
Completes assigned homework Obeys school rules Participates in class discussion Completes laboratory work Volunteers for special tasks Shows interest in subject Enjoys helping others	Answers, assists, complies, conforms, discusses, greets, helps, labels, performs, practices, presents, reads, recites, reports, selects, tells, writes
Demonstrates belief in the democratic process Appreciates good literature (or art or music) Appreciates the role of science (or other subjects) in everyday life Shows concern for the welfare of others Demonstrates problem-solving attitude Demonstrates commitment to social improvement	Completes, describes, differentiates, explains, follows, forms, initiates, invites, joins, justifies, proposes, reads, reports, selects, shares, studies, works
Recognizes the need for balance between freedom and responsibility in a democracy Recognizes the role of systematic planning in solving problems Accepts responsibility for his or her own behavior Understands and accepts his or her own strengths and limitations Formulates a life plan in harmony with his or her abilities, interests, and beliefs	Adheres, alters, arranges, combines, compares, completes, defends, explains, generalizes, identifies, integrates, modifies, orders, organizes, prepares, relates, synthesizes
Displays safety consciousness Demonstrates self-reliance working independently Practices cooperation in group activities Uses objective approach in problem solving Demonstrates industry, punctuality, and self-discipline Maintains good health habits	Acts, discriminates, displays, influences, listens, modifies, performs, practices, proposes, qualifies, questions, revises, serves, solves, uses, verifies

Reprinted with permission of Macmillan Publishing Company from *Stating Objectives for Classroom Instruction*, 3d ed. by Norman E. Gronlund. Copyright © 1985 by Norman E. Gronlund.

The problem with affective objectives is in finding some way to measure the outcome. In some cases, such measurement may be possible, as when a student shows a choice of helping another person rather than just passing someone who is injured. On the other hand, it is not always easy to measure these objectives in behavioral terms, although an attempt can be made. For example, we may look for changes in a child's behavior. If we want students to appreciate art, we might say, "After instruction, students will choose artistic endeavors over other choices in a free-time period." We may also use a systematic rating scale, either forms that allow the teacher to rate students on behaviors that reflect the value—for example, interpersonal relationships—or self-report forms on which students are asked to state their attitudes or values (Hughes & Frommer, 1982; Anderson & Anderson, 1982). Some forms are commercially available, while teachers may want to develop some attitude surveys on their own.

An affective objective that is rarely stated but is important is developing a student's attitude towards a subject. Mager (1984) noted that students should, at the least, like a subject as much when they end it as they did when they began it.

Educational Objectives in the Psychomotor Domain

Psychomotor activities are basic to physical education, industrial arts, home economics, some music and art classes, and typing. Some laboratory skills also fall under this category. There are a number of categorization systems, and they differ from each other. Simpson's (1972) **taxonomy of educational objectives for the psychomotor domain** is representative and consists of seven levels: perception, set, guided response, mechanism, complex overt response, adaptation, and origination.

Perception. At the first level, a person receives information that will guide his or her motor performance through the sense organs.

Set. This level refers to a readiness to take part in some type of motor activity. The student is mentally, physically, and emotionally ready to act.

Guided Response. This involves simply imitating a response made by a teacher. Many errors are made at this stage.

Mechanism. At this level, the movements are well practiced, and teachers are more concerned with

Many subjects have psychomotor objectives, but they are most obvious in some areas, such as keyboarding.

the level of performance than with the actual learning of the basic skill.

Complex Overt Response. Students at this level are very skilled in their responses and have no uncertainty. The movements at this level are complex.

Adaptation. Students at this high level can modify the responses to fit the nature of the situation.

Origination. At this highest level, students can produce new and creative patterns that fit the situation.

As you can see, the lower levels involve understanding what is necessary to perform the behavior. The middle levels require guided response and practice until one becomes proficient. At a higher level, one can adapt a skill to changing circumstances, for example, adapt swimming strokes to fit the roughness of the water. The highest level is origination, which involves creating new patterns such as inventing a new dance step. Note that the hierarchy begins at a level of knowing how, continues through motor response and practice, and finally reaches the level of originality.

taxonomy of educational objectives (psychomotor domain) A hierarchical listing of educational objectives covering the psychomotor domain, which involves movement and manual skills.

It is not difficult to create a behavioral objective in the psychomotor area, and some descriptive phrases for this area are found in Table 11.4. We may say, for example, "After instruction, the students will be able to run the track for five minutes" or "After taking four weeks of lessons, the child will be able to play a particular musical piece with three or fewer errors."

Robert Gagné's Learning Outcomes and Learning Hierarchy

The outcomes of learning can be looked at in many ways. According to the prominent psychologist, Robert Gagné, there are five varieties of learning: verbal information, intellectual skills, motor skills, attitudes, and cognitive strategies (Gagné, 1977). Verbal information involves acquiring facts and organized bodies of knowledge. The second class of learning—intellectual skills—involves skills that allow people to function well in society and that range from analyzing a newspaper story to measuring the area of a room for a new carpet. It includes knowing how to do something rather than knowing some fact.

Gagné has offered a learning hierarchy for intellectual skills, with mastery of one intellectual skill forming the base for mastering a more complex skill. Four types of intellectual skills are discrimination learning, concept learning, rule learning, and higher-order

---

Table 11.4 Examples of General Instructional Objectives and Clarifying Verbs for the Psychomotor Domain

Illustrative General Instructional Objectives	Illustrative Verbs for Stating Specific Learning Outcomes
Recognizes malfunction by sound of machine Relates taste of food to need for seasoning Relates music to a particular dance step	Chooses, describes, detects, differentiates, distinguishes, identifies, isolates, relates, selects, separates
Knows sequence of steps in varnishing wood Demonstrates proper bodily stance for batting a ball Shows desire to type efficiently	Begins, displays, explains, moves, proceeds, reacts, responds, shows, starts, volunteers
Performs a golf swing as demonstrated Applies first-aid bandage as demonstrated Determines best sequence for preparing a meal	Assembles, builds, calibrates, constructs, dismantles, displays, dissects, fastens, fixes, grinds, heats, manipulates, measures, mends mixes, organizes, sketches, works
Writes smoothly and legibly Sets up laboratory equipment Operates a slide projector Demonstrates a simple dance step	Assembles, builds, calibrates, constructs, dismantles, displays, dissects, fastens, fixes, grinds, heats, manipulates, measures, mends mixes, organizes, sketches, works
Operates a power saw skillfully Demonstrates correct form in swimming Demonstrates skill in driving an automobile Performs skillfully on the violin Repairs electronic equipment quickly and accurately	Assembles, builds, calibrates, constructs, dismantles, displays, dissects, fastens, fixes, grinds, heats, manipulates, measures, mends mixes, organizes, sketches, works
Adjusts tennis play to counteract opponent's style Modifies swimming strokes to fit the roughness of the water	Adapts, alters, changes, rearranges, reorganizes, revises, varies
Creates a dance step Creates a musical composition Designs a new dress style	Arranges, combines, composes, constructs, designs, originates

Reprinted with permission of Macmillan Publishing Company from *Stating Objectives for Classroom Instruction*, 3d ed. by Norman E. Gronlund. Copyright © 1985 by Norman E. Gronlund.

rule learning, or problem solving. Discrimination involves making distinctions, as when we distinguish between colors or shapes. This is a prerequisite for the next level, that of learning concepts. A concept is a generalized idea that allows one to classify objects or events on the basis of some common property that each shares. It requires a person to recognize similarities and ignore differences. For example, a concept of a car involves noticing that a car has four wheels and travels on the road while ignoring the fact that cars differ in length and color. Concepts are related to one another through rules. Students learn the rules for composing music by relating notes, rhythm, and other musical concepts to each other. Higher-level rule learning, another name for problem solving, occupies the highest level of intellectual learning and involves using a number of rules to solve a particular problem.

Motor skills, the third class of learning, relate to the smooth movement needed for such functions as getting dressed, playing sports, or writing. The fourth class of learning is attitudes, which influence the choices an individual makes. For example, a student with a poor attitude toward reading will be more likely to choose a different activity. Last, Gagné argues that cognitive strategies control the outcomes of learning. That is, students learn to control their own learning through a number of strategies in the areas of memory, reasoning, and study skills (discussed in Chapters 3 and 4).

For Gagné, learning in each of these outcomes is cumulative, with more complex learning resting upon simpler learning. Gagné argues that all five learning outcomes are important goals for school learning. For the most part, though, the curriculum focuses on verbal information and intellectual skills, and performance objectives are important in both areas.

Gagné's views are important because Gagné plainly lists the five outcomes of learning that cut across disciplines and grade levels. In addition, note that the highest level of outcome is problem solving.

The five outcomes of learning are distinguished by five different capabilities (see Table 11.5). We can write performance objectives covering each of these areas of learning. Gagné's system offers us another way to view the outcomes of learning.

Table 11.5   Five Major Categories of Learned Capabilities, Including Subordinate Types, and Examples of Each
Robert Gagné's list of learning capabilities cuts across various disciplines.

Capability (Learning Outcome)	Examples of Performance Made Possible
Intellectual skill	Demonstrating symbol use, as in the following:
Discrimination	Distinguishing printed *m*'s and *n*'s
Concrete concept	Identifying the spatial relation "underneath"; identifying a "side" of an object
Defined concept	Classifying a "family," using a definition
rule	Demonstrating the agreement in number of subject and verb in sentences
Higher-order rule	Generating a rule for predicting the size of an image, given the distance of a light source and the curvature of a lens
Cognitive strategy	Using an efficient method for recalling names; originating a solution for the problem of conserving gasoline
Verbal information	Stating the provisions of the first Amendment to the U.S. Constitution
Motor skill	Printing the letter *R* Skating a figure eight
Attitude	Choosing to listen to classical music

Table 2.1 from *The Conditions of Learning*, 3d ed. by R. M. Gagné. Copyright © 1977 by Holt, Rinehart, and Winston Inc. Reprinted by permission from the publisher.

PART IV
Effective Teaching Techniques

What Instructional Objectives Mean to the Teacher

After this discussion of instructional objectives, the natural question to ask is, Does it make any difference whether instructional objectives are used? In other words, is student achievement any higher when such objectives are used? Evidence here is mixed, with many studies—but certainly not all—showing advantages to the use of such objectives (Roberts, 1982; Melton, 1978). The objectives seem more helpful for pupils of average ability than for higher or lower ability students (White & Tisher, 1986; Melton, 1978).

One reason for the inconclusive results is the many variables involved. For instance, most studies that show that instructional objectives are effective used objectives that were very clear. In addition, these objectives were communicated to students and referred to so that students were always aware of them (Melton, 1978). A policy of using vaguely stated objectives or just handing students lists of objectives will not lead to the use of such objectives and is unlikely to show much advantage. In addition, if objectives are very easy or extremely difficult, they will have less of a positive impact on students.

Another important issue is how the objectives are used. If a teacher writes a reasonable objective but fails to teach to it, the objective becomes meaningless. For example, if my objective states, "After reading a story, students will summarize the story in writing in their own words," but I do not teach students how to summarize or organize their thoughts, the failure lies not in the objective but in the teaching procedures used. Last, the objectives must be evaluated. This can be accomplished through some sort of testing program or even through observation. If we write a reasonable objective, teach in a way that satisfies the objective, and then do not use the objective as the basis for evaluation, the process has little purpose.

With this research in mind, the following points may help you not only to write better objectives but also to increase the probability that the objectives will improve student achievement.

1. **Instructional objectives are part of the teaching process, whether stated or implied.** Every teacher has objectives when he or she steps into the classroom to give a lesson. Putting them in written form improves organization and clarity. However, the exact form and structure of the ob-jectives is flexible and should be adapted to individual needs (Roberts, 1982).

2. **The taxonomies are useful because they broaden the teacher's scope of teaching, constantly reminding the instructor that many different types of objectives exist.** Whether you agree that they are hierarchies or would rather conceive of them as parallel, a variety of skills are required in education, and lessons should reflect this. If all we are demanding is knowledge, we may choose to expand our lessons into such areas as comprehension and application.

3. **Objectives are a vital part of the planning process.** The process might look something like this. First identify the major goals of instruction and then write instructional objectives for a content area consistent with the goals and student abilities. The instructional methods used depend upon the objectives adopted. Assessment is part of the process and should, again, be directed by your goals. Testing will then also show whether there is a need for more instruction (Montague, 1987). This may also give you an idea of what changes you might consider for next year's teaching of this unit.

4. **Instructional objectives do not have to be seen as limiting a teacher, nor are they anything etched in stone.** You may find that as you begin to teach a particular unit, some areas of interest to students arise. The use of instructional objectives should not stop a teacher from delving into a new area, especially since one of education's goals, whether stated or not, is to increase student intrinsic motivation and interest in the subject matter. You may also find that students need training in some area that you thought they knew and that you may need to change your objectives.

5. **Objectives are most effective as aids when they are communicated clearly to students and when students are aware of them.** Many students ignore these objectives because they are unaware of them or because objectives have been ignored in the past. Objectives must also be clear and reasonable to be effective.

6. **Remember the importance of affective objectives.** Although much more difficult to evaluate, affective objectives have their place in all subjects and should be a part of a unit's instructional objectives.

When objectives are written clearly, used correctly, and communicated to students, they can serve as aids in planning and improving student achievement. However, they should not be viewed as rigid directives that retard spontaneity in the classroom and prevent teachers from exercising their decision-making power to follow a course that they think will be educationally valuable.

True or False   Instructional objectives should not influence testing procedures because their primary purpose is to introduce a new unit of study.

THE GOAL IS MASTERY: MASTERY LEARNING

Would you be satisfied if 50 percent of your students achieved your goals? If not, would you feel successful if 75 percent did? If your answer is that all students should achieve your goals, is this a realistic objective?

It is almost an axiom that a teacher will not be successful with all students. However, one type of learning approach, called **mastery learning,** disputes this belief, if we define success as reaching particular goals that are well defined. Under this system of learning, every student is normally expected to reach highly specified goals (Guskey, 1988).

Mastery learning arises from Carroll's (1963) argument that differences in achievement are not so much due to innate ability as to children's different needs for the amount of time required to learn. In other words, almost every student can learn if given sufficient time. Benjamin Bloom (1968, 1981) developed this idea into a system called mastery learning, in which every student is expected to master specifically defined material to a high level of proficiency. This system requires constant feedback, corrective instruction, and enrichment for those who master the skill before others.

To master a particular skill, each student must perform adequately on tests that measure specific learning outcomes (Horton, 1981). Bloom's model assumes that if students do not achieve mastery, they should receive additional instructional time until they do. This is especially important, because mastery of certain skills is a prerequisite for mastery of more involved skills. It is a grave mistake, then, for students who do not have proficiency in elementary work to be passed on to learning other, more involved work.

Mastery learning also requires well-defined behavioral or instructional objectives and the structuring of learning in a logical and sequential manner. In mastery learning, the amount of learning time is varied according to the needs of the individual. The process operates in this manner. The teacher first formulates specific learning objectives. The students are then given an initial assessment to discover their competence. The pretest determines a student's initial level of knowledge so that the student can be placed in the best learning sequence and given the most effective instruction. A student who obtains nine of ten correct probably can be given a wide range of application work, while an individual obtaining only one or two correct needs a different type of instruction.

The third element is instruction, and here no single strategy is advanced. Mastery learning does not demand that teachers use any particular method of instruction. Although whole-group instruction is possible, individualized worksheets and, at times, small-group work are used as well (Stallings & Stipek, 1986). During the instruction, students are given brief diagnostic tests that they may score themselves. This shows both the students and their teacher the progress and leads to corrective instruction. These correctives are not more of the same but are individual assignments, small-group study, peer tutoring, programmed instruction, or whatever is required to help students reach mastery.

Students who master the unit quickly receive enrichment, and students continue this diagnostic-assessment procedure until they have achieved mastery, which is defined by the teacher as some high level of knowledge or skill. Grades are not competitive, and any student mastering the curriculum is given an A. Until a child demonstrates mastery, he or she is given an incomplete.

Although mastery learning is appealing, it has its critics. For one thing, it requires a very well defined curriculum with very well defined objectives and levels of mastery. Not all school content, especially at higher grades, can be placed into such a design. Second, since there is a time differential among students—that is, some students master the information

mastery learning   A program designed so that students reach a high level of competence in certain well-defined skills.

or skill faster than others—enrichment is important, but it is not very easy to design. There is some concern that brighter students may be penalized because so much teacher time is devoted to students needing corrective work. If teachers do not proceed to the next skill until nearly all students have achieved mastery, high-achieving students may have to wait and may suffer unless the enrichment is challenging.

Mastery learning's supporters claim that the time differences between higher- and lower-achieving students are not very great, but that remains a controversial claim. In addition, many critics believe that mastery-based programs are too structured and rigid, while still other critics believe that requiring 95 percent of the students to achieve very high rates of proficiency places too high a demand on the average teacher (Cox & Dunn, 1979; Horton, 1979). Last, in such a system, the recordkeeping, testing, and need for individual correctives is very high, and the resources for such individual corrective instruction may not be available.

The main questions, though, are, Does it work? and Is it worth the effort? The evidence in this regard is largely favorable. Most studies (but not all) find advantages for students who are taught using mastery learning over more traditional approaches (Block & Burns, 1976). There is also some evidence that mastery learning has a mildly positive effect on student attitudes towards learning (Stallings & Stipek, 1986). However, until the criticisms described above are satisfied, mastery learning will probably not be widely used in classrooms (Horton, 1981).

TEACHING STRATEGIES

Once the objectives are determined, the next decision concerns the teaching methods to use. Should you lecture, use demonstrations, plan for discovery sessions, or use questioning to teach your students? How much homework should you give? What type of practice should you assign? How will you help students who are having difficulty with the material? These are basic questions.

Each subject and grade level has specific teaching techniques that are especially relevant. Although it would be impossible to describe all of them, research in educational psychology has been especially productive in evaluating the strengths and weaknesses of the major teaching methods, some of which are de-scribed in the following sections. As you read about these methods, ask yourself how you would present some lesson in your own discipline using each of these particular methods.

Direct Instruction

How would you teach students the causes of the Civil War, how to solve mathematical word problems requiring addition and subtraction, or how to summarize a story? The goal in each of these is to convey to students a body of information or a particular skill. For this purpose, **direct instruction** has demonstrated its effectiveness (Borich, 1988). Sometimes people mistake direct instruction for a simple college type of lecture in which the teacher talks for fifty minutes or so about a topic and students take notes. It isn't.

True or False The form of teaching called direct instruction is another name for lecture.

direct instruction A type of instructional method especially useful for conveying information that includes setting clear goals, presenting a sequence of well-organized assignments, explaining material to students, presenting examples, asking frequent questions, and giving frequent practice in what the students have learned.

Unfortunately, direct instruction is sometimes confused with straight lecture. Direct instruction is quite different.

The basic components of direct instruction are setting clear goals and communicating them to students, presenting a sequence of well-organized assignments, giving students clear and concise explanations and illustrations of the subject matter, asking frequent questions to ascertain student understanding, and giving students frequent practice in what they have learned (Judy et al., 1988; U.S. Department of Education, 1987a).

The specific activities or instructional functions connected with such teaching can be found in Table 11.6. A lesson might begin with some review of the previous day's work, including homework and reteaching if necessary. An overview of the new material is given, with the material so structured that it is taught in small steps at a rapid pace. A great deal of interaction takes place between students and teachers, much of it involving questions asked by teachers.

Guided practice and applications are included with corrections and reteaching. Finally, independent seatwork is assigned when students know their work, and students receive weekly and monthly reviews. Evaluation is done through classroom achievement tests (Womack, 1989).

The first reaction of many students to this description of direct instruction is, "That's the way we learned when I was in school. It's boring and repetitive." Studies have demonstrated, however, that direct instruction is not used very much (Gaskins, 1988). Students are rarely told what they are going to do or why, how, and when to apply the skill. A careful review of Table 11.6 may be enough to convince you that direct instruction is rarely practiced. This is unfortunate, because it can be effective when the aim is to transmit a body of information and skills to students (Shapiro, 1988), and it is particularly effective when teaching

---

Table 11.6 Instructional Functions
Direct instruction follows a logical sequence. As you can see, it is anything but straight lecture.

1. Daily review, checking previous day's work, and reteaching (if necessary)
   Checking homework
   Reteaching areas where there were student errors
2. Presenting new content/skills
   Providing overview
   Proceeding in small steps (if necessary), but at a rapid pace
   If necessary, giving detailed or redundant instructions and explanations
   Phasing in new skills while old skills are being mastered
3. Initial student practice
   Allowing high frequency of questions and overt student practice (from teacher and materials)
   Providing prompts during initial learning (when appropriate)
   Providing all students with a chance to respond and receive feedback
   Checking for understanding by evaluating student responses
   Continuing practice until students are firm
   Maintaining a success rate of 80% or higher during initial learning

4. Feedback and correctives (and recycling of instruction, if necessary)
   Giving feedback to students, particularly when they are correct but hesitant
   Allowing student errors to provide feedback to the teacher that corrections or reteaching is necessary
   Making corrections by simplifying question, giving clues, explaining or reviewing steps, or reteaching last steps
   When necessary, reteaching using smaller steps
5. Independent practice so that students' responses are firm and automatic
   Using seatwork
   Teaching unitization and automaticity (practice to overlearning)
   Allowing a need for procedure to ensure student engagement during seatwork (i.e., teacher or aide monitoring)
   Maintaining 95% correct or higher
6. Weekly and monthly reviews
   Reteaching, if necessary

Note: With older, more mature learners (1) the size of steps in the presentation is larger, (2) student practice is more covert, and (3) the practice involves covert rehearsal, restating, and reviewing (i.e., deep processing or "whirling").

Adapted from "Teacher Functions in Instructional Programs" by B. Rosenshine. In *Elementary School Journal* 83:4, 338–351 (1983). Copyright © 1983 University of Chicago Press.

new material to disadvantaged, young, poor students, or learning-disabled students (U.S. Department of Education, 1987b; Duffelmeyer & Baum, 1987).

Direct instruction has its limitations and its critics. It seems very regimented and is associated with a great deal of teacher talk and memorization and an emphasis on learning facts (Jarolimek & Foster, 1989). Sometimes it can degenerate into straight lecture. Two specific assumptions are made in direct instruction. First, there is a common body of knowledge that all learners need to know. Second, learners know about the same amount of material as they enter the learning situation (Womack, 1989). The first assumption is one that is easily met, while the second is rarely met. If direct instruction is to succeed, teachers must be certain that students are ready for the information they are going to teach. This involves doing some assessment before teaching a unit to find out what skills students have.

››› CONNECTIONS

Teachers and Direct Instruction

Direct instruction is a challenge for the teacher, not because the techniques are so difficult, but because it is so easy to fall into bad habits and simply lecture. For some, such a teacher-dominated scheme is something to be avoided entirely. However, too much research demonstrates the effectiveness of direct instruction for transmitting information and skills to simply push it aside. The following suggestions may help in implementing direct instruction.

1. **Understand where your students are.** Before planning any lesson or unit, it is important that you gauge the skills the students will require and the knowledge they already have. This can sometimes be discovered through a pretest or by looking at scores on specific standardized tests.

2. **Plan the lesson by using an outline of the steps required in direct instruction.** These steps involve daily review and checking previous work, providing an overview, planning the presentation in small steps, making certain one point is mastered before the next, modeling the skill when appropriate, having many varied examples, giving detailed explanations, checking for student understanding, asking questions, providing guided practice, and then slowly allowing the students to take responsibility for their own practice.

3. **State the objectives of the lesson as specific or behavioral objectives and communicate them to the students.** Since the material to be transmitted by direct instruction is usually basic, it is not difficult to write objectives. The objectives should be communicated to the students to provide them with some understanding of what and why they are going to learn the material.

4. **Try to anticipate where student problems will be.** This is, admittedly, difficult for new teachers, but it is still possible. If you can foresee where students may have problems, you can, among other things, proceed more slowly in these spots, give more practice, break the material down to smaller portions, and give more examples.

5. **Remember to question students repeatedly about the information.** Don't just ask, "Do you understand?" because, as noted repeatedly in this text, students often don't know that they know or don't know, and most students will not want to look foolish in front of their classmates and admit that they do not understand. Frequently asking questions of students during the lesson to ascertain understanding is vital to the success of direct instruction. The art and science of asking questions is discussed in Chapter 9, but one hint here is important. Many students have told me that they do not ask questions or admit they do not know something because in the past the teacher has not reacted positively to their revelation. Sometimes their question or admission was greeted with impatience or, even worse, ridicule. Accept questions willingly and be especially careful that your gestures and facial expressions do not show impatience.

6. **A summary or some statement that a topic is now completed is in order.** It is a wise move to give some closure to the lesson and summarize what the students have learned.

7. **Guided practice is important.** We will look into seatwork later in the chapter. Teachers often assign seatwork after teaching some part of a lesson, only to find students do not understand what they are to do or how to do it. Students should be guided through a few examples.

8. **Watch your pacing.** The pacing should be reasonably rapid. It is true that sometimes teachers go too fast, but it is equally true in direct instruction that it is possible to go too slowly.

9. **Adapt the size of the steps to the developmental level of the students.** For students who are very slow or young, very small steps may be required.

If you teach older students or students of higher ability, the steps should be larger.

10. **Watch for boredom.** Direct instruction does not mean that the materials used in the presentation cannot be varied. Films and demonstrations can be used as well. If students are becoming bored, you may be going too slowly, presenting material in steps that are too small, not challenging students, or not presenting interesting applications.

11. **Make certain students experience success.** One of the most impressive aspects of direct instruction is that students can experience success as they do well on their practice sheets and more formal evaluations that come directly from the instructional goals. Teacher praise, having parents sign papers that are well done, and other reinforcement procedures can help students, especially slow learners, achieve a feeling of success that they may never have felt before.

12. **Beware of using the technique incorrectly.** Direct instruction is useful in some areas but not in others. Not everything can be taught in this way, as we shall soon see. In addition, it is very easy to fall into a pattern of simply lecturing, which defeats the purpose of direct instruction.

Direct instruction is not a panacea for everything that is wrong with education, nor is it the deadening, cold, dry type of instruction some of its detractors claim it to be. It can be effectively used to transmit to students a body of information and skills if it is well paced, the teacher interacts well with the class, and the students are given enough feedback and experience success.

Indirect Methods of Instruction

The class was divided into couples, one boy and one girl. The couples were told that they were married and were given an amount of money and told to live on it. They were to meet and discuss their money situation, shop together to find out how much basic items cost, investigate housing alternatives, and then work out a budget.

Students were told that they were to adopt an egg—a raw egg that represented a baby. For a week they had to carry the egg around with them. When not cared for by the "parent," the egg had to be taken care of by someone special. The egg could not be left by itself. The students were told that this was their baby and that they were responsible for its welfare.

Students—just twenty-six of them—were told that they were marooned on a desert island. There was enough to eat and drink but little hope of help coming. The students would have to exist on the island, probably for many years. They had to determine some rules and some way to govern themselves.

Each of the above assignments demonstrates **indirect methods of instruction.** These methods are sometimes called inquiry learning, learning through problem solving, or discovery learning. Actually, the process of learning in these cases is through inquiry, the context is problem solving, and the result is discovery (Borich, 1988). The inquiry method involves asking questions, seeking information, and carrying on investigations (Jarolimek & Foster, 1989). Learners therefore must be very involved in the learning process and responsible for providing ideas and questions to be explored, proposing hypotheses, organizing information to test, and reaching conclusions. For example, a problem may be to find out how different metals are affected by temperature. Students might suggest taking four different metals and exposing them first to ice and then to heat. From their observations, the students make conclusions. Teachers might ask thought questions and help the students form their own questions. Students discover things for themselves, and such inquiry teaching provides experience for learners to develop the independent and critical learning skills necessary for problem solving. Inquiry learning focuses on process. The search and experience are just as important as the end product. Students must take responsibility in directing their own learning, which often involves a great deal of independent activity (Blair, 1988).

Indirect instruction is most appropriate if the goals of learning are more experiential, less objective, and more process oriented or if the desire is to teach students to develop critical thinking or problem-solving skills. Figure 11.1 shows some of the differences between direct and indirect instructional methods.

indirect methods of instruction (inquiry learning, discovery learning) A group of techniques often involving questioning and conducting investigations in which the content of what is to be learned must be discovered by the student before it can be made part of the student's cognitive structure.

Direct = √   Inquiry = ×

Teacher Control of the Class

No Control						Firm
			×		√	
1	2	3	4	5	6	7

Who Directs the Learning?

Teacher						Students
√				×		
1	2	3	4	5	6	7

Amount of Student Movement in Class

None						Much
	√				×	
1	2	3	4	5	6	7

Social Interaction

None						Much
	√				×	
1	2	3	4	5	6	7

Who Controls the Pacing of Instruction?

Teacher						Students
√					×	
1	2	3	4	5	6	7

Noise in the Classroom

Very Noisy						Silence
			×		√	
1	2	3	4	5	6	7

Who Decides What the Instructional Activities Will Be?

Teacher						Students
√			×			
1	2	3	4	5	6	7

Amount of Independent Practice

None						Much
		√			×	
1	2	3	4	5	6	7

Monitoring of Student Progress

None						Much
			×			√
1	2	3	4	5	6	7

Level of Comprehension Questions

Exclusively Factual						Exclusively Critical
	√			×		
1	2	3	4	5	6	7

Figure 11.1   Direct Versus Inquiry Instruction
How does direct instruction differ from inquiry methods? This figure rates these teaching methods in ten different areas.

Adapted from *Emerging Patterns of Teaching* by T. R. Blair. Copyright © 1988 Merrill Publishing Company, Columbus, Ohio. Reprinted by permission of Merrill Publishing Company.

The role of the teacher using indirect methods is often misunderstood. It would be inaccurate to say that students are simply handed a problem and allowed to use their own devices to solve it. This is not so, nor would it be desirable. Chapter 4 described an assignment I once gave my eighth-grade students to design a city using certain financial constraints. Before being allowed to work on this project, the students had to understand the basics of urban life and be able to keep track of money and write a report. The project could not be a free-for-all. Students cannot discover things unless they have the skills and knowledge necessary to do so. A discovery lesson in the biology lab has meaning only if the students know how to use the microscope and understand what they are looking for.

True or False Teachers using the discovery method of teaching give students a problem and then allow students to solve it in their own way without interfering with student activity.

One common mistake made by people using indirect methods is to assume that no direction is required. Often, direct instruction in some fashion may need to precede discovery learning. A student planning a cross-country trip, mapping it out, pricing it, and working out a budget must be able to read maps, send letters, and work with numbers, all of which may require directive instruction. In addition, even after students are ready for the discovery experience, they may need help formulating questions or require guidance in some form or another. The teacher might divide the class into small groups and allow each group to follow its own course to find the answer. Often, there is more than one answer to or way to solve a problem. However, the teacher does not remain passive. After being certain that students have the skills necessary to solve the problem, the teacher must be sure that they can obtain the needed materials and must help them clarify the problem. The teacher may then ask, "How do you want to go about finding this out?" The teacher also must keep the groups working on the task and help those who are having difficulty.

It is more difficult to use discovery than direct instruction as a method, perhaps because we ourselves were more likely to have been exposed to a more direct method (though probably not direct instruction) and are apt to teach as we were taught (Womack,

1989). It is not easy to leave gaps and allow students to think for themselves and act as a guide rather than simply give information. The goals of discovery learning are different, and it takes much longer to use this method.

Inquiry Learning

The inquiry method places a great emphasis on process. Students learn by conducting an investigation. The *experience* itself is important. Some inquiry experiences involve classroom or library work. Others might require field trips, which allow students to ask questions, find their answers, and thus develop their problem-solving abilities. However, not every experience a student may have can be subsumed under inquiry. Just taking students to the zoo and letting them run around is not inquiry. There is no problem formed, no questions asked, and no collection of data. This does not mean that a trip or an experience does not have value for its own sake. Taking students to a ballet to be exposed to the performance or to a play for the sheer joy of seeing it certainly has some value. However, for an experience to be considered inquiry or discovery, there must be some greater focus on problem and process.

One of the great strengths of inquiry is its emphasis on experience. When two students are asked to investigate the possibility of living on a budget, they must do their own research, and the experience itself is of value. I have known high school students for whom this exercise not only was enjoyable but also opened their eyes to the realities of life. No lecture and no direct learning method could have matched the experience.

Students react positively to experiential programs. In an interesting study, Gary Peltier (1987) asked 500 college students to write about their most potent learning experiences. Most of the described experiences were incidental or spontaneous, such as dealing with the death of people very close, or involved interpersonal relationships. Of those related to formal learning activities, most could be considered experiential learning. Activities such as student community service projects and field trips were most prominent. Other studies have also demonstrated that perhaps schools should do more with experiential learning. Informal student surveys indicate high ratings for make-believe marriages, adopting a raw egg, being

Although a trip to the zoo itself may be worthwhile, if students have questions to answer or things to discover, the trip will have even more value.

preschool helpers, and taking field trips, but such learning activities must be integrated into the regular curriculum. The possibilities are endless. Producing one's own local radio or television news program and participating in beautification programs, action-oriented environmental programs, consumer economics projects, and tutorial programs are just some of the many possibilities. Such action learning can involve spending time with political leaders or donating time to a charity. This is well in keeping with the suggestion made in the chapter on moral and ethical development in which putting one's values into action instead of just talking about them was advocated. Obviously, such experiences can be useful in meeting objectives in the affective domain, as attitudes are often affected by these experiences.

Indirect methods of teaching have their drawbacks, however. First, discovery is not a very time efficient method of learning compared with direct instruction. Of course, one could argue the meaning of efficiency when the goal is to learn something about a process or to change attitudes. However, it takes more time for students to discover something by themselves than it takes to be told about it. Students might take more time to find the information that answers their question than if they were simply given the information. Therefore, adoption of the inquiry method does not mean abandonment of direct instruction, which is useful in many areas and may even serve an introductory function in inquiry learning.

Another problem is that it takes a considerable amount of planning to use an inquiry approach. This approach requires more patience as well, since students may take the wrong turn while trying to find ways to answer the questions. As noted, when a more involved procedure is to be used, students must be prepared for it. In addition, giving some control to students does not come easy for some teachers. Teachers are more used to teacher-dominated, teacher-controlled classrooms. So are students, and it is not unusual to be disappointed at the beginning, since students are not used to having to generate questions, focus on process, and do something themselves.

Jerome Bruner and Discovery Learning

One of the best known advocates of discovery learning is Jerome Bruner. Bruner argued that education should emphasize the structure of a particular discipline and important cases rather than facts (1960; 1966; 1970). The student who is studying chemistry is, for that moment, a chemist, and the student who is studying geography, a geographer. It does not matter whether the student is in fourth grade or is a senior in high school. Bruner advocated that students be taught the structures of academic disciplines that include their major concepts, principles, and methods of inquiry. Each field has its own way of thinking and of going about solving problems. It is this approach that is so important for students to understand.

For Bruner, the teaching of isolated facts does not help students understand or solve problems in various disciplines. Nor will it lead to effective transfer of information to other areas. Instead, Bruner emphasizes the importance of teaching concepts and modes of inquiry within a context of the discipline. Bruner (1971) uses geography as an example. In a geography text, students are told that the world is divided into three zones—temperate, torrid, and frigid—and the ensuing discussion tries to make the categorization obvious. There is no discussion of the geographer's problem of how to characterize the world's climates, and geography becomes nothing more than a game of names.

There are a number of advantages to Bruner's approach. One is that by organizing courses in a manner in which the structure of various disciplines is made clear, students are provided with the scaffolding on which they can organize information and encode new information. Another advantage is that the student who understands the basics of the discipline has a sense of control over it. The student has some mastery, develops self-confidence, and can solve problems in the field. Bruner's approach also gives the student an understanding of how the practitioner in the field can use these methods to solve problems. Finally, students come to better understand the nature and purpose of the discipline itself, since they have an overall understanding of the ideas that comprise the discipline. For instance, when talking about small groups, the basic concepts are norms, sanctions, and roles. When teaching a lesson or unit on small groups, the teacher would build the course around these concepts. Each area has its own concepts or overall principles. The aim, then, is to design lessons that allow students to better understand the overall structure of the field and its concepts. This is nicely illustrated in the teaching of the metric system. The underlying principles of the system are metric units. If students learn the concepts of meter, liter, and gram, they can generalize the information to other metric units (millimeter, centimeter, etc.). Students first understand the value of these units and their relationship to one another. They then can use their learning. The central concept is the basis from which other content is built (Thornburg, 1984).

How can students learn the concepts, the central principles that the discipline comprises, and the modes of inquiry? Bruner believes that students can do it if they are allowed to approach learning in a context of discovery. He believes that discovery learning is a potent motivator and more satisfying to the student than other methods of instruction. Bruner notes that relatively little research has been performed on curiosity and a great deal on reward and punishment. He understands the importance of reinforcement but argues that the learner should be encouraged to develop a self-directed reward system and view a sense of accomplishment as being more important than external rewards.

Principles and concepts learned through discovery will also be more useful in solving problems. As Bruner states, "Practice in discovering for oneself teaches one to acquire information in a way that makes that information more readily viable in problem solving" (Bruner, 1961, p. 26). Discovery learning, then, will improve problem solving. If a student has discovered some principle, the principle should be more readily transferred to new areas.

Bruner argues that lessons must be structured so that students can actively use their cognitive abilities to learn new material. This is well in keeping with what Bruner sees as the normal pattern of how the mind works. The mind seeks to reduce the complexity of the world and to order its experience through categorization. The mind edits, selects, connects information to what is already known, and seeks patterns. It accomplishes this through the formation of concepts.

Bruner advocates using inductive reasoning in discovery learning. Inductive reasoning occurs when, after being given many examples, a student formulates an overall rule or principle. Put another way, the student discovers the principle. For example, a student will form the concept and understand the principle of buoyancy when given enough examples and experiences that show the phenomenon.

Perhaps one of Bruner's most engaging ideas is that students should be encouraged to use their intuition to guess about how to solve a problem or explain why some particular phenomenon occurred. Bruner (1970) noted that it is rare for anyone to ever have full evidence, and the shrewd guess and fertile hypothesis are very valuable. Heuristic techniques (refer to Chapter 4) can be used to give a person a good estimate on less than full evidence.

There are usually two approaches to study in any given field: one intuitive, the other analytic. Intuitive approaches are less rigorous with respect to proof, are more oriented toward solving the whole problem, and are based upon an ability to operate with insufficient data. Analytic reasoning follows the scientific method. The scientific discoveries that have shaped our lives are not solely the result of analytic reasoning; intuitive reasoning has its place in such discoveries. Intuition is especially helpful when we are given a problem and must begin the process of solving it. In many cases, it takes a hunch to figure out how to use whatever analytical skills we have. Intuition, then, is a good opening approach to problem solving. However, schools rarely value intuitive approaches (Bruner, 1971). Students are rarely told to use their intuition, hypothesize, or go beyond the information given. There is no reward for clever guessing and use of imagination. Bruner, though, is quick to point out that intuition yields a solution that is incomplete and must be followed up by more analytical means.

What can teachers take from Bruner's ideas? First, Bruner's argument that students should be taught key principles and concepts certainly deserves attention. Teachers, then, must organize their materials around central concepts and principles, connected in a meaningful manner. Second, Bruner's idea that students should be allowed to discover principles inductively leads to a particular way of teaching concepts (discussed a little later in the chapter). Third, Bruner reminds us of the need to consider intrinsic motivation along with extrinsic rewards (refer to Chapter 8). Fourth, Bruner emphasizes the importance of prob-lem solving. The teacher does not answer all the questions for the student. Students must be allowed to suggest ways to answer the questions or solve problems themselves. Students might be asked, "How can I find out what the effects of cold might be on plants?" or "How would you design a house for a child who cannot see?" Last, Bruner believes that intuitive guessing and conjuring up hypotheses are beneficial and educationally valuable practices. This leads to the suggestion that asking students to consider guessing what could happen to a character in a story or why they think New York or Los Angeles became such big cities is educationally sound.

▶▶▶ CONNECTIONS

The Teacher and Inquiry

The following suggestions may make a beginning attempt at inquiry learning somewhat easier.

1. **Know what you want to accomplish.** One common mistake is thinking that inquiry is a free-for-all. It isn't. Your goals may involve cognitive and/or affective outcomes and should be explicitly stated.

2. **Be certain students have the knowledge and skills necessary to learn something through inquiry.** Suppose you want to begin with some simple inquiry-based learning, such as investigating animals of different continents. You have certain cognitive goals and process goals, one of which may involve knowing how to find appropriate library materials. Students may need lessons in library skills to be successful.

3. **Explain the process of inquiry but do not give all the answers.** The process of asking questions and then finding some ways of answering them is basic to this process. Students may be divided into groups and allowed to construct questions and suggest ways of answering the questions. This may not be sufficient, however. Students may need help clarifying the specific questions and forming a plan of action. If there is a constant throng of students around the teacher's desk, inadequate instruction may be the problem (Womack, 1989).

4. **All groups or individuals should be monitored.** To be certain that students are progressing, constant monitoring is required. If a group is having difficulty, extra attention must be paid to that group. Such attention should facilitate the group's activities but should not give the group the answers.

5. **The teacher must provide the resources necessary for successful completion of the project.** If library material is required, students must be able to get to the library. If interviews are required, students may need some help in conducting them.

6. **Students must be encouraged to focus on their work.** If students are frustrated, do not know what to do next, or are turning group work into a strictly social hour, something is wrong. Although inquiry often means that there is somewhat more noise and more individual activity, the activity should be directed toward learning, and students' on-task behavior should be monitored.

7. **Consider whether inquiry is the right strategy.** As noted, the inquiry mode is better for some objectives than for others. Always using the inquiry mode can be inefficient in teaching more factual areas. In addition, since this method takes more time, teachers should be certain that state and locally mandated content is covered.

8. **Evaluation should be considered part of the plan.** Evaluating students in the inquiry method is just as important as it is in direct instruction. It is good practice to tell students how they will be evaluated before the project begins. Evaluation can take various forms, including paper and pencil tests, but can also include written papers that describe the process and demonstrate the thinking skills that went into the work.

MEANINGFUL LEARNING

Whenever describing these two major modes of teaching, the question of meaningfulness is always raised. Certainly we want our students to find their learning meaningful, since there is no doubt that they remember meaningful learning far longer than they remember learning that is not meaningful to them. Does direct instruction involve nothing more than rote learning, which essentially is not meaningful to the student? Is discovery learning always, by its very nature, meaningful?

Reception Learning

One important theorist who looked at this problem was David Ausubel (1969; 1977; 1978), whose work on advance organizers was discussed in Chapter 3. Aus-

ubel argued that we must make a distinction between reception and discovery learning and between rote and meaningful learning. In **reception learning,** the entire content of what is to be learned is presented to the student in its final form. The learner is expected to learn the material so that it can be retrieved when appropriate. In discovery learning, on the other hand, the content of what is to be learned must be discovered by the student before it can be made part of the student's cognitive structure. The information is not given to the student in its final form. In **guided discovery,** teachers are active in organizing activities so that students can discover concepts and principles. This differs from the more autonomous discovery learning in which much less teacher involvement is present. Most classrooms are organized along the reception lines. Reception learning does not have to be simple and discovery learning complex. When students learn advanced algebra in high school through reception learning, the learning is certainly complex.

Note that the distinction between reception and discovery learning does not indicate that one is more meaningful than the other. The other dimension—meaningful versus rote learning—stands on its own. Ausubel sharply disputes the commonly held belief that the only type of knowledge one really has and understands is that which he discovers by himself. Both reception and discovery learning may vary along the meaningful-rote continuum as shown in Figure 11.2.

But what does it mean for learning to be meaningful or rote? Meaningful learning occurs if the learning task is related in some nonarbitrary way to what the learner already knows. In other words, to be meaningful, the new learning must be able to be connected to learning that the learner already possesses. Meaningful learning also depends upon the learner's willingness to make such connections. Meaningful learning re-

reception learning   A type of learning described by David Ausubel in which the entire content of what is to be learned is presented to the student.

guided discovery   A type of discovery in which the teacher is active in focusing student attention on the important areas and structuring the problem and problem-solving activities so that students can discover the solution to a problem.

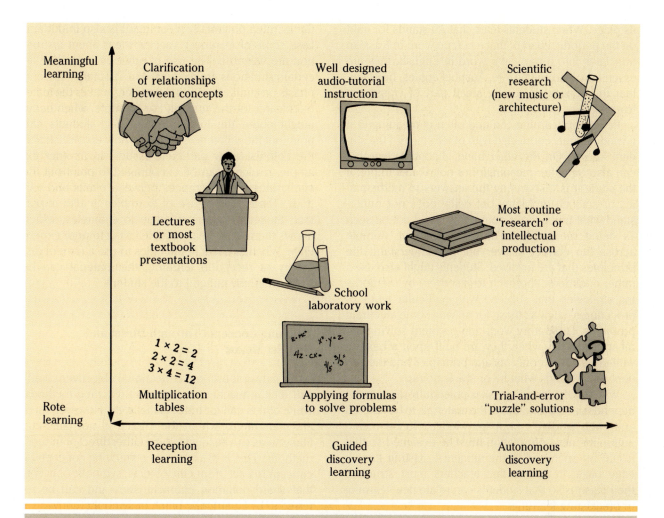

Figure 11.2 Continuum of Reception and Discovery Learning
According to David Ausubel and colleagues, learning varies across the meaningful-rote continuum and the reception-discovery continuum.

Adapted from Figure 1.1 (p. 25) in *Educational Psychology: A Cognitive View*, 2d ed., by D. P. Ausubel, J. D. Novak, and H. Hanesian. Copyright © 1978 by Holt, Rinehart, and Winston, Inc. Reprinted by permission of the publisher.

quires that the learner have a disposition or a learning set to relate the new material to what he or she already knows. No matter how potentially meaningful a particular concept may be, if the student is disposed to just memorize details, the concept's potential meaning will not matter. On the other hand, if the student is ready to relate the new material to previously learned material but the learning is not potentially meaningful, meaningful learning will not result. For example, a student may be willing and ready to relate to his or her past learning the physical law that states that force equals mass times acceleration, but if the student does not understand what force, mass, and acceleration are, meaningful learning cannot result. Students may develop a rote set to potentially meaningful learning if they have had the experience of not receiving credit for their answers that are correct even though not exactly like their teacher's answers or if they lack confidence in their ability or are very anxious.

Rote learning occurs if the learning task consists of arbitrary associations or is not related to the student's prior knowledge or if a student adopts an attitude towards the task that he or she merely wants to encode the task through rote memorization. Rote learning has its place. When students learn that Au stands for gold on the periodic chart or that a certain word in Russian translates into a particular word in English, they are essentially learning by rote. Ausubel argues, however, that this makes up a very small part of classroom learning.

Reception learning can and often is meaningful if it is adequately connected with other material the student knows. On the other hand, discovery learning can also be either meaningful or not. For example, if the student is discovering the answers to mathematics or science problems but really does not understand what he or she is doing, this could not be seen as being meaningful. The student might stumble across the correct answer but not understand the principles that are involved. Students might also use a rather cookbook approach to discovery by memorizing strategies that succeed with particular types of procedures, such as those for solving some algebraic problems. Laboratory work and problem solving are meaningful only when they are built upon a base of well-understood concepts and principles and the student understands what he or she is doing.

Whether the learning task is potentially meaningful depends upon the nature of the materials to be learned and each student's prior knowledge. To be meaningful, the new information must be designed so that it can be anchored to the student's existing knowledge base. It follows that teachers must structure their lessons so that students can relate new learning to preexisting learning.

Ausubel suggests a method of teaching called **expository teaching,** which involves presenting the main ideas before going into any of the details, using advance organizers that give students an organizational framework that provides them with the cognitive scaffolding on which to place new learning, and pointing out similarities and differences throughout the lesson. In an expository lesson, the teacher begins with an advance organizer, presents the content using many examples, and discusses similarities to and differences from other material. The new information is then related back to the advance organizer, and students are asked questions and are encouraged to ask their own questions.

Ausubel's ideas remind us not to make assumptions about the meaningfulness of material learned through reception or discovery learning. Ausubel's emphasis on relating present learning to the student's prior experience and learning that will serve to make the learning potentially meaningful is also important. Last, some of Ausubel's specific ideas about instruction are valuable. The use of advance organizers in certain situations are discussed in Chapter 3. The emphasis on similarities and differences makes the material clearer for the student. For example, when being taught about the Revolutionary War, students can point out the differences between how the British and the colonists saw particular issues. In another example, students can be encouraged to point out the similarities and differences between plants and animals. The extensive use of examples is also important. Students can often relate to examples, which allows them to relate present learning to prior experience. Whether a teacher decides to use a form of discovery or reception learning, the material can be made more meaningful to the student.

Teaching Concepts Through Direct and Indirect Means

As already noted, some educational objectives clearly call for the teacher to use direct teaching methods, while others call for indirect methods. However, there are many areas where the choice is not clear-cut. Many areas can be taught using either direct or indirect methods. This is the case when teaching concepts. A **concept** is a set of specific objects, symbols, or events that share common characteristics and can be referred to by a particular name or symbol (Tennyson & Park, 1980). Jazz, modern art, democracy, and science are all concepts. The use of concepts makes our thinking clearer and more efficient. For example, a person who categorizes a particular musical piece as jazz knows a great deal about the music. He or she understands something of the music's structure,

expository teaching   An approach to teaching described by David Ausubel which involves reception rather than discovery learning. It involves presenting the main ideas before any details, using advance organizers, and pointing out similarities and differences.

concept   A set of specific objects, symbols, or events that share common characteristics and can be referred to by a particular name or symbol.

rules, and style as well as how the piece relates to other types of music. On a simpler level, classification of an object as a ball because it is round and bounces allows a child to infer that the object can be used to play games, that it can be kicked and thrown, and even, perhaps, that it was manufactured by human beings and sold at a store.

Concepts allow us to go beyond our perceptual information (Dodd & White, 1980). Concepts also make our environment a more organized and simpler place in which to live. When we place different objects into the same category, we can respond to them as a member of a particular category rather than as something that is distinct and new. For example, we may encounter balls of many different colors and shapes and still interpret them as objects with which we can play.

Concepts also facilitate our ability to identify objects in the environment (Bruner et al., 1956). We can assign similar objects and ideas to already existing categories. For instance, if we see a small ball that is red and a larger one that is blue and white, we can place both balls in our concept of ball and understand the properties each share.

Concept formation can be seen as a process whereby people learn the attributes of a particular category in terms of the category's attributes. There are two kinds of attributes. **Variable attributes** are general properties that define a concept but do not differentiate it from all other concepts. For example, an airplane is a mode of transportation. While this is true, so are boats and automobiles. **Critical attributes** are those properties that differentiate a concept from other concepts that share some similarities. Airplanes are manufactured objects that fly through the air.

One view of concept learning notes that people form concepts through their experiences in which they abstract similarities from different objects. After a number of experiences with airplanes, children learn which attributes define an airplane and which do not. We form concepts, then, as we find and abstract common features from the various stimuli in our environment.

There are some difficulties with this view, though, and the view has recently been challenged for a number of reasons. First, not everything has well-defined critical attributes. Second, people are quite certain they understand a concept but often have difficulty explaining the rules they use to classify a particular object (Best, 1986). The simple concept of table can demonstrate these problems. You can probably think of some attributes of a table, but listing critical attributes is very difficult. If you try it, you may find that there are several tables that do not fit in well and other items that are not tables that do. Yet you are probably convinced that you know what a table is.

According to some cognitive psychologists, people form a **prototype,** or the most typical instance of a category, and compare other instances to the category. Rosch (1975) found that people formed prototypes of many categories, including color, birds, and vegetables. When asked to classify whether new items fit into these categories, they compared the new stimuli to the prototypes. Some examples are better prototypes than others. For instance, robins are better prototypes of birds than turkeys or penguins. How well a particular example fits a prototype affects how fast we process information. People are faster classifying a robin than a penguin as a bird. According to this theory, then, students may develop a prototype as representative for a concept and, when faced with a new stimulus, compare it to their prototype.

Teachers are often called upon to teach concepts. The strategies used for teaching concepts are still based upon the attribute model, probably because research into prototypes is still fairly new. Concepts may be taught in one of two ways. In the more direct method, six steps are required (Montague, 1987, p. 151):

1. Select the concept or generalization and identify the critical attributes.
2. Identify prerequisite knowledge and assess students.
3. Introduce the definition to students.
4. Introduce examples and nonexamples as needed, usually three or four.
5. Introduce examples and nonexamples simultaneously.
6. Provide practice.

variable attributes   General properties that define a concept but do not differentiate it from all other concepts.

critical attributes   Those properties that differentiate a concept from other concepts that share some similarities.

prototype   The most typical instance of a category.

Note that the teacher presents a definition to the students that contains the attributes of the concept. This is one of the keys to this strategy, and research shows that the strategy can be very helpful to students. In one study, Johnson and Stratton (1966) defined an altercation as a "social interaction characterized by a heated exchange of opposing arguments." Students who were given this definition performed much better on classification of new examples than students not given the definition first. Providing the definition reduces the number of examples the students require to master the concept (Tennyson & Park, 1980). One definite challenge here is to use terminology that is appropriate for the developmental level of the student and that is easily understood. Often, definitions are too abstract or are difficult to understand. When a teacher gives a definition, the critical attributes should stand out and the students should be able to grasp the definition easily and quickly.

A second strategy is more experiential and indirect. It involves providing students with some direct experience and then using questions about their experience that leads them to identify the critical attributes themselves. Seven steps are required in this method (Montague, 1987):

1. Select the concept or generalization and identify the critical attributes.
2. Identify prerequisite knowledge and assess students.
3. Provide a hands-on activity that provides experience with critical attributes.
4. Use questioning to analyze the experience.
5. Use a combination of questioning and presentation to identify the critical attributes.
6. Identify the symbol or symbols used to represent the concept or generalization.
7. Provide practice.

Two excerpts from *Fundamentals of Secondary Classroom Instruction* by Earl J. Montague. Copyright © 1987 by Merrill Publishing Company, Columbus, Ohio. Reprinted by permission.

Although this strategy gives students the opportunity to discover the concept for themselves, the teacher may also direct student attention and guide students toward the discovery of attributes by focusing student attention on specific elements of the material the students are examining. For instance, when learning the concept of a plant, students can examine a number of plants and actively search for similarities and differences. Teachers may want to be somewhat more active and focus student attention on the roots, leaves, or stem of a plant. Another important aspect of this method is the use of questions after the students have completed whatever activity is planned. Questions encourage students to discuss what they have experienced, recognize the similarities and differences among plants, and draw conclusions. The concept is then summarized.

The advantages and limitations of direct and indirect methods have already been discussed. The teacher must decide which method to adopt when teaching a particular concept. This decision will be based upon a number of considerations, including the objectives of the unit or lesson.

The Demonstration Mode

A teacher wanted to demonstrate how to use a particular piece of laboratory equipment. He performed the correct sequence of actions and then turned to the students and said, "Okay, now you do it." He was surprised when the students didn't do it correctly.

A demonstration is certainly an effective learning technique. A music teacher may demonstrate a way to play a song; a social studies teacher, a technique of analyzing a map; an English teacher, a technique for skimming some reading material. Demonstrations involve modeling a particular behavior. They dramatically illustrate a point. For example, one could lecture on how to use a jigsaw or how to use subheads as organizers when reading, but demonstrations can effectively and efficiently do the same job while increasing interest.

As the teacher at the beginning of this section discovered, however, demonstration involves much more than simply doing something. It involves showing, doing, and telling (Jarolimek & Foster, 1989). For a demonstration to be useful, a teacher must prepare students for what they are going to see or hear, specifically describe what is going on while they are doing it, and even tell students why they did something one way rather than another. Student attention is drawn to the most important aspects of the demonstration. A demonstration requires a teacher to plan the sequence very carefully. It may require repetition and active hands-on practice as well. The demonstration method may stand alone, but it is also used with both directive and inquiry methods. Students' under-

Demonstrations involve showing, doing, and telling about something.

standing of demonstrations can be measured not only through written tests but also through their ability to perform a particular activity if they have been given practice in it.

True or False While conducting a demonstration, teachers should tell their students why they have chosen to do it one way rather than another.

 CONNECTIONS

If You Are Going to Use the Demonstration Method

The following points may help make your demonstrations more valuable.

1. **Plan the demonstration sequences carefully.** If the demonstration is rather complicated, a step-by-step approach (first we do A, then B) may be required.

2. **Make certain that the demonstration is planned at a developmentally appropriate level.** Obviously, a demonstration and the student practice that follows must be safe. The speed of the demonstration, the size of the steps in which the demon-stration is performed, and the amount of practice required depend upon the developmental level of the students and the students' experience with the material.

3. **Prepare students for the demonstration.** The students should be told what they will see and why it is important and be introduced to the materials that will be used in the demonstration. Student attention should be directed toward the most important areas of the demonstration.

4. **Don't just show the students what you are doing, explain what you are doing as well.** Demonstrations are much more effective when explanations are given as the demonstration is taking place. Also, you may want to cover mistakes that are commonly made and tell students why you chose to do something one way and not another.

5. **The teacher may choose whether to have students state hypotheses and give conclusions or do so him or herself.** A teacher may want students to answer the questions, What happened? What does this show us? What conclusions can we make? The teacher may also decide to be more directive and state hypotheses and conclusions him or herself.

6. **Sometimes it is effective to allow students to see and describe mistakes.** After students know what they are seeing—and especially if it is a bit complicated—it may be useful to incorrectly demonstrate something and ask the students what you did wrong. (Of course, safety considerations are always paramount.) If a student is performing a demonstration, you may want to correct a mistake, but it should be done with sensitivity.

7. **Give students practice.** If students are supposed to be able to do the demonstrated activity, they need practice. In addition, if the material is complex or requires steps, both verbal and written prompts may be required. For instance, if something takes ten steps, you may want to demonstrate it and then allow for guided practice, talking students through the steps. You may then want to use fading (refer to Chapter 5), in which you give students fewer and fewer prompts as they become more familiar with the material.

PRACTICE

It isn't enough to teach something well. Students also require practice. Practice improves not only accuracy but also speed. When practice is given, both students and teachers become aware of what the students know and what they do not know. The most common methods used to give students practice are seatwork and homework. In addition, peer tutoring is sometimes used to improve student skills.

Seatwork

What is the one academic activity that students engage in most in elementary school? If you said **seatwork,** you're correct. Although the percentage of time devoted to seatwork differs among teachers, the figure is commonly given as 60 percent (Doyle & Carter, 1987). Even in junior high school, seatwork is plen-

seatwork Exercises that are designed for students to perform independently as a form of practice after they have learned the work.

tiful. The results of a study of time use in fifty-two mathematics and fifty English classes in eleven junior high schools in a large Southwestern city found that seatwork averaged about twenty minutes out of the thirty-nine and a half minutes of academic time for both mathematics and English (Sanford & Evertson, 1983). There can be no doubt that seatwork is an important activity.

Two different types of seatwork are found in classes. The first, and most common, is supervised study, in which students work independently on exercises while the teacher walks around helping individual students. The students are all engaged in seatwork but may not be engaged in the same exercises. The other possibility occurs when the teacher works with a small group while the other students are engaged in seatwork.

Is seatwork an effective method of giving practice? Although it can be, some research has questioned its effectiveness. Often students do not understand why they are doing it, and both good students and poor students tend to try to finish it as fast as possible. Accuracy does not seem to be very important. In addition, students are not as attentive during seatwork as during instruction (Rosenshine & Stevens, 1986). De-Voss (1979) described the rhythm of seatwork. Student attention to their seatwork waxes and wanes, and noise levels increase with time. Many socialize, walking around the room and sometimes taking their work with them to make their social journeys appear work related. Others daydream and doodle. When the noise becomes too great, the teacher intervenes and restores attention, and students begin working again. The cycle repeats itself. If the teacher will be collecting the work, a spurt of activity occurs at the end of the work period, and students rapidly finish the work, often because of a warning that there are only a few minutes left.

If this analysis of seatwork appears rather critical, it does not mean that seatwork is of no value. There is a great deal of interaction that goes on between students and teachers that allows teachers to give individual attention and to deal with student misunderstandings (Doyle & Carter, 1987). Seatwork can also be collected and feedback given, which encourages correction. If a particular mistake is found, the teacher can reteach the material. Seatwork also gives students a feeling of success if they can do it correctly.

Most of the difficulties involved in seatwork can be corrected, and in fact, it is not very difficult to do so.

Seatwork is most effective when students *can* do the work. It is not an exercise in self-teaching. Students who cannot do the work or who do not know what to do often act out or spend less time on a task. Seatwork is designed to be performed after the skill is taught. Therefore, to avoid problems, students should receive seatwork only when there is an excellent chance that they will get all the problems correct or, at the very least, 80 percent of them. Students should be taught a procedure for requesting help, perhaps involving nothing more than raising their hand. If more than one student does so, the teacher should give feedback by saying, "Sally, Pedro, Wallace." This is the order in which the teacher helps each student. If too many students are having difficulty, it shows a lack of understanding either of the seatwork assignment itself or of the material that was taught. Students who do not understand what they are supposed to do are often the source of noise in the classroom and lost time on a task. The best procedure here is to do a few of the problems with students so that they will know what they are supposed to do. Feedback is important because it gives students the information necessary to improve their performance.

True or False Seatwork is actually a type of self-teaching.

▷▷▷ CONNECTIONS

Effective Seatwork

Seatwork gives teachers an opportunity to give individualized attention, to diagnose problems, and to help students solidify their skills. However, these goals can be reached only if students are engaged on a task. The following suggestions may improve seatwork.

1. **Use guided practice and spend more time explaining the work.** This remedies the common problem of students not understanding the nature of the seatwork or not successfully being able to complete the work on their own. Seatwork is individual practice. If most students cannot do the work on their own, the teacher cannot give adequate individual attention to those students who may be having difficulty. Do some problems with the class so that the students will have a better idea of what is expected of them.

2. **Design the seatwork so that students can do at least 80 percent of it correctly.** Anything less than 80 percent correct indicates a need for teaching the material over or a need to evaluate the seatwork assignment.

3. **Make sure the seatwork follows directly from the instruction and guided practice.** The purpose of seatwork is to help students solidify their skills. Therefore, it should be directly related to the work in class.

4. **Actively monitor seatwork.** When everyone is doing seatwork, monitoring is not as difficult as when the teacher is working with a reading group while others are doing seatwork. Active monitoring keeps students on a task.

5. **Give students feedback and corrections.** Seatwork is more effective if students know it will be checked. Giving feedback allows students to correct their misconceptions.

6. **If necessary, break instruction into smaller units followed by seatwork.** If the material you are teaching is complex, break it up into smaller chunks, teach each chunk, and follow it with seatwork.

7. **Manage the seatwork by circulating among students, providing feedback, asking questions, and giving short explanations when necessary.** When students have contact with teachers, their engagement rate increases. Contacts can be relatively short, averaging half a minute or less.

8. **When instructing a small group and the rest of the class is working on seatwork, arrange the seats so that you can face both the small group and the students working independently.** This is one way to monitor students in a difficult situation.

9. **Establish a set routine to be used during seatwork activities.** For example, have students who have completed exercises turn them in and work on other assignments or do free reading. Students may check their exercises with other designated students. Students who need help are to approach the teacher between, not during, small-group activities.

10. **Try to make seatwork interesting.** Although seatwork is not self-teaching, the questions, problems, or paragraphs to be read can be interesting and require students to apply what they have learned.

True or False Seatwork should be assigned as long as students are certain to get half of the examples or problems correct.

Homework

How did you feel about homework when you were in elementary or secondary school? If you are like most students, you didn't want much. If your parents were like most parents, they wanted more, and they partially judged teachers by the amount of homework assigned. Homework is a commonly used activity for giving students practice. However, homework has other functions as well. Homework may be assigned to give students an opportunity to apply their learning to the real world, to individualize learning for both slower and more advanced students, and to enable students to complete work not finished in school. Homework also teaches independent study skills and work habits. It can communicate to parents the nature of the material being taught if a teacher requires that homework assignments be signed by parents (Salend & Schliff, 1988).

Homework fits into three categories: practice, preparation, and extension (LaConte & Doyle, 1986). Only the first type is designed for the express purpose of helping students solidify their learning of a particular skill. It is the most common type of homework. After the student has learned something about photosynthesis, he or she is required to answer questions on the topic. After learning about the exports of Brazil, the student is asked to study and memorize them. Although this is the most common type of homework, it can be boring, and many students simply go through

Homework can be used as practice, preparation for new information, or an extention of classroom learning.

the motions. Practice is much better if students are asked to apply their knowledge. For example, after students are taught about different kinds of plants, they may be asked to find photographs of plants in magazines and to identify some of them.

Homework is also used as preparation. For example, students may be asked to read the chapter on the War of 1812 and answer the first four questions. This type of homework is more commonly used in the upper grades. By having the students prepare for the lesson, the teacher hopes that the students will have a background in the material and will be able to comprehend the lesson better. For this to be effective, students must be given some idea of the elements of the assignment they are to focus on. For example, what should the students pay attention to when reading Chapter 7 in their social studies books? In addition, if students are asked to answer only some questions, why are the others being left out? In other words, if students are to profit from preparation, they must be able to focus on the relevant aspects and ignore some of the others. Other preparatory work might include an activity such as measuring a room and later using the measurements to find the room's area or perimeter.

The last type of homework is extension, which takes the individual beyond what was done in class. This is often used on long-term projects. For example, if the class is studying various countries, the students may be asked to choose a country and discuss a certain aspect of it, perhaps its economy. Students have some choice in extension types of activities. The activity may also be problem oriented, allowing the students to show their creativity in solving a problem.

Extension homework might not always be creative. When a student is asked to find out the names of all the past presidents, the assignment is rather technical and routine. This more routine type of extension often requires only that the student have available the resources necessary to answer the question, perhaps a dictionary, an encyclopedia, or an almanac. The more creative type of homework may require more planning and may take additional time to explain. If it is a long-term project, the assignment should be given not only orally but also in writing. The assignment sheet should describe the project in detail, including its due date, format, and purpose, as well as the teacher's willingness to help. Progress should be checked periodically. Some students may begin the assignment very late; others may just ignore it because they do not know how to begin or are too embarrassed to ask questions. Periodic check points are thus important.

Does Homework Help?

The amount of homework assigned by both elementary and secondary schoolteachers has increased greatly in recent years (Palardy, 1988). The question is, How effective is it in accomplishing its purposes, and do students who are assigned homework and do it show achievement gains? A number of studies show that homework has a positive effect on grades (U.S. Department of Education, 1987a: Keith, 1982). Of great interest is the compensatory effect that homework seems to have. When low-ability students do homework, their grades are as high as average students who do not do homework, and when average students do homework, they do as well as high-ability students who do not do it (U.S. Department of Education, 1987a). In an analysis of fifteen studies concerning homework, a moderately large positive effect was found for academic achievement, and the effect was greatest when homework was collected, feedback was given, and the homework was graded (Paschal et al., 1985). Although studies have generally found a positive link between homework and achievement (LaConte & Doyle, 1986), some studies have questioned the benefit of homework (Barber, 1986). However, most of the studies which raise doubts about the benefits of homework focus on homework designed to supply routine practice rather than homework assigned to prepare students for new lessons.

True or False The amount of homework assigned by teachers has increased in the past decade.

Research on homework shows some surprises. One study of 693 middle-school students in Kentucky found that only 11 percent of the students always write their assignments down and 64 percent always try to remember them without writing them down. Sixty-eight percent report that their parents do not look at their assignments. Students, however, do think that homework is valuable, as 65 percent said that homework assignments are always or usually helpful (Yarbro, 1988). It is obvious that students need to be taught to organize their assignments. There is little research showing that routine homework is effective or appropriate in the primary grades (LaConte & Doyle, 1986). Teachers show a recognition of this, as they do

not assign homework regularly until the fourth grade (England & Flatley, 1985). As students mature, the evidence for the effectiveness of homework increases. Research also shows that able students are more likely to do routine homework but profit from it less, whereas slow students are less likely to do it, but if they do it, they are more likely to profit from it (LaConte & Doyle, 1985).

Teachers sometimes have difficulty gauging how much time it will take students to do their homework (LaConte & Doyle, 1986). Teachers may face some diligent students who spent considerably more time doing the assignment than the teacher thought necessary. If a teacher continually has a parade of parents complaining about the amount of homework being assigned, it would be wise for him or her to reconsider the quantity of work assigned. Another difficulty is the failure of the teacher to communicate the assignment to the students. Students may not understand what they are supposed to do and therefore fail to complete their assignments. (Turner, 1987). Evaluation is very important. Students will be motivated to do their homework carefully if they know it will be looked at by the teacher. Homework that is collected and checked will have a greater impact on a student's achievement. The homework may be collected and checked by the teacher on a variable interval basis (refer to Chapter 5); at other times, it may be checked in class.

Although homework can be used as a component of a student's final grade, it can present a problem. Practice is, after all, just practice, and students who are afraid of making errors get someone else to do the work for them. This raises an interesting point. Parents are great supporters of homework. They expect teachers to give it (Palardy, 1988), and they are often willing to check and sign homework papers. It is a good idea for teachers to communicate their homework policy to both students and their parents. Some teachers send policy statements home at the beginning of the term. These statements inform both the student and the parents of how often homework will be assigned, the proper form for homework, how it will count in grading (if at all), and perhaps the amount of time each night students should devote to it. The teacher is responsible for telling parents when a child has not done his or her homework. Many parents become angered when they learn that their children have been penalized for not doing fifteen homework assignments when they were not informed that their child had failed to do even one assignment. As noted previously, though, students often do their homework in school. If parents are told to check the homework regardless of where it is done, the results will be better. However, not all parents have the ability or the interest to check homework. Teachers cannot always depend upon parents for help.

True or False Most parents want teachers to assign homework regularly.

One last consideration is the use of homework as punishment. Some teachers use homework as punishment. For example, if students misbehave they may have to write sentences containing specific vocabulary words. This is poor practice, and schoolwork should not be used as punishment.

▶▶▶ CONNECTIONS

Homework That Works

Sufficient research exists to show that homework can be valuable, although the results of research studies are not unanimous in this conclusion. Educators would like students to do their work carefully and to benefit from it. Research points to policies that can successfully achieve positive results.

1. **Introduce your homework policy to both students and parents—early in the term—as early as the first day.** Include why you give homework, how you expect it to look, and the consequences for doing or not doing it. Your policy should be explained in writing. Asking parents to sign a tear-off portion at the bottom of the sheet is an excellent practice (Canter, 1988). Also parents should be told to what extent the teacher would like them to be helping their children.

2. **Develop a systematic and regular schedule for giving homework.** If homework is given only once in a while, it can be difficult for a parent or a student to plan the time needed to do it. I know of some teachers who rarely give homework, but when they do, it takes students hours to finish. This is a poor practice.

3. **Give the assignment in a standard manner.** The homework should be given both orally and in writing, perhaps on the blackboard in a particular space at a particular time.

4. **Make certain the homework assignment is clear and that the students have the ability and**

resources to do it. If you are giving practice sheets for homework, make certain each sheet contains the directions. If you are assigning something that will require unusual materials, make certain students have access to them. In fact, if your subject regularly requires any particular resources, send a list of resources home at the beginning of the term, but be aware that the financial situation of many families is limited. Allow students to ask questions about the assignments. It is good policy to explain to students exactly how you want the homework done, the purpose of the assignment, the materials necessary for completion, and the due date (Salend & Schliff, 1988).

5. **Have a realistic idea about how much time the assignment will take.** Evidence demonstrates that many students require more time to complete their assignments than the teacher estimates. You can monitor this by asking students or their parents how much time the students spend on your assignments. Of course, the ability level and study skills of students will determine to some extent how much time the assignments will take to complete.

6. **Discuss with younger students what to do with their homework.** "I forgot it" is a common answer to the question, Why didn't you do your homework? Other answers can be amusing (many pets and younger siblings have voracious appetites for paper). Young students should be told to place their completed homework in a folder in their backpacks or with their schoolbooks. If a student is excused from doing homework because of a family emergency, some communication with the parents will be required.

7. **Check the work.** Homework is most effective in helping students if the students receive feedback about their work. It is possible to incorporate homework into a grading system, but teachers need to remember that in many cases, homework is practice and practice may mean errors. Some teachers give extra credit for not missing assignments while taking away points for missing too many.

8. **Practice assignments should obviously come from the work taught in class.** Such practice can reinforce skills and material taught and can offer students an opportunity to apply the new information.

9. **Preparation type of homework assignments should be focused for the student.** Just telling a

student to read a chapter is not sufficient. Students should be told what aspects to attend to. They need to be specifically informed if they are expected to master special terminology.

10. **Long-term assignments should be given in writing and discussed with the class.** More extensive assignments often are to be done over a period of time, and students may not be skilled at scheduling their time. Teachers should help students to schedule their work time and periodically check students' progress. If the assignment is a major paper, the teacher should ask for an outline.

11. **Discuss with students where they do their homework and how.** One must be careful when discussing where students should do their homework. It is commonly thought that students should do their homework on a desk and in a quiet place. However, new knowledge of learning styles has shown us that this is not necessarily true. Some children like to do their homework on their beds, others on the floor. Some like to do their homework with music in the background, others in quiet places. The teacher should encourage students to get to know under what circumstances they study and learn best when at home.

12. **Homework is not punishment.** Homework is not punishment and should not be given as punishment for misbehavior.

13. **Anticipate possible problems and solve them.** Sometimes a teacher can look at a homework assignment and anticipate where students might have difficulties. For example, when giving an assignment, the teacher might tell the students that they can review the types of clouds on page 57 of their textbook.

14. **Communicate with parents when students do an excellent job on their homework and when they do not.** Parents deserve to know when their children miss their assignments as well as when their children do well.

15. **Individualize homework when appropriate.** Although homework is often given on a group basis, there are times when homework can be individualized.

16. **Coordinate homework with other teachers.** Sometimes teachers of each subject in secondary school will give major assignments at the same time, making it difficult for students. When you are giving a major assignment, tell other teachers.

Peer Tutoring

One technique gaining popularity in the search for better methods of giving students practice is **peer tutoring.** In such tutoring, one student helps another to master some information or skill. There are a number of variations. Sometimes, the tutor is in the same class, while at other times the tutor is older. Such cross-age tutoring is especially popular today. Peer tutors are rarely, if ever, younger.

The student who tutors sometimes has greater knowledge than the student who is being tutored. Sometimes, however, the tutoring is so structured that any student can serve in the role of either the tutor or the tutee. For example, in one tutoring scheme, students were randomly chosen to be on one of two teams that competed for highest total points in social studies. The reward was a citation in the school weekly bulletin and bonus points on grades. Students were then randomly selected within teams to be either a tutor or a tutee. The tutoring included the tutors dictating study guide questions to the tutees, who then wrote the answer. The tutors said that the answer was either correct or incorrect and then provided the tutees with the correct answer. The tutees then had to write the correct response three times. The process lasted fifteen minutes, after which the tutoring pairs were reversed.

The research on the effectiveness of peer tutoring in quite impressive (Topping, 1987). Relatively simple tutoring procedures have been quite successful, and such tutoring has shown great promise when applied to both mildly handicapped and low-achieving students in both elementary and secondary school (Maheady et al., 1988; Pickens & McNaughton, 1988). The evidence for its effectiveness with disadvantaged students is especially noteworthy (Shapiro, 1988; Greenwood et al., 1987). The effects are found in academic achievement in general and in reading and mathematics in particular (Hedin, 1987). Evidence indicates that cross-age tutoring increases the confidence of younger tutees, who then feel more comfortable around older students in the school (Raschke

peer tutoring An active, structured learning situation in which one student helps another student master some aspect of schoolwork.

et al., 1988). Other benefits sometimes (but not always) found are increased motivation and task involvement. Benefits for the cross-age tutors are not always consistent, but they are more pronounced when the tutoring lasts for an extended time, the tutors are underachievers who are several years older, and the tutors are carefully trained and regularly supervised (Hartup, 1983).

True or False   *Peer tutoring is an effective way of providing practice for students.*

What tutoring arrangements work best? When cross-age tutoring is used, children prefer to teach younger children and to be taught by older children. In fact, achievement gains are somewhat better when the tutor is older, although same-age tutoring can also be effective. Children prefer same-sex tutors over opposite-sex tutors, although no evidence exists for differential effectiveness. Tutors don't like to participate in the evaluation of their tutees. Children's attitudes about tutoring and its success are related to tutor competence and motivation in both partners (Hartup, 1983).

The tutors themselves should not be rewarded according to how well their tutees do or be given money for their efforts. Garbarino (1975) compared tutors who were promised tickets to the theatre for their sixth-grade tutee's success with tutors who were not promised a reward. The tutors who were to be rewarded with tickets were far more critical and more demanding and, interestingly enough, did not use their time as efficiently as those in the no-reward group. In addition, in the no-reward group, the social interaction between the tutors and tutees was more positive, and learning was more rapid. This does not mean that tutors should not receive anything for tutoring, only that what they receive should not be based upon the progress of the tutees. About eight percent of the public schools offer school credit for community service, and students who volunteer to tutor younger students could receive school credit (Hedin, 1987).

True or False   *One of the most effective methods of peer tutoring is apportioning rewards to the tutor on the basis of how well the tutee performs on an examination.*

A tutoring program can be formed as an after-school program, but it is probably better to schedule tutoring during class time to be certain that those who need it will receive it. This is somewhat easier to do with same-age, same-class tutors than with cross-age tutors who may come from another school.

CONNECTIONS

Beginning a Tutoring Program

The success of any tutoring program depends upon five principal factors: class preparation, selection of tutors, preparation of tutors, monitoring by the teacher, and assessment (Casanova, 1988).

1. **Explain the nature of peer tutoring to the class to prepare the students for the experience.** The emphasis should be placed on the cognitive rather than social nature of these interactions and on what the students playing either of these roles are expected to do.

2. **Select tutors with care.** Here, there is a difference between programs that use tutors and tutees of the same age and programs that use tutors and tutees of different ages, called cross-age tutoring. In cross-age tutoring, tutors might be selected according to interest and skills in working with younger children. An older student who does not have very good grades should not be eliminated from consideration, however, since some of these students can make very good tutors. In-class tutors are somewhat different. If the tutoring is very structured—that is, if students are told exactly what to do and how to do it—there is no reason that roles cannot be reversed. If the type of peer interaction is less structured and some extra knowledge is required, reversing the roles of tutor and tutee may not be possible. Tutors, though, should be compatible, and two students who do not really like each other should not be placed together. Doing so will not lead to improvements in their interpersonal relationships.

3. **Prepare the tutors.** For tutors to be effective, they need to be trained. The degree of training depends upon the age of the tutors and the degree of structure in the tutoring assignment as well as on the type of work assigned. For example, if a student is to listen to another student read a sentence, wait for the end of the sentence, and then stop and correct any words incorrectly read, relatively little training is necessary, at least in cognitive instructional skills. However, if problem-solving skills such as those in mathematics are being tutored, some additional training is necessary to be certain that the tutor knows how to break the problem-solving process into manageable bites. One of

the most effective techniques for preparation is modeling, that is, teaching a skill publicly to one student while other students watch and discuss what is going on. Attention to the noncognitive aspects of tutoring, especially how to handle errors and give praise, is necessary.

4. **Monitor the tutoring process.** During the tutoring sessions, the teacher should walk around and listen to what is going on. In some schemes, the teacher awards extra points for good tutoring (Greenwood et al., 1987). This monitoring requires some sensitivity, since the teacher does not want to be seen as looking over the tutors' shoulders.

5. **Assess both the tutors' and tutees' achievements.** Frequent assessment in peer tutoring is important. Both tutors and tutees (in same-age tutoring) should be given short quizzes on the lesson content, and progress can be visibly demonstrated through graphs.

Peer tutoring is a useful method of providing practice for students. Students are often receptive to the idea, and such tutoring provides both variety for the student and flexibility for the teacher.

GROUPING

Thus far we've considered teaching decisions in the areas of objectives and modes of presentation. Another area of decision making for the teacher is whether to present the material in a whole-class framework, in a small-group framework, or on an individualized basis. Sometimes time constraints, inadequate resources, or the nature of the material to be taught forces a particular grouping. It is probably easier and more efficient to give instruction to the entire class about how to behave on the school lunch line. As noted earlier, direct instruction in a whole-class setting is an effective type of teaching when conveying a logical set of facts or concepts that every student must know (Ornstein & Levine, 1981).

The teacher faces a number of difficulties when teaching the whole group. Although the teacher can survey the class and monitor students, the problem of individual needs and participation is difficult to handle in a whole-class situation. Pacing is another problem. It is difficult to completely meet the needs both of students who are slower and of those who learn more quickly. After all, if you go too slowly, you

Teachers often use small-group instruction when their students read at substantially different levels.

lose the quicker students; if you go too fast, you leave your slower students behind. Although special assignments, good questioning, and the judicious use of seatwork can help, it remains difficult to give the individual attention necessary and to take individual needs into consideration. Also, in a whole-class situation, it is sometimes difficult to keep track of who participated and who did not. Some students feel inhibited about talking out and answering questions in front of an entire class. Partially to remedy these problems, teachers sometimes use small groups.

Consider an elementary schoolteacher with students in her class who span many reading levels. Some are more advanced than others. Teaching from the same reader at the same speed would not be appropriate. The students' skill levels are different, and their needs are varied. Such differences occur in other areas besides reading. Sometimes a teacher may find that some of her students have a better background in a particular subject than others and may need to group her students to adequately serve them. In addition, some inquiry techniques and some cooperative learning experiences (refer to Chapter 8) may require small-group instruction, which allows the teacher to give more individual instruction. For instance, we know that especially in the primary grades, the best format is one-to-one instruction. It offers the most individualized practice and feedback (Brophy, 1982). The problem is that it is very difficult, if not impossible, to give the necessary one-to-one attention during whole-class instruction. However, more individual attention is possible in small groups.

Small-group work is often challenging. The preparation is more difficult because different groups may be working at different levels. In addition, students may require training in how to solve problems or to work cooperatively. Because some groups may complete their assignments before others, students must be well trained on what to do after they have completed their work (Houston et al., 1988). Small-group instruction is a management challenge as well. The teacher must spend time with each group and monitor the progress and conduct of the other groups when not working directly with them, keeping students on the task. Despite all these concerns, small-group instruction is desirable and makes up part of the day for most elementary schoolteachers.

Few, if any, studies have compared instruction in small groups with whole-class instruction. Therefore, any generalization about the effectiveness of either one over the other is very difficult (Brophy & Good, 1986). In addition, teachers use the two types of instruction for different purpose, and we may, then, not be able to directly compare them.

True or False Small-group instruction is usually superior to whole-class instruction.

Clements and Evertson (1982) compared teachers who were better managers of small groups with those who were poor managers and found that the better managers excelled in three areas. First, better managers set the stage by making sure the students knew what they were supposed to be doing in the small groups. They consistently monitored the class, did not start group work until all movement in the class had stopped, and made special rules concerning conduct and work in small groups. Such rules involved instruction on how to gain the teacher's attention and when the students were allowed to leave their seats.

Second, better managers maintained the pace of instruction while keeping an eye on the class. Before leaving a group, the teachers gave members a seat-work assignment to be completed when the group broke up. Finally, better managers were skilled in responding to inappropriate behavior.

THE EFFECTIVE TEACHER

This chapter has looked at some ways that various methods of teaching can be used effectively to meet educational goals in the cognitive, affective, and psychomotor domains. In one sense, this entire text has been devoted to effective teaching. As you glance through the table of contents, you will note that each chapter investigates some important aspect of teaching and that specific teacher behaviors that influence student learning are emphasized.

What is it about the teacher that makes him or her more effective? An expert in the field, Madeline Hunter, notes that "studies are showing that it is not what a teacher is, or how a teacher feels, but what a teacher does that has the potential for affecting students' achievement" (1979, p. 62). But what are these behaviors? Studies of specific behaviors that differentiate more effective from less effective teachers are plentiful. Gary Borich (1988) argues that effective teaching can be viewed in terms of five types of behavior: teacher clarity, variety, task orientation, engagement in learning, and introducing a high success rate into the classroom (Table 11.7). Other researchers have sought to describe teacher behaviors that are most effective in specific settings. A respected authority in the field, Jere Brophy, listed the following eight teacher behaviors that have been found effective for teaching inner-city children (1982).

1. Effective teachers believe that students are capable of learning, show a willingness to try different methods, and treat failure as a challenge.
2. Effective teachers allocate most of the available class time to instruction.
3. Effective teachers demonstrate superior classroom management and organization (refer to Chapter 10).
4. Effective teachers proceed rapidly but in small steps and generate a very high rate of success.
5. Effective teachers use an active teaching method

Table 11.7 Characteristics of Effective Teaching

There are many ways of listing characteristics of effective teaching. Gary Borich classifies these characteristics under five categories.

Clarity

To be clear in the classroom, the effective teacher

- informs the learners of the objective
- provides learners with advance organizers
- checks for task-relevant prior learning and reteaches, if necessary
- gives directives slowly and distinctly
- knows the ability level of learners and teaches to those levels
- uses examples, illustrations, and demonstrations to explain and clarify text and workbook content
- provides a review or summary at the end of each lesson

Variety

To have variety in the classroom, the effective teacher

- uses attention-gaining devices
- shows enthusiasm
- varies mode of presentation
- mixes rewards and reinforcers
- varies types of questions and probes
- uses student ideas

Task Orientation

To be task oriented in the classroom, the effective teacher

- develops unit and lesson plans that reflect the curriculum
- handles administrative and clerical interruptions efficiently
- stops or prevents misbehavior with a minimum of class disruption
- selects the most appropriate instructional model for the objectives being taught
- establishes cycles of review, feedback, and testing

Engagement in Learning

To engage students in the learning process, the effective teacher

- elicits the desired behavior
- provides opportunities for feedback in a nonevaluative atmosphere
- uses group and individual activities as motivational aids when necessary
- uses meaningful verbal praise
- monitors seatwork and checks for practice

Introduction of Success into the Class

To establish moderate-to-high rates of success in the classroom, the effective teacher

- establishes unit and lesson content that reflects prior learning
- corrects partially correct, correct but hesitant, and incorrect answers
- divides instructional stimuli into bite-sized pieces at the learners' current level of functioning
- changes instructional stimuli gradually
- varies the instructional pace or tempo to create momentum

Adapted from *Effective Teaching Methods* by Gary D. Borich. Copyright © 1988 Merrill Publishing Company, Columbus, Ohio. Reprinted by permission of Merrill Publishing Company.

involving direct instruction, using both large and small groups.

6. Effective teachers provide many opportunities for practice and application, monitor student progress, provide feedback and remedial instruction, and make certain that basic skills have been mastered.
7. Effective teachers understand the different needs of students at different grade levels.
8. Effective teachers provide a supportive learning environment.

There are some problems with any listing approach, however. The relationships between listed behaviors and student achievement are positive but relatively low. However, the most serious problem is the natural tendency to add up all these behaviors to create the effective teacher. It simply does not work that way. These behaviors must be integrated by the teacher with the instructor's style and ability to develop a relationship with students, and other not-so-easy-to-describe variables enter into the equation.

MAKING DECISIONS

One of the teacher's most important roles is that of instructional expert. Teachers are trained instructional experts, knowing what to present and how to present it. It is difficult to talk about the methods used to present material unless one also stipulates the goals of instruction. Teachers choose their instructional methods to match educational and instructional goals as well as to offer variety in the classroom experience. In addition, in this chapter, the methods were described in relatively pure form. In practice, teachers adapt these methods to meet their own needs and abilities as well as those of their students.

The goal of the research on instructional objectives, instructional methods, and effective teaching is not to standardize teaching so it becomes automatic and repetitive. What the research yields is some valuable suggestions that may help both new and experienced teachers become more organized and more effective. The creativity of a teacher, the need to adapt methods to the instructor's particular style, and student needs remain vital to a teacher's success. However, when a teacher adopts one goal over another or one method of teaching over another or one grouping method over another, the teacher has made a choice. That choice should be an informed one made after considering a number of other ways that the lesson could be presented. The choice reflects the particular and definitive skills of the teacher in the role of instructional expert.

SUMMARY

1. Educational goals are broad statements of purposes. Instructional objectives are descriptions of what students are expected to be able to do following instruction. These objectives provide direction for instruction, provide guidelines for testing, and allow teachers to tell others what they are trying to accomplish. General instructional objectives state the general learning outcomes expected after a unit has been taught. Behavioral objectives contain the condition under which the behavior will occur, the expected behavior that is described in measurable terms, and the criterion for success. Not all objectives can be easily measured.

2. There are three domains of interest in education. The cognitive, or intellectual, domain; the affective domain, which consists of attitudes and values; and the psychomotor domain, which involves body movement. A taxonomy—a list of objectives ranging from least to most complex and from least to most difficult for each of these domains—has been formulated. The most widely used is the taxonomy of educational objectives in the cognitive domain written by Benjamin Bloom and colleagues.

3. Robert Gagné argued that there are five varieties of learning: verbal information, intellectual skills, motor skills, attitudes, and cognitive strategies. He has arranged intellectual skills into a learning hierarchy, with problem solving (higher rule learning) occupying the highest level in the hierarchy.

4. Many studies, but not all, have found that the use of objectives improve learning. To be effective, the objectives must be communicated to the student, be appropriate for the developmental level of the student, and be used as the basis of instruction and evaluation.

5. In mastery learning, each student is expected to master a particular skill to a relatively high degree of proficiency. This system requires constant feedback, corrective instruction, and enrichment for those who master the skill more quickly than others. Mastery learning requires highly defined objectives and criteria. Critics of mastery learning claim that the method penalizes very bright students, because enrichment after a student finishes the unit successfully is not easy; requires too much paperwork; is too structured; and requires individual corrective work, which may be difficult to implement.

6. Direct instruction is particularly effective when the teacher wants to convey a body of knowledge to students. The basic components of direct instruction are setting clear goals and communicating them to students, presenting a sequence of well-organized assignments, giving students clear and concise explanations and illustrations of the subject matter, asking frequent questions to ascertain student understanding, and giving students frequent practice in what they have learned.

7. Indirect methods of teaching, sometimes called discovery or inquiry methods, require students to be active in formulating questions and problems, gathering data, and answering the questions. The

teacher acts as a guide, helping students clarify the problem and seek out ways of solving it. Inquiry methods emphasize the importance of process and student experience during learning. Inquiry learning takes more time than direct instruction.

8. Jerome Bruner argues that students must learn the basic principles and problem-solving techniques in the area in which they are studying. He argues that discovery learning can be conducted in an inductive manner in which students extract a principle or a concept from many different examples. Bruner also encourages teachers to value intuitive reasoning.

9. David Ausubel argues that distinctions must be made between reception learning and discovery learning. Reception learning involves presenting the material to students in its final form, while in discovery learning the content must be discovered by the student. Another distinction must be made between meaningful and rote learning. To be meaningful, the new material must be related in a nonarbitrary way to knowledge the student already has. Ausubel recommends a type of teaching called expository learning.

10. A concept is a set of specific objects, symbols, or events that share common characteristics and can be referred to by a particular name or symbol. Concepts can be formed by extracting the similarities from a number of instances or through the formation of a prototype—an example that best typifies the category. Concepts can be taught either directly, by giving students a definition and then following it with examples and nonexamples of the concept, or through indirect means in which students are given hands-on experiences that allow them to discover, by themselves or with the guidance of the teacher, the attributes that define the concept.

11. The demonstration mode can be used by itself or as an adjunct to other types of instruction. It is important to plan demonstrations carefully, directing student attention, giving students practice when appropriate, and telling students why you performed one behavior rather than another.

12. Elementary school students spend more time doing seatwork than any other activity. Seatwork is most effective if the students can successfully do the problems, understand what they are to do and why, and receive feedback on the seatwork.

13. Homework may be used as practice, as preparation for future work, or as an extension of the work of the classroom to real-world situations outside the classroom. Homework is most effective if the teacher informs the students of its purpose and how it is to be done, if it flows directly from the work, if it is checked, and if students receive feedback.

14. Peer tutoring takes many forms. It can involve two students in the same class or older students tutoring younger students. Some tutoring techniques are so structured that either student may be the tutor or the tutee. The evidence for the effectiveness of peer tutoring is very impressive. Tutors need preparation, both in the process of tutoring and in how to correct mistakes.

15. Teachers must often make the decision of whether to teach material to an entire class, to a small group, or on an individual basis. Teaching to the whole class is best when the same material is required of each student and if the students have the necessary skills to master the material. Small-group work is best when students' skill levels are so varied that different material must be taught to several groups of students. Many inquiry techniques and cooperative learning techniques also require small groups, and during small-group work, it is possible to give more individual attention to students who may require it.

16. Much research has sought to differentiate between more and less effective teaching techniques. These studies have emphasized the importance of particular teacher behaviors to student achievement.

ACTIVITIES AND EXERCISES

1. **Formulating Instructional Objectives.** The text mentions both general instructional objectives and behavioral objectives. Choose two units in your area of instruction and write both general instructional objectives and behavioral objectives for each unit. If you have difficulty writing the behavioral objectives, refer to Table 11.1 for help.

2. **Using the Taxonomies.** Three taxonomies are discussed in the text, covering cognitive, affective, and psychomotor skills. Choose a unit that you may be going to teach and write instructional objectives that involve various levels of the cognitive

and affective domains. If your specialty will involve the psychomotor domain, include objectives from this domain as well.

3. **Direct Instruction.** Direct instruction is a type of instruction very useful when imparting a definite set of facts or skills to students. Using the guidelines discussed in the text, ask a teacher if you can tutor a few students who were absent and have missed some work. Using a direct instructional approach, teach these students the required material.

4. **Planning Inquiry or Discovery Lessons.** Most of us have been extensively taught through direct methods, and it is not easy to design and execute indirect strategies. In addition, students are not used to having to clarify problems or seek out their own answers. Identify two lessons in your specialty that you believe could be best taught through the inquiry method and write a plan for each of them.

5. **Experiential Learning.** Students often remember and value experiential learning. In the text, adopting an egg, helping others, and a few other ideas were noted. Jot down a few experiential learning experiences that you remember from your elementary and secondary school days. Ask others about their experiences with such learning activities and jot them down as well.

6. **Design an Experience.** Designing a lesson so that it will give students some experience of value is not easy. However, as noted in the text, students often appreciate and enjoy such a lesson. Plan out a lesson or a project that would involve active experience.

7. **A Field Trip.** Students love field trips. Although just going to the zoo may have some value, it is educationally more significant if students must focus on some aspect of their experience. One simple way is to have students formulate questions to answer during their trip, another is simply to give students questions to answer, and still a third would have students write their thoughts on something that is connected with the trip. Choose a field trip that is appropriate for your level of teaching and specialty and note ways it can be made more educationally valuable.

8. **Plan a Demonstration.** Most teachers will use demonstrations at some time or another in their classroom presentation. Choose a demonstration that you would be likely to present to your students and carefully list the steps you would take to make it more effective. If you can, try it out on a colleague.

9. **Considering Seatwork.** Seatwork takes up a major proportion of the time students spend actively engaged in academic work. Different teachers have their own ways of handling seatwork. Interview teachers on their seatwork procedures, with an eye to gaining helpful hints about managing seatwork that you may be able to use. If you can, observe some teachers using seatwork.

10. **Homework Policy.** Many teachers require students to take home a formal explanation of a teacher's homework policies, procedures, and rules and have the parents sign it. Ask some teachers if they do this and, if they do, ask them for a copy of their rules. Then write your own note to parents.

11. **Different Types of Homework.** Homework may be used for practice, for preparation, and as extension. The first two are relatively easy and common. However, extension is not. Write five extension-type homework assignments in your area of specialization.

12. **Train a Peer Tutor.** One of the most interesting and effective methods of giving students practice is through peer tutoring. Choose two students and teach each how to tutor the other. This should be done in a very structured situation (spelling words, mathematics facts, social studies facts, etc.). Your instruction should also involve teaching the students how to correct and praise each other. The students should be able to reverse roles when appropriate. One hint is to demonstrate the behaviors you want.

13. **Observe Small-Group Instruction.** Small-group instruction is a common practice, especially in elementary school. Observe a teacher using small-group instruction, perhaps in reading. Specifically look at how the teacher manages the groups and what rules are being used. In addition, ask the teacher to show you plans for the different groups.

14. **Rules for Small-Group Instruction.** Students must be taught rules and skills for small-group instruction. List the rules and skills that you think students need to learn and develop a list that could be given to students.

Here are ten scenarios. Try to apply the information you have learned in the chapter to each situation.

1. Mr. Tabler is a great believer in homework. He argues that students cannot possibly do everything in class, that practice is necessary, and that preparation is required. Students in his sixth-grade class, he believes, should spend forty minutes or so every day doing their homework. Each day he assigns what he believes is a reasonable amount of homework. He collects the homework in a different subject each day and reviews all the homework in class. His students complain, claiming that he gives more homework than any other teacher, that they should not receive homework on weekends, and that they spend two hours or more doing homework, which they do not believe is fair. After all, they want to play, too. Mr. Tabler is in a bind of sorts. Every so often a parent will send a letter saying that a student could not do all his homework, but he has received no other feedback. He is afraid that if he reduces the amount of homework, student academic achievement will suffer and he will be reinforcing student complaining. On the other hand, students are complaining about their work more and more. What would you suggest Mr. Tabler do both about the amount of homework he assigns and the class's constant complaints?

2. Mrs. Cohen teaches a third-grade class. She does not believe in giving much homework and gives it only sparingly. Her school has a night during which parents are invited to come to school to meet the teachers. After a few minutes of introduction and a discussion of her instructional objectives and procedures, a parent asks about homework. When Mrs. Cohen tells the parents she does not believe in regular homework assignments for third-graders, the parents are concerned. Many state their belief that such assignments help their children and a few note that this is really the only direct way they know what students are learning in class. Despite the parents' doubts, Mrs. Cohen still does not want to assign much, if any, homework. What can she do to allay parents' fears and answer parents' objections to her policy?

3. Ever since Mr. Ash attended a seminar on direct instruction he has become aware of the difference between direct instruction and regular, conventional lecture strategies. Although he does not view direct instruction as appropriate in every area, he believes it would be superior to a straight lecture in many instances. He has tried to use the direct instructional framework, but unfortunately, he seems to revert back to a strict lecture format, which he knows to be less effective. He asks you, his colleague, for help in this regard. What suggestions could you give Mr. Ash concerning how to avoid regressing to a lecture format?

4. Ms. Bass gives a moderate amount of homework and has never had any difficulty with student or parent complaints. The problem she has with her seventh-grade class is students not doing their assignments. She does not have the time to collect the assignments each night and mark them. In addition, when she goes around the room checking to see if students have done them, she is concerned that they are just writing down anything so that they will not get a zero for not doing their homework. She really has two problems, then. First, some students (five to be exact) simply are not doing their homework on a regular basis. The other problem is that she believes that very few students are doing their mathematics homework with much care. She has a policy that if you miss three homework assignments you fail, and a number of students have already gone over that line. This is especially a problem with one of her students who is actually doing well on tests. Ms. Bass feels she must fail the student anyway, because her rules were given at the beginning of the term. Evaluate Ms. Bass's problems and suggest ways she could improve her students' accuracy in doing their homework. Do you think Ms. Bass should fail the student who is doing well on the tests but failed to do three homework assignments? Why or why not? Would you make any changes in Ms. Bass's homework policies?

5. Mr. Wong has always found seatwork difficult. He uses it as a sort of practice but finds that he is having a great deal of difficulty keeping order and encouraging the students to stay on the task. At the beginning of the term, he told the students that when they are assigned seatwork they are to do it quietly, if they have any difficult they are

to raise their hand and wait, after they have finished they are to do something such as read, and they are not to get out of their seats without permission. He finds that there is a great deal of noise, especially when he is working with a small group of students while the others are doing some seatwork assignments. At times, students seem to daydream, and some even do their homework during these practice sessions. The students do not seem to do the seatwork until Mr. Wong warns them that they have only a few minutes left, after which they just put anything down on the paper. Mr. Wong is continually interrupted by students with seatwork problems while dealing with other groups and is unnerved by the extra noise and activity and what he sees as a lack of attention to the practice. If you were Mr. Wong, what would you do to correct the situation?

6. Miss Largo would like to begin a peer tutoring group in her class. Most of her students are about six months to a year behind in English and are not doing very well. They rarely raise their hands to answer questions, and although they do their seatwork and homework, their work is of relatively poor quality. Many of her students simply do not practice the skills they learn in school, making mastery very difficult. Her students' parents are interested, but generally cannot offer much help. The areas Miss Largo would like her students to practice most are spelling, vocabulary words, and social studies and mathematics facts. Miss Largo believes that a peer tutoring program might give students the individual practice they require in a different format. She has introduced the idea to the class, telling them that she will form teams through a lottery system and within each team, students will be chosen to be tutors and tutees, and the roles will then be reversed. The reward for the winning team will be additional points on their grades and special mention in the school newspaper and PTA newsletter. Both teams can win if they score above an 85 percent on the test. She models to her students the way they should ask the questions, the amount of time to wait for answers, and how to check the papers. Students were excited, and Miss Largo is hopeful that the program will work. She feels, however, that she may have forgotten something. If she were to ask you for suggestions,

what changes or additions would you make in her procedures?

7. Your principal has just sent around a memo stating that she expects all teachers to have instructional goals that can be presented to students and parents. Although slavish devotion to these goals is not expected or desired, the principal has left no doubt that she expects teachers to show some tangible progress in terms of satisfying the goals. This directive has met with some resistance from the staff, who complain that these objectives are generally not useful and are difficult to write. The principal replied that they can be valuable if they are communicated to students and used as a basis for evaluation. She asks for your opinion concerning whether instructional objectives lead to better student achievement. How would you answer the principal's question?

8. You are a high school social studies teacher. Your normal goals are arranged along the cognitive dimension and do, indeed, run into the higher level objectives involving analysis, synthesis, and evaluation. Lately there has been an emphasis in your district on constitutional rights, prejudice, discrimination, and citizenship, and you find that although you have no difficulty listing cognitive goals, you are having some difficulty with the affective goals. For instance, you would like students to feel pride in their citizenship and in their school, to empathize with the victims of prejudice, and to appreciate the importance of keeping individual rights. You can also list a number of other affective objectives. Your problem is evaluating these objectives. You find it rather easy to evaluate cognitive areas of learning, even the more advanced ones. However, you feel that you must find some way to accurately evaluate these more affective areas. The other difficulty is how to use such an evaluation. Even if you evaluate the affective component, can you and should you use it as a basis of a grade? If you do, aren't you just asking students to agree with you? How would you evaluate the affective component of your work, and would you use it as any part of the grading system? Why or why not? If you would, how would you go about it?

9. Your sixth-grade class consists of twenty-five students whose reading and mathematics scores range from two years ahead to one and a quarter

years behind in grade equivalent scores. The students' percentile ratings range from the 95th percentile in reading and mathematics to a low of the 30th percentile in these subjects. In other words, the range of abilities in your class is extreme. There are some children achieving in the average range (twelve to be exact), but six are quite a bit above average while seven score below the mean in the two subjects. When you use a direct instructional approach, you find that it sometimes works, but at other times, the lower ability students do not seem ready for the work. Your pacing is also a problem, as the higher level students do not seem to work up to their potential and are sometimes bored. Very simply, you must find a way to work with the slower students, to keep the average students on track, and to challenge the students of higher ability. What procedures would you use in teaching such a diverse group of students?

10. Mrs. Simonetti is an eighth-grade science teacher who has decided that some long-term project would be desirable for her class. After all, such a long-term project will teach students responsibil-

ity, teach them certain research and writing skills, and enable them to choose and delve more deeply into specific areas of interest. Mrs. Simonetti first puts together a list of thirty or so projects and reports that students can do but also tells students that they may also think about a different project or report as long as she approves it. Some of the projects are experiments or experiential, such as interviewing scientists. Others involve reports that require more than an encyclopedia, such as looking for trends in technology. She has different directions for each type of assignment and has allowed some students to work in small groups if the project is large enough. She has given each student a due date and material about form and has answered some student questions. The material is due in a month.

A month later, when Mrs. Simonetti looks at the projects, some are excellent, others look like the students' parents have done them, some student projects are poor, while a few students have not done the work. How could Mrs. Simonetti have improved her procedures?

Are These Statements True or False?

Turn the next page for the correct answers. Each statement is repeated following the paragraph in which the information can be found.

1. Instructional television has been a remarkable failure in the schools, with very few classes using it on a regular basis.
2. Computers are not used extensively as instructional aids in regular academic classes.
3. Computer literacy courses today place more emphasis on computer applications than on how a computer works.
4. There is less emphasis on teaching programming skills to students today than existed a decade ago.
5. The most popular instructional use of computers by classroom teachers is to provide drill and practice for students.
6. Programs of drill and practice should not be used unless the student has already been taught the material.
7. Computer simulations and computer-generated problem-solving programs should not be used by the classroom teacher because they are very complicated and should be run only by experts in the field of computer-generated graphics.
8. When computers are used in regular academic classes such as mathematics, social studies, or science, students' attitudes toward the subject itself become more positive.
9. Live television programs allow for more classroom interaction than programs that are shown on videotape.
10. Students should not be informed of the educational value of an instructional television program, because this will interfere with students' enjoyment of the program.
11. Students should not be encouraged to take extensive notes while they watch an educational film.
12. The overhead projector should not be used by most teachers, because the equipment is difficult to operate and the medium lacks flexibility.

The Use of Technology in Education

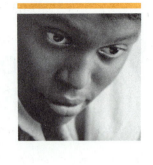

Answers to True-False Statements

1. *False* Correct statement: Instructional television may not have revolutionized education, but it is extensively used in the classroom and cannot be labeled a failure.

2. *True*

3. *True*

4. *True*

5. *True*

6. *True*

7. *False* Correct statement: Many of these programs are user friendly, and they are meant to be used by both regular classroom teachers and students.

8. *False* Correct statement: Although there are many advantages to using computers in regular academic classes, computer use does not lead students to develop a more positive attitude toward the subject itself.

9. *False* Correct statement: Just the opposite is true. Videotapes allow more classroom interaction than live television shows do, because videotapes can easily be stopped at appropriate times and teachers can ask and answer questions.

10. *False* Correct statement: Students should be told why the program is of value.

11. *True*

12. *False* Correct statement: The overhead projector is both easy to use and very versatile.

Fifteen new computers just arrived at the school. There is some excitement as one teacher comments, "Thank goodness, they're finally here. I can't wait to use them." Another teacher shakes his head and remarks, "I think they're a fad, just as educational television was. It was going to save the classroom teacher. Now it's gone. Computers will go the same way."

A teacher sets up a projector and is ready to show a film that fits perfectly into his unit on weather. He has previewed the film and prepared the class for the movie. The teacher is unnerved when his students ask, "Are we responsible for the material the film covers?" When he answers in the affirmative, the class groans.

THE USE OF TECHNOLOGY IN EDUCATION

The first scenario is occurring all over the United States, and the views expressed show both extremes of teacher attitudes toward computers. The use of technology in education is not new. Films have been around for generations, and instructional television since the 1960s. Each time a new technology is introduced, some authorities claim that it will revolutionize education, others say that it will have no effect, and still others believe that it is fraught with danger.

In the past, technology has not revolutionized education, nor has it adversely affected education. The overhead projector, slide, filmstrip, and movie projector, videocassette recorder (VCR), record player, radio, and tape recorder have become commonplace in most classrooms and are accepted as ways to help improve classroom learning (AECT, 1977). Other types of technology, including the programmed "teaching machines" and instructional television of the 1960s, were touted by some of their proponents as being capable of serving as the primary source of instruction in some areas. This has not generally occurred, although they too are seen as useful instructional and learning aids. Today, computer technology is the focus of attention, and teachers are grappling with some very interesting questions about the best way to use computers. Will the computer become another instructional and learning aid, or will its flexibility and distinctive capabilities permit it to become more than that?

Teachers now entering the profession usually have access to a number of technological aids, and many practical questions surround these aids. How can a teacher use a computer to help teach science in high school? How should a film be used in English? Other more basic questions are also being raised, including, Why should a teacher use these technological innovations? and Under what circumstances should they be used? In this chapter, we will try to answer both these fundamental questions as well as many of the practical questions classroom teachers have about the use of technology in education.

Some Necessary Limitations

The use of technology in education is a large and varied area. It would be impossible to review every available technology or every subtype of a particular technology. For example, we could look at commercial television, closed-circuit television, and cable and satellite television. However, all share some similarities, and we will explore their use under the main heading of instructional television.

We will also limit our focus to the use of technology in instruction. This does not deny the usefulness of technology as a management tool. For example, the computerization of some management functions, such as programs to keep track of students' grades, the use of data bases for compiling lists of students, and marking multiple-choice tests by computer, may well reduce the time it takes to do paperwork, thus allowing for more interaction with students. Thus, the computerization of some management functions may contribute to educational productivity (Trollip & Alessi, 1988). However, in this chapter, we will focus on the possibilities of using the computer for instructional purposes.

Judging Success and Failure

Before looking at different types of technological aids, two additional considerations need to be raised. Both our optimist and our cynic in the opening vignette can make some strong arguments. The optimist can't wait to adapt a new vehicle to her teaching; the cynic believes the new technology will go the way of other fads and specifically mentions instructional television. How do we judge whether or not a technology has been successful?

Let's look at instructional television (ITV) to demonstrate the problems that exist when judging the success or failure of a technology. ITV was introduced with much fanfare in the 1960s, and some touted it as a revolutionary technology. Today, we do not see it as that. Does that mean it has failed?

No, according to one expert in the field, Saul Rockman (1985), who notes that one third of the students in school today use instructional television on a fairly regular basis as part of the educational process. Is this, then, a success or a failure? Those who believed that it would revolutionize education or change the relationship between the classroom teachers and their students have not been proven correct. On the other hand, ITV's use by one third of the students makes it difficult to label it a failure. If a technology becomes just a part of the instructional process, can we consider it successful, or does it have to measurably increase efficiency in learning or perhaps reduce the cost of educating students? If it becomes what Rockman calls a "weapon in the educational arsenal," is that sufficient? These are questions that are difficult to answer and depend mostly on one's point of view.

True or False Instructional television has been a remarkable failure in the schools, with very few classes using it on a regular basis.

Let's begin our investigation of the use of technology in education by considering the most controversial modern technology—the computer. We will then consider the use of instructional television and a number of audio-visual aids and glance at some of the technology currently being introduced into the schools. As we do this, consider how you as a classroom teacher may profitably use these technological aids to improve both your teaching and your students' learning.

COMPUTERS IN THE CLASSROOM

The number of computers in schoolrooms is staggering. There were one million computers in use in the schools in 1985, two million in 1986, and four million in 1987 (Callison, 1988). The increasing numbers of computers can also be seen in the ratio of the number of students to computers available. In 1983–1984, each computer had to serve about 125 students, while in the following year the figure stood at 75. During the 1985–1986 year, there was one microcomputer for every fifty students (Houston et al., 1988). However, access and usage are extremely uneven. Alfred Bork (1988) notes that there are still schools that have no computers and some with only one or two machines. The estimated average at the present time is only 20

There has been a substantial increase in the number of computers in the schools. The major question is, How should they be used?

per school. In addition, some schools use their computers extensively while others very little.

How Are Computers Used in School?

Computers are more available for use in schools now than at any other time. Local districts and states are concerned that their students obtain adequate knowledge of computers as well as actual experience using them. Computers are used in the schools as a means to deliver drill to students, are able to serve a tutorial function, are used for word processing and data base functions, and are used as a means of presenting students with problems and simulations. They are also used, of course, for teaching students programming skills.

At this point, however, the computer has not made much of an impact as a teaching aid in the daily presentation of academic subjects. Computers are not extensively used for simulations or as instructional aids. About 70 percent of eleventh-grade students questioned in one survey had never used a computer in mathematics class, and 85 percent had never used

it in science (Lapointe & Martinez, 1988). In the same survey, only 25 percent of the third-graders and 17 percent of the eleventh-graders said that they had ever used a computer in reading or English.

True or False Computers are not used extensively as instructional aids in regular academic classes.

Computer Literacy and the Use of Computers in Instruction

To better understand how the educational process is being affected by computers, we must look at two specific areas of concern. The first area includes the concept of learning about the computer in order to have some basic knowledge of what a computer does. This is sometimes called computer literacy. The second area includes the use of the computer for such things as simulations and games, drill, and tutorials and as an instructional aid in the classroom. This can be considered under the general heading of instructional use. The use of the computer as a tool for word processing can be placed under both headings.

Computer Literacy

What should a student know about the computer to be able to function in society? The computer has obviously affected many areas of life and will continue to do so in the future. It is estimated that 75 percent of the jobs within a few years will involve the use of computers (Troyer, 1987). If one of the purposes of education is to prepare students for the world of the future, some knowledge of computers is required. One of the recommendations in the famous report discussed in Chapter 1 *A Nation at Risk* (1983), was a call for a fourth basic skill besides reading, writing, and arithmetic—competence in the use of computers.

Unfortunately, many studies have indicated that students know very little about computers. For instance, one report from the National Assessment of Educational Progress (NAEP) investigated three areas: knowledge of computer technology, understanding computer applications, and understanding computer programming. The results showed a general lack of knowledge about what computers can do and how they work (Bracey, 1988b).

The term computer literacy means different things to different people. A reasonably good general definition is that **computer literacy** consists of the skills and knowledge that will allow a person to function successfully in an information-based society (Upchurch & Lockhead, 1987, p. 152).

There is very little doubt that students should know something about computers, but what specific elements does computer literacy comprise? Suggestions include knowledge of computer terminology and operations and the ability to program computers. Other areas of interest include understanding the use of computers in solving problems, the computer's capabilities and limitations, and the impact computers have on society. Computer literacy can be divided into knowledge of and performance with computers. Under the knowledge area, topics that may be taught

are familiarity with the components of a computer system (hardware and software) and how they work, information about the history of computing, awareness of the current and projected uses of computers in society, the possible implications of those uses, and knowledge about job opportunities associated with computers. In the performance area, we may want the student to be able to use software, write a simple program in one or two languages, and use the computer to solve problems (Brownell, 1987).

The focus of attempts to develop computer literacy has changed within the past decade. Early attempts stressed computer history, terminology, internal operations, and programming. Although these are still taught to some extent, the focus has changed from learning how a computer works to how computers can be used to help solve problems. In other words, applications are stressed. Discussions of how computers are used in our society to solve problems, the computer's possible effect on society, and computer abuse and ethics are now emphasized. This focus on problem solving and application is noticeable in the performance area, as many students are now given some experience in using the computer for word processing and are introduced to data bases and spread sheets. Little or no emphasis is now placed on programming.

True or False   Computer literacy courses today place more emphasis on computer applications than on how a computer works.

True or False   There is less emphasis on teaching programming skills to students today than existed a decade ago.

Computer literacy can be taught in many ways. Some schools may offer one-semester courses, others nine-week minicourses. At other times, elements of computer literacy are integrated into the regular academic classroom. One such curriculum for grades kindergarten through eight is found in Table 12.1.

Programming

Perhaps the most controversial change is the de-emphasis of programming skills. Is it necessary for students to learn to program, and should programming be an integral part of computer literacy? Students may be required to write programs because people believe that there is some equivalence between

---

computer literacy   A term used to describe general knowledge about computers that includes some technical knowledge of hardware and software, the ability to use computers to solve problems, and an awareness of how computers affect society.

Table 12.1   Overview of the Computer Curriculum

In an effective computer curriculum, students learn how to use the computer in a developmentally appropriate manner beginning in kindergarten.

Strands	Grades K–2	Grades 3–4	Grades 5–6	Grades 7–8
		Teach Students To:		
Procedures	■ Follow a procedure for a familiar task ■ Modify a procedure ■ Show different procedures can produce the same outcome ■ Find and correct errors in a procedure ■ Describe procedures used to perform a task	■ Help to develop a procedure involving repetition, decision making, and variables ■ Find and correct errors in a procedure ■ Develop a procedure; demonstrate that it works ■ Use procedures to perform new tasks	■ Apply procedures skills to new problems ■ Note differences between procedures for people and procedures for computers ■ Break problem into subproblems: plan procedures and subprocedures ■ Develop procedures for organizing data	■ Apply procedure skills to new problems ■ Choose the best aid for solving a problem: calculator, computer, pencil
Using Programs	■ Use computer drills and games ■ Operate equipment; load and run programs ■ Recognize the computer needs instruction	■ Read documentation that describes programs and tells how to use them ■ Select and operate programs without teacher's help ■ Select and use a program to solve a specific problem	■ Use simulations as an aid in learning ■ Demonstrate learning from a simulation ■ Retrieve information from a computer data base ■ Apply skills in using equipment, programs, and documentation	■ Use word processor to improve writing ■ Use more complex simulations ■ Use new methods to retrieve information
Fundamentals	■ Understand that computer instructions are contained in a program	■ Understand that the computer is a general purpose machine	■ Recognize tasks for which computer speed is needed ■ Recognize tasks requiring repetition ■ Recognize tasks requiring large amounts of data	■ Apply knowledge of fundamentals to new situations
Applications	■ Discover computer applications in homes and neighborhoods	■ Know about computer applications in school and local government ■ Compare fictional and real computers	■ Understand one or more ways information retrieval is used in diverse fields ■ Understand how scientists might use computers	■ Recognize uses of word processor ■ Recognize uses of computer in business and manufacturing ■ Recognize use of computer systems in large organizations ■ Recognize main components of computer systems

Table 12.1 Continued

Strands	Grades K–2	Grades 3–4	Grades 5–6	Grades 7–8
			Teach Students To:	
Impact	■ Follow rules for using equipment and programs	■ Follow rules for using equipment and programs	■ Understand reasons to restrict access to data bases and programs ■ Understand advantages and disadvantages of particular uses of information retrieval	■ Become aware of new social issues created by computers ■ Appreciate social dependence on computers ■ Understand effects of computer failures ■ Understand the kinds of computer skills needed in diverse careers ■ Become aware of computer professions
Writing Computer Programs	(Note: For grades K–6, objectives and activities related to computer programming are reflected in the Procedures, Using Programs, and Fundamentals strands.)			■ Modify programs ■ Code programs ■ Write documentation ■ Test and debug programs ■ Plan and develop programs

Adapted from Beverly Hunter, *My Students Use Computers: Learning Activities for Computer Literacy.* Copyright © 1983, pp. 12–13. Reprinted by permission of Prentice-Hall, Inc., Englewood Cliffs, New Jersey.

computer program writing and computer literacy, that learning to program a computer gives an individual more control over the machine, and that writing programs is a useful experience. Some argue that there are jobs in programming and add this as a reason, although it is uncertain whether introductory programming skills will be of great vocational use in the future. In addition, computer literacy includes general skills and should not be thought of as vocational in nature. Others argue that programming can teach problem-solving skills and enhance thinking skills (Upchurch & Lockhead, 1987). However, considerable conflict surrounds the usefulness of elementary programming for teaching problem-solving skills.

The three programming languages most often used when teaching programming are LOGO, BASIC, and Pascal. **LOGO** comes from the Greek word *logos,* meaning a word. LOGO is an attempt to give young children the experience of programming and to make mathematics and computer programming more attractive to children. It was designed to be easy for children to use and to allow students to do things with the computer that they find interesting. **BASIC,** an acronym for Beginner's All-purpose Symbolic Instruction Code, was developed in the mid 1960s to help students learn to program. It is the most popular

LOGO An education-oriented programming language designed to easily enable children to begin to program and communicate with computers.

BASIC Beginner's All-purpose Symbolic Instructional Code, an easy-to-learn programming language widely used by students, educators, and owners of personal computers.

Should students be required to learn basic programming as part of computer literacy? The teaching of computer programming has been deemphasized over the past decade.

We will concentrate here on LOGO because it is often the first computer language students are introduced to in schools and it has sparked a good deal of research. LOGO was formulated by Seymour Papert (1980), who worked with Jean Piaget for a number of years. Papert agrees with Piaget that children must actively interact with the environment in order to learn. Papert also argues that students require experiences that encourage them to explore their own thinking and that they should be exposed to problem-solving strategies associated with·learning to program a computer (Brownell, 1987). Such experiences can be enjoyable. If students enjoy using computers, they will acquire the skills needed to use them more effectively. They will want to learn the computer language to make the computer obey their desires (Graham, 1989). Papert also claims that experience with LOGO will improve student thinking and that such improvements will be maintained and transferred to situations outside the computer domain. Papert, then, argues that there are important intellectual thinking and problem-solving skills to be gained when a child learns to use LOGO.

LOGO is best known for its graphics capability that allows students to create their own designs using the computer language (see Figure 12.1). It does so by means of a turtle that leaves tracks on the computer screen when given specific, relatively simple commands. For example, the command FORWARD 30 means that the turtle moves forward thirty steps. All commands are composed of very descriptive words. A set of commands can be grouped together to form a new word, called a procedure.

Although LOGO is a fairly simple language, still some students may have difficulty learning it (Lehrer, 1986). Fay and Mayer (1987) suggest that children approach programming with some misconceptions and confusions that can make learning LOGO difficult. For example, many children have an egocentric concept of space. When they use commands such as RIGHT and LEFT, they do so with respect to their own bodies or perhaps with the screen rather than with respect to the turtle. If a child writes LEFT 90, it means that whatever direction the turtle is facing, the turtle turns 90 degrees to its left. Second, children have difficulty discriminating commands such as turning and moving. They sometimes believe that turning LEFT 40 means turning LEFT 40 degrees and moving forward.

For students to learn a computer language, they must acquire an understanding of the concepts of the

language for microcomputers because it is relatively simple and flexible and does not require much memory (Mandell & Mandell, 1989). It can be used for solving a wide variety of problems.

Pascal was also developed for teaching programming concepts. It is the most popular language for computer science students. It is a very powerful language and can perform very sophisticated mathematical operations. High school students planning to take the Advanced Placement Test offered by the Educational Testing Service, College Entrance Examination Board, must know Pascal.

Pascal   A high-level programming language developed for instructional purposes and now commonly used in a wide variety of applications.

Figure 12.1　Pictures Drawn Using LOGO
One of the most prominent features of LOGO is its graphics abilities

language. For LOGO graphics, two of the more important concepts are the ability to take the turtle's frame of reference into consideration and the ability to discriminate commands. Fay and Mayer suggest that students should be observed as they are learning LOGO to determine their understanding of these concepts. If they do not understand the concepts, an attempt should be made to introduce students to them.

As noted earlier, a number of reasons have been advanced for teaching programming. The most controversial is the claim that it will improve students' thinking and problem solving outside the computer situation. Much of the research in this area has investigated the relationship between learning LOGO and the transfer of thinking and problem-solving skills.

Some studies have found such improvements in problem-solving skills (Clements & Gullo, 1984; Lehrer & Randle, 1987). Most controlled studies have not been successful, however, in showing any long-term effects on higher-order cognitive skills (Pea et al., 1985). The most common finding is that learning LOGO does not lead to a generalization of skills to other problem-solving contexts (Dalbey & Linn, 1985). Therefore, although there may be some minimal support for the notion that learning LOGO develops thinking and problem-solving skills that generalize to other contexts, most of the literature is not positive.

Before explicitly saying that learning computer programming does not lead to developing more sophisticated cognitive skills that transfer, we must recognize that computer programming is a fairly new area. We need more research if we are to understand how students learn to program and what the best way is to teach them programming skills that may have an impact on their cognitive skills. There are enough promising results to warrant further study (Mayer & Fay, 1987).

At the present time, we can only say that the early hopes that learning computer programming would in some way help develop higher-order cognitive skills have not yet been realized. However, because some research has found positive results, we cannot yet make any definitive statement. It may be that computer programming taught in a specific manner will provide these benefits. At this point, though, we are only beginning to understand how this might be accomplished.

The tide seems to be turning against teaching computer programming, especially in secondary schools. Only students who may either need the skill because of a scientific interest or feel they will need programming in their future vocation are encouraged to learn to program (Trollip & Alessi, 1988). While students certainly do not have to know how to program to use computers effectively, questions concerning the possible benefits from learning to program require further investigation.

Do Students Need Hands-on Experience?

If programming is deemphasized, how much hands-on experience is necessary? It can be argued that one can learn about computers and their impact on society by reading about them, discussing them, visiting places where they are used, and perhaps through seeing them demonstrated. Therefore, only a few strategically placed computers are necessary (Stallard, 1987). Others disagree and maintain that hands-on experience is vital if students are to feel comfortable with computers. Eliminating all performance requirements is undesirable. Students cannot learn everything they need to know about computers by talking about them or seeing them demonstrated.

Are students getting hands-on experience? The National Assessment of Educational Progress (NAEP) survey of 1985–1986 showed that about one third of the students never used computers and 75 percent of the seventh- and eleventh-graders used a word processor either less than once a week or not at all. Students want to spend more time on computers (Bracey, 1988b). In the NAEP survey, 91.2 percent of the third-graders and 86 percent of the seventh-graders said they wanted to work with computers more often.

The need to prepare students to function in an information rich environment is obvious. Most people acknowledge the need to teach students what computers can and cannot do, how computers are affecting and will affect their lives, and some aspects of computer terminology. Although there are contrary voices, there is a need for actual hands-on experience

with computers as well. The extent to which computer literacy requires programming is a point of controversy at the present time. Computer literacy will continue to be an educational concern well into the next century.

The Computer as a Teaching and a Learning Tool

Whereas computer literacy involves learning and teaching about computers, the use of computers as instructional and learning tools comprise another area of interest. **Computer-aided instruction** (CAI) can be defined as the use of computers as a tool to increase student learning (Long, 1985). For our purposes, we will divide CAI into three areas. In the first area, the computer is used to deliver drill, practice, and tutorials. In the second area, computers can be of aid in the classroom by presenting the class with simulations and games that can help students sharpen their problem-solving skills. In the third area, computers can be used as tools to improve research and writing skills and to actually enhance the creative process.

Drill and Tutorials

The most popular use of computers as tools of instruction is to provide drill and practice. Computer drills can be similar to flashcards, or they can be much more involved. In the simplest drills, a computer might generate mathematics questions concerning basic facts, the student responds, and the computer gives immediate feedback. Those questions that are answered incorrectly can be placed in a file and presented after all the other examples are tendered to the student. This is similar to the strategy one might use with flashcards. Drill and practice are useful in mathematics, social studies, and foreign language, and although we may argue that the procedure can be overused, there is no doubt that it has its place.

True or False The most popular instructional use of computers by classroom teachers is to provide drill and practice for students.

computer-aided instruction The use of computers as a tool to increase student learning.

The use of the computer for drill and practice purposes has drawn criticism. However, drill and practice do have their place in education.

A reasonable question to ask is why the computer is more effective than simply drilling a student yourself or having parents do it. This can be answered in several ways. First, individual drill takes a considerable amount of time and is labor intensive. Teachers may not have the time to give individual drill. When it is given in a group situation, the drill presented may not match the speed or need of certain students. Parents may not have the time to drill their children, and students may not be able to drill themselves. The seemingly simple strategies of retesting those items that a student gets wrong may not be present in some younger students, and computerized drill is very effective for those students who may lack these self-learning strategies (Salisbury, 1988).

The ability to program drill and practice goes beyond simple strategies, however. Some drill and practice activities have been written so that they make better use of the computer's capabilities. One is the corrective feedback paradigm (CFP) (Siegel & Misselt, 1984). Several features are added to the familiar flashcard drill to improve it. First, the type of feedback offered depends upon the type of mistake made. For instance, consider a drill involving the elements of the periodic table. What if the computer shows "Mg" and the student types in "metal." If the student response is not the answer to another drill question, the computer gives the correct answer, "magnesium." However, what if the student types "manganese." The feedback the computer provides is that Mg is magnesium and Mn is manganese. The computer has told the student the question the student responded to as well as the correct answer to the original question.

Students are also given discrimination training, as the item missed and the confused item are presented simultaneously so that students can see the items' similarities and differences. For instance, if the student answered with magnesium for Mg and Mn, they would be presented together and the student made aware of the difference between them. The student would then need to correctly respond to both items before the drill continued.

In addition, in the normal flashcard procedure, an error is placed at the end of the pile and then presented again after the student has answered all the other questions. By that time, the student may have forgotten the correct answer. This problem is avoided using what is called increased ratio review. In this more complicated drill, if the student makes a mistake and receives feedback and possibly discrimination training, the missed items reappear according to a spaced review schedule that is determined by the teacher before the drill begins. The missed item may appear after three more items. If it was answered correctly, it appears after six more and then finally after ten more items. An incorrect response indicates a need for more review. This is similar to placing the error into the middle of the deck of flashcards according to a prearranged schedule. It can be done by hand, but it would be difficult.

The teacher may also decide on the number of times an item is to be answered correctly before it is no longer asked. This rule is called a retirement criterion. For example, the teacher may decide that if the item is answered correctly twice, it can be dropped from the drill. The teacher may decide five correct answers are necessary. Of course, the computer has no difficulty counting how many times the item has been presented and answered correctly, whereas we would find such bookkeeping rather difficult.

Computer drills can be used in a number of areas, including biology, spelling, arithmetic, foreign language, social studies, and English as a second language. These techniques are superior to more traditional methods of review (Siegel & Misselt, 1984). One caution is necessary, however. Computerized drill and practice are meant for review purposes and as a way of perhaps increasing response speed. They are not meant as a way to introduce students to new material. If students do not have a basic knowledge of the material, they will find the drill program very frustrating.

True or False Programs of drill and practice should not be used unless the student has already been taught the material.

Unlike practice and drill, tutorials are designed to introduce students to new material. The computer acts as a tutor, with the student directly interacting with the computer to learn new material. The computer is programmed to present material and to react to student responses and questions with prearranged questions and responses. It is very similar to the programmed learning materials described in Chapter 5 (Percival & Ellington, 1988). Tutorials have the advantage of being easily individualized and tailored to meet the needs of the learner. The timing of the presentation of any new material is contingent upon student responses to tutorial questions. Tutorials are interactive, requiring active participation, and provide immediate feedback for the student (Lepper & Gurtner, 1989). They are especially effective in helping students who have missed several days because of illness to catch up.

Computerized tutorials differ, however, from the older programmed material in a number of ways. Again, the flexibility of the computer adds something substantial to modern tutorials. For example, in earlier models, the student would be directed immediately to a remedial exercise if he or she answered something incorrectly. The modern computer can keep track of responses over a long period of time—perhaps a full lesson—and direct students to remedial loops, depending upon the total pattern of student responses. In addition, earlier types of programs may have required students to choose one answer using a multiple-choice format, whereas newer packages allow students to respond in their own words and even to type in questions (Percival & Ellington, 1984).

Figure 12.2 shows a possible dialogue between a student and a computer that is assisting the student in

You are required to investigate experimentally the chemical equilibrium of the system $Fe^{3+} + SCN \rightleftharpoons FeNCS^2$ to discover how the equilibrium constant varies as a function of the ionic strength. You need a method that is both sensitive and discriminating. Which method(s) do you suggest?

I'm sorry, but I haven't a clue

You first need to consider the physical properties of the individual species, or of the system as a whole, that you might use.
What feature do all the species involved have in common?

They are all ionic

Good!
So what method or methods might you choose that make use of this property?

Conductivity methods

Yes—a conductance method.
Is a conductance method sensitive? (Very, Fairly, Not Very, Not at All)

Very

No. A conductance method is only fairly sensitive.
Is it a discriminating method?

Yes

Conductance methods are only really discriminating when applied to H^+ ions: for all other ions, the readings are rather similar.
Do you want to consider this method further?

No

What other method(s) might be more discriminating and sensitive?

Possibly a colorimetric method

Good. Are colorimetric methods sensitive?

and so on

Figure 12.2 Extract from a Tutorial Dialogue
Tutorial programs engage students in a structured dialogue.

Adapted from *A Handbook of Educational Technology* by F. Percival and H. Ellington. Copyright © 1988 by Nichols Publishing.

planning a chemistry experiment. Newer tutorial systems now pose more complex tasks for students, providing further instruction or assistance based upon student inquiries and may use graphics to demonstrate a point. In addition, the branching programs used are more involved. The computer not only notes that an answer is wrong but also, depending upon the type of incorrect answer, directs the student to a different remedial subprogram (*Education Week,* April 15, 1987). Just as in the area of drill, computerized tutorials now use more flexible and effective strategies.

Computer Simulations and Games

Students are asked to produce ammonia in a computer-simulated laboratory—a process that requires a very high pressure. Students are able to understand the effects of altering temperatures, pressure, and concentration ratio on the efficiency of the process (Percival & Ellington, 1988).

Simulations and games are perhaps the most original uses for computer technology. Consider the student learning about the flow of blood in the human body, the food chain in a pond, the life cycle of a frog, or cell division (Harty et al., 1988). Computer simulations allow students to view a graphic action sequence and to alter particular variables and see what happens. The computer simulation allows students to perform experiments that cannot be done in the classroom, to actively apply knowledge to a problem scenario, and to graphically see the results of changing elements of a situation. The possibility of simulating labs is important, as such "dry labs" allow students to work on laboratory exercises that would not be feasible for practical reasons (Pogrow, 1985). Because students do not have to set up the experiment and pour the chemicals, they can participate in more labs (Vockell, 1987). Obviously, computer simulations will not take the place of all labs, since the physical setup of the labs and actual hands-on experience are of value. Students can also run these computer-simulated experiments several times, investigating different hypotheses.

Many simulations can be used to teach problem solving. For example, computers can generate a graph, and students can vary the value of x and y. Rules for solving problems in mathematics can be applied to business decisions (Pogrow, 1985).

Learning games have been used in the classroom for many years. Computer games have been created for many subjects, including language, mathematics, logic, physics, chemistry, biology, economics, business, medicine, and geology (Tolman & Allred, 1987). Games can take many forms. Some games pit student against student but are losing favor, as the competition may not be desirable. Others pit student against the computer. More and more, though, games require some cooperative effort. Two students might play against the computer. In one game, students must use almanacs and travel guides to find thieves that go from place to place to avoid arrest (Brownell, 1987).

The use of computerized simulations and games is becoming more popular. Such programs allow for the effective presentation of problems to students and provide opportunities for students to try to solve the problems, many of which are realistic but cannot be practically presented in the classroom in any other manner. They may be used for demonstration purposes as well. For instance, a teacher may show the class how things change in the ammonia experiment when temperature and pressure are altered. Used in this way, the computer simulation becomes a part of the daily lesson and an aid in presenting new material to the entire class.

True or False Computer simulations and computer-generated problem-solving programs should not be used by the classroom teacher because they are very complicated and should be run only by experts in the field of computer-generated graphics.

The Computer as a Tool for Students

The third way of using the computer is as an aid for students doing research or as a tool for enhancing creativity. Word processing is a good example of this. Consider for a moment the student who is writing a composition. The student writes it and then realizes that it must be edited. Editing is the most important part of writing, and revision the most difficult (Daigon, 1982). It is this rewriting that forms the drudgery of writing. Word processing allows students to do this more easily. In one study of writing classes, students who had access to computers and word processors rewrote their work more effectively, especially in the areas of organizing and expanding ideas (Vockell, 1987). Students without computers must spend more time recopying text and may not want to revise the composition because it requires so much effort.

One of the most popular applications for the computer is in word processing.

Many word-processing programs have the capacity to check for spelling errors and contain a thesaurus that allows students to easily find synonyms for words. Students can make their changes directly on the computer, moving paragraphs, looking up words in the thesaurus when necessary, and adding sentences where appropriate. Word processing makes writing reports, compositions, and letters easier for students and editing and revising less of a chore.

Computers are also useful as information storage and retrieval systems for students doing research. Many libraries now have data bases that allow students to do research in a quicker, more efficient manner. Students may also use the computer's graphics and sound capabilities as aids in both art and musical composition (Lepper & Gurtner, 1989). In this way, the computer can be an aid in students' creative endeavors.

When to Use a Computer

While describing these three specific areas of computer use, care was given to demonstrating the advantages for using the computer over more traditional methods. A computer may not always be better than other methods of instruction. The question, Under what circumstances should computers be used?

was addressed by Stanley Trollip and Stephen Alessi (1988), who listed six such circumstances:

1. Computers should be used when material is difficult to teach using other media. For example, some material may be presented using simulations that cannot easily be otherwise shown.
2. Computers should be used when a great deal of individualized student practice is required. This uses the computer's ability to deliver effective drill and practice. There are times when computerized drill is superior to workbooks or class drill led by the teacher. Workbooks often provide little or no feedback, and the teacher may find it difficult to provide individualized drill to an entire class of students.
3. Computers should be used when normal instruction may not be safe. A number of experiments in chemistry and physics have some real danger attached to them. Students using "dry labs" or computer simulations can do experiments safely and efficiently.
4. Computers should be used when other forms of instruction are too costly. Although the computer should not be thought of educationally as a cost-saving device, in some situations, such as driver education or learning auto mechanics, computer-based simulations may be less expensive than

working with the actual object. Of course, computerized simulations do not entirely take the place of hands-on experience, which will be necessary at some point.

5. Computers should be used when other forms of instruction do not motivate students. Motivation is a factor in learning, as discussed in Chapter 8. Students like working with computers. At times, they may feel more comfortable making mistakes in the privacy of a one-to-one computer-learner situation. Students often show positive attitudes towards computer use, and computers may serve a motivational function (Tollman & Allred, 1987). This is especially noticeable for students who have been frustrated after repeated failure in classrooms. Malone (1981) claims that the three elements of computer programs that gain and keep attention are challenge, fantasy, and curiosity. Software that contains these elements appeals to learners. Computers, then, can be seen as a motivational aid in the classroom. However, much depends upon the software available. If the software is poor, students will reject the program, and the program will not enhance their motivation.

6. Computers should be used when it is logistically difficult to teach a topic. Sometimes it is not possible to show something in the classroom setting. Some labs, especially those concerning heredity, are difficult. In addition, it may not be possible for students to travel to places where certain equipment, such as expensive power tools, is available. Computer simulations and graphics allow for realistic and controlled demonstrations that would otherwise be difficult to do.

Is CAI Effective?

Any new mode of instruction must be evaluated. On the surface, it would seem easy to answer the question of whether CAI is more effective than traditional methods of instruction. However, this is not the case, for many reasons. First, CAI is really in its infancy, and it may not be fair to make categorical statements about such a new technology. Second, it is difficult to know what to measure. True, measuring academic achievement is important, but so might be affective goals, such as interest and motivation. If a student shows an interest in science and goes to the library to find out more about the heart because of a simulation but does not do any better on a test in biology, has

CAI been successful? Third, the research in the field, while plentiful, is of relatively poor quality (Lepper & Gurtner, 1989; Bracey, 1988c).

Many studies that try to evaluate CAI do not use control groups. Also, the studies often use very short time periods, and sometimes teachers are not given enough time to become comfortable with their new teaching tool (Marshall, 1988). Studies have so many weaknesses that one researcher, Henry Becker, found it necessary to discard seventeen of fifty-one studies conducted after 1984 on the effectiveness of computers. In addition, the area is changing so fast that studies might become outdated very quickly. After all, the materials available twenty years ago are not anything like the relatively inexpensive yet very powerful microcomputers available today. And finally, the use of computers is software specific. In other words, if I try a software package and get poor results, does this say something about CAI or about the specific software I am using?

Even taking these serious problems into consideration, there is much evidence pointing to the positive influence CAI can have on student achievement. A review of 199 studies conducted by James Kulik and Chen-Lin Kulik (1987) found that students generally learned more in classes where computers were used. On the average, computer use raised scores from the 50th to the 61st percentile. Students also learned their lessons with less instructional time, and their attitude towards computers improved. However, the use of computers did not lead to positive changes in student attitude towards the subject matter itself. Another analysis of forty-three studies comparing computer-based instruction with traditional instruction in grades seven through twelve also found achievement gains when the content of the CAI was part of the curriculum itself. The improvement was similar to that found in the Kulik study, as the student who would have scored in the 50th percentile now scored in the 63rd percentile (Samson et al., 1986).

True or False When computers are used in regular academic classes such as mathematics, social studies, or science, students' attitudes toward the subject itself become more positive.

Specific evaluations of computer-based tutorials and drill and practice have found that such programs have a moderately strong positive effect on academic achievement. Evidence is more positive for tutorials than for drill, perhaps because it has been only recently that the computer's abilities have been used to write more effective drill programs. The positive results are stronger for younger than older students and for students of lower ability. There is some evidence that students learn more quickly using CAI (Lepper & Gurtner, 1989). There is especially strong research suggesting that the use of a computer as an aid in addition to a traditional program is very effective (Burns & Bozeman, 1981). However, it ought to be noted that in 72 percent of these studies on drill and tutorials, students were not randomly assigned to the treatment group (the group that received CAI) and the control group (the group that did not receive CAI). Also, in 51 percent of the studies, the amount of instructional time was not controlled (Lepper & Gurtner, 1989).

The research on games and simulations shows a positive trend as well. Of course, the research here is complicated by the fact that there are so many games and simulations, and making any generalization is difficult. Few simulations or games have been subjected to multiple evaluations. Still, studies have demonstrated the potential for benefits. A number of studies have concluded that students taught through games and simulations learn more, while a few studies show no differences (Heitzmann, 1987). Games can also be used as effective means of giving drill and practice (Kraus, 1981).

Reviewing the effectiveness of games and simulations, Thomas Butler (1988) concluded that students using CAI generally acquire at least equal knowledge and intellectual skills as those not using it. The information is learned faster, although the amount of information is not significantly greater. Students of low academic ability often improve their performance because of an increase in interest, and some improvement in problem-solving ability is found. Again, students' interest in the subject itself may not be improved even if students want to participate. Games can also promote socialization.

Despite the problems in evaluation discussed earlier, some authorities have tried to draw general conclusions from the research. One such summary was formulated by Slesnick (1986). First, CAI does not replace traditional instruction. In most studies where it has, no difference in achievement has been found, although there is no evidence of its being detrimental. CAI, however, is consistently found to be an effective supplement to instruction, although many supplements are effective whether computer based or not.

Drill and practice in arithmetic improves achievement, although, again, drill leads to better achievement whether it is computerized or not. There is some evidence that the rate of learning through computerized drill of rote knowledge is better with CAI, although there remains some question about retention. CAI improves the attitude of students toward the computer but not toward the subject matter.

If the computer encourages academic achievement, Edward Vockell (1987) suggests it does so by increasing effective academic learning time, defined as the time students spend actively attending to important instructional tasks with success (Perkins, 1988). Computers can improve achievement by focusing student attention on the relevant areas of concern and by reducing the extraneous activities, such as setup time in the laboratory and the drudgery of rewriting an English composition by hand.

Contrary Voices and Responses

A pause is necessary here. Much of the research on the use of computers is positive, and the reasons for using computers in the classroom appear compelling. However, there are voices that warn against a headlong rush into the use of computers and technology in general. Despite the overall optimism, it is not difficult to find dissenting voices. Some of the dissenters are reacting to the statements that computers will cause a revolution in education. At least until now, this has not been the case. Although computer use has increased, there is no evidence of a revolution in education where computers will somehow replace the traditional classroom teacher's duties. However, these contrary voices raise some serious points that should be taken into consideration by classroom teachers who may want to use computer technology.

One real concern is the possible lack of social interaction that could occur if computers are used too much. Consider a student who spends hours at a computer on various subjects. The student may not be involved with other students (Bork, 1988). This lack of interaction may cause difficulties in learning social skills. This is a concern at all grade levels, but the use of computers with very young students has led some to complain that children may fail to learn social skills because of the decrease in social interaction (Karger, 1988).

At the present time, since most schools do not use computers all that much, it is not necessarily an important issue. However, some schools are beginning to become more dependent on technology. For example, a school in St. Paul, Minnesota, called the Saturn School of Tomorrow, makes extensive use of technology for its fourth-, fifth-, and sixth-graders. These students are grouped according to their skills rather than by grade level. With the aid of very sophisticated computer software, the students help to determine their educational goals and track their progress. The students will spend at least one third of their day using computers and other equipment (West, 1989). However, even in this experimental environment, the students will spend one third of their day in cooperative learning situations and the balance in teacher-led discussions or field trips.

Human interaction is recognized as important. In addition, some cooperative computer programs allow more than one student to work with a computer, thereby ensuring social interaction. Students work as teams to solve a problem. Social interaction, then, can be built into the use of computers in the classroom.

Another concern surrounding the increased use of CAI involves the possible dehumanization of the classroom environment. How will computerization affect the role of both teacher and student? Will teachers be more limited in the way they teach, becoming managers more than teachers? Will the curriculum become subservient to the computer? Could a student's role be reduced to one of answering computer-generated questions? These questions demonstrate the importance of objectively evaluating the psychological effects of computerization within the society in general and on the educational process in particular.

Financial considerations are also a cause for concern. Even though microcomputers have declined in price, they are expensive (Apple, 1987). The software required to run them effectively is also costly. New furniture is needed, and more security and a number of other financial considerations make computers an expensive addition (Jorde, 1986). One concern is whether the money spent on computerization could be more profitably spent elsewhere. The problem of access is also often raised when considering the financial aspects of computerization in schools. Less affluent school districts often do not have the money to provide computers for their students compared with more affluent districts. Students from poor families, therefore, may not obtain the access to computers that may be desirable (Bork 1988).

Perhaps the most cutting criticisms, though, come from Michael Streibel (1986), who argues that the two main uses for computers in instruction—drill and tutorials—have a very narrow focus. Drill and practice software "convert the learning process into a form of work that tries to maximize performance-gains, and restricts individualism to rate of progress and level of difficulty (and ultimately to individualized levels of productivity)" (Streibel, 1986, p. 147). Streibel warns that nonbehavioral goals will be ignored as objectives that can be reached through CAI are preferred. Streibel evaluates tutorial computer programs as narrow and mechanized. He criticizes the use of the computer simulations and problem-solving exercises because they are limited to quantitative reasoning and do not develop the qualitative or experiential domains. He also questions whether the programs really teach problem solving. Others have complained that many computerized drills and practice exercises are nothing more than electronic workbooks (Hlebowitsh, 1988).

Robert Heinich (1988) replied to these criticisms by noting that teachers use various instructional modes to teach students, and CAI is simply one of them. For instance, he describes his experience learning Chinese. During the class, he engaged in a number of procedures, including drill and practice in learning the words, practice in writing the words on prepared worksheets, and practice using a computer. He also listened to Chinese dialogues in the language lab and to explanations in class and participated in conversations in small, supervised groups. The question, as he notes, is one of mix, not exclusivity. In addition, he points out, students do go beyond the problems generated by the computer, and nothing stops the teacher from talking to students about other nonquantitative factors regarding the problems. The controversy surrounding tutorial and drill is one of purpose. The methods can be useful if not overused but should not be thought of as a total instructional program.

Another criticism is that although the computer is touted as an interactive medium, the amount of active interaction is sometimes minimal (Thompson & Jorgensen, 1989). Students may interact merely by pressing A or B, certainly not a very involving interaction. This issue is really one of software quality and can be reduced if more sophisticated software is used.

You may have noticed that many of these criticisms, especially those involving the lack of flexibility and narrowness of focus, could also be made concerning the use of workbooks, certain readers, and a number of other instructional approaches and materials. These might be considered general issues that are appropriately raised with many approaches to instruction. The criticisms, however, are often focused on the use of the computer, although they are just as relevant to discussions of many other school practices.

Can Students Become Too Dependent on Technology?

A very difficult question involves the use of technology which, according to some, may hamper or interfere with the development of academic skills. For example, should students learning word processing be allowed to use spelling checkers and grammar checkers? Should students working with mathematical computations be allowed to use a calculator? Would such aids interfere with a student's ability to spell, learn grammar, or perform mathematical computations without technological help?

In some schools, the students are not allowed to use spelling checkers at all. The use of calculators has recently been the source of considerable dispute. A task force of the National Academy of Sciences urged schools to give all students from kindergarten through grade twelve access to calculators and computers in mathematics class. The task force claims that mathematics education is often nothing more than doing calculations. The new look in mathematics, which emphasizes reasoning and problem solving, could be enhanced through the use of calculators (Rothman, 1988). Obviously, this is a very controversial suggestion. The same controversy exists in other fields, as some advocate giving students pocket spellers (West, 1989). Others claim that the use of such instruments in school could lead to a condition in which students will become overly dependent on technology and will not learn how to calculate, spell, or use correct grammar.

The questions and criticisms raised certainly must be considered. Being aware of the subtle changes in the educational process that may occur if CAI is extensively used is one step in the right direction, as is developing better, more interactive software. However, it is also important to actively document whether these changes are really occurring or if they are merely theoretically possible. This will require additional research.

> ### ▶▶▶ CONNECTIONS
>
> #### What to Do When the Computers Arrive
>
> As we've seen, computers can be valuable instructional and learning tools. But how does one start to use them? The following suggestions may be helpful.
>
> 1. **Get to know what your district or school has available.** Many districts or schools have computer coordinators who can help the regular classroom teacher discover what is available for his or her grade level or subject. If you have a specific need for software, discuss it with the coordinator. There are many catalogues that describe the software available (see the following Connections on how to evaluate software). In addition, you can contact teachers at other schools who are using computers and obtain very useful advice and information.
> 2. **Consider what you might want to use the computer for in the classroom, what your goals are, and how much time you are willing and able to devote to computer use.** As noted, computers can be used for many purposes. The idea is to use computer-aided learning where it fits best into your course work. The goals of any computer program usually do not find their way onto the screen. However, they are described in the documentation that accompanies the software. Compare your goals with those noted in the documentation.
> 3. **Decide how many computers you will need and how many are available at the school.** If you decide you want a mathematics program that will allow students to see what happens graphically when values for a certain equation are changed, you must decide whether you want simply to demonstrate it using one computer in front of the classroom or whether you want all the students to conduct a form of laboratory experiment by themselves or together in small groups. The availability of computers may limit your options in this area. There are aids available today that will project what is on the computer screen to a larger motion picture screen so that the entire class can easily see.
> 4. **Familiarize yourself with how the computers available in your school operate.** Once you

know what is available and that it fits your needs, you must know how to use the hardware and the software. Many school districts hold seminars or minicourses to educate teachers on the use and operation of the computer. In some schools, the computer coordinator will help teach the class to use the computers.

5. **Keep in mind that the computer is not a toy and that the work done on the computer is part of the required course work.** Students may enjoy the computer simulations and find the drill games interesting. Using the computer may also improve student motivation. No matter how the computer is used, however, students need to know that they are responsible for the material presented via computer.

6. **Overcome your own and your students' computer phobia.** For some teachers and students, computers are forbidding machines. The symptoms of computer phobia are negative attitudes about computers and technology, a fear of touching a computer, a feeling that you'll somehow ruin or damage the computer, or a feeling of being threatened by the computer (Jay, 1986). There are a number of ways to reduce anxiety, including reading about computers, obtaining hands-on experience guided by the coordinator, and attending seminars on computer usage.

7. **Understand that the computer does not take the place of books and other forms of instruction.** Some authorities advocate CAI as a principal method of instruction, while others see it as an aid. No one argues, however, that computer-aided instruction takes the place of books, newspapers, or other materials.

8. **Consider what is required if you are using the computer for drill.** The computerized drill must cover the appropriate material. In addition, a good program will make use of computer abilities by employing the more sophisticated drill techniques described earlier. Students will stay with it longer if the program is interesting. Also remember that drill is not meant to introduce new concepts to students but to let students practice material they have already learned (Goldman & Pellegrino, 1986).

9. **Decide how you will use the computer as a tutor.** In deciding whether or not to use a tutorial, consider whether the subject needs to be introduced by personal teaching rather than by a computerized tutorial. Perhaps the tutorial should be used for students who need to make up work or who require more time to learn the material. Tutorials should be previewed to ascertain whether they proceed logically and emphasize the most important material. Teachers may also want to look at whether the tutorial allows for a variety of learning speeds and encourages active involvement.

10. **If using the computer for simulations or problem-solving exercises, consider whether the simulation or exercise is clear.** Also know how to operate the program well before trying it out in the classroom. If students are required to solve computer-generated problems, remember that they need time to learn how to use the program. This learning time must be included in your lesson plan.

11. **If using computer games, consider whether the game is effective in teaching the learning objective, and if it is educationally valuable.** Students may enjoy games but the purpose of the game must fit with the teacher's learning objectives.

12. **If using computers for word processing or as a research tool, consider obtaining the help of the computer coordinator.** Also consider the time it may take for students to learn the word-processing capabilities or to use a data base.

13. **Monitor your students' use of the computers.** Studies indicate that teachers typically do not actively monitor students during CAI, and this is unfortunate (Haynes & Malouf, 1986). To be certain that the computers are being used correctly, student use must be monitored. If students are making mistakes or are getting frustrated in their use of the software, you may need to intervene and spend some additional time teaching them how to use it. In addition, computers cannot tell whether students who are taking a long time to answer are doing so because they are working on the problems or because they are not engaged in learning (Goldman & Pellegrino, 1986). However, a teacher can make that distinction and correct the situation.

14. **Teach students how to transfer knowledge and skills.** Even if students can solve computer-generated problems, they may fail to solve problems in the classroom under other circumstances (Perkins, 1988). Teachers can improve transfer and generalization by modeling problem solving (thinking aloud) and helping students to understand the connection between solving problems

on the computer and solving problems in other situations (refer to Chapter 4).

The computer can be an instructional aid and sometimes a primary source of instruction for some material. However, it has its limitations, and its effective use requires planning and knowledge. Computer use will not automatically end the problems of the teacher or the learner. However, it does have the potential for being an important instructional aid if used appropriately.

 CONNECTIONS

Evaluating the Software

The effectiveness of computers in the classroom depends upon the quality of the software. There is much to choose from—about 8,000 educational packages are available (Davis et al., 1988). But how can one evaluate software? The following suggestions may be useful.

1. **Analyze your needs and those of your students.** What do you want the software to do? What is it you want to demonstrate? No matter what the purpose of the computer usage, the software must fit your needs to be useful.

2. **The level must be appropriate.** If the software requires reading, it must be at a level that your students can easily handle. The graphics must be suitable as well.

3. **Consider the values that are transmitted by the program.** (Mandell & Mandell, 1989) One of the problems with some computer software is violence. Some software shows people being disintegrated when the user responds incorrectly. This may be inappropriate. If a game program fosters too much competition between students, it may not be useful.

4. **Consider the accuracy of the material.** Teachers should check the accuracy of statements made in the program. Students sometimes think that just because the material is presented by a computer, it is accurate.

5. **Determine the ease of use.** You want to run the program, not spend hours trying to master it. Most educational programs are user friendly. A user-friendly program operates easily and gives prompts to tell you what to do. See if the documentation explaining it is written at a level that you can understand.

6. **Consider the software's variety and interest level.** One of the advantages of computer drill is that some of the games may add to student interest and encourage student participation. If you wish to use a problem-solving type of program, you may want variety in the problems presented. Flexibility may be a concern as well. Some programs are suitable only for small groups, large groups, or individuals, while others allow for more flexible usage.

7. **Consider who controls the program and how interactive it really is.** Does the student or the computer control the sequence of the instruction? Can the student move backwards or forwards, make choices, or control the speed? Does the program move faster students along at a faster pace? One of the major advantages of the computer is its ability to allow students to actively interact. But sometimes interaction means just answering A or B. If this is acceptable to you, then that is fine. However, if you want students to be able to type their own answers, this requires a more sophisticated program.

8. **Consider practical factors.** These are not just financial. For example, some programs have copy protection (a control that does not allow you to make extra copies), and most have copyright protection. This may prevent you from using the program with an entire class. You should also check that the memory requirements of the software match the computers available at the school.

9. **Preview the software.** This is very important although sometimes difficult. Vendors are aware of pirating and are very reluctant to send a copy for preview. It may be possible for you to preview the program if you know someone who already has it, perhaps in another school district. In addition, because vendors are aware of the teacher's need to preview their material, they will send software for a small price on approval or have demonstration discs available.

THE SCREEN COMES ALIVE

Instructional television, videotapes, and films are used extensively in schools today. They add a realistic dimension to lessons and a visual quality that can enhance student learning.

Instructional Television

Children are comfortable with television. Since they watch a great deal of it in their homes, it makes sense to use television in the classroom. Instructional television (ITV) began in the 1960s (Smith, 1987) and was hailed as a revolution. Today, it has lost some of its luster. Although it has not revolutionized—and will not revolutionize—education, more than half the teachers in the United States use television for instruction. It is estimated that 14.5 million students use television as a regular part of their instructional day (Rockman, 1985).

ITV has had its greatest impact on science and social studies classes (Clark & Salomon, 1986). The advantages of using ITV are considerable. It can be a

Although instructional television has not revolutionized education, it is used by about one third of all students on a fairly regular basis.

highly effective way to introduce new material if the content and level are appropriate. It can provide interesting and visually effective case studies and background material and can stimulate discussion. ITV can offer a combination of a good narrator or teacher conducting an experiment or interviewing an important person that can be of great value to students. Many of these programs are produced by public television stations and are of high quality.

The use of ITV does not end in the school. Ninety eight percent of all American households have television sets, and 52 percent have more than one, the extra set for the children (Parke & Slaby, 1983). The success of programs such as "Sesame Street" and "Mr. Rogers Neighborhood" shows that this is a medium capable of being entertaining and stimulating as well as educational.

Although ITV is useful, it has its weaknesses and limitations. First, the programs are sometimes used to keep students quiet and to fill time, just as parents at times use television as an electronic babysitter. Second, it is sometimes difficult to preview television shows to be certain the content is appropriate. You may receive some background information, but if it is being aired on television for the first time, it is difficult to be certain that it will be of value to your students. It may be best to tape the show, preview it, then use it in instruction. Many producers realize that television shows used in schools need to be previewed and have made arrangements making such previewing possible. Of course, legal aspects of taping should be reviewed with your school administrator.

The third difficulty is that programs are often shown at times that are inconvenient during the day or even during the school year. You may not be covering the War of 1812 the week that a program about the event is being telecast. Or a program that would be appropriate for class viewing is shown during a school holiday. This problem can partially be solved by renting a tape of the show, which is usually available at a very reasonable price. Television shows also can be videotaped; more than 90 percent of the schools and 60 percent of all homes have a video recorder. However, there are legal problems here, and a teacher should consult the audio-visual coordinator or supervisor about the practice. Some schools have been sued for taping programs and showing them at different times. Another difficulty with ITV is that some of the programs that are rebroadcast become outdated.

The last, and perhaps most serious, difficulty is that most programs are not interactive. Students listen and watch, but there is little or no response during the program itself. The teacher sits at the back of the room, and the television program proceeds at its own rate. One cannot tell the program to stop so that teachers can answer or ask a question. The class must wait for the program to end unless time is provided for this purpose within the program itself. This is one problem that the video cassette recorder solves, as discussed later.

Even though many teachers use instructional television, some still doubt the usefulness of educational television programs. The medium has so long been associated with commercials and programs of little or no educational value that some believe that the medium itself is the problem. In short, Milton Chen and William Marsh (1989) suggest people mistake ITV for MTV. They note three misconceptions concerning instructional television.

First, people think of television as a passive medium, both physically and cognitively. As noted, this is a major limitation. However, Chen and Marsh claim that ITV shows can involve young children in physical activities such as singing, clapping, and even exercising. Cognitive involvement can be provided by leaving time within the program for student responses. This was done by the children's program, "The Electric Company," a reading series produced by the Children's Television Workshop in the 1970s and still in use. Within the context of the program, children were encouraged to practice reading words aloud. This is more a design problem for the television show than a problem with the medium.

Second, people sometimes believe that television viewing is a demon causing students to read less. This argument as applied to ITV is invalid. In fact, television programs with educational value can motivate students to read. After watching a television program on a subject, students may be motivated to read about the subject. The program may provide the background needed to allow students to find areas of interest. In a more direct manner, some programs deal with interviews of authors or highlight books. Such programs have been very successful, and the books highlighted on television are very much in demand.

A third myth is that ITV is an old or failed technology. As noted, it will not revolutionize education, but it is used by many teachers.

ITV is a very useful medium for presenting material to students in an effective manner. When a show about the American Revolution fits into the course you are teaching, it may bring Thomas Jefferson and Alexander Hamilton to life, allowing them to be seen as real people coping with real and difficult conflicts. In addition, with the aid of the video cassette recorder, some of the interactive problems can be resolved.

Video Cassette Recorders

The video cassette recorder (VCR) has great advantages over live television. In fact, many instructional television productions are available on videotape free of charge or for a small fee. Most schools have at least one VCR; some have more than one. One advantage is the ability to show a program at a time when it is convenient for the teacher. Videotapes can be stored (if owned by the school) or easily rented when needed.

The greatest benefit of the VCR is the ability to stop the tape and make comments, ask questions, or field questions from the students. Such a technique—called actively viewed video by Chen and Marsh—allows the teacher to remain in front of the classroom or walk around with a remote control, interrupt the program or use only a small part of it, call out questions, or engage students in a dialogue.

True or False   Live television programs allow for more classroom interaction than programs that are shown on videotape.

A videotape also allows more flexibility in programming. It is possible to set up a scenario on the program in a way that is not possible in the classroom, such as showing a historic situation using actors discussing their choices and then at the appropriate time turning to the class and asking students to consider the situation, allowing students to take all the time necessary to discuss the historical context and alternatives. This demonstrates a way that the medium can be used to encourage thinking in the classroom.

Having a VCR also allows the teacher to preview the material. There are times when a teacher may want to show only one part of a program, and previewing saves class time by not having to show the entire program to the class.

The advantage of the video cassette recorder is that the teacher can stop the tape to answer questions or comment on the program.

Last, videotapes can be used to tape a lecture or a class session, allowing students who are absent to hear the lecture when they return to school or students who require a review to watch the lesson again. In some colleges, telecourses are offered in which programs on a particular subject are viewed on television at scheduled times and on a supplemental basis on videotape in the college library. Students can attend supplemental classes as well, but the bulk of the teaching is conducted through television and tape. These courses have become popular, especially for people who have schedules that do not allow them to be on a college campus at the same time each week for a class.

Films

Films have been used in education for quite some time. As is the case with television programs, some films are excellent, while others are poorly produced. Films share some of the same features as ITV. Films, just as television programs and videotapes, can effectively communicate complicated phenomena, for example, fusion. They can visually overcome physical barriers and recreate situations. Films can be used to introduce a topic, perhaps a controversial one. They can also be used to visually demonstrate what has been discussed in the classroom. Last, they can be used as a motivator, encouraging students to look more deeply into some element of what is being shown in the film. For instance, a film on Native American customs can be connected with an assignment to research the customs of different Native American tribes.

Films are widely available for a reasonable rental, and many schools have procedures for renting films. Some films are owned by the school. When using those that are owned by the school, the teacher needs to be especially careful to look at the publication date. Some films are very old and out of date. For example, a mathematics film may emphasize calculation rather than problem solving or application. Some films are, of course, timeless. Rentals have the added disadvantage that they have time limitations. Because a film may have to be rented some time before it is to be shown, planning becomes more complicated.

Classic films are also available and can be used in a number of subjects, especially English and social studies. For example, after reading the play *Twelve Angry Men,* one of my daughters watched the movie and discussed similarities and differences between the movie and the play. Other films on controversial topics can spark discussions and serve as a basis for additional study.

Films suffer from the same limitations as ITV. Although they can be stopped for questions, it is difficult to do so. Of course, many films are now found on videotape, thereby allowing more flexible usage. However, when showing a film, one should be aware of stopping too often and interfering with the film's total impact.

▶▶▶ CONNECTIONS

The Teacher and Visual Media

Suppose that you were an eighth-grade social studies teacher about to show a film or videotape about World War I. How can you help your students get the most out of the presentation? The following suggestions may be of help.

1. **Know why you are showing the film.** As in any other educational endeavor, you should have solid reasons for choosing to show a film instead of presenting material using some other format. You should communicate your goals to the students.

2. **Be certain the program or film is suitable and appropriate for your students.** Films and ITV programs are directed at many levels, and although the title of a show ("WWI: Life in the Trenches") is of interest, the program may be pegged at too high or too low a level.

3. **Be sure the film or program fits into your curriculum.** Technology should not determine the curriculum. Rather, it should blend with the curriculum, allowing increased flexibility.

4. **Consider the practical difficulties.** Practical problems can prevent the use of all technological aids. If a television show is televised at ten o'clock but you teach the class at two, it may not be possible to use the program. Also consider the problem of students who may be absent on the day the program is shown. Is there any way for them to see the presentation? If not, how will the material learned in the film be presented to them?

5. **Preview the material.** Many instructional television shows have written summaries or introductions available. Teachers can preview videotapes, and they can determine if they want to use some of a tape or all of it. They can also determine in advance if and when they want to stop the tape to ask questions or check student understanding.

6. **Introduce the material and integrate it into your current unit.** Students need some orientation to the program. They need to know what to focus on during the program or film. Some teachers present questions for the students to answer that function as a guide. The students should know the title of the film. After giving the students some introduction to the film, you may want to ask them to write down three or four questions they might want answered. If there are new terms or vocabulary in the program, introduce them to the students and write them on the blackboard.

7. **Discuss material after the show.** If time is available, post-program discussions are very valuable. They can be used to tie the film to the entire unit or to raise controversial points. They also can be used to summarize what ideas students have learned from watching the program or film.

8. **Plan follow-up activities.** Programs can be used as a basis for homework. The homework may involve answering questions based on the program or even writing a review of the movie (Miller, 1979). Younger students can be asked to retell the program's story in their own words. A caution is necessary on the use of questions. If too much emphasis is placed on questions, students may be so busy writing down the answers as they watch the program that they miss other information. In fact, notetaking during the film should not be encouraged. If students ask if they should take notes, you might say, "Only if you feel it is necessary." However, you may want to point out that too much notetaking can be counterproductive.

9. **Plan the seating arrangements.** Seating arrangements for television viewing can be a problem. Before the program begins, the television set should be placed in a position that allows all students to see it. Sometimes a few students may have to change their seats.

10. **Try to prevent equipment problems.** Equipment should be checked out before the show begins. It is frustrating for the teacher and the class when equipment is defective, and while the teacher is fixing the equipment, some students may begin to act out.

11. **Let the students know that they are responsible for learning the material in the film or program.** Students may ask, "Will we be tested on this material?" This question indicates that many

---

students do not understand the way films fit into the educational process. That is understandable. The media are not used as a source of education very much in students' daily lives. Even in some classrooms, they may not be linked to what is being studied very well, or students may not have been responsible for learning from films in the past. However, if films or television programs are to be educationally valid, students must be made to realize that they are being shown for a valid purpose and are part of the educational experience. You can help students, though, by discussing why you are showing the film and noting some content areas on which the students can focus.

12. **Show the most important part of a film or tape a second time if necessary and if it is feasible to do so.** If there is a part of the tape that is most important or controversial and time permits, you may find it valuable to show the five-minute segment again. This is easiest with a videotape, less possible with film, and impossible with a live television show. In addition, some shows have transcripts that are available at a reasonable cost. These allow the teacher to read through the most important parts of the program with the students.

13. **Assess the strengths and weaknesses of the presentation, both from your own and your students' viewpoints.** (Brown et al., 1973) You may want to write down the strengths and weaknesses of the program and any additional explanation on a particular point that is needed. In one of the videotapes that I show in class, a very important statement is made in one sentence and can easily be lost by students. The film covers a particular psychological theory and does a very nice job of integrating it with an experiment. However, an important qualifier that demonstrates that the theory is not predictive in a fairly large minority of cases is presented very quickly. I stop the video at that time to highlight the statement and discuss it with the students, since I know that the students will not pay attention to it unless I emphasize it.

14. **Discuss the program with the students, having them rate what they learned from it and evaluate its value.** As the program is shown, observe your students. If they are interested and motivated, their behavior will show it. If they are restless and bored, that is a definite strike against the program. Although students do not have to be wildly excited about a program, attention and interest are certainly two criteria for using it.

15. **Keep an audio-visual file.** A small file box with index cards is sufficient for this purpose. It may be difficult to keep track of the films or videotapes you use and their strengths and weaknesses, especially if you teach a number of different courses or grade levels. If you note the name of the film or program, its date of issue, its strengths and weaknesses, any pre- or post-program activities that have been successful, and even perhaps the address of the distributor, the information will save you time later when you want to use it again.

16. **Search for audio-visual programs of value.** Catalogs are freely available. Some stations (especially public television stations) will send advanced announcements of programs if you are on their mailing list. You can also learn about other worthwhile programs through discussions with your colleagues.

17. **Most students have television sets available, and you can assign students to watch a particular television show at home.** However, a number of things can interfere with a student's ability to watch the program. The time may not be convenient, or a student may have other scheduled activities or may not be able to convince siblings that he or she needs to watch the program. It is reasonable to ask for a note from a parent if a student was not able to watch the program, but giving a student a poor grade or penalizing the student for not watching (especially if a note is received) will pit the teacher against a parent.

18. **Use media as a challenge for integrating writing into the curriculum.** There is a movement to integrate writing into every class. (See Chapter 9.) Television and films can be used as a base for such an activity (Miller, 1979). Allowing students to choose topics for research related to the program is another possibility.

The television and film area is a powerful one. However, to be useful, programs must be integrated into the curriculum, and teachers must carefully prepare students for the use of such programs. Television and films can add an extra dimension, making the educational experience more realistic and more varied for students at all levels.

True or False   Students should not be informed of the educational value of an instructional television program, because this will interfere with students' enjoyment of the program.

EVERYDAY CLASSROOM AIDS

When people think of technology in education, the computer and instructional television come to mind. However, there are a number of other technological devices that teachers use to make their presentations more effective.

The Overhead Projector and Transparencies

One of the most popular and versatile technological aids is the overhead projector. These projectors are easy to operate and are useful. They project onto a screen or a white background whatever is drawn on the transparency. Teachers can use the transparency as they would a blackboard and write on the trans-

parency while teaching. The great advantage is that the teacher continues to face the class. In addition, after one transparency is finished being used, it can be saved and referred to again and again.

Besides using the transparency as a substitute blackboard, teachers can prepare visual displays on transparencies ahead of time. Teachers can therefore have someone else who is perhaps a better artist draw diagrams for them. Transparencies also allow the teacher to use overlays (Brown et al., 1973). That is, the teacher can show a diagram of what the United States looked like in 1783, then place other transparencies over the first to show the country's growth through the years. The ability to prepare such displays in advance allows for better planning. Transparencies also can be easily duplicated. In addition, there are many professionally produced transparen-

Overhead projectors can be used as substitute blackboards. The transparencies can be prepared by the teacher before the class session, or a number of excellent commercially produced transparencies can be used.

cies on the market that are very well done. They are compact and easy to store and save, and a person can develop his or her own library of transparencies or create departmental libraries for collective use.

One interesting technique that can be used with transparencies is to cover all the material except what is immediately being explained and to slowly uncover the remaining material as it is being explained. This is especially important with prepared transparencies that sometimes have just too much information on them for students to follow at one time. Students can also be given handouts that are similar to the diagrams. For instance, a map of the colonies can be drawn on a transparency and a work sheet given to students. As the lesson unfolds, the colonies are labeled by both teacher and students. Students giving reports might want to make their own transparencies.

The overhead projector has its limitations and potential problems. First, it can produce an annoying glare because the bulb is so strong, interfering with a teacher's ability to see and monitor students (Doyle & Carter, 1987). Second, to be used properly, the overhead projector requires a screen or a white background, something that may or may not be readily available. Third, there is a tendency to write too much information on one transparency, which can confuse students.

When using prepared transparencies, planning is the key. Not only do the transparencies have to be prepared in advance and integrated into the lesson, but they must be organized in such a way that the teacher can easily get to them. Trying to look around to see where you put that transparency of the peripheral nervous system now that you have finished talking about the central nervous system means time wasted and possible student behavior problems.

The overhead projector is a widely accepted technological aid that is available in most schools. With some planning, it can be a useful instructional aid.

Filmstrips, Slides, and Photographs

There is an old saying that a picture is worth a thousand words. Whether or not this is so, pictures do stimulate student interest and help students understand and remember material (Brown et al., 1973). Sometimes filmstrips are available that are accompanied by an audio narrative. These filmstrips allow the presentation to proceed at a prearranged rate or to be interrupted by the teacher to emphasize a point. For example, a filmstrip explaining prenatal development may require additional explanation at certain times, and this can be accomplished through the judicious use of the pause button.

A number of slide presentations of good quality are commercially available. For example, perceptual illusions are very effective as slides. Teachers may also take their own slides and use them. One teacher took pictures of various trees and bushes that he used to demonstrate local flora.

Pictures taken from books, magazines, and newspapers are also used frequently. The problem here is that they may not be large enough to show to the entire class. Opaque projectors can be used to project such pictures onto a screen, but they require almost total darkness, and not all schools have this type of projector.

Slide and filmstrip projectors suffer from some technical problems that can become very annoying.

Pictures are very useful, but all students must be able to see them.

For example, slides are sometimes out of focus; filmstrips are easily destroyed, and their sequence cannot be altered. Filmstrips are also less flexible than slides and can be out of date because of a single frame (Percival & Ellington, 1988). However, if the equipment is in proper condition, these visual aids can be quite useful to the classroom teacher.

Audio Aids

Radios, tape recorders, and record players are indispensable in subjects such as music. However, they are also useful in other subjects, such as English and social studies. Through these aids, one can listen to John Kennedy giving his inaugural address or a dramatic reading of a poem. Students can also be involved in making and using audio recordings. A student's speech can be taped, or students might be asked to do a radio play. Spelling lists can be recorded, giving students practice (Brown et al., 1973). Introductions to laboratory exercises can be recorded that are especially useful for students who have to make up labs. In the area of foreign language, tapes allow students an opportunity to hear the language and replay a sentence again and again. Students can also tape themselves speaking the foreign language and play it back.

Audio projects are also possible. Students can be asked to function as newspeople and write a skit or roleplay interviews of famous people. Simulating radio news broadcasts encourages writing skills, and creating sound effects adds an enjoyable dimension to such projects. Audio aids frequently require imagination. Students can conjure up the scenes in a play, or in the younger grades, they can draw something connected to what they are hearing. Some students, especially in high school and college, may ask to tape class sessions. It is certainly a teacher's prerogative to say yes or no, but such tapes can aid students who need the repetition.

Audio aids have some potential problems. The most devastating is the tendency of these aids to be unclear and distorted. Simply stated, the quality may not be good. If students cannot understand what is being said, the teacher will probably encounter student restlessness and behavioral problems. Second, tapes tend to be too long. Some lectures are so long that students lose interest. Therefore, when using

audio equipment, one must watch for signs of boredom and uneasiness and perhaps play only part of the material.

▶▶▶ CONNECTIONS

The Teacher and Audio-Visual Aids

In using any media presentation, a basic five-step plan is to prepare yourself, prepare the environment, prepare the class, use the item, and follow up the item's use (Brown et al., 1973).

1. **Prepare yourself.** This involves planning the way the aid will be used, preparing questions you may want to ask the students, and previewing the material.

2. **Prepare the environment.** Arrange for the necessary materials and make certain they are in proper working order. Also be sure that each student can see or hear the material and that the equipment is operating safely.

3. **Prepare the class.** The material should be introduced and students told why it is being used and given some idea about what material to focus on. Students should understand that the use of the media is part of the educational process.

4. **Use the item.** While using the item, monitor student attention. If necessary and practical, interrupt to emphasize points or to answer questions.

5. **Follow up.** Ask questions, review the lesson, perhaps use the material as a basis for further study, or in some way follow up the experience with related activities. Also assess the presentation's value.

The use of audio-visual aids can complement many lessons. Tapes, slides, pictures, and transparencies can make presentations more effective. Audio-visual aids can make lessons more appealing and more realistic, add variety, and sometimes explain difficult material more effectively. They can add another dimension to the educational process.

The preceding suggestions deal with how teachers can use audio-visual aids in their lessons. However, students can produce their own audio and video materials. They can create their own slide shows, do interviews, and make transparencies. Such student-produced programs often add interest to reports and assignments and can serve to motivate students.

TRENDS

It is difficult to predict trends in the use of technology in the classroom. It is difficult to predict what may or may not find acceptance in educational circles. Computers that are faster and that store more material and produce better graphics, as well as improved software will become available. Funding is one big question, however, that affects the use of any new technology. Teacher acceptance and teacher training are other important variables. Unless teachers are well trained in the use of any new technology and are willing to accept it, the technological aid will not be extensively used in the classroom.

One interesting innovation is the use of distance learning. Imagine a teacher in one classroom—perhaps in one state—presenting a lesson to students in another locality connected by both visual and auditory links allowing for two-way communication (Snider, 1987). This technology allows students to have interactions with an expert who does not have to leave his or her school. This is already available in some areas of the country.

There will also be more sharing of information among teachers. Teachers will be able to communicate with one another through the use of a modem, a device that allows computers to communicate with each other over telephone lines. Many electronic bulletin boards will permit greater sharing of information.

The new technology that has incredible possibilities is the interactive video. This is basically the marriage of video cassette recorders or videodisc players and the computer. The aim of the combination is to provide interactive teaching programs through the computer and the best visual and sound characteristics through the video cassette recorder or videodisc. Interactive video merges graphics and sound with computer-generated text. The videodisc player will probably be used more than the video cassette recorder, because it allows for easier access to specific parts of the program and discs are more durable than tapes, can store more material, and can store both motion pictures and slides. The quality of the videodisc is better than that of tapes, and the videodisc permits very precise computer control (Schneider &

This student is using an interactive video system that presents lessons, references and corrections on computer, interspersed with video clips from a laser disk for lesson presentation and review.

Bennion, 1981). In the past, videodiscs have been used mostly for very high quality music recordings, but they can also store color graphics, images, and animation (Mandell & Mandell, 1989).

The interactive process involves the user responding to computer-generated questions and making inquiries into the system. Schneider and Bennion (1981) show how this can be used in simulations. They discuss a program that simulates a visit to a Mexican village, beginning with a complete view of the plaza of the town. From the corner a man approaches the camera, and when he arrives, he asks in Spanish, "You're an American tourist, aren't you?" His image freezes. If the question is understood, the student indicates this, and the computer controlling the disc writes a number of possible answers in English. If the question is not understood, the scene is repeated. The student chooses an answer, translates it into Spanish, and actually may speak it into a microphone that is connected to a voice-activated recorder. The student indicates which answer he or she wants to use and then sees him or herself on the screen giving the answer to the man who originally asked the question. The dialogue then continues. When the session ends, the audiotape can be given to the teacher for review. The simulation includes a number of other possible scenarios, including a visit to the market, bargaining to purchase something, and a taxi ride. Since the program has one starting point but eight different end points, the student can explore the entire village.

The capabilities of this medium are fantastic. Figure 12.3 compares interactive video with other media. The student can be presented with a lesson that involves actual film footage, animation, or pictures projected onto a television monitor. Then the computer can ask the student questions and by judging the responses replay part of the lesson or branch to the most appropriate material (Brownell, 1987). The videodisc is flexible, and a person can watch news footage of historical events, learn about the most recent advances in science, and listen to music of great composers or speeches of famous people, all by giving a command through the computer.

TECHNOLOGY: A RATIONAL APPROACH

A remarkable new technology is introduced into the school system and experts predict education will be revolutionized. The technology will, as never before, allow the widespread dissemination of new concepts and ideas that will stimulate young minds and free the teacher for more creative pursuits. Yet the magic fails to materialize, and within a few years articles appear in the popular press asserting that the failure obviously arises from teachers not being skilled enough in the new technology.

The above scenario actually describes the introduction of the blackboard in the 1840s. Such a scenario occurred again with the introduction of film in

FILM & TELEVISION

Visual format may vary with use of audio and motion.
Easily available with limited variety of programing to user/learner.
May display photography, print and other static/dynamic information.
Traditional passive information system with limited user/learner control.
Unique contributions to learning process but limited in depth of instruction.
Serial information presentation traditionally with varying quality of format.
Learner/user productivity limited by lack of direct random access.

COMPUTER

Rapid direct random access to predominantly printed information.
Relatively poor quality presentation format.
Interactivity can be maximized for learner/user.
Limited motion, audio, and photography quality display.
Relatively expensive for individual learner/user.
Flexible learner/user monitoring with feedback capabilities.
Excellent learner/user productivity with varying entry levels.

**INTERACTIVE VIDEODISC/
MICROCOMPUTER**

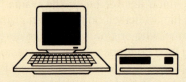

Can combine user/learner strengths of other media, such as variety of information displays with print, photography, multiple-audio tracks, and languages, freeze-frame and rapid accurate direct random access, with maximized learner/user control to vary nonserially presented displays.

Figure 12.3 Media Comparisons by Formats
Adapted with permission from "High Technology: An Assessment of Its Potential for Instruction" by R. K. Wood in *Videodisc/Microcomputer Courseware Design*, by M. L. DeBloois. Copyright © 1982 by Educational Technology Publications.

1900, when Edison predicted motion pictures would so excite students they would have to be kicked out of school. It happened again with radio, again with television, and yes, yet again, with personal computers (Lewis 1988, p. 15).

Lewis's statement is essentially correct. Today much of the emphasis is on the use of computers; tomorrow computer/videodisc technology may add a dimension to learning. These are the latest in a long line of technological improvements that add to a teacher's ability to present material effectively and in a varied manner. The newer technologies seem to have the power to actually create a dialogue with students.

In the past, each technological improvement has been greeted with predictions from its advocates that it will radically change education. On the other hand, its critics have cringed at the thought of the lack of human interaction and the possibility that students will be tied to machines for hours at a time, as if chained to oars in a boat. These dreams and fears have proved to be unfounded.

The new technology certainly can deliver an interactive learning experience, and we are just beginning to make use of its potential. New technologies will enable machines to respond in a more realistic fashion, and the new movement toward artificial intelligence may find its way into machines that can interact in a more sophisticated manner (*Education Week*, Dec. 10, 1986).

The computer's integration into the classroom, however, has been painfully slow (Trollip & Alessi, 1988). Even if its usage increases, there is no reason to believe that it will take the place of the classroom experience or replace the intensive human interaction that is part of the educational process at its best. The successful and effective utilization of these technologies requires that a teacher understand how to employ the technology.

Technology exists to serve the student and the teacher. While we must recognize the limitations of technology in education, we must also try to be open to innovation and use the technology to its fullest potential.

SUMMARY

1. Many technological devices are available as instructional aids. Some authorities not only see new technologies such as the microcomputer as being useful instructional aids but also believe they may serve as the primary mode of instruction in some areas.

2. The number of computers available in schools across the United States has risen greatly. Computer literacy consists of the skills and knowledge that will allow a person to function successfully in an information-based society. These skills and knowledge include some understanding of computer terminology, an ability to use software, and knowledge about computer applications, how the computer affects society, and the computer's potential and limitations. While some authorities believe knowing how to program computers is an important component of computer literacy, many do not, and programming is being deemphasized.

3. Computer-aided instruction (CAI) involves the use of computers as an instructional tool to increase learning. The computer can be used to deliver drill, practice, and tutorials to students, to provide students through simulations and games with problem-solving exercises, and as a research and writing aid using word processing programs.

4. The most popular use of the computer as an instructional tool is to deliver drill and practice to students. Drill delivered via computer can be especially effective if the computer's special abilities are utilized. Tutorials carefully introduce students to new concepts. Simulations and problem-solving programs permit the teacher to show involved demonstrations to the class and allow students to work individually or in groups to solve computer-generated problems. Computers can help students write more effectively through the use of word-processing programs.

5. Computers should be used when the material to be taught is difficult to teach using other media, when a great deal of individualized practice is needed, when normal instruction may not be safe, when other forms of instruction are more costly or do not motivate students, and when it is logistically difficult to demonstrate a phenomenon of interest.

6. It is difficult to determine the effectiveness of computer-aided instruction because, although the research is plentiful, it is of relatively poor quality. However, much of the research that is available is positive. Computer-aided instruction has been found to be especially effective when combined with traditional approaches to learning.

7. Some authorities warn about the possible negative effects computers may have on education. They argue that human interaction may be decreased, teaching may be dehumanized, we may become overdependent upon technology, and many of the popular drill and tutorials are very narrow. Proponents of CAI dispute these claims.

8. Instructional television (ITV) is used by more than half the teachers in the United States. It can sometimes serve as the primary source of information on an issue, or it can be used to provide interesting and visually effective case studies and background material. The main objection to the use of ITV is that most live programs do not allow for active student interaction. The use of the video cassette recorder can remedy this problem, as it allows the teacher to stop the tape and discuss the material or answer a question. Films have also been used extensively in schools.

9. Overhead projectors are versatile instructional aids. They project onto a screen whatever is drawn on transparencies. They can be used as a substitute for the blackboard. However, the transparencies can be prepared before the class session, and many commercially prepared materials are available. The use of slides, photographs, and pictures can add much to a lesson.

10. Audio aids such as radios, record players, and tape recorders can be useful, not only in music but also in English and social studies. Some recordings of famous speeches are available, and poetry and literature readings can be useful. In addition, students may roleplay interviews with famous people or organize simulated news programs.

11. When using any media presentation, a basic five-step plan is to prepare yourself, prepare the environment, prepare the class, use the item, and follow up on the item's use.

12. In some schools, students can view a teacher giving a lesson in another locality and actually interact with the instructor. In addition, teachers will share more information concerning their lessons through electronic bulletin boards. The combination of a computer and a videodisc player will allow for extensive interaction between learner and machine. Interactive video combines computer-generated text with excellent graphics and video capabilities of the videodisc player.

ACTIVITIES AND EXERCISES

1. **Help for the Inexperienced.** If you have not had any experience with computers, it is time to start. Gain access to a computer, either in a public school or college. The computer coordinator can help you. Some public libraries even have computers available, and some computer stores give very inexpensive training courses. Ask for a software package that might be interesting. If you are working in a school, some drill or tutorials are usually available. Try to learn the basics of computer use, including how to turn the computer on, how to load the disk into the disk drive, how to use the keyboard, and how to operate the program. If the computer is connected to a printer, find out how the printer operates as well. There is no substitute for hands-on experience.

2. **Computer Simulations.** The use of computer simulations, both to demonstrate some phenomenon to the class and as a possible laboratory activity, was discussed in the chapter. Choose two specific subjects in your area of expertise and describe in detail a simulation for both that would be helpful. If any simulation software is available, ask the computer coordinator to show it to you, even if it is not in your subject area.

3. **Interviewing the Computer Coordinator.** Many districts and some schools have computer coordinators. In addition, most colleges have professionals who are responsible for this area. Find out what materials are available, what new ideas in software are coming out, how the computer is now used, and what training is available.

4. **Visiting a Classroom in Which CAI Is Used.** Find out which teachers in your school district use CAI. Then interview a teacher to find out how CAI is used, why the teacher uses it, and what the teacher has learned since beginning to use it. It would be helpful if you could gain permission to watch the teacher using CAI.

5. **Observing a Computer Class.** Most schools hold some classes to introduce students to computers. Some of these classes emphasize the use of the computer as a word processor; others focus on other applications, such as data bases

and spread sheets. Obtain permission to observe a class getting its first experiences with using computers as a tool. Take note of the problems that students seem to have and how the teacher works with them. This may help you gain insight into how you might introduce your classes to computer use.

6. **Reviewing Software.** The key to CAI is good software. You can have the most powerful computer, and it will not help if the software you are using is poor. Ask to see the documentation for some software available at the school. If possible, review it using the questions raised in the text and any others you might think appropriate.

7. **Computer Magazines and Information.** There are many useful computer magazines available. Some review both hardware (different computers) and software. In addition, many companies have catalogs describing the software they are offering. Obviously, they will promote their own products, but they do give you some idea of what is available. The computer coordinator may have some of these publications available for you to look through. The public library will also have some of this material. Read through a few of these catalogs and magazines, making note of those you think would be most helpful.

8. **Instructional Television Usage.** The audio-visual coordinator in any school will know what programs are used in the school. Ask the coordinator what programs are the most popular. If you can find out who is using them, discuss their use with the teacher, including why they are used and how the teacher integrates them into his or her unit.

9. **ITV and You.** Find out what ITV programs are available that might be relevant to your subject. This can be done while discussing ITV usage with the audio-visual coordinator. In addition, public television stations often have literature available. View one show and describe how you could use it in a class. Take special note of any problems you think you might encounter, such as any particularly difficult segments or statements made during the program that can be misconstrued.

10. **Preparing Transparencies.** The overhead projector is one of the easiest devices to operate and one of the most useful instructional aids. It can be used as a blackboard, or transparencies can be prepared ahead of time. Choose two lessons that you might give in your specialty and prepare a few transparencies for use. In addition, find out if any of your colleagues have examples of commercially prepared transparencies in your area. Look them over and consider whether they would add anything to your lessons.

11. **Using Audiovisual Aids.** A number of audio-visual aids were discussed in the chapter. The college or public library may have audio-visual catalogs available that describe these aids. Describe two different lessons in which you would use some of these aids and how the aids would fit into the lesson.

12. **The Five-Step Process.** A five-stage process for working with audio-visual aids was discussed, including preparing yourself, preparing the environment, preparing the class, using the item, and following up on the item's use. Write a lesson plan that entails using a film, videotape, or audiotape showing your preparation, how you would prepare the class, and any follow-up ideas you may have.

SCENARIOS

Here are ten scenarios. Try to apply the information you have learned in the chapter to each situation.

1. Mr. Terranova teaches third grade. He believes that it is important for his students to be introduced to the use of computers, and he is determined to do so. He has investigated the availability of computers and finds that he has enough for students to get some practice on them. In addition, he is assured that he can usually get one for his classroom if he needs it. He doesn't know where to go from here. He knows vey little about computers, although he is certainly not a "computer phobic." What specifically can Mr. Terranova do? Where should he start?

2. The junior high in which you teach has very few computers available and almost no software. The principal has been asking the board of education for money to buy more computers and appropriate software. Finally, the board has asked the principal to make a presentation on why computers should be provided in the junior high school, and the principal has called a staff meeting. He must convince the board members that computers are needed. He must both prepare a presentation

and predict the questions that might be asked so that he can prepare for them as well. He asks you to help him, perhaps because you have stated a desire for more computers and software. Briefly outline a presentation, answering the following questions: Why are computers needed? How will they be used? How many are needed? What types of software are required? How will the staff be trained? (If you will be teaching at either the elementary or the high school level, prepare a similar presentation relevant for either of these levels.)

3. Mrs. Timmons uses the computers that are available mostly for drill and practice of mathematics facts. She uses a computer program that is not very sophisticated but delivers the needed practice. Her elementary school students appear enthusiastic, and the program allows the students to control the speed of presentation. One of her colleagues asks Mrs. Timmons whether it is more effective than the more traditional methods of drill, such as using flashcards or worksheets. Mrs. Timmons knows that this is an important issue. She also knows that it is more effective for some students than for others. How can she realistically investigate the effectiveness of the computerized drill she is using?

4. Mr. Ramirez is having difficulty with his eighth-grade social studies class. The students are a tough bunch who fool around a great deal. Unfortunately, Mr. Ramirez did not begin the term with the students. He was hired after the originally scheduled teacher became very ill and needed to have surgery. The school had a number of substitutes before Mr. Ramirez was finally hired as the permanent teacher. The behavioral problems become worse when Mr. Ramirez must write something on the blackboard. As soon as he turns toward the blackboard, he hears more talking. When he faces the class, the talking stops. One of his colleagues suggests that he use the overhead projector instead of the blackboard. Evaluate the suggestion and note the pros and cons of using this instructional aid.

5. "I don't like computers," Mark tells you. Mark is an eighth-grader who looks at computers with disdain. He has successfully avoided them throughout his early schooling but now finds there is no way out. The local school board demands some computer literacy skills, and hands-on performance objectives are part of the curriculum. Mr.

Bishop is responsible for introducing Mark to the world of computers. He finds that most students are very happy to work with computers, but a few like Mark seem to begin with a negative attitude and a certain amount of anxiety. Mr. Bishop knows that he cannot excuse Mark from the work, nor does he believe it would be desirable to do so. He must deal with the problem. Discuss ways that Mr. Bishop could reduce Mark's fears.

6. Mrs. Cartier is using what she feels is an excellent film on the Civil War. She has previewed the film, and it looks excellent. She is in the middle of her unit on the war, and the film fits in beautifully. She introduces the film to her students, telling them that it is an excellent discussion and recreation of events from the Civil War. Students seem attentive during the film. After the film ends, Mrs. Cartier asks for questions. Getting none, she begins to ask some of her own that directly relate to the film. She is astonished that her students do not seem to have grasped the main points of the film or the film's overall theme. It was not a particularly difficult film and definitely was on their level. What could Mrs. Cartier have done to prevent this problem?

7. An instructional television series on dinosaurs was fantastic, and Mr. Chin feels it will be of value to his sixth-grade class. The series consists of three programs and covers the types of dinosaurs living in different periods of time, how they lived, how we know about them, and, of course, possible reasons for their extinction. The series is available for a very reasonable rental, and Mr. Chin has arranged for it. He has spent one lesson discussing dinosaurs and is ready to show the series. Unfortunately, some of the language used in certain parts of the series is a little above his students, but overall, the series is good. Mr. Chin introduces the students to the program, and although most of the students are enjoying it and seem to be learning from it, there are a few students who look bored and do not seem to be getting anything from it. Mr. Chin would like to continue using the tapes because most students are enjoying the experience and are involved in the discussions that follow. However, he is not pleased that these few students are not benefiting from the videotape. What can Mr. Chin do for those students who do not seem to be benefiting from the experience?

8. Mickey's reports and homework are always neatly and accurately done. In class, though, Mickey has difficulty with spelling but can multiply and divide. Mrs. Epstein finds that Mickey uses a word processor with a spelling checker at home as well as a calculator to do his seventh-grade homework. However, Mickey has now asked to use a calculator and a hand-held spelling checker at school. He claims that he cannot spell very well, that his father always uses a spelling checker at work, and that his writing grades should not suffer just because he doesn't spell very well. He also claims that he should be able to use a calculator, because it would make the work go more quickly and would reduce the number of "stupid mistakes" he makes. Some of Mickey's classmates are awaiting Mrs. Epstein's ruling on the matter. Mrs. Epstein is concerned that these technological devices will become crutches and that her students will not know how to calculate or spell. On the other hand, Mickey's points do make some sense. If you were in Mrs. Epstein's position, what decision would you make? Why?

9. There aren't enough computers in the school for all your students to use them at the same time. You are told that within a few years the school expects to have enough computers to allow an entire class to participate in some activity, but for the present time, only eight are available. You have an excellent program showing the food chain that also gives students an opportunity to see what happens when certain events such as pollution and overfishing occur. The graphics are excellent, and students can vary elements, make decisions about how to intervene to clean up the environment, and generally, learn a great deal about ecology. You want to use the program but have twenty-one students in your class. Sharing the computers—that is, assigning three students to each computer—would seem a reasonable approach. However, you want each student to answer certain questions and write a report. Discuss ways that you could give each student an opportunity to participate in this activity.

10. Mr. Kotlowitz believes very strongly in the power of instructional television, videotapes, and films to bring an educationally valuable message to his class. He uses these media whenever possible, sometimes three times a week. His students liked it at first but became somewhat disenchanted when they realized that they had to learn something from the programs. However, they did finally accept this as Mr. Kotlowitz's style of teaching. Some of Mr. Kotlowitz's colleagues believe that he uses too many films and that the films lose their effectiveness after a while. Mr. Kotlowitz replies that all the programs he uses cover relevant topics, that he prepares the class, discusses the material shown in the tapes or films, and then uses them as a basis for homework. Still, some colleagues are not convinced. You are asked for your opinion. Is there any such thing as using too much audio-visual material? In addition, how could Mr. Kotlowitz demonstrate the effectiveness of his integration of a large number of programs into his teaching?

13

Are These Statements True or False?

Turn the next page for the correct answers. Each statement is repeated following the paragraph in which the information can be found.

1. About one child in ten is considered disabled and requires special education services.
2. By law, every disabled child must be mainstreamed—that is, placed in a class with nondisabled students.
3. Most learning-disabled students show hyperactivity.
4. Hyperactivity can be cured through correct use of medication.
5. Children with speech problems should be seated as close to the teacher as possible so the teacher can monitor the student's speech on an ongoing basis.
6. Children who act aggressively are not very popular with their peers.
7. Subnormal intellectual ability is the sole criterion for being labeled mentally retarded.
8. The majority of the legally blind have some remaining vision.
9. Students who lip-read can understand only about half of what is said.
10. Cerebral palsy is caused by a virus that is transmitted in a way unknown to medical science at the present time.
11. Students who are intellectually gifted tend to be well adjusted and have good interpersonal relationships.
12. Changing test conditions for a disabled student, such as giving a learning-disabled student more time to complete a classroom test, is an acceptable procedure.

Teaching the Child with Exceptional Needs in the Regular Classroom

1. *True*
2. *False* Correct statement: The law demands that the child be placed in the "least restrictive environment." This may or may not mean the regular classroom setting.
3. *False* Correct statement: Most learning-disabled students do not show hyperactivity.
4. *False* Correct statement: Medication may reduce the symptoms, but it does not cure the disorder.
5. *False* Correct statement: Children with speech problems should be seated in the middle of the classroom so they can converse with other students.
6. *True*
7. *False* Correct statement: Subnormal intellectual functioning is only one of the criteria for labeling a child mentally retarded.
8. *True*
9. *True*
10. *False* Correct statement: Cerebral palsy is caused by brain damage, most often at birth.
11. *True*
12. *True*

Lisa is a fifth-grade student with a learning disability. She has difficulty comprehending what she reads in your class. She is frustrated by her inability to perform and is keenly aware of her problem.

Hector is a legally blind eighth-grader in your class. He cannot read regular print but is eager to begin his studies.

Michael is a very slow student who has been labeled mildly retarded. He spends some of his time in your regular fourth-grade class.

Jill is a very bright girl who shows a special talent for mathematics. She finishes her assigned work very quickly and almost always obtains a perfect score.

Ian stutters badly. He does not volunteer often to answer questions in class. When called upon, it takes him some time for him to express his thoughts, and the class becomes tense and uncomfortable.

THE CHILD WITH EXCEPTIONAL NEEDS

What would you do if you walked into your classroom and were confronted with any of these children? Of the 45 million children in public schools today, a little over 10 percent are disabled. Of these, 85 to 90 percent are mildly disabled (Lewis, 1988). Most of these students will spend at least half their day in the regular classroom. Since about two thirds of the disabled students served in public schools are under twelve years of age, elementary schoolteachers are somewhat more likely than secondary schoolteachers to teach disabled students. However, every teacher will encounter disabled students sometime in the course of his or her teaching career, and many will find disabled students in their classes every year. The trend toward placing disabled students in the regular classroom is increasing (Viadero, 1988a; Lloyd et al., 1988).

True or False About one child in ten is considered disabled and requires special education services.

The classroom teacher's responsibility in educating the disabled student is to teach the normal subject matter. The special educator has the responsibility of remediating a particular disability and for providing the support necessary for the child to function in the regular classroom environment.

The purpose of this chapter is to introduce you to the most common exceptionalities (see Table 13.1) and describe some practical and realistic methods of adapting instruction to meet the needs of these students in the regular classroom. Both the teacher's time and the resources within the classroom are limited. Elaborate techniques sometimes used by special educators are not described in this chapter, nor are

Table 13.1 Public Elementary and Secondary Students in Educational Programs for the Handicapped, by Type of Handicap: 1978 to 1987

Using this table you can note the changes in the percentage of disabled students (with various types of conditions) attending public schools. Especially noteworthy is the increase in the percentage of learning disabled students.

Item	1978	1979	1980	1981	1982	1983	1984	1985	1986	1987
All conditions (1,000)	**3,751**	**3,889**	**4,005**	**4,142**	**4,198**	**4,255**	**4,298**	**4,315**	**4,317**	**4,374**
PERCENT DISTRIBUTION										
Learning disabled	25.7	29.1	31.9	35.3	38.6	40.9	42.0	42.4	43.1	43.6
Speech impaired	32.6	31.2	29.6	28.2	27.0	26.6	26.2	26.1	26.1	25.8
Mentally retarded	24.9	23.2	21.7	20.0	18.7	17.8	16.9	16.1	15.3	15.0
Emotionally disturbed	7.7	7.7	8.2	8.4	8.1	8.3	8.4	8.6	8.7	8.7
Hard of hearing and deaf	2.3	2.2	2.0	1.9	1.8	1.7	1.7	1.6	1.5	1.5
Orthopedically handicapped	2.3	1.8	1.6	1.4	1.4	1.3	1.3	1.3	1.3	1.3
Other health impaired	3.6	2.7	2.6	2.4	1.9	1.2	1.2	1.6	1.3	1.2
Visually handicapped	.9	.8	.8	.8	.7	.7	.7	.7	.6	1.6
Multihandicapped	(NA)	1.3	1.5	1.6	1.7	1.5	1.5	1.6	2.0	2.2
Deaf-blind	(NA)	.1	.1	.1	.1	.1	.1	.1	(Z)	(Z)

NA Not available.   Z Less than .05 percent.

U.S. Dept. of Education, Office of Special Education Programs, *Annual Report to Congress*. No. 233. PI380 from Statistical Abstracts of the United States, 1989.

strategies that require specific training not easily available to the classroom teacher. The emphasis here is on the classroom adaptations that can successfully be made by the classroom teacher so that disabled children can succeed in the regular classroom.

Defining Terms

The terms *exceptional, disabled,* and *handicapped* are often used interchangeably and incorrectly. An **exceptional child** is a child whose intellectual, emotional, or physical performance falls far above or below that of his or her "normal" peers (Haring, 1982). Everyone deviates from this mythical average, but there is a range of normal performance expected from children at particular stages in their lives, and children who deviate appreciably from the norm are considered exceptional. Exceptional children require educational modifications to optimize their achievement in school.

The term **disabled** refers to a total or partial behavioral, mental, physical, or sensorial loss of function-

ing (Mandell & Fiscus, 1981), whereas the term **handicapped** refers to the difficulty a disabled person may have in adjusting to the environment (Haring, 1982). The term handicapped is often used in connection with an environmental restriction that results from the exceptionality and may well depend on the individual situation. A child who must spend his or her day in a wheelchair is certainly disabled, but if ramps are available, the child need not be handicapped in entering and leaving a building. A general principle involved in serving the disabled is to manipulate the

exceptional child A child whose intellectual, emotional, or physical performance falls substantially above or below that of "normal" peers.

disability A total or partial behavioral, mental, physical, or sensorial loss of functioning.

handicap The difficulty a disabled person has in adjusting to the environment.

Over 10 percent of the 45 million children in public schools today are disabled.

learning environment and mode of presentation in such a way that disabilities do not become handicaps.

The Law and the Exceptional Child

Years ago, children with disabilities were often denied an education, given an inferior education, or simply separated from the mainstream of children as a matter of policy. But this is no longer the case. Beginning in the late 1960s, a number of court decisions resulted in improvements in conditions for exceptional children across the United States. Then, in 1975, Congress passed the most important legislation for children with disabilities. Public Law 94–142, also called the Education For All Handicapped Children Act, brought about considerable change for both these children and the regular classroom teacher. The law calls for all children to receive a free, appropriate education and provides for procedures to safeguard the rights of disabled children. The most important provisions of the Act are summarized in Table 13.2.

A school district can no longer claim that programs are unavailable for a disabled child or that a child cannot be educated. It is the district's responsibility to educate the child. In addition, the guarantee that due process be used in placing a child in some educational program means not only that a legal procedure must be followed but also that all testing must be nondiscriminatory. A Spanish-speaking child can no longer be given an intelligence test written in English, nor can only one test be relied on for any decision. The law also requires educational accountability, because educators must develop what is called an **individualized education program (IEP)**, which states the goals of the child's schooling and the methods for attaining them. Parents also have the right to participate in all phases of their children's placement and education. Finally, the law mandates that each child be placed in the **least restrictive environment.**

Figure 13.1 shows various classroom placement alternatives. The most restrictive are found at the top, while integration into the normal classroom is considered the least restrictive possible. Alternatives 1 through 5 deal with regular classroom placement. When alternative 2 (regular class placement with consulting teacher assistance) is used, the child is not taken out of the regular classroom environment; rather, a specialist is available to help the regular classroom teacher. The consultant may answer questions and supply teaching aids and materials. Alternative 3 (regular class placement with itinerant specialist assistance) involves taking a student out of the regular classroom for a minimum of time for tutorial or remedial work. These itinerant teachers often work in a number of schools within the district, spending only a day or so in each school. Alternative 4 (regular class placement with resource room assistance) involves a more structured program in which students leave their regular classroom for some time on a regular basis. Resource rooms are usually small classrooms where disabled students receive remedial and tutorial help, usually on a regular basis. In alternative 5, students share their time in school between special classes and regular classes, whereas in alternative 6, students spend all their time in special classes. When disabled children are placed in a regular classroom, they are said to be mainstreamed (discussed later).

individualized education program (IEP) An individual plan outlining educational goals for a student and methods for attaining them.

least restrictive environment The placement in which a disabled student can be educated with no more restriction than is absolutely necessary.

Table 13.2 Major Provisions of PL 94–142

PL94-142 is the most important law protecting the rights of the disabled student to gain an education.

Each state and locality must have a plan to ensure the following:

Child identification	Extensive efforts must be made to screen and identify all handicapped children.
Full service, at no cost	Every handicapped child must be assured an appropriate public education at no cost to the parents or guardians.
Due process	The child's and parent's rights to information and informed consent must be assured before the child is evaluated, labeled, or placed, and the child and parents have a right to an impartial due process hearing if they disagree with the school's decisions.
Parent/parent surrogate consultation	The child's parents or guardian must be consulted about the child's evaluation and placement and the educational plan; if the parents or guardian is unknown or unavailable, a surrogate parent to act for the child must be found.
LRE	The child must be educated in the least restrictive environment that is consistent with his or her educational needs and, insofar as possible, with nonhandicapped children.
IEP	A written individualized education program must be prepared for each handicapped child. The plan must state present levels of functioning, long- and short-term goals, services to be provided, and plans for initiating and evaluating the services.
Nondiscriminatory evaluation	The child must be evaluated in all areas of suspected disability and in a way that is not biased by the child's language or cultural characteristics or handicaps. Evaluation must be by a multidisciplinary team, and no single evaluation procedure may be used as the sole criterion for placement or planning.
Confidentiality	The results of evaluation and placement must be kept confidential, though the child's parents or guardian may have access to the records.
Personnel development, in-service	Training must be provided for teachers and other professional personnel, including in-service training for regular teachers, in meeting the needs of the handicapped.

There are detailed federal rules and regulations regarding the implementation of each of these major provisions. The definitions of some of these provisions—LRE and nondiscriminatory evaluation, for example—are still being clarified by federal officials and court decisions.

From Hallehan and Kauffman, *Exceptional Children: Introduction to Special Education*, 4th ed. Copyright © 1988, p. 31. Reprinted with permission of Prentice-Hall, Inc., Englewood Cliffs, N.J.

Recently there has been a call for identifying and educating disabled toddlers and preschoolers. A new law—PL99–457—encourages states to begin early intervention with infants and toddlers and requires that services be extended to three- to five-year-olds (Viadero, 1987).

THE TEACHER'S ROLE IN THE PROCESS

Much confusion exists concerning the role of the regular classroom teacher in the process of serving the child with exceptional needs. The confusion revolves about three areas: referral and labeling, the individualized education program, and the issue of mainstreaming the disabled child into the regular classroom.

The Referral Process

The referral process is the first stage in helping a student who may have a disability, and the regular classroom teacher is the source of referral for the overwhelming majority of children (Lewis & Doorlag, 1987). This is only natural, since the teacher sees these students every day, and the challenges of schoolwork often force a disability to show itself. For example, a child with a learning disability that results in difficulty in learning to read may show this problem

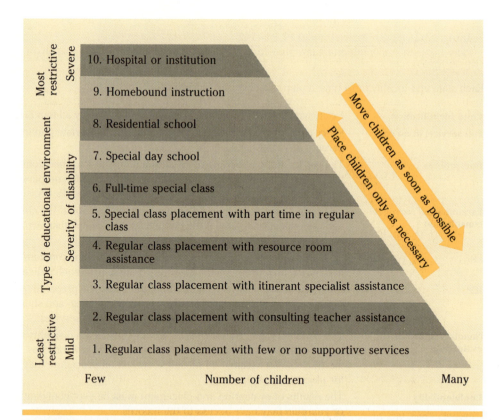

Figure 13.1   A Continuum of Educational Services
This figure shows the many alternatives available for placing disabled children. Notice the continuum of services ranging from placing the child in a regular classroom with few or no supportive services (1) to placement in a hospital or institution (10). Children are placed in the least restrictive environment in which they can effectively function.

From "Instructional Alternatives for Exceptional Children," by E. Deno. Council for Exceptional Children, 1973. Reprinted with permission of the Council for Exceptional Children and the author.

only when presented with tasks requiring reading. Federal law requires that each school system have a referral system but does not mandate a specific referral procedure, and districts vary widely in their procedures and forms. One such referral form is found in Figure 13.2. It is estimated that 92 percent of all children who are referred for special education consideration are evaluated, and of all those evaluated, 73 percent are accepted into special education programs (Algozzine et al., 1982).

The question of when to refer a student is often asked by classroom teachers. Bill Gearheart and colleagues suggest that teachers ask themselves, Does this student need special help beyond that which is normally provided in the regular classroom? (1988, p. 40). If the answer is yes, a referral may be required.

In some districts, prereferral programs exist in which teachers are asked to bring their observations to the attention of a committee of professionals who then suggest ways to help the child before referring the student for formal evaluation. Although more research on such programs is needed, the results are promising (Lloyd et al., 1988; Kerr et al., 1987).

The Controversy Surrounding Labeling

For students to be adequately served, they must be tested and evaluated and their specific problem diagnosed. Although regular classroom teachers may be asked to evaluate the child's present functioning in the classroom, the entire process of evaluation is per-

Referring Agent: _____

Child's Name: _____

Child's Age: _____

Child's Date of Birth: _____

1. Please describe, being brief but specific, academic and/or behavior problems evidenced by the child being referred.

2. Under what conditions does the problem exist?

3. What methods have you tried to solve the problem(s)?

4. What do you see as this particular child's strengths?

5. Additional information from school records and/or comments:

_____
Referring Agent, Signature

(This form is to be completed and returned to the committee chairperson.)

Figure 13.2   Sample Referral Form

From *Functions of the Placement Committee in Special Education,* 1976, by the National Association of State Directors of Special Education, p. 57. Reprinted by permission.

formed by a special multidisciplinary team that specifically categorizes children and determines the best educational alternatives. The process of categorization is required by law but is rather controversial, since labeling children—especially at young ages—is a serious concern.

Labeling does have its benefits. Without labeling a child as visually impaired or learning disabled, it would be difficult to create the educational programs appropriate for the child (Kirk & Gallagher, 1989). Labeling also allows us to estimate the number of children who have certain problems, thus enabling us to provide the necessary resources. Funding depends partly on how many students a school district has in particular categories. In addition, it allows parents who have children with similar problems to band together and enables school districts to run effective and relevant programs for these children.

Labeling has significant disadvantages, however. Some children have been mislabeled, and these in-

correct labels can stay with a child forever (Haring, 1986). Labeling can also affect many areas of a child's life. A label of emotional disturbance or mental retardation can adversely affect a child's self-concept and how other people think about the child. The label can also become a self-fulfilling prophecy in that a child might act according to the label and people aware of the diagnosis might act in a way that limits the child's achievement. Labeling also focuses our attention on the child's deficiencies and not the child's strengths.

Most often, regular classroom teachers are given some diagnostic information. They are told, for example, that a student is learning disabled, visually handicapped, or emotionally disturbed. This type of communication is probably unavoidable, since different changes in the environment are required for each type of disability. However, the diagnosis itself simply gives the teacher some idea of the child's condition but says nothing about the child as an individual or about the child's interests and strengths. It may not even say much about the abilities of the child. For instance, a child labeled as learning disabled may have difficulties in some areas and be gifted in others. A child who has a severe visual problem may actually achieve more in class than a child with a moderate visual impairment. Although categorization is a requirement, it should be done with care, and it should not be used to limit the child.

The Classroom Teacher and the IEP

When a student is evaluated as needing special educational services, an individualized education program (IEP) must be written. All individualized education programs must provide a statement of the child's current level of educational achievement, annual goals, short-term objectives, specific services required for the child to be educated, dates when the services will begin, and methods for evaluating the effectiveness of the planned services (Mandell & Gold, 1984). These are minimum standards, and other state and local standards may be added. Figure 13.3 shows an IEP.

Some misunderstanding exists about what the IEP really is. It is *not* a contract, and federal law is quite specific that it is no guarantee that the objectives will be met. It is, rather, a good-faith educational plan (Gearheart et al., 1988). According to law, the child's teacher must be present at the IEP meeting, although which teacher—the regular classroom teacher or the special education teacher—is not stated. It is the duty of the special education teacher to make certain that the procedure matches federal and state law. However, the classroom teacher may attend IEP meetings and conferences, since the success or failure of the educational program rests with the classroom teacher. Unfortunately, many elementary schoolteachers are not very involved in the process. A student in secondary school may have many teachers, making direct involvement on the part of all teachers concerned even more difficult. However, some participation on the part of the regular classroom teacher is desirable, and consultation and communication between the regular classroom teacher and the special education coordinator is necessary if the child is to be best served.

Mainstreaming: Problems and Potential

The most controversial part of Public Law 94–142 involves the practice of **mainstreaming.** Actually, main-

mainstreaming The term used to describe the process by which exceptional children are integrated into classes with "normal" peers.

streaming is not really part of the law at all. The law mandates that a child be placed in the least restrictive environment, but it does not require that all children be mainstreamed. Still, for many children, the law has meant integration into regular classrooms. In fact, about two thirds of all children with disabilities receive at least part of their education in regular classrooms. About one quarter are educated in separate classrooms within a regular school; a bit more than one in twenty of the most severe disabilities are educated in special schools; and about one percent are educated at home or in hospitals (Heward & Orlansky, 1988).

The great majority of disabled students are integrated into the regular classroom environment.

School District

Name and Number: Summit

School Building: Mead Elementary

Name of Student: Stuart Williams

Date of Birth: 9-20-76   **Age:** 12   **Grade:** 6

Hours per Week in Regular Classroom: 32

Summary of Present Levels of Student Performance:
WRAT (Aug. 1981)

Reading	3.6
Spelling	3.8
Mathematics	5.8

Program Goals	Special Education and/or Support Services	Professional Person(s)	Hours Weekly	Methods and Materials	Objective Evaluation Criteria
Reading					
■ Will increase reading comprehension skills. ■ Will increase knowledge of CVCV patterns and digraphs.	resource room	Mr. Davis	4	Adapted material from SRA reading series.	Adapted test material from reading text (90% accuracy).
Spelling					
■ Will increase spelling skills emphasizing the use of plurals, prefixes, and suffixes.	resource room	Mr. Davis	4	Teacher-made multi-sensory material.	Weekly teacher-made test (100% accuracy).
Science					
■ Will be able to understand concept of classification and will be able to conduct an experiment.	resource help to the regular classroom	Mr. Davis Mrs. Johnson	3	Adapted science material. Use of peer tutor	Unit test to be given orally (80% accuracy). Successfully complete an experiment (100% accuracy).

Description of Placement Recommendations
Placement in resource room for one period a day, four days a week.

Starting Date: September 5, 1989

Ending Date: June, 1990

Review Date: June, 1990

Date of Placement Committee Meeting: 9-1-89

Placement Committee Members Present:

Figure 13.3 Sample Individualized Education Program
Notice that the IEP is very specific and lists the goals, services to be rendered, and methods and materials to be used.

Adapted from *Understanding Exceptional People* by C. J. Mandell and E. Fiscus, pp. 84–85. Copyright © 1981 by West Publishing Company. All rights reserved.

Position	Signature
Mr. Davis (resource teacher)	_____
Ms. Fine (school psychologist)	_____
Ms. Johnson (regular teacher)	_____
Mr. & Ms. S. Williams (parents)	_____
Ms. Reynos (principal)	_____

Name of Student: Stuart Williams

Resource Teacher: Mr. Davis

Date: From Sept. 5 to Sept. 8

Program Goals	Instructional Objectives and Techniques	Criteria for Evaluation	Reinforcement
Will increase reading comprehension skills	After reading a short story, will identify the main character(s) and the main idea	Teacher-made questions (100% accuracy)	Earn two minutes of free time to be taken at end of hour in the resource room
	When reading a short story will identify the sequence of events	Teacher-made material (80% accuracy)	Same as above
	Will answer multiple-choice question on the literal interpretation of a short story	Teacher-made questions (100% accuracy)	Same as above

Weekly program changes (outline any changes made in weekly instruction): _____

_____

_____

_____

Figure 13.3 Continued

True or False By law, every disabled child must be mainstreamed—that is, placed in a class with non-disabled students.

The thinking behind such integration is obvious. First, many people were dissatisfied with the practice of placing disabled children into special classes. The thinking behind segregation was that students needed to be protected from repeated failure, that they would be shunned by their nondisabled peers, and that they needed a slower, more direct type of instruction not available in the regular classroom.

A number of arguments are made, however, against separation and in favor of mainstreaming. Most studies do not find that students achieve more in segregated settings (Hallahan & Kauffman, 1988). In addition, separation itself can stigmatize students and tracks them on the bottom. The isolation deprives them of contact with brighter students (Leinhardt & Pallay, 1982). If we want the disabled child to grow up and take his or her place in normal society and if we wish the nondisabled to respect the rights of their disabled peers to live in mainstream society, it makes sense to encourage the two groups to associate with one another as they grow up. Both the disabled and the nondisabled benefit from being exposed to and interacting with one another. The disabled child learns to live in the nondisabled world and gains the social skills necessary for independent living. The nondisabled child becomes more accepting of and less prejudiced toward the disabled. A strong case, then, can be made for mainstreaming.

Mainstreaming has brought problems, however. Teachers sometimes walk into classrooms to find they have disabled children to teach but little or no training or information about how to meet the special needs of these children. Little, if any, time is included in the day to work with experts in special education. Nor is the exceptional child given much preparation for entering the mainstream (Tolkoff, 1981). There is also some doubt about the reason some children are mainstreamed. Recent studies have demonstrated that educating students all day in the regular classroom is much less expensive than educating students in a resource room setting and costs less than half of what it would cost to place students in special classes (Viadero, 1988b). There is now some concern that students who should not be in regular classes will be placed in them and that some additional services, such as counseling and access to social workers, will be reduced. This may not be a violation of the law, but it would reduce the out-of-classroom services available to the students (Flax, 1988).

It is difficult to evaluate mainstreaming for many reasons. Some districts are more careful about mainstreaming than others. Some provide better support services. The question of which exceptionalities do better in which environment is an important question whose answer is still unclear. It may turn out that it is not the setting itself that makes as much difference as the type of teaching to which the student is exposed (Hallahan & Kauffman, 1988). Disabled children do best when they are taught in reasonably small classes that allow regular monitoring of their progress, when mastery learning systems are used, and when learning proceeds in small steps at a brisk pace. They also

do well when cognitive activities are stressed, when substantial practice is given, when frequent questioning and correction are planned, and when a formal management system is used that allows for better organization (Rosenshine, 1983; Leinhardt & Pallay, 1982). Successful programs also have goals and objectives that are clearly specified.

Mainstreaming, however, was also touted as a way of socially integrating students into the mainstream. In this area, more needs to be done, because the evidence is not very encouraging. Mainstreaming has apparently not led to reduced prejudice or increased acceptance on the part of the nondisabled (Gresham, 1982). In preschool programs, the evidence for improved social integration between disabled and nondisabled youngsters is more encouraging (Esposito & Reid, 1986). In other words, despite being part of the regular class, exceptional children have not been effectively integrated into the social framework of the classroom.

Does this mean that mainstreaming or the concept of the least restrictive environment has failed? No. All it means is that we cannot merely place disabled students into regular classrooms and expect events to take their course. Proximity only gives us an opportunity to help; it does not insure a better outcome. Strategies aimed at enhancing cooperation between the disabled and nondisabled are required. In addition, exceptional children must be taught appropriate social skills, including conversation and listening skills, so that they can handle social situations (Wanat, 1983). Perhaps all children could use a dose of such training, but it is vital to the success of the exceptional child who may be negotiating a new situation at an initial disadvantage. The most successful mainstreaming programs have (1) developed specific criteria indicating who should and should not be mainstreamed and to what extent, (2) prepared disabled students and their nondisabled peers, (3) promoted communication among educators, and (4) continually evaluated the progress of exceptional children and provided teacher in-service training to enable teachers to deal better with the challenge of serving students with exceptional needs (Salend, 1984).

When most people think of a child with exceptional needs, the child who is blind, deaf, or orthopedically handicapped comes to mind. However, the percentage of students who suffer from these disabilities is small. The two most common types of exceptionalities

Communication between the special educator and the regular classroom teacher is an important key to the successful education of the disabled student.

found in regular classes are the learning-disabled and speech- and language-impaired, who account for 43.6 percent and 25.8 percent of all disabled children. Of these, 77 percent with learning disabilities and 93 percent with speech or language impairments spend most of their day in regular classrooms (Heward & Orlansky, 1988).

THE CHILD WITH LEARNING DISABILITIES

No matter how hard Carla tries, she can't seem to learn to read. She often mispronounces words, cannot differentiate sounds, and lags behind in most subjects. As her attempts meet with failure, Carla feels very discouraged and stops trying. School is a painful experience, and Carla considers herself a disappointment to her family.

Richard has had little success in learning to read. Now, at the end of second grade, he has been sent for testing by the school psychologist. She noted that there is a great discrepancy between what Richard's intelligence says he should be doing and his actual achievement.

Carla and Richard have a learning disability. There have always been children who, despite their best efforts, simply could not achieve in schools. Today, we are beginning to understand the strange malady called learning disabilities.

One of the greatest frustrations is attempting to define a learning disability. Many definitions compete with one another, and numerous labels have been used. For instance, children who show problems in school achievements—most often associated with lack of progress in reading—have been designated perceptually handicapped, having a minimal brain dysfunction, or being dyslexic, or they have been put into at least thirty-eight other categories (Cruickshank & Paul, 1980).

Today the term **learning disabilities** refers to a group of disorders marked by significant difficulties in acquiring and using listening, speaking, reading, writing, or reasoning skills or mathematics. These disorders are intrinsic to the child and are presumed to be the result of central nervous system dysfunction (Hammill et al., 1981). In other words, children with learning disabilities do not achieve up to their age and ability in some basic skill. This problem is not the result of sensory handicaps such as blindness, mental retardation, or emotional disturbances or due to environmental, cultural, or economic disabilities (*Federal Register*, 1977). When diagnosing learning disabilities, three factors stand out: (1) there are academic problems, (2) there is a discrepancy between ability and performance, and (3) these problems are not the result of the exclusions noted previously (Mercer et al., 1985).

The learning-disabled child experiences great difficulties in learning to read and developing other academic skills. In addition, children with learning disabilities often experience social problems. They may be rejected because of the way they interact with others (Vaughn, 1985). Learning-disabled children often do not interpret verbal communications properly and often respond in ways that may not be appropriate or sensitive. Their parents rate them significantly lower

learning disabilities   A group of disorders marked by significant difficulties in acquiring and using listening, speaking, reading, writing, reasoning skills, or mathematics.

in social competence and social involvement and claim that they display more behavior problems than do the parents of non-learning disabled children (McConaughty & Ritter, 1985). These children are keenly aware of their deficits (Cohen, 1983).

Learning disabilities is a global term, and there are so many learning disabilities that it is hard to list them all. Learning-disabled children are a heterogeneous group, and no one individual has all the symptoms that might be listed under the heading of learning disabilities. Individuals who have a learning disability might have visual, tactual, or movement and coordination problems. For example, they may have difficulty perceiving the letters and discriminating a *P* from a *B*, or they may not perceive the position of the stimuli correctly, reversing letters or words and reading saw for was. These problems are common in young children, but they persist in the learning disabled.

Another problem involves attentional problems and hyperactivity. Learning-disabled children may have difficulty focusing their attention on the task or selectively attending to relevant aspects, be impulsive, and have difficulty maintaining attention (Keller & Hallahan, 1987). The relationship between hyperactivity, learning disabilities, and attentional problems is complex. Almost all children who are diagnosed hyperactive have attentional problems, although many, but certainly not all, children with attentional problems show hyperactivity. In one study of 500 learning-disabled children, about one quarter were hyperkinetic (Klasen, 1972), so most learning-disabled children are not hyperactive.

True or False Most learning-disabled students show hyperactivity.

Learning-disabled children also can show cognitive disabilities involving disorders of memory and thinking. They do not use memory strategies such as rehearsal when appropriate, and they show poor organization skills. They also have metacognitive problems; that is, they have difficulty monitoring their knowledge and knowing what they do or do not know. This is often shown on tests, as they are less likely to select and utilize appropriate strategies, often interpret test questions incorrectly, and are more likely to be influenced by misleading distractors on test questions (Scruggs et al., 1985). Such problems in attention, memory, visual perception, perceptual motor skills, and language are commonly called **developmental learning disabilities** because they are devia-

developmental learning disabilities Deviations from the normal development of psychological or linguistic functions.

tions from the normal development of psychological or linguistic functions. They are often, but not always, associated with problems in academic achievement.

Learning-disabled students also have academic disabilities that take the form of an inability to read, difficulty in expressing themselves, problems in written expression, poor vocabulary, and difficulties in mathematics.

Obviously, with this number of possible problems, the classroom situation can get confusing, which is why teachers and special educators must ascertain the exact nature of the student's problem. The diagnosis of learning disabilities with no other explanation is hardly helpful to the teacher.

▶▶▶ **CONNECTIONS**

What Regular Classroom Teachers Can Do to Help the Learning-Disabled Child

To effectively teach a child with a learning disability, the regular classroom teacher must be acquainted with the child's specific strengths and weaknesses. The nature of the child's specific strengths and weaknesses determines the most effective way to present the material (Moskowitz, 1988). For example, the teacher must help students who have organizational deficits to organize their work, perhaps by providing them with a sequential list of things they have to do, giving them clues to identify which is the most important work, periodically checking their progress on long-term assignments, and even teaching them to organize their notebooks. If a child has an auditory processing deficit, the teacher should avoid giving verbal directions and show the child what to do, provide outlines, and ask the student to repeat the question before answering it. If the child has a visual or visual motor deficit, the teacher may have the child use a tape recorder, reinforce visual directions with verbal ones, and use an index card for keeping the child's place. If the child has a language impairment, it may be necessary to explain idioms and vocabulary before beginning a chapter and have the student repeat directions in his or her own words. The classroom teacher can find ways to present the material that allows this student to learn. In addition, the following general strategies are useful.

1. **Use a multimedia approach when teaching concepts.** Learning-disabled students may do better if they can use their strengths rather than tax their weaknesses. This is well in line with our new understanding of learning styles. Using tapes, films, supplementary readings, and the like instead of lectures may be required. When a teacher does lecture, it may be best to hand out an outline of the lecture. Such a procedure is described at the end of the chapter.

2. **Give students practice using many different formats.** The learning-disabled student benefits when given practice in different formats, such as take-home projects, group assignments, and worksheets (Ludlow, 1982).

3. **Offer different evaluation methods when required.** It is useless to give learning-disabled students a written test that they cannot read and to infer from that examination that they do not know their science or social studies. Oral examinations, projects, and numerous other types of graded assignments can be used.

4. **Try to avoid distractions.** Many learning-disabled children are easily distracted, and minimizing distractions by having them sit farther from the windows or directly in front of you may be advisable.

5. **Avoid criticizing learning-disabled students.** These students should be praised when they perform adequately or show initiative. Unfortunately, they are used to criticism and may give up easily. Bringing attention to their strengths can encourage them to work harder. Contingency reinforcement and token reinforcement are especially useful.

6. **Peer tutoring helps.** The research on peer tutoring shows that it can be of help in academic areas, although its effects on social areas are still subject to question (Keller & Hallahan, 1987). If a teacher elects to use peer tutoring, the tutoring must be highly structured and the required responses rather simple. Tutors must be trained for their role and monitored, both of which take time.

7. **Cooperative learning strategies can be useful.** These strategies can help, especially in the social areas where learning-disabled students may not be well accepted.

8. **Analyze material whenever possible.** When material is presented too fast, a learning-disabled student may simply give up. If an assignment requires ten steps, a learning-disabled student may have difficulty with only one or two steps yet may not be able to do the assignment. Breaking assignments down into easy-to-understand steps makes it easier for the learning-disabled student. For example, consider the assignment to draw a map of a particular country. The first step may be to have the student go to the library and find an atlas. The student may then be told to find the page with the map on it, trace the map, find the country's capital next to the star, and find the country's principal mountains by their color. Each step is outlined.

9. **Encourage learning-disabled students to express their thoughts.** Many learning-disabled students have problems with word ordering, word endings, word meanings, and language rules and can benefit from a rich language environment. This involves creating opportunities for learning-disabled students to talk about things that are of interest to them (Dudley-Marling & Searle, 1988).

10. **Closely monitor student progress.** This is certainly a reasonable suggestion for all students, but it is of utmost importance for the learning-disabled. One study found that even after being identified and receiving special services, six and seven-year-old learning-disabled children fell progressively farther behind their classmates in reading comprehension over the three years that they were studied (McKinney & Feagans, 1984). If a student is not progressing adequately, it may be necessary to change strategies.

11. **Help students develop metacognitive abilities.** Many learning-disabled students have difficulty with the metacognitive aspects of reading. Such techniques as reciprocal teaching and teaching the student self-questioning methods can help (Keller & Hallahan, 1987).

12. **Use direct instruction, with considerable opportunities for practice.** Research suggests that direct instruction along with drill and practice activities that provide immediate feedback and correction is the most effective method of teaching new concepts to learning-disabled students (Lawrence, 1988). Seatwork, workbook assignments, and other types of independent work should be assigned after the student understands the concept and will get at least 80 percent of the material in the practice exercises correct (Lawrence, 1988).

HYPERACTIVITY

If you spend a few minutes with a hyperactive child, you begin to appreciate the patience and skill required for dealing with such children. **Hyperactive** children are impulsive, easily distracted, and inattentive and show a great deal of inappropriate behavior (Ross & Ross, 1976). They have difficulty in school, and their relationships with their teachers are often strained. They are considered aggressive and annoying and are not accepted by their peers. Their parents find them less compliant and less responsive to their questions, and parents report many more conduct problems than they do for their nonhyperactive children (Tarver-Behring et al., 1985).

Three basic approaches are being used to treat hyperactivity. Hyperactive children are often treated with stimulant medications to reduce the symptoms of the disorder. Under such medication, these children become calmer and more attentive (Forness & Kavale, 1988). Some people have criticized the use of these drugs because the drugs treat only the symptoms, not the underlying cause, and may produce unpleasant side effects. FInding the correct dosage for a particular child is often a problem, too (Varley & Trupin, 1983).

No one claims that drug therapy will improve intelligence, or even schoolwork, but the medication may reduce the symptoms so that the child can learn. An analysis of 135 studies of stimulant use with hyperactive youngsters concluded that stimulants are effective (Kavale, 1982). This does not mean that drug therapy is always the treatment of choice. The very idea of a child's taking medication over a period of years should make us cautious. Some authorities claim that such treatment should be used only as a last resort, and then always in combination with another type of treatment. In any event, because medication only reduces the symptoms of hyperactivity, other techniques must be used to compensate for the child's academic and social problems. Often, teachers will be asked to monitor the behavior of students who are taking medication for both improvements and side effects. A child taking medication who looks and acts lethargic should be reported at once.

True or False Hyperactivity can be cured through correct use of medication.

One popular nondrug treatment is the **Feingold diet,** named after the physician who developed it, Dr.

hyperactivity A term used to describe the behavior of children who are impulsive, overly active, easily distracted, and inattentive.

Feingold diet A diet developed by Dr. Benjamin Feingold for the treatment of hyperactivity, consisting mainly of the elimination of preservatives and artificial colors and flavors.

Benjamin Feingold. Feingold noted that hyperactivity was related to the consumption of food additives such as preservatives and artificial colors and flavors. Even some natural chemicals, such as salicylates, might be implicated, and Feingold suggested that children might be genetically predisposed to react to these chemicals. He claimed that if hyperactive children were put on a diet free of these compounds, a significant number would improve (Johnson, 1981; Feingold, 1975).

Although some clinical support for the Feingold diet has been found (Holborow et al., 1981), controlled studies have been difficult to conduct, and each has been criticized on methodological grounds. Jean Johnson (1981) suggests that a scarcely significant relationship exists between diet and hyperactivity, especially among young children, and that the success rate with the diet is lower than claimed. Others argue that the diet is generally ineffective or note that it is successful in only a small number of cases (Kavale & Forness, 1983; Mattes, 1983), but some authorities argue that this negative assessment is premature and may be inaccurate (Rimland, 1983). More research is needed in this area. At this point, it is reasonable to conclude that the diet may be effective for some children but not for as many as was first thought.

Elementary schoolteachers can become involved in diet treatment in three ways. One is monitoring the diet's effectiveness. The second is making certain that the diet is not broken by the school. For example, suppose a school party is being planned. The child on any special diet may not be able to eat particular foods brought by other children. It is a good idea to check with parents about food allergies anyway. However, during such parties, it is especially easy for children to go off their diet. A good policy for children on any type of special diet is to encourage their parents to send substitutes for the forbidden foods so that the children will not feel left out of the party. Third, teachers can become a party to the diet; that is, they can be given some responsibility to ensure that the student stays on the diet. Teachers are not law enforcement agents and cannot and should not be responsible for a child's staying on a diet. As teachers, we can watch to the best of our ability and encourage a child to stay on a diet, but we cannot stop a child from taking a potato chip or a cookie. Teachers should make their limitations clear to parents who ask the impossible of teachers.

The third approach to treating hyperactivity (which may be used in combination with either of the first two) involves manipulating the environment and its reinforcements. For example, providing structure and solid routines and using positive reinforcement are helpful (Walden & Thompson, 1981). Some claim that behavior intervention is superior to medication (Gadow, 1983). Chapters 5 and 10 and have discussed some of the behavioral and cognitive behavioral techniques—including contingency reinforcement, token reinforcement and self-statements—that may be helpful in this regard.

⋙ CONNECTIONS

The Regular Classroom Teacher and the Hyperactive Child

Hyperactive children can be a problem in the classroom in two ways. First, their behavior may interfere with the learning of others. Second, their lack of attention and inability to stay on a task inhibit their own learning. In addition to working with the special educator to devise behavioral and cognitive behavioral methods to reduce the inappropriate behavior and increase time on a task, using the following suggestions may help.

1. **Reduce distractions as much as possible.** Place the student away from windows and doors if possible (Moskowitz, 1988).
2. **Limit the amount and type of materials at the student's desk.** This can be accomplished by using a storage and checkout procedure controlled by the teacher (Gearheart et al., 1988).
3. **Use cues to gain students' attention.** To improve attention, gives students a cue to alert them that something important is coming, such as saying "Listen" or "Ready" (Lewis & Doorlag, 1987).
4. **Make certain that students are attentive when giving directions.** Ask the hyperactive student to

repeat the directions back and establish eye contact whenever possible (Moskowitz, 1988).
5. **Make certain that your attention or reinforcement is contingent on attending behavior.** Give the student attention and positive reinforcement for attending.
6. **Use physical proximity when possible.** Being close to the student can allow the teacher to react appropriately to the hyperactive student's behavior while continuing the lesson.
7. **Avoid dwelling on the students' problems, especially their need for movement.** These movements may include getting out of their seat, chewing a pencil, or doodling (Moskowitz, 1988). Of course, if a student's behavior is bothering others, the teacher must attend to it. However, the behavior may not cause any further problems, in which case teachers should not become over-involved.

There is no single answer for the difficulties displayed by the hyperactive child. Such a child requires structure, understanding, and consistency to improve.

COMMUNICATION DISABILITIES

Dean is quiet and shy in class. When he does speak he stutters, and it takes him quite a while to express himself. Sam also has a problem. His language is immature, and his grammar and vocabulary are well below what would be expected of him.

Communication disabilities can be divided into two categories. **Speech disorders** involve problems in the physical reproduction of speech. They include articulation disorders where students mispronounce words. Some students make omissions, such as saying sow instead of slow. Or, they make substitutions, such as saying tar instead of car. Other forms of articulation disorders are distortions, such as an initial lisping sound and additions that involve adding an irrelevant sound like washish the doggog instead of wash the dog (Mandell & Fiscus, 1981). Voice disorders involve difficulties in voice quality. The student with a

speech disorders Problems in the physical reproduction of speech.

hoarse or a very squeaky voice may have a voice disorder. The third category of speech disorders is dysfluencies, which include stuttering and stammering.

The second class of communication disabilities is **language disabilities,** which involve problems with the proper use of words, poor grammar, and delayed language. Speech and language disorders are the second most common exceptionality. Since almost all students with these disorders are mainstreamed, certainly the classroom teacher can expect to find these students in his or her classroom. Such students do not usually require much content change in what is being taught. Most of these students will be seen by specialists in the areas of speech and language. The main job of the regular teacher is to follow the directions of the speech and language therapist concerning the child's need to practice the skills taught by the specialist.

Teachers may refer children for a speech or language problem if they believe that the child's communication patterns are not age appropriate. For example, dysfluencies are common in preschoolers but should become less so in early elementary school. If the pattern continues, it should be reported. Voice disorders are rather obvious and should be reported if the quality of the speaker's voice is poor. A child whose language is inappropriate and immature for his or her age should also be referred for evaluation. However, teachers should understand that accents and dialects are not considered disorders.

Many children with speech problems find it embarrassing to talk. Since in the past these children may have been ridiculed, they begin to withdraw. As children age, they become very aware of their dysfluencies; many stutterers become proficient at synonyms so they can use words that they can pronounce. Providing an accepting atmosphere for these students in which they can be involved in class discussions and question-and-answer sessions is important.

⟫⟫ CONNECTIONS

The Classroom Teacher and the Child with a Communication Problem

Children with communication impairments will spend almost all their schoolday in the regular classroom. Some general suggestions for working with children with a communication problem follow.

1. **Listen to students with communication impairments.** Both teachers and students should listen to the child even if the child's speech problem is obvious or it takes longer for the child to get the statement out. The child's statements should not be repeated unless absolutely necessary and, if necessary, should be paraphrased by saying, "So you are saying. . . ."

2. **Do not criticize speech errors.** You may, however, demonstrate the correct speech. For example, if a student says, "A rabbit is an *aminal,*" the teacher may say, "That's right, a rabbit is an animal." Do not draw attention to the child's problem.

3. **Seat speech-impaired students with other students and encourage interaction.** Since these children are often reluctant to communicate, it is appropriate to place them in the midst of the class. It is common for some teachers to have students with exceptional needs sit near them for extra support and help. With these children, it is better to have them sit where they are assured an opportunity to interact.

4. **Encourage the student who has a language disorder to ask about words he or she does not understand.** This can be done by asking the student to find three words he or she does not understand and discussing their meaning.

5. **Provide opportunities for verbal practice.** All students need such opportunities, but the speech- and language-impaired need more of them. However, such opportunities must take place in an atmosphere of acceptance.

Communication-impaired students are likely to be frustrated at their inability to communicate well. Understanding and building a strong relationship with these children are necessary preconditions if the students are to participate in class discussions.

True or False   Children with speech problems should be seated as close to the teacher as possible so the teacher can monitor the student's speech on an ongoing basis.

---

language disabilities   Problems with the proper use of words, poor grammar, or delayed language.

THE BEHAVIORALLY DISORDERED STUDENT

Learning-disabled and communication-impaired children are the two most common expectionalities found in the schools. However, if we consider teachers' estimates, the most common exceptionality would be the behaviorally disordered child. About two percent to three percent of the children in elementary school have persistent behavioral difficulties that require attention (Cullinan & Epstein, 1986). In fact, teachers are likely to prefer that the behaviorally disordered and the mentally retarded—more than any other exceptionality—be placed in separate classrooms (Johnson, 1987).

Public Law 94–142 specifically uses the word *serious* to describe behavior disorders. The category covers children who have one or more of the following characteristics that exist over a long period of time and to a marked degree and that adversely affect these children's ability to learn (*Federal Register,* 1977).

> A. An inability to learn which cannot be explained by intellectual, sensory and health factors.
> B. An inability to build or maintain satisfactory interpersonal relationships with peers and teachers.
> C. Inappropriate types of behavior or feelings under normal circumstances.
> D. A general pervasive mood of unhappiness or depression; or
> E. A tendency to develop physical symptoms or fears associated with personal or school problems.

Behaviorally disordered children may be aggressive, show disruptive or destructive behavior, be discourteous, and throw temper tantrums. However, these students may also be overly anxious, depressed, or withdrawn. It is the aggressive, acting-out student who is most likely to be identified as behaviorally disturbed, because his or her behavior cannot easily be ignored and the pattern of behavior forces itself on the teacher's attention. These students often do poorly in their schoolwork. In determining whether a student is behaviorally disordered, three questions need to be asked (Nelson, 1985).

1. Does the behavior deviate significantly from what should be expected for a child of that age?
2. How frequent and intense is the behavior?
3. How long has the behavior been manifested?

As a rule, before a student is considered behaviorally disordered, the teacher should try everything reasonable to modify the student's behavior (Mandell & Fiscus, 1981).

There are many ways to categorize these students, but for the classroom teacher, the child who acts out, the withdrawn child, and the anxious child are three types that are seen most often.

The Child Who Acts Out

The child who acts out is disruptive, discourteous, aggressive, and destructive; talks back; moves around the room "looking for trouble"; curses; shouts out; and performs other behaviors that make it difficult, if not impossible, for learning to occur. This student's behavior is a definite problem in the classroom. Sometimes the behaviors are related to a desire to belong to a group that reinforces them. This student's behavior when actual standards and laws are violated, the children who manifest the behaviors may be called socially maladjusted (Cullinan & Epstein, 1986). Children in this group are specifically eliminated from consideration as emotionally or behaviorally disturbed, although it is hard to find socially maladjusted children who do not show at least one of the five criteria noted previously.

Children who are aggressive are easy to identify and receive an enormous amount of criticism and rejection. They may be attracted to others who act like them, since they are rejected by many of their peers. These children must be told exactly what types of behavior will and will not be tolerated, and the classroom must be structured so that their behavior can be monitored continuously. A favorite strategy is to place these students near the teacher.

True or False Children who act aggressively are not very popular with their peers.

Trying to build a supportive relationship by speaking with these students when they have not been disruptive can help. You might want to converse with students on a topic of interest to them, such as music or sports. Also, since most of the interactions that students have had with teachers have been negative, it is important to emphasize the positive things that they have done. These students rarely see their progress, and showing them how they have improved is appropriate. Since young students may not be able to wait for teacher assistance, it has been suggested that signs be made and placed on their pencils that say "don't forget me," which may help cut down on these problems, especially when the student is frustrated (Gearheart et al., 1988).

Some of the more common problems arise during transitions, and well-organized teachers may find they have fewer problems. However, the problems of tardiness, verbal outbursts, and aggressiveness may best be handled by behavioral and cognitive behavioral means. Such techniques as behavior contracts and time-out described in Chapters 5 and 10 offer hope. It is also necessary to arrange for communication between the responsible special educator and the parent to constantly monitor the behavior of these students.

The Withdrawn or Depressed Student

Children who are withdrawn or depressed do not stand out. They may go unnoticed because they do not disturb the class. Their work may be acceptable, though they never volunteer and may even refuse to answer questions in class. They may show symptoms of depression and have poor interpersonal relationships. These children need to form a close, trusting relationship with an adult and to develop social skills. A trusting teacher may rehearse an answer with a child and then, when appropriate, call on that child. Such children require patience and should be brought along slowly. Many such children are afraid of rejection and failure and may need to practice how to converse with others. The social environment of the school, with its competition for attention, may be overwhelming for them. Making friends in the context of an activity in which a child excels may be best. A child in the band may feel more confident in that environment and find it easier to strike up a conversation and make friends there.

A child who shows such symptoms as a loss of interest in activities, expressions of worthlessness or guilt, unhappiness, loss of energy, and even expression of suicidal thoughts requires immediate attention. All suicidal expressions should be immediately

While the student who acts out is often the prototype of the behaviorally disordered student, pupils who are withdrawn also require attention.

reported to the appropriate supervisor (refer to Chapter 7 for signs of potential suicide). The teacher can help the student who shows depression first by building a relationship with the child. Again, social skills may be the key, since poor social skills can maintain depression in students (Epstein & Cullinan, 1986). Depressed students may not try to interact very much, and if they are rebuffed, they may say to themselves, "You see, it doesn't work. I can't make friends." Obviously, the depression could be the result of home difficulties, such as the death of someone or a divorce, and communication with the parents may be necessary. Teachers may also reinforce positive behaviors, and attention should be paid to students for positive interactions. Some cognitive techniques, such as positive self-statements, can also help (Bauer, 1987).

The Anxious Child

Anxious children certainly need help, too. Often, these children have not lived up to expectations or are afraid of failing. They show a number of nervous habits and react to pressure in a self-defeating manner. They may also show physical symptoms when

Children who are overly anxious may be afraid of failing or not living up to standards. They may react to pressure in a self-defeating manner.

under pressure. For such children, reducing the pressure they feel and working with their parents can be helpful. These children can be helped by a number of behavioral approaches that can be used by the school psychologist and guidance counselor. For example, in systematic desensitization, the student is exposed in small, gradual steps to the feared stimulus while in a relaxed state. Modeling procedures consist of an individual, such as a teacher, engaging in the behavior that produces anxiety in the student and showing how he or she deals with it. For example, a teacher may handle a spider or react to making a mistake on the blackboard in a calm manner. A number of self-control methods that might involve becoming aware of negative thinking styles, learning and using a number of specific self-statements or strategies, and learning specific adaptive and behavioral skills may help (Morris & Kratochwill, 1987). The teacher may be asked by the counselor to remind students to follow these procedures.

MENTAL RETARDATION

Years ago, children who were mildly mentally retarded were educated in special classes using special curricula. Today, the situation has changed, and many mentally retarded students are being mainstreamed, not just in music, art, and physical education but also in science, social studies, and reading. Some of the increase in the number of students reported as learning-disabled may be an attempt not to designate students as mildly retarded. There may be some stigma to being learning-disabled, but there is much more of a stigma to being called retarded. In the future, more mentally retarded students will be placed in regular classrooms because of concerns about incorrect diagnoses, the funds required to keep students in special classrooms, and the lack of evidence that special classrooms are better for these students.

To be considered **mentally retarded,** three criteria must be met. First, the individual must show an intelligence score of below 70 on an individualized intelli-

mental retardation   A condition marked by subnormal intellectual functioning and adjustment difficulties that occur before a person is 18 years of age.

gence test given in the child's primary language. Second, the retardation must occur before the age of 18. Third, a substantial failure in adjustment must be present (President's Commission on Mental Retardation, 1977). Some explanation here is necessary. Intelligence testing is not an exact science, and a child's intelligence score can change over time. Since significant gains in intelligence have been noted after periods of intensive instruction, borderline children should be labeled with care. In addition, some authorities argue that even our best intelligence tests are culturally biased against minority children. Thus, defining anyone as mentally retarded simply on the basis of intelligence is dangerous. The requirement that there be some adjustment problem is based on more subjective evaluations. Although some objective tests measure adjustment problems, they are of questionable validity (Brown, 1983). Even so, this criterion is important because adjustment problems relate to the individual's performance in the areas of social responsibility and self-sufficiency (Grossman, 1973). A child who shows a lack of reasoning or an inability to communicate with others certainly has an adjustment problem.

True or False Subnormal intellectual ability is the sole criterion for being labeled mentally retarded.

Years ago, the mentally retarded were classified into the categories of idiot, imbecile, and moron, which have rather obvious negative connotations. Then the terms educable, trainable, and custodial were introduced, and they are still in use. The problem here is the implication that children who are trainable cannot be educated. Today, many authorities use the terms mild, moderate, severe, and profound to indicate levels of retardation. Even so, you may find the older titles—educable, trainable, and custodial—still being used. About 85 percent of the mentally retarded are in what was called the educable category, about 12 percent are deemed trainable, and three percent are categorized as custodial. The great majority of those diagnosed as mentally retarded are found in the upper levels, near normal intelligence.

Most mildly retarded individuals do not look any different from the general population, although both their gross motor skills, such as jumping, and their fine motor skills, such as those involved in finger dexterity, often lag behind normal children (Watson, 1977). These children have difficulty with abstractions and show slower cognitive development (Kirk &

Gallagher, 1989). Most mildly retarded children are diagnosed in school when it becomes more obvious that they perform on a lower academic level. They perform poorly both on verbal and nonverbal intelligence tests, have poorer memories, and have difficulty with concepts and generalizations. Their attention span is short, and they have difficulty with transfer. Many also suffer from adaptive problems, and mentally retarded children often have a low self-concept and low frustration tolerance. These children may withdraw and become passive-resistant, refusing to participate, or become destructive, possibly because they are always the people who can't do something or who always fail.

Despite these problems, if the mentally retarded receive a good education and proper social and vocational training, many mildly retarded people can learn to lead independent lives (see Table 13.3). Vocational training is important in secondary school. The mildly retarded can successfully work in unskilled or semi-skilled jobs, and research shows them to be effective workers (Brickley & Campbell, 1981).

Regular teachers will see only the mildly mentally retarded in their classrooms, as more seriously retarded children are not usually mainstreamed. The teacher may become concerned, since these students learn at a slower rate, and their capacity, especially when dealing with more difficult concepts, is limited. Some experts flatly state that the educable mentally retarded child cannot reach the same level of achievement as the nonretarded, noting that they can be expected to achieve at approximately three-fourths the rate of the nonretarded (Watson, 1977). Placing a limit is poor practice, however, since individual differences should be taken into account. The mildly retarded can be expected to learn basic academic skills.

The regular classroom teacher and the special educator dealing with the educable mentally retarded must realize their tendency to treat mentally retarded students as younger than they are because their academic skills are limited. This is a concern throughout these students' school years but becomes more of a problem as the children become older. A twelve-year-old mentally retarded student may not be reading well and may have many academic difficulties but is still twelve years old with the developmental interests of a twelve-year-old. Whatever curricula modifications that must be made should be appropriate to the student's mental abilities and developmental age. Asking a twelve-year-old to read a story that is simplified for the

Table 13.3   Educational Achievement Among the Mentally Retarded
The mentally retarded are frequently able to surprise people with what they can achieve if given the best educational and familial environments possible.

Degree of Mental Retardation	Potential for Educational Achievement	Potential for Adult Functioning
Mildly retarded: IQ approximately 51–65	"Educable"; capable of third- to sixth-grade educational achievement; able to read and write and use basic mathematics.	Able to be independent personally and socially; able to be self-supporting; frequently lose identification as retarded and blend into "normal" population.
Moderately retarded: IQ approximately 36–50	"Trainable"; capable of kindergarten through third-grade achievement; typically not able to read and write.	Able to be employed in unskilled occupations if supervision available; typically incapable of independent living or marriage.
Severely retarded: IQ approximately 21–35	Able to acquire some self-care skills; able to talk and express self; unable to acquire any academic skills.	Need permanent care from family or society; some are capable of performing simple chores under total supervision.
Profoundly retarded: IQ approximately 20 or lower	Unable to speak; some are capable of self-ambulation, but many remain bedridden throughout their lives.	Incapable of any self-maintenance; require permanent nursing care.

From *Special Children: An Integrative Approach* by Bernard G. Suran and Joseph V. Rizzo. Copyright © 1983, 1979 by Scott, Foresman, and Company. Reprinted by permission.

student is certainly appropriate, but that story must also be age appropriate and deal with areas of interest to the student.

In addition, motivation is a major problem. This child has learned to fail. When given a new task, he or she may desperately try to avoid failure, not to achieve success (Watson, 1977). The child does not trust his or her own skills and looks to others to imitate. Since there is a lack of confidence, showing the child that he or she has made progress is especially important.

►►► CONNECTIONS

How Classroom Teachers Can Help the Mentally Retarded

The special educator can help the regular classroom teacher adapt materials for the use of the mentally retarded. The following suggestions may also be helpful.

1. **Use individualized instruction materials.** This includes programmed workbooks and readers with simple vocabularies. Remember that subject matter must be geared to the child's interests.

2. **Use individual work centers when appropriate.** Sometimes special space in the classroom is established for various materials, and students proceed from one area to another to do their mathematics, science, or reading. This method is useful for students of all levels, because each child can work at his or her own level and speed. Such learning centers foster self-reliance and initiative (Watson, 1977).

3. **Watch closely for student rejection.** Mentally retarded students are not as often rejected for their slow acquisition of academic subjects as they are for their inability to behave in an age-appropriate manner. They may need help to develop social skills, and special care must be taken to integrate the child socially into the class.

4. **The material taught should be concrete, not abstract, and must be presented in a detailed manner so that no gaps are left.** Programmed materials that break subjects down and present them in small bits of information are useful.

5. **Frequent rewards may be required.** The very slow student is easily frustrated and used to failure. Reinforcement can be of enormous help.

6. **Watch for transfer difficulties.** A mentally retarded child might learn that three plus three is six yet not understand that three toys and three toys equal six toys. Teachers must include as many examples as possible and activities that encourage low-road transfer (refer to Chapter 4).

7. **Give the child a chance for verbal expression.** Mentally retarded children should be required to answer appropriate questions in class and encouraged to verbalize their interests and needs.

8. **Be aware of their special abilities.** Even though these children may be slow, they may have areas of considerable ability. Be on the lookout for these areas and then use them to introduce new material.

9. **Frequent review is necessary.** These students require review that should also include examples showing simple application.

10. **Simplify directions.** Make certain directions are simplified and understood before beginning a task.

11. **Use peer tutoring.** Peer tutors may be helpful, especially with exercises that provide practice or drill. However, as noted previously, tutors need training.

THE VISUALLY IMPAIRED

The visually handicapped category comprises legally blind and partially sighted children. The definition of blindness and visual impairment is based on visual acuity—the ability to see an object well at prescribed distances—and/or disturbances in an individual's field of vision. Almost everyone is familiar with the Snellen Chart. A person stands at a distance of 20 feet and is asked to read the letters on the chart. The letters get smaller and smaller with each line. Average vision is considered 20/20, meaning that the person can see at 20 feet what most people can see at that distance. To be considered **legally blind,** a person would have to have 20/200 vision in the better

legal blindness   A person with a visual acuity of 20/200 in the better eye with correction or with peripheral vision that covers less than 20 degrees of the field of vision.

eye, even with correction. In other words, a legally blind person would see at 20 feet what most people see at 200 feet. The vision of the partially sighted falls between 20/70 and 20/200 in the better eye, with correction.

An individual may, however, have 20/20 eyesight and still be legally blind. Some people have such poor peripheral vision that it is as if they are seeing through a keyhole. If a child's entire field of vision is less than 20 degrees, the child is also considered legally blind (Ashcroft et al., 1980). Most blind people have at least some sight and can see something. This residual vision is of great importance today, for the trend is to teach the partially sighted and legally blind to use what they can see to the utmost. The problem with these definitions is that they may not be as educationally valid as we might like. For instance, near point vision—the ability to see very close, as would be required in reading—is required to be measured in only a few states (Lewis & Doorlag, 1987).

True or False   The majority of the legally blind have some remaining vision.

Visual impairment is not a common childhood disability, and most teachers will meet few of these students. It is more a condition of the elderly than of children. In addition, many children have visual problems that can be corrected to an extent to which special education is not required.

One would think that a relationship exists between the degree of visual impairment and the child's educational handicap—the worse the vision, the lower the child's academic achievement. But this is not necessarily the case with the visually impaired. Remember that the vast majority of visually impaired children have some sight. According to Barraga (1976), some children use their residual sight better than others, and one cannot determine what aid a visually impaired child requires just by considering his or her visual acuity.

Blind children have difficulty both in mobility and in orientation. Getting around the classroom is a simple matter for most students, but not for the blind. This is true for all novel environments. In addition, since people obtain most of their information from their sense of vision, blind children will not have the same experiences as their sighted peers. Blind children may also lose orientation easily. If a sighted student wants to take something from a cubbyhole, it is a simple task. However, a blind student who is disoriented could be an inch away and might not be able to negotiate the situation.

The extent to which blind children have social difficulties is controversial and depends to some extent upon the nature and breadth of their social experiences. Some people are uncertain about how to treat a blind person, and a number of blind people have told me that people talk louder to them than to sighted people. Some blind children are sheltered by their parents and are not permitted to interact with other youngsters, reducing their social experiences. Whatever social problems that blind children have are probably not inevitable (Jan et al., 1977).

The blind require mobility training and help in becoming comfortable in the classroom. In addition, alternative testing procedures are a necessity, since these students may not be able to read print. The need for educational intervention depends upon the individual needs of the child. For some visually impaired, a magnifying glass or some technological aid may be sufficient. For others, audio tapes and large-type books and readers may be needed. The visually impaired need to be taught typing skills at a very early age, as early as the third grade. The teacher must find out to what extent these students can deal with printed material.

Teaching the visually impaired does not usually require much of a modification in content. The larger problem is working out the logistics surrounding how the material can be presented to the student. If the blind student requires tapes, someone must read into a tape recorder. If a visually impaired student requires large type, the books need to be located. Some distinctly visual skills, such as map reading or reading graphs, may be inappropriate for the blind, but they are exceptions to the rule. Teachers of the visually impaired must be certain to present the material as much as possible using the senses of hearing and touch.

⟩⟩⟩ CONNECTIONS

Helping the Visually Impaired Student to Achieve

The classroom teacher should be alert to signs that a child may have a visual problem. The National Society to Prevent Blindness (1977) suggests that students who rub their eyes continually; have difficulty reading or doing close classwork; blink more than usual; squint or frown; shut or cover one eye; appear cross-eyed; show red, encrusted, or swollen eyes; or complain of itching, burning, the inability to see well, or blurred or double vision should be referred immediately for a visual examination.

Generally, children who are visually impaired can participate in all class discussions and can do almost all class assignments. Substitute assignments are necessary only when the original assignment entails such reliance on visual abilities that no auditory translation is possible. For example, a student who cannot see may be told what is in a painting but cannot evaluate the artistic style. Such cases are rare. The following suggestions can help these students to achieve.

1. **Find out as much about the child's functioning as possible.** The teacher must know whether the student must use a magnifying device, a tape recorder, or large-type books. If the student requires more time to read material, this must be planned.

2. **Help the visually impaired travel from one classroom to another.** Some sort of buddy system often works. This system, often used with students using crutches, allows other students to help find the proper rooms and seats. It may also open up a possibility for new friendships.

3. **Allow blind and partially sighted students to become oriented and to explore.** This requires eliminating obstacles, informing the student of environmental changes, and physically showing the child any changes in room arrangement.

4. **Watch for glare.** High-gloss surfaces or light coming at an uncomfortable angle and reflecting off surfaces can be a major problem.

5. **Inform the special educator of your academic plans.** If large-type or braille material is available, the special educator may need time to obtain them.

6. **Make certain visually disabled children have access to a typewriter.** Typing is a necessity for visually disabled children, who should be encouraged to type their assignments.

7. **When writing on the blackboard, verbally explain what it is that you are writing.** A visually impaired student may not be able to read what is written on the blackboard and may not always ask for verbal explanation. Therefore, the teacher must explain it without being specifically asked to do so.

8. **Do not raise your voice when talking to a blind student.** Also look at the student as you would any other child. Gain the student's attention by calling him or her by name.

9. **The visually handicapped can participate in almost every classroom activity.** Call on this student just as you would any other student.

10. **Gain parental help when assigning material to read.** If large-type books or tapes are not available, the parents may need to read the assignment to the child.

Despite the fact that people normally take in so much of their information by visual means, most classrooms are auditory experiences, and with the proper adaptations, there is little reason that the visually impaired cannot succeed in a regular classroom.

THE HEARING IMPAIRED

Put your hands over your ears tightly and ask a friend to talk to you in a moderately low voice. Now try reading your friend's lips. Your friend should speak in a normal manner. After a couple of minutes, repeat what you think was said.

If you do this exercise, you may begin to appreciate what it is like to be hearing impaired. Reading lips is not easy, and although you may improve with practice, even experienced lip readers can understand only about 50 percent of what they see. Because sounds in English are sometimes very similar to each other in physical production (viewed from the outside), it is estimated that a deaf listener can perceive only 30 percent to 40 percent of the sounds spoken by a speaker (Gallaudet College, 1975). The hearing-impaired person obtains some additional meaning from gestures and contextual cues.

True or False Students who lip-read can understand only about half of what is said.

In many ways, a hearing impairment is more of a liability than a visual impairment, since it often leads to speech and language difficulties. To learn to communicate using speech, children need to listen to and become actively involved in conversation. Children who cannot hear human speech do not receive this stimulation. They cannot hear themselves talk, and the natural process by which speech is developed does not occur.

Most deaf people use sign language to communicate with the outside world. This is very limiting, however, since relatively few hearing people understand sign language. The hearing impaired spend a large part of their day interacting with people who do not know sign language and do not have much experience interacting with them.

Hearing impairment is normally looked at in terms of time of onset, type of loss, and severity. The onset can be at the prelingual or postlingual stage. The distinction is crucial. Children who lose their hearing at age seven or eight still have had the opportunity to develop reasonably mature speech patterns, but a child who is born deaf (congenitally deaf) or becomes deaf from an accident or illness at a very early age does not have these language experiences and has a more difficult time developing speech.

Hearing losses are also classified as to type. Hearing problems that are due to mechanical problems in the ear, called **conductive hearing losses,** can often be helped by a hearing aid. **Sensorineural hearing losses** involve nerve damage, and hearing aids are relatively ineffective in reducing these hearing problems. Table 13.4 shows the effects of hearing impairment on a child's abilities and the educational programming most often used. As with visual impairment, a hearing-impaired child must learn to use any residual ability to the utmost.

The deaf and severely hard of hearing show such great delays in language acquisition that they are readily identified, but many children suffering from less severe hearing deficits compensate for their problem. They may be labeled very slow or even mentally retarded and then later discovered to suffer from a hearing disability (Mollick & Etra, 1981). The lack of attention to what is said and the processing of partial information lead one to suspect mental retardation. One child's parents were not aware of the child's auditory problem until her mother noticed that she always switched the telephone from her right ear to her left even though she was right-handed. These children often receive negative feedback for their inattention and delayed development. In some cases, hearing loss is never discovered.

conductive hearing losses   Hearing losses caused by mechanical problems in conducting vibrations within the ear.

sensorineural hearing losses   Hearing problems caused by nerve damage.

Table 13.4 Hearing Loss: Effects of Degree and Type

Hearing loss may affect speech and the ability to communicate.

Average Hearing Loss (500–2000 Hz)	Probable Causes	Ability to Hear Speech Without a Hearing Aid	Extent of Communicative Handicap	Auditory Rehabilitative Considerations
0–20 dB *Normal Range*	May have slight, fluctuating conductive loss. Child with central auditory disorder will show normal hearing.	No difficulty in any conversational setting. Child with central auditory disorder will seem to hear but not understand.	None, except for child with central auditory disorder or with speech/language disorders from other causes.	Probably needs no rehabilitative treatment. Child with central auditory disorder will need intensive therapy.
20–40 dB *Mild Loss*	Most likely conductive from otitis media. Sensorineural loss may result from mild illness or disease.	Hears in most settings, misses soft or whispered speech, will hear vowels but may miss unvoiced consonants, says "huh?", wants TV turned up loud.	Mild handicap, may have speech disorder or mild language delay, may omit final and unvoiced consonants.	If conductive and medically or surgically treatable, needs favorable classroom seating. Child with sensorineural problem may need hearing aid, speech reading, and auditory training.
40–60 dB *Moderate Loss*	Conductive from otitis media or middle ear problem; maximum conductive loss is 60 dB. Sensorineural loss from ear disease or illness.	Hearing is a problem in most conversational settings and groups or when there is background noise; hears louder voiced consonants, may need TV and radio turned up loud, and may have difficulty on the phone.	Possible disorder in auditory learning, mild to moderate language delay; articulation problems with final and unvoiced consonants; may not pay attention.	All of the above may apply. May also need special class for the hearing impaired or special tutoring.
60–80 dB *Severe Loss*	Probably sensorineural, although mixed is also possible. Rubella, meningitis, Rh, heredity are possible causes.	Misses all but very loud speech, unable to function in conversation without help, can't use telephone.	Probably severe language and speech disorder; learning disorder; may have no intelligible speech.	All of the above may apply. May need placement in school for the deaf.
80 dB or more *Profound Loss*	Sensorineural, or mixed with large sensorineural component. Rubella, meningitis, Rh, heredity, ear disease, etc., are causes.	Unable to hear speech except loud shout, does not understand spoken language, can't hear TV or radio, can't use the telephone.	Severe speech and language deficit, probably no oral speech, learning disorder, "deaflike" speech and voice.	All of the above may apply. Will need placement in deaf-oral school or school for the deaf.

From *An Introduction to Special Education,* 2d ed., by William H. Berdine and A. Edward Blackhurst. Copyright © 1985 by William H. Berdine and A. Edward Blackhurst. Reprinted by permission of Scott, Foresman and Company.

Because deafness affects communication so greatly, one would expect deaf pupils to have difficulty in school and in social adjustment, and this is so. The deaf often suffer from language deficits (Green, 1981). Although they have normal abilities, their communication deficits cause them much difficulty in school. Those with milder disorders usually do better than those with more severe disorders, because they suffer a smaller language deficit (Davis et al., 1981). Deaf students' progress in reading lags as well.

A major question facing the education of the deaf involves what the phrase "least restrictive environment" really means. More than any other exceptional child, deaf students are socially isolated. The least restrictive environment has always been interpreted to be the regular classroom, but there is some doubt as to whether this is true for the deaf. Is it really the least restrictive environment if students cannot adequately communicate with others, have difficulty participating in extracurricular activities, and do not have their social needs met (Champie, 1986). It is possible that the regular classroom environment cannot be called least restrictive when little interaction between hearing and deaf children takes place and when what does occur requires the mediation of sign-language interpreters.

Another question surrounding the education of the deaf is how to teach language? One school of thought argues that the deaf need a language of their own to communicate with the outside world and that sign language is the most practical method. Others argue that sign language is reasonable when communicating with other deaf children but that the hearing world does not understand sign language. These authorities emphasize the oral method—teaching the deaf to speak. The third school, known as total communication, combines the two. Today, most deaf students are taught using the total communication method.

CONNECTIONS

Helping the Hearing Impaired in the Regular Classroom

As in the case of visual abilities, it is important to identify hearing problems early. Teachers should be especially aware of children who do not seem to pay attention when called on, frequently lose their place, turn their head to the source of a sound to get one ear closer to the sound, complain of discomfort in their ears, show delays in speech and language, turn the volume up on the television or radio, complain they cannot hear, or frequently ask the teacher to repeat things (Stephens et al., 1982). In fact, a hearing assessment should be made for children who are thought to be learning disabled, behaviorally disabled, or mentally retarded, since hearing loss may be the problem.

Classroom adaptations for the hearing impaired are numerous.

1. **If an interpreter is necessary, make certain you speak to the child, not to the interpreter.** Tell other students they should do the same.

2. **Introduce vocabulary and important terms ahead of time.** Write them on the blackboard or give the students an outline (Schultz & Turnbull, 1983).

3. **Do not talk to the blackboard.** If a hearing-impaired student is trying to lip-read, the results are disastrous. In addition, try to remain stationary and watch for glare in the room. Using an overhead projector instead of the blackboard increases the amount of time a teacher can spend looking at the students.

4. **Use visual aids.** Visual aids are very helpful and should be used as often as possible.

5. **Speak in a normal fashion.** Don't exaggerate lip movements, speech rate, or voice volume.

6. **Organize a system to help hearing-impaired students get classroom notes.** Hearing-impaired students cannot take notes as they watch your lips or look at an interpreter. Have another student take notes and photocopy them for the student.

7. **Seat deaf students between five and ten feet from the teacher.** This makes lip reading easier (Mandell & Fiscus, 1981).

8. **Encourage the child to ask for clarification whenever necessary.** Rephrase the material, especially if the child is trying to lip-read.

9. **Encourage the hearing-impaired child to express him or herself.** However, understand that the language deficit and hearing impairment will affect vocabulary and syntax.

10. **Watch for fatigue.** Deaf children have a tendency to become fatigued, since their concentration needs to be total. Brief rest periods may be required.

11. **Make sure a child's hearing aid is working.** Hearing aids should be checked periodically.

12. **Get the hearing-impaired person's attention before speaking.** Face the person and maintain eye contact. Stand close to the deaf person with no obstructions and stand in a well-lighted place. Background noise can be annoying, so try to limit it. In addition, do not shout, since this distorts sound, and use facial expressions and body language liberally.

13. **Involve the hearing-impaired person in group activities.** Deaf children tend to be quite isolated. Group work and cooperative learning strategies may help integrate these students into the mainstream.

CHILDREN WITH PHYSICAL AND HEALTH PROBLEMS

When asked to describe a handicapped child, many people picture a youngster in a wheelchair. Orthopedic disabilities can be the result of cerebral palsy, spina bifida, or an accident. Spina bifida is a congenital malformation of the spine that often allows a protrusion of the spinal cord into a sac at the base of the spine (Mandell & Fiscus, 1981). The disabilities vary greatly, ranging from minor motor loss to paralysis. Cerebral palsy is a disorder that results from brain damage. It can be caused by infection, trauma, or a lack of oxygen at birth. The damage shows itself in a number of possible symptoms, including motor problems, paralysis, lack of coordination, and poor speech. It may or may not result in losses in intelligence. The severity of the disorder differs widely. Some victims require braces, speak clearly, and are gifted; others must spend their days in wheelchairs and have severe intellectual and speech problems. The vast majority are somewhere in the middle. In addition, there is no relationship between the extent of physical impairment and intellectual performance, and some individuals with severe motor involvement are gifted (Lewis & Doorlag, 1987). The disorder does not get worse with time; that is, it is not progressive.

True or False   Cerebral palsy is caused by a virus that is transmitted in a way unknown to medical science at the present time.

The greatest problem the physically challenged (a term preferred over the word *handicapped*) face is

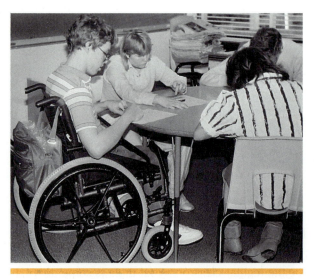

The most important thing a teacher can do for the student with an orthopedic disability is to remove architectural barriers.

their lack of mobility. The importance of removing architectural barriers is obvious. In addition, some children may shun people because of fear, lack of knowledge, or simply not knowing how to react.

The second category includes the relatively small number of children who have significant health problems, such as heart and respiratory problems or diabetes, that affect their schooling. The academic problems of these children are due to their frequent absences from school and fatigue. Their absences make educational continuity very difficult. Home tutoring may not be the answer, because some of these students are absent for a few days at a time, then return to school, then are absent a few more days. Some means to communicate with the parents about their work is absolutely necessary. This may be arranged through the guidance office in the secondary school. The fatigue factor makes it vital to place the more difficult academic subjects in the morning for these children.

There is no substitute for adequate information. If a student has diabetes or epilepsy, the teacher must be told what to expect and what the side effects are of any medication that the child may be taking. The teacher must know what restrictions the child has on his or her activities.

The Regular Classroom and the Physically Challenged

Generally, this group of disabled children requires no content modifications or changes in how material is presented in the classroom. Many will require modifications in physical education. However, if a child is in a wheelchair, some attention to the physical environment is in order. The aisles must be large enough, and all areas of the room should be accessible. Other necessary arrangements will depend upon the unique nature of the child's disability.

Since children with health impairments are so varied, generalizations are difficult, and what needs to be done depends upon the nature of the illness. Again, information is the key, and the special educator, parent, and child must be consulted. Any limitations, such as the need for more rest periods, must be planned into the day. If medication is to be taken, the side effects must be understood, and if certain emergencies are likely to occur, the teacher should ask how they are to be handled.

Physically challenged students can be integrated into the mainstream, but sometimes younger, non-disabled students experience some apprehension and avoid them. It may be necessary to give the class information about the problem, stressing that these students are no different except that they cannot walk or run or whatever. Sometimes films are available for this purpose, and some attention to social integration is necessary. Again, the buddy system and group or cooperative learning strategies may help.

THE GIFTED AND TALENTED

Until now we have looked at exceptionalities covered by PL94–142. However, there are other children whose exceptionalities are not considered disabilities and who are not protected by federal law. Some children are gifted and require changes in curricula to reach their potential.

At first glance, defining **giftedness** would seem to be an easy task. The gifted, most people think, are those who have a very high intelligence. Children who score considerably above average on intelligence tests are indeed gifted, but is that all there is to it? What of the child who is artistically gifted? What of the child who is very creative? What of the child who,

gifted students Students who have either demonstrated or seem to have potential for high capabilities in general intellectual ability, specific academic aptitude, creative or productive thinking, leadership ability, or the visual or performing arts.

because of his or her cultural background, does not score high on an intelligence test yet shows flashes of brilliance in the classroom?

Older definitions considered giftedness only in terms of intelligence, but newer definitions have greatly expanded the concept (Passow, 1981). After all, if giftedness is defined simply in terms of an intelligence score in the top 20 percent—a very liberal criterion—about 75 percent of those children who score very high on tests of creativity would not be identified (Torrance, 1962). The federal government defines a gifted child as any child who either has demonstrated or seems to have the potential for high capabilities in general intellectual ability, specific academic aptitude, creative or productive thinking, leadership ability, or the visual and performing arts (Gifted and Talented Children's Act of 1978). Thus, not only general intellectual abilities but also specific aptitude, creative thinking, leadership ability, and talent are considered in this definition (Torrance, 1980). Federal laws do not guarantee every gifted child the same rights as laws that mandate special education programs for these children and many districts have instituted such programs on their own. The basic assumption is that the unique skills of these children require special curricular alterations (Hershey, 1988).

Stereotypes of the gifted sometimes prevent society from meeting the special needs of such children (Treffinger, 1982). For example, many people believe that the gifted are socially backward, have little or no common sense, and look down on other people (Rickert, 1981). These stereotypes should be laid to rest. The gifted tend to be fast learners and interested in school but also to be well adjusted, energetic and physically healthy, intuitive, perceptive, a bit rebellious, and original (MacKinnon, 1978; Terman & Oden, 1959; Terman, 1925). The intellectually gifted show superior concentration skills and field independence, tend to be reflective, have an internal locus of control (i.e., they feel in control), are active in their

Gifted students also need special educational services. This gifted fourth-grader is solving a difficult problem in a workshop setting especially designed for gifted students.

tricts offer much in the area of leadership training. Many use group intelligence and achievement tests to identify the gifted, but this may penalize those who have abilities in a single area, who underachieve, or who are culturally disadvantaged or disabled. Other programs use individual intelligence tests or tests of creativity. Still others allow nominations by parents, teachers, peers, or the student him or herself for inclusion into the program. It is best to use multiple criteria and not rely solely on standardized tests.

Two general approaches are taken to the education of the gifted. **Acceleration** involves skipping a grade or a particular unit and placing the child in a more challenging situation. It may involve a student working at his or her own pace who may finish two years of work in one. Advanced placement and extra classes for extra credit are also classified under acceleration (Correll, 1978). **Enrichment** involves staying at the grade level but assigning work that goes beyond the usual. Children may either be kept in their normal classroom, be placed in a special room for a few hours a day, or even be placed in separate classrooms.

learning, and are persistent (Scott, 1988). The gifted usually have a positive self-concept (Maddux et al., 1982), and most have good interpersonal relationships (Austin & Draper, 1981).

True or False Students who are intellectually gifted tend to be well adjusted and have good interpersonal relationships.

Any pictures of the gifted, however, must be drawn with care. The gifted are not a homogeneous population (Juntune, 1982), and even though most seem well adjusted, others are not. Some overgeneralizations can be harmful. For example, although most gifted children are quick learners, we should not equate being smart with being fast (Sternberg, 1982). Very intelligent people may spend more time planning how they are going to solve a problem instead of merely jumping into a solution.

The identification of the gifted is a controversial process, and each school district or school has its own way of doing so. Although the federal definition involves five categories of giftedness, most districts' programs are meant for the intellectually gifted. Those who have talent in the visual or performing arts are identified by their teachers in these areas and then may be encouraged to develop their abilities. Few dis-

⟫ **CONNECTIONS**

The Classroom Teacher and the Gifted and Talented Student

The classroom teacher is more likely to be involved in enrichment than in acceleration, which is more likely to be a district policy or program. It is important to understand that enrichment does not just mean "more." The work must be qualitatively different. Assigning a gifted child five stories to read instead of three is not enrichment. Giving a gifted child twenty-five mathematics examples instead of the class's fifteen is not enrichment. Extra work may even be seen by the child as a type of punishment. Some areas of enrichment include presenting material with a higher degree of complexity, the introduction of content beyond the prescribed curriculum, student-selected projects, or field trips (Tuttle et al., 1988). Since most gifted children have the ability to work independently, enrichment within the regular classroom need not be excessively time consuming.

The following suggestions for working with the gifted may be helpful.

1. **Challenge students.** Gifted students may seem gifted only when they are challenged. In addition,

often a student will show his or her talents only when he or she is exposed to initial training in an area. Therefore, students should be exposed to many experiences and must be challenged so that they can show their talents.

2. **Recognize extra effort.** If teachers assign enriched assignments, students must be recognized for their effort in doing them.

3. **Encourage independent study.** Many gifted students are relatively quick, and if they finish their assignments, independent study and projects can keep them interested.

4. **Allow students to go beyond the regular work.** This is true for all students, but encouraging students to follow their interests is especially important for the gifted.

5. **Don't use grades and material rewards.** The classroom teacher should aim at encouraging student interest and using the student's intrinsic motivation.

6. **Be aware of your own attitudes towards the gifted.** Some teachers do not like to have their best students removed for gifted programs or hold negative stereotypes of the gifted. This may prevent the teacher from encouraging the gifted to achieve.

7. **Encourage questioning and reasoning.** Gifted students may question an assumption or seek clarification about your reasoning. This can lead to interesting discussions that can be a rewarding experience for all the students.

The Gifted Minority Student

People often believe in what Samuel Kirk and James Gallagher (1989) call the cannonball theory, which states that the gifted will eventually show themselves

---

acceleration A program in which a gifted student skips a grade or a particular unit or in which material is presented much more quickly than it would be for an average student.

enrichment An educational program in which a gifted student is given special, challenging work that goes beyond the usual.

---

and do well no matter what impediments are placed in their way. Just like a cannonball, the gifted cannot be stopped. However, this is simply not the case. There are gifted who are never identified, because they belong to a minority group or are disabled.

The gifted minority student may not be identified, especially if the same cutoff points are used in aptitude and achievement tests as are used with nonminority students. Many doubt the usefulness of these tests with minority students, claiming that their backgrounds make it more difficult to test them. The underrepresentation of minority students in programs for the gifted may also be due to the highly verbal nature of many criteria.

A number of approaches attempt to deal with these problems. First, it is important to be aware of the problem and actively search for gifted minority students who may not show their talents on tests (Wolf & Stephans, 1986). However, even with teacher nominations and increased awareness of the problem, a more objective system is required. One promising approach is to use an equalizing factor, such as the system of multicultural pluralistic assessment, called SOMPA, which makes allowances in intelligence scores by taking into consideration socioeconomic status. For example, a child in a low-income area with an intelligence score of 111 would have an estimated learning potential of 134 (Mercer & Lewis, 1981). This is a controversial procedure, and doubts have been voiced about its assumptions and validity. Still another promising approach identifies the top 15 percent to 24 percent of those who perform well on tests or in the regular classroom environment, and enrichment activities are scheduled for them (Reiss & Renzulli, 1982).

The problem of identification is also found with the gifted disabled student. For example, a learning-disabled student may be gifted and may not be identified as such (Gunderson et al., 1987). Some of these students are not even identified as learning disabled, because they compensate for their disability and are achieving normally. Some students are receiving special services that, while remediating the child's weaknesses, may overlook the child's strengths.

Women are also sometimes underrepresented among the gifted, especially in mathematics and science. This is particularly true in secondary schools. In elementary school, at least half the identified gifted are female, but in junior high school, less than a quarter are still identified as gifted (Noble, 1987). As noted in Chapter 8, some gifted females may experience social pressures to hide their abilities. It may be necessary to actively search for female students with high mathematics and science abilities and encourage them to continue their studies in these areas.

ADAPTING LESSONS TO ACCOMMODATE MAINSTREAMED STUDENTS

Teachers formulate their lesson plans to meet the needs of all the students in the classroom. For a number of reasons, the regular classroom teacher cannot and should not be expected to write and formulate different lesson plans for disabled students. First, it would be very time consuming, especially if a teacher finds two or three children in a class with different disabilities. Second, it is not necessary. The regular classroom teacher may need, however, to adapt his or her lessons to meet the needs of these students, and this can be accomplished with relative ease.

As discussed in Chapter 11, there are a number of methods that a teacher may use when teaching a particular unit. The teacher may use direct instruction, lecture, or adopt an inquiry method involving the joint search for the answers to particular questions. The teacher might also use a demonstration, engage in group work, or any number of approaches. Each may be adapted to the needs of the disabled student.

Perhaps the most popular methods of teaching are lecture and direct instruction. These may cause difficulty for students who have auditory processing problems, such as an inability to recall information. One possible and relatively easy way of helping these students is to use a multisensory approach, which might include distributing lecture outlines or even audiotaping lectures so that children can review materials with which they are having difficulty. Using an overhead projector for presenting the main ideas and using graphic materials and bulletin boards can also help.

The easiest method is simply to give the student a **slot outline**—an outline that provides spaces in which

children can take notes (see Figure 13.4) (Wood & Rosbe, 1985). Students can be trained to take notes using a slot outline by showing them what a possible completed outline looks like and comparing their notes to this completed form. After students become adept at a slot outline, a normal lecture outline might be sufficient.

MUSCLES

I. Definition: Muscles are _____ that move body parts.

II. Numbers: About ___ muscles in human body
About ___ % of male weight
About ___ % of female weight

III. Types: Voluntary ___ be controlled
ex. _____
_____ cannot be controlled
ex. _____

14:5 Three Kinds of Muscles

I. Smooth Muscles
A. Involuntary
B. Line walls of internal _____
C. Ex. _____

II. Striated Muscles
A. _____
B. Have bands called _____
C. Also called _____
D. Attached to bones by _____
E. Move bones and limbs by _____ and relaxing

III. Heart (_____) muscles
A. Involuntary
B. Has _____
C. Only in _____
D. Contracts and relaxes to _____
_____

Figure 13.4   Slot Outline
Teachers can help learning disabled students through the use of slot outlines which provide spaces for students to take notes.

From "Adapting the Classroom Lecture for the Mainstreamed Student in the Secondary School" by J. W. Wood and M. Rosbe. *The Clearing House*, 1985, 58, 354–358. Reprinted with permission of the Helen Dwight Reid Educational Foundation. Published by Heldref Publications, 4000 Albemarle St., N.W., Washington, D.C. 20016. Copyright © 1985.

slot outline   An outline that provides spaces in which students can take notes.

When asking a question, the teacher must be certain that the question matches the cognitive level of the student. The teacher should call on the student before asking the question, and depending upon the disability, pause longer for a response (Wood & Miederhoff, 1988). The demonstration mode involving showing, doing, and telling is especially useful for disabled students. Peer tutoring, using simulations and relevant games, and taking field trips in which specific questions are to be answered are appropriate. Teachers may find that using roleplaying, helping to prepare exhibits, and selecting activities in which students can succeed can be useful too. No matter which modes are used, the adaptations required do not have to be time consuming or difficult. However, if disabled students are to achieve, their lessons must be adapted to give them a chance to succeed.

ALTERNATIVE TESTING

One area of special adaptation for the student with special needs is alternative testing. Consider the plight of the blind student in school. This student cannot read the material, and if she is to be tested, someone must read it to her. It may not be possible to test her knowledge of graphs, except in the most general manner. The hyperactive child may not be able to sit still long enough to finish a unit test, and the child

Alternative testing procedures can be used to help students show their knowledge in a setting more conducive to success.

who cannot read but "knows his science" may also need **alternative testing**.

Alternative testing does not mean that a student is given easier tests. The student does not "get out of" doing anything. The testing simply shows that we recognize that the student's difficulties require us to change the way we test so that we may validly measure the student's knowledge. Two types of alternative testing techniques are commonly used. The first type involves modifications that alter the testing procedures but not the pupil skills being tested. For example, some children may require more time than we would normally give a class. Children with learning disabilities or who are hyperactive may need more time, and since most tests are power tests, not speed tests, this should not be much of a problem. Other students may require removal to another location for testing. Some students may not be able to use computer answer sheets and may require some other means of marking their answers.

True or False   Changing test conditions for a disabled student, such as giving a learning-disabled student more time to complete a classroom test, is an acceptable procedure.

The second type involves modifications to testing procedures so that the skills being tested are somewhat different from those intended when the test was prepared. For example, some students may require the use of a calculator, while others may not be able to complete particular questions because of the item format, such as dictation in some spelling tests (New York State Department of Education, 1982). Perhaps a visually impaired student needs someone to read the questions to him or her.

Alternative testing needs are listed on the IEP. If it is a severe problem, the teacher may be helped by a resource room volunteer. In one of the junior high schools in which I taught, the exams were proctored by a volunteer in the resource room who would do whatever was appropriate to allow the student a chance to show his or her knowledge. Alternative testing procedures need not take much teacher time

alternative testing   A special adaptation of the testing program for disabled students that involves modifications to the testing procedures themselves or to the skills that are being tested.

but may help exceptional children show their knowledge in an appropriate manner.

EQUALITY AND FAIRNESS

This chapter has dealt with the child with exceptional needs and what the classroom teacher can do to help the child achieve. Increasingly, it is the classroom teacher who will have the responsibility for educating these children. To do this, the teacher needs the active help, involvement, and encouragement of both the school administration and the special educator.

It is quite normal for teachers to have doubts about confronting children who present so many challenges, and some have doubted the wisdom of spending the necessary amount of time and resources for these children to succeed. However, we are driven to do so by the research that shows that most educationally handicapped children belong in regular classrooms for at least part of the day and by a basic humanity that says that even though these children may need more, they deserve a chance for success.

The question often comes down to determining what equal treatment really means. Does equal treatment mean spending the same amount of money and time on each child? Or does equal treatment mean spending the money and time that are necessary to meet the educational needs of all children? Indeed, parents face this problem when one of their children, for whatever reason, requires more of their time or resources. Most people would agree that equal treatment requires us to give children whatever is necessary to give them an opportunity to succeed. The classroom teacher can help accomplish this, and it is only fair to make the reasonable adaptations necessary to give children with exceptional needs an opportunity to succeed in school.

SUMMARY

1. A little more than 10 percent of all students are categorized as disabled. The overwhelming majority of such students have mild disabilities and spend at least part of their time in regular classrooms.
2. A disability is a total or partial loss of functioning. A handicap refers to the difficulty a disabled person has in adjusting to the environment. An ex-

ceptional child is one whose intellectual, physical, or emotional performance falls either much above or below that of his or her peers.
3. Public Law 94–142 requires school districts to provide an appropriate free education for every child. It also mandates nondiscriminatory testing and educational accountability through an individualized education program (IEP). Finally, it requires that children be placed in the least restrictive educational environment. Mainstreaming is the process by which disabled children are placed in the regular classroom.
4. Each school district has its own policies concerning referral. Some schools have pre-referral committees that try to help teachers deal with a child's specific needs before formal evaluation. There are positive and negative aspects to labeling.
5. The IEP is a good-faith educational plan, but it is no guarantee that its objectives will be reached. The IEP is written by the special education teacher, and the classroom teacher may or may not have much of a role in the process.
6. Research does not support the academic benefits of special classes for the mildly disabled. Research indicates that disabled students are not well integrated into the social fabric of the classroom, and more attention must be devoted to this goal.
7. The most common disabilities today are learning disabilities. Children with learning disabilities do not achieve up to their age and ability in a particular skill. The problem is not the result of sensory handicaps, mental retardation, or cultural or economic disadvantage. Some possible symptoms include perceptual problems, attention deficits and hyperactivity, cognitive disabilities in memory and organization, and metacognitive problems. These children also have difficulties in reading, writing, or expressing themselves. The approaches used to teach the learning-disabled student depend upon the child's specific strengths and weaknesses.
8. Hyperactive children are impulsive and easily distracted. They are treated by medication, changes in diet, and behavior modification.
9. Speech disorders involve problems in the physical production of speech sounds. They include articulation, voice, and fluency disorders. Language disabilities include problems in the proper use of words, poor grammar, and delayed language. It is

important to provide an atmosphere of acceptance where these children can practice their language skills without fear of being ridiculed.

10. Only students who show the most severe behavioral problems are categorized under the law as behaviorally disordered. Behavior modification and cognitive behavior techniques have shown promise in dealing with these children.

11. Most retarded individuals are mildly retarded. To be considered mentally retarded, the individual must show an intelligence score of below 70 on an individualized intelligence test given in the child's primary language, the retardation must occur before the age of 18, and a substantial failure in adjustment must be present. Mentally retarded children learn slowly and may become easily frustrated. Curricular modifications must take into account not only the abilities of the child but the child's age as well.

12. A child is legally blind if he or she has 20/200 vision in the better eye with correction or severely restricted peripheral vision. Mobility and orientation are the biggest problems for such a child. Children who are visually impaired require few modifications of curricular content, but some changes in the way in which the material is presented may be required.

13. Students who are deaf often have difficulty learning to talk. Most schools for the deaf teach both sign language and oral communication. Many deaf students require the services of an interpreter to communicate with the outside world. There is a major controversy concerning the meaning of the phrase least restrictive environment with the deaf, since they have such difficulty communicating with the hearing world.

14. Cerebral palsy is a disorder resulting from brain damage, usually at birth, causing motor problems, poor speech, and sometimes retardation. Other orthopedic disabilities can be caused by spina bifida or accidents. Eliminating architectural and environmental barriers is necessary if these children are to participate in school activities. Children with disabilities from diseases resulting in cardiac or respiratory problems often have difficulties in school because of excessive absence and fatigue.

15. The federal government defines a gifted child as any child who either has demonstrated or seems to have the potential for high capabilities in general intellectual ability, specific academic aptitude, creative or productive thinking, leadership ability or the visual and performing arts. The gifted are generally well adjusted. The two most common approaches to educating the gifted involve acceleration and enrichment. Educators have become increasingly alert to the problem of identifying gifted minority students, gifted disabled students, and especially in the areas of science and mathematics, gifted female students.

16. Relatively simple adaptations to each of the different methods of teaching can be made so that the disabled student can achieve in school.

17. Alternative testing may be required for those disabled students for whom the usual methods of testing are not valid.

ACTIVITIES AND EXERCISES

1. **Volunteer to Tutor a Special Education Student or Work in a Resource Room.** There is no substitute for actual experience, and the need for volunteers is great. If you can spend a few hours in a resource room, you will become acquainted with how it is run, what services are provided, and the strengths and weaknesses of the resource-room approach. Tutoring a student who has a disability can give you some valuable experience, and at the same time, you will be helping a student.

2. **What Services Are Available for the Exceptional Student in Your District?** Interview a special educator or school psychologist in your district and find out what services are available for the disabled student. Ask about the criteria used to mainstream students, the strengths and weaknesses of the program, and any new directions the program is taking.

3. **Visit a Classroom with Mainstreamed Students.** Obtain permission to observe a few classes in which disabled students are mainstreamed. As you observe each class, pay particular attention to any modifications or accommodations that are made for the children. If possible, discuss any modifications in presentation or curricula.

4. **How Do Teachers Feel About Mainstreaming?** Ask teachers in elementary, junior high, and high school about their attitudes towards mainstreaming versus special classes. What do they see as

the benefits and drawbacks of the practice? In addition, ask these teachers which types of disabled students are best mainstreamed and which, in general, more often belong in special classes.

5. **What Were Your Experiences in School?** Speak to college students or adults who are disabled and ask them about their experiences in school. Were they placed in special classes or mainstreamed? Were they accepted by their classmates? What were their greatest problems? It would be interesting to see if the experiences of the younger adults differ from those who were educated earlier.

6. **Social Integration of the Disabled into the Regular Classroom.** One of the arguments for mainstreaming is that disabled children and their nondisabled peers would both benefit from interacting with one another. Unfortunately, the evidence is not encouraging. Many disabled children are isolated in the classroom, and little interaction takes place between disabled and nondisabled children. It has been suggested that activities need to be designed that encourage interaction. If you were a teacher and one student in your class has a particular disability (choose any disability), design some activities that might integrate the student socially into the fabric of the class.

7. **Spend a Day in a Wheelchair.** You will become aware of the many architectural barriers that make full participation difficult for the orthopedically disabled. Some of these barriers are obvious, such as the lack of building ramps, elevators, or sidewalk ramps. Others are more subtle, such as classroom or store aisles that are not wide enough. Look around your school and see if any architectural barriers exist. Speak to a few orthopedically disabled people and ask them what particular architectural problems they find most offending and common.

8. **Interview with the Speech-Language Specialist.** Almost all speech- and language-impaired students are mainstreamed. Traditionally, the speech-language specialist has traveled from school to school within a district, taking the students in need of help out of class for remediation. Speak to one or two such teachers and ask them how the classroom teacher can help the communication impaired student. In addition, ask the specialist what the benefits and drawbacks are to working in a number of schools.

9. **The IEP.** The special educator is responsible for formulating the IEP. Ask a special educator how he or she devises an IEP and to what extent the regular classroom teacher is involved in the process. If possible, review a few such programs with the special education teacher.

10. **Parents of Exceptional Children and the School.** Interview some parents of disabled children about their perception of the process of referral, evaluation, and placement as well as the experiences of their children within the special education program. Ask them the following three questions. What problems do they see? What would they like to see changed? What is their relationship with the classroom teacher?

11. **A Deaf Educator Speaks.** The question of how deaf students should be educated is very controversial at the present time. Many communities have special schools for the deaf. Visit such a school and ask the educators both how the regular classroom teacher can help integrate the deaf child into the regular classroom and how the educator feels about mainstreaming.

12. **Identifying the Gifted.** Find out how the gifted are identified in your district or school. In addition, ask an administrator the following questions:
    1. What services are available for the gifted?
    2. Are there any special programs for identifying the gifted minority student?
    3. What are the goals of education for the gifted in the school?

13. **Attitudes Towards the Gifted.** There are many stereotypes of the gifted. Devise a questionnaire to measure the extent to which these stereotypes are believed. Some possible statements that you might include are as follows:
    1. The gifted are generally socially backward.
    2. Gifted students can be identified by intelligence testing alone.
    3. Gifted students tend to be frail and not athletic.
    4. Gifted students tend to be interested only in their schoolwork.
    5. Gifted students have poor self-concepts.
    6. People who are gifted consider themselves superior to everyone else.

Many other statements are possible. It is interesting to add in a few truthful statements, such as

"The gifted tend to be intuitive and perceptive." In addition, add some statements measuring people's attitudes towards educating the gifted. For example, "The gifted should be educated in separate classes." "The gifted should be pulled out of their regular classrooms once a week for enrichment." "The gifted should receive no extra services." Ask people if they strongly agree, mildly agree, are neutral, mildly disagree, or strongly disagree with these statements.

14. **Disabled People on Television.** For a few weeks, watch television with an eye towards the way people who have disabilities are treated. Keep a log of the characters and how they are portrayed. It is also interesting to see how the gifted are portrayed on television.

15. **Enrichment.** One of the strategies used to further the education of the gifted is enrichment. Choose a unit that you might teach and outline specific ways you would enrich the unit to meet the needs of a gifted student in your class.

16. **Preparing a Slot Outline.** The use of a slot outline is recommended for students who have a number of disabilities. Prepare a slot outline for a lesson you might be teaching in your subject matter.

SCENARIOS

Here are twelve scenarios. Try to apply the information you have learned in the chapter to each situation.

1. Lynnette is a fourth-grader. She has spent the past three years in a special school for children with physical disabilities. Lynnette suffers from cerebral palsy and must spend her days in a wheelchair. She can read and write and is now ready for mainstreaming. Her parents are a bit concerned, and Lynnette is nervous. It was really the parents' choice to mainstream the child. Lynnette has not been exposed to a complicated situation like this before, and her parents are not sure whether it was the right decision. Unfortunately, Lynnette could not attend her new class for the first two weeks of the fall semester. Now a decision must be made. Ms. Peña, her teacher, met her in the morning before school and introduced herself. The principal of the school asked Ms. Peña how she plans to introduce Lynnette to the class. Ms. Peña isn't sure. Should she explain Lynnette's condition to the class, since perhaps some students will think that what she has is catching and will avoid her? Should she do nothing and allow Lynnette to make her own way? (Why raise questions that may not be in the other students' minds?) If you were Lynnette's teacher, what would you do?

2. Barry has never been a problem in school, if you define problems in terms of overt behavior. On the contrary, he is a pleasant ten-year-old who always has a smile on his face. But Barry is bored in school. He daydreams constantly and finishes his work quickly but often in a sloppy manner. Yet he usually does well on tests and reads at a high level. His scores on intelligence tests show him to be intellectually gifted. Barry's report card is good but not great, and Barry is not achieving as much as his teacher thinks he should. Each time his teacher succeeds in motivating him, she is surprised by the boy's excellent analytical mind and ability to solve unusual problems. She suggests that Barry be put in a class for very bright children. This class meets three mornings a week, while the rest of the time is spent in the regular classroom. However, Barry's parents are not certain this is the right course of action. Although they know Barry is bright, his grades do not show it. They also believe that the same problems of boredom, disinterest, and daydreaming will haunt him in the gifted program. They also admit to some social concerns. Barry is not the most popular student in class, because he is not athletic. He has been taunted as "The Brain" in previous years' classes, which bothered him a lot. Barry's parents even caught him making mistakes on his homework, seemingly on purpose so as not to appear too smart. They are afraid that placing him in the class would accentuate the problem. If you were Barry's teacher, would you recommend such a placement alternative. If your answer is positive, how would you allay Barry's parents' fears? If your answer is no, state your reasons for opposing special placement.

3. Mr. Jacobsen is an eighth-grade teacher of social studies. He has been told that Jay is learning disabled and has difficulty reading. That is the only information he has received. He looks up Jay's grades from seventh grade and finds that they are

poor and just barely passing. When Mr. Jacobsen speaks to Jay, he finds the student courteous but rather quiet and a bit shy. He receives one-word answers. Mr. Jacobsen does not know where to begin. He knows that if he does not do anything Jay will repeat his performance of barely passing. What can Mr. Jacobsen do?

4. Eileen is a mentally retarded third-grader who has been placed in Mrs. Levy's class. The student is polite and cooperative but, as you would expect, rather slow. The real problem, though, is her frustration. She gets frustrated very easily and then either refuses to do the work, demands immediate attention, or just doodles. She has a poor self-concept as well. She has a couple of friends in the class who have tried to help her. Eileen's parents are concerned people who believe that Eileen belongs in a mainstreamed classroom. They are willing to help and look towards Mrs. Levy for guidance. If you were Mrs. Levy, how would you handle the situation?

5. Mike is a student in Mr. Linsky's second-grade class. He has a severe visual impairment and cannot read print. He is the first severely visually impaired student Mr. Linsky has had in his class, and Mr. Linsky is not certain what changes he should make. He is also concerned that the student will take so much of his time that he will not be fair to his twenty-seven other students, some of whom are slow and in need of one-to-one help. He asks you, his colleague, what he needs to do to meet the needs of this student? How would you answer him?

6. When Ms. O'Hara was told that she would have two deaf students in her classroom, she was truly looking forward to the challenge. An interpreter was supplied for her students, and she met with the interpreter and discussed the interpreting procedures. She realizes that she should talk to the students, not the interpreter, and can talk at her usual pace. Despite some reading comprehension problems, the students are doing nicely. However, they are completely isolated in the classroom, and after some investigation, Ms. O'Hara has discovered they do not participate in after-school clubs, teams, or any other activities. She would like to integrate them into the class but does not know how it can be done. How can Ms. O'Hara accomplish this?

7. When Mr. Mason was told that he was going to have Len in his sixth-grade class, he was so upset that he ran down to the principal's office to complain. Len is a behaviorally disordered child who acts out in class. He is discourteous, gets into arguments with other students, and generally makes it difficult to teach. Although Mr. Mason has not had Len previously in his class, the boy's reputation precedes him. Len's home life is terrible, with an alcoholic father and a mother who can't handle the problems and works full-time at a job she hates. His siblings have been in trouble with the law, and he spends most of his time being cared for by an elderly grandmother who is not up to it. The principal told Mr. Mason that the boy is receiving help from a social worker and that, although bothersome, the boy has never done anything so dangerous as to make him a safety problem in the classroom. He tells Mr. Mason to "make the best of it." With no other choice, Mr. Mason must find some way of dealing with Len. If he asked you to suggest an approach that will work, what would you tell him?

8. Nobody really notices Keith. After all, why should they notice a high school sophomore who never opens his mouth, is always alone, never speaks to anyone, and is generally considered odd by the other students? If called upon in class, Keith gives short answers in a low voice. He always completes his work, although at times he does not appear to be paying attention. He sits at the back of the classroom and causes no difficulty. Still, his teacher, Mr. Simone is concerned. He believes that Keith is becoming more and more unhappy and isolated and would like to help him. When Mr. Simone spoke to Keith, Keith simply said that he has no friends in the class and that he had problems, but he refused to go into any details. Mr. Simone has discovered that Keith has no friends in any of his other classes. In your opinion, should Mr. Simone refer the child for evaluation? In addition, how can Mr. Simone help Keith?

9. You are asked by your principal to prepare the school for the mainstreaming of some children who are visually impaired and orthopedically handicapped. The key word is accessibility. How would you proceed?

10. Sarah has a moderate speech impediment. She

is an eighth-grade student who stutters and has difficulty expressing herself. She will not raise her hand to participate in class but does all her work. She has a few friends in class, and her family is very supportive of her efforts to improve. She is receiving help from a qualified specialist. The problem is how to handle the question-and-answer sessions that her teacher, Mrs. Campello, always has in class. If her teacher calls on her, it takes her quite a while for her to answer the question, and during this time, tension increases in the classroom. Although the students do not laugh or taunt Sarah, she feels their discomfort. If Mrs. Campello does not call on Sarah, she is afraid that this may cause worse problems. What should Mrs. Campello do?

11. Geraldo suffers from a cardiac problem that keeps him out of school for days at a time. He may be in school for a few weeks, then be out of school for three or four days, come back for a day, and be out again. When he comes back to school, he is lost. He is a high school freshman who is falling behind. His parents are cooperative but do not know the work. For example, they can't help teach him algebra, because they don't remember it themselves. What can the school do to help Geraldo keep up with his work?

12. Miss Muñoz is a high school science teacher. She teaches a number of disabled students. One such student has a learning disability that makes it difficult for him to read the material quickly. Miss Muñoz allows this student more time on tests. Another learning-disabled student cannot write well enough to do an essay, so Miss Muñoz allows oral presentations. Miss Muñoz also permits two foreign-born students to use dictionaries during their science exams, with the promise that they will not look up their science vocabularies. A few of the teachers think that Miss Muñoz is wrong to allow these changes with both groups. They claim that she is giving these students an advantage over the "regular students." They ask you for your opinion. Should Miss Muñoz continue with these alternative testing procedures? If your answer is yes, why should she do so, and are there any limits to alternative testing? If your answer is no, explain your response and discuss if there are any instances in which you believe alternative testing should be used.

Measuring Outcome

14

Are These Statements True or False?

Turn the next page for the correct answers. Each statement is repeated following the paragraph in which the information can be found.

1. Most standardized tests compare the test taker's score to a score considered passing by experts in the field.
2. Standardized tests are more likely to be used as a measure of a school's effectiveness today than twenty years ago.
3. A student taking a particular standardized test in Boston, Massachusetts, will receive the same instructions and the same amount of time to complete it as a student taking the test in Little Rock, Arkansas.
4. A student who takes a standardized test of reading achievement on Tuesday and again on Wednesday should score exactly the same on both tests.
5. Teachers are proficient at predicting how their students will answer questions on standardized tests.
6. A child who scores in the 45th percentile has answered 45 percent of the questions correctly.
7. A third-grade student who scored a grade equivalent of 5.5 (fifth grade, fifth month) on a reading exam is ready for fifth-grade reading work.
8. The most commonly administered standardized tests are achievement tests.
9. As minimum competency tests are given year after year in a particular state, more and more students fail them.
10. Scores on intelligence tests are poor predictors of academic achievement.
11. Students can learn to improve their test-taking techniques, and this leads to some improvement in their test scores.
12. On multiple-choice tests, students are more likely to change their answers from wrong to right than from right to wrong.

Standardized Tests

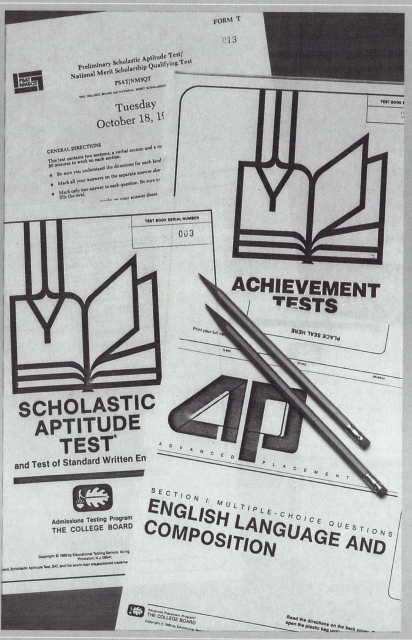

Answers to True-False Statements

1. *False* Correct Statement: Most standardized tests compare the test taker's score to those of other students who have taken the test at an earlier time.

2. *True*

3. *True*

4. *False* Correct Statement: Every test has some error, and some relatively small variation should be expected.

5. *True*

6. *False* Correct Statement: Percentile ranks are not percentages, and if a child scored in the 45th percentile, it means that the student scored equal to or better than 45 percent of the students in the group on which the test was normed.

7. *False* Correct Statement: All we can say is that this student is reading above grade level, not that the student is ready for fifth-grade work.

8. *True*

9. *False* Correct Statement: Fewer students fail minimum competency tests as the tests are given year after year in a particular state.

10. *False* Correct Statement: Scores on intelligence tests are good but not perfect predictors of academic achievement.

11. *True*

12. *True*

Ms. Garcia has just received the results of a standardized achievement test administered to her class. They contain grade equivalents and percentile rankings for her students. How should Mrs. Garcia use this information?

Mr. Davis knows that his high school students will have to take a minimum competency examination in order to obtain a high school diploma. Should this fact affect what he teaches and how long he spends on each topic?

Amalia is an eighth grade student who suffers from very intense test anxiety. According to her own reports, she freezes on tests and her memory of the studied material becomes a blur. What can her teachers do to help her?

TODAY'S TEST MANIA

More than 100 million standardized tests are administered each year to elementary and secondary students in the United States (Fiske, 1988). The popularity of these tests is increasing as federal, state, and local authorities seek an objective way to measure how effective schools are in educating their students. These test results are being used not only to determine whether a student should be promoted, receive a diploma, or be placed in a particular educational program but also as tools to evaluate curricula. The success or failure of a school district is often measured in terms of the reading and mathematics scores its pupils achieve on standardized tests.

This chapter looks at some of the benefits and drawbacks of using standardized tests. It also examines the unique qualities of standardized tests and then reviews four types of standardized tests that classroom teachers are most likely to encounter.

Before we begin, it is important to clear up one misconception. The terms *evaluation, testing,* and *measurement* are often used incorrectly. **Evaluation** is a systematic process of judging the quality, value, or worth of some performance or program (Brown, 1983). Evaluations are based upon many sources of information, only one of which is test data. **Measurement** involves the quantitative description of student behavior and is usually accomplished through testing

> **evaluation** A systematic process of judging the quality, value, or worth of some performance or program.
>
> **measurement** The quantitative description of student behavior, usually accomplished through testing.

(Gronlund, 1976). Tests are only one form of measurement; others include questionnaires and rating scales. While tests are fact oriented—that is, they measure a specific area objectively—evaluation contains a judgmental component and may deal with qualitative aspects of the situation (Houston et al., 1988). For example, a student might receive a 70 percent score on a test, measuring his or her knowledge of a particular area. However, the decision as to whether this translates into successful completion of the course involves evaluation. Evaluations can depend upon the teacher's estimate of the student's ability, the scores of other students, and standards established by the school district or state.

What Is a Standardized Test?

What makes a test qualify as a standardized test? All **standardized tests** are instruments that contain a specific set of items and give definite and standardized directions for administration and scoring (Reisman & Payne, 1987). They are commercially prepared by experts in the field of testing and allow the measurement of some sample of behavior under uniform procedures (Mehrens & Lehmann, 1987). For example, every student taking a particular standardized test will be given the same directions and the same amount of time to finish the test and will have their answers scored in the same manner. Most, but not all, of these tests have been administered to a norm group so that the test taker's score is compared to the performance of others.

WHAT DOES A 75 MEAN?

Consider a student who takes a spelling test and correctly spells fifteen of the twenty words on the test. She has spelled 75 percent (15/20) of the words correctly. What does this really mean? Is it better than most other students her age? Is it good enough for her to be considered knowledgeable in spelling? It certainly would matter whether it was an easy or a difficult test. It's conceivable that a student could score 50 percent on a hard test and know more spelling than a student who receives 80 percent on an easier test. The fact that the student achieved a 75 percent score tells us very little. We need a frame of reference

to interpret these scores, and two such frameworks are available.

Norm-Referenced Tests

Norm-referenced tests are those in which the score of the test taker is compared to the scores of other students who took the test when it was developed. The student's score is reported in terms of where the student stands in comparison with the nationally normed reference group. If a student scored in the 60th percentile in social studies, we could say that she scored equal to or better than 60 percent of the people in the norm group.

The overwhelming majority of standardized tests are norm-referenced. Notice that in norm-referenced tests (NRTs) we can easily rank students; that is, we can say that if Paul scored in the 85th percentile on a biology test and Edward scored in the 75th percentile, Paul knows more biology than Edward, assuming, of course, that the test truly measures what it is supposed to be measuring. NRTs do not tell us how much biology Paul or Edward knows, for they do not give an absolute score. They only compare the students' scores to those scores achieved by the standardized norm group. NRTs can provide information concerning student achievement levels and can serve as tools to help in the selection of students for particular programs. They are also useful in program evaluation (Shepard, 1979).

True or False Most standardized tests compare the test taker's score to a score considered passing by experts in the field.

Norm-referenced tests are very useful, but a number of objections and cautions surround their use. The first is that such a test's usefulness depends greatly on the characteristics of the group on which the test was standardized. For example, what if we

---

standardized tests Instruments that contain a specific set of items and give definite and standardized directions for administration and scoring.

norm-referenced tests Tests in which the score of the test taker is compared to the scores of other students who took the test when it was developed.

Millions of standardized tests are administered each year in schools.

compared the scores of a student from a very poor socioeconomic background to the national norm and found that the student had achieved the 55th percentile on mathematics skills? It is well-known that students from poverty-stricken backgrounds tend not to do as well as students from middle-class backgrounds. Now, what if we were told that compared to other students in this student's district or community the student would score in the 90th percentile? To whom should we compare the student's achievement—to the student's local peers or to a nationwide sample? Perhaps both should be used. The most pressing question here is whether the norm group bears a relationship to the group being tested. For example, there is some question as to the use of some standardized tests for children with exceptional needs, since not all tests provide information as to whether the norm group contained such children (Fuchs et al., 1987). Today, great care is taken in selecting and describing the norm group, yet obviously

each test is standardized on a different group of students, and the students to whom one's students are being compared make all the difference.

Another argument is that to be economically successful, test publishers have to sell a large number of tests and thus must publish national tests that people in a rural area of Nebraska as well as those in New York City can use. Yet the curricula in these areas may differ widely. It is impossible for such tests to reflect these different curricula emphases. There may, then, be a possible mismatch between what is taught and what is tested.

In addition, because most NRTs test rather broad skills and knowledge, they contain relatively few items that measure each skill or behavior. How many examples of addition of two numbers can there be in a general test of mathematics skills? If a student does not answer one or two questions correctly, we might assume he or she does not possess the skill. Yet this may not be true.

Another problem is the need for norm-referenced tests to contain items that result in response variance among students. If everyone in the norm group answered every question correctly, we would find it impossible to compare a test taker to the group. Therefore, test items that everyone answers correctly or incorrectly are not used in NRTs. However, these items may reflect the information and skills that teachers around the country think are most important and spend the most time on in their classrooms (Popham, 1978).

Other questions surround the possible cultural bias in these tests and the fact that the tests may enforce curricula conformity, since teachers would be asked to teach only those skills that would be measured on these national tests.

It would only be fair to indicate that those who support NRTs answer each and every charge. For example, the question of bias is answered by noting that if a group does not do well on a test, it may be not that the test is poor but rather that the group as a whole has not received the necessary education and experience in the area tested. Supporters of NRTs also note that curricula are more common around the country than their detractors think (Ebel, 1977). The elimination of items answered correctly by almost everyone is defended on many grounds, including the argument that these items may actually reflect common knowledge rather than academic learning (Ebel, 1978). The controversy surrounding the use of NRTs is ongoing, and no definite conclusion can be reached at this point. However, keeping in mind the controversies surrounding NRTs may help teachers understand the nature and problems involved in their use.

Criterion-Referenced Tests

The second method of interpreting test scores compares a student's achievement level against some standard of proficiency in the area of content. If the student's score equals or surpasses a particular criterion, the student is said to be proficient or to have mastered the skill. If not, more work is required. Suppose Glenn takes a test on the addition of two numbers and correctly answers 18 of 25 questions. If the criterion for success is 20 correct, Glenn lacks proficiency or mastery of the skill.

On a different level, **criterion-referenced tests** (CRTs) can tell teachers what students can and cannot do. A mathematics test report states the *kinds* of mathematics operations the student can do and their difficulty level. The interpretation of a CRT is not dependent upon some comparison with a norm group but rather is made in terms of the test's content meaning. When a teacher receives feedback about the class, the number and percentage mastering or not mastering a particular objective are noted, and the teacher can use this information to plan remediation. The skills that are measured are specific and detailed. For example, a language test may offer measurements of a child's specific skills in the areas of written composition, capitalization, punctuation, spelling, correct English usage, sentence structure, and proofreading (Houston et al., 1988). These areas can be broken down even further.

Such tests can be used to improve instruction, since the teacher now knows exactly what skills the student has and has not learned well. Since the criterion-referenced test specifically spells out what is being measured, there is less chance for misunderstandings as to the meaning of a particular subtest, and a substantial number of test items are devoted to each

measured category. CRTs do not need variation in scores, since we would ideally like each student to attain the criterion. Therefore, if an item is considered valid, it is maintained even if each student gets it right (Popham, 1978). To construct such a test, we must have a very well defined domain and be able to break up the domain into smaller units that reflect instructional objectives, such as multiplying three-digit numbers by two-digit numbers. CRTs are especially useful in testing basic skills (Anastasi, 1988).

CRTs have their limitations, however. They are useful in areas where the domain of knowledge is well established, but there is doubt as to their usefulness in measuring more advanced levels of knowledge typified by critical thinking (Anastasi, 1988). Many CRTs do not offer appropriate data on how they were formulated. In addition, the question of establishing ground rules for reporting that a student has mastered an objective remains unanswered. For example, why should the cutoff be nine correct answers out of eleven questions: why not eight? Last, the problem of educating to minimum levels is raised. If we are just interested in students being educated to reach a particular standard in specific and narrow areas, then CRTs are useful. However, CRTs measure only the extent to which students have minimal competency in such areas. Often we want students to go beyond these minimal standards.

CONTROVERSIES SURROUNDING THE USE OF STANDARDIZED TESTS

Both NRTs and CRTs, then, can be useful. Which should be used depends upon what the educator wants to know. If we want to know generally how a student stacks up against others, NRTs are most useful. If we want to know whether a student has mastered very specific content material, CRTs are better. However, the question of why we are testing at all must be answered. What benefits are there to testing students, and what drawbacks are inherent in such testing? The answers to these questions should determine the type and quantity of the testing to be performed in the schools.

The Uses of Standardized Tests

Standardized tests provide valuable information that aids educators in making decisions in the instructional,

criterion-referenced tests   Tests in which student scores are compared to a particular criterion or absolute standard.

guidance, and administrative areas. Under the instructional heading, tests can help evaluate learning outcomes, teaching, and curricula and diagnose learning problems. In the guidance area, certain standardized tests of occupational interest and aptitude are helpful. In the administrative area, some tests can serve as tools to help in the selection, classification, and placement of students (Mehrens & Lehmann, 1987). Some states have adopted elaborate testing programs to screen students for summer school remediation and grade retention (Gold, 1988).

Standardized tests give us an objective tool in comparing student achievement. Imagine that you want to determine whether students in your district are improving in some skill—perhaps reading. Since each teacher's tests are different and some are easier than others, it is difficult to determine how these students are really doing. It is also difficult to determine how your school district matches up against others, or whether some area of the curriculum is not being emphasized sufficiently. Standardized tests help keep everyone concerned fixed on the main targets of the learning process (Ebel, 1977).

Today, there is a great emphasis on educational accountability. The schools are under increasing scrutiny to demonstrate their effectiveness. But how can one compare and evaluate unless there is some measuring instrument that is given to students across the country in a uniform manner? Indeed, the use of tests for educational accountability and curricula reform is increasing rapidly, and there is clamor for more. For example, some states partly base state financial aid to schools on deficiencies in student test scores (Rothman, 1987). Principals wait nervously to see how their students will do on standardized reading tests, and many in the community view the scores on these tests as a measuring rod against which the effectiveness of the school is gauged. This move towards testing is encouraged by the U.S. Department of Education, which certainly advocates such tests' usage. In one of its publications it notes the following:

Standardized tests apply similar gauges to everyone in a specific grade level. By giving standardized tests, school districts can see how achievement progresses over time. Such tests also help schools find out how much of the curriculum is actually being learned. Standardized tests also reveal problems in the curriculum itself. For example, a recent international mathematics test showed that U.S. students had encountered only 70 percent of what the test covered (1987, p. 54).

From this statement, we can conclude that American students not only will be tested to determine their achievement against their American peers but also will now be compared to other students in other developed countries!

True or False   Standardized tests are more likely to be used as a measure of a school's effectiveness today than twenty years ago.

Cautions and Doubts About the Use of Standardized Tests

Not everyone is enamored of the use of standardized tests. There is another side to the story. Many standardized tests measure knowledge but do not look at higher level skills. This encourages teachers only to instruct students on facts and to avoid the difficult task of teaching students to think—a skill that is not easily tested (Perrone, 1977). After all, most tests use a multiple-choice format, which assumes only one correct answer, and do not encourage complex answers. They essentially test recognition and superficial learning. They do not ask students to solve problems independently or to use their creative faculties. Even their timing is criticized, since they place value on thinking quickly, not profoundly (Fiske, 1988).

The usefulness of these tests for placement programs is also attacked, since labeling a child on the basis of test scores and sending the child to remedial classes may result in the child's viewing him or herself as a failure. There is concern that very young children may be labeled too early and that this label may follow them through school.

As noted when discussing NRTs, there is also concern about the match between local curricula and national tests. A student whose teacher has concentrated on a different area may find him or herself at a competitive disadvantage. The test may not bear a strong relationship to some local programs, especially if the programs stress higher levels of individualization and flexibility of objectives (Perrone, 1977).

Other technical objections involve the time it takes to prepare a standardized test. The items have to be developed based upon what is being taught nationally at the time. It may take years to develop such a test, during which time a gap may develop between the curricula assumptions of the test and the curricula at the time the test is given (Perrone, 1977).

Others argue that although testing is often thought of as a driving force behind school reform and educational accountability, it may actually retard school reform, because teachers may teach to the test and ignore everything else. Especially if students will be promoted partially on the basis of their test scores, the test becomes the most important educational event of the semester. New curricula that may not match the test are resisted, and tests that were once servants become the masters of education.

The Lake Wobegon Challenge

The most recent challenge to the use of standardized tests—especially achievement tests—is the Lake Wobegon Report. The question asked by the report's author, a pediatrician from West Virginia, is, How can all fifty states score above the national average in academic achievement? After looking at the data, John Cannell noted that 90 percent of the school districts report being above average. Although there are a number of technical inaccuracies in Cannell's work, some authorities believe he has identified a problem—that current NRTs overstate achievement levels in schools, districts, and states. This appears to be due both to inaccurate initial norms and the process of teaching to the test.

It can be argued that the norms are dated. Students appear to be improving their mastery of skills, but when compared to these older norms, the improvement looks greater than it is. In reality, the school districts are just keeping pace with the national rise in scores, allowing them to appear above average because the average is now out of date. In addition, most school districts try to choose tests that match rather closely their curricula—a sensible practice. However, remember that the norming sample is nationally representative and was not chosen because it had been taught those exact skills. When students who have been taught the exact skills are compared to the naive-normed group, the students taking the test have an unfair advantage and look even brighter than they really are. Sometimes test publishers provide districts with customized tests that exactly match the curriculum of the district, and naturally, the district's scores are compared to the original national norms. This is a misleading procedure. Another possible contributing factor is that the district itself decides which students will or will not be tested. Some

districts may exclude poor students, thus inflating a district's scores.

Sometimes after giving the tests over and over again, teachers become acquainted with what will be asked and teach specifically those skills. It can become ridiculous. In one state, a district's mathematics supervisor discovered that the state's minimum competency test used shaded figures for problems involving areas and unshaded figures for perimeters. She told a number of teachers to give their students a rule: multiply if shaded, add if not (Koretz, 1988). It is difficult to give an exact answer to the question of how closely a teacher should gauge his or her teaching to the test, since teaching to the test can lead to superficial learning and an educational aim of simply passing the test. When students were taught to convert Roman to Arabic numerals, the Roman numerals always came first, as they usually did on the test. When the test was changed so that Arabic numerals were given first, the average score dropped by 40 percent (Koretz, 1988). Then there are those who argue that normed achievement tests may be "dumbed down" to make student achievement look better. In other words, reading comprehension tests have become easier, and so students seem to be doing better when really they are not (Rothman, 1988b).

Defenders of these tests deny these charges, and besides emphasizing inaccuracies and statistical mistakes in Dr. Cannell's argument (he admits to not being an expert in statistics), test manufacturers argue that student achievement gains are real.

What Does the Debate over Standardized Testing Mean to the Teacher?

Cannell's assertions together are impressive, although they more strongly argue for caution in using and interpreting tests rather than for the elimination of standardized testing altogether. Standardized tests are valuable if used and interpreted wisely. However, viewing such test scores as the single greatest outcome of educational instruction ignores affective and higher level cognitive goals and gives tests a power over educational reform and instruction that may go beyond common sense. It remains for each district to be certain that the content of such tests matches the curricula. Each district must decide why it is going to test and what use each test will be put to. I once had the opportunity to question the superintendent of a school district as to why a certain test was given and how it was used. The superintendent simply told me that testing was deemphasized. That was not an answer, but it may have been the best information he had. When I asked a principal why teachers required IQ scores, he shrugged his shoulders. Despite the problems involved, standardized tests have certain qualities that enable them to provide educators with valuable information. The role of the teacher is to understand the meaning of these tests and to make certain the tests are used responsibly.

QUALITIES OF STANDARDIZED TESTS

To better understand the nature, potential, and limitations of standardized tests, three concepts must be discussed: standardization, validity, and reliability.

Standardized Procedures and Norms

The term **standardization** has two different meanings. It first refers to the specific rules for administering and scoring a test. Every test taker receives the same amount of time and the same instructions. All the relevant information is supplied in the manual that accompanies the test. Any deviation from established standards would seriously threaten the usefulness of the test.

> *True or False*   A student taking a particular standardized test in Boston, Massachusetts, will receive the same instructions and the same amount of time to complete it as a student taking the test in Little Rock, Arkansas.

The other meaning of standardization involves the process by which norms are formulated for norm-referenced tests. The characteristics of the norm group, the year of the testing, and the procedures should all be available for examination. Since NRTs compare the student taking the test to this norm group, information about the norm group is critical to the accurate interpretation of the test.

Validity

A test is **valid** if it measures what it intends to measure. A test that is supposed to cover biology must cover the subject. If it covers chemistry or physics, it

is not valid. However, tests are not simply valid or invalid. Tests are valid for a specific purpose and for use with a given population. Let's say that you wanted to give a group of non-English speaking students who have just arrived in the United States a test to measure their intelligence. Would it be valid to administer a normal intelligence test written in English, even if we know that the test correctly measures intelligence? Of course not, for these students would not adequately understand the material. Validity is not, then, an all-or-nothing element of a test.

There are three major types of validity, all of which may be important at some time or another. Different types of validity are used for different purposes. Table 14.1 shows how a single arithmetic test requires different evidence of validity depending upon how it is to be used (Anastasi, 1988, p. 162).

Content Validity

Content validity, which indicates that the test covers the domain it is intended to cover, is crucial to the usefulness of achievement tests. Content validity is found by carefully examining the test questions to be certain they reflect the objectives of the course. Content validity deals only with whether the test covers the material; it does not indicate if the items are poorly written or the reading level is inappropriate. Content validity is not indicated by any mathematical expression. It is assured by preparing a table that includes the major objectives, breaking the objectives down to smaller areas, and allotting a sufficient number of questions to cover each objective. The use of such a table for a teacher-made test is discussed in Chapter 15. The test manual should discuss the pro-

---

standardization   The specific rules for administering and scoring a standardized test to ensure that everyone taking the test does so under the same conditions. It also refers to the process by which norms are formulated for norm-referenced tests.

validity   A quality of a test when it measures what it is designed to measure.

content validity   A type of validity that indicates that the test covers the domain it is intended to cover.

Table 14.1   Validation of a Single Arithmetic Test for Different Purposes
When a test is being used for different purposes, it requires different evidence for its validity.

Testing Purpose	Illustrative Question	Evidence of Validity
Achievement test in elementary school arithmetic	How much has Dick learned in the past?	Content-related
Aptitude test to predict performance in high school mathematics	How well will Jane learn in the future?	Criterion-related: predictive
Technique for diagnosing learning disabilities	Does Bill's performance show specific disabilities?	Criterion-related: concurrent
Measure of quantitative reasoning	How can we characterize Helen's cognitive processes?	Construct-related

Reprinted with permission of Macmillan Publishing Company from *Psychological Testing*, 6th ed. by Anne Anastasi. Copyright © 1988 by Anne Anastasi.

cedures that have been used by the test constructors to ensure content validity, including when the items were chosen and which texts or curricula were used as the basis for developing the questions.

Criterion-Related Validity: Predictive and Concurrent Validity

When a test uses **criterion-related validity,** scores from a test are correlated with some external criterion. There are two types of criterion-related validity: predictive and concurrent.

Sometimes tests are used for predicting success in some future endeavor. For example, some aptitude tests are given for purposes of predicting which students have a better chance of succeeding in a particular program. **Predictive validity** is found by first describing the behavior that is to be predicted—called the criterion—and comparing it to the test—called the predictor. Let's say we wanted to design a test that would predict the chances of success in college. For such a test, grade-point average would be a reasonable criterion. To find the predictive validity, all we have to do is administer the test, wait for the behavior that was predicted to occur, measure the criterion, and correlate the two sets of scores (Gay, 1985). In the previous example, after administering the test, we would wait for our test takers to proceed through college before finding the relationship between their test scores and their grade point averages. The resulting validity coefficient would indicate the predictive power of the test. A high correlation shows good pre-

dictability, while a low correlation shows poor predictability. Predictive validity is most important for tests that will be used in the selection of students (Anastasi, 1988).

Concurrent validity is very similar to predictive validity except that all the data for validity are collected at the same time. In concurrent validity, we often seek to substitute a shorter, easier-to-administer test for an older, more lengthy test. Let's say that there exists an accepted but very lengthy test that will demonstrate whether a child will succeed in kindergarten. If a publisher formulates a simpler, faster test, one way of showing the test's validity is to show that it correlates highly with the accepted test (Kubiszyn & Borich, 1987).

criterion-related validity   A type of validity in which scores from a test are correlated with some external criterion. Predictive and concurrent validity are two types of criterion-related validity.

predictive validity   A type of criterion-related validity in which a test demonstrates the ability to predict some behavior.

concurrent validity   A type of criterion-related validity in which a test is validated against an external criterion such as another test that we already know is valid.

Construct Validity

Construct validity indicates whether the test corresponds well to a theory or to some hypothetical construct (Gay, 1985). One popular construct is intelligence. If some students learn better and faster, we may believe that the construct of intelligence underlies the difference and develop tests that measure how much of this construct a student possesses. Indeed, students who score high on intelligence tests tend to do better in school (Gay, 1985). Construct validity is also used for tests of creativity and motivation. Suppose we want to measure the construct creativity. We believe that under certain circumstances, people with the construct creativity will behave differently from those who do not have it. Using this construct, we create a theory to account for these different behaviors. Now we can identify creative people by identifying the observable behavior and classify these people according to the theory. We might, in the case of creativity, imagine that creative people will be able to come up with many alternative uses for a product or to generate more different ideas about how to solve some problem. In fact, one way of testing for creativity involves asking students to name as many uses as possible for different items. Of course, tests based upon construct validity are valid only if the construct involved is valid. To validate a construct is not easy, since deductions from the theory must be tested and demonstrated.

Reliability

Another important element of standardized testing is reliability. What if you gave an achievement test in science to a student who scored in the 60th percentile on Thursday of last week. Today you give the same test, and the student receives a score in the 85th percentile. How much science does the student really know?

For a test to be useful, it must be **reliable;** that is, it must yield consistent scores. Since standardized tests are often used as a basis for making decisions such as where to place students, tests must be dependable. What could cause a test to lack reliability? Perhaps the test taker was ill or had something else on his or her mind, or perhaps the conditions under which the test was taken did not match those under which it was standardized. Errors can be introduced through

> **construct validity** A type of validity that indicates whether the test corresponds well to a theory or to some hypothetical construct.
>
> **reliability** The quality of a test when it yields consistent scores.

poorly worded or tricky questions, unrealistic time limitations, or scoring errors (Montague, 1987). Reliability can be measured in a number of ways, three of which are described in the following paragraphs.

Test-Retest Reliability

The reliability of a test is often measured by giving the test to a group, waiting a specified period of time and administering the test again, and then determining the relationship between the two sets of scores. If the scores on the test are very similar, the test is reliable. Of course, there could be a problem if much learning took place between the first and the second administration of the test or if students remember the test problems. Whenever this type of reliability is used, the interval should be appropriate. After only a day's wait, the estimate may be artificially high; after two months it may be artificially low.

True or False A student who takes a standardized test of reading achievement on Tuesday and again on Wednesday, should score exactly the same on both tests.

Equivalent Forms Reliability

The problems cited in test-retest reliability are eliminated by using alternate forms of the test. These equivalent forms are the same in every way except that the actual test items differ. The tests have the same number of items and level of difficulty and use the same directions. If a group receives form A and then form B and the scores correlate well, it would indicate that the test is reliable. This type of reliability is most important when the test takers might recall responses and the test is to be given more than once. We want to be sure that it won't make much difference whether form A or form B is used. The major problem is that there may not be alternate forms available, and it is relatively difficult to produce two or more alternate forms.

Split-Half Reliability

Split-half reliability involves the extent to which a test has internal consistency. Because this type of reliability requires only one test administration, there is no worry about differences in testing conditions. The test is divided into two comparable halves, often in terms of odd and even numbers, and the score on the two halves are correlated.

The Standard Error of Measurement

If a student scored 112 on an intelligence test today and 110 next Tuesday, what meaning would that have? No test is absolutely free of error, and the standard error of measurement reflects the degree of variation in a score we can expect. Put another way, the standard error of measurement gives us an estimate of how much difference we could expect between the obtained scores and the true score. A small standard error indicates high reliability; a large standard error indicates low reliability. If the standard error of measurement was five and the student scored 85 on the test, we could say that we are fairly confident that the student's score falls between 80 and 90.

⟫⟫ CONNECTIONS

Validity, Reliability, Standardization, and the Teacher

Sometimes, a discussion of the basic qualities of standardized tests seems divorced from the real world of the teacher. After all, most teachers do not determine which standardized tests to administer to their students. However, teachers must use the information that they receive from these tests. Therefore, they need to be able to interpret the tests' meaning. In addition, they sometimes must explain the meaning to parents who may have many questions about their children's test scores. The following suggestions reflect some of the practical implications of these basic qualities of standardized tests for the classroom teacher.

1. **Thoroughly examine the test materials.** A great deal of information is usually contained in the materials that accompany the test booklets. This material gives directions for administering the test and information on the tests' validity, reliability, and standardization procedures. It is a good idea for teachers to familiarize themselves with this material so that when they administer the test, they will not make mistakes.

2. **Make certain every student has a fair chance to do well on the test.** Every standardized test contains involved directions for administering the test. For example, there are time limits for each part. Students must be allowed the proper amount of time for each section. In addition, the noise level should be controlled. Too much outside noise will interfere with a student's ability to concentrate.

3. **Consider the characteristics of the group on which the test was standardized.** Most standardized tests are norm referenced tests which compare your students to another group of students. Some understanding of how this group was selected, their characteristics as well as when the test was standardized should be taken into consideration when interpreting the test results. For example, if the test was standardized many years ago, the curriculum may have changed.

4. **Examine the test for content that has not been taught.** The most common standardized tests are those measuring achievement, for which content validity becomes crucial. For a test to be fair to students, it must cover what has been taught. If some element of the test has not been taught, the unfamiliar material should be taken into consideration when the test is interpreted. For instance, one school found that its students did very poorly on the map skills portion of a social studies test. That topic had not been taught, and parents were informed of this fact. The curriculum for this district introduced map skills the following year.

5. **Reliability estimates should be quite high.** What should a reliability coefficient be for a test to be considered useful? It is difficult to give an exact number since many factors including the length of the test and amount of time between a first and second testing may affect the test's reliability. However, in a standardized test, coefficients should be high (.85 and up) (Anastasi, 1988). It is not unusual to find such reliability estimates in the .90 range. If the measure is to be used to help make decisions about individuals, it should be more reliable than if it is used to make decisions about groups (Mehrens & Lehmann, 1987). Many achievement and aptitude tests have subtests, and their reliabilities should be noted. They may be somewhat lower, but if a test manual just says they are acceptable, this should cause some concern.

6. Watch for unusual declines in test scores. What if a student had an excellent score on one achievement test and then did much worse on a test taken somewhat later? Teachers are relatively good at estimating how students will answer questions on standardized tests (Coladarci, 1986) and in predicting students' scores on such tests (Hoge & Butcher, 1984). If students' scores do not match their performance in the past, it is wise to consider a second testing, perhaps with an alternate form, if available. Although each test has some error and no test is perfectly reliable, there is no reason to accept widely differing scores without further investigation.

True or False Teachers are proficient at predicting how their students will answer questions on standardized tests.

HOW TO INTERPRET STANDARDIZED TESTS

The language of test interpretation is sometimes difficult to understand. Most teachers are not given a choice of exams, and they must administer the exams chosen by the district administration. However, they are offered reports of their students' progress and need to understand what the results mean before they can use the information. Teachers are also often confronted by parents who may not understand the meaning of their children's test scores. These scores are often reported in statistical form, and a knowledge of what the statistics actually mean can help reduce the problems in interpretation that often arise.

Mean, Median, and Mode: Measures of Central Tendency

Perhaps the most widely used statistics are measures of central tendency. These measures identify the typical or central value in a set of scores (Gronlund, 1976). The most commonly used measure of central tendency is the **mean**—the arithmetic average obtained by summing all the scores and dividing by the number of scores. The problem with using the mean is that it can be affected by extremely high or low scores. For example, if most of the students do very well or very poorly, the average will be somewhere in

the middle and will give the evaluator a false idea of how the typical student performed on the test.

This is not the case with another measure of central tendency, called the **median**—the point in a distribution above and below which an equal number of scores fall. It is the midpoint when scores are arranged in numerical order. In a distribution in which there is an odd number of scores, the median is the middle score. For example, in the distribution 90, 85, 75, 73, 63, 52, 12, the median of the seven scores is the fourth score, or 73. Note that the extremely low score of 12 does not affect the median. In a distribution containing an even number of scores, the point halfway between the two middle scores is the median. In the distribution 90, 85, 75, 73, 63, 52, the median would fall between 75 and 73 ($[75 + 73] \div 2$), or 74. The median does not have to be an actual score in the distribution.

The **mode** is the score that people obtain more than any other score. All one has to do is look at the scores and choose the score that appears most often. Since a set of scores can have more than one mode and gives only limited information, this measure is not used very often.

Variability

Measures of central tendency are valuable descriptions of test scores but do not tell us everything we may want to know. Look at the following distributions:

A: 65, 67, 69, 71, 73, 75, 77
B: 38, 58, 63, 71, 82, 90, 95

If you calculate the mean (average), it is 497/7 = 71 for both distributions. The median (midpoint) is the fourth score, or 71. However, the two distributions are very different. In A, all the scores cluster closely around the mean, while in B they are spread out. To adequately describe these distributions, we must

mean The arithmetic average.

median The point in a distribution above and below which an equal number of scores fall.

mode The score obtained by more people than any other score.

characterize how spread out the scores are, which is called the **variability.** There are two commonly used ways of measuring variability: the range and the standard deviation.

The Range

The range is the difference between the highest and the lowest scores. In distribution A, the range is 12 ($77 - 65$), while in distribution B, it is 57 ($95 - 38$). In distribution A, the range is small, while in distribution B, it is quite large. The range gives us a quick, rough estimate of variability, but the amount of information it gives is limited, since the very highest and lowest scores may be atypical and all the other scores may hover near the mean. It does not take into consideration each score.

The Standard Deviation

The most appropriate measure of variability is called the standard deviation and is frequently reported for standardized tests. It takes into consideration every score. To find the **standard deviation,** we first calculate the mean and then find how far each score differs from the mean by subtracting the mean from each score. Then we square the difference, add up all the squares, and divide by the number of scores. This gives us a quantity called the variance. To obtain the standard deviation we take the square root of the variance (see Figure 14.1). If we know the mean and standard deviation, we have a good idea of what the distribution looks like, and these two scores can help us understand how tests are normed.

The Normal Curve

If every eight-year-old child in the United States were to receive an intelligence test, how would you expect the distribution to look? Most scores would probably cluster around the middle, with fewer scores being found at each extreme. There are far fewer geniuses or mentally retarded people than people of relatively average intelligence. In fact, such a distribution is called the **normal curve.** Many human characteristics are normally distributed; that is, they fit well on a normal curve. Very few people are really very tall or very short. Most hover about the mean. If we plotted these

Suppose a group's test scores were the following: 95, 94, 86, 83, 82, 79, 77, 76, 62, 56. How would you go about finding the standard deviation?

Use these six steps to calculate the standard deviation.

1. Find the mean. Sum all scores and divide by the number of scores. In this example the sum of the scores is 790. When this is divided by the number of scores (10), it yields a mean of 79.
2. Find the difference (deviation) between each score and the mean. Subtract each score from the mean ($95-79$, $94-79$. . . . .)
3. Square the deviations (16×16, 15×15. . . . . .)
4. Find the sum of the squared deviations. Add these squared deviations. The sum is 1386 in this case.
5. Divide by the number of scores. $1386/10 = 138.6$
6. Calculate the square root to find the standard deviation. The square root of 138.6 is 11.77.

Test Scores	Deviations	Squared Deviations
95	$-79 = $ 16	256
94	$-79 = $ 15	225
86	$-79 = $ 7	49
83	$-79 = $ 4	16
82	$-79 = $ 3	9
79	$-79 = $ 0	0
77	$-79 = $ -2	4
76	$-79 = $ -3	9
62	$-79 = $ -17	289
56	$-79 = $ -23	529
790		1386

Sum of scores = 790   Variance = $1386/10 = 138.6$
Mean = $790/10 = 79$ Standard deviation = $\sqrt{138.6} = 11.77$

Figure 14.1   Calculating the Standard Deviation

variability   The extent to which scores in a distribution are spread out about or lie close to the mean.

standard deviation   One measure of a distribution's variability.

normal curve (normal distribution)   A bell-shaped distribution in which scores occur symmetrically about the mean, and the mean and median are the same. It is very useful for understanding the distribution of many human traits.

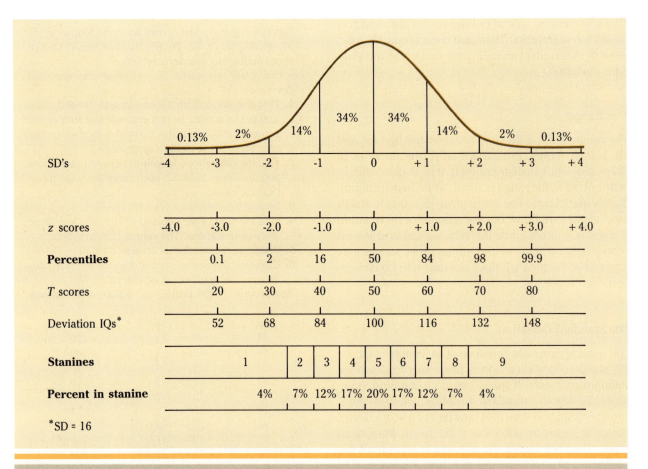

Figure 14.2   Normal Curve and Corresponding Scores and Percentiles

Reprinted with permission of Macmillan Publishing Company from *Measurement and Evaluation in Teaching,* 5th ed. by Norman E. Gronlund. Copyright ©
1985 by Norman E. Gronlund.

scores and drew a curve, it would look like the one in Figure 14.2.

The normal curve has certain properties. It is centered at the mean of the population. The right half of the curve represents all the scores above the mean, and the left half represents all the scores below the mean. A vital characteristic of the normal curve is that we know the percentage of scores that will fall between the mean and different places on the curve that are marked by standard deviations. For example, we know that 34.13 percent of the scores will fall between the mean and one standard deviation above the mean and 34.13 percent of all the scores will fall between the mean and one standard deviation below the mean. If the mean for an intelligence test is 100, we would place that at the center. Let's say that the

standard deviation is 16. Then 34.13 percent of the scores would fall between 100 and 100 plus 16, or 116. Therefore, 34.13 percent of the population has an intelligence between 100 and 116. We would find that most students score between one standard deviation above and one standard deviation below the mean. In other words, most students score between $100 + 16 = 116$ and $100 - 16 = 84$. In fact, we can predict that 68.26 percent of the scores would fall between 84 and 116 (34.13 + 34.13).

What percentage of the scores fall between plus and minus two standard deviations from the mean? We can calculate that 13.59 percent of the scores lie between one and two standard deviations above the mean and the same percentage lie between one and two standard deviations below the mean. For our intelligence test, we can calculate that 95.44 percent of the scores lie between plus and minus two deviations from the mean (34.13 + 34.13 + 13.59 + 13.59). On our intelligence test, 95 percent of the scores will fall between 132 and 68 (100 + 16 + 16 = 132 and 100 − 16 − 16 = 68) (see Figure 14.2).

Not all attributes and test scores will fit well into the normal curve. However, many attributes approximate the normal curve, and when they do, this situation allows us to make comparisons among scores. Some characteristics such as intelligence, most kinds of achievement, and most physical characteristics fit well into the normal curve, and it serves as a useful model for interpreting test results.

Derived Scores

As we've seen, a raw score such as 55 correct on a test means very little unless we can compare it to something else. We can transform these raw scores into something more useful that indicates the relative position the child has attained compared to others by converting them into **derived scores.** There are many types of derived scores, but percentiles, standard scores, stanines, and grade equivalents are the most popular. Not only do these scores allow us to compare a student with his or her peers, but they allow us to compare a student's performance on two different tests. For example, if a student's raw score is 55 on a mathematics test but 43 on a test of English skills, it does not necessarily mean that the student is better at mathematics than English, since we must take into consideration the mean and standard deviations of the test scores. Derived scores are often reported to teachers and parents when the results of the test are announced, and they are often misunderstood.

Percentile Ranks

Figure 14.3 shows the reported profile for a third-grade student on the California Achievement Test (CAT). Notice the column marked NP. This reports the national **percentile ranking** of the child in various subtests of the CAT, the child's total language, reading, and mathematics percentiles, and the score for the total battery. The percentile rank indicates the percentage of peers nationwide who scored at or below the child's score. This child scored in the 85th

percentile in word analysis. We could say that the child scored higher or equal to 85 percent of the norm group in word analysis. This child scored in the 54th percentile in science and we could say that his or her score was equal to or higher than 54 percent of the norm group in science. Another way of looking at this child's scores is that 15 percent of the norm group performed better in word analysis and 46 percent performed better in science. Note that the raw scores are so meaningless that they are not even included in this report. With this information, a teacher might realize that this child has some interesting strengths and weaknesses. The child needs work on mathematical computations, but her percentile ranking in other areas would indicate strengths that might be encouraged.

Percentile ranks are very useful, but they have their limitations. First, they are too often confused with percentages. They do not mean that the child knows 85 percent of his work in word analysis or 54 percent of his science work. This problem can be easily alleviated through a simple explanation. However, more difficult to explain is the fact that equal increases in raw scores do not necessarily mean equal increases in percentile ranking. For example, an increase in raw scores for those whose scores fall around the median will increase the percentile rankings much more than an equal increase in raw scores at the highest and lowest ends of the distribution. This is because, as would be expected in a normal distribution, most scores tend to fall in the middle ranges and fewer at the extremes. Thus, one cannot say that an increase of 4 points in raw scores will always mean a particular increase in percentile ranking.

True or False A child who scores in the 45th percentile has answered 45 percent of the questions correctly.

derived scores The transformation of raw scores into more usable measures that indicate the relative position of the student. Derived scores include percentiles, standard scores, stanines, and grade equivalents.

percentile ranking Scores indicating the percentage of peers who scored at or below the student's score.

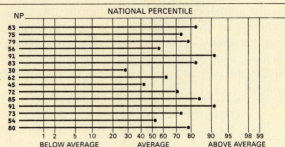

Figure 14.3 Sample Report Form for California Achievement Test

Reproduced by permission of the publisher, CTB, 2500 Garden Road, Monterey, California 93940. Copyright © 1985 by McGraw-Hill, Inc. All rights reserved.

Standard Scores

A **standard score** is one that expresses how far a given raw score is from the mean in standard deviation units (Gay, 1985). One advantage of using a standard score is that it allows scores from different tests to be compared easily. Given two scores on different tests, standard scores allow us to make a statement about whether a student is better in mathematics or science. The simplest standard score is the z score, found by calculating the difference between the raw score and the mean and then dividing the difference by the standard deviation.

> **standard score** A measure that expresses how far a given score is from the mean in standard deviation units.

Let's take a real problem. If Zachary received a raw score of 48 in mathematics and 45 in reading, is he better in reading or mathematics? Of course, since raw scores tell us nothing, we might ask for other information. If we are told that the mean of the mathematics test is 56 and standard deviation is 8, and that the mean of the reading test is 40 and the standard deviation is 10, we could find Zachary's z-score for both subjects. For mathematics, it would be

$$\frac{(48 - 56)}{8} = \frac{-8}{8} = -1$$

In reading it would be

$$\frac{(45 - 40)}{10} = \frac{5}{10} = .5$$

Zachary is actually scoring one standard deviation below the mean in mathematics and one-half a standard deviation above the mean in English.

Working with z scores often involves negative numbers, something that is somewhat of a public relations problem. Parents do not like to hear that their son or daughter scored −1.5. As a result, some publishers use a T score which is calculated by multiplying the z score by 10 and adding 50. If a z score is 0 (the mean), the T score would be 10 times 0 plus 50, or 50. A z score of −1 would be 10 times −1, or −10, plus 50, or 40. The T score distribution has a mean of 50 and a standard deviation of 10. For Zachary's mathematics score, it would be 10 times −1 plus 50, or 40, while for reading, the score would be 10 times .50 plus 50, or 55.

A derived score that is gaining some popularity is the stanine, which is short for standard nine and divides the distribution into nine parts. To calculate the stanine for a test score, we first find the z-score, double it, add 5, and round the score to the nearest whole number. Fixed percentages of scores fall within these stanines. Stanine 5 includes 20 percent of the scores, stanines 4 and 6 each contain 17 percent, stanines 3 and 7 each contain 12 percent, stanines 2 and 8 each contain 7 percent, and stanines 1 and 9 each contain approximately 4 percent. Stanine 5 is located precisely in the middle of the distribution. (The distribution of stanines in the normal curve and the percentage of cases are shown in Figure 14.2.) One definite advantage of stanines is that their interpretation is simple, and when one says that Bobby scored in the second stanine, there is apt to be little misinterpretation.

Grade Equivalents

Grade equivalents are the most commonly used method of comparison and unfortunately the most misleading and misunderstood. **Grade equivalents** are derived by assigning to the median score of a fourth-grade norm population a grade level equivalence of 4.0. Scores above or below the median are then assigned grade equivalents. A score of 4.3 means that the student taking the test scored the same as an average person in the fourth grade in the third month of the term. You can readily see a problem. If a fourth-grade student scores 7.2, a parent might believe that the child is ready for seventh-grade work, which is nonsense. All a score of 7.2 means is that this is the test publisher's estimate of what the typical seventh-grader during the second month would score on the test. The fourth-grader is not ready for seventh-grade work. We can conclude that the student is far above average, but that is about all. What if a seventh-grader received a grade equivalent of 5.4? Does this mean that the student reads only as well as a fifth-grader in the fourth month? No, it doesn't, because the seventh-grader is taking a test specifically normed for seventh-graders. A seventh-grader who took a test normed for fourth-graders might score very high. All we can say about our seventh-grader who received a grade equivalent of 5.4 is that the student is reading far worse than we might hope, and any additional interpretation is unwarranted.

True or False A third-grade student who scored a grade equivalent of 5.5 (fifth grade, fifth month) on a reading exam is ready for fifth-grade reading work.

Most tests meant for fourth-graders are not administered to students too far above or below the intended grade. A fourth-grade test might be administered to third- and fifth-graders but probably not to seventh-graders (Kubiszyn & Borich, 1987). Thus, these grade equivalents are actually estimates. In addition, the score of 7.3 suggests a great deal more precision than is actually true. A test may be given in the beginning and end of the year to the norm group, but any values in between are merely estimates. Many people also think that all students in the third month of the fifth school year should be reading at 5.3. However, grade equivalents are norms and not standards.

grade equivalents A measure of grade level derived by assigning to the median score on a test a particular grade level equivalent and comparing other scores to it.

Last, equal differences in scores do not reflect equal differences in achievement. The growth from 3.4 to 4.4 is not always the same amount of growth as from 5.5 to 6.5. Grade equivalents are not equal unit scores.

Many professionals, including some test publishers, have called for an end to the use of grade equivalents. Indeed, with all the difficulties in interpreting them, we would probably be better off not using them (Perrone, 1977). However, they remain popular and probably will continue to be used even though other reporting devices described earlier are better.

What Statistical Measures Mean to Teachers and Parents

Throughout this discussion of interpretation we've been concerned with overinterpretation and misinterpretation of data, not only by teachers but also by parents. If norms are considered standards or raw scores are misunderstood, the child will suffer. If derived scores are misinterpreted, again, the child may suffer. Most authorities argue that percentiles and stanines are the easiest derived scores to understand.

Most test publishers have devised relatively simple explanatory reports that are sent to parents. Even so, the untutored parent may not fully understand the meaning of the test scores, and especially what some of the subtests measure. Teachers can help by discussing the scores during parent-teacher conferences. Encouraging parents to make an appointment with the teacher to review the meaning of the test reports is a viable way of being certain that parents do not misinterpret the scores. During the interview, special attention should be paid both to strengths and weaknesses. Teachers should be armed with suggestions for improving skills in which the child is weak and should encourage the student to continue developing his or her strengths.

FOUR TYPES OF TESTS TEACHERS ENCOUNTER MOST OFTEN

Most teachers will have contact with four types of exams: standardized achievement tests, minimum competency tests, readiness tests, and ability and aptitude tests. As these tests are discussed, keep in mind the benefits and drawbacks of using tests as well as the qualities that make a test valid and reliable.

Standardized Achievement Tests

The most commonly administered standardized tests are achievement tests. **Standardized achievement tests** measure the student's knowledge of a specific subject, such as reading or mathematics. There are three types of achievement tests: achievement batteries, single-subject achievement tests, and diagnostic achievement tests. The determination of their validity is based upon content validity. For example, one of the most popular achievement batteries—the Metropolitan Achievement Test (MAT)—was developed after extensive analyses of texts, syllabi, state guidelines, and other curricular sources. All items were also reviewed by a panel of minority educators to detect cultural and gender biases. Since curricular content can vary locally, the MAT provides a detailed listing of all instructional objectives (Anastasi, 1988). Reliabilities are typically high on these batteries. The scales include measurements of vocabulary, word recognition skills, reading comprehension, mathematics concepts, problem-solving computation, spelling, language (use of grammar, dictionary skills, etc), science, and social studies. Other achievement batteries, such as the California Achievement Test (CAT), are also carefully prepared. Achievement batteries measure normative performance, although some of the newer batteries are also concerned with CRT performance. Most batteries are available for use over a wide variety of school grades.

True or False The most commonly administered standardized tests are achievement tests.

The second type of achievement test—single-content area tests—are available in every area imaginable, although the most common measure achievement in reading and mathematics. The most popular are the Gates MacGintie Reading Tests and the Modern Math Understanding Test (MMUT). These single-subject tests are given when all we want to know is the child's reading or mathematics achievement. It is not cost effective to give an entire battery, and survey

standardized achievement tests Tests that measure a student's knowledge of a particular subject.

batteries are not as thorough in their coverage of any single subject as are single-content area tests.

The third type of achievement test is given specifically to diagnose weaknesses. Some of the achievement batteries, such as the MAT and CAT, provide an analysis of errors and some diagnostic help. However, special diagnostic tests offer more information that specifically can be used to help teachers remediate difficulties in many areas, such as mathematics, language, writing, and listening skills. For example, a diagnostic test of reading may give specific information concerning auditory discrimination, knowledge of syllables, beginning and end sounds, and blending. Many offer specific, detailed information regarding instructional planning for remediation.

Minimum Competency Testing

The most controversial type of achievement testing is minimum competency testing. **Minimum competency tests** are intended to ensure that each graduate has certain basic skills. These tests are an outgrowth of

Proficiency tests are now given by many states as part of an attempt to improve standards for graduation.

> **minimum competency tests** Tests intended to ensure that each graduate possesses particular skills at a basic level.

the movement of the 1970s and 1980s to improve educational accountability and be certain that a high school diploma certifies some basic knowledge. The great majority of states now require some form of minimum competency test, although the tests vary in what they measure and in the cutoff for success (Riegel & Lovell, 1980).

Minimum competency tests have explicit standards for acceptable performance (Perkins, 1982). Therefore, they can be categorized as criterion-referenced tests. They are the ultimate in pass/fail tests, since the consequences of passing or failing are definite. They can be used to determine whether a student will receive a high school diploma or be promoted from grade to grade. Students who fail minimum competency tests are usually given extra help.

The interpretation of these tests goes beyond the individual student. The tests are also used as a yardstick to measure the quality of education and the effectiveness of instructional programs and school personnel (Riegel & Lovell, 1980). A school in which many students do not pass these tests is likely to be seen as one in which the instruction is ineffective. Whether this is true or not is debatable, but it is the perception that counts. Indeed, one of the forces behind the minimum competency movement is the perception that students are not being taught what they need to do well in the outside world and that achievement in high school is declining—both of which, again, can be debated (Riegel & Lovell, 1980). Sometimes the state mandates the standards, while at other times, local standards are allowed. Sometimes the state constructs the test; sometimes it is left to the local districts to do so.

The supporters of minimum competency testing argue that it increases public confidence in the diploma, encourages the involvement of the public in education, improves teaching and learning, places emphasis on educational accountability, and serves a diagnostic and remedial function (Perkins, 1982). Its detractors argue that it will lead to schools changing their curricula to satisfy the test requirements, therefore encouraging schools to concentrate on minimums. They also argue that it will cause less attention to be paid to the more difficult to measure learning outcomes, that teachers will teach only to the test, that the tests may be unfair to some minority students, and that the tests will lead to a narrowing of the curriculum.

Whatever one's basic outlook on minimum competency testing, some test-related issues should be understood. First, if we are to give a valid test, we must define what we mean by minimum competency. Some have argued simply that it translates into competency in reading, mathematics, and writing. Others, however, have argued that it is appalling when a high school graduate can't make change or fill out a form because he or she lacks these practical skills. They advocate a test that would measure survival skills, social responsibility, social studies and natural science knowledge, and functional literacy. Many people feel that knowledge and skills other than reading and mathematics should be required for a high school diploma (Schab, 1984). However, the further we travel away from the basic school subjects, the more difficult it is to measure minimum competency. If some of these additional skills are to be required, the curriculum must reflect the change. The validity of any achievement test depends upon the test's relationship to the goals of education. The better defined the goals, the better the chance that validity will be high. In addition, even if we measure just the basic skills, we are faced with the problem of where to place the cutoff for success. Should a student be awarded a diploma if he or she reads at the eighth-grade level or at the tenth or at the twelfth?

A potentially serious problem may arise if the skills being measured are not taught in the individual classroom. As with any achievement test, we are assuming that students are taught this material. However, with minimum competency examinations, the consequences are much greater than with the average standardized achievement test, and thus the issue takes on greater importance. This problem has given rise to a relatively new term, **instructional validity,** which indicates whether the test is measuring those skills taught in the classroom. It would hardly be fair to deny a diploma to a student who did not receive the requisite training. In a landmark case, a Florida court noted that its test passed the requirement of instructional validity (Linn, 1986). However, the issue still lingers.

> **instructional validity** A term used to describe whether a test is measuring skills taught in the classroom.

How do students do on such tests? Evidence suggests that as the test continues to be given to graduating class after graduating class, the percentage of students who fail decreases dramatically. If the test requirement in Florida had gone into effect as planned in 1979, about six percent of the students would have failed. But by the time diplomas were denied on the basis of the test in 1983, only 1.4 percent of the class had failed (Linn, 1986). These results would seemingly be impressive, but they leave many questions unanswered. How specific are the gains? Do they generalize from this test to others or to other situations? In addition, there is little research showing what influence the program has had on instruction. Are teachers simply teaching to the test? Are higher order skills that are not measured on such tests being neglected? Without more research, these and many other questions remain unanswered.

True or False As minimum competency tests are given year after year in a particular state, more and more students fail them.

Minimum competency tests will continue to be a source of controversy. It is difficult to separate the politics and the public relations issues from what is educationally sound. The tests are quite popular with the public, with some studies showing an 80 percent approval rating (Riegel & Lovell, 1980). On the other hand, can a single test really measure minimum competency? Whether or not one favors the approach, the validity of the test and its interpretation must be carefully watched to be certain it remains educationally valid and reflects the aims and goals of the educational system.

Readiness Tests

What if you began to teach a child to read before the child could tell the difference between the *b* and *p* sounds, recognize shapes, and visually differentiate between *b* and *d*? What if you tried to teach a child

Often, young children are given readiness tests. However, there has been some concern expressed over the use of standardized tests with children so young.

subtraction before the child really understood the concept of quantity? It would be inappropriate, because the child does not have the skills necessary to succeed. This is exactly where readiness tests enter the picture. **Readiness tests** are used to assess whether a student has the necessary skills to master a new skill, for example, reading. They are given prior to instruction and measure particular skills that are deemed necessary for success (DeLawter & Sherman, 1978). Most readiness tests involve reading and mathematics readiness and are administered during kindergarten and first grade. To be useful, a readiness test must measure very detailed and important skills that are necessary for success. Many reading-readiness tests measure visual discrimination, identification of differences and similarities in written words or figures and in spoken words, auditory discrimination, verbal comprehension, recognition of letters, recognition of words that may have been taught in sample lessons, and skill in drawing or copying (Gronlund, 1976). If a teacher receives information that a student does not have a particular skill, some program might be instituted to help the child develop the skill.

Despite the usefulness of these tests, however, their interpretation should be made with care. Scoring well on a reading-readiness test does not mean that reading success is assured since the readiness test measures neither attitudes nor attention span. In addition, some children who do not do particularly well on reading-readiness tests do learn to read for reasons

that are uncertain (DeLawter & Sherman, 1978). Still, readiness tests can yield important information for the teacher.

Aptitude Tests

Aptitude tests describe a general category of measuring instruments that include intelligence tests as well as tests of cognitive, perceptual, and reasoning skills and whose basic purpose is to predict a student's future behavior (Hobbie, 1988) or success in a future endeavor. If student A scores high on a mechanical aptitude test and student B scores low on the test, we should be able to predict that student A would find it easier to succeed and be more likely to do well than student B in a task that requires mechanical skills if both were given training.

The differences between aptitude and achievement tests are not always clear. As previously discussed, achievement tests measure the level of a student's knowledge at the time the student takes the test, whereas the function of aptitude tests is to predict some future behavior. It is sometimes stated that achievement tests measure learning while aptitude tests measure innate capacity, but we know today that this is not true and that both achievement and aptitude tests depend greatly on learning. Many tests that measure intellectual competence have changed their names to avoid the many problems of using the terms *intelligence* and *mental ability,* which are often seen by the general public as denoting innate capacity. For example, the Otis-Lennon Mental Ability Test is now call the Otis-Lennon School Ability Test, and the Cognitive Abilities Test was once called an intelligence test (Mehrens & Lehmann, 1987).

Chapter 4 looked at various definitions of intelligence. If intelligence testing is to be considered aptitude testing, what does it predict? The answer is academic achievement. There is a relatively high

readiness tests   Tests that measure whether a student has attained the skills necessary to master a new skill.

aptitude tests   Tests that predict how well a student will perform in a future endeavor.

correlation between school achievement and intelligence—about .60 with grades; that is, children who score high on intelligence tests are more likely to do better in school. The correlation between IQ tests and standardized achievement test scores generally falls within a range of .70 to .90 (Kubiszyn & Borich, 1987). Intelligence tests, then, have predictive power in the area of school success. However, notice that the correlation is not perfect (1.00), which indicates that other factors, including motivation, background, and the nature of the test setting, affect how a child performs on the test. In fact, some psychologists believe that such factors as motivation and adjustment must be assessed if we are to measure the intellectual competence of children (Scarr, 1981).

True or False   Scores on intelligence tests are poor predictors of academic achievement.

Intelligence tests can be divided into **individual intelligence tests** and group tests. An individual test is administered by a school psychologist on a one-to-one basis and can take anywhere from forty-five minutes to an hour and a half. Group intelligence tests are pencil-and-paper tests that are distributed in class like any other test, collected as a group, and usually scored by a computer.

Individual Intelligence Tests

In the early 1900s, Alfred Binet was asked to create a test that would identify students who could not benefit from traditional education. Binet used a series of tests that measured a sample of children's abilities at different age levels. At each level, some children performed better than others. Binet simply compared children's performance on these tests to that of others in the same age group. If a child had less knowledge than the average child of the same age level, the child had less intelligence; if the child knew more, the child's intelligence was higher. Binet used the term **mental age** to describe the age at which the child was functioning. Later, another psychologist, William Stern, proposed the term intelligence quotient (IQ), in which the mental age of a child is divided by the child's chronological age (age since birth) and then multiplied by 100 to remove the decimal. The problem with the IQ is that it assumed a straight-line (linear) relationship between age and intelligence. This is not the case, especially after age 16.

individual intelligence tests   Intelligence tests that are administered by a psychologist on a one-to-one basis.

mental age   The age at which an individual is functioning.

Today, a more statistically sophisticated way of calculating the intelligence score—called a deviation IQ—is used. This is based on the normal curve with a mean of 100 and a standard deviation of about 15 or 16, although different IQ tests have different standard deviations, indicating that we should be careful in comparing IQ scores from different tests. The original Binet has gone through a number of revisions, and today it is called the Stanford-Binet Intelligence Test.

Beginning in the 1930s, David Wechsler began to develop another set of individualized intelligence tests. The Wechsler Intelligence Scale for Children (revised edition), known as the WISC, contains a number of subtests that can be divided into two categories—verbal and performance. The five verbal subtests are information, similarities, arithmetic, vocabulary, and comprehension. The five performance subtests are picture completion (pointing out what is missing in the picture), picture arrangement (arranging a group of pictures in sequential order), block design (copying a pattern with blocks), object assembly (putting together puzzle pieces), and coding (a test in which people are asked to translate one set of symbols into another). Two additional subtests—one verbal and one performance—are sometimes used: digit span (a test of immediate recall in which the test taker is asked to repeat random series of digits sometimes in forward order and sometimes in reverse order) and mazes. A composite, or total, intelligence score can also be obtained.

The Binet and Wechsler tests differ in a number of ways. The Wechsler tests are arranged by subject, while the Binet tests are given by age level. The Binet is more heavily verbal (Brown, 1983). The subtests of the Wechsler tests provide additional information about the student's strengths and weaknesses, which may give it some advantage over the Stanford-Binet in some circumstances. The correlation between the two tests varies, but for the full scale, it is .73. Thus, the tests do not tap identical skills.

The Wechsler Intelligence Scale for Children (WISC) is a popular individual intelligence test. As in all individual intelligence tests, it must be administered on a one-to-one basis by a psychologist.

These intelligence tests do predict, although imperfectly, academic achievement. The Wechsler's various subtests also offer useful diagnostic information, although IQ tests cannot be considered primarily diagnostic. Michael Petti (1987, 1988) has suggested that performance on each of the subtests of the WISC has a number of educational implications. For example, a teacher may assume that a student knows certain facts. However, if this student scores low on the WISC subtest of information, the teacher will now understand that the student lacks the knowledge base and the teacher can respond accordingly. If a student does poorly on digit span, it might indicate a short-term memory problem, and the student may have difficulty in remembering what she has just heard and in following directions. A student who is weak in finding missing details in pictures may overlook arithmetic signs and punctuation marks. Therefore, at times, an individual intelligence test may point to specific strengths and weaknesses in addition to predicting academic achievement. Such individual intelligence tests are also used to satisfy one of the criteria for placement of students into classes for the mentally retarded, although their use in this area has been under legal scrutiny for a number of years.

Group Intelligence Tests and Tests of Academic Ability

Group intelligence tests and most tests of academic or cognitive ability are designed to be given in a group setting. Therefore, they do not require the presence of a psychologist and can be given to many people at one time. For example, the Cognitive Abilities Test measures verbal, quantitative, and nonverbal abilities and was normed along with the Iowa Tests of Basic Skills, which makes aptitude-achievement comparisons easier. These tests are easily administered and scored and allow the testing of many students at once.

How Intelligence Tests Can Be Misused

In recent years, much controversy has arisen over the use of intelligence tests. Group intelligence tests are a problem specifically because young children may

group intelligence tests   Intelligence tests that are designed to be administered to a group of students at one time, as in a class situation.

not understand the directions and may be afraid to ask questions. Because no psychologist is watching them, the children may go astray or give unusual answers that may make sense but still may be marked wrong. The interpretation and use of such tests in placement has also come under fire (Kaplan, 1977). The tests are also used to categorize children prematurely. For instance, one of my acquaintances was shocked when her child's fifth-grade teacher told her that her son was doing fine, considering he had an IQ of "only" 105! Under such circumstances, the self-fulfilling prophecy may operate to the detriment of the individual child.

These tests are not even the best predictor of school achievement available. Richard Antonak and his colleagues (1982) found that the best predictor of school achievement at grade four was not a group intelligence test but rather early school achievement, and he concluded that there is no longer any reason for schools to give these group tests.

Much criticism has been directed at individual intelligence tests as well, especially for cultural bias against minorities. In 1971, a group of parents of black children who were placed in classes for the retarded sued in federal court, claiming that the placements were discriminatory because they were based on intelligence tests that were culturally biased. Eight years later, the court ruled that IQ tests were culturally biased. This famous case—*Larry P.* v. *Riles*—is well-known, and in 1986, a federal judge approved an agreement between the California State Department of Education and the parents that standardized individual tests of intelligence can no longer be administered to black students for any purpose (Dent et al., 1987a). In another case, *Pase* v. *Hannon,* after hearing similar testimony and looking over the test one question at a time, a judge decided that individual intelligence tests, when used with other criteria for determining educational placement, were not discriminatory (Bersoff, 1981a, 1981b). Some psychologists argue that these tests do not show consistent bias against minorities, while others disagree. Even if the tests do not show such bias, the lack of bias does not make the test socially beneficial, and even the *appearance* of bias—as when more minority students are placed in classes for the retarded—is undesirable.

New classification procedures that do not require the use of intelligence tests have been advanced (Dent, 1987b). In addition, because these tests are highly verbal, they may be inappropriate for children

The use of intelligence tests has been the subject of a number of lawsuits.

for whom English is not the primary language (Heward & Orlansky, 1984). In an attempt to free standardized tests from any bias, culture-free or culture-fair tests have been formulated. These tests depend less on language abilities and speed of responding, and they eliminate items that reflect differential cultural or social experiences. Such tests use matching, picture completion, copying block designs, analogies, spatial relationships, and the ability to see relations between patterns (Brown, 1983). But a test that is perfectly culture-free has yet to be invented. Even if it is formulated, it is questionable whether it will predict school performance as well as our present standardized tests.

Another problem is the interpretation of intelligence as if it were fixed quality etched in stone. It isn't. Intelligence scores become more stable as children age. The intelligence scores for younger children are far less reliable and more subject to error than the IQ scores for older children and adults. The correlation is best at about ten years of age. Even after that age, however, intelligence can change with experience. Finally, although scores on an intelligence test correlate with academic achievement, there is a tendency to overrate the test's predictive abilities and to rigidly categorize children (Kaplan, 1977). The use of intelligence tests in schools, then, remains controversial, and the supporters and detractors of the tests have been arguing for a number of years. It is hoped that the discussion will lead to better measuring instruments and improvements in the use of these tests.

A LOOK AT THE STUDENT DURING TESTING

So far, we've focused on the nature of tests and how tests are interpreted. But it is the students who must take the tests, and their experiences with test anxiety and test-taking skills unfortunately are often forgotten. If tests are to accurately measure student skills, these facets of the test situation must be understood.

Test Anxiety

"I knew the material before I took the test. I sat down and I just drew a blank."

"I get so nervous and anxious on tests that I freeze, and when the tests are returned, I find the answers were obvious, but I got them wrong."

There are few teachers who haven't heard students pine that they knew the material before they took the test and then went blank during the test. Almost every student experiences some anxiety concerning tests; after all, taking tests is not the most pleasant experience. However, there are some students who, because of test anxiety, do not seem able to show their knowledge.

Many studies have related test anxiety to decreases in student performance on a number of different types of tests (Covington & Omelich, 1987; Naveh-Benjamin et al., 1987). One might think that if we could relax

Many students suffer from test anxiety. The negative affect of this anxiety can be reduced through instruction in study skills as well as relaxation techniques.

students and reduce their anxiety, students' performance on tests would improve significantly. Unfortunately, despite its logic, this approach has been relatively unsuccessful (Allen et al., 1980). In fact, although relaxation exercises have been successful in reducing test anxiety, very few studies have shown that they lead to improvement in academic performance (Tryon, 1980; Benjamin et al., 1981). Even more confusing are the findings that the relationship between self-reported test anxiety and scores on achievement tests and grades is positive but generally relatively small (Rocklin & Thompson, 1985; Tryon, 1980). In other words, not everyone who reports being very anxious does poorly on tests. Although there is a relationship between test anxiety and poor performance, it would not appear to be straightforward or simple.

Test anxiety is often divided into emotionality and the cognitive component of worry. Most early studies of test anxiety focused on the emotional and physiological reactions students have to the test, but more recently the worry component has taken center stage. Students with high test anxiety focus wholly on the negative aspects of the test, with beliefs that they will fail, cannot handle the situation, and don't do well on objective tests. These self-statements are accompanied by intense self-awareness and preoccupation with themselves (Wine, 1980). Students with high test anxiety experience more of these negative thoughts during exams than students with low test anxiety (Hunsley 1985; 1987). Worry interferes with performance by reducing the student's concentration and diverting attention from the task at hand (Sarason, 1984). In other words, worry interferes with test performance.

There is another element to consider, however. Studies have consistently shown that high test-anxious students have significantly lower levels of study skills competency when compared to low test-anxious students (Culler & Holahan, 1980). They have poorer grades as well. Teaching study skills is one possible way, then, of dealing with the problem of test anxiety. However, just as in the case of the emotional component of test anxiety, improving study skills itself does not automatically lead to a reduction in test anxiety or an improvement in academic performance (Paulman & Kennelly, 1984). Perhaps we have to combine both approaches to understand the problem. It may be that some high test-anxious students may have difficulty encoding information because of poor study skills, while others may find that their worry interferes with their retrieval of information during the test (Naveh-Benjamin et al., 1987).

Although test anxiety is not a tenable explanation for failure for the majority of students, it is a problem for some. What approaches are likely to be successful? One approach uses a multimodal model for understanding test anxiety that views test anxiety as a chain of events and does not focus on a single cause (Russo, 1984). The student is challenged with an exercise. The test-anxious student experiences a great many negative thoughts in response to being evaluated. He or she imagines failure and a loss of self-esteem, loses concentration, and attends to irrelevant stimuli. All of these factors may be accompanied by physical reactions.

Successful intervention may be applied anywhere throughout this scheme. For example, we might concentrate on giving students sets of suggestions to reduce self-centered worry, such as reminding students to stop thinking about themselves and to concentrate and not to allow themselves to get flustered by errors and difficult items. It is also possible to alter cognitions by encouraging the student to replace negative statements with positive self-statements. In the imagery area, it may be possible for the guidance counselor or teacher to help the student imagine a pleasant task outcome. In the behavioral area, poor preparation must be reduced. Since there is evidence that high test-anxious students have poor test-taking skills (Kirkland & Hallandsworth, 1980), it is reasonable to help students develop good test-taking skills as well. Last, although relaxation may not be very effective on its own, relaxation exercises may be helpful as an adjunct to this program. It may be necessary to use a number of these strategies to counter test anxiety, and some research shows that combined treatment programs that include the reduction of emotionality and worry and improvement in study skills and test-taking skills may be the best solution (Anastasi, 1988).

Test-Taking Skills

Some students seem to have better test-taking skills than others. **Testwiseness** is defined as "the capacity to utilize the characteristics and formats of the test and/or test taking situation to receive a high score" (Millman et al., 1965, p. 707). It can be divided into two elements. First, there are those skills that are in-

> **testwiseness** A student's ability to utilize the characteristics and format of a test or the test-taking situation to receive a high score.

dependent of the test itself, such as knowing how to use time effectively, strategies for avoiding errors, sensible guessing tactics, and the use of deductive reasoning to eliminate alternatives in multiple-choice tests (Koenke, 1987; Mehrens & Lehmann, 1987). The second type of testwiseness involves the use of information in one test question to answer another correctly. Such errors in test construction are much more likely to occur on teacher-made tests than on standardized tests, and ways to avoid them are discussed in Chapter 15.

The evidence is overwhelming that testwiseness is a skill that can be taught and that it can lead to small score increases on achievement tests (Kalechstein et al., 1981). Testwiseness is especially important for multiple-choice tests. For example, a number of people may not know how to limit choices through deductive reasoning. Sometimes conventional wisdom leads to test-taking conclusions that are false. It has become common knowledge that one's first answer is usually correct, and therefore students are advised not to change answers. However, studies show that more answers are changed from wrong to right than from right to wrong (Feder, 1979; Hanna, 1989).

True or False Students can learn to improve their test-taking techniques, and this leads to some improvement in their test scores.

True or False On multiple-choice tests, students are more likely to change their answers from wrong to right than from right to wrong.

Familiarity with tests and test procedures is also important. In one study, Melanie Dreisbach and Barbara Keough (1982) familiarized kindergarten students from Mexican-American backgrounds with test-taking procedures. They introduced the children to the test booklet and explained the purpose of testing, familiarized them with the testing vocabulary, practiced three different responses required in the readiness test (circle, underline, and mark through the answer), and emphasized the importance of following directions. The students scored much better than untrained children in both English and Spanish-translated readiness tests. There is evidence that training in these skills especially helps below-average readers and generalizes to different test situations (Ritter & Idol-Maestas, 1986). Experience with tests themselves contributes to modest improvements in scores. Many tests use computer answer sheets, and students who are unfamiliar with them begin the test at a disadvantage.

What does teaching test-taking skills or giving students practice in taking certain types of tests do to the validity of the test? It actually increases the test's validity (Anastasi, 1988). A test is valid if it measures what it is designed to measure. A student who does not know how to take a test or does not have sufficient test-taking strategies will not be able to show his or her true level of knowledge. So, if students possess good test-taking skills, they should be encouraged to use them. If students do not have such skills, the skills should be taught.

One such training program uses the mnemonic device called SCORER (Carman & Adams, 1972). Students are taught to <u>S</u>chedule their time; note the <u>C</u>lue words, especially in directions; <u>O</u>mit difficult questions; <u>R</u>ead carefully; <u>E</u>stimate the answers; and <u>R</u>eview their work.

▶▶▶ CONNECTIONS

The Teacher's Perspective on Test Anxiety and Test-Taking Skills

The experience of test anxiety is natural, and most students cope with it well. The question is what to do with students who tell you that they are unable to function in the test situation or always freeze. The evidence indicates that students who are affected greatly by test anxiety do not all respond in the same way. Some become so worried that it interferes with concentration; others lack study skills and do not adequately know the material even before they enter the room. Still others lack test-taking skills. In addition, there is always the possibility that the student is using test anxiety as a rationalization for his or her poor performance. The following are some suggestions concerning what the teacher can do to help students experiencing high test anxiety.

1. **Reduce the anxiety level in the classroom.** This can be accomplished by assuming a pleasant manner and not overemphasizing the importance of the test.

2. **Remember that relaxation may not in itself lead to improved achievement.** It is natural to counter student test anxiety by helping students to relax both before and during the test. Though relaxation may decrease the anxiety somewhat, research shows that this may not lead to improvement in academic performance. Therefore the teacher must do more than relax students.

3. **Adopt a multi-faceted program to help test-anxious students.** Such a program would contain teaching students better study skills (see Chapter 3), better test-taking skills, positive self-statements to counter the negative ones, as well as relaxation training.

4. **Severe cases of test-anxiety should be referred to the guidance counselor or school psychologist.** If the problem of test anxiety is very serious, a referral to the appropriate school personnel is required.

5. **Make a list of the test taking skills that your students require.** You can discover which skills students lack by observing the class while taking a test and talking to students individually. Ask a few students to read a question to you and work the question orally. This will show you how these students deal with the problem. You may find that your students do not use all the information available or skip over important words.

6. **Train students in test-taking skills.** Students require training in such skills, and such training does not adversely affect the validity of a test. Teachers should be active in familiarizing students with different types of test questions and in teaching test-taking skills. For example, some students may add when they should subtract because they do not check for signs, or they miss words like *almost, always,* and *not* on multiple-choice tests. Students should be taught to read the questions carefully. There are many test taking skills, for example, budgeting one's time, deducing the correct answer in a multiple-choice test, reviewing work, and knowing when to change answers. Each can be addressed. Strategies such as planning one's time and skipping very difficult questions and coming back to them later, are sometimes helpful. Teachers can and should teach these strategies to students.

CURRENT AND FUTURE ISSUES IN TESTING

Despite the problems inherent in standardized testing, it is doubtful that any movement that wishes to do away with these tests will succeed. If anything, the pressure towards more testing will be great. Educators and administrators see the tests as useful, although they often view them as useful for someone else. Educators see them as useful for administrators, while administrators tend to think teachers would miss them if they were eliminated (Dreher & Singer, 1984). Most teachers are aware of the possibilities of bias or misinterpretation, although few want to see such tests completely abolished. However, teachers seem to be dissatisfied with the information provided to them by these tests.

In the future, the reporting of test results may include not only the usual percentiles and stanines but also content information, such as an example of the most difficult test question that the student successfully answered. In addition, to show individual progress, some self-comparison may be provided. It is important to see how the child is progressing from year to year rather than always showing how the child compares to the normed group. For example, suppose a student scored in the 45th percentile on a third-grade reading test and also in the 45th percentile on a fourth-grade reading test. It appears he hasn't learned anything new, but this is not true. One suggestion is that the fourth-grader take both the third- and the fourth-grade tests to show that he is making progress. By taking both tests, the student will show that he has mastered the material he could not do in the previous year. He may score in the 90th percentile on last year's test, thereby showing progress. He still requires extra help in reading, but it more accurately shows his progress. Teachers, principals, parents, school superintendents, and school board members all note a desire for a combination of both self- and norm comparison information (Dreher & Singer, 1984).

Another area of change involves the legal aspects of testing. Some states have passed truth-in-testing laws. The New York statute requires testing companies to make standardized tests for admission to post-secondary and professional schools available to examinees and to permit students to see their graded tests and correct answers (Bersoff, 1981). Of course, the publishers claim that the requirement would violate test security and increase costs. It remains to be seen how far these laws will go in protecting the student. The legal challenge to intelligence tests and the search for ways to evaluate without bias is ongoing, and more legal challenges can be expected.

In the immediate future, however, the question of how tests ought to be used will be debated from many points of view. The recent movement to improve schooling and for increased accountability is essentially test driven. As we've seen, such issues as teaching to the test, curricula matching, and the evaluation of schools and teachers on the basis of student scores on achievement tests are now getting considerable attention. As schools are increasingly evaluated as good or poor on the basis of their students' test scores, will teachers be forced to teach only what is on the test, to ignore higher order skills, or to give students practice that is so close to the test item that the meaningfulness of the test is compromised? Will students be judged solely on how they do on multiple-choice pencil-and-paper tests? These questions remain to be answered.

The crucial question surrounding standardized tests is how these tests are going to be used. Standardized tests are useful tools if they are interpreted and used properly. The question is whether they will be servant—or master.

SUMMARY

1. The popularity of standardized testing is increasing, as such tests are being used to determine whether a student should be promoted, awarded a diploma, or placed in a particular program. Standardized tests are also used to evaluate curricula and instructional effectiveness.

2. Evaluation is a systematic process of judging the quality, value, or worth of some performance or program, while measurement refers to a quantitative description of student behavior and is usually accomplished through testing.

3. All standardized tests contain a specific set of items and offer standardized directions for administration and scoring. They are commercially prepared by experts in the field of testing and measure behavior under unvarying procedures.

4. A norm-referenced test is one in which the test is first given to a representative group of people and the test taker's score is compared against the group's scores. These tests provide teachers and administrators with data that compare students' scores. They do not, however, tell us about the absolute level of knowledge acquired

by a student. Some authorities object to them, since the norm group may not be representative of the group being tested, the test may not match the local curricular needs, and teachers may be pressed to teach to the test. Each of these objections can be answered by those in favor of norm-referenced tests.

5. Criterion-referenced tests (CRTs) compare the student's score to a standard of acceptable performance in the content area. CRTs yield useful information concerning the skills the student has and has not mastered. They are especially useful in testing well-defined basic skills but not as useful in measuring upper-level cognitive skills or skills that involve critical thinking. In addition, the level for achieving proficiency may be arbitrary.

6. Standardized tests are used in education because they allow for objective comparisons across schools and districts. However, their interpretation is difficult, they may be biased, cause teachers to resist new curricula that may not be reflected on the test, and may test superficial knowledge. Lately, people have become concerned that standardized achievement tests may be overestimating achievement, since the norms may be out of date and teachers may be teaching to the test itself.

7. Standardization refers both to the fact that standardized tests have specific rules for their administration and scoring and to the process by which the norm group is tested and norms are established that then serve as the basis for comparison.

8. A test is valid if it measures what it is supposed to measure. Content-related validity is established when the content of the test covers the domain it is designed to cover. It is most important for achievement tests. There are two types of criterion-related validity: predictive and concurrent. If the test relates to a later event, such as academic achievement in college, it has predictive validity. If the test results correlate well with another accepted test in the area, the test has concurrent validity. A test has construct validity if it corresponds well to a theory or hypothetical construct.

9. A test is reliable if it yields consistent scores. Test-retest reliability can be determined by giving the test once and then repeating it. Alternate form reliability involves using two different forms of the test and then determining how closely related the scores are. The internal consistency of a test is measured through split-half reliability, in which the test is divided in half and the scores on both halves are correlated. The standard error of measurement is a statistic that allows us to estimate the error in an individual score. If the standard error is three points, we can be reasonably certain that the true score lies within three points of the obtained score in either direction.

10. Various statistics are often used to interpret test scores. The mean is the arithmetic average, the median is the middle score, and the mode is the score that occurs the most often. The range and standard deviation yield information as to the variability of the scores in the distribution. The normal distribution is an ideal distribution in which we know the percentage of scores that fall between the mean and different points along the curve marked by standard deviations. It is useful as a model for interpreting test results.

11. To interpret raw scores easily, they are often converted into derived scores, such as percentiles, z scores, or grade equivalents. Percentile rankings show the percentage of students that scored on or below the student's score. A standard score demonstrates how far a given raw score is from the mean in standard deviation units. Standard scores include z scores, T scores, and stanines. Grade equivalents are derived by assigning the median score of a norm group, for example, fourth-graders, as 4.0, and assigning scores above and below appropriate values. They are easily misunderstood.

12. The most commonly administered standardized tests are those measuring achievement. Some achievement batteries measure global skills, others are specific in that they measure only one area, such as reading, while still others are diagnostic in nature. Minimum competency tests indicate whether an individual has achieved proficiency so that he or she will receive a diploma or be promoted. Readiness tests measure the extent to which a student has the required skills to learn a new skill.

13. An aptitude test is one that is given to predict success in a particular area when given training. Scores on intelligence tests predict academic achievement but are far from perfect predictors. Intelligence is related to school achievement, but

other factors, such as motivation and adjustment, are important. Individual or group tests of intelligence and cognitive ability are sometimes used in the schools. Both individual and group tests have been criticized for a variety of reasons, and their usefulness is still being debated.

14. Although there is a relationship between test anxiety and decreased test scores, just reducing the anxiety does not seem to lead to improved scores. Test anxiety involves both emotionality and the cognitive component of worry. Students with high test anxiety are distracted from the test by their self-doubts. High test-anxious students tend not to have good study skills. A multifaceted program, including altering self-statements, relaxation, and teaching better test-taking and study skills, holds the most promise for helping students suffering from high test anxiety.

15. Testwiseness involves, among other skills, being able to use time effectively, strategies for avoiding errors, sensible guessing tactics, and the use of deductive reasoning to eliminate alternatives in multiple-choice tests. Testwiseness is a skill that can be taught.

16. In the future, tests will provide more meaningful information to teachers, including examples of the most difficult questions that students answered correctly on a test. The legal aspects will also become more salient, as will questions concerning the use and abuse of these tests.

ACTIVITIES AND EXERCISES

1. **Evaluating a Standardized Test.** Ask to see a copy of the manual for a standardized test and examine it thoroughly. Specifically, look at such information as the procedures used for standardizing the test, the validity and reliability estimates, and the characteristics of the norm group. If you can obtain a copy of a second test that measures the same characteristics (such as two achievement batteries), compare them.

2. **How Does a District Use Standardized Tests?** The text emphasizes the importance of determining the uses for standardized tests before such tests are given. Interview a school principal, a district superintendent, or a professional responsible for designing a test program and ask him or her to give you an idea of the total test program in the district or school and how standardized tests are used. Then interview some teachers and ask them how they use test data.

3. **Testing and the Media.** The "new" push towards school reform is certainly test driven. Not only are students now tested to show their own progress and achievement, but their test scores are frequently used in the public relations and political arena to demonstrate the effectiveness or ineffectiveness of instruction and curricula. Scan the newspapers and popular magazines for articles relating to testing and note their political overtones and importance.

4. **The Popularity of Minimum Competency Testing.** Take a poll of high school teachers, students, and parents to discover their views on minimum competency testing. The following are just some of the questions you may want to include on your questionnaire:

   Do you agree that to graduate and receive a diploma, students should have to take a minimum competency test that measures their knowledge of reading and mathematics?

   Should the test measure more than the basic skills? If your answer is yes, what else should it measure?

   If you believe that reading should be included on such a test, what level of reading proficiency should be used as the criterion (8th grade, 9th grade, 10th grade, 11th grade, 12th grade)?

5. **Teaching to the Test.** Ask a number of teachers at all levels of teaching whether they prepare their students for standardized tests by specifically teaching to the test. This is especially important for high school teachers whose students may have to pass minimum competency tests.

6. **Statistics and Testing.** Given the following test scores, calculate the mean, median, mode, range and standard deviation: 37, 46, 46, 46, 48, 52, 50, 53, 53, 59, 60.

7. **Readiness Tests in Kindergarten.** Visit a kindergarten classroom and speak to the teacher about readiness testing and readiness skills for reading. Specifically ask the teacher how he or she rates readiness tests, whether they are useful, and whether he or she uses them to plan activities.

8. **Individual Intelligence Tests.** The most commonly used individual intelligence test is proba-

bly the Wechsler Intelligence Scale for Children (revised edition). The school psychologist usually has a copy of the test and extensive experience in administering it. Ask the psychologist to show you the subtests. In addition, ask his or her opinion of the use of the test as a diagnostic tool and whether he or she shares the findings with teachers.

9. **What Do You Do to Counter Anxiety?** Some test anxiety is natural, and most people cope well with it. Ask a number of your fellow students how they deal with test anxiety. Try to get them to specifically describe the coping mechanisms they use.

10. **Test-Taking Skills.** Testwiseness involves both knowing how to take a test and using the test questions themselves as a source of information for answering other questions. Write down your own rules for taking multiple-choice tests. They may include rules for deductive reasoning (eliminating alternatives), using time, and skipping difficult items. Ask your fellow students for their rules and compare them to your own.

11. **Teaching Skills to Students Who Lack Them.** You are placed in charge of a program that is to teach test-taking skills to (a) junior high school students who do not have them or (b) students who are returning to college after being away from school for twenty years. Briefly describe a program that will enable these students to improve their test-taking skills.

12. **The Normal Curve.** You are told that an aptitude test has a mean of 100 and a standard deviation of 12. How would this test look on the normal curve? Now consider the scores of two students in your class, John whose score was 94 and Rachel whose score was 112. Convert these raw scores to z scores and T scores. What percentage of scores lies between 88 and 124 and between 76 and 100?

13. **Did Kim Perform Better in Mathematics or Reading?** Kim achieved a raw score of 25 on a mathematics test and 32 on a reading test. The mean on the mathematics test was 10 and on the reading test, 6. Did Kim perform better on the mathematics test or the reading test?

14. **Grade Equivalent.** One of the problems with using grade equivalents is the lack of understanding the public has about their meaning. Ask parents and teachers whether the following are true or false.

If a student in the fifth grade receives a 4.5 grade equivalent on a reading test, it means that she is reading as well as a fourth-grader in January.

If a sixth-grade student reads at 7.5, it means he is ready for seventh-grade reading work.

SCENARIOS

Here are eleven scenarios. Try to apply the information you have learned in the chapter to each situation.

1. Mr. Leonard has just received the results of an achievement battery his fourth-grade class took last month. He has an appointment with Jay's parents to discuss Jay's achievement test scores. Using the CAT scores in Figure 14.3. How would you interpret these scores to Jay's parents?

2. Ms. McKenzie teaches English and mathematics to a third-grade class. She would like to measure the students' competency in particular skills to discover their level of achievement so that she can adjust her teaching to her students' strengths and weaknesses. She is not very familiar with types of standardized tests and asks you, her colleague, what type of test she should use. How would you respond, and why would you make that particular suggestion?

3. Mr. Lang is the parent of a fifth-grade student, Peter, who is not doing very well in class. Peter's teacher, Mr. Jimenez, is aware that Mr. Lang is not happy with Peter's achievement. On reading and mathematics achievement tests, Peter's grade equivalents and percentile ranking were the following:

Reading: Grade equivalent 4.3; percentile ranking 34

Mathematics: Grade equivalent 4.6; percentile ranking 43

Mr. Lang told Mr. Jimenez that his son seems to be reading only as well as a fourth-grader in November of that year and correctly answered only 34 percent of the questions on the reading test. He also notes that his son is achieving in mathematics only as well as a fourth-grader tested in February and answered only 43 percent of the math questions correctly. He is annoyed that his son last year received a percentile ranking of 33 in reading and 41 in mathematics and it seems that Peter knows less now than he did last year. If you were Mr. Jiminez, how would you answer Mr. Lang's statements?

4. Recently, Mrs. Powers was required to give her seventh-grade class a standardized test battery. She was told by her supervisor that she would receive the results of the tests a month or so later and was given a booklet containing the standardized instructions, time limits, etc. Six weeks later, she received the results for each student and her class. The information received included stanines and percentile rankings. Mrs. Powers looked over the questions and had some doubts about the test. It didn't seem to cover some of the curriculum, while it emphasized some areas that she and her colleagues do not stress much. What information should Mrs. Powers request from her supervisor, and how could she use this information in the interpretation of the test scores?

5. Mr. Tanner administered an achievement test to his ninth-grade science class. He looked over the questions, and they seemed reasonable. He was really surprised when Ursula, an A student in his class, did very poorly on this seemingly valid test. He spoke to a colleague, Mr. Smith, who told him, "You can never tell. You can't predict how students will do on standardized achievement tests." Still Mr. Tanner is not certain what to do. If you were in Mr. Tanner's position, what would you do? Also evaluate Mr. Smith's position as to a teacher's ability to predict student performance on achievement tests.

6. There is an argument brewing at Jefferson Junior High. The question is, What statistical information should teachers and parents receive concerning students' performance on standardized tests? Some teachers want as much information as they can get, while others claim that all these statistics just serve to confuse the matter. If you were a teacher at Jefferson Junior High School, what statistical information would you want, and why would it be helpful? Should parents routinely be sent the same information? Why or why not?

7. Miss Kramer is getting her class ready to take the minimum competency test in mathematics. She knows how important the test is to her students but is not certain how much she should "teach to the test." She's fairly new to teaching and has seen only one of these tests. One of her colleagues, Ms. Kent has been teaching for quite a number of years, knows the test well, and seems to present the mathematics problems almost exactly in the manner that they appear on the test (just with different numbers). Miss Kramer is not certain that this strategy is the best, since it may compromise the meaning of the test. She has found that Ms. Kent's students often are well drilled on solving the problems in the exact manner they are given on the test but that any significant variation would mean failure, since they do not necessarily understand the work. Yet, she appreciates the fact that if too many of her students do not pass the test, she will stand out and her teaching ability will be questioned. She asks you, her colleague, how you handle these competency tests. What would you say?

8. Mr. Craig has a problem with Ken, a student in the eighth grade. One of the requirements for admission to a particular program is taking a group IQ test. Ken is a bright student but did not make the cutoff for the special program. His parents demanded to see his record, and of course, they were given access to it. They were floored when they saw that he had an IQ of 107. They thought it was much higher. When Ken found out about it, he became lethargic and apathetic about his schoolwork. He is disappointed in himself and feels that now he cannot hope to become a doctor. If you were Mr. Craig, how would you handle the situation?

9. Ms. Allenson is concerned about Jamie, a student in her high school European history class. Jamie seems to have difficulty taking tests. Although she answers questions correctly in class and seems to spend a great deal of time studying, she makes careless mistakes on the tests and complains of being so anxious that she can't think or respond properly. What can be done to help Jamie with her problem?

10. Ms. Steele doesn't really know much about Randy's achievement in science. Just about every other teacher is in the same boat. Randy is very quiet in class, and although he does his homework carefully, he does not do well on tests. Normally, the conclusion would be that he doesn't know his work, but some strange things seem to happen when he is confronted with a test. He often adds on mathematics tests when he should

subtract. He seems to interpret questions incorrectly on social studies tests, not taking into account such terms as *never* or *sometimes*. He often does not finish his science tests. Randy reads at grade level, and he seems to understand his work but doesn't seem to be able to show it on tests. What can Ms. Steele and the rest of his teachers do to help him?

11. Mr. Bates teaches science in a low socioeconomic area where many students are not reading at grade level. He is a good teacher and is concerned since he believes his students know their work but still do poorly on the standardized exam in eighth-grade because they don't read well. He decides to show how well his students know science by reading the test to them. This infuriates his colleagues and his supervisor. He claims that this is the only fair way to test them. Evaluate Mr. Bates's conduct and the reactions of his colleagues.

15

Are These Statements True or False?

Turn the next page for the correct answers. Each statement is repeated following the paragraph in which the information can be found.

1. Testing and grading take up a total of about five percent of a teacher's professional time.
2. A good test will contain items that no one in the class answers correctly.
3. Longer tests tend to be more valid and reliable than shorter tests.
4. When writing a multiple-choice test, a few of the choices should be made humorous to reduce the tension in the classroom.
5. There is a tendency for the true statements to be longer than the false statements in true-false question tests.
6. Matching exercises are not valid for measuring knowledge and should not be used.
7. Most teacher-made tests measure only factual knowledge.
8. Giving students a choice of essay questions reduces the validity of the test.
9. It is best to minimize the importance of a test to students so as to reduce anxiety.
10. Both high-achieving and low-achieving students have a more positive attitude toward school if they attend schools in which grades are not assigned.
11. A student's conduct should not be taken into consideration when grading a student's achievement.
12. Pass/fail grading systems lead to higher student achievement levels when compared with courses in which a traditional grading system is used.

Teacher-made Tests

Answers to True-False Statements

1. *False* Correct statement: It is estimated that between 20 percent and 30 percent of a teacher's professional time is spent in assessment-related activities.
2. *False* Correct statement: Tests should not contain items that no one in the class answers correctly.
3. *True*
4. *False* Correct statement: Humorous distractors should not be used, since all they do is increase the student's ability to guess the correct answer.
5. *True*
6. *False* Correct statement: Matching exercises are useful for testing factual knowledge of a single domain.
7. *True*
8. *True*
9. *False* Correct statement: Teachers should neither minimize the importance of a test nor make the test seem more important than it really is.
10. *False* Correct statement: Low-achieving students have a better attitude towards school if they attend schools in which grades are not used, but high-achieving students have a more positive attitude if they attend schools in which they are graded.
11. *True*
12. *False* Correct statement: Pass/fail systems do not lead to higher student achievement levels when compared with courses in which a traditional grading system is used.

Mr. Kandinsky must write a social studies unit test for his seventh grade students. In the past, he has found that some of his tests were not as complete as he would have liked. How can he make certain that his tests cover the material that has been taught and assigned?

Ms. Henriques is writing questions for a science midterm. She does not wish the questions to be tricky and wants students to perceive the test as fair. Should she use multiple choice questions, true-false questions, fill-in items, essay questions, or some combination of these items?

Dr. Hill has been having difficulty with Dennis for some time. Dennis is disruptive and often calls out in class. Dennis' grades are passing, but Dr. Hill wonders whether he should subtract points for poor conduct. Should Dr. Hill take conduct into consideration when calculating student grades?

ADVENTURES IN TESTING AND GRADING

"But it isn't fair." "You never taught us that." "The test questions were tricky." These are three common complaints students voice, especially while a test is being reviewed. Testing and evaluation are two areas of the educational process disliked by both teachers and students—and with good reason. Constructing good tests and devising a reasonable grading system are difficult tasks that require a great deal of time. Between 20 percent and 30 percent of a teacher's professional time is spent directly involved in assessment-related activities. The anxiety many students suffer when taking tests and the feeling of vulnerability they experience as they are evaluated by the teacher are most unpleasant.

True or False Testing and grading take up a total of about five percent of a teacher's professional time.

This chapter investigates the nature of teacher-made tests and discusses one evaluation process—grading. It concentrates on measuring the cognitive outcomes of learning, although this is certainly not the only sphere of interest in education. Teachers may also wish to measure psychomotor skills, which involve physical skills and coordination, and affective outcomes, which involve the development of certain basic attitudes (refer to Chapter 11). However, teachers spend most of their assessment time measuring the cognitive outcomes of learning.

The Purposes of Testing and Evaluation

If you asked students to name the most common reason for testing, the overwhelming majority would say, "So that the teacher can give grades." For the most part, students would be correct. Yet, there are many reasons for giving tests and evaluating students. These purposes can be broadly placed into four distinct classes (Blue, 1986). First, there is **diagnostic evaluation.** Diagnostic evaluations are best known in the context of special education, where strengths and weaknesses are extensively tested and evaluated to determine whether children are eligible for special education and, if they are, what program would be best suited to their needs (Kirk & Gallagher, 1986). Standardized tests are often used. However, diagnostic tests may be administered by teachers in the classroom setting to diagnose the strengths and weaknesses of a student in a particular area and to discover exactly where a child's problem lies so that the teacher can adjust teaching strategies to the individual needs of the student.

A second type of evaluation, **placement evaluation,** aims at discovering whether students have the necessary skills to succeed or whether they may have already achieved the objectives before the unit is taught (Sparks, 1987; Gronlund, 1976). A key question to be answered is, Are students ready for the unit the teacher intends to teach? A student who does not know the letters of the alphabet will not be able to learn to read; a student who cannot multiply two numbers will not be able to multiply four numbers. The data from placement tests are used to place students in the proper mathematics or reading groups and to help teachers decide where to start when planning a unit.

The third type of evaluation is called **formative evaluation** and consists of an assessment of progress as the teaching is taking place. Teachers use this type of evaluation when they are questioning students during the class to discover whether the students truly understand what is being taught. However, sometimes a more systematic approach is desirable, and the use of tests to provide feedback for the teacher may be helpful as a means of modifying instruction while the unit is still being taught. Formative evaluation invites teachers to continuously evaluate their methodology and answers the question, Am I succeeding in teaching _____ to my students? Armed

with this knowledge, teachers can change their teaching strategies if necessary. The students are told that the test is being given to indicate what has been mastered and what still needs to be worked on. The tests are scored, and students receive feedback about their progress. In one program, students who have mastered the material as demonstrated on such tests either do enrichment work or serve as peer tutors, while those who have not achieved mastery work in groups or individually towards this goal (Conner et al., 1985). Such formative tests may also help students discover the areas in which they must allocate additional study time, and evidence indicates that such tests can help improve student achievement (Foos & Fisher, 1988). The tests may also motivate pupils, as students sometimes require short-term goals, which doing well on formative tests may provide. This type of evaluation is not often used to grade students but rather is used to indicate whether alternative strategies might be necessary.

By far the most common type of classroom evaluation is **summative evaluation,** which aims at determining whether the instruction has been successful. Summative tests are most often used as the basis for grading. These tests answer the question, Has the student learned what he or she is accountable for learning? Of course, this can be turned around and asked in a more teacher-oriented manner, as in Has my teaching of the unit on _____ been successful? These tests are administered at the end of the instruction and are of less value for directing current learning (Brown, 1983). However, they often can be used to

---

diagnostic evaluation Evaluations in which the strengths and weaknesses of a student are measured, often to determine the student's eligibility for special programs.

placement evaluations Evaluations that aim at discovering whether students have the necessary skills to succeed or whether they have already achieved objectives.

formative evaluations Assessments of progress as the teaching of a particular unit is taking place.

summative evaluation Evaluations that aim at determining whether instruction has been successful.

Teachers spend between 20 percent and 30 percent of their professional time in assessment-related activities.

change instruction for the following year. Perhaps a teacher is disappointed with her students' performance on the test on the Industrial Revolution and seeks a way to improve performance for the coming year. If the scores on the test are very poor, a teacher may choose to spend additional time on the material. However, with the time constraints that exist, this may not be possible.

In some areas, students must demonstrate a particular level of mastery before being allowed to advance. **Mastery tests** measure proficiency at a particular skill. The most common cover mathematics skills, where tests of specific skills are administered. The

mastery tests   Tests that measure a student's proficiency at a particular skill. Scores are reported in terms of the percentage needed for mastery and the percentage a student answered correctly.

scores needed for success are usually rather high. Students are informed ahead of time that these tests will be administered and are advised of the score needed for success. The scores are reported in terms of the percentage needed for mastery and the percentage the student answered correctly. A student's progress on specific skills is often reported to the parents. Mastery tests can serve a formative function as well, for if a student does not achieve this level, more instruction may be required.

Good and Bad Tests

Think back on the hundreds of tests you have taken. Do a few very poor ones stand out? If they do, what made them so poor? If you are like most students, you can remember tests that were not fair, that you did not have the time to finish even though you were supposed to, or that concentrated on minor areas rather than areas that the teacher stressed as important during instruction. Educational psychologists are not naive. They do not claim that creating a quality test will make students enjoy taking tests. However, formulating a test that is fair is more likely to serve the teacher's purposes and will make the chore of returning and reviewing a test less troublesome. The following ten factors suggested by Robert Ebel (1965) can form the basis for judging good tests from bad ones:

1. **Relevance.** Each test item should directly relate to the objectives of the unit being tested, and its relevance should be obvious to the student. This is another way of saying the test must be valid, that is, that it measures what it is designed to measure.
2. **Balance.** The proportion of items on the test should match the emphasis the teacher has placed on the material. Students often complain that something that was not stressed by the teacher received too much emphasis on a test, while the test items did not reflect the amount of time spent on a particular area.
3. **Efficiency.** The test must be long enough to measure what the teacher is trying to test but short enough to fit into the time allotted for it. There is a developmental aspect here. Young elementary school students will need more time to answer questions, and since their attention span is limited, shorter tests are necessary (Green, 1963).

4. **Objectivity.** The questions must be clear and the answers definite so that someone knowledgeable in the field would get an excellent score. Ambiguous or tricky questions should not be asked. There must be a right answer to every objective question. Students will often try to defend their incorrect answer when reviewing a test in class. When constructing a test, it is good practice to be certain that only one correct answer is present and to imagine yourself "defending" against a question as to why choice A or B is not correct. Although the range of acceptable answers to essay tests is greater, such tests often can be constructed to yield responses that are correct or incorrect.

5. **Specificity.** In the ideal test, students in the class who know the material very well should receive excellent scores, while students who know nothing about the material should receive chance scores (the scores students would receive if they guessed on the questions). No clues to the answer should be found in the question.

6. **Difficulty.** Some teachers write tests that are so easy that everyone does well whether they know a great deal of the material or not. Others create tests that are so difficult that no one does well. In most cases, the test should be constructed in such a way that each item is passed by at least half the students. When hardly any student gets a certain item correct, the fault may lie with the item.

True or False A good test will contain items that no one in the class answers correctly.

7. **Discrimination.** The test should discriminate between students who know their work and students who do not. If there are items in which students who did poorly on the test as a whole answer correctly but students who did well on the test did not, the item is not very useful.

8. **Reliability.** The key question here is whether the test scores agree with those obtained from equally good independent measurements of the same achievement. If a student does very well on a standardized reading test but poorly on your test, you may need to do some investigating. In some cases, reliability, or the degree to which a test yields consistency, is difficult to assess in a classroom test.

9. **Fairness.** The test should be constructed and administered so that each student has an equal chance to demonstrate knowledge. Sometimes teachers give out test papers slowly, allowing those who received them first to begin as soon as they receive them. This places the students at the back of the room at a disadvantage and increases students' anxiety level.

10. **Speededness.** There are generally speaking two types of tests. A test is a *speed test* if accuracy within a predetermined time is measured. This time limit usually is insufficient to allow students to finish all items on the test. Tests of filing and typing are speed tests. In a *power test,* time does not play a significant role, although there are almost always time constraints. Generally speaking, time should not be much of a factor in classroom achievement tests, although if a student consistently lags behind the other students on most tests, the teacher should look into the situation.

THE PROCESS OF TESTING

Classroom tests differ greatly from the standardized tests that were discussed in Chapter 14 (see Table 15.1). However, most of these characteristics of good tests, with the possible exception of reliability, can easily be achieved by the individual teacher if the test is correctly planned, constructed, administered, and interpreted. Good tests don't just happen; they are the result of planning and experience. At first, creating a good test will take considerable time and effort, but it will become easier and less time consuming with experience.

Planning the Test

The first step in planning the test involves delineating the content to be tested. Some boundaries must be placed on the test, which is a simple process during which the teacher notes what generally will be covered on the test. If the test is a weekly social studies quiz, writing down the topics to be covered is sufficient. The second step involves making a more detailed outline of what was taught. If the specific objectives are already written, the teacher is ready for the next step. If only a content outline is available, the objectives must be specified. Remember that we not only are interested in communicating facts or knowledge to our students but also may be concerned with

Table 15.1 Characteristics of Teacher-made and Standardized Tests
Teacher-made tests differ from standardized tests in many ways, some of which are noted in this table.

Characteristic	Teacher-made	Standardized
Relevance	Measures objectives for the class.	Measures achievement for typical classes.
Balance	Measures objectives in same proportion as time spent on instruction.	Measures a large variety of objectives.
Difficulty	Is geared to the group being tested.	May vary; usually averages around 50 percent passing for all items.
Reliability	Usually not calculated; normally very low but can be as high as standardized tests if carefully planned.	Usually high; normally .85 and above.
Speededness	Sufficient time usually given for completion of test.	Strict time limits typical.
Discrimination	Each question helps to differentiate between high- and low-scoring students if differentiation is goal; if testing for mastery, this characteristic is meaningless.	Attempts to find individual differences between students, with each question contributing to differentiation of those scoring high and low.
Specificity	Measures specific learnings.	Attempts to measure specific learning.
Objectivity	Agreement among experts on answers to items chosen.	Answers usually checked by subject-matter experts.

Reprinted by permission from *The Science Teacher,* a publication of The National Science Teachers Association, 1972.

comprehension, application, and some of the higher order cognitive skills found in Bloom's taxonomy (refer to Chapter 11). A teacher writing a test on evaporation may want students to know what the term means, to be able to determine whether evaporation is occurring given a number of examples of physical phenomena, and perhaps even to design an experiment to demonstrate the phenomenon.

The third step involves selecting the test content. Since it is usually impossible to test everything, most tests measure a sample of behaviors. For example, what if your students were asked to remember the capitals of all the countries in the world that belong to the United Nations. There are about 150 such countries. Most teachers wouldn't test all 150 items. Instead, they would choose a representative sample of items. This should not be done randomly, or the teacher might end up with ten out of twenty items covering African countries. Most teachers would rather choose some countries from each continent.

When planning which questions should be asked, there is no substitute for creating a table of specifications, which is really a blueprint for the test (Gay, 1985). Table 15.2 shows a table of specifications of a

fourth-grade science unit on weather. The topics are listed in the left-hand column. At the top are the headings that reflect the objectives of the unit. Note that on this test only three of Bloom's taxonomy are listed, as the objectives did not cover the others. The numbers in the grid show the number of questions used to evaluate this content/objective pairing. For example, two questions cover knowledge of condensation, and one question covers applications relating to condensation. The totals at the right side illustrate the total number of items relating to each topic and the percentage of the test devoted to that topic. The tabulations at the bottom show the number of items covering each of the objectives and the percentage of the test devoted to each objective. Five items cover the topic of evaporation, or 16.5 percent of the test. Eight items cover comprehension, which accounts for 26.5 percent of the test. In some tables of specifications, the objectives can be broken down even further. The knowledge component could be divided to include knowledge of common terms and knowledge of specific facts.

There are various ways of forming these tables. Sometimes, only a one-way table of specifications is

Table 15.2   Table of Specifications for a Unit on Weather for Fourth-Grade Students
Creating a table of specifications is an important step in the formulation of a fair and comprehensive test.

Topics	Behavior			Total Number of Items	Percentage of Test
	Knowledge	Comprehension	Application		
1. Evaporation	3		2	5	16.5
2. Condensation	2	1	1	4	13.5
3. Wind	2	1	1	4	13.5
4. Temperature	3	3	3	9	30
5. Clouds	2	3	3	8	26.5
Total Number of Items	12	8	10	30	
Percentage of Test	40	26.5	33.5	100	

From *Elementary Education: A Basic Test* by F. Reisman and B. Payne, Copyright © 1987 Merrill Publishing Company, Columbus, Ohio. Reprinted by permission.

required, as shown in Table 15.3. Here, the objectives are clearly noted, and the teacher has decided on the emphasis placed on each objective. When the teacher has determined the desired length of the test (60 questions in this case), he or she can multiply the relative emphasis in percentage and the total number of items and determine how many items should be placed on the test. For example, 30 percent of the test will cover identification of coniferous trees by cones and needles. When 60 is multiplied by .30, we find that 18 items ought to be devoted to this objective.

The length of a test is determined by the subject being tested, the time available, and the developmental level of the students. As a rule, longer tests tend to be more valid and reliable. However, there is no set rule or magic formula for determining the number of items that should be included on the test, and each teacher must determine the optimum length for a particular test.

True or False   Longer tests tend to be more valid and reliable than shorter tests.

Table 15.3   Example of a One-way Table of Specifications
When objectives are already clearly written, a one-way table of specifications can be used in the formation of a test.

Topic	Amount of Emphasis	Number of Points
Define "coniferous tree"	5%	3
Describe structural parts & functions	20%	12
Reproductive cycle	10%	6
Coniferous trees of Oklahoma	10%	6
Identify coniferous trees by cones & needles	30%	18
Identify coniferous trees in slides	10%	6
Economic uses of coniferous trees	15%	9
Total	100%	60

From "Measures of Validity, Reliability and Item Analysis for Classroom Tests" by D. N. Nimmer, *The Clearing House,* 58, 3, 138–140, November 1984. Reprinted with permission of the author.

Constructing the Test

Do you prefer essay tests or short-answer tests? If the teacher gave you a choice of taking a multiple-choice test or a test constructed of true-false questions, which would you choose? Your answer to these questions

may have little to do with the actual difficulty of these different types of tests, for each can be made as easy or as difficult as the teacher wishes. Instead, your decision will probably be influenced by your subjective experience with different types of tests. You may find that essay tests are easier for you because you write well or because you are successful in skirting the answers—you embellish well. On the other hand, you may find multiple-choice questions easier because you can reason out the answers. Of the four alternatives, you may be able to eliminate two as ridiculous and then have, at worst, a 50 percent probability of success. On the other hand, you may dislike multiple-choice questions because you find them tricky. As we examine each type of test question, think about the tests you've taken in the past and reflect on how they could have been improved.

Objective Test Items

Objective test items are those in which a student must either recognize the correct answer or supply a one- or two-word answer to a question. The answers are either right or wrong. Objective test items include multiple-choice questions, true-false questions, matching exercises, and fill-in questions.

Multiple-Choice Questions

Multiple-choice questions are the most widely used objective questions (Houston et al., 1988). They consist of an incomplete statement or a question followed by a number of alternatives. The test taker has to choose the number or the letter of the alternative that either completes the sentence or answers the question. The question or incomplete statement is called the stem, while the incorrect alternatives are called distractors.

The advantages of multiple-choice tests are many. They are very flexible in that they can measure outcomes that cut across all of Bloom's taxonomy with the exception of synthesis (Montague, 1987). A teacher can give students a large number of multiple-choice questions, allowing for a more representative sampling of the material. The scoring is simple and straightforward and can be done by computer if special, relatively inexpensive answer sheets are provided, making statistical analysis much easier. Unlike the essay, it does not take much time to respond to the question, once the student has figured out the correct answer.

Multiple-choice questions have some disadvantages, however. They take quite a bit of time to construct, and it is very difficult to conjure up three or four good, solid distractors that are plausible yet not so close to the correct answer as to confuse students. Another problem is that although theoretically multiple-choice items can measure a variety of learning outcomes, in practice they are often used to test only a student's knowledge of terms and definitions. In addition, multiple-choice items require considerable reading ability, and this may cause problems, especially for young or poor readers. Students may know the material, yet the lack of reading skills may not allow them to show this. To reduce this problem, it is reasonable to help define a word or interpret a statement for any student who does not understand the question, providing the word or the statement is not the one being tested. In this way, a student who does not understand the word *validate* or *circumnavigate* or has difficulty understanding an item can ask a question. Of course, any student who continually requires assistance may require special help. Perhaps the student's reading skills are very poor or the student has a learning disability that requires alternative testing. Not all students will take advantage of such a policy. Very young students or pupils who are very frightened or shy may not ask questions, and the teacher may need to investigate the possibility that reading ability has unduly influenced the results of the test.

 **CONNECTIONS**

Practical Suggestions for Writing Multiple-Choice Questions

Constructing multiple-choice questions is a skill. The following points and examples can improve your skills in formulating these questions.

1. **Try to use a four- or five-option multiple-choice format and use the same number of options throughout the test.** If you must switch from a four- to a five-option question, make the switch very clear to students or you may find students placing a (D) as the last choice for the five-choice format when they really mean (E). By using at least four choices, the effect of guessing is reduced. For example, in a ten-item multiple-choice test with four alternatives, the chances of obtain-

ing a score of seven by chance alone is one in one thousand (Reisman & Payne, 1987).

2. **Avoid using any one choice as the correct answer too often.** One student told me, "When in doubt, always choose C." He was talking about a science class where the teacher used C as the correct answer more often than he should have. After a while, some members of the class realized this. On the other hand, there is nothing wrong with occasionally having three or even four correct answers in a row being the same (for example, four D's).

3. **Don't let one multiple-choice question give a clue to answering another question.** Sometimes teachers will ask one question that gives some information in the stem of the question and then ask another question requiring this knowledge. This is poor form, since it allows a testwise student to show his or her ability to gather information from the test but does not demonstrate knowledge of the subject being tested.

4. **Place as much of the text in the stem as possible and include in the stem any words that would be repeated in each response.** With the exception of definitions, using longer stems and shorter alternatives is the best source.

For example, consider this multiple-choice question:

Stalin

a. was the chief Soviet scientist involved in the Russian atom bomb project.

b. was the leader of the Soviet Union during WWII.

c. was a general in the Soviet Air Force during WWII.

d. was the admiral of the Soviet fleet during WWII.

Notice that the words *was* and *during WWII* are repeated. Students must take unnecessary time to read these repeating phrases. In addition, the stem gives little information about what is desired. When the stem does not present much information, the alternatives must be read before the student can understand what the teacher is looking for (Gronlund, 1976). A better form would be the following:

What position did Stalin hold during WWII?

a. chief Soviet scientist involved in the Russian atom bomb project

b. leader of the Soviet Union

c. general in the Soviet Air Force

d. admiral of the Soviet fleet

The rule that the stem should contain as much information as possible is broken when testing a definition. When doing so, a simple question such as Which of the following statements defines the term *culture*? is best. This discourages guessing and is better suited to testing the knowledge students have of the term.

5. **Watch your grammar, especially the use of *a/an*.** Consider the following incomplete statement:

The person who drives a train is called an:

a. brakeman

b. engineer

c. conductor

d. driver

The answer is obviously b, because there is no other choice that begins with a vowel. The use of *an* gave it away. Simply using *a/an* will solve this problem easily.

6. **Avoid making the correct answers longer or more complete than other answers.** This is a common problem among inexperienced test writers, and testwise students will look for these hints.

7. **Avoid negatively stated items as much as possible.** (Green, 1963) The use of such statements as All of the following are correct except? and Which is not a factor? can be tricky, especially for younger students, and test student reading ability. When it is necessary to use such terms, print them boldly or in all capital letters.

8. **Be very careful in your use of *all of these* or *none of these*.** (Miller & Erickson, 1985) There is some disagreement concerning the use of these alternatives. They may be reasonable alternatives as long as they are used as the correct answer only once in a while. Remember that a student answering "none of the above" may not know the correct answer but may know that the ones presented do not answer the question. Do not use *none of these* if the question is phrased in a negative way. This becomes very confusing for students.

9. **All distractors must be reasonable.** We've all taken multiple-choice tests where a distractor such as Yogi Bear or Mickey Mouse was used. Although these provide humor, they also reduce the number of alternatives, thereby increasing the chances that students can guess the answer.

In addition, sometimes teachers may be testing knowledge of some concept but the distractors give away the answer. For example:

Which man was president of the United States during WWI?
a. Bertrand Russell
b. René Descartes
c. Woodrow Wilson
d. Zane Grey

The answer is obviously Woodrow Wilson, but a student might answer this question correctly not because he or she knows the right answer but because none of the other three was president of the United States.

10. **Arrange alternatives in logical order and list them vertically.** Look at the following multiple-choice item:

Approximately what percentage of mothers with children under one year of age is in the work force? a. 40 b. 65 c. 20 d. 33 e. 50

The horizontal format makes reading more difficult, and this is especially a problem if the distractors are very long. Second, the random presentation of the alternatives does not allow students to quickly and easily find the answer they are looking for. It would be better if the percentages were arranged from smallest to greatest. In other types of alternatives, alphabetical listings are possible.

It takes much time and effort to produce good multiple-choice questions, but these test items have so many advantages that the effort is worth the time.

True or False   When writing a multiple-choice test, a few of the choices should be made humorous to reduce the tension in the classroom.

True-False Questions

Most people are familiar with true-false tests. The test taker must determine whether a statement is true or false, correct or incorrect. The test can be varied somewhat by requiring the student who marks an item "false" to supply the correct answer as in:

Thomas Jefferson was the second president of the United States. T. F.

The word that is underlined draws the student's attention, and if the answer is false, the student must write the correct answer (third) in the space provided. Most true-false items are simpler, however, requiring only that the student answer true or false.

True-false questions can be used for purposes other than measuring achievement. They are useful in surveying students to discover to what extent they believe common myths (Reisman & Payne, 1987). For example, consider the statement, "Cerebral palsy is a progressive, communicative disease." This is false, and if students believe the statement, some instruction is necessary.

True-false questions can also be used as motivational devices. Pretests using true-false questions can heighten interest as students discover how much they know or don't know about a subject. However, here we are interested only in their use in measuring achievement.

The advantages of true-false items are obvious. They are easy to score, can sample a tremendous amount of content, and require little response time. They take less time to construct than multiple-choice items, but many more true-false questions are needed to cover the same amount of material. It takes about five true-false items to measure what three multiple-choice items can measure (Ebel, 1975).

True-false questions have their limitations. Most things are neither right or wrong nor true or false all the time. The only way to compensate for this absolute bias in true-false questions is to use what psychologists call specific determiners, which include such terms as *only, all, none, always, sometimes, never, might,* or *would.* These often confuse students and cause problems. If something can occur under extreme circumstances is "sometimes" the right answer? If someone stated that the correlation between smoking and cancer was substantial, a student must know what substantial means.

In addition, guessing is a distinct problem. Unless the scoring system is changed so that there is a penalty for guessing—something that is difficult to do in a classroom test—the naive student has a fifty-fifty chance of getting an item correct. In a four-alternative multiple-choice item, the chance is 25 percent. Ideally, true-false questions can measure most levels of achievement. In reality, though, they are limited to the more elementary learning outcomes, which limits their usefulness.

**Practical Suggestions for Writing
True-False Questions**

The following guidelines may help teachers construct true-false questions:

1. **Construct the items so that the true and false statements are of about equal length.** There is a tendency for the true statements to be longer than the false statements (Gay, 1985).

2. **Avoid the use of specific determiners as much as possible.** In addition, some determiners such as *always* and *none* are usually false, while the terms *generally* and *usually* are often true.

3. **Avoid testing irrelevant information.** Consider this example:

   The painting called *Sunflowers* was painted by Victor van Gogh.

   The answer is false, since the artist was Vincent van Gogh. However, a teacher must ask herself whether she really wants to test her students' knowledge of first names. In addition, it is very easy for a student who knows the right answer to simply read over the Victor as Vincent.

4. **Avoid having two ideas in one statement unless the statement involves cause and effect.** For example:

   Seals are mammals and are the most intelligent animals on this planet.

   There are two statements here. Seals are mammals, which is true, while the second statement that they are the most intelligent animals on this planet is false.

5. **The number of true and false questions should be approximately equal.** It is best if students do not develop a bias of responding true, or false, to your test questions.

6. **Unless you are measuring the ability to identify whether or not something is fact or opinion, always specify the source of the opinion.** For example:

   The best way to ensure peace is through a powerful nuclear deterrent.

   Not only is this an opinion question, but the question of "according to whom" is begged.

7. **Avoid sentences in excess of about twenty words.** Long sentences become cumbersome and may include many complicated clauses and phrases (Miller & Erickson, 1985).

True or False   There is a tendency for the true statements to be longer than the false statements in true-false question tests.

Matching Exercises

Suppose you want to test your students' ability to recognize the capitals of specific states. You could use a multiple-choice format or even a true-false format. However, since the domain of knowledge to be tested is uniform (capitals and states), it is more efficient to use a matching format. Matching tests involve constructing two columns. In this case, the left-hand column would contain the names of the states, while the right-hand column would list the state's capital cities. The students must match the cities to the states in which they are located. Generally, more choices appear in the right-hand side of the matching exercise so that the exercise does not turn into a process of elimination. The items in the column for which the match is sought are called premises, and the items in the columns from which the selection is made are called responses (Gronlund, 1976). The premises are often, but not always, longer than the responses. Matching exercises are effective and efficient whenever the ability to identify the relationship between two things is being tested and a number of similar premises and responses are available. Matching exercises can also be used with pictorial materials, as when different types of geometric figures are matched with their names.

The advantages of the matching format are its very compact format and its thorough testing of a fairly large set of items in a very efficient manner. It is easy to construct, and it is an effective way of measuring factual knowledge. It can sometimes be used to test more sophisticated levels of understanding, such as measuring students' understanding of cause and effect (Reisman & Payne, 1987).

True or False   Matching exercises are not valid for measuring knowledge and should not be used.

Matching exercises are limited in their usefulness, however. It is often difficult to devise matching questions that test higher level cognitive skills. If the factual knowledge to be tested comes from a variety of areas, matching questions are inappropriate. For example, matching exercises should not quiz knowledge about explorers and scientists. However, if we only want to test students' knowledge of explorers and their achievements, matching is a possibility.

Practical Suggestions for Constructing Matching Exercises

The following suggestions for constructing matching exercises may be helpful:

1. **Matching exercises should be complete on one page.** I remember taking three such exercises, and the third one was completed on the back of the page. Students wasted much time turning the paper over and looking at a second page.

2. **Use responses that are homogeneous but different enough from one another so that they do not confuse students.** It is not a good policy to mix dates, names, and vocations on responses.

3. **Arrange both premises and responses in logical order.** The order can be alphabetical or chronological, but some order makes it easier for students to respond. For instance, if the responses are dates, placing them in chronological order is reasonable; if they are cities, alphabetical order is helpful.

4. **There should be more responses than premises.** This limits guessing and eliminates the possibility that students will arrive at their answers through a process of elimination.

5. **Use the developmental level of the students to determine the number of items.** For elementary school students, five or six items is sufficient. For older students, the number may be increased.

6. **The directions should clearly state the basis for matching.** Directions should not say match column B with column A but rather should give overall organization to the exercise by telling students to match the inventions in column A with the inventors in column B.

Fill-in Items

The name of the fourth president of the United States is _____.

If you mix red and blue together you get the color _____.

The _____ River is the longest river in the United States.

What is the technical term for a mathematical average?

Who wrote *Uncle Tom's Cabin*?

These are examples of fill-in or short-answer items. As you probably noticed, there is little difference between leaving a dash for the correct answer or simply asking a question that requires a one- or two-word response. Unlike other objective test items, fill-in or short-answer questions measure recall, not recognition. The student is asked to supply the right answer from memory, not to recognize the right answer from among a group of answers.

Short-answer questions are flexible in that they can be written in question form or simply as statements in which an important word is omitted. The answer required can be one word or, in the case of a question, an entire sentence. Such questions have the advantage of reducing guessing to a minimum, since the student must supply the correct answer. It is very useful in measuring factual recall, and the construction of such items is rather easy, allowing many areas of knowledge to be tested in a short time.

The disadvantages of fill-in items involve the difficulty of composing items that measure more than memorized material. In addition, it is tempting to use the exact wording from a text, which is a problem, since it measures only rote memorization, not understanding (Anderson, 1972). It is best, but not always easy, to paraphrase. It is also sometimes difficult to write unambiguous items, and misinterpretation is rather common (Montague, 1987). For example, look at this fill-in item:

The third president of the United States was _____.

I am looking for the person's name, but what if a student wrote "elected in 1800"? This is technically correct, and I would have difficulty marking it wrong. The final difficulty involves scoring. Fill-in questions must be scored by hand, making it more difficult to statistically analyze how the class performed on the question. A teacher would have to write down all the wrong answers to find out where the students made their mistakes, a very time consuming process, although it certainly yields some very useful information.

Practical Suggestions for Writing Fill-In and Short-Answer Questions

The following guidelines can be helpful in constructing fill-in questions or short-answer objective items.

1. **The statements used must stand on their own.** They should not need to be viewed in the context of any other statements.

2. **Avoid more than one blank per sentence.** However, it may be necessary to use more than one blank if a teacher wants to ask for items that belong together. For example:

   Two states that border Washington are _____ and _____.

   This situation is an exception to the rule.

3. **Whenever possible, place the blank or blanks at the end of the sentence.** This makes the sentence more readable.

4. **Construct each statement so that the range of student responses is minimized.** The clearer and less ambiguous the statements, the more easily students will understand what you are looking for and supply the desired answer.

5. **The omitted item should refer to something that is important and obviously the focus of the sentence.** Avoid testing unimportant information.

6. **Construct items to be explicit enough to elicit the correct type of response (Green, 1963) and make certain the vocabulary is appropriate.** The only reason a student should answer a question incorrectly is lack of knowledge. If the item is too vague or the vocabulary too difficult, the student may not understand it.

7. **Keep the blanks uniform length.** Short blanks give clues that the answer is short and long blanks that the answer is long.

8. **If you are using short-answer questions requiring a full-sentence answer, make certain students know that you expect a full sentence in response.** This can be explained in the test instructions.

Essay Exams

Essay tests are traditionally grouped into two categories. *Restricted-response essays* are those in which the length of a student's essay is limited by the teacher. A student may have to describe the causes of the Civil War in three pages or the central theme of a novel in two. An *extended-response essay* exam allows the student to choose the optimal length of the answer. Extended-response essays may be more useful for take-home tests or term paper assignments, since the amount of organization and planning is so great and they tend to be longer (Kubiszyn & Borich, 1987). Some students panic without some idea as to how long their answer should be. They are afraid that their two-page answer, although it may answer the question, will be less acceptable than a ten-page answer. Therefore, it is reasonable to provide some guidance for an essay exam, perhaps saying that the usual answer is between three and five pages, although fewer or more pages will be acceptable. Since time constraints may operate in the classroom, some care as to the number of extended-response items should be used. After all, how many such items can be answered reasonably in one hour by the average student in your class. If extended essay questions are to be used, such practical considerations are important. On the other hand, the teacher must take care that restricted-response items are not so restrictive that they cannot be adequately answered in the space permitted. Otherwise, they become little more than lists.

Essays are most useful for measuring higher level cognitive skills, especially synthesis and evaluation

Essay tests are especially useful for measuring higher level cognitive skills.

(Gay, 1985). Essays allow teachers to test skills involved in criticizing or defending a statement, describing strengths and weaknesses, or designing experiments or courses of action (Gronlund, 1976). Essay questions require that students have other skills besides recalling information. Students must also organize the information and write it in a coherent manner. This requires thought and much planning. Unfortunately, many essays and most teacher-made tests do not tap these advanced skills. Benjamin Bloom suggests that 95 percent of all the items on teacher-made tests require merely a recollection of facts (Chance, 1987). That is, they do not measure upper level skills.

True or False Most teacher-made tests measure only factual knowledge.

Essays offer a number of advantages. They give the teacher an opportunity to evaluate learning outcomes not easily measured by objective short-answer tests. They are adaptable to areas in which freedom of expression, depth of analysis, and scope of knowledge are desirable (Green, 1963). It may be possible to test whether a student has read a particular book using objective test items, but if a teacher wants to go beyond this, essay tests are necessary, especially in the humanities and social sciences. In recent years, public pressure has arisen to demand more writing, and essay tests are in keeping with this movement (Coker et al., 1988). Essay tests also avoid the problem of guessing, often a concern with multiple-choice and true-false questions. Last, essay items are much easier to construct and require less time to write than multiple-choice items.

Essays also have their limitations. Their scoring lacks reliability (Coker et al., 1988; Coffman, 1971). Simply stated, two teachers may not grade the essay the same way, and evidence exists that the same teacher may grade an essay differently, at different times, depending upon many factors. These factors include the emotional and physical state of the grader, the handwriting of the student, the paper's neatness, and the teacher's expectations for a particular student, to name just a few (Chase, 1968, 1979; Hughes et al., 1983). This problem can be greatly reduced, as discussed later in the chapter (Broyles, 1985), but it is doubtful it can completely be eliminated. Another problem is the time it takes to grade essays. If a teacher has three classes of thirty students each taking this particular examination and each test contains two essays, the teacher has to mark 180 essays. The third limitation is that since essay tests take so long to answer, a teacher may not be able to sample a wide range of material covered in the class (Gronlund, 1976). Despite these rather serious limitations, essay tests are important vehicles for measuring more sophisticated learning outcomes. They are sometimes used in tandem with objective test questions. A test might contain thirty multiple-choice questions and two essays, the multiple-choice questions examining the more factual areas and the essays demonstrating other learning outcomes.

>>> CONNECTIONS

Practical Suggestions for Writing Essay Questions

Consider the following essay questions:

What are the major food groups? Name two foods from each group.

Compare Jefferson's and Hamilton's ideas.

Describe five ways in which genetic endowment affects development.

Each of these essay questions has flaws that limit its usefulness. The first question is really a misuse of the essay test format, a situation that is relatively common. Essay tests can be used to measure knowledge and comprehension, but they are less efficient than objective test items for this purpose. The first question requires the student to simply name the food groups and to name a couple of foods for each group. This type of learning would be more efficiently measured by fill-in or multiple-choice questions.

Writing essay questions requires skill. Although writing essay questions is certainly easier than writing multiple-choice questions, many essay questions are poorly written. The second question, Compare Jefferson's and Hamilton's ideas, begs the question, About what? Essay tests are often ambiguous or do not provide the student with enough information about what the teacher wants. The third question looks reasonable but can cause problems. A student could simply name five genetic diseases and answer the question instead of discussing what the teacher wants, that is, a discussion of how genetics affects growth, intelligence, personality, and the like.

The following suggestions for writing essay questions can be helpful in constructing essays:

1. **Write the question so that what you want is very clear.** Ambiguous questions are likely to re-

duce the reliability of the test, and students' answers will be disappointing. If the questions are ambiguous, the teacher can never be certain whether the results obtained are due to faulty learning or misinterpretation of the question. The best way to clarify the questions is to present students with a definite task (Gronlund, 1976). Thus, to be clear, essay questions can be longer and explain what is desired in more detail. For example: Alexander Hamilton and Thomas Jefferson held different beliefs in a number of areas. Compare their beliefs about government, people's rights, and foreign policy during Washington's presidency.

2. **Let your students know the criteria you will use to grade the essays.** Will spelling count? Does neatness count? Students are justifiably annoyed when they do not know the basis on which they will be graded. This is a special case of ambiguity discussed above. Some teachers consider spelling and grammar important elements in grading an essay, while other teachers may argue that students do not have the time to read their papers over, and they excuse such errors. Some teachers will emphasize the importance of organization and clarity of expression, others may not. Whatever the criteria for grading, they should be communicated to the student.

3. **Do not compose a question that allows a student to muddle through the answer.** One student told me that he loved essay tests. He'd look for a question that allowed him to state his opinion. He'd always use one or two things he heard the teacher say and end it with some massive generality that agreed with the teacher's bias. Student opinion and evaluations of issues can be tapped without allowing students full reign to duck questions. This is accomplished by asking students to back up their opinions with material from their text or outside required readings. Students should be told that the evidence in support of their position rather than the position itself will be graded.

4. **Essay items should reflect the most important learning outcomes.** Since the number of essays that can be required on a test is limited, only the most important outcomes should be measured.

5. **The specific wording of the question should reflect the learning objectives being measured.** If synthesizing is required, a phrase such as "Describe a plan for proving that _____" is required.

6. **Do not allow choice or use take-home tests.** These are admittedly unpopular suggestions. Students want some choice. However, authorities agree that giving students a choice of questions can reduce the validity of the test results, as students will avoid certain questions and may prepare answers on a few topics in advance (Gronlund, 1976). Another problem is the tendency to reduce the number of learning objectives measured. Perhaps you have four learning objectives that are best measured in essay form and allow a student to do only two or three essays. You do not know whether the student knows the material on the omitted essay, and you will have difficulty comparing students, since some may omit one essay while others omit a different one. Take-home essays may serve a function as a learning

It is important for teachers to circulate around the room while students are taking tests to be certain students are following directions.

device, but they fail as measuring instruments. They do not aid poorer students, because better students are more familiar with the work and do better anyway (Gronlund, 1976). Most importantly, a teacher may not be certain of the authenticity of a student's work. More than one parent has "helped" his or her child write an essay.

7. **Try to start the essay with phrases that indicate that you want something more than the recall of factual material.** For example, such phrases as compare, contrast, give original examples, and predict what would happen are better than what, who, when, or list (Kubiszyn & Borich, 1987).

8. **In most cases, give the students some idea of how long the answer should be or how much time should be spent on each item.** This information is necessary for students to plan their time. The following instructions is one example. "Each of the following four questions has a value of 20 points. Spend approximately the same amount of writing time on each question. Since the organization of your answers will be a factor in your grade, you should spend the first few minutes outlining your answers before you begin to write" (Green, 1963, p. 61).

9. **Pupils require practice and training in taking essay tests.** Frequently, students do not know how to answer a question, and teaching students how to plan an answer, write it out, and edit it within a specified amount of time is good practice.

10. **Essay tests can be used with low-achieving students.** Too often, students in high-achieving classes are given essay tests, while those in lower achieving classes are not. This is understandable, as the problems of poor writing and difficulty in planning an answer haunts lower achieving students. However, it is wrong to assume that only those students who are very bright can be taught higher cognitive skills (Chance, 1987), and not giving lower achieving students training and practice in essay writing on tests does nothing to improve these skills.

11. **Watch the timing of the test.** Essay tests are not speed tests, and forcing students to write at breakneck speeds may reduce the validity of the test. Consider the student who wants to plan the essay for five minutes before writing it down. If he is under too much time pressure, he may omit this reasonable procedure in order to finish the test.

True or False Giving students a choice of essay questions reduces the validity of the test.

CONNECTIONS

Grading Essay Tests

Grading essay tests can be a complicated activity. There is no single correct procedure to follow, but there are some practical ways to reduce the subjectivity of essay scoring.

1. **Grade the essay without knowing who wrote it.** This can be accomplished by folding the name flap down, having students sign their names at the end of the exam, or even assigning numbers to students.

2. **Grade one essay at a time.** Grade essay one for the entire class, then turn to essay two, and so on. This will improve reliability, as you will be using the same criteria to grade all student essays number one and so on.

3. **Formulate a written answer and determine the number of points for each item.** This involves outlining what the ideal answers might be. There is frequently more than one acceptable answer on an essay test. The ideal answers must be outlined, for if they are not, there is a tendency to grade the first papers you read differently from the last papers. An example of this process is found in Figure 15.1. There are two traditional ways to score essays. One is to use analytic scoring, in which important elements of the ideal answer are identified and scored more or less separately. If they do not contain errors, the more of these elements a student has in the paper, the greater his or her score (Ebel, 1965). Global quality scoring is more subjective and less reliable and is more frequently used when a great number of students are involved (Gay, 1985). It involves judging the project as a whole rather than assigning point values for various aspects of the responses. The teacher still must write out an ideal answer, but no point values are assigned to particular elements of the essay.

4. **Determine how the essay is to be scored before presenting it to the students.** If a particular element in an essay will be worth 3 points and another 10, this should be stated. In addition, if organization is to be important in grading, this also should be noted.

5. **Shuffle the papers after grading each essay.** This will make certain that the same students' essays are not graded last or first.

6. **Consider what part factual knowledge demonstrated in the essay will play in the scoring system.** When essays are being used to measure

higher order cognitive processes, factual knowledge may still be important but ought not to be the entire grade. After all, asking students for recommendations, hypotheses, creative application, and the like means that there are other areas of importance besides factual content.

What Does Our Knowledge of Test Construction Mean to Teachers?

Multiple-choice, true-false, matching, fill-in, and essay questions all have their advantages and disadvantages, and each can be useful. If we look closely, though, some general rules for test construction carry over from one type of test to another.

The central idea of testing is not to trick or confuse students but rather to measure the extent of their learning. Therefore, choosing the most important areas to test, providing clear instructions, writing questions in an understandable manner, and being present to respond to problems during the test are parts of the process.

Student perception of the test as fair and relevant is another element in the testing process. Most teachers review the test with the class, thus integrating testing into the learning process. Whenever constructing a test, it is wise to remember that you will have to review the test with the students. Handling such student complaints as an item wasn't taught, you spent only a few minutes in class discussing something that was worth 50 points on the test, or the question was tricky can make returning the tests a tense session.

Robert Ebel's ten criteria for devising a good test as discussed at the beginning of the chapter can give an overall analysis of a test. If your tests follow all the criteria, you can be reasonably certain that your tests are good ones and will accurately and fairly measure the learning outcomes in which you are most interested.

Administering the Test

The test is planned and constructed. The next step is to administer it. The guiding principle in test administration is that every student should have a fair chance to show his or her knowledge on the test (Gronlund, 1976).

A number of things can be accomplished the day before the test. Test-taking procedures can be discussed, and students should be informed of the materials required, such as pencils and paper. Young children may require some practice in test-taking procedures, such as clearing their desks and taking out paper and pencils. Some discussion of lateness and cheating may also be necessary.

Students should be protected from too many interruptions while taking the test. Since both the physical and psychological atmosphere of the testing situation can affect the test takers, some attention should be paid to providing proper lighting, comfortable temperatures, adequate work space, and a quiet atmosphere. Teachers should neither minimize the importance of the test ("Don't worry, it doesn't mean anything") nor overemphasize the importance of the test ("If you fail this, you'll be left behind").

Teachers administering a test should do so in an unobtrusive way, yet active proctoring is necessary. In the younger grades, the proctor must circulate around the room to be certain that the students are following directions correctly. In addition, the teacher should be available to answer the students' questions.

Last, a word on cheating. Nothing minimizes cheating as much as active surveillance on the part of the teacher. It may be possible to separate desks and tell students to cover their papers. Even a talk on honesty the day before the test may be in order. However, for some students, the temptation to cheat is strong, and actively watching students taking the test is required. Other ways to reduce cheating are to assign seats instead of allowing students to choose their own seats and to rearrange both the questions and answers on multiple-choice tests (Houston, 1986).

Evaluating the Test Items

After the test papers are graded, how can you be certain that the test items were fair? Chapter 14 discussed some of the main statistical techniques that are helpful in evaluating students' test scores. Here we concentrate on how to evaluate the test questions themselves. This is especially important when dealing with the most common types of objective-answer questions.

The Item-Response Profile

If you gave a multiple-choice test, how would you know if the distractors you composed were reasonable, too difficult, or too easy? An item-response profile offers the teacher such information. The teacher simply counts the number of students who select a particular choice in each question. Take a look at the following profiles (* indicates the correct answer):

Response Profile for Question 1

Choices	1	2	3	4*
	0	6	6	18

Since no student chose alternative 1, the teacher should revise this alternative.

Response Profile for Question 2

Choices	1*	2	3	4
	12	10	4	4

In the response profile for question 2, almost the same number of students answered with choice 2 as with choice 1 (the correct answer). This would indicate that something is wrong. The choices may be too similar or the question ambiguous.

By performing an item-response profile, you might even discover that a particular question was answered incorrectly by the majority of the class and be able to see where the misunderstanding came from and correct it.

Item Difficulty: The Easiness Index

The easiness index indicates the proportion of students who answered an item correctly. It is found by dividing the number of students correctly responding to an item by the number of students in the class. If there are thirty students in the class and all of them answered the item correctly (30/30), the index is 1; if none of the students answered it correctly, the index would be 0 (0/30). Obviously, the index will usually fall somewhere in the middle. Looking at the response profile for question 1, eighteen of the thirty students answered the question correctly, yielding .60 (18/30). By doing this simple statistical index, a teacher can see which questions are the most difficult and which are the easiest. If the index is .70 or greater, the item has a low difficulty; .30–.70, moderate difficulty; and .30 or lower, high difficulty (Miller & Erickson, 1985).

Item Discrimination

Now that we've looked at the item profile and easiness index, one task remains. Look at the following item profile:

Choice	1*	2	3	4
No. Students Choosing	18	4	4	4

On the surface this looks like a reasonable distribution, and the item difficulty is moderate (18/30 = .60). However, what if you were told that of the twelve students who answered the question incorrectly, ten of them received 85 or better on the test, and of the eighteen who answered correctly, ten received a grade of 70 or less on the test? Now the question does not appear as good as it did a while ago. Why would the best students get the question wrong and the students who know less of the material answer the question correctly? Teachers can determine whether an item on a test distinguishes between the highest and lowest scoring students by performing a statistical test called an item discrimination. The formula for this measure is

> Item Discrimination equals H-L divided by K, where H is the number of highest scoring students responding correctly to the item, L is the number of lowest scoring students responding correctly to the item, and K is the number of students making up 25 percent of the class.

To perform item discrimination

1. Arrange the scores in order from highest to lowest.
2. Determine the number of students that make up 25 percent of the class (K).
3. Determine the scores that make up the highest 25 percent of the class and the lowest 25 percent.
4. Determine the number of students from the highest 25 percent who responded correctly to the test item (H).
5. Determine the number of students from the lowest 25 percent who responded correctly to the test item (L).
6. Substitute the appropriate figures into the formula.

A test item may have a positive, a negative, or no discrimination and is expressed in terms of a scale ranging from -1.00 to $+1.00$. If an item has a positive discrimination, more students in the highest quarter responded correctly to the item than students in the lowest quarter. An item discriminates negatively if more lowest scoring students than highest scoring students responded correctly. A zero discrimination would indicate that an equal number of highest and lowest scoring students responded correctly. Items that either score 0 or negatively discriminate should be examined and rewritten, since this shows that something is wrong. If the discrimination index is .40 or greater, it is highly discriminative; .30–.40, moderately discriminative; and .20 or less, not very discriminative (Miller & Erickson, 1985).

The Validity of Classroom Tests

To be fair to students and to provide useful data for evaluation, classroom tests must possess content validity. A test must measure the areas that have been taught. The best way to be certain that a test is valid is to use a table of specifications when constructing the test (refer to Table 15.2). If the table has been formulated correctly, the proper number of items will be used to measure the various learning outcomes, and the test will be valid.

GRADING

Most teachers use tests as the basis for their grades. Grading involves an evaluation of a student's progress in a particular area. Yet, who among us cannot recall receiving a grade that we thought was unfair? Our annoyance or even anger at the wrong done to us may have been caused by any of a number of factors. We may not have been adequately warned that the two quizzes that didn't seem so important accounted for half of our grade. We may not have known that the teacher was going to collect and grade our biology notebook. We may have objected to the fact that attitude and conduct were considered in receiving that unfair grade.

Grading is one of the more difficult parts of the teaching process, and there has been much discussion concerning doing away with grades or trying to find alternatives to grading (Driscoll, 1986). In the earliest years of elementary school, some schools allow teachers to be more descriptive and do not use letters or numbers. They may allow teachers to check whether students are mastering specific areas of work or to write comments describing a student's progress. However, grading is part of the educational process, and although there are periodic movements to change the basic system, the grading process appears to be here to stay. Most parents want to receive some easily understandable report that reflects their child's progress. In addition, with the increased emphasis on accountability and testing, it is doubtful that grades will be abolished. However, as we will see, some modifications to the standard grading system are possible. Generally, it may be more realistic to talk in terms of making grading fairer and communicating the meaning of grades more accurately to parents than to talk in terms of the abolition of grades.

Most people understand that grades do more than objectively give an evaluation of the achievement of a student in a subject. Grades affect every aspect of a child's experience and self-esteem. Grading affects motivation (Butler & Nisan, 1986), satisfaction with school (Colton & White, 1985), and one's self-concept (Bachman & O'Malley, 1986). Students often believe that a grade reflects not just how they do in a particular subject but their adequacy as people. Of course, the student who does poorly in school is most adversely affected by his or her grades. When comparing students in schools that use grades with those

Students who feel that their good grades mirror their achievement and work experience pride.

attending schools that do not use grades, Betty Yarborough and Roger Johnson (1980) found that bright pupils from graded schools had a more positive attitude towards school than brighter pupils in schools where grades were not used. However, slower pupils from the schools that did not use grades had more positive attitudes than slower pupils from graded schools. The slower student in a graded atmosphere is constantly reminded of his or her inadequacy. So are the student's parents. Parents are likely to make the same mistake, believing that grades reflect more about their children than they actually do. Any discussion of grading must keep in mind its potent effects on the child's attitude towards school and towards him or herself.

True or False   Both high-achieving and low-achieving students have a more positive attitude toward school if they attend schools in which grades are not assigned.

Principles of Grading

Each teacher has his or her own personal way of grading students. This individuality has its advantages, as teachers can flexibly construct a grading system that is most meaningful to them and reflects their requirements and objectives. On the other hand, it makes it difficult to compare students taught by different teachers. Is a 90 percent or an A from Mrs. Green's class equivalent to a 90 percent or an A from Mr. Brown's class? Often, the standards for grading differ substantially from one teacher to another, and students are correct when they argue that some teachers are "easier" graders than others. However, whatever your particular standards, they will become more meaningful if you are consistent and follow some rather simple, although often violated, principles that are illustrated by the following common student complaints.

"But you never said that our notebooks were important." Bill had been doing well in biology only to find out that one third of his grade would be based upon his biology notebook, which included some homework problems. This is not an uncommon problem and one that can easily be avoided by teachers. Students have a right to know on what basis they will be graded. Students often do not have a good idea of how their final grades will be arrived at and often see them as arbitrary and unfair (Evans & Engelberg, 1988). It is poor practice to wing it, that is, to figure out how the grades will be determined as you go along.

"But we had only one test." When only one or two tests are given, students often feel that they have not had an adequate opportunity to show what they know. Grading is more reliable when a number of measurements are used.

"All we ever get is multiple-choice questions and big unit tests." Whenever possible, it is best to include a variety of questions on tests and grade using measurements taken from a number of different measuring instruments. Short quizzes, unit tests, homework problems, lab reports, and the like are possibilities. This enables students to show their knowledge in a number of ways.

"What does my conduct have to do with my grade?" It is tempting to punish a child who is misbehaving by reducing his or her grade. However, the overwhelming number of authorities disagree with this practice (Gay, 1985). If the purpose of grading is to present feedback about a student's achievement, including conduct in the grade is poor practice. Many school districts have an additional space for a conduct grade, and it is here where such a grade should be noted.

True or False   A student's conduct should not be taken into consideration when grading a student's achievement.

"Why did I receive such a poor grade since I tried so hard?" It is emotionally taxing for a teacher to assign a poor grade to a student who the teacher knows is trying. Yet it isn't fair to this student or to the other students in the class to inflate a grade just because a student is trying. If grades are to reflect achievement, parents will receive the wrong impression from such an inflated grade. The practice of factoring effort into the grade is more understandable in the very early elementary grades. Some districts have a grading system for effort from one to five, where one means maximum effort and five means little effort. If a student is working very hard and not succeeding, some diagnostic work and special attention may well be required.

One somewhat popular way of rewarding effort is through extra-credit assignments and projects. Students willing to work hard on a project or extra assignment of value may then be rewarded not only for their effort but also for their additional learning. The benefits of such assignments are that they may encourage students to perform a challenging assignment and may allow students who have not performed as well as desired on a test to improve their grade through some meaningful activity. On the other hand, extra-credit assignments have some definite limitations. First, to be useful, the assignment must reflect some meaningful cognitive exercise. Extra credit in English for producing a nicely colored cover for a book report is poor practice, for it does nothing to improve the child's English. In addition, if the extra-credit assignment covers work that is important, why shouldn't it be given as a regular assignment to the class? If it does not, it is difficult to support its inclusion into the grade. Therefore, although extra-credit assignments such as an extra book report may have some validity, extra-credit assignments should be used with care, to stimulate and to motivate. They may be sometimes used to add a point or two to a grade, but their weight should be limited.

"Why did I receive only 3 of 5 points for class participation? Although tests may be objective, they are not the only measurement included in a grade. Some marks, by their very nature, are somewhat more subjective. For example, class participation ratings tend to be quite subjective as does marking notebooks and reaction papers. This subjectivity can be reduced by writing a criterion for grading and making it known to the students. For example, under class participation, asking questions about how many pages are required on a book report may not be considered, while asking a question about Edgar Allen Poe's writing style probably is. Subjectivity in these instances cannot completely be eliminated, and teachers should understand that this subjectivity brings with it student complaints, especially from those students who may measure their participation differently.

"He grades everything." The call for a number of different types of measurements does not mean that everything should be used in figuring grades. Students sometimes need practice on problems and opportunities to make mistakes that will not affect their grades. The feedback they receive on these assignments can help them correct their mistakes in preparation for a test that may be included into the determination of their grades.

Types of Grading Systems Used

With these principles in mind, what types of grading systems are used and which type is best? The search for the ultimate grading system is ongoing, but teachers have a number of systems from which to choose. As we shall see, each has its advantages and its drawbacks.

Comparisons with Other Students

One method of grading uses what is commonly called a curve. Under such a system, one's grade depends upon how one's achievement compares with that of other students in the class (Kubiszyn & Borich, 1987). This ensures that the best students in the class, regardless of their absolute scores on examinations, will receive A's in the class; it also assures that the lowest achieving students, regardless of their absolute scores on exams, will fail. Usually, marking on the curve begins with some decision concerning what percentage of the students will receive an A, B, C, D, or F. This percentage may be based upon some statistical model but may also be relatively arbitrary. A common distribution is 7 percent A, 23 percent B, 40 percent C, 23 percent D, and 7 percent F (Gay, 1985). In a class of thirty, then, seven percent, or two students, will receive A's.

Although this type of system may simplify marking, since the standard is predetermined, it has some serious faults. First, it is based upon the assumption that in each class some students will score well, some poorly, and some in between (Montague, 1987). What if everyone does poorly or everyone does well? Such a curve may work reasonably well if there is a nice range and distribution, but I can remember one college course in which a 92 on a test was a C because everyone had done so well. This hardly seems fair. In addition, the type of class a students finds him or herself in may affect the student's grade. If Jim is in a class for the gifted, his 75 may not measure up well against his classmates, but if he is in a slow class or even an average class, 75 may well be a B or an A. In addition, this type of system tells the teacher little about how much the student really knows about social studies or mathematics. Consider the fact that a student who receives a 50 on an exam or combination of exams may well receive an A if she is in the top seven percent. This doesn't communicate much to parents or students.

One can readily see the deadening effect that this type of grading system has on slower students. Let's say that a slow student works very hard and receives a 70 percent score on a test. This still may not be passing if he finds himself in the bottom seven percent anyway. The percentage is also somewhat arbitrary, and it is reasonable to ask why five percent or three percent shouldn't receive F's or A's. Last, it is frustrating for teachers. No matter how hard they work, some students must fail, and the distribution always looks very similar. Such grading systems may also increase competition among students and reduce cooperation, since what one student scores on a test affects another student's grades.

To make marking on the curve a bit more palatable, some teachers allow passing to be based upon some criterion (such as getting 65 on tests) no matter what their score means in comparison to their peers. They also will look for normally occurring clusters of grades instead of using a rigid "20 percent get B, 10 percent receive A" concept. For instance, if the cutoff for an A is an 86 and one student received an 85 but the next closest student was an 81, the student with the 85 would receive an A. This seems fair, but such clusters may not appear in some classes, making such subjective groupings difficult.

Comparisons with Some Established Criterion

In this method of grading, student grades are dependent upon the students' reaching predetermined levels of achievement as defined by a particular standard. The teacher chooses the standard, and the student grades are determined solely by whether the students attain the levels demanded. This method can be used in a number of different ways. It is the type of grading used with mastery learning (refer to Chapter 11). If a student attains the criterion (perhaps 80 percent correct), the student has mastered that skill. In this case, the report sent home reflects the skills mastered and those that remain to be mastered, the level of mastery required, and the level attained.

Criterion grading can be translated into letter grades as well. The teacher determines what score will be an A, a B, and down the line. Perhaps achieving a 90 percent correct level will be considered an A, 80 percent a B, and so on. But there is nothing sacred about the 90 percent level for an A; the level could be higher or lower. This, of course, differs from the mastery usage but retains the criterion-related grading format.

The advantages of such grading systems are obvious. Unlike norm-referenced systems, under a crite-

Testing is part of the educational process. The feedback students receive on tests can help them correct their misconceptions and improve their writing skills.

rion system, every student could pass and, ideally, every student could achieve a grade of A if everyone were to reach that level of achievement. It is relatively simple and automatic to use and allows a teacher to see improvements if students have studied more or if the teacher has tried some new teaching method. It is also fairly easy to understand how the student is achieving in a particular skill, since the standard is objective. Last, competition among students does not arise from this grading system, since one child's grade does not influence another child's grade. This allows for the relatively easy use of cooperative learning strategies.

There are difficulties with criterion systems, however. One glaring problem is knowing what standards to use. Why use 80 percent as your standard? Why not use 90 percent or 65 percent? In addition, it is possible for one teacher to use one mastery level or one criterion for an A, B, or C, while another teacher adopts a different one. Also remember that in theory, every student could receive an A if all the students achieve extremely well in the subject. How would administrators and parents react if every student received an excellent grade or, for that matter, failed? Although we applaud a system that allows each student to achieve the highest grade, it may be a problem if all actually do. Last, think of the tendency for teachers—when each student has met the criterion and is doing well—to increase the difficulty of the test or the stan-

dard for receiving a particular grade. These shifting standards could be a problem for students.

Basing Grades upon Ability, Effort, or Improvement

It seems unfair that a high ability student could do little work and get a good grade while a student of lesser ability sweats for a C. One way to reduce this seeming inequity is to take ability level into consideration when grading. A student with average ability who achieves at a high level would be given a high grade, whereas a student with high ability who achieves below his or her ability would be given a low grade. A student of poor ability who achieves much would receive a very high grade.

This leads to some serious problems, however. A low-ability student who achieved much might receive an A, while a child of superior ability who scored the same might receive a C. Interpreting grades is impossible. A B for a high-aptitude student might indicate an 85 percent mastery, while a B for an average student might represent 80 percent, and perhaps a B for a low-achieving student, even lower. The same grade means different things to different students. There are other problems, some of them technical and statistical. Defining ability in a fair and operational way can be difficult. Although tests and criteria can be formulated, there will always be questions about the cutoff points, and it would be to the student's benefit not to be considered overly bright. The entire system may be seen by students as unfair, since bright students may claim that they did better than other students but still received lower grades.

Teachers like to reward students who show effort, but basing a grading system on effort leads to difficulties. It is very difficult to operationally define effort. In addition, such a system rewards those who require a great deal of time to catch on and punishes those who are quick. Last, the purpose of grading is to give an accurate report to students and parents about achievement, and effort, unfortunately, does not always correlate perfectly with achievement.

How about grading students on improvement? Under such a system, the grade would be calculated by comparing a student's knowledge or skills on the pretest administered before the unit is taught and at the end on the post-test. Students who progress the most get the highest grade. The problem here is that this penalizes students who know a great deal about a subject at the beginning of the unit. Eventually, such students will catch on and will purposely do poorly on the pretest.

All three of these systems require a great deal of recordkeeping and suffer from statistical problems. For example, it is much more difficult for a student who is very bright or who received a 90 percent on a pretest to improve or to work up to his or her potential. It is much easier for an average student or a student who performed in an average manner on a test to improve because there is simply more room for improvement.

Percent Grading

Percent grading involves averaging scores and converting them to a percentage. It can be reported as a percentage (Wayne received 83 percent in mathematics) or converted into a letter grade (B). Percent grading has the advantage of being swift and certain and is a commonly used method. However, it has a number of disadvantages. Unlike a criterion-related grading system, the 83 percent in mathematics tells us very little about what Wayne actually learned in school, and unlike norm-referenced grading, one doesn't know if that is the lowest or the highest grade in the class. Is this a low level of achievement, a middle level, or a high level? In addition, a teacher may easily influence the range of grades by giving easy, moderately difficult, or very difficult tests. A 60 percent on the first test, which was difficult when averaged with an 80 percent on an easier test, does not indicate the amount of knowledge a student possesses in the subject. For percentages to be meaningful, we would have to be assured that an 85 percent on a test or a series of tests means that the student knows 85 percent of the work in that area. We would have to be able to define the total amount of knowledge in the subject and create a test that absolutely measures it. This is very difficult and rarely occurs. The true meaning of a percentage grade is difficult to determine.

Alternatives to Grading: Multiple Grades, Contracted Learning, and Pass/Fail Systems

The evidence that grades affect so many areas of the self-concept, may not reflect actual achievement, and engender so much anxiety has led some to argue that alternatives must be found to number or letter grading systems. Some modifications to grading and some alternative structures may be practical in some specific circumstances. One useful modification is multiple grades, in which students are given grades not only for their knowledge but also for noncognitive outcomes such as initiative and group leadership (Malehorn, 1984). This gives parents a more complete evaluation of their child's progress.

In contracted learning, the teacher provides students with the standards required for a particular grade, and the student contracts with the teacher to do the amount of work required to receive the grade. The student chooses the grade he or she wants, and if the student fulfills the requirements for receiving that grade, the student gets the grade. The requirements for receiving an A are higher than for receiving a B, and so forth. The student, therefore, chooses his or her goals and can follow an individual study plan. Students know what is required of them and can work towards their own self-chosen goals. This system presents some difficulties, however. It is often based upon the sheer volume of work rather than quality. It is ideally possible in a criterion-related grading system for everyone to receive an A, but it is highly improbable. In a contract learning system, it can happen. What if each student contracts for an A and does the necessary work? This may mean that the work levels for receiving the desired grades are too low. It would be prudent to talk over any contract system with your supervisor and receive his or her approval before beginning such a project. However, in some instances, such a contract system may be valuable.

One alternative system that has not worked is the pass/fail system. Under such a system, students are graded only on whether they have passed or failed the course. The requirements for passing are often criterion related but can also be norm referenced. Such grading exists in colleges and in some high schools. The basic theory is that this would reduce pressure on students and allow them to explore other areas. However, studies show that this system results in a reduction in achievement, and students are less motivated to do well in pass/fail courses (Gay, 1985). Since students often will spend less time on the pass/fail course and more time on their graded courses, unless the system is used across the board, there is a possibility that it will simply lead to less achievement in some classes.

True or False Pass/fail grading systems lead to higher student achievement levels when compared with courses in which a traditional grading system is used.

A RATIONAL LOOK AT TESTING AND GRADING

There are no perfect ways to test or grade. Each type of test and grading system has its own advantages and disadvantages. But whatever system of testing and grading a teacher embraces, both practices should foster achievement as well as measure and evaluate it. Just as teachers are accountable for teaching, students are accountable for learning. But students must believe that they will get at least an average grade if they do their work. The average student who works in class and finishes the assignments in a reasonable manner should be able to achieve an average grade in the subject. This is based upon the ideal that students are able to do the work if they are taught reasonably well and are willing to put forth some effort themselves.

Grading is not a way of rewarding or punishing students. It is a form of information transmitted to the student and others that reflects the student's achievement. Nor is it an absolute standard. A test on state and local government may not measure a change in attitude, a rising spark of interest within a student, or any of a number of important affective changes. The fact that grades have such a general effect on a student's self-concept and satisfaction with school indicates that they are misunderstood and misinterpreted by the general public. It may be important to enlarge our grading systems to more accurately assess the cognitive outcomes not only by being more specific and listing the objectives mastered but also by noting some admittedly subjective evaluations of such areas as effort, conduct, and attitude.

Testing does not have to be tinged with charges of unfairness, and grading does not have to lead to charges of arbitrariness. Few students or, for that matter, teachers will enjoy testing or grading. With time, effort, knowledge, and skill, however, we can make the process of evaluation less anxiety provoking, less arbitrary, and fairer for the student and can transmit information that is more objective, more accurate, and more useful for everyone concerned.

SUMMARY

1. Teachers give tests for many reasons. Diagnostic tests are those in which student strengths and weaknesses are evaluated before the unit is taught. They are administered for the purpose of helping teachers create a program to remediate some of these weaknesses. Placement testing is used to discover what students do or do not know so that the teacher can begin his or her teaching at the right level. Formative testing is performed during the teaching process and gives the teacher some understanding of how the students are learning the unit, while summative testing is performed at the end of a unit and is most often used for grading purposes.

2. Robert Ebel has suggested ten factors that are useful in evaluating tests: relevance, balance, efficiency, objectivity, specificity, difficulty, discrimination, reliability, fairness, and speededness.

3. The first stage in planning a test involves delineating the scope of the material to be tested. Then, a table of specifications is required. This table indicates the content to be tested and the objectives of the unit, allowing the teacher to determine the number of items required to adequately test each area. There are various ways such a table can be constructed. The test items are written using this table of specifications as the basis for ensuring fair and adequate coverage of the material.

4. Multiple-choice questions are the most common type of objective items used by teachers. Multiple-choice questions have the advantages of being flexible, being easy to score, and requiring little response time so that many can be asked. The disadvantages include their reliance on the student's reading ability and the difficulty in constructing reasonable distractors. True-false questions have the advantages of being easy to construct, taking little time to answer so that many can be asked, and being easy to mark. However, they encourage guessing and can be very tricky if specific determiners such as *sometimes, almost,* and *never* are used. Matching exercises allow a teacher to efficiently test a great deal of factual information on a single topic. They are very compact and easy to construct and allow for a thorough testing of a specific domain of knowledge. Their usefulness is limited to testing factual information within one domain. Fill-in questions allow the teacher to test recall rather than recognition, reduce the problem of guessing, and are flexible. The disadvantages are that they are

difficult to construct if we wish to measure higher level knowledge, there is a tendency to use the exact wording in a text in the question, and misinterpretations of the items are relatively common.

5. Essay tests can measure higher level cognitive skills. Students must show such skills as organization, planning, and writing. The advantages of essay tests are that they can test a wide range of cognitive outcomes, require students to show important writing skills, eliminate the problem of guessing, and are easier to construct than multiple-choice questions. However, the scoring of essays is often unreliable, it takes considerable time to mark essays, and since it takes so long for students to answer these essays, the sample of material that can practically be tested in one testing period is limited. In a restricted-response essay, the teacher determines the length of the answer, while in an extended-response essay, the student decides how long the essay should be. Although essays can be used to measure knowledge and comprehension, they are not as efficient as objective questions for doing so. The grading of essay tests can be made more reliable if the teacher grades all students on one essay before going on to the next, takes steps to ensure the anonymity of the student while grading the test, outlines what a correct answer is, and determines (before giving the test) the number of points to be given for each part of the essay.

6. The guiding principle in test administration is that each student should be given an equal opportunity to show how much he or she knows. To do this, the teacher must be certain that the students have the necessary materials, provide a quiet, well-lighted room for the students, and neither minimize the importance of the test nor cause so much anxiety that students cannot function.

7. In an item-response profile, the teacher counts the number of students who selected a particular choice for each question. This will indicate if any of the choices on a multiple-choice item either were not useful or confused the students. The easiness index indicates the proportion of students who answered an item correctly. Teachers can determine whether an item on a test distinguishes between the highest and lowest scoring students by performing a statistical test called an item discrimination. The content validity of a test can be assured through the judicious use of a table of specifications.

8. Grading involves the evaluation of a student's progress in a specific area. It is usually based upon tests but can contain other components, including homework assignments and papers. Grades affect a student's self-concept, motivation, and satisfaction with school.

9. Students should know on what basis they will be graded. Grades are more accurate if a number of measuring instruments are used and a number of different types of items are used within the tests. Conduct should not be factored in as part of the achievement grade, nor should effort be a factor in such evaluation. Teachers need not grade all the students' work, as students should have an opportunity to learn from mistakes without having to always pay a penalty for them. Teachers should be aware that some areas of evaluation, such as class participation and grading notebooks, are more subjective. Although the subjectivity cannot completely be eliminated, some criteria should be established for such grading procedures.

10. One type of grading involves using a curve. Under such a system, a student's grade depends upon how his or her achievement compares with that of other students in the class. This ensures that the best students in the class, regardless of their absolute scores on examinations, will receive A's in the class; it also assures that the lowest achieving students, regardless of their absolute scores on exams, will fail. Although this system ensures a reasonable distribution of grades, it does not allow all students who do well on a test to receive a good grade, and a student who does reasonably well in an excellent class is likely to get a lower grade than a student who did reasonably well in a low-achieving class, even if the two students scored the same on the test. In a criterion-based grading system, students' grades are dependent upon their reaching predetermined levels of achievement as defined by a particular standard. The teacher chooses the standard, and the student grades are determined solely by whether the students attain the levels demanded. Under such a system, everyone can receive a good or a poor grade, improvement is easily reflected in one's

grade, and competition is reduced. The disadvantages are that we may not agree on the standards to use, and there may be difficulties with administrators and parents if every student achieves an A. Grading systems based upon ability, effort, or improvement are not recommended. Percent grading involves averaging scores and converting them to a percentage. Percent grading is easy and efficient but really does not tell us much about the student's actual level of achievement.

11. Such modifications as multiple grades in which students receive not only a grade that reflects their achievement but also grades for attitude, effort, conduct, leadership ability, etc., are reasonable, since they give parents a more complete picture of their child's progress. In a contract learning approach, the teacher decides the amount and quality of work needed for a student to receive a particular grade, and the student decides which grade he or she will work for. Pass/fail systems have not been very successful, since students tend to put less work into these classes and more into those in which a standard grading system is used.

ACTIVITIES AND EXERCISES

1. **Why Were These Tests Objectionable?** Almost every student has had poor experiences with classroom testing sometime in his or her school career. Choose three such experiences and evaluate the tests' problems using Ebel's ten elements of a quality test (discussed at the beginning of the chapter).

2. **Tables of Specifications.** Create a table of specifications concerning some relatively small unit in your area of expertise. List in the left-hand column the topics and across the top those learning outcomes from Bloom's taxonomy that are relevant. If you have the written objectives of such a unit already available from your work in Chapter 11, you may be able to write out a one-way table such as the one in Table 15.3.

3. **Writing Objective Test Items.** Choose a topic in your area of expertise and write ten multiple-choice questions that cover the area. If your major is elementary education, choose some topic in social studies or science. Exchange your

multiple-choice questions with a classmate's and critique them. Do the same for true-false and fill-in or short-answer questions and create a matching exercise.

4. **What's Wrong with These Items?** The following five multiple-choice test items all have some rather important flaws. Critique these items.
    1. The first aviator to fly solo from North America to Europe was
        a. Alexander Hamilton
        b. Charles Lindbergh
        c. Andrew Jackson
        d. Superman
    2. Florence Nightingale
        a. was a famous educator in early America.
        b. was a nurse during the Crimean War.
        c. was a great entertainer during WWI.
        d. was a member of Congress responsible for Medicare legislation.
    3. Which of the following is not a metal?
        a. oxygen
        b. nitrogen
        c. sulphur
        d. None of these
    4. A fertilized egg is called a
        a. ovum
        b. amnion
        c. zygote
        d. ellipse
    5. The Normans conquered England in
        a. 1944
        b. 866
        c. 1066
        d. 1492

   Do the same for the following true-false questions:
    1. All poetry has to rhyme.
    2. Dan Milton wrote *Paradise Lost.*
    3. Capital punishment is a deterrent to violent crime.
    4. Michael Faraday was a distinguished American scientist who correctly estimated the speed of light.
    5. Operant conditioning is the learning process whereby behavior is governed by its consequences, while classical conditioning is the learning process by which a neutral stimulus is paired with a stimulus that always causes a certain response until the stimulus that was originally neutral now causes that response.

   What's wrong with these fill-in and short-answer questions?
    1. The war between _____ and the U.S. ended in 1945.
    2. Why does the sky appear blue?

3. The term "RAM" means _____.
4. Christopher Columbus was a _____ who discovered _____.
5. B. F. Skinner is a famous _____.

5. **Writing Essay Exams.** Essay tests are most useful for measuring higher cognitive outcomes. Choose a topic in your area of expertise and write five essay questions.

6. **What's Wrong with These Essay Questions?** Critique the following three essay questions.
   1. Compare Eugene O'Neill's and Arthur Miller's styles.
   2. List ten elements from the periodic table and name two products containing each element.
   3. Should the electoral college be abolished?

7. **Interview Teachers Concerning Testing and Grading.** Throughout this text, it has been suggested that new teachers gather as much information as possible about various aspects of teaching by tapping the experience of more experienced teachers. There is no area where this is more appropriate than testing and grading. Ask these experienced teachers to show you their tests, ask them for hints about testing, and discuss their grading systems with them.

8. **Computing the Easiness Index.** Using the following information, compute and evaluate the easiness index for the following two items:

Question One	1	2*	3	4
	6	12	3	4
Question Two	1	2	3*	4
	1	2	20	2

9. **Classroom Placement and Diagnostic Tests.** Many elementary schoolteachers and some secondary schoolteachers (especially in mathematics) give placement and diagnostic tests. Contact some teachers who use such tests and ask them to show them to you. Some of the tests are commercially available, while others are written by the teachers themselves.

10. **Directions.** Directions must be written so that they are clear and simple to understand. Write a set of directions for multiple-choice questions, true-false questions, a matching exercise, and fill-in or short-answer questions covering a particular domain of interest. In addition, write directions for an essay test.

11. **A Scoring Guide for an Essay Question.** Write an essay question and a scoring guide for the essay question. Assume that the essay question is worth 20 points.

SCENARIOS

Here are thirteen scenarios. Try to apply the information you have learned in the chapter to each situation.

1. Mr. Okamoto believes that essay exams are necessary in his class. He gives essay tests but finds that he has two difficulties. First, the time it takes to grade the tests is excessive and does not leave him with enough time to plan his lessons effectively. Second, his students complain about the subjectivity of his grading, and they often ask him to grade their papers over. What can Mr. Okamoto do to reduce these problems?

2. Mrs. Engel does not know how to grade Richard, a nicely behaved student who has done poorly on his tests but who seems to try very hard. He just does not seem to be catching on despite the effort he is obviously putting into the class. Richard has done a number of minor extra-credit assignments, but his general achievement in the subject is not passing. Mrs. Engel feels that effort should be rewarded but does not know if she should pass Richard on the basis of effort and the extra-credit assignments. If she consulted you, what advice would you give her?

3. Mr. Warren has had difficulty coping with his science class. This group of bright students continues to complain that the multiple-choice portions of his tests are tricky and do not emphasize the material he has taught or assigned. How could Mr. Warren analyze these complaints?

4. Ms. Perkins has given three tests this quarter in mathematics. On the first test, the class average was 55; on the second, 60; and on the third, 58. On the basis of their absolute grades, the class's failure rate would be very high. Ms. Perkins asks you whether she should curve the grades and, if so, what the advantages and disadvantages of the practice would be. How would you advise her, and how would you answer her questions.

5. Mr. Lee has decided to use a contract system for grading his reading class. He has composed different standards for each grade and has discussed the practice with his students. To his surprise, all the students have chosen to do A work, and most are doing the necessary work. He believes that if this continues, he will have to give A's to twenty of the twenty-five students in the class. Did anything go wrong with Mr. Lee's con-

tract learning system? If so, how could he rectify the situation?

6. Miss Cook, a seventh-grade science teacher, likes to use only objective test questions on tests. She uses a variety of such questions, including multiple-choice, true-false, matching, and fill-in questions. She claims that these tests do not have the difficulty of being subjective. She bases her grades on two such tests each term. Discuss and evaluate Miss Cook's testing and grading system.

7. Mr. Santos believes that he ought to give some form of essay on his tests but has been bitterly disappointed by the poor writing and organizational skills showed by the students in one of his low-ability, low-achieving classes. He is considering not giving essay tests to these students. Discuss Mr. Santos's problem and some ways he might be able to reduce it.

8. Mrs. Williams, a high school social studies teacher, has just given an essay test composed of four essay questions. She told her students that each essay is worth 25 percent. She grades all the essays of a particular student first and then goes on to the next paper. She makes a habit of looking at the name of the student who wrote the essay for two reasons. First, she claims that by the handwriting alone she would know the student's identity most of the time anyway and, second, by knowing the student's name, she can take into consideration the student's writing skills and ability. Assuming that her essay questions are valid and well constructed, discuss her procedures for administering and grading the tests.

9. One of Mr. Kenny's students, named Deborah, claims that her grade on her mathematics test should not be used and she should be given another test. It seems that during the test a great commotion occurred outside the classroom, Mr. Kenny ran out of test papers and Deborah had to wait five minutes for her paper, the lights went out for a few minutes, and it was very warm despite the fact that Mr. Kenny had opened the window. Mr. Kenny claims that Deborah is wrong because all the students were under the same disadvantages, and that makes the test valid. Evaluate Deborah's complaints and Mr. Kenny's answer. How would you handle such a situation?

10. Ms. Moore gave her class an English test. It was clear from the beginning that the students hadn't studied and weren't doing well. However, Ms. Moore graded the tests, gave them back, and told the students that because they had done so poorly she was giving them another test in two days and that they should study this time. Martin was livid. He had studied and had achieved a grade of 96 percent on the test. He wants his test grade to stand. Ms. Moore tells him that he'll have to take another test but not to worry, because he'll probably do just as well. Martin isn't satisfied. He does not think he will attain that grade again and believes that he is being treated unfairly just because the other students did not study. Do you agree with Ms. Moore's handling of the situation? If so, why? If not, what would you do differently?

11. Mr. McPhee has had it with Jon. Jon is always on time for the class but always fools around and talks out. He is doing 70 percent work but talks back and has a smart answer for everything. He sometimes gets out of his seat. Mr. McPhee wants to fail Jon and has told him that he intends to do so. Jon claims that he can't do that, since he has passed his tests and has done his homework. Mr. McPhee believes that he can't pass someone with Jon's attitude while he fails students who are well behaved and try so hard. Analyze Mr. McPhee's and Jon's points of view.

12. Ms. Campo believes that objective tests and essays communicate only one small part of the picture to parents. She bases ten percent of her grade on class participation, ten percent on an evaluation of students' notebooks, ten percent on students' attitude, and five percent on attendance. She argues that these are important elements in the learning situation. Evaluate Ms. Campo's system and point of view and outline the advantages and disadvantages of Ms. Campo's grading system.

13. Mr. Davis makes it a habit to give a test while he is teaching a unit. He claims that these tests, which are not used to grade students, give him information as to how students are doing and allow him to change strategy if need be. His classes have been doing much better since he started using this procedure. His friend and colleague, Ms. Collins, claims that these tests merely give students a good idea of what questions will appear on the unit test and that is why his classes are doing better. Evaluate Mr. Davis's use of formative testing and Ms. Collins's rejoinder.

Research Methods

Many students ask why a knowledge of research methods is important. "It's the information that matters," they say. "Why worry about how the researcher got it?" This attitude misses the point. The way a researcher obtains the information—the research methods—largely determines the legitimacy of the study's conclusions. A poorly designed study will produce invalid results.

Knowing about research methods will both allow students to better understand the research available to teachers and give students a background for evaluating information. We live in an information-rich environment. Daily we read new findings concerning what works in a school system or in an individual classroom. Not all studies that lead to these reports are carefully designed or unbiased. A knowledge of research methods can help students determine which information deserves attention and which should be ignored. This is important in keeping well informed.

Research in educational psychology can be loosely divided into two categories: descriptive and experimental. The aim of **descriptive research** is to objectively describe what is presently going on during the educational process (Borg, 1987). We may be interested in describing the factors associated with a particular type of behavior, such as teacher praise or student attentiveness. On the other hand, we may be interested in discovering what would happen if we varied the amount of praise a teacher gives to his or her class. We then manipulate the amount of teacher

praise and see what the effects might be. This would allow us to make a statement about cause and effect. **Experimental research** aims at discovering what will happen if certain variables are manipulated and allows the researcher to make cause-and-effect statements (Best & Kahn, 1989). Each type of research has its place.

DESCRIPTIVE METHODS

Descriptive research is vital to progress in educational psychology. Before we can make any statement about what is going on in the classroom, we must be able to answer such questions as How much praise do teachers give their students? and How do teachers use praise? These and other questions must also be answered before we can make any statement concerning changes that need to be made in the classroom. There are many descriptive methods, including observation, surveys and interviews, causal-comparative research, and correlational research. Each has its advantages and its disadvantages.

Observation

Let's concentrate on teacher praise. How could we find out to what extent praise is used in the class-

descriptive research Research whose aim is to objectively describe what is presently going on during the educational process.

experimental research A research strategy using controls that allows the researcher to discover cause-and-effect relationships.

room? One way would be to observe the teacher in action. We might sit at the back of the room and **observe** how often the teacher uses praise. Of course, we would have to define praise in a way that could easily be recorded. We could accomplish more if we also observed under what circumstances the teacher praised students and perhaps even which students were praised. We could tabulate the results and evaluate them.

On the surface, observation appears to be a simple process, but it really isn't. Consider the question of determining whether a particular statement is actually praise. Two observers may differ in their assessments. To be useful, observation must be both systematic and objective. It must be systematic in that all data are recorded in the same way. It must be objective in that (1) it should make little difference which trained observers are present and (2) bias has been eliminated as much as possible. (Experimenter bias is discussed later in detail.)

In addition, would you act the same way if you knew you were being observed? Probably not. The observer should be as unobtrusive as possible. Today, the advent of videotaping might to some extent reduce the problem of a stranger in the classroom influencing both teachers' and students' behavior. This is not a total answer, however, and the problem still remains. Another difficulty is trying to observe too much. There are limits to the number of interactions that an observer can process, and the more data that have to be recorded, the greater the chance for error. In our praise study, it may be possible for the observer to record the instances of praise and to note who was being praised and perhaps the type of statement that was made.

It would be difficult, however, especially without videotaping, to discover all the circumstances that surround the praise. Sometimes we run the danger of fragmenting the interaction or the lesson. To keep the observations systematic and objective, we must pay attention to a small number of occurrences and record them. It is possible that by doing so we miss the larger picture. This is basically what happened when administrators were asked to use certain checklists to evaluate teacher behaviors that were considered important to keeping students on a task. The administrators spent so much time marking the checklist that they were unable to evaluate the teacher's overall performance. Despite such problems, observations

can be useful if they are systematic and objective and the limitations of the method are understood.

Surveys and Interviews

Why not just ask the teachers and the students about teachers' use of praise? It would seem a much simpler strategy. You construct a questionnaire or conduct some short interviews and gather your data. In a **survey** or an interview, researchers ask a large number of people questions about their own behavior or that of others and the answers are tabulated and reported. Most of us are familiar with attitude surveys, such as those conducted by the Gallup organization. Chapter one presented the Gallup Poll on the public's attitudes toward education. Surveys have the advantage of providing the researcher with tremendous amounts of data in a brief period of time.

The survey approach has its problems, however. If we ask teachers and students questions about teacher-student interaction, we can never be absolutely certain that they will tell us the truth—or even know the truth. In addition, let us presume that some students and teachers refuse for a variety of reasons to fill out the questionnaire. Can we be certain that the teachers and students who filled out the questionnaire are similar to those who refused? Perhaps only the more secure teachers answered our questions. Another problem is generalizability. If we looked at the teacher-student use of praise in two schools in Lansing, Michigan, could we make any statement about the use of praise in schools in Boston or in a suburban Atlanta community? It would be difficult to do so. If we take a survey of elementary schoolteachers, we would have difficulty automatically generalizing to secondary schoolteachers. For the survey to be useful, the people responding to the questionnaire—called the sample—must be representative of

---

observation A research method in which the researcher objectively and systematically records the behavior of subjects.

survey A method of study in which data are collected from a number of people through written questionnaires or oral interviews.

the population in which the researcher is interested (discussed later). Last, constructing a fair and un-biased questionnaire is not easy. The researcher must be careful about the wording of the questions. For example, imagine asking parents questions concerning their use of discipline or punishment. You might get one answer to the question, How often do you spank your child?, but you would probably receive a very different answer to the question, How often do you beat your child?

Surveys and interviews are useful in obtaining a great deal of data in a relatively short time, but they must be constructed with care, and attention must be paid to how representative the sample of the population is.

Causal-Comparative Research

Until now, we've concentrated on simply describing the use of praise through observation and survey methods. Perhaps we are more interested in finding out what conditions or types of behavior are associated with praise. For example, do students who receive a great deal of praise differ in their academic achievement or their attitude towards school from those who do not? This type of study is called a **causal-comparative study.** Note that we are not going to tell the teachers whom to praise. We are dealing essentially with events that have already happened. In fact, these studies are sometimes called ex post facto (after the fact) studies (Best & Kahn, 1989). To conduct such a study, the researcher must find a sample of students who were praised extensively and then compare a sample of similar children who were not given much praise on some variable of interest, perhaps academic achievement.

Causal-comparative research is very useful, especially when variables cannot be manipulated. For example, we would use this type of research if we were

interested in comparing the academic abilities of sixth-grade students who have over the past six years had nutritionally deficient diets with similar students who have had nutritionally adequate diets (Borg, 1987). If we wanted to look at the personality characteristics of students who do not like school and compare them to a group who say they enjoy school, causal-comparative research would be the method to use.

Causal-comparative research can offer us some ideas about causation but cannot really demonstrate cause and effect. Let's say that we've isolated our group of highly praised students and non-praised students and we find that the highly praised students are more likely to do their homework. Could we make a statement concerning cause and effect? Can we say that praise in class caused the students to do more homework? Not really, because there are other competing hypotheses. Perhaps the fact that the children did their homework led to the students knowing more material, volunteering more in class, and receiving praise. As we shall see, experimental research is needed to establish cause and effect.

Often, causal-comparative research is used to look for these possible explanations, and then experimental studies discover which cause-and-effect relationships really exist (Borg, 1987). Occasionally, when experimental studies cannot be performed for ethical or practical reasons, causal-comparative research can be used to approximate a cause-and-effect relationship. This occurs when a number of research studies are performed by different researchers and result in the same conclusions, when all competing hypotheses have been eliminated, and when variable A could cause variable B but variable B could not cause variable A. A good example of such research would be the effects of severe malnutrition on academic achievement. Because we would not deliberately place children into such circumstances we must use ex post facto research. After exhausting all alternative hypotheses, we may make the tentative statement that malnutrition led to poor academic achievement.

causal-comparative study A method of research in which a researcher compares a group of subjects who have a particular characteristic to a group that does not possess the characteristic on a variable of interest.

Correlational Research

Often, researchers involved in collecting and analyzing data seek to discover the relationships between two elements in the environment. For instance, there is a relationship between scores on intelligence tests and school achievement. Higher intelligence scores are related to higher achievement levels in school. Psychologists use the term **correlation** to describe such a relationship.

A correlation can be positive, negative, or zero. A positive correlation indicates that relatively large scores on one factor are associated with large scores on another and relatively small scores on one factor are associated with small scores on another. As intelligence increases, so does academic achievement. A perfect positive correlation is expressed as +1.00. A zero correlation indicates that there is no relationship between the two factors, for example, between body weight and intelligence (Best & Kahn, 1989). A negative correlation indicates that relatively large scores on one factor are related to relatively small scores on another. For example, there is a negative correlation between academic achievement and the number of hours per week of television viewing—the more television viewing the lower the academic achievement. A perfect negative correlation is expressed as −1.00.

Correlations are usually far from perfect, however. The correlation between scores on an intelligence test and achievement in school hovers at about +.60 to .70 (depending upon the measure used) which is high but not anywhere near perfect. Other factors besides intelligence, such as motivation and perseverance, are involved in school success. The correlation between television viewing and academic achievement is not perfect either, as some very good students may watch a great deal of television. Correlations do not indicate cause and effect. The important facts to remember about a correlation is that it tells us that a relationship exists, the direction of the relationship (whether it is positive or negative), and the magnitude of that relationship.

Correlational research is similar to causal-comparative research. However, the studies are conducted differently. In causal-comparative research, two groups of individuals are selected because they are similar in every way except for one characteristic, such as experiencing a great deal of praise. After selecting groups that differ on only this variable, the researcher studies the groups to determine how they differ on other variables.

In correlational research, instead of selecting only subjects who either have or do not have a characteristic, a sample is selected that is likely to have scores that lie at all levels on the characteristic. Subjects are measured on both the variable being studied (amount of praise received) and the other factors the researcher believes may be related, such as academic achievement. A correlation coefficient is computed, and the extent of the relationship is established. Causal-comparative studies are typically looking for differences, while correlational studies are typically searching for relationships.

EXPERIMENTAL RESEARCH

Descriptive research is useful, but as we've seen, it does not normally allow us to make cause-and-effect statements. If we want to state that under particular circumstances praise causes some specific outcome—perhaps attentiveness to work in school—we must perform an experimental study. The watchword of the experimental approach is control. We must choose two groups (or more) that are equivalent and do something to one group and not to the other. We must control for every factor possible to make certain that the only difference between the two groups is the amount of praise they receive.

The factors of an experiment that are manipulated are called **independent variables,** while the factors that are measured are called **dependent variables.** In our study, the independent variable is the amount of praise a child receives, while the dependent variables include measures of attentiveness.

Experimental research typically entails selecting a sample of subjects, randomly assigning these subjects to experimental and control groups, exposing only the experimental group to a treatment that serves as the independent variable while the other group (called the control group) is not exposed to such treatment, and finally measuring the dependent variable and comparing the groups. In some studies, the

correlation A term denoting a relationship between two variables.

independent variable The factor in a study that will be manipulated by the researcher.

dependent variable The factor in a study that will be measured by the researcher.

control group is exposed to an alternative treatment, while in others, the treatment is withheld from the control group. If, for practical reasons, we cannot randomly assign students to these different groups, the study is called **quasi-experimental.**

An experiment begins with a question of some interest to the researcher. The question must be worded in such a way that it can be answered experimentally. For example, What do we mean by praise? What kind of statements comprise praise? We must also define a way of measuring the dependent variable. All past relevant research must be searched to learn what is already known about the question. This ensures that our research rests on solid ground. It also would allow us to make hypotheses (educated predictions) about what will happen in our experiment.

Now we are ready to choose our sample. Since we want both the experimental group and the control group to be similar, we would try to randomly assign students to either the praised or the non-praised group. Each student chosen for the experiment has the same opportunity to be placed in the experimental group and receive praise or in the control group and not receive praise. We tell the teachers in the experiment to praise certain students at defined times (perhaps when they answer questions or turn in homework), while not praising other students. After a stated amount of time, the researcher evaluates the groups on attentiveness. If we find significant differences, we can then make a causal statement that praise caused better grades. The reasoning is simple. Randomizing allows us to say that both groups were the same at the beginning of the experiment, and because the only difference was the treatment (praise), any differences at the end must be due to the treatment.

It is very difficult to do experimental research. First, we can't always turn the school upside down to randomly assign students to various treatments. For example, what if we wanted to evaluate two different methods of teaching sex education and want to randomly assign sixth-grade students to one of two treatments. This would entail breaking up classes and sending students from one classroom to another. Just using classes instead of randomly assigning students may mean that we are not starting with equal groups. Perhaps one class is more knowledgeable than the other. Furthermore, to be really scientific, we should also randomly assign teachers to teach method one or method two or allow one teacher to teach method one while the other is busy teaching method two and

then to switch teachers the next term. Experimental studies require the experimenter to exercise great control over the environment. However, the extra effort is often worth the trouble, since experimental studies allow us to demonstrate cause-and-effect relationships.

ACTION RESEARCH

Many teachers and administrators face questions that are of local importance and may be interested in using a research strategy to discover something of specific interest to their school or district. Perhaps a teacher would like to know which type of questioning leads to greater student participation in his or her classroom or an administrator would like to discover whether reading program A or B leads to better results. This type of research, which does not purport to generalize beyond the classroom or school or district, is called **action research.** Its purpose is to collect evidence that can help school professionals make informed decisions about local problems (Borg, 1987). The teacher or administrator defines the variables and designs the experiment. Frequently, no randomization occurs, and the stringent standards applied to scientific research are somewhat eased. This type of research has been criticized, since action research lacks the controls that more scientifically conducted research has. However, action research has its place, and if it is designed properly and coupled with a knowledge of other, more scientifically conducted research, it can provide some basis for making local and individual educational decisions.

THREE RESEARCH PROBLEMS

Researchers face a number of decisions as to how to approach their research. Should they use observations, conduct a survey, or design an experimental

quasi-experimental study A study in which an experimental and a control group are used but in which random assignment to these groups is not performed.

action research Research whose purpose is immediate application to a particular local problem.

study? What dependent variables should they use? All studies, however, share a number of problems. Three of the most common are sampling, researcher bias, and interpretation.

Sampling

Suppose you are a teacher who has been asked to determine how parents view the elementary school's new super-improved reading program. How would you go about doing so? Constructing a questionnaire is a reasonable approach. Your problem is how to get the questionnaire to the people, completed, and returned to you.

You could get a list of all the children in the school and give each child the questionnaires to take home. This is a disastrous approach, if you remember anything about your old school days. Only a small number of children take the notices home. Most of the questionnaires end up in the wastebasket, become paper airplanes, or lie in the middle of notebooks for weeks before accidentally being discovered.

To avoid this problem, mailing questionnaires to the parents might be advisable. But then the wait begins. Many parents will not return the questionnaires. They simply can't be bothered with them, even though filling them out would take only a minute and you have provided a stamped, addressed envelope. In addition, you cannot be certain that those parents who do respond really represent the opinion of the community at large. That is, do the 30 percent or so who spend the time and effort necessary to fill out the questionnaire differ from those who do not? Perhaps these people are actively involved in their child's education and know all about the new reading program, while the others don't have the faintest idea that it exists. Merely sending out questionnaires may not yield the definitive results you are hoping for.

What about taking a telephone poll and reading the questions to parents? This makes some sense, but it is expensive and time consuming. In addition, you will not be able to find everyone at home, and some parents won't want to be bothered with your questions. If you call during the day, you have just eliminated many working people. In addition, using the telephone could be a problem if you teach in a poor neighborhood where not everyone has a phone.

Finding a representative sample of some larger group (called a population) is not easy. It is important, however, because in any experiment you want to be able to infer what you find out about the sample to the population. In the reading program survey, you might attempt to send out the questionnaire to the entire population of the school with the hope that the portion who returned the completed forms correctly mirrored the opinions of the entire school district. In most studies, since it is impossible to work with an entire population, the researcher tries to find a fraction of the population (called a sample) that will be representative of the larger group. The best way to do this is to choose subjects from the population at random. For many practical reasons, this is not always possible. In some experimental studies, the researcher matches samples; that is, an attempt is made to demonstrate that the experimental and control groups are similar on important factors such as grade point average or IQ scores. In some survey studies, an attempt may be made to show that the sample that answered the questionnaire is similar to the general population. Still, the more representative the sample is of the population being studied, the more useful the research results will be.

Researcher Bias

Imagine you are a science teacher who has just been informed that your students are going to take a statewide examination designed to measure their knowledge of science. Your students are very poor readers, but you believe they know their science. What would you do? If you do nothing, your students will fail the science test, because they cannot read well.

Let's say you decide to read the questions to the students, although this is a clear violation of the rules. When the test results are returned, your students have performed much better than others in the same grade who had to read the questions themselves. A group of teachers asks you to demonstrate the manner in which you administered the test. You stand up in front of the room and read the questions aloud. When giving the correct answer in the multiple-choice portion, your right hand rises slightly and your voice changes somewhat. Your students may have picked up these nonverbal clues, and you may have inadvertently given away some of the answers to the test.

A similar phenomenon occurs in research. When researchers seek the answer to a question, they often make a tentative guess about the results of the study (called a hypothesis). Could the researcher's opinion bias the results? The answer is a definite yes! In one study, Robert Rosenthal and Kermit Fode (1963) led students to believe that the rats they were running through mazes were either dull or bright. Actually, there were no differences between the groups. The rats had been randomly assigned to the students. However, the students who thought that their rats were bright experienced greater success in training than those who were dealing with rats labeled dull. In fact, students working with the "bright" rats claimed that their rats were gentler, easier to work with, and generally more cooperative. The students' expectations that their rats were bright or dull somehow influenced the rats' behavior, enough to bias the results of the study.

In an experiment described in detail in Chapter 8, Robert Rosenthal and Lenore Jacobson (1968) demonstrated that expectancy effects exist in the field as well as in the laboratory. The results of experiments are often explained by referring to the **self-fulfilling prophecy,** a phenomenon in which the expectation that something will occur affects the probability of its occurrence. In other words, if you expect something to happen, it has a better chance of taking place. It is probable that the students in the previously described experiment were not even aware that they treated their rodents differently. Yet, it is possible that researchers will influence their subjects through nonverbal behavior, and they need to make efforts to eliminate such a problem.

Subtle researcher bias can affect the results of any study. If the subjects are treated differently, the results may be nullified. Thus, many researchers have chosen to use **blind experimental designs,** in which the re-

searcher is not aware of the group a subject belongs to while working with that subject. For example, suppose you were attempting to discover the effects of peer tutoring on children who come from poor or middle-class backgrounds. To counter the problem of bias, the tutors should not know the background of the child being tutored. In this way, blind experimental designs reduce the problem of bias.

Interpretation of Data

Once a science-minded young man spent the entire night drinking Scotch and soda. The next morning he awoke painfully aware of his overindulgence. He decided not to repeat his mistake, so the next night he drank bourbon and soda. The following morning his head was splitting and he couldn't feel his tongue, so he decided again not to repeat the mistakes of the past. The third evening was spent drinking gin and soda. The next morning was the worst of all, and he sat down to evaluate the disaster. He asked himself what had been common to all three evenings, and suddenly it hit him. Each night he had been drinking soda, and he solemnly promised himself he would never drink soda again (after McGraph, 1964).

The young man made what must seem an obvious mistake. Of course, the other factor common to each evening was alcohol, but this conveniently slipped his mind. Reaching such an unfortunate conclusion is not the sole province of people who drink too much and think too little, like this young man. Researchers must be careful not to incorrectly interpret the data from their studies. Two possible sources of error have already been noted—sampling and researcher bias—but there are other sources of error.

Consider the problem of a researcher trying to investigate the effectiveness of two different types of teaching strategies. Everything is done to control the situation, but while one room is quiet, students in the other room must contend with a great deal of street noise. Because the noise is not a variable included in the research design, it could confound the results of the experiment, making interpretation difficult. Studies using very young children often suffer from these difficulties, as such youngsters are easily distracted and can lose interest very quickly.

Another source of interpretation error involves the attention subjects receive in an experiment. Suppose

self-fulfilling prophecy The concept that a person's expectations concerning some event affect the probability of the event's occurrence.

blind experimental designs An experimental design in which researchers do not know whether a subject they are working with belongs to the experimental group or the control group.

you're trying to discover whether first-graders who engage in a special program that involves readiness exercises will perform better than those who do not participitate in such a program. You supervise the exercises with one group and leave the other group as is. You then measure the two groups and discover that your special group is more advanced. You conclude that your special exercises have great benefit. But wait a minute! While your special group was receiving this training, what was the other group doing? It could be that the special attention itself rather than the new exercise program created the disparity between the groups. Such factors as attention, improved social relationships, and creation of an atmosphere in which the subjects are made to feel special can cause differences between groups. This is often called the **Hawthorne effect,** after a study performed on workers in the early twentieth century. In that study, a number of changes in the work environment boosted productivity. The factor that was important was the change in workers' attitudes and their social relationships with other workers (Maier & Verser, 1982). It may be that subjects in a study show change because they are the center of attention and feel special.

How can this attentional factor be controlled? One method is to equalize the attention. For example, the control group in the above-mentioned study could have received simple practice in pre-reading skills, thereby equalizing the amount of attention given to each child.

GOOD RESEARCH: DIFFICULT BUT POSSIBLE

After reading all the things that can go wrong in an experiment, it must seem as if performing good research is very difficult. It is, but it is not impossible. No experiment is perfect, nor can one experiment be designed to answer all our questions. Many of the problems can be reduced or eliminated by carefully

---

Hawthorne effect The tendency for people to act differently when extra attention is paid to them.

---

choosing samples, reducing researcher bias, and controlling the research environment.

As we've noted throughout the text, research can be of enormous help to the classroom teacher if it is conducted properly. Chapter 1 offered a list of nine questions that can serve as a guide in helping students to differentiate good from poor research. In this overview of research methods and problems, we've noted the advantages and disadvantages of using each of these methods. We've also described some of the problems that researchers must overcome if their research results are to be useful to other researchers, public officials, and classroom teachers. Conducting research in education is a challenging and rewarding activity, and the research results obtained through such endeavors offer the possibility of helping to improve teaching and learning in the classroom.

SUMMARY

1. Some understanding of research methods is important, for it allows an individual to judge the value of a particular study and provides tools for evaluating information in general.
2. Research in educational psychology can be divided into two categories. Descriptive research objectively describes what is going on in the educational process, while experimental research aims at discovering what will happen if certain variables are manipulated and makes it possible for researchers to make cause-and-effect statements.
3. Observation can be very valuable if it is systematic and objective. Problems can arise if observers are asked to observe too much, and the observers' presence itself can lead to changes in behavior.
4. A survey allows the experimenter to obtain a great deal of information in a short amount of time. Not all people answer the questions accurately, and great care must be taken in formulating the questions, since the wording of the questions can bias the answers. The most important problem, though, is obtaining a representative sample of some population so that the results can be generalized.
5. If a researcher is interested in what conditions or types of behavior are associated with other behaviors, a causal-comparative study would be performed. In such studies, students who do and do not have a particular trait are compared or some

behavior. For example, students who have had deficient diets might be compared in some measure of behavior—perhaps reading ability—with students who have had nutritious diets.

6. A correlation indicates a relationship between two factors, for instance, intelligence and academic achievement. A correlation indicates the existence of a relationship, the direction of the relationship, and the magnitude of the relationship. Correlational studies search for relationships, while causal-comparative studies look for differences.

7. Researchers using the experimental method must control the environment, allowing only the desired variables to vary. Such experiments can demonstrate cause and effect.

8. Sometimes, teachers or school district officials conduct research relating to local problems called action research. This research does not always provide for the controls of more scientifically based research, but it still can be useful.

9. Researchers face numerous problems. Three important concerns are choosing a representative sample, eliminating researcher bias, and correctly interpreting results.

ACTIVITIES AND EXERCISES

1. **Observation: Easy or Difficult?** Observation is often thought of as relatively simple, but after observing in a systematic and objective manner, some of the difficulties can be appreciated. Observe a class and concentrate on an area of interest. For example, consider observing the teacher's use of praise or criticism or the teacher's method of handling transitions. Decide on a definition of the term in question that can be measured and devise an objective rating scale that might help you record teacher-student interactions.

2. **Devise a Questionnaire.** Constructing a questionnaire is a skill. Choose a topic within the domain of educational psychology and write at least eight questions. In addition, describe the sample you would like to give the questionnaire to. For example, if you wanted to discover how people over age 40 and under age 40 view a particular issue, your sample would have to include a reasonable number of people above and below that age. If you want to note differences between how high school students and other people view a particular problem, you would need to obtain a sample of both high school students and others. After formulating your questions and your plan, you may want to ask one of your fellow students to review your questionnaire and suggest ways to improve it. Last, use the questionnaire and tabulate and interpret the results.

3. **How Is Research Treated in the Media?** Oftentimes, newspapers or television news shows will discuss educational and psychological research. While no one expects the media to completely investigate the research methods behind the study's results, it is incredible how often important facts are omitted. After reading or hearing about a study, list the questions that you think have been omitted that might lead a person to an inaccurate conclusion. For example, did the article mention how the sample was obtained? Did the newspaper article make sweeping generalizations about the implications of the study?

4. **The Misunderstood Correlation.** Of all the concepts of research, perhaps correlation is the most confused and misunderstood. Too often a correlation is immediately interpreted as demonstrating cause and effect. As you read newspapers and magazines, be especially aware of the reporting of correlations (relationships between two elements). Follow up these statements to see if they are interpreted as demonstrating cause and effect.

5. **Action Research.** Some school districts have an individual or several people who are involved in doing research for the local district. Sometimes teachers are involved as well. Find out whether any action research is taking place within the district or has taken place in the past and discuss the research with the people who have been involved.

Glossary

acceleration A program in which a gifted student skips a grade or a particular unit or in which material is presented much more quickly than it would be for an average student.

accommodation The process by which one's existing structures are altered to fit new information.

action research Research whose purpose is immediate application to a particular local problem.

active listening Providing the student with feedback that demonstrates that the teacher understands the student's message.

activity reinforcers Any reinforcer that allows students to engage in a preferred activity as a reward for the desired behavior.

adolescent egocentrism The adolescent failure to differentiate between what one is thinking and what others are considering.

advance organizers Topical introductions that orient students to the subject matter and relate new learning to material students already know.

algorithm A procedure that guarantees a solution to a problem but may not be the most efficient way to do so.

alternate response training A self-control procedure in which students are taught to use responses that either interfere with or replace an undesirable response.

alternative testing A special adaptation of the testing program for disabled students that involves modifications to the testing procedures themselves or to the skills that are being tested.

animism The preschooler's belief that inanimate objects are conscious or alive.

aptitude tests Tests that predict how well a student will perform in a future endeavor.

artificialism The belief that natural phenomena are caused by human beings.

assimilation The process by which information is altered to fit into one's already existing structures.

attribution theory An approach that seeks to explain how people make sense of events occurring both within and about the individual by ascribing the causes of these events.

backup reinforcers The reinforcers that can be purchased by students who have earned tokens in a token economy.

baseline A measure of the frequency in which a specific behavior is demonstrated.

BASIC Beginner's All-Purpose Symbolic Instructional Code, an easy-to-learn programming language widely used by students, educators, and owners of personal computers.

behavior modification The use of the principles of learning theory to alter behavior.

behavioral objectives Specific statements of learning outcomes defining the behavior expected of students after completing a unit in observable terms, the conditions under which the behavior is to be shown, and the criterion for successful performance.

being needs (growth needs) Maslow's term for needs that are associated with a person's fulfillment of potential.

bilingual A term describing people who can communicate in more than one language.

Black English A dialect spoken throughout the United States by lower-income blacks.

blind experimental designs An experimental design in which researchers do not know whether a subject they are working with belongs to the experimental group or the control group.

brainstorming A technique for generating a large number of solutions to a problem in which people suggest many possible solutions that are not evaluated until the group (or individual) is finished proposing solutions.

causal-comparative study A method of research in which a researcher compares a group of subjects who have a particular characteristic to a group that does not possess the characteristic on a variable of interest.

centering The tendency to be able to concentrate on only one dimension at a time.

child abuse A general term used to denote an injury that is intentionally perpetrated on a child.

chunking A technique for remembering many bits of information by combining them.

classical conditioning A learning process in which a neutral stimulus is paired with a stimulus that elicits a response until the originally neutral stimulus elicits that response.

classification The process of placing objects in different groupings.

cognition The process of thinking, knowing, or processing information.

cognitive style The characteristic manner in which people perceive, organize, and evaluate information.

combinational logic The ability to produce all the possible alternatives to answer a problem.

computer-aided instruction The use of computers as a tool to increase student learning.

computer literacy A term used to describe general knowledge about computers that includes some technical knowledge of hardware and software, the ability to use computers to solve problems, and an awareness of how computers affect society.

concept A set of specific objects, symbols, or events that share common characteristics and can be referred to by a particular name or symbol.

conceptual conflict Conflict that occurs when there is a disagreement over philosophy or content.

concrete operational stage Piaget's third stage of cognitive development—lasting from about seven through eleven years of age—in which children develop the ability to perform logical operations, such as conservation.

concurrent validity A type of criterion-related validity in which a test is validated against an external criterion such as another test that we already know is valid.

conditioned response The learned response to the conditioned stimulus.

conditioned stimulus The stimulus that is neutral before conditioning and after being paired with the unconditioned stimulus will elicit the desired response by itself.

conductive hearing losses Hearing losses caused by mechanical problems in conducting vibrations within the ear.

conservation The principle that quantities remain the same despite changes in their appearance.

construct validity A type of validity that indicates whether the test corresponds well to a theory or to some hypothetical construct.

content validity A type of validity that indicates that the test covers the domain it is intended to cover.

contingency contract A contract between teacher and student specifically noting the exact behavior desired and the consequences for performing and not performing the behavior.

continuous reinforcement A reinforcement schedule that involves reinforcing each instance of the desired behavior.

conventional level Kohlberg's second level of moral reasoning in which conformity to the expectations of others and society in general serves as the basis for moral decision making.

convergent thinking A type of thinking in which people solve problems by integrating information in a logical manner.

cooperative learning strategies Learning strategies that require two or more students to work together to reach some academic goal.

correlation A term denoting a relationship between two variables.

creativity The production of a novel re-sponse that appropriately solves a given problem.

criterion-referenced tests Tests in which student scores are compared to a particular criterion or absolute standard.

criterion-related validity A type of validity in which scores from a test are correlated with some external criterion. Predictive and concurrent validity are two types of criteron-related validity.

critical attributes Those properties that differentiate a concept from other concepts that share some similarities.

critical thinking Thinking that involves analyzing and focusing on what to believe or do in a particular situation.

cue (prompt) Any event that helps initiate a desired response.

dangle An instructional behavior in which students are left dangling while teachers talk about something essentially unconnected with the lesson.

deficiency needs (maintenance needs) Maslow's term for needs that disrupt a person's psychological or biological balance, causing the individual to respond to the discomfort.

dependent variable The factor in a study that will be measured by the researcher.

derived scores The transformation of raw scores into more usable measures that indicate the relative position of the student. Derived scores include percentiles, standard scores, stanines, and grade equivalents.

descriptive research Research whose aim is to objectively describe what is presently going on during the educational process.

developmental learning disabilities Deviations from the normal development of psychological or linguistic functions.

diagnostic evaluation Evaluations in which the strengths and weaknesses of a student are measured, often to determine the student's eligibility for special programs.

differential reinforcement of an incompatible behavior (DRI) A process in which a reinforcer is delivered after a response that is incompatible with the target response.

differential reinforcement of low rates of responding (DRL) A process in which the reinforcer is delivered for a reduction in the frequency in the target behavior.

differential reinforcement of other (DRO) A process in which the rein-forcer is delivered after any response other than the target response is shown.

direct instruction A type of instructional method especially useful for teaching facts that includes setting clear goals, presenting a sequence of well-organized assignments, explaining material to students, presenting examples, asking frequent questions, and giving frequent practice in what the students have learned.

disability A total or partial behavioral, mental, physical, or sensorial loss of functioning.

divergent thinking A type of thinking marked by the ability to see new relationships between things that are still appropriate to the situation.

edible reinforcers Reinforcers that involve any type of food.

educational psychology A field of psychology that applies psychology to education. It is concerned with the development, evaluation, and application of theories and principles of learning and instruction that can enhance lifelong learning.

egocentrism A thought process in which young children believe everyone is experiencing the environment the same way they are. Children who are egocentric have difficulty understanding someone else's point of view.

elaborative rehearsal A type of rehearsal in which information is processed in some meaningful way.

emotional abuse (psychological maltreatment) Psychological damage perpetrated on the child by parental actions which often involves rejection, isolation, terrorizing, ignoring, or corrupting.

enrichment An educational program in which a gifted student is given special, challenging work that goes beyond the usual.

epigenetic principle The preset developmental plan in Erikson's theory consisting of two elements: personality develops according to maturationally determined steps and each society is structured to encourage challenges that arise during these times.

episodic memory Memories concerning specific events that happened to a person at a specific time or place.

equilibration The process by which children seek a balance between what they know and what they are experiencing.

evaluation A systematic process of judging the quality, value, or worth of some performance or program.

exceptional child A child whose intellectual, emotional, or physical performance falls substantially above or below that of "normal" peers.

experimental research A research strategy using controls that allows the researcher to discover cause-and-effect relationships.

expository teaching An approach to teaching described by David Ausubel which involves reception rather than discovery learning. It involves presenting the main ideas before any details, using advance organizers, and pointing out similarities and differences.

extinction The weakening and disappearance of a learned response.

extinction burst An increase in the frequency of the response that often occurs when an extinction procedure is begun.

extrinsic motivation Motivation that comes from outside the individual, as when a student does his work to get a reward from his teacher.

fading The gradual removal of a prompt or reinforcer.

feedback Information that helps a student correct his or her behavior.

Feingold diet A diet developed by Dr. Benjamin Feingold for the treatment of hyperactivity, consisting mainly of the elimination of preservatives and artificial colors and flavors.

field dependent cognitive style (global cognitive style) The use of information absorbed from the environment as the principal guide in processing information.

field independent cognitive style (analytic cognitive style) The use of internal, independent factors as guides in processing information.

fixed interval reinforcement schedule A partial reinforcement schedule in which the reinforcer is administered following a fixed period of time after the previous reinforcer has been delivered.

fixed ratio reinforcement schedule A schedule of partial reinforcement in which a predetermined number of responses must be made before the reinforcer is administered.

flip-flop A term used to describe an instructional behavior in which a teacher goes from one topic to another and then returns to the first.

formal operational stage The last Piagetian stage of cognitive development, in which a person develops the ability to deal with abstractions and reason in a scientific manner.

formative evaluations Assessments of progress as the teaching of a particular unit is taking place.

fragmentation The tendency to have students learn something individually that could better be learned in a group context.

general instructional objectives Statements of the general learning outcomes expected after teaching a particular unit.

gifted students Students who have either demonstrated or seem to have potential for high capabilities in general intellectual ability, specific academic aptitude, creative or productive thinking, leadership ability, or the visual or performing arts.

grade equivalents A measure of grade level derived by assigning to the median score on a test a particular grade level equivalent and comparing other scores to it.

group intelligence tests Intelligence tests that are designed to be administered to a group of students at one time, as in a class situation.

growth needs See being needs.

guided discovery A type of discovery in which the teacher is active in focusing student attention on the important areas and structuring the problem and problem-solving activities so that students can discover the solution to a problem.

handicap The difficulty a disabled person has in adjusting to the environment.

Hawthorne effect The tendency for people to act differently when extra attention is paid to them.

heuristic A rule of thumb for solving problems or for reasoning in everyday situations.

high road transfer Transfer that requires the abstraction of a principle from one context and the conscious application of the principle to another context.

higher order reasoning skills (higher order thinking skills) Term used to describe elaborate and complex thinking skills such as analyzing, inferring, and evaluating.

holophrase One word used to stand for an entire thought.

hyperactivity A term used to describe the behavior of children who are impulsive, overly active, easily distracted, and inattentive.

hypothetical-deductive reasoning The ability to form a hypothesis, scientifically test the hypothesis, and draw conclusions using deductive logic.

identity The sense of knowing who you are.

identity achievement An identity status in which a person has developed a solid, personal identity.

identity diffusion An identity status resulting in confusion, aimlessness, and a sense of emptiness.

identity foreclosure An identity status marked by a premature identity decision.

identity moratorium An identity status in which a person is actively searching for an identity.

ill-defined problems Problems whose descriptions are vague or for which the information needed to solve them is not directly available.

imaginary audience A term used to describe an adolescent's belief that he or she is the focus of attention and is being evaluated by everyone.

impulsive cognitive style A cognitive style marked by cursory examination of a problem and answering questions very quickly.

independent variable The factor in a study that will be manipulated by the researcher.

indirect methods of instruction (inquiry learning, discovery learning) A group of techniques often involving questioning and conducting investigations in which the content of what is to be learned must be discovered by the student before it can be made part of the student's cognitive structure.

individual intelligence tests Intelligence tests that are administered by a psychologist on a one-to-one basis.

individualized education program (IEP) An individual plan outlining educational goals for an individual and methods for attaining them.

information processing approach An approach to cognition which investigates the way people take in information, process it, and act on the information.

instructional objectives Descriptions of what students are expected to do after completing some unit of instruction.

instructional validity A term used to describe whether a test is measuring skills taught in the classroom.

intelligence The ability to profit from experience. A cluster of abilities, such as reasoning and memory. In the Piagetian view, any behavior that allows the individual to adapt to the environment.

interpersonal conflict Conflict arising from differences in style or personality.

intrinsic motivation Motivation that flows from within the individual.

jigsaw technique A method of instruction in which students from different ethnic groups work cooperatively to learn new material.

language disabilities Problems with the proper use of words, poor grammar, or delayed language.

latchkey children (self-care children) Elementary schoolchildren who must care for themselves after school hours. (Some add junior high school students to the defintion.)

learned helplessness The learned inability to overcome obstacles that involves the belief that one cannot do anything to improve one's lot.

learning disabilities A group of disorders marked by significant difficulties in acquiring and using listening, speaking, reading, writing, reasoning skills, or mathematics skills.

learning style Normal variations in internal and external preferences for the setting and manner in which learning takes place.

least restrictive environment The placement in which a disabled student can be educated with no more restriction than is absolutely necessary.

legal blindness A person with a visual acuity of 20/200 in the better eye with correction or with peripheral vision that covers less than 20 degrees of the field of vision.

levels of processing view A view of memory as a system with many levels of processing. How well an item is remembered is purported to be a function of how deeply and elaborately information is processed.

linguistic deficit hypothesis The belief that a dialect such as Black English is a hindrance to learning.

linguistic difference hypothesis The belief that a dialect such as Black English is different from Standard English but not a deficit.

logico-mathematical knowledge Knowledge acquired through creating and inventing relationships between objects and symbols.

LOGO An education-oriented programming language designed to easily enable children to begin to program and communicate with computers.

long-term memory Memory storage that has a large—perhaps an unlimited—capacity and a long duration.

low road transfer The transfer that occurs spontaneously when material learned in one circumstance is carried over to very similar situations.

mainstreaming The term used to describe the process by which exceptional children are integrated into classes with "normal" peers.

maintenance needs See deficiency needs.

maintenance rehearsal A type of rehearsal in which information is simply repeated.

mastery learning A program designed so that students reach a high level of competence in certain well-defined skills.

mastery tests Tests that measure a student's proficiency at a particular skill. Scores are reported in terms of the percentage needed for mastery and the percentage a student answered correctly.

maturation A term used to describe changes that are due to the unfolding of the genetic plan.

mean The arithmetic average.

measurement The quantitative description of student behavior, usually accomplished through testing.

median The point in a distribution above and below which an equal number of scores fall.

mental age The age at which an individual is functioning.

mental retardation A condition marked by subnormal intellectual functioning and adjustment disabilities that occur before a person is 18 years of age.

metacognition The conscious monitoring and regulation of the way people approach and solve a problem or challenge.

metamemory A person's knowledge of his or her own memory process.

minimum competency tests Tests intended to ensure that each graduate possesses particular skills at a basic level.

mnemonic device Memory aid that helps to organize new material and make it more meaningful through interactive imagery or by relating it to existing, well-learned information.

mode The score obtained by more people than any other score.

moral realism The Piagetian stage of moral reasoning during which rules are viewed as sacred and justice is whatever the authority figure says.

moral reasoning An approach to the study of moral development stressing the importance of the child's ideas and reasoning about justice and right and wrong.

moral relativism The Piagetian stage of moral reasoning in which children weigh the intentions of others before judging their actions as right or wrong.

motivation The process by which behavior is activated and directed towards some goal.

multiethnic education (multicultural education) Multidisciplinary approach to education that aims at teaching students about the cultural heritage of various groups and the many contributions each group makes to society.

nativist approach An explanation of language development based on biological or innate factors.

negative reinforcement A type of reinforcement in which the reward for the desired behavior is a reduction or elimination of an aversive condition.

neglect A term used to describe a situation in which the care and supervision of a child is insufficient or improper.

norm-referenced tests Tests in which the score of the test taker is compared to the scores of other students who took the test when it was developed.

normal curve (normal distribution) A bell-shaped distribution in which scores occur symmetrically about the mean, and the mean and median are the same. It is very useful for understanding the distribution of many human traits.

object permanence The understanding that an object exists even when it is out of one's visual field.

observation A research method in which the researcher objectively and systematically records the behavior of subjects.

observational learning Learning by observing others.

operant conditioning The learning process in which behavior is governed by its consequences.

operation An internalized action that is part of a child's cognitive structure.

overdwelling Teacher behavior that involves spending too much time on a small point.

overextension A type of error in which children apply a term more broadly than it should be.

overgeneralization A type of error in which children overuse the basic rules of language. For instance, once they learn to use plural nouns they many say "mans" instead of "men."

overjustification effect The loss of interest that occurs when an individual shifts from an intrinsic to an extrinsic motivational orientation.

overlapping Jacob Kounin's term for a teacher's ability to do more than one thing at a time.

overlearning Practicing a learned response after it is already mastered.

partial reinforcement schedules A group of reinforcement schedules in which the reinforcer is administered after a portion of the total responses in a particular situation rather than after every response.

Pascal A high-level programming language developed for instructional purposes and now commonly used in a wide variety of applications.

peer tutoring An active, structured learning situation in which one student helps another student master some aspect of schoolwork.

percentile ranking Scores indicating the percentage of peers who scored at or below the student's score.

personal fable The adolescent's belief that his or her experiences are unique and original.

physical knowledge Knowledge about objects acquired through acting on objects and observing the result of the actions.

placement evaluations Evaluations that aim at discovering whether students have the necessary skills to succeed or whether they have already achieved objectives.

postconventional level Kohlberg's third level of moral reasoning in which moral decisions are made on the basis of individual values that have been internalized.

preconventional level Kohlberg's first level of moral reasoning in which satisfaction of one's own needs and rewards and punishment serve as the bases for moral decision making.

predictive validity A type of criterion-related validity in which a test demonstrates the ability to predict some behavior that will occur at a later date.

Premack principle A principle of learning that states that a behavior that appears more often can be used as a reinforcer for a behavior that occurs less often.

preoperational stage Piaget's second stage of cognitive development, marked by the appearance of language and symbolic function and the child's inability to understand logical concepts, such as conservation.

procedural conflict Conflict over what action is necessary to reach an agreed-upon goal.

procedural memory Memories concerning how to do something.

programmed instruction A self-instructional process in which material is presented to students in a step-by-step progression from easier to more difficult and provides students with immediate feedback.

Project Head Start A federally funded education program aimed at reducing or eliminating the differences in educational achievement between poor and middle-class youngsters.

proposition The smallest unit of knowledge that can either be true or false.

prototype The most typical instance of a category.

quasi-experimental study A study in which an experimental and a control group are used but in which random assignment to these groups is not performed.

reactivity Changes that occur when people monitor their own behavior.

readiness tests Tests that measure whether a student has attained the skills necessary to master a new skill.

recall A method of testing retrieval in which the subject must produce the correct response given very limited cues.

reception learning A type of learning described by David Ausubel in which the entire content of what is to be learned is presented to the student.

reciprocal teaching An approach to teaching reading strategies that involves summarizing, question generating, clarifying, and predicting and requires students and teacher to enter into a dialogue for discovering the meaning of a written passage.

recognition A method of testing retrieval in which the subject is required to choose the correct answer from a group of choices.

reflective cognitive style A cognitive style marked by first thoroughly exploring the problem, then considering various alternatives, and finally answering the question or performing the task.

reinforcement An event that increases the likelihood that the behavior that preceded it will recur.

relearning A method of testing retrieval in which students learn material and then relearn the same material after an interval. Retention is measured in the savings in time or trials on the second learning.

reliability The quality of a test when it yields consistent scores.

response cost A procedure in which a positive reinforcer is lost if an undesirable behavior is exhibited.

reversibility Beginning at the end of an operation and working one's way back to the beginning.

ripple effect The effect that a teacher's behavior towards one student has on other students.

SQ3R A commonly used reading and studying technique consisting of five steps: survey, question, read, recite and review.

scheme (Piagetian Theory) An organized system of actions and thoughts useful for dealing with the environment that can be generalized to many situations.

schema (information processing) An organized body of knowledge which functions as a framework describing objects and relationships that generally occur.

script A structure that describes an appropriate sequence of events in a particular context.

seatwork Exercises that are designed for students to perform independently as a form of practice after they have learned the work.

selective attention The capacity to focus attention on a narrow band of sensory stimulation.

self-concept The picture people have of themselves.

self-efficacy A term describing people's beliefs about what they can and cannot do.

self-esteem The value people place on various aspects of the self.

self-fulfilling prophecy The concept that a person's expectations concerning some event affect the probability of the event's occurrence.

self-monitoring An activity in which students keep track of some aspect of their own behavior.

self-reinforcement A process in which students reinforce themselves for desired behaviors.

self-worth theory A theory of achievement motivation whose central postulate is that students need to protect their own sense of worth or personal value and will act in a way that minimizes the implications of failure with respect to ability.

semantic memory Memories consisting of general knowledge.

sensorimotor stage The first stage in Piaget's theory of cognitive development, in which the child discovers the world using the senses and motor activity.

sensorineural hearing losses Hearing problems caused by nerve damage.

sensory register A type of memory that retains an almost complete representation of sensory stimulation for a very brief period of time.

seriation The process of placing objects in size order.

sex roles Behaviors expected of people in a given society based on one's gender.

short-term memory A type of memory that has a short duration and a very limited capacity.

slot outline An outline that provides spaces in which students can take notes.

social-arbitrary knowledge Knowledge acquired from other people including their customs, language, and values.

social learning theory A theory of learning emphasizing the importance of imitation and observational learning.

social reinforcers Behaviors such as praise and attention that can be used as reinforcers.

social skills Skills necessary for good interpersonal relations, including the ability to follow instructions, accept criticism, disagree appropriately, greet someone, make a request, and reinforce and compliment others.

speech disorders Problems in the physical reproduction of speech.

spontaneous recovery The phenomenon in which after extinction has taken place and a rest period ensues, the response thought to be extinguished returns.

standard deviation One measure of a distribution's variability.

standard score A measure that expresses how far a given score is from the mean in standard deviation units.

standardization The specific rules for administering and scoring a standardized test so that every person taking the test does so under the same conditions. It also refers to the process by which norms are formulated for norm-referenced tests.

standardized achievement tests Tests that measure a student's knowledge of a particular subject.

standardized tests Instruments that contain a specific set of items and give definite and standardized directions for administration and scoring.

stimulus bound Jacob Kounin's term for a state in which teachers react to anything that momentarily enters their mind.

stimulus discrimination The process by which a person learns to differentiate among stimuli.

stimulus generalization The tendency of an organism that has learned to associate a certain behavior with a particular stimulus to show this behavior when confronted with similar stimuli.

student-owned problems Problems in which a student's needs are frustrated by other people or events that do not directly involve the teacher.

study skills Methods students use to study.

style flexing A term used to describe the use of a variety of teaching techniques to accommodate varying student cognitive and learning styles.

substantive conflict Conflict that occurs when people disagree over goals.

summative evaluation Evaluations that aim at determining whether instruction has been successful.

survey A method of study in which data are collected from a number of people through written questionnaires or oral interviews.

symbolic function The ability to use one thing to stand for another.

tangible reinforcers Material reinforcers such as stickers.

taxonomy of educational objectives (affective domain) A hierarchical listing of education objectives covering the affective domain (attitudes, values, and emotions).

taxonomy of educational objectives (cognitive domain) Bloom's hierarchical listing of educational objectives covering the cognitive (intellectual) domain.

taxonomy of educational objectives (psychomotor domain) A hierarchical listing of educational objectives covering the psychomotor domain, which involves movement and manual skills.

teacher-owned problems Problems in which student behavior interferes with teachers meeting their own needs and at times cause the teacher to feel frustration or anger.

telegraphic speech Sentences in which only the basic words necessary to communicate meaning are used, with helping words such as *a* or *to* left out.

testwiseness A student's ability to utilize the characteristics and format of a test or the test-taking situation to receive a high score.

Theory of Multiple Intelligences A conception of intelligence advanced by Howard Gardner, who argues that there are seven different types of intelligence.

Three-dimensional discipline A system of classroom management based upon the establishment and refinement of classroom rules that form the basis for a contract binding both students and the teacher.

thrusts Any intrusion whether internal or external that unnecessarily disrupts the lesson.

time out A technique in which a student who misbehaves is placed for a short period of time in a less reinforcing environment.

token economy (token reinforcement system) A system of reinforcement in which students receive a token (such as a star) for performing the desired behavior and can either use it immediately or save it and add it to previously earned tokens to "purchase" reinforcers.

Torrance Tests of Creative Thinking A test of creativity that measures the fluency, flexibility, ability to elaborate, and originality of a person's thinking.

transfer Learning in one situation that is carried over to another situation.

Triarchic Theory of Intelligence A theory of intelligence based on information processing considerations advanced by Robert Sternberg, who postulates the following mechanisms of intellectual functioning: metacomponents, which involve the individual's skills used in planning and decision making; performance components, which relate to the basic operations involved in actually solving the task; and knowledge acquisition components, which involve processes that are used in acquiring new knowledge.

unconditioned response The response to the unconditioned stimulus.

unconditioned stimulus The stimulus that originally elicits the response.

underextension A type of error in which children apply a term more narrowly than it should be.

validity A quality of a test when it measures what it is designed to measure.

variability The extent to which scores in a distribution are spread out or lie close to the mean.

variable attributes General properties that define a concept but do not differentiate it from all other concepts.

variable interval reinforcement schedule A partial reinforcement schedule in which the time period between the administration of reinforcers is varied.

variable ratio reinforcement schedule A partial reinforcement schedule in which the number of responses required to obtain a reinforcer varies.

well-defined problems Problems that are explicitly described and whose end states and constraints are clearly defined.

withitness Jacob Kounin's term for teachers who constantly know what is going on in the classroom.

References

CHAPTER 1

Albrecht, J. E. (1984). A nation at risk: Another view. *Phi Delta Kappan, 65,* 684–685.

Anderson, L. M. (1981). Student responses to seatwork: Implications for the study of students' cognitive processing. Cited in Educational Psychology Returns to School by L. S. Schulman. In *The G. Stanley Hall Lecture Series,* Vol. 2 (A. G. Kraut, editor). Washington, DC: American Psychological Association, 1982, 73–119.

Anderson, L., Evertson, C., & Brophy, J. (1979). An experimental study of effective teaching in first-grade reading groups. *Elementary School Journal, 79,* 193–223.

Ash, M. J., & Love-Clark, P. (1985). An historical analysis of the content of educational psychology textbooks, 1954–1983. *Educational Psychologist, 20,* 47–55.

Ayers, W. (1987, November 25). What do 17-year-olds know? A critique of recent research. *Education Week,* p. 18.

Bardon, J. I. (1989). Relations with other disciplines. In M. C. Wittrock & F. Farley (Eds.), *The future of educational psychology* (pp. 131–145). Hillsdale, NJ: Erlbaum.

Berliner, D. C. (1987). But do they understand. In V. Richardson-Koehler (Ed.), *Educators' handbook,* pp. 259–295. New York: Longman.

Billups, L. H., & Rauth (1987). M. Teachers and research. In V. Richardson-Koehler (Ed.), *Educators' handbook* (pp. 624–641). New York: Longman.

Brophy, J. (1981). Teacher praise: A functional analysis. *Review of Educational Research, 51,* 1069–1078.

Brophy, J. E., & Good, T. L. (1986). Teacher behavior and student achievement. In M. C. Wittrock (Ed.), *Handbook of research on teaching* (pp. 328–376) New York: Macmillan.

Brownell, G. (1987). *Computer and teaching.* St. Paul, MN: West.

Callison, W. (1988, February/March). Future of computers in classrooms. *Thrust,* pp. 36–37.

Chase, C. I. (1986, September/October). How 2,000 teachers view their profession. *Journal of Educational Research,* pp. 12–18.

Emmer, E., Evertson, C. M., & Anderson, L. M. (1980). Effective classroom management at the beginning of the school year. *The Elementary School Journal, 80,* 219–231.

Erickson, F. (1986). Qualitative methods in research on teaching. In M. C. Wittrock (Ed.), *Handbook of research on teaching* (pp. 119–162). New York: Macmillan.

Evertson, C. M. (1987, Winter) Creating conditions for learning: From research to practice. *Theory into Practice,* pp. 44–50.

Feder, B. (1979). *The complete guide to taking tests.* Englewood Cliffs, NJ: Prentice-Hall.

Finn, C. E. (1988). What ails educational research. *Educational Researcher, 17,* 5–8.

Finn, C. E., & Ravitch, D. (1987, October). What our 17-year-olds don't know. *The American School Board Journal,* pp. 31–33.

Flanagan, J. C. (1983). The contribution of educational institutions to the quality of life of Americans. *International Review of Applied Psychology, 32,* 275–288.

Gallup, A. M. & Elam, S. M. (1988, September). The 20th annual poll of the public's attitudes toward the public schools. *Phi Delta Kappa,* pp. 33–46.

Hanna, G. S. (1989). To change answers or not to change answers: That is the question. *The Clearing House, 62,* 414–416.

Heward, W. L., & Orlansky, M. D (1988). *Exceptional Children* (3rd ed.). Columbus, OH: Merrill.

Isakson, R. L., & Ellsworth, R. (1979). The measurement of teacher attitudes toward educational research. *Educational Research Quarterly, 4,* 12–17.

Jones, B. (1986, April). Quality and equality through cognitive instruction. *Educational Leadership,* pp. 4–11.

Jones, B. F. (1989). Educational psychologists where are you? Toward closing the gap between research and practice. In M. C. Wittrock & F. Farley (Eds.), *The future of educational psychology* (pp. 145–173). Hillsdale, NJ: Erlbaum.

Kearney, P., Plax, T. G., Sorensen, G., & Smith, V. R. (1988, April). Experienced and prospective teachers' selections of compliance—Gaining messages for "common" student misbehavior. *Communication Education,* pp. 150–164.

Lepper, M. R. (1985). Microcomputers in education: Motivation and social issues. *American Psychologist, 40,* 1–18.

Letteri, C. A. (1985, Spring). Teaching students how to learn, *Theory into Practice,* pp. 112–122.

Lynn, S. (1986). Experienced teachers share their insights. *Instructor, 96,* 54–56.

Marso, R. N. and Pigge, F. L. (1987, November/December). Differences between self-perceived job expectations and job realities of beginning teachers. *Journal of Teacher Education, 38,* 53–56.

Myers, M. (1986). When research does not help teachers. *American Educator, 10,* 18–23.

Ornstein, A. (1985). The national reports on education: Implications for directions and aims. *Kappa Delta Pi Record, 21,* 58–64.

Rosenshine, B. & Stevens, R. (1986). Teaching functions. In M. C. Wittrock (Ed.), *Handbook of Research on Teaching* (3rd ed.) (pp. 376–392). New York: Macmillan.

Rothman, R. (1988, March 9). U.S. fares poorly on science test. *Education Week.* p. 4.

Rubin, L. (1983, January). Artistry in teaching. *Educational Leadership,* pp. 44–49.

Schulman, L. S. (1982). Educational psychology returns to school. In A. G. Kraut, *The G. Stanley Hall Lecture Series* (Vol. 2) (pp. 73–119). Washington, DC: American Psychological Association.

Stedman, L. C. and Kaestle, C. F. (1985). The test score decline is over—but now what. *Phi Delta Kappan, 67,* 204–210.

Turner, R. R. (1987a). What are the critical problems in teaching and how can they be solved. *Learning, 15,* 58–63.

Turner, R. R. (1987b). *Learning, 15,* 55–57.

U.S. Department of Education (1987). What works: Research about teaching and learning (2nd ed.). Washington, DC: U.S. Department of Education.

U.S. math education just doesn't add up. . . . and in other bad news (1989, January 27). pp. 5, 15.

U.S. News and World Report (1987, September 28). What Americans should know, 86–94.

U.S. News and World Report (1988, August 1). Putting kids first, p. 62.

Veenman, S. (1984). Perceived problems of beginning teachers. *Review of Educational Research, 54,* 143–178.

Wittrock, M. C., & Farley, F. (1989). Toward a blueprint for educational psychology. In M. C. Wittrock & F. Farley (Eds.), *The future of educational psychology* (pp. 193–199). Hillsdale, NJ: Erlbaum.

CHAPTER 2

Adelson, J. (1972). The political imagination of the young adolescent. In J. Kagan & R. Coles, *Twelve to Sixteen: Early adolescence.* (pp. 106–144). New York: Norton.

Adelson, J., & O'Neil, R. P. (1966). Growth of political ideas in adolescence: The sense of community. *Journal of Personality and Social Psychology, 4,* 295–306.

Anglin, J. M. (1977). *Word, object, and conceptual development.* New York: Norton.

Arlin, P. K. (1981). Piagetian tasks as predictors of reading and math readiness in grades K–1. *Journal of Educational Psychology, 73,* 712–721.

Ault, R. (1977). *Children's cognitive development.* New York: Oxford University Press.

August, D. L. (1986, May). Bilingual Education Act, Title 2 of the Education Amendments of 1984. *Washington Report,* Washington Liaison Office of the Society for Research in Child Development.

Baker, K. A., & de Kanter, A. A. (1981). *Effectiveness of bilingual education: A review of the literature.* Washington, DC: U.S. Department of Education, Office of Planning, Budget and Evaluation.

Bloom, L. M. (1975). Language development. In F. D. Horowitz (Ed.), *Review of child development research,* Vol. 4. Chicago: University of Chicago Press.

Bott, R., Hitchfield, E. M., Davies, M. P., Johnson, J. E., Glynne-Jones, M. L., & Tamburrini, J. R. (1970). *The teaching of young children: Some applications of Piaget's learning theory.* New York: Schocken Books.

Bruner, J. (1978, September). Learning the mother tongue. *Human Nature,* 11–19.

Bullock, M. (1985). Animism in childhood thinking: A new look at an old question. *Developmental Psychology, 21,* 217–226.

Bybee, R. W., & Sund, R. B. (1982). *Piaget for Educators* (2nd ed.). Columbus, OH: Merrill.

Chomsky, N. (1972). *Language and mind* (Enl. Ed.). New York: Harcourt Brace Jovanovich.

Christensen, C. M. (1960). Relationships between pupil achievement, pupil affect-need, teacher warmth, and teacher permissiveness. *Journal of Educational Psychology, 51,* 169–174.

Clark, H. H., & Clark, E. V. (1977). *Psychology and language: An introduction to psycholinguistics.* San Diego: Harcourt Brace Jovanovich.

Confrey, J. (1987). Mathematics Learning and Teaching. In V. Richardson-Koehler (Ed.). *Educators' handbook.* New York: Longman, 3–26.

Cooper, P., & Stewart, L. (1987). *Language Skills in the Classroom.* Washington, DC: National Education Association.

Copeland, R. W. (1984). *How children learn mathematics: Teaching implications of Piaget's research* (4th ed.). New York: Macmillan.

Crawford, J. (1987, April 1). Bilingual education: Language, learning, and politics. *Education Week* (Special Report, pp. 19–50.

de Villiers, J. G., & de Villiers, P. A. (1978). *Language Acquisition.* Cambridge, MA: Harvard University Press.

DeVries, R., with L. Kohlberg (1987). *Programs of early education: The constructivist view.* New York: Longman.

Diaz, R. M. (1985). Bilingual cognitive development: Addressing three gaps in current research. *Child Development, 56,* 1376–1388.

Duckworth, E. (1964). Piaget rediscovered. In R. E. Ripple & U. N. Rockcastle (Eds.), *Piaget Rediscovered.* Ithaca, NY: Cornell University Press.

Educating the melting pot (1986, March 31).

U.S. News and World Report, pp. 20–21.

Elkind, D. (1987). *Miseducation.* New York: Knopf.

Flavell, J. H. (1982). On cognitive development. *Child development, 53,* 1–10.

Flavell, J. H. (1985). *Cognitive development* (2nd ed.). Englewood Cliffs, NJ: Prentice-Hall.

Flavell, J. H. (1986). The development of children's knowledge about the appearance-reality distinction. *American Psychologist, 41,* 418–426.

Flavell, J. H. (1977). *Cognitive development* (2nd ed.). Englewood Cliffs, NJ: Prentice-Hall.

Flavell, J. H., (1975). *Development of role-taking and communication skills in children.* Huntington, NY: Krieger.

Forman, G. E., & Kuschner, D. S. (1977). *The child's construction of knowledge: Piaget for teaching children.* Monterey, CA: Brooks/Cole.

Gallatin, J., and Adelson, J. (1971). Legal guarantees of individual freedom: A cross-national study of the development of political thought. *Journal of Social Issues, 227,* 93–108.

Goodluck, H. (1986). Language acquisition and linguistic theory. In P. Fletcher & M. Garman (Eds.), *Language Acquisition* (2d ed., pp. 44–49). London: Cambridge University Press.

Gorman, R. M. (1972). *Discovering Piaget: A guide for teachers.* Columbus, OH: Merrill.

Griffiths, P. (1986). Early vocabulary. In P. Fletcher & M. Garman (Eds.). *Language Aquisition.* London: Cambridge University Press.

Harter, S. (1983). Developmental perspective on the self-system. In P. H. Mussen (Ed.) *Handbook of child psychology* (4th ed.), *4,* 275–387. New York: Wiley.

Hoff-Ginsberg, E. (1986). Function and structure in maternal speech: Their relation to the child's development of syntax. *Developmental psychology, 22,* 155–163.

Harter, S. (1983). Developmental perspective on the self-system. In P. H. Mussen (ed). *Handbook of child psychology* (4th ed.), *4,* 275–387. New York: Wiley.

Hough, R. A., Nurss, J. R., & Wood, D. (1987, November). Tell me a story: Making opportunities for elaborated language in early childhood classrooms. *Young Children,* pp. 6–12.

Inhelder, B., & Piaget, J. (1964). *The early growth of logic in the child.* New York: Norton.

Inhelder, B., & Piaget, J. (1958). *The growth of logical thinking.* New York: Basic Books.

Karplus, R., & Arnold, S. M. (1982). The development of reasoning (editorial). In R. W. Bybee & R. B. Sund, *Piaget for educators* (2d ed.) (p. 39). Columbus, OH: Merrill.

Kegan, R. (1982). *The evolving self: Problem and process in human development.* Cambridge, MA: Harvard University Press.

King, M. L. (1987). Language insights from acquisition. *Theory into Practice, 26,* 358–363.

Koslowski, B. (1980). Quantitative and qualitative changes in the development of seriation. *Merrill-Palmer Quarterly, 26,* 391–405.

Kuhn, D. (1979). The application of Piaget's theory of cognitive development to education. *Harvard Educational Review. 49,* 340–360.

Labov, W. (1977). *The study of nonstandard english.* In V. P. Clark, P. A. Eshholz, & A. F. Rosa (Eds.) *Language* (2nd ed., pp. 439–450). New York: St. Martin's Press.

Mandler, J. M. (1983). Representation. In P. H. Mussen (Ed.), *Handbook of child psychology,* Vol. 3 (4th ed.), (pp. 420–495). New York: Wiley.

McKinney, J. P., Fitzgerald, H. E., & Strommen, E. A. (1982). *Developmental psychology: The adolescent and young adult* (2nd ed.). Homewood, IL: Dorsey Press.

McLaughlin, B. (1977). Second language learning in children. *Psychological Bulletin, 84,* 438–459.

McLaughlin, B. (1978). *Second-language acquisition in childhood.* Hillsdale, NJ: Erlbaum.

Menyuk, P. (1977). *Language and maturation.* Cambridge, Mass: M.I.T. Press.

Merelman, R. M. (1971). The development of policy thinking in adolescence. *American Political Science Review, 65,* 1033–1047.

Miller, P. H. (1989). *Theories of developmental psychology* (2nd ed.). New York: Freeman.

Molfese, D. L., Molfese, V. J., & P. L. Carroll. (1982). Early language development. In B. B. Wolman (Ed.), *Handbook of developmental psychology* (pp. 301–323). Englewood Cliffs, NJ: Prentice-Hall.

Morrison, G. S. (1988). *Early childhood education today* (4th ed.). Columbus, OH: Merrill.

Nelson, K. (1973). Structure and strategy in learning to talk. *Monograph of the society for research in child development, 38,* 1–2, serial no. 149.

New York Times (1988, July 28). Americans falter on geography test, p. A16.

Oken-Wright, P. (1988). Show-and-tell grows up. *Young Children,* pp. 52–58.

Olim, E. G., Hess, R. D., & Shipman, V. C. (1967). Role of mothers' language styles in mediating their preschool children's development. *School Review, 75,* 414–425.

Peters, A. M. (1986). Early syntax. In P. Fletcher & M. Garman (Eds.), *Language acquisition* (2d ed.) (pp. 307–326). London: Cambridge University Press.

Peterson, R., & Felton-Collins, V. (1986). *The Piaget handbook for teachers and parents.* New York: The Teacher's College Press.

Phillips, J. L. (1975). *The origins of intellect: Piaget's theory* (2nd ed.). San Francisco: W. H. Freeman.

Piaget, J. (1952). *The Child's conception of number.* New York: Humanities Press.

Piaget, J. (1954). *The construction of reality in the child.* New York: Basic Books.

Piaget, J. (1967). *Six Psychological Studies.* New York: Random House.

Piaget, J. (1970). *Science of education and the psychology of the child.* New York: Orion Press.

Piaget, J. (1972). *Principles of genetic epistemology.* New York: Basic Books.

Piaget, J. (1973). *To understand is to invent.* New York: Grossman Press.

Piaget, J. (1974). *To understand is to invent.* New York: Viking Press.

Piaget, J. (1983). Piaget's theory. In P. H. Mussen (Ed.), *Handbook of child psychology,* Vol. 1, pp. 103–129. New York: Wiley. (Originally published in Carmichael's Manual of Child Psychology, 2d ed., 1970).

Piaget, J., & Inhelder, B. (1969). *The psychology of the child.* New York: Basic Books.

Pulaski, M. A. S. (1980). *Understanding Piaget: An introduction to children's cognitive development* (Rev. Ed.). New York: Harper & Row.

Raloff, J. (1982). Reports from the 1982 Meeting of the American Speech Language Hearing Association's Meeting in Toronto, Canada. *Science News, 122,* 360.

Raspberry, W. (1970, April). Should ghettoese be accepted? *Today's Education,* pp. 30–31, 34–41.

Renner, J., Stafford, D., Lawson, A., McKinnon, J., Friot, F., & Kellogg, D. (1976). *Research, teaching, and learning with the Piaget model.* Norman, OK: University of Oklahoma Press.

Salkind, N. J. (1981). *Theories of human development.* New York: Van Nostrand.

Segalowitz, N. S. (1981). Issues in the cross-cultural study of bilingual development. In H. C. Triandis & A. Heron (Eds.), *Handbook of cross-cultural psychology,* Vol. 4 (pp. 55–93). Boston: Allyn & Bacon.

Siegler, R. S. (1986). *Children's thinking.* Englewood Cliffs, NJ: Prentice Hall.

Skinner, B. F. (1957). *Verbal Behavior.* New York: Appleton-Century-Crofts.

Smith, R. M., & Neisworth, J. T. (1983). *The exceptional child: A functional approach* (2nd ed.). New York: McGraw-Hill.

Sprinthall, N. A., & Collins, W. A. (1984). *Adolescent psychology: A developmental view.* New York: Random House.

Thomas, R. M. (1979). *Comparing theories of child development.* Belmont, CA: Wadsworth.

Trehub, S. (1973). Infants' selectivity to vowel and tonal contrasts. *Developmental Psychology, 9,* 81–96.

Vernon, P. E. (1976). Environment and intelligence. In V. P. Varma & P. Williams, *Piaget: Psychology and education* (pp. 31–43). Itasca, IL: F. E. Peacock.

Wadsworth, B. (1978). *Piaget for the classroom teacher.* New York: Longman.

Wadsworth, B. (1971). *Misinterpretations of Piaget's theory.* New York: McKay.

Whitehurst, G. J. (1982). Language development. In B. B. Wolman (Ed.). *Handbook of developmental psychology,* pp. 367–384. Englewood Cliffs, NJ: Prentice-Hall.

Willig, A. E. (1985). A Meta-analysis of selected studies on the effectiveness of bilingual education. *Review of educational research, 55,* 269–317.

CHAPTER 3

Aiken, E. G., Thomas, G. S., & Shennum, W. A. (1975). Memory For a lecture: Effects of notes, lecture rate, and informational density. *Journal of Educational Psychology, 67,* 439–444.

American College Dictionary (1969). New York: Random House.

Anderson, D. R., & Field, D. E. (1983). Children's attention to television: Implications for production. In M. Meyer (Ed.), *Children and the formal features of television.* New York: Sauer.

Anderson, D. R., & Lorch, E. P. (1983). Looking at television: Action or reaction? In J. Bryant & D. R. Anderson (Eds.), *Children's understanding of television* (pp. 1–30). New York: Academic Press.

Andre, T. (1979). Does answering higher-level questions while reading facilitate productive learning? *Review of Educational Research, 49,* 280–318.

Atkinson, R. C., & Shiffrin, R. M. (1968). Human memory: A proposed system and its control processes. In W. K. Spence & J. T. Spence (Eds.), *The psychology of learning and motivation: Advances in research and theory* (pp. 89–195). New York: Academic Press.

Ausubel, D. P. (1968). *Educational psychology: A cognitive view.* New York: Holt, Rinehart and Winston.

Badderly, A. D. and Dale, H. C. (1966). The effect of semantic similarity on retroactive interference in long- and short-term memory. *Journal of verbal learning and verbal behavior, 5,* 417–420.

Barnett, J. E., Di Vesta, F. J., & Rogozinski, J. T. (1981). What is learned in note taking? *Journal of Educational Psychology, 73,* 181–193.

Berliner, D. C. (1987). But do they understand? In V. Richardson-Koehler, *Educators' handbook* (pp. 259–295). New York: Longman.

Best, J. B. (1986). *Cognitive development.* St. Paul: West.

Borich, G. D. (1988). *Effective teaching methods.* Columbus, OH: Merrill.

Bretzing, B. H., & Kulhavy, R. W. (1979). Note taking and depth of processing. *Contemporary Educational Psychology, 4,* 145–153.

Bretzing, B. H., & Kulhavy, R. W. (1981). Note-taking and passage style. *Journal of Educational Psychology, 73,* 242–251.

Brown, A. L., Bransford, J. D., Ferrara, R. A., & Campione, J. C. (1983). Learning, remembering, and understanding. In J. H. Flavell & E. M. Markman (Eds.), *Handbook of child psychology* (4th ed.) (pp. 77–167). New York: Wiley.

Brown, A. L., & Smiley, S. S. (1977). Rating the importance of structural units of prose passages: A problem of metacognitive development. *Child Development, 48,* 1–8.

Carrier, C. A. and Titus, A. (1981). Effects of notetaking presentation and test model expectations on learning for lectures. *American Education Research Journal, 18,* 385–397.

Carter, J. F., & Van Matre, N. H. (1975). Note taking versus note having. *Journal of Educational Psychology, 67,* 900–904.

Carter, V., & Good, B. (Eds.). (1973). *Dictionary of education.* New York: McGraw-Hill.

Chi, M. T. H., & Glaser, R. (1985). Problem solving ability. In R. J. Sternberg (Ed.),

Human abilities: An information processing approach. New York: Freeman.

Cohn, M. (1979). *Helping your teen-age student: What parents can do to improve reading and study skills.* New York: E. P. Dutton.

Corkill, A. J., Glover, J. A., Bruning, R. H., & Krug, D. (1988). Advance organizers: Retrieval context hypotheses. *Journal of Educational Psychology, 80,* 304–311.

Craik, F. I. M., & Lockhart, R. S. (1972). Levels of processing: A framework for memory research. *Journal of Verbal Learning and Verbal Behavior, 11,* 671–684.

Cross, D. R., & Paris, S. G. (1988). Developmental and instructional analyses of children's metacognition and reading comprehension. *Journal of Educational Psychology, 80,* 131–142.

Daehler, M. W., & D. Bukatko (1985). *Cognitive Development.* New York: Knopf.

Dirks, J., & Neisser, U. (1977). Memory for objects in real scenes: The development of recognition and recall. *Journal of Experimental Child Psychology, 23,* 315–328.

Di Vesta, F. J., & Gray, G. S. (1972). Listening and note taking. *Journal of Educational Psychology, 63,* 8–14.

Doctorow, M., Wittrock, M. C., & Marks, C. (1978). Generative processes in reading comprehension. *Journal of Educational Psychology, 70,* 109–118.

Eggen, P. D., Kauchak, D., & Harder, R. J. (1979). *Strategies for teachers: Information processing models in the classroom.* Englewood Cliffs, NJ: Prentice-Hall.

Ellis, H. C., & Hunt, R. R. (1989). *Fundamentals of human memory and cognition* (4th ed.). Dubuque, IA: Wm. C. Brown.

Fitzgerald, J. (1983). Helping readers gain self-control over reading comprehension. *The Reading Teacher, 37,* 249–254.

Flavell, J. H. (1985). *Cognitive development* (2nd ed.). Englewood Cliffs, NJ: Prentice-Hall.

Flavell, J. H., Beach, D. H., & Chinsky, J. M. (1966). Spontaneous verbal rehearsal in a memory tasks as a function of age. *Child Development, 37,* 283–299.

Flavell, J. H., Friedrichs, A. G., Hoyt, J. D. (1970). Developmental changes in memorization process. *Cognitive Psychology, 1,* 324–340.

Flavell, J. H., & Wellman, H. M. (1977). Metamemory. In R. V. Kail & J. W. Hagen (Eds.), *Perspectives on the development of memory and cognition.* Hillsdale, NJ: Erlbaum.

Glover, J. A., Timme, V., Deyloff, D., Rogers, M., & Dinell, D. (1987, September/Oc-

tober). Oral directions: Remembering what to do when. *Journal of Educational Research,* pp. 33–40.

Gray, M. J. (1987, September). Comprehension monitoring: What the teacher should know. *The Clearing House,* pp. 38–41.

Holt, J. (1964). *How children fail.* New York: Pitman.

Houston, W. R., Clift, R. T., Freberg, H. J., & Warner, A. R. (1988). *Touch the future: Teach!* St. Paul: West.

Istomina, Z. M. (1975). The development of voluntary memory in preschool-age children. Cited in S. G. Paris & B. K. Lindauer, The development of cognitive skills during childhood. In B. B. Wolman, *Handbook of developmental psychology* (pp. 333–349). Englewood Cliffs, NJ: Prentice-Hall.

Jones, B. F., & Hall, J. W. (1982). School applications of the mnemonic keyword method as a study strategy by eighth graders. *Journal of Educational Psychology, 74,* 230–237.

Justice, E. (1985). Categorization as a preferred memory strategy: Developmental Psychology, 21, 1105–1110.

Kail, R., & Hagen, J. W. (1982). Memory in childhood. In B. B. Wolman (Ed.), *Handbook of developmental psychology* (pp. 350–367). Englewood Cliffs, NJ: Prentice-Hall.

Keeney, T. J., Cannizzo, S. R., & Flavell, J. H. (1967). Spontaneous and induced verbal rehearsal in a recall task. *Child Development, 38,* 953–966.

Klatzky, R. L. (1980). *Human memory: Structure and processes* (2nd ed.). San Francisco: W. H. Freeman.

Kloster, A. M., & Winne, P. H. (1989). The effects of different types of organizers on students' learning. *Journal of Educational Psychology, 81,* 9–15.

Koran, J. J., & Lehman, J. R. (1981, January). Teaching children science concepts: The role of attention. *Science and Children.*

Lewis, R. B., & Doorlag, D. H. (1987). *Teaching special students in the mainstream.* (2nd ed.). Columbus, OH: Merrill.

Lindberg, M. A. (1980). Is knowledge base development a necessary and sufficient condition for memory development? *Journal of Experimental Child Psychology, 30,* 401–410.

Mandler, J. M. (1983). Representation in P. H. Mussen (ed.). *Handbook of child psychology,* (4th ed.), *3.* New York: Wiley, 420–495.

Mandler, J., & Johnson, N. (1977). Remembrance of things passed: Story structure and recall. *Cognitive Development, 9,* 111–151.

Markman, E. M. (1973). Facilitation of part-whole comparisons by use of the collective noun "Family." *Child Development, 44,* 837–840.

Mayer, R. E. (1979). Can advance organizers influence meaningful learning? *Review of Educational Research, 49,* 371–383.

Miller, G. A. (1956). The magical number seven, plus or minus two: Some limits on our capacity for processing information. *Psychological review, 632,* 485–491.

Muth, K. D., Glynn, S. M., Britton, B. K., and Graves, M. F. (1988). Thinking out loud while studying text: Rehearsing key ideas. *Journal of Educational Psychology, 80,* 315–318.

Nelson, K. (1978). How children represent knowledge of their world in and out of language: A preliminary report. In R. S. Siegler (Ed.), *Children's thinking: What develops.* Hillsdale, NJ: Erlbaum.

Nelson, K., & Gruendel, J. (1981). Generalized event representations: Basic building blocks of cognitive development. In M. E. Lamb & A. L. Brown (Eds.), *Advances in developmental psychology,* Vol. 1. Hillsdale, NJ: Erlbaum.

Norman, D. A. (1982). *Learning and memory.* San Francisco: W. H. Freeman.

Paivio, A. (1971). *Imagery and Verbal Processes.* New York: Holt, Rinehart and Winston.

Paivio, A., & Desrochers, A. (1981). Mnemonic techniques in second-language learning. *Journal of Educational Psychology, 73,* 780–795.

Paris, S. G. & Lindauer, B. K. (1982). The development of cognitive skills during childhood. In B. B. Wolman, *Handbook of developmental psychology* (pp. 333–349). Englewood Cliffs, NJ: Prentice-Hall.

Peper, R. J., & Mayer, R. E. (1978). Note taking as a generative activity. *Journal of Educational Psychology, 70,* 514–522.

Percival, F., & Ellington, H. (1988). *A handbook of educational technology* (2nd ed.). London: Kogan Page.

Peterson, L. R., and Peterson, M. T. (1959). Short-term retention of individual verbal items. *Journal of experimental psychology, 58,* 193–198.

Pressley, M., & Dennis-Rounds, J. (1980). Transfer of a mnemonic keyword strategy at two age levels. *Journal of Educational Psychology, 72,* 575–583.

Pressley, M., & Levin, J. R. (1986). Elaborative learning strategies for the inefficient reader. In S. J. Ceci (Ed.), *Handbook of cognitive, social and neuropsychological aspects of learning disabilities,* (pp. 258–280). Hillsdale, NJ: Erlbaum.

Recht, D. R., & Leslie, L. (1988). Effect of prior knowledge on good and poor readers' memory of text. *Journal of Educational Psychology, 80,* 16–20.

Rogoff, B., Newcombe, N., & Kagan, J. (1974). Planfulness and recognition memory. *Child Development, 45,* 972–977.

Salomon, G. (1983). Television watching and mental effort: A social psychological view. In J. Bryandt & D. R. Anderson (Eds.), *Children's understanding of television* (pp. 181–196). New York: Academic Press.

Schank, R. C., & Abelson, R. P. (1977). *Scripts, plans, goals, and understanding.* Hillsdale, NJ: Erlbaum.

Schmidt, C. M., Barry, A., Maxworthy, A. G., and Huebsch, W. R. (1989, February). But I read the chapter twice. *Journal of Reading,* pp. 428–432.

Shavelson, R. J., Webb, N. M., & Burstein, L. (1986). Measurement of teaching. In M. C. Wittrock (Ed.), *Handbook of research on teaching* (3rd ed., pp. 50–92). New York: Macmillan.

Short, E. J., & Ryan, E. B. (1984). Metacognitive differences between skilled and less skilled readers: Remediating deficits through story grammar and attribution training. *Journal of Educational Psychology, 76,* 225–235.

Shriberg, L. K., Levin, J. R., McCormick, C. B., & Pressley, M. N. (1982). Learning about "famous" people via the keyword method. *Journal of Educational Psychology, 74,* 238–248.

Sternberg, R. J. (1985). General intellectual ability. In R. J. Sternberg (Ed.), *Human abilities: An information processing approach* (pp. 5–31). New York: Freeman.

Tulving, E. (1983). *Elements of episodic memory.* Oxford: Clarendon Press: Oxford University Press.

Tulving, E. (1972). Episodic and semantic memory. In E. Tulving and W. Donaldson (Eds). *Organization of memory.* New York: Academic Press.

U.S. Department of Education (1987). *What works: Research about teaching and learning* (2nd ed.). Washington, DC: Department of Education.

Veit, D.T., Scruggs, T. E., & Mastropieri, MA. (1986). Extended mnemonic instruction with learning disabled students. *Journal of Educational Psychology, 78,* 300–308.

Vurpillot, E. (1968). The development of scanning strategies and their relation to visual differentiation. *Journal of Experimental Child Psychology, 6,* 632–650.

Vurpillot, E., & Ball, W. A. (1979). The concept of identity and children's selective attention. In G. Hale & M. Lewis (Eds.), *Attention and cognitive development.* New York: Plenum.

White, R. T., & Tisher, R. P. (1986). Research on natural sciences. In M. C. Wittrock (Ed.), *Handbook of research on teaching* (3rd ed.) (pp. 874–906). New York: Macmillan.

Williams, J. W., & Stith, M. (1980). *Middle Childhood: Behavior and Development* (2nd ed.). New York: Macmillan.

Wimmer, H. (1979). Processing of script deviations by young children. *Discourse Processes, 2,* 301–310.

Wimmer, H. (1980). Children's understanding of stories: Assimilation by a general schema for actions or coordination of temporal relations? In. F. Wilkening, J. Becker, & T. Trabasso (Eds.), *Information integration by children.* Hillsdale, NJ: Erlbaum.

Wingfield, A., & Byrnes, D. E. (1981). *The psychology of human memory.* New York: Academic Press.

CHAPTER 4

Armento, B. J. (1986). Research on teaching social studies. In M. C. Wittrock (ed.). *Handbook of research on teaching,* (3rd ed.). New York: MacMillan, 942–952.

Armstrong, C. (1987). On learning styles. *The Clearing House, 61,* 157–161.

Bell-Gredler, M. E. (1986). *Learning and instruction.* New York: Macmillan.

Best, J. B. (1986). *Cognitive psychology.* St. Paul, Minnesota: West.

Beyer, B. K. (1987). Practice is not enough. In M. Heiman & J. Slomianko (Eds.), *Thinking skills instruction: Concepts and techniques* (pp. 77–87). Washington, DC: National Education Association.

Bien, E. C. (1980). The relationship of cognitive style and structure of arithmetic materials to performance in fourth grade arithmetic. Cited in Cognitive development and cognitive style as factors in mathematics achievement by S. Vaidya & N. Chansky. *Journal of Educational Psychology, 72,* 326–330.

Bireley, M., & Hoehn, L. (1987). Teaching implications of learning styles. *Academic Therapy, 22,* 437–441.

Blackman, S., & Goldstein, K. M. (1982). Cognitive styles and learning disabilities.

Journal of Learning Disabilities, 15, 106–115.

Borkowski, J. G., Peck, V. A., Reid, M. K., & Kurtz, B. E. (1983). Impulsivity and strategy transfer: Metamemory as mediator. *Child Development, 54,* 459–473.

Bondy, E. (1984, March/April). Thinking about thinking. *Childhood Education,* pp. 234–238.

Borton, T. (1986). 8 ways to encourage inventive thinking. *Learning, 15,* 94–96.

Bransford, J. D., Sherwood R. D. and Sturdevant, T. (1987). Teaching thinking and problem solving. In J. B. Baron and R. J. Sternberg (Eds.). *Teaching thinking skills: Theory and practice.* New York: W. H. Freeman, 162–182.

Bush, E. S., & Dweck, C. S. (1975). Reflections on conceptual temp: Relationship between cognitive style and performance as a function of task characteristics. *Developmental Psychology, 11,* 567–574.

Carbo, M. (1982). *Reading style inventory.* Roslyn Heights, NY: Learning Research Associates.

Carbo, M., & Hodges, H. (1988, Summer). Learning styles strategies can help students at risk. *Teaching Exceptional Children,* pp. 55–58.

Carbo, M., R. Dunn, & K. Dunn. (1986). *Teaching students to read through their independent learning styles.* Englewood Cliffs, NJ: Prentice-Hall.

Chi, M. T. H. and Glaser R. (1985). Problem solving ability. In R. J. Sternberg (ed.) *Human abilities: An information processing approach.* 227–251. New York: W. H. Freeman.

Cornett, C. E. (1983). What you should know about teaching and learning styles. Bloomington, IN: Phi Delta Kappa Educational Foundation.

Costa, A. L. (1984). Mediating the metacognitive. *Educational Leadership, 42,* 57–67.

Cotterell, J. (1982). Matching teaching to learners: A Review of a decade of research. *Psychology in the Schools, 19,* 106–112.

Covington, M. V., Crutchfield, R. S., & Davies, L. (1966). *The productive thinking program.* Berkeley: Educational Innovation, Inc.

Cross, D. R., & Paris, S. G. (1988). Developmental and instructional analyses of children's metacognition and reading comprehension. *Journal of Educational Psychology, 80,* 131–142.

Cuccia, A. (1986, August/September). Developing a learning styles classroom from A to Z. *Early years,* pp. 81–85.

de Bono, E. (1983). The Direct teaching of thinking as a skill. *Phi Delta Kappan, 64,* 703–708.

Doebler, L. K., & Eike, F. J. (1979). Effects of teacher awareness of the educational implications of field-dependent/field-independent cognitive style on selected classroom variables. *Journal of Educational Psychology, 71,* 226–232.

Duemler, D., & Mayer, R. E. (1988). Hidden costs of reflectiveness: Aspects of successful scientific reasoning. *Journal of Educational Psychology, 80,* 419–423.

Dunn, R., & Bruno, A. (1985). What does the research on learning styles have to do with Mario? *The Clearing House, 59,* 9–12.

Dunn, R., & Dunn, K. (1978). *Teaching students through their individual learning styles.* Jamaica, NY: Learning Styles Network, St. John's University.

Eisner, E. W. (1988). The celebration of thinking. *National Forum,* pp. 30–33.

Ennis, R. H. (1987). Critical thinking and the curriculum. In M. Heiman & J. Slomianko, *Thinking skills instruction: Concepts and techniques* (pp. 40–49). Washington, DC: National Education Association.

Feldhusen, J. F., & Clinkenbeard, P. A. (1987). Creativity instructional materials: A review of research. *Journal of Creative Behavior, 20,* 1153–1182.

Feldhusen, J. F., Treffinger, D. J., & Bahlke, S. J. (1970). Developing creative thinking: The purdue creativity program. *Journal of Creative Behavior, 4,* 85–90.

Feuerstein, R., Miller, R., Hofman, M. B., Rand Y., Mintzker, Y., & Jensen, M. R. (1981). Cognitive modifiability in adolescence: Cognitive structure and the effects of intervention. *Journal of Special Education,* pp. 269–287.

Fry, P. S. & Lupart, J. L. (1987). *Cognitive processes in children's learning.* Springfield, Illinois: Charles C. Thomas.

Gardner, H. (1987a). Beyond the IQ: Education and human development. *Harvard Educational Review, 57,* 187–193.

Gardner, H. (1987b). The theory of multiple intelligences. *Annals of Dyslexia, 37,* 19–35.

Gardner, H. (1983). *Frames of mind.* New York: Basic Books.

Getting smart about IQ. (1987, November 23). *U.S. News and World Report,* pp. 53–55.

Glaser, E. M. (1985). Critical thinking: Educating for responsible citizenship in a democracy. *National Forum, 65,* 24–27.

Grice, G. L., & Anway Jones, M. (1989). Teaching thinking skills: State mandates and the K–12 curriculum. *The Clearing House, 62,* 337–341.

Guilford, J. P. (1967). *The nature of human intelligence.* New York: McGraw-Hill.

Halpern, D. F. (1987). Thinking across the disciplines: Methods and strategies to promote higher-order thinking in every classroom. In M. Heiman & J. Slomianko (Eds.), *Thinking skills instruction: Concepts and techniques,* (pp. 69–77). Washington, DC: National Education Association.

Heiman, M. (1987). Learning to learn: Improving thinking skills across the curriculum. In M. Heiman & J. Slomianko (Eds.), *Thinking skills instruction: Concepts and techniques,* (pp. 87–92). Washington, DC: National Education Association.

Heiman, M., & Slomianko, J. (1986). *Critical thinking skills.* Washington, D.C.: National Educational Association.

Heiman, M., & Slomianko, J. (1987). *Thinking skills: How parents can help.* Washington, DC: NEA Professional Library.

Hennessey, B. A., & Amabile, T. M. (1987). *Creativity and learning.* Washington, DC: National Educational Association.

Kagan, D. M. (1987). Cognitive style and instructional preferences: Some inferences. *Educational Forum, 51,* 393–401.

Kagan, J. (1965). Reflectivity-inpulsivity and reading ability in primary grade children. *Child Development, 36,* 609–628.

Kail, R., & Pellegrino, J. W. (1985). *Human intelligence: Perspectives and prospects.* New York: Freeman.

Karmos, J. S. & Karmos, A. H. (1987). Strategies for active involvement in problem solving. In M. Heiman & J. Slomianko (eds.). *Thinking skills instruction: Concepts and techniques.* Washington, DC: National Education Association, 99–111.

Keating, D. P. (1980). Four faces of creativity: The continuing plight of the intellectually underserved. *Gifted Child Quarterly, 24,* 56–61.

Klahr, D. & Robinson, M. (1981). Formal assessment of problem solving and planning processes in preschool children. *Cognitive Psychology, 13,* 113–148.

Kogan, N. (1983). Stylistic variation in childhood and adolescence: Creativity, metaphor and cognitive style. In P. H. Mussen

(Ed.), *Handbook of child psychology* (4th ed.). New York: Wiley.

Kuchinskas, G. (1979). Whose cognitive style makes the difference. *Educational Leadership,* pp. 269–271.

Levitsky, R. (1987). Simulation and thinking. In M. Heiman & J. Slomianko (Eds.). *Thinking skills instruction: Concepts and techniques* (pp. 262–272). Washington, DC: National Education Association.

Levy, J. (1984, May). Right brain, left brain: Fact and fiction. *Psychology Today,* pp. 42–44.

Lipman, M. (1987). Some thoughts on the foundations of reflective education. In J. B. Baron & R. J. Sternberg (Eds.), *Teaching thinking skills: Theory and practice* (pp. 151–162). New York: Freeman.

Mannies, N. (1986). Brain Theory and learning. *The Clearing House, 60,* 127–130.

Mansfield, R. S., Busse, T. V., & Krepelka, E. J. (1978). The effectiveness of creativity training. *Review of Educational Research, 48,* 517–536.

Matthews, D. B., & Lin-Odom, B. (1988). Can intelligence be taught? *Middle School Journal, 19,* 22–23.

McTighe, J. J. (1987). Teaching for thinking, of thinking, and about thinking. In M. Heiman & J. Slomianko (Eds.), *Thinking skills instruction: Concepts and techniques.* Washington, DC: National Educational Association, pp. 24–30.

Meichenbaum, D. H., & Goodman, J. (1971). Training impulsive children to talk to themselves: A means of developing self-control. *Journal of Abnormal Psychology, 77,* 115–126.

Messer, S. (1976). Reflection-impulsivity: A review. *Psychological Bulletin, 83,* 1026–1052.

Montague, E. J. (1987). *Fundamentals of secondary classroom instruction.* Columbus, OH: Merrill.

Navarick, D. J. (1979). *Principles of learning: From laboratory to field,* Reading, MA: Addison-Wesley.

Nickerson, R. S. (1987). Why teach thinking? In J. B. Baron & R. J. Sternberg (Eds.), *Teaching thinking skills* (pp. 27–39). New York: Freeman.

Owings, R. A., Petersen, G. A., Bransford, J. D., Morris, C. D., & Stein, B. S. (1980). Spontaneous monitoring and regulations of learning: A comparison of successful and less successful fifth-graders. *Journal of Educational Psychology, 72,* 250–256.

Packer, J., & Bain, J. D. (1978). Cognitive style and teacher-student compatibility.

Journal of Educational Psychology, 70, 864–871.

Palincsar, A. S. (1986). The role of dialogue in providing scaffolded instruction. *Educational Psychologist, 21,* 73–98.

Palincsar, A. S., & Brown, A. L. (1984). The reciprocal teaching of comprehension—Fostering and comprehension-monitoring activities. *Cognition and Instruction, 1,* 117–175.

Palincsar, A. S., & Brown, A. L. (1988). Teaching and practicing thinking skills to promote comprehension in the context of group problem solving. *Remedial and Special Education, 9,* 53–59.

Paris, S. G., & Jacobs, J. E. (1984). The benefits of informed instruction for children's reading awareness and comprehension skills. *Child Development, 55,* 2083–2093.

Paris, S. G., & Myers, M. (1981). Comprehension monitoring. Memory and study strategies of good and poor readers. *Journal of Reading Behavior, 13,* 5–22.

Paris, S. G., & Oka, E. R. (1986). Children's reading strategies, metacognition and motivation. *Developmental Review, 6,* 22–56.

Paul, R. W. (1988, April). Critical thinking in the classroom. *Teaching K–8,* pp. 49–51.

Penrod, S. (1986). *Social psychology* (2nd ed.). Englewood Cliffs, NJ: Prentice-Hall.

Perkins, D. N. (1986, May). Thinking frames. *Educational Leadership,* pp. 4–10.

Perkins, D. N. (1987). Knowledge as design: Teaching thinking through content. In J. B. Baron & R. J. Sternberg (Eds.), *Teaching thinking skills: Theory and practice* (pp. 62–86). New York: Freeman.

Presseisen, B. Z. (1986). *Thinking skills: Research and practice.* Washington, DC: National Education Association.

Presseisen, B. Z. (1987). Thinking and curriculum: Critical crossroads for educational Change. In M. Heiman & J. Slomianko (Eds.), *Thinking skills instruction: Concepts and techniques* (pp. 31–40). Washington, DC: National Educational Association.

Roetter, P. (1987, April/May). The positive approach in the classroom. *The High School Journal,* pp. 47–49.

Saracho, D. N., & Dayton, C. M. (1980). Relationship of teacher's cognitive styles to pupil's academic achievement gains. *Journal of Educational Psychology, 72,* 544–549.

Springer, S. P., & Deutsch, G. (1981). *Left brain, right brain.* San Francisco: Freeman.

Sternberg, R. J. (1985). General intellectual ability. In R. J. Sternberg (Eds.), *Mechanisms of cognitive development* (pp. 163–187). New York: Freeman.

Sternberg, R. J. (1987). Teaching intelligence: The application of cognitive psychology to the improvement of intellectual skills. In J. B. Baron & R. J. Sternberg (Eds.), *Teaching thinking skills: Theory and practice* (pp. 182–219). New York: Freeman.

Strahan, D. B. (1986). Guided thinking: A research-based approach to effective middle grades instruction. *The Clearing House, 60,* 149–155.

Stuart, A., & Pumfrey, P. D. (1987). Reflectivity-impulsivity and problem-solving by primary school children. *Research in Education, 38,* 27–50.

Thurstone, L. L. (1938). Primary mental abilities. *Psychometric Monographs,* No. 1.

Vaidya, S., & Chansky, N. (1980). Cognitive development and cognitive style as factors in mathematics achievement. *Journal of Educational Psychology, 72,* 326–330.

Weisberg, R. W. (1986). *Creativity: Genius and other myths.* New York: Freeman.

Whimbey, A. (1985). You don't need a special "reasoning" test to implement and evaluate reasoning training. *Educational Leadership, 43,* 37–39.

Witkin, H. A., & Moore, C. A. (1981). Cognitive style and the teaching-learning process. Cited in M. H. Dembo, *Teaching for learning: Applying educational psychology in the classroom.* Santa Monica, CA: Goodyear.

CHAPTER 5

Atkeson, B. M., & Forehand, R. (1979). Home-based reinforcement programs designed to modify classroom behaviors: A review and methodological evaluation. *Psychological Bulletin, 86,* 1298–1308.

Axelrod, S. (1983). *Behavior modification for the classroom teacher* (2nd ed.). New York: McGraw-Hill.

Ayllon, T., & Roberts, M. D. (1974). Eliminating discipline problems by strengthening academic performance. *Journal of Applied Behavior Analysis, 7,* 71–76.

Bandura, A. (1977). *Social learning theory.* Englewood Cliffs, NJ: Prentice-Hall.

Bandura, A. (1986). *Social Foundations of thought and action: A social cognitive theory.* Englewood Cliffs, NJ: Prentice-Hall.

Barrish, H., Saunders, M., & Wolf, M. (1969). Good behavior game: Effects of individual contingencies for group consequences on disruptive behavior in a classroom. *Journal of Applied Behavior Analysis, 2,* 119–124.

Borich, G. D (1988). *Effective Teaching Methods.* Columbus, OH: Merrill.

Broden, M., Bruce, M. A., Mitchell, A., Carter, V., & Hall, R. V. (1970). Effects of teacher attention on attending behavior of two boys at adjacent desks. *Journal of Applied Behavior Analysis, 3,* 199–203.

Chilcoat, G. W. (1988). Developing student achievement with verbal feedback. *NASSP Bulletin, 72,* 8–13.

Dickerson, E. A., & Creedon, C. F. (1981). Self-selection of standards by children: The relative effectiveness of pupil-selected and teacher-selected standards of performance. *Journal of Applied Behavior Analysis, 14,* 425–433.

Dietz, S. M., & Repp, A. C. (1974). Differentially reinforcing low rates of misbehavior with normal elementary school children. *Journal of Applied Behavior Analysis, 7,* 622.

Drabman, R. S., & Lahey, B. B. (1974). Feedback in classroom behavior modification: Effects on the target and her classmates. *Journal of Applied Behavior Analysis, 7,* 591–598.

Egel, A. L. (1981). Reinforcer variation: Implications for motivating developmentally disabled children. *Journal of Applied Behavior Analysis, 14,* 345–350.

Emery, J. R. (1969). Systematic desensitization: Reducing test anxiety. In J. D. Krumboltz & C. E. Thoresen (Eds.), *Behavioral Counseling* (pp. 267–289). New York: Holt.

Fink, W. T., & Carnine, D. W. (1975). Control of arithmetic errors using information feedback and graphing. *Journal of Applied Behavior Analysis, 8,* 461.

Forman, S. G. (1987). Affective and social education. In C. A. Maher & S. G. Forman (Eds.), *A behavioral approach to education of children and youth* (pp. 75–109). Hillsdale, NJ: Erlbaum.

Glover, J., & Gary, A. L. (1976). Procedures to increase some aspects of creativity. *Journal of Applied Behavior Analysis, 9,* 79–84.

Glynn, E. L. & Thomas, J. D. (1974). Effect of cueing on self-control of classroom behavior. *Journal of Applied Behavior Analysis, 7,* 299–306.

Gnagey, W. J., (1981). *Motivating classroom discipline.* New York: Macmillan.

Goldiamond, I. (1976). Self-reinforcement. *Journal of Applied Behavior Analysis, 9,* 509–514.

Gresham, F. M., & Lemanek, K. L. (1987). Parent education. In C. A. Maher & S. G. Forman (Eds.), A *Behavioral approach to education of children and youth* (pp. 153–183). Hillsdale, NJ: Erlbaum.

Graham-Clay, S. L., & Reschly, D. (1987). Legal and ethical issues. In C. A. Maher & S. G. Forman (Eds.), *Behavioral approach to education of children and youth* (pp. 289–306). Hillsdale, NJ: Erlbaum.

Hamlet, C. C., Axelrod, S., & Kuerschner, S. (1984). Eye contact as an antecedent to compliant behavior. *Journal of Applied Behavior Analysis, 17,* 553–557.

Harris, A. L., & Harris, J. M. (1987). Reducing mathematics anxiety with computer assisted instruction. *Mathematics and Computer Education, 21,* 1–8.

Haskett, G. J., & Lenfestey, W. (1974). Reading-related behavior in an open classroom: Effects of novelty and modelling on preschoolers. *Journal of Applied Behavior Analysis, 7,* 233–241.

Hering, K., & Nys, P. (1988). Positive reinforcement—Catch kids being good. *Middle School Journal, 20,* 24–25.

Jones, F. H., & Miller, W. H. (1974). The effective use of negative attention for reducing group disruption in special elementary school classrooms. *The Psychological record, 24,* 435–448.

Kazdin, A. E. (1982). The token economy: A decade later. *Journal of Applied Behavior Analysis, 15,* 431–445.

Kazdin, A. E. (1984). *Behavior modification in applied settings* (3rd. ed.). Homewood, IL: Dorsey Press.

Keller, F. S. (1968). Good-bye teacher . . . . . . *Journal of Applied Behavior Analysis, 1,* 79–89.

Kelley, M. L., & Stokes, T. F. (1982). Contingency contracting with disadvantaged youths: Improving classroom performance. *Journal of Applied Behavior Analysis, 15,* 447–454.

Kerr, M. M., & Nelson, C. M. (1983). *Strategies for managing behavior problems in the classroom.* Columbus, OH: Merrill.

Kirby, F. D., & Shields, F. (1982). Modification of arithmetic response rate and attending behavior in a seventh grade student. *Journal of Applied Behavior Analysis, 5,* 79–84.

Kistner, J., Hammer, D., Wolfe, D., Rothblum, E., & Drabman, R. S. (1982). Teacher

popularity and contrast effects in a classroom token economy. *Journal of Applied Behavior Analysis, 15,* 85–96.

Kulik, J. A., Chen-Lin, C., & Cohen, P. A. (1979). A meta-analysis of outcome studies of Keller's personalized system of instruction. *American Psychologist, 34,* 307–319.

Lahey, B. B., Gendrich, J. G., Gendrich, S. I., Schnelle, J. F., Gant, D. S., & McNees, M. P. (1977). An evaluation of daily report cards with minimal teacher and parent contacts as an efficient method of classroom intervention. *Behavior Modification, 1,* 381–394.

Long, J. D., & Williams, R. L. (1973). The comparative effectiveness of group and individual contingent free time with innercity junior high school students. *Journal of Applied Behavior Analysis, 6,* 465–473.

Maher, C. A., Cook, S. A., & Kruger, L. J. (1987). Human resource development. In C. A. Maher & S. G. Forman (Eds.), *A behavioral approach to education of children and youth* (pp. 221–253). Hillsdale, NJ: Erlbaum.

Maher, C. A., & Forman, S. G. (1987). The behavioral approach to education of children and youth: Overview and orientation. In C. A. Maher & S. G. Forman (Eds.), *A behavioral approach to education of children and youth* (pp. 1–18). Hillsdale, NJ: Erlbaum.

McClenaghan, B. A., & Ward, D. S. (1987). Health and physical education. In C. A. Maher & S. G. Forman (Eds.), *A behavioral approach to education of children and youth* (pp. 131–153). Hillsdale, NJ: Erlbaum.

McDaniel, T. R. (1987). Using positive reinforcement. *The Clearing House, 60,* 389–392.

Mercer, C. D. (1986). Learning disabilities. In N. G. Haring & L. McCormick (Eds.), *Exceptional children and youth* (4th ed.) (pp. 119–153). Colombus OH: Merrill.

Nelson, C. M. (1987). Behavioral interventions: What works and what doesn't. *The Pointer, 31,* 45–50.

Piersel, W. C. (1987). Basic skills education. In C. A. Maher & S. G. Forman (Eds.). *A behavioral approach to education of children and youth* (pp. 39–75). Hillsdale, Erlbaum.

Premack, D. (1965). Reinforcement theory. In D. Levine (Ed.), *Nebraska symposium on motivation* (pp. 123–180). Lincoln, NB: University of Nebraska Press.

Presbie, R. J., & Brown, P. L. (1985). *Behav-*

ior modification (2nd ed.). Washington, DC: NEA Professional Library.

Rapport, M. D., Murphy, A., & Bailey, J. S. (1978). The effects of a response cost treatment tactic on hyperactive children. Journal of School Psychology, 18, 98–110.

Raybould, T. (1984). Precision teaching. In D. Fontana (Ed.), Behaviorism and learning theory in education (pp. 43–75). Edinburgh, Scotland: Scottish Academic Press.

Reese, H. W., & Lipsitt, L. (1970). Experimental child psychology. New York: Academic Press.

Repp, A. C., Barton, L. E., & Brulle, A. R. (1983). A comparison of two procedures for programming the differential reinforcement of other behaviors. Journal of Applied Behavior Analysis, 16, 435–445.

Repp, A. C., & Deitz, S. M. (1974). Reducing aggressive and self-injurious behavior of institutionalized retarded children through reinforcement of other behaviors. Journal of Applied Behavior Analysis, 7, 313–325.

Ringness, T. A. (1975). The affective domain in education. Boston: Little, Brown.

Robinson, P. W., Newby, T. J., & Ganzell, S. L. (1981). A token system for a class of underachieving hyperactive children. Journal of Applied Behavior Analysis, 14, 307–315.

Saudargas, R. W., Madsen, C. H., Scott, J. W. (1977). Differential effects of fixed and variable-time feedback on production rates of elementary school children. Journal of Applied Behavior Analysis, 10, 673–678.

Schumaker, J. B., Hovell, M. F., & Sherman, J. F. (1977). An analysis of the effect of teacher aides in an open-style classroom. Journal of Applied Behavior Analysis, 10, 449–464.

Skinner, B. L. (1968). The technology of teaching. New York: Appleton-Century-Crofts.

Skinner, B. F., (1986). Programmed instruction revisited. Phi Delta Kappan, 68, 103–110.

Skinner, B. F. (1987). Upon further reflection. Englewood Cliffs, NJ: Prentice-Hall.

Stephens, T. M., & Cooper, J. O. (1980). The token economy: An affirmative perspective. The Educational Forum, 37, 124–129.

Taylor, W. F., & Hoedt, K. L. (1966). The effect of praise upon the quality and quantity of creative writing. Journal of Educational Research, 60, 80–83.

Tribble, A., & Hall, R. V. (1972). Effects of peer approval on completion of arithmetic assignments. Cited in S. Axelrod, (1983). Behavior modification for the classroom teacher (2nd ed.). New York: McGraw-Hill.

Van Houten, R., Hill, S., & Parsons, M. (1975). An analysis of a performance feedback system: The effects of timing and feedback, public posting, and praise upon academic performance and peer interaction. Journal of Applied Behavior Analysis, 8, 449–457.

Van Houten, R., & Nau, P. A., Mackenzie-Keating, S. E., Sameoto, D., & Colovecchia, B. (1982). An analysis of some variables influencing the effectiveness of reprimands. Journal of Applied Behavior Analysis, 15, 65–83.

Walker, H. M. (1979). The acting-out child: Coping with classroom disruption. Boston: Allyn & Bacon.

White, M. A. (1975). Natural rates of teacher approval and disapproval in the classroom. Journal of Applied Behavior Analysis, 8, 367–372.

CHAPTER 6

Abarbanel, A. (1979). Shared parenting after separation and divorce: A study of joint custody. American Journal of Orthopsychiatry, 49, 320–329.

Allport, G. W. (1954). The nature of prejudice. Reading, MA: Addison-Wesley.

Archer, S. L. (1982). The lower boundaries of identity development. Child Development, 53, 1555–1556.

Aronson, E., & Osherow, N. (1980). Cooperation, prosocial behavior and academic performance. In L. Bickman (Ed.), Applied social psychology annual (Vol. 1). Beverly Hills, CA: Sage.

Aronson, E., Stephan, C., Sikes, J., Blaney, N., & Snapp, M. (1978). The jigsaw classroom. Beverly Hills, CA: Sage.

Asher, S. R., Oden, S. L., & Gottman, J. M. (1981). Children's friendship in school settings (1977). Cited in M. Putallaz & J. M. Gottman, Social skills and group acceptance in school setting. In S. R. Asher and J. M. Gottman (Eds.), The development of children's friendships (pp. 116–149). Cambridge: Cambridge University Press.

Asher, S. R., & Renshaw, P. D. (1981). Children without friends: Social knowledge and social skill training. In S. R. Asher & J. M. Gottman (Eds.), The development of children's friendships (pp. 273–297). Cambridge: Cambridge University Press.

Banks, M. W. (1977). Multiethnic education: Practices and promises. Bloomington, IN: Phi Delta Kappan Educational Foundation.

Barney, J., & Koford, J. (1987, October). Schools and single parents. The Education Digest, pp. 40–43.

Belsky, J., & Steinberg, L. D. (1978). The effects of daycare: A critical review. Child Development, 49, 929–949.

Belsky, J., & Steinberg, L. D (1979, July–August). What does research teach us about day care? Children Today, 21–26.

Benjamin, S. (1985). Cultural diversity: What are the implications for teacher? The Clearing House, 59, 80–83.

Bernard, M. E., Elsworth, G., Keefauver, L. W., & Naylor, F. D. (1981). Sex-role behavior and gender in teacher-student evaluations. Journal of Educational Psychology, 73, 681–696.

Berndt, T. (1979). Developmental changes in conformity to peers and parents. Developmental Psychology, 15, 608–617.

Berndt, T. J. (1981). Relations between social cognition, nonsocial cognition and social behavior: The case of friendship. In J. H. Flavell & L. Ross (Eds.), Social cognitive development. Cambridge: Cambridge University Press.

Berndt, T. J., & Hoyle, S. G. (1985). Stability and change in childhood and adolescent friendship. Developmental Psychology, 21, 1007–1015.

Bierman, K. L., & Furman, W. (1984). The effects of social skills training and peer involvement on the social adjustment of preadolescents. Child Development, 55, 151–162.

Blaney, N. T., Stephan, C., Rosenfield, D., Aronson, E., & Sikkes, J. (1977). Interdependence in the classroom: A field study. Journal of Educational Psychology, 69, 139–146.

Block, J. H., Block, J., & Gjerde, P. F. (1986). The personality of children prior to divorce: A prospective study. Child Development, 57, 827–840.

Brody, G. H., & Forehand, R. (1988). Multiple determinants of parenting: Research findings and implications for the divorce process. In E. M. Hetherington and J. D. Arasteh (Eds.), Impact of divorce, single parenting, and stepparenting on children (pp. 117–135). Hillsdale, NJ: Erlbaum.

Burns, R. B. (1979). The self-concept: Theory, management, development, and behavior. London: Longman.

Busch-Rossnagel, N. A., & Vance, A. K. (1982). The impact of the schools on social and emotional development. In B. B. Wolman (Ed.), *Handbook of developmental psychology* (pp. 452–471). Englewood Cliffs, NJ: Prentice-Hall.

Byrne, D. (1961). Interpersonal attraction and attitude similarity. *Journal of Abnormal and Social Psychology, 62,* 713–715.

Cairns, R. B., Cairns, B. D., Neckerman, H. J., Gest, S. D., & Gariepy, J. L. (1988). Social networks and aggressive behavior: Peer support or peer rejection. *Developmental Psychology, 24,* 815–823.

Campbell, L. P., & Flake, A. E. (1985). Latchkey children—What is the answer? *The Clearing House, 58,* 381–383.

Carlson, C. I. (1987). Helping students deal with divorce-related issues. *Special Services in the Schools, 3,* 121–138.

Clarke-Stewart, A. (1982, September). The day-care child. *Parents.*

Clarke-Stewart, A., & Fein, G. G. (1983). Early childhood programs. In M. M. Haith & J. J. Campos (Eds.), *Handbook of child psychology* (vol. 2. pp. 917–1001). New York: Wiley.

Clingempeel, W. G., & Segal, S. (1986). Stepparent-stepchild relationships and the psychological adjustment of children in stepmother and stepfather families. *Child Development, 57,* 474–484.

Cole, J. D., & Dodge, K. A. (1988). Multiple sources of data on social behavior and social status in the school: A cross-age comparison. *Child Development, 59,* 815–829.

Cole, J. D., & Kupersmidt, J. B. (1983). A behavioral analysis of emerging social status in boys' groups. *Child Development, 54,* 1400–1416.

Cooke, R. E. (1979). Introduction in E. Zigler & J. Valentine (Eds.), *Project Head Start: A legacy of the war on poverty.* New York: The Free Press.

Corsaro, W. A. (1981). Friendship in the nursery school: Social organization in a peer environment. In S. R. Asher & J. M. Gottman (Eds.), *The development of children's friendships* (pp. 207–242).

Darlington, R. B., Royce, J. M., Snipper, A. S., Murray, H. W., & Lazar, I. (1980). Preschool programs and the later school competence of children from low-income families. *Science, 208,* 202–204.

Dion, K. K. (1973). Young children's stereotyping of facial attractiveness. *Developmental Psychology, 9,* 183–188.

Donovan, J. M. (1985). Identity status and interpersonal style. *Journal of Youth and Adolescence, 4,* 37–55.

Egertson, H. A. (1987, May 20). Recapturing kindergarten for 5-year-olds. *Education Week,* pp. 28, 29.

Eisele, J., Hertsgaard, D., & Light H. K. (1986). Factors related to eating disorders in young adolescent girls. *Adolescence, 21,* 283–290.

Elkind, D. (1967). Egocentrism in adolescence. *Child Development, 38,* 1025–1034.

Elkind, D. (1987). *Miseducation.* New York: Knopf.

Elkind, D., & Bowen, R. (1979). Imaginary audience behavior in children and adolescence. *Developmental psychology, 15,* 38–44.

Emery, R. E. (1982). Interparental conflict and the children of discord and divorce. *Psychological Bulletin, 92,* 310–330.

Entwisle, D. R., Alexander, K. L., Pallas, A. M., & Cadigan, D. (1987). The emergent academic self-image of first graders: Its response to social structure. *Child Development, 58,* 1190–1206.

Entwisle, D. R., & Baker, D. P. (1983). Gender and young children's expectations for performance in arithmetic. *Developmental Psychology, 19,* 100–209.

Epstein, M. H., & Cullinan, D. (1987). Effective social skills curricula for behaviorally disordered students. *The Pointer, 31,* 21–24.

Erikson, E. H. (1963). *Childhood and society.* New York: Norton.

Erikson, E. H. (1968). *Youth and crisis.* New York: Norton.

Erikson, E. H. (1981). The problem of ego identity. In L. D. Steinberg (Ed.), *The life cycle: Readings in human development* (pp. 189–198). New York: Columbia University Press.

Etaugh, C. (1980). Effects of nonmaternal care on children: Research evidence and popular views. *American Psychologist, 35,* 309–319.

Etaugh, C., & Hughes, V. (1975). Teachers' evaluations of sex-typed behaviors in children: The role of teacher sex and school setting. *Developmental Psychology, 11,* 394–395.

Fagot, B. I. (1977). Influence of teacher behavior in the preschool. *Developmental Psychology, 9,* 198–206.

Faust, M. S. (1960). Developmental maturation as a determinant in prestige of adolescent girls. *Child Development, 31,* 173–184.

Fennema, E. (1987). Sex-related differences in education: Myths, realities, and interventions. In V. Richardson-Koehler (Ed.), *Educator's handbook* (pp. 329–348). New York: Longman.

Finkelstein, N. W. (1982). Aggression: Is it stimulated by day care? *Young Children, 37,* 3–9.

Flax, E. (1987, September 9) Teachers cite latchkey situations as cause of learning distress. *Education News,* p. 17.

Forehand, R., Long, N., & Brody, G. (1988). Divorce and marital conflict: Relationship to adolescent competence and adjustment in early adolescence. In E. M. Hetherington & J. D. Arasteh (Eds.), *Impact of divorce, single parenting, and stepparenting on children* (pp. 155–168). Hillsdale, NJ: Erlbaum.

Forehand, R., Middleton, K. & Long, N. (1987). Adolescent functioning as a consequence of recent parental divorce and the parent-adolescent relationship. *Journal of Applied Developmental Psychology, 8,* 305–315.

Forgatch, M. S., Patterson, G. R., & Skinner, M. L. (1988). A mediational model for the effect of divorce on antisocial behavior in boys. In E. M. Hetherington & J. D. Arasteh (Eds.), *Impact of divorce, single parenting, and stepparenting on children* (pp. 135–155). Hillsdale, NJ: Erlbaum.

Froming, W. J., Allen, L., & Jensen, R. (1985). Altruism, role-taking, and self-awareness: The acquisition of norms governing altruistic behavior. *Child Development, 56,* 1223–1228.

Furman, W., & Bierman, K. L. (1983). Developmental changes in young children's conception of friendship. *Child Development, 54,* 549–556.

Furman, W., & Buhrmester, D. (1985). Children's perceptions of the personal relationships in their social networks. *Developmental Psychology, 21,* 1016–1024.

Glick, P. C. (1984). Marriage, divorce, and living arrangements: Prospective changes. *Journal of Family Issues, 47,* 481–517.

Goleman, D. (1988, September 22). Studies play down dangers to latchkey children. *New York Times,* p. 12.

Grant, C. L., & Fodor, I. G. (1986). Adolescent attitudes toward body image and anorexic behavior. *Adolescence, 21,* 269–281.

Gray, E., & Coolsen, P. (1987, July/August). How do kids really feel about being home alone? *Children Today,* pp. 30–32.

Gronlund, N. E. (1959). *Sociometry in the classroom.* New York: Harper.

Gurney, P. (1987). Self-esteem enhancement in children: A review of research findings. *Educational Research, 29,* 130–135.

Hamachek, D. E. (1988, April). Evaluating self-concept and ego development within Erikson's psychosocial framework: A formulation. *Journal of Counseling and Development,* pp. 354–360.

Harter, S. (1983). Developmental perspectives on the self-system. In E. M. Hetherington (Ed.), *Handbook of child psychology* (pp. 103–197). New York: Wiley.

Hartup, W. W. (1970). Aggression in childhood: Developmental perspectives. In P. Mussen (Ed.), *Carmichael's manual of child psychology* (3rd ed.). New York: Wiley.

Hartup, W. W. (1983). Peer reactions. In P. H. Mussen (Eds.), *Handbook of child psychology: Socialization, personality and social development, Vol. 4* (4th ed.) (pp. 103–197). New York: Wiley.

Haskins, R. (1985). Public school aggression among children with varying daycare experience. *Child Development, 56,* 689–703.

Hatch, J. A. (1987). Peer interaction and the development of social competence. *Child Study Journal, 17,* 169–183.

Hernandez, D. J. (1988). Demographic trends and the living arrangements of children. In E. M. Hetherington & J. D. Arasteh (Eds.), *Impact of divorce, single parenting, and stepparenting on children* (pp. 3–23). Hillsdale, NJ: Erlbaum.

Hetherington, E. M. (1979). Divorce: A child's perspective. *American Psychologist, 34,* 851–859.

Hetherington, E. M., Cox, M. & Cox, R. (1978). The aftermath of divorce. In J. H. Stevens & M. Mathews (Eds.), *Mother-child/father-child relations.* Washington, DC: National Association for the Education of Young Children.

Howes, C. (1988). Relations between early child care and schooling. *Developmental Psychology, 24,* 53–58.

Hymes, J. L. (1987). Public school for four-year-olds. *Young Children, 62,* 51–52.

Jennings, S. (1975). Effects of sex typing in children's stories on preference and recall. *Child Development, 46,* 220–223.

Jones, M. C. (1949). Adolescence in our society: Anniversary papers of the community service society of New York. In *The family in a democratic society* (pp. 70–82). New York: Columbia University Press.

Jones, M. C., & Bayley, N. (1950). Physical maturing among boys as related to behavior. *Journal of Educational Psychology, 41,* 129–148.

Jones, M. C., & Mussen, P. H. (1958). Self conceptions, motivations and interpersonal attitudes of early- and late-maturing girls. *Child Development, 29,* 491–501.

Kagan, S. I. (1985, December 11). Four-year-olds in the public schools. *Education Week,* p. 24.

Kail, C. J., Downs, J. C., & Black, D. D. (1988). Social skills in the school curriculum: A systematic approach. *NASSP Bulletin, 72,* 107–110.

Kaplan, P. S. (1988). *The human odyssey: Life-span development.* St. Paul: West.

Kaplan, P. S., & Stein. J. (1984). *Psychology of adjustment.* Belmont, CA: Wadsworth.

Keefe, C. H. (1988). Social skills: A basic subject. *Academic Therapy, 23,* 367–373.

Kelly, J. B., & Wallerstein. J. S. (1976). The effects of parental divorce: Experiences of the child in early latency. *American Journal of Orthopsychiatry, 46,* 20–33.

Krogman, W. M. (1980). *Child Growth.* Ann Arbor: University of Michigan Press.

Kurdek, L. A. (1981). An integrative perspective on children's divorce adjustment. *American Psychologist, 36,* 855–866.

Lazar, I, Darlington, R., Murray, H., Royce, J., & Snipper, A. (1982). Lasting effects of early education: A report from the Consortium of Longitudinal Studies. *Monographs of the Society for Research in Child Development, 47* (2–3, Serial No. 195).

Lee, V. E., Brooks-Gunn, J., & Schnur, E. (1988). Does Head Start work? A 1-year follow-up comparison of disadvantaged children attending Head Start, no preschool, and other preschool programs. *Developmental psychology, 24,* 210–222.

Magee, D. (1987). Nurturing self-esteem, *Guidance and Counseling, 2,* 35–39.

Manning, M. L. (1986, January). How teachers can help the child nobody likes. *Education Digest,* pp. 49–51.

Manning, D. T., & Wooten, M. D. (1987). What stepparents perceive schools know about blended families. *The Clearing House, 60,* 230–235.

Marcia, J. (1967). Ego identity status: Relationship to change in self-esteem "general maladjustment," and authoritarianism. *Journal of Personality, 35,* 118–133.

Marcia, J. (1980). Identity in adolescence. In J. Adelson (Ed.). *Handbook of adolescent psychology.* New York: Wiley.

Marcia, J., & Friedman, M. L. (1970). Ego identity status in college women. *Journal of Personality, 38,* 249–263.

Maymi, C. R. (1982, April). Women in the labor force. In P. W. Berman & E. R. Ramey (Eds.), *Women: A developmental perspective.* Washington, DC: U.S. Department of Health and Human Services, Public Health Services, NIH Pub. No 82-2298.

McClinton, B. S., & Meier, B. G. (1978). *Beginnings: The psychology of early childhood.* St. Louis: C. V. Mosby.

McGuinness, D. (1979). How schools discriminate against boys. In S. Hochman & P. Kaplan (Eds.), *Reading in psychology: A soft approach* (Rev. Ed) (pp. 74–79). Lexington, Mass: Ginn.

Mergendoller, J. R., & Marchman, V. A. (1987). Friends and associates. In V. Richardson-Koehler (Ed.), *Educator's handbook* (pp. 297–329). New York: Longman.

Miller, J. P. (1978). Piaget, Kohlberg and Erikson: Developmental implications for secondary education. *Adolescence, 13,* 237–250.

Minuchin, P. P., & Shapiro, E. K. (1983). The School as a context for social development. In E. M. Hetherington (Ed.), *Handbook of child psychology: Socialization, personality, and social development* (4th ed) (Vol. 4, pp. 197–275). New York: Wiley.

Mitman, A., & Packer, M. (1982). Concerns of seventh-graders about their transition to junior high school. *Journal of Early Adolescence, 2,* 319–338.

Muuss, R. E. (1982). *Theories of adolescence* (4th ed.). New York: Random House.

Nash, S. C. (1979). Sex role as a mediator of intellectual functioning. In M. A. Wittig & A. C. Petersen (Eds.), *Sex related differences in cognitive functioning.* Orlando, FL: Academic Press.

Oshman, H. P., & Manosevitz, M. (1976). Father absence: Effects of stepfathers upon psychosocial development in males. *Developmental Psychology, 12,* 479–480.

Osofsky, J. L., Marcia, J. E., & Lesser, I. M. (1973). Ego identity status and the intimacy versus isolation crisis of young adulthood. *Journal of Personality and Social Psychology, 27,* 211–219.

Paulsen, K., & Johnson, M. (1983). Sex role attitudes and mathematical ability in 4th-, 7th-, and 11th-grade students from a high socioeconomic area. *Developmental Psychology, 19,* 210–214.

Peel, E. A. (1969). Intellectual growth during adolescence. In R. E. Grinder (Ed.), *Studies in adolescence* (2nd ed.) (pp. 486–497). New York: Macmillan.

Pellegrini, A. D. (1988). Elementary-school children's rough-and-tumble play and social competence. *Developmental Psychology, 24,* 802–806.

Peskin, H. (1973). Influences of the development schedule on learning and ego functioning. *Journal of Youth and Adolescence, 2,* 273–280.

Petitpas, A. (1978). Identity foreclosure: A unique challenge. *American Personnel and Guidance Journal, 56,* 558–562.

Phillips, D., McCartney, K., & Scarr, S. (1987). Child-care quality and children's social development. *Developmental Psychology, 23,* 537–544.

Richmond-Abbott, M. (1983). *Masculine and feminine.* Reading, MA: Addison-Wesley.

Robison-Awana, P., Kehle, T. J., & Jenson, W. R. (1986). But what about girls? Adolescent self-esteem and sex role perceptions as a function of academic achievement. *Journal of Educational Psychology, 78,* 179–183.

Rodman, H., Pratto, D. J., & Nelson, R. S. (1985). Child care arrangements and children's functioning: A comparison of self-care and adult-care children. *Developmental Psychology, 21,* 413–418.

Rubin, Z. (1980). *Children's friendships.* Cambridge, MA: Harvard University Press.

Santrock, J. W. (1972). Relation of type and onset of father absence to cognitive development. *Child Development, 43,* 455–469.

Schau, C. G., & Scott, K. P. (1984). Impact of gender characteristics of instructional materials: An integration of the research literature. *Journal of Educational Psychology, 76,* 183–193.

Schofield, L. W. (1981). Complementary and conflicting identities: Images and interaction in an interracial school. In S. R. Asher & J. M. Gottman (Eds.), *The development of children's friendships* (pp. 53–91). Cambridge: Cambridge University Press.

Searey, S. (1988). Developing self-esteem. *Academic Therapy, 23,* 453–460.

Serbin, L. A., O'Leary, K. D., Kent, R. N., & Tonick, I. J. (1973). A comparison of teacher response to the preacademic and problem behavior of boys and girls. *Child Development, 44,* 796–804.

Shantz, C. U. (1983). Social Cognition. In P. H. Mussen (Ed.), *Handbook of child psychology: Cognitive development* (Vol. 4) (4th ed.) (pp. 495–556). New York: Wiley.

Shapiro, J., Kramer, S., & Hunerberg, C. (1981). *Equal their chances: Children's activities for non-sexist learning.* Englewood Cliffs, NJ: Prentice-Hall, 1981.

Silvernail, D. L. (1987). *Developing positive student self-concept* (2nd ed.). Washington, DC: National Education Association.

Staffieri, J. R. (1972). Body build and behavioral expectancies in young females. *Developmental Psychology, 6,* 125–127.

Steinberg, L. (1986). Latchkey children and susceptibility to peer pressure: An ecological analysis. *Developmental Psychology, 22,* 433–440.

Steinberg, L. (1988). Simple solutions to a complex problem: A response to Rodman, Pratto, and Nelson. *Developmental Psychology, 24,* 295–296.

Steinberg, L., & Silverberg, S. B. (1986). The Vicissitudes of autonomy in early adolescence. *Child Development, 57,* 841–851.

Stephan, W. G. (1978). School desegregation: An evaluation of predictions made in Brown v. Board of Education. *Psychological Bulletin, 85,* 1161–1167.

Tanner, J. M. (1970). Physical growth. In P. H. Mussen (Ed.), *Carmichael's manual of child development* (3rd ed.) (pp. 77–155). New York: Wiley.

Tuma, N., & Hallinan, M. T. (1979). The effects of sex, race and achievement in school children's friendships. *Social Forces, 57,* 1265–1285.

U.S. Bureau of Labor Statistics. (1987). Employment in perspective: Women in the labor force 1987, Report 740. Washington, DC.

Vandell, D. L., Henderson, V. K., & Wilson, K. S. (1988). A longitudinal study of children with day-care experiences of varying quality. *Child Development, 59,* 1286–1292.

Wallerstein, J. S. (1983). Children of divorce: The psychological tasks of the child. *American Journal of Orthopsychiatry, 53,* 230–243.

Wallerstein, J. S., Corbin, S. B., & Lewis, J. M. (1988). Children of divorce: A 10-year study. In E. M. Hetherington & J. D. Arasteh (Eds.), *Impact of divorce, single parenting, and stepparenting on children* (pp. 197–215). Hillsdale, NJ: Erlbaum.

Wallerstein, J. S., & Kelly, J. (1980). Effects of divorce on the visiting father-child relationship. *American Journal of Psychiatry, 137,* 1534–1539.

Washington, V. (1985). Head Start: How appropriate for minority families in the 1980s. *American Journal of Orthopsychiatry, 55,* 577–590.

Waterman, A. S., & Waterman, C. K. (1971). A longitudinal study of changes in ego identity status during the freshman year at college. *Developmental Psychology, 5,* 167–173.

Watkins, H. D., & Bradbard, M. R. (1984, Fall). The social development of young children in day care: What practitioners should know. *Child Care Quarterly, 11,* 169–187.

Weatherley, D. (1964). Self-perceived rate of physical maturation and personality in late adolescence. *Child Development, 35,* 1197–1210.

Weigel, R. H., Wiser, P. L., & Cook, S. W. (1975). The impact of cooperative learning experiences on cross-ethnic relations and attitudes. *Journal of Social Issues, 31,* 219–245.

Weyant, J. M. (1986). *Applied social psychology.* New York: Oxford University Press.

Williams, J. W., & Stith, M. (1980). *Middle childhood: Behavior and development* (2nd ed.). New York: Macmillan.

Zigler, E., & Berman, W. (1983). Discerning the future of early childhood intervention. *American Psychologist, 38,* 894–907.

CHAPTER 7

Adelson, J. (1972). The political imagination of the young adolescent. In J. Kagan & R. Coles (Eds.), *Twelve to sixteen: Early adolescence* (pp. 106–144). New York: Norton.

Adelson, J., & O'Neil, R. P. (1966). Growth of political ideas in adolescence: The sense of community. *Journal of Personality and Social Psychology, 4,* 295–306.

Allen, B. P. (1987). Youth suicide. *Adolescence, 22,* 271–288.

Altman, D. (1986). *AIDS in the mind of America.* Garden City, NY: Anchor/Doubleday.

American Humane Association (1987). *Highlights of official child neglect and abuse reporting.* Denver, CO: American Humane Association.

Bandura, A. (1977). *Social learning theory.* Englewood Cliffs, NJ: Prentice-Hall.

Bandura, A. (1986). *Social foundations of thought and action: A social cognitive theory.* Englewood Cliffs, NJ: Prentice-Hall.

Barron, J. The teen drug of choice: Alcohol. *New York Times Education Life.* August 7, 1988, 41–44.

Barron, J. Sex Education programs that work in public schools. *New York Times.* November 8, 1987, Section 12, 16–19.

Bauer, G. (1987, March). Teaching morality in the classroom. *Education Digest.* 2–5.

Baumrind, D. (1986). Sex differences in moral reasoning: Response to Walker's (1984) conclusion that there are none. *Child development, 57,* 511–521.

Bernhardt, G. R., & Praeger, S. G. (1985). Preventing child suicide: The elementary school death education puppet show. *Journal of Counseling and Development, 63,* 311–312.

Blasi, A. (1980). Bridging moral cognition and moral action: A critical review of the literature. *Psychological Bulletin, 88,* 1–45.

Brenna, H. B. (1983). Empirical foundations of family based approaches to adolescent substance abuse. In T. J. Glynn et al. (Eds.), *Preventing adolescent drug abuse: Intervention strategies,* Washington DC: NIDA U.S. Government Printing Office 1983.

Camblin, L. D., Jr., & Prout, H. T. (1983, May). School counselors and the reporting of child abuse: A survey of state laws and practices. *The School Counselor, 30,* 358–367.

Carroll, J. L., & Rest, J. R. (1982). Moral Development. In B. B. Wolman (Ed.), *Handbook of human development,* 435–451. Englewood Cliffs, NJ: Prentice-Hall.

Chandler, M., & Boyes, M. (1982). Social-cognitive development. In B. B. Wolman (Ed.), *Handbook of Developmental Psychology* (pp. 387–400). Englewood Cliffs, NJ: Prentice-Hall.

Child Welfare League (1986). *Too young to run: The status of child abuse in America.* New York: Child Welfare League of America.

Compton, N., Duncan, M., & Hruska, J. (1987). *How schools can help combat student pregnancy.* Washington, DC: NEA Professional Library.

Dale, G., & Chamis, G. C. (1981). Cited in P. Scales, Sex education and the prevention of teenage pregnancy: An overview of policies and programs in the United States. In T. Ooms (Ed.), *Teenage pregnancy in a family context: Implications for policy* (pp. 2133–2153). Philadelphia: Temple University Press.

DeLora, J. S., Warren, C. A. B., and Ellison, C. R. (1981). *Understanding Sexual Interaction* (2nd ed.). Boston: Houghton Mifflin.

Dreyer, P. H. (1982). Sexuality during adolescence. In B. B. Wolman (Ed.), *Handbook of developmental psychology* (pp. 559–602). Englewood Cliffs, NJ: Prentice-Hall.

Drotman, P., & Viadero, D. (1987, September 30). Expert's answers to frequently asked questions about AIDS. *Education Week,* p. 6.

Education Week. Nov 25, 1987b, (Forum) p. 9.

Education Week. (1987, September 16). Child abuse and neglect: What to watch for, what to do, p. 21.

Farberow, N. L. (1985). Youth suicide: A summary. In L. L. Peck, N. L. Farberow, & R. E. Litman (Eds.), *Youth suicide* (pp. 191–205). New York: Springer.

Ferguson, T. J., & Rule, B. G. (1982). Influence of inferential set, outcome intent, and outcome severity on children's moral judgments. *Developmental Psychology, 18,* 843–851.

Fischer, T. D. (1986). Parent-child communication about sex and young adolescents' sexual knowledge and attitudes. *Adolescence, 21,* 517–527.

Flax, E. (1987, June 24). Koop warns of an explosion of AIDS among teen-agers. *Education Week.*

Forbes, D. (1987). Saying no to Ron and Nancy: School-based drug abuse prevention programs in the 1980s. *Journal of Education, 169,* 80–90.

Frederick, C. J. (1985). An introduction and overview of youth suicide. In M. L. Peck, N. L. Farberow, & R. E. Litman (Eds.), *Youth suicide* (pp. 1–19). New York: Springer.

Friedland, G. H., Saltzman, B. R., Rogers, M. F., et al. (1986). Lack of transmission of HTLV-111/LAV infection to household contacts of patients with AIDS or AIDS-related complex with oral candidiasis. *New England Journal of Medicine, 314,* 344–349.

Furstenberg, F. F., et al. (1985). Sex education and health experience among adolescents. *American Journal of Public Health, 75,* 1331.

Gallatin, J., & Adelson, J. (1971). Legal guarantees of individual freedom: A cross-national study of the development of political thought. *Journal of Social Issues, 27,* 93–108.

Garbarino, J., Guttman, E., & Seeley, J. (1986).

The psychologically battered child: Strategies for identification, assessment, and intervention. San Francisco: Jossey-Bass.

Gilligan, C. (1982). *In a different voice.* Cambridge: Harvard University Press.

Ginnott, H. G. (1969). *Between parent and teenager.* New York: Macmillan.

Gispert, M., Wheeler, K., Marsh, L., & Davis, M. S. (1985). Suicidal adolescents: Factors in evaluations. *Adolescence, 20,* 753–762.

Goldberg, K. Values said key factor in teenage pregnancy. *Education Week.* Jan. 21, 1987b, p. 5.

Goldberg, K. Consensus is sought on instilling moral values. *Education Week,* May 6, 1987, p. 9.

Goldberg, K. Educators' role in abuse cases questioned after child's death. *Education Week,* Nov. 25, 1987, p. 9.

Gong, V. (1985). *AIDS-defining the syndrome,* 1–10, New Brunswick, NJ: Rutgers University Press.

Goodstadt, M. S. (1987, February) School-based drug education: What is wrong? *Education Digest,* pp. 44–47.

Gordon, S. (1981). Preteens are not latent, adolescence is not a disease. In *Sex education in the eighties,* edited by L. Brown (pp. 83–101). New York: Plenum.

Hart, S. N. (1987). Psychological maltreatment in schooling. *School Psychology Review, 16,* 169–180.

Hart, S. N., & Brassard, M. R. (1987). A major threat to children's mental health: Psychological maltreatment. *American Psychologist, 42,* 160–166.

Heron, B. (1988). Eliminating drug abuse among students. *The Clearing House, 61,* 215–216.

Hersch, R. H., Paolitta, D. P., & Reimer, J. (1979). *Promoting moral growth: From Piaget to Kohlberg.* New York: Longman.

Hobart, T. Y. (1986, October 13). Helping the young defeat the scourges of drugs, alcohol and suicide. *New York Teacher.* p. 10.

Hotelling, K., & Forrest, L. (1985, November). Gilligan's theory of sex-role development: A perspective for counseling. *Journal of Counseling and Development,* pp. 183–186.

Kohlberg, L. (1969). Stage and sequence: The cognitive developmental approach to socialization. In D. A. Goslin (Ed.), *Handbook of socialization theory and research.* Chicago: Rand-McNally.

Kohlberg, L. (1987). The development of moral judgment and moral action. In L. Kohlberg (Ed.), *Child psychology and* childhood education: A cognitive-developmental view (pp. 259–328). New York: Longman.

Kohlberg, L., Colby, A., Gibbs, J., Speicher-Dubin, B., & Powers, C. (1978). Assessing moral development stages: A manual. Cambridge, MA: Center for Moral Education.

Kohlberg, L., & Kramer, R. (1969). Continuities and discontinuities in childhood and adult moral development. Human Development, 12, 83–120.

Kohlberg, L., & Lickona, T. (1987). Moral discussion and the class meeting. In R. DeVries with L. Kohlberg, Programs of early education (pp. 143–188). New York: Longman.

Learning. An exchange of opinion between Kohlberg and Simon (1973). In H. Kirschenbaum & S. B. Simon, Readings in values clarifications (pp. 62–64). Minneapolis: Winston Press.

Maccoby, E. E. (1980). Social development: Psychological growth and the parent-child relationship. New York: Harcourt Brace Jovanovich.

Malinowski, C. I., & Smith, C. P. (1985). Moral reasoning and moral conduct: An investigation prompted by Kohlberg's theory. Journal of Personality and Social Psychology, 49, 1016–127.

McCormick, K. (1987, September). AIDS instruction: A troubling test for educators. Education Digest. pp. 56–59.

McGuire, D. (1983). Teenage suicide: A search for sense. International Journal of Offender Therapy and Comparative Criminology, 27, 211–217.

Meddin, B. J., & Rosen, A. L. (1986, May). Child abuse and neglect: Prevention and reporting. Young Children, pp. 26–30.

Miller, P. M., Danaher, D. L., & Forbes, D. (1986). Sex-related strategies for coping with interpersonal conflict in children aged five and seven. Developmental Psychology, 22, 543–548.

Mills, R. K. (1987). Traditional morality, moral reasoning and the moral education of adolescence. Adolescence, 22, 371–375.

Minix, N. A. (1987). Drug and alcohol prevention education: A developmental social skills approach. The Clearing House, 61, 162–165.

Moline, J. (1983, Spring). The moral of the story. American Educator, 7, 25–32.

Morrison, D. M. (1985). Adolescent contraceptive behavior: A review. Psychological Bulletin, 98, 538–568.

Mussen, P. H., & Eisenberg-Berg, N. (1977). Roots of caring, sharing and helping. San Francisco, CA: Freeman.

Muuss, R. E. (1988). Carol Gilligan's theory of sex differences in the development of moral reasoning during adolescence. Adolescence, 23, 235–243.

Nelson, F. L. (1987). Evaluation of a youth suicide prevention school program. Adolescence, 22, 813–825.

Nevi, C. (1988). Fornication: To teach or not to teach. The Clearing House, 61, 244.

People. (1985, February 18). pp. 76–89.

Perry, D. G., Perry, L. C., & Rasmussen, P. (1986). Cognitive social learning mediators of aggression. Child Development, 57, 700–711.

Pestrak, V. A., & Martin, D. (1985). Cognitive development and aspects of adolescent sexuality. Adolescence, 20, 981–987.

Piaget, J. (1965). The moral judgment of the child (M. Gabain, Trans.). New York: The Free Press (originally published 1932).

Pinching, A. J., & Jeffries, D. (1985). AIDS and HTLV-111/LAV infection. Consequences for obstetrics and perinatal medicine. British Journal of Obstetrics and Gynecology, 92, 1211.

Power, C., & Kohlberg, L. (1987, May). Using a hidden curriculum for moral education. Education Digest, pp. 10–13.

Raths, L. E., Harmin, M., & Simon, S. B. (1966). Values and teaching. Columbus, OH: Charles E. Merrill.

Read, D. A., Simon, S. B., & Goodman, J. B. (1977). Health education: The search for values. Englewood Cliffs, NJ: Prentice-Hall.

Rest, J. R. (1983). Morality. In P. H. Mussen (Ed.), Handbook of child psychology: Cognitive development (4th ed.) (Vol. 3). (pp. 556–630). New York: Wiley.

Rinck, C., Rudolph, J. A., & Simkins, L. (1983). A survey of attitudes concerning contraception and the resolution of teenage pregnancy. Adolescence, 72, 923–929.

Ringness, T. A. (1975). The affective domain in education. Boston: Little, Brown.

Rodman, B. (1987, May 27). Diverse group urges instruction in democratic values. Education Week, p. 5.

Rosenberg, M. S. (1987). New directions for research on the psychological maltreatment of children. American Psychologist, 42, 166–172.

Rothman, R. (1988, March 16). Schools must teach values, says A.S.C.D. Education Week, p. 7.

Ryan, K. (1981). Questions and answers on moral education, Bloomington, IN: Phi Delta Kappa Educational Foundation.

Ryan, K. (1986, November). The new moral education. Phi Delta Kappan, pp. 228–233.

Sagor, R. (1987). Looking for peace in the war on drugs. NASSP Bulletin, 71, 84–87.

Sarafino, E. P. (1979, February). An estimate of nationwide incidence of sexual offenses against children. Child Welfare, pp. 127–135.

Scales, P. (1982). Offset outrage: Let parents help land your sex education program. American School Board Journal, 7, 32–33.

Scales, P. (1978). Sex education policies and the primary prevention of teenage pregnancy. Cited in E. R. Allgeier & A. R. Allgeier, Sexual interactions. Lexington, MA: D. C. Heath.

Schram, N. R. (1986, August 10). AIDS: 1991. Los Angeles Times Magazine, pp. 10–16.

Schultz, L. G., & Jones, P. (1983, March/April). Sexual abuse of children: Issues for social and health professionals. Child Welfare, pp. 99–109.

Select Committee on Children, Youth and Families. (1985). Teen pregnancy: What is being done? A state-by-state look. Washington, DC: U.S. Government Printing Office.

Shafii, M., Carrigan, S., Whittinghill, J. R., & Derrick, A. (1985). Psychological autopsy of completed suicide in children and adolescents. American Journal of Psychiatry, 142, 1061–1064.

Snarey, J. R., Reimer, J., & Kohlberg, L. (1985). Development of social-moral reasoning among kibbutz adolescents: A longitudinal cross-cultural study. Developmental Psychology, 21, 3–18.

Snider, W. (1987, March 4). Study finds rise in cocaine smoking. Education Week, p. 9.

Sorenson, R. C. (1973). The Sorenson Report: Adolescent sexuality in contemporary America. New York: World.

Starr, R. Y. (1979). Child abuse. American Psychologist, 34, 872–878.

Tatum, M. L. (1981). Sex education in the public schools. In L. Brown (Ed.), Sex education in the eighties (pp. 137–145). New York: Plenum.

Tower, R. L. (1987a). How schools can help combat student drug and alcohol abuse. Washington, DC: NEA Professional Library.

Tower, R. L. (1987b). How schools can help combat child abuse and neglect (2nd ed.). Washington, DC: NEA Professional Library.

Turbett, J. P., & O'Toole, R. (1983, December). Teachers' recognition and reporting of child abuse. *JOSH,* pp. 605–609.

Tyson-Bernstein, H. (1987, Fall). The values vacuum. *American Educator, 11,* p. 14+.

U.S. Department of Education (1987a). *What works: Schools without drugs.* Washington, DC: U.S. Department of Education.

U.S. Department of Education (1987a). *What works: Schools without drugs.* Washington, DC: U.S. Department of Education.

U.S. Department of Education (1987b). *What works: Research about Teaching and Learning* (2nd ed.). Washington, DC: U.S. Department of Education.

U.S. Department of Education (1988). *Aids and the education of our children.* Washington, DC: U.S. Department of Education.

U.S. News and World Report (1987, January 12). AIDS: At the dawn of fear, 60–70.

Viadero, D. (1987a, April 1). Principals say drug education should begin early. *Education Week,* p. 6.

Viadero, D. (1987b, June 15). Youth actions seen unchanged by AIDS scare. *Education Week,* p. 16.

Viadero, D. (1987c, October 28). Studies shed new light on teen-age suicides. *Education Week,* p. 7.

Viadero, D. (1987d, January 28). Panel to develop model suicide-prevention program for schools. *Education Week,* p. 5.

Walker, L. J. (1982). The sequentiality of Kohlberg's stages of moral development. *Child Development, 53,* 1330–1336.

Walker, L. J. (1984). Sex differences in the development of moral reasoning: A critical review. *Child Development, 55,* 667–691.

Walker, L. J. (1986). Sex differences in the development of moral reasoning: A rejoinder to Baumrind. *Child Development, 57,* 522–526.

Wattleton, F. (1987). American teens: Sexually active, sexually illiterate. *Journal of School Health, 57,* 379–380.

Wenar, C. (1982). *Psychopathology from infancy through adolescence.* New York: Random House.

Wilcox, R. T. (1988). Indoctrination is not a four-letter word. *The Clearing House, 61,* 249–252.

Wurtele, S. K., & Miller-Perrin, C. L. (1987a). Sexual abuse prevention: Are school programs harmful? *Journal of School Health, 57,* 228–231.

Wurtele, S. K., & Miller-Perrin, C. L. (1987b). Harmful effects of school-based sexual abuse prevention programs? Reassure the parents. *How schools can help combat child abuse and neglect* (2nd ed.), by C. C. Tower. (pp. 146–153). Washington, DC: NEA Professional Library.

Zabin, L. S., Hirsch, M. B., Smith, E. A., Street, R., & Hardy, J. B. (1986, May/June). Evaluation of a pregnancy prevention program for urban teenagers. *Family Planning Perspective,* pp. 119–126.

Zabin, L. S., Kantner, J. L., & Zelnik, M. (1979). The risk of adolescent pregnancy in the first months of intercourse. *Family Planning Perspectives, 4,* 215–222.

Zelnik, M., & Kim Y. J. (1982, May–June). Sex education and its association with teenage sexual activity, pregnancy, and contraceptive use. *Family Planning Perspectives,* pp. 117–126.

CHAPTER 8

Ames, C., & Ames, R. (1978). The thrill of victory and the agony of defeat: Children's self and interpersonal evaluations in competitive and noncompetitive learning environments. *Journal of Research and Development in Education, 12,* 79–87.

Anderson, R., Manoogian, S. T., & Reznick, J. S. (1976). The undermining and enhancing of intrinsic motivation in preschool children. *Journal of Personality and Social Psychology, 34,* 915–922.

Andrews, R. G., & Debus, R. L. (1978). Persistence and causal perceptions of failure: Modifying causal attributions. *Journal of Educational Psychology, 70,* 154–166.

Atkinson, J. W. (1964). *An introduction to motivation.* Princeton, NJ: Van Nostrand Reinhold.

Balk, D. (1983, August). Learned helplessness: A model to understand and overcome a child's extreme reaction to failure. *JOSH,* pp. 365–370.

Bandura, A. (1977). Self-efficacy: Toward a unifying theory of behavioral change. *Psychological Review, 84,* 191–215.

Bandura, A. (1982). Self-efficacy mechanism in human agency. *American Psychologist, 37,* 122–147.

Bandura, A. (1986). *Social foundations of thought and action: A social cognitive theory.* Englewood Cliffs, NJ: Prentice-Hall.

Bandura, A., & Walters, R. H. (1963). *Social learning and personality development.* New York: Holt, Rinehart and Winston.

Bar-Tal, D. (1978). Attributional analysis of achievement-related behavior. *Review of Educational Research, 48,* 259–271.

Bardwell, R. (1984a). Failure: Facilitating or debilitating. *Journal of Experimental Education, 52,* 192–194.

Bardwell, R. (1984b). The learning of expectations and attributions. *Education and Treatment of Children, 7,* 237–245.

Bates, J. A. (1979). Extrinsic reward and intrinsic motivation: A review with implications for the classroom. *Review of Educational Research, 19,* 557–576.

Beery, R. G. (1975). Fear of failure in the school experience. *Personnel and Guidance Journal, 54,* 190–206.

Bigelow, B. J. (1977). Children's friendship expectations: A cognitive developmental study. *Child Development, 48,* 246–253.

Birney, R. C. (1968). Research on the achievement motive. In E. F. Borgatta & W. W. Lambert (Eds.), *Handbook of personality theory and research* (pp. 857–890). Chicago: Rand McNally.

Blanck, P. D., Reis, H. T., & Jackson, L. (1984). The effects of verbal reinforcements on intrinsic motivation for sex-linked tasks. *Sex Roles, 10,* 369–387.

Block, J. H., Block, J., & Gjerde, P. F. (1986). The personality of children prior to divorce: A prospective study. *Child Development, 57,* 827–840.

Boggiano, A. K., & Barrett, M. (1985). Performance and motivational deficits of helplessness: The role of motivational orientations. *Journal of Personality and Social Psychology, 49,* 1753–1761.

Brombacher, B. (1983, November). Getting students involved in decisions about learning. *Education Digest,* pp. 44–45.

Brophy, J. E. (1983). Research on the self-fulfilling prophecy and teacher expectations. *Journal of Educational Psychology, 75,* 631–661.

Brophy, J. E., & Good, T. L. (1974). *Teacher-student relationships.* New York: Holt, Rinehart and Winston.

Burka, J. M. & Yuen, L. M. (1982). Mind games procrastinators play. *Psychology Today,* 32–37.

Butkowsky, I. S., & Willows, D. M. (1980). Cognitive-motivational characteristics of children varying in reading ability: Evidence of learned helplessness in poor readers. *Journal of Educational Psychology, 72,* 408–422.

Butler, R., & Nissan, M. (1986). Effects of no feedback, task-related comments, and grades on intrinsic motivation and performance. *Journal of Educational Psychology, 78,* 210–216.

Chaikin, A., Sigler, E., & Derlega, V. (1974). Nonverbal mediators of teacher expectancy effect. *Journal of Personality and social psychology, 30,* 144–149.

Cherry, F., & Deaux, K. (1981). Fears of success versus fear of gender-inconsistent behavior: A sex similarity. Cited in K. F. Schaffer, *Sex roles and human behavior.* Cambridge, MA: Winthrop.

Collins, J. L. (1986). Self-efficacy and ability in achievement behavior. Cited in A. Bandura, *Social foundations of thought and action.* Englewood Cliffs, NJ: Prentice-Hall.

Condry, J. C. (1977). Enemies of exploration: Self-initiated versus other-initiated learning. *Journal of Personality and Social Psychology, 35,* 459–477.

Condry, J., & Dyer, S. (1976). Fear of success: Attribution of cause to the victim. *Journal of Social Issues, 32,* 63–83.

Cook, E. A., & Chandler, T. A. (1984). Is fear of success a motive? An attempt to answer criticisms. *Adolescence, 19,* 667–674.

Cooper, H. M. (1979). Pygmalion grows up: A model for teacher expectation communication and performance influence. *Review of Educational Research, 49,* 389–410.

Cooper, H. M., & Tom, D. Y. H. (1984). Teacher expectation research: A review with implications for classroom instruction. *Elementary School Journal, 85,* 77–89.

Covington, M. V. (1984). The self-worth theory of achievement motivation: Findings and applications. *Elementary School Journal, 85,* 5–20.

Covington, M. V., Beery, R. (1976). *Self-worth and school learning.* New York: Holt, Rinehart and Winston.

Covington, M. V., & Omelich, C. L. (1979). Effort: The double-edged sword in school achievement. *Journal of Educational Psychology, 71,* 169–182.

Covington, M. V., & Omelich, C. L. (1981). As failures mount: Affective and cognitive consequences of ability demotion in the classroom. *Journal of Educational Psychology, 73,* 796–808.

Covington, M. V., & Omelich, C. L. (1979). It's best to be able and virtuous too: Student and teacher evaluative responses to success effort. *Journal of Educational Psychology, 74,* 688–700.

Crano, W., & Mellon, P. (1978). Causal influences of teachers' expectations on children's academic performance: A cross-lagged panel analysis. *Journal of Educational Psychology, 79,* 39–49.

Craske, M. L. (1985). Improving persistence through observational learning and attribution retraining. *British Journal of Educational Psychology, 55,* 138–147.

deCharms, R. (1976). *Enhancing motivation: Change in the classroom,* New York: Irvington.

deCharms, R. (1980). The origins of competence and achievement motivation in personal causation. In L. J. Fyans (Ed.), *Achievement motivation: Recent trends and theory,* New York: Plenum.

deCharms, R., & Muir, M. S. (1978). Motivation: Social approaches. *Annual Review of Psychology, 29,* 91–113.

Deci, E. L., Schwartz, A. J., Sheinman, L., & Ryan, R. M. (1981). An instrument to assess adults' orientations toward control versus autonomy with children: Reflections on intrinsic motivation and perceived competence. *Journal of Educational Psychology, 73,* 642–650.

Desmond, S. M., & Price, J. H. (1988). Self-efficacy and weight control. *Health Education, 19,* 12–18.

Diener, C., & Dweck, C. S. (1978). An analysis of learned helplessness: Continuous changes in performance, strategy, and achievement cognitions following failure. *Journal of Personality and Social Psychology, 36,* 451–462.

Downing, C. J. (1986, February). Affirmations: Steps to counter negative, self-fulfilling prophecies. *Elementary School Guidance and Counseling,* pp. 174–179.

Dunn, H. (1981, November/December). Listen to kids! *Today's Education,* p. 37.

Dusek, J. B., & Joseph, G. (1983). The bases of teacher expectancies: A meta-analysis. *Journal of Educational Psychology, 75,* 327–346.

Eccles, P. J. (1983). Expectancies, values, and academic behaviors. In J. T. Spence (Ed.), *Achievement and achievement motives,* San Francisco: W. H. Freeman.

Emery, R. E. (1982). Interparental conflict and the children of discord and divorce. *Psychological Bulletin, 92,* 310–330.

Ericksen, S. C. (1984). *The essence of good teaching.* San Francisco: Jossey-Bass.

Feather, N. T. (1975). *Values in education and society.* New York: The Free Press.

Fennema, E. (1987). Sex-related differences in education: Myths, realities, and interventions. In V. Richardson-Koehler (Ed.), *Educators' handbook: A research perspective* (pp. 329–347). New York: Longman.

Fiske, S. T., & Taylor, S. E. (1984). *Social*

Cognition. Reading, MA: Addison-Wesley.

Fleming, E., & Anttonen, R. (1971). Teacher expectancy as related to the academic and personal growth of primary-age children. Monographs of the Society for Research in Child Development, 36 (Serial No. 145).

Fredericks, A. D. (1984, December). You've got to motivate parents. *Early Years,* pp. 22+.

Geen, R. G. (1984). Human motivation: New perspectives on old problems. In A. M. Rogers & C. J. Scheirer (Eds.), *The G. Stanley Hall lecture series* (Vol. 4) (pp. 9–57). Washington, DC: American Psychological Association.

Gibbons, P. A., & Kopelman, R. E. (1977). Maternal employment as a determinant of fear of success in females. *Psychological Reports, 40,* 1200–1202.

Gleason, J. J. (1983). ABCDs of motivating adolescent LD students. *Academic Therapy, 19,* 53–55.

Gnagey, W. J. (1981). *Motivating classroom discipline,* New York: Macmillan.

Good, T. (1981). Teacher expectations and student perceptions: A decade of research. *Educational Leadership, 38,* 415–421.

Gottfried, A. E. (1985). Academic intrinsic motivation in elementary and junior high school students. *Journal of Educational Psychology, 77,* 631–645.

Gottfried, A. E. (1983). Intrinsic motivation in young children. *Young Children,* 64–73.

Graham, S., & Long, A. (1986). Race, class and attributional process. *Journal of Educational Psychology, 78,* 4–13.

Gray, J. M. (1981, November/December). Enjoy yourself and be flexible: Motivation, a symposium. *Todays Education.* pp. 34–35.

Greene, D., & Lepper, M. R. (1974a, September). Intrinsic motivation: How to turn play into work. *Psychology Today,* pp. 49–52.

Greene, D., & Lepper, M. R. (1974b). Effects of extrinsic rewards on children's subsequent intrinsic interest. *Child Development, 45,* 1141–1145.

Harter, S. (1981). A new self-report scale of intrinsic versus extrinsic orientation in the classroom: Motivational and informational components. *Developmental Psychology, 17,* 300–312.

Hiebert, E. H., Winograd, P. N., & Danner, F. W. (1984). Children's attributions for failure and success in different aspects of reading. *Journal of Educational Psychology, 76,* 1139–1148.

Horner, M. (1968). Sex differences in achievement motivation and performance in competitive and non-competitive situations. Unpublished doctoral dissertation, University of Michigan.

Hoy, C. (1986). Preventing learned helplessness. *Academic Therapy, 22,* 11–18.

Jackson, P. (1979). Cited in J. G. Nicholls, Quality and equality in intellectual development: The role of motivation in education. *American Psychologist, 34,* 1071–1084.

Jamieson, D. W., Lydon, J. E., Stewart, G., & Zanna, M. P. (1987). Pygmalion revisited: New evidence for student expectancy effects in the classroom. *Journal of Educational Psychology, 79,* 461–466.

Johnson, D. W., & Johnson, R. T. (1974). Instructional goal structure: Cooperative, competitive, or individualistic. *Review of Educational Research, 44,* 218–240.

Johnson, D. W., Johnson, R., & Maruyama, G. (1983). Interdependence and interpersonal attraction among heterogeneous and homogeneous individuals: A theoretical formulation and a meta-analysis of this research. *Review of Educational Research, 53,* 5–54.

Johnson, P. B. (1981). Achievement motivation and success: Does the end justify the means? *Journal of Personality and Social Psychology, 40,* 374–375.

Jones, R. S. (1985). Teachers who stimulate curiosity. *Education, 101,* 158–165.

Kaplan, P. S., & Stein, J. (1984). *Psychology of adjustment.* Belmont, CA: Wadsworth.

Kazdin, A. E. (1984). *Behavior modification in applied settings* (3rd ed.). Homewood, IL: The Dorsey Press.

King-Stoops, J., & Meier, W. (1978). Teacher analysis of the discipline problem. *Phi Delta Kappan, 59,* 354.

Klienke, C. L. (1978). *Self-perception: The psychology of personal awareness.* San Francisco: Freeman.

Knight, C. J., Peterson, R. L., & McGuire, B. (1982, May). Cooperative learning: A new approach to an old idea. *Teaching Exceptional Children,* pp. 233–238.

Kreitler, S., Zigler, E., & Kreitler, H. (1975). The nature of curiosity in children. *Journal of School Psychology, 13,* 185–200.

Kukla, A. (1972). Attributional determinants of achievement-related behavior. *Journal of Personality and Social Psychology, 21,* 166–174.

Kukla, A. (1975). Preferences among impossibly difficult and trivially easy tasks: A review of Atkinson's theory of choice. *Journal of Personality and Social Psychology 32,* 338–345.

Lambiotte, J. G., Dansereau, D. F., O'Donnell, A. M., Hall, R. H., & Rocklin, T. R. (1987). Manipulating cooperative scripts for teaching and learning. *Journal of Educational Psychology, 79,* 424–431.

Lepper, M. R., Greene, D., & Nisbett, R. E. (1973). Undermining children's intrinsic interest with extrinsic rewards: A test of the "overjustification" hypothesis. *Journal of Personality and Social Psychology, 28,* 129–137.

Liebert, R. M. & M. D. Spiegler. (1987). *Personality: strategies and issues.* Homewood, Illinois: The Dorsey Press.

Lockheed, M. (1976). Some determinants and consequences of teacher expectations concerning pupil performance. In *Beginning teacher evaluation study: Phase 2.* Princeton, NJ: Educational Testing Service.

Maslow, A. H. (1968). *Toward a psychology of being* (2nd ed.). New York: D. Van Nostrand Company.

Maslow, A. H. (1970). *Motivation and personality* (2nd ed.). New York: Harper & Row.

McClelland, D. C., Atkinson, J. W., Clark, R. A., & Lowell, E. L. (1953). *The achievement motive.* New York: Appleton-Century-Crofts.

McDaniel, T. R. (1985, September). The ten Commandments of motivation. *The Clearing House,* pp. 19–23.

McLloyd, V. C. (1979). The effects of extrinsic rewards of differential value on high and low intrinsic interest. *Child Development, 50,* 1010–1019.

Michaels, J. W. (1977). Classroom reward structures and academic performance. *Review of Educational Research, 47,* 87–98.

Miller, A. (1986). Performance impairment after failure: Mechanism and sex differences. *Journal of Educational Psychology, 78,* 486–491.

Morgan, M. (1984). Reward-induced decrements and increments in intrinsic motivation. *Review of Educational Research, 54,* 5–30.

Motowidlo, J. S. (1980). Effects of traits and states: Subjective probability of task success and performance. *Motivation and Emotion, 4,* 247–262.

New York Times (1987, October 17). The $100,000 final exam, p. 30.

Parsons, J., & Ruble, D. (1977). The development of achievement-related expectancies. *Child Development, 48,* 1075–1079.

Phares, E. J. (1988). *Clinical psychology* (3rd ed.). Chicago: The Dorsey Press.

Pittman, T. S., Emery, J., & Boggiano, A. K. (1982). Intrinsic and extrinsic motivational orientations: Reward induced change in preference for complexity. *Journal of Personality and Social Psychology, 42,* 789–797.

Popp, G. E., & Muhs, W. F. (1982). Fear of success and women employees. *Human Relations, 35,* 511–519.

Proctor, C. P. (1984, March). Teacher expectations: A model for school improvement. *Elementary School Journal.* pp. 469–481.

Raschke, D., Dedrick, C., & Thompson, M. (1987, winter). Reluctant learners: Innovative contingency packages. *Teaching Exceptional Children,* pp. 18–21.

Rosenholtz, S. J., & Rosenholtz, S. H. (1981). Classroom organization and the perception of ability. *Sociology of Education, 54,* 132–140.

Rosenthal, R. (1976). *Experimental effects in behavioral research* (2nd ed.). New York: Irvington.

Rosenthal, R., & Jacobson, L. (1968). *Pygmalion in the classroom: Teacher expectation and pupils' intellectual development.* New York: Holt, Rinehart and Winston.

Rutter, M., Maughan, E., Mortrimore, P., Ousteon, J., & Smith, A. (1979). *Fifteen thousand hours: Secondary schools and their effects on children.* Cambridge, MA: Harvard University Press.

Ryan, R. M., & Grolnick, W. S. (1986). Origins and pawns in the classroom: Self-report and projective assessments of individual differences in children's perceptions. *Journal of Personality and Social Psychology, 50,* 550–558.

Schunk, D. H. (1981). Modeling and attributional effects on children's achievement: A self-efficacy analysis. *Journal of Educational Psychology, 73,* 93–106.

Schunk, D. H. (1982). Effects of effort attributional feedback on children's perceived self-efficacy and achievement. *Journal of Educational Psychology, 74,* 548–556.

Seligman, M.E.P. (1975). *Helplessness.* San Francisco: Freeman.

Skon, L., Johnson, D. W., & Johnson, R. T. (1981). Cooperative peer interaction versus individual competition and individualistic efforts: Effects on the acquisition of cognitive reasoning strategies. *Journal of Educational Psychology, 73,* 83–92.

Slavin, R. E. (1983). *Cooperative Learning.* New York: Longman.

Slavin, R. E. (1984). Students motivating students to excel: Cooperative incentives, cooperative tasks and student achievement. *Elementary School Journal, 85,* 53–63.

Slavin, R. E., Madden, N. A., & Leavey, M. (1984). Effects of team assisted individualization on the mathematics achievement of academically handicapped and nonhandicapped students. *Journal of Educational Psychology, 76,* 813–819.

Snow, R. (1969). Unfinished Pygmalion. *Contemporary Psychology, 14,* 197–199.

Sowa, C. J., & Burks, H. M. (1983). Comparison of cognitive restructuring and contingency-based instructional models for alleviation of learned helplessness. *Journal of Instructional Psychology, 10,* 186–191.

Spielberg, F. (1981, November/December). Be Funny!: Motivation, a symposium. *Today's Education,* p. 40.

Stephens, T. M., & Cooper, J. O. (1980). The token economy: An affirmative perspective. *In Annual Editions: Educational Psychology, 82/83,* 95–97.

Strecher, V. J., Develles, B. M., Becker, M. H., & Rosenstock, I. M. (1986). The role of self-efficacy in achieving health behavior change. *Health Education Quarterly, 13,* 73–91.

Teevan, R. C., & McGhee, P. E. (1972). Childhood development of fear and failure motivation. *Journal of Personality and Social Psychology, 21,* 345–348.

Tresemer, D. W. (1977). *Fear of success: An intriguing set of questions.* New York: Plenum Press.

Van Oudenhoven, J. P., Van Berjum, G., & Swen-Koopmans, T. (1987). Effect of cooperative and shared feedback on spelling achievement. *Journal of Educational Psychology, 79,* 92–94.

Warring, D., Johnson, D. W., Maruyama, G., & Johnson, R. (1985). Impact of different types of cooperative learning on cross-ethnic and cross-sex relationships. *Journal of Educational Psychology, 77,* 53–59.

Weiner, B. (1972). Attribution theory, achievement motivation and the educational process. *Review of Educational Research, 42,* 203–215.

Weiner, B. (1979). A theory of motivation for some classroom experiences. *Journal of Educational Psychology, 71,* 3–25.

Weiner, B., Graham, S., Taylor, S. E., & Meyer, W. U. (1983). Social cognition in the classroom. *Educational Psychologist, 18,* 109–124.

Weinstein, R., & Middlestadt, S. (1979). Student perceptions of teacher interactions with male high and low achievers. *Journal of Educational Psychology, 71,* 421–431.

Weyant, J. M. (1986). *Applied social psychology,* New York: Oxford University Press.

Whitehead, G. I., Anderson, W. F., & Mitchell, K. D. (1987). Children's causal attributions to self and other as a function of outcome and task. *Journal of Educational Psychology, 79,* 192–194.

Wlodkowski, R. J. (1981). Making sense out of motivation: A systematic model to consolidate motivational constructs across theories. *Educational Psychologist, 16,* 101–110.

Zuckerman, M., & Wheeler, L. (1975). To dispel fantasies about the fantasy-based measure of fear of success. *Psychological Bulletin, 82,* 932–946.

CHAPTER 9

Adams, R., & Biddle, B. (1970). *Realities of Teaching: Explorations with videotape.* New York: Holt, Rinehart and Winston.

Anderson, E. J., & Fowler, H. S. (1978). The effects of selected entering behaviors and different cognitive levels of behavioral objectives on learning and retention performance in a unit on population genetics. *Journal of Research in Science Teaching, 15,* 373–379.

Anderson, L., Evertson, C., & Brophy, J. (1979). An experimental study of effective teaching in first-grade reading groups. *Elementary School Journal, 79,* 193–223.

Bank, B. J., Biddle, B. J., & Good, T. L. (1980). Sex roles, classroom instruction, and reading achievement. *Journal of Educational Psychology, 72,* 119–132.

Bayes, M. A. (1979). An investigation of the behavioral cues of interpersonal warmth. Cited in Nonverbal communication in teaching, by H. A. Smith. *Review of Educational Research, 49,* 631–672.

Becker, H. J., & Epstein, J. L. (1982). Parent involvement: A survey of teacher practices. *Elementary School Journal, 83,* 85–102.

Bengfort, A. (1987). Teaching students how to ask for help. *Academic Therapy, 23,* 185–188.

Benjamin, A. (1974). *The Helping Interview* (2nd ed.). Boston: Houghton Mifflin.

Berliner, D. C. (1987). But do they understand? In V. Richardson-Koehler (Ed.), *Educators' Handbook* (pp. 259–295). New York: Longman.

Bolton, R. (1979). *People skills,* Englewood Cliffs, NJ: Prentice-Hall.

Borich, G. D. (1988). *Effective teaching methods.* Columbus, OH: Merrill.

Brookover, W. B., et al. (1979). *School social systems and student achievement: Schools can make a difference.* New York: Praeger.

Brooks, D. M., & Wilson, B. J. (1978). Teacher verbal and nonverbal behavioral expression toward selected pupils. *Journal of Educational Psychology, 70,* 147–153.

Brophy, J. (1981). Teacher praise: A functional analysis. *Review of Educational Research, 51,* 5–32.

Brophy, J. (1986). Teacher influences in student achievement. *American Psychologist, 41,* 1069–1078.

Brophy, J. E., & Good, T. L. (1974). *Teacher-student relationships: Causes and consequences.* New York: Holt, Rinehart and Winston.

Busch-Rossnagel, N. A., & Vance, A. K. (1982). The impact of the schools on social and emotional development. In B. B. Wolman (Ed.), *Handbook of developmental psychology,* Englewood Cliffs, NJ: Prentice Hall. 452–465.

Byers, P., & Byers, H. (1972). Nonverbal communication and the education of children. In C. Cazden, V. John, & D. Hymes (Eds.), *Functions of language in the classroom* (pp. 3–31). New York: Teachers College Press.

Cantrell, R., Stenner, A., & Katzenmeyer, W. (1977). Teacher knowledge, attitudes, and classroom teaching correlates of student achievement. *Journal of Educational Psychology, 69,* 172–179.

Casanova, U. (1987). Ethnic and cultural differences. In V. Richardson-Koehler (Ed.), *Educators' handbook* (pp. 370–394). New York: Longman.

Chernow, F. B., & Chernow, C. (1981). *Classroom discipline and control: 101 practical techniques.* New York: Parker.

Cruickshank, D. R. (1985). Applying research on teacher clarity. *Journal of Teacher Education, 36,* 44–48.

Daigon, A. (1982, December). Toward righting writing. *Phi Delta Kappan,* pp. 242–246.

Davis, G. L. (1979). Nonverbal behavior of

the first grade teachers in different socio-economic level elementary schools. Cited in Nonverbal communication in teaching, by H.A. Smith. *Review of Educational Research, 49,* 631–672.

Delamont, S. (1976). *Interaction in the classroom.* London: Methuen.

Dillon, J. T. (1982). The multidisciplinary study of questioning. *Journal of Educational Psychology, 74,* 147–165.

Dillon, J. T. (1984, November). Research on questioning and discussion. *Educational Leadership,* pp. 50–56.

Doyle, J. A. (1985). *Sex and Gender.* Dubuque, IA: Wm. C. Brown.

Doyle, W. & Carter, K. (1987). Choosing the means of instruction. In V. Richardson-Koehler (Ed.). *Educators' handbook.* New York: Longman, 188–207.

Dweck, C. S. (1986). Motivational processes affecting learning. *American Psychologist, 41,* 1040–1049.

Dweck, C., Davidson, W., Nelson, S., & Enna, B. (1978). Sex differences in learned helplessness: The contingencies of evaluative feedback on the classroom: An experimental analysis. *Developmental Psychology, 14,* 268–274.

Epstein, J. L., & Becker, H. J. (1982). Teachers' reported practices of parent involvement: Problems and possibilities. *Elementary School Journal, 83,* 103–113.

Etaugh, C., & Hughes, V. (1975). Teachers' evaluations of sex-typed behaviors in Children: The role of teacher sex and school setting. *Developmental Psychology, 11,* 394–395.

Evertson, C. M., Anderson, C., Anderson, L., & Brophy, J. (1980). Relationships between classroom behaviors and student outcomes in junior high mathematics and English classes. *American Educational Research Journal, 17,* 43–60.

Fagot, B. I. (1977). Consequences of moderate cross gender behavior in preschool children. *Child Development, 13,* 166–167.

Fairbairn, D. M. (1987). The art of questioning your students. *The Clearing House, 61,* 19–22.

Feiman-Nemser, S., & Floden, R. E. (1986). The cultures of teaching. In M. C. Wittrock (Ed.), *Handbook of research on teaching* (3rd ed.) (pp. 505–527). New York: Macmillan.

Feldman, R. S., & Donohoe, L. F. (1978). Nonverbal communication of affect in interracial dyads. *Journal of Educational Psychology, 70,* 979–987.

Fennema, E. (1987). Sex-related differences

in education: Myths, realities, and interventions. In V. Richardson-Koehler (Ed.), *Educators' handbook* (pp. 329–348). New York: Longman.

Flanders, N. (1970). *Analyzing teacher behavior.* Reading, MA: Addison-Wesley.

Florio-Ruane, S., & Dunn, S. (1987). Teaching writing: Some perennial questions and some possible answers. In V. Richardson-Koehler (Ed.), *Educators' handbook: A research perspective* (pp. 50–84). New York: Longman.

Friedman, P. (1976). Comparisons of teacher reinforcement schedules for students with different social class backgrounds. *Journal of Educational Psychology, 68,* 286–292.

Gall, M. D. (1984, November). Synthesis of research on teachers' questioning. *Educational Leadership,* pp. 40–47.

Gall, M. D. (1970). The use of questions in teaching. *Review of Educational Research, 40,* 707–721.

Galloway, C. (1970). Teaching is communicating: Nonverbal language in the classroom. Washington DC: National Education Association Bulletin No. 29.

Gazda, G. M., et al. (1977). *Human relations development: A manual for educators* (2nd ed.). Boston: Allyn & Bacon.

Ginott, H. (1969). *Parent and child.* New York: Macmillan.

Ginott, H. (1972a). *Teacher and child.* New York: MacMillan.

Ginott, H. (1972b). Even praise has its pitfalls. *Early Years, 1,* 43–45.

Good, T. L. (1983). Classroom research: A decade of progress. *Educational Psychologist, 18,* 127–144.

Good, T. L., Sikes, N., & Brophy, J. E. (1973). Effects of teacher sex and student sex on classroom interaction. *Journal of Educational Psychology, 65,* 74–87.

Good, T. L., Slavings, R. L., Harel, K. H., & Emerson, H. (1987). Student passivity: A study of question asking in K–12 classrooms. *Sociology of Education, 60,* 181–199.

Gordon, T. (1974). *T.E.T. teacher effectiveness training.* New York: McKay.

Hall, E. T. (1969, March). Listening behavior: Some cultural differences. *Phi Delta Kappan,* 345–348.

Hall, E. T., & Hall, M. R. (1987). Nonverbal communication for educators. *Theory into practice, 26,* 364–367.

Hayes, J. R., & Flower, L. S. (1980). Writing as problem solving. *Visible Language, 14,* 388–399.

Heller, M. S., & White, M. A. (1975). Rates of

teacher verbal approval and disapproval to higher and lower ability classes. *Journal of Educational Psychology, 67,* 796–800.

Hillocks, G. (1984). What works in teaching composition: A meta-analysis of experimental treatment studies. *American Journal of Education, 93,* 133–170.

Hines, C., Cruickshank, D., & Kennedy, J. (1985). Teacher clarity and its relationship to student achievement and satisfaction. *American Educational Research Journal,* p. 22.

Hunter, M. (1982). *Mastery Teaching.* El Segundo, CA: TIP Publications.

Hurt, H. T., Scott, M. D., & McCroskey, M. C. (1978). *Communication in the classroom.* Reading, MA: Addison-Wesley.

Kaplan, P. S. (1986). *The child's odyssey.* St. Paul: West.

Kounin, J. S. (1970). *Discipline and group management in classrooms.* New York: Holt, Rinehart and Winston.

Leinhardt, G., Seewald, A. M., & Engel, M. (1979). Learning what's taught: Sex differences in instruction. *Journal of Educational Psychology, 79,* 432–439.

Lightfood, S. L. (1978). *Worlds apart.* New York: Basic Books.

Losen, S. M., & Diament, B. (1978). *Parent conferences in the schools.* Boston: Allyn & Bacon.

Madsen, C. H., Becker, W. C., & Thomas, D. R. (1968). Rules, praise, and ignoring: Elements of elementary classroom control. *Journal of Applied Behavior Analysis, 1,* 139–150.

McCullough, D., & Findley, E. (1983, March). Teaching: How to ask effective questions. *Arithmetic Teacher,* pp. 8–9.

Moles, O. C. (1982, November). Synthesis of recent research on parent participation in children's education. *Educational Leadership,* pp. 44–47.

Montague, E. J. (1987). *Fundamentals of secondary classroom instruction.* Columbus, Ohio: Merrill.

NEA (1982). *Productive relationships: Parent-school-teacher:* Washington, DC: National Education Association.

O'Leary, K. D., & O'Leary, S. G. (1977). *Classroom management* (2nd ed.) New York: Pergamon Press.

Petti, M. (1987). Helping pupils handle criticism. *Academic Therapy, 23,* 75–78.

Philips, S. U. (1987). *The invisible culture: Communication in classrooms and community on the Warm Springs Indian reservation.* New York: White Plains, NY: Longman. Cited in U. Casanova, Ethnic and cultural differences. In V. Richardson-Koehler (Ed.), *Educators' handbook* (pp. 370–394). New York: Longman.

Redfield, D. L., & Rousseau, E. W. (1981). A Meta-analysis of experimental research on teacher questioning behavior. *Review of Educational Research, 51,* 237–245.

Richmond-Abbott, M. (1983). *Masculine and feminine.* Reading, MA: Addison-Wesley.

Rosenshine, B., & Stevens, R. (1986). Teaching functions. In M. C. Wittrock (Ed.), *Handbook of research on teaching* (3rd ed.) (pp. 376–392). New York: Macmillan.

Rotter, J. C., Robinson, E. H., & Fey, M. A. (1987). *Parent-teacher conferencing* (2nd ed.). Washington, DC: NEA Professional Library.

Rotter, J. C., & Robinson, E. H. (1982). *Parent-teacher conferencing.* Washington, D.C.: National Education Association.

Rowe, M. B. (1974). Pausing phenomena: Influence on the quality of instruction. *Journal of Psycholinguistic Research, 3,* 203–223.

Rowe, M. B. (1978, May). Give students time to respond. *Education Digest.*

Rowe, M. B. (1986). Wait time: Slowing down may be a way of speeding up. *Journal of teacher education, 37,* 43–50.

Rubin, Z. (1973). *Liking and loving: An invitation to social psychology.* New York: Holt, Rinehart and Winston.

Scardamalia, M., & Bereiter, C. (1986). Research on written composition. In M. C. Wittrock (Ed.), *Handbook of research on teaching* (3rd ed.) (pp. 778–804). New York: Macmillan.

Schmuck, R. A., & Schmuck, P. A. (1983). *Group processes in the classroom.* Dubuque, IA: Wm. C. Brown.

Schwebel, A., & Cherlin, D. (1972). Physical and social distancing in teacher and pupil relationships. *Journal of Educational Psychology, 63,* 543–550.

Serbin, L., & O'Leary, K. (1975, December). How different nursery schools teach girls to shut up. *Psychology Today,* pp. 57–58+.

Serbin, L., O'Leary, K., Kent, R., & Tonick, I. (1973). A comparison of teacher responses to the preacademic and problem behavior of boys and girls. *Child Development, 44,* 796–804.

Sherman, E. (1973). Listening comprehension as a function of proxemic distance and eye-contact. *Graduate Research in Education and Related disciplines, 7,* 5–34.

Slater, C. (1982, October). Writing: The experience of one school district. *Journal of Reading,* pp. 24–32.

Smith, H. A. (1979). Nonverbal communication in teaching. *Review of Educational Research, 49,* 631–672.

Susskind, E. (1969). The role of question-asking in the elementary school classroom. In F. Kaplan & S. B. Sarason (Eds.) *The psychoeducational clinic.* Yale University Department of Psychology and Massachusetts Department of Public Health Monograph Series, No. 4. New Haven, CT: Yale University Press.

Swift, J. N., & Gooding, C. T. (1983). Interaction of wait time feedback and questioning instruction on middle school science teaching, *Journal of research for science teaching, 20,* 721–730.

Tangri, S., & Moles, O. (1987). Parents and the community. In V. Richardson-Koehler (Ed.), *Educators' handbook* (pp. 519–551). New York: Longman.

Tobin, K. G., & Capie, W. (1982). Relationships between classroom process variables and middle school science achievement. *Journal of Educational Psychology, 14,* 441–454.

U.S. Department of Education (1987). *What works: Research about teaching and learning.* Washington, DC: U.S. Department of Education.

Van der Meij, H. (1988). Constraints on Question Asking in Classrooms. *Journal of Educational Psychology, 80,* 401–405.

Williams, D. L. (1982, November). Final interim report: Southwest Parent Education Research Center. Austin, TX: Southwest Educational Development Laboratory. Cited in O. C. Moles, Resource information service. *Educational Leadership,* pp. 44–47.

Winne, P. H. (1979). Experiments relating teachers' use of higher cognitive questions to student achievement, *49,* 13–48.

Wittrock, M. C. (1986). Students' thought processes. In M. C. Wittrock (Ed.) *Handbook of Research on Teaching* (3rd ed.) (pp. 247–315). New York: MacMillan.

Woolfolk, A. E., & Brooks, D. M. (1985). The influence of teachers' nonverbal behavior on student perception and performances. *Elementary School Journal, 85,* 513–528.

Woolfolk, A. E., & Brooks, D. M. (1982). Nonverbal communication in teaching (Chapter 5). In *Review of Research in Education, 10,* 103–149.

CHAPTER 10

Adamson, D. R. (1987). 10 ways to master classroom discipline. *Learning, 16,* 48–50.

Arlin, M. (1979). Teacher transitions can disrupt time flow in classrooms. *American educational Research Journal, 16,* 42–56.

Axelrod, S. (1983). *Behavior modification for the classroom teacher* (2nd ed.). New York: McGraw-Hill.

Behnke, G. J. (1979). *Coping with classroom distractions: The formal research study.* San Francisco: Far West Laboratory.

Bergmann, C., Bernath, L., Hohmann, I., Krieger, R., Mendel, G., & Theobald, G. (1984). Cited in S. Veenman, Perceived problems of beginning teachers. *Review of Educational Research, 54,* 143–178.

Borg, W. R., & Ascione, F. R. (1982). Classroom management in elementary mainstreaming classrooms. *Journal of Educational Psychology, 74,* 85–96.

Bornstein, P. H., & Quevillon, R. P. (1976). The effects of a self-instructional package on overactive preschool boys. *Journal of Applied Behavior Analysis, 9,* 179–188.

Bristol, M. M. (1976). Control of physical aggression through school- and home-based reinforcement. In J. D. Krumboltz & C. E. Thoresen (Eds.), *Counseling methods.* New York: Holt, Rinehart and Winston.

Brooks, D. M. (1985). Beginning the year in junior high: The first day of school. *Educational Leadership, 42,* 76–78.

Brophy, J. E. (1983). Classroom organization and management. *Elementary School Journal, 83,* 265–286.

Brophy, J. E., & Good, T. L. (1986). Teacher behavior and student achievement. In M. C. Wittrock (Ed.), *Handbook of research on teaching* (3rd ed.) (pp. 328–376). New York: Macmillan.

Brophy, J. E., & Rohrkemper, M. M. (1981). The influence of problem ownership on teachers' perceptions of and strategies for coping with student problems. *Journal of Educational Psychology, 73,* 295–311.

Cruickshank, D. R., Kennedy, J. J., Sanford, J. P. & Evertson, C. M. (1981). Evaluation of reflective teaching outcomes. *Journal of educational research, 75,* 26–32.

Curwin, R., Mendler, A., & Culhane, B. (1980, February). Kids and teachers discipline one another. *Learning.*

Doyle, W. (1979). Making managerial decisions in classrooms. In D. L. Duke (Ed.), *Classroom management: The seventy-eighth yearbook of the National Society for the Study of Education* (Part 2). Chicago: University of Chicago Press.

Doyle, W. (1984). How order is achieved in classrooms: An interim report. *Journal of Curriculum Studies, 16,* 259–277.

Doyle, W. (1985). Recent research on classroom management: Implications for teacher preparation. *Journal of Teacher Education, 37,* 31–35.

Doyle, W. (1986). Classroom organization and management. In M. C. Wittrock (Ed.), *Handbook of research on teaching* (3rd ed.) (pp. 392–432). New York: Macmillan.

Doyle, W., & Carter, K. (1987). Choosing the means of instruction. In V. Richardson-Koehler (Ed.), *Educators' handbook: A research perspective* (pp. 188–207). New York: Longman.

Emmer, E. T. (1987). Classroom management and discipline. In V. Richardson-Koehler (Ed.), *Educators' handbook: A research perspective* (pp. 233–258). New York: Longman.

Emmer, E. T., Evertson, C. M., & Anderson, L. M. (1980). Effective classroom management at the beginning of the school year. *Elementary School Journal, 80,* 219–231.

Emmer, E. T., Evertson, C. M., Sanford, J. P., Clements, B. S., & Worsham, M. (1984). *Classroom management for secondary teachers.* Englewood Cliffs, NJ: Prentice-Hall.

Emmer, E., et al. (1982). *Organizing and managing the junior high classroom.* Washington, DC: U.S. Department of Education.

Evertson, C. (1982). Differences in instructional activities in higher and lower achieving junior high English and math classes. *Elementary School Journal, 82,* 329–350.

Evertson, C. M. (1985). Training teachers in classroom management: An experimental study in secondary school classrooms. *Journal of Educational Research, 79,* 51–58.

Evertson, C. M., & Emmer, E. T. (1982). Effective management at the beginning of the school year in junior high classes. *Journal of Educational Psychology, 74,* 485–498.

Evertson, C. M., Emmer, E. T., Sanford, J. P., & Clements, B. S. (1983). Improving classroom management: An experiment in elementary school classrooms. *Elementary School Journal, 84,* 173–188.

Fisher, C. W., Berliner, D. C., Filby, N. N., Marliave, R., Cahen, L. S., & Dishaw, M. M. (1980). Teaching behaviors, academic learning time, and student achievement: An overview. In C. Denham & A. Liebersman (Eds.), *Time to learn.* Washington, DC: U.S. Government Printing Office.

Gelfand, D. M., Jenson, W. R., & Drew, C. J. (1982). *Understanding child behavior disorders.* New York: Holt, Rinehart and Winston.

Glickman, C. D., & Wolfgang, C. H. (1979). Dealing with student misbehavior: An eclectic view. *Journal of Teacher Education, 30,* 7–13.

Gnagey, W. J. (1981). *Motivating classroom discipline,* New York: MacMillan.

Gordon, T. (1974). *Teacher effectiveness training,* New York: David McKay.

Harter, S. (1983). Developmental perspectives on the self-system. In P. H. Mussen (Ed.), *Handbook of child psychology* (4th ed.) (pp. 275–287). New York: Wiley.

Houston, W. R., Clift, R. T., Freiberg, H. J., and Warner, A. R. (1988). *Touch the future: Teach.* St. Paul: West.

Humphrey, L. L., Karoly, P., & Kirschenbaum, D. S. (1978). Self-management in the classroom: Self-imposed response cost versus self-reward. *Behavior Therapy, 9,* 592–601.

Kaplan, P. S. (1986). *A child's odyssey.* St. Paul: West.

Kindsvatter, R., & Levine, M. A. (1980, June). The myths of discipline. *Phi Delta Kappan 61,* 690–693.

Kohut, S., & Range, D. G. (1986). *Classroom Discipline: Case studies and viewpoints* (2nd ed.). Washington, DC: National Education Association.

Kounin, J. S. (1970). *Discipline and group management in classrooms.* New York: Holt, Rinehart and Winston.

Kounin, J., & Doyle, P. (1975). Degree of continuity of a lesson's signal system and the task involvement of children. *Journal of Educational Psychology, 67,* 159–164.

Kounin, J., & Gump, P. (1987). Signal systems of lesson settings and task related behavior of preschool children. *Journal of Educational Psychology, 66,* 554–562.

Kounin, J. S., Gump, P. V., & Ryan, J. J. (1961). Exploration in classroom management. *Journal of Teacher Education, 12,* 235–246.

Lasley, T. J. (1987). Classroom management: A developmental view. *The Educational Forum, 51,* 286–296.

Levin, J., Nolan, J., & Hoffman, N. (1985). A strategy for classroom resolution of chronic discipline problems. *NASSP Bulletin, 69,* 11–18.

McDaniel, T. R. (1986). School discipline in perspective, *The Clearing House, 59,* 369–370.

McLaughlin, T. F. (1976). Self-control in the classroom. *Review of Educational Research, 46,* 631–663.

McLaughlin, T. F., & Scott, J. W. (1981). The use of response cost to reduce inappropriate behavior in educational settings. Cited in W. J. Gnagey, *Motivating classroom behavior.* New York: Macmillan.

Meichenbaum, D., & Goodman, J. (1971). Training impulsive children to talk to themselves. *Journal of Abnormal Psychology, 77,* 115–126.

Morris, R. C. (1981). Better teaching fosters better classroom control. *Education, 107,* 135–138.

Moskowitz, G., & Hayman, J. (1976). Success strategies of inner-city teachers: A year-long study. *Journal of Educational Research, 69,* 283–289.

O'Leary, K., & Dubey, D. (1979). Applications of self-control procedures by children. *Journal of Applied Behavior Analysis, 12,* 449–465.

Partin, R. L. (1987). Minimizing classroom interruptions. *The Clearing House, 61,* 29–31.

Patterson, C. J., & Mischel, W. (1975). Plans to resist distraction. *Developmental Psychology, 11,* 369–378.

Robin, A. (1976). The turtle technique: An extended case study of self-control in the classroom. *Psychology in the Schools, 13,* 449–453.

Rosenbaum, M. S., & Drabman, R. S. (1979). Self-control training in the classroom: A review and critique. *Journal of Applied Behavior Analysis, 12,* 467–485.

Rosenfield, P., Lambert, N. M., & Black, A. (1985). Desk arrangement effects on pupil classroom behavior. *Journal of Educational Psychology, 77,* 101–108.

Short, P. M., & Short, R. J. (1987). Beyond technique: Personal and organizational influences on school discipline. *The High School Journal, 37,* 31–36.

Smith, R. O. (1987). Discipline in the middle school. *Middle School Journal, 18,* 23–25.

Spettel, G. B. (1983). Classroom discipline— Now? *The Clearing House, 56,* 266–268.

Spiegler, M. D. (1983). *Contemporary behavioral therapy.* Palo Alto, CA: Mayfield.

Tjosvold, D. (1980, January). Control, conflict, and collaboration in the classroom. *The Educational Form,* 195–203.

Veenman, S. (1984). Perceived problems of beginning teachers. *Review of Educational Research, 54,* 143–178.

Weber, T. R., & Sloan, C. A. (1986). How does high school discipline in 1984 compare to previous decades? *The Clearing House, 59,* 326–329.

CHAPTER 11

Anderson, L. W., & Anderson, J. C. (1982, April). Affective assessment is necessary and possible. *Educational Leadership,* pp. 524–525.

Ausubel, D. P. (1977). The facilitation of meaningful verbal learning in the classroom. *Educational Psychologist, 12,* 162–178.

Ausubel, D. P., Novak, J. D., & Hanesian, H. (1978). *Educational psychology: A cognitive view* (2nd ed.). New York: Holt, Rinehart and Winston.

Barber, B. (1986). Why students don't need more homework. *Educational Leadership, 43,* 55–57.

Best, J. B. (1986). *Cognitive psychology.* St. Paul: West.

Blair, T. R. (1988). *Emerging patterns of teaching.* Columbus, OH: Merrill.

Block, J. H., & Burns, R. B. (1976). Mastery learning. In L. S. Shulman (Ed.), *Review of research in education,* Vol. 4. Itasca, IL: Peacock.

Bloom, B. S. (1968, May). Learning for mastery, *Evaluation Comment 1,* pp. 1–12.

Bloom, B. S. (1981). *Evaluation to improve learning,* New York: McGraw-Hill.

Bloom, B. S., Englehart, M. D., Furst, E. J., Hill, W. H., & Krathwohl, D. R. (1956). *Taxonomy of educational objectives, Handbook 1: Cognitive domain.* New York: Longmans Green.

Borich, G. D. (1988). *Effective teaching methods.* Columbus, OH: Merrill.

Brophy, J. (1982, April). Successful teaching strategies for the inner-city child. *Phi Delta Kappan,* pp. 527–530.

Brophy, J. E., & Good, T. L. (1986). Teacher behavior and student achievement. In M. C. Wittrock (Ed.), *Handbook of research on teaching* (pp. 328–376). New York: Macmillan.

Bruner, J. S., Goodnow, J. J., & Austin, G. A. (1956). *A study of thinking.* New York: Wiley.

Bruner, J. S. (1960). *The process of education.* Cambridge: Harvard University Press.

Bruner, J. S. (1961). The act of discovery. *Harvard Educational Review, 31,* 21–32.

Bruner, J. S. (1966). *Toward a theory of instruction.* New York: Norton.

Bruner, J. S., & Hall, E. (1970, December). Bad education: A conversation with Jerome Bruner. *Psychology Today,* 115–118.

Bruner, J. S. (1971). *The relevance of education.* New York: Norton.

Canter, L. (1988, September). Homework without tears. *Instructor,* pp. 28–32.

Carroll, J. B. (1963). A model of school learning. *Teachers College Record, 65.* 722–733.

Casonova, U. (1988, January). Peer tutoring: A new look at a popular practice. *Instructor,* pp. 14–15.

Cox, W. F. & Dunn, T. G. (1979). Mastery learning: A psychological trap? *Educational psychologist, 14,* 24–29.

deVoss, G. G. (1979). The Structure of major lessons and collective student activity. *Elementary School Journal, 80,* 8–18.

Dodd, D. H., & White, R. M. (1980). *Cognition: Mental structures and processes.* Boston: Allyn & Bacon.

Doyle, W., & Carter, K. (1987). Choosing the means of instruction. In V. Richardson-Koehler (Ed.), *Educators' handbook.* New York: Longman.

Duffelmeyer, F. A., & Baum, D. D. (1987). Reading comprehension: Instruction vs. practice. *Academic Therapy, 23,* 53–59.

England, A., & Flatley, J. (1985). *Homework-and-why.* Phi Delta Kappa Fastback. Bloomington, IN: Phi Delta Kappa.

Furst, E. J. (1981). Bloom's taxonomy of educational objectives for the cognitive domain: Philosophical and educational issues. *Review of Educational Research, 51,* 441–453.

Gagné, R. M. (1977). *The conditions of learning* (3rd ed.). New York: Holt, Rinehart and Winston.

Garbarino, J. (1975). The impact of anticipated reward upon cross-age tutoring. *Journal of Personality and Social Psychology, 32,* 421–428.

Gaskins, R. W. (1988). The missing ingredients: Time on task, direct instruction, and writing. *The Reading Teacher, 41,* 750–755.

Greenwood, C. R., Dinwiddie, G., Bailey, V., Carta, J. J., Dorsey, D., Kohler, F. W., Nelson, C., Rotholz, D., & Schulte, D. (1987). Field replication of classwide peer tutoring. *Journal of Applied Behavior Analysis, 20,* 151–160.

Gronlund, N. E. (1985). *Stating objectives for classroom instruction* (3rd ed.). New York: Macmillan.

Guskey, T. R. (1988). Mastery learning and mastery teaching. *Principal, 68,* 6–8.

Hartup, W. W. (1983). Peer relations. In P. H. Mussen (Ed.), *Handbook of child psychology* (4th ed.) (pp. 103–196). New York: Wiley.

Hedin, D. (1987). Expanding the use of cross-age peer tutoring. *The Clearing House,* pp. 39–41.

Horton, L. (1981). *Mastery learning.* Phi Delta Kappa Fastback. Bloomington, IN: Phi Delta Kappa.

Horton, L. (1979). Mastery learning: Sound in theory, but ... *Educational leadership, 37,* 154–156.

Houston, W. R., Clift, R. T., Freiberg, H. J., & Warnner, A. R. (1988). *Touch the future: Teach.* St. Paul: West.

Hughes, A. L., & Frommer, K. (1982, April). A system for monitoring affective objectives. *Educational Leadership,* pp. 521–523.

Hunter, M. (1979, October). Teaching is decision making. *Educational Leadership,* pp. 62–67.

Jarolimek, J., & Foster, C. D., Sr. (1989). *Teaching and learning in the elementary school* (4th ed.). New York: Macmillan.

Johnson, D. M., & Stratton, R. P. (1966). Evaluation of five methods of teaching concepts. *Journal of Educational Psychology, 57,* 48–53.

Judy, J. E., Alexander, P. A., Kulikowich, J. M., & Wilson, V. L. (1988). Effects of two instructional approaches and peer tutoring on gifted and nongifted sixth-grade students' analogy performance. *Reading Research Quarterly, 23,* 236–256.

Keith, T. Z. (1982). Time spent on homework and high school grades: A large-sample path analysis. *Journal of Educational Psychology, 74,* 248–254.

Krathwohl, D. R., Bloom, B. S., & Masia, B. B. (1964). *Taxonomy of educational objectives, handbook 2: Affective domain.* New York: David McKay.

LaConte, R. T., & Doyle, M. A. (1986). *Homework as a learning experience* (2nd ed.). Washington, DC: National Educational Association.

Mager, R. F. (1975). *Preparing instructional objectives* (2nd ed.). Belmont, CA: Fearon.

Mager, R. F. (1984). *Developing attitudes toward learning* (2nd ed.). Belmont, CA: David S. Lake.

Maheady, L., Sacca, M. K., & Harper, G. F. (1988). Classwide peer tutoring with mildly handicapped high school students. *Exceptional children, 55,* 52–59.

Melton, R. F. (1978). Resolution of conflicting claims concerning the effect of behavioral objectives on student learning. *Review of Educational Research, 48,* 291–302.

Montague, E. J. (1987). *Fundamentals of secondary classroom instruction.* Columbus, OH: Merrill.

Moore, D. S. (1982). Reconsidering Bloom's taxonomy of educational objectives, cognitive domain. *Educational Theory, 32,* 29–34.

Ornstein, A. C., & Levine, D. U. (1981, April). Teacher behavior research: Overview and outlook. *Phi Delta Kappan,* pp. 592–596.

Palardy, J. M. (1988). The effect of homework policies on student achievement. *NAASP Bulletin,* pp. 14–17.

Paschal, R. A., Weinstein, T., & Walberg, H. J. (1985). The effects of homework on learning: A quantitative synthesis. *Journal of Educational Research, 78,* 97–104.

Peltier, G. L. (1987). Is action learning another dead horse to beat? *The Clearing House, 60,* 247–249.

Pickens, J., & McNaughton, S. (1988). Peer tutoring of comprehension strategies. *Educational Psychology, 8,* 67–80.

Raschke, D., Dedrick, C., Strathe, M. , Yoder, M., & Kirkland, G. (1988). Cross-age tutorials and attitudes of kindergarterners toward older students. *The Teacher Educator, 23,* 10–18.

Reisman, F., & Payne, B. (1987). *Elementary education: A basic text.* Columbus, OH: Merrill.

Ringness, T. A. (1975). *The affective domain in education.* Boston: Little, Brown.

Roberts, W. K. (1982, July). Preparing instructional objectives: Usefulness revisited. *Educational Technology,* pp. 15–19.

Rosch, E. (1975). Cognitive representations of semantic categories. *Journal of Experimental Psychology: General. 104,* 192–233.

Rosenshine, B., & Stevens, R. (1986). Teaching functions. In M. C. Wittrock (Ed.), *Handbook of research on teaching* (pp. 376–392). New York: Macmillan.

Salend, S. J., & Schliff, J. (1988). The many dimensions of homework. *Academic Therapy, 23,* 397–403.

Sanford, J. P., & Evertson, C. M. (1983). Time use and activities in junior high classes. *Journal of Educational Research,* pp. 140–147.

Shapiro, E. S. (1988). Preventing academic failure. *School Psychology Review, 17,* 601–613.

Simpson, E. J. (1972). The classification of educational objectives in the psychomotor domain. *The Psychomotor Domain,* Vol. 3. Washington, DC: Gryphon, House.

Stallings, J. A., & Stipek, D. (1986). Research on early childhood and elementary school teaching programs. In M. C. Wittrock (Ed.), *Handbook of research on teaching* (pp. 727–754). New York: Macmillan.

Tennyson, R. D., & Park, O. C. (1980). The teaching of concepts: A review of instructional design research literature. *Review of Educational Research, 50,* 55–70.

Thornburg, H. D (1984). *Introduction to educational psychology.* St. Paul: West.

Topping, K. (1987). Peer tutored paired reading: Outcome data from ten projects. *Educational Psychology, 7,* 133–145.

Turner, T. N. (1987, January). Coping with the ways students cope with homework. *Educational Digest,* pp. 32–33.

U.S. Department of Education. (1987a). *What works: Research on Teaching.* Washington, DC: U.S. Department of Education.

U.S. Department of Education (1987b). *What works: Schools that work: Educating disadvantaged children.* Washington, DC: U.S. Department of Education.

White, R. T., & Tisher, R. P. (1986). Research on natural sciences. In M. C. Wittrock (Ed.), *Handbook of research on teaching* (pp. 874–906). New York: Macmillan.

Womack, S. T. (1989). Modes of instruction. *The Clearing House, 62,* 205–210.

Yarbro, R. (1988). The home-study environment of middle school children. *Middle School Journal, 19,* 30–31.

CHAPTER 12

AECT Task Force (1977). *The definition of educational technology.* Washington, DC: Association for Educational Communications and Technology.

Apple, M. W. (1987, October). Hidden effects of computers on teachers and students. *Educational Digest,* pp. 2–6.

Artificial intelligence may improve computer-aided instruction (1986, December 10). *Education Week,* p. 9.

Balajthy, E. (1988, December). Results of the first national assessment of computer competence. *The Reading Teacher.* p. 242.

Bork, A. (1980). Computers in continuing education. In M. N. Chamberlain (Ed.), (pp. 79–85). San Francisco: Jossey-Bass.

Bork, A. (1989). Ethical issues associated with the use of interactive technology in learning environments. *Journal of Research on Computing in Education, 21,* 121–128.

Bracey, G. W. (1988, October). Computers and learning: The research jury is still out. *Electronic Learning,* pp. 8, 28+.

Branched programming gives new life to outmoded teaching machines (1987, April 15). *Education Week,* p. 18.

Brown, J. W., Lewis, R. B., & Harcleroad, F. F. (1973). *AV instruction, technology media and methods.* New York: McGraw-Hill.

Brownell, G. (1987). *Computers and teaching.* St. Paul: West.

Burns, P. K., & Bozeman, W. C. (1981, October). Computer-assisted instruction and mathematics achievement: Is there a relationship? *Educational Technology,* pp. 32–39.

Butler, J. T. (1988). Games and simulations: Creative educational alternatives. *Tech Trends,* 20–23.

Callison, W. (1988, February/March). Future of computers in classrooms. *Thrust,* pp. 36–37.

Chen, M., & Marsh, W. (1989, May 24). Myths about instructional television: A riposte. *Education Week,* p. 32+.

Clark, R. E., & Salomon, G. (1986). Media in teaching. In M. C. Wittrock (Ed.), *Handbook of research on teaching* (3rd ed.) (pp. 464–479). New York: Macmillan.

Clements, D. H., & Gullo, D. F. (1984). Effects of computer programming on young children's cognition. *Journal of Educational Psychology, 76,* 1051–1058.

Daigon, A. (1982, December). Toward right writing. *Phi Delta Kappan,* pp. 242–246.

Dalbey, J., & Linn, M. C. (1985). The demands and requirements of computer programming: A literature review. *Journal of Educational Computing Research, 1,* 253–274.

Davis, B. J., Redmann, D. H., & Seaward, M. R. (1988). Selecting and evaluating software. *Journal of Education for Business, 64,* 81–85.

Doyle, W., & Carter, K. (1987). Choosing the means of instruction. In V. Richardson-Koehler (Ed.), *Educators' Handbook* (pp. 188–207). New York: Longman.

Fay, A. L., & Mayer, R. E. (1987). Children's naive conceptions and confusions about logo graphics commands. *Journal of Educational Psychology, 79,* 254–268.

Goldman, S. R., & Pellegrino, J. (1986). Microcomputer: Effective drill and practice. *Academic Therapy, 22,* 133–140.

Graham, N. (1989). *The mind tool* (5th ed.). St. Paul: West.

Harty, H., Kloosterman, P., & Matkin, J. (1988, Summer). Computer applications for elementary science teaching and learning. *Journal of Computers in Mathematics and Science Teaching,* pp. 26–29.

Haynes, J. A. and Malouf, D. B. (1986). Computer assisted instruction needs help. *Academic Therapy. 22,* 157–164.

Heinich. R. (1988). The use of computers in education: A response to Streibel. *Educational Communication and Technology, 36,* 143–145.

Heitzmann, W. R. (1987). *Educational games and simulations.* Washington, DC: National Education Association.

Hlebowitsh, P. S. (1988). Technology in the classroom. *The Clearing House, 62,* 53–56.

Houston, W. R., Clift, R. T., Freiberg, H. J., & Warner, A. R. (1988). *Touch the future: Teach!.* St. Paul: West.

Jay, T. B. (1986). Computerphobia: What to do about it. In D. O. Harper & J. H. Stewart, *Run: Computer education* (2nd ed.) (pp. 94–95). Monterey, CA: Brooks/Cole.

Jorde, P. (1986, Summer). Microcomputers and the pro-innovation bias. *Education, 106,* 388–393.

Karger, H. J. (1988, December). Children and microcomputers: A critical analysis. *Educational Technology,* pp. 7–11.

Kraus, W. H. (1981, March). Using a computer game to reinforce skills in addition basic facts in second grade. *Journal for Research in Mathematics Education,* 152–155.

Kulik, J. A., & Kulik, C. L. C. (1987). Review of recent research literature on computer-based instruction. *Contemporary Educational Psychology, 12,* 222–230.

Lapointe, A. E., & Martinez, M. E. (1988, September). Aims, equity, and access in computer education. *Phi Delta Kappan,* pp. 59–61.

Lehrer, R. (1986). Logo as a strategy for developing thinking? *Educational Psychologist, 21,* 121–137.

Lehrer, R., & Randle, L. (1987). Problem solving, metacognition and composition: The effects of interactive software for first-grade children. *Journal of Educational Computing Research, 3,* 409–427.

Lepper, M. R., & Gurtner, J. L. (1989). Chil-dren and computers: Approaching the twenty-first century. *American Psychologist, 44,* 170–179.

Long, C. (1985). How are today's elementary schools using computers? *Educational Technology, 25,* 27–29.

Malone, T. (1981). Towards a theory of intrinsically motivating instruction. *Cognitive Science, 4,* 333–369.

Mandell, C. J., & Mandell, S. L. (1989). *Computers in Education Today.* St. Paul: West.

Marshall, G. (1988, October). Evaluating research on school computer use. *The Executive Educator, 10,* 22–23.

Mayer, R. E., & Fay, A. L. (1987). A chain of cognitive changes with learning to program in logo. *Journal of Educational Psychology, 79,* 269–279.

Miller, H. E. (1979). *Films in the classroom: A practical guide.* Metuchen, NJ: Scarecrow Press.

Papert, S. (1980). *Mindstorms.* New York: Basic Books.

Parke, R. D., & Slaby, R. G. (1983). The development of aggression. In E. M. Hetherington (Ed.), *Handbook of child psychology* (4th ed.) (pp. 547–643). New York: Wiley.

Pea, R. D., Kurland, D. M., & Hawkins, J. (1985). Logo and the development of thinking skills. In M. Chen & W. Paisley (Eds.), *Children and microcomputers* (pp. 193–212). Beverly Hills: Sage.

Percival, F., & Ellington, H. (1988). *A Handbook of educational technology* (2nd ed.). London: Kogan Page.

Perkins, V. L. (1988). Effective instruction using microcomputers. *Academic Therapy, 24,* 129–135.

Pogrow, S. (1985). Using computers to teach problem-solving skills. *NAASP Bulletin, 69,* 47–54.

Rockman, S. (1985). Success or failure for computers in the schools. *Educational Technology, 25,* 48–50.

Rothman, R. (1988, April 20). Computers, calculators in math urged. *Education Week,* p. 9.

Salisbury, D. F. (1988, December). When is a computer better than flashcards? *Educational Technology,* pp. 26–32.

Samson, G. E., Niemiec, R., Weinstein, T., & Walberg, H. J. (1986, Summer). Effects of computer-based instruction on secondary school achievement: A quantitative synthesis. *AEDS Journal,* pp. 312–326.

Schneider, E. W., & Bennion, J. L. (1981). *The instructional media library: Videodiscs.* Englewood Cliffs, NJ: Educational Technology Publications.

Siegel, M. A., & Misselt, A. L. (1984). Adaptive feedback and review paradigm for computer-based drills. *Journal of Educational Psychology, 76,* 310–318.

Smith, T. E. C. (1987). *Introduction to education.* St. Paul: West.

Snider, W. (1987, October 14). March of school technologies proceeding—but slowly. *Education Week.* p. 1+.

Stallard, C. K. (1987). Computers for education: On what basis do we proceed? *Computer Education, 61,* 154–156.

Streibel, M. J. (1986). A critical analysis of the use of computers in education. *Education Communication and Technology, 34,* 137–161.

Thompson, J. G., & Jorgensen, S. (1989, February). How interactive is instructional technology? Alternative models for looking at interactions between learners and media. *Educational Technology,* pp. 24–27.

Tolman, M. N., & Allred, R. A. (1987). *The computer and education.* Washington, DC: National Education Association.

Trollip, S. R., & Alessi, S. M. (1988, Fall). Incorporating computers effectively into classrooms. *Journal of Research on Computing in Education, 22,* 70–81.

Troyer, M. B. (1987). Issues and problems in teacher computer literacy education. *Journal of Research on Computing in Education, 21,* 141–154.

Upchurch, R. L., & Lochhead, J. (1987). Computers and higher-order thinking skills. In V. Richardson Koehler (Ed.), *Educators' Handbook* (pp. 139–165). New York: Longman.

Vockell, E. L. (1987). The computer and academic learning time. *The Clearing House, 61,* 72–75.

West, P. (1988, December 7). Electronic spelling aids gaining toehold in schools. *Education Week,* p. 7.

West, P. (1989, June 7). St. Paul District touting saturn school as model for technology in education. *Education Week,* p. 6.

CHAPTER 13

Algozzine, B., Christenson, S., & Ysseldyke, J. E. (1982). Probabilities associated with the referral to placement process. *Teacher education and special education. 5,* 19–23.

Ashcroft, S. C., & Zambone-Ashley, K. (1980). Mainstreaming children with visual impairments. *Journal of Research and Development, 13,* 22–36.

Austin, A. B., & Draper, D. C. (1981). Peer relationships of the academically gifted: A review. *Gifted Child Quarterly, 25,* 129–133.

Barraga, N. (1976). *Visual handicaps and learning: A developmental approach.* Belmont, CA: Wadsworth.

Bauer, A. M. (1987). A teacher's introduction to childhood depression. *The Clearing House, 61,* 81–84.

Brickey, M., & Campbell, K. (1981). Fast food employment for moderately and mildly mentally retarded adults. *Mental Retardation, 19,* 113–116.

Brown, F. G. (1983). Principles of educational and psychological testing. New York: Holt, Rinehart and Winston.

Champie, J. (1986, November). Least restrictive environments for the deaf. *Educational Digest,* pp. 43–45.

Cohen, R. L. (1983). Reading disabled children are aware of their cognitive deficits. *Journal of Learning Disabilities, 16,* 286–289.

Correll, M. M. (1978). *Teaching the gifted and talented.* Bloomington, IN: Phi Delta Kappan.

Cruickshank, W. M., & Paul, J. L. (1980). The psychological characteristics of children with learning disabilities. In W. M. Cruickshank (Ed.), *Psychology of exceptional children and youth* (pp. 497–542). Englewood Cliffs, NJ: Prentice-Hall.

Cullinan, D., & Epstein, M. H. (1986). Behavior disorders. In N. G. Haring & L. McCormick (Eds.), *Exceptional children and youth* (pp. 161–201). Columbus, OH: Merrill.

Davis, J. M., Shepart, N. P., Stemachowicz, P. G., & Gorga, M. P. (1981). Characteristics of hearing-impaired children in the public schools. *Journal of Speech and Hearing Disorders, 25,* 130–143.

Dudley-Marling, C., & Searle, D. (1988). Enriching language learning environments for students with learning disabilities. *Journal of Learning Disabilities, 21,* 140–143.

Esposito, B. G., & Reed, T. M. (1986). The effects of contact with handicapped persons on young children's attitudes. *Exceptional Children, 53,* 224–229.

Federal Register (1977). *Education of handicapped children,* U.S. Office of Education. *Federal Register, 42,* 650082–65085.

Federal Register (1977, August 23). Washington, DC: U.S. Government Printing Office.

Feingold, B. F. (1975). Hyperkinesis and learning disabilities linked to artificial food flavors and colors. *American Journal of Nursing, 75,* 797–803.

Flax, E. (1988, December 7). Rising enrollment and costs threaten special-education gains, study finds. *Education Week,* p. 6.

Forness, S. R., & Kavale, K. A. (1988). Psychopharmacological treatment: A note on classroom effects. *Journal of Learning Disabilities, 21,* 144–147.

Gadow, K. D. (1983). Effects of stimulant drugs on academic hyperactive and learning disabled children. *Journal of Learning Disabilities, 16,* 290–293.

Gallaudet College (1975). *Deafness briefs: Information on deaf adults.* Washington, DC: Gallaudet College.

Gearheart, B. R., & Weishahn, M. W., & Gearheart, C. J. (1988). *The exceptional student in the regular classroom* (4th ed.). Columbus, OH: Merrill.

Gifted and Talented Children's Act of 1978: PL 95-561. Section 902.

Green, W. W. (1985). Hearing disorders. In W. H. Berdine & A. E. Blackhurst (Eds.). *An introduction to special education* (2nd ed.). Boston: Little, Brown, 183–245.

Gresham, F. M. (1982). Misguided mainstreaming: The case for social skills training with handicapped children. *Exceptional Children, 48,* 4223–430.

Grossman, H. J. (Ed.) (1973, 1977). *Manual on terminology and classification in mental retardation.* Washington, DC: American Association on Mental Deficiency.

Gunderson, C. W., Maesch, C., & Rees, J. W. (1987). The gifted/learning disabled student. *Gifted Children Quarterly, 31,* 158–160.

Hallahan, D. P., & Kauffman, J. M. (1988). *Exceptional children: Introduction to special education* (4th ed.). Englewood Cliffs, NJ: Prentice-Hall.

Hammill, D. D., Leigh, J. E., McNutt, G., & Larsen, S. C. (1981). A new definition of learning disabilities. *Learning Disability Quarterly, 4,* 372–382.

Haring, N. G. (1986). Introduction in N. G. Haring (Ed.). *Exceptional children and youth.* (4th ed.), 2–39, Columbus, OH: Merrill, 1986.

Haring, N. G. (Ed.) (1982) *Exceptional children and youth.* Columbus, OH: Merrill.

Hershey, M. (1988, February). Gifted child education. *The Clearing House* pp. 280–282.

Heward, W. L., & Orlansky, M. D. (1988). *Exceptional children* (3rd ed.). Columbus, OH: Merrill.

Holborow, P., Elkins, J., & Berry, P. (1981). The effect of the Feingold diet on "normal" school children. *Journal of Learning Disabilities, 14,* 143–147.

Jan, J. E., Freeman, R. D., & Scott, E. P. (1977). *Visual impairment in children and adolescents.* New York: Grune and Stratton.

Johnson, A. B. (1987). Attitudes toward mainstreaming: Implications for inservice training and teaching the handicapped. *Education, 107,* 229–233.

Johnson, J. A. (1981). The etiology of hyperactivity. *Exceptional Children, 47,* 348–354.

Juntune, J. (1982). Myth: The gifted constitutes a single homogeneous group! *Gifted Child Quarterly, 26,* 9–10.

Kavale, K. (1982). The efficacy of stimulant drug treatment for hyperactivity: A meta-analysis. *Journal of Learning Disabilities, 15,* 280–289.

Kavale, K., & Forness, S. R. (1983). Hyperactivity and diet treatment: A meta-analysis of the Feingold hypothesis. *Journal of Learning Disabilities, 16,* 324–330.

Keller, C. E., & Hallahan, D. P. (1987). *Learning disabilities: Issues and instructional interventions.* Washington, DC: National Education Association.

Kerr, M. M., Nelson, C. M., & Lambert, D. L. (1987). *Helping adolescents with learning and behavior problems.* Columbus, OH: Merrill.

Kirk, S. A., & Gallagher, J. J. (1989). *Educating exceptional children* (6th ed.). Boston: Houghton Mifflin.

Klasen, E. (1972). *The syndrome of specific dyslexia.* Baltimore: University Park Press.

Lawrence, P. A. (1988). Basic strategies for mainstream integration. *Academic Therapy, 23,* 349–355.

Leinhardt, G., & Pallay, A. (1982). Restrictive educational settings: Exile or haven? *Review of Educational Research, 52,* 557–578.

Lewis, P. H. (1988, November 6). A Great equalizer for the disabled. Education Life. *The New York Times,* Section 4A, pp. 61–67.

Lewis, R. B., & Doorlag, D. H. (1987). *Teaching special students in the mainstream* (2nd ed.). Columbus, OH: Merrill.

Ludlow, B. L. (1982). *Teaching the learning disabled.* Bloomington, IN: Phi Delta Kappa.

Maddux, C. D., Scheiber, L. M., & Bass, J. E. (1982). Self-concept and social distance in gifted children. *Gifted Child Quarterly, 26,* 77–81.

Mandell, C. J., & Fiscus, E. (1981). *Understanding exceptional people*. St. Paul: West.

Mandell, C. J., & Gold V. (1984). *Teaching handicapped students*. St. Paul: West.

Mattes, J. A. (1983). The Feingold diet: A current reappraisal. *Journal of Learning Disabilities, 16*, 319–323.

MacKinnon, D. (1978). *In search of human effectiveness*. Buffalo: Creative Education Foundation.

McConaughty, S. H., & Ritter, D. R. (1985). Social competence and behavioral problems of learning disabled boys aged 6–11. *Journal of Learning Disabilities, 18*, 547–553.

McKinney, J. D., & Feagans, L. (1984, Summer). Academic and behavioral characteristics of learning disabled children and average achievers: Longitudinal studies. *Learning Disabilities Quarterly*, pp. 251–265.

Mercer, C. D., Hughes, C., & Mercer, A. R. (1985). Learning disabilities definitions used by state education departments. *Learning Disability Quarterly, 8*, 45–55.

Mercer, J., & Lewis, J. (1981). *System of multicultural pluralistic assessment*. New York: Psychological Corporation.

Mollick, L. B., & Etra, K. S. (1981). Poor learning ability . . . or poor hearing. *Teacher, 98*, 42–43.

Morris, R J., & Kratochwill, T. R. (1987). Dealing with fear and anxiety in the school setting: Behavioral approaches to treatment. *Special Services in the Schools, 3*, 53–68.

Moskowitz, C. (1988). Strategies for mainstreamed students. *Academic Therapy, 23*, 541–547.

National Society to Prevent Blindness. (1977). *Signs of possible eye trouble in children*. New York: National Society to Prevent Blindness, Pub G.112.

Nelson, C. M. (1985). Behavior disorders. In W. H. Berdine & A. E. Blackhurst (Eds.), *An introduction to special education* (2nd ed.) (pp. 427–469). Boston: Little, Brown.

New York State Department of Education. (1982, March). *Alternative testing techniques for Children with Handicapping Conditions*. Albany, NY: New York State Department of Education.

Noble, K. D., (1987). The dilemma of the gifted woman. *Psychology of Women Quarterly, 11*, 367–378.

Passow, A. H. (1981). The nature of giftedness and talent. *Gifted Child Quarterly, 25*, 5–10.

President's Commission on Mental Retardation. (1977). *Mental retardation: Past and present*. Washington, DC: U.S. Government Printing Office.

Reiss, S. M., & Renzulli, J. S. (1982). A case for a broadened conception of giftedness. *Phi Delta Kappan, 63*, 619–620.

Rickert, E. S. (1981). Media mirrors of the gifted: E. Susanne Richert's review of the film *Simon*. *Gifted Child Quarterly, 25*, 3–4.

Rimland, B. (1983). The Feingold diet: An assessment of the reviews by Mattes, by Kavale and Forness and others. *Journal of Learning Disabilities, 16*, 331–333.

Rosenshine, B. (1983). Teaching functions in instructional programs. *Elementary School Journal, 83*, 335–354.

Ross, D. M., & Ross, S. A. (1976). *Hyperactivity: Research, theory and action*. New York: Wiley.

Salend, S. J. (1984). Factors contributing to the development of a successful mainstreaming program. *Exceptional Children, 50*, 409–416.

Schulz, J. B., Turnbull, A. P. (1983). *Mainstreaming Handicapped Students*. Boston: Allyn & Bacon.

Scott, M. E. (1988, Spring). Learning strategies can help. *Teaching Exceptional Children*. pp. 30–34.

Scruggs, T. E., Bennion, K., & Lifson, S. (1985). Learning disabled students' spontaneous use of test-taking skills on reading achievement tests. *Learning Disability Quarterly, 8*, 205–210.

Stephens, T., Blackhurst, A., & Magliocca, L. (1982). *Teaching mainstreamed students*. New York: Wiley.

Sternberg, R. J. (1982). Lies we live by: Misapplication of tests in identifying the gifted. *Gifted Child Quarterly, 26*, 157–161.

Tarver-Behring, S., Barkley, R. A., & Karlsson, J. (1985). The mother-child interactions of hyperactive boys and their normal siblings. *American Journal of Orthopsychiatry, 55*, 202–209.

Terman, L. M. (1925). *Mental and physical traits of a thousand gifted children*. Stanford, CA: Stanford University Press.

Terman, L. M., & Oden, M. H. (1959). *Genetic studies of genius, 1: Mental and physical traits of a thousand gifted children*. Stanford, CA: Stanford University Press.

Tolkoff, E. (1981). Mainstreaming: A promise gone awry. Albany, NY: New York State United Teachers.

Torrance, E. P. (1962). *Guiding creative talent*. Englewood Cliffs, NJ: Prentice-Hall.

Torrance, E. P. (1980). Psychology of gifted children and youth. In W. M. Cruickshank (Ed.), *Psychology of exceptional children and youth* (4th ed.) (pp. 469–497). Englewood Cliffs, NJ: Prentice-Hall.

Treffinger, D. J. (1982). Demythologizing gifted education: An editorial essay. *Gifted Child Quarterly, 26*, 3–8.

Tuttle, F. B., Beckler, L. A., & Sousa, J. A. (1988). *Program design and development for gifted and talented students* (3rd ed.). Washington, DC: National Education Association.

Varley, C., & Trupin, E. W. (1983). Double-blind assessment of stimulant medication for attention deficit disorder: A model for clinical application. *American Journal of Orthopsychiatry, 53*, 542–547.

Vaughn, S. (1985). Why teach social skills to learning disabled students? *Journal of Learning Disabilities, 18*, 588–591.

Viadero, D. (1987, April 1). Most states adopting programs for handicapped preschoolers. *Education Week*, pp. 1, 57.

Viadero, D. (1988a, March 2). Study documents jump in special-education enrollment. *Education Week*, p. 17.

Viadero, D. (1988b, August 3). Least restrictive class found cheapest for handicapped. *Education Week*, p. 7.

Walden, E. L., & Thompson, S. A. (1981). A review of some alternative approaches to drug management of hyperactivity in children. *Journal of Learning Disabilities, 4*, 213–217.

Wanat, P. E. (1983). Social skills: An awareness program with learning disabled adolescents. *Journal of Learning Disabilities, 16*, 35–38.

Watson, M. (1977). *Mainstreaming*. Washington, DC: National Education Association.

Wolf, J. S., & Stephens, T. M. (1986). Gifted and talented. In N. G. Haring & L. McCormick, *Exceptional children and youth* (pp. 475–505). Columbus, OH: Merrill.

Wood, J. W., & Miederhoff, J. W. (1988). Adapting lesson plans for the mainstreamed student. *The Clearing House, 61*, 269–276.

Wood, J. W., & Rosbe, M. (1985). Adapting the classroom lecture for the mainstreamed student in the secondary schools. *The Clearing House, 58*, 354–358.

CHAPTER 14

Allen, G. J., Elias, N. J., & Zlotlow, S. F. (1980). Behavioral interventions for alleviating test anxiety: A methodological overview of current therapeutic practices. In I. G. Sarason (Ed.). *Test anxiety: Theory, research and applications* (pp. 155, 186). Hillsdale, NJ: Erlbaum.

Anastasi, A. (1988). *Psychological testing* (6th ed.). New York: Macmillan.

Antonak, R. F., King, S., & Lowy, J. J. (1982). Otis-Lennon Mental Ability Test, Stanford Achievement Test, and three demographic variables as predictors of achievement in grades 2 and 4. *Journal of Educational Research, 75,* 366–373.

Benjamin, M., McKeachie, W. J., Lin, Y. G., & Holinger, D. P. (1981). Test anxiety: Deficits in information processing. *Journal of Educational Psychology, 73,* 816–824.

Bersoff, D. N. (1981a). Testing and the law. *American Psychologist, 36,* 1047–1057.

Bersoff, D. N. (1981b). Test bias: The judicial report card. *New York University Educational Quarterly, 13,* 2–9.

Brown, F. G. (1983). *Principles of educational and psychological testing.* New York: Holt.

Carman, R. A., & Adams. W. R. (1972). *Study skills: A student's guide to survival.* New York: Wiley.

Coladarci, T. (1986). Accuracy of teacher judgments of student responses to standardized test items. *Journal of Educational Psychology, 78,* 141–146.

Covington, M. V., & Omelich, C. L. (1987). "I knew it cold before the exam": A test of the anxiety-blockage hypothesis. *Journal of Educational Psychology, 79,* 393–400.

Covington, M. V., Omelich, C. L., & Schwarzer, R. (1986). Anxiety, aspirations and self-concept in the achievement process: A longitudinal model with latent variables. *Motivation and Emotion, 10,* 71–88.

Culler, R. E., & Holahan, C. J. (1980). Test anxiety and academic performance: The effects of study-related behaviors. *Journal of Educational Psychology, 72,* 16–20.

DeLawter, J., & Sherman, B. W. (1979). Skirting the perils of testing. *Learning, 8,* 98–100.

Dent, H. E. (1987). The San Francisco Public Schools experience with alternatives to I.Q. testing: A model for non-biased assessment. *The Negro Educational Review. 38,* 146–162.

Dent, H. E., Mendocal, A. M., Pierce, W. D., & West, G. I. (1987). Court bans use of I.Q. tests for blacks for any purpose in California state schools. Press release by Law Offices of Public Advocates, Inc., San Francisco, CA: *The Negro Educational Review, 38,* 190–199.

Dreher, M. J., & Singer, H. (1984). Making standardized tests work for you. *National Association of Elementary School Principles, 63,* 20–24.

Dreisbach, M., & Keogh, B. K. (1982). Test-wiseness as a factor in readiness test performance of young Mexican-American children. *Journal of Educational Psychology, 74,* 224–229.

Ebel, R. L. (1977). The uses of standardized testing (*Fastback* 93), Bloomington, IN: Phi Delta Kappa Educational Foundation.

Ebel, R. L. (1978). The case for norm-referenced measurements. *Educational Researcher, 7,* 3–5.

Feder, B. (1979). *The complete guide to taking tests.* Englewood Cliffs, NJ: Prentice-Hall.

Fiske, E. B. (1988, April 10). America's test mania. *New York Times Education Life,* pp. 16–18+.

Fuchs, D., Fuchs, L. S., Benowitz, S., & Barringer, K. (1987). Norm-referenced tests: Are they valid for use with handicapped students? *Exceptional Children, 54,* 263–271.

Gay, L. R. (1985). *Educational evaluation and measurement* (2nd ed.). Columbus, OH: Merrill.

Gold, D. L. (1988, March 30). Early testing said to have "long-term negative effects." *Education Week,* p. 6.

Gronlund, N. E. (1976). *Measurement and evaluation in teaching* (3rd ed.). New York: Macmillan.

Heward, W. L., & Orlansky, M. D. (1984). *Exceptional children* (2nd ed.). Columbus, OH: Merrill.

Hobbie, F. R. (1988, April 10). The quizzes of a lifetime. *New York Times Education Life,* p. 20.

Hoge, R. D., & Butcher, R. (1984). Analysis of teacher judgments of pupil achievement levels. *Journal of Educational Psychology, 76,* 777–781.

Houston, W. R., Clift, R. T., Freiberg, H. J., & Warner, A. R. (1988). *Touch the future: Teach!* St. Paul: West.

Hunsley, J. (1985). Test anxiety, academic performance, and cognitive appraisals. *Journal of Educational Psychology, 77,* 678–682.

Hunsley, J. (1987). Cognitive processes in mathematics anxiety and test anxiety: The role of appraisals, internal dialogue, and attributions. *Journal of Educational Psychology, 79,* 388–392.

Kalechstein, P., Kalechstein, M., & Docter,
R. (1981). The effects of instruction on test taking skills in second-grade black children. *Measurement and Evaluation in Guidance, 13,* 198–202.

Kaplan, P. S. (1977, March 13). It's the I.Q. tests that flunk. *New York Times,* p. 26.

Kirkland, K., & Hallandsworth, J. G. (1980). Effective test taking: Skills-acquisition versus anxiety-reduction techniques. *Journal of Consulting and Clinical Psychology, 48,* 431–439.

Koenke, K. (1987). Test wiseness: Programs and problems. *ERIC/RCS.*

Koretz, D. (1988). Arriving in Lake Wobegon: Are standardized tests exaggerating achievement and distorting instruction? *American Educator, 12,* 8–16+.

Kubiszyn, T., & Borich, G. (1987). *Educational testing and measurement* (2nd ed.). Glenview, IL: Scott Foresman.

Linn, R. L. (1986). Educational testing and assessment: Research needs and policy issues, *American Psychologist, 41,* 1153–1161.

Mehrens, W. A., & Lehmann, I. J. (1987). *Using standardized tests in education* (4th ed.). New York: Longman.

Millman, J., Bishop, C. H., & Ebel, R. (1965). An analysis of test-wiseness. *Educational and Psychological Measurement, 25,* 707–726.

Montague, E. J. (1987). *Fundamentals of secondary classroom instruction.* Columbus, OH: Merrill.

Naveh-Benjamin, M., McKeachie, W. J., & Lin, Y. G. (1987). Two types of test-anxious students: Support for an information processing model. *Journal of Educational Psychology, 79,* 131–136.

Paulman, R. G., & Kennelly, K. J. (1984). Test anxiety and ineffective test taking: Different names, same construct. *Journal of Educational Psychology, 76,* 279–288.

Perkins, M. R. (1982). Minimum competency testing: What? why? why not? *Educational Measurement: Issues and Practice, 1,* 5–9.

Perrone, V. (1977). *The abuses of standardized testing* (Fastback 92). Bloomington, IN: Phi Delta Kappa Educational Foundation.

Petti, M. (1987). Educational implications of the nonverbal WISC-R. *Academic Therapy, 23,* 177–181.

Petti, M. (1988). Educational implications of the verbal WISC-R. *Academic Therapy, 23,* 279–286.

Popham, W. J. (1978). The case for criterion-referenced measurements. *Educational Researcher, 7,* 6–10.

Reisman, F., & Payne, B. (1987). *Elementary education: A basic text.* Columbus, OH: Merrill.

Riegel, R. P., & Lovell, N. B. (1980). *Minimum competency testing* (Fastback 137). Bloomington, IN: Phi Delta Kappa Educational Foundation.

Ritter, S., & Idol-Maestas, L. (1986). Teaching middle school students to use a test-taking strategy. *Journal of Educational Research, 79,* 350–357.

Rocklin, T., & Thompson, J. M. (1985). Interactive effects of test anxiety, test difficulty, and feedback. *Journal of Educational Psychology, 77,* 368–372.

Rothman, R. (1987, November 19). Test scores tied to state aid in Connecticut plan. *Education Week,* p. 1.

Rothman, R. (1988a, February 10). Questions about normed tests spur meeting, *Education Week,* p. 1+.

Rothman, R. (1988b, April 20). Bennett is urged to probe "dumbing down" of tests. *Education Week,* pp. 1, 22.

Russo, T. J. (1984). Multimodal approaches to student test anxiety. *The Clearing House, 58,* 162–166.

Sarason, I. G. (1984). Stress, anxiety, and cognitive interference: Reactions to tests. *Journal of Personality and Social Psychology, 46,* 929–938.

Scarr, S. (1981). Testing for children: Assessment and the many determinants of intellectual competence. *American Psychologist, 36,* 1159–1167.

Schab, F. (1984). Minimum competency: A comparison of reactions of southern black high school students, their parents and black teachers. *Adolescence, 73,* 107–112.

Shepard, L. (1979). Norm-referenced vs. criterion-referenced tests. *Educational Horizons, 58,* 21–32.

Tryon, G. S. (1980). The measurement and treatment of test anxiety. *Review of Educational Research, 50,* 343–372.

U.S. Department of Education (1987a). *What works: Research about teaching and learning* (2nd ed.). Washington, DC: U.S. Department of Education.

U.S. Department of Education (1987b). *What works: Schools that work: Educating disadvantaged children.* Washington, DC: U.S. Department of Education.

Wine, J. D. (1980). Cognitive-attentional theory of test anxiety. In I. G. Sarason (Ed.), *Test anxiety: Theory, research and application* (pp. 349–385). Hillsdale, NJ: Erlbaum.

Zigler, E., & Berman, W. (1983). Discerning the future of early childhood intervention. *American Psychologist, 38,* 894–907.

CHAPTER 15

Anderson, R. C. (1972). How to construct achievement tests to assess comprehension. *Review of Educational Research, 42,* 145–170.

Bachman, J. G., & O'Malley, P. M. (1986). Self-concept, self-esteem, and educational experiences: The frog pond revisited (again). *Journal of Personality and Social Psychology, 50,* 35–46.

Blue, T. W. (1986). *The teaching and learning process.* Washington, DC: National Education Association.

Broyles, B. (1985). Another look at grading essays. *The Clearing House, 59,* 127–128.

Brown, F. G. (1983). *Principles of educational and psychological testing.* New York: Holt.

Butler, R., & Nisan, M. (1986). Effects of no feedback, task-related comments, and grades on intrinsic motivation and performance. *Journal of Educational Psychology, 78,* 210–216.

Chance, P. (1987, April). Master of mastery. *Psychology Today,* pp. 43–46.

Chase, C. I. (1968). The impact of some obvious variables on essay test scores. *Journal of Educational Measurement, 5,* 315–318.

Chase, C. I. (1979). The impact of achievement expectations and handwriting quality on scoring essay tests. *Journal of Educational Measurement, 16,* 39–42.

Coffman, W. E. (1971). Essay examinations. In R.L. Thorndike (Ed.), *Educational Measurement* (Chapter 10). Washington, DC: American Council on Education.

Coker, D. R., Kolstad, R. K., & Sosa, A. H. (1988). Improving essay tests. *The Clearing House, 61,* 253–255.

Colton, J. A., & White, M. A. (1985). High school student satisfaction and perceptions of the school environment. *Contemporary Educational Psychology, 10,* 235–248.

Conner, K. Hairston, J., Hill, I., Kopple, H., Marshall, J., Scholnick, K., & Schulman, M. (1985, October). Using formative testing at the classroom, school, and district levels. *Educational Leadership,* pp. 63–67.

Driscoll, M. P. (1986). The relationship between grading standards and achievement: A new perspective. *Journal of Research and Development in Education, 19,* 13–17.

Ebel, R. L. (1965). *Measuring educational achievement.* Englewood Cliffs, NJ: Prentice-Hall.

Ebel, R. L. (1975). Can teachers write good true-false test items? *Journal of Educational Measurement, 12,* 31–35.

Evans, E. D., & Engelberg, R. A. (1988). Student perceptions of school grading. *Journal of Research and Development in Education, 21,* 45–54.

Foos, P. W., & Fisher. R. P. (1988). Using tests as learning opportunities. *Journal of Educational Psychology, 80,* 179–183.

Gay, L. R. (1985). *Educational evaluation and measurement* (2nd ed.). Columbus, OH: Merrill.

Green, J. A. (1963). *Teacher-made tests.* New York: Harper & Row.

Gronlund, N. E. (1976). *Measurement and evaluation in teaching* (3rd ed.). New York: Macmillan.

Houston, J. P. (1988). Classroom answer copying: Roles of acquaintanceship and free versus assigned seating. *Journal of Educational Psychology, 78,* 230–232.

Houston, W. R., Clift, R. T., Freiberg, H. J., & Warner, A.R. (1988). *Touch the future: Teach!* St. Paul, MN: West.

Hughes, D. C., Keeling, B., & Tuck, B. F. (1983). Effects of achievement expectations and handwriting quality on scoring essays. *Journal of Educational Measurement, 20,* 65–70.

Kirk, S. A., & Gallagher, J. J. (1986). *Educating exceptional children* (5th ed.), Boston: Houghton Mifflin.

Kubiszyn, T., & Borich, G. (1987). *Educational testing and measurement* (2nd ed.). Glenview, IL: Scott-Foresman.

Malehorn, H. (1984). Ten better measures than giving grades. *The Clearing House, 57,* 256–257.

Miller, P. W., & Erickson, H. E. (1985). *Teacher-written student tests.* Washington, DC: National Education Association.

Montague, E. J. (1987). *Fundamentals of secondary classroom instruction.* Columbus, OH: Merrill.

Reisman, F., & Payne, B. (1987). *Elementary education: A basic text.* Columbus, OH: Merrill.

Sparks, W. G. (1987). The art of writing a test. *The Clearing House, 61,* 175–178.

Yarborough, B. H., & Johnson, R. A. (1980, April). Research that questions the traditional elementary school marking system. *Phi Delta Kappan,* pp. 527–528.

APPENDIX

Best, J. W., & Kahn, J. V. (1989). *Research in education* (6th ed.). Englewood Cliffs, NJ: Prentice-Hall.

Borg, W. R. (1987). *Applying educational research.* (2nd ed.). New York: Longman.

McGraph, J. E. (1964). *Social psychology: A brief introduction.* New York: Holt.

Maier, N. R. F., & Verser, G. C. (1982). *Psychology in industrial organizations* (5th. ed.). Boston: Houghton Mifflin.

Rosenthal, R., & Fode, K. L. (1963). The effect of experimenter bias on the performance of the albino rat. *Behavioral Science, 8,* 183–189.

Rosenthal, R., & Jacobson, L. F. (1968). Teacher expectations for the disadvantaged. *Scientific American Offprints, 218,* 3–7.

Name Index

Graham, N. 414
Graham, S. 261
Graham-Clay, S.L. 161, 168
Grant, C.L. 193
Gray, E. 204
Gray, G.S. 94
Gray, J.M. 279
Gray, M.J. 89
Green, W.W. 469
Green, J.A. 522, 527, 531, 532, 534
Greene, D. 260, 285
Greenwood, C.R. 397
Gresham, F.M. 161, 453
Grice, G.L. 110
Griffiths, P. 56
Grolnick, W.S. 283
Gronlund, N.E. 197, 363, 365, 367, 369, 371, 487, 496, 498, 501, 521, 527, 529, 532, 533, 534, 535
Grossman, H.J. 463
Gruendel, J. 81
Guilford, J.P. 127
Gullo, D.F. 415
Gump, P. 341
Gunderson, C.W. 473
Gurney, P. 187, 192
Guskey, T.R. 374

H

Hagen, J.W. 87
Hall, E. 309, 310
Hall, J.W. 82
Hall, M. 309, 310
Hall, R.V. 152
Hallahan, D.P. 447, 452, 453, 455, 456
Hallandsworth, J.G. 510
Hallinan, M.T. 198
Halpern, D. 113
Hamachek, D.E. 188, 189
Hammill, D.D. 454
Hamlet, C.C. 163
Hanna, G.S. 8
Haring, N.G. 445, 449
Harris, A.L. 149
Harris, J.M. 149
Hart, S.N. 240
Harter, S. 43, 190, 275, 348
Hartup, W.W. 197, 396
Harty, H. 419
Haskett, G.J. 190
Haskins, R. 201
Hatch, J.A. 187
Hayes, J.R. 315
Haynes, J.A. 425
Hayman, J. 332
Hedin, D. 395, 396
Heiman, M. 114, 116, 121
Heitzmann, W.R. 422

Heller, M.S. 307
Hennessey, B.A. 127, 128
Hering, K. 152
Hernandez, D.J. 186
Heron, B. 236
Hersh, R.H. 229
Hershey, M. 471
Heth, E.M. 204, 205
Hetherington, E.M. 200
Heward, W.L. 16, 450, 454, 508
Hiebert, E.H. 261
Hillocks, G. 315
Hines, C. 295
Hlebowitsh, P.S. 423
Hobart, T.Y. 243
Hobbie, F.R. 505
Hodges, H. 134
Hoedt, K.L. 152
Hoehn, L. 130
Hoff-Ginsberg, E. 58
Hoge, R.D. 496
Holborow, P. 457
Holahan, C.J. 509
Holt, J. 89
Horner, M. 258
Horton, L. 374, 375
Hotelling, K. 225
Hottinger, W. 32
Hough, R.A. 59
Houston, J.P. 536
Houston, R., 335
Houston, W.R. 11, 73, 369, 398, 409, 487, 489, 526
Howes, C. 201
Hoy, C. 264
Hughes, A.L. 320
Hughes, D.C. 532
Hughes, V. 208, 311
Humphrey, L.L. 347
Hunsley, J. 509
Hunt, R.R. 78
Hunter, B. 413
Hunter, M. 299, 398
Hurt, H.T. 309, 312
Hymes, J.L. 202

I

Idol-Maestas, 511
Inhelder, B. 34, 39, 44
Isakson, R.C. 18
Istomina, Z.M. 87

J

Jackson, P. 257
Jacobs, J.E. 125
Jacobson, L. 270, A-7
Jamieson, D.W. 274

Jan, J.E. 466
Jarolimek, J. 362, 377, 378, 388
Jay, T.B. 425
Jeffries, D. 238
Jennings, S. 208
Johnson, A.B. 460
Johnson, D.M. 388
Johnson, D.W. 279, 280, 281
Johnson, J. 457
Johnson, M. 208
Johnson, N. 81
Johnson, R. 538
Johnson, R.T. 280, 457
Jones, B.F. 6, 9, 10, 84
Jones, F.H. 166
Jones, M. 110
Jones, M.C. 193
Jones, P. 240, 243
Jones, R.S. 276, 277
Jorde, P. 423
Jorgensen, S. 423
Joseph, G. 272
Judy, J.E. 376
Juntune, J. 472
Justice, E. 87

K

Kaesle, C.F. 14
Kagan, D.M. 133
Kagan, J. 130, 133
Kagan, S.I. 202
Kahn, J. A-1, A-3, A-4
Kail, R. 87, 107
Kain, C.J. 199
Kalechstein, P. 510
Kaplan, P.S. 190, 201, 254, 299, 331, 352, 508
Karger, H.J. 422
Karmos, A.H. 119, 120
Karmos, J.S. 119, 120
Karplus, R. 53
Kauffman, J.M. 447, 452, 453
Kavale, K.A. 457
Kazdin, A.E. 155, 159, 160, 283
Kearney, P. 14
Keating, D. 128
Keefe, C.H. 199
Keeney, T.J. 87
Kegan, R. 44
Keith, T. 393
Keller, C.E. 455, 456
Keller, F.S. 175
Kelly, J. 206
Kelly, J.B. 204
Kelly, M.L. 160
Kennelly, K.F. 509
Keough, B. 510
Kerr, M.M. 166, 448
Kim, Y.J. 234, 235

Kindsvatter, R. 331
King, M.L. 59
King-Stoop, J. 254
Kirby, F.D. 155
Kirkland, K. 510
Kistner, J. 159
Kirk, S.A. 449, 462, 473, 521
Klahr, D. 119
Klasen, E. 455
Klatsky, R.L. 71, 77, 79
Klienke, C.L. 258
Kloster, A.M. 83, 84
Knight, C.J. 281
Koenke, K. 510
Koford, J. 200
Kogan, N. 127
Kohlberg, L. 29, 223, 224, 225, 226, 228, 229
Kohut, S. 331
Kopelman, R. 259
Koran, J.J. 74
Koretz, D. 491
Koslowski, B. 55
Kounin, J. 307, 335, 338, 339, 341
Kramer, R. 225
Krathwohl, D.R. 368
Kratochwill, T.R. 462
Kraus, W.H. 422
Kreitler, S. 276
Krogman, W.M. 192
Kubiszyn, T. 493, 501, 506, 531, 534, 540
Kuchinskas, G. 134
Kuhn, D. 55
Kukla, A. 258
Kilhavy, R.W. 95
Kulik, J.A. 175, 421
Kulik, C.L. 421
Kupersmidt, J.B. 199
Kurdek, L.A. 204
Kuschner, D.S. 43

L

LaConte, R.T. 392, 393
Labov, W. 60
Lahey, B.B. 161, 164
Lambiotte, J.G. 282
Lapointe, A.E. 410
Lasley, T.J. 331
Lawrence, P.A. 456
Lazar, I. 202
Lee, V.E. 202
Lehmann, I.J. 487, 490, 494, 505, 510
Lehrer, R. 414, 415
Lehman, J.R. 74
Leingardt, G. 311
Leinhardt, G. 453
Lemanek, K.L. 161
Lenfestey, W. 170
Lepper, M.R. 7, 284, 285, 418, 420, 421, 422

Letteri, C.A. 9
Levin, J.R. 86
Levine, D.V. 397
Levitsky, R. 114
Levy, J. 136, 138
Lewis, P.H. 444
Lewis, R.B. 447, 458, 465, 470, 473
Lickona, T. 229
Liebert, R.M. 257
Lightfoot, S.L.
Lin-Odom, B. 110
Lindauer, B.K. 87
Lindberg, M.A. 87
Linn, M.C. 415
Linn, R.L. 504
Lipman, M. 116
Lipsett, L. 148
Lloyd, J.W. 444, 448
Lockhart, R.S. 82
Lockhead, J. 411, 413
Lockheed, M. 271
Long, A. 261
Long, C. 416
Long, J.D. 156
Lorch, E.P. 73
Loser, A.S. 320
Lovell, N.B. 503
Ludlow, B.L. 456
Lupart, P.S. 119, 122
Lynn, S. 17

M

MacKinnon, D. 471
Maccoby, E.E. 226
Madsen, C.H. 306
Magee, D. 192
Mager, R.F. 364, 370
Maheady, L. 395
Maher, C.A. 147, 174, 175
Maier, N.R.F., A-8
Malehorn, H. 542
Malinowski, C.I. 226
Malouf, D.B. 425
Mandell, C.J. 426, 435
Mandell, S.L. 426, 435, 445, 450, 451, 458, 460, 461, 470
Mandler, J. 38, 81
Mannies, N. 136, 137
Manning, D.T. 199, 200, 206
Manosevitz, M. 205
Mansfield, R.S. 128, 129
Marchman, V.A. 199, 200
Marcia, J. 195
Markman, E.M. 88
Marsh, W. 428
Marshall, G. 421
Marso, R.N. 14, 15
Martin, D. 234

Martinez, M.E. 410
Masia, B.B. 368
Maslow, A.H. 255, 256
Mattes, J.A. 457
Matthews, D.B. 110
Mayer, R.E. 94, 133, 414
Mayer, R.E. 84
Maymi, C.R. 200
McClelland, D.C. 258
McClinton, B.S. 202
McConaughty, S.H. 455
McCormick, K. 239
McDaniel, T.R. 155, 275, 278, 330, 331
McGhee, P. 259
McGraph, J.E. A-7
McGuinness, D. 208
McGuire, D. 244
McKinney, J.D. 456
McKinney, J.P. 48
McLaughlin, B. 62
McLaughlin, T.F. 346, 347
McLenaghan, B.A. 163
McLloyd, V.C. 285
McNaughton, S. 395
McTighe, J.J. 114
Meddin, B.J. 239
Mehrens, W.A. 487, 490, 495, 505, 510
Meichenbaum, D.H. 133, 348
Meier, B.G. 202
Meier, W. 254
Mellon, P. 271
Melton, R.F. 373
Menyuk, P. 58
Mercer, C.D. 177, 473
Merelman, R.M. 50
Mergendoller, J.R. 199, 200
Messer, S. 133
Michaels, J.W. 280
Middlestadt, S. 272
Miederhoff, J.W. 475
Miller, A. 263
Miller, G.A. 77
Miller, H.E. 430, 431
Miller, J.P. 296
Miller, P.H. 33
Miller, P.M. 225
Miller, P.W. 527, 529, 536, 537
Miller, W.H. 166
Miller-Perrin, C.L. 243
Millman, J. 510
Mills, R.K. 230
Minix, N.A. 236, 237
Minuchin, P.P. 187, 201, 205
Mischel, W. 348
Mitman, A. 187
Misselt, A.L. 417, 418
Molfese, D.L. 55
Moles, O. 320
Moline, J. 230

Subject Index

Item-response profile, 536
Itinerant specialist, 446

J

Jigsaw approach, 211
Junior high school
  and attention, 72–73
  discipline, 353
  and formal operational reasoning, 48–52
  homework, 393
  and moral development, 222–224, 226
  and physical development, 192–193
  reasoning, 193–194
  rule making, 335–336
  seating plans, 333
  seatwork, 390
  and self-concept, 187–188
  time constraints for lessons, 339–340

K

Keller Plan, 175
Keyword method (mnemonic device), 84
Knowledge (as educational objective), 366, 367
Kohlberg's theory of moral reasoning, 222–225
  program to promote moral reasoning, 228–230

L

Labeling in special education, 448–450
Lake Wobegon challenge to standardized tests, 491
Language development, 55–62
  development of, 55–57
  teachers and, 58–59
  theories of language learning, 57–58
Language disorders, 459
Larry P. vs. Riles, 508
Latchkey children, 8, 203–204
Learning, *See also,* teaching and teachers
  and attention, 73–74
  about computers, 410–411
  and curiosity, 276–277
  through direct instruction, 375–377
  and discipline, 353–354
  and experiences, 380–381
  and homework, 393
  and indirect methods, 381
  and memory, 90–91
  and use of questions, 301
Learned helplessness, 262–263
Learning disabilities, 454–457
  teaching students with learning disabilities, 455–456

Learning and memory strategies, 82–87, 91–97
Learning styles, 130–132
Learning theory, *See also,* behaviorism, operant conditioning
Learning to Learn Program, 116
Legal blindness, 465
Levels of processing model, 82
Linear programming, 174
Logico-mathematical knowledge, 30–31
LOGO, 413, 414–416
Long-term memory, 78–79
Low road transfer, 123

M

Maintaining behavior change, 167
Maintenance rehearsal, 78
Mainstreaming, 450, 452–454
Maintenance needs, 255, 257
Mastery learning, 374–375
Maslow, Abraham, 255–258
Mastery learning, 265, 374–375
Mastery tests, 522
Matching questions, 529–530
Mathematical reasoning, 46–47
Maturation, 32
  early and late maturation, 193
Mean, 496
Means/ends analysis, 120
Meaningful learning, 277, 384–386
Measures of central tendency, 496
Median, 496
Memory, 74–79
  development of strategies, 82, 86–88
  long-term, 78–81
  measuring retrieval, 75
  and metamemory, 88–89
  model of human, 76–78
  schemata and scripts, 79–81
  sensory, 77
  short-term, 77–78
  and teaching strategies, 90–91
Memory processes, 82–85
Mental age, 506
Mental retardation, 462–464
Metacognition, 124–125
  learning disabled students, 455, 456
  and reading, 124–125
Metamemory, 88–90
Metropolitan Achievement Test, 502
Minimum competency testing, 503–504
Minority group
  effective teaching techniques with, 398–399
  and giftedness, 473–474
  and identity statuses, 196
  and integration, 211
  and multicultural education, 210–211

and non-verbal behavior, 309
  and self-concept, 187
Misbehavior
  behavioral methods, 345–348
  cognitive-behavioral methods, 348–349
  dealing with, 341–355
  general principles, 341–342
  non-intrusive methods, 344
  problem ownership, 343–344
  slightly intrusive methods, 344–345
Mnemonic devices, 84–86
Mode, 496
Model of memory, 75–76
Models, 172
Momentum, 339
Moral behavior, 226–227
Moral development and the schools, 221–244
  approaches, 223–233
  evaluating programs, 221–222
  programs to encourage, 228–230
  See also, health concerns
Moral reasoning, 222–224
  and gender, 225–26
  and moral behavior, 226
Moral realism, 222–223
Moral relativism, 222–223
Moral/Values education, 16–17
  See also, moral development, teachers and moral development
Motivation, 254–285
  achievement need, 258
  attribution theory, 260–262
  behavioral views, 266–269
  cognitive views, 260–262
  and competition, 279–280
  and cooperation, 280–282
  curiosity and, 276–277
  definition, 254
  and expectations, 270–273
  extrinsic motivation, 283–285
  fear of failure, 259–260
  and lessons, 275–279
  fear of success, 258–259
  humanistic approach, 255–258
  intrinsic motivation, 275–279
  and parents, 273–274
  self-worth theory, 264–266
  social learning approach, 266–269
Motivational processes (in social learning theory), 171–172
Motor reproduction (in social learning theory), 171
Multimedia approach, 456
Multiple-choice tests, 518–526
Multiple grading, 542
Multicultural education, 210
Multiethnic education, 210